CARSWELL

PERSONAL TAX RETURN GUIDE

2018 TAXATION YEAR

Paula Ideias

BA, LLB, LLM (Tax)

Reflecting developments to December 31, 2018
(unless otherwise noted)

THOMSON REUTERS®

ISBN 978-0-7798-8816-0

Printed in the United States by Thomson Reuters.

THOMSON REUTERS CANADA, A DIVISION OF THOMSON REUTERS CANADA LIMITED

One Corporate Plaza
2075 Kennedy Road
Toronto, Ontario
M1T 3V4

Customer Relations
Toronto 1-416-609-3800
Elsewhere in Canada/U.S. 1-800-387-5164
Fax 1-416-298-5082
www.carswell.com
E-mail www.carswell.com/email

SUMMARY TABLE OF CONTENTS

Introduction and What's New v
Glossary vii
Detailed Table of Contents xi

Chapter 1   Personal Tax Filing and Payment Requirements 1

Chapter 2   Employment Income and Deductions 47

Chapter 3   Dividend, Interest, and Other Investment Income 135

Chapter 4   Capital Gains and Losses 177

Chapter 5   Rental Income 263

Chapter 6   Business and Professional Income 295

Chapter 7   Depreciation, Amortization, and Resource Deductions 337

Chapter 8   Pensions and Other Income 409

Chapter 9   Other Deductions 441

Chapter 10   Federal Non-Refundable Tax Credits 489

Chapter 11   Calculation of Net Federal Tax 563

Chapter 12   Provincial and Territorial Taxes and Credits............................ 599

Chapter 13   Completing the Québec Income Tax Return (Form TP-1) 677

Chapter 14   Assessments, Audits, and Avoidance Rules 735

Chapter 15   Canadian Taxation of Non-Residents and Deemed Residents 795

Chapter 16   Tax Planning, Registered Plans, and U.S. Tax Considerations 819

Appendix A   Medical Expense Credit Quick Reference Table......................... 853

Appendix B   Tax Reference Tables 921

Topical Index 939

INTRODUCTION

Introduction

The *Personal Tax Return Guide — 2018 Taxation Year* ("T1 Guide") is intended to answer many questions associated with completing the 2018 federal T1 Personal Income Tax and Benefit Return ("T1 return") and the 2018 Québec Income Tax Return ("TP-1 return"). Tax practitioners can also rely on the T1 Guide to answer personal tax questions at any time of the year. In addition to covering all aspects of preparing personal tax returns, the T1 Guide also discusses other personal tax compliance requirements and personal taxation issues. Material is logically arranged to reflect the personal tax return process. References are provided to tax return lines, related tax forms, and schedules. Text boxes and quick reference tables are used throughout to highlight key concepts, tips, and traps. The T1 Guide provides an easily understood description of technical tax legislation. Extensive references are made to legislative provisions, court cases, tax return schedules, tax forms, Canada Revenue Agency (CRA) publications, and other sources.

What's New in this Edition

The T1 Guide has been updated to reflect legislative and administrative developments since the last edition, including the 2018 federal budget measures contained in Bill C-74 (*Budget Implementation Act, 2018, No. 1*) and Bill C-86 (*Budget Implementation Act, 2018, No. 2*), and other federal and provincial legislative and administrative measures. The T1 Guide has also been updated to reflect the latest court cases, government publications, and changes to both federal and provincial personal tax credits, tax deductions, and threshold amounts for 2018. Extensive sources have been consulted when updating the T1 Guide, including documents posted to Taxnet Pro during the year, to ensure that the latest personal tax developments are reflected.

Below are some of the personal income tax developments that are reflected in this edition of the T1 Guide:

- Changes to the Voluntary Disclosure Program (¶1510)

- Elimination of the election to exclude work in progress from income (¶6220)

- Accelerated Investment Initiative for capital cost allowance (¶7006)

- Expansion of the medical expense tax credit in respect of specially trained service animals (¶10195.7)

- Extension of eligibility for the mineral exploration tax credit (¶11033)

- Changes to the federal dividend tax credit rate (¶11080)

- Changes to the Working Income Tax Benefit (¶11290)

- Expansion of the scope of the tax on split income (¶14210)

- Extension of the registered plan anti-avoidance rules (¶16250)

Glossary

Glossary

ABIL	Allowable business investment loss
ACB	Adjusted cost base
ACCA	Accelerated capital cost allowance
ADR	American depository receipts
AIIP	Accelerated investment incentive property
AIP	Accumulated income payments
AMT	Alternative minimum tax
BIL	Business investment loss
BYOD	Bring your own device
CCA	Capital cost allowance
CCB	Canada child benefit
CCPC	Canadian-controlled private corporation
CDA	Capital dividend account
CDB	Child disability benefit
CDE	Canadian development expenses
CDSB	Canada disability savings bond
CDSG	Canada disability savings grant
CEC	Cumulative eligible capital
CEE	Canadian exploration expenses
CESG	Canada education savings grant
CFA	Controlled foreign affiliate
CICA	Canadian Institute of Chartered Accountants
CNIL	Cumulative net investment loss
COGPE	Canadian oil and gas property expense
CPI	Consumer Price Index
CPP	Canada Pension Plan
CRA	Canada Revenue Agency
CRCE	Canadian renewable and conservation expenses
CTF	Canadian Tax Foundation
DIC	Deposit insurance corporation
DPSP	Deferred Profit Sharing Plan
EAP	Educational assistance payment
ECP	Eligible capital property
EI	Employment Insurance
ELHT	Employee Life and Health Trust
EPSP	Employee Profit Sharing Plan
Exch	Exchequer Court of Canada
FAPI	Foreign accrual property income
FA	Foreign affiliate

FCA	Federal Court of Appeal
FCTD	Federal Court — Trial Division
FMV	Fair market value
FTC	Foreign tax credit
FTS	Flow-through share
GAAP	Generally accepted accounting principles in Canada
GAAR	General anti-avoidance rule
GIS	Guaranteed income supplement
GRIP	General rate income pool
GST	Goods and services tax
HATC	Home accessibility tax credit
HBP	Home Buyers' Plan
HRSDC	Human Resources and Skills Development Canada
HST	Harmonized sales tax
IC	Information Circular
IRA	Individual retirement account
IT	Interpretation Bulletin
ITA	*Income Tax Act* (Canada), R.S.C. 1985, c. 1 (5th Supp.)
ITAR	*Income Tax Application Rules* (federal), R.S.C. 1985, c. 2 (5th Supp.)
ITC	Investment tax credit
ITR	*Income Tax Regulations* (federal)
ITTN	Income Tax Technical News
JV	Joint venture
LLP	Lifelong learning plan
LP	Limited partnership
LPP	Listed personal property
LRIP	Low rate income pool
LSVCC	Labour-sponsored venture capital corporation
M&P	Manufacturing and processing
MURB	Multiple unit residential building
NAICS	North American Industry Classification System
NCBS	National child benefit supplement
NISA	Net Income Stabilization Account
NOA	Notice of assessment
NOO	Notice of objection
NOR	Notice of reassessment
OAS	Old Age Security
OIFP	Offshore investment fund property
PA	Pension adjustment
PAC	Price adjustment clause
PE	Permanent establishment
PRPP	Pooled Registered Pension Plan
PSB	Personal services business
PUC	Paid-up capital for income tax purposes
QDOT	Qualified domestic trust
QPIP	Quebec parental insurance plan
QPP	Quebec Pension Plan
QSBC	Qualified small business corporation
RCA	Retirement Compensation Arrangement

RDTOH	Refundable dividend tax on hand
RDSP	Registered Disability Savings Plan
REIT	Real estate investment trust
REOP	Reasonable expectation of profit
RESP	Registered Education Savings Plan
RPP	Registered Pension Plan
RRIF	Registered Retirement Income Fund
RRSP	Registered Retirement Savings Plan
SBC	Small business corporation
SBD	Small business deduction
SCC	Supreme Court of Canada
SIFT trust	Specified investment flow-through trust
SPC	Single purpose corporation
SPP	Saskatchewan Pension Plan
SR&ED	Scientific research and experimental development
T1	Personal Income Tax and Benefit Return
TAB	Tax Appeal Board
TCC	Tax Court of Canada
TCP	Taxable Canadian property
TDD	Tax Data Delivery
TEI	Tax Executive Institute
TFSA	Tax-free Savings Account
TIEA	Tax information exchange agreement
TSO	Tax Services Office
UCC	Undepreciated capital cost
UCCB	Universal child care benefit
VD	CRA Views Document (available on *Taxnet Pro*)
V-Day	Valuation day (FMV at end of 1971)
VDP	Voluntary Disclosure Program
WITB	Working Income Tax Benefit

Detailed Table of Contents

Chapter 1 — Personal Tax Filing and Payment Requirements

¶1000 Introduction to Canadian Income Tax

¶1010 Sources of Tax Law

¶1020 Liability for Canadian Tax

¶1100 Filing Requirement

¶1110 Requirement to File

¶1120 Method of Filing

¶1130 Filing Tax Elections

¶1140 Filing Due Date

¶1150 Identification Information

¶1200 Instalments and Balance-Due Payments

¶1210 Instalment Methods

¶1220 Interest Charges on Late or Deficient Tax Instalments

¶1230 Balance-Due Day and Interest Charges on Outstanding Payments

¶1240 My Account and Authorized Representatives

¶1300 Other Tax Compliance Requirements

¶1310 Foreign Investment and Income Information Reporting

¶1320 Reporting Tax Avoidance Transactions

¶1330 Claim for Tax Shelter Loss or Deduction

¶1400 Filing Due Dates, Forms, Remitting and Penalties

¶1410 Filing Requirements Quick Reference Table

¶1420 Penalties Quick Reference Table

¶1430 Third-Party Penalties

¶1500 Taxpayer Relief Provisions

¶1510 Voluntary Disclosures

¶1520 Requests for Taxpayer Relief

Chapter 2 — Employment Income and Deductions

¶2000 Employment Income (T1: Lines 101, 102, 104)

¶2005 Income from an Office or Employment

¶2010 Loss from an Office or Employment

¶2015 Employee vs. Independent Contractor

¶2020 Salary Deferral Arrangements

¶2025 Professional Athletes

¶2100 Taxation of Employment Benefits and Allowances (T1: Lines 101, 102, 104)

¶2105 Accumulated Vacation and Sick Leave Credits

¶2110 Advances

¶2115 Aircraft (personal use of)

¶2120 Allowances

¶2125 Apprenticeship Incentive Grant

¶2130 Automobile and Motor Vehicle Benefits and Allowances

¶2135 Board and Lodging

¶2140 Cellular Phones, Computers and Internet

¶2145 Child Care Expenses

¶2150 Commissions

¶2155 Counselling Services

¶2160 Deferred Salary Payments

¶2165 Directors' Fees

¶2170 Disability-Related Employment Benefits

¶2175 Discounts on Merchandise and Commissions from Personal Sales

¶2180 Employee Benefit Plans

¶2185 Employee Health and Welfare Trusts/Employee Life and Health Trusts

¶2190 Employee Profit Sharing Plans

¶2195 Employment Insurance Premiums

¶2200 Flexible Benefit Plans

¶2205 Gifts, Awards and Long-Service Awards

¶2210 Government Grants

¶2215 Gratuities and Tips

¶2220 Group Life Insurance Premiums

¶2225 Income Tax Paid by Employer

¶2230 Injury Leave Pay

¶2235 Loans — Interest-Free and Low-Interest

¶2240 Loyalty and Other Points Programs

¶2245 Meals

¶2250 Member of Legislative Assembly (MLA) Expense Allowance

¶2255 Miscellaneous Employee Benefits

Detailed Table of Contents

¶2260 Moving Expenses

¶2265 Municipal Officer's Expense Allowance

¶2270 Parking

¶2275 Private Health Services Plan Premiums

¶2280 Prizes and Awards

¶2285 Professional Membership Dues

¶2290 Provincial Hospital or Health Care Plan Premiums

¶2295 Recreational Facilities and Club Dues

¶2300 Reimbursements and Awards

¶2301 Research Grants

¶2305 Retirement Compensation Arrangements (RCAs)

¶2310 Scholarships, Fellowships and Bursaries

¶2315 Security Options Benefit

¶2320 Service Pension or Allowance

¶2325 Social Events

¶2330 Special Payments by Employers

¶2335 Statutory Exemptions

¶2340 Strike Pay

¶2345 Tool Reimbursement or Allowance

¶2350 Transportation

¶2355 Tuition and Training Fees

¶2360 Uniforms and Special Clothing

¶2365 Vacations (Employer-Paid)

¶2370 Workers' Compensation Payments

¶2400 Deductions from Employment Income

¶2401 Employee and Partner GST/HST Rebate (T1: Line 457)

¶2405 Annual Union, Professional and Membership Dues (T1: Line 212)

¶2410 Apprentice Mechanics' Tools Deduction (T1: Line 229)

¶2415 Apprenticeship Incentive Grant Repayment (T1: Line 232)

¶2420 Artists' Employment Expenses (T1: Line 229)

¶2425 Canadian Forces Personnel and Police Deduction (T1: Line 244)

¶2430 Clergy Residence Deduction (T1: Line 231)

¶2435 Commission Sales Employees (T1: Line 229)

¶2440 Employee Home Relocation Loan Deduction (T1: Line 248)

¶2445 Employee Profit Sharing Plans (T1: Line 232)

¶2450 Legal Fees (T1: Line 232)

¶2455 Motor Vehicle (or Aircraft) Expenses (T1: Line 229)

¶2460 Musical Instrument Expenses (T1: Line 229)

¶2465 Northern Residents' Deduction (T1: Line 255)

¶2470 Office Rent and Home Office Expenses (T1: Line 229)

¶2475 Overseas Employment Tax Credit (T1 Schedule 1: Line 426)

¶2480 Power Saw Operators (T1: Line 229)

¶2485 Railway Employees' Expenses (T1: Line 229)

¶2490 Reimbursement of Disability Payments (T1: Line 232)

¶2495 Reimbursement of Salary (T1: Line 232)

¶2500 Retirement Compensation Arrangement (RCA) (T1: Line 232)

¶2505 Salary Paid to a Substitute or Assistant (T1: Line 229)

¶2510 Security Options Deduction (T1: Line 249)

¶2515 Supplies (T1: Line 229)

¶2520 Tradesperson's Tools Deduction (T1: Line 229)

¶2525 Transport Employees' Expenses (T1: Line 229)

¶2530 Travelling Expenses (T1: Line 229)

Chapter 3 — Dividend, Interest, and Other Investment Income

¶3100 Dividend Income (Schedule 4: Part I, Line 120)

¶3105 Meaning of Taxable Dividend

¶3110 Dividends from Canadian Corporations

¶3115 Dividends from Non-Resident Corporations

¶3120 Dividends Received by Spouse or Common-Law Partner

¶3125 Capital Dividends

¶3130 Deemed Dividends

¶3135 Dividends in Kind

¶3140 Stock Dividends

¶3145 Patronage Dividends

¶3150 Capital Gains Dividends

¶3155 Demutualization Benefits

¶3160 Securities Lending Arrangements

¶3165 Dividend Rental Arrangements

Detailed Table of Contents

¶3200 Interest Income (Schedule 4: Part II, Line 121)

¶3205 Taxation of Interest Income (Accrual Rules)

¶3210 Definition of Interest

¶3215 Canada Savings Bonds

¶3220 Treasury Bills

¶3225 Indexed, Prescribed and Deep Discount Debt Obligations

¶3230 Interest on Bonds Transferred between Interest Dates

¶3235 Blended Payments

¶3245 Interest on Tax Refunds

¶3250 Interest Included in Damage Awards

¶3300 Other Investment Income (Schedule 4: Part II, Line 121)

¶3305 Annuities

¶3310 Life Insurance

¶3315 Mutual Fund Income

¶3320 Income Trusts and Specified Investment Flow-Through Trusts

¶3325 Royalties and Payments Based on Production or Use

¶3330 Loans to Shareholders

¶3335 Loans to Non-Arm's Length Individuals

¶3340 Transfer of the Right to Income

¶3400 Income from Trusts and Estates (Schedule 4: Part II, Line 121)

¶3410 Taxation of Trust Distributions to Beneficiaries

¶3420 Non-Resident Beneficiaries

¶3430 Non-Resident Trusts

¶3500 Foreign Investment Income (Schedule 4: Part II, Line 121)

¶3510 Offshore Investment Fund Property

¶3520 Foreign Accrual and Property Income (FAPI)

¶3530 Foreign Investment and Income Information Reporting

¶3600 Net Partnership Income: Limited or Non-Active Partners Only (T1: Line 122)

¶3610 Limited Partner Definition

¶3620 At-Risk Amount

¶3700 Deductions in Computing Investment Income (Schedule 4: Part III, Line 221)

¶3710 Carrying Charges

¶3720 Interest Expense

Chapter 4 — Capital Gains and Losses

¶4000 Dispositions of Capital Property

¶4005 Capital Gains and Losses (Sch. 3)

¶4010 Capital Gains versus Income

¶4015 Adventure or Concern in the Nature of Trade

¶4100 Computation of Capital Gains and Losses

¶4110 Proceeds of Disposition (Sch. 3: Col. 2)

¶4120 Adjusted Cost Base (ACB) of Capital Property (Sch. 3: Col. 3)

¶4130 Total Capital Gains (Sch. 3: Line 191)

¶4140 Capital Gains Reserves (Sch. 3: Line 192)

¶4200 Qualified Dispositions (Sch. 3: Parts 1 and 2)

¶4210 Lifetime Capital Gains Exemption

¶4220 Qualified Small Business Corporation Shares (Sch. 3: Part 1)

¶4230 Qualified Farm or Fishing Property (Sch. 3: Part 2)

¶4240 Cumulative Net Investment Loss (CNIL)

¶4250 Surplus Stripping

¶4300 Disposition of Publicly Traded Shares, Mutual Fund Units, Deferral of Eligible Small Business Corporation Shares and Other Shares (Sch. 3: Part 3)

¶4310 Disposition of Mutual Fund Units or Shares

¶4315 Disposition of Digital Currencies

¶4320 Employee Security Options

¶4330 Donations of Capital Property

¶4340 Capital Gains Deferral for Eligible Small Business Corporation Shares

¶4350 Proceeds of Disposition of Securities: Special Rules

¶4360 Investments in a Bankrupt Corporation: Deemed Disposition of Shares

¶4370 Convertible Shares or Debt

¶4400 Disposition of Real Estate, Depreciable Property and Other Properties (Sch. 3: Part 4)

¶4410 Disposition of Land and Building

¶4420 Disposition of Depreciable Property

¶4430 Principal Residence Exemption

¶4500 Disposition of Bonds, Debentures, Promissory Notes and Other Properties (Sch. 3: Parts 5–8)

¶4510 Bonds, Debentures, Treasury Bills, Promissory Notes and Similar Properties (Sch. 3: Part 5)

¶4520 Debts Held on Capital Account (Bad Debts) (Sch. 3: Part 5)

¶4530 Foreign Exchange Gains and Losses on Capital Account (Sch. 3: Part 5)

¶4540 Options to Buy or Sell Property (Sch. 3: Part 5)

¶4550 Other Capital Properties (Sch. 3: Part 5)

¶4560 Other Mortgage Foreclosures and Conditional Sales Repossessions (Sch.3 Part 6)

¶4570 Personal-Use Property (Sch.3: Parts 7 and 8)

¶4600 Allowable Business Investment Losses (ABILs)

¶4610 Deductibility of ABILs (T1: Lines 217 and 228; Sch. 3: Line 178)

¶4620 Small Business Corporation Definition

¶4630 Guarantees of Debt

¶4700 Replacement Property Rules

¶4710 Former Business Property

¶4720 Replacement Property (Involuntary Dispositions)

¶4730 Applicable Rollover Rules Where Election is Filed

¶4740 Disposition of Land and Building: Reallocation of Proceeds

¶4800 Miscellaneous Loss Denial and Limitation Rules

¶4810 Losses on Transfers between Affiliated Persons

¶4820 Dividend Stop-Loss Rules

Chapter 5 — Rental Income

¶5000 Rental Income (T1 Lines 126 and 160)

¶5005 U.S. Rental Income

¶5100 Real Property Rental: Business or Property Income?

¶5110 Nature of Rental Income

¶5120 Income Tax Consequences

¶5200 Rental Expenses

¶5210 Current vs. Capital Expense

¶5220 Deductible Rental Expenses

¶5230 Non-Deductible Expenses

¶5240 Capital Cost Allowance (CCA) (Form T776: Lines 9936, 9947, 9948, Charts A-F)

¶5250 Rental Expenses: Special Situations

¶5300 Rental Losses

¶5400 Principal Residence: Change-in-Use Rules

¶5410 Change in Use from Personal to Income Producing

¶5420 Change in Use from Income-Producing to Personal

¶5430 Partial Changes in Use

¶5500 Non-Residents Electing under Section 216

    ¶5510 Alternative re Rents

    ¶5520 Meaning of "Timber Royalty"

    ¶5530 Optional Method of Payment

    ¶5540 Subsequent Sale of Canadian Property

    ¶5550 Rental or Other Business

¶5600 Completing Form T776, *Statement of Real Estate Rentals*

    ¶5610 Identification and Details of Other Co-Owners

    ¶5620 Rental Income (Form T776: Lines 8141, 8230, 8299)

    ¶5630 Rental Expenses

Chapter 6 — Business and Professional Income

¶6100 Business Income (T1: Lines 135, 162)

    ¶6110 Determining Business Income

    ¶6120 Limitations on Deductibility of Expenses

    ¶6130 Allowable Deductions for Expenses

    ¶6140 Non-Allowable Deductions for Expenses

    ¶6150 Capital Cost Allowance (CCA)

    ¶6160 Eligible Capital Expenditures

    ¶6170 Special Situations

¶6200 Professional Income (T1: Lines 137, 164)

    ¶6210 Determining Professional Income

    ¶6220 Election to Exclude Work in Progress

    ¶6230 Professional Expenses

    ¶6240 Incorporation of a Professional Practice

    ¶6250 Service and Management Corporations

¶6300 Farming and Fishing Income (T1: Lines 141, 143, 168, 170)

    ¶6310 Computing Farming and Fishing Income

    ¶6320 Definition of Farming and Fishing

    ¶6330 Other Considerations

    ¶6340 Net Income Stabilization Account (NISA)

    ¶6350 Farming Losses

Detailed Table of Contents

Chapter 7 — Depreciation, Amortization, and Resource Deductions

¶7000 Depreciable Property Quick Reference Table

¶7005 CCA Class Summary Table

¶7006 Accelerated Investment Incentive for Capital Cost Allowance (ACCA)

¶7100 Capital Cost Allowance (CCA)

¶7105 General Rules Applicable to Depreciable Property

¶7110 CCA Claim for the Year (Form T776 or T2125: Part A)

¶7115 Depreciable Property Additions (Form T776 or T2125: Part A, Column 3)

¶7120 Adjustment for Current-Year Additions (Form T776 or T2125: Part A, Column 6)

¶7125 Available-For-Use Rules

¶7130 Depreciable Property — Special Situations

¶7135 Dispositions of Depreciable Property (Form T776 or T2125: Part A, Column 4)

¶7140 Half-Year Rule (Form T776 or T2125 Part A: Column 6)

¶7145 CCA Recapture (Form T776: Line 9947, Form T2125: Line 8230)

¶7150 Terminal Losses (Form T776: Line 9948, Form T2125: Line 9270)

¶7155 Property included in a Separate Class

¶7160 "Luxury" Passenger Vehicles (Class 10.1)

¶7165 Rental Properties

¶7170 Revising CCA Claims

¶7200 Special Depreciable Property Rules

¶7205 Patents, Franchises, Concessions, and Licences

¶7210 Leasehold Interests (Class 13)

¶7215 Specified Leasing Property

¶7220 Lease Transactions

¶7225 Mining Projects (Classes 41, 41.2)

¶7230 Oil Sands Projects (Classes 41, 41.1)

¶7235 Clean Energy Equipment (Classes 43.1, 43.2)

¶7300 Eligible Capital Property

¶7305 Eligible Capital Property Additions (Applicable before 2017)

¶7310 Eligible Capital Amounts (Applicable before 2017)

¶7315 Gain on Dispositions of Eligible Capital Property (Applicable before 2017)

¶7320 Restrictive Covenants

¶7325 Class 14.1

¶7400 Resource Pools

¶7405 Canadian Exploration Expenses (CEE) (Form T1229: Parts II and III)

¶7410 Canadian Development Expenses (CDE) (Form T1229: Parts II and III)

¶7415 Canadian Oil and Gas Property Expenses (COGPE) (Form T1229: Parts II and III)

Chapter 8 — Pensions and Other Income

¶8000 Pensions and Other Income

¶8100 Pension Income (T1: Lines 113–116)

¶8110 Old Age Security Pension (T1: Line 113)

¶8120 CPP/QPP Benefits (T1: Line 114)

¶8130 Other Pensions or Superannuation (T1: Line 115)

¶8140 Elected Split-Pension Amount (T1: Line 116)

¶8200 Other Income (T1: Lines 117–130)

¶8210 Universal Child Care Benefit (T1: Line 117)

¶8220 Employment Insurance & Other Benefits (T1: Line 119)

¶8230 Registered Disability Savings Plan Income (T1: Line 125)

¶8240 Support Payments Received (T1: Line 128)

¶8250 RRSP Income (T1: Line 129)

¶8260 Other Income (T1: Line 130)

¶8300 Workers' Compensation and Other Benefits (T1: Lines 144, 145, 146)

¶8310 Workers' Compensation Benefits (T1: Line 144)

¶8320 Social Assistance Payments (T1: Line 145)

¶8330 Net Federal Supplements (T1: Line 146)

Chapter 9 — Other Deductions

¶9000 Other Deductions

¶9010 Personal Tax Deductions Quick Reference Table

¶9100 Deductions from Total Income (T1: Lines 205–235)

¶9105 PRPP Employer Contributions (T1: Line 205)

¶9110 Pension Adjustment (T1: Line 206)

¶9120 Registered Pension Plan Deduction (T1: Line 207)

¶9130 RRSP and PRPP Deduction (T1: Line 208)

¶9140 Deduction for Elected Split-Pension Amount (T1: Line 210)

¶9150 Annual Union, Professional or Like Dues (T1: Line 212)

¶9160 Universal Child Care Benefit Repayment (T1: Line 213)

¶9170 Child Care Expenses (T1: Line 214)

¶9180 Disability Supports Deduction (T1: Line 215)

¶9190 Business Investment Loss (T1: Line 217)

¶9200 Moving Expenses (T1: Line 219)

¶9210 Support Payments Made (T1: Line 220)

¶9220 Carrying Charges & Interest Expenses (T1 Line 221)

¶9230 Deduction for CPP or QPP Contributions on Self-Employment and Other Earnings (T1: Line 222)

¶9240 Exploration & Development Expenses (T1: Line 224)

¶9250 Other Employment Expenses (T1: Line 229)

¶9260 Clergy Residence Deduction (T1: Line 231)

¶9270 Other Deductions (T1: Line 232)

¶9280 Social Benefits Repayment (T1: Line 235)

¶9300 Deductions from Net Income (T1: Lines 244–256)

¶9310 Canadian Forces Personnel and Police Deduction (T1: Line 244)

¶9320 Employee Home Relocation Loan Deduction (T1: Line 248)

¶9330 Security Options Deductions (T1: Line 249)

¶9340 Other Payments Deduction (T1: Line 250)

¶9350 Limited Partnership Losses of Other Years (T1: Line 251)

¶9360 Non-Capital Losses of Other Years (T1: Line 252)

¶9370 Net Capital Losses of Other Years (T1: Line 253)

¶9380 Capital Gains Deduction (T1: Line 254)

¶9390 Northern Residents Deduction (T1: Line 255)

¶9400 Additional Deductions (T1: Line 256)

Chapter 10 — Federal Non-Refundable Tax Credits

¶10000 Federal Non-Refundable Tax Credits (T1 Schedule 1: Lines 300–398)

¶10005 Personal Tax Credits Quick Reference Table

¶10010 Basic Personal Amount (T1 Schedule 1: Line 300)

¶10020 Age Amount (T1 Schedule 1: Line 301)

¶10030 Spouse or Common-Law Partner Amount (T1 Schedule 1: Line 303)

¶10035 Canada Caregiver Amount for Spouse or Common-Law Partner, or Eligible Dependant Age 18 or Older (T1 Schedule 1: Line 304)

¶10040 Amount for an Eligible Dependent (T1 Schedule 1: Line 305)

¶10050 Amount for Infirm Dependants Age 18 or Older (T1 Schedule 1: Line 306)

¶10055 Canada Caregiver Amount for Other Infirm Dependants Age 18 or Older (T1 Schedule 1: Line 307)

¶10060 CPP/QPP Contributions through Employment (T1 Schedule 1: Line 308)

¶10070 CPP/QPP Contributions on Self-Employment and Other Earnings (T1 Schedule 1: Line 310)

¶10080 Employment Insurance Premiums through Employment (T1 Schedule 1: Line 312)

¶10090 Adoption Expenses (T1 Schedule 1: Line 313)

¶10100 Pension Income Amount (T1 Schedule 1: Line 314)

¶10110 Caregiver Amount (T1 Schedule 1: Line 315)

¶10120 Disability Amount (for self) (T1 Schedule 1: Line 316)

¶10130 Employment Insurance Premiums on Self-Employment (T1 Schedule 1: Line 317)

¶10140 Disability Amount Transferred from a Dependant (T1 Schedule 1: Line 318)

¶10150 Interest Paid on Your Student Loans (T1 Schedule 1: Line 319)

¶10160 Tuition, Education and Textbook Amounts (T1 Schedule 1: Line 323)

¶10170 Tuition Amounts Transferred from a Child (T1 Schedule 1: Line 324)

¶10180 Amounts Transferred from Spouse or Common-Law Partner (T1 Schedule 1: Line 326)

¶10190 Medical Expenses for Self, Spouse and Dependent Children (T1 Schedule 1: Line 330)

¶10200 Medical Expenses for Other Dependants (T1 Schedule 1: Line 331)

¶10210 Donations and Gifts (T1 Schedule 1: Line 349)

¶10220 Volunteer Firefighters' Amount (T1 Schedule 1: Line 362)

¶10230 Canada Employment Amount (T1 Schedule 1: Line 363)

¶10240 Public Transit Amount (T1 Schedule 1: Line 364)

¶10250 Children's Fitness Amount (T1 Schedule 1: Line 365)

¶10260 Canada Caregiver Amount for Infirm Children Under 18 Years of Age (T1 Schedule 1: Line 367)

¶10270 Home Buyers' Amount (T1 Schedule 1: Line 369)

¶10280 Children's Arts Amount (T1 Schedule 1: Line 370)

¶10290 Search and Rescue Volunteers Tax Credit (T1 Schedule 1: Line 395)

¶10300 Home Accessibility Tax Credit (T1 Schedule 1: Line 398)

Chapter 11 — Calculation of Net Federal Tax

¶11000 Calculation of Net Federal Tax (T1 Schedule 1: Lines 405–427)

¶11010 Federal Foreign Tax Credit (T1 Schedule 1: Line 405)

¶11020 Federal Political Contribution Tax Credit (T1 Schedule 1: Line 410)

¶11030 Investment Tax Credit (T1 Schedule 1: Line 412)

¶11040 Labour-Sponsored Funds Tax Credit (T1 Schedule 1: Lines 413, 414)

¶11050 Working Income Tax Benefit Advance Payments (T1 Schedule 1: Line 415)

¶11060 Special Taxes (T1 Schedule 1: Line 418)

¶11065 Family Tax Cut Credit (T1 Schedule 1: Line 423)

¶11070 Federal Tax on Split Income (T1 Schedule 1: Line 424)

¶11080 Federal Dividend Tax Credit (T1 Schedule 1: Line 425)

¶11090 Overseas Employment Tax Credit (T1 Schedule 1: Line 426)

¶11100 Minimum Tax Carryover (T1 Schedule 1: Line 427)

¶11200 Calculation of Refund Due or Balance Owing (T1: Lines 420–486)

¶11210 CPP Contributions Payable on Self-Employment and Other Earnings (T1: Line 421)

¶11220 Social Benefits Repayment (T1: Line 422)

¶11230 EI Premiums Payable on Self-Employment and Other Earnings (T1: Line 430)

¶11240 Total Income Tax Deducted (T1: Line 437)

¶11250 Refundable Quebec Abatement (T1: Line 440)

¶11260 CPP Overpayment (T1: Line 448)

¶11270 Employment Insurance Overpayment (T1: Line 450)

¶11280 Refundable Medical Expense Supplement (T1: Line 452)

¶11290 Working Income Tax Benefit (T1: Line 453)

¶11300 Refund of Investment Tax Credit (T1: Line 454)

¶11310 Part XII.2 Trust Tax Credit (T1: Line 456)

¶11320 Employee and Partner GST/HST Rebate (T1: Line 457)

¶11325 Children's Fitness Tax Credit (T1: Lines 458, 459)

¶11330 Eligible Educator School Supply Tax Credit (T1: Lines 468, 469)

¶11340 Tax Paid by Instalments (T1: Line 476)

¶11350 Refund or Balance Owing (T1: Lines 484, 485)

Chapter 12 — Provincial and Territorial Taxes and Credits

¶12010 Provincial Tax Overview

¶12020 Provincial Residence

¶12030 Provincial or Territorial Tax (Form T1: Line 428)

¶12040 Provincial or Territorial Credits (Form T1: Line 479)

¶12050 Administration and Enforcement

¶12100 Alberta

¶12110 Liability for Tax

¶12120 Tax Rate

¶12130 Tax on Split Income (Form AB428: Line 34)

¶12140 Additional Minimum Tax (Form AB428: Line 42)

¶12150 Non-Refundable Tax Credits

¶12160 Other Tax Credits, Benefits and Incentives

¶12200 British Columbia

¶12210 Liability for Tax

¶12220 Tax Rates

¶12230 Tax on Split Income (Form BC428: Line 42)

¶12240 Additional Minimum Tax (Form BC428: Line 50)

¶12250 Non-Refundable Tax Credits

¶12260 Other Tax Credits, Benefits and Incentives

¶12300 Manitoba

¶12310 Liability for Tax

¶12320 Tax Rates

¶12330 Tax on Split Income (Form MB428: Line 43)

¶12340 Additional Minimum Tax (Form MB428: Line 51)

¶12350 Non-Refundable Tax Credits

¶12360 Other Tax Credits, Benefits and Incentives

¶12400 New Brunswick

¶12410 Liability for Tax

¶12420 Tax Rates

¶12430 Tax on Split Income (Form NB428: Line 39)

¶12440 Additional Minimum Tax (Form NB428: Line 48)

¶12450 Non-Refundable Tax Credits

¶12460 Other Tax Credits, Benefits and Incentives

¶12500 Newfoundland and Labrador

¶12510 Liability for Tax

¶12520 Tax Rates

¶12530 Tax on Split Income (Form NL428: Line 42)

¶12540 Additional Minimum Tax (Form NL428: Line 50)

¶12550 Non-Refundable Tax Credits

¶12560 Other Tax Credits, Benefits and Incentives

¶12600 Northwest Territories

¶12610 Liability for Tax

¶12620 Tax Rates

¶12630 Tax on Split Income (Form NT428: Line 39)

¶12640 Additional Minimum Tax (Form NT428: Line 47)

¶12650 Non-Refundable Tax Credits

Detailed Table of Contents

¶12660 Other Tax Credits, Benefits and Incentives

¶12700 Nova Scotia

  ¶12710 Liability for Tax

  ¶12720 Tax Rates

  ¶12730 Tax on Split Income (Form NS428: Line 41)

  ¶12740 Additional Minimum Tax (Form NS428: Line 49)

  ¶12750 Non-Refundable Tax Credits

  ¶12760 Other Tax Credits, Benefits and Incentives

¶12800 Nunavut

  ¶12810 Liability for Tax

  ¶12820 Tax Rates

  ¶12830 Tax on Split Income (Form NU428: Line 40)

  ¶12840 Additional Minimum Tax (Form NU428: Line 48)

  ¶12850 Non-Refundable Tax Credits, Benefits and Incentives

  ¶12860 Other Tax Credits

¶12900 Ontario

  ¶12910 Liability for Tax

  ¶12920 Tax Rates

  ¶12930 Tax on Split Income (Form ON428: Line 40)

  ¶12940 Additional Minimum Tax (Form ON428: Line 48)

  ¶12950 Non-Refundable Tax Credits

  ¶12960 Other Tax Credits, Benefits and Incentives

¶121000 Prince Edward Island

  ¶121010 Liability for Tax

  ¶121020 Tax Rates

  ¶121030 Tax on Split Income (Form PE428: Line 41)

  ¶121040 Additional Minimum Tax (Form PE428: Line 49)

  ¶121050 Non-Refundable Tax Credits

  ¶121060 Other Tax Credits, Benefits and Incentives

¶121100 Saskatchewan

  ¶121110 Liability for Tax

  ¶121120 Tax Rates

  ¶121130 Tax on Split Income (Form SK428: Line 45)

  ¶121140 Additional Minimum Tax (Form SK428: Line 53)

  ¶121150 Non-Refundable Tax Credits

¶121160 Other Tax Credits, Benefits and Incentives

¶121200 Yukon

¶121210 Liability for Tax

¶121220 Tax Rates

¶121230 Tax on Split Income (Form YT428: Line 45)

¶121240 Additional Minimum Tax (Form YT428: Line 53)

¶121250 Non-Refundable Tax Credits

¶121260 Other Tax Credits, Benefits and Incentives

Chapter 13 — Completing the Québec Income Tax Return (Form TP-1)

¶13000 Introduction

¶13010 Overview and New for 2018

¶13020 Who Must File a Québec Income Tax Return

¶13030 Definition of Spouse

¶13040 Definition of Business Establishment

¶13050 Residency

¶13060 Filing Deadline and Penalties

¶13070 Solidarity Tax Credit

¶13100 Calculating Total Income (Form TP-1: Lines 96–199)

¶13105 Overview

¶13110 Income from Transferred Property

¶13115 Employment Income (Form TP-1: Line 101)

¶13120 Retirement Income Transferred by a Spouse (Form TP-1: Line 123)

¶13125 Dividends from Taxable Canadian Corporations (Form TP-1: Lines 128, 166, 167)

¶13130 Interest and Other Investment Income (Form TP-1: Line 130)

¶13135 Rental Income (Form TP-1: Lines 136, 168)

¶13140 Capital Gains (Form TP-1: Line 139)

¶13145 Support Payments (Form TP-1: Line 142)

¶13150 Income Replacement Indemnities and Net Federal Supplements (Form TP-1: Line 148)

¶13155 Other Income (Form TP-1: Line 154)

¶13160 Business Income (Form TP-1: Line 164)

¶13200 Calculating Net Income (Form TP-1: Lines 201 to 275)

¶13205 Deduction for Workers (Form TP-1: Line 201)

¶13210 Registered Pension Plan Deduction (Form TP-1: Line 205)

¶13215 Employment Expenses and Deductions (Form TP-1: Line 207)

¶13220 RRSP Deduction (Form TP-1: Line 214)

¶13225 Support Payments (Form TP-1: Line 225)

¶13230 Moving Expenses (Form TP-1: Line 228)

¶13235 Carrying Charges and Interest Expenses (Form TP-1: Line 231)

¶13240 Business Investment Loss (Form TP-1: Line 234)

¶13245 Deduction for Residents of Designated Remote Areas (Form TP-1: Line 236)

¶13250 Deduction for Exploration and Development Expenses (Form TP-1: Line 241)

¶13255 Deduction for Amounts Contributed to the QPP and the QPIP on Income from Self-Employment (Form TP-1: Line 248)

¶13260 Other Deductions (Form TP-1: Line 250)

¶13265 Carry-Over of the Adjustment of Investment Expenses (Form TP-1: Line 252)

¶13270 Adjustment of Investment Expenses (Form TP-1: Line 260)

¶13300 Calculating Taxable Income (Form TP-1: Lines 276–299)

¶13305 Adjustment of Deductions (Form TP-1: Line 276)

¶13310 UCCB and Income from a Registered Disability Savings Plan (Form TP-1: Line 278)

¶13315 Deduction for Strategic Investments (Form TP-1: Line 287)

¶13320 Non-Capital Losses from Other Years (Form T-1: Line 289)

¶13325 Net Capital Losses from Other Years (Form TP-1: Line 290)

¶13330 Capital Gains Deduction (Form TP-1: Line 292)

¶13335 Deduction for an Indian (Form TP-1: Line 293)

¶13340 Deductions for Certain Income (Form TP-1: Line 295)

¶13345 Miscellaneous Deductions (Form TP-1: Line 297)

¶13400 Non-Refundable Tax Credits (Form TP-1: Lines 350–399)

¶13405 Basic Personal Amount (Form TP-1: Line 350)

¶13410 Age Amount, Amount for a Person Living Alone, and Amount for Retirement Income (Form TP-1: Line 361)

¶13415 Amount for Dependants and Amount Transferred by a Child 18 or over Enrolled in Post-Secondary Studies (Form TP-1: Line 367)

¶13420 Union, Professional or Other Dues (Form TP-1: Line 373)

¶13425 Amount for a Severe and Prolonged Impairment in Mental or Physical Functions (Form TP-1: Line 376)

¶13430 Expenses for Medical Services Not Available in your Area (Form TP-1: Line 378)

¶13435 Medical Expenses (Form TP-1: Line 381)

¶13440 Tuition or Examination Fees (Form TP-1: Line 384)

¶13445 Interest Paid on a Student Loan (Form TP-1: Line 385)

¶13450 Tuition or Examination Fees Transferred by a Child (Form TP-1: Line 387)

¶13455 Tax Credit for Volunteer Firefighters (Form TP-1: Line 390)

¶13460 Tax Credit for Workers 65 or Older (Form TP-1: Line 391)

¶13465 Tax Credit for Recent Graduates Working in Remote Resource Regions (Form TP-1: Line 392)

¶13470 Donations and Gifts (Form TP-1: Line 393)

¶13500 Income Tax and Contributions (Form TP-1: Lines 401–450)

¶13505 Income Tax on Taxable Income (Form TP-1: Line 401)

¶13510 Tax Adjustment (Form TP-1, Schedule E: Line 402)

¶13515 Foreign Tax Credit (Form TP-1, Schedule E: Line 409)

¶13520 Tax Credit for the Beneficiary of a Designated Trust (Form TP-1: Line 411)

¶13525 Tax Credit for Contributions to Authorized Québec Political Parties (Form TP-1: Line 414)

¶13530 Dividend Tax Credit (Form TP-1: Line 415)

¶13535 Tax Credit for the Acquisition of Capital Régional et Coopératif Desjardins Shares (Form TP-1: Line 422)

¶13540 Tax Credit for a Labour-Sponsored Fund (Form TP-1: Line 424)

¶13545 Credits Transferred from One Spouse to the Other (Form TP-1: Line 431)

¶13550 Alternative Minimum Tax (Form TP-1: Line 432, Schedule E)

¶13555 Special Taxes (Form TP-1: Line 443)

¶13560 Health Contribution (Form TP-1: Line 448)

¶13600 Calculating Refund or Balance Due (Form TP-1: Lines 451–479)

¶13605 Tax Credit for Childcare Expenses (Form TP-1: Line 455)

¶13610 Tax Credits Respecting the Work Premium (Form TP-1: Line 456)

¶13615 Tax Credit for Home-Support Services for Seniors (Form TP-1: Line 458)

¶13620 QST Rebate for Employees and Partners (Form TP-1: Line 459)

¶13621 — Tax Shield (Form TP-1: Line 460)

¶13625 Other Credits (Form TP-1: Line 462)

¶13630 Refund (Form TP-1: Line 474)

¶13635 Transfer to Spouse (Form TP-1: Lines 476, 477)

¶13700 Assessment

¶13710 Assessment

¶13720 Recourse

Chapter 14 — Assessments, Audits, and Avoidance Rules

¶14000 Adjustments, Assessments, and Objections

¶14010 Adjusting a Filed T1 Return

¶14020 Assessments and Reassessments

¶14030 Assessment Checklist

¶14040 Waivers

¶14050 Objections

¶14100 Audits and Investigations

¶14110 Tax Audits

¶14120 Books and Records

¶14130 Investigations and Inspections

¶14140 Solicitor-Client Privilege

¶14200 Income Splitting and the Attribution Rules

¶14210 Tax on Split Income (TOSI)

¶14220 Transfers and Loans to Spouse or Common-Law Partner and Minors

¶14230 Attribution of Gains/Losses to Spouse or Common Law Partner

¶14240 Transfers and Loans to a Trust

¶14250 Transfers and Loans to a Corporation

¶14260 Transfers of Property to a Reversionary Trust

¶14270 Income Splitting Strategies

¶14300 Other Avoidance Rules

¶14310 Benefit Conferred (Indirect Payments or Transfers)

¶14320 Transfer of Income Rights

¶14330 Non-Arm's Length Loans

¶14340 Inadequate Consideration

¶14350 Shareholder Benefits and Loans

¶14360 Non-Arm's Length Sale of Shares (Surplus Stripping)

¶14400 General-Anti Avoidance Rule (GAAR)

¶14410 Consequences of GAAR Applying

¶14420 Series of Transactions

¶14430 Post-Canada Trustco GAAR Cases

Chapter 15 — Canadian Taxation of Non-Residents and Deemed Residents

¶15100 Determining Residency for Tax Purposes

¶15110 Common Law Rules

¶15120 Deeming Rules

¶15130 Ceasing Canadian Residency

¶15140 Part-Year Residents

¶15200 Dispositions of Taxable Canadian Property

    ¶15210 Excluded Dispositions

    ¶15220 Certificates of Compliance

¶15300 Payments Subject to Withholding Tax

    ¶15310 Interest Payments

    ¶15320 Dividend Payments

    ¶15330 Rents and Royalties

    ¶15340 Pensions and Other Benefits

¶15400 Filing Requirements for Non-Residents & Deemed Residents

    ¶15410 Elective Returns for Non-Residents

¶15500 Emigration and Immigration

    ¶15510 Emigrating from Canada

    ¶15520 Immigrating to Canada

Chapter 16 — Tax Planning, Registered Plans, and U.S. Tax Considerations

¶16100 Tax Planning

    ¶16110 Owner-Manager Remuneration Planning

    ¶16120 Post-Mortem Tax Planning and Elections

¶16200 Registered Plans

    ¶16210 Tax-Free Savings Accounts (TFSAs)

    ¶16220 Registered Education Savings Plans (RESPs)

    ¶16230 Registered Disability Savings Plans (RDSPs)

    ¶16240 Comparing Registered Plans

¶16300 U.S. Tax Considerations for Canadians with U.S. Connections

    ¶16310 U.S. Income Tax

    ¶16320 U.S. Estate Tax

    ¶16330 U.S. Filing Due Dates, Forms, Remitting, and Penalties

Appendix A — Medical Expense Credit Quick Reference Table

Appendix B — Tax Reference Tables

B-1   Federal and Provincial/Territorial Income Tax Rates and Brackets — 2018

B-2   Federal and Provincial/Territorial Non-Refundable Tax Credit Rates and Amounts for 2018

B-3   Québec Non-Refundable and Refundable Tax Credit Rates and Amounts for 2018

B-4   Combined Top Marginal Tax Rates for Individuals — 2018

Detailed Table of Contents

B-5   Retirement and Savings Plans — Contribution Limits
B-6   Automobiles — Deductions and Benefits

Chapter 1 — Personal Tax Filing and Payment Requirements

Contents

¶1000 Introduction to Canadian Income Tax

    ¶1010 Sources of Tax Law

    ¶1020 Liability for Canadian Tax

¶1100 Filing Requirement

    ¶1110 Requirement to File

    ¶1120 Method of Filing

    ¶1130 Filing Tax Elections

    ¶1140 Filing Due Date

    ¶1150 Identification Information

¶1200 Instalments and Balance-Due Payments

    ¶1210 Instalment Methods

    ¶1220 Interest Charges on Late or Deficient Tax Instalments

    ¶1230 Balance-Due Day and Interest Charges on Outstanding Payments

    ¶1240 My Account and Authorized Representatives

¶1300 Other Tax Compliance Requirements

    ¶1310 Foreign Investment and Income Information Reporting

    ¶1320 Reporting Tax Avoidance Transactions (Form RC312)

    ¶1330 Claim for Tax Shelter Loss or Deduction

¶1400 Filing Due Dates, Forms, Remitting and Penalties

    ¶1410 Filing Requirements Quick Reference Table

    ¶1420 Penalties Quick Reference Table

    ¶1430 Third-Party Penalties

¶1500 Taxpayer Relief Provisions

    ¶1510 Voluntary Disclosures

    ¶1520 Requests for Taxpayer Relief

¶1000 — Introduction to Canadian Income Tax

The Canadian income tax system is based on self-assessment. Taxpayers must file their returns, and voluntarily report all income and expenses and calculate any amounts of tax owing. Each calendar year, individuals are required to compute their tax liability and file (either by mail, delivery, or electronically) a personal tax return with the Canada Revenue Agency (CRA). The CRA is the government agency responsible for administering income taxes in Canada.

The main purpose of the income tax is to raise revenue to finance government spending. However, income tax also serves other important functions, including promoting the redistribution of income, regulating private economic activity, and promoting economic and social policies, such as home ownership, retirement savings, post-secondary education, environmental protection, and entrepreneurship.

¶1010 — Sources of Tax Law

Canadian federal income tax is imposed by the *Income Tax Act* (ITA). In addition, the *Income Tax Regulations* (ITR) that are authorized under the ITA contain much of the detail of income tax law. Since the ITRs do not have to be enacted by Parliament, they can be changed more easily than the ITA; however, they generally have the same force of law as the ITA itself. Court decisions assist in interpreting the ITA in circumstances where the ITA is silent, incomplete, or unclear. Additionally, tax treaties are agreements entered into by Canada with other countries to coordinate the tax treatment of cross-border transactions. Tax treaties are used to avoid double taxation and to prevent fiscal evasion. Treaties are "relieving" in nature as they reduce taxes imposed under domestic law. Where the ITA conflicts with a treaty, the treaty prevails.

The provinces and territories also have their own income tax acts. All of the provinces and territories, other than Quebec, have entered into tax collection agreements with the federal government under which the federal government collects the provincial income tax, and, in return, the province agrees to accept most of the rules of the federal Act for taxing but sets its own provincial rates of tax and tax credits for its residents. Chapter 12 discusses provincial and territorial taxes and credits. Chapter 13 discusses completing the Québec income tax return.

The CRA also issues various administrative publications which do not have the force of law but are considered secondary sources of tax law. These publications express the CRA's position with respect to a particular issue. They are not legally binding on the CRA; however, it is generally the CRA's policy to assess taxpayers in accordance with the opinions or positions expressed in its publications. These publications include the following:

- *Interpretation Bulletins (IT Bulletins)* — Interpretation bulletins explain the CRA's interpretations of many of the provisions of the Act. The courts look at interpretation bulletins as a persuasive aid to interpretation but are not bound by the CRA's opinion, and do not always follow them.

- *Information Circulars (ICs)* — Information circulars are designed to provide information on administrative and procedural matters. They cover the CRA's organization and procedures and other useful information.

- *Advance Income Tax Rulings (ATRs)* — An advance income tax ruling is issued at the request of a taxpayer, who pays a fee for the service. The purpose of a ruling is to explain to the taxpayer how the CRA will assess a transaction that is contemplated by the taxpayer.

- *Income Tax Technical News (ITTNs)* — Income tax technical news publications announce changes in the CRA's administrative policy or interpretative views resulting from new case law and other developments.

- *Income Tax Folios (Folios)* — CRA is currently in the process of replacing its IT Bulletins and ITTNs with web-based tax publications called the Income Tax Folios. The Folios are organized by subject matter into Series. Each Folio within a Series represents a broad subject relevant to that Series, and is subdivided into more topic-specific chapters. Generally, a chapter of a Folio is an updated version of the technical content in one or more IT Bulletins or ITTNs. Current IT Bulletins and ITTNs will continue to be available on the CRA website until the technical content is updated and published in a Folio, at which time the related IT Bulletin or ITTN will be cancelled. CRA expects the update process to take several years.

- *Tax Guides and Pamphlets* — The CRA's tax guides and pamphlets are easy to read and are meant for use by the general public. For example, CRA Guide 5000-G, *General Income Tax and Benefit Guide* (T1 Guide), assists individuals in completing their T1 return.

- *Technical Interpretations* — Technical interpretations are also called CRA Views documents (VDs) and are available on Taxnet Pro and Tax Partner. CRA VDs are CRA's written response to taxpayers or their advisors on a certain subject matter or provision of the ITA for which the taxpayer or advisor has requested an interpretation. They may clarify tax issues for which the legislation or CRA's interpretative views or administrative policies are unclear. The final two characters of a VD number indicate the type of document as follows: C6, Conference; A11, Consultation with Appeals; E5, Interpretation — external; I7, Interpretation — internal; M4, Ministerial correspondence; R3, Ruling; Z0, Other document; and X0, Other document (replaced Z0 in 2009).

¶1020 — Liability for Canadian Tax

Canadian resident individuals are subject to Canadian income tax on their worldwide income. Taxable income includes worldwide income from employment, business, property, and capital gains.

The ITA does not define what constitutes residence in Canada but generally relies on the meaning attributed to residence in common law (i.e., case law). Under Canadian common law, many factors are looked at when determining residency for tax purposes. In addition to the amount of time spent in Canada, some of the other factors considered include whether an individual maintains a residence in Canada, has relatives in Canada, has bank accounts in Canada, or has other social or economic ties to Canada. There are also circumstances in which an individual will be deemed to be resident in Canada for Canadian tax purposes. For example, a person who is not a resident of Canada for any part of the year, but who visits Canada for a total of 183 days or more in a year, may be deemed to be a resident of Canada and subject to Canadian income tax on worldwide income for the entire year.

For income tax purposes, deemed resident persons are essentially treated in all respects as if they were actually resident in Canada and must file Canadian tax returns and pay tax accordingly. Generally, non-residents of Canada are only subject to Canadian tax on income from employment in Canada, income from a business carried on in Canada, taxable capital gains from the disposal of taxable Canadian property, and the taxable part of Canadian scholarships, fellowships, bursaries, and research grants. In addition, non-residents of Canada are subject to withholding tax on certain types of income, such as dividends, interest, and royalties received from sources in Canada. Non-residents and deemed residents may or may not have to file a Canadian tax return. See 2017 Chapter 15 for more information on residency and the Canadian taxation of, and filing requirements for non-residents and deemed residents of Canada.

ITA 2, 3, Guide 5000-G, Guide 5013-G, Guide T4131, Fact Sheet T4133, IT-171R2 (cancelled): *Non-resident Individuals — Computation of Taxable Income Earned in Canada and Non-refundable Tax Credits*, Folio S5-F1-C1: *Determining an Individual's Residence Status*

¶1100 — Filing Requirements

¶1110 — Requirement to File

CRA Guide 5000-G, *General Income Tax and Benefit Guide* (T1 Guide) provides that individuals are required to file a T1 General Income Tax and Benefit Return (T1 return) for the taxation year if any of the following situations apply:

- You have to pay tax for the taxation year;

- The CRA sent you a request to file a return;

- You and your spouse or common-law partner elected to split pension income for the taxation year;

- You received Working Income Tax Benefit (WITB) advance payments in the taxation year;

- You disposed of capital property in the taxation year or you realized a taxable capital gain;

- You have to repay all or part of your old age security or employment insurance benefits;

- You have not repaid all amounts withdrawn from your Registered Retirement Savings Plan (RRSP) under the Home Buyers' Plan or the Lifelong Learning Plan;

- You have to contribute to the Canada Pension Plan; or

- You are paying employment insurance premiums on self-employment and other eligible earnings.

Even if none of the above applies, individuals may choose to file a return if any of the following apply:

- You want to claim a refund;

- You want to claim the WITB;

- You want the CRA to determine if you are eligible for the GST/HST credit (including any related provincial credits);

- You or your spouse or common-law partner wants to begin or continue receiving Canada child benefit payments including related provincial or territorial benefit payments;

- You have incurred a non-capital loss in the taxation year that you want to be able to apply in other years;

- You want to carry forward or transfer any unused part of your tuition fees;

- You want to report income for which you could contribute to an RRSP in order to keep your RRSP deduction limit for future years current; or

- You want to carry forward the unused investment tax credit on expenditures you incurred during the current year.

Although typically not required, it can be beneficial to file a tax return for minors. In particular, if the minor has a part-time job, filing a return will create registered retirement savings plan (RRSP) room. Also, certain provincial refundable tax credits are available to low-income minors where a return is filed (for example, the federal GST/HST credit is available to low or no income persons over 18 years of age; see ¶1153).

ITA 150(1)(d), Guide 5000-G

¶1120 — Method of Filing

Individuals can file their T1 return as a paper return by mail or delivery to the CRA, or over the Internet using CRA's NETFILE system, or by EFILE. In addition, beginning in 2018, eligible individuals can file their T1 return by telephone using the CRA's "File My Return" service.

In 2018, CRA launched the "File My Return" service, which allows eligible individuals with low income or a fixed income that is unchanged year-to-year to file their tax returns by answering a few questions over the telephone through an automated phone service. See: canada.ca/en/revenue-agency/campaigns/file-my-return.html for more information on the File My Return service.

¶1121 — *Paper Returns*

Paper returns filed by first class mail (or its equivalent) are deemed to be received by the CRA on the date on which the return was mailed. Individuals who file their T1 return by mail should include one copy of each information slip (see ¶1124 for when to attach other supporting documents such as certificates, forms, schedules, or official receipts).

Beginning with the 2017 tax year, taxpayers who filed using paper tax forms in previous years will receive a tax package by mail. The forms can also be downloaded from canada.ca or call 1-800-959-8281 to have a tax package mailed.

Canadian resident individuals filing their T1 return by mail should send it to the appropriate Tax Centre as follows:

Mail your return to:	For individuals who live in the following provinces, territories, or areas of Ontario or Quebec as shown below:
Winnipeg Tax Centre Post Office Box 14001, Station Main Winnipeg MB R3C 3M3	Alberta, British Columbia, Manitoba, Saskatchewan, Northwest Territories, Yukon Ontario: Hamilton, Kitchener, Waterloo, London, Thunder Bay, Windsor
Sudbury Tax Centre 1050 Notre Dame Avenue Sudbury ON P3A 5C2	New Brunswick, Newfoundland and Labrador, Nova Scotia, Nunavut, Prince Edward Island Ontario: Barrie, Belleville, Kingston, Ottawa, Peterborough, St. Catharines, Sudbury, Toronto
Jonquière Tax Centre 2251 René-Lévesque Boulevard Jonquière QC G7S 5J2	Quebec: Montréal, Outaouais, Sherbrooke Quebec: all areas other than Montréal, Outaouais or Sherbrooke

Non-resident individuals who are required to file a T1 return should mail their return to the appropriate Tax Centre as follows:

Mail your return to:	For non-resident individuals who live in the following countries:
Winnipeg Tax Centre Post Office Box 14001, Station Main Winnipeg MB R3C 3M3 Canada	United States, United Kingdom, France, Netherlands, or Denmark
Sudbury Tax Centre 1050 Notre Dame Avenue Sudbury ON P3A 5C2 Canada	Countries other than the United States, United Kingdom, France, Netherlands, or Denmark

¶1122 — *NETFILE*

NETFILE enables individuals to file returns directly over the internet using CRA-certified software or a web application that the CRA has certified for NETFILE. Taxpayers who are planning to NETFILE their tax return should ensure that they prepare it using "NETFILE-certified" tax preparation software or a "NETFILE-certified" tax preparation web application, which means that the developer of the tax preparation software has gone through a process with the CRA to verify that their product is compatible with the CRA NETFILE electronic tax filing service.

Individuals who file their T1 return by NETFILE do not need to send a printed return or information slips to CRA; however, the T1 return and all of the backup documentation for the return must be kept for at least six years. There are many free certified software packages and web products available for taxpayers to file their income tax return online. For more information on NETFILE, to obtain a NETFILE access code, and for a full list of the certified software for the NETFILE Program, see netfile.gc.ca/.

ITA 150.1, Guide RC4018, Form T183

¶1123 — *EFILE*

EFILE is an automated service that permits those who prepare and file taxes on behalf of others (e.g., an accounting firm) to electronically file the current year tax return via the internet. To become a registered electronic filer, a tax preparer must register/renew their application with the CRA each year; visit: canada.ca/en/revenue-agency/services/e-services/e-services-individuals/efile-individuals.html.

Both individual taxpayers and authorized representatives can use "Auto-fill my return" with EFILE and NETFILE-certified software to automatically fill in parts of the personal tax return. Auto-fill my return is a secure CRA service that allows an individual taxpayer or his/her authorized representative to electronically request and receive tax information that the CRA has available at the time of filing, to help fill in certain parts of the taxpayer's income tax return. CRA will have most tax information slips and other tax-related information, such as T4, RRSP information and carry forward amounts. To use this service, taxpayers must be registered with My Account, and be using a certified software product that offers this service. For more information, see: canada.ca/en/revenue-agency/services/e-services/about-auto-fill-return.html.

The ReFILE service allows individuals and EFILE service providers to send T1 adjustments electronically, and is intended to replace the filing of T1 adjustments by paper. For more information on ReFILE, see: canada.ca/en/revenue-agency/services/e-services/e-services-businesses/refile-online-t1-adjustments-efile-service-providers.html.

Like NETFILE, individuals who file their T1 return by EFILE do not need to send a printed return or information slips to CRA; however, the T1 return and all of the backup documentation for the return must be kept for at least six years. A T1 return cannot be filed electronically in any of the following situations (see: canada.ca/en/revenue-agency/services/e-services/e-services-businesses/efile-electronic-filers/file-returns.html#h4 for a full list of EFILE exclusions):

1. The taxpayer is a deemed resident (not subject to provincial or territorial tax)

2. The taxpayer died prior to the current tax year

3. The taxpayer's social insurance number begins with 0

4. The taxpayer is coded bankrupt according to CRA's records and is filing an in-bankruptcy or post-bankruptcy return

5. The taxpayer is an emigrant or a non-resident

6. The taxpayer's address is outside Canada

7. The taxpayer is filing Form RC199, Voluntary Disclosures Program (VDP) Taxpayer Agreement or making a request to the Voluntary Disclosures Program

ITA 150.1, Guide RC4018, Form T183

¶1123.1 — *Mandatory Electronic Filing for "Tax Preparers"*

Professional tax preparers who prepare more than ten individual income tax returns in the year are required to e-file the returns (although the preparer can file up to ten returns by other means). Employees of the tax preparer are excluded from these requirements and there are certain exceptions, such as returns that are not permitted to be efiled. A penalty may be assessed if a "tax preparer" fails to EFILE a T1 return. The penalty is $25 for each failure to file a T1 return in paper format rather than electronic format. For this purpose, a "tax preparer" is defined for a calendar year as a person or partnership that accepts consideration to prepare more than ten T2 returns or more than ten T1 returns. A corporate employee that prepares a T1 return in the course of performing employment duties is not considered a "tax preparer" for this purpose.

In VD 2012-0445451E5, the CRA confirmed that a return filed in either electronic or paper format is still a validly-filed return for the purposes of the general requirement to file a return in ITA 150(1) and the related penalty provisions; however, if the return is filed other than by way of electronic filing, a taxpayer may be subject to a penalty. As well, the penalty could apply where a tax preparer prepares a return for consideration, but the individual decides to file the return in paper format. However, the $25 penalty would not apply in respect of an unfiled return.

Answers to frequently asked questions with respect to the requirements for tax preparers to EFILE returns can be found at: canada.ca/en/revenue-agency/services/e-services/e-services-tax-preparers/mandatory-electronic-filing-tax-preparers.html.

ITA 150.1(2.2)–(2.4), 162(7.3), ITR 205.1(2)

¶1124 — *Tax Return Schedules, Forms, and Other Supporting Documents*

For T1 returns that are filed electronically, attachments such as information slips and receipts are not submitted with the return. However, these supporting documents must be kept on file for six years, since the CRA may request to see them. For T1 returns that are filed by mail (or by delivery to the CRA), the following schedules, forms and statements, information slips, and other receipts are required to be filed with the T1 return (as applicable):

T1 Jacket and Federal Schedules

- Schedule 1 — Federal Tax
- Schedule 2 — Federal Amounts Transferred From Your Spouse or Common-Law Partner
- Schedule 3 — Capital Gains (or Losses)
- Schedule 4 — Statement of Investment Income
- Schedule 5 — Amounts for Spouse or Common-Law Partner and Dependants
- Schedule 6 — Working Income Tax Benefit
- Schedule 7 — RRSP and PRPP Unused Contributions, Transfers, and HBP or LLP Activities
- Schedule 8 — Canada Pension Plan Contributions and Overpayments
- Schedule 9 — Donations and Gifts
- Schedule 11 — Tuition, Education, and Textbook Amounts
- Schedule 12 — Home Accessibility Expenses
- Schedule 13 — Employment Insurance Premiums on Self-Employment and Other Eligible Earnings
- Schedule A — Statement of World Income
- Schedule B — Allowable Amount of Non-Refundable Tax Credits
- Schedule C — Electing Under Section 217 of the *Income Tax Act*

Information Slips and Other Receipts

- T3, T4, T4A, T4A(OAS), T4A(P), T4A-RCA, T4E, T4PS, T5, T101, T5003, T5006, T5007, T5013, T5013A, T4RSP, T4RIF

- RRSP contribution receipts

Forms and Statements

- Provincial Form 428, Provincial Tax

- Provincial Form 479, Provincial Credits

- T1-OVP, Individual Tax Return for RRSP Excess Contributions

- T1A, Request for Loss Carryback

- T691, Alternative Minimum Tax

- T746, Calculating Your Deduction for Refund of Unused RRSP, PRPP and SPP Contributions

- T776, Statement of Real Estate Rentals

- T777, Statement of Employment Expenses

- T778, Child Care Expenses Deduction

- T1032, Joint Election to Split Pension Income

- T1043, Deduction for Excess Registered Pension Plan Transfers You Withdrew From an RRSP or RRIF

- T1158, Registration of Family Support Payments

- T1198, Statement of Qualifying Retroactive Lump-Sum Payment

- T1206, Tax on Split Income

- T1212, Statement of Deferred Security Options Benefits

- T1229, Statement of Resource Expenses and Depletion Allowance

- T2036, Provincial or Territorial Foreign Tax Credit

- T2038(IND), Investment Tax Credit (Individuals)

- T2042, Statement of Farming Activities

- T2121, Statement of Fishing Activities

- T2125, Statement of Business or Professional Activities

- T2201, Disability Tax Credit Certificate

- T2203, Provincial and Territorial Taxes — Multiple Jurisdictions

- T2205, Amounts from a Spousal or Common-Law Partner RRSP, RRIF or SPP to Include in Income

- T2209, Federal Foreign Tax Credits

- T2222, Northern Residents Deductions

- T3012A, Tax Deduction Waiver on the Refund of Your Unused RRSP, PRPP or SPP Contributions from your RRSP

- T5004, Claim for Tax Shelter Loss or Deduction

For T1 returns that are filed by mail (or by delivery to the CRA), the following forms, worksheets, and receipts are NOT required to be filed with the paper-filed return, but must be retained by the taxpayer in case the CRA requests to see them:

- T1-M, Moving Expenses
- T929, Disability Supports Deduction
- T1223, Clergy Residence Deduction
- T2202A, Tuition and Enrolment, Certificate
- TL11A, Tuition and Enrolment, Certificate — University Outside Canada
- TL11B, Tuition and Enrolment, Certificate — Flying School or Club
- TL11C, Tuition and Enrolment, Certificate — Commuter to the U.S.
- T2210, Verification of Policy Loan Interest by the Insurer
- Receipts for union, professional or other dues (Line 212)
- Receipts for child care expenses (Line 214)
- Receipts for the disability supports deduction (Line 215)
- Receipts for moving expenses (Line 219)
- Receipts and cancelled cheques for supports payments made (Line 220)
- Receipts for carrying charges and interest expenses (Line 221)
- Receipts for expenses paid to earn employment income, such as legal fees (Line 229)
- Receipts for any other deductions claimed (Line 232)
- Receipts for adoption expenses (Line 313)
- Receipts for interest paid on student loans (Line 319)
- Receipts for tuition amounts (Line 323)
- Medical expense receipts (Lines 330, 331)
- Charitable donation receipts (Line 349)
- Supporting documents for the home buyers' amount (Line 369)

¶1125 — Registration of Tax Preparers Program ("RTPP")

In early 2014, as part of a larger initiative to improve compliance and provide support to the small and medium-sized business community, a consultation process was initiated with taxpayers and the tax preparer community on the proposed Registration of Tax Preparers Program (RTPP). Under the proposed RTPP, all tax preparers who prepare an individual or corporate income tax return for a fee would be required to register. The tax preparer community was asked to provide feedback and suggestions on various issues with respect to the design of the RTPP.

At the 2017 STEP Canada CRA Roundtable, the CRA stated that it is not going forward with the RTPP, based on the input of tax preparers and the legislative and system requirements needed to implement the program. The CRA is considering other options that would serve to implement the objectives of the proposed RTPP through existing CRA programs and initiatives at lower costs (see VD 2017-0698971C6).

ITA 150.1(2.1), VD 2014-0523051C6, Kim G C Moody, "Canada's new Registration of Tax Preparers Program", Moodys Gartner Tax Law LLP Newsletter (available on Taxnet Pro), Jan. 18, 2014, Sal Amodeo, "Registration of Tax Preparers Program", Canadian Tax Highlights, Vol. 22-6, June 2014

¶1130 — Filing Tax Elections

If an individual is filing a certificate or an election with his or her return and is filing the return electronically and the election or the certificate has a prescribed form, send the election or certificate to the individual's CRA Tax Centre. Many elections and designations are not made using a prescribed form (i.e., the CRA has not provided a prescribed form for the purposes of making some elections and designations). The CRA has stated that if the ITA requires that "the taxpayer elects in the taxpayer's return of income" for the year and a prescribed form is not available, the election is required to be submitted in writing. As well, paragraph 42 of IC 97-2R10, the CRA states that "if you are making an election, note it prominently in the relevant area of the return and schedules, or attach a note."

At the 2012 CTF Atlantic Tax Conference, the CRA provided the following update with respect to making elections when a tax return is filed electronically (VD 2012-0465981C6):

> The CRA's goal is to expand the NETFILE and EFILE programs to remove most exclusions and barriers to electronic filing. This includes adding the ability for taxpayers to file forms and elections electronically. However, we are not yet at a point where this can be done. Until then, for returns that are filed electronically, all elections, including the supporting documentation, must be submitted to us in writing, unless otherwise indicated . . . As explained in RC4018, *Electronic Filers Manual*, electronic filers are required to inform their clients that elections, designations, agreements, waivers, and special elective returns must be submitted in paper format by the appropriate due dates as established in the *Income Tax Act*. A taxpayer can indicate in the software that they are making an election and the software will build an Election indicator field. This is there for EFILE as well. Completion of this field code does not constitute an election; it is designed only to inform us that an election form or a letter/note containing the required information is being submitted in paper format.

In *Dhaliwal*, 2012 CarswellNat 769 (TCC), the Court found that a taxpayer had elected in his electronically-filed personal tax return to have the deemed disposition rule in ITA 50(1) apply to a bad debt merely by claiming the loss (see also *Roy*, [2004] 2 CTC 2519 (TCC) and *Anderson*, 1992 CarswellNat 397 (TCC)). The taxpayer recorded the capital loss in his tax return but did not specify that an election was being made under ITA 50(1) in any other manner (for example, a letter was not sent to the taxpayer's TSO indicating the election was being made). The Court highlighted that the CRA does not have a recommended form available for the election and that tax returns developed by the CRA do not have a space to expressly indicate an election to have ITA 50(1) apply. The Court was critical of the CRA's policies with respect to tax election filing requirements (see, in particular, paras. 22, 32, 35). Nonetheless, when asked at the 2012 CTF Ontario Tax Conference how an election under ITA 50(1) should be made when filing electronically in light of the decision in *Dhaliwal*, the CRA stated "[f]or returns that are filed electronically, all elections, including subsection 50(1) elections, together with the supporting documentation, must be submitted to us in writing, unless otherwise indicated" (see also VD 2012-0454041C6).

Rectification is generally not an available remedy to amend a previously filed tax election (see MacKnight, "Rectification and Amending Elections", Tax for the Owner-Manager, Vol. 14-3, July 2014).

October 2010 Alberta CAs CRA Roundtable, albertacas.ca, q. 16, VD 2010-0381311E5, Yager, "E-Filer Makes ABIL Election", *Canadian Tax Highlights*, Vol. 20, No. 5, May 2012, Friedlan "Subsection 50(1) Election and an E-Filed Return", *Tax for the Owner-Manager*, Vol. 12, No. 3, July 2012

¶1131 — *Late-Filed Elections*

In respect of certain tax elections, the CRA has the discretion, upon an application by the taxpayer, to extend the time for making an election or designation or to grant permission to amend or revoke an election or designation under a prescribed provision even though the normal deadline for making such an election or designation has passed and no election or designation has been made. However, a taxpayer may not late-file an election, or amend or revoke a valid election previously made, in respect of a taxation year more than 10 calendar years after the end of that taxation year. Appendix A of IC 07-1R1 includes a summary of the elections that may be accepted by the CRA when late-filed. When amending an election or late-filing an election, IC 07-1R1 states that a taxpayer should make a request in writing, and file it either electronically using "My Account" or by mail to the taxpayer's CRA Taxation Centre. Part III (paragraphs 45 to 63) of IC 07-1R1 discusses the CRA's guidelines for accepting late, amended or revoked elections.

By virtue of ITA 220(3.5), a taxpayer granted an extension or permission with respect to a late-filed or amended election is liable to a penalty equal to $100 multiplied by the number of complete months from the date on which the election was required to be made to the date a proper request was made. Such a penalty may not exceed $8,000. A taxpayer may request that the penalty be waived, which the CRA will consider in limited circumstances.

When a late-filed or amended election is accepted by the CRA, the election or designation is deemed to have been made properly and on a timely basis. In the case of an amendment to an election or designation, the earlier election or designation is considered not to have been made. The normal reassessment limits are overridden for this purpose and the CRA is required to make any assessment of tax, interest, or penalties that is necessary to take into account the accepted late-filed or amended election. The CRA is also required to examine each late-filed or amended election, assess any penalty payable in respect thereof, and send a related notice of assessment to the taxpayer. The taxpayer is "forthwith" required to pay any unpaid balance of an assessed penalty. The provisions of the ITA concerning returns, assessments, payment, objections, and court appeals apply as if the assessment had been made in the normal manner.

There are many elections and designations in respect of which the applicable provision of the ITA does not specify a filing-due date. In *Hayes*, [2005] 3 C.T.C. 241 (FCA), the Court found that the late-filing of a personal tax return did not invalidate an election under ITA 39(4). The Court noted that neither ITA 39(4) nor 150(1)(d) provide that if a personal tax return in which an election is included is late-filed, the election is invalid. In *Loewen (H.R.)*, [1993] 1 C.T.C. 212 (FCTD), the Court found that an election under ITA 39(4) filed after a personal tax return was filed for a particular taxation year was invalid because ITA 39(4) does not provide for the late-filing of the election.

Citing the decision in *Hayes*, in VD 2013-0487871I7, the CRA states that an election will not be considered late-filed where a filing-due date for the election is not specified in the ITA or ITR, the election is required to be filed "in the taxpayer's return of income for the year", and the election is filed in the taxpayer's tax return, either before *or* after the filing-due date of the return (i.e., if both the return and the election are late-filed at the same time, the election will be valid). The CRA further stated that if an election is filed after the taxpayer's tax return is filed, the election will technically be considered late-filed even if it is filed before the filing-due date of the tax return. However, if the return is filed electronically, the CRA will generally grant an administrative concession if a related election is filed after the filing of the tax return in cases where the election must be submitted to the CRA in writing.

The CRA will generally not accept late-filed elections that are not referred to in ITR 600; see, for example, In VD 2010-0381311E5.

ITA 161(11)(c), 165(1.1), 220(3.1)–(3.7), ITR 600, IC 07-1, VDs 2010-0381311E5, 2009-0343601I7, 2007-024411117, 2000-EM20425, ITTN-7

¶1140 — Filing Due Date

The T1 return for a taxation year must be filed (and any balance of tax must be paid) by April 30 of the following year. If the taxpayer or his or her spouse or common-law partner carried on a business in the year, the taxpayer and the taxpayer's spouse's or common-law partner's returns are not due until June 15 of the following year; however, the taxpayer's and the taxpayer's spouse's or common-law partner's tax owing is still due by April 30 of the following year.

For a deceased person, the T1 return is due as follows:

• Death in the first 10 months of a year — the final T1 return is due by April 30 of the following year;

- Death in the first 10 months of a year of an individual who carried on a business in the year (or for a spouse or common-law partner of such an individual) — the final T1 return is due by June 15 of the following year;

- Death in November or December in the year — the final T1 return is due before the later of the day by which the return would otherwise be required to be filed, and the day that is six months after the day of death.

If the filing due date falls on a Saturday, Sunday, or a statutory holiday, the CRA considers the return to be filed on time if it is received or postmarked on the next business day.

ITA 150(1)(d), 248(1)"filing due-date", Guide T4011

¶1150 — Identification Information

¶1151 — *Information about your Residence*

Individuals are required to enter information about their residence on the last day of the taxation year. Individuals who became a resident of Canada or ceased to be a resident of Canada for income tax purposes in the year should enter the date of their move to or from Canada. The special tax rules relating to immigrants, emigrants, part-year residents, non-residents, and deemed residents are discussed in Chapter 15.

¶1152 — *Marital Status & Spouse/Common-Law Partner Information*

Tick the box that applies to the individual's marital status on the last day of the taxation year.

For tax purposes, a spouse is a person to whom the taxpayer is legally married. A common-law partner is a person with whom the taxpayer is living in a conjugal relationship and one of the following applies: 1) the taxpayer has been living with the person in a conjugal relationship for at least one continuous year; 2) the person is the parent of the taxpayer's child by birth or by adoption; or 3) the person has custody and control of the taxpayer's child (or had custody and control immediately before the child turned 19) and the child is wholly dependent on the person for support. See also, Form RC65, *Marital Status Change*. Twelve continuous months includes any period the taxpayer was separated from the person for less than 90 days because of a breakdown in the relationship.

Individuals must provide the following information for their spouse or common-law partner: social insurance number, first name, net income from Line 236 of the spouse or common-law partner's return, or the amount it would be if he or she filed a return (enter even if it is zero). The net income information is required to calculate the GST/HST credit and certain other credits and benefits.

ITA 248(1)"common-law partner", 252(3)

¶1153 — *GST/HST Credit Application*

Individuals must file a T1 return to apply for the GST/HST credit (for taxation years before 2014, individuals were required to tick the GST/HST credit check box on the first page of the T1 return to apply for the credit). Individuals must file a T1 return to receive the GST/HST credit, even if the individual received it in the previous year. The credit is calculated based on the individual's net income (and, where applicable, the net income of the individual's spouse or common-law partner and the number of children an individual has). Individuals who have a spouse or common-law partner must provide information regarding the spouse's social insurance number, first name, and net income amount (even if it is zero). The CRA will automatically determine if the individual is eligible to receive the GST/HST credit, and send a notice of determination to each eligible individual. In the case of eligible couples, the GST/HST credit will be paid to the spouse or common-law partner whose income tax return is assessed first. This means that spouses do not have the ability to choose which one receives the credit (other than by ensuring they are the first spouse to file). Notices of determination will not be sent to ineligible individuals; however, an ineligible individual can obtain a notice of determination upon request, which will preserve their right to object to the determination.

Generally, Canadian residents age 19 or older are eligible to receive the GST/HST credit, which is paid quarterly to eligible recipients. Those under 19 may be eligible, if they have a spouse or common-law partner, or if they are a parent who resides with their child. Individuals who are 18 years of age or older should file a T1 return even if they have no income in order to apply for the GST credit. New residents of Canada can apply for the GST/HST credit in the year that they become a resident of Canada, using Form RC151, *GST/HST Credit Application for Individuals Who Become Residents of Canada*.

See the CRA GST/HST Guideline Tables at: canada.ca/en/revenue-agency/services/child-family-benefits/goods-services-tax-harmonized-sales-tax-gst-hst-credit/gst-hst-credit-guideline-tables.html for information on the amounts of GST/HST credits received at various income levels.

For more detailed information on the GST/HST credit, see Booklet RC4210, *GST/HST Credit including related provincial credits and benefits*.

¶1154 — *Foreign Property*

Answer the question on page 2 of the T1 return about owning or holding specified foreign property at any time in the taxation year. This refers to specified foreign property the taxpayer owned and the taxpayer's share of specified foreign property in which the taxpayer had an interest. For these purposes, specified foreign property does not include property in the taxpayer's RRSP, RRIF or RPP; mutual funds registered in Canada that contain foreign investments; property used or held exclusively in the course of carrying on an active business; or personal-use property. Tick "Yes" if the total cost of specified foreign property owned or held by the taxpayer was more than CAN$100,000 at any time in the taxation year and attach a completed copy of Form T1135, *Foreign Income Verification Statement*, to the T1 return. Individual taxpayers can file Form T1135 electronically for 2014 and later taxation years.

The CRA has implemented changes to Form T1135 for the 2015 and subsequent taxation years. For taxpayers with an interest in specified foreign property with a total cost in excess of $100,000 but less than $250,000, there is a simplified reporting method available (Form T1135 Part A). Taxpayers who own specified foreign property with a total cost of $250,000 and above will continue to be subject to detailed information reporting requirements (Form T1135 Part B). See ¶3531 for information on completing and filing Form T1135.

¶1200 — Instalments and Balance-Due Payments

¶1210 — Instalment Methods

Individuals who earn income that is not subject to withholding at source may be required to pay tax by instalments. Instalments are periodic income tax payments that individuals have to pay to the CRA on certain dates to cover tax that they would otherwise have to pay in a lump sum on April 30 of the following year. Instalments are not paid in advance; they are paid throughout the calendar year in which the taxable income is earned. If an individual still owes tax at the end of a taxation year, the remainder is due on or before the balance-due date, which is generally April 30 in the following year (see ¶1230).

Generally, individuals are required to pay income tax by instalments for the year if the individual's taxes payable are more than $3,000 ($1,800 for Quebec residents) in both the current year, and in either of the two preceding taxation years. Tax payable for a tax year for purposes of computing instalments is the total tax payable for the year before taking into consideration "specified future tax consequences" for the year. "Specified future tax consequences" are adjustments arising because of the carryback of losses, tax credits or similar amounts, or because of corrections of certain amounts renounced in connection with the issue of flow-through shares. Taxes payable includes both federal and provincial or territorial income taxes. Refundable and non-refundable federal, provincial, and territorial tax credits should be included in the calculation of instalment payments (use estimated credits for the current year to calculate instalment payments).

For individuals (other than farmers and fishers; see ¶1214) quarterly instalments are due on March 15, June 15, September 15, and December 15. The CRA charges arrears interest on late or deficient instalments according to the prescribed interest rate (see ¶1220). When instalment interest owed is more than $1,000, the CRA may charge an instalment penalty (see ¶1420).

ITA 248(7) deems anything, other than a remittance of source deductions or an amount payable by a corporation, sent by first class mail or its equivalent (which includes lettermail, registered mail, or courier service), to have been received by the Receiver General on the day that it was sent. Therefore, an instalment payment from an individual, sent to the Receiver General by first class mail or its equivalent, is considered to have been received on the day that it was sent (VD 2013-0481351I7).

Taxes paid by instalments should be reported on Line 476 of the T1 return (see ¶11340).

For more information on paying your tax by instalments, see: canada.ca/en/revenue-agency/services/tax/individuals/topics/about-your-tax-return/making-payments-individuals/paying-your-income-tax-instalments.html.

ITA 153, 155, 156, 156.1, 161(2), (11), 163.1, ITR 5300, Pamphlet P110

¶1211 — No-Calculation Method

Under the no-calculation method, CRA determines the suggested instalments on the basis of the individual's net taxes payable (including any CPP contributions and voluntary EI premiums payable) for the two previous years. The individual's March 15 and June 15 instalments are based on the individual's taxes payable for the second preceding taxation year, and the September 15 and December 15 instalments are based on the excess of the individual's taxes payable for the preceding taxation year over the taxes payable for the second preceding taxation year. For example, for 2019, the March 15 and June 15 instalments would be calculated as one-quarter of the balance due for 2017, and the September 15 and December 15 instalments would be calculated by subtracting the total of the first two 2019 suggested instalments from the individual's 2018 balance due. Each of the final two instalments would be one-half of this amount.

The no-calculation method is best for taxpayers whose income, deductions, and credits stay about the same from year to year. The CRA will automatically provide taxpayers with instalment amounts based on the no-calculation method in instalment reminders sent in February and August. Taxpayers who use the no-calculation method and make the instalment payments shown on the instalment reminders by their due dates will not be subject to interest or penalties on deficient instalments, even if an individual's final tax payable is higher than the suggested instalments paid for the year. However, if an individual's income for the year is expected to be significantly lower than in the previous two years, the no-calculation method may result in excessive instalments, and one of the other methods discussed below may be more appropriate.

Following is an example illustrating the no-calculation method:

Example

Jake is self-employed and has to make instalment payments in 2017. His income increased slightly over the last two years, and he expects it will increase again in 2017. Jake also decided to pay voluntary EI premiums on his self-employed income for 2016. Jake's net tax owing and CPP contributions payable were $6,000 for 2015, and his net tax owing, CPP contributions payable, and voluntary EI premiums payable were $6,600 for 2016.

The CRA calculates Jake's March and June instalment payments for 2017 each as one quarter of his net tax owing and CPP contributions payable for 2015.

The CRA calculates his September and December 2016 payments by subtracting the first two instalment payments calculated above from his net tax owing, CPP contributions payable, and voluntary EI premiums payable for 2016 and dividing the result by two.

Using the no-calculation option, Jake makes the four instalment payments shown on his 2017 reminders, as follows:

		Instalment payments
March 15	($6,000 ÷ 4)	$1,500
June 15	($6,000 ÷ 4)	$1,500
September 15	($6,600 - $3,000) ÷ 2	$1,800
December 15	($6,600 - $3,000) ÷ 2	$1,800
Total		*$6,600*

ITA 153, 155, 156, 156.1, ITR 5300, Pamphlet P110

¶1212 — *Prior-Year Method*

Under the prior-year method, instalments are based on the individual's net taxes payable for the preceding taxation year. Using this method, each instalment is calculated as one-quarter of the total balance due in the immediately preceding taxation year.

The prior-year method is best for individuals whose income, deductions, and credits for the year will be similar to the immediately preceding year, but significantly different from the second preceding year. However, an individual may be subject to interest charges if this method results in an underpayment of the taxes due (see ¶1220).

Following is an example illustrating the prior-year method:

Example

Gayle has to pay her tax by instalments in 2017. She retired at the end of 2015 and her 2017 pension income will be close to what it was in 2016, but much less than her employment income was in 2015. Using her 2016 income tax and benefit return and the calculation chart, she calculates that her total instalment amount due is $4,000.

Using the prior-year option, Gayle makes four instalment payments in 2017, based on her calculations, as follows:

	Instalment payments
March 15	$1,000
June 15	$1,000
September 15	$1,000
December 15	$1,000
Total	*$4,000*

¶1213 — *Current-Year Method*

Under the current-year method, instalments are based on the individual's estimated taxes payable for the current taxation year. Using this method, each instalment is calculated as one-quarter of the total balance due in the current year.

The current-year method is best for individuals whose current year income, deductions, and credits will be significantly different from those in both the preceding and second preceding taxation year. However, an individual may be subject to interest charges if this method results in an underpayment of the taxes due (see ¶1220).

Following is an example illustrating the current-year method:

Example

Jesse has to pay his tax by instalments in 2017. However, since Jesse's investment income decreased this year, he knows he will owe less tax in 2017, and as a result, he can make lower instalment payments than he did in 2015 and 2016. Using a 2016 income tax and benefit return, the calculation chart, and his 2017 income estimates, he calculates that his total instalment amount due will be $5,000.

Using the current-year option, Jesse makes four instalment payments in 2017, based on his calculations, as follows:

	Instalment payments
March 15	$1,250
June 15	$1,250
September 15	$1,250
December 15	$1,250
Total	*$5,000*

¶1214 — *Instalment Requirements for Farmers and Fishermen*

Since the annual income for farmers and fishermen is likely to remain uncertain until near the end of the year, and profits may vary greatly from year to year, farmer and fishermen are not required to make quarterly tax instalment payments. Instead, farmers and fishermen are permitted to delay their first instalment payment until December 31. At that time they have the choice of paying 2/3 of either: (1) the amount they estimate to be their taxes payable for that taxation year; or (b) the taxes payable for the preceding taxation year. The remainder of taxes owing are due at the time the T1 return is filed.

Taxes payable for a tax year for purposes of computing instalments is the total tax payable for the year before taking into consideration "specified future tax consequences" for the year. "Specified future tax consequences" are adjustments arising because of the carryback of losses, tax credits or similar amounts, or because of corrections of certain amounts renounced in connection with the issue of flow-through shares. Taxes payable includes both federal and provincial or territorial income taxes. Refundable and non-refundable federal, provincial and territorial tax credits should be included in the calculation of instalment payments (use estimated credits for the current year to calculate instalment payments).

ITA 155, 156.1, Pamphlet P110

¶1215 — *Making Tax Instalment Payments*

Taxpayers should use Form INNS3, *Instalment Remittance Voucher*, when paying an instalment in-person at their financial institution or when sending an instalment payment by mail. Form INNS3 includes two tear-off voucher sections. Taxpayers can also pay by online banking, debit card, credit card or pre-authorized debit. For more information on using alternate methods of payment, see: canada.ca/en/revenue-agency/services/make-a-payment-canada-revenue-agency.html.

Interest and penalties apply to late or deficient instalments or final tax payments (see ¶1220 and ¶1420). To not be considered late, instalment payments and final tax payments are required to be made on or before the due date either by mailing a cheque payable to the Receiver General or by paying directly through a Canadian financial institution.

ITA 248(7) deems anything, other than a remittance of source deductions or an amount payable by a corporation, sent by first class mail or its equivalent (which includes lettermail, registered mail, or courier service), to have been received by the Receiver General on the day that it was sent. Therefore, an instalment payment from an individual, sent to the Receiver General by first class mail or its equivalent, is considered to have been received on the day that it was sent (VD 2013-0481351I7). Where the instalment due date falls on a Saturday, Sunday, or a statutory holiday, the payment is considered to be made on time if it is received or postmarked on the next business day.

ITA 161, 248(7), *Interpretations Act* sections 26 and 35(1)"holiday", Pamphlet P110

¶1220 — Interest Charges on Late or Deficient Tax Instalments

The CRA charges interest according to the prescribed rate if an individual makes late or insufficient instalment payments. Interest compounds daily according to the taxpayer's instalment requirements for the taxation year. Prescribed interest rates are available on the CRA's website at: canada.ca/en/revenue-agency/services/tax/prescribed-interest-rates.html.

The CRA uses the offset method to calculate instalment interest (i.e., the contra-interest method) in accordance with the rules contained in the ITA. Thus, the CRA gives credit when an individual prepays or overpays instalments and this can reduce or eliminate interest charges on late or insufficient payments; however, the CRA does not refund any excess of this credit (i.e., the offset method is used for purposes of calculating instalment interest charges only). When using the offset method, the interest rate is the same on prepayments as it is on underpayments. When instalment interest is more than $1,000, the CRA may charge an instalment penalty (see ¶1420).

The contra-interest rules are beneficial as they ensure the same interest rate is applied to both deficient payments and overpayments and because instalment interest charges are not deductible in computing income for tax purposes (normally, the interest rate applied to deficient payments is 4% higher than the interest rate applied to amounts due to a taxpayer from the CRA).

The CRA generally does not pay refund interest where excessive instalments have been made. Also, the CRA will not refund instalment payments until they have assessed the return for the year in question. At such time, the CRA will refund any overpayment.

ITA 156(1), 161(2)–(2.2), 163.1, 164(1), 248(11), ITR 4300–4302, Pamphlet P110

¶1230 — Balance-Due Day and Interest Charges on Outstanding Payments

Generally, the "balance-due day" for an individual's taxes owing for the year is April 30 of the following year. Where an individual or his or her spouse or common-law partner carried on a business in the year, the return must be filed on or before June 15 of the following year; however, the individual still must pay any balance owing for the year on or before April 30 of the following year. ITA 248(7) deems anything, other than a remittance of source deductions or an amount payable by a corporation, sent by first class mail or its equivalent (which includes letter-mail, registered mail, or courier service), to have been received by the Receiver General on the day that it was sent. Therefore, a payment of tax owing from an individual, sent to the Receiver General by first class mail or its equivalent, is considered to have been received on the day that it was sent (VD 2013-0481351I7). Where the due date falls on a Saturday, Sunday, or a statutory holiday, the payment is considered to be made on time if it is received or postmarked on the next business day.

An individual may pay the balance of tax owing electronically, or in person at a financial institution in Canada by cheque or money order made out to the Receiver General. For additional information about payments options, see: canada.ca/en/revenue-agency/services/make-a-payment-canada-revenue-agency.html. Below is a summary of when payment is considered to be made for the various types of payment methods:

Method of payment	Date when payment considered to be made
In person at financial institution	Date stamped on remittance voucher
Mail	Date of mailing (CRA considers a tax payment made in respect of an individual to be received on the day it is mailed to the CRA, provided it is sent by first-class mail or equivalent)
Online banking	Date when financial institution credits CRA with payment
Post-dated cheque or pre-authorized debit	Date when payment is negotiable

The CRA charges compound daily interest on unpaid taxes according to the prescribed rate, beginning on the day after the return is due, on any unpaid amounts owing, including any balance owing if the T1 return is reassessed by the CRA. The CRA also charges interest on any penalties, beginning the day after the return is due. Where the penalty is for failure to file a return when due or for filing an incomplete return or a return containing false statements, the penalty bears interest from the date when the return was required to be filed. A list of prescribed interest rates for current and previous years can be found at: canada.ca/en/revenue-agency/services/tax/prescribed-interest-rates.html.

ITA 156.1, 161, 248(1)"balance-due day", 248(7), Form T7DR, Pamphlet P110

¶1240 — My Account and Authorized Representatives

¶1241 — *My Account for Individuals*

The CRA's *My Account* service allows individuals to view up-to-the-minute information about their tax refund or balance owing; direct deposit; RRSP, Home Buyers' Plan, and Lifelong Learning Plan; Tax-Free Savings Account; tax returns and carryover amounts; tax information slips; disability tax credit; account balance and payments on filing; instalments; Canada Child Benefit, GST/HST credit, account balances, and statements of account; Working Income Tax Benefit advanced payments; pre-authorized payment plan; authorized representative; addresses and telephone numbers; and marital status.

With My Account, individuals can also manage their personal income tax and benefit information online by changing their return(s); changing their address or telephone numbers; applying for child benefits; arranging for direct deposit; authorizing a representative; setting up a payment plan; formally disputing an assessment or determination; changing marital status; and ordering remittance voucher(s).

For more information on *My Account*, visit: canada.ca/en/revenue-agency/services/e-services/e-services-individuals/account-individuals.html.

¶1242 — *Authorized Representatives (Form T1013)*

A taxpayer can authorize a representative to discuss the individual's T1 return for any year with the CRA or cancel the authorization given to a representative by using either the "Authorize my representative" service online in My Account or by completing Form T1013: *Authorizing or Cancelling a Representative*. At least annually, a taxpayer should verify if the list of authorized representatives is up-to-date and, if applicable, modify or cancel authorized representatives. My Account allows an individual to authorize a new representative, and to view, update, and cancel authorizations of existing representatives.

For authorized representatives, the CRA offers a service referred to as Represent a Client, available at: canada.ca/en/revenue-agency/services/e-services/represent-a-client.html. Represent a Client provides advisors online access to tax information on behalf of individuals (and businesses). To use the service, a person is required to register as a representative. A business, such as a professional tax services firm, can also register with the service to be a representative of an individual (or a business). Online access to tax information only becomes effective after a registered representative is authorized by the individual (or business).

ITA 241(5), Form T1013

¶1300 — Other Tax Compliance Requirements

¶1310 — Foreign Investment and Income Information Reporting

In addition to filing the appropriate T1 return and schedules, individuals may be required to file one or more information returns. Below are some of the more common information returns:

- Form T1135, *Foreign Income Verification Statement* — required if, at any time in the year, the total cost of all specified foreign property the taxpayer owned or held a beneficial interest in was more than $100,000 (see ¶1154 and ¶3531);

- Form T1134, *Information Return Relating to Controlled and Not-Controlled Foreign Affiliates* — required to be filed for each foreign affiliate (i.e., a non-resident corporation or non-resident trust) of the taxpayer that is either a controlled foreign affiliate or non-controlled foreign affiliate at any time in the year (see ¶3532);

- Form T1141, *Information Return in Respect of Transfers or Loans to a Non-resident Trust* — required to be filed by Canadian residents who have transferred or loaned property to a non-resident trust that has a Canadian beneficiary, or a non-resident corporation controlled by the trust (see ¶3533); and

- Form T1142, *Information Return in Respect of Distributions from and Indebtedness to a Non-resident Trust* — required to be filed where a taxpayer is beneficially interested in a non-resident trust (excluding a non-resident estate) at any time in the taxation year, and has received a distribution from, or was indebted to, that non-resident trust (see ¶3534).

Form T1134 is due within 15 months after the end of the individual's taxation year for filings related to taxation years before 2020; 12 months after the end of the year for filings related to 2020; and 10 months after the end of the year for filings related to 2021 and later taxation years. Forms T1135, T1141 and T1142 are due on or before the due date of the individual's T1 return. See ¶3531–¶3534 for details on completing and filing these information returns.

¶1320 — Reporting Tax Avoidance Transactions (Form RC312)

Taxpayers, advisors and promoters who engage in certain tax avoidance transactions are subject to certain reporting requirements. The intention of the reporting regime is to identify to the CRA certain types of potentially abusive tax avoidance transactions that were not formerly subject to any specific information reporting requirements.

ITA 237.3 applies in respect of avoidance transactions entered into after 2010, as well as to avoidance transactions that are part of a series of transactions that commenced before 2011 and are completed after 2010. Information return RC312: *Reportable Transaction Information Return*, is due on or before June 30 of the calendar year following the calendar year in which the avoidance transaction first became a reportable transaction for the person. Failure to file Form RC312 could result in denial of the tax benefit and a penalty.

For taxation years ending after March 20, 2013, where Form RC312 has not been filed as required, the reassessment period is extended by three years after the date, if any, that the information return has been filed; and a waiver of this extended reassessment period maybe filed with the CRA within this additional three year period. The scope of an assessment, reassessment, or additional assessment of a taxpayer's taxation year during the extended reassessment period is limited to what can reasonably be regarded as relating to the tax benefit.

For purposes of these reporting rules, an "advisor" is defined as any person who, in respect of a transaction or a series of transactions, provides directly or indirectly in any manner whatever, any contractual protection in respect of the transaction or series, or any assistance or advice with respect to creating, developing, planning, organizing or implementing the transaction or series, to another person. A person can be an advisor to a particular person who enters into a transaction and for whom a tax benefit could result from the transaction or series, or to a person who enters into a transaction for the benefit of another person. A person can also be an advisor in respect of a transaction if that person provides contractual protection, assistance or advice to any promoter or any other advisor in respect of the transaction or series of transactions, even though the person does not provide contractual protection, assistance or advice directly to the person who entered into the transaction (i.e., although an advisor would generally be a person whose business is to provide professional services or contractual protection to a person entering into a transaction or series, other persons can also be considered to be an advisor in respect of a transaction or series). More than one person may be an advisor in respect of a transaction. A person or partnership that provides advice or representation to a person only in respect of an audit or tax dispute in relation to a particular transaction or series of transactions, and that, in respect of that transaction or series, was neither involved in the creation, development, planning, organizing or implementation of the transaction or series, nor in the providing of contractual protection, would not be an advisor in respect of that transaction or series for the purposes of ITA 237.3.

A "promoter" is defined as any person who, in respect of a transaction or series of transactions, promotes or sells an arrangement where it can reasonably be considered that the arrangement includes or relates to the transaction or series. A person is also a promoter if the person makes a statement or representation that a tax benefit could result from the arrangement, or accepts consideration in respect of the promotion or sale of the arrangement, or for the making of a statement or representation that a tax benefit could result from the arrangement. More than one person may be a promoter in respect of a transaction. The "promoter" definition includes any person engaging in these activities or receiving such consideration whether as principal or agent and whether directly or indirectly.

A transaction is reportable only if it is an "avoidance transaction" as defined in ITA 245(3) for purposes of the GAAR. An "avoidance transaction" is defined to mean either:

1. A transaction that (but for GAAR) would directly or indirectly result in a tax benefit, unless the transaction may reasonably be considered to have been undertaken or arranged primarily for *bona fide* purposes other than to obtain the tax benefit; or

2. A transaction that is part of a series of transactions which series (but for GAAR) would result, directly or indirectly, in a tax benefit unless the transaction may reasonably be considered to have been undertaken or arranged primarily for *bona fide* purposes other than to obtain a tax benefit.

For GAAR to apply to a transaction, there is an additional "misuse" or "abuse" test that must be met. A "tax benefit" is defined broadly in ITA 245(1) to mean a reduction, avoidance or deferral of tax or other amount payable under the ITA, or an increase in a refund of tax or other amount under the ITA, including such a reduction, avoidance, or deferral or increase in a refund as a result of a tax treaty. The references to "other amount" extend to interest, penalties, remittances of amounts withheld from salary or from certain payments to non-residents as well as any other amounts that are not taxes. It does not extend to taxes or other amounts payable or refundable under some other Canadian or foreign legislation.

A reportable transaction does not include a transaction that is, or is part of a series of transactions that includes, the acquisition of a tax shelter or issuance of a flow-through share for which an information return has been filed with the CRA under ITA 237.1(7) or 66(12.68).

The filing of an information return by any person that provides a full and accurate disclosure of all the transactions in a series would be considered to have been made by every person who has a reporting obligation in respect of any transaction of the series.

ITA 237.3, Forer et al., "Recent Legislative and Administrative Developments in Federal and Provincial Tax Law," 2011 Prairie Provinces Tax Conference, (Toronto: Canadian Tax Foundation, 2011), 2:1–53, Jang, "Aggressive Transaction Reporting Revisited" (2011) vol. 1, no. 3 Canadian Tax Focus, 5-6

¶1321 — *Reportable Transactions*

Form RC312 is required to be filed in respect of a "reportable transaction". An avoidance transaction is a "reportable transaction" if at least two of the following three hallmarks exists:

1. The promoter or advisor has or had an entitlement to certain types of "fees";

2. The promoter or advisor has or had "confidential protection" with respect to the transaction; and/or

3. The taxpayer or the promoter or advisor who entered into the transaction for the benefit of the taxpayer has or had obtained a "contractual protection" for the transaction (otherwise than as a result of certain types of "fees").

Each transaction that is part of a series of transactions that includes an avoidance transaction is a separate reportable transaction (this is also the case where a series of transactions includes more than one avoidance transaction). The fact that a transaction is an avoidance transaction and bears two hallmarks from the perspective of one party to a transaction does not necessarily mean that it is a reportable transaction to the other party to the transaction; whether a transaction is a reportable transaction to either of the parties to a transaction is to be determined from the perspective of each party.

A person who is a lawyer and acting solely in the capacity of an advisor to a client in respect of a reportable transaction does not have a reporting obligation in respect of prescribed information to be provided about the transaction if, after having taken reasonable steps and based on reasonable grounds, the advisor determines that solicitor-client privilege exists in respect of the information. Such a person is expected to provide information for which solicitor-client privilege does not exist, and would be expected to keep proper records of information in respect of which the person asserts the existence of solicitor-client privilege, as well as to present an explanation supporting such an assertion, in the event that the assertion is challenged by the CRA.

(1) — Fees Hallmark

The fees hallmark is met in circumstances in which an "advisor" or "promoter", or any person not dealing at arm's length with an advisor or promoter, is entitled to any of three types of "fees". A "fee" is defined as any consideration that is, or could be, received or receivable, directly or indirectly and in any manner whatever, by an advisor or promoter in respect of an avoidance transaction, or a series of transactions that includes the avoidance transaction, for providing advice or an opinion with respect to the transaction or series; creating, developing, planning, organizing, or implementing the transaction or series; promoting or selling an arrangement, plan, or scheme that includes, or relates to, the transaction or series; preparing the documents supporting the transaction or series, including tax returns or any information returns to be filed under the ITA; or providing "contractual protection". The three types of fees that cause the hallmark in (1) to be met include:

1. A fee of an advisor or promoter in respect of a transaction the computation of which is to any extent based on the amount of a tax benefit that could result from an avoidance transaction or series of transactions that include the avoidance transaction (for example, where the advisor or promoter sets a fee the amount of which is based on a percentage of the amount of the tax benefit from a transaction or series of transaction). A fee based solely on the value of the services provided in respect of a transaction or series, determined without reference to the tax results of the transaction or series, would not cause the hallmark in (1) to be met;

2. A fee for which the advisor or promoter has or had an entitlement that is contingent upon the obtaining of, or the failure to obtain, a tax benefit from an avoidance transaction. A fee could be considered to be contingent if the entitlement of the advisor or promoter to the fee under the relevant legal agreement arises upon the filing of an income tax return, when the tax benefit is confirmed by the CRA after audit, if any court confirms the tax benefit in whole or in part, or upon the expiration of the applicable assessment periods (or a shorter, agreed to, period) that apply to the taxation year. A fee may also be considered to be contingent if it may be refunded, recovered or reduced, in any manner whatever, based upon the failure of a person to obtain a tax benefit from the avoidance transaction (for example, if the tax benefit is denied on audit). A fee would not cause hallmark (1) to be met if no portion of the fee to which the advisor or promoter is entitled is dependent on the taxpayer obtaining any tax benefit. The hallmark also would not be met merely because a fee to which an advisor or promoter is entitled depends on whether a transaction or series is completed provided that the fee is not dependent on any tax benefit from the transaction or series; or

3. A fee that is attributable to the number of persons who enter into an avoidance transaction or series (or a similar transaction or series), or who have been provided access to advice or an opinion given by the advisor or promoter regarding the tax consequences from the avoidance transaction or series (or a similar transaction or series). Similar transactions include transactions having the same or similar structure and entered into by different taxpayers, when the objective of those transactions or series is to result in similar tax benefits, even if those transactions may involve different properties or obligations. For example, a broadly marketed scheme in which different taxpayers acquire and finance property separately, but where the property that each taxpayer acquires is similar in nature and where the financing structure that each taxpayer enters into is similar, may be considered similar avoidance transactions.

(2) — Confidential Protection Hallmark

The "confidential protection" hallmark would exist in respect of an avoidance transaction if an advisor or promoter in respect of the transaction has or had anything that would prohibit the disclosure to any person or to the CRA of details or the structure of the avoidance transaction (this is in contrast to a situation in which a client of an advisor benefits from solicitor-client privilege in respect of information regarding the avoidance transaction or series of transactions, and which would not give rise to a hallmark in respect of the transaction). The disclaiming or restricting of an advisor's liability is not considered confidential protection for this purpose if there is no prohibition of the disclosure of details or the structure of the avoidance transaction. For example, a standard provision found in many tax opinions limiting an adviser's liability solely to its client and disclaiming liability to any third parties would not be considered confidential protection. Also, "confidential protection" is only relevant as a hallmark in respect of an avoidance transaction if an advisor or promoter has such protection in respect of the avoidance transaction. For example, rights of confidentiality of a person who enters into a transaction will not be a hallmark where those rights protect the confidentiality entitlement of a person against the person's advisors, such as the rights of a client vis-à-vis a legal advisor.

(3) — Contractual Protection Hallmark

The "contractual protection" hallmark would exist in respect of an avoidance transaction if one of several persons had "contractual protection" in respect of the avoidance transaction otherwise than as a result of a fee described in (1) above. The applicable persons that may have "contractual protection" include: a person for whom a tax benefit could result from the avoidance transaction (the "particular person"); another person who entered into the avoidance transaction for the benefit of the particular person; or any other person who does not deal at arm's length with the particular person. "Contractual protection" in respect of a transaction is defined as including:

1. Any form of insurance (other than standard professional liability insurance) or other protection (including an indemnity, compensation, or a guarantee) that, either immediately or in the future and either absolutely or contingently, either protects a person against a failure of the avoidance transaction to achieve any tax benefit or pays for or reimburses any expense, fee, tax, interest, penalty, or similar amount that may be incurred by a person in the course of a dispute in respect of a tax benefit from the avoidance transaction, and

2. Any form or undertaking provided by a promoter, or by any person who does not deal at arm's length with the promoter, that provides, either immediately or in the future and either absolutely or contingently, assistance, directly or indirectly in any manner whatever, to a person in the course of a dispute in respect of a tax benefit from the transaction or series.

The first type of contractual protection concerns tax-result protection under which the taxpayer is compensated or indemnified should the tax benefit from the avoidance transaction not be achieved. Examples of such protection may include situations where a taxpayer would be entitled to be compensated for any fees to be incurred during the course of an audit, an objection to an assessment, reassessment, additional assessment, an appeal of an assessment to the Tax Court of Canada, or any other subsequent appeal to a court of higher jurisdiction in respect of a tax benefit that could result from an avoidance transaction or series. An advance income tax ruling obtained from the CRA is not considered contractual protection for this purpose.

The second type of contractual protection concerns situations where, in respect of a transaction, a promoter (or a person who does not deal at arm's length with the promoter) provides an undertaking to assist a person in the course of a dispute in respect of a tax benefit from the transaction or series, even if done for no consideration. This would include situations where the promoter offers to provide to a taxpayer relevant documentation and guidance to dispute an assessment or file an appeal of any court's decision in respect of the transaction or series.

Fees that are contingent upon the obtaining of a tax benefit by a person are excluded from the application of hallmark (3) to preclude a double recognition of such fees. In the absence of this specific exclusion, an advisor's or a promoter's fee might be considered as both a type of contractual protection as well as the type of fee referred to in hallmark (1) above.

An advisor or promoter (for example, a promoter or an insurer) entitled to a "fee" for providing contractual protection in respect of an avoidance transaction may have a reporting obligation in respect of the avoidance transaction along with the taxpayer who could benefit from the avoidance transaction. For example, if in respect of an avoidance transaction a taxpayer obtains "contractual protection" from the advisor or promoter that the taxpayer will be compensated for all or a portion of a denied tax benefit or litigation costs (including a refund of any portion of a fee charged by the advisor or promoter), two hallmarks will exist if any portion of the advisor or promoter's fees were contingent on the tax benefit not being denied (i.e., as hallmarks (1) and (3) would be met).

¶1322 — *Penalties for Failure to Report Avoidance Transactions*

If a complete and accurate Form RC312 is not filed as and when required, the CRA may impose a late-filing penalty on the persons who have failed to satisfy their reporting obligations and re-determine the tax consequences of any person for whom a tax benefit could result from the undisclosed reportable transaction or series that includes that transaction. The redetermination may be made as if the GAAR was deemed to apply to the transaction(s). The tax benefit resulting from the reportable transaction may be denied until the required Form RC312 has been filed and any related penalty and interest have been paid. Where the latter conditions are met, the CRA may allow a tax benefit from a reportable transaction disclosed after the filing deadline to be claimed if the tax benefit satisfies all of the requirements of the ITA, including the GAAR. The amount of the penalty for failure to file Form RC312 is equal to the total of all the fees for the transaction that the promoter or advisor was entitled to receive. Every person who is subject to a penalty under these rules is jointly and severally, or solidarily, liable to pay the penalty. However, under ITA 237.3(10), an advisor or a promoter, or a person who is not dealing at arm's length with the advisor or promoter, in respect of a reportable transaction that was not reported as and when required under section 237.3 is jointly and severally, or solidarily, liable to pay the penalty under ITA 237.3(8) only to the extent of the fees that the particular advisor or promoter, or non-arm's length person, is entitled to receive in respect of the undisclosed reportable transaction or the series that includes that transaction, and that is included in the amount of that penalty. A due diligence defence is available for persons who could be subject to the reporting requirements; if such a defence is successfully raised, penalties will not apply.

Even if an advisor has fulfilled his/her reporting obligation in respect of a reportable transaction and is not liable to the penalty, the fees that advisor is entitled to receive can be included in the amount of the penalty to which a taxpayer may be liable if the taxpayer fails to satisfy its reporting obligation in respect of other reportable transactions that are part of the same series of transactions.

A taxpayer will not be liable to a penalty if it is determined that the taxpayer has exercised the degree of care, diligence, and skill to prevent the failure that a reasonably prudent person would have exercised in comparable circumstances (i.e., a due diligence defence applies; see ITA 237.3(11)). The October 2012 Technical Notes state that it is intended that the application of the due diligence defence for the purpose of ITA 237.3 be based on the jurisprudence that applies in respect of similar defences for the purposes of other provisions of the ITA.

The normal reassessment period is extended to three years after the date Form RC312 is filed if the form is not filed as and when required (see ITA 152(4)(b.1)).

¶1330 — Claim for Tax Shelter Loss or Deduction

If an individual is claiming a loss or deduction from an interest in a tax shelter, file Form T5004 with the tax return. The promoter of the tax shelter is required to prepare Form T5003, *Statement of Tax Shelter Information*, and send copies to each investor. Attach copy 2 of Form T5003 to the T1 return (if the return is filed electronically, send the documents to the taxpayer's tax centre; see ¶1121). If the taxpayer is a limited partner of a partnership that invested in a tax shelter, complete Line 122 (see ¶3600). Otherwise, claim the amounts on the Line of the T1 return that corresponds with the type of loss or deduction that is being claimed. For example, claim a rental loss on Line 126 (see ¶5300), business loss on Line 135 (see ¶6100), farming loss on Line 141 (see ¶6450), business investment loss on Line 217 (see ¶4600), carrying charges and interest expenses on Line 221 (see ¶3710), exploration and development expenses on Line 224 (see ¶9240), and other deductions on Line 232 (see ¶9270).

A "tax shelter" is generally defined as (a) a "gifting arrangement" (as described in paragraph (b) of that definition) and (b) a "gifting arrangement" (as described in paragraph (a) of that definition) or any property (except certain specified property) in respect of which, on the basis of statements or representations made or proposed to be made, the total of losses and other amounts represented to be deductible in respect of the gifting arrangement or the interest in the property for taxation years ending on or before the end of four years after the date of entering the arrangement or acquiring the interest in the property would be expected to equal or exceed the cost of the property acquired under the arrangement or of the property interest, less certain prescribed benefits in respect of the property or property interest (such as contingent liabilities or limited recourse debt) that reduce the risk of loss in respect of the property or property interest. Complex rules apply to investments or arrangements that meet the definition of "tax shelters". The amount of an expenditure that is the cost of a tax shelter investment may be reduced by several amounts, such as "at-risk adjustments" or "limited recourse" amounts that relate to the expenditure. These reductions may also apply to persons that do not deal at arm's length with the investor. For examples of cases in which investments were found to meet the definition of tax shelter, see *Labelle*, [2004] 2 C.T.C. 3053 (TCC) and *Bernier*, [2005] 1 C.T.C. 125 (FCA).

A "promoter" (essentially an issuer, broker, sales agent, or advisor) in respect of a tax shelter is required to apply to the CRA and obtain an identification number before selling or issuing (either as a principal or as an agent) an interest in a tax shelter, or accepting consideration in respect of such an interest. The promoter is then required to make reasonable efforts to ensure that the identification number is provided to every person who acquires an interest in the tax shelter. In addition to these requirements, a promoter from whom an interest is acquired or who accepts consideration or acts as a principal or agent in respect of an acquisition of an interest is required to file an annual information return containing the name, address, and either the Social Insurance Number or business number, as well as other information required in a prescribed form concerning each person who acquired an interest. The CRA may invoke any of the procedures in ITA 231 to 231.3 (see ¶14100) to verify or ascertain any information in respect of the tax shelter. The CRA can also audit the tax shelter's books and records maintained by a taxpayer for the shelter at any time after application for an identification number has been made.

Applicable for amounts assessed for 2013 and later taxation years, where an amount in dispute is in respect of an assessment of tax, interest, or penalties that results from the disallowance of a deduction or tax credit claimed in respect of a tax shelter that involves a charitable donation, the CRA is allowed to collect 50 percent of the taxes, interest, and penalties in dispute.

Applicable to taxation years that end after March 20, 2013, the normal reassessment period is extended to three years after the date a tax shelter information return (Form T5003) is filed if the return is not filed on time.

ITA 237.1, IC 89-4, Pamphlet P113, Guide RC4407, *Kinglon Investments*, 2014 CarswellNat 1431 (TCC); rev'd 2015 CarswellNat 1636 (FCA) ("tax shelter" definition)

¶1400 — Filing Due Dates, Forms, Remitting, and Penalties

¶1410 — Filing Requirements Quick Reference Table

The ITA and ITRs impose many filing and payment obligations on individuals, and penalties and interest apply in respect of compliance infractions. The Filing Requirements Quick Reference Table below is intended to assist individuals meet tax payment and filing obligations imposed under the ITA. Requirements beyond those applicable to personal income tax returns are addressed.

Due Date	Form	Description	Comments	Reference
1-Jan	NR6	Undertaking to File a Tax Return by a Non-Resident Receiving Rent from Real Property or Receiving a Timber Royalty	A non-resident person may file Form NR6 on or before January 1 of the year in question (or before the first rental payment for the year is due). By filing Form NR6, the non-resident is undertaking to file a T1 return within 6 months after the end of the taxation year (regardless of whether there is a profit or loss). The election allows the agent (a resident of Canada to whom the rental payments are paid or credited on behalf of the non-resident) to withhold and remit at the applicable rate on the net amount (rather than the gross amount) of the rents or royalties received for remittance to the non-resident (i.e., on the excess of rents or royalties over disbursements for items such as repairs and maintenance, property taxes, property management fees and interest charges relating to the property in question). Tax withheld is applied against the non-resident's taxes payable for the year (due April 30 of the following year).	¶15311, ITA 216(4), Guide T4144
1-Jan	T1287	Non-resident actors	A non-resident actor who receives payments for acting services rendered in Canada who intends to file an income tax return in Canada can apply to the CRA for a reduction in the non-resident tax withheld from payments. Form T1287 should be filed before a payment is received for the year.	¶15313, ITA 216.1(1), Guides T4058, 5013-G
30-Jan	N/A	Family loans; interest payment deadline	ITA 74.1 is designed to prevent an individual from splitting income with family members to reduce the total amount of tax otherwise payable on income from property. ITA 74.1 does not apply, however, to loans of property that bear a commercial rate of interest provided the annual interest is paid in the year or within 30 days after the end of the year.	¶14220, ITA 74.1(2), 74.5(1), IT-511R
30-Jan	N/A	Employee loans; interest payment deadline	The amount of a taxable employment benefit attributable to a low-interest employee loan is the interest for the period of the loan or debt at the prescribed rate less the interest actually paid during the year or not later than 30 days after the end of the year.	¶2235, ITA 80.4(1), IT-421R2
31-Jan	TD1X	Commission employees; election to reduce taxes withheld at source	A commission-remunerated employee may elect under ITR 107(2) for source deductions to be reduced in respect of the employee's expenses, including estimated deductions under ITA 8(1)(f), (h) and (j) (i.e., sales, travel, and vehicle employment expenses). The election must be filed with an employer by January 31 if the individual had the same employer in the previous taxation year.	¶2435, ITR 107(2), Guide T4001

Due Date	Form	Description	Comments	Reference
14-Feb	N/A	Deadline to reimburse an employer for personal-use of company vehicle	Where an employer pays automobile operating expenses (including gas, insurance, and maintenance costs) relating to the personal use of an automobile by an employee, the payment is a taxable benefit to the employee under ITA 6(1)(k) or (l). Any reimbursements to the payer in respect of operating expenses reduce the amount included in employment income to the extent that the reimbursements are made in the year or within 45 days after the end of the year.	¶2130, ITA 6(1)(k), Guide T4130
1-Mar	N/A	RRSP contribution deadline in respect of prior year	The RRSP contribution deadline for contributions to be deductible in respect of a particular taxation year is 60 days after the end of the year. As such, the deadline is normally March 1st (in a leap year, the deadline is normally February 29th, unless February 29th falls on a Saturday or a Sunday).	¶9130 ITA 146(5)
15-Mar	INNS3, Instalment Remittance Voucher	First instalment due (individuals other than farmers and fisherman)	Instalments are generally required where an individual's "net tax owing" (as defined in ITA 156.1(1)) for the current taxation year or for each of the two preceding taxation years exceeds $3,000 (or $1,800 in Quebec). If the payment due date falls on a Saturday, Sunday, or a statutory holiday, the payment will be considered as having been received on time if it is received the first business day after the due date.	¶1210 ITA 156(1), Pamphlet P110
31-Mar	T1134	Foreign affiliate reporting	An individual with foreign affiliates at any time in a taxation year must file Form T1134: *Information Return Relating to Controlled and Not-Controlled Foreign Affiliates* within 15 months after the end of the taxation year (reduced to 12 months for 2020 and 10 months after 2020). A separate form must be filed for each foreign affiliate.	¶3532, ITA 233.4
Mar. 31	NR4 Summary and Slips	Amounts paid or credited by residents of Canada to non-resident persons	Form NR4 must be filed by a taxpayer who makes payments to non-residents of Canada of income such as interest, dividends, rents, royalties, and pensions. Form NR4: *Statement of Amounts Paid or Credited to Non-Residents of Canada* and Form NR4 *Summary: Return of Amounts Paid or Credited to Non-Residents of Canada* must be filed if the total annual amount paid or credited to a non-resident is $50 or more. The forms must be filed on or before the last day of March following the calendar year to which the information return applies.	¶15300, ITR 202, Guide T4061

Due Date	Form	Description	Comments	Reference
31-Mar	T1-OVP	Tax Return in respect of RRSP Excess Contributions	Where an individual makes excess contributions to an RRSP, the contributions are non-deductible and a special penalty tax of 1% per month may apply to the "cumulative excess amount" (basically the amount by which an individual's undeducted RRSP premiums at the relevant time exceed his/her RRSP deduction limit for the year) at the end of the month under Part X.1. The first $2,000 of overcontributions is not subject to the special tax. Although Part X.1 tax is calculated on a monthly basis, it is payable annually. Form T1-OVP must be filed within 90 days after the end of the year.	¶9135, ITA 204.3(1), Guide T4040
31-Mar	N/A	Special taxes in respect of excess TFSA contributions (Part XI.01)	If in a calendar month there is an "excess TFSA amount" in an individual's TFSA account, the individual may be subject to a penalty tax of 1% of the highest such amount in that month. A penalty tax may also apply if a prohibited investment or a non-qualified investment is acquired by the TFSA (or if property held in the TFSA becomes such a property). The TFSA holder may be entitled to a refund of taxes paid on non-qualified investments or prohibited investments if the TFSA trust sells the property (or if the property ceases to be a non-qualified or prohibited investment) before the end of the calendar year following the calendar year in which the tax arose. A tax may also be applied in certain other situations, such as when an "advantage" is conferred. A person liable to pay Part XI.01 tax is required to file a return in prescribed form within 90 days after the end of the year and to pay the tax to the Receiver General.	¶16210, ITA 207.07(1), Guide RC4466
31-Mar	N/A	Special taxes in respect of Registered Disability Savings Plans (Part XI)	A tax may be payable in respect of an RDSP where the trust acquires property that is a non-qualified investment or where property within the RDSP becomes a non-qualified investment. Also, a tax may be payable if an individual receives an "advantage" in respect to an RDSP or if the trust disposes of property and receives inadequate consideration. Each person who is a holder of an RDSP at the time that a tax is imposed in connection with the plan is jointly liable to pay the tax. If there is a tax liability, an individual is required to pay the Part XI tax no later than 90 days following the end of the calendar year for which the tax is applicable and to file a corresponding return; a form has not been prescribed for this purpose.	¶ 16230, ITA 207(1), Guide RC4460

Due Date	Form	Description	Comments	Reference
30-Apr	T1	Income tax and benefit return	April 30 is the regular filing due date for an individual's tax return (Form T1). See the comments to June 15 for a self-employed taxpayer. In the case of a deceased individual or a cohabiting spouse or "common-law partner" of a deceased individual, where the individual passes away after October in the year, Form T1 is due 6 months after the day of the individual's death.	¶1140, ITA 150(1)(b), (d), Guides 5000-G, T4058, T4011
30-Apr	T7DR — Remittance Voucher	Remainder of taxes payable	Every individual is required to pay to the Receiver General, on or before his/her "balance-due day" for each taxation year, the amount (if any) by which his/her Part I tax payable for the year exceeds the total of all amounts deducted or withheld under ITA 153 and all other amounts paid to the Receiver General on account of the individual's Part I tax payable for the year. Note that individuals reporting business income that have a filing due date of June 15th also must pay their balance of taxes due by April 30.	¶1230, ITA 156.1(4)
30-Apr	T183	Information Return for Electronic Filing of an Individual's Income Tax and Benefit Return	For EFILED returns, Form T183 must be completed in duplicate and signed by the client (the person required to file the return) before the return is transmitted. The use of signature labels on Form T183 is not acceptable. A signature other than the client's is acceptable if a power of attorney exits. Both the preparer and client are required to retain a copy of Form T183. Form T183 must be retained for at least six years following the date that the return was filed. If the return as originally transmitted is not accepted and the changes required for retransmission alter the refund or balance owing by more than $300, a new Form T183 is required to be completed and signed.	¶1123, ITA 150.1(4)
30-Apr	T1A	Request for Loss Carryback	To make a carryback claim, a taxpayer essentially amends his/her return for the earlier taxation year when taking the deduction. The taxpayer must have filed a return for the earlier year to make a carryback claim. A claim may be made by filing Form T1A no later than the date on or before which the taxpayer is required to file the return for the taxation year in which the loss was incurred (normally April 30).	¶9360, ¶9370, ITA 152(6)
30-Apr	T1135	Foreign Income Verification Statement	An individual is required to file Form T1135: *Foreign Income Verification Statement*, if, at any time in the year, the total cost of all specified foreign property the individual owned or held a beneficiary interest in was more than $100,000. Form T1135 is required to be filed with Form T1 on or before the individual's tax return filing-due date for the year (normally April 30).	¶1154, ¶3531, ITA 233.3

Due Date	Form	Description	Comments	Reference
30-Apr	T1136	Old Age Security Return of Income	A non-resident of Canada receiving OAS pension payments is required to file Form T1136; otherwise, OAS payments may not be received by virtue of ITA 180.2(4)(b)(ii). The CRA uses Form T1136 to determine the amount of OAS recovery tax, if any, an individual is subject to; recovery tax is calculated based on net world income. The OAS return does not have to be filed if a regular T1 return has been filed for the base year.	¶ 8110, ¶ 15230, ITA 180.2(5), Guide T4155
30-Apr	T1141	Transfers or loans to a specified foreign trust	Form T1141: *Information Return in Respect of Transfers or Loans to a Non-Resident Trust*, must be filed if an individual (or a controlled foreign affiliate of the individual) has transferred or loaned property to a specified foreign trust or a non-resident corporation controlled by the trust. Form T1141 must be filed on or before the individual's tax return filing-due date for the year (normally April 30).	¶3533, ITA 233.2
30-Apr	T1142	Distributions from or indebtedness to a non-resident trust	Form T1142: *Information Return in Respect of Distributions from and Indebtedness to a Non-Resident Trust* must be filed by an individual that: 1) is a beneficiary of a non-resident trust (other than an excluded trust) at any time in the year, and 2) received a distribution from or was indebted to the non-resident trust in the year. Form T1142 must be filed on or before the individual's tax return filing-due date for the year (normally April 30).	¶3534, ITA 233.6
30-Apr	T1	Non-resident actor electing under section 216.1; return due	Subsection 212(5.1) requires a non-resident actor to pay an income tax of 23% on every amount paid or credited (or provided as a benefit) to or on behalf of the person for the provision in Canada of the actor's acting services in a film or video production. ITA 216.1(1) enables such recipients to file a Part I return and elect therein to pay tax at marginal rates on net income (instead of 23% on the gross amount). A non-resident actor who receives payments for acting services rendered in Canada that intends to file an income tax return in Canada can apply to the CRA for a reduction in the non-resident tax withheld from payments (see Form T1287). For a self-employed actor, a tax return is due on or before June 15.	¶15313, ITA 216.1(1), Guides T4058, 5013-G

Due Date	Form	Description	Comments	Reference
30-Apr	T1172	Additional Tax on Accumulated Income Payments from RESPs	A person liable to pay Part X.5 tax for a taxation year is required to file a Part X.5 return. RESP promoters report accumulated income payments (AIPs) in Box 40 of Form T4A. The recipient has to include the AIP as income on his/her tax return in the year the AIP is received. Form T1172 is required to be filed on or before the individual's tax return filing-due date for the year (normally April 30). Part X.5 tax, if any, is normally due by April 30 of the year that follows the year in which the individual receives the AIP.	¶11060, ITA 204.94(3)
30-Apr	T1198	Statement of Qualifying Retroactive Lump-Sum Payment	ITA 110.2(2) allows a deduction in respect of a qualifying retroactive amount. Generally, the individual's taxable income is reduced by the principal portion of the payments relating to previous years and a tax adjustment is calculated under ITA 120.31 in respect of such amounts. The recipient of the payment is required to attach Form T1198 to his/her return filed for the year in which the retroactive lump-sum payments were received for the special rules to apply. If the tax computed using the special calculation is less than the amount calculated under the normal tax rules, the recipient of the payment is required to pay only the lesser amount. When an individual attaches Form T1198 to his or her tax return, the CRA will only apply the special tax calculation if it is beneficial to the taxpayer.	¶8221, ¶8242, ¶9212, ITA 110.2(2)
30-Apr	T661	SR&ED Expenditures Claim	In order to deduct an amount as an SR&ED expenditure under ITA 37(1), a taxpayer is required to file Form T661 with the CRA within one year of the taxpayer's filing-due date for the year in which the expenditure was incurred. In other words, individuals normally have until April 30 from the calendar year following the calendar year in which the expenditures were incurred to file an SR&ED claim. A provincial claim form may also be required.	¶11032, ITA 37(11), Guides T4012, T4088, Form T2038 (IND)
31-May	N/A	EPSP and DPSP contribution deadline	To be deductible, contributions to an Employee Profit Sharing Plan or a Deferred Profit Sharing Plan are required to be paid to the trustee during the year or within 120 days thereafter.	ITA 144(5), 147(8), IT-280R
15-Jun	INNS3, Instalment Remittance Voucher	Second instalment due (individuals other than farmers and fisherman)	See comments under March 15. If the payment due date falls on a Saturday, Sunday, or a statutory holiday, the payment will be considered as having been received on time if it is received the first business day after the due date.	¶1210 ITA 156(1)

Due Date	Form	Description	Comments	Reference
15-Jun	T1	Income tax and benefit return (self-employed taxpayers)	In the case of an individual who carried on a business in the year or a person who was at any time in the year a cohabiting spouse or common-law partner of such an individual, a personal tax return (Form T1) is due on or before June 15 (note that the balance of taxes payable were due on April 30).	¶1140, ITA 150(1)(d)
28-Jun	N/A	Unpaid bonus or other employee remuneration	In the case of unpaid remuneration in respect of an office or employment, deductibility is generally limited to amounts paid within 180 days after the end of the taxation year in which the expense was incurred. If the amount is not paid within these 180 days, ITA 78(4) permits the employer to deduct an amount only in the taxation year in which it is actually paid. ITA 78(4) expressly provides that it does not apply to reasonable vacation or holiday pay or to a deferred amount under a salary deferral arrangement. This provision may apply, for example, to an owner-manager bonus accrued at year-end.	ITA 78(4)
30-Jun	T1	Non-resident electing under section 217	ITA 217(2) provides that no Part XIII tax is payable in respect of a non-resident person's "Canadian benefits" (generally pension or similar payments) for a taxation year provided the non-resident both files a Part I return for the year within 6 months after the end of the year and elects in that return to have ITA 217 apply. A non-resident intending to make a section 217 election on eligible income that has not yet been received may apply to reduce the tax the payer would otherwise be required to withhold at source (see Form NR5). A non-resident is required to file a section 217 return if Form NR5 is filed. For Quebec residents, see also Form TP-1016-V.	¶15312, ITA 217(2), Guide 5013-G, Pamphlet T4145
30-Jun	T1159	Non-resident electing under section 216	Where a non-resident has filed Form NR6: *Undertaking to File an Income Tax Return by a Non-Resident Receiving Rent from Real Property or Receiving a Timber Royalty for Tax Year*, the non-resident is required to file a return under ITA 216 (see Form T1159) within 6 months after the end of the taxation year.	¶15311 ITA 216(4), Guide T4144
15-Sep	Instalment Remittance Voucher	Third instalment due (individuals other than farmers and fisherman)	See comments under March 15. If the payment due date falls on a Saturday, Sunday, or a statutory holiday, the payment will be considered as having been received on time if it is received the first business day after the due date.	¶1215 ITA 156(1)

Due Date	Form	Description	Comments	Reference
30-Sep	N/A	Last day to purchase a qualifying home under HBP	Where an individual makes an RRSP withdrawal under the Home Buyers' Plan (HBP), the qualifying home must be acquired by October 1 of the calendar year following the calendar year of the withdrawal (unless the individual dies before the end of that following calendar year); see the definition "completion date" in ITA 146.01(1).	¶9130, ITA 146.01(1)
1-Oct	NR5	Application for a Reduction in the Amount of Non-Resident Tax Required to be Withheld	A non-resident intending to make a section 217 election on eligible income that has not yet been received may apply to reduce the tax the payer would otherwise be required to withhold at source (see Form NR5). ITA 217 generally applies to a non-resident who receives pension or similar payments. The CRA uses Form NR5 to determine if an election under ITA 217 would be beneficial for an individual. If Form NR5 is approved, the CRA advises the payer to reduce the rate at which tax is withheld. The CRA has stated that Form NR5 should be filed by October 1 before the taxation year in question or before the first payment for the year is made to the non-resident.	¶15312, ITA 217(2), Pamphlet T4145
1-Dec	N/A	Consider selling securities with accrued losses before end of year	Generally, if an individual disposes of securities held on capital account (outside of an RRSP) with an accrued loss on or before December 31 of a calendar year, subject to the application of the superficial loss rules, the capital loss may be applied to reduce capital gains realized in the year (or in any of the three preceding years). A superficial loss generally arises on the disposition of a property when the same or identical property is acquired within 30 days before or after the disposition by the individual, the individual's spouse or common-law partner or by a corporation controlled, directly or indirectly in any manner whatever, by the individual. An unused portion of a capital loss may be carried forward indefinitely.	¶4812, ITA 39(1)
1-Dec	N/A	Consider sale of non-qualifying RRSP investments before end of year	Where RRSP funds are used to acquire a non-qualified investment, the fair market value of the investment at the time of its acquisition is required to be included in computing the annuitant's income for the year. Where an amount is included in an RRSP annuitant's income under ITA 146(10) on money used by the trustee to purchase a non-qualified investment, the annuitant may deduct that amount to the extent that it is recovered on the sale of the non-qualified investment.	¶9130, ITA 146(6), Guide T4079

Due Date	Form	Description	Comments	Reference
1-Dec	N/A	Consider sale of non-qualifying RDSP investments before end of year	A penalty tax may apply if a non-qualified investment is acquired by an RDSP (or if property held in the trust becomes such a property). Where this tax is paid, a refund may be claimed if the non-qualified investments are sold before the end of the calendar year following the calendar year in which the tax arose or if the property ceases to be a non-qualified or prohibited investment before the end of the calendar year following the calendar year in which the tax arose.	¶16230, ITA 207(2)
1-Dec	N/A	Consider sale of non-qualifying TFSA investments before end of year	A penalty tax may apply if a prohibited investment or a non-qualified investment is acquired by a TFSA (or if property held in a TFSA becomes such a property). The TFSA holder may be entitled to a refund of taxes paid on non-qualified investments or prohibited investments if the TFSA trust sells the property before the end of the calendar year following the calendar year in which the tax arose or if the property ceases to be a non-qualified or prohibited investment before the end of the calendar year following the calendar year in which the tax arose.	¶16210, ITA 207.01(2)
15-Dec	INNS3, Instalment Remittance Voucher	Fourth instalment due (individuals other than farmers and fisherman)	See comments under March 15. If the payment due date falls on a Saturday, Sunday, or a statutory holiday, the payment will be considered as having been received on time if it is received the first business day after the due date.	¶1210 ITA 156(1)
15-Dec	N/A	Consider paying deductible expenses or making donations or contributions before the end of year	Certain amounts are required to be paid by December 31 to claim a deduction or credit. For example, the following amounts must be paid (or gifted) by the end of a calendar year to receive a related credit or deduction: interest incurred to earn investment income, investment counsel fees, spousal support payments, moving expenses, child care expenses, certain amounts paid by a disabled individual in respect of which a disability supports deduction may be claimed, adoption expenses, donations, medical expenses, tuition fees, student loans interest, political contributions, and contributions to a registered pension plan. Note that eligible medical expenses paid by an individual within any selected period of 12 consecutive months the last day of which falls within a particular calendar year may qualify for purposes of the medical expense credit in that year. Donations can generally be carried forward for five taxation years during which a credit may be claimed.	20(1)(c), 20(1)(bb), 60(b), 62(1), 63(1), 64(a), 118.01(2), 118.03(2), 118.1(3), 118.2(2), 118.5(1), 118.62, 127(3), 147.2(4), Guide 5000-G

Due Date	Form	Description	Comments	Reference
31-Dec	INNS3, Instalment Remittance Voucher	Instalment due (farmers and fisherman)	ITA 155 permits farmers and fishermen to delay their first instalment payment until December 31, at which time they have the choice of paying 2/3 of either: 1) the amount they estimate to be their Part I tax payable for that taxation year, or 2) the "instalment base" for the preceding taxation year. They are then given until their "balance-due day" (normally April 30) for the year to pay the remainder.	¶1210 ITA 155(1)
31-Dec	N/A	Shareholder debt; repayment within one year to avoid deemed dividend treatment	If a corporation or partnership in the chain of related parties contemplated by ITA 15(2) makes a loan to one of the corporation's shareholders or a "connected person", the amount of the loan must be included in computing the income of that shareholder or connected person for the year in which the loan is received. However, no loan or indebtedness will give rise to an income inclusion under ITA 15(2) if it is repaid within one year after the end of the lender's taxation year in which the loan was made or the indebtedness arose, provided the repayment was not part of a series of loans and repayments.	¶14352 ITA 15(2.6), IT-119R4
31-Dec	N/A	Election for vehicle operating expense benefit to equal one-half of standby charge	ITA 6(1)(k) provides for two methods of determining the benefit in respect of operating costs paid for by the employer in respect of an employer provided vehicle. If the automobile is used more than 50% for employment purposes, the employee has the option of using as the operating expense benefit one-half of the standby charge reduced by any reimbursements of expenses in respect of the operation of the automobile repaid to the employer in the year or within 45 days after the end of the year. To choose this option, the employee is required to notify his/her employer in writing before the end of the year. Where the optional method is not chosen, the operating expense benefit is generally determined by multiplying the total number of km that the automobile is driven for personal use by a prescribed amount and subtracting reimbursements paid to the employer in the year or within 45 days after the end of the year.	¶2130, ITA 6(1)(k), ITR 7305.1, IT-63R5

Due Date	Form	Description	Comments	Reference
31-Dec	N/A	Non-arm's length corporate loans; interest payment deadline	ITA 74.4 is intended to prevent an individual from splitting income with family members by lending or transferring property to a corporation where the individual's spouse or common-law partner or certain minors have at any time thereafter, directly or indirectly, an interest in the corporation. Any income attributed to a taxpayer under ITA 74.4(2) is reduced by the amount of interest received in the year by the individual who transferred property or lent amounts to the corporation.	¶14250, ITA 74.4(2)
31-Dec	N/A	Consider making RESP contribution	Generally, the government provides a grant of 20% of the first $2,500 of annual RESP contributions for a qualifying beneficiary. No CES grant may be paid in respect of a contribution for a beneficiary unless the beneficiary's Social Insurance Number is provided and the beneficiary is resident in Canada at the time the contribution is made. The maximum lifetime grant that a beneficiary born after 1997 may receive is $7,200 (see 5(10) of the CESA). These grants are paid directly to the trustee of the RESP and are paid out to the beneficiary as part of his/her educational assistance payments.	¶16220, 5(2) and (3) of the *Canada Education Savings Act*
31-Dec	N/A	Consider making RDSP contribution	Generally, the government may pay a Canada Disability Savings Grant (CDSG) into an RDSP in respect of any contribution made to the RDSP. The amount of a CDSG for a particular year depends on family income levels; generally, the maximum grant is $3,500 for low-income families and $1,000 for high income families. Not more than $70,000 in CDSGs may be paid in respect of a beneficiary during the beneficiary's lifetime. Pursuant to ss. 7(1) of the CDSA, the Minister may also pay a Canada Disability Savings Bond (CDSB) into an RDSP of a beneficiary. The maximum annual CDSB is $1,000 and the maximum lifetime CDSB payments that may be paid in respect of a beneficiary is $20,000.	¶16230, 6 and 7 of the *Canada Disability Savings Act*

Due Date	Form	Description	Comments	Reference
31-Dec	NR7-R	Application for Refund of Part XIII Tax Withheld	Any non-resident person on whose behalf tax has been withheld under Part XII.5 or XIII of the Act may recover any such tax for which the person is not liable by making written application to the Minister no later than 2 years after the end of the calendar year in which the amount was paid. The application for a refund is made by filing Form NR7-R. It should be noted that tax required to be withheld from the purchase price of certain property under ITA 116 does not fall within these provisions. The non-treaty reduced withholding tax rate applicable to amounts paid to non-residents under Part XIII is 25%; this rate is reduced to 10% under most treaties in respect of interest and to 15% in respect of dividends.	ITA 227(6), VD 2007-0253901E5
31-Dec	NR7-R	Application for refund of withholding tax paid	If a dividend is deemed to have been paid to a non-resident under subsection 15(2), subsection 227(6.1) provides for a refund of Part XIII tax paid when that loan or indebtedness is repaid. In order to obtain the refund, the repayment cannot have been made as part of a series of loans and repayments. Where only a portion of the loan has been repaid, the amount of the refund is based on the tax that was paid on that portion of the loan or indebtedness. The refund is limited to the lesser of: 1) the tax originally paid in respect of the amount of the loan repaid, and 2) the Part XIII tax that would be payable at the time of the repayment if a dividend equal to that amount were paid to the non-resident at that time. In order to obtain the refund, an application must be made to the CRA within 2 years after the end of the calendar year in which the repayment is made.	¶14352, ITA 227(6.1)
10th day after the disposition	T2062	Request by a Non-Resident for a Certificate related to Disposition of a Taxable Canadian Property	Generally, Canadian income tax is payable by a non-resident on taxable capital gains realized on the disposition of "taxable Canadian property" (defined in ITA 248(1)) other than "treaty-protected property" (see ITA 2(3) and 115(1)(b)). When a non-resident of Canada disposes of "taxable Canadian property", the non-resident is required to notify the CRA of the proposed or actual disposition on Form T2062. On a proposed disposition, the seller may either prepay or provide security for the tax that may be payable. If the non-resident does not notify the CRA of the proposed disposition or if the information about the proposed disposition changed, the seller has 10 days after the disposition to advise the CRA.	ITA 116(1), (3)

¶1420 — Penalties Quick Reference Table

Form	Infraction	Penalty	Reference
T1	Late-filed tax return	The late-filing penalty is based on the unpaid amount of Part I tax payable for the year at the time the return was required to be filed. The penalty is calculated on the Part I tax payable before any reduction as a result of the application of any subsequent carrybacks and is equal to 5% of the unpaid amount, plus 1% for each complete month the return was late, to a maximum of 12 months. This is not a discretionary penalty and is automatically calculated and applied on assessment or reassessment. The maximum late-filing penalty under ITA 162(1) is 17% (5% + 12%) of the tax that was unpaid at the time the return was required to be filed. If the T1 return is filed by the deadline, penalties will not apply even if the taxpayer has an outstanding balance of taxes payable in respect of the taxation year. A higher penalty applies to repeat offenders — see below.	¶1140 ITA 162(1)
T1	Late-filed tax return; repeated failure to file	For individuals who have failed to file a T1 return as and when required, where a demand for the return has been served under ITA 150(2), and before the time of the failure to file as required by ITA 150(1), a penalty was payable under ITA 162(1) or (2) in respect of a tax return for any of the three preceding taxation years, an increased penalty applies equal to the total of 10% of the Part I tax payable for the year unpaid at the time the return was required to be filed plus 2% of such unpaid tax multiplied by the number of complete months, not exceeding 20, from the date on which the return was required to be filed to the date on which the return was actually filed.	¶1140 ITA 162(2), *Hughes*, 2017 CarswellNat 2535 (TCC)
T1	Failure to file electronically	A "tax preparer" may be assessed a penalty for a failure to file a tax return by way of electronic filing as required by ITA 150.1(2.3). The penalty is $25 for each failure to file an individual return in electronic format (and $100 for each failure to file a corporate return in electronic format).	¶1123.1 ITA 162(7.3)
N/A	Late payment of balance of taxes due	Where the balance of tax an individual owes for a taxation year is paid late, interest applies. Interest commences to run from the taxpayer's "balance-due day" for the taxation year. The rate of interest is prescribed by Part XLIII of the ITR.	¶1230 ITA 161(1)
N/A	Late or deficient tax instalments	The CRA charges arrears interest on late instalments according to the prescribed interest rate (ITR 4301). Arrears interest is compounded daily on any unpaid balance from the balance due date to the date of payment. When instalment interest owed is more than $1,000, the CRA may charge an instalment penalty. The penalty is computed by subtracting from the instalment interest the greater of: 1) $1,000, and 2) 25% of the instalment interest calculated if no instalment payment had been made for the year. One-half of the difference is the amount of the penalty. The CRA also charges interest on any instalment penalty from the balance due date to the date it is paid.	¶1220 ITA 161(2), (11), 163.1

Form	Infraction	Penalty	Reference
N/A	Late payment of a penalty	Pursuant to ITA 161(11), where a penalty is payable under ITA 162, 163 or 235, interest at the prescribed rate is payable on any unpaid penalty from the day on or before which the taxpayer's return of income for the year was required to be filed (or would have been required to be filed if tax were payable under Part I) until payment interest is charged on penalties until the date that they are paid.	ITA 161(11), VD 2009-0335321E5
N/A	Failure to provide information required on form	In addition to penalties referred to above, where a person has filed a return of income but has failed to complete the information required by a prescribed form made pursuant to the ITA or an ITR, ITA 162(5) imposes a penalty of $100 for each such failure. By virtue of ITA 220(3.1), the CRA has the power to cancel or waive all or any portion of the penalty. The penalty under ITA 162(5) cannot be imposed if the information was in respect of another person or partnership and a reasonable effort was made to obtain it from that person or partnership.	ITA 162(5)
Various	Failure to file information return	Applicable to returns required to be filed on or before a day that is after 1997 and to duties and obligations first imposed after 1997, failure by a person to file any information return as and when required by the ITA or ITRs or to comply with any duty or obligation imposed thereunder renders that person liable to a penalty equal to the greater of: 1) $100, and 2) $25 multiplied by the number of days of failure (to a maximum of 100 days). ITA 162(7) is only applicable where another provision of the ITA (other than ITA 162(10) or (10.1) or 163(2.22)) sets out a penalty for the failure. Where a non-resident fails to file a return as and when required by ITA 150(1) but no tax is payable for the period and ITA 162(2.1) does not apply, a parallel penalty under paragraph 162(7)(b) applies.	ITA 162(7), *Exida*, [2010] 5 C.T.C. 149 (FCA), *Douglas*, 2012 CarswellNat 479 (TCC) (penalty waived)
Various	Intentional or negligent false statements or omissions	The penalty is equal to the greater of: i) $100 and ii) 50% of the understatement of tax and/or the overstatement of credits related to the false statement or omission. For ITA 163(2) to apply, there must be: a) a liability for tax; b) a false statement or omission in a return filed as required by or under the ITA or an ITR; c) knowledge or gross negligence by the person in the making of a false statement or omission; d) an understatement of income for a year, as defined by ITA 163(2.1), that is reasonably attributable to the false statement or omission. In applying the penalty, total unreported income may be reduced by the total of amounts deductible, but not deducted from than income; however, no deduction is allowed if part of the deduction relates to reported income.	ITA 163(2), *Roy*, [2001] 3 C.T.C. 226 (FCA), VD 2009-0344291I7

Form	Infraction	Penalty	Reference
T1	Failing to report income in a tax return	In addition to the penalties referred to above in respect of late-filed returns, a taxpayer may be subject to other penalties. For example, where an individual who files a T1 return fails to report an amount required to be included in income of at least $500, the individual will be subject to a penalty of 10% of the amount that should have been reported if the individual had previously failed in any return for any of the three preceding taxation years to report an amount required to be included in computing income. A taxpayer is entitled to a due diligence defense when assessed a penalty under ITA 163(1).	ITA 163(1), (1.1), VD 2010-035636117
T1-OVP	Late filed return, late payment	The penalty for late-filing Form T1-OVP is 5% of the balance owing, plus 1% of the balance owing for each month that the return is late, to a maximum of 12 months. The late-filing penalty may be higher if CRA charged the individual a late-filing penalty on Form T1-OVP return for any of three previous years.	¶9135 161(11), 162(1), 204.3(2)
T1134	Late-filed	The penalty for a late-filed T1134 is $25 for each day of default with a minimum penalty of $100 and a maximum penalty of $2,500 (ITA 162(7)). ITA 162(10.1) imposes a penalty in cases where a person or partnership is liable for a penalty under ITA 162(10) and the return is more than 24 months late. The penalty is basically 5% of the greatest total cost amount to the person or partnership of the shares and debt of the affiliate. The penalty under ITA 162(10.1) is "in addition to" the penalty under ITA 162(10), but the amount of the penalty under ITA 162(10.1) is reduced by the total penalties to which the person or partnership is liable under ITA 162(7) and (10) in respect of the return.	¶3532 ITA 162(7), (10.1), VD 2014-053770117
T1134	Failure to furnish foreign-based information	Every person or partnership who, knowingly or under circumstances amounting to gross negligence, fails to file a T1134 or comply with a demand to file such a return is subject to a penalty of $500 or $1,000 per month, depending on the circumstances set out in paragraphs 162(10)(a) and (b). The penalty is computed based on a maximum of 24 months (minus the penalty in ITA 162(7)). See also ITA 163(2) and (2.4) (penalty for false statements or omissions) and ITA 238 and 239 (offenses).	¶3532 ITA 162(10), VD 2014-053770117
T1135	Late-filed	The penalty for a late-filed T1135 is $25 for each day of default with a minimum penalty of $100 and a maximum penalty of $2,500. ITA 162(10.1) imposes a penalty in cases where a person or partnership is liable for a penalty under ITA 162(10) and the return is more than 24 months late. The penalty is basically 5% of the greatest total cost amount to the person or partnership of specified foreign property in the year or period. The penalty under ITA 162(10.1) is "in addition to" the penalty under ITA 162(10), but the amount of the penalty under ITA 162(10.1) is reduced by the total penalties to which the person or partnership is liable under ITA 162(7) and (10) in respect of the return.	¶1154, ¶3531 ITA 162(7), (10.1), *Douglas*, 2012 CarswellNat 479 (TCC) (penalty waived) VDs 2015-057277117, 2016-0641511C6

Form	Infraction	Penalty	Reference
T1135	Failure to furnish foreign-based information	Every person or partnership who, knowingly or under circumstances amounting to gross negligence, fails to file a T1135 or comply with a demand to file such a return is subject to a penalty of $500 or $1,000 per month, depending on the circumstances set out in paragraphs 162(10)(a) and (b). The penalty is computed based on a maximum of 24 months (minus the penalty in ITA 162(7)). See also ITA 163(2) and (2.4) (penalty for false statements or omissions) and ITA 238 and 239 (offenses).	¶1154, ¶3531 ITA 162(10)
T1141	Late-filed	The penalty for a late-filed T1141 is $25 for each day of default with a minimum penalty of $100 and a maximum penalty of $2,500. ITA 162(10.1) imposes a penalty in cases where a person or partnership is liable for a penalty under ITA 162(10) and the return is more than 24 months late. The penalty is basically 5% of total fair market value of the minimum transfer or loan that necessitated the filing of the return. The penalty under ITA 162(10.1) is "in addition to" the penalty under ITA 162(10), but the amount of the penalty under ITA 162(10.1) is reduced by the total penalties to which the person or partnership is liable under ITA 162(7) and (10) in respect of the return.	¶3533 ITA 162(7), (10.1)
T1141	Failure to furnish foreign-based information	Every person or partnership who, knowingly or under circumstances amounting to gross negligence, fails to file a T1141 or comply with a demand to file such a return is subject to a penalty of $500 or $1,000 per month, depending on the circumstances set out in paragraphs 162(10)(a) and (b). The penalty is computed based on a maximum of 24 months (minus the penalty in ITA 162(7)). See also ITA 163(2) and (2.4) (penalty for false statements or omissions) and sections 238 and 239 (offenses).	¶3533 ITA 162(10)
T1142	Late-filed	The penalty for a late-filed T1142 is $25 for each day of default with a minimum penalty of $100 and a maximum penalty of $2,500.	¶3534 ITA 162(7)
T1159	Late filed	If a non-resident does not file a section 216 return by the due date, the election is invalid. If the payer did not withhold the correct amount of non-resident tax, the CRA will issue a non-resident tax assessment to the non-resident. Also, if the non-resident person fails to file the return, or fails to pay the tax in respect thereof on time, the Canadian resident or agent must thereupon pay the full tax which would be payable under ITA 212(1)(d) and (e) on the gross amount, minus the tax already remitted in the year under the alternative arrangement.	¶15311 ITA 216(4)

Form	Infraction	Penalty	Reference
T2062	Failure to withhold non-resident withholding tax	If the non-resident seller does not prepay or provide security for the tax payable, the purchaser of taxable Canadian property may have to pay any tax owing by the seller. Generally, this tax is 25% of the cost of the property sold (or if the CRA issued a certificate for a proposed disposition under ITA 116(2), the tax is 25% of the cost minus the proceeds of disposition (certificate limit) fixed by that certificate). The buyer is required to send this amount to the CRA no later than 30 days after the end of the month in which the property was acquired. The buyer is entitled to recover the tax paid on behalf of the seller and can withhold amounts from any later payments to the seller. The buyer is not liable for the seller's tax if the CRA issued a certificate under ITA 116(4) to the non-resident seller and the buyer for the actual disposition.	ITA 116(5)
Form RC312	Failure to Report Tax Avoidance Transaction	Where the transaction is not reported, the CRA can deny any tax benefit that could result from the reportable transaction. Also, the CRA may impose a joint and several (or solidarity) penalty on every person who failed to report any reportable transaction generally equal to the total fees paid to an advisor or a promoter related to the transactions.	¶1320

¶1430 — Third Party Penalties

A penalty may be charged if a person counsels or assists a corporation in filing a false return or knowingly allows a taxpayer to submit false tax information. In recent years, there has been a significant rise in third-party penalty assessment activity.

Relevant factors the CRA considers in determining whether to apply a penalty under ITA 163.2 include:

- Whether the position taken is obviously wrong, unreasonable, and/or contrary to well-established case law;

- Considering the advisor's experience with the relevant subject matter and knowledge of the taxpayer's specific circumstances, the extent of knowing or deliberate participation in false statements;

- The degree to which the culpable conduct represents the most aggressive and blatantly abusive behaviour;

- The extent to which there is a pattern of repeated abuse; and

- Whether the reduction of taxes is significant.

The following types of cases have been reviewed by the third-party penalty committee: fictitious amounts (including with respect to T4s, business, farming and rental losses, and employment expenses); appropriations of funds and invalid journal entries; abusive donation schemes; RRSP stripping arrangements; transactions reported based on "deceptive" valuations; and SR&ED claims.

In *Guindon*, 2012 CarswellNat 3708 (TCC), the Tax Court found that the penalty imposed under ITA 163.2 is a criminal rather than a civil penalty such that an assessed individual is entitled to the same constitutional protections as those charged with a criminal offence. However, this decision was overturned by the Federal Court of Appeal (2013 CarswellNat 1832), which held that it was not open to the TCC to find that ITA 163.2 was the equivalent of being "charged with a criminal offence" since a notice of constitutional question had not been served. Even if the notice had been served, the FCA stated that the assessment of a penalty under ITA 163.2 is not the equivalent of being charged with a criminal offence (paras. 37, 41, 54–59). The decision of the FCA was unanimously upheld by the Supreme Court of Canada (2015 CarswellNat 3231), which noted that the standard for assessing a preparer penalty under ITA 163.2 was at least as high as the standard for assessing a gross negligence penalty under ITA 163(2) (para. 61). *Guindon* dealt with a typical unsuccessful leveraged donation scheme in respect of which Ms.

Guindon (a family law lawyer) provided a tax opinion and acted as the president of the charity in question, signing some of the charitable donation receipts issued. The penalty assessed for Ms. Guindon's role in signing the donation receipts was $547,000.

In IC 01-1, the CRA clarifies that third party penalties are not intended to be applied to tax planning arrangements that comply with the law, honest mistakes, or differences of interpretation where the jurisprudence is not well-settled. Additionally, third party penalties will generally not be applied to arrangements that are subject to the application of the GAAR or to an advisor who discusses a possible voluntary disclosure with a client who ultimately decides not to proceed with the voluntary disclosure (the CRA's position is that the advisor would be "expected to rectify the situation to the extent that the false statement affects the tax return of the current year").

In *Ploughman*, 2017 CarswellNat 1819 (TCC), the Court held that the good faith defense under ITA 163.2(6) is only available in respect of information on which the advisor relies that is provided by the person who ultimately makes the false statement (or by someone acting on behalf of that person). See also Oh, "Administrative Penalty Assessed for False Statements on Donation Receipts", Charity & NFP Law Update (Carters Professional Corporation), May 2017 and Richardson-Scott, "*Ploughman v. R*, — Third Party Civil Penalties after Guindon", Canadian Tax Controversy & Tax Litigation (Taxnet Pro), Nov. 2017.

ITA 163.2, IC 01-1, May 2016 Alberta CPA/CRA Roundtable (cpaalberta.ca/Members/Advisories), Q.13 (taxpayer relief provisions of ITA 220(3.1) may be available to an individual assessed a civil penalty), Russell, "*Guindon* — Civil or Criminal Tax Penalty?", *Tax Hyperion* (Taxnet Pro), Vol. 12-8, Aug. 2015

¶1500 — Taxpayer Relief Provisions

¶1510 — *Voluntary Disclosures (RC199: Voluntary Disclosures Program (VDP) Taxpayer Agreement)*

A taxpayer can apply for relief from potential penalties in respect of compliance infractions through the CRA's Voluntary Disclosures Program (VDP) where certain conditions are met. Under the VDP, taxpayers can make disclosures to correct inaccurate or incomplete information, or disclose information not previously reported. Generally, relief under the VDP may be considered if a taxpayer failed to fulfill their obligations under the ITA, failed to report any taxable income they received, claimed ineligible expenses on a tax return, failed to remit source deductions of their employees, failed to file information returns, or failed to report foreign sourced income that is taxable in Canada.

Information Circular IC 00-1R6: *Voluntary Disclosures Program* sets forth new VDP policies that apply to VDP applications made after February 28, 2018. The revised VDP has two tracks for income tax disclosures:

1) the General Program, under which accepted applications are eligible for penalty relief and partial interest relief, and

2) the Limited Program, under which applicants will not be referred for criminal prosecution with respect to the disclosure (i.e. for tax offences) and will not be charged gross negligence penalties, even where the facts establish that the taxpayer is liable for such penalties (however, the taxpayer will be charged other penalties as applicable under the Limited Program).

The determination of whether an application will be processed under the General or Limited Program is made on a case-by-case basis using the following criteria (IC 00-1R6, paras. 20–22):

In general terms, the Limited Program provides limited relief for applications that disclose non-compliance where there is an element of intentional conduct on the part of the taxpayer or a closely related party. The following factors may be considered: efforts were made to avoid detection through the use of offshore vehicles or other means, the dollar amounts involved, the number of years of non-compliance, the sophistication of the taxpayer, the disclosure is made after an official CRA statement regarding its intended specific focus of compliance (for example, the launch of a compliance project or campaign) or following broad-based CRA correspondence (for example, a letter issued to taxpayers working in a particular sector about a compliance issue). For example, a taxpayer who opened an offshore bank account in 2010 and has been transferring undeclared business income earned in Canada to that account since that time would not normally qualify under the General Program. Generally, applications by corporations with gross revenue in excess of $250 million in at least two of their last five taxation years, and any related entities, will be considered under the Limited

Program. The existence of a single factor will not necessarily mean that a taxpayer is eligible only for the Limited Program. For example, a sophisticated taxpayer may still correct a reasonable error under the General Program.

If a VDP application is accepted under the General Program, the taxpayer will not be charged penalties (subject to the limitation period explained in para. 17 of IC 00-1R6) or be subject to criminal prosecution with respect to the disclosure (IC 00-1R6, para. 13). Interest relief under the General Program is limited and is at the discretion of the CRA. Generally, 50% of applicable interest will be forgiven for years prior to the three most recent years of tax returns that are the subject of the application and the full amount of interest will remain payable for the three most recent years of tax returns being filed (IC 00-1R6, para. 15).

If a VDP application is accepted under the Limited Program, the taxpayer will not be referred for criminal prosecution with respect to the disclosure and will not be charged gross negligence penalties; however, the taxpayer will be charged other penalties as applicable (IC 00-1R6, para. 14). No interest relief is granted in respect of an application accepted under the Limited Program (IC 00-1R6, para. 16). Also, where an application is accepted under the Limited Program, a taxpayer is required to waive its right to "object and appeal in relation to the specific matter disclosed in the VDP application and any specifically related assessment of taxes[;] however, this waiver will not prevent a taxpayer from filing a Notice of Objection in circumstances where the assessment includes a calculation error, relates to a characterization issue (such as income versus capital gain treatment), or relates to an issue other than the matter disclosed in the VDP application" (IC 00-1R6, para. 66 — such a requirement did not exist under the former VDP).

Certain applications will generally not be accepted under the revised VDP, including (IC 00-1R6, paras. 23-24):

- applications that relate to income tax returns with no taxes owing or with refunds expected; these would be handled using normal processing procedures.

- elections; there are provisions within the various acts administered by the CRA which entitle taxpayers to choose or "elect" specific treatment of certain tax transactions, e.g. section 216 returns under the ITA. For more information about late, amended, or revoked elections, see IC 07-1R1, *Taxpayer Relief Provisions*;

- applications relating to an advance pricing arrangement (an agreement with a taxpayer that confirms the appropriate transfer pricing methodology);

- applications that depend on an agreement being made at the discretion of the Canadian competent authority under a provision of a tax treaty, e.g. S-corporation agreements under Article XXIX(5) of the Canada-US Treaty;

- applications where a person is in receivership or has become bankrupt;

- post-assessment requests for penalty and interest relief; these requests will be considered to be retroactive tax planning.

For a voluntary disclosure to be accepted, the application must: 1) be voluntary; 2) be complete; 3) involve the application or potential application of a penalty; 4) include information that is at least one year past due; and 5) include payment of the estimated tax owing. Each of the latter criterions is discussed in paragraphs 29–40 of IC 00-1R6. Notably, the fifth criterion did not exist under the former VDP. Regarding this criterion, paragraphs 39-40 of IC 00-1R6 state:

39. Subject to paragraph 40, the taxpayer must include payment of the estimated tax owing with their VDP application.

40. When the taxpayer does not have the ability to make payment of the estimated tax owing at the time of the VDP application, they may request to be considered for a payment arrangement subject to approval from CRA Collections officials. The taxpayer will have to make full disclosure and provide evidence of income, expenses, assets, and liabilities supporting the inability to make payment in full. In some cases, the payment arrangement will need to be supported by adequate security.

Paragraph 11 of IC 00-1R6 confirms that if relief is denied under the VDP, the CRA will provide the taxpayer with an explanation of the reasons for the decision and relief of arrears interest and any penalties payable may be requested and considered in accordance with the taxpayer relief provisions described in IC 07-1R1: *Taxpayer Relief Provisions*.

Under the former VDP, a taxpayer making a disclosure was not necessarily precluded from making a second disclosure in respect of the same period. However, under the revised program, "[a] taxpayer is generally entitled to obtain the benefits of the VDP only once" and "[a] second application from the same taxpayer will normally only be considered by the CRA if the circumstances surrounding the second application are both beyond the taxpayer's control and related to a different matter than the first application" (IC 00-1R6, para. 25).

A taxpayer who is unsure if he or she wants to proceed with a VDP application is permitted to engage in an anonymous discussion with the CRA (IC 00-1R6, paras 41-42). Such discussions are informal, non-binding, and general in nature; the discussions do not constitute acceptance into the VDP and have no impact on CRA's ability to audit, penalize, or refer a case for criminal prosecution. The "no name" submission procedure under the former VDP has been eliminated.

Paragraph 44 of IC 00-1R6 provides that if a taxpayer received assistance from an advisor in respect of the subject matter of a VDP application, "the name of that advisor should generally be included in the application". Furthermore, paragraphs 45–47 of IC 00-1R6 state:

> It is expected that taxpayers and/or their representatives will co-operate in the voluntary disclosure process. While the VDP application is being evaluated, the CRA official may request documents, records, books of account, as well as other additional specific documentation, for example information relating to foreign accounts and assets, financial institutions and advisers. The taxpayer must comply with such requests within the stipulated timeframes, and provide sufficient detail to allow the facts of the case to be verified. If a taxpayer refuses to provide complete documentation or if the CRA is not satisfied that the application is complete, then the taxpayer will in most cases not be eligible for relief. Due to the nature of a particular application, referrals to other programs within the CRA may be necessary in order to fully analyze the application. Furthermore, applications involving complex issues or large dollar amounts will be reviewed for completeness by a specialist area prior to the VDP application being accepted. The taxpayer's authorized representative can submit the application for relief under the VDP. In this case, both the taxpayer and the authorized representative must sign the VDP application.

The former VDP did not make reference to a taxpayer's advisors.

Paragraph 33 of IC 00-1R6 provides that a request for an additional specified period of time to make a disclosure must be made in writing at the time the application is submitted. It will likely be common for a taxpayer to request additional time to make a full disclosure at the time a VDP application is made since gathering all pertinent information can be time-consuming and protection is not available until an application has been filed.

Even if a VDP application is accepted, the CRA may subsequently audit the taxation years in question. According to paragraph 12 of IC 00-1R6: "The CRA reserves the right to audit or verify any information provided in a VDP application whether it is accepted under the VDP or not. If the CRA finds there is any misrepresentation due to neglect, carelessness, wilful default, or fraud, a reassessment can be issued at any time for any tax year to which the misrepresentation relates, not just those years included in the VDP application. Furthermore, any relief that may have been granted under the VDP will be cancelled as a result of the misrepresentation."

Overall, the revised VDP is significantly more restrictive than the pre-March 2018 program. Under the former program, relief offered was the same, regardless of the nature or scale of the non-compliance, and restrictions on the waiver of penalties and interest were less rigid. There is also increased uncertainty under the new VDP as to whether a particular application will be accepted (for example, it is unclear what constitutes a "sophisticated" taxpayer or a "large" dollar amount).

In *Worsfold*, 2012 CarswellNat 2218 (FC), the Court found that a taxpayer's disclosure was voluntary, although a related corporation was under audit. The Court was satisfied that the taxpayer did not know of the audit at the time the disclosure was made and it was also not clear whether the audit of the related corporation would have led to the discovery of the information disclosed. As well, in *Matthew Boadi Prof. Corp.*, 2018 CarswellNat 55 (FC), the taxpayer's disclosure was found to be voluntary, since the Court concluded that the demand to file enforcement action by the CRA for separate taxation years was unlikely to have uncovered the taxpayer's delinquent Form T1135 filing obligations. However, in *Livaditis*, [2012] 4 C.T.C. 108 (FCA), a disclosure was found not to be voluntary where, immediately prior to the disclosure, the CRA had called the taxpayer requesting additional information related to the underreported income in question. The Court found that as a result of the phone call, the taxpayer was aware an enforcement action was set to commence.

In *Bozzer*, [2011] 5 C.T.C. 1 (FCA), the Court found that the CRA was incorrect in refusing to consider applications for interest relief where the underlying tax debt arose more than ten years before the application for relief; rather, the Court stated the CRA has the statutory authority to cancel interest to the extent that it accrued during the ten taxation years preceding a taxpayer's application for interest relief. The CRA now considers requests for the cancellation or waiver of interest that accrues during the 10 calendar years preceding the calendar year in which the request for relief is made, regardless of the year in which the tax debt arose (see para.18 of IC 00-1R6, para. 15 of IC 07-1R1, and canada.ca/en/revenue-agency under "Revised 10-year limitation period for interest relief").

In *Takenaka*, 2018 CarswellNat 1897, 2018 FC 347 (FC), the Federal Court quashed a CRA decision to impose a late-filing penalty in respect of late-filed Form T1135s filed by a taxpayer who had no income. See also *Douglas*, 2012 CarswellNat 479 (TCC) and *Fiset*, 2017 CarswellNat 8928 (TCC).

ITA 220(3.1), *Sifto Canada*, 2014 CarswellNat 1865 (FCA), *Stemijon Investments*, 2011 CarswellNat 4372 (FCA), *334156 Alberta Ltd.*, [2007] 1 C.T.C. 110 (FC), *Karia*, [2005] 3 C.T.C. 98 (FC), IC 00-1R6: *Voluntary Disclosures Program*, IC 07-1R1: *Taxpayer relief provisions*; VDs 2016-0632811E5, 2014-0537701I7, 2012-0434071E5, 2012-0434071E5, 2006-0185642C6, 9217287, canada.ca/en/revenue-agency under "Taxpayer relief provisions", Rabinovitch et al., "Voluntary Disclosures", *Practical Insights* (Taxnet Pro), June 2018, Lindsay et al., "VDP Report" (2017) 25:2 *CTH* 1-2; Sorensen, "CRA Finalizes New Information Circular for Income Tax Voluntary Disclosures Program", Gowling WLG, Dec. 18, 2017, Joint Committee Submission 2017-08-08: *Proposed Changes to the Voluntary Disclosure Program Announced June 9, 2017*

¶1520 — Requests for Taxpayer Relief

In certain circumstances, penalties or interest charges in respect of a failure to make a payment or to file a personal tax return may be waived if the reason for late-filing or not making a payment was beyond the taxpayer's control. The types of situations in which a penalty or interest charge may be waived include: natural or human-made disasters, such as floods or fires; civil disturbances or disruptions in services, such as postal strikes; serious illness or accident suffered by the person who is responsible for filing the taxpayer's return; and the taxpayer receiving the wrong information, either in a letter from the CRA or in one of the CRA publications. If a taxpayer is in one of these situations and needs an extension for filing a return because of extraordinary circumstances, or if a taxpayer believes there is a valid reason for cancelling a penalty or interest charge, complete Form RC4288: *Request for Taxpayer Relief* or send the CRA a letter explaining why it was not possible to file a personal tax return or make a payment on time. For relief to be granted, the CRA requires a taxpayer to have taken a reasonable amount of care in attempting to comply with the ITA and efforts must have been taken to avoid or reduce the delay in complying or paying. In addition, the delay should have been remedied within a reasonable time. Penalties or interest resulting from neglect or lack of awareness will not be waived.

The CRA's discretion on an application for relief must be based on the purposes of the Act, the fairness purposes encompassed by ITA 220(3.1), and a rational assessment of all the relevant circumstances of the case. The CRA's discretion must be genuinely exercised and must not be fettered or dictated by policy statements such as those in IC 07-1R1, which may be used as guidelines only (see, for example, *Stemijon Investments Ltd*, 2011 FCA 299 (F.C.A.) at para. 27, and para. 24 of IC 07-1R1). On an application for judicial review from an ITA 220(3.1) decision, the Federal Court may quash unreasonable exercises of discretion by the CRA (i.e., exercises of discretion that fall outside the range of the acceptable and defensible on the facts and the law: *New Brunswick (Board of Management) v. Dunsmuir*, 2008 SCC 9, [2008] 1 S.C.R. 190 (SCC)).

ITA 220(3.1), *Taylor*, [2012] 6 C.T.C. 143 (FC), *3500772 Canada Inc.*, [2008] 4 C.T.C. 1 (FC), *Spence*, 2010 CarswellNat 70 (FC), *Toronto Dominion Bank v. BC*, 2017 BCCA 159, *Slau Ltd.*, [2010] 1 C.T.C. 15 (FCA), *Nixon*, [2008] 5 C.T.C. 263 (FC), *Ross*, [2006] 3 C.T.C. 42 (FC), *Vitellaro*, [2005] 3 C.T.C. 88 (FCA), *Elwell*, [2004] 4 C.T.C. 263 (FC), *Robertson*, [2003] 2 C.T.C. 78 (FCTD), *Edison*, [2001] 3 C.T.C. 233 (FCTD), IC 07-1R1, canada.ca/en/revenue-agency under "Taxpayer relief provisions", CRA Taxpayer Relief Procedures Manual (*Taxnet Pro*), Guide RC4540: *Complaints and disputes*, Sittler, "Review of Penalty and Interest Relief Requests Under the *Income Tax Act*," *Report of the Proceedings of the Sixty-Seventh Tax Conference*, 2015 Conference Report (Toronto: Canadian Tax Foundation, 2016)

Chapter 2 — Employment Income and Deductions

Contents

¶2000 Employment Income (T1: Lines 101, 102, 104)

¶2005 Income from an Office or Employment

¶2010 Loss from an Office or Employment

¶2015 Employee vs. Independent Contractor

¶2020 Salary Deferral Arrangements

¶2025 Professional Athletes

¶2100 Taxation of Employment Benefits and Allowances (T1: Lines 101, 102, 104)

¶2105 Accumulated Vacation and Sick Leave Credits

¶2110 Advances

¶2115 Aircraft (personal use of)

¶2120 Allowances

¶2125 Apprenticeship Incentive Grant

¶2130 Automobile and Motor Vehicle Benefits and Allowances

¶2135 Board and Lodging

¶2140 Cellular Phones, Computers and Internet

¶2145 Child Care Expenses

¶2150 Commissions

¶2155 Counselling Services

¶2160 Deferred Salary Payments

¶2165 Directors' Fees

¶2170 Disability-Related Employment Benefits

¶2175 Discounts on Merchandise and Commissions from Personal Sales

¶2180 Employee Benefit Plans

¶2185 Employee Health and Welfare Trusts/Employee Life and Health Trusts

¶2190 Employee Profit Sharing Plans

¶2195 Employment Insurance Premiums

¶2200 Flexible Benefit Plans

¶2205 Gifts, Awards and Long-Service Awards

¶2210 Government Grants

¶2215 Gratuities and Tips

¶2220 Group Life Insurance Premiums

¶2225 Income Tax Paid by Employer

¶2230 Injury Leave Pay

¶2235 Loans — Interest-Free and Low-Interest

¶2240 Loyalty and Other Points Programs

¶2245 Meals

¶2250 Member of Legislative Assembly (MLA) Expense Allowance

¶2255 Miscellaneous Employee Benefits

¶2260 Moving Expenses

¶2265 Municipal Officer's Expense Allowance

¶2270 Parking

¶2275 Private Health Services Plan Premiums

¶2280 Prizes and Awards

¶2285 Professional Membership Dues

¶2290 Provincial Hospital or Health Care Plan Premiums

¶2295 Recreational Facilities and Club Dues

¶2300 Reimbursements and Awards

¶2301 Research Grants

¶2305 Retirement Compensation Arrangements (RCAs)

¶2310 Scholarships, Fellowships and Bursaries

¶2315 Security Options Benefit

¶2320 Service Pension or Allowance

¶2325 Social Events

¶2330 Special Payments by Employers

¶2335 Statutory Exemptions

¶2340 Strike Pay

¶2345 Tool Reimbursement or Allowance

¶2350 Transportation

¶2355 Tuition and Training Fees

¶2360 Uniforms and Special Clothing

¶2365 Vacations (Employer-Paid)

¶2370 Workers' Compensation Payments

¶2400 Deductions from Employment Income

¶2401 Employee and Partner GST/HST Rebate (T1: Line 457)

¶2405 Annual Union, Professional and Membership Dues (T1: Line 212)

¶2410 Apprentice Mechanics' Tools Deduction (T1: Line 229)

¶2415 Apprenticeship Incentive Grant Repayment (T1: Line 232)

¶2420 Artists' Employment Expenses (T1: Line 229)

¶2425 Canadian Forces Personnel and Police Deduction (T1: Line 244)

¶2430 Clergy Residence Deduction (T1: Line 231)

¶2435 Commission Sales Employees (T1: Line 229)

¶2440 Employee Home Relocation Loan Deduction (T1: Line 248)

¶2445 Employee Profit Sharing Plans (T1: Line 232)

¶2450 Legal Fees (T1: Line 229)

¶2455 Motor Vehicle (or Aircraft) Expenses (T1: Line 229)

¶2460 Musical Instrument Expenses (T1: Line 229)

¶2465 Northern Residents' Deduction (T1: Line 255)

¶2470 Office Rent and Home Office Expenses (T1: Line 229)

¶2475 Overseas Employment Tax Credit (T1 Schedule 1: Line 426)

¶2480 Power Saw Operators (T1: Line 229)

¶2485 Railway Employees' Expenses (T1: Line 229)

¶2490 Reimbursement of Disability Payments (T1: Line 232)

¶2495 Reimbursement of Salary (T1: Line 232)

¶2500 Retirement Compensation Arrangement (RCA) (T1: Line 232)

¶2505 Salary Paid to a Substitute or Assistant (T1: Line 229)

¶2510 Security Options Deduction (T1: Line 249)

¶2515 Supplies (T1: Line 229)

¶2520 Tradesperson's Tools Deduction (T1: Line 229)

¶2525 Transport Employees' Expenses (T1: Line 229)

¶2530 Travelling Expenses (T1: Line 229)

¶2000 — Employment Income (T1: Lines 101, 102, 104)

¶2005 — Income from an Office or Employment

Income from an office or employment includes all amounts received in the year as salary, wages, commissions, director's fees, bonuses, gratuities, honoraria, certain GST/HST rebates, and the value of all monetary and non-monetary benefits. See under ¶2100 for a discussion of the taxation of employment benefits and allowances. All receipts and benefits are taxable in the year they are actually received or enjoyed by the individual. For example, bonuses and retroactive salary increases would be included in income in the year received (subject to certain rules which may apply to retroactive lump-sum payments).

The terms "office" and "employment" are defined in ITA 248(1). "Office" means the position of an individual entitling the individual to a fixed or ascertainable stipend or remuneration and includes a judicial office, the office of a minister of the Crown, the office of a member of the Senate or House of Commons of Canada, a member of a legislative assembly, or a member of a legislative or executive council and any other office, the incumbent of which is elected by popular vote or is elected or appointed in a representative capacity, and also includes the position of a corporate director. An "officer" is a person holding such an office. "Employment" is defined to mean the position of an individual in the service of some other person (including Her Majesty, or a foreign state, or sovereign) and "servant" or "employee" means a person holding such a position.

Income received from an office or employment will generally be reported on a taxpayer's T4 slip. On Line 101, individuals should report the total of the amounts shown in Box 14 of all T4 slips. On Line 102, individuals should report the total commissions in Box 42 of all T4 slips. This amount is already included in income on Line 101, so it should not be added again for purposes of calculating total income on Line 150.

Individuals may receive other employment income and miscellaneous amounts in the year that will not be reported on a T4 slip. On Line 104, individuals should report other employment income that is not reported on a T4 slip and miscellaneous amounts that are not income from employment, including the following:

- Employment income not reported on a T4 slip, such as tips and occasional earnings;

- Foreign employment income — report in Canadian dollars. If the amounts on a U.S. W-2 slip have been reduced by contributions to a 401(k), 457 or 403(b) plan, *US Medicare* or *Federal Insurance Contributions Act* (*FICA*), include the contributions in income on Line 104 (see Line 207 at ¶9120 to determine whether the contributions are deductible);

- GST/HST and QST rebates — include the amount of rebate for an employee who paid and deducted employment expenses in 2017 and received a GST/HST or QST rebate in 2018; see also ¶2401;

- Royalties received for a work or invention; see also ¶3325 (Line 121) and ¶6100 (Line 135);

- Clergy's housing allowance (T4 Box 30); see ¶2430 for discussion of the clergy residence deduction;

- Amounts received as a research grant (T4A Box 104); see ¶2301;

- Payments from a wage-loss replacement plan (T4A Box 107);

- Medical premium benefits (T4A Box 118);

- Taxable benefit for premiums paid to insure the individual under a group term life insurance plan (T4A Box 119); see ¶2220;

- Veteran's benefits (T4A Box 127);

- Amounts received under the Wage Earner Protection Program (T4A Box 132);

- Amounts received under a supplementary unemployment benefit plan (T4A Box 152);

- Amounts received under a bankruptcy settlement (T4A Box 156);

- Amounts received from an employee profit-sharing plan (T4PS Box 35); see ¶2190.

Note that even though some of the Line 104 income items may not be reported on an information slip, they are still required to be included in employment income.

Guide T4044, Guide 5000-G, IT-428: *Wage Loss Replacement Plans*

¶2010 — Loss from an Office or Employment

An individual may have a loss from an office or employment where the allowable deductions under ITA 8 exceed employment income. The loss is deductible from the taxpayer's income from other sources in the year in determining net income from all sources for the year. If there is no income from any other source, or to the extent that the loss exceeds other income for the year, the loss is a non-capital loss that may be carried back three years and forward 20 years to reduce taxable income in those years (see Line 252 at ¶9360).

ITA 5(2), 111(1)(a), 111(8)

¶2015 — Employee vs. Independent Contractor

An individual's income may arise from a contract for service, implying the existence of an employer-employee relationship, or from a contract for services where the recipient of the income is in a freelance or independent contractor relationship with the payer. In the latter case, the income is not from an office or employment but is income from a business and, as such, is subject to the rules that govern business and professional income. Business and professional income are calculated on Form T2125, *Statement of Business or Professional Activities*, and reported on Lines 135 and 162 for business income or Lines 137 and 164 for professional income (see Chapter 6, "Business and Professional Income").

It is sometimes difficult to determine whether amounts are received by an individual under an express or implied contract for service, and thus constitute income from an office or employment, or whether they are received under an express or implied contract for services, and thus represent income from a business or a profession. The question generally depends on whether or not a master/servant relationship exists between the payer and the payee. The distinction is important for many purposes, including the deductibility of expenses, the basis for which is much broader in computing business and professional income than in computing income from an office or employment, and source deduction requirements.

¶2016 — Determining Factors

There are many court cases that deal with the determination of employee status. The leading cases for determining employee and independent contractor status are *Wiebe Door Services Ltd.*, [1986] 2 C.T.C. 200 (FCA) and *671122 Ontario Ltd. v. Sagaz Industries*, [2001] 4 C.T.C. 139 (SCC), in which the Supreme Court of Canada outlined the factors to be considered as follows (at para. 47):

> The central question is whether the person who has been engaged to perform the services is performing them as a person in business on his own account. In making this determination, the level of control the employer has over the worker's activities will always be a factor. However, other factors to consider include whether the worker provides his or her own equipment, whether the worker hires his or her own helpers, the degree of financial risk taken by the worker, the degree of responsibility for investment and management held by the worker, and the worker's opportunity for profit in the performance of his or her tasks.

Therefore, the courts generally look at the following factors to determine whether a worker is an employee or is self-employed:

- Control — does the employer control (or have the right to control) the worker's hours and working conditions?

- Tools and equipment — does the worker use the employer's tools, equipment, and facilities?

- Subcontracting work or hiring assistants — can the worker subcontract work or hire assistants?

- Financial risk — does the worker share the employer's risk?

- Responsibility for investment and management — is the worker an integral part of the business?

- Opportunity for profit — does the worker have a chance of profit or risk of loss?

The above factors are not exhaustive; in some circumstances, the subjective intention of the parties may also be considered. The Federal Court of Appeal recently clarified the consideration that should be given to the subjective intention of the parties when determining whether a worker is an employee or an independent contractor (*1392644 Ontario Inc. v. MNR*, 2013 FCA 85). The Court concluded that the determination is a two step process — the first step is to determine the subjective intent of each party and the second step is to determine whether the objective reality sustains the subjective intent of the parties, applying the above factors from *Weibe Door* and *Sagaz Industries*. However, a shared, subjective intention is not determinative where the objective factors otherwise yield a clear result. For a comprehensive discussion of the rules governing the determination of an employee's status, see the Practical Insight, "Employee or Independent Contractor" by Karen Stilwell on *Taxnet Pro*.

Guide RC4110: *Employee or Self-Employed?* is intended to assist employers and employees in determining a worker's status, and the implications that result from that status. Guide RC4110 provides the following indicators for each of the tests used by the courts for determining a worker's status as an employee or an independent contractor:

Control

...

Indicators showing that the worker is an employee

- The relationship is one of subordination. The payer will often direct, scrutinize, and effectively control many elements of how and when the work is carried out.

- The payer controls the worker with respect to both the results of the work and the method used to do the work.

- The payer chooses and controls the method and amount of pay. Salary negotiations may still take place in an employer-employee relationship.

- The payer decides what jobs the worker will do.

- The payer chooses to listen to the worker's suggestions but has the final word.

- The worker requires permission to work for other payers while working for this payer.

- Where the schedule is irregular, priority on the worker's time is an indication of control over the worker.

- The worker receives training or direction from the payer on how to do the work. The overall work environment between the worker and the payer is one of subordination.

Indicators showing that the worker is a self-employed individual

- A self-employed individual usually works independently.

- The worker does not have anyone overseeing his or her activities.

- The worker is usually free to work when and for whom he or she chooses and may provide his or her services to different payers at the same time.

- The worker can accept or refuse work from the payer.

- The working relationship between the payer and the worker does not present a degree of continuity, loyalty, security, subordination, or integration, all of which are generally associated with an employer-employee relationship.

Tools and equipment

...

Indicators showing that the worker is an employee

- The payer supplies most of the tools and equipment the worker needs. In addition, the payer is responsible for repair, maintenance, and insurance costs.

- The worker supplies the tools and equipment and the payer reimburses the worker for their use.

- The payer retains the right of use over the tools and equipment provided to the worker.

Indicators showing that the worker is a self-employed individual

- The worker provides the tools and equipment needed for the work. In addition, the worker is responsible for the costs of repairs, insurance, and maintenance to the tools and equipment.

- The worker has made a significant investment in the tools and equipment and the worker retains the right over the use of these assets.

- The worker supplies his or her own workspace, is responsible for the costs to maintain it, and does substantial work from that site.

Subcontracting work or hiring assistants

...

Indicators showing that the worker is an employee

- The worker cannot hire helpers or assistants.

- The worker does not have the ability to hire and send replacements. The worker has to do the work personally.

Indicators showing that the worker is a self-employed individual

- The worker does not have to carry out the services personally. He or she can hire another party to either do the work or help do the work, and pays the costs for doing so.

- The payer has no say in whom the worker hires.

Financial risk

Indicators showing that the worker is an employee

- The worker is not usually responsible for any operating expenses.

- Generally, the working relationship between the worker and the payer is continuous.

- The worker is not financially liable if he or she does not fulfill the obligations of the contract.

- The payer chooses and controls the method and amount of pay.

Indicators showing that the worker is a self-employed individual

- The worker hires helpers to assist in the work. The worker pays the hired helpers.

- The worker does a substantial amount of work from his or her own workspace and incurs expenses relating to the operation of that workspace.

- The worker is hired for a specific job rather than an ongoing relationship.

- The worker is financially liable if he or she does not fulfill the obligations of the contract.

- The worker does not receive any protection or benefits from the payer.

- The worker advertises and actively markets his or her services.

Responsibility for investment and management

...

Indicators showing that the worker is an employee

- The worker has no capital investment in the business.

- The worker does not have a business presence.

Indicators showing that the worker is a self-employed individual

- The worker has capital investment.

- The worker manages his or her staff.

- The worker hires and pays individuals to help do the work.

- The worker has established a business presence.

Opportunity for profit

. . .

Indicators showing that the worker is an employee

1. The worker is not normally in a position to realize a business profit or loss.

2. The worker is entitled to benefit plans that are normally offered only to employees. These include registered pension plans, and group accident, health, and dental insurance plans.

Indicators showing that the worker is a self-employed individual

- The worker can hire a substitute and the worker pays the substitute.

- The worker is compensated by a flat fee and incurs expenses in carrying out the services.

ITA 5, *In re Hutton ex parte Benwell* (1844), 14 Q.B.D. 301, IT-525R (C): *Performing Artists*, Pamphlet RC4110: Employee or Self-Employed?; Revenu Quebec, IN-301-V, Employee or Self-Employed Person?; Geoffrey A Garland, CA and Paul K Grower, "Employee and Independent Contractor — Where Are We Now?", *2004 Prairie Provinces Tax Conference*, (Toronto: Canadian Tax Foundation, 2004) 7:1–55; Lara Friedlander, "What Has Tort Law Got To Do with It? Distinguishing Between Employees and Independent Contractors in the Federal Income Tax, Employment Insurance and Canada Pension Plan Contexts" (2003) vol. 51, no. 4 *Canadian Tax Journal*, 1467–1519; Alain Gaucher, "A Worker's Status as Employee or Independent Contractor," *Report of Proceedings of Fifty-First Tax Conference, 1999 Tax Conference* (Toronto: Canadian Tax Foundation, 2000) 33:1–98; Joanne Magee, "Whose Business Is It?" 45(3) *Canadian Tax Journal* 583–603 (1997)

¶2020 — Salary Deferral Arrangements

There are special rules for the taxation of remuneration for services rendered by an employee where receipt of such remuneration is postponed and it is reasonable to consider that one of the main purposes of the postponement is to defer the tax payable by the employee. The postponed amount is referred to as a "deferred amount", and these types of arrangements are called "salary deferral arrangements". A "deferred amount" also includes an amount a person has the right to receive in a subsequent year where the amount is contributed to, or agreed to be contributed to, a trust under a salary deferral arrangement. Increments to the deferred amounts by way of interest or similar amounts are treated as deferred amounts except in the case of a trust under a salary deferral arrangement. These special provisions are designed to prevent the receipt of compensation from being deferred to enable postponement of tax on the deferred compensation and on increments to the deferred compensation.

> A salary deferral arrangement is, in essence, an arrangement under which any person has a right to receive an amount in a future year, and it is reasonable to consider that one of the main purposes for the creation or existence of the right is to postpone tax payable in respect of an amount that is (or is in lieu of) salary or wages for services rendered in the year or a previous year.

A salary deferral arrangement may exist even if such a right is subject to one or more conditions, unless there is a "substantial risk" that any one of the conditions will not be satisfied. While the ultimate decision as to the existence of such a substantial risk rests with the courts, as a general rule, a substantial risk of forfeiture would arise if the condition imposes a significant limitation or duty which requires a meaningful effort on the part of the employee to fulfil, and creates a definite and substantial risk that forfeiture may occur. Examples of cases where substantial risk of forfeiture would not likely be considered to occur are as follows:

- receipt of the deferred amount is contingent on the employee abstaining from competition or making himself available for advice and consultations following retirement or termination;

- receipt of the deferred amount is contingent on the employee refraining from transferring or encumbering his interest in the deferred amount;

- receipt of the deferred amount is contingent on the employee not being dismissed for cause or the commission of a crime; or

- receipt of the deferred amount is contingent on the employee remaining as an employee for a minimum period, say three years, unless there is definite and substantial risk that the employment may be terminated before that time in circumstances beyond the control of the employee.

A salary deferral arrangement arises only where one of the main purposes of the arrangement is to postpone tax in respect of an amount that is, or is on account of or in lieu of, "salary or wages". "Salary or wages" means the income of a taxpayer from an office or employment, and includes all fees received for services not rendered in the course of the taxpayer's business, but does not include superannuation or pension benefits or retiring allowances.

A "superannuation or pension benefit" includes any amount received out of or under a superannuation or pension fund or plan; any payment made to a beneficiary under the fund or plan; and any payment to an employer or former employer of the beneficiary under the fund or plan in accordance with the terms of the fund or plan, resulting from an amendment to or modification of the fund or plan, or resulting from the termination of the fund or plan. The term is not limited to a registered superannuation or pension plan and may extend to a contractual unfunded arrangement. A "retiring allowance" is an amount received on or after retirement of a taxpayer from an office or employment in recognition of the taxpayer's long service, or in respect of a loss of an office or employment of a taxpayer, whether or not received as, on account or in lieu of payment of, damages or pursuant to an order or judgment of a competent tribunal, by the taxpayer or, after the taxpayer's death, by a dependant or a relation of the taxpayer or by the legal representative of the taxpayer.

The following are specifically excluded from the definition of a salary deferral arrangement:

- a registered pension fund or plan,

- a disability or income maintenance insurance plan under a policy with an insurance corporation,

- a deferred profit sharing plan,

- an employee profit sharing plan,

- an employee trust,

- a group sickness or accident insurance plan,

- a supplementary unemployment benefit plan,

- a vacation pay trust described in ITA 149(1)(y),

- a plan or arrangement the sole purpose of which is to provide education or training for employees of an employer to improve their work or work-related skills and abilities,

- a plan or arrangement established for the purpose of deferring the salary or wages of a professional athlete for his services as such with a team that participates in a league having regularly scheduled games,

- a plan or arrangement under which a taxpayer has a right to receive a bonus or similar payment in respect of services rendered by him in a taxation year to be paid within three years following the end of the year, or

- a prescribed plan or arrangement (as defined in ITR 6801).

Certain leave-of-absence arrangements qualify as a prescribed plan or arrangements to be excluded from the definition of salary deferral arrangements. Generally, up to one-third of regular salary or wages may be deferred for a period of not longer than six years where the employee undertakes to return to employment with his/her employer or an employer that participates in the same or a similar arrangement, for a period at least as long as the leave-of-absence period. The minimum leave-of-absence period is six consecutive months, except that a period of three consecutive months is sufficient where the leave is for the purpose of enabling full-time attendance by the employee at a designated educational institution. The arrangement must be in writing and is subject to certain conditions.

The CRA has commented that where an employee has entered into a salary deferral arrangement with the intention of not returning to work after his or her leave of absence (for example, where the employee is retiring), the plan would not qualify as a prescribed plan under ITR 6801(a) and any deferred salary would be taxable in the year earned rather than in the year received. (see VD 2004-0069211E5). The CRA has also commented that where an arrangement meets the criteria of ITR 6801(a) at the time it is established, but, at some later time, the employee decides not to return to work, then the arrangement will cease to meet the requirements at that point in time and any amounts not previously paid out should be paid to the employee and included in the employee's income (see VD 2003-0003705).

¶2021 — *Deferred Amounts*

Under ITA 6(1)(a), an amount equal to the "deferred amount" at the end of the year under a salary deferral arrangement in respect of a taxpayer is deemed to have been received by the taxpayer in the year as a benefit in respect of an office or employment to the extent that it was not already otherwise included in income in the year or a previous year. The "deferred amount" at the end of the taxation year under a salary deferral arrangement in respect of a taxpayer means the amount that any person has a right under the arrangement at the end of the year to receive after the end of the year. However, in the case of a trust governed by a salary deferral arrangement in respect of a taxpayer, the deferred amount is any amount that a person has a right under the arrangement at the end of the year to receive after the end of the year where the amount has been received, is receivable or may become receivable by the trust as, on account of or in lieu of salary or wages of the taxpayer for services rendered in the year or a previous taxation year.

For the purposes of the definition of a "deferred amount", a right under the arrangement includes a right that is subject to one or more conditions unless there is a substantial risk that any one of those conditions will not be satisfied. This provision is similar to that found in the definition of a "salary deferral arrangement", discussed above.

Tax in respect of a deferred amount under a salary deferral arrangement may be payable by the taxpayer even though some other person has the right to such amount. For example, if a salary deferral arrangement exists in respect of an employee, but the right to receive the deferred amounts rests with his or her spouse or some other person, the employee will be taxed. As well, where any person has a right under a salary deferral arrangement (except a trust governed by a salary deferral arrangement) in respect of a taxpayer to receive a deferred amount, any interest or other additional amount that accrued to that person in the year is deemed to be a deferred amount to which the person had the right to receive. This means that such a deferred amount will be included in the taxpayer's income at the end of each year. The exact scope of the words "interest or other additional amount that accrued" to a person under a salary deferral arrangement is not clear. It likely includes increments equivalent to interest, but any such additional amount must have "accrued" to the person at the end of the year. Thus, if an additional amount is not ascertainable in the year because it is based, for example, upon the value of the employer's shares in the future, there can probably be no year-by-year accrual of additional deferred amounts.

Generally, the current taxation of deferred amounts does not apply in the case of deferred amounts under a salary deferral arrangement established primarily for the benefit of one or more non-resident employees for services to be rendered outside Canada. As well, if an employee is not resident in Canada during the period of the services with respect to which the amounts are deferred, current taxation will not apply even if such services are rendered in Canada, provided that the arrangement was established primarily for the benefit of one or more non-resident employees for services rendered outside Canada.

When a deferred amount under a salary deferral arrangement with respect to any person has been included in the income of that person, the employer or former employer of that person may claim a deduction of that amount as an expense in computing income from a business or property. This deduction is available for the taxation year that includes the end of the taxation year of the employee or former employee in which the deferred amount was included in income.

¶2022 — *Salary Deferral Arrangement Payments*

Under ITA 6(1)(i), where there is a salary deferral arrangement in respect of a taxpayer, any amount received by any person as a benefit (except an amount received by or from a trust governed by a salary deferral arrangement) in the year out of or under the salary deferral arrangement is to be included in the taxpayer's income to the extent that it exceeds:

> 1. the aggregate of all deferred amounts thereunder and included in his income under ITA 6(1)(a) for preceding taxation years, reduced by

> 2. the aggregate of: (a) all deferred amounts received by any person in preceding taxation years out of or under the arrangement, and (b) all forfeited deferred amounts under the arrangement deducted under ITA 8(1)(o) in computing the taxpayer's income for the year or a previous year.

The purpose of this provision is to provide a catch-all for receipts out of or under a salary deferral arrangement, except to the extent that the deferred amounts have already been included in income.

ITA 6(1)(a), 6(1)(i), 6(11)–(14), 8(1)(o), 12(1)(n.2), 12(11), 18(1)(o.1), 20(1)(oo), 20(1)(pp), 56(1)(w), 248(1)"amount", 248(1)"deferred amount", 248(1)"salary deferral arrangement", 248(1)"salary or wages", ITR 6801, IT-529: *Flexible Employee Benefit Programs*, ATR-39, *Specht v. R.*, [1975] C.T.C. 126 (FCTD)

¶2025 — Professional Athletes

Generally, professional athletes, whether resident or non-resident, are not taxed differently than other persons under the ITA. The remuneration of professional athletes who are players and other employees or officers of football, hockey, and similar clubs includes the following items: salaries, wages, and other remuneration including gratuities; bonuses for performance, all-star rating, signing contracts, etc.; fees for scouting, refereeing, special coaching, etc.; living allowances to players or officers during and after the training and tryout period (other than accommodation provided or expenses reimbursed during that period as explained in IT-168R3); honoraria and stipends; payment for time lost from other employment; commuting expenses; use of automobiles; payment of income taxes or related equalization; payment of fines; awards, including cash and value of bonds, automobiles and other merchandise; and agent's fees, legal fees, or other amounts paid on the employee's behalf.

Non-accountable allowances paid to or on behalf of players during the training and tryout period before contracts are signed are income for the purposes of the ITA. Where a reimbursement is made of actual expenses that are reasonable and supported by vouchers, or where the club provides a living accommodation, the value of living expenses during the training and tryout period is not income to the players. After a player is signed, however, benefits of this nature are considered to be income from employment.

ITA 5(1), 6(1)(a), (b), (c), Canada-U.S. Tax Treaty:Art. XVI, *Bure*, [2000] 1 C.T.C. 2407 (TCC) (payment by club of agent's fees was taxable benefit to player), IT-168R3: *Athletes and Players Employed by Football, Hockey and Similar Clubs*, IT-420R3: *Non-Residents — Income Earned in Canada*, Guide T4130 under "Board and lodging allowances paid to players on sports teams or members of recreation programs", Jadd, et al., "Performing in Canada: Taxation of Non-Resident Artists, Athletes and Other Service Providers", 56(3) Canadian Tax Journal 589–638 (2008), Bruce Sprague, "Taxation of Professional Athletes: Cross-Border Perspectives", 54(2) Canadian Tax Journal 477–506 (2006)

¶2100 — Taxation of Employment Benefits and Allowances (T1: Lines 101, 102, 104)

ITA 6(1)(a) provides that all benefits and allowances received or enjoyed by an employee from an office or employment are taxable unless specifically excluded by another provision of the ITA. The scope of this provision is very broad; in *Blanchard*, [1995] 2 C.T.C. 262 (FCA), the Court stated (para. 4):

> Paragraph 6(1)(a) is an all-embracing provision ... The section casts a wide net, incorporating two broadly worded phrases. The first is "benefits of any kind whatever." The scope contemplated by this phrase is plain and unambiguous: all types of benefits imaginable are to be included.

Where something is provided to an employee primarily for the benefit of the employer, it will generally not be a taxable benefit if any personal enjoyment is merely incidental to the business purpose. It is often difficult, however, to determine whether an item gives rise to a taxable employment benefit as jurisprudence on the issue has been somewhat inconsistent. In *Hoefele*, [1996] 1 C.T.C. 131 (FCA), the Court stated (paras. 9 and 10):

> The classic statement of what comprises a taxable benefit derives from the Supreme Court of Canada case, *R v Savage*, [[1983] 2 S.C.R. 428 (SCC)]. In that case Mr. Justice Dickson, as he then was, explained the principle which distinguishes taxable from non-taxable receipts: "If it is a material acquisition which confers an economic benefit on the taxpayer and does not constitute an exemption, e.g., loan or gift, then it is within the all-embracing definition of section [6]".

According to the Supreme Court of Canada, then, to be taxable as a "benefit", a receipt must confer an economic benefit. In other words, a receipt must increase the recipient's net worth to be taxable. Conversely, a receipt which does not increase net worth is not a benefit and is not taxable. Compensation for an expense is not taxable, therefore, because the recipient's net worth is not increased thereby.

Many cases have applied the broad concept of "benefit" established in *Savage*. For example, in *Norman*, [1987] 2 C.T.C. 2261 (TCC), an amount received from a taxpayer's employer to settle a grievance under a collective agreement was held to be a benefit in respect of employment. Also, in *Dumas*, [2001] 1 C.T.C. 2490 (TCC), the Court conceded that the settlement amount in question was not taxable under ITA 6(1)(f) as it was not paid or received "on a periodic basis"; however, relying on the broad concept of "benefit" in *Savage*, the Court held that there was a taxable benefit equal to the settlement amount received minus the costs incurred in order to obtain it.

The amount to be included in income in respect of an employment benefit is generally the fair market value of the benefit. In Guide T4130, the CRA states:

> Once you determine that the benefit is taxable, you need to calculate the value of the specific benefit. The value of a benefit is generally its fair market value (FMV). This is the price that can be obtained in an open market between two individuals dealing at arm's length. The cost to you for the particular property, good, or service may be used if it reflects the FMV of the item or service. You must be able to support the value if you are asked.

Below is a comprehensive listing of various payments, benefits and allowances an individual may receive from an office or employment and a discussion of their treatment for tax purposes. See 2017 Chapter 8, "Other Income", for non-employment amounts included in income, such as retiring allowances, death benefits, pension benefits, unemployment benefits, etc.

ITA 5(1), 6(1)(a), Guide T4001, Guide T4044, Guide T4130, VDs 2010-0385881E5, 2010-0360261E5

¶2105 — Accumulated Vacation and Sick Leave Credits

A payment received from an employer in respect of accumulated vacation leave or sick leave while employed is income from an office or employment and taxable under ITA 5(1) in the year the payment is received. However, an amount received upon or after retirement in respect of unused sick leave credits qualifies as a retiring allowance where the payment is received on or after retirement in recognition of long service or in respect of loss of employment (see Folio S2-F1-C2, *Retiring Allowances* and *Harel v. DMR* (Que.), [1977] C.T.C. 441 (SCC)).

Folio S2-F1-C2, *Retiring Allowances*, Folio S3-F9-C1, *Lottery Winnings, Miscellaneous Receipts and Income (and Losses) from Crime*, VDs 2011-0404361E5, 2009-0342701E5

¶2110 — Advances

A payment on account of future earnings is included in an employee's income in the year it is received. Where an employee is taxed on an advance and is required to reimburse an employer for part or all of the balance outstanding by reason of not having performed the anticipated services, the amount repaid ordinarily is deductible from income for the year of repayment. If the amount repaid exceeds the advances received in that year, the excess is deductible from income of the preceding year. An advance is not equivalent to a loan. In IT-222R (cancelled), the CRA states "[a]n advance on account of future earnings is a payment for salary, wages, or commissions that the employee is expected to earn by his future services and, in theory, the employee is not entitled to any further payment until services of a value greater than the amount of the advance have been rendered".

An amount paid in error is not salary or wages of the officer or employee receiving it, nor is it an advance to the officer or employee; and therefore, is not included in income for the year of receipt. In the event that the employee is required to repay the amount in the same or another year, no deduction from income is allowable with respect to the repayments made (whether made by payroll deduction or in some other manner).

> Normally, a reimbursement or an accountable advance (i.e., an amount given by an employer to an employee for expenses to be incurred by the employee on the employer's business and to be accounted for by the production of vouchers and the return of any amount not so spent) for travel expenses is not income for the employee receiving it unless it represents payment of the employee's personal expenses (see ¶2530).

ITA 6(1)(a), 8(1)(n), (n.1), CRA Guide T4130, IT-222R (cancelled), IT-421R2: *Benefits to Individuals, Corporations and Shareholders from Loans or Debt*, IT-522R: *Vehicle, Travel and Sales Expenses of Employees*, VDs 9815507, 9903997

¶2115 — Aircraft (Personal Use of)

An employee who uses an aircraft for personal purposes that is owned (either directly or indirectly) or leased by the taxpayer's employer is considered to have derived a taxable benefit under ITA 6(1)(a), unless the employee pays or reimburses the employer an amount equal to the fair market value of that benefit. If the employee is also a shareholder and the aircraft is used substantially for private use, the benefit is considered taxable as a shareholder benefit under ITA 15(1) (see ¶14350).

The taxable benefit for the personal use of an aircraft provided by an employer is determined based on the value of the benefit, which generally corresponds to the amount the employee would have paid under similar circumstances to receive the same benefit from an arm's length party for whom the individual is neither a shareholder nor employee. Generally, the method for determining the value of the benefit does not depend on the purpose for which the property was acquired, but rather the manner in which the property was used. The CRA provides the following guidance on its website with respect to the proper method to use to compute the benefit (see canada.ca under "Taxable benefit for the personal use of an aircraft"):

> In computing the value of the taxable benefit arising from the personal use of a corporation's or employer's aircraft by its shareholders and/or employees, there are three main scenarios to consider:
>
> 1. Where the shareholder or employee takes a flight on the aircraft in circumstances where there is a business purpose for the flight and their presence on the flight, and there is a personal purpose for others taking the flight, the value of the taxable benefit for the personal use would be equal to the highest priced ticket available in the marketplace for an equivalent commercial flight.
>
> 2. Where the shareholder or employee takes a flight on the aircraft in circumstances where there is no business purpose for the flight, the value of the taxable benefit would be equal to the price of the charter of an equivalent aircraft for an equivalent flight.
>
> 3. Where the shareholder or employee uses the aircraft primarily for personal purposes relative to the aircraft's total use during the calendar year ("primary purpose test"), either alone, or in combination with other persons not dealing at arm's length, the value of the taxable benefit is equal to the personal use portion of the aircraft's operating costs plus an imputed available-for-use amount.

The value of the taxable benefits arising under any of the above scenarios are computed on a calendar basis and included in the employee's income, reduced by the amount paid as a reimbursement to the employer (or related party) for personal use of an aircraft within the calendar year, or 45 days immediately following the year. The employer, as well as the individual taxpayer, are required to maintain adequate records, logs or other evidence to substantiate whether instances of aircraft travel, and travel by the passengers on that aircraft, were for business or personal reasons.

For more information on computing the value of the taxable benefit for personal use of an aircraft, see canada.ca under "Taxable benefit for the personal use of an aircraft".

ITA 5, 6(1)(a), 15(1), *Fingold*, 1997 CarswellNat 1412 (FCA), *Youngman*, 1990 CarswellNat 323 (FCA), IT-160R3 (cancelled), VD 2011-0405391E5

¶2120 — Allowances

Subject to items expressly excluded from employment income, any non-accountable allowance (i.e., an allowance for which an employee does not have to provide details or submit receipts to justify amounts paid), including an allowance for personal or living expenses received by an officer or employee incidental to an office or employment, is generally included in income. However, a reimbursement of *bona fide* expenses incurred by an employee in the course of performing duties or on behalf of an employer is not income of the employee. Where a personal or living expense of an employee is reimbursed (including housing or utility expenses, tools owned by the employee, or travel costs between home and work), however, the amount is a taxable employment benefit.

Certain allowances are specifically excluded as taxable benefits under ITA 6(1)(b) and are not included in computing employment income. Excluded allowances include:

- A travelling or personal or living expense allowance expressly fixed in an Act of Parliament or paid under the authority of the Treasury Board to a person in respect of the discharge of duties relating to an appointment or engagement pursuant to the *Inquiries Act*;

- A travelling or separation allowance received under service regulations as a member of Canadian armed forces;

- A "representation or other special allowance" (see VD 2012-043530117, 2011-039317117 and 2005-0158871E5 for interpretations of this phrase) received in respect of a period abroad by a member of the Canadian forces; an ambassador, minister, high commissioner, officer or servant of Canada, or an agent-general, officer or servant of a province who was resident in Canada immediately prior to the appointment or employment, or received representation allowances in respect of the year; a person while performing services abroad under a prescribed international development assistance program participated in by Canada, provided the person resided in Canada at any time during the three months preceding the commencement of services abroad; or by a member of the overseas Canadian Forces school staff who has elected under ITA 250(1)(d.1) to file returns as a resident of Canada;

- A representation or other special allowance received by an agent-general of a province in respect of a period in Ottawa in such capacity;

- A reasonable travelling expense allowance received by an employee from an employer in respect of a period when the employee was employed in connection with the selling of property or negotiating of contracts for the employer (in IT-522R, the CRA states this provision does not apply to bill-collectors, maintenance or servicepersons, or to salespersons when engaged in any duties other than selling);

- An allowance for room and board to a maximum of $300 per month (as indexed) paid to persons who are participants or members of a sports team or recreational program whose participation is restricted to persons under 21 provided other conditions are satisfied (in *Grenier*, 2006 CarswellNat 5744 (TCC), the Court found that an amateur hockey team's allowance and stipend paid to a player were not taxable);

- A reasonable transportation expense allowance received by a clergyman in charge of or ministering to a diocese, parish, or congregation in connection with duties performed (see ¶2121, "Travel Allowances");

- A reasonable travelling allowance (other than allowances for the use of a motor vehicle) received by an employee in the performance of employment duties while absent from the municipality where the employer's establishment at which the employee ordinarily worked or reported for duty is located, and away from the metropolitan area, if any, where it is located (see ¶2121, "Travel Allowances");

- A reasonable allowance solely for the use of an automobile for travelling in the performance of carrying out employment duties (see ¶2122, "Motor Vehicle Allowances"); and

- A reasonable allowance received by an employee from an employer for a child living away from home and in full-time attendance at school, provided the school is in a community not farther from the employee's home than the nearest community having suitable boarding facilities and providing instruction in the official language of Canada primarily used by the employee, provided a suitable school is not available where the employee is required to live, and the school uses the child's primary language as the language of instruction.

Unless one of the above exceptions is met, an allowance received by an employee generally must be included in employment income by virtue of ITA 6(1)(a).

The exclusions referred to above apply to "reasonable" allowances. With respect to allowances the CRA considers to be unreasonably high, in IT-522R, the CRA states:

41. If the Department considers that an allowance, which is claimed to be non-taxable under subparagraph 6(1)(b)(v), (vi), (vii) or (vii.1), is unreasonably high, the employee is required to provide vouchers or other acceptable evidence to show that the allowance is not in excess of a reasonable amount. Where the employee is unable to show that the allowance is reasonable, the whole amount of the allowance is included under paragraph 6(1)(b) in computing the employee's income and, if the employee qualifies, an amount may be deducted under paragraph 8(1)(f), (h), (h.1) or (j), depending on the circumstances, as discussed in 31 through 38 above. An allowance for travel expenses is not considered unreasonable merely because the employee's total expenses for business travel exceed the total travel allowances received in the year . . .

50. In this bulletin, "reimbursement" and "accountable advance" have the following meanings:

(a) a reimbursement means a payment by an employer to an employee to repay the employee for amounts spent by the employee on the employer's business. Where an employee receives a reasonable allowance to cover particular "motor vehicle" expenses and for other "motor vehicle" expenses the employee charges the cost to the employer (for example, the employee uses the employer's credit card), the amount charged to the employer does not represent a reimbursement. Where subparagraphs 6(1)(b)(x) and (xi) do not apply (see 42 above) and the conditions in subparagraph 6(1)(b)(vii.1) are satisfied (see 49 above), the allowance is excluded from income under subparagraph 6(1)(b)(vii.1); and

(b) an accountable advance means an amount given by an employer to an employee for expenses to be incurred by the employee on the employer's business and to be accounted for by the production of vouchers and the return of any amount not so spent.

51. Usually a reimbursement or an accountable advance for travel expenses is not income in the hands of the employee receiving it, unless it represents payment of the employee's personal expenses. For example, a reimbursement or accountable advance for expenses incurred in travelling between home and the employer's place of business at which the employee ordinarily reports for work is included in income.

52. Where a spouse accompanies an employee on a business trip, the payment or reimbursement by the employer of the spouse's travel expenses is a taxable benefit to the employee, unless the spouse was, in fact, engaged primarily in business activities on behalf of the employer during the trip.

Special rules applicable to meals, moving, and remote workplace allowances, which are discussed below under ¶2245 "Meals", ¶2260 "Moving expenses", and ¶2136 "Special Work Sites and Remote Locations".

ITA 6(1)(a), 6(1)(b), VDs 2011-0395471E5 (book allowance), 2011-040258117 (home office allowance), 2010-0371001E5 (education allowance), 2010-0384711E5 (equipment allowance), 2009-0306351E5 (allowance to cover the Ontario Drug Benefit Plan)

¶2121 — *Travel Allowances*

As noted above, an allowance (other than for the use of a motor vehicle) received by an employee (other than one employed in connection with the selling of property or negotiating of contracts for the employer) for travel expenses is taxable unless the conditions of ITA 6(1)(b)(vii) are satisfied. With respect to traveling allowances, the CRA states as follows in Guide T4130:

Salesperson and clergy

You may pay a reasonable travel allowance for expenses other than for the use of an automobile (such as meals, lodging, per diem allowance) to a salesperson or member of the clergy. You do not have to include the allowance in the employee's income if it was for expenses related to the performance of duties of the office or employment and the employee is either: an agent selling property or negotiating contracts for the employer; or a member of the clergy.

Other employees

You have to include reasonable travel allowances in the income of employees, other than a salesperson or member of the clergy, who travel to perform the duties of the office or employment, unless the allowances are received by the employee for travelling away from the municipality and the metropolitan area where the employer's establishment is located and where the employee ordinarily works or reports.

In some situations, you may provide an allowance to your employee for travel (other than an allowance for the use of a motor vehicle) within a municipality or metropolitan area so your employee can complete his or her duties in a more efficient way during a work shift.

This allowance is not a taxable benefit and can be excluded from the employee's income if all of the following conditions are met:

- The employee travels away from the office.

- The allowance is reasonable. We generally consider a value of up to $17 for the meal portion of the travel allowance to be reasonable.

- You are the primary beneficiary of the allowance.

- The allowance is not an additional form of remuneration.

This means that you do not have to include this type of travel allowance if its main reason is so that your employee's duties are completed in a more efficient way during a work shift.

Reasonable travel allowances

Whether an allowance for travel expenses is reasonable is a question of fact. You should compare the reasonable costs for travel expenses that you would expect your employee to incur against the allowance you pay to the employee for the trip. If the travel allowance is reasonable, you do not have to include it in your employee's income. If it is not reasonable, the allowance has to be included in your employee's income.

In paragraph 47 of IT-522R, the CRA states that where an employee referred to in ITA 6(1)(b)(v), (vi), (vii) or (vii.1) receives an allowance for travel expenses that is "unreasonably low", the allowance is technically required to be included in income; however, the CRA will not insist upon the inclusion in income of the allowance, provided that no amount is claimed for travel expenses by the employee under ITA 8(1)(h) or (h.1) (see ¶2530).

It is generally accepted that travel expenses incurred by a taxpayer in traveling to and from home to a place of employment are considered personal expenses and not traveling costs encountered in the course of the taxpayer's duties. The CRA's position is that travel between an employee's home and regular place of employment is personal, even in situations where an employee has a home office that is also a regular place of employment (VD 2005-0164431E5). For example, in VD 2012-0432671E5, the CRA states:

> In general, travel between an employee's home and regular place of employment ("RPE") is considered personal. Where an employee receives a reimbursement from, or is provided with an allowance by an employer in respect of personal or living expenses, the amount is generally taxable under paragraph 6(1)(a) or 6(1)(b) of the *Income Tax Act* (the "Act"), respectively, unless it falls within the exceptions listed in subparagraphs 6(1)(a)(i) to (v) or 6(1)(b)(i) to (ix) of the Act.

> While it is always a question of fact whether a particular location is considered a RPE for an employee, it is the view of the Canada Revenue Agency that a particular location may be considered a RPE even though the employee may only report to work at that particular location on a periodic basis (e.g., once or twice a month) during the year. However, depending on the circumstances and facts, a location may not constitute a RPE for an employee if, for example, the employee works at that particular location only once during the year or perhaps for only a few days in the year.

> Where an employee (as required by the employer or with the employer's concurrence) proceeds directly from home to a point of call other than the employee's RPE, or returns home from such a point, such travel is generally considered employment-related. In such situations, reasonable travel allowances provided to an employee for using his or her own vehicle in connection with or in the course of performing his or her employment duties and reimbursements made to an employee for reasonable meal and lodging costs incurred in such situations may not be a taxable benefit, provided that certain conditions are met [(see the conditions in Guide T4130 listed above)].

In VD 2005-0152401E5, the CRA states travel between work locations during the course of a workday is likely employment related travel. However, this position does not apply if the client location is regularly visited as it is the view of the CRA that any location to which an employee regularly reports for work or performs the duties of the office or employment is considered to be a regular place of employment. In VD 2009-0313371E5, the CRA states "[w]here an employee reports to work at a particular work location or at more than one particular work location for an extended period of time or frequency, each such work location will likely be considered as that employee's regular place of employment".

Reasonable travel and automobile allowances paid to an employee of a corporation are not taxable merely because the employee is also a shareholder of the corporation (VD 2005-0141491E5).

ITA 6(1)(b), 8(1)(h), (h.1), *Daniels*, [2004] 2 C.T.C. 377 (FCA), *O'Neil*, [2001] 1 C.T.C. 2091 (TCC), VD 2005-0124101E5, 2006-0185481E5, 2008-0276131E5, 2008-0278661E5, 2009-034550117, 2010-0359491E5, 2010-0362781E5, 2011-0400141E5, 2011-0427831E5, 2011-0428741E5, 2009-0313371E5, 2009-0311091E5, 2009-0339891E5, 2011-0400901E5

¶2122 — *Motor Vehicle Allowances*

In order to be considered reasonable, an allowance for automobile expenses must be based solely on the number of kilometres for which the vehicle is used for employment purposes; otherwise, the allowance will be included in the employee's income as a taxable benefit. If the employee receives a non-taxable allowance, as well as being reimbursed either in whole or in part for automobile expenses (except for supplementary business insurance, parking, toll, or ferry charges), and the allowance was determined without taking into consideration those reimbursed expenses, the full amount of the allowance will be considered not to be a reasonable amount and must be included in the employee's income as a taxable benefit. In such a case, the employee may be entitled to deduct related travelling expenses (see ¶2455 and ¶2530).

The CRA's view on motor vehicle allowances is contained in Chapter 2 (Automobile and motor vehicle benefits and allowances) of CRA Guide T4130, excerpts from which are reproduced below:

Automobile and motor vehicle allowances

An allowance is any payment that employees receive from an employer for using their own vehicle in connection with or in the course of their office or employment without having to account for its use. This payment is in addition to their salary or wages. An allowance is taxable unless it is based on a reasonable per-kilometre rate. This section explains common forms of automobile and motor vehicle allowances. Employees receiving a taxable allowance may be able to claim allowable expenses on their income tax and benefit return.

Reasonable per-kilometre allowance

If you pay your employee an allowance based on a per-kilometre rate that we consider reasonable, *do not deduct* CPP contributions, EI premiums, or income tax.

The type of vehicle and the driving conditions usually determine whether we consider an allowance to be reasonable. The per-kilometre rates that we usually consider reasonable are the amounts prescribed in section 7306 of the *Income Tax Regulations*. Although these rates represent the maximum amount that you can deduct as business expenses, you can use them as a guideline to determine if the allowance paid to your employee is reasonable.

We consider an allowance to be reasonable if *all* the following conditions apply:

- The allowance is based only on the number of business kilometres driven in a year.

- The rate per-kilometre is reasonable.

- You did not reimburse the employee for expenses related to the same use of the vehicle. This does not apply to situations where you reimburse an employee for toll or ferry charges or supplementary business insurance, if you determined the allowance without including these reimbursements.

When your employees complete their income tax and benefit return, they do not include this allowance in income . . .

Per-kilometre allowance rates that we do not consider reasonable

If you pay your employee an allowance based on a per-kilometre rate that we do not consider reasonable because it is either too high or too low, it is a taxable benefit and has to be included in the employee's income.

Flat-rate allowance

If you pay your employee an allowance based on a flat rate that is not related to the number of kilometres driven, it is a taxable benefit and has to be included in the employee's income.

Combination of flat-rate and reasonable per-kilometre allowances

If you pay your employee an allowance that is a combination of flat-rate and reasonable per-kilometre allowances that cover the *same use* for the vehicle, the total combined allowance is a taxable benefit and has to be included in the employee's income.

Example 1

You pay an allowance to your employee as follows:

- a flat per-diem rate to offset the employee's fixed expenses for each day the vehicle is required; and

- a reasonable per-kilometre rate for each kilometre driven to offset the operating expenses. The flat per-diem rate compensates the employee for some of the same use on which the reasonable per-kilometre allowance is based. That is, the fixed expenses incurred by the employee to operate the vehicle.

The combined amount is considered one allowance and therefore taxable, since it is not based only on the number of kilometres the vehicle is used for employment purposes.

Example 2

You pay an allowance to your employee as follows:

- a flat-rate per month for travel inside the employment district; and

- a reasonable per-kilometre rate for employment-related travel outside the employment district.

Since the flat-rate allowance does not cover any of the same use of the vehicle on which the reasonable per-kilometre allowance is based, the allowances are considered separately.

The reasonable per-kilometre allowance paid for travel outside the district is *not included in income*. The amount based on a flat-rate paid for travel inside the district is *taxable*, since it is not based only on the number of kilometres for which the vehicle is used in connection with the employment.

Only the total of the monthly flat-rate allowance has to be reported in Box 14, "Employment income," and in the "Other information" area under code *40* at the bottom of the employee's T4 slip.

Reimbursement or advance for travel expenses

A *reimbursement* is a payment you make to your employees as a repayment for amounts they spent (such as gas and meals) while conducting your business. Generally, the employee completes a claim or expense report detailing the amounts spent. Do not include a reasonable reimbursement (which is part of your business expenses) in the employee's income.

An *advance* is an amount you give to employees for expenses they will incur on your business. An *accountable advance* is one that you give to an employee who has to account for his or her expenses by producing vouchers and return any amount he or she did not spend.

Usually, a reimbursement or an accountable advance for travel expenses is not income for the employee receiving it unless it represents payment of the employee's personal expenses.

Averaging allowances

To comply with the rules on reasonable per-kilometre allowances, employees have to file expense claims with you on an ongoing basis, starting at the beginning of the year.

A flat-rate or lump-sum allowance that is not based on the number of kilometres driven cannot be averaged at the end of the year to determine a reasonable per-kilometre rate and then be excluded from the employee's income.

We understand the administrative problems that can result from this. As a result, we are giving you a choice. If you make accountable advances to employees for vehicle expenses, you do not have to include them in the employee's income if *all* the following conditions are met:

- There is a pre-established per-kilometre rate that is not more than a reasonable amount.

- The rate and the advances are reasonable under the circumstances.

- You document this method in the employee's record.

- No other provision of the *Income Tax Act* requires you to include the advances in the employee's income.

Employees have to account for the business kilometres they travelled and any advances they received. They have to do so on the date their employment ends in the year, or by the calendar year-end, whichever is earlier.

At that time, you have to pay any amounts you owe the employee and the employee has to repay any amount over actual expenses. Where no repayment occurs, you cannot simply report the excess advances on the employee's T4 slip.

Reducing tax deductions at source on automobile or motor vehicle allowances

In many cases, allowances that are not based only on a reasonable per-kilometre rate can later be substantially offset by the employees' expense deductions on their income tax and benefit returns. In these situations, employees can ask to reduce their tax deductions on their remuneration by filling out and sending in a Form T1213, *Request to Reduce Tax Deductions at Source*, or a written request to any tax services office along with the following information:

- the type of employment for which the employee will receive the allowance;

- an estimate of the total vehicle allowances the employee will receive in the year;

- an estimate of the business kilometres the employee will drive in the year;

- an estimate of the employee's vehicle expenses for the year; and

- the amount for which the employee is requesting the waiver.

If you have a number of employees in the same situation, you can get a bulk waiver for the group. This way, every employee does not have to make an individual request.

See also the commentary under ¶2130 "Automobile and Motor Vehicle Benefits and Allowances" and the annual car expense and benefit guide published by PwC, available at: pwc.com/ca/carexpenses.

¶2123 — *Part-Time Employees*

A part-time employee who has to travel between jobs and who might be compensated for such travelling by one of the employers may not claim tax relief because the expenses are not incurred in the performance of the duties of any one employment (ITA 6(1)(b)). However, in certain circumstances, an allowance or reimbursement received by the employee might be exempt from tax under the more general provision of ITA 81(3.1). In Guide T4130, the CRA states:

You may give a part-time employee a reasonable allowance or reimbursement for travelling expenses incurred by the employee going to and from a part-time job. If so, and you and the part-time employee are dealing at arm's length, you do not have to include that amount in the employee's income. This applies to:

- teachers and professors who work part-time in a designated educational institution in Canada, providing service to you as a professor or teacher, and the location is not less than 80 kilometres from the employee's home; and

- a part-time employee who had other employment or carried on a business, and he or she did the duties at a location no less than 80 kilometres from both the place of the employee's home and the place of the other employment or business.

ITA 6(1)(b)(x), (xi), 8(1)(f), (h), Guide T4130, S2-F3-C2, *Benefits and Allowances Received from Employment*, IT-522R: *Vehicle, Travel and Sales Expenses of Employees*, VDs 2011-0411941C6, 2007-024170117, 2006-0216791E5, 2008-030000117, 2006-0200171E5

¶2125 — Apprenticeship Incentive Grant

A taxpayer must include in income amounts received under the Apprenticeship Incentive Grant or the Apprenticeship Completion Grant programs which are administered by Employment and Social Development Canada (see canada.ca/en/employment-social-development.html). This is a cash grant of $1,000 per year to apprentices in the first two years of an apprenticeship program in one of the red seal trades and certain other programs.

If a taxpayer makes a repayment under the Apprenticeship Incentive Grant program of an amount that was included in computing income pursuant to ITA 56(1)(n.1) for the taxation year or a preceding taxation year, the taxpayer is allowed to claim a deduction in respect of the total of all such repayments paid in the taxation year (see ¶2415).

ITA 56(1)(n.1), 60(p)

¶2130 — Automobile and Motor Vehicle Benefits and Allowances

When an employee (or person related to the employee) is regularly allowed the personal use of an automobile belonging to the employer or to a person related to the employer, the employee is considered to have a taxable benefit. The taxable benefit to the employee may include: a standby charge based on the cost or lease cost of the automobile to the employer or person related to the employer, as provided in ITA 6(1)(e); an automobile operating expense benefit as determined under ITA 6(1)(k) or (l); and other personal benefits (e.g., in respect of parking costs) that are not excluded by ITA 6(1)(a)(iii).

¶2131 — *Standby Charge*

The minimum standby charge is determined according to a formula that in part depends on whether the automobile is owned or leased by the employer (or related person). If it is owned, the standby charge is 2% of the automobile's capital cost to the employer for each month during which it was available for the personal use of the employee or a related person. This calculation is made on the basis of the number of days made available, divided by 30 (adjusted to the nearest whole number) and multiplied by 2%. The result is that percentage of the automobile's capital cost that is deemed to be the minimum standby charge. For example, if an automobile owned by the employer had a cost of $20,000 and was made available part time for the personal use of an employee from January 1 to July 8, the factor would be 189/30 or 6.3, which is rounded to 6, and the standby charge would be $6 \times 2\% \times \$20,000$, or $2,400.

Where the automobile is leased, the minimum standby charge is 2/3 of the amount payable by the employer to the lessor (exclusive of damage and liability insurance) for the number of days during which the vehicle was made available for the personal use of the employee or related person.

The standby charge may be reduced if the employee is able to establish that the degree of personal use was less than 1,667 km per month (or 20,000 km per year). However, this reduction is available only where the automobile (based on distance travelled) is primarily used in the course of employment and the employee has only limited personal use of the automobile. The CRA generally considers "primarily" to mean more than 50%. The reduced standby charge is determined by multiplying the formula referred to above by the fraction C/D, where C is the number of kilometres driven for personal use and D is 1,667 multiplied by the number of months of personal use determined as explained above.

At the option of the employer, the standby charge for employees employed principally in selling or leasing automobiles may be computed on the basis of 1.5% of the cost of the automobile (instead of 2%). The cost is determined as the greater of the average cost to the employer of all new automobiles purchased·by the employer during the year and the average cost of all automobiles acquired by the employer for sale or lease. Accordingly, this calculation accommodates circumstances where the employer sells or leases only used automobiles.

In the case of an employee who has different automobiles available for personal use out of a large fleet owned by the employer, the CRA will accept calculations based on the average cost of such automobiles.

There is no standby charge or operating expense benefit to an employee in respect of the use of a vehicle that is excluded from the definition of "automobile" in ITA 248(1). Pick-up trucks and vans are included in the definition of "automobile" unless either: 1) they have a seating capacity for not more than a driver and two passengers and are used in the taxation year of acquisition or lease primarily for the transportation of goods or equipment in the course of gaining or producing income, or 2) "all or substantially all" (considered to mean at least 90% by the CRA) of their use in that taxation year is for the transportation of goods, equipment or passengers in the course of gaining or producing income (see VD 2007-0238631E5).

¶2132 — *Operating Expense Benefit*

An actual payment by an employer of an employee's personal operating expenses of an automobile is a taxable benefit based on the actual operating costs and the number of kilometres driven for personal use. Operating expenses include gasoline, insurance, and maintenance costs (parking is not an operating cost but would be included as a benefit under ITA 6(1)(a); see ¶2270). Alternatively, where the employee notifies the employer in writing before the end of the year, the benefit relating to operating costs will be computed as one-half of the standby charge, reduced by any amount that the employee reimburses to the employer within 45 days after the end of the year. This election is available only where the automobile is used primarily (i.e., at least 50%) in the course of the employee's office or employment.

Where the employee or a person related to the employee is provided with an automobile, either by the employer or by a person related to the employer, in the absence of the above-noted election, the operating expense benefit is determined by a formula. The amount of the benefit is based on the number of kilometres driven for personal use during the period in the year while the automobile is available to the employee.

The prescribed kilometer rate is provided in ITR 7305.1(b). Updated rates are also provided by the CRA at: canada.ca/en/revenue-agency/services/tax/businesses/topics/payroll/benefits-allowances/automobile/automobile-motor-vehicle-benefits.html. The fixed rate for 2018 is 26¢ per kilometre of personal use. In the case of a taxpayer in the business of reselling or leasing automobiles, the prescribed kilometre rate is lower (23¢ in 2018). The computed benefit is reduced by any reimbursements made within 45 days of the end of the year to the employer relating to operating expenses. The prescribed benefit is considered to include any GST component. No benefit will arise if the employee repays the employer for all personal use operating expenses, including GST.

In circumstances where only nominal operating costs are paid for by the employer (for example, the annual licensing fee), it would generally be advisable for the employee to repay these amounts to the employer. In order to avoid an income inclusion, an employer must be repaid in the year or within 45 days thereafter (i.e., by February 14 of the immediately following year).

ITA 6(1)(l) includes in computing employment income the value of any benefit received for automobile operating expenses attributable to personal use except where ITA 6(1)(k) applies or would apply if the amounts had not been fully reimbursed within the required time limit. ITA 6(1)(l) could apply, for example, where an employee receives a payment (other than an allowance included in income under ITA 6(1)(b)) for operating expenses of the employee's own automobile because of his/her employment or office, and where an employee of a partner in a partnership receives a payment from the partnership for operating expenses of an automobile provided by the partner (see paragraph 22 of IT-63R5).

It is generally accepted that travel expenses incurred by a taxpayer in traveling to and from home to a place of employment are considered personal expenses (see, for example, *Daniels*, [2004] 2 C.T.C. 377 (FCA) and *O'Neil*, [2001] 1 C.T.C. 2091 (TCC)). In certain cases, however, the court has found that an employee receives no benefit in relation to kilometers driven between work and home generally where: 1) the vehicle is provided because the employee is required by the employer to be available for work (ie, on-call) in case of emergencies, and 2) the employee is prohibited from driving the vehicle for personal purposes (see *Hudson*, [2008] 3 C.T.C. 2178 (TCC), *MacMillan*, [2005] 4 C.T.C. 2463 (TCC), *Fox*, [2003] 4 C.T.C. 2224 (TCC), and *Anderson*, [2002] 4 C.T.C. 2008 (TCC)). Despite the latter decisions, the CRA's position remains that an employee who uses an employer-provided vehicle to travel between home and work without paying for the use of the vehicle has received a benefit, regardless of whether the conditions of employment require the employee to take the vehicle home.

When a vehicle is used partially for business purposes and partially for other purposes, the expenses relating to its use must be apportioned to determine the amount of taxable employee benefits. The proration should normally be determined based on distances driven. To support a deduction or claim, the CRA requires taxpayers to retain logbook records. The CRA Notice, "Documenting the use of a vehicle", explains the ways in which a person who uses a vehicle in a business can keep track of business travel (canada.ca/en/revenue-agency/services/what-s-new/documenting-use-a-vehicle.html).

Kilometres driven by an employee between a special work site or remote work location and his or her principal place of residence are not considered personal use for the purpose of computing a standby charge and operating benefit if all the conditions specified under ITA 6(6) are met (see VD 2005-0164991E5). See ¶2136 below.

When calculating the standby charge where an automobile is made available to more than one driver or where more than one automobile is made available to an employee, see VD 2006-0214581C6.

> The CRA provides a calculator on its website to allow employers to estimate automobile benefits for withholding purposes. Employees can also use the calculator to estimate the taxable benefit related to a company provided automobile. See: canada.ca/en/revenue-agency/services/e-services/e -services-businesses/automobile-benefits-online-calculator-disclaimer.html.

ITA 6(1)(k), 6(2), 6(2.1), Form RC18, Guide T4130 (Chapter 2, Automobile and motor vehicle benefits and allowances), IT-63R5: *Benefits, Including Standby Charge for an Automobile, from the Personal Use of a Motor Vehicle Supplied by an Employer — after 1992*, VDs 2010-0353961E5, 2008-0285351C6, 2007-0231311E5, 2005-0158771C6, 2005-0162611E5

¶2135 — Board and Lodging

The value of board and lodging received or enjoyed in the year by a taxpayer in respect of, in the course of, or by virtue of an office or employment must be included in income. This would include the value of meals and accommodation regularly furnished as a perquisite of the employment; for example, in the case of hotel employees or domestic help. The CRA does not attempt to place fixed, nationwide values upon board and lodging, but expects the employer to report as part of the employee's income an amount relating to the cost of the board (food plus preparation and serving costs) and the fair market value of the lodging provided. The CRA's assessment practices respecting the valuation of board and lodging (including board and lodging furnished as a perquisite of the employment, such as for certain hotel employees) supplied to employees is set out in Folio S2-F3-C2 and Guide T4130 under "Board and lodging". The value of an employment benefit in respect of rent-free housing may be reduced where the employee's privacy is disrupted or where the employee's presence provides security if the location is a worksite.

In *Cameron*, [2008] 3 C.T.C. 2363 (TCC), employer-paid rent to allow an employee to live closer to work in a second residence in another city was held to give rise to a taxable benefit.

An employee is deemed to receive a taxable benefit when the employee receives a housing subsidy or is allowed to occupy premises provided by the employer either rent-free, or at a rent substantially below fair market value. The amounts contemplated would include employer-sponsored subsidies such as mortgage interest payments and bridge financing. See also ¶2238 "Home Purchase and Home Relocation Loans".

> As an exception to the above rules, board and lodging supplied to an individual employed away from home at a special work site or remote location is not included in income (see ¶2136 below).

ITA 6(1)(a), 6(6), 6(23), *Schutz*, [2009] 2 C.T.C. 2183 (TCC), *Potvin*, [1990] 2 C.T.C. 2381 (TCC), VDs 2005-0147831E5, 2010-0382541E5 and 2005-0144811E5). Guide T4130, IT-91R4: *Employment at Special Work Sites or Remote Work Locations*, VDs 2010-0354771E5, 2009-0346161E5, 2009-0318781M4, 2007-0262851E5

¶2136 — *Special Work Sites and Remote Locations*

In certain circumstances, employees at a special or remote work site may exclude from income the value of board and lodging supplied during that interval or a reasonable allowance received to cover the cost of board and lodging. To qualify for this exemption, an employee must either:

- be temporarily engaged in duties at a special work site too far distant from the place where the employee maintains a "self-contained domestic establishment" (defined in ITA 248(1) as a dwelling house, apartment or other similar place of residence in which place a person as a general rule sleeps and eats) as the principal place of residence to enable the employee to return home daily, provided the other residence is available for occupancy and is not rented out to any person, or

- be employed (whether temporarily or regularly) at a place so remote from any established community that the employee could not reasonably be expected to maintain a self-contained domestic establishment there.

This exemption does not apply in respect of any period involving absence from the taxpayer's principal place of residence for less than 36 hours.

Where an employee who is eligible for this exemption in respect of board and lodging also receives a travelling allowance to cover transportation for the same period between the principal place of residence and the special or remote work site and a location in Canada (or country in which he or she is employed), the allowance or the value of the transportation supplied is also exempt.

Fishers and other seamen are considered to be employed at a special work site and may qualify for a deduction under this provision if required by their duties to be on the ship for a period of not less than 36 hours. If, however, this provision does not apply, the employee will be taxable on the value (or cost to the employer) of the employee's quarters and food. In some cases, a seafarer may be required to pay the employer for the value of food and quarters supplied, and under the arrangement have ordinary salary or wages increased by an amount equal to the value of such food and quarters. In that case, the seafarer is subject to tax on the total salary or wages paid but may be entitled to a deduction in respect of payments for food and quarters under ITA 8(1)(g), provided the employee otherwise qualifies.

ITA 5, 6(6), IT-91R4: *Employment at Special Work Sites or Remote Work Locations*, IT-254R2 (archived), Guide T4130 under "Board, lodging, and transportation — Special work sites and remote work locations", VDs 2010-0354771E5, 2009-0346161E5, 2009-0318781M4 and 2007-0262851E5

¶2140 — Cellular Phones, Computers and Internet

> Employer-provided cellular phones and computers generally do not give rise to a taxable benefit, provided that the employee's personal use is incidental and the device is provided to the employee principally for the employer's benefit. However, there is an exception for reimbursements under "bring your own device" plans.

Certain employers implement "bring your own device" (BYOD) policies with respect to computer equipment and cellular phones under which an employee can purchase a device and be reimbursed for the lesser of a maximum amount and the actual cost of the equipment. At the 2011 CTF Annual Conference (see VD 2011-0425801C6), the CRA stated a reimbursement under a BYOD plan should be included in employment income unless, upon reimbursement, the employee transfers ownership of the computer equipment to the employer and the use of the equipment is primarily for employment purposes (the CRA's position is questionable; arguably, the value of any reimbursement included in employment income should be reduced to reflect the employment use of the device).

In a "bring your own device" arrangement where the employer reimburses employees up to a fixed rate per month for a cell phone plan that is reflective of the employment requirements in terms of data and voice use, and where the employer does not reimburse the employees for any hardware costs, the employer does not pay any additional charges unless the charges are business related, and the employee has title to the cell phone will not result in a taxable benefit to employees because the employer is not reimbursing the cost of the device (VD 2013-0489981E5). It is also the CRA's view that a monthly payment of a fixed amount made to employees who use their personal cell phone in the performance of their duties is considered an allowance. The payment cannot be treated as a reimbursement of expenses because no detailed receipts are required; the fact that the contract with the service provider must be given to the employer is not a proof of payment (VDs 2014-0552731E5, 2015-0588201E5).

Where an employer provides an employee with internet service at home to carry out the employee's employment duties, the business use is not a taxable benefit. However, the value of any personal use is required to be included in the employee's income as a taxable benefit based on the fair market value of the service less any amounts the employee reimburses to the employer. The employer is responsible for determining the percentage of business use and the fair market value.

In CRA Guide T4130, the CRA states:

Cellular phone and Internet services

If you provide your employee with a cellular phone (or other handheld communication device) or Internet service at home to help carry out his or her duties, the business use is not a taxable benefit. If part of the use of the phone or Internet service is personal, you have to include the value of the personal use in your employee's income as a taxable benefit. The value of the benefit is based on the fair market value (FMV) of the service, minus any amounts your employee reimburses you. You can only use your cost to calculate the value of the benefit if it reflects the FMV.

For cellular phone service only, we do not consider your employee's personal use of the cellular phone service to be a taxable benefit if all of the following apply:

- The plan's cost is reasonable.

- The plan is a basic plan with a fixed cost.

- Your employee's personal use of the service does not result in charges that are more than the basic plan cost.

You, as the employer, are responsible for determining the percentage of business use and the FMV. You have to be prepared to justify your position if we ask you to do so.

Note

If you give your employee an allowance for cellular phone or Internet services, the allowance must be included in the employee's income.

Regarding computers provided to employees, the CRA provides the following example in Folio S2-F3-C2:

An employee buys a new home computer for her family's use. The employee occasionally uses the computer to check her office email account. Her employer reimburses part of the cost of the computer. As noted in ¶2.15, an employee receives an economic advantage when reimbursed, in whole or in part, for the purchase of a personally-owned asset, even if it is used for employment purposes. In this case, the employee has received an economic advantage and is the primary beneficiary. The reimbursement is included in her income under paragraph 6(1)(a).

Folio S2-F3-C2, Guide T4130 under "Cellular phone and Internet services", VDs 2005-0155975E5, 2011-0399171E5

¶2145 — Child Care Expenses

Employer paid child care expenses generally give rise to taxable employment income. Such taxable benefits are considered to have been paid by the employee for purposes of the child care expense deduction in ITA 63 (see ¶9170). As an exception to this general rule, it is the CRA's administrative policy that child care is not taxable if all of the following conditions are met: the services are provided at the employer's place of business; the services are managed directly by the employer; the services are provided to all of the employees at minimal or no cost; and the services are not available to the general public, only to employees. If the facilities are available to non-employees for a higher rate than employees are charged, the CRA considers the difference in rates to be a taxable benefit for the employee. Also, if an employer subsidizes a facility operated by a third party in exchange for subsidized rates for employees, the amount of the subsidy is considered a taxable benefit by the CRA to the employee.

In VD 2008-0297761E5, the CRA states that in circumstances where an employee is required to be away from home due to unusual overtime demands and as a result is unable to supervise young children or provide physical care for dependent family members, if the employee has no choice but to incur an expense for such care and the employer pays the incremental cost, the payment "may not be an employment benefit".

Amounts paid by an employee for child care expenses, including babysitting, day nursery services, and services provided at a boarding school or camp, may be deductible where the employee (or his or her spouse or common-law partner) pays for someone to look after their child in order to earn income. See ¶9170.

Guide T4130 under "Child care expenses", VDs RCT 5-8359, 2002-0161525, 2005-0124661E5, 2010-0390931E5, 2014-0528601C6

¶2150 — Commissions

Commissions received by an employee, including a commission based on the volume of sales made or contracts negotiated, are income from employment. However, ITA 8(1)(f) allows the deduction of expenses incurred in earning commission income (see ¶2435).

¶2155 — Counselling Services

Financial counselling services and income tax return preparation services provided to an employee at the employer's expense are normally considered to be taxable employment benefits to the employee.

However, where an employer provides or pays for counselling services to an employee in respect of the mental or physical health of either the employee or a person related to the employee, these amounts are not included in the employee's income as a taxable benefit unless the amount related to an expense incurred by the employer to provide recreational facilities or pay membership fees or dues for a dining, recreational, or sporting facility described in ITA 18(1)(l) (see ¶2295). Similarly, counselling services in connection with either the re-employment or retirement of the employee are not considered taxable benefits.

ITA 6(1)(a)(iv), S2-F3-C2: *Benefits and Allowances Received from Employment* (paras. 2.46–2.48), Guide T4130 under "Counselling services", VD 2000-0042265

¶2160 — Deferred Salary Payments

A taxpayer who receives a large sum as arrears of salary owed for prior periods is taxable for the year of receipt, subject to the rules that apply to retroactive lump-sum payments. However, the taxpayer will be considered to have constructive receipt and be taxable in the year of constructive receipt where the unpaid amount is freely available. For example, an amount that is credited to the employee's account but which remains undrawn would be considered to be received in the year credited. Similarly, where a cheque issued in payment of salary is not immediately cashed, the taxpayer will be considered to have received salary in the year made available by way of cheque. For more information, see ¶2020, "Salary Deferral Arrangements".

ITA 110.2

¶2165 — Directors' Fees

By definition, an office includes the position of a corporation director. As such, directors' fees are income from an office or employment.

Directors' fees paid to a non-resident for services performed in Canada should be reported on a T4 slip. Where a non-resident director does not attend any meeting or perform any other related functions in Canada, the remuneration is not subject to withholdings; however, if services are partly performed in Canada, the CRA's position is that the employer is responsible for apportioning that part of the annual fee paid to the non-resident director for the services performed in Canada and to withhold in respect of that portion of the fees (see VD 2009-0345151E5).

In VD 2009-0308041E5, the CRA states that while director's fees are normally included in the computation of the income of the individual director, the CRA will in certain circumstances permit the fees to be considered the income of a partnership or corporation.

Where a director directs an amount of remuneration to be paid directly to a charity, the CRA's position is that the donated amount is included in the employment income of the director (VD 2010-0367781E5). As such, the payer of the remuneration would be required to withhold in respect of the payment donated to charity.

ITA 6(1)(c), 56(2), 248(1)"office", ITR 104(2), IT-377R (cancelled), Guide T4001 under "Director's fees", Guide T4061, VD 2003-0020315, Arthur Drache, "Diverting Directors' Fees", xxxi(24) *The Canadian Taxpayer* (Carswell) 191-92 (Dec 8, 2009)

¶2170 — Disability-Related Employment Benefits

If an employer provides transportation to and from work or special parking near the work location for either blind employees or employees with severe and prolonged mobility impairments, the employee is not considered to receive or enjoy a taxable benefit. Similarly, there is no taxable benefit if the employer provides an attendant to assist an employee who has a severe and prolonged mental or physical impairment in the performance of that employee's duties.

In VD 2003-0033715, the CRA states that an individual who is blind is not in receipt of a taxable benefit if the employer pays the travel expenses of the individual's spouse, provided that the spouse is travelling solely to perform the functions of an attendant to assist the individual in the performance of his or her duties of employment.

ITA 6(16), VDs 2003-0014615, 2001-0110095

¶2175 — Discounts on Merchandise and Commissions from Personal Sales

The CRA's longstanding administrative position generally exempts from an employee's income the benefit derived from employee-only discounts on the employer's merchandise, provided that the employee paid at least the employer's cost of the merchandise. Specifically, the CRA's position, as stated in T4130 *Employer's Guide*, is as follows:

Discounts on merchandise and commissions from personal purchases

If you sell merchandise to your employee at a discount, the benefit he or she gets from this is not usually considered a taxable benefit.

However, we consider discounts to be taxable in all the following situations:

- You make a special arrangement with an employee or a group of employees to buy merchandise at a discount.

- You make an arrangement that allows an employee to buy merchandise (other than old or soiled merchandise) for less than your cost.

- You make a reciprocal arrangement with one or more other employers so that employees of one employer can buy merchandise at a discount from another employer.

If you determine the discount is taxable or you sell merchandise to your employee below cost, the taxable benefit is the difference between the fair market value of the goods and the price the employees pay.

However, in Folio S2-F3-C2, *Benefits and Allowances Received from Employment*, the CRA revised the wording of its administrative position on the taxable benefit treatment of employee benefits to limit the administrative exemption outlined above. Specifically, Folio S2-F3-C2 provides that where "an employee receives a discount on merchandise because of their employment, the value of the discount is generally included in the employee's income under paragraph 6(1)(a)." As a result of criticism to this revised administrative position, the CRA removed Folio S2-F3-C2 from its website, and is conducting an internal review on the wording change followed by a consultation. At the time of writing, the internal review and consultation was ongoing, and the CRA instructs employers to "follow current practices consistent with the information available in Guide T4130, *Employers' Guide — Taxable Benefits and Allowances*".

Company point systems are discussed under ¶2205 "Gifts, Awards, and Long Service Awards".

S2-F3-C2: *Benefits and Allowances Received from Employment*, VDs 2011-0431701E5, 2011-0409721E5, 2011-0407121E5, 2011-0399661E6, 2010-0388111M4, 2009-0316531I7, 2007-0260051E5, 2005-0154061E5, Dereka Thibault, FCA, "Life Insurance Taxation: An Update," *2010 Prairie Provinces Tax Conference*, (Toronto: Canadian Tax Foundation, 2010), 9:1–16)

¶2180 — Employee Benefit Plans

An amount received out of an "employee benefit plan" as defined in ITA 248(1) is included in computing the recipient's income from employment, regardless of whether the recipient is an employee, former employee, or an individual not dealing at arm's length with the employee or former employee, unless the amount is paid as a death benefit, contributed to the plan by the recipient or by a deceased employee, and the recipient is the heir or legal representative, or a pension benefit attributable to service rendered by any person in a period throughout which that person was a non-resident of Canada.

The following types of plans or arrangements are specifically excluded from the definition of an "employee benefit plan": a deferred profit sharing plan; an employee life and health trust; a group sickness or accident insurance plan; a group term life insurance policy; a registered pension fund or plan; a private health services plan; a supplementary unemployment benefit plan; an employees' profit sharing plan; a vacation pay trust described in ITA 149(1)(y); an employee trust; a salary deferral arrangement; a retirement compensation arrangement; a plan or arrangement the sole purpose of which is to provide education or training for employees to improve their work-related skills and abilities; and a prescribed arrangement (as defined in ITR 6800).

ITA 6(1)(g), 248(1)"employee benefit plan", ITR 6800, IT-502: *Employee Benefit Plans and Employee Trusts*, VDs 2005-0129961E5, 2008-0265651E5, 2009-0308741E5, 2010-0373561C6, Samantha Hans, "Employee Benefit Plans: Tips and Traps", 13(3) *Taxation of Executive Compensation and Retirement* (Federated Press) 31–34 (Oct. 2001), Scott Sweatman & Brandon Hodge, "Employee Benefit Plans and Employee Profit Sharing Plans", 16(9) TECR 539-47 (May 2005)

¶2185 — Employee Health and Welfare Trusts/Employee Life and Health Trusts

Health and welfare benefits for employees are sometimes provided through a trust arrangement under which the trustees receive contributions from the employer to provide agreed-upon benefits including life insurance, sickness or accident insurance, wage continuation payments during illness, and similar benefits. Employer contributions made to the trustees under a health and welfare trust are deductible by the employer and are not considered a taxable benefit to the employees until the trustees make a payment or defray a premium for which the employee is otherwise liable. The trust in such an arrangement is taxable on the income derived from invested funds and is required to file a T3 trust return for each calendar year.

An "employee life and health trust" (ELHT) is a taxable *inter vivos* trust established by one or more employers after 2009 that meets a number of conditions under ITA 144.1(2). ELHTs are designed to replace the health and welfare trust, and the rules governing them are contained in ITA 144.1. The only purpose of an ELHT is the payment of a designated employee benefit (DEBs) for employees and certain related persons. Employers can deduct contributions made to the trust, as long as they are for DEBs and meet the conditions in ITA 144.1(4). Employee contributions are permitted, but are not deductible. However, employee contributions may qualify for the medical expense tax credit, to the extent that they are made to a private health services plan. Any amount received from an ELHT must be included in income, unless the amount was received as the payment of a DEB.

ITA 144.1, IT-85R2: *Health and Welfare Trusts for Employees*

¶2190 — Employee Profit Sharing Plans

Amounts allocated to an employee, whether contingently or absolutely, in the year by a trustee under an "employee profit sharing plan" are required to be included in employment income. Generally, employees who are members of the plan are taxable on amounts allocated to their account in the year of such allocation and the amount on which the employee has paid tax in the year of allocation is not taxed again when the employee actually receives the money. A corporation is required to file a Form T4PS: *Statement of Employee Profit-Sharing Plan Allocations and Payments* in Information return and send the T4PS slips to payment recipients on or before the last day of February following the calendar year to which the in formation return applies.

ITA 6(1)(d), 144(1), IT-379R: *Employees Profit Sharing Plans — Allocations to Beneficiaries*, Finance Release 2011-08-30: *Consultations on the Tax Rules for Employee Profit Sharing Plans*

¶2195 — Employment Insurance Premiums

Under ITA 6(1)(a), an individual employee is not considered to receive any immediate benefit from the general contributions made by his/her employer under a group sickness or accident insurance plan, employee life and health trust, private health services plan, or supplementary unemployment benefit plan. However, where an employee is covered under a sickness or accident insurance plan, a disability insurance plan, or an income maintenance insurance plan (or any of those described plans that is administered or provided by an "employee life and health trust") under which the employer pays part or all of the premiums, the amount of any insurance proceeds received by the employee on a periodic basis constitutes income from employment to the extent it exceeds the total of all amounts contributed by the employee by way of premiums. The employee may deduct the cumulative total of premiums paid in the first year in which insurance benefits are received under the plan provided the amount deductible does not exceed the benefits received in the year and the premium paid is not deducted twice. After a deduction is claimed, the accumulation starts over again. Where a plan is entirely employee funded, no amount is included in income.

> Applicable in respect of employer contributions made after March 28, 2012 to the extent that the contributions relate to coverage after 2012, as an exception to the above rules, employer contributions to a group sickness or accident insurance plan are considered a taxable benefit under ITA 6(1)(e.1) to the extent that the contributions are not in respect of a wage loss replacement benefit payable on a periodic basis and must be reported as income on an employee's T4 slip for the year the contributions are made. Formerly, no amount was included in an employee's income, either when employer contributions were made or benefits were received, to the extent that benefits were not payable on a periodic basis or benefits were payable in respect of a sickness or accident when there was no loss of employment income (see CRA Q&A 2012-03-30A: *Budget 2012: Group Sickness or Accident Insurance Plan*).

¶2196 — *Employer Contributions*

Once the employer has contributed to the plan, all benefits received are taxable notwithstanding that contributions have been made by the employee (*Schuett*, [1980] C.T.C. 2185 (TRB)).

The treatment of payments and benefits under wage loss replacement plans differs from the treatment of payments and benefits under the *Unemployment Insurance Act* or the *Employment Insurance Act*. Although payments received under these Acts are taxable, they are not income from an office or employment but rather are included in income under ITA 56(1)(a)(iv) (see Line 119 at ¶8220). Similarly, benefits received under a registered supplementary unemployment benefit plan are taxable under ITA 56(1)(g). Premiums paid by the employee are deductible annually in computing income from employment.

In VD 2005-0121521E5, the CRA takes the position that a lump-sum payment in respect of future benefits under an employer long-term disability plan constitutes proceeds of disposition of a capital property that must be included in computing the recipient's taxable capital gain resulting from the disposition. The CRA's view is that ITA 6(1)(f) applies to all employees even if employer premiums are only paid in respect of certain employees (VDs 2006-0172261E5 and 2009-0347621E5).

In VD 2005-0125791C6, the CRA states that where the terms of a taxable wage loss replacement plan are changed to provide that all future contributions to the plan will be 100 percent funded by employees and it can be shown that all previous employer contributions to the plan are exhausted (e.g., where the plan is in a deficit position), the CRA will not only consider all payments of liabilities that occur after the purification to be paid under an employee-pay-all plan, but also all payments for liabilities that arose before the purification.

ITA 6(1)(f), 8(1)(k), IT-428: *Wage Loss Replacement Plans*, VDs 2005-0160551E5, 2006-0182841M4, 2009-0343571E5

¶2200 — Flexible Benefit Plans

In response to the significant increase in the use of flexible employee benefit arrangements often referred to as "flexible benefit plans" or "cafeteria plans", IT-529: *Flexible Employee Benefit Programs* was issued to discuss the tax treatment of such plans. Flexible benefit plans are usually designed so that both taxable and non-taxable benefits may be provided. Although the ITA does not contain provisions that specifically apply to these programs as a whole, the design of the plan must satisfy certain conditions in order to avoid adverse tax consequences for all benefits provided under the plan. Provided the latter conditions are satisfied (as discussed in IT-529), the various benefit components under the plan are subject to specific provisions of the ITA in the same manner as if they were offered outside of the plan (i.e., depending on the particular benefit and how it is paid for, it may result in a taxable or non-taxable benefit to the employee).

The conversion of salary and/or vacation entitlements to flex credits after the initial commencement of a flexible employee benefits program will normally give rise to a taxable employment benefit (VDs 2009-0342701E5 and 2011-0404361E5).

TFSAs may be part of a flexible employee benefit program wherein the employee can use flex credits to contribute to a TFSA or direct their employer to contribute the amounts to a TFSA on the employee's behalf (VD 2008-0272891E5).

An amount paid to employees to compensate the employer's unilateral decision to reduce non-taxable benefits would be a taxable employment benefit (VD 2009-0329441E5).

VDs 2006-0187401E5, 2007-0238961E5, 2002-0123617

¶2205 — Gifts, Awards, and Long-Service Awards

Bonuses paid to employees in recognition of employment services rendered are taxable when received. Following is an excerpt from Guide T4130 providing the CRA's administrative policy for cash and non-cash gifts, awards and long-service awards:

Rules for gifts and awards

A gift has to be for a special occasion such as a religious holiday, a birthday, a wedding, or the birth of a child.

An award has to be for an employment-related accomplishment such as outstanding service or employees' suggestions. It is recognition of an employee's overall contribution to the workplace, not recognition of job performance. Generally, a valid, non-taxable award has clearly defined criteria, a nomination and evaluation process, and a limited number of recipients.

An award given to your employees for performance-related reasons (such as performing well in the job he or she was hired to do, exceeding production standards, completing a project ahead of schedule or under budget, putting in extra time to finish a project, covering for a sick manager/colleague) is considered a reward and is a taxable benefit for the employee.

If you give your employee a non-cash gift or award for any other reason, this policy does not apply and you have to include the fair market value of the gift or award in the employee's income.

The gifts and awards policy does not apply to cash and near cash items or to gifts or awards given to non-arm's length employees, such as your relatives, shareholders, or people related to them.

. . .

Policy for non-cash gifts and awards

You may give an employee an unlimited number of non-cash gifts and awards with a combined total value of $500 or less annually. If the FMV of the gifts and awards you give your employee is greater than $500, the amount over $500 must be included in the employee's income. For example, if you give gifts and awards with a total value of $650, there is a taxable benefit of $150 ($650 - $500).

Items of small or trivial value do not have to be included when calculating the total value of gifts and awards given in the year for the purpose of the exemption. Examples of items of small or trivial value include: coffee or tea, T-shirts with employer's logos, mugs, plaques or trophies

Long-service awards

As well as the gifts and awards in the policy stated above, you can, once every five years, give your employee a non-cash long-service or anniversary award valued at $500 or less, tax free. The award must be for a minimum of five years' service, and it has to be at least five years since you gave the employee the last long-service or anniversary award. Any amount over the $500 is a taxable benefit.

If it has not been at least five years since the employee's last long-service or anniversary award, then the award is a taxable benefit. For example, if the 15 year award was given at 17 years of service, and then the next award is given at 20 years of service, the 20 year award will be a taxable benefit, since five years will not have passed since the previous award.

The $500 exemption for long-service awards does not affect the $500 exemption for other gifts and awards in the year you give them. For example, you can give an employee a non-cash long-service award worth $500 in the same year you give him or her other non-cash gifts and awards worth $500. In this case, there is no taxable benefit for the employee.

The CRA's administrative policy does not apply to cash or near-cash gifts, such as gift certificates or "company bucks" (VDs 2011-0394901E5, 2007-0247981E5 and 2005-0153611E5). The CRA's policy also does not apply to a company points system where an employee earns points and can redeem them for items from a catalogue; the CRA considers such points to be a near-cash item (VD 2012-0440731E5). Furthermore, the CRA's policy does not apply to performance-based bonuses and awards (VDs 2011-0405361E5 and 2011-0423981E5).

The CRA considers gifts provided to an employee by a customer of the employer to be taxable as employment income (VD 2010-0388581E5, *Robinson v MNR*, [1970] Tax A.B.C. 1287).

As an administrative concession, employees are not taxed on gifts of a nominal value, such as coffee and tea mugs, T-shirts with employer logos, plaques, trophies, etc. are not considered taxable benefits. With respect to employer draws or lotteries, see ¶2280, "Prizes and Awards".

ITTN-15, S2-F3-C2: *Benefits and Allowances Received from Employment*, Guide T4130 under "Gifts, awards, and long-service awards", VDs 2010-0359501E5, 2005-0153611E5

¶2210 — Government Grants

Where an individual's employment is financed directly or indirectly and either wholly or in part by a government grant, such financial assistance is considered income from employment. For example, a university professor may have been employed on the basis of a Canada Council grant awarded to the university specifically for the purpose of engaging the professor's services. Therefore, the professor's remuneration would be taxable as employment income pursuant to ITA 5(1).

ITA 5(1), IT-257R: *Canada Council Grants*, VDs 2004-0076661E5, 2002-0125695

¶2215 — Gratuities and Tips

Gratuities are income from employment even though they may not be received from the employer. The CRA's general position is that taxes should be withheld from tips and gratuities in cases where the employer has control over the how the tips will be paid. In Guide 5000-G, the CRA states "[i]f tips you received through employment are not shown on your T4 slips, report them on Line 104". If the recipient is self-employed (such as an independent taxi operator), gratuities and tips are income from business.

ITA 5(1), VD 2006-0202891E5

¶2220 — Group Life Insurance Premiums

Pursuant to ITA 6(1)(a)(i), the benefit which an employer confers on employees through the payment of group term life insurance premiums as an inducement to enter and continue in employment is not included in the employees' income. However, employer paid life insurance benefits, other than group term life insurance benefits, are included in employment income, unless the employees are required to work in a high-risk zone that nullifies the employees' own life insurance.

ITA 6(4) includes in income employment benefits arising out of a group term life insurance policy. Where insurance is provided by an employer under which a payment on death is payable only where the death occurs as a result of an accident, the CRA will not impute a benefit to an employee under ITA 6(4).

ITA 6(1)(a), 6(4), 6(5) (repealed), 248(1)"group term life insurance policy", ITR 2700–2704, Guide T4130 under "Group term life insurance policies — Employer-paid premiums", VDs 2009-0322781E5, 2008-0278501E5, 2008-0265651E5

¶2225 — Income Tax Paid by Employer

Income tax of an employee paid by an employer is included in the income of the employee. As an exception, the CRA has stated that payments from a fund established and fully funded by employees who are assigned to various countries to help equalize the effect of differing tax rates would not constitute a taxable employment benefit.

Salter, [1947] C.T.C. 29, *Hartland v Diggines*, [1926] A.C. 289, VDs 2006-0188141E5, 2003-0020053

¶2230 — Injury Leave Pay

Salary or wages received by an employee while on leave as a result of injury or sickness are taxed as a benefit from employment; however, where salary or wages so received and included in income are subsequently reimbursed to the employer by or on behalf of the employee (for example, from the proceeds of a workers' compensation award), the employee is allowed a deduction for such repaid amounts (see ¶2490 and ¶2495). Amounts received as personal injury damages on account of accrued or future lost wages are normally excluded from income. See also ¶2370 "Workers' Compensation Payments".

ITA 6(1)(f), 8(1)(n), Guide T4130 under "Income maintenance plans and other insurance plans", IT-428: *Wage Loss Replacement Plans*, VD 2010-0388721E5

¶2235 — Loans — Interest-Free and Low-Interest

¶2236 — *Employee Loans*

Where a loan is made to an employee, the amount received by the employee is not included in income from an office or employment. Only those earnings that are applied against the loan plus any other salary, wages, or commissions that are paid to the employee should be included in income.

Where the balance of a genuine loan is not repaid, the forgiven amount is included in the employee's income from an office or employment as income arising on the settlement or extinguishment of the loan. The forgiven amount is defined as the lesser of the principal amount of the obligation and the amount for which it was issued, minus any amount paid in satisfaction of the principal amount and any other adjustments reflecting the extent to which the unpaid amount has been dealt with for tax purposes. However, the forgiven amount does not include any amount included in computing income as a result of the settlement, nor is it reduced to reflect the extent to which it was otherwise applied under ITA 79(3) in determining the proceeds of disposition of a property (see ¶4112). Any interest payable on the principal amount is not taken into account in determining the forgiven amount.

For these purposes, the value of the benefit is considered to be the amount of the obligation that was forgiven. For example, if an employee repays only $2,000 of a loan where the amount originally advanced was $10,000, the value of the benefit would be the $8,000 forgiven by the employer. Otherwise, ITA 80 (debtor's gain on settlements of debts) will apply on the settlement of the debt (see ¶4112).

ITA 6(1)(a), 6(15), (15.1), 80, IT-421R2: *Benefits to Individuals, Corporations and Shareholders from Loans or Debt*

¶2237 — Interest Benefit

Pursuant to ITA 80.4, a taxable benefit is imputed to an employee on low interest or interest-free loans or other advances to the employee regardless of whether the loan is made as a consequence of a prior, current, or future employment. For these purposes, a loan or debt is deemed to be received or incurred by reason of the employment relationship if it is reasonable to conclude that either the terms of the debt would have been different or the loan would not have been made in the absence of the employment relationship. The intended use of the funds by the individual is irrelevant in determining whether the loan was made as a result of employment. An imputed benefit is included in income as income from an office or employment.

The amount of the benefit is the difference between the interest that would be payable on the loan or indebtedness at the prescribed rate, and the interest actually paid by the employee during the year or not later than 30 days after the end of the year. For an example of the computation of a deemed interest benefit, see IT-421R2 or VD 2009-0331661E5.

No benefit is imputed if the rate of interest payable on the loan or debt was equal to or greater than the rate that would have been agreed upon at the time the loan was received between arm's length parties had the loan not arisen in an employer-employee relationship and if part of the ordinary business of the lender or debtor is the lending of money. This relief is forfeited, however, if interest is paid on the loan or debt by a person other than the debtor. In addition, no benefit will be attributed to a loan or debt that was included in the income of the debtor.

Where a benefit is included in income by virtue of this provision, the amount is considered interest expense for the purposes of ITA 8(1)(j)(i) (interest deduction for loans to acquire an aircraft or motor vehicle; see ¶2455) and ITA 20(1)(c) (see ¶3720).

ITA 6(9), 80.4, 80.5, ITR 4301(c), Guide T4130 under "Loans — interest-free and low-interest"

¶2238 — Home Purchase and Home Relocation Loans

A "home purchase loan" is a loan received by virtue of employment where the proceeds are used to acquire, or repay a loan incurred to acquire, a dwelling or a share in the capital stock of a co-operative building. The dwelling must be for the habitation of the individual employee or specified shareholder of a corporation carrying on a personal services business, or a person who is related to such person. In the case of a co-operative corporation, the debt must be incurred to acquire a share of a co-operative housing corporation entitling the purchaser or a related person to inhabit a dwelling unit owned by the corporation. For the CRA's interpretation of "home purchase loan", see paragraph 19 of IT-421R2.

As proposed in the 2017 Federal budget, the employee home relocation loan deduction is eliminated, effective for benefits arising in 2018 and subsequent taxation years.

A home relocation loan is one that is received by an individual or the individual's spouse or common-law partner where the person has moved from one residence in Canada to another by reason of taking up employment in Canada. In order to qualify as a home relocation loan:

- the distance between the individual's old residence and the new work location must be, at least 40 kilometres greater than the distance between the new residence and new work location;

- the loan must be used to acquire a dwelling for the individual where the individual will ordinarily reside, or to acquire a share of the capital stock of a co-operative housing corporation entitling the purchaser to inhabit a dwelling unit owned by the corporation again where the individual will ordinarily reside;

- the loan must be received by virtue of employment as described in ITA 80.4(1) or would have been so received if ITA 80.4(1.1) had applied; and

- the individual must designate the loan as a home relocation loan. No more than one loan in respect of a particular move, nor at a particular time, may be designated.

In the case of a home relocation loan, the taxpayer may claim a corresponding deduction in respect of the amount included as a taxable benefit to the extent that the benefit does not exceed the benefit that would be calculated on a $25,000 interest-free loan (see ¶2440). The deduction may be claimed throughout the duration of the loan, but in no case for more than five years. A loan that is received to repay a home relocation loan is considered to be the same loan as the original relocation loan.

The prescribed rate for purposes of determining the benefit on a home purchase or a home relocation loan cannot exceed the prescribed rate at the time the loan was received or the debt incurred. If the prescribed rate falls during the term of the loan, the benefit will be reduced. If the term of the home purchase or home relocation loan exceeds five years, the balance at the end of five years is treated as a new loan at that time and the benefit after that date is calculated on the prescribed rate then in force. This adjustment is required every five years throughout the term of the loan.

ITA 6(9), 6(15), 80.4, 80.5, 110(1)(j), 110(1.4), 248(1)"home relocation loan", ITR 4301(c), IT-421R2: *Benefits to Individuals, Corporations and Shareholders from Loans and Debt*, Guide T4130 under "Loans — interest-free and low-interest"

¶2240 — Loyalty and Other Points Programs

It is the CRA's administrative policy not to assess a taxable benefit in respect of frequent flyer points earned on an employee's personal credit card used for business travel and reimbursed by the employer, unless any of the following applies: the points are converted to cash, the plan or arrangement between the employer and the employee seems to be a form of remuneration, or the plan or arrangement is a form of tax avoidance. Note, however, *Giffen*, [1995] 2 C.T.C. 2767 (TCC), where the Court held that free travel rewards constitute benefits received or enjoyed in respect of employment.

The CRA has also stated a reimbursement of travel reward points used by an employee for business travel would be deductible by the corporation and non-taxable to the employee where it is clearly established that the employee used his/her personal Air Miles to pay for business travel and the reimbursement does not exceed the fair market value of the tickets (VD 2010-0378631E5).

Guide T4130 under "Loyalty and other points programs", VDs 2002-0168007, 2010-0353041E5, 2010-0378631E5, 2010-0383501E5

¶2245 — Meals

The Courts have generally found that meals provided to employees give rise to a taxable benefit. However, the following exceptions are noted in Guide T4130 under "Meals":

Overtime meals or allowances

If you provide overtime meals, or an allowance for overtime meals, there is no taxable benefit if *all* of the following conditions apply:

- The allowance, or the cost of the meal, is reasonable. We generally consider a value of up to $17 to be reasonable. We will consider higher amounts reasonable if the relative cost of meals in that location is higher, or under other significant extenuating circumstances.

- The employee works two or more hours of overtime right before or right after his or her scheduled hours of work.

- The overtime is not frequent and is occasional in nature (usually less than three times a week).

If overtime occurs frequently or becomes the norm, we consider the overtime meals or allowances to be a taxable benefit, since they start to take on the characteristics of additional remuneration. [See also VDs 2011-0398021E5 (the $17 allowance is per meal), 2009-0336061E5 (the CRA does not require proof that a meal was actually consumed by the employee) and 2006-0215801E5.]

Subsidized meals

If you provide subsidized meals to an employee (such as in an employee dining room or cafeteria), these meals are *not* considered a taxable benefit if the employee pays a reasonable charge. A reasonable charge is one that covers the cost of the food, its preparation, and service. If the charge is not reasonable, the value of the benefit is the cost of the meals, *minus* any payment the employee makes. Include the taxable benefit in Box 14, "Employment income," and in the "Other in Formation" area under code 40 at the bottom of the employee's T4 slip.

In *Morissette*, 2012 CarswellNat 379 (TCC), a $20 meal allowance for employees working overtime was found to be reasonable and not to constitute a taxable benefit.

It is also important to highlight that employer paid travel, including meal allowances, does not confer a taxable employment benefit provided the amounts are paid primarily for the benefit of the employer.

See ¶2136 for special rules relating to employment at a special work site or remote location.

Lavoie, [1978] C.T.C. 2452 (TRB), *McGoldrick*, [2004] 3 C.T.C. 264 (FCA), *Shell Canada Ltd*, [1999] 4 C.T.C. 313 (SCC), S2-F3-C2: *Benefits and Allowances Received from Employment*, VDs 2009-0348151E5, 2009-0333541E5

¶2250 — Member of Legislative Assembly (MLA) Expense Allowance

For taxation years before 2019, ITA 81(2) provides that allowances received by an elected member of a provincial legislature, for expenses related to the discharge of the member's duties, are not required to be included in computing the member's income, to the extent that they do not exceed one-half the amount payable by way of salary, indemnity and other remuneration. This exemption has been repealed for 2019 and later taxation years, such that the full amount of non-accountable allowances paid to these officials will be included in income. The reimbursement of employment expenses will remain a non-taxable benefit to the recipient.

ITA 81(2), IT-266 (cancelled), VD 2000-0048324

¶2255 — Miscellaneous Employee Benefits

The treatment of various miscellaneous employee benefits is outlined below in alphabetical order:

- *Criminal Background Checks*: Non-taxable if required to employ a person (VD 2002-0133095).

- *Grievance Settlement*: Normally taxable; however, may not be taxable if the amount can be established as reasonable compensation for damages due to the employer's negligence (VDs 2010-037383117, 2009-0322501E5).

- *Leased Vehicle Purchased by Employee*: An employee benefit arises equal to the excess of the automobile's fair market value over the purchase price paid by the employee for the automobile (VD 2010-0370211E5).

- *Legal Expenses*: Generally, where personal legal expenses of an employee are paid or reimbursed by the employer, the CRA considers the amount paid to be a taxable employment benefit. However, the CRA does not consider a taxable benefit to arise where the legal expenses primarily benefit the employer and the expenses are incurred by reason of employment (VDs 2003-0035475, 2010-0391441E5, 2011-0406611I7 and 2011-0408071E5, IT-99R5 (paras. 30–32)).

- *Licensing and Testing Fees*: Such fees paid by the employer are non-taxable if the costs are incurred as a condition of employment or for the maintenance or upgrading of employment-related skills (VD 2010-0377631E5)

- *Rental Cars*: A taxable benefit does not arise where an employee is reimbursed for the cost of a rental car used to travel between the employee's temporary office and hotel (VD 2004-0084201E5).

- *Sports Clubs*: Various income arrangements common to football, hockey and similar clubs are discussed in IT-168R3: *Athletes and Players Employed by Football, Hockey and Similar Clubs* (see also ¶2025 and Guide T4130 under "Board and lodging allowances paid to players on sports teams or members of recreation programs")

Guide T4130: *Employers' Guide — Taxable Benefits and Allowances*, S2-F3-C2: *Benefits and Allowances Received from Employment*

¶2260 — Moving Expenses

When an employer bears the cost of moving an employee and the employee's family and household possessions from one location to another (including in respect of relocations from outside Canada) during or prior to employment, the employee is not considered to receive a taxable benefit. However, if the employer pays a further allowance, commonly referred to a "household adjustment allowance", in recognition of intangible expenses and inconveniences, the amount of such additional payment is generally taxable.

If the moving expenses are borne by the employee, they may be deductible under ITA 62 (see Line 219 at ¶9200).Where an employee receives from an employer an allowance for, rather than a reimbursement of, moving expenses, the employee may claim a deduction only for moving expenses incurred to the extent that the allowance is included in computing income.

The CRA's position is that where an employer pays or reimburses an employee for relocation expenses other than those that would qualify as deductible moving expenses under ITA 62, a taxable benefit arises. As an exception, in Guide T4130, the CRA states:

> A non-accountable allowance is an allowance for which an employee does not have to provide details or submit receipts to justify amounts paid. We consider a non-accountable allowance for incidental relocation or moving expenses of $650 or less to be a reimbursement of expenses that the employee incurred because of an employment-related move. Therefore, this type of allowance is not taxable. For us to consider it as a reimbursement for incidental expenses, the employee has to certify in writing that he or she incurred expenses for at least the amount of the allowance, up to a maximum of $650.

In *Suffolk*, [2010] 5 C.T.C. 2414 (TCC), employer reimbursements of certain household items purchased in the course of a move were held to be taxable benefits since the taxpayer was found to be better off economically.

As a special rule, the reimbursement by an employer of a housing loss (other than an "eligible housing loss") suffered by the employee on the sale of a home upon being transferred or relocated is a taxable benefit received by reason of office or employment. For these purposes, a housing loss is the amount by which the greater of the adjusted cost base or the highest fair market value of the house within a period of six months that ends at that time exceeds the lesser of the proceeds of disposition or fair market value of the house (if the residence was disposed of before the end of the first taxation year beginning after that time) or in any other case, the fair market value at that time.

An "eligible housing loss" is defined as the housing loss relating to one residence which occurs during the period while the taxpayer has an "eligible relocation". An "eligible relocation" is generally a relocation that enables the employee to be employed at a location in Canada if both the employee's old residence and the employee's new residence are in Canada and the distance between the old residence and the new work location is not less than 40 kilometres greater than the distance between the new residence and the new work location. The employee must designate the residence that relates to the eligible loss. No more than one residence may be designated by a taxpayer in respect of an eligible relocation (for example, an employee could not designate both a house and a cottage). In the case of an eligible housing loss, only one-half of any amount that exceeds $15,000 of amounts paid by the employer in respect of the loss is considered an employment benefit.

Where an employer pays an amount to assist an employee to acquire or use a residence, that amount paid or the value of assistance provided is considered an employment benefit.

ITA 6(1)(a), 6(19)–6(23), 62, 248(1)"eligible relocation", S2-F3-C2: *Benefits and Allowances Received from Employment*, Guide T4130 under "Moving expenses and relocation benefits", VDs 2009-0331701E5, 2008-0276771E5, 2011-0427911E5, 2011-0413871E5, 2009-0313341E5 and 2006-0202091E5

¶2265 — Municipal Officer's Expense Allowance

For taxation years before 2019, the following types of municipal officials may receive a tax-free allowance of up to one-half the amount of their stipend: an elected officer of an incorporated municipality; an officer of a municipal utilities board, commission or corporation, or any other similar body, if elected by popular vote; and a member of a public or separate school board.

The *Municipal Act* of some provinces provides that a proportion of the total amount paid (i.e., as salary plus non-accountable allowances) to an elected member of a municipal council is deemed to be an allowance for expenses. In this case, it is the policy of the CRA that the proportion deemed to be an expense allowance (up to one-third of the total paid) will be considered as an expense allowance notwithstanding that local by-laws may specifically allocate portions of the total to salary, indemnity, allowance, or other remuneration.

When there is no deeming provision in the *Municipal Act* of a province, the CRA will consider one-third of the total amount received to be an expense allowance and two-thirds to be salary or other remuneration. However, where the expense allowance actually paid is less than one-third of the total received, the actual amount will be used.

ITA 81(3), IT-292, VDs 2006-0212631E5, 2011-0398781I7

¶2270 — Parking

ITA 6(1.1) provides that benefits in respect of the use of a motor vehicle do not include any amount or benefit related to the parking of the vehicle, such that benefits in respect of personal parking expenses are included in computing the employee's income under ITA 6(1)(a).

Employer-provided parking normally constitutes a taxable benefit based on the fair market value of the parking, minus any payment the employee makes to use the space (see, for example, *Anthony*, 2011 CarswellNat 5125 (FCA)). However, it is the CRA's position that there is no taxable benefit where: free parking is available to the public (e.g, a shopping centre); parking is provided for business purposes and employees are "regularly" (i.e., for more than half the week's workdays) required to use their cars for employment; or where only scramble parking is provided (see VDs 2011-0422901E5, 2008-0286381E5, 2008-0288491E5 and 2006-0187401E5). The CRA defines scramble parking as follows:

> Scramble parking is where there are significantly fewer parking spaces than there are employees who want parking. In other words, on any given day, whether or not an employee is able to find a parking spot is random or uncertain.

Whether or not scramble parking is in effect is determined by the number of parking spaces regularly needed to accommodate employees desiring a parking space, not by the number of parking passes issued.

In the following cases, employer-provided parking was found to be a taxable employment benefit: *Bernier*, 2009 CarswellNat 1477 (TCC), *Toronto Parking Authority*, [2010] 5 C.T.C. 2456 (TCC), *Richmond*, [1998] 3 C.T.C. 2552 (TCC), *Adler*, [2007] 4 C.T.C. 2205 (TCC) *Schroter*, [2010] 4 C.T.C. 143 (FCA) (in this case, one employee was found to have a taxable benefit, while a second employee was found not to have a taxable benefit because the employee was required to travel for his duties) and *Smith*, 2017 TCC 62.

In the following cases, employer-provided parking was found not to be a taxable benefit: *Long*, [2010] 5 C.T.C. 2185 (TCC), *Chow*, [2001] 1 C.T.C. 2741 (TCC), *Saskatchewan Telecommunications*, [1999] G.S.T.C. 69 (TCC), and *Stauffer*, [2002] 4 C.T.C. 2608 (TCC).

ITA 6(1.1), Guide T4130 under "Parking", 2016-0645911E5

¶2275 — Private Health Services Plan Premiums

When an employer pays premiums under a "private health services plan" for the benefit of employees, the benefit is specifically excluded from income by ITA 6(1)(a)(i) (for public plans, see under ¶2290). A private health services plan ("PHSP") is defined in ITA 248(1) as:

(a) a contract of insurance in respect of hospital expenses, medical expenses, or any combination of such expenses, or

(b) a medical care insurance plan or hospital care insurance plan or any combination of such plans,

except any such contract or plan established by or pursuant to:

(c) a law of a province that establishes a health care insurance plan as defined in section 2 of the *Canada Health Act*, or

(d) an Act of Parliament or a regulation made thereunder that authorizes the provision of a medical care insurance plan or hospital care insurance plan for employees of Canada and their dependants and for dependants of members of the Royal Canadian Mounted Police and the regular force where such employees or members were appointed in Canada and are serving outside Canada.

Generally, a PHSP includes extended health plans, drug plans and dental plans (see IT-339R2). It also includes a "Health Care Expense Account" and a medical/dental spending account employment benefit (see VDs 9629843, 2003-0051591R3, 2004-0091211R3, 2004-0105181E5). As of 2015, the CRA accepts that a plan is a PSHP if "all or substantially all" (normally 90% or more) of the premiums paid under the plan relate to medical expenses that are eligible for the medical expense tax credit (METC) under ITA 118.2(2) (see VD 2015-0610751C6). The expenses that are not eligible for the METC, but covered under a plan (i.e., the 10% coverage) must be a medical or hospital expense or an expense that is incurred in connection with a medical or hospital expense, and must be incurred within a reasonable time period following the medical or hospital expense (VD 2016-0636871E5).

For more information, see: canada.ca/en/revenue-agency/news/whats-new/new-position-on-private-health-services-plans-questions-answers.html.

If the employee pays the premiums in respect of themselves, their spouse or common-law partner, or member of the household with whom the employer is connected by blood, marriage, common-law partnership or adoption, they are treated as medical expenses except to the extent that the premium contribution or consideration is deducted pursuant to ITA 20.01(1) in computing business income. In either case, medical costs paid for under such plan, or to which the employee or person related to the employee is entitled to reimbursement by such a plan, may not be claimed as medical expenses to the extent that the reimbursed amount is not required to be included in computing income. See ¶10190 for a full discussion of medical expenses that can be claimed for purposes of the medical expense tax credit. In respect of an employee that is also a shareholder, if the employee has received coverage in his or her capacity as a shareholder, a benefit in respect of such coverage arises under ITA 15(1). See ¶14351 for a discussion of shareholder benefits.

In VD 2010-0385181R3, the CRA concluded that payments in lieu of continued private health service plan coverage for retirees of an employer that entered insolvency were non-taxable. A private health services plan is normally designed as traditional plan (i.e., a plan that does not have dollar limits for most categories of expenses) or as a flexible health care spending account (i.e., a plan that normally sets caps for all categories of expenses). Prior to 2013, the CRA's administrative position was that an employee could redirect a portion of his/her bonus to obtain additional flex credits in a health care spending account on a tax-free basis (see, for example, VD 2007-0257631R3). However, at the 2011 Annual CTF Conference CRA Roundtable, the CRA announced that effective January 1, 2013, such redirected amounts are taxable as employment income (see VD 2011-0397751R3).

In VD 2016-0633741C6, the CRA concluded that a plan for one plan member (which could include coverage for his or her spouse and members of his or her household), who is the company's sole employee and who deals at arm's length with the company, may qualify as a PHSP.

ITA 6(1)(a)(i), 118.2(2)(q), 118.2(3)(b), 248(1)"private health services plan", Guide T4130 under "Private health services plan premiums", IT-339R2: *Meaning of "Private Health Services Plan"*, VDs 2006-0175931E5, 2009-0322451E5, 2010-0368871E5, Jeanne Cheng & Sonal Shah, "Private Health Services Plans for Small Businesses", 5(4) Canadian Tax Focus (ctf.ca) 52-3 (Nov. 2015), Darren Bank, "Deferred Income Plans for the Owner Manager," *2009 British Columbia Tax Conference*, (Vancouver: Canadian Tax Foundation, 2009), 13:1–37, Frank Baldry, "Too Good to be True?", 1(1) *It's Personal* (Carswell) 5 (Nov. 2007)

¶2280 — Prizes and Awards

When an employee competes among fellow employees for a prize for outstanding performance, such as a free holiday trip, the value of the prize, measured by its cash equivalent, is income from employment.

CRA provides the following comments regarding the taxation of prizes in paragraphs 3.53 to 3.55 of Folio S1-F2-C3:

> 3.53 Subparagraph 56(1)(n)(i) includes in computing a taxpayer's income, the amount of a prize for achievement in a field of endeavour ordinarily carried on by the taxpayer (other than a prescribed prize). A prize can be considered to be an award to a particular person selected from a group of potential recipients and given for something that is accomplished, attained or carried out successfully. However, the type of prize contemplated in subparagraph 56(1)(n)(i) is restricted. The criteria for awarding the prize must be such that a recipient is rewarded for success in an area in which the recipient regularly applies effort. Therefore, an amount generally qualifies as a prize for purposes of subparagraph 56(1)(n)(i) if it is paid in recognition of a genuine accomplishment in a challenging area, whether it be of an academic, vocational or technical nature. A prize that is not described by subparagraph 56(1)(n)(i) is considered to be a *windfall* and is not required to be included in income unless it is also a business receipt (see ¶3.55) or income from employment (see ¶3.54). The following points indicate how subparagraph 56(1)(n)(i) applies to certain situations.

> - An award of damages to an injured party. This is not considered to be a prize.

> - Lottery winnings. Although this is a prize, the recipient is not being recognized for an accomplishment nor are the winnings likely to relate to a field of endeavour ordinarily carried on by the recipient. As a result, subparagraph 56(1)(n)(i) does not apply.

> - An award by a professional institution to the candidate obtaining the highest marks in examinations set by the institution. This is a prize subject to the provisions of subparagraph 56(1)(n)(i).

> 3.54 If an employee receives, from his or her employer, a prize or other award related to sales or other work performance (such as exceeding sales targets, success in examinations, suggestion awards or exceptional service), the fair market value of such an incentive is regarded as remuneration for services that must be included in the individual's employment income under subsection 5(1). Similarly, the fair market value of a prize or award that is not regarded as remuneration, but is considered to have been received by an employee in respect of, in the course of, or by virtue of the employee's office or employment, is included in income from an office or employment under paragraph 6(1)(a), subject to certain exceptions for small non-cash gifts and awards. A prize or other award that is considered to be income from an office or employment for purposes of subsection 5(1) or paragraph 6(1)(a), will be excluded from paragraph 56(1)(n).

> 3.55 If there is no employer-employee relationship between the payer and the recipient of an amount and it can be established that the amount is a business receipt, it should be included in the recipient's business income under subsection 9(1). However, if the amount received is a prize for achievement in a field of endeavour ordinarily carried on by the taxpayer and it cannot be regarded as a business receipt (and is not a prescribed prize), the amount should be used in computing the recipient's income under subparagraph 56(1)(n)(i).

The CRA's policy with respect to employer draws and lotteries is set forth in VD 2008-0293781E5:

- An item given to one employee by an employer via a prize draw — a taxable benefit is something that an employee gains by virtue of his or her employment. If the draw is only open to employees of the company, then any item won is a benefit of employment, and therefore, is taxable.

- An item paid for by the employer and given via a draw to an employee of a high-performing team — In this example, the prize takes on the nature of performance pay, or a thanks for a job well done, and as such, is a taxable benefit to the employee.

- An item paid for by a social committee and given via a draw — our policy applies specifically to employer/employee relationships, and a social committee may be outside that. If the social committee is not funded and controlled by the employer, a prize won via lottery from the social committee is considered to be a windfall. If the employer does fund or exercise control over the social committee, the prize may be taxable.

S1-F2-C3: *Scholarships, Research Grants and Other Education Assistance, S3-F9-C1: Lottery Winnings, Miscellaneous Receipts, and Income (and Losses) from Crime*, IT-316: *Awards for Employees' Suggestions and Inventions* (archived)

¶2285 — Professional Membership Dues

Professional membership fees paid by an employer are non-taxable if the employer is the primary beneficiary. On the other hand, the CRA considers employer-paid professional initiation or admission fees to give rise to a taxable benefit, although it is arguable that the payment of such fees primarily benefits the employer (VD 2004-0058301E5).

ITA 8(1)(i)(i), Guide T4130 under "Professional membership dues", ITTN-15, IT-158R2: *Employees' Professional Membership Dues*, S2-F3-C2: *Benefits and Allowances Received from Employment*, VD 2008-0267901E5

¶2290 — Provincial Hospital or Health Care Plan Premiums

The contributions of an employer under a group sickness or accident insurance plan or private health services plan set up for employees are specifically excluded from the category of taxable benefits under ITA 6(1)(a) (see ¶2275). However, where an employer pays all or part of an employee's premiums under a provincial hospital insurance plan or a provincial medical care insurance plan, the amount so paid is considered to be a taxable benefit to the employee.

ITA 6(1)(a), *Rymer* (1966), 41 Tax A.B.C. 343, *Salter*, [1947] C.T.C. 29, *Dorval*, [1979] C.T.C. 2888 (TRB), S2-F3-C2: *Benefits and Allowances Received from Employment*, Guide T4130 under "Premiums under provincial hospitalization, medical care insurance, and certain Government of Canada plans", VDs 2006-0181751E5, 2011-0404371E5

¶2295 — Recreational Facilities and Club Dues

When an employer pays for a social or athletic club membership for an employee for business purposes, the employee is not considered to receive a taxable benefit. However, if the membership is principally for the benefit of the employee, there will generally by a taxable benefit regardless of whether the employer also enjoys an indirect benefit. Recreational facilities provided by an employer for use by all staff are likewise not considered to confer a taxable benefit.

In Guide T4130, the CRA sets forth its policy with respect to employer-paid recreation and club dues as follows:

The use of a recreational facility or club is a taxable benefit for an employee in any of the following situations:

- You pay, reimburse, or subsidize the cost of a membership at a recreational facility, such as an exercise room, swimming pool, or gymnasium.

- You pay, reimburse, or subsidize the cost of memberships to a business or professional club (that operates fitness, recreational, sports, or dining facilities for the use of their members but their main purpose is something other than recreation).

- You pay, reimburse, or subsidize the cost of membership dues in a recreational facility of the employee's choice, up to a set maximum. In this case it is the employee who has paid for the membership, owns it, and has signed some kind of contract with the company providing the facility.

- You pay, reimburse, or subsidize the employee for expenses incurred for food and beverages at a restaurant, dining room lounge, banquet hall, or conference room of a recreational facility or club.

- You provide recreational facilities to a select group or category of employees for free or for a minimal fee, while other employees have to pay the full fee. There is a taxable benefit for employees who do not have to pay the full fee.

However, the use of a recreational facility or club does not result in a taxable benefit for an employee in any of the following situations:

- You provide an in-house recreational facility and the facility is available to all your employees. This applies whether you provide the facilities free of charge or for a minimal fee. [See also VDs 2009-0330341C6 and 2011-0427381E5. In VD 2011-0431681E5, the CRA states a taxable benefit will generally arise where the use of an in-house recreational facility is not made available to all employees.]

- You make an arrangement with a facility to pay a fee for the use of the facility, the membership is with you and not your employee and the facility or membership is available to all your employees. Membership will be considered to be made available to all employees as long as each employee can use the membership even if an employee chooses not to.

- You provide your employee with a membership in a social or athletic club and it can be clearly demonstrated that you are the primary beneficiary of the membership. The membership is a taxable benefit to your employee if the membership in or use of the club's facilities provides only an indirect benefit to you. This would be the case where the employee becomes physically healthier as a result of using the club's facilities and becomes generally better able to perform his or her duties (for example, fewer sick days, less downtime, remain fit for duty).

With respect to demonstrating that a membership is principally for an employee's advantage, in VD 2006-0216251E5, the CRA states:

Generally, we would not consider that the employer is the primary beneficiary where the employee's membership in a fitness club or fitness training course provides an indirect benefit to the employer. This would be the case where the employee becomes physically healthier as a result of utilizing the club's facilities and consequently becomes generally better able to perform his or her duties (e.g. is sick less often). In such situations, the employee is regarded as being the primary beneficiary and would be in receipt of a taxable benefit described in paragraph 6(1)(a) of the Act.

However, there may be situations in which the nature of the particular employment and/or the terms of the employment contract require that an employee meet certain stringent fitness standards, and if it can be demonstrated that a particular fitness training course or fitness club membership fulfills this specific employment requirement, it may be considered that the primary beneficiary is the employer. In such a situation, the amounts paid by the employer for the program or membership would not represent a taxable benefit to the employee under paragraph 6(1)(a) of the Act.

The CRA does not consider an employee to receive a taxable benefit where an employer simply arranges for a third party to provide discounted fitness passes to a group of employees and the employer does not absorb the discount (VD 2005-0154061E5).

In VD 2005-0109731E5, the CRA takes the position that an employer funded weight loss program would give rise to a taxable benefit even if the program is made available to all employees.

Regarding employer-paid golf club membership fees, in VD 2007-0226111I7, the CRA states:

Generally, the cost of a golf club membership provided to an employee is considered to be a taxable benefit included at 100% of fair market value in the employee's income, even though the dues or fees are not deductible by the employer pursuant to paragraph 18(1)(l) of the Act. However, if the employer and employee can establish that the membership is primarily for the employer's advantage, no taxable employment benefit will arise. This policy on golf club memberships can apply to employees in public relations or those who network with and entertain clients where it can be demonstrated that such work primarily benefits the employer. Further, even where the employer's business is unrelated to the golf business, the primary beneficiary of the membership may still be the employer.

In *Rachfalowski*, [2009] 1 C.T.C. 2073 (TCC), the Court found that an employer-paid golf club membership did not give rise to a taxable employment benefit since the membership was mainly for the benefit of the employer and the employee's use of the membership was minimal. In the case, the employee's preference would have been to convert the membership into cash and the Court noted that from the taxpayer's point of view "the membership was clearly not an advantage to him" (para. 23).

IT-148R3: *Recreational Properties and Club Dues*

¶2300 — Reimbursements and Awards

When a taxpayer is entitled to claim a deduction under ITA 8(1) in connection with certain reimbursements and awards, the amounts must be included in computing the taxpayer's income. Generally this would apply to a reimbursement or award of legal expenses incurred to collect wages or salary that are otherwise deductible under ITA 8(1)(b). A similar provision is provided in ITA 56(1)(l.1) with respect to awards and reimbursements of legal expenses incurred to collect or establish a right to a retiring allowance or certain pension benefits.

ITA 6(1)(j)

¶2301 — Research Grants

Under ITA 56(1)(o), an individual must bring into the computation of his/her income on Line 104 any grant received in the year to enable the individual to carry on research or any similar work. This would include, for example, a Canada Council grant. Reasonable expenses incurred in connection with the research project are eligible for deduction, although expenses cannot exceed the amount of the grant received. For purposes of reporting, individuals should subtract the allowable expenses from the research grant received and report the net amount on Line 104. Individuals filing a paper return should attach the list of expenses to the T1 return. Individuals filing electronically should keep the list of expenses in case the CRA requests it at a later date.

Eligible expenses include the cost of a research assistant, capital expenses such as a computer, and travel expenses incurred while away from home and in the course of carrying out the research, including meals and lodging. Expenses not eligible for deduction include the individual's personal or living expenses (except while travelling in the course of carrying on the work), expenses for which the individual has been reimbursed (except amounts included in income as part of the grant received), and expenses that are otherwise deductible in computing the individual's income for the year. Generally, an individual must deduct eligible expenditures in the year that the expenditures are incurred and the research grant is received. However, administratively, CRA allows an individual to deduct expenses incurred up to one year before or one year after the year the grant is received, although prior-year expenses incurred by an individual before being notified of the grant award are not deductible.

CRA's administrative position on the taxation of research grants under ITA 56(1)(o) is set out in paragraphs 3.58 to 3.65 of Folio S1-F2-C3, *Scholarships, Research Grants and Other Education Assistance*, as follows:

Research Grants

3.58 Amounts received in a tax year to enable a taxpayer to carry on research or any similar work are included in income as a research grant under paragraph 56(1)(o). However, such research grants are only included in income to the extent that they exceed the total of the allowable expenses (see ¶3.73–3.78) incurred by the taxpayer in the year for the purpose of carrying on the work. A research grant is generally a sum of money given to enable the recipient to pay expenses necessary to carry out a research project. The grant may also include an element of remuneration to the recipient. It is the nature and terms of the grant, rather than the name given to it, that determine whether it is taxed as a scholarship under paragraph 56(1)(n) or as a research grant under paragraph 56(1)(o).

Meaning of "research"

3.59 For the purposes of paragraph 56(1)(o), research involves a critical or scientific inquiry aimed at the discovery of new facts, or the development of new interpretations or applications. In *Ghali v. The Queen*, 2004 FCA 60, 2005 D.T.C. 5472, the Federal Court of Appeal stated that "the words "research or any similar work" in paragraph 56(1)(o) may be defined as: a set of scientific, literary and artistic works and activities having as its purpose the discovery and development of knowledge."

3.60 It does not include research carried out for the sake of acquiring the experience or skill of conducting research, as may be the case with research carried out by undergraduate students. In order for a payment to be considered a research grant, the terms of the payment must establish that its primary purpose is to enable the recipient to carry out research (see the comments in ¶3.32). The following factors may be helpful in this context:

- If only one of the major purposes of the grant is to enable the recipient to carry out a research project, this does not in itself establish the primary purpose. The comments in ¶3.33 should be referred to in cases where a grant has more than one major purpose;

- The term or terms relating to the research requirements for the grant must be specific. Vague and general references, such as *including research*, do not of themselves bring the grant within paragraph 56(1)(o);

- Generally, awards to undergraduates are taxed under paragraph 56(1)(n), even though some research for essays, projects, etc., is required as part of the course requirements; and

- If the terms of the grant do not mention research, paragraph 56(1)(n) applies, even if a great deal of research is in fact done.

Research grants awarded to non-employees

3.61 A corporation or other entity (such as a university or college) may decide to give a grant to a person outside its own organization to do specific research. Where this is done, the grant is considered to be a research grant to the recipient for purposes of paragraph 56(1)(o) whether the results of the research belong to the grantor or the recipient.

Research grants awarded to employees

3.62 If the recipient is an employee of the grantor and is retained on part salary while undertaking a specific research project that is unrelated to the recipient's normal employment duties, the part salary is included in the recipient's employment income under subsection 5(1). Any amount received as a research grant (net of allowable expenses) is included in income under paragraph 56(1)(o). This would arise, for instance, where a university faculty member has been granted sabbatical leave by his or her employer to carry out research. Under such arrangements, an employee usually receives a full or partial continuation of salary throughout the leave period that is taxable as employment income under subsection 5(1). The employee is usually not under the direction of the employer during the sabbatical leave period despite the fact that the employee continues to receive such salary. Amounts received during the sabbatical leave period to enable the employee to carry on the research (for example, payments that have been approved by the university as approved expenses under the employee's research program) will generally be considered research grants for purposes of paragraph 56(1)(o). See *Ghali*, wherein the Federal Court of Appeal considered the taxability of amounts received by a University professor from his employer while on a sabbatical leave.

3.63 Individuals (such as university faculty members) whose duties of employment include research responsibilities are not entitled to treat a portion of their regular salaries as a research grant when they engage in the type of research work ordinarily expected of them under their terms of employment. For example, an individual employed by a university to teach a course as well as conduct research, will be considered to receive employment income in respect of both activities as each fall within his or her normal employment duties.

Amounts not received as a research grant

3.64 For the purposes of paragraph 56(1)(o), a research grant is not considered to be *received* at any time if all of the following circumstances apply:

- The funds are made available to an individual who holds an academic appointment at a university, hospital, or similar institution, to enable the individual to carry on research or similar work;

- the funds are paid directly to the university, hospital, or similar institution;

- the funds are provided only to pay for the costs of the research project; and

- the funds were not used by the individual and were not otherwise available for the personal benefit of the individual.

3.65 In some cases, part of the research grant may be paid to a researcher or may otherwise be made available for the researcher's personal benefit, but the remaining funds meet the criteria listed above. If so, only that part of the grant actually paid to, or otherwise available for the researcher's personal benefit, will be considered for purposes of paragraph 56(1)(o) to have been *received* by the researcher as a research grant.

In *Subbarao*, [1986] 2 C.T.C. 2089, an associate professor on a research trip to India was not entitled to deduct travel expenses for his wife and two children because the travel expenses permitted as deductions under ITA 56(1)(o) were held by the Tax Court of Canada to refer only to the taxpayer's own expenses.

In *Ghali*, [2003] 3 C.T.C. 2513 (TCC) the taxpayer was a university professor who, while taking a year of sabbatical, received payments from the university to cover certain expenses incurred during his leave. The Tax Court of Canada held that, while the amounts received by the professor related entirely to research activities conducted during his sabbatical, the funds were taxable as employment income and not as a research grant under ITA 56(1)(o) so that he could not deduct his related research expenses. Further, in VD 2006-020415117, in determining whether an amount was received as a bursary or a research grant, the CRA stated that "the particular treatment depends upon the primary purpose for which a fellowship was granted as determined by reference to the terms and conditions attached to the award. If the primary purpose of a particular award is to further the education and training of the recipient in his or her individual capacity, such as studying for a doctoral degree, the award is included under subparagraph 56(1)(n)(i), even though research is undertaken as a means to achieve that purpose. If the awarding of a fellowship is primarily for the purpose of research, a detailed description of the term or terms relating to the research requirements would normally be provided". See also VD 2008-0276691E5.

In *Amyot*, [1976] C.T.C. 352, the taxpayer sought to characterize a $4,500 award from the Canada Council as a research grant under ITA 56(1)(o) so as to permit the deduction of expenses. Reversing a decision by the Tax Review Board, the Federal Court held that the object of the grant was not the taxpayer's contribution to the general body of knowledge but was assistance for him towards his doctorate, so that the amount was taxable as a fellowship under ITA 56(1)(n). The CRA's administrative views on the difference between a fellowship and a research grant are contained in paragraphs 3.31 and 3.32 of Folio S1-F2-C3:

Amounts determined to be fellowship income

3.31 If the primary purpose of the award is to further the education and training of the recipient in his or her individual capacity, such as studying for a doctoral degree (as opposed to post-doctoral work which is discussed in ¶3.36), the award will be characterized as a fellowship for income tax purposes. It would be used in computing the income of the recipient under subparagraph 56(1)(n)(i) even though research is undertaken as a means to achieve that purpose.

Amounts determined to be research grants

3.32 If the primary purpose of the award is to carry out research for its own sake (for example, to further knowledge in a particular field by discovering new facts, or by reinterpreting existing knowledge), the award is considered to be a research grant for income tax purposes and should be included in the recipient's income under paragraph 56(1)(o). Where the recipient's education and training is also furthered by such research, such a benefit does not invalidate the primary purpose of the grant provided the benefit could be considered to be a secondary purpose of the grant or an inevitable but incidental benefit. See ¶3.58 for further discussion on research grants.

In some circumstances, a research grant received by an individual may have to be repaid if the individual fails to satisfy some condition attached thereto. The amount of such a repayment, to the extent it represents an amount included in computing the individual's income in a preceding taxation year under ITA 56(1)(o), may be deducted by the individual under ITA 60(q) in computing income for the year of repayment.

ITA 56(1)(o), 60(q), Pamphlet P105, Folio S1-F2-C3

¶2305 — Retirement Compensation Arrangements (RCAs)

A retirement compensation arrangement (RCA) is a plan or arrangement under which payments are made either by an employer (or former employer) or by a person with whom the employer does not deal at arm's length to a custodian on or in contemplation of the retirement of the employee or the severance of the employment relationship. Other plans recognized under the ITA, such as deferred profit sharing plans, are specifically excluded from the "retirement compensation arrangement" definition. The general purpose of the RCA rules is to prevent any tax deferrals or other tax advantages inherent in unregistered pension or retirement arrangements.

ITA 56(1)(x), (y), (z), 248(1)"retirement compensation arrangement", Guide T4041: *Retirement Compensation Arrangements*

¶2306 — *Income Inclusion*

When a taxpayer or any other person receives benefits out of an RCA that are related to the employment of the taxpayer, ITA 12(1)(n.3) includes those amounts in the taxpayer's income for the year in which the payments are received. Excluded, however, are amounts that represent a return of contributions or other amounts paid to the employer, another person who carried on a business that was acquired by the taxpayer, or persons not at arm's length with such persons, and which are included in the income of the taxpayer pursuant to ITA 12(1)(n.3).

Also included in the taxpayer's income are proceeds from the disposition of an interest in an RCA, net of the cost of acquiring the interest. Specifically, ITA 60(u) allows the taxpayer to deduct the purchase price paid for the interest in the RCA together with the amount of any non-deductible contributions (the available deduction does not include contributions that were otherwise deductible by the taxpayer as an amount that the taxpayer is required by the terms of employment to make to the plan). The amount of the deduction, however, cannot exceed the proceeds of disposition required to be included in the taxpayer's income under ITA 56(1)(y) and must be net of any such amounts previously deducted pursuant to ITA 60(u).

A taxpayer must also include in income amounts received out of an RCA that relate to the employment of another person unless those amounts have been included in the income of that other person either pursuant to ITA 56(1)(x), 70(2), or 12(1)(n.3). RCA amounts are also required to be included in the income of the taxpayer if they relate to the employment of the taxpayer, even though such amounts were actually paid to another person (for example, a spouse or common-law partner). Where the recipient of the RCA benefit is a non-arm's length person, the recipient is jointly and severally liable for tax attributable to such benefit. This is similar to the joint and several liability in respect of payments out of an RRSP after death or in respect of inter-spousal or common-law transfers.

In the event of the employee's death, RCA payments may be made to the employee's estate or beneficiary. Pursuant to ITA 70(2), the payments are included in the deceased's income for the year of death.

An employee may not deduct the amount of contributions made to an RCA. The employee may, however, recoup contributions made to an RCA and, in the case of a Canadian resident, recover the amount paid to acquire an interest in an RCA prior to being taxable on amounts paid out of the arrangement. That is, where a taxpayer is required to include the RCA benefits in income, the taxpayer may deduct an amount equal to the contributions and the purchase price for the interest. However, no deduction may be made for contributions that were otherwise deductible by the taxpayer as an amount that the taxpayer is required by the terms of employment to make to the plan.

When an RCA trust buys, sells, or permits the use of property for a price other than fair market value with the result that the value of the trust is reduced, the difference between the price and fair market value is considered to be received under the arrangement by the person who bought, sold, or used the property. Accordingly, the amount is taxable to the person who would otherwise be taxable on distributions from the arrangement.

When an RCA trust makes a distribution to a beneficiary, the trust is deemed to have disposed of any property distributed at its fair market value at that time and the recipient is deemed to have acquired the property at that fair market value. On distribution, the trust may realize a gain or loss in respect of the property. As a consequence of the distribution, the beneficiary will be deemed to have disposed of an interest in the trust and to have received proceeds of disposition equal to the adjusted cost base to the beneficiary of such interest. Accordingly, the beneficiary will not realize either a gain or loss on the disposition.

When the property distributed by the trust to the beneficiary is depreciable capital property, the capital cost of which to the trust exceeds its fair market value at the time of distribution, special rules apply. The capital cost of the property to the recipient is deemed to be the same as that of the trust and any difference between the capital cost and fair market value is deemed to have been previously allowed to the recipient as capital cost allowance. Accordingly, on a subsequent disposition of the depreciable property, the recipient could be taxable on recapture in respect of capital cost allowance previously claimed by the trust.

In some circumstances, a plan might be characterized as a combination of an employee benefit plan, salary deferral arrangement and an RCA. In those cases, the RCA portion is considered a separate arrangement. Any payments out of a combination plan are considered to be made first out of the salary deferral arrangement part of the plan and then out of the RCA, unless the plan provides a different ordering. Accounting records must be maintained that separate the RCA portion.

ITA 8(1)(m.2), 56(1)(x), (y), (z), 56(10), 56(11), 60(t), 60(u), 107.2, 160.3

¶2307 — *Refundable Tax*

Custodians of an RCA are subject to a 50 percent refundable tax pursuant to Part XI.3 of the ITA. A refundable tax account must be maintained for the RCA and specific filings are required. It is the responsibility of the custodian of the RCA to ensure that all amounts of refundable tax owing are properly remitted to the Receiver General.

Refundable tax at the end of a particular year is equal to:

- 50% of all contributions to the RCA while it was an RCA up to that time;

plus

- 50% of the amount by which income (excluding the amount of the dividend gross-up) and capital gains of the RCA exceed its losses and capital losses for that year and any preceding year;

less

- 50% of all benefits paid as distributions under the RCA except benefits paid as part of a series of contributions and refunds.

The custodian of an RCA must pay refundable tax pursuant to Part XI.3 equal to the amount by which refundable tax for the year exceeds the refundable tax for the preceding year. Similarly, where the custodian has filed an RCA Part XI.3 tax return within three years after the end of the year and the refundable tax at the end of a preceding year exceeds the refundable tax for the particular year, the excess must be refunded to the custodian of the RCA by the CRA. The RCA Part XI.3 tax return must be filed and any refundable tax must be paid within 90 days after the end of the taxation year of the RCA. Specific administrative, collection, and appeal provisions are applicable to the RCA refundable tax.

An employer making contributions to an RCA must withhold 50 percent tax at source and remit the amount withheld directly to the Receiver General. The remittance must be made no later than the 15th day of the month following that in which the deduction is made. If the employer fails to deduct and remit the refundable tax, the employer may be assessed an amount equal to the amount of contribution made to the custodian. Withholding is also required on distributions under an RCA that are paid by a custodian. A person who makes a payment on account of the purchase price of an interest in an RCA is required to withhold the 50 percent refundable tax and remit that amount to the Receiver General. Penalties and interest are levied for failure to comply with these provisions.

ITA 153(1)(p), (q), (r), 207.5–207.7, 227(8.2), ITR 100–108

¶2308 — *Special Rules*

There are a number of special rules that affect RCAs, including the following:

- a custodian may recover refundable tax where the RCA realizes investment losses or where the RCA is terminated by electing to use a special method of determining its refundable tax at the end of the year;

- where an RCA is established without the creation of a trust, an *inter vivos* trust is deemed to be created that would constitute an RCA trust for the purposes of the Part XI.3 provisions;

- where a life insurance policy or annuity is acquired in connection with an RCA, the person who acquires the policy is considered to be the custodian of the RCA with the result that an employer paying the premiums would be required to withhold and remit tax in connection with the RCA contribution;

- special rules preclude the use of personal service corporations for the purpose of avoiding the RCA rules; and

- special rules apply where an employee benefit plan becomes an RCA by virtue of the custodian changing its residence or ceasing to carry on business through a fixed place in Canada.

Foreign plans are precluded from being used to provide retirement benefits for Canadian resident employees so as to avoid the RCA rules. Contributions made in such circumstances (referred to as "resident's contributions") together with any investment income earned on the amounts are subject to RCA tax. A resident's contribution is defined as that part of a contribution that is not a prescribed contribution and that can reasonably be considered to be in respect of services rendered by an individual in a period when the individual was resident in Canada and the services were rendered primarily in Canada or in connection with a business carried on in Canada by the employer. If the employee were resident in Canada for fewer than five of the preceding six years, contributions are excluded if the employee was a member of the plan before becoming a Canadian resident. A resident's contributions may also include amounts paid by persons other than the employer, for example, a parent corporation of the employer.

ITA 56(1)(x), (y), (z), 207.5–207.7, 248(1)"retirement compensation arrangement", Guide T4041: *Retirement Compensation Arrangements*

¶2310 — Scholarships, Fellowships, and Bursaries

Scholarships, fellowships, and bursaries, as well as prizes for achievement in an individual's ordinary field of endeavour (except for prescribed prizes) are included in income; however, there is an exclusion for amounts received in the year on account of scholarships, fellowships, and bursaries received in connection with the taxpayer's enrolment in an elementary or secondary school educational program.

As well, under ITA 6(3), certain related payments, such as a payment made prior to employment as an inducement to enter into the employment, or one made after termination of the employment in consideration of a covenant not to compete, are considered income from the employment. The CRA provides the following administrative guidance in Folio S1-F2-C3 regarding the tax implications in these situations:

Scholarship or bursary awarded to a current or former employee

3.11 During or immediately after a period of employment, employees and employers sometimes make agreements under which an employer agrees to pay all or a portion of an employee's education costs on the condition that the employee returns to work for the employer when the education is completed. In such cases, the education-related expenses paid by the employer will be considered to have been received in respect of, in the course of or by virtue of an office or employment and will not be included in computing the student's income under subparagraph 56(1)(n)(i).

3.12 The education-related expenses paid by the employer will be taxable to the student as employment income under section 6, subject to the exception where the course or training is determined to be primarily for the benefit of the employer (see ¶3.23 for further information). This will be the case notwithstanding any commitment of the student to repay all or a portion of the expenses paid by the employer in the event that they do not satisfy the terms and conditions of an employment agreement (for example, the student does not work for the employer for the requisite period after graduation).

3.13 Where a student is required to repay an employer for education expenses the employer previously incurred on their behalf, the student will be entitled to deduct the repayment under paragraph 8(1)(n) where the repayment is made by or on behalf of the student in the year pursuant to an arrangement requiring the reimbursement of any amounts received for a period throughout which the student did not perform the duties of the office or employment. However, the deduction under paragraph 8(1)(n) will be limited to the extent that:

- the amounts received were included in computing the student's employment income; and

- the total reimbursements do not exceed the total of the amounts received by the student for the period throughout which the student did not perform the employment duties.

Scholarship or bursary awarded prior to employment relationship

3.14 If an employer-employee relationship has not yet been established and a student receives a scholarship or bursary in return for undertaking to commence employment with the person granting the award after completion of the studies or course of training, the payments received would normally be considered to be scholarship or bursary income under paragraph 56(1)(n).

3.15 The determination of whether an employer-employee relationship exists at the time an award is granted is a question of fact. Payments received by the student after an employer-employee relationship has been established, should generally be treated in accordance with the comments in ¶3.11.

3.16 Where the student is committed to return all or a portion of the scholarship or bursary in the future under certain circumstances (e.g., as a result of a breach of an employment agreement), the amount received will be considered a repayable award. This is discussed in more detail at ¶3.49.

ITA 6(1)(a) was amended to "clarify" that all employment benefits received by a person who does not deal at arm's length with the employee are included in the employee's income, other than those benefits specifically excluded. Specifically, ITA 6(1)(a)(vi) excludes from employment income any benefit received or enjoyed by a person who is not the employee under a program provided by the employer that is designed to assist individuals to further their education. This exception only applies, however, if the benefit is not a substitution for salary, wages, or other remuneration of the employee, and only if the employee deals at arm's length with the employer. The amendments were made in response to the decisions in *Bartley*, [2008] 5 C.T.C. 2403 (TCC) and *DiMaria*, 2008 CarswellNat 595 (TCC), both affirmed by [2009] 2 C.T.C. 73 (FCA). In these cases, the Court found that scholarships paid by employers to an employee's children did not constitute employment benefits in the hands of the employees. In response to the decisions, the CRA revised its views on scholarships and bursaries paid to the family members of employees (see VD 2008-0296041E5, 2009-0312451E5, 2010-0364111E5).

The CRA provides the following guidance in Folio S1-F2-C3 regarding the tax implications when an employer awards a scholarship or bursary to family members of employees:

Employer and employee dealing at arm's length

3.17 Where an arm's length employer provides a post-secondary scholarship, bursary or free tuition to the family member of an employee under a scholarship program, the amount will be included in computing the particular student's income under subparagraph 56(1)(n)(i) provided the employee's salary was not decreased to fund or partially fund the amount. If the student is eligible to claim the education tax credit under subsection 118.6(2) in respect of the program, the entire amount may be exempt from tax pursuant to the scholarship exemption provided in subsection 56(3) (this is discussed further in ¶3.90). The employee will not be considered to have received a taxable employment benefit under paragraph 6(1)(a) with respect to the award, regardless of the criteria used to award the particular amount. This income tax treatment has been adopted as a result of the Federal Court of Appeal decisions in *R v DiMaria* and *R v Bartley*, 2008 FCA 390, 2009 D.T.C. 5019.

3.18 Under subparagraph 6(1)(a)(vi), any benefit received or enjoyed on or after October 31, 2011 by the family member of a taxpayer under a program offered by the taxpayer's employer that is designed to assist the family member in furthering his or her education, will not be included in the taxpayer's income as an employment benefit, where:

- the employer and the taxpayer deal with each other at arm's length; and

- it is reasonable to conclude that the benefit is not a substitute for salary, wages or other remuneration of the taxpayer.

Subparagraph 6(1)(a)(vi) applies to benefits received or enjoyed by the family member with respect to the family member's attendance at an elementary, secondary or post-secondary school (private or otherwise), including tuition discounts provided by educational institutions to the family members of its employees. The amount of the benefit received or enjoyed by the family member under these programs will be included in computing the family member's income under subparagraph 56(1)(n)(i). Subsection 56(3) may permit an exemption from the family member's income for some or all of the benefit amount. The exemption is discussed at ¶3.90.

Where the family member of an employee was provided with a scholarship, bursary or free tuition by an arm's length employer for attendance at an elementary or secondary school (private or otherwise) before October 31, 2011, the amount will be included in the employee's income as a taxable benefit under paragraph 6(1)(a), regardless of the criteria used to award the particular amount. As such, no amount will be included in the family member's income pursuant to paragraph 56(1)(n).

Employer and employee not dealing at arm's length

3.19 Where an employer provides an elementary, secondary or post-secondary school scholarship or bursary, or free tuition, to the family member of an employee under a scholarship program and the employer and employee are not dealing at arm's length, the income tax treatment will generally be as follows:

- if the employee is not a shareholder of the employer, or the benefit is not considered to be provided to the family member in the employee's capacity as a shareholder of the employer, the value of the benefit should be included in the employee's income pursuant to paragraph 6(1)(a). The employer will not be precluded from deducting the scholarship or bursary in computing its taxable income by virtue of paragraph 18(1)(a). Subject to satisfying the necessary requirements, the family member may also be eligible to claim the education tax credit under subsection 118.6(2) in respect of the program.

- if the employee is a shareholder of the employer (i.e., the Corporation) and it is determined that the benefit provided to the family member is by virtue of the employee's interest in the Corporation as a shareholder (or in contemplation of the employee becoming a shareholder), the value of the benefit must be included in the employee-shareholder's income under subsection 15(1). In addition, the amount of any scholarship or bursary provided will not be deductible by the Corporation for income tax purposes pursuant to paragraph 18(1)(a). Subject to satisfying the necessary requirements, the family member may also be eligible to claim the education tax credit under subsection 118.6(2) in respect of the program.

3.20 The determination of whether an employer and employee are dealing at arm's length, or whether a benefit is received by an employee-shareholder in his or her capacity as an employee or as a shareholder, involves findings of fact. There is a general presumption that an individual receives a benefit by virtue of his or her shareholdings in those situations where the shareholder, or shareholders, can significantly influence business policy, except where the individual is able to establish otherwise. Exceptions to this presumption would be a situation where the benefit is available to all employees of the Corporation under the same or similar circumstances, or a situation where the benefit is comparable in nature and quantum to benefits generally offered to employees who perform similar services and have similar responsibilities for other employers of a similar size.

The value of tuition assistance benefits provided under a collective agreement to an employee's family member can be excluded from the employee's income under ITA 6(1)(a)(vi) if it is reasonable to conclude that the tuition assistance is not a substitute for an employee's salary, wages, or other remuneration, and if the employee deals at arm's length. However, the amount may be included in the family member's income to the extent that it exceeds any scholarship exemption (VD 2015-0623221E5).

ITA 56(1)(n), 56(3), Guide T4130 under "Scholarships, bursaries, tuition, and training", *Savage*, [1983] C.T.C. 393 (SCC), Folio S1-F2-C3, *Scholarships, Research Grants and Other Education Assistance*, IC 75-23, *Tuition Fees and Charitable Donations Paid to Privately Supported Secular and Religious Schools*

¶2315 — Security Options Benefit

Corporations may provide incentives to employees by granting an option to purchase securities of the corporation at a stipulated price within a specified period of time in accordance with a formal agreement. In some circumstances, the securities to be issued are not those of the corporation granting the option, but of another corporation with which the employer does not deal at arm's length. Also, in some cases, the employee is not employed by the corporation granting the option, but by another corporation that is non-arm's length to the corporation granting the option. In either situation, if the employee derives a financial benefit from the arrangement, that benefit will be included in the employee's income in accordance with ITA 7.

ITA 7 only applies to the issuance of treasury shares (*Tomkins*, [1963] C.T.C. 258) (Ex Ct)). In addition, a security option must be received by a taxpayer by virtue of employment for ITA 7 to apply. An option received by a taxpayer by virtue of holding shares in a corporation would not, for example, be taxable under ITA 7 (in such a case, the shareholder benefit rules in ITA 15(1) would apply; see also *Bernstein*, [1977] C.T.C. 328 (FCA)). However, a shareholder who is also a director of a company meets the definition of an "employee". Where a security option benefit is received otherwise than in respect of, in the course of, or by virtue of employment, a taxpayer will not be entitled to a security option deduction in respect of the option benefit (see ¶2510, "Security Options Deduction"). An employee whose employment ceases prior to the exercise or transfer of a right contemplated by ITA 7 is treated as if he/she were still an employee. Also, it is CRA's view that ITA 7 applies to a security option included in an offer of employment to a prospective employee (VD 2000-0035405).

Where security options are issued to a consultant as consideration for services rendered immediately before the options were granted, the CRA's position is that ITA 9 applies to include in income the fair market value of the option at the time of the grant (see VD 2002-0151247).

For cases that consider whether an "agreement" exists for purposes of the security options rules in ITA 7, see *G G Smith*, [1969] Tax A.B.C. 217; *Fowler* (1963), 32 Tax A.B.C. 353; *Chrysler Canada*, [1992] 2 C.T.C. 95; and *McAnulty*, [2002] 1 C.T.C. 2035 (TCC). In addition, see paragraphs 6 to 12 of IT-113R4.

A deduction may be claimed in respect of the fair market value of treasury shares issued as compensation for past employment services under purely discretionary stock bonus plans (as a result of *Transalta Corp.*, 2012 CarswellNat 773 (TCC)).

If a taxpayer disposes of shares acquired under an option agreement as a result of a repurchase of the shares by the employer, a deemed dividend may arise, and the employee may incur a capital loss that cannot be applied to offset the dividend (see VDs 2003-0008805 and 2003-0008795).

ITA 7, 84(3), IT-113R4: *Benefits to Employees — Stock Options*, Ryan Keey, "Share Based Compensation: Fairness Restored?", *Tax Times* 2012–15 (Carswell), August 2012

¶2315.1 — *Income Triggering Events*

Where ITA 7 applies, except in the special case relating to shares in a CCPC (see ¶ 2315.3), a benefit received by an employee pursuant to a securities option plan is taxed as follows:

(a) if the employee acquires securities pursuant to the agreement, the employee is taxed in the year of acquisition on the excess of the value of the securities when acquired over the amount paid or to be paid for them and any amount paid to acquire the option (ITA 7(1)(a));

(b) if instead of exercising the option the employee disposes of it in an arm's length transaction, the employee is deemed to have received a benefit by virtue of employment in the year of the disposition equal to the value of the consideration received less the amount paid by the employee to acquire the option (ITA 7(1)(b));

(c) if the option is disposed of in one or more non-arm's length transactions and is exercised by the new holder, the employee is deemed to receive a taxable benefit in the year the securities are acquired by that person on the excess of their value over the price paid or to be paid to the corporation for them and as any amount paid to acquire the option (ITA 7(1)(c)); and

(d) if the option is not exercised by the last holder referred to in (c) but is disposed of in an arm's length transaction, the employee is deemed to have received a taxable benefit at that time equal to the value of the consideration received less the amount paid by the employee to acquire the option (ITA 7(1)(d)).

In summary, the employee's tax situation is normally not affected until he or she exercises or disposes of the option. If an option is exercised and a security is acquired at less than its fair market value, the employee receives a taxable employment benefit equal to the difference between the fair market value of the security acquired and the amount paid or to be paid for the security, including any amount paid for the rights to acquire the security. An employee may also realize a taxable benefit when the rights under the agreement are transferred or sold (see, for example, VD 2008-0279251E5).

> If an employee exercises a stock option granted by a CCPC, the taxable benefit is instead included in the employee's income in the year that the employee disposes of the shares acquired under the option agreement and not when the employee exercises the option, if certain conditions are met (see ¶ 2315.3).

An acquisition of shares will occur when title passes, or, if title remains with the vendor as security for the unpaid balance, when all the incidents of title (such as possession, use, and risk) pass (see paragraph 10 of IT-113R4 and VD 2008-0279251E5).

A change to the vesting period of options or to the share appreciation rights under a security option plan will normally not result in the disposition of any rights under the plan by an employee for purposes of the security option rules (see VD 2001-0084013, 2004-0073821R3 and *Amirault*, [1990] 1 C.T.C. 2432 (TCC)).

Where the employee is deceased at the time securities are acquired in circumstances described in (c) or (d) above, the amount of the benefit is included in the income of the non-arm's length transferee as deemed employment income. Where the employee was employed primarily in Canada, this provision will apply equally to a non-resident transferee. Where, at the time of death, an employee held an unexercised option to acquire securities, the employee is considered to realize a benefit in the taxation year in which the employee died equal to the value of the option immediately after death less the amount paid to acquire the option. Where this provision applies, the rules that might otherwise apply to transfers where the employee is deceased would not apply.

Where a disposition occurs as a result of an amalgamation of the corporation granting the option, and upon the amalgamation the option is exchanged for an option in the newly amalgamated company, the new option is considered a continuation of the old one. This rollover treatment also applies where employee securities options are exchanged in the course of a reorganization or restructuring within a non-arm's length group of corporations or trusts. However, the employee may not receive consideration on the exchange other than a new option, nor can the exchange result in an economic advantage to the employee. This is determined by comparing the fair market value of the new securities less the new option price to the fair market value of the old securities less the old option price.

ITA 7(1)(a)–(e), (1.4), IT-113R4: *Benefits to Employees — Stock Options* (paras. 15 and 18)

¶2315.2 — *Withholding Taxes Applicable to Option Benefits*

An amount in respect of the employment benefit associated with a security option is required to be withheld and remitted to the CRA by the employer. For this purpose, the employment benefit realized on the exercise of a security option is treated as a cash bonus. If the employee stock option benefit deduction requirements are met at the time that the securities are acquired (see ¶2510), the amount of the employment benefit may be reduced in determining the amount of tax to be withheld.

Where it is not possible to increase withholdings from regular remuneration to meet withholding obligations, there are several other alternatives an employer may consider. Security option plans may include tax withholding provisions applicable on an exercise of options that require an option holder to pay any required withholding amount (i.e., in addition to the exercise price, the employee could be required to pay a sufficient amount to permit the required tax remittance). Alternatively, the option plan could permit the employer to sell a portion of the securities issued on the exercise of options to fund withholding requirements. However, the sale of a portion of the shares acquired under an option agreement may not be feasible for non-CCPC private company shares for which there is no active market (in respect of CCPC shares, an option benefit deferral is available until the shares are sold; see ¶2315.3).

When an employee immediately sells shares acquired under an option agreement to fund withholding obligations, the employee should consider filing a designation under ITA 7(1.31) to avoid the adjusted cost base averaging rules (see ¶2315.5). By making this designation, the adjusted cost base of the shares sold will not be averaged with the adjusted cost base of shares of the employer already owned by the employee before the exercise of the option.

ITA 153(1.01), (1.31), ITR 103(1), (2), Guide T4001 (Chapter 6), ITTN-41, VDs 2009-0316621C6, 2M0333A

¶2315.3 — *Shares in a Canadian-Controlled Private Corporation*

An exception to the taxation of security options under ITA 7 occurs for shares of a CCPC acquired under a stock option agreement. If the employee is dealing at arm's length with the CCPC immediately after the agreement is made, no benefit is deemed to have been received by the employee until the employee disposes of or exchanges the shares. Instead, the employment benefit, calculated based on the value of the shares at the time the option was exercised, is included in the employee's income in the taxation year in which the shares are disposed of or exchanged. Provided certain conditions are met, one-half of such benefit may be deducted in computing taxable income in respect of the shares acquired (see ¶2511). Alternatively, if the conditions for the CCPC option benefit deduction are not met (for example, the shares are not held for at least two years), a deduction may be available under the general security option benefit deduction provision where the conditions of that provision are met (see ¶2510).

¶2315.4 — *Order of Disposition of Securities*

For the purposes of determining the timing of any employment benefit that would otherwise be realized on the disposition of shares acquired pursuant to an employee security option plan, the employee is deemed to dispose of identical shares in the order in which they were acquired. As a result, the employment benefit is deferred until the employee disposes of the security in respect of which the benefit arises. This rule is also relevant for the purposes of determining whether the disposition of the share in question gives rise to a capital gain in addition to any employment benefit. Since a share of a CCPC must be held for at least two years in order for the employee security option deferral to apply, this disposition rule is also relevant in determining whether the particular share in question has satisfied the holding period requirement.

Where a taxpayer holds securities that have been acquired pursuant to an employee security option plan that otherwise qualify for an employment income deferral and acquires identical shares that do not qualify for the deferral, the taxpayer is deemed to acquire the non-deferral shares immediately before the first of the deferral shares were acquired. As a result, on a disposition of securities, the taxpayer is deemed to dispose of the non-deferral shares first and may avoid any recognition of the employment benefit until all non-deferral shares are disposed of.

Where a taxpayer has been granted a number of security options over a period of time and acquires several identical securities at the same time based on those options, the taxpayer is deemed to acquire the securities in the same order as when the options were granted. Consequently, when the taxpayer disposes of the securities, they are deemed to be disposed of in the same order in which the options were granted.

Where securities acquired pursuant to an employee stock option plan are eligible for deferral by reason of ITA 7(1.1), (1.5), or (1.31), or former ITA 7(8), they are deemed not to be identical properties. Accordingly, in determining any capital gain or loss on the disposition of such securities, each is considered to have its own particular adjusted cost base regardless of any other identical securities held (i.e., the cost-averaging rule does not apply in these circumstances).

The entire benefit (i.e., not one-half of the benefit) as determined under ITA 7(1) increases the adjusted cost base of the securities acquired under an option agreement. The employment benefit is added to the adjusted cost base of the securities in the year in which the employment benefit is deemed to have been received, regardless of whether the income inclusion in respect of the benefit is deferred.

ITA 7(1.3), 7(1.31), 47(3), 53(1)(j), VD 2001-0064025

¶2315.5 — *Designation of Share Disposed Of*

A taxpayer may designate a security most recently acquired by the taxpayer pursuant to an option agreement to be the security that is disposed of where: 1) the disposition occurs within 30 days of the acquisition of the security; 2) no other identical securities have been acquired within the intervening period; 3) the designation is made in the tax return filed for the year of disposition; and 4) the particular security may not have been designated in connection with the disposition of any other security. Such a designation may be relevant where an employee acquires a security under an option agreement and within 30 days after acquisition donates the security to a qualifying charity. In such circumstances, the employee can claim part of the employment benefit as a deduction. Also, a designation may be made in these circumstances if securities recently acquired under an option agreement have a higher adjusted cost base than identical securities held that would otherwise be deemed to be disposed of. This may be the case, for example, when some of the securities acquired under an option agreement are immediately disposed of to meet withholding tax funding requirements.

ITA 7(1.31)

¶2315.6 — *Shares in a Non-Canadian-Controlled Private Corporation*

Prior to Budget 2010 amendments, the income inclusion in respect of both CCPC and non-CCPC employee options could be deferred until the security acquired was disposed of when certain conditions were met. However, applicable in respect of rights exercised after March 4, 2010, the deferral available in respect of non-CCPC options was repealed. As a result, under current rules, employees who exercise options to acquire publicly-traded securities or securities of private corporations other than CCPCs are taxed on the employment benefit in the year in which the options are exercised.

An employee who acquired securities subject to the deferral under the former rules is required to file Form T1212, *Statement of Deferred Security Options Benefits*, with their personal income tax return providing information with respect to the acquisition and disposition of the deferred securities. Form T1212 must be filed regardless of whether the taxpayer has deferred any security options benefits in the particular year or has disposed of any securities in the particular year relating to a security option benefit that was previously deferred.

Where a capital loss is incurred on the disposition of a security acquired under an option agreement, the capital loss cannot be applied to offset the employment benefit realized on the acquisition or the disposition of the optioned security (see, for example, VD 2003-0007795). As such, an employee may be in a position where an election was filed to defer a security option benefit and the fair market value of the securities acquired under the agreement are less than the tax liability outstanding in respect of the deferred option benefit. Prior to Budget 2010 amendments, Finance had reviewed this issue and concluded that amendments to the ITA were not required (VD 2003-0007795). However, ITA 180.01 was added effective March 4, 2010 to allow for special elective tax treatment to apply to a taxpayer who deferred a security option benefit under the former rules and experienced financial difficulties as a result of a decline in the value of the optioned securities.

To qualify for the special elective tax treatment, a taxpayer must have made an election under the former rules and the securities must be disposed of before 2015. If the taxpayer disposed of the securities before 2010, the taxpayer is required to file Form RC310, *Election for Special Relief for Tax Deferral Election on Employee Security Options*, on or before the filing-due date for the taxpayer's 2010 tax return. In any other case (i.e., in respect of dispositions after 2009 and before 2015), Form RC310 is due on or before the filing-due date for the taxation year of the taxpayer in which the disposition of the securities occurs.

Where the election is filed, taxpayers may eliminate their deferred employee security option benefit income inclusion and replace it with a deemed capital gain equal to the lesser of the security option benefit and the capital loss on the disposition of the optioned securities. Any unused allowable capital losses arising on the disposition of the optioned securities can be used to offset the deemed capital gain. In lieu of the elimination of the employment benefit, any proceeds received by the taxpayer on the disposition of the optioned securities is payable as a special tax. The special tax is equal to the proceeds received, except in the case of a taxpayer resident in the Province of Quebec at the end of the year, in which the tax is equal to two-thirds of the taxpayer's proceeds of disposition.

An election under ITA 180.01 will generally be beneficial if the securities acquired under an employee option agreement have declined in value to the extent that the proceeds of disposition in respect of the securities is (or was) insufficient to pay the tax that was deferred on the benefit. However, the election may not be beneficial if the capital loss realized on the disposition of the securities is (or has already been) partially or fully utilized to offset other capital gains. In such a case, any additional taxes payable on the deemed capital gain would need to be considered in determining whether to file the election.

ITA 7(8)–(15) (repealed), 7(16), 180.01

¶2320 — Service Pension or Allowance

A pension or allowance under the *Pension Act*, the *Civilian War related Benefits Act*, or the *War Veterans' Allowance Act*, an amount received under the *Gallantry Awards Order*, or compensation under regulations made under section 9 of the *Aeronautics Act*, is not included in income. Also exempt are certain pensions under the *Royal Canadian Mounted Police Pension Continuation Act* and the *Royal Canadian Mounted Police Superannuation Act* and to certain war-time pensions received from countries allied with Canada during the war if that country grants substantially similar relief to a person receiving certain service pensions referred to in ITA 81(1)(d).

ITA 81(1)(d), (e), (i)

¶2325 — Social Events

The CRA's administrative position is that an employer-provided party or other social event that is generally available to all employees (such as an employer Christmas party) is not a taxable benefit, provided the cost per employee is $150 or less ($100 or less for taxation years before 2018). Additional costs, such as transportation home, taxi fare, and overnight accommodation are not included in the $150 per person amount. If the cost of the party is greater than $150 per person, the entire amount, including the additional costs, is a taxable benefit.

Guide T4130 under "Social events", ITTN-15, S2-F3-C2: *Benefits and Allowances Received*

¶2330 — Special Payments by Employers

All payments received by an employee from an employer in consideration for entering into a contract of employment, for services thereunder, or for a covenant (such as a non-competition agreement) relating to the employee's activities after termination of employment are included in income under ITA 6(3). The CRA's position respecting the timing of income recognition of payments caught by this provision is set out in Folio S2-F3-C1: *Payments from Employer to Employee*.

A payment that is made to induce an employee to terminate employment is considered to be in the nature of general income relating to the prospective use of the taxpayer's experience and capabilities. However, this is the case only if the payment is not made by an employer or by a person who becomes the employer. Paragraph 1.7 of Folio S3-F9-C1, *Lottery Winnings, Miscellaneous Receipts and Income (and Losses) from Crime* provides as follows:

> 1.7 When an employee receives an amount which is intended as an inducement to leave his or her present employment and accept new employment, the payment is included in the recipient's income. Subsection 6(3) will normally apply to include in income such an inducement paid to an employee by a prospective employer. Furthermore, regardless of who pays the amount, any payment received by an employee as an inducement to accept new employment is considered to be for the purpose of acquiring that taxpayer's experience and capabilities and to be by its nature an income item. For example, in a situation in which a payment is made by a shareholder to induce an individual to resign a managerial position and accept new employment, the payment would be included in the individual's income.

ITA 6(3), Folio S2-F3-C1: *Payments from Employer to Employee*, Folio S3-F9-C1: *Lottery Winnings, Miscellaneous Receipts and Income (and Losses) from Crime*

¶2335 — Statutory Exemptions

An amount that is exempt from income tax by any other legislation of the Parliament of Canada (for example, the *Indian Act*) is not required to be included in income for purposes of the ITA. This provision ensures that there is no conflict between the ITA and other federal legislation.

Section 87 of the *Indian Act* exempts from taxation the personal property of an individual Indian or an Indian band situated on a reserve. Also, no Indian or Indian band is subject to taxation in respect of personal property situated on a reserve.

Amounts exempt from Canadian tax by virtue of one of Canada's tax treaties are considered "income" for purposes of the ITA; however, such amounts are deductible in computing taxable income under ITA 110(1)(f)(i) (see under ¶9400, Line 256). As such, treaty exempt income may affect the computation of income-tested benefits and credit.

ITA 81(1)(a), IT-397R: *Amounts Excluded from Income — Statutory Exemptions and Certain Service or RCMP Pensions, Allowances and Compensation*

¶2340 — Strike Pay

Strike pay (payments by a union to its members while on strike) has traditionally not been taxed, but in *Ferris v. Minister of National Revenue*, [1977] C.T.C. 2034, the Tax Review Board asserted that there appeared to be no statutory sanction for not taxing it. "This [strike] fund is built up from . . . the union dues paid by each member," the Board stated, "and the contributor is allowed to deduct amounts paid as union dues from his income. In the case of pension plans [etc], when the amounts contributed by a taxpayer are deductible from his income when paid, they are also taxable as income when they are paid out to the taxpayer at some future date." What was in issue in that case, however, was not the basic strike pay (which was not taxed) but "supplementary strike pay" derived from the publishing of a newspaper by the union members, the profits from which were received by the union and then distributed to the members. The Minister considered such payments taxable as arising from a joint business venture, and the assessment was upheld by the Board, which held that by placing "taxable income from a commercial venture within the four walls of a union and then getting it back by way of a distribution" did not render that income tax-exempt.

However, in considering substantially the same issue in *O'Brien v. R.*, [1985] 1 C.T.C. 285, the Federal Court — Trial Division found otherwise. In reviewing the decision in the Ferris case, the Court noted that if there were simply a flow-through from profits of the newspaper to the individual members of the unions through the intermediary of the unions themselves, the conclusion in the Ferris case could be accepted, but the factual situation was much more complex. In this case, the Court found that not all of the profits were distributed, and that a small part of the profits came from other sources (donations and contributions from other unions); furthermore, the individuals had no right to claim the funds and were dependent on the unions with respect to the amounts of such profits distributed as supplementary strike benefits. The Court found that the unions operated the newspaper for the benefit of their members but not as agents of the members or under the members' direction. Consequently, the profits from the operation were tax-exempt in the hands of the unions and the distribution of the profits was held not to be taxable in the hands of the individual members since those individuals were not engaged in a business. Thus, the supplementary strike benefits were not taxable.

In *R. v. Fries*, [1986] 1 C.T.C. 4, the Federal Court — Trial Division held amounts received by a Liquor Board employee out of a strike fund to be income not exempt from tax. The fact that it had never been the Department's policy to tax strike pay was held to have no real bearing on the issue. Mr. Justice Collier could find no statutory basis for exempting strike pay. The Federal Court of Appeal (at [1989] 1 C.T.C. 471) affirmed the trial judge's decision that the amounts paid by the union were income in nature within the meaning of paragraph 3(a) and that nothing in the Act exempts strike pay. However, on appeal to the Supreme Court of Canada (*R. v. Fries*, [1990] 2 C.T.C. 439), the Court reversed the decision of the Federal Court of Appeal. In ruling that the amounts received out of the strike fund were not taxable, the Court stated:

> We are not satisfied that the payments by way of strike pay in this case come within the definition of "income . . . from a source" within the meaning of section 3 of the *Income Tax Act*. In these circumstances the benefit of the doubt must go to the taxpayers.

The CRA's administrative position following the *Fries* decision is provided in paragraph 1.10 of Folio S3-F9-C1, *Lottery Winnings, Miscellaneous Receipts and Income (and Losses) from Crime*, as follows:

Payments from a union

1.10 A union member who is on strike or locked out need not include strike pay in income. This is the case, even if the member performs picketing duties as a requirement of membership. In the decision of the Supreme Court of Canada in *Wally Fries v. The Queen*, [1990] 2 C.T.C. 439, 90 D.T.C. 6662, payments of strike pay were held not to be *income from a source*. On the other hand, payments made by a union to its members for services performed during the course of a strike are included in income if the member is employed by or is a consultant to the union whether permanently, as a member of a temporary committee, or in some other capacity. Regular salary, wages, and benefits received by employees of unions are subject to tax in the usual manner.

Folio S3-F9-C1, *Lottery Winnings, Miscellaneous Receipts and Income (and Losses) from Crime*, *Sénéchal*, 2011 CarswellNat 4217 (TCC), *Vachon*, 2009 CarswellNat 4682 (FCA)

¶2345 — Tool Reimbursement or Allowance

Amounts received by a person who was entitled to an apprentice mechanic tool deduction (see ¶2410) or tradesperson tool deduction (see ¶2520), or who does not deal at arm's length with such apprentice mechanic or tradesperson, as consideration for the sale of such property must include such amounts in income. The amount included in income is the amount by which the proceeds exceed the cost of the eligible tool (as determined under ITA 8(7)).

ITA 8(1)(r), 8(1)(s), 56(1)(k)

¶2350 — Transportation

¶2351 — *Transportation Passes*

An employee receives a benefit if transportation passes are provided from an employer. In Guide T4130, the CRA sets forth its policy with respect to such benefits as follows:

If you pay for or provide your employee with public transit passes, it is usually a taxable benefit for the employee. Public transit includes transit by local bus, streetcar, subway, commuter train or bus, and local ferry.

Transit passes — employees of a transit company

If your company is in the business of operating a bus, streetcar, subway, commuter train or bus, or ferry service, and you provide free transit passes to your employees or their families, special rules apply.

If you provide free or discounted passes to an employee or retired employee who works in one of the businesses mentioned above, and the passes are only for the employee's use, there is no taxable benefit for the employee . . .

If you provide free or discounted passes to a member of your employee's or retired employee's family, the fair market value (FMV) of the pass is a taxable benefit for the employee . . .

Note

If you provide free or discounted passes to an employee who works in an area other than the transportation business or its operations, their FMV is a taxable benefit for the employee. For example, if a city owns a transit company, the FMV of a pass given to an employee who works in the city's accounting department would be a taxable benefit, while a pass given to an employee who works in the accounting department of the transit business operations would not be a taxable benefit.

The use of airline passes available to airline employees becomes taxable only if the employee travels on a space-confirmed basis and is paying less than 50 percent of the economy fare available on that carrier for that trip on the day of travel. In such a case, the employee is considered to have received a taxable benefit equal to the difference between 50 percent of the economy fare and any amount reimbursed to the carrier for that trip.

Any allowance or reimbursement paid to an employee for transportation to or from the employee's job must be included in income (see ¶2121), although exceptions exist for certain part-time employees (see ¶2123), employees employed at special work sites or remote locations (see ¶2136), and certain disabled individuals (see ¶2170).

A group discount on transit passes would normally not be a taxable employment benefit where the employer purchases and distributes the passes and then recovers 100 percent of the cost from the employees through payroll deductions (VD 2011-0394411E5).

S2-F3-C2: *Benefits and Allowances Received from Employment*, Guide T4130 under "Transit passes", VD 2008-0267971E5, 2008-0298021E5, 2011-0411941C6, 2006-0216791E5, Antonio Di Domenico, "Employer-Provided Benefits and the Environment: Transit Passes and Parking," (2006), vol. 54, no. 1 *Canadian Tax Journal*, 115–141

¶2352 — *Transportation to and from Home*

As a general rule, any allowance or reimbursement paid to an employee for transportation to or from a work location must be included in income. However, if transportation between an employee's home and a regular place of employment is provided by an employer for security reasons, or if public and private vehicles are not allowed or practical, then such travel is not considered personal (for examples of situations where transportation to and from home is considered a taxable benefit, see: canada.ca/en/revenue-agency/services/tax/businesses/topics/payroll/benefits-allowances/automobile/transportation-home/examples-transportation-home.html). As well, exceptions apply for part-time employees (see ¶2123), employees employed at special work sites or remote locations (see ¶2136), and certain disabled individuals (see ¶2170). The CRA normally considers a work location to be remote when it is 80 kilometres or more from the nearest established community with a population of at least 1,000 people.

As a further exception, where occasional commuting assistance is provided by an employer, in VD 2004-0076281E5, the CRA states:

> [E]mployer-paid or reimbursed commuting expenses are not a taxable employment benefit where an employee is required to work overtime under certain conditions, as follows: the employee is required to work at least three hours in addition to and immediately subsequent to the regular hours of work; public transportation is not available or the physical safety of the employee is at risk at the time of travel; and the occurrence of such overtime is occasional.

ITA 6(6), 6(16), 81(3.1), S2-F3-C2: *Benefits and Allowances Received from Employment*, Guide T4130, VDs 2011-0411941C6, 2006-0216791E5

¶2355 — Tuition and Training Fees

As a general rule, tuition fees paid by an employer on behalf of an employee are a taxable benefit to the employee unless the course is taken on the initiative of, and for the benefit of, the employer rather than of the employee. Therefore, it is necessary to determine whether the training is taken primarily for the benefit of the employer or primarily for the benefit of the employee.

Generally, the CRA considers that courses taken to maintain or upgrade employment-related skills are mainly for the employer's benefit when it is reasonable to assume that the employee will resume his or her employment for a reasonable period of time after he or she finishes the course. For example, tuition fees and other associated costs such as books, meals, travel, and accommodation that an employer pays for courses leading to a degree, diploma, or certificate in a field related to the employee's current or future responsibilities in the business are not a taxable benefit. As well, other business-related courses, although not directly related to the employer's business, are taken mainly for the employer's benefit (e.g., fees paid by the employer for stress management, employment equity, first aid, and language courses are not a taxable benefit). However, courses for personal interest or technical skills not related to the employer's business are taken mainly for the employee's benefit and, therefore, are a taxable benefit.

In *Spence*, [2011] 5 C.T.C. 188 (FCA), the Court found that an employment benefit attributable to reduced school tuition fees should be valued at fair market value as opposed to the cost of the employer providing the services.

If a tuition amount paid by an employer is included in the employee's income, the employee either will be able to claim a tuition credit under ITA 118.5 in respect of the fees paid by the employer, or may transfer the unused portion of the credit to a spouse or a supporting person (see ¶10166). Where tuition fees are paid for or reimbursed by the employer and the employee has not received a taxable benefit, the employee is not entitled to claim the tax credit (see VDs 2004-0071261E5 and 9707727).

In VD 2006-0172701E5, the CRA concluded that amounts for tuition fees reimbursed by a professional development fund created under a collective agreement were not required to be included in the employee's income since it was apparent that the courses taken were directly related to employment (see also VD 2009-0308741E5). On the other hand, in VD 2010-0371431E5, the CRA stated that an annual amount provided by an employer to an employee for expenses related to professional development would be taxable if the payment was made regardless of whether any professional development costs would be incurred (i.e., if the payment did not represent a reimbursement of actual costs or an accountable advance), and regardless whether such professional development was primarily for the benefit of the employee.

The CRA's position is that the reimbursement of tuition fees incurred by a student before being employed by a new employer would normally represent a benefit conferred to that employee where the reimbursement occurs after the student starts working for the employer (VD 2011-0424601E5).

In *Detchon*, [1996] 1 C.T.C. 2475 (TCC), a case involving teachers employed at a private secondary school that provided free tuition to their children, the Court found that the teachers had received a taxable benefit from employment. The CRA's policy with respect to education allowances for children of employees and subsidized school services is contained in Guide T4130 (see also VDs 2009-0320591E5, 2010-0372541E5 and 2004-0088561E5). Other than in the case of remote areas, subsidized school services for employee's children are generally taxable employment benefits.

Free tuition for an employee's dependant where the employee is working in a foreign country is not a taxable employment benefit since there is no economic advantage conferred on the employee (VD 2004-0088561E5).

A reimbursement of tuition in respect of a student from a family member's employer will not preclude the student from claiming the education tax credit when the reimbursement is included in the employee's income as an employment benefit (VD 2009-0307721E5).

ITTN-13, S2-F3-C2: *Benefits and Allowances Received from Employment*, Guide T4130 under "Education benefits", VDs 2004-0088561E5, 2009-0320591E5, 2010-0372541E5, 2010-0371431E5, 2008-0267551E5, 2008-0295321E5, 2006-0172701E5

¶2360 — Uniforms and Special Clothing

An employee is not considered to receive a taxable benefit from the use of uniforms or other specialized clothing supplied by an employer. Likewise, no taxable benefit arises when the employer pays the cost of laundering and dry cleaning such clothing.

Shoveller, [1984] C.T.C. 2207 (TCC), *Huffman*, [1989] 1 C.T.C. 32 (FCTD), S2-F3-C2: *Benefits and Allowances Received from Employment*, Guide T4130 under "Uniforms and special clothing", VDs 2004-0060001E5, 2004-0098471E5, 2006-0168521E5, 2007-0237891E5

¶2365 — Vacations (Employer-Paid)

A vacation with expenses paid by the employer is considered a taxable benefit measured by the fair market value of the trip or vacation. If the employer pays a third party for the holiday, the value of the benefit is considered to be the cost of the holiday to the employer. If the employee is granted use of a vacation property owned by the employer, the employee realizes a taxable benefit equal to the amount the employee would have to pay a third party for equivalent accommodation, less any amount the employee pays the employer for the use of the property.

Where there is an element of business mixed in with the holiday, the taxable benefit may be something less than the whole value (*Philp*, [1970] C.T.C. 330 (Exct)). Also, in *Lowe*, [1996] 2 C.T.C. 33 (FCA), the taxpayer was found not to have received a taxable employment benefit in respect of a vacation taken with clients since any personal benefit from the trip was found to be incidental in nature.

In *Hale*, [1968] C.T.C. 477 (Exch), the attendance of an employee's wife at a sales conference at the expense of the employer was held not to be a taxable benefit since the Court found that the attendance of the taxpayer's spouse at the conference was tantamount to being obligatory and that the spouse actively participated in the conference. The spouses were expected to attend all planned business sessions at the conference, some of which were devoted to matters of special interest to spouses of insurance salesmen. Also, the taxpayer's wife acted as the taxpayer's hostess at informal gatherings arranged by her husband and generally worked with him in the supervision and guidance of his branch delegation to the conference. In the earlier case of *Paton*, [1968] Tax A.B.C. 200 (TAB), the Court imputed a taxable benefit to the taxpayer with respect to expenses attributable to the accompaniment of the taxpayer's wife on a business trip where the employer requested that the taxpayer's wife accompany the taxpayer. In this case, the Court found that in essence, the spouse's only role was to provide companionship to the taxpayer at various social functions that were arranged during the trip.

IT-131R2: *Convention Expenses*, S2-F3-C2: *Benefits and Allowances Received from Employment*, Guide T4130 under "Travel assistance benefits", VDs 2010-0374311E5, 9905737

¶2370 — Workers' Compensation Payments

Workers' compensation payments are effectively excluded from taxation in the employee's hands through the combined operation of ITA 56(1)(v) and 110(1)(f)(ii). An amount is included in income on Line 144 (see ¶8310), but a deduction is available on Line 250 (see ¶9340), such that the only effect is on net income, which affects income-tested benefits such as the age credit, Canada Child Benefit, GST/HST credit, medical expense credit, and the ability of another person to claim the taxpayer as a dependant. Workers' compensation also affects OAS benefits (*Dupuis*, 2011 CarswellNat 4936 (TCC)), which can result in adverse tax consequences where a payment covering several years of benefits is received and included in income in the same year (see *Franklin*, [2004] 1 C.T.C. 2062 (TCC)).

In *Québec (Ville)*, 2007 CarswellNat 5250 (TCC), the employer was not liable for source deductions when it reduced injured employees' pay to net pay while they were off work.

The policy of the CRA is not to include lump sum workers' compensation benefit payments received on death in the net income of the recipients, provided a Form T5007 is not issued (VD 2006-0191501I7).

Amounts received from a U.S. workers' compensation program are normally not taxable in Canada by virtue of the Canada-U.S. Tax Treaty (VD 2010-0389831E5).

See Guide T4001 under "Workers' compensation claims" for more information.

Nicholson, [2006] 5 C.T.C. 2359 (TCC), IT-202R2, VDs 2009-0324731I7, 2011-0411231M4

¶2400 — Deductions from Employment Income

This section discusses the deductions allowed in computing a taxpayer's income for a taxation year from an office or employment. These are generally contained in section 8 of the ITA. There are also other deductions that can be claimed regardless of the source of income, including contributions to an RPP or RRSP, child care expenses, moving expenses, and certain support payments. These are discussed in Chapter 9, "Other Deductions". Note that, unlike employees, self-employed individuals earning business or professional income can deduct any expenses to earn business or professional income that are not specifically prohibited — such individuals are discussed in Chapter 6, "Business and Professional Income".

As discussed below in the "Claiming and Filing" section under each applicable heading, employees must complete and file Form T777, *Statement of Employment Expenses*, with their T1 return in order to claim certain deductions. As well, for certain deductions, Form T2200, *Declaration of Conditions of Employment*, must be completed and signed by the employer to certify that the employee meets the requirements of the relevant provision. The CRA has stated that an employer must be reasonably certain that an employee meets the specified conditions before signing Form T2200. Also, even where Form T2200 is completed, an employee may be required by the CRA to provide additional evidence that the information provided on the form is valid.

ITA 8, *Schnurr*, [2005] 1 C.T.C. 2213 (TCC), *Potter*, [2008] 5 C.T.C. 2303 (TCC), *Fitzgerald*, [2009] 5 C.T.C. 2286 (TCC), VD 2012-0437201E5

¶2401 — Employee and Partner GST/HST Rebate (T1: Line 457)

Employees who deduct expenses from employment income on Line 212 (Annual union, professional or like dues; see ¶2405) or Line 229 (Other employment expenses; see ¶9250) and partners who deduct expenses from partnership income on Lines 135 to 143 may be eligible for a rebate of the GST/HST they paid on those expenses. Individuals can claim this rebate if either of the following applies: the individual's employer is a GST/HST registrant, other than a listed financial institution, or the individual is a member of a GST/HST-registered partnership and has reported their share of the income from that partnership.

The amount of GST/HST rebate received by an employee for the expenses deducted from employment income should be included in income on Line 104 (Other income) in the year it is received.

Taxpayers can claim a GST/HST rebate based on the amount of capital cost allowance (CCA) the taxpayer claimed on motor vehicles and musical instruments on which the taxpayer paid GST/HST. If a taxpayer claims CCA on more than one property of the same class, the part of the CCA for the property that qualifies for the rebate must be separated from the CCA for the other property. If any part of the GST/HST rebate is for a vehicle or musical instrument purchased by the taxpayer, the undepreciated capital cost of the vehicle or musical instrument should be reduced by the amount of the rebate at the beginning of the year in which the rebate is received. Do not include that part of the rebate on Line 104.

Expenses that are not eligible for the GST/HST rebate include the following:

- Expenses on which GST/HST was not paid (e.g., groceries, most expenses incurred outside Canada, medical underwriting fees, insurance premiums, bonding premiums, mortgage interest, residential rents, interest, motor vehicle licence, and registration fees, salaries, etc.)

- Expense incurred when the employer was not a GST/HST registrant

- Any personal-use part of an eligible expense

- 50 percent of the GST/HST paid on eligible expenses for food, beverages, and entertainment

- An expense or part of an expense for which the taxpayer was reimbursed or is entitled to be reimbursed by his or her employer

Both employees and partners should calculate the GST/HST rebate on Form GST370, *Employee and Partner GST/HST Rebate Application*, and file it with their T1 return. For more information, employees should see Guide T4044, *Employment Expenses*, and partners should see Guide RC4091, *GST/HST Rebate for Partners*.

¶2405 — Annual Union, Professional, and Membership Dues (T1: Line 212)

¶2406 — *Professional Dues*

A professional person deriving income as a salaried employee may deduct on Line 212 annual professional membership dues required to maintain a professional status recognized by statute. Entrance fees paid to such an association are not deductible under this provision. Also, the fees must be necessary for the maintenance of a professional status (see, for example, VD 2006-0185911E5) and the professional status must be one recognized by provincial statute (for example, the medical, dental, nursing, legal, engineering, and accounting professions). Dues paid to a professions board, for example, L'Office de professions du Québec, are also deductible where the payment is required by provincial law.

A real estate appraiser was allowed a deduction in *Montgomery*, [1999] 2 C.T.C. 196 (FCA) since it is not required that a statute regulate the particular profession.

The CRA considers annual membership fees paid by pastors and ministers to qualify for deduction if the provincial marriage legislation recognizes their professional status (VD 2006-0168311E5). Also, the CRA considers the cost of medical malpractice insurance that an employee is required to pay by virtue of the conditions of his or her employment to be deductible (VD 2005-0163641E5).

The CRA does not consider amounts expended on professional development courses to qualify as professional membership dues even if the profession imposes continuing education requirements (VD 2001-0112695). Such costs were, however, deductible by a pharmacist in *Bornstein*, [2002] 3 C.T.C. 2163 (TCC).

In paragraph 8 of IT-158R2, the CRA takes the position that dues paid by students before becoming members of a professional organization are not deductible. Such fees may be eligible for a tuition credit (see, for example, VD 2009-0338271E5).

The CRA does not consider mess dues paid by members of the Canadian Forces to be deductible as professional dues (VD 2007-0227181M4).

In Guide 5000-G, the CRA states:

Line 212 — Annual union, professional, or like dues

Claim the total of the following amounts *related to your employment* that you paid (or that were paid for you and reported as income) in the year:

- annual dues for membership in a trade union or an association of public servants [see commentary below];

- professional board dues required under provincial or territorial law;

- professional or malpractice liability insurance premiums or professional membership dues required to keep a professional status recognized by law; and

- parity or advisory committee (or similar body) dues required under provincial or territorial law.

Annual membership dues do not include initiation fees, licences, special assessments, or charges for anything other than the organization's ordinary operating costs. You cannot claim charges for pension plans as membership dues, even if your receipts show them as dues.

Any portion of the membership dues that is for superannuation, insurance (other than professional or malpractice liability insurance as noted below), savings or other purposes not directly connected with the ordinary expenses of the professional association, is not deductible as membership dues. Also, if an employee is wholly or partly reimbursed for the membership dues paid, a deduction may be claimed only for the portion of the unreimbursed dues. However, if such amounts are paid on behalf of an employee and included in computing the employee's income, an offsetting deduction may be claimed.

Dues in respect of professional or malpractice insurance that is necessary to maintain statutory professional status are allowed as a deduction.

An employed professional may also deduct dues required by the laws of a province to be paid to a professions board. A self-employed professional person carrying on business in a professional practice can deduct professional membership dues in computing income from that business or practice (see Chapter 6, "Business and Professional Income").

ITA 8(1)(i), 8(5), Guide T4044, IT-158R2: *Employees' Professional Membership Dues*

¶2407 — *Union Dues*

Annual membership dues in a trade union are deductible by an employee in computing employment income on Line 212. A deduction is also allowed where the employee is not a union member but where, pursuant to a collective agreement, union dues are retained from pay by the employer and paid over to a trade union. Dues which an employee is obliged by provincial law to pay to a parity or advisory committee or similar body are also deductible.

No deduction is allowed for dues or membership fees where the employee is reimbursed for such amounts.

In VD 2008-0304301E5, the CRA takes the position that dues paid to an "independent workers association" do not qualify as annual dues to a trade union for purposes of the deduction since the "provision generally contemplates organizations that negotiate collectively with employers for improvements in their members' working conditions". Also, in VD 2009-0346331E5, the CRA takes the position that dues paid to an association of non-unionized employees do not qualify for deduction, stating:

> It is our view that this provision generally contemplates organizations that negotiate collectively with employers for improvements in their members' working conditions. Since the Association does not negotiate collectively, nor does it negotiate terms and conditions of employment, it is our view that it would not qualify as a trade union. Subparagraph 8(1)(i)(iv) of the Act also allows an employee to deduct from income amounts paid as annual dues to maintain membership in an association of public servants the primary object of which is to promote the improvement of the members' conditions of employment or work. While it remains a question of fact what the primary purpose of the Association is, from our review of the documentation provided, it does not appear that the condition in subparagraph 8(1)(i)(iv) has been met. The documents do not clearly demonstrate that the primary purpose of the Association is to promote the improvement of the members' conditions of employment or work. Accordingly, it is our view that membership dues would not qualify for deduction under this provision.

Union dues may be reported on the taxpayer's T4 slip in Box 44. Generally, the amounts shown in T4 Box 44 or on receipts will include any GST/HST paid.

ITA 8(1)(i), 8(5), Guide T4044, IT-103R: *Dues paid to a Union or to a Parity or Advisory Committee*

¶2408 — *Public Servants Association Dues*

Annual membership dues paid by federal, provincial, or municipal government employees to employees' associations are deductible in computing employment income on Line 212. The primary object of the association must be to promote the improvement of the members' conditions of employment or work. Any part of the dues which is for superannuation, insurance, savings, or other purposes not directly connected with the ordinary expenses of the association is not deductible as membership dues; however, additional dues paid to fund a strike are generally deductible (*Lucas*, [1987] 2 C.T.C. 23 (FCTD)). In *Crowe*, [2003] 3 C.T.C. 271 (FCA), the Court concluded the term "public servants" does not include judges or other independent office holders but approximates to "civil servants" or "government employees".

ITA 8(1)(i)(iv), 8(5), VDs 2006-0182451E5, 2007-0261121E5

¶2410 — Apprentice Mechanics' Tools Deduction (T1: Line 229)

An eligible apprentice mechanic may claim a deduction in respect of the cost of eligible tools on Line 229 of the T1 return. An eligible apprentice mechanic is a taxpayer who is registered under a federal or provincial program whereby the taxpayer is licensed to repair self-propelled motorized vehicles and is employed as an apprentice mechanic. An eligible tool (including ancillary equipment such as a tool box) is a tool which is acquired for use in connection with employment as an apprentice mechanic; is new and not previously used; is certified by the taxpayer's employer as being required to be provided by the taxpayer as a condition of, and for use as, an apprentice mechanic; and is not an electronic communications device (i.e., a cell phone) or electronic data processing equipment, unless it can be used only for measuring, locating, or calculating. A taxpayer who was an eligible apprentice mechanic can carry over unused amounts to other years and deduct such amounts from employment income.

¶2411 — *Deduction for Tools*

The maximum deduction for the cost of eligible tools is equal to (A - B) + C, where:

A = the total cost of eligible tools purchased in the year (if the taxpayer became employed as an eligible apprentice mechanic for the first time during the year, the taxpayer can claim the cost of eligible tools bought during the last three months of the prior year)

B   = the lesser of:

    1. the total cost of eligible tools purchased in the year (A); and

    2. the greater of:

        a. $500 + the Canada employment amount claimed on Line 363 (max. $1,195 for 2018 and $1,178 for 2017); and

        b. 5% of: the taxpayer's employment income as an eligible apprentice mechanic and the net amount received in the year under the Apprenticeship Incentive Grant and the Apprenticeship Completion programs; less any claim made for the tradesperson's tools deduction (see ¶2520)

C   = the amount, if any, of the eligible tools carryforward

The claim cannot create a non-capital loss. Taxpayers should enter their claim on Line 9131, "Apprentice mechanic tools expenses", on Form T777, *Statement of Employment Expenses.*

An example illustrating the calculation of the tools deduction is contained in CRA Guide T4044.

¶2412 — *Disposition of Tools*

If the taxpayer disposes of an eligible tool for proceeds of disposition in excess of the cost of the tool (as adjusted), the excess amount is included in computing the taxpayer's income for the year of the disposition. The original cost of each eligible tool purchased must be adjusted using the following formula: $D - (D \times [E/A])$, where:

D   = the original cost of each eligible tool purchased in the year

E   = the total of the tradesperson's tools deduction (see ¶2520) and apprentice mechanics' tools deduction claimed in the year (for the apprentice mechanics' tools deduction, always assume that C = 0 when calculating E)

A   = the total cost of all eligible tools purchased in the year (where the taxpayer made a claim for both the tradesperson's tools deduction (see ¶2520) and the apprentice mechanics' tools deduction, use the value of A that is greater)

Complete a separate calculation for each eligible tool purchased in the year.

¶2413 — *Claiming and Filing*

Taxpayers should enter their claim for apprentice mechanics' tool costs on Line 9131 of Form T777, which should be filed with the taxpayer's T1 return. The total employment expenses on Line 9368 of Form T777 should be entered on Line 229 of the taxpayer's T1 return.

Also, in order to claim the apprentice mechanics' tools deduction, the taxpayer's employer must complete and sign Form T2200. In particular, the employer must complete question 12 in Part B to certify that the employee bought and provided the tools that are being claimed by the employee. The taxpayer should attach to Form T2200 a list of the tools being claimed, as well as the related receipts. Form T2200, the list of tools and receipts are not required to be filed with the taxpayer's T1 return, but should be retained by the taxpayer in case the CRA requests them.

ITA 8(1)(r), 8(6), 8(7), 56(1)(k), 56(1)(n.1), Guide T4044 (Chapter 7), Form T777, Form T2200, 2006-0175501E5

¶2415 — Apprenticeship Incentive Grant Repayment (T1: Line 232)

A repayment of an amount under the Apprenticeship Incentive Grant program that was included in the taxpayer's income under ITA 56(1)(n.1) for the taxation year or for a previous year may be claimed as a deduction on Line 232 (Other deductions) of the T1 return.

ITA 60(p), canada.ca/en/employment-social-development/services/apprentices/grants.html

¶2420 — Artists' Employment Expenses (T1: Line 229)

An employed artist who incurs expenses in connection with earning income from artistic activities may claim a deduction for such expenses. Artistic activities for these purposes would include the following activities:

- creating a painting, etching, drawing, sculpting, or similar work of art (reproducing these items is not an artistic activity for income tax purposes)

- composing a dramatic, musical, or literary work

- performing as an actor, dancer, singer, or musician in a dramatic or musical work

The amount that may be deducted is the lesser of $1,000 and 20% of the employee's employment income (from all employers) earned from the artistic activity. The amount otherwise deductible is reduced by any amounts claimed in respect of interest or capital cost allowance in respect of a motor vehicle (see ¶2456) or amounts claimed in respect of musical instrument expenses (see ¶2460).

Expenses that cannot be claimed as a result of the 20% or $1,000 limit may be carried forward and deducted from artistic income earned in a future year as long as the total expenses are within the required limits for that year.

See CRA Guide T4044 for an example illustrating the calculation of this deduction.

¶2421 — *Claiming and Filing*

Taxpayers claiming artists' employment expenses should enter their claim on Line 9973 of Form T777, which should be filed with the taxpayer's T1 return. Total employment expenses from Line 9368 of Form T777 should be entered on Line 229 of the taxpayer's T1 return.

ITA 8(1)(q), IT-504R2: *Visual Artists and Writers*, IT-525R: Performing Artists, Guide T4044 (Chapter 6)

¶2425 — Canadian Forces Personnel and Police Deduction (T1: Line 244)

For taxation years before 2017, employment income earned by a member of the Canadian Forces or a police officer while serving on a deployed international operational mission (as determined by the Department of National Defence (DND)) that was assessed for risk allowance at level 3 or higher, a prescribed mission assessed for risk allowance at level 2, or any other prescribed mission, was deductible in computing taxable income. (ITR 7500 prescribes missions for these purposes). For 2017 and later taxation years, this tax deduction is extended to all Canadian Forces members and police officers serving on deployed international operational missions (as determined by the DND), the Minister of Public Safety and Emergency Preparedness, or designate), without the requirement that a particular risk score be associated with the mission.

The deduction is limited to the lesser of the employment income while serving on the mission and the income that would have been earned if the taxpayer was paid the maximum rate of pay that applied during the mission to a non-commissioned member of the Canadian Armed Forces. Civilian members of the RCMP are not entitled to this deduction (VD 2006-0215221E5).

¶2426 — *Claiming and Filing*

The amount of the Canadian Forces personnel and police deduction will generally be reported in Box 43 of the individual's T4 slip and should be entered on Line 244 of the T1 return.

ITA 6(1)(b)(ii), 6(1)(b)(iii), 110(1)(f)(v), ITR 102(6), 7500

¶2430 — Clergy Residence Deduction (T1: Line 231)

The clergy residence deduction allows certain members of the clergy to deduct an amount in respect of their living accommodations from their remuneration from office or employment (including taxable benefits included in income; see VD 2011-0413541E5). The purpose of the deduction is to provide a subsidy for the use of a clergyperson's home. To qualify for the clergy residence deduction, an individual must satisfy both the "status test" and the "function test". The status test requires individuals seeking to claim the deduction to be "members of a clergy or of a religious order or a regular minister of a religious denomination." The function test requires the individual to be in charge of, or ministering to a diocese, parish or congregation or "engaged exclusively in full-time administrative service by appointment of a religious order or religious denomination."

The deduction is limited to the least of the following:

1. the individual's remuneration for the year from the office or employment,

2. the greater of 1/3 of the individual's total remuneration from the employment for the year, and $1,000 per month (to a maximum of ten months) in the year during which an individual meets the conditions set out in ITA 8(1)(c)(i) and (ii), and

3. the actual rent and eligible utilities paid (where the residence is rented) or the fair market rental value plus utilities (where the residence is owned).

Where the living accommodation is supplied by virtue of the employment, the amount of the deduction is equal to the value of the benefit derived from the supply of the living accommodation to the extent that the value is already included in income under ITA 6. It is the CRA's view that a dormitory room meets the definition of a "living accommodation", provided that the individual resides or lives in the dormitory and the dormitory includes access to shared facilities, and that fees paid for use of a dormitory room could be considered rent for the purposes of calculating the clergy residence deduction (VD 2015-0569011I7).

The clergy residence deduction is not available to a self-employed clergyman (*Abrahams*, 2013 CarswellNat 4688 (TCC), VDs 2007-0221471I7 and 2009-0350821E5) or a retired member of the clergy with no income (VDs 2009-0314611E5, 2010-0382791E5). However, it is available where the clergyman provides services through his corporation, which pays him employment income (*Moerman v. R,,* 2015 TCC 295).

With respect to determining whether an organization is a religious order, see *McGorman*, [1999] 3 C.T.C. 2630 (TCC), *Zylstra*, [1997] 2 C.T.C. 203 (FCA), VDs 2013-0494611I7, 2012-0467711E5, 2012-0451081E5, 2012-0436451E5, 2011-039555117, 2010-355231I7, 2010-0383881E5, 2010-0363501E5, 2009-0339731I7, 2009-0369281I7, 2009-0305761I7 and 2008-0301781E5 and paragraph 9 of IT-141R(C), *Clergy Residence Deduction*.

For the meaning of a "member of the clergy", see *Pereira*, [2007] 4 C.T.C. 2410 (TCC), *Lefebvre*, 2009 CarswellNat 3417 (FCA), *Proulx*, 2010 CarswellNat 3705 (FCA), *Tidd*, 2011 CarswellNat 5790 (TCC), *Moerman*, 2015 TCC 295 and VDs 2003-0026465, 2003-0046121E5, 2004-0055401M4, 2004-0067671M4, 2004-0091791E5, 2005-0160401M4, 2006-0178781I7, 2007-0223581E5, 2007-0227951E5, 2007-0228421E5, 2007-0241541E5, 2008-0264171E5, 2008-0299791E5, 2010-0358181I7, 2010-0370201E5, 2011-0394061E5, 2011-0422771I7, 2012-0436101E5, 2012-0447881E5, 2015-0576461E5, 2015-0598631E5 and 2015-0620371E5.

For the meaning of "ministering to a congregation", see *Alemu*, [1999] 2 C.T.C. 2245 (TCC), *McGorman, Tidd*, *Lichtman*, 2017 CarswellNat 7304 (TCC), and VDs 2004-0055131E5, 2006-0186041I7, 2009-0310621I7, 2010-0387251E5, 2011-039555117, 2011-0404771I7, 2012-0436101E5, 2012-0447881E5, 2015-0576461E5 and 2015-0598631E5.

For administrative personnel qualifying under ITA 8(1)(c)(ii)(C), see *Fitch*, [1999] 2 C.T.C. 2419 (TCC) and VDs 2008-0270131E5, 2009-0307291E5, 2010-0363501E5 and 2012-0436451E5.

¶2431 — *Claiming and Filing*

Taxpayers claiming the clergy residence deduction must complete Form T1223, *Clergy Residence Deduction*, to calculate and claim the deduction. Form T1223 is not required to be filed with the taxpayer's return but the taxpayer must provide a completed and signed Form T1223 at the CRA's request. Taxpayer's should enter their claim for the clergy residence deduction on Line 231 of the T1 return.

ITA 4(3), 8(1)(c), 8(10), Form T1223, IT-141R(C): *Clergy Residence Deduction*

¶2435 — Commission Sales Employees (T1: Line 229)

Commissioned sales employees who meet all the following requirements can deduct expenses paid to earn commission income:

- The employee is required to pay his or her own expenses under the employment contract;

- The employee is normally required to work away from the employer's place of business;

- The employee is paid in whole or in part by commissions or similar amounts which are based on the volume of sales made or the contracts negotiated; and

- The employee did not receive a non-taxable allowance for travelling expenses (generally, an allowance is non-taxable as long as it is a reasonable amount; for example, an allowance for the use of a motor vehicle is usually non-taxable when it is based solely on a reasonable per-kilometre rate).

> Generally, if a commission sales employee receives a non-taxable allowance from the employer to cover travel expenses, the allowance is not included in income (see ¶2120, "Allowances"), but the sales employee *may not* claim any employment expenses for tax purposes.

Expenses that may be deducted by a commissioned sales employee include the following:

- Accounting and legal fees — includes reasonable fees paid by the employee for help preparing and filing their T1 return and legal fees paid in the year to collect or establish a right to collect salary or wages (see ¶2450)

- Advertising and promotion expenses — includes amounts paid for business cards, promotional gifts, and advertisements

- Allowable motor vehicle expenses including capital cost allowance (see ¶2456)

- Computers, cell phones, and other equipment — the portion of the lease cost that relates to earning commission income

- Annual licence fees if the employee is required to have a licence to perform their duties (e.g., real estate and insurance salespeople)

- Food, beverages, and entertainment expenses (see ¶2530)

- Home office expenses — if the home office is where the employee mainly does his or her work or if the employee uses the home office on a regular and continuous basis for meeting clients and customers; see ¶2470 for a discussion of the allowable expenses

- Office rent paid to earn commission income (see ¶2470)

- Parking — parking costs related to earning commission income, not including the cost of parking at the employer's office or the cost of traffic tickets (see ¶2455)

- Salaries paid to a substitute or assistant (see ¶2505)

- Supplies — the cost of supplies that the sales employee paid for, including stationery items, stamps, toner, ink cartridges, maps and directories, and long distance calls that relate to commission income (see ¶2515)

- Training Costs — costs incurred for courses to maintain, upgrade or update the employee's existing employment skills or qualifications; training costs are not deductible if the course is for personal reasons or the employee receives a lasting benefit from the course (e.g., the course is towards a degree or professional qualification)

- Travel Expenses — where the employee's work conditions require travel away from the employer's place of business and the employee pays his or her own travel fare and lodging expenses (see ¶2530)

Following are some of the limitations for claiming expenses by a commissioned sales employee:

- Expenses claimed may not be of a capital nature (except as permitted in respect of interest expense or capital cost allowance on the acquisition of a motor vehicle or aircraft used for employment purposes; see ¶2456);

- Expenses claimed may not be greater than the amount of commission income received in the year (except for interest and capital cost allowance);

- Expenses claimed may not be for the use or maintenance of a recreational property or for membership dues for a dining, recreational, or sporting club;

- A deduction is not allowed for an amount paid by an employee, the effect of which is to reduce a standby charge which would otherwise be included in the employee's income (see ¶2131); and

- Expenses may not exceed a reasonable amount.

> If a commission employee's total commission expenses are more than the commissions received by the employee, it may be more advantageous for the commission employee to instead claim expenses as a salaried employee because the claim would not be limited to commissions received in the year. However, the commission employee would only be allowed to claim travelling expenses (see ¶2530), motor vehicle expenses (see ¶2455), and certain other expenses, such as the cost of supplies (see ¶2515), and office rent/home office expenses (see ¶2470). Generally, commission employee must meet the same conditions that a salaried employee must meet for claiming these expenses.

¶2436 — *Claiming and Filing*

Commission employees should calculate their total allowable expenses on Form T777 and enter the amount calculated on Form T777 on Line 229 of the T1 return. Also, the taxpayer's employer must complete the applicable portions of Form T2200 and sign it. Form T2200 is not required to be filed with the taxpayer's T1 return, but should be retained by the taxpayer in case the CRA requests it.

ITA 8(1)(f), IT-352R2: *Employee's Expenses, Including Work Space in Home Expenses*, IT-357R2: *Expenses of Training*, IT-522R: *Vehicle, Travel and Sales Expenses of Employees*, Guide T4044 (Chapter 2)

¶2440 — Employee Home Relocation Loan Deduction (T1: Line 248)

> As proposed in the 2017 Federal budget, the employee home relocation loan deduction is eliminated, effective for benefits arising in 2018 and subsequent taxation years.

An individual employee (or shareholder) who, by virtue of employment (or shareholdings), receives a low-interest or non-interest bearing loan, must include an imputed interest benefit into income, computed in relation to the prescribed rate of interest (see ¶2235, "Loans — Interest-Free and Low-Interest"). However, if the loan qualifies as a "home relocation loan", the employee can claim a deduction on Line 248 equal to the benefit that would be received if the loan were $25,000, and were extinguished on the earlier of five years after the day on which it was made and the day on which it was extinguished. This means that the taxpayer will not have to pay any tax in respect of an imputed interest benefit equal to the prescribed interest on $25,000 of an interest-free home relocation loan, during the first five years that the loan is outstanding. The deduction is limited not by the actual amount of the loan, but by the amount of the imputed interest or the prescribed interest on $25,000 of a home relocation loan, whichever is less.

Generally, a "home relocation loan" is a loan received by an individual employee or shareholder (or the individual's spouse or common-law partner) where the individual relocates within Canada, either to maintain existing employment or to begin a new job. The loan must be designated by the individual as a home relocation loan and the individual is only allowed to have one such loan at a particular time. The individual's new residence must be at least 40 kilometers closer to the new work location than the old residence and must be the individual's ordinary place of residence.

¶2441 — *Claiming and Filing*

The amount of the employee home relocation loan deduction will generally be reported in Box 37 of the individual's T4 slip and should be entered on Line 248 of the T1 return.

ITA 80.4(4), 110(1)(j), 110(1.4), 248(1)"home relocation loan", ITR 4301(c), Guide T4130, IT-421R2, *Benefits to individuals, corporations and shareholders from loans or debt*

¶2445 — Employee Profit Sharing Plans (T1: Line 232)

Where an employee ceases to be a beneficiary under an employee profit sharing plan, amounts which have otherwise been allocated to the employee and previously included in income but which the employee has not received, nor is entitled to receive, may be deducted in computing income from employment on Line 232. This treatment is parallel to that under ITA 6(1)(d), under which allocations under an employee profit sharing plan are included in computing an individual's income from an office or employment (see ¶2190).

ITA 8(1)(o.1), IT-379R: *Employees Profit Sharing Plans — Allocations to Beneficiaries*, Finance Release 2011-08-30: *Consultations on the Tax Rules for Employee Profit Sharing Plans*

¶2450 — Legal Fees (T1: Line 229)

Legal expenses incurred by an employee in collecting or establishing a right to an amount owing by an employer or former employer which, if received, would be included in computing income from an office or employment, are deductible in computing income from the office or employment for the year in which those legal expenses were paid (ITA 8(1)(b)). Fees deductible under this provision are not limited to those paid to a lawyer (see IT-99R5).

Recent amendments to ITA 8(1)(b) addressed concerns that where an amount is not owed to the employee directly by the employer, any legal expenses incurred by the taxpayer would not have been deductible under this provision, even though the amount, when received, would be taxable as employment income. The amendment applies, for example, to allow for a deduction of legal fees incurred by a taxpayer to collect insurance benefits under a sickness or accident insurance policy provided through an employer.

In *Loo*, [2004] 3 C.T.C. 247 (FCA), this provision was found to apply in respect of fees incurred by a taxpayer attempting to establish entitlement to more than the taxpayer had been paid. In respect of this decision, in VD 2009-0310391I7, the CRA states:

> Essentially, the FCA found that the legal expenses fell squarely within the words of paragraph 8(1)(b) of the Act because Mr. Loo was trying to establish, by litigation, that in respect of the services he already rendered to his employer, the law may require that he be paid more than he was already paid. The FCA also noted that paragraph 8(1)(b) of the Act has two branches. The first branch permits a deduction for legal expenses incurred in an action to collect salary or wages owed (i.e. it contemplates litigation resulting from the failure of an employer to pay the salary or wages due to an employee). In these circumstances, there may be no dispute as to the amount of salary or wages that the employee is entitled to be paid for the services the employee has performed, but there may be a factual dispute as to how much of the salary or wages remains unpaid . . .

The second branch contemplates a situation in which the matter in controversy is the legal entitlement to the salary claimed and applies if, for example, an individual incurs legal expenses in litigating a factual dispute as to whether he or she has actually performed the services required by the contract of employment, or a dispute as to the rate of salary payable for services performed (ie this would include, for example, a dispute as to the terms and conditions of employment).

In *Chagnon*, 2011 CarswellNat 1759 (TCC), a company's ex-President was permitted to deduct legal fees incurred to defend a claim by the company for a reimbursement of previously paid salary (see also *Fenwick*, 2008 CarswellNat 1258 (TCC); aff'd [2009] 2 C.T.C. 184 (FCA)).

It is the CRA's position that legal fees incurred to obtain an insurance settlement that would be taxable under ITA 6(1)(f) are deductible (VD 2009-034554117).

Legal fees relating to inappropriate termination notice and negotiating a settlement are not deductible under ITA 8(1)(b) (see VD 2005-0113991E5, *Fenwick*, [2009] 2 C.T.C. 184 (FCA), *Jazairi*, [2001] 2 C.T.C. 28 (FCA) and *Turner-Lienaux*, [1997] 2 C.T.C. 344 (FCA)). However, note that where expenses are incurred in order to establish a right to damages for wrongful dismissal rather than for salary or wages, ITA 60(o.1), rather than ITA 8(1)(b), may be applicable.

Legal fees that cannot be deducted due to insufficient income may create an employment loss which can be carried back or forward as a non-capital loss (VD 2006-0176951E5).

It is not necessary for the legal action to be successful for the legal fees to be deductible (VD 2006-0179401E5).

A taxpayer is required to include in computing employment income any amounts received in the year as an award or reimbursement of legal expenses.

¶2451 — *Claiming and Filing*

Legal fees paid to collect (or establish a right to) salary or wages are deducted on Line 229 of the T1 return.

The following legal fees are deductible on Line 232 (see ¶9271):

- Legal fees paid for advice or assistance responding to the CRA as a result of its review of the individual's income, deductions, or credits for a year, or to object to or appeal an assessment or decision under the ITA the *Unemployment Insurance Act*, the *Employment Insurance Act*, the Canada Pension Plan, or the Quebec Pension Plan;

- Legal fees paid to collect or establish a right to a retiring allowance or pension benefit up to the amount of retiring allowance or pension income received in the year (less any part of these amounts transferred to an RRSP or RPP); and

- Legal fees paid to try to make child support payments non-taxable (see ¶8244).

Legal fees relating to support payments that the individual's current or former spouse or common-law partner, or the parent of the individual's child paid to the individual must be deducted as carrying charges on Line 221 (see under ¶3700). Legal fees incurred to obtain a separation or divorce, to establish custody of or visitation arrangements for a child, or to establish, negotiate, or contest the amount of support payments cannot be claimed as a deduction for tax purposes.

ITA 8(1)(b), IT-99R5: *Legal and Accounting Fees*, Guide T4044 under "Accounting and legal fees", VDs 2011-0423761E5, 2009-031039117, 2008-0302451E5, *Guenette*, [2004] 2 C.T.C. 2861 (TCC), *Bonsma*, 2010 CarswellNat 1781 (TCC), *Blackburn*, [2006] 4 C.T.C. 2377 (TCC) (deduction not allowed for legal fees in criminal and disciplinary proceedings), *Blackburn*, [2004] 2 C.T.C. 2787 (TCC) (establishment of right to salary or wages upon the reinstatement of a police officer deductible), *Blagdon*, [2003] 4 C.T.C. 107 (FCA) (legal fees paid to maintain an employee's position or right to earn income are not deductible), *Cimolai*, [2006] 1 C.T.C. 2410 (TCC); aff'd [2007] 1 C.T.C. 268 (FCA) (fees paid to preserve taxpayer's professional reputation not deductible), *Esposito*, [2004] 2 C.T.C. 2840 (TCC) (legal fees incurred by police officer to protect future source of income not deductible), *Guenette*, [2004] 2 C.T.C. 2861 (TCC) (legal fees paid in a suit for wrongful dismissal not deductible), *Kaushik*, [2006] 1 C.T.C. 2273 (TCC) (expenses incurred in course of protecting professor's academic reputation not deductible), *Shapiro*, 2011 CarswellNat 222 (TCC) (legal fees to defend a director's liability assessment for a corporation's unremitted GST were not deductible)

¶2455 — Motor Vehicle (or Aircraft) Expenses (T1: Line 229)

An employee may claim motor vehicle expenses where the employee meets all of the following requirements:

- the employee is required under the contract of employment to pay his or her own motor vehicle expenses incurred in the performance of the employment duties;

- the employee is ordinarily required to carry out his or her employment duties away from the employer's place of business or in different places (see ¶2120, "Allowances" and ¶2530, "Travelling Expenses" regarding this condition);

- the employee did not receive a non-taxable allowance for motor vehicle expenses (generally, an allowance is non-taxable as long as it is a reasonable amount; for example, an allowance for motor vehicle expenses is usually non-taxable when it is based solely on a reasonable per-kilometre rate); and

- the employee did not claim a deduction for the year for travelling expenses (see ¶2530).

Deductible motor vehicle operating expenses include: fuel (gasoline, propane, oil), repairs and maintenance, insurance, licence and registration fees, capital cost allowance, eligible interest paid on a loan used to buy the motor vehicle, and eligible leasing costs. Only motor vehicle expenses that are reasonable and supported by receipts may be deducted; the deduction cannot be based on a per kilometer rate.

> Where a vehicle is used for personal and business purposes, it is important to maintain a mileage log distinguishing between personal and business kilometers travelled. The CRA explains how a person who uses a vehicle in a business can keep track of business travel at canada.ca/en/revenue-agency/services/what-s-new/documenting-use-a-vehicle.html.

The CRA's general position is that travel between an employee's home and the employer's business location is personal, even when the employee has a home office that is a regular place of employment (see under ¶2120 "Allowances").

In VD 2011-0392721E5, the CRA indicates that motor vehicle expenses can include parking. In Guide T4044, the CRA states:

> You can deduct parking costs related to earning your commission income. Generally, you cannot deduct the cost of parking at your employer's office, such as monthly or daily parking fees or the cost of traffic infractions such as speeding tickets. These are personal costs. Do not include parking costs as part of your allowable motor vehicle expenses. Enter them on the "Parking" line on Form T777.

Expenses incurred to run a motor vehicle to earn employment income are discussed further in Chapter 8 of Guide T4044, excerpts of which are reproduced below:

Joint ownership

> If you and somebody else own or lease the same passenger vehicle, the limits on CCA, interest, and leasing costs still apply. The total amount the joint owners can claim cannot be more than the amount that would be allowed if only one person had owned or leased the vehicle.

Employment use of a motor vehicle

If you use a motor vehicle for both employment and personal use, you can deduct only the percentage of expenses related to earning income. To support the amount you can deduct, keep a record of both the total kilometres you drove and the kilometres you drove to earn employment income. We consider driving back and forth between home and work as personal use. If you use more than one motor vehicle to earn employment income, calculate the expenses for each vehicle separately.

When a motor vehicle or aircraft is used both for pleasure and for the purpose of earning income, the employee is required to apportion the operating expenses, interest, and capital cost allowance on a reasonable basis. See CRA Release, "Documenting the use of a vehicle", dated June 28, 2010, which explains the CRA's policies on kilometer tracking requirements (canada.ca/en/revenue-agency/services/what-s-new/documenting-use-a-vehicle.html).

Note that an employee who is a commission salesperson can deduct amounts expended for the purpose of earning employment income, including motor vehicle expenses, where the salesperson did not receive a non-taxable travel allowance and was required by his or her employment contract to pay the expenses and carry on the duties of employment away from the employer's place of business (see ¶2435). The scope of deductions available under this provision is broad; however, such deductions are limited to the extent of commission income earned from the employment.

¶2456 — *Capital Cost Allowance, Interest, and Leasing Costs*

Capital cost allowance and interest expense on a motor vehicle or aircraft can be deducted by an employee who is entitled to a deduction for sales expenses of commission employees (see ¶2435), travel expenses (see ¶2530), or motor vehicle expenses (see ¶2455). Such expenses would not otherwise be eligible for deduction since ITA 20(1)(a) (capital cost allowance) and 20(1)(c) (interest expense) are limited to the computation of income from a "business or property."

Regardless of whether expenses are deducted under either ITA 8(1)(f) (limited to commission income) or ITA 8(1)(h) or (h.1) (not limited to commission income, but more restricted), capital cost allowance will also be deductible under ITA 8(1)(j) since the capital cost allowance deduction is not limited to commission income in either case (see VD 2006-0203361E5 and the example in Chapter 2 of Guide T4044).

Deductions available in respect of capital cost allowance, interest, and lease costs depend on whether the vehicle is a motor vehicle or a passenger vehicle for tax purposes. A motor vehicle is defined for tax purposes as an automotive vehicle designed or adapted for use on highways and streets (it is not a trolley bus, or a vehicle designed or adapted to be operated exclusively on rails). A passenger vehicle is defined as a motor vehicle designed or adapted primarily to carry people on highways and streets that seats a driver and no more than eight passengers.

Most cars, station wagons, mini-vans, vans, and some pick-up trucks are passenger vehicles for tax purposes. A passenger vehicle does not include an ambulance; police and fire emergency-response vehicles; emergency medical services vehicles used to carry paramedics and their emergency medical equipment; a motor vehicle purchased to use mainly (more than 50%) as a taxi, a bus to transport passengers, or a hearse in a funeral business; a motor vehicle purchased to sell, rent, or lease in a motor vehicle sales, rental, or leasing business; a motor vehicle (except a hearse) purchased in a funeral business to transport passengers; and certain vans and pick-up trucks.

Pick-up trucks or vans are passenger vehicles for tax purposes unless either: 1) they have a seating capacity for not more than a driver and two passengers and are used in the taxation year of acquisition or lease primarily for the transportation of goods or equipment in the course of gaining or producing income, or 2) "all or substantially all" of their use in the taxation year is for the transportation of goods, equipment or passengers in the course of gaining or producing income. Pick-up trucks used in the taxation year of their acquisition or leasing primarily for the transportation of goods, equipment or passengers in the course of earning or producing income at one or more remote or special work sites in Canada that are at least 30 kilometres from the nearest urban area having a population of at least 40,000 individuals as determined in the last census published by Statistics Canada are also excluded from being passenger vehicles. The "used primarily" test is generally considered to be met where more than 50 percent of the distance travelled is for the stated purpose, while "all or substantially all" is normally interpreted to mean at least 90 percent.

Capital cost allowance on a passenger vehicle may be claimed only up to a prescribed limit of the cost of the automobile. For vehicles acquired after 2000, the prescribed ceiling is $30,000 plus federal and provincial sales taxes. Such vehicles must each be included in a separate Class 10.1. Class 10.1 assets are depreciated at a rate of 30 percent per annum on a declining balance basis. Because each passenger vehicle costing over the prescribed amount is prescribed to be a separate class of Class 10.1 property, no capital cost allowance would be available under the general rules in respect of such a vehicle disposed of during the year. However, a taxpayer who owns such a vehicle at the beginning of a year and disposes of it before the end of the year is entitled to a deduction equal to 50 percent of the capital cost allowance deduction that would have been available in respect of the vehicle for that year if it had not been disposed of. Also, Class 10.1 passenger vehicles are excepted from the application of the recapture provisions, and a terminal loss cannot be realized on the disposal of such a vehicle.

Similar deduction limitations to those applicable to passenger vehicle capital cost allowance claims also apply if a passenger vehicle is leased for use by an employee.

ITA 67.2 applies to limit the amount of interest that may be deducted on money borrowed or owing in respect of the acquisition of a "passenger vehicle". The amount of interest paid or payable for a period on money borrowed for the acquisition of a "passenger vehicle" is deemed to be the lesser of the actual amount paid or payable and $300 (or other prescribed amount) divided by 30 and multiplied by the number of days in the period in respect of which interest was paid or payable.

The following interest expense deduction chart is provided in Chapter 8 of CRA Guide T4044:

> You can deduct interest you paid on money you borrowed to buy a motor vehicle or passenger vehicle that you use to earn employment income. Include the interest you paid when you calculate your allowable motor vehicle expenses.
>
> If you use a *passenger vehicle* to earn employment income, there is a limit on the amount of interest you can deduct. Use the "Available interest expense for passenger vehicles chart" to calculate the amount you can deduct. Enter your available interest expense amount on Line 10 of Form T777.

Available interest expense for passenger vehicles chart	
Total interest paid in the year	$ A
$10* × the number of days for which interest was paid	$ B
The available interest expense is the *lower of* amount A and amount B.	

Note:

* Use $8.33 for passenger vehicles bought *between* December 31, 1996, and January 1, 2001. In *all* other cases, use $10.

In the case of an aircraft, the aggregate deduction for operating expense, interest and capital cost allowance may not exceed what is reasonable in the circumstances having regard to the cost and availability of other modes of transportation.

Claiming and Filing

Taxpayers should calculate and report their total allowable motor vehicle expenses, including any capital cost allowance, on Form T777 and enter the amount calculated on Form T777 on Line 229 of the T1 return. Employees should also have their employer sign and complete the applicable portions of Form T2200. Form T2200 is not required to be filed with the taxpayer's T1 return, but should be retained by the taxpayer in case the CRA requests it.

ITA 8(1)(h.1), 8(1)(j), 8(9), 13(1), 13(2), 20(16.1), ITR 1100(2.5), 1101(1af), 7307, IT-63R5: *Benefits, Including Standby Charge for an Automobile, from the Personal Use of a Motor Vehicle Supplied by an Employer* (paras. 6, 12, 23), IT-522R: *Vehicle, Travel and Sales Expenses of Employees* (para. 30), Guide T4044 (Chapters 2, 8, 9), VD 2004-0057251E5, 2006-0203361E5, 2007-0238631E5, 2008-0270191E5, 2009-0310401E5, 2012-0442381E5, PwC, "Car Expenses and Benefits: A Tax Guide" (pwc.com/ca/carexpenses), *Tax Hyperion*, Vol. 7 No. 8 (Carswell, August 2010)

¶2460 — Musical Instrument Expenses (T1: Line 229)

A taxpayer who is employed as a musician and who must provide a musical instrument for a period in the year as a condition of employment may deduct expenses incurred to maintain, insure, or rent the instrument for the periods during the year while employed as a musician. The amount of deductible expenses may not, however, exceed income for the year from employment as a musician. An employed musician may also claim capital cost allowance with respect to the instrument not exceeding 20% calculated on a declining balance basis. A computer was considered to be a musical instrument in *Belkin*, [2006] 1 C.T.C. 2399 (TCC).

If the taxpayer uses the musical instrument for both employment and other purposes, divide the total instrument expenses among the different uses. For example, if the taxpayer is using the instrument for employment, self-employment, and personal purposes, separate all three uses. Personal expenses cannot be deducted.

¶2461 — *Claiming and Filing*

Taxpayers claiming musical instrument expenses should enter their claim on Line 1776, "Musical instrument expenses", and Line 1777, "Capital cost allowance for musical instruments", of Form T777, which should be filed with the taxpayer's T1 return. Capital cost allowance can be calculated on the back of Form T777. Total employment expenses from Line 9368 of Form T777 should be entered on Line 229 of the taxpayer's T1 return.

ITA 8(1)(p), IT-525: *Performing Artists*, Guide T4044 (Chapters 6, 9)

¶2465 — Northern Residents' Deduction (T1: Line 255)

Under ITA 110.7, individuals who reside in a "prescribed northern zone" or a "prescribed intermediate zone" for at least six months beginning or ending in the year are entitled to claim special deductions in computing taxable income for a specified percentage of employee travel and housing benefits. Where the taxpayer moves from one qualifying area to another, the combined consecutive months will satisfy the six-month test.

Examples of prescribed northern zones are Yukon, Nunavut, the Northwest Territories, Labrador, and the northern parts of Manitoba, Ontario, and Quebec. Examples of prescribed intermediate zones are the Queen Charlotte Islands (BC), Magdalen and Anticosti Islands (QC), Sable Island (NS), the northern parts of British Columbia, Alberta, and Saskatchewan, and designated areas of Manitoba, Ontario, and Quebec.

¶2466 — *"Qualifying Period" of Residence*

The "qualifying period" consists of not less than six consecutive (calendar) months beginning or ending in the taxation year. For the purpose of determining an individual's residence for the purposes of this deduction, a special rule contemplates dual residence (i.e., a principal place of residence outside the prescribed area or zone and a temporary residence throughout the qualifying period at a remote work site within a prescribed area or zone). Moreover, in *Morecroft v MNR*, [1991] 2 C.T.C. 2265, the Tax Court of Canada stated (at pp 2267):

> Section 110.7 does not restrict a taxpayer to reside in only one area. He need only reside in a prescribed area throughout a period of six months to be eligible to claim a deduction; there is nothing in the provision prohibiting him from residing at the same time in another area.

Although the Court noted that the word "throughout" means continuously or without interruption, it considered that residence does not require a person's constant and uninterrupted presence in a particular area. Thus, the fact that the taxpayer left the prescribed area for two days at a time to purchase supplies and visit his family was held not to destroy the continuity of his residence in the prescribed area for purposes of the deduction. In the CRA's view, the following factors may suggest that an absence from a prescribed zone is temporary: the individual intended to return to his or her residence when leaving the prescribed zone; the individual actually returned to his or her residence in the prescribed zone; there was a reasonable expectation that the individual would return to his or her residence in the prescribed zone; the individual's family remained at the residence in the prescribed zone; the individual did not establish another residence outside the prescribed zone, change his or her mailing address, move household effects or belongings; and the individual's residence in the prescribed zone was available for his or her use throughout the absence period. However, the longer the duration of an absence, the more likely these factors may change and indicate that the absence is no longer temporary (VD 2015-0582091E5).

For a case where the six month requirement was not considered to be met, see *Sigouin v The Queen*, [1997] 2 C.T.C. 2308 (TCC). Also see *McCombie v. R.*, [2000] 4 C.T.C. 2251 (TCC) in which the taxpayer's residence in the Northwest Territories from June 18, 1997 to December 9, 1997 was considered not to meet the six month requirement. The Court reasoned that such condition required a full six months of residence, not parts of calendar months.

An individual residing in more than one particular area on any day is deemed to reside in only one such area on that day for the purposes of the Northern residents' deduction.

¶2467 — *Travel Benefits Deduction*

The deduction for travel expenses is available to an employee (meeting the residence and filing requirements) who received an amount or received or enjoyed a benefit in the year from an employer with whom he/she was dealing at arm's length in respect of travel expenses incurred during the relevant period by the employee or a member of the employee's household, provided the amount does not exceed a prescribed amount, and is included and not otherwise deducted in computing the taxpayer's income for any taxation year. Furthermore, the expenses must have been incurred in respect of trips made in the year by the taxpayer or by another member of the taxpayer's household during the relevant period of residence. Any number of trips may be made for the purpose of obtaining medical services not locally available, but no more than two trips per year can qualify.

Taxpayers cannot claim the Northern residents' deduction in respect of amounts claimed for purposes of the medical expense tax credit for any taxation year. Also, the Northern residents' deduction cannot be claimed to the extent that either the taxpayer or a member of his or her household is entitled to any reimbursement or assistance in respect of the travelling expenses, unless such reimbursement or assistance is included in computing the income of the taxpayer or the household member.

If an individual lives in a prescribed northern zone, the maximum deduction that may be claimed for each eligible trip is limited to the least of the following amounts:

- the travel benefits received from the employer for the trip that are included in income and not otherwise deducted;

- the total travel expenses for the trip; and

- the cost of the lowest return airfare available between the airport closest to the individual's residence and the nearest designated city (see Form T2222, *Northern Residents Deductions*, for a list of designated cities).

If an individual lives in a prescribed intermediate zone, the deduction is 50% of the deduction (as calculated above) that would be available if the individual lived in a prescribed northern zone.

An optional simplified method for calculating travel expenses for the Northern residents' deduction, under which supporting receipts are not required, may be used to calculate meal and vehicle expenses. Under the simplified method, a flat rate of $17 per meal (to a maximum of $51 per day, per person) may be claimed without receipts. Similarly, an individual may opt to claim vehicle expenses by multiplying the number of qualifying kilometres driven by the cents per kilometre rate for the province or territory from which the travel begins. The flat rate for vehicle expenses (per number of kilometers travelled in the course of the trip) varies depending on the province or territory from which the travel begins.

¶2468 — *Housing Deduction*

A deduction of $11.00 ($8.25 before 2016) may also be claimed for each day that an individual resides in a prescribed area. If a self-contained domestic establishment is maintained and inhabited in the area, an additional deduction of $11.00 ($8.25 before 2016) per day may be claimed, provided no other person residing in the same establishment also claims the deduction in respect of that day. A self-contained domestic establishment is defined as a house, apartment, or similar place of residence in which a person as a general rule eats and sleeps. The maximum deduction available in relation to living costs is limited to 20% of net income for the year. As above, for persons residing in prescribed intermediate zones, the rates are reduced by 50%.

In certain cases, where an individual is residing in a hotel room under circumstances similar to that of residing in an apartment, the CRA may consider that the individual meets the test of residing in a self-contained domestic establishment for purposes of claiming the Northern residents' deduction (see VD 2005-0127641E5).

For taxpayers who qualify for both the housing benefits deduction and the tax exemption for board and lodging at a remote work site (see ¶2136), the amount of the housing deduction is reduced by the value of any non-taxable benefits received relating to the board and lodging at a remote work site. However, the receipt of amounts for food, beverages or entertainment at a remote work site are not taken into account in computing the employee's Northern residents' deduction.

¶2469 — *Claiming and Filing*

Generally, an individual's T4 slip will indicate travel assistance benefits in Box 32. The medical portion of the travel assistance is reported in Box 33, as well as in Box 32. To claim the Northern residents' deduction, taxpayers must complete CAIXFORM Form T2222, *Northern Residents Deductions* and attach it to their T1 return. The Northern residents' deduction calculated on Form T2222 should be entered on Line 255 of the T1 return.

ITA 6(6)(a)(i), 110.7, 248(1)"self-contained domestic establishment", ITR 7303.1, 7304, T4 boxes 31, 32, 33, Form T2222, Guide RC4054, Guide T4130, IT-91R4, *Employment at Special Work Sites or Remote Work Locations*, VDs 2005-0136061E5, 2005-0146421E5, 2006-0197431R3, 2007-0235791E5, 2007-0239391E5, canada.ca/en/revenue-agency/services/tax/individuals/segments/northern-residents.html

¶2470 — Office Rent and Home Office Expenses (T1: Line 229)

An employee who is required by a contract of employment to pay office rent may deduct those payments to the extent that the employee is not reimbursed or entitled to be reimbursed. Office rent does not include mortgage interest, property taxes or insurance expenses. Where the office is part of a house or an apartment rented by the employee (i.e., a home office), one of the following conditions must be met for expenses to be deductible:

- the work space is where the employee principally does his or her work; or,

- the employee uses the work space only to earn income from an office or employment, and uses it on a regular and continuous basis for meeting clients or customers in the course of performing those duties.

The CRA's position is that the term "principally" for the purposes of claiming home office expenses means more than 50 percent of the time (see VD 2009-0329111E5).

Where one of the above conditions is satisfied, the employee may deduct a reasonable portion of expenses consumed directly in the performance of employment duties, including expenses incurred for the maintenance of the premises, fuel, electricity, and cleaning materials. Expenses which are not otherwise specifically provided for may not be deducted. Therefore, where an employee (other than a commissioned sales employee) provides office space in a property owned by the employee, expenses on account of capital cost allowance, property taxes, property insurance and mortgage interest may not be deducted.

As an exception, commission sales employees may claim an appropriate portion of property taxes and insurance paid on the home, but not mortgage interest or capital cost allowance (see also ¶2435).

Allowable expenses may be deducted to the extent of the employee's income from the office or employment. Any undeducted expenses may be carried forward indefinitely for deduction against income from the same office or employment.

In Guide T4044, under "Work-space-in-the-home expenses", the CRA states:

> To calculate the percentage of work-space-in-the-home expenses you can deduct, use a reasonable basis, such as the area of the work space divided by the total finished area (including hallways, bathrooms, kitchens, etc.). For maintenance

costs, it may not be appropriate to use a percentage of these costs. For example, if the expenses you paid (such as cleaning materials or paint) were to maintain a part of the house that was not used as a work space, then you cannot deduct any part of them. Alternatively, if the expenses you paid were to maintain the work space only, then you may be able to deduct all or most of them.

If your office space is in a rented house or apartment where you live, deduct the percentage of the rent and any maintenance costs you paid that relate to the work space . . . You can only deduct work space expenses from the income to which the expenses relate, and not from any other income. If you cannot deduct all your work space expenses in the year, you can carry forward the expenses. You can deduct these expenses in the following year as long as you are reporting income from the same employer. However, you cannot increase or create a loss from employment by carrying forward work space expenses.

¶2471 — *Claiming and Filing*

Taxpayers should calculate their claim for home office expenses on Form T777 in the area "Calculation of workspace-in-the-home expenses" and enter their claim on Line 9945 of Form T777. The total employment expenses on Line 9368 of Form T777 should be entered on Line 229 of the taxpayer's T1 return. Form T777 should be filed with the taxpayer's T1 return.

Also, the taxpayer's employer must complete and sign Form T2200. In particular, the employer must complete question 10 in Part B to certify that the employee was required to use a portion of his or her home for work. Form T2200 is not required to be filed with the taxpayer's T1 return, but retained by the taxpayer in case the CRA requests it.

ITA 8(1)(i)(ii), 8(1)(i)(iii), 8(1)(l.1), 8(1)(l.2), 8(2), 8(7), 8(10), 8(13), *Horbay*, [2003] 2 C.T.C. 2248 (TCC), *Lester*, 2011 CarswellNat 4943 (TCC), Guide T4044 under "Work-space-in-the-home expenses", IT-352R2: *Employee's Expenses, Including Work Space in Home Expenses*, Greg Crowell, "Home Office Expenses of Employees", 8(6) *Tax Hyperion* (Carswell, June 2011)

¶2475 — Overseas Employment Tax Credit (T1 Schedule 1: Line 426)

An employee who is abroad for a period of time in connection with a work project of an employer is generally considered a resident of Canada during the period of temporary absence and is liable to tax on income earned while abroad. However, for taxation years before 2016, employees could claim an Overseas Employment Tax Credit (OETC) against tax otherwise payable. Before 2013, the OETC was equal to the proportion of the employee's tax otherwise payable that is the lesser of $80,000 or 80 percent of net overseas income taxable in Canada of the total income for the year.

> The OETC was gradually phased out from 2013 to 2015. During the phase-out period, the factor applied to an employee's qualifying foreign employment income in determining the employee's OETC was reduced to 60% for the 2013 taxation year, 40% for the 2014 taxation year, and 20% for the 2015 taxation year. Similarly, the maximum qualifying foreign employment income eligible for the OETC was correspondingly reduced. *For all employees, the OETC is eliminated for taxation years after 2015.*

¶2476 — *Claiming and Filing*

For taxation years before 2016, the OETC was claimed on Line 426 of Schedule 1 of the T1 return. Taxpayers claiming the OETC for taxation years before 2016 should complete and attach Form T626, *Overseas Employment Tax Credit*, to their T1 return.

ITA 122.3, IT-497R4: *Overseas Employment Tax Credit*, Guide T4001 under "Overseas employment tax credit", Form T626, CRA Q&A Release 2012-03-30B: Budget 2012: Overseas Employment Tax Credit (OETC) — Phase Out

¶2480 — Power Saw Operators (T1: Line 229)

Employees who work in forestry operations and are required to supply their own power saws and pay for their operation can deduct the expenses of purchasing and using the power saw if the employee is not reimbursed for the expenses. Each employee will be required to file, with their T1 return, a statement setting out in detail the actual cost of operating the power saw. Receipts and vouchers must be available to support these expense claims if requested by the CRA.

While an employee is not specifically prohibited from claiming capital cost allowance on a power saw, the CRA takes the position that such saws have a very short life. Accordingly, a sufficiently broad interpretation can be made to allow an employee to deduct the actual cost of a saw purchased during the year in addition to the operating expenses. Each claim for deduction of the cost of a saw must be set out clearly in the statement of expenses filed with the T1 return, and this cost must be reduced by the trade-in value or sale price received from the disposal of saws during the year.

Travelling expenses are generally not deductible by power saw operators since the CRA considers that such expenses are for the purpose of travelling from home to the cutting site, from home to a woods camp, or from a woods camp to the cutting site. Such costs are personal or living expenses and not deductible in the computation of income for tax purposes. The cost of horses and harness is also not deductible but are considered capital expenditures.

Employers of power saw operators should ensure that total earnings reported on the T4 slip have not been reduced in any way by the cost or value of saws, parts, gasoline, or any other materials supplied to the employee. Employers are not required to report separately the amount of rent paid to employees for the use of power saws. Rental payments should be included in total earnings.

¶2481 — *Claiming and Filing*

The deduction for power saw expenses should be entered on Line 229 of the taxpayer's T1 return. In order to claim a deduction for power saw expenses, the employee is required to file a statement setting out in detail the actual cost of operating the power saw with the employee's T1 return. Also, the taxpayer's employer must complete and sign Form T2200. In particular, the employer must complete question 12 in Part B. Receipts and vouchers must be available to support the expense claims if requested by the CRA. Form T2200 and the receipts and vouchers are not required to be filed with the taxpayer's T1 return, but should be retained by the taxpayer in case the CRA requests them.

ITA 8(1)(i)(iii), CRA Guide T4044 (Chapter 5)

¶2485 — Railway Employees' Expenses (T1: Line 229)

Railway employees can deduct in computing income amounts paid for meals and lodging where the employee meets one of the following conditions:

- the employee works away from home for a railway company as a telegrapher or station agent in a relief capacity, or to carry out maintenance and repair work for the railway company, or

- the employee works away from the municipality or metropolitan area where the employer's home terminal is located, and at such a distant location that it is unreasonable for the employee to return home every day, to the place where the employee supports a spouse or common-law partner, or a dependant related to the employee.

Taxpayers must reduce their claim for meal and lodging expenses by any non-taxable allowance or reimbursement they receive or are entitled to receive from their employer.

¶2486 — *Claiming and Filing*

Taxpayers should complete Form TL2, *Claim for Meals and Lodging Expenses*, and enter their deduction on Line 229 of the T1 return. Form TL2 is not required to be filed with the T1 return but the taxpayer should keep it on file in case the CRA requests it.

ITA 8(1)(e), 8(1)(g), IC 73-21R9, *Claims for Meals and Lodging Expenses of Transport Employees*, Form TL2, *Claim for Meals and Lodging Expenses*, CRA Guide T4044 (Chapter 4)

¶2490 — Reimbursement of Disability Payments (T1: Line 232)

An employee may deduct an amount paid by or on behalf of the employee to an employer or former employer as a reimbursement of a "top-up disability payment".

A top-up disability payment is one which is made by an employer to replace a periodic disability payment which would otherwise be made by an insurer but the insurer has become insolvent. If the employee receives payments from the insurer which are included in the employee's income pursuant to ITA 6(1)(f), but which must be paid to the employer as a reimbursement of the top-up payment previously received, the employee may claim a deduction equal to the amount included in the employee's income. If the disability plan was not funded by the employer, there would be no income inclusion by the employee pursuant to ITA 6(1)(f); and therefore, no deduction for the reimbursement payment made. However, if the disability plan was partially or totally funded by the employer, then a part or all of the reimbursement amount would be deductible to the employee. The deduction is generally claimed in the year in which the reimbursement payment is made unless the payment is made within sixty days after the year in which the employee receives the payment from the insurer. In that case, the deduction may be claimed for the same year that the employee received the payment from the insurer.

¶2491 — *Claiming and Filing*

The deduction for a reimbursement of disability payments should be specified and entered on Line 232 of the T1 return.

ITA 6(17), 8(1)(n.1)

¶2495 — Reimbursement of Salary (T1: Line 232)

Salary received by an employee and later refunded to the employer pursuant to an arrangement to do so, if it related to a period during which no duties were performed, may be deducted in computing the employee's income from an office or employment for the year in which it is repaid. The amount deducted must have been included in the taxpayer's income and cannot exceed the amount otherwise received by the taxpayer while not performing services. This would apply, for example, where an employee receives ordinary pay during a period of sickness or disability, but is required to reimburse the employer from proceeds received under an insurance policy or workers' compensation. However, this does not apply to certain arrangements that are a "top-up disability payment" (see ¶2490).

The CRA acknowledges that an annual bonus and relocation payment (that was previously included in employment income) repaid to the employer when the employee terminates his/her employment contract early is deductible. For example, in VD 2010-0385801I7, the CRA states:

> One of the requirements to qualify for the deduction under paragraph 8(1)(n) of the Act is that the taxpayer is required to reimburse any amount paid to him/her for a period throughout which the taxpayer did not perform the duties of the employment. In our view, "the period throughout which the taxpayer did not perform the duties of the office or employment" refers to the critical day or days under a contract or specified time period (herein referred to as contract) that the employee must have worked to retain a relocation/bonus payment. In a situation where an employee is required to repay the entire relocation/bonus payment if he did not work the very last day of the contract, then that day is the critical "period throughout which" he did not perform the duties of the office or employment which gives rise to the repayment. Where the repayment would be prorated, then the period of the contract not worked which gives rise to the partial repayment is the critical period referred to in paragraph 8(1)(n) of the Act.

> Since in [the current situation under consideration,] the individual did not perform the duties of the office or employment on the last day of the contract, the repayment would relate to a period "throughout which" he did not perform the duties of the office or employment within the meaning of that phrase in paragraph 8(1)(n) of the Act. Therefore, the requirements of paragraph 8(1)(n) would be met and the taxpayer should be permitted to claim a deduction for the relocation/bonus repayment (assuming all other conditions are met).

The Court has found that this provision allows a deduction only for amounts actually paid, not amounts payable (*Lunn*, 2011 CarswellNat 4944 (TCC)).

The CRA does not consider this provision to apply where an employee inadequately performs the duties of office or employment. For example, in VD 2005-0116061E5, the CRA states:

> One of the requirements to qualify for the deduction under paragraph 8(1)(n) of the Act is that the taxpayer is required to reimburse any amount paid to the taxpayer for a period throughout which the taxpayer did not perform the duties of the employment. As indicated in the Department of Finance Explanatory Notes, this would apply, for example, where an employee receives his ordinary remuneration during a period of sickness or disability but is required to reimburse his employer out of any proceeds he may receive under an insurance policy or workmen's compensation plan.
>
> Accordingly, it is our view that this paragraph would not permit a deduction where an employee did perform the duties of his office or employment, albeit inappropriately.

¶2496 — *Claiming and Filing*

The deduction for a reimbursement of salary should be specified and entered on Line 232 of the T1 return.

ITA 6(17), 8(1)(n)

¶2500 — Retirement Compensation Arrangement (RCA) (T1: Line 232)

A deduction is allowed in computing employment income in respect of employee pension plan contributions if the contributions are qualifying contributions and the plan is an RCA with a Canadian resident custodian, or the contributions are made to a prescribed pension plan established by the federal or a provincial government. An employee can only claim a deduction for contributions to an RCA to the extent that they do not exceed contributions by any other person in respect of the taxpayer. If the registration of a plan has been revoked, a qualifying contribution would include amounts contributed in accordance with the plan as last registered unless the plan was revoked as of its original registration day. See ¶2305 for a discussion of the tax rules governing RCAs.

¶2501 — *Claiming and Filing*

The deduction for RCA contributions should be specified and entered on Line 232 of the T1 return.

ITA 8(1)(m.2), Guide T4041: Retirement compensation arrangements under "Receiving employee contributions"

¶2505 — Salary Paid to a Substitute or Assistant (T1: Line 229)

An employee who is required by his or her employment contract to pay salary to an assistant or substitute may deduct those payments to the extent that the employee is not reimbursed or entitled to be reimbursed. The employee may also deduct the amounts paid as an employer's contribution under the *Canada Pension Plan* or *Quebec Pension Plan*, as an employer's premium under the *Employment Insurance Act*, and as an employer's premium under the Quebec Parental Insurance Plan in respect of such assistant or substitute.

The assistant can be the taxpayer's child (see *Aprile*, [2005] 2 C.T.C. 2425 (TCC) (deduction allowed) and *Zepotoczny*, [2008] 4 C.T.C. 2213 (TCC) (deduction not allowed as evidence provided was not credible).

¶2506 — *Claiming and Filing*

Taxpayers should enter their total employment expenses on Line 229 of the T1 return. Also, the taxpayer's employer must complete and sign Form T2200. In particular, the employer must complete question 9 in Part B to certify that the employee was required to pay for a substitute or assistant. Form T2200 is not required to be filed with the taxpayer's T1 return, but is retained by the taxpayer in case the CRA requests to see it.

ITA 8(1)(i)(ii), Guide T4044 under "Other expenses", IT-352R2: *Employee's Expenses, Including Work Space in Home Expenses*

¶2510 — Security Options Deduction (T1: Line 249)

Generally, an employee who acquires securities of his or her employer is required to include a stock option benefit into employment income equal to the difference between the fair market value of the shares at the time of exercise and the amount paid by the employee to acquire the shares and options (see ¶2315).

If the shares are of a CCPC, the benefit is automatically deferred until the employee disposes of the shares, provided that the employee and the corporation are at arm's length on the grant date.

For publicly-traded shares, a special election can be made to defer inclusion of all or part of the benefit until the time the shares are sold. However, this election for publicly-traded shares was repealed for options exercised after March 4, 2010; therefore, the election is only available to defer the employment benefit for options of publicly-traded shares which are exercised on or before March 4, 2010. Publicly-traded share options that were exercised after March 4, 2010 do not qualify for the special election for deferral.

Pursuant to ITA 110(1)(d) and (d.1), in the year that the stock option benefit is included in income, the employee can claim a security options deduction on Line 249 equal to one-half of the related employment benefit (reported on Line 101 or Line 104), provided that all of the following conditions are met:

- The employer corporation (or a corporation not at arm's length with the employer) is the seller or issuer of the shares or units;

- The shares qualify as prescribed shares (generally, this means that the shares must have the characteristics of common shares); and

- The amount payable at the time the employee acquired the shares is at least equal to the fair market value of the shares at the time the option was granted, minus any amount paid by the employee to acquire the option.

A non-resident who computes taxable income earned in Canada under ITA 115 is also entitled to the security options deduction under ITA 110(1)(d) and (d.1).

¶2511 — *CCPC Security Options Deduction*

There is an exception to the above requirements where the shares are of a CCPC that are held for at least two years prior to sale, and the employee and employer are at arm's length immediately after the option agreement is made. In this case, one-half of the benefit still qualifies for the security option deduction, even if the price paid for the shares was less than the fair market value of the shares on the date the employee was granted the option. In all other circumstances, the above-noted conditions must be met to claim the security options deduction.

In applying the two-year rule, if the shares are held in trust for the employee, the employee is deemed to have acquired them when acquired by the trustee. As such, a security option trust may be utilized to begin the two year clock ticking before the shares are acquired by the employee. Also, an exchange of shares by reason of an amalgamation or share exchange will not be considered a disposition for the purposes of the two-year rule. A rollover is also available where the employee's shares that were acquired under the option are exchanged in the course of any corporate reorganization or restructuring within a non-arm's length group of corporations, provided the employees receive only shares as a result of the exchange. These provisions apply equally where there are several share exchanges. However, the fair market value of the new shares immediately after the exchange cannot exceed the total fair market value of the shares immediately before the exchange. Rollover rules also apply to an exchange of the options.

The net employment benefit in respect of an option does not qualify for the lifetime capital gains exemption. However, any gains in respect of the share that accrue after the acquisition of the share will generally be considered a capital gain that may be eligible for the lifetime capital gains exemption if the shares are qualifying small business corporation shares (see ¶4220). This rule also applies where shares are held by a trustee for the employee.

¶2512 — *Stock Option Cash-Out Rights*

Some stock option plans contain cash-out rights whereby the employee can elect to either exercise the option in the ordinary course and receive the shares, or receive a cash payment equal to the in-the-money amount of the option. The security option deduction discussed above is also generally available where the employee exercises the cash-out right, provided that the option itself qualifies for the deduction. In certain circumstances, the CRA allows employers to claim a deduction for the full amount of the cash payment paid to an employee upon exercise by the employee of a cash-out right. However, for options exercised (or cash-out rights exercised) on a cash-out basis after March 4, 2010, the employee cannot claim the security option deduction unless the employer elects to forego its deduction in respect of the cash-out payment. Essentially, this means that for options that are cashed out after March 4, 2010, either the employee can claim the 50 percent security option deduction or the employer can claim a deduction on the cash-out payment, but not both. The rule applies to options exercised after March 4, 2010, regardless of when the underlying option was granted.

Evidence of the employer's election must be filed by the employee with his or her tax return claiming the stock option deduction. The T4 slip serves as the required "evidence" for both the employee and the employer. The employer reports what portion of the reported stock option benefit relates to the employer's election in T4 Box 86, "Security Options Election". Since the employer files the T4 with CRA and provides a copy to the employee, the requirements of the election will be considered to have been met. The employer should advise the employee of the election before or at the time of the cash-out, since the decision to elect will affect the level of withholdings required. Where the election has not been filed, the employee cannot claim the security option deduction and the stock option benefit would be taxed in the same manner as other employment income. However, the employer would be allowed to claim a deduction for the cash paid to the employee in exchange for the option rights.

ITA 7(1.4), 7(6), 110(1)(d), 110(1.1), (1.2), (1.7), (1.8), *No 179 v MNR* (1954), 11 Tax A.B.C. 76, *Steen v The Queen*, [1988] 1 C.T.C. 256 (FCA), IT-113R4: *Benefits to Employees — Stock Options* (paras. 8, 11), VDs 2001-0084013, 2005-0112901E5, 2005-0132991C6, 2008-0279251E5, 2004-0093241E5

¶2513 — *Claiming and Filing*

Employers are required to calculate the stock option benefit and deduction and report the amounts on the employee's T4 slip in Box 39 or 41 (although, for stock options granted by foreign corporations, the amounts may not be reported on a T4 slip). The portion of the stock option benefit that relates to the employer's election is reported in T4 Box 86, Security Options Election.

If the taxpayer has disposed of the securities for which the taxable benefit has been deferred, claim 50 percent of the amount from Line 4 of Form T1212, *Statement of Deferred Security Options Benefits*. If the taxpayer is electing for the special relief in respect of gains from a disposition of eligible securities for which an election was made to defer inclusion of the taxable benefit, complete Form RC310, *Election for Special Relief for Tax Deferral Election on Employee Security Options*, to calculate the amount that can be claimed on Line 249. This special relief is only available for security options that were exercised on or before March 4, 2010.

ITA 7(1), 7(1.1), 7(1.4), 7(1.5), 7(6), 110(1)(d), 110(1)(d.1), IT-113R4: *Benefits to Employees — Stock Options* (paras.13, 14, 19), VD 2002-0167465

¶2515 — Supplies (T1: Line 229)

A salaried employee who is required by a contract of employment to pay for supplies used directly in the performance of duties may deduct the cost of those supplies from the employee's employment income. The amount which may be deducted is "the cost of supplies that were consumed directly in the performance of the duties of the office or employment and that the officer or employee was required by the contract of employment to supply and pay for".

The CRA's position is that this provision does not allow for a deduction of special clothing, haircuts, tools, safety gear, equipment required for work, or monthly phone costs. However, in paragraph 9 of IT-352R2, the CRA states that it considers the word "supplies" to include the following: the cost of gasoline and oil used in the operation of power saws owned by employees in woods operations; dynamite used by miners; bandages and medicines used by salaried doctors; telegrams, long-distance telephone calls, and cellular telephone airtime that reasonably relate to the earning of employment income; and various stationery items (other than books) used by teachers, such as pens, pencils, paper clips, and charts.

Note that for 2016 and later taxation years, teachers and early childhood educators can claim a $150 refundable tax credit for the cost of eligible teaching supplies paid in a taxation year. See ¶11330 for more information on this tax credit, called the eligible educator school supply tax credit.

¶2516 — *Claiming and Filing*

Taxpayers should enter their claim for supplies on Line 8810 of Form T777, which should be filed with the taxpayer's T1 return. The total employment expenses on Line 9368 of Form T777 should be entered on Line 229 of the taxpayer's T1 return. In order to claim a deduction for supplies, the taxpayer's employer must complete and sign Form T2200. In particular, the employer must complete question 9 in Part B to certify that the employee was required to pay for supplies that the employee used in his or her work. Form T2200 is not required to be filed with the taxpayer's T1 return but should be retained by the taxpayer in case the CRA requests it.

ITA 8(1)(i)(iii), *Luks*, [1958] C.T.C. 345 (Exch. Ct.), *Cuddie*, [1998] 3 C.T.C. 2232 (TCC), *Ellis*, [1998] 4 C.T.C. 2373 (TCC), *Crawford*, [2003] 2 C.T.C. 2169 (TCC), IT-352R2: *Employee's Expenses, Including Work Space in Home Expenses*, Guide T4044 under "Supplies", VDs 2003-0052451M4, 2006-0186091E5, 2008-0276151E5, 2009-0317611E5, 2011-0403621M 4

¶2520 — Tradesperson's Tools Deduction (T1: Line 229)

A taxpayer who is employed as a tradesperson may deduct up to $500 in respect of the cost of eligible tools. The maximum deduction for eligible tools is the lesser of:

(a) $500; and

(b) The amount, if any, determined by the formula: A - $1,195 (for 2018), where A = the lesser of: 1) the cost of eligible tools purchased in the year; and 2) income from employment as a tradesperson for the year (including the net amounts received in the year under the Apprenticeship Incentive Grant and the Apprenticeship Completion programs).

For the purposes of this deduction, an eligible tool (including associated equipment such as a toolbox) is a tool that is acquired for use in connection with employment as a tradesperson, has not been used for any other purpose before being acquired, is certified by the employer as being required as a condition of and for use in the taxpayer's employment as a tradesperson, and is not an electronic communication device (e.g., a cell phone), or electronic data processing equipment (unless the device or equipment can be used only for the purpose of measuring, locating or calculating).

With respect to the meaning of the term "tradesperson", in VD 2006-0216591I7, the CRA states:

> Since there is no definition of "tradesperson" in the Act, we are of the view that this term should be interpreted using its ordinary or everyday meaning. For example, The Concise Oxford Dictionary (8th edition) defines a "tradesman" as "a person engaged in trading or a trade, esp. a shopkeeper or skilled craftsman" and a "trade" as "a skilled handicraft esp. requiring an apprenticeship." The Dictionary of Canadian Law defines a "tradesperson" as "a person other than an

apprentice, who works for remuneration at any designated trade, including an employer who so works" and a "trade" as "includes industry, craft, and business, and any branch of any industry, craft or business."

Notwithstanding the latter definition of the term "tradesperson" above, we are doubtful whether any inference can be made that there is a requirement that a tradesperson be registered. In our view, the new provision would contain such a requirement if that were the intention, similar to the apprentice mechanics' tools deduction under paragraph 8(1)(r) of the Act. Accordingly, it is our view that any person engaged in an occupation that demands a certain level of skill may be considered a tradesperson for purposes of the deduction, whether the person is registered or not.

Although, in theory, a distinction could be drawn between tradespersons, as defined above, and unskilled workers who may not qualify for the new tradesperson's tool expenses deduction, in practice, it may not be necessary to be overly concerned about this issue. Namely, only tradespersons would ordinarily be required by their employers to purchase "eligible tools" that would exceed a total cost of $1,000 in a year.

¶2521 — *Claiming and Filing*

Taxpayers should enter their claim for tradesperson's tools expenses on Line 1770 of Form T777, which should be filed with the taxpayer's T1 return. The total employment expenses on Line 9368 of Form T777 should be entered on Line 229 of the taxpayer's T1 return.

In order to claim the tradesperson's tools deduction, the taxpayer's employer must complete and sign Form T2200. In particular, the employer must complete question 11 in Part B to certify that the employee bought and provided the tools that are being claimed by the employee. The taxpayer should attach to Form T2200 a list of the tools being claimed, as well as the related receipts. Form T2200, the list of tools and receipts are not required to be filed with the taxpayer's T1 return, but should be retained by the taxpayer in case the CRA requests them.

ITA 8(1)(s), 8(6.1), 8(7), Guide T4044 (Chapter 7)

¶2525 — **Transport Employees' Expenses (T1: Line 229)**

Where a taxpayer is an employee of an employer whose principal business is the transportation of goods, passengers or both (e.g., airline, railway, bus, and trucking companies), and whose duties of employment require:

- regular travel away from the municipality and metropolitan area (if there is one) where the employer's regular establishment (i.e., home terminal) is located in vehicles used by the employer to transport the goods or passengers, and

- regular disbursements for "meals and lodgings" (i.e., the employee must be required to pay for both meals and lodging) while away from such municipality and metropolitan area,

the amount so disbursed may be deducted from employment income to the extent the employee is not reimbursed and not entitled to be reimbursed.

A taxpayer claiming travel expenses is required to maintain sufficient records and vouchers to substantiate the amount claimed and to make these available for review if requested. The deduction in respect of meals is limited to 50 percent of the expense incurred by virtue of ITA 67.1. Also, the CRA does not consider expenses incurred in getting to the place where an employee normally discharges his or her duties or the cost of travelling between two or more concurrent employments to be deductible under this provision.

A deduction under this provision is permitted if the employee is required to stay away overnight and stays in their own truck (*Kasaboski*, [2005] 3 C.T.C. 2370 (TCC), VD 2005-0149621E5). In-flight meals that a pilot brought from home were found to be non-deductible in *Elwood*, 2012 CarswellNat 4196 (TCC) since the disbursements were not made "while away from the municipality". Paramedics do not qualify for a deduction under this provision according to the CRA (VD 2006-0175771E5).

As an exception to the above rules, the amount paid or payable by a "long-haul truck driver" during an "eligible travel period" is deemed to be 80 percent of the amount paid rather than 50 percent of the amount (i.e., 20 percent of an amount paid by a "long-haul truck driver" in respect of the consumption of food or beverages during an "eligible travel period" is deductible). A "long-haul truck driver" is defined as an individual whose principal business or principal duty of employment is driving a "long-haul truck" that transports goods. A "long-haul truck" is defined in ITA 67.1(5) as a truck or a tractor that is designed for hauling freight and that has a "gross vehicle weight rating" or "GVWR" that exceeds 11,788 kilograms. Pursuant to the *Motor Vehicle Safety Regulations*, GVWR means the value specified by the vehicle manufacturer as the loaded weight of a single vehicle. The *Motor Vehicle Safety Act* and the *Motor Vehicle Safety Regulations* are available on Transport Canada's website (tc.gc.ca/eng/menu.htm).

The CRA sets forth the following policies in paragraphs 3 and 8 of IC 73-21R9:

3. Employees of employers whose principal business is to transport goods, passengers, or both (such as, airline, railway, bus and trucking companies), who in the course of their work, must regularly travel away from the municipality and the metropolitan area, if there is one, where their employer's establishment to which they report for work is located, on vehicles used by the employer to transport goods or passengers, may deduct amounts they pay for meals and lodging while so away, to the extent they have not been reimbursed and are not entitled to be reimbursed for any part of the amounts deducted. This deduction is authorized by paragraph 8(1)(g) of the *Income Tax Act*.

Paragraph 8(1)(g) of the *Income Tax Act* contemplates journeys of such substantial distance and duration as to require disbursements for both meals and lodging while away from the relevant municipality and metropolitan area, if there is one. Therefore, to make a claim under paragraph 8(1)(g) of the *Income Tax Act*, employees must generally be away from home overnight in the performance of their employment duties. The deduction claimed under paragraph 8(1)(g) of the *Income Tax Act* is not intended for employees who return to their homes at the end of each day, and make disbursements for meals only as a matter of course.

However, the CRA is prepared to allow a deduction for meals only, even though no disbursement has been made for lodging, provided the duties of employment required the employee to stay away overnight and the employee can demonstrate that, rather than paying for lodging, he or she used other facilities. This may be the case where a transport employee uses a truck equipped with a sleeper cab.

A deduction for meals only may also be allowed (to the extent of a reasonable number of meals) where a transport employee, although regularly required to travel away on journeys of substantial distance and duration so as to require disbursements for both meals and lodging, occasionally travels, as part of the employment, on journeys of shorter distance and duration not requiring him or her to stay away from home overnight. Where the shorter journey is scheduled for ten hours or less, the CRA would expect the transport employee to eat breakfast and dinner meals at home, as is the case with most other employees. Accordingly, only one meal per day, namely lunch, will be permitted in these circumstances and only to those transport employees claiming meal expenses under paragraph 8(1)(g) of the Act.

When making a claim under paragraph 8(1)(g) of the *Income Tax Act*, transport employees must use Form TL2, *Claim for Meals and Lodging Expenses*, to summarize trip information. Both the employee and the employer should complete this form.

Where the conditions of paragraph 8(1)(g) of the *Income Tax Act* have not been met, the transport employee may be entitled to claim a deduction for travel expenses under paragraph 8(1)(h) of the *Income Tax Act* if all the conditions of that provision have been met . . .

8. The cost of a meal may only be claimed and a portion allowed as a deduction if the meal has, in fact, been paid for. Generally, neither paragraphs 8(1)(e), 8(1)(g) nor 8(1)(h) of the *Income Tax Act* permit a deduction for meals consumed by individuals who, though they may otherwise qualify under either of these provisions, do not pay for meals but instead carry a lunch from home to work.

For those transport employees described in paragraphs 3, 4, 5, and 6, the amount they may deduct in respect of food or beverages consumed after February 1994 is limited to 50 percent of the lesser of: the actual cost less reimbursements and non-taxable allowances, as explained in paragraph 7 above, and an amount that is reasonable in the circumstances . . .

The above limitations (in this Circular referred to as the "50 percent limitation") are in accordance with section 67.1 of the *Income Tax Act*. If the cost of food or beverages is part of a package price that includes amounts not subject to the 50 percent limitation, the employee will have to determine the value or make a reasonable estimate of the amount subject to the 50 percent limitation.

In Chapter 4 (Transportation employees) of Guide T4044, the CRA states:

To calculate your meal expenses, you can use either the simplified or detailed method, or in certain situations, the batching method. These methods are explained in this section.

The most you can deduct for meal expenses is 50% of your claim (unless you are a long-haul truck driver claiming meals for an eligible trip, as explained on the next page under "Meal expenses of long-haul truck drivers"). For example, if you use the simplified method, which is based on a daily meal rate of $17 per meal, the most you can deduct is $8.50 ($17 × 50%) for each meal.

Under either the simplified or detailed method, you can claim one meal after every four hours from the departure time, to a maximum of three meals per day. For the purposes of calculating the maximum number of meals allowed, a day is considered to be a 24-hour period that begins at the departure time.

The simplified method — This is the easiest way to calculate your meal expenses since you do not have to keep receipts for your meals, although you do have to keep a detailed list of the trips you take in a record or log book.

The simplified method is based on a meal rate of $17 for each meal. Multiply the actual number of meals you ate by $17 (to a maximum of three meals per day) and report that amount on Form TL2, *Claim for Meals and Lodging Expenses*, in the "Meals bought" column of Part 2 — Trip and expense summary . . .

The detailed method — If you choose to use the detailed method to calculate your meal expenses, you have to keep a log or record book itemizing each expense. You also have to keep receipts to support the amount you deduct. Report the actual amount you spent on meals on Form TL2 in the "Meals bought" column of Part 2 — Trip and expense summary . . .

The batching method — When you are part of a work crew, such as on a train, your employer may provide you with cooking facilities. If you buy groceries and cook meals either by yourself or as a group, each person can claim up to $34 for each day. As long as you do not claim more than this amount, you do not have to keep receipts. Report this amount on Form TL2 in the "Meals bought" column of Part 2 — Trip and expense summary.

In *Kasaboski*, [2005] 3 C.T.C. 2370 (TCC) and *Beach*, [2009] 5 C.T.C. 2001 (TCC), the Court allowed a larger per day claim than that allowed under the CRA's policy. However, in other cases, such as *Neault*, 2009 CarswellNat 3721 (TCC), *McKay*, 2009 CarswellNat 4123 (TCC) and *Kozmeniuk*, [2006] 2 C.T.C. 2356 (TCC), the CRA's rate was considered to be reasonable by the Court.

The simplified method cannot be used by self-employed truckers (see, for example, VDs 2011-0392521E5 and 2011-0392961E5).

The deductibility of travelling expenses of employees other than those working in the transport business is discussed under ¶2530 "Travelling Expenses".

¶2526 — *Claiming and Filing*

Taxpayers should complete Form TL2, *Claim for Meals and Lodging Expenses*, and enter their deduction on Line 229 of the T1 return. Form TL2 is not required to be filed with the T1 return but should be retained by the taxpayer in case the CRA requests it.

ITA 8(1)(e), 8(1)(g), IC 73-21R9: *Claims for Meals and Lodging Expenses for Transport Employees, Renko and Crawford*, [2003] 4 C.T.C. 8 (FCA), *Pepper*, [1984] C.T.C. 2694 (TCC), *Creamer*, [1976] C.T.C. 676 (FCTD), VD 2006-0174671E5

¶2530 — Travelling Expenses (T1: Line 229)

Reasonable travelling expenses paid by an employee in the course of employment may be deducted from salary or wages in certain circumstances. Travelling expenses include food, beverage, and lodging expenses, but do not include motor vehicle expenses (see ¶2455). An employee who receives a motor vehicle expense allowance is not prevented from deducting travelling expenses; however, the employee must also satisfy all of the following conditions to deduct travelling expenses:

- the employee was ordinarily required to carry on the duties of the employment away from the employer's "place of business" or in different places;

- the employee was required to pay his or her travelling expenses under the employee's contract of employment;

- the employee did not receive a tax-free allowance for travelling expenses (i.e., as a salesperson, clergyperson, or employee); and

- the employee did not claim an expense deduction for the year as a railway employee, commission salesperson, or transport employee.

The CRA provides the following guidance in paragraph 32 of IT-522R with respect to the meaning of "ordinarily required to carry on the duties of the office or employment away from the employer's place of business or in different places" for the purposes of ITA 8(1)(h) or (h.1):

(a) "ordinarily" means "customarily" or "habitually" rather than "continually," but there should be some degree of regularity in the travelling that the employee is required to do,

(b) "required" means that the travelling is necessary to the satisfactory performance of the employee's duties (it does not necessarily imply that the employer must order the employee to travel),

(c) "place of business" generally is considered to have reference to a permanent establishment of the employer such as an office, factory, warehouse, branch or store, or to a field office at a large construction job, and

(d) "in different places" generally refers to the situation where the employer does not have a single or fixed place of business. For example, a school inspector who has a number of schools to supervise and is required to travel from school to school meets this requirement. Similarly, an employee who is required to travel from building to building within the boundaries of the employer's property meets this requirement if the employer's property is very large and the distance between buildings is sufficient to justify the use of a "motor vehicle." On the other hand, where the employee is employed on a ship, the ship is the employer's place of business where the employee is ordinarily required to carry on the duties, and the fact that the ship may travel to different places is insufficient to meet this requirement ...

In paragraph 34 of IT-522R, for the purposes of ITA 8(1)(h) and (h.1), the CRA states:

(a) where for one type of travel expense, an employee receives an allowance that is excluded from income by virtue of paragraph 6(1)(b), but the employee must pay a second type of travel expense for which no allowance or reimbursement is received, the second type of travel expense will not be disallowed provided it is otherwise deductible under paragraph 8(1)(h) or (h.1). For example, where an employee while on an out-of-town business trip receives a daily meal allowance that is excluded from income by virtue of subparagraph 6(1)(b)(vii) and the employee must bear the cost of "motor vehicle" expenses, the employee will not be prevented from claiming the vehicle expenses if they are otherwise allowable under paragraph 8(1)(h.1), and

(b) where an employee receives an allowance for travel expenses that must be included in income, the employee may claim actual expenses under paragraph 8(1)(h) or (h.1) (and capital cost allowance and interest under paragraph 8(1)(j)) if the other requirements of paragraph 8(1)(h) or (h.1), and the requirement of subsection 8(10) as discussed in 58 below, are met.

In *Imray*, [1998] 4 C.T.C. 221 (FCTD), the Court held that attendance at a teachers' convention which occurred only once per year could be described as "ordinarily". In VD 2009-0334751E5, the CRA states:

In *Imray*, the taxpayer had claimed deductions for travel expenses for attending an annual teachers' convention. The CRA had taken the position that the taxpayer was not "ordinarily" required to carry on the duties of his employment away from his employer's place of business or in different places because the required level of frequency of travel did not occur. The court found that even though the taxpayer only travelled once in the particular year for employment-related purposes, the travel expenses were incurred pursuant to legal and professional obligations under the *Alberta School Act* (1988) and the taxpayer's employment contract to participate in the conference for professional development purposes. Based on these facts, in the court's view, the taxpayer met the "ordinarily" requirement and his expenses were deductible. Accordingly, where an employee in circumstances comparable to those in *Imray*, is required by his or her employer to attend an annual conference or convention for work-related purposes, reasonable motor vehicle or travel expenses will be deductible from employment income provided the other requirements under the Act are otherwise met.

It is not required that there be a written contract of employment in order for an employee to qualify for making deductions for travelling expenses; however, this provision was strictly interpreted by the Federal Court of Appeal to require a taxpayer to establish that he is contractually bound to pay the travelling expenses in question in *Cival*, [1983] C.T.C. 153 (FCA); rev'g [1981] C.T.C. 392 (FCTD).

The cost of meals is not allowed as a travelling expense under this provision, unless consumed while away for a period of at least 12 hours from the metropolitan area or municipality where the employer's establishment is located. In addition, the deduction in respect of meals is limited to 50 percent of the expense incurred by virtue of ITA 67.1. A taxpayer claiming travel expenses is required to maintain sufficient records and vouchers to substantiate the amount claimed, and to make these available for review if requested. An employee can use the simplified method described under ¶2525 "Transport Employees' Expenses" to compute meal expenses where a deduction is permitted.

In *Strong*, [2004] 5 C.T.C. 2095 (TCC), the Court held that while "travel expenses" could not include entertainment expenses (such as tickets to a sporting or cultural event, a fishing trip, or a cruise), the provision was broad enough to include the food and beverage expenses of business guests while staying away from home.

An employee cannot deduct the cost of dog boarding, lawn care, snow removal, and home security incurred while travelling for employment purposes as travelling expenses (VD 2006-0190481E5).

Unlike the provision which permits commissioned sales employees to deduct "expenses" incurred in the course of employment up to the amount of commission earned, only expenses for "travelling" may be deducted under this provision. As noted in ¶2435, "Commission Sales Employees", rather than deducting expenses to the extent of commission earnings for the year, a commissioned employee can alternatively deduct expenses under ITA 8(1)(h) (travelling expenses) and (h.1) (motor vehicle expenses) and not be limited by the amount of commission income earned. However, in such a case, the employee is limited to claiming only travelling expenses; the scope of expenses permitted under ITA 8(1)(f) (sales expenses of commission employees) is much broader. See ¶2435 for further information.

¶2531 — *Claiming and Filing*

Taxpayers should calculate their total allowable travelling expenses on Form T777 and enter the amount calculated on Form T777 on Line 229 of the T1 return. Employees should also have their employer sign and complete the applicable portions of Form T2200. Form T2200 is not required to be filed with the taxpayer's T1 return but should be retained by the taxpayer in case the CRA requests it.

ITA 6(1)(b), 8(1)(h), 8(4), 8(10), 67.1, *Dionne*, [2006] 2 C.T.C. 292 (FCA), Guide T4044 (Chapter 3), IT-522R: *Vehicle, Travel and Sales Expenses of Employees*, VD 2007-0245181E5

Chapter 3 — Dividend, Interest, and Other Investment Income

Contents

¶3100 Dividend Income (Schedule 4: Part I, Line 120)

¶3105 Meaning of Taxable Dividend

¶3110 Dividends from Canadian Corporations

¶3115 Dividends from Non-Resident Corporations

¶3120 Dividends Received by Spouse or Common-Law Partner

¶3125 Capital Dividends

¶3130 Deemed Dividends

¶3135 Dividends in Kind

¶3140 Stock Dividends

¶3145 Patronage Dividends

¶3150 Capital Gains Dividends

¶3155 Demutualization Benefits

¶3160 Securities Lending Arrangements

¶3165 Dividend Rental Arrangements

¶3200 Interest Income (Schedule 4: Part II, Line 121)

¶3205 Taxation of Interest Income (Accrual Rules)

¶3210 Definition of Interest

¶3215 Canada Savings Bonds

¶3220 Treasury Bills

¶3225 Indexed, Prescribed and Deep Discount Debt Obligations

¶3230 Interest on Bonds Transferred between Interest Dates

¶3235 Blended Payments

¶3245 Interest on Tax Refunds

¶3250 Interest Included in Damage Awards

¶3300 Other Investment Income (Schedule 4: Part II, Line 121)

¶3305 Annuities

¶3310 Life Insurance

¶3315 Mutual Fund Income

¶3320 Income Trusts and Specified Investment Flow-Through Trusts

¶3325 Royalties and Payments Based on Production or Use

¶3330 Loans to Shareholders

¶3335 Loans to Non-Arm's Length Individuals

¶3340 Transfer of the Right to Income

¶3400 Income from Trusts and Estates (Schedule 4: Part II, Line 121)

¶3410 Taxation of Trust Distributions to Beneficiaries

¶3420 Non-Resident Beneficiaries

¶3430 Non-Resident Trusts

¶3500 Foreign Investment Income (Schedule 4: Part II, Line 121)

¶3510 Offshore Investment Fund Property

¶3520 Foreign Accrual and Property Income (FAPI)

¶3530 Foreign Investment and Income Information Reporting

¶3600 Net Partnership Income: Limited or Non-Active Partners Only (T1: Line 122)

¶3610 Limited Partner Definition

¶3620 At-Risk Amount

¶3700 Deductions in Computing Investment Income (Schedule 4: Part III, Line 221)

¶3710 Carrying Charges

¶3720 Interest Expense

¶3100 — Dividend Income (Sch. 4: Part I, Line 120)

Taxable dividends received from taxable Canadian corporations are reported on Line 121 in Part II of Schedule 4, *Statement of Investment Income*, and carried to Line 121 of the T1 return.

Generally, taxable dividends will be reported on the following information slips: Boxes 11 and 25 of Form T5, *Statement of Investment Income*; Boxes 25 and 31 of Form T4PS, *Statement of Employee Profit-Sharing Plan Allocations and Payments*; Boxes 32 and 50 of Form T3, *Statement of Trust Income Allocations and Designations*; Boxes 51-1 and 52-1 of Form T5013, *Statement of Partnership Income*, and Form T5013A, *Statement of Partnership Income for Tax Shelters and Renounced Resource Expenses*.

¶3105 — Meaning of Taxable Dividend

ITA 82(1), in conjunction with ITA 12(1)(j), includes in the income of a taxpayer for a taxation year all amounts received in the year from Canadian resident corporations as, on account or in lieu of payment of, or in satisfaction of, taxable dividends.

In ITA 89(1), a "taxable dividend" is defined to mean any dividend other than:

1. a dividend in respect of which the corporation paying the dividend has elected in accordance with ITA 83(1) as it read prior to 1979 or in accordance with ITA 83(2), and

2. a qualifying dividend paid by a public corporation to shareholders of a prescribed class of tax-deferred preferred shares of the corporation within the meaning of ITA 83(1).

Thus, all dividends or deemed dividends constitute taxable dividends unless they have been paid out of the corporation's tax-paid undistributed surplus on hand, 1971 capital surplus on hand, or capital dividend account. It should also be noted that an eligible dividend must also be a "taxable dividend".

The ITA does not define what is meant by a "dividend" for the purposes of ITA 82, except to state that it includes a stock dividend (other than a stock dividend paid to a corporation or to a mutual fund trust by a non-resident corporation).

An eligible dividend is defined as a taxable dividend received by a person resident in Canada, paid after 2005 by a corporation resident in Canada, and designated to be an eligible dividend in the manner provided in ITA 89(14) (i.e., it is the designation by the corporation that makes a taxable dividend an eligible dividend). A dividend that has not been designated as an eligible dividend is considered an ordinary dividend (also referred to as an "ineligible dividend" or "non-eligible dividend").

The day on which a dividend is to be regarded as "received" for the purposes of the ITA is the date of actual receipt rather than the date on which it is declared or the record date on which shareholders become entitled to receive it (*Robwaral Limited v MNR*, [1960] C.T.C. 16, *Caldwell Trust v MNR*, [1990] 1 C.T.C. 2310 (TCC), *Horkoff v The Queen*, [1996] 3 C.T.C. 2737 (TCC)). See also *Barker v The Queen*, [1998] 4 C.T.C. 2137 (TCC) for receipt of a dividend by a person who is a beneficial but not a legal owner of the share. In *Banner Pharmacaps NRO Ltd. v. R.*, [2004] 1 C.T.C. 111 (FCA), the Federal Court of Appeal held that a dividend paid by the delivery of a promissory note was received for the purposes of former clause 82(1)(a)(ii)(A) as that was the intention of the note's maker.

ITA 12(1)(j), 82(1), 121, 248(1)"dividend"

¶3110 — Dividends from Canadian Corporations

The personal income tax system provides for reduced taxes payable by individuals in respect of dividends received from taxable Canadian corporations through a "gross-up" and dividend tax credit mechanism (provided for in ITA 82 and 121 respectively). The dividend tax credit is intended to represent a credit in respect of taxes paid at the corporate level. An enhanced gross-up and dividend tax credit is available in respect of "eligible dividends" paid to individual shareholders resident in Canada by taxable Canadian corporations. The eligible dividend rules were introduced in 2006 to eliminate double taxation in respect of distributions of corporate income subject to the general rate of corporate tax and to provide comparable tax treatment in respect different business structures.

As a result, the tax treatment of taxable dividends received or deemed to be received by an individual from a Canadian resident corporation depends on whether the dividend is an eligible dividend or non-eligible dividend.

¶3111 — *Taxable Dividends other than Eligible Dividends*

Individuals who receive a taxable dividend other than an eligible dividend (i.e., a "non-eligible" or "small business dividend) from a Canadian resident corporation in 2018 must gross up the amount of the dividend actually received by 16%. The grossed-up amount of the dividend is reported on Line 120. The individual may then claim a non-refundable dividend tax credit equal to 8/11 of the amount of the gross-up (or 10% of the amount of the grossed-up dividend). The dividend tax credit is reported on Line 425 (see ¶11080).

As a result of the reduction in the small business tax rate for 2018 and subsequent taxation years, the gross-up factor for non-eligible dividends decreased to 16% for the 2018 taxation year, and to 15% for 2019 and subsequent taxation years. The dividend tax credit rate decreased to 10% for the 2018 taxation year, and to 9% of taxable dividends for 2019 and subsequent taxation years. These changes are illustrated in the following table:

Non-Eligible Dividends	2017	2018	2019+
Dividend gross-up	17%	16%	15%
Dividend tax credit	10.5%	10%	9%

¶3112 — *Eligible Dividends*

For 2012 and later taxation years, individuals who receive an eligible dividend from a Canadian resident corporation must gross up the amount of the dividend actually received by 38%. The grossed up amount of the dividend is reported on Line 120. The individual may then claim a non-refundable dividend tax credit equal to 6/11 the amount of the gross up (or 15.02% of the amount of the grossed up dividend). The dividend tax credit is reported on Line 425 (see ¶11080).

Canadian-controlled private corporations (CCPCs) and certain deposit insurance corporations (DICs) can pay eligible dividends to the extent that the corporation has a "general rate income pool" (GRIP) balance at the end of the taxation year in which the eligible dividends are paid. The GRIP is generally intended to represent taxable income that was subject to the general corporate tax rate. If a corporation is neither a CCPC nor a DIC, the corporation can generally pay eligible dividends to the extent the corporation does not have a "low rate income pool" (LRIP) balance at the time the eligible dividends are paid. The LRIP is generally intended to represent taxable income that was not subject to the general rate of corporate tax.

An "eligible dividend" is defined in ITA 89(1) as "an amount that is equal to the portion of a taxable dividend that is received by a person resident in Canada, paid by a corporation resident in Canada and designated under subsection (14) to be an eligible dividend". Thus, for a dividend to be an eligible dividend, the dividend must be: (1) a "taxable dividend", (2) received by an individual resident in Canada, (3) paid by a corporation resident in Canada, and (4) designated as an eligible dividend in accordance with the manner set forth in ITA 89(14).

Before March 29, 2012, former paragraph (a) of the "eligible dividend" definition provided that an "eligible dividend" was a taxable dividend received by a person resident in Canada, paid after 2005 by a corporation resident in Canada and designated, as provided under ITA 89(14), to be an eligible dividend. Based on this definition, the CRA's position was that for taxation years after 2006, a corporation could not designate a fraction of a dividend paid to each shareholder to be an eligible dividend (see VDs 2006-0217891Z0 and 2010-0387541E5). As a result of amendments to ITA 89(14) and the "eligible dividend" definition, applicable to dividends paid after March 28, 2012, a portion of a taxable dividend can be designated as an eligible dividend.

Since a "taxable dividend" is defined as a dividend other than a capital dividend, a capital dividend cannot be an eligible dividend. A capital gains dividend also cannot be an eligible dividend since a capital gains dividend is deemed not to be a dividend (ITA 130.1(4)(b) and 131(1)(b)). However, under the definition of "dividend" in ITA 248(1), a stock dividend can be an eligible dividend, and where all the requirements of being an eligible dividend are met, a deemed dividend can be an eligible dividend as well. Certain dividend compensation payments are also deemed to be eligible dividends pursuant to ITA 260(1.1) and (5).

A dividend received by a beneficiary of a trust can qualify as an eligible dividend in the hands of the beneficiary. ITA 104(19) provides that where certain conditions are met, a taxable dividend received by a trust from a taxable Canadian corporation can be deemed for purposes of the ITA to be a taxable dividend received by the beneficiary of the trust from the corporation paying the dividend. Thus, an eligible dividend received by a trust can be flowed out from the trust to a beneficiary as an eligible dividend. Similarly, an eligible dividend received by a partnership can be flowed out to the partners of the partnership as an eligible dividend in the hands of the partner (ITA 96(1)(f)).

¶3112.1 — *Eligible Dividend Designation*

For a dividend to meet the definition of an "eligible dividend", among other requirements, the dividend must be designated to be an eligible dividend as provided under ITA 89(14). Pursuant to ITA 89(14), "[a] corporation designates a portion of a dividend it pays at any time to be an eligible dividend by notifying in writing at that time each person or partnership to whom the dividend is paid that the portion of the dividend is an eligible dividend". Subject to the ability to late-file a designation under ITA 89(14.1), the shareholder notification must be made when the eligible dividend is paid.

Applicable to dividends paid after March 28, 2012, ITA 89(14) was amended by replacing "designates a dividend it pays" with "designates a portion of a dividend it pays" to allow for a portion of a taxable dividend to be designated as an eligible dividend.

Applicable to dividends paid after March 28, 2012, ITA 89(14.1) was added to allow a corporation that has not made an eligible dividend designation in respect of a taxable dividend that it has paid to make a late-filed eligible dividend designation where the following conditions are met:

1. the corporation makes the designation within the three-year period immediately following the day on which the designation was first required to be made; and

2. the CRA is of the opinion that accepting the late designation would be just and equitable in the circumstances.

When determining whether to accept a late-filed designation, the Supplementary Information (Annex 4) to Budget 2012 stated that the CRA should take into account the interests of affected shareholders and the extent to which the corporation actually had income taxed at the general corporate income tax rate when the dividend was paid. In VD 2012-0445661C6, the CRA states that ITA 89(14.1) "was designed to allow relief for situations where, for example: there have been tax consequences not intended by the taxpayers and there is evidence that the taxpayers took reasonable steps to comply with the law; the request for late designation arises from circumstances that were beyond the taxpayers' control; or the taxpayers can demonstrate that they were not aware of the election provision, but took a reasonable amount of care to comply with the law and took remedial action as quickly as possible". See also VDs 2013-0495771C6 and 2013-0475261E5.

The CRA's policy related to the shareholder notification requirements is outlined in VD 2006-0217891Z0. The CRA's policies vary depending on the status of the corporation (i.e., public versus private) and the year in which the dividend is paid. In the CRA's view, a notification method that does not provide each shareholder with the exact amount of the eligible dividends to be received at the time the dividends are paid does not meet the designation requirements of ITA 89(14) (VD 2007-0249941E5). The fact than an eligible dividend must be designated at the time of payment (subject to the ability to late-file a designation) can create uncertainty since a CCPC may not know what its GRIP balance will be until the end of a taxation year. The CRA does not consider written notification on T3 and T5 slips as sufficient notification pursuant to ITA 89(14) for the payment of eligible dividends (VDs 2009-0309111E5 and 2006-0217891Z0).

ITA 12(1)(j), 82(1), 83(2), 89(1), 121, IT-67R3: *Taxable Dividends from Corporations Resident in Canada*, Gosselin, "Late-Filed Eligible-Dividend Designations Subject to Strict Three-Year Window", *Tax for the Owner-Manager*, Vol. 15-3, July 2015

¶3115 — **Dividends from Non-Resident Corporations**

A dividend received by an individual from a foreign corporation (i.e., a corporation not resident in Canada) is not grossed-up and no dividend tax credit may be claimed.

Individuals should report foreign dividend income on Line 121 in Canadian dollars. To exchange the foreign amounts into Canadian dollars, use the Bank of Canada exchange rate that was in effect on the day the income was received, or the average annual rate if the amount was paid at various times throughout the year.

Individuals who paid foreign tax on foreign investment income may claim the foreign tax as a foreign tax credit on Line 405 (see ¶11010). To the extent that the foreign withholding tax exceeds 15% of dividends paid, the excess is not deductible as a foreign tax credit; however, the amount can be claimed as a deduction from income on Line 232 (see under ¶9273).

ITA 20(11), 82(1)(b), 90, 121, 126(1), Form T2036, Form T2209

¶3120 — Dividends Received by Spouse or Common-Law Partner

An individual who is married or is in a common-law partnership can claim a tax credit in respect of a spouse or common-law partner whom the taxpayer supports. The amount of the tax credit is reduced if the taxpayer's spouse or common-law partner has income in excess of a stipulated limit (see ¶10030). ITA 82(3) permits a taxpayer whose spouse or common-law partner has earned dividends, including eligible dividends, from taxable Canadian corporations to elect to have those dividends included in the taxpayer's own income rather than in the income of the spouse or "common-law partner", thereby maximizing the spousal tax credit.

The election must be filed by the filing-due date of the taxpayer's return of income for the year; however, the election may be filed late in certain circumstances (see ITA 220(3.2) and (3.5)). In this way, the taxpayer may exclude from the income of his/her spouse or common-law partner the dividends in question and thereby take the best advantage of the spousal/common-law partner tax credit and the dividend tax credit. If an election is made under ITA 82(3), it must be in respect of *all* the taxable dividends received by the spouse or common-law partner from Canadian resident corporations; an election in respect of only part is not acceptable (*Gillis v. R.*, [1977] C.T.C. 343 (FCTD)).

ITA 82(3), 118(1), 118.8, IT-295R4: *Taxable Dividends Received after 1987 by a Spouse*, Folio S1-F4-C1: *Basic Personal and Dependant Tax Credits*

¶3125 — Capital Dividends

Generally, the non-taxable portion of certain gains of a private corporation may be accumulated in a capital dividend account and distributed tax-free to Canadian resident shareholders. A capital dividend can be paid in cash, in kind, or by way of a stock dividend. A private corporation's "capital dividend account" is defined in ITA 89(1), and is made up of the following items:

(a) one-half of the amount by which the corporation's capital gains exceed its capital losses;

(b) capital dividends received from other private corporations;

(c) one-half of net gains realized on the sale of goodwill and other "nothings"; and

(d) certain life insurance proceeds paid to the corporation;

(e) less, the total of all capital dividends previously payable by the corporation.

Capital dividends received by a Canadian resident individual are not taxable and can be excluded from income, providing the corporation paying the dividend makes a valid election under ITA 83 (the prescribed form for making a capital dividend election is Form T2054: *Election for a Capital Dividend under Subsection 83(2)*). In addition, the payment of a capital dividend does not give rise to a reduction of the adjusted cost base of the shares on which the dividend is paid.

Non-resident shareholders receiving a capital dividend from a private corporation are liable for withholding tax on the dividend (ITA 212(2)).

ITA 83, Folio S3-F2-C1: *Capital Dividends*

¶3130 — Deemed Dividends

ITA 84(1)–(4) trigger deemed dividends upon certain corporate transactions by Canadian resident corporations involving alterations of paid-up capital (PUC), distributions on winding-up, or upon the redemption, acquisition, or cancellation of shares. A deemed dividend is considered a regular dividend under the ITA and should be reported on Schedule 4.

¶3131 — *Capitalization of Surplus*

Any transaction, the effect of which is to increase the PUC of the shares of a Canadian resident corporation by more than the corresponding increase in its net assets is deemed to be a dividend paid at that time on the issued shares of the particular class. The purpose of this rule is to ensure that an increase in the PUC of a Canadian resident corporation will be treated as a dividend if such increase is accomplished otherwise than by means of a stock dividend, by a corresponding increase in the value of the corporation's net assets or decrease in net liabilities, or by a corresponding decrease in the PUC of all other classes of shares.

By way of exception, a deemed dividend does not arise upon the conversion of contributed surplus into PUC provided the contributed surplus arose on the issuance of shares (other than an issuance to which certain rollover provisions apply); on the acquisition of property from a shareholder of that class as long as the shares were not received by the shareholder as consideration for the disposition; or, on a reduction of PUC otherwise allowed by ITA 84(10) where the amount of contributed surplus converted does not exceed the amount by which the PUC was previously reduced.

The amount of contributed surplus of a public corporation that can become PUC of shares without triggering a deemed dividend is limited. Capitalized contributed surplus cannot include any amount in respect of which a dividend was paid to the shareholders of the corporation. Further, contributed surplus is reduced by the amount of any dividends paid by the corporation in excess of its retained earnings.

ITA 84(1), (10), (11), 89(1)"paid-up capital", 186(4), 53(1)(b), IT-463R2: *Paid-up Capital*, VDs 2010-0360501R3, 2010-0372181R3

¶3132 — *Distribution on Winding-Up, etc.*

If a Canadian resident corporation discontinues its business, or is wound-up, or reorganizes, and distributes any of its funds or other property to the shareholders of any class of its capital stock, those shareholders are deemed to have received a dividend from the corporation equal to the amount by which the amount or value of funds distributed exceeds the amount by which the PUC in respect of the shares of that class has been reduced by reason of the distribution. A particular shareholder's portion of such a deemed dividend is proportionate to the shareholder's holdings in the relevant class of stock. If the distribution includes a share of the corporation's own stock, the PUC of that share at that time is included in computing the value of the property distributed.

On the winding-up of a Canadian corporation, special rules under ITA 88(2)–(2.3) may apply in respect of the deemed dividend that arises under ITA 84(2). IT-126R2 discusses the meaning of "winding-up".

ITA 84(2), (5), (6), VDs 2010-0389551R3, 2010-0370551E5, 2008-0289331R3

¶3133 — *Redemption or Acquisition of Shares, etc.*

If a Canadian resident corporation redeems, acquires, or cancels in any manner any of its shares of any class (otherwise than by way of a distribution on wind-up described above), it is deemed to have paid a dividend equal to the amount by which the payment for the shares exceeds the PUC in respect of those shares, and each individual shareholder of the class is deemed to have received a dividend equal to the part of the excess that is proportionate to the shareholder's holdings in respect of that class. On a redemption, acquisition, or purchase for cancellation, the shareholder is deemed to have disposed of the share to the corporation. The shareholder may, therefore, realize a capital gain. However, the shareholder's proceeds of disposition are reduced by the amount of any deemed dividend arising on the disposition.

This provision does not apply in the case of an ordinary purchase by the corporation of its shares on the open market if the corporation acquired the shares in the manner in which the shares would be purchased by any member of the public in the open market. Also, the provision will not apply to deem a dividend to have been paid or received where shares of a predecessor corporation are converted into shares of the new corporation on an amalgamation.

ITA 84(3), (5), (6), (9), 87, 54"proceeds of disposition"(j), *943963 Ontario Inc.*, [1999] 4 C.T.C. 2119 (TCC), ITTN-33, IT-269R4, IT-291R3, Folio S4-F7-C1, VDs 2005-0112921E5, 2003-0050601R3

¶3134 — *Reduction of Paid-Up Capital*

If a Canadian resident corporation (other than a public corporation) reduces the PUC in respect of any class of its shares otherwise than by way of a redemption, acquisition, or cancellation of any shares of that class or a transaction described in ITA 84(2) or (4.1), it is deemed by ITA 84(4) to have paid a dividend to the extent that the amount paid by the corporation exceeds the amount by which the PUC in respect of those shares has been reduced. Each shareholder of that class is deemed to receive a dividend proportionate to the shareholder's holdings in respect of that class.

ITA 84(4.1) treats a payment on a reduction of PUC by a public corporation as a dividend, except where the payment is made by way of a redemption, acquisition, or cancellation of a share, or in the course of a transaction described in ITA 84(2) or 86. An exception also applies where the amount paid on a reduction of PUC may reasonably be considered to be a distribution of proceeds of disposition realized from a transaction that did not occur in the ordinary course of the corporation's business and those proceeds were derived from a transaction that occurred no more than 24 months before the return of the PUC. The rule in ITA 84(4.1) is a departure from the normal rule that PUC may generally be distributed as a return of capital.

ITA 84(4.2) and (4.3) extend deemed dividend treatment to certain transactions involving term preferred shares and guaranteed shares to which ITA 112(2.2), (2.4), or (4) apply.

ITA 84(4)–(4.4), 248(1)"specified financial institution"

¶3135 — Dividends in Kind

Dividends in kind are those paid out in the form of assets other than cash (e.g., a promissory note). The amount of a dividend in kind is considered to be equal to the fair market value of the transferred assets. A dividend in kind is a taxable dividend and is taxed as such under the ITA. The gross-up and credit mechanism applicable to taxable dividends also apply to dividends in kind, including the enhanced gross-up and dividend tax credit.

¶3140 — Stock Dividends

A stock dividend is a dividend paid by the issuance of shares of any class of the capital stock of the paying corporation (ITA 248(1) "stock dividend"). The "amount" of a stock dividend for tax purposes is generally equal to the greater of the increase in the paying corporation's paid-up capital by virtue of the payment of the stock dividend, and the fair market value of the shares paid as a stock dividend at the time of the payment (except in the case of dividends to which ITA 112(2.1), (2.2) or (2.4), 187.2 or 187.3, 258(3) or (5), or 191.1 applies).

The amount of a stock dividend is included in the shareholder's income as an ordinary taxable dividend and is subject to the gross-up and dividend tax credit provisions. Shares received as a result of a stock dividend are deemed to have been acquired at a cost equal to the amount of the stock dividend. Stock dividends are reported on a T5 information slip. Taxpayers are required to report the taxable amount of the dividend into income on Line 120.

Where a dividend is paid partly in the form of shares of the paying corporation and partly in the form of cash, the stock portion constitutes a stock dividend. The cash portion, including cash paid in lieu of the issuance of a fractional share, is subject to the usual rules regarding cash dividends.

Where shares received as a stock dividend may be "identical" to shares which the shareholder already owns, the identical property provisions in ITA 47 will be applicable for the purposes of computing the adjusted cost base of the shares (see ¶4121). Thus, the cost determined under ITA 52(3) of shares received as a stock dividend will be averaged under these rules with the adjusted cost base of other identical shares.

Where it may reasonably be considered that one of the purposes of the payment of the stock dividend was to alter significantly the value of the interest of any specified shareholder of the payer corporation, the fair market value of a share received as a stock dividend may be included in a shareholder's income under ITA 15(1.1), if, and to the extent that, such fair market value exceeds the amount of the stock dividend included in income under ITA 82(1)(a). Subject to various deeming provisions, a "specified shareholder" is a taxpayer who owns, directly or indirectly, at any time in the year, not less than 10% of the issued shares of any class of the capital stock of the corporation, or any corporation that is related to the corporation.

Shareholders may participate in a dividend reinvestment program in which the corporation does not pay dividends in cash to participating shareholders but, instead, invests the dividend in shares of the corporation on behalf of the shareholders. In these cases, shares of the corporation issued to shareholders pursuant to a dividend reinvestment program do not constitute stock dividends. The amount of the dividend that would have been paid in cash to or on behalf of a particular shareholder, if the shareholder had not participated in the program, is grossed up and included in the shareholder's income for the taxation year of the shareholder in which the cash dividend would have been paid.

In contrast to a stock dividend, a stock split is not taxable. In a stock split, there is an increase in the number of shares accompanied by a proportional decrease in the paid-up capital per share so that neither the total amount of paid-up capital nor the total amount of surplus available for distribution as a dividend changes. See IT-65: *Stock Splits and Consolidations*, for more information on stock splits.

¶3145 — Patronage Dividends

A patronage dividend is an amount paid by a cooperative corporation to customers as "allocations in proportion to patronage" (defined in ITA 135(4)). An "allocation in proportion to patronage" entitles a customer to receive payment calculated at a rate relating to the quantity, quality, or value of either goods or products sold or services rendered. A cooperative corporation is a corporation that is established for the purpose of: marketing natural products belonging to or acquired from its members or customers; purchasing supplies, equipment or household necessaries for or to be sold to its members or customers; or performing services for its members or customers (ITA 136(2)).

A patronage dividend constitutes income of the customer for the year in which it is received (subject to ITA 135.1(2) in respect of the payments of tax-deferred patronage dividends by agricultural cooperative corporations). If payment is effected by the issuance of a certificate of indebtedness or a share, it constitutes income when the certificate or share is received and not when it is subsequently redeemed. Notwithstanding this general rule, a patronage dividend does not constitute income if it relates to goods and services the cost of which was not deductible by the recipient of the dividend in computing income from a business or property.

Where tax has been withheld at source from a patronage dividend, it is the gross amount and not the net after-tax amount that constitutes the "payment". A withholding tax of 15% applies on patronage dividends in excess of $100 paid to a resident of Canada except a person exempt from tax under ITA 149 (subject to ITA 135.1(6) for payments of tax-deferred patronage payments by agricultural cooperative corporations). This tax is then applied against the customer's eventual tax liability for the year. A refund would be available if the tax withheld exceeds that liability. Patronage payments to non-residents are subject to non-resident tax under Part XIII of the ITA.

Patronage dividends are required to be reported on Form T4A slip in Box 30 — Patronage allocations (ITR 218). The amount should be included in income on Line 130, Other income (see ¶8260). Patronage dividends should not be reported as dividends and do not qualify for the dividend tax credit.

ITA 135(6), (7), 136(2), 149, 212(1)(g), *Lantagne*, [1978] C.T.C. 2233 (TRB), CRA Guide RC4157, IT-362R: Patronage Dividends

¶3150 — Capital Gains Dividends

Amounts paid to shareholders as a capital gains dividend from a mutual fund corporation, investment corporation, mortgage investment corporation, mutual fund trust, or other trust are given capital gains treatment. Therefore, these amounts should be reported on Schedule 3, not on Schedule 4, and no dividend tax credit may be claimed for the capital gains dividend (see ¶4310). Generally, capital gains dividends are dividends paid by mutual fund corporations, investment corporations, mortgage investment corporations, mutual fund trusts, or other trusts that the corporation or trust has elected to treat as a distribution out of its pool of realized capital gains.

ITA 131, ITR 2104

¶3155 — Demutualization Benefits

Demutualization is a process whereby a mutual insurance corporation converts into a corporation with share capital (i.e., policyholders become shareholders). Generally, the rules allow policyholders to receive shares in place of their ownership interest on a tax-free basis and the cost of the shares received is deemed to be nil. Cash payments and other non-share benefits ("taxable conversion benefits") received in connection with a demutualization are treated as taxable dividends paid by the insurance corporation, and therefore are eligible for the gross-up and credit mechanism.

Mutual insurance corporations that have demutualized include Canada Life, Industrial-Alliance Life, Manufacturer's Life, Mutual Life, and Sun Life.

ITA 139.1

¶3160 — Securities Lending Arrangements

A "securities lending arrangement" typically involves a borrowing of shares or debt securities to cover a "short position" or a transaction failure, which arises when securities are sold that the vendor does not own. A vendor enters into a short sale to profit from an expected decline in the value of the relevant securities. In effect, the vendor sells the securities for a specified price on a specified date, with the intention of subsequently acquiring those securities at a lower price. A short sale is thus the converse of the familiar transaction in which an investor acquires securities with the intention of selling them subsequently at a higher price.

The need to borrow securities arises on a short sale because the purchaser to whom the vendor has sold short will require delivery of the securities on the closing date. In order to make delivery without actually acquiring the securities, the vendor will borrow them from a third party lender. The borrowed securities are ultimately returned to the lender when the borrower/vendor actually acquires the securities and eliminates the short position.

Where shares have been transferred or loaned as part of a securities lending arrangement, the borrower will normally be required to provide compensation payments to the lender for taxable dividends paid on the borrowed shares during the term of the loan. In certain circumstances, ITA 260(5) applies to deem such compensation payments to be received by the lender as a taxable dividend on borrowed shares. Where this provision applies, there is a corresponding exclusion from income of a borrower who is a Canadian resident individual.

In particular, for individual taxpayers, the amount included in computing income under ITA 82(1)(a)(i) is reduced by the total of all amounts paid by the taxpayer in the taxation year that are deemed by ITA 260(5) to have been received by another person as taxable dividends. This exclusion ensures that taxable dividends received on borrowed shares by a borrower during the term of the loan are taxed only to the lender on the receipt of compensation payments.

ITA 260

¶3165 — Dividend Rental Arrangements

A dividend rental arrangement is an arrangement, the main reason for which is to enable a person to receive a dividend on a share that has been borrowed from another person, but any increase or decrease in the value of the shares is for the benefit of another person. In other words, dividend rentals involve the transfer of the right to receive a dividend on a share without also transferring all of the risk of loss and opportunity for gain in respect of the share. Dividends received on prescribed shares defined in paragraph (e) of the definition of "term preferred share", or an amount deemed to be received as a dividend in respect of an income bond or income debenture as provided in ITA 15(3), are not included in dividends subject to the dividend rental arrangement rule.

Prior to the introduction of this rule, under dividend rental arrangements, a·taxpayer that normally would invest in interest-yielding short-term debt would instead borrow or purchase for a short period a share scheduled to pay a dividend. After receipt of the dividend, the share would be returned, together with a fee for its use, to the original owner whose tax circumstances are such as to be indifferent to the form of payment (i.e., a non-taxable entity). Under the arrangement, the purchaser would not be at risk as to the value of the share and would receive a higher after-tax rate of return since the dividend would generally be received tax-free.

> Where a transaction is considered to be a dividend rental arrangement, the taxpayer is denied the gross-up and tax credit with respect to the taxable dividend received under the arrangement. As a result, the taxpayer is denied the preferential tax treatment afforded to dividends and is taxed at their normal marginal tax rate on the dividend received under a rental arrangement.

ITA 248(1)"dividend rental arrangement"

¶3200 — Interest Income (Sch. 4: Part II, Line 121)

Interest income is reported on Line 121 in Part II of Schedule 4, *Statement of Investment Income*, and carried to Line 121 of the T1 return. For most investments, interest must be reported each year as it is earned.

Interest received on bank deposits and on money loaned or invested in bonds (including Canada Savings Bonds), debentures, mortgages, promissory notes, treasury bills, guaranteed investment certificates, and similar instruments must be included in computing income (ITA 12(1)(c)). As well, transactions on account of income for debt obligations in bearer form are reported as interest income on Line 121 (e.g., where an individual keeps a treasury bill issued at a discount until it matures, the difference between the issue price and the amount cashed in is interest income).

Banks, financial institutions, and other payers of interest income are required to provide taxpayers with an information slip where the payer has paid more than $50 of interest to a taxpayer in the year. Generally, interest income from these type of investments will be reported on the following information slips: Box 26 of Form T3, *Statement of Trust Income Allocations and Designations*; Box 13 of Form T5, *Statement of Investment Income*; Boxes 50 and 55 of Form T5013, *Statement of Partnership Income*; or in Boxes 50 and 55 of Form T5013A, *Statement of Partnership Income for Tax Shelters and Renounced Resource Expenses*. Taxpayers are still required to report interest paid or credited to them in the year, even if it is not reported on an information slip. For example, interest earned on a bank account may not be reported on an information slip if it is less than $50 but it must still be included in income.

Taxpayers should report their share of interest from an investment owned jointly based on how much each taxpayer contributed to the investment. The following example is provided in the CRA T1 Guide:

Example

Sally and Roger received a T5 slip from their joint bank account showing the $400 interest they earned in 2018. Sally had deposited $4,000 and Roger had deposited $1,000 into the account.

Roger reports $80 interest, calculated as follows: $1,000 (his share)/$5,000 (total) × $400 (total interest) = $80

Sally reports $320 interest, calculated as follows: $4,000 (her share)/$5,000 (total) × $400 (total interest) = $320

Where a parent invests their own money in a child's name, the parent must report the income from those investments. However, if a parent deposited Canada child benefit payments into a bank account or trust in a child's name, the interest earned on those payments is the child's income.

Where interest is derived from foreign sources and is paid in foreign currency, it must be reported in Canadian dollars using the Bank of Canada exchange rate in effect on the day the interest was received (www.bankfocanada.ca). Taxpayers can use the annual exchange rate where amounts were paid at various times throughout the year. Interest reported from foreign sources should not be reduced by foreign taxes withheld. Instead, a foreign tax credit may be claimed for foreign taxes paid (See ¶11010).

¶3205 — Taxation of Interest Income (Accrual Rules)

Individuals must report accrued interest on "investment contracts" on an annual basis based on interest accrued to the "anniversary day" of the contract. The anniversary day of a contract is defined as one year after the day immediately preceding the date of issue and each successive one-year interval, as well as the day on which the contract is disposed of. If the investment contract is disposed of, any income earned from the previous anniversary to the date of disposition must be reported as interest in the year of disposition.The CRA's views on when interest "accrues" are set out in IT-396R: *Interest Income*.

Generally, an "investment contract" is defined as any debt obligation that is not specifically excluded by the definition provided in the ITA (as outlined below). "Debt obligation" is not defined in the ITA or at common law. Black's Law Dictionary defines a debt as a "liability on a claim; a specific sum of money due by agreement or otherwise"; and an obligation as "a formal, binding agreement or acknowledgement of a liability to pay a certain amount". Notes, bonds, and debentures would be considered debt obligations.

The following debt obligations are specifically excluded as investment contracts:

- salary deferral arrangements, as well as certain obligations specifically excluded from the definition of salary deferral arrangement in ITA 248(1);

- retirement compensation arrangements, as well as certain obligations specifically excluded from the definition of retirement compensation arrangement in ITA 248(1);

- employee benefit plans;

- foreign retirement arrangements;

- income bonds, income debentures, small business bonds, and small business development bonds;

- obligations on which an individual has earned interest on an annual or other basis, provided the individual has included the accrued interest in income at least annually;

- obligations in respect of a net income stabilization account (NISA);

- indexed debt obligations (see ¶3226); and

- prescribed contracts

The bonus or premium received on the maturity of investments such as treasury bills, stripped coupon bonds, or other discounted obligations must also be reported annually on an accrual basis.

Also included in income under the interest accrual rules are amounts that may not be identified as interest but which are received in lieu of payment of interest, or in satisfaction of interest, or on account of interest. Whether an amount is "interest" is relevant in determining whether the income accrual rules apply and in computing the capital gain or loss on a disposition of a debt. Interest need not be paid at a fixed rate, nor does the payment need to be described as interest in order to be included in income on an accrual basis. Whether an amount is in the nature of interest is dependent upon the facts of each case.

ITA 12(1)(c), 12(4), 12(11), IT-396R: *Interest Income*

¶3210 — Definition of Interest

The term "interest" is not defined in the ITA. In most cases there will be little difficulty in identifying an amount as "interest"; however, determining whether an amount is "interest" may be difficult in certain cases, such as those involving issue discounts and premiums. The CRA discusses its views on the meaning of the term interest in Folio S3-F6-C1 and VDs 2006-0180221E5, 2005-0152201E5, 2005-0154191E5, and 2000-0062337. Specifically, in paragraph 1.1 of Folio S3-F6-C1, the CRA states:

> "Interest" is not defined in the Act but has been addressed in several court decisions, including *Shell Canada Limited v The Queen*, [1999] 3 SCR 622, 99 D.T.C. 5669 (Eng.); *The Queen v. Sherway Centre Ltd.*, [1998] 2 C.T.C. 343, 98 D.T.C. 6121 (FCA); and *Miller v The Queen*, [1985] 2 C.T.C. 139, 85 D.T.C. 5354 (FCTD). As in *Miller*, interest for tax purposes is generally accepted to mean an amount that has met three criteria. The amount must be:
>
> • calculated on a day-to-day accrual basis,
>
> • calculated on a principal sum (or a right to a principal sum), and
>
> • compensation for the use of the principal sum (or the right to the principal sum).

In VD 2005-0154191E5, the CRA states:

> To be referable to a principal sum, amounts are usually determined by applying a percentage to that principal. In our view, an amount that is determined on the basis of other criteria (such as cash flow, revenue, or net profit) is not referable to a principal sum. While it is possible to create formulae under which amounts calculated on the basis of those other criteria are expressed as a percentage of the principal sum, the mere expression of such an amount in this manner does not necessarily qualify the amount as interest. Whether an "excluded amount" would be considered interest is a question of fact that would require a review of the documentation relating to a particular debt obligation.

ITA 12(1)(c), 12(3)–(9.1), Folio S3-F6-C1: *Interest Deductibility*, IT-114 (Cancelled), *Shell Canada Limited*, [1999] 4 C.T.C. 313 (SCC), *Sherway Centre Ltd.*, [1998] 2 C.T.C. 343 (FCA), *Miller*, [1985] 2 C.T.C. 139 (FCTD), *Melford Dev. Inc.*, [1982] 2 S.C.R. 504, [1982] C.T.C. 330, 82 D.T.C. 6281 (SCC), VDs 2006-0180221E5, 2005-0152201E5, 2000-0062337

¶3215 — Canada Savings Bonds

Generally, there are two types of Canada Savings Bonds: those that pay full interest every year ("R bonds") and those on which the holder does not receive the interest until the bond is cashed ("C bonds"). Taxpayers must report and pay tax on all interest accrued annually on Canada Savings Bonds, regardless of whether the taxpayer owns R bonds or C bonds. The interest will be reported in Box 13 of Form T5, *Statement of Investment Income*, received from the Bank of Canada.

Holders of Canada Savings Bonds may be entitled to a "cash bonus" or "bonus" interest, that effectively represents an increase in the interest rate payable in respect of the bond over the actual interest rate stipulated on the bond. Taxpayers must include in income an amount equal to one-half of the cash bonus, which allows the recipient to effectively treat the bonus as a capital gain taxable at a 50% rate.

ITA 12(1)(c), 12.1, IT-396R: *Interest Income*, csb.gc.ca/

¶3220 — Treasury Bills

Treasury Bills ("T-bills") are short-term debt securities issued by federal or provincial governments. T-bills are purchased at less than face value (at a discount) and mature at their face value. The difference between the value of the T-bill at maturity and the purchase price is taxed as interest income. In other words, when a taxpayer holds the debt until maturity, the difference between the purchase price and the amount the taxpayer cashes in is considered interest.

If an individual sells a T-bill before it matures, the individual may have a capital gain or loss in addition to the interest accrued at that time. The individual is required to determine the amount of interest accumulated to the date of disposition, subtract the interest from the proceeds of disposition, and then calculate the capital gain or loss in the usual way.

Example

A T-bill with face value of $20,000 is purchased on June 1, with a maturity date of September 1 (92 days). The purchase price is $19,750, giving a yield of 5.022%. The interest income is $250 if the T-bill is held to maturity. The T-bill is sold on August 1 after being held for 61 days, for proceeds of $19,975.

Interest income can be calculated in 2 ways — using the yield rate, or using the number of days:

$$\text{Yield Rate: interest income} = \$19{,}750 \times 5.022\% \times 61\text{days}/365 \text{ days} = \$165.76$$

$$\text{Number of Days: interest income} = \$250 \times 61 \text{ days}/92 \text{ days} = \$165.76$$

The capital gain or loss is calculated as follows:

Proceeds	$	19,975.00
Less: interest	($	165.76)
Net Proceeds	$	19,809.24
Adjusted Cost Base	$	19,750.00
Capital Gain	$	59.24

ITA 12(9), ITR 7000(2), IT-396R, CRA Guide T4037

¶3225 — Indexed, Prescribed, and Deep Discount Debt Obligations

¶3226 — *Indexed Debt Obligations*

ITA 16(6) and ITR 7001 govern the tax treatment of payments indexed for inflation under an "indexed debt obligation". The provisions treat the amount of any inflation adjustment under an indexed debt obligation as interest for both the holder and the debtor. Where there is an increase in an amount payable under an indexed debt obligation because of a decline in the purchasing power of money, the indexed amount is deemed to be received and receivable by the holder in the relevant taxation year as interest in respect of the obligation. The same amount is deemed to be payable in respect of the year by the debtor as interest in respect of the obligation. These deeming provisions ensure that the holder of an indexed debt obligation is required to include the indexed amount in income as interest under ITA 12(1)(c), while the debtor may deduct the same amount as interest provided the conditions in ITA 20(1)(c) are satisfied (in particular, the debtor is required to use the borrowed money for the purpose of earning business or property income).

Interest is not included in the taxpayer's income under these rules for any period of the taxation year in which the indexed debt obligation is impaired.

ITA 16(6), 16(7), 248(1)"indexed debt obligation", ITR 7001

¶3227 — *Deep Discount Debts Issued by Tax-Exempt Entities*

Pursuant to ITA 16(3), where a bond is issued by a tax-exempt body (such as a municipality) at a deep discount (other than an obligation that is a prescribed debt obligation for the purposes of ITA 12(9)), the first taxpayer that purchases the bond as a capital property is required to include the discount in computing income for the taxation year in which the purchaser acquires the obligation.

ITA 16(3) applies to obligations issued by tax-exempt entities, by non-resident persons (if not carrying on business in Canada), or by governmental authorities. In respect of tax-exempt entities, the issuance of an obligation at a discount at the expense of a higher rate of interest does not pose any adverse tax issues. Where ITA 16(3) applies, the first Canadian resident owner of the obligation is required to include in computing income for the year in which the obligation is acquired (whether directly from the issuer or from a previous ineligible owner) the full amount of the difference between the "principal amount" of the obligation and the amount for which it was issued. The income inclusion is limited to the first Canadian-resident who acquires a discount obligation as capital property.

ITA 16(3) only applies where the yield on a debt obligation exceeds 4/3 of the stated interest rate and, thereby, effectively controls the "depth" of the discount that may be offered by certain tax-exempt issuers. The provision would apply, therefore, to a debt obligation issued at a discount where no interest rate is stipulated. However, this type of obligation is also a "prescribed debt obligation" under ITR 7000(1)(a) such that a resident holder is required to include the amount of the discount in income on an annual accrual basis over the term of the obligation. To avoid double taxation, ITA 16(3) only applies to debt obligations other than those that are prescribed for the purpose of ITA 12(9).

ITA 16(3), ITR 7000

¶3228 — *Prescribed Debt Obligations*

Accrued interest determined in a prescribed manner in respect of "prescribed debt obligations" is required to be included in income for tax purposes. "Prescribed debt obligations" are defined in ITR 7000, which mandates specific accrual rules for such instruments. Prescribed debt obligations generally include bonds, debentures, notes, mortgages, or similar obligations of, or guaranteed by, the Government of Canada or similar obligations of the Government of a Province. Generally, there are four types of prescribed obligations and each type has a different formula for calculating the deemed interest. The formula determines both the amount and the timing of the deemed interest, which is treated as accruing to the taxpayer in each year the taxpayer holds an interest in the prescribed obligation and, therefore, is taxable under ITA 12(3) or (4), as applicable.

Since the rules for prescribed debt obligations bring into income on an anticipatory basis amounts that will be received or become receivable in a subsequent year, there may be an issue concerning the treatment of such amounts in the year of receipt. To avoid any double inclusion as income or capital gain that might otherwise result, amounts included in income pursuant to the rules for prescribed debt obligations will be added to the taxpayer's cost of the debt obligation (see ¶4120).

The four types of debt obligations prescribed by ITR 7000 are as follows:

(a) Non-interest bearing debt obligation — this is an obligation under which no interest is stipulated to be payable on the principal amount (e.g., zero coupon bonds, which are bonds with no coupon that are issued at a discount to face value) (ITR 7000(1)(a));

(b) Coupon-stripping and similar transactions — this is an obligation under which the taxpayer is entitled to be paid a proportion of principal that differs from the proportion of interest to which the taxpayer is entitled (e.g., stripped bonds, where the interest coupon is detached from the bond and the two are sold separately) (ITR 7000(1)(b));

(c) Deferred interest — this is an obligation under which it can be determined, at the time of acquisition by the taxpayer, that the maximum amount of interest payable in a year ending after that time is less than the maximum amount of interest payable in a subsequent year (e.g., step-up bonds or escalating term deposits, where the interest payable increases over the term of the obligation) (ITR 7000(1)(c)); and

(d) Contingent interest — this is an obligation under which the amount of interest to be paid for a taxation year depends on a contingency that exists after the year (ITR 7000(1)(d)).

¶3230 — Interest on Bonds Transferred between Interest Dates

When a bond or similar instrument is transferred from one owner to another at some time between the dates on which interest is payable on it, ITA 20(14) requires the transferor to include in computing income the interest imputable to the period following the preceding interest-paying date, computed on a pro-rata daily basis, and the transferee may deduct a corresponding amount from the interest included in the income of the transferee in respect of the bond. For purposes of ITA 12(1)(c), as well as ITA 20(14), it must be clearly established that the individual has become the legal owner of a bond in order for the individual to claim interest income therefrom and, concomitantly, to deduct interest accrued before the time of transfer or legitimate interest expenses.

ITA 12(1)(c), 20(14), *Antosko*, [1994] 2 C.T.C. 25 (SCC), *Trzop*, [2002] 1 C.T.C. 227 (FCA), VD 9228680

¶3235 — Blended Payments

A blended payment is a payment that is partly of capital nature and partly of the nature of interest or other income, such as a mortgage payment. A payment is considered "blended" only where its principal and interest components are mixed so as to be inseparable and indistinguishable. Therefore, where an arithmetic calculation will establish with certainty the respective amounts of the principal and interest components of a payment, it will not be considered "blended".

Where a portion of a payment received or to be received can reasonably be considered to be in part interest (or other amount of an income nature) and in part a capital amount, an income inclusion may arise for tax purposes. Specifically, the part of a blended payment that can reasonably be regarded as interest is deemed to be interest on a debt obligation held by the person to whom the amount is paid or payable (ITA 16(1)(a)). As a result, the amount is included in the payee's income under ITA 12(3) or (4), as applicable. The most common example of this type of payment is an instalment payment in settlement of a real estate transaction.

ITA 16

¶3245 — Interest on Tax Refunds

Interest received on overpayments of income tax refunded is required to be included in income for tax purposes.

ITA 9(1), *Terra Nova Properties Ltd*, [1967] C.T.C. 82, *Irving Oil*, [2002] 1 C.T.C. 191 (FCA); *Munich Reinsurance*, [2002] 1 C.T.C. 199 (FCA); *3850625 Canada Inc.*, 2010 CarswellNat 330 (TCC)

¶3250 — Interest Included in Damage Awards

When interest is awarded as part of a settlement for damages, the tax authorities have tended to regard it as income under ITA 12. The CRA's position with respect to interest in respect of damage awards is set out in paragraphs 12 to 14 of IT-396R and in IT-365R2. Paragraph 4 of IT-365R2: Damages, Settlements and Similar Receipts, provides as follows:

> Where an amount in respect of damages for personal injury or death has been awarded by a Court or resolved in an out-of-court settlement, no part of such amount will be income to the recipient even though the amount includes or is augmented by an amount which, pursuant to the terms of the Court order or the settlement agreement, is referred to as interest. However, where an amount that has been awarded for damages is held on deposit, the amount of interest earned will be included in the income of the injured taxpayer unless paragraph 81(1)(g.1) or (g.2) has application (see 6 below).

Where an amount that has been awarded for damages is held in trust, any interest earned on the amount is income of the trust or of the beneficiary, depending on the circumstances.

Paragraph 12 of IT-396R: *Interest Income*, provides, in part, as follows:

> Consequently, it is the Department's position that where, after 1983, an award for damages is made either by a court or by means of an out-of-court settlement which includes, or is augmented by, an amount stated, either by the court or in the terms of the settlement, to be in fact interest on all or a portion of the award, such amount will constitute interest income in the hands of the recipient thereof for all purposes of the Act. This position arises from the fact that a liability for damages is considered to originate on the date on which an injury occurred and there is therefore an amount owing to, or belonging to, the injured party from that date. It is immaterial that the amount owing was not determinable until a later date because once the right to receive damages has been established, that right exists from the time at which the injury giving rise to those damages occurred.

ITA 16(1)(a), IT-365R2: *Damages, Settlements and Similar Receipts*, IT-396R: *Interest Income*, S3-F6-C1: *Interest Deductibility*

¶3300 — Other Investment Income (Sch. 4: Part II, Line 121)

¶3305 — Annuities

Amounts received in the year as annuity payments are required to be included in income and subject to a deduction in respect of the capital element of the annuity (see discussion below). Generally, the holder of an annuity contract must include in income an amount equal to the accrued income on the contract at the end of the year. Accrued investment income on such contracts up to the annual anniversary date of the contract must be included in income in the taxation year in which the anniversary date falls. The amount of the income inclusion is equal to the accumulating fund at the end of the year in respect of the contract less the adjusted cost basis of the contract. Note that certain annuities are exempt from tax, and others are partially exempt.

Income-averaging annuity contracts were formerly available as a means of averaging certain types of income over a selected number of future years. Whenever an income-averaging annuity is sold, redeemed or otherwise disposed of, the entire proceeds are included in income for the year. Similarly, if for any reason an income-averaging annuity contract ceases to qualify as such, it is deemed to have been disposed of at that time for proceeds equal to its fair market value at that time.

As an exception to the above rules, individuals are not required to report income on an accrual basis in respect of "prescribed annuity contracts". All payments made under a prescribed annuity contract are included in income under ITA 56(1)(d) and a deduction equal to the amount of the capital element of each payment is permitted under ITA 60(a). Generally, a prescribed annuity contract for a taxation year includes an annuity contract purchased pursuant to any of the following: a registered pension plan, a registered retirement savings plan, a registered retirement income fund, a deferred profit sharing plan, a tax-free savings account, a "revoked plan", an income-averaging annuity contract, and an annuity contract, where the payment for the contract was deductible in computing the taxpayer's income by virtue of ITA 60(l) or where the contract was acquired in circumstances to which ITA 146(21) applied (i.e., acquired with funds paid out of a specified pension plan).

¶3306 — *Capital Element in Annuities*

Where the full amount of an annuity payment is included in computing the recipient's income under the above rules, ITA 60(a) permits the deduction of any portion of the payment which is considered a return of capital (the capital element). Payments from a pension plan, under a registered retirement savings plan, a registered retirement income fund or an income-averaging annuity contract, or annuities purchased for the beneficiary by the trustee under a deferred profit sharing plan (or revoked plan) have no capital element for tax purposes. If the annuity was paid under a contract, the amount considered a return of capital is determined by ITR 300. If the annuity was paid under a will or trust, the deduction will be that amount which the recipient can establish as not having been paid out of the income of the estate or trust.

ITA 12.2, 20(20), 138(12), 146(1), 146(21), 147, 148(1)(c), (e), 148(9), ITR 300–310

¶3310 — Life Insurance

Generally, interest accruing on life insurance policies is required to be reported on an annual basis unless the policy is an "exempt policy", which is designed to be exempt from the accrual provisions of life insurance policies. The "exempt policy" definition is generally intended to apply where the policy has been acquired primarily for purposes of insurance protection, as opposed to earning investment income. The amount of investment income that can be earned and accumulated in an exempt policy on a tax-deferred basis is limited.

The amount of the income inclusion is equal to the "accumulating fund" in respect of the insurance policy at the end of the year less the adjusted cost basis of the interest in the policy. For life insurance policies acquired or materially altered after 1989, investment income accrued up to the annual anniversary date of the contract must be included in income in the taxation year in which the anniversary date falls. The anniversary day of a life insurance policy is defined as one year after the policy was issued and each successive one-year interval. Where a rider is added to an insurance policy that was acquired prior to 1990, and as a consequence the insured is covered by additional life insurance, the rider is considered to be a separate insurance policy issued at the same time as the rider, unless the policy was an exempt policy acquired after December 1, 1982 and the only additional life insurance is for accidental benefit.

When a life insurance policy is disposed of other than on death, the taxpayer's actual earnings in respect of the policy may be less than the total of accrued income taxed under the accrual rules referred to above. In that case, the amount of over-accrual may be deducted in computing income in the year of the disposition. This provision applies to accrued but unreceived income where, at the time of disposition, annuity payments have already commenced.

ITA 12.2, 20(20), 148, ITR 300–310

¶3315 — Mutual Fund Income

Mutual funds are investment vehicles made up of a pool of funds collected from many investors for the purpose of investing in securities such as stocks, bonds, money market instruments, and similar assets. Mutual funds are operated by money managers, who invest the fund's capital and attempt to produce income and capital gains for the fund's investors. A mutual fund's portfolio is structured and maintained to match the investment objectives stated in its prospectus.

Income earned on the investments held in a mutual fund may include interest, dividends, foreign income, and capital gains. Income earned on the investments held in a mutual fund is allocated annually to unitholders and taxed in their hands. Income allocated to an individual unitholder from a mutual fund must be included in income, even if the distributions are not received by the individual because the individual has chosen to have them automatically reinvested in the same fund. Where the mutual fund is organized as a trust, the income will be reported on a T3 slip. Where the mutual fund is organized as a corporation, the income will be reported on a T5 slip.

An individual may also realize a capital gain or loss from mutual funds by the sale or redemption of fund units or shares (see ¶4121).

ITA 132, Info Sheet RC4169: *Tax Treatment of Mutual Funds for Individuals*

¶3316 — *Segregated Funds*

Segregated funds are a type of mutual fund, which include an insurance element that guarantees the return of principal on maturity or death. Generally, the investor purchases a contract with the segregated fund, which owns units of a mutual fund trust. Segregated funds allocate to contract holders distributions from the underlying mutual fund, as well as capital gains or losses realized from the sale of underlying mutual fund units. Unlike mutual funds, segregated funds may allocate capital losses to contract holders.

¶3320 — Income Trusts and Specified Investment Flow-Through Trusts

Publicly-traded income trusts and publicly-traded limited partnerships holding a significant amount of "non-portfolio properties" are classified as specified investment flow-through entities (SIFTs). Generally, "non-portfolio properties" include investments in Canadian real estate and Canadian resource property where the total fair market value of all such properties is greater than 50% of the total value of the SIFT entity's holdings. Cash distributions from income trusts can be made up of interest and other income, taxable Canadian dividends, capital gains, or a return of capital. The percentages allocated to each type of income may change over time. The tax treatment of cash distributions are reported to unitholders on a T3 slip and the history of taxable distributions can usually be found on the income trust's website.

Amendments were made to the taxation of SIFT trusts, applicable beginning in the 2007 taxation year for income trusts that began trading publicly after October 2006, and in the 2011 taxation year for income trusts that were traded publicly prior to November 2006. Under the old rules applicable to SIFT trusts, income trusts could deduct the income and capital gains paid to unitholders for purposes of calculating taxable income. Any remaining taxable income was taxed at the highest personal tax rate, plus applicable provincial taxes.

Under the current rules, SIFT trusts cannot deduct most of these amounts (called "non-portfolio earnings"). However, the tax rate that is applied to the "distributed non-portfolio earnings" of a SIFT trust is reduced to a rate equivalent to the corporate tax rate plus 13% for provincial taxes. The distributed non-portfolio earnings of a SIFT trust are taxed in the hands of investors as Canadian dividends eligible for the enhanced dividend tax credit (see ¶3112).

Undistributed taxable income of a SIFT trust will still be taxed at the old rates. Distributions of return of capital are not deductible to the trust and not taxable when received by investors. The treatment of a return of capital did not change (i.e., the return of capital amounts reduce the cost basis of the investor's holdings of the trust). Generally, under the current rules, SIFT trusts are taxed at a rate equivalent to the general corporate tax rate. Therefore, the effect of the new tax is to treat SIFT trusts more like corporations and eliminate their tax advantage.

A trust that meets the definition of a "real estate investment trust" (REIT) in ITA 122.1(1) is specifically excluded from the definition of a SIFT trust. As such, the prior rules continue to apply to qualifying REITs.

ITA 104(6)(b)(iv), 104(16), 120(3)(d), 122(1)(b), 122.1(1), (2)

¶3325 — Royalties and Payments Based on Production or Use

Income from royalties may be either investment income or business income. For example, where an individual receives royalties from a patent that the individual purchased as an investment, the royalties will be considered investment income and reported on Line 121 of Schedule 4. However, where an individual receives royalties as an author, the royalties will generally be considered business (or employment) income. Royalties may be reported on a T5 slip. Payments received by individuals for the use of their real estate should be reported as real estate income (see Chapter 5).

Generally, amounts received in the year by a taxpayer that are dependent on the use of, or production from, property must be included in the taxpayer's income for the year under ITA 12(1)(g), regardless of whether the amount is an instalment of the sale price of the property (except for an instalment of the sale price of agricultural land).

Although proceeds from the sale of property are normally treated as capital receipts, if proceeds are not ascertainable at the time of sale because they are calculated according to future use, ITA 12(1)(g) may apply to treat the amounts as income rather than capital. A taxpayer may enter a variety of different arrangements under which sale proceeds of property are calculated according to production or use. Paragraph 5 of IT-462: *Payments Based on Production or Use*, provides the tax consequences resulting from those arrangements:

> 5. When paragraph 12(1)(g) requires proceeds of dispositions of property to be included wholly or partly as income, subject to 3 above, the following rules apply when calculating what is income and what is on account of capital
>
> > (a) Where the payments under the agreement for sale are all based on production or use, all amounts received by the taxpayer are brought into income under paragraph 12(1)(g).

(b) Where the agreement for sale provides for payments based on production or use plus a fixed sum, the former are brought into income under paragraph 12(1)(g) and the latter is treated as proceeds of disposition.

(c) Where the agreement for sale provides for a fixed sum, with an additional amount being payable in the event that production or use exceeds a stipulated figure, the fixed sum is treated as proceeds of disposition and the additional amount, if any, is brought into income under paragraph 12(1)(g).

(d) Where the agreement for sale provides for payments based on production or use but also stipulates that there is to be a minimum sale price (or minimum annual payments), the payments based on production or use are brought into income under paragraph 12(1)(g) regardless of whether they are less than, or in excess of, the minimum. However any other payments which must be made to meet the minimum requirements are treated as proceeds of disposition.

ITA 12(1)(g), IT-462: *Payments Based on Production or Use*

¶3330 — Loans to Shareholders

Where a corporation makes a loan to a shareholder and the loan is not repaid within one year after the end of the corporation's year in which the loan was made, the amount of the loan must be included in computing the shareholder's income for the year in which it was received, unless the loan was made for one of the specific purposes referred to in ITA 15(2.2)–(2.6) (e.g., where the loan was made in the ordinary course of business and *bona fide* arrangements were made for repayment within a reasonable time). Upon repayment of the loan by an individual who was taxed on the loan, the amount of the repayment may be deducted. For a further discussion of shareholder benefits and loans, see ¶14350.

ITA 15(2), 20(1)(j)

¶3335 — Loans to Non-Arm's Length Individuals

Where an individual makes a loan to a non-arm's length individual or to a trust in which the particular individual is beneficially interested and income is earned either from the property which is loaned or from property for which it is substituted, the income may be taxed to the lender rather than to the borrower. This rule also applies where an individual or trust becomes indebted to a non-arm's length individual, for example, where property is transferred for a promissory note which bears little or no interest.

The provision applies if it is reasonable to assume that one of the main reasons for making the loan was to reduce or avoid tax by causing income on the loaned property, property that the loan or indebtedness enabled the individual to acquire, or property that the loan enabled a trust in which the individual was beneficially interested to acquire, to be included in the income of the non-arm's length individual. It also applies to substituted property. However, the rule will not apply if ITA 74.1 (the general attribution rules relating to spouses, common-law partners or minor children) applies. Further, it does not apply where there is an outright transfer or gift of property rather than a loan or transfer for debt.

Where a trust receives a loan from or becomes indebted to an individual, income that is taxable to the trust is not attributed to the individual unless the trust income is flowed through to a person beneficially interested in the trust with whom the individual does not deal at arm's length. A person is considered beneficially interested in a trust if they have any right to receive income or capital from the trust, either directly, or indirectly.

Where a trust loans funds to an individual or the individual otherwise becomes indebted to the trust and property has been transferred to the trust by another individual with whom the debtor does not deal at arm's length, the attribution rules will apply if it may reasonably be considered that one of the main reasons for the transaction was to reduce or avoid tax. The attribution rule only applies for those periods during which the trust is a Canadian resident. Although this rule does not ordinarily apply where the other attribution rules apply, income earned by a trust may be attributed to a contributor to the trust where the reversionary trust rule in ITA 75(2) applies.

If the loan or indebtedness bears interest, this attribution rule does not apply. The rate of interest charged must at least be equal to the lesser of the rate prescribed by the CRA at the time the loan was made and the rate that would have been agreed upon had the parties been acting at arm's length. Interest must be paid in respect of the loan for each year by no later than 30 days after the end of each year.

This attribution rule will apply to a loan used to repay money that was borrowed either to acquire property or to reduce an amount payable for property in the same way as if the property had been acquired directly with borrowed funds. If a loan is made on commercial terms for the purpose of allowing the borrower to repay a previous loan from the same non-arm's length lender, the attribution rules will continue to apply.

The CRA has stated that providing collateral to secure a joint line of credit for a spouse will not trigger the application of ITA 56(4.1).

For a complete discussion of the various attribution rules in the ITA, see under ¶14200. For further discussion of other avoidance rules in the ITA, including those applicable to indirect payments or transfers, non-arm's length loans, and inadequate consideration, see under ¶14300.

ITA 56(4.1), 56(4.3), ITR 4301(c)

¶3340 — Transfer of the Right to Income

Where a taxpayer has transferred or assigned the right to income to a non-arm's length person, without transferring or assigning the ownership of the property producing such income, the taxpayer is taxed on the income as if the transfer had not been made. This provision does not apply, however, where a retirement pension is assigned to a spouse or common-law partner pursuant to section 65.1 of the *Canada Pension Plan Act* or similar provincial pension plan. In such circumstances, the assigned income would be taxable to the recipient spouse or common-law partner. For a further discussion of the rules that apply to a transfer of income rights, see ¶14320.

ITA 56(2), 56(4), IT-440R2: *Transfer of Rights to Income*, VDs 2002-0149781R3, 2007-0238221E5

¶3400 — Income from Trusts and Estates (Sch. 4: Part II, Line 121)

This section contains a general discussion of the taxation of an individual's income from personal trusts that are set up during an individual's lifetime (known as *inter vivos* trusts) for family and estate planning purposes, and trusts that arise on the death of an individual (testamentary trusts).

For 2015 and earlier taxation years, a personal trust is defined for tax purposes as either a testamentary trust, or an *inter vivos* trust in which no beneficial interest was acquired for consideration. However, for 2016 and later taxation years, as a result of the elimination of graduated rate taxation for testamentary trusts, a personal trust is defined as a "graduated rate estate", or a trust in which no beneficial interest was acquired for consideration. Generally, a graduated rate estate is the estate that arises on an individual's death, and can exist for no more than 36 months. A deceased individual can only have one graduated rate estate. A testamentary trust cannot be a graduated rate estate (see VD 2014-0553181E5).

Personal trusts can be contrasted with the various types of public or commercial trusts, such as mutual fund trusts and income trusts that were discussed above.

¶3410 — Taxation of Trust Distributions to Beneficiaries

¶3411 — *Income Distributions to Beneficiaries*

Income earned in a personal trust, such as a family trust, will be taxable to the beneficiary if the income is paid to the beneficiary in the year, or the income becomes "payable" to the beneficiary in the year. Income becomes "payable" to a beneficiary when the beneficiary is entitled to enforce payment of the income, although the beneficiary does not need to actually enforce the payment. Generally, income is payable where the beneficiary has the absolute right to the income, and there is no restriction on its disposition, use or enjoyment. In order to determine whether the income of a trust has become payable to its beneficiaries, it is necessary to examine the trust document to determine whether payments of income are discretionary or non-discretionary.

An income distribution is discretionary where the terms of the trust do not force the income to be distributed or withheld but, instead, confer the authority on the trustees to make a distribution. Where a distribution of income is discretionary, income is payable to a beneficiary if the following conditions are met:

- The trustees have exercised their discretion before the end of the trust's taxation year,

- The exercise of discretion is required to be irrevocable with no conditions attached to the beneficiaries' entitlement to enforce payment of the amount in the year,

- The allocation to each of the various beneficiaries, where applicable, must have been set (whether as a fixed percentage, a fixed amount, or all of the income), and

- The beneficiaries must have been advised of the trustees' decision during the taxation year.

An income distribution is non-discretionary where the trustees are expressly obliged under the terms of the trust to distribute income or to withhold income in some measure.

Generally, where a trust provides that the income of the trust must be paid to a beneficiary, the income is payable at the time the payment must be made, regardless of whether the trustees make the payment. However, if the amount cannot be ascertained during the taxation year due to a contingency or event occurring after that time, then the income will not be payable. In the case of an estate, income will be payable where the income is in the estate, and the only reason that the beneficiary cannot claim the income is because it is the first 12 months of the administration of the estate (i.e., the "executor's year"). Income will not be treated as payable where the income is in the estate, but the administration of the estate is not complete, or if the estate or trust is not able to distribute income as a result of an ongoing dispute.

If the trust document confers a power on the beneficiary to force the trustee to pay out income from the trust, the existence of that power will not make the income of the trust payable. Similarly, a clause that confers a power on the beneficiary to amend the trust deed to allow access to income will not, by itself, make the income payable. As well, where a beneficiary has the right to demand payment which is subject to the approval of a third party appointed under the terms of a trust, then income will not be payable. In each of these instances, however, the income would become payable upon the exercise of the discretion or power.

¶3412 — Capital Distributions to Beneficiaries

Generally, distributions of capital made by a personal trust (other than a qualified spousal or common-law partner trust) to a Canadian resident beneficiary in satisfaction of the beneficiary's capital interest in the trust are not taxable; and, therefore, are not required to be reported by the beneficiary on his or her T1 return. In other words, capital property is allowed to "roll-out" of the trust on a tax-deferred basis to Canadian resident beneficiaries.

A Canadian resident beneficiary is deemed to have acquired the property at the trust's adjusted cost base for non-depreciable capital assets, and at the UCC for depreciable capital assets, which are received as a distribution in satisfaction of the beneficiary's capital interest. Specifically, the capital beneficiary is deemed to have acquired depreciable capital property at its original cost to the trust and to have deducted the CCA which the trust deducted. As a result, capital gains and recaptured CCA on the property will not be realized for tax purposes until the beneficiary disposes of the property.

There is an exception to the "roll-out" of capital property when a Canadian resident trust distributes property, including certain types of taxable Canadian property, to a non-resident beneficiary in satisfaction of all or part of the non-resident beneficiary's capital interest in the trust. In this case, the trust is deemed to have disposed of the property for proceeds equal to the fair market value of the property at the time of the disposition. This ensures that gains which accrue in the trust while the property is owned in Canada do not escape Canadian tax.

¶3413 — *Flow Through of Income*

Generally, for Canadian income tax purposes, income that flows through a trust to a Canadian resident beneficiary loses its character unless a specific provision allows the income to maintain its character in the beneficiary's hands. There are various provisions in the ITA which allow trustees to make a designation for income such as capital gains and dividend income to retain its character in the hands of a beneficiary.

Taxable capital gains earned by a Canadian resident trust can be designated as being the taxable capital gains of a beneficiary under ITA 104(21), thereby retaining their character when distributed to beneficiaries. Retaining the character of taxable capital gains may be advantageous where the beneficiary has capital losses in the year, or the property disposed of by the trust is qualified farm property or qualifying small business corporation shares and the capital gains exemption is available for use by the beneficiary. To be eligible for the designation, both the trust and beneficiary must be resident in Canada, and the income must be paid or payable to the beneficiary in the year. The designation does not have to be for the full amount of the taxable capital gains but can be for a portion only.

Taxable dividends paid to a trust by a taxable Canadian corporation can be designated to a Canadian resident beneficiary, and thereby, retain their character as taxable dividends. The designation to the beneficiary cannot be contrary to the terms of the trust and must be reasonable in the circumstances. The dividends retain their character for the purposes of dividend gross-up and dividend tax credit. The dividends do not retain their character for the purpose of non-resident withholdings when distributed to non-resident beneficiaries. It is not required to designate taxable dividend income on a pro-rata basis to beneficiaries unless required to do so under the terms of trust.

Capital dividends can also be designated to a beneficiary, and thereby, retain their character as capital dividends.

¶3414 — *Designation of Income under 104(13.1) or (13.2)*

As discussed above, income paid out by a trust to a Canadian resident beneficiary is generally included in the beneficiary's income for tax purposes (and deducted from the income of the trust). As an exception, the ITA contains provisions that allow income to be paid out to an individual, while a designation is made under which the income is deemed to be retained and taxed in the trust, rather than to the individual who received the income.

ITA 104(13.1) and (13.2) provide a mechanism for Canadian resident trusts to designate to beneficiaries their share of the portion of the trust's actual income or capital gains distributions which have not been deducted in calculating its income for the year. Such designated amounts are deemed not to have been paid or payable in the year by the trust for tax purposes, with the result that such amounts will neither be deductible to the trust nor taxable in the hands of the beneficiaries.

> New ITA 104(13.3) provides that a designation by a trust under ITA 104(13.1) or (13.2) to tax distributed income or capital gains in the trust rather than in the beneficiaries' hands can only be used after 2015 to the extent that the trust's taxable income will remain nil. As a result, for 2016 and later taxation years, a trust can only make a designation under ITA 104(13.1) or (13.2) to tax distributed income or capital gains in the trust to the extent that the trust has unutilized loss carryforwards.

ITA 104(13.1)–(13.3), (19)–(21), Part XIII, Guide T4013, IT-286R2: *Trusts — Amount Payable*, IT-381R3: *Trusts — Capital Gains and Losses and the Flow-Through of Taxable Capital Gains to Beneficiaries*, IT-524: *Trusts — Flow-through of taxable dividends to a beneficiary after 1987*

¶3420 — Non-Resident Beneficiaries

¶3421 — *Income Distributions*

Income paid or distributed from an estate or trust to a non-resident beneficiary does not retain its identity or character. Such amounts are treated as income from an estate or trust.

Part XIII of the ITA imposes a 25% withholding tax on payments of income from an estate or trust to a non-resident beneficiary. The withholding tax must be withheld by the trustees and remitted to the Receiver General by the fifteenth of the month following the month of payment. The 25% withholding tax may be reduced where Canada has a tax treaty with another contracting state. For example, the Canada-U.S. Tax Convention reduces the withholding tax on estate and trust income to 15%. No withholding is required on distributions to U.S. residents where the income is earned from a source outside Canada.

ITA 212(1)(c), 212(11), 215(1), IT-465R: *Non-Resident Beneficiaries of Trusts*

¶3422 — *Capital Distributions*

When a non-resident beneficiary receives property in satisfaction of all or part of his income interest in a Canadian resident trust, the proceeds of disposition in excess of the cost of the interest is generally considered to be income to the non-resident beneficiary.

Similarly, where trust property is distributed to a non-resident beneficiary in satisfaction of all or part of the non-resident beneficiary's capital interest in the trust, the trust is deemed to have disposed of such property at its fair market value and the beneficiary is similarly deemed to have acquired the property at fair market value. There is no tax-deferred roll-out of capital property to a non-resident beneficiary, as there would be to a Canadian resident beneficiary. As a result of the distribution, the non-resident beneficiary has a disposition of their capital interest in the trust, which is generally subject to 25% withholding tax by the trustee.

ITA 107(5), 115(1)(a)(iv), 227(9), VD 2004-0083201E5

¶3430 — Non-Resident Trusts

A trust which is a non-resident of Canada based on common law may be deemed to be Canadian resident under ITA 94.

¶3431 — *Former Section 94*

Former ITA 94 was applicable to trust taxation years ending before January 1, 2007. Generally, former ITA 94 deemed a non-resident trust to be a Canadian resident trust, and therefore, subject to Canadian tax on its worldwide income, where the non-resident trust met both of the following two conditions: (1) the trust had a Canadian resident beneficiary; and (2) there was a Canadian resident contributor to the trust who was related to a Canadian resident beneficiary or was an uncle, aunt, niece, or nephew of a Canadian resident beneficiary. Both conditions must have been met at some time in the taxation year of the trust to result in the trust being deemed resident in Canada. There was an exemption for Canadian resident contributors who were resident in Canada for less than 60 months in total or who were not resident in Canada at any time in the prior 18 months.

¶3432 — *Current Section 94*

Generally, current ITA 94 applies to trust taxation years ending after December 31, 2007. Under current ITA 94, a non-resident trust is deemed to be a Canadian resident trust, and therefore, subject to tax on its worldwide income, where the trust meets either of the following conditions: (1) the trust has a Canadian resident beneficiary; or (2) there is a Canadian resident contributor to the trust. Where the trust has received contributions from both Canadian residents and non-residents, then only income in respect of property received from Canadian residents (the "resident portion") will be taxable.

A "resident contributor" to a trust at any time is a person, that is, at that time, both resident in Canada and has made a contribution to the trust. However, it does not include an individual who has not, at that time, been resident in Canada for more than 60 months.

A "contribution" is defined as a transfer or loan (other than an arm's length transfer) of property to the trust by the particular person. A transfer includes a gift as well as a sale for consideration. The definition of "contribution" is extremely broad, such that it appears to include almost any transaction whereby value is created for the benefit of a trust, with the exception of an "arm's length transfer". Generally, the definition of an "arm's length transfer" requires not only arm's length terms, but also a situation analogous to an arm's length relationship.

Generally, a "resident beneficiary" is a person that is a Canadian resident beneficiary of the trust, where at that time there is a "connected contributor" to the trust. A "connected contributor" to a trust is a person (including a person who has ceased to exist) who has made a contribution to the trust, but does not include: (1) an individual who was resident in Canada for less than 60 months in total during the individual's lifetime; or (2) a person whose contribution is made at a "non-resident time", which is a time at which the person is non-resident and has not been a Canadian resident for the preceding five years, and does not become a Canadian resident within five years (reduced to 18 months for testamentary trusts). There are various limited exceptions (e.g., for foreign commercial trusts).

A trust ceases to be resident in Canada at any time where there is neither a resident contributor nor a resident beneficiary.

¶3433 — *Taxation of Non-Resident Trusts*

A non-resident trust that is not deemed to be resident in Canada under ITA 94 is taxed in Canada only on income from businesses carried on by the non-resident trust in Canada and taxable capital gains from the disposition of taxable Canadian properties (other than treaty protected properties). However, where a non-resident trust is deemed to be resident in Canada under ITA 94, the non-resident trust will be subject to Canadian tax on its worldwide income as if it were a Canadian resident person.

For purposes of calculating the trust's income, where a trust has received contributions from both Canadian residents and non-residents, the trust's property will be divided between the "resident portion" and "non-resident portion". The "non-resident portion" of a trust means all property held by the trust to the extent that it is not at that time part of the "resident portion" of the trust. Generally, contributions to the trust will form part of the "resident portion" of the trust to the extent that they were made by current or former residents of Canada. Special rules apply for purposes of computing the foreign tax credit and foreign tax deduction of a deemed resident trust.

Like normal Canadian resident trusts, deemed resident trusts can claim a deduction for amounts that are paid or payable to a beneficiary; however, the amount of deductions that may be claimed by a deemed resident trust is limited if the distribution is made to a non-resident beneficiary.

ITA 94, 104, 115, Folio S6-F1-C1: *Residence of a Trust or Estate*

¶3500 — Foreign Investment Income (Sch. 4: Part II, Line 121)

Foreign interest and dividend income received by an individual are reported on Line 121 in Canadian dollars. The individual may use the Bank of Canada exchange rate that was in effect on the day he or she received the income, or the average annual rate if the amount was paid at various times throughout the year (www.bankofcanada.ca).

Income from foreign investments may be reported on another type of information slip (e.g., U.S. investment income is reported on IRS Form 1099). Where a taxpayer paid foreign tax on foreign investment income, the taxpayer can claim the foreign tax as a foreign tax credit on Line 405 (see ¶11010), or as a deduction from income on Line 232 (see ¶9273). It is generally more advantageous to claim the foreign tax as a tax credit. Because both the credit and the deduction are subject to limitations, taxpayers should make sure that the rate used to calculate foreign tax withheld does not exceed the applicable treaty rate.

¶3510 — Offshore Investment Fund Property

In certain circumstances, an individual who holds an interest in an offshore investment fund property must include an amount in income on Line 121 in respect of the property even if there is no income distribution from the foreign investment. The rules governing investments in offshore investment fund properties are contained in ITA 94.1. Generally, ITA 94.1 is an anti-avoidance provision directed at taxpayers who invest in offshore investment funds that derive their value primarily from certain portfolio investments, where one of the main reasons for the investment in the fund is to reduce or defer the tax which would otherwise have applied in respect of the portfolio income had such income been earned directly by the taxpayer. Where the conditions for the application of ITA 94.1(1) are met, the taxpayer is required to include in computing income for the year an amount equal to the "designated cost" of the investment in the offshore investment fund at the end of each month multiplied by a prescribed rate of interest under Part XLIII of the ITR for the relevant period plus 2%.

ITA 94.1(1) applies where three conditions are met:

1. a taxpayer holds or has an interest in a share of the capital stock of, an interest in or a debt of a "non-resident entity" (ITA 94.1(2)), or an interest in or a right or option to acquire such a share, interest or debt (para. (a));

2. the above described property may reasonably be considered to derive its value, directly or indirectly, primarily from specified portfolio investments listed in ITA 94.1(1)(b) (para. (b)); and

3. it may reasonably be concluded, having regard to all the circumstances, including those enumerated in ITA 94.1(1)(c) to (e), that one of the main reasons for the taxpayer's acquiring, holding or having an interest in the offshore investment fund property was to derive a benefit from portfolio investments in specified assets in such manner that the taxes, if any, on the income, profits and gains from such assets for any particular year are significantly less than the tax that would have been applicable under Part I of the Act if the income, profits and gains had been earned directly by the taxpayer (para. (c)).

In *Gerbro Holdings*, 2016 CarswellNat 3955 (TCC), the Court found that a significant reduction of Canadian tax was not "one of the main reasons" that a privately-held Canadian investment company made certain offshore hedge fund investments. In the case, the Court held that the hedge fund investments at issue primarily derived their value from portfolio investments, even though the investment portfolio was actively managed using sophisticated trading strategies. After concluding that the tests in ITA 94.1(1)(a) and (b) were met, the Court stated that the motive test in ITA 94.1(1)(c) is not a purely subjective test, and that "a finding as to intention and the importance of an intention is a factual determination intrinsically linked to the evidence provided at trial" (para. 115). With respect to the case at hand, the Court concluded that the dominant reasons for Gerbro's offshore hedge fund investments were "compelling business reasons" (see paras. 168–173) as well as the fund managers' reputations (para. 159). Thus, the Court found that "[t]he nature, organization and operation of the Funds and the characteristics of Gerbro's interests therein [did] not clearly point to tax deferral being a main reason for investing", such that ITA 94.1 did not apply (para. 160). Notably, the hedge funds invested in companies resident in low tax-rate jurisdictions.

ITA 94.1, Leslie, "*Gerbro* — Makes a Strong Case for Documenting "Main Reasons"", *Tax Hyperion* (Taxnet Pro), Vol.13-9, Sept. 2016, Rabinovitch, "*Gerbro Holdings* case", McCarthy Tétrault *International Tax Newsletter* (Taxnet Pro), Nov. 2016

¶3520 — Foreign Accrual Property Income (FAPI)

The "foreign affiliate" (FA) taxation regime governs the tax treatment of earnings of, and distributions from, an FA of a Canadian-resident taxpayer. The FA regime has two main components; the surplus rules and the "foreign accrual property income" (FAPI) rules. ITA 95 provides definitions applicable to the FA taxation regime and also contains the rules concerning what types of income constitute FAPI. ITA 91 contains the rules that impute FAPI to a Canadian resident taxpayer and the rules that provide recognition for foreign taxes already imposed on FAPI, generally ensuring that FAPI is not taxed a second time when it is distributed to the Canadian taxpayer. The surplus rules govern the tax treatment of dividends received by a Canadian-resident corporate shareholder from an FA.

The FAPI rules are generally intended to thwart the use of so-called tax havens to avoid Canadian tax on passive income earned by certain FAs. The FAPI rules also apply to certain income generally considered to have been diverted from Canada (these rules are commonly referred to as the base erosion rules). Generally, where a non-resident corporation is a "controlled foreign affiliate" (CFA) of a Canadian taxpayer, the Canadian taxpayer (whether corporate or individual) is deemed to have earned FAPI of that CFA as it is earned. In other words, Canadian taxation may arise in respect of FAPI of a CFA even if the income has not been distributed by the CFA to the Canadian taxpayer (by way of a dividend or otherwise).

The FAPI rules are not intended to apply to legitimate active business operations of FAs; however, many of the rules are broad in scope and can impede *bona fide* business transactions.

Generally, with certain exceptions, FAPI is computed in accordance with the rules under the ITA. FAPI includes income from property that is not incidental to an active business; income from property (such as interest, dividends, royalties, and rents) that is derived from an "investment business" (which is a business with fewer than six full-time employees actively engaged in the business, the principal purpose of which is to derive income from property); certain types of income considered to be diverted from Canada and deemed to be income from a business other than an active business under the base erosion rules; one-half of capital gains realized on the disposition of property other than "excluded property" (excluded property generally includes property principally used in an active business of an FA); and income from a "non-qualifying business" (which is income earned in a country with which Canada has neither a tax treaty nor a comprehensive tax information exchange agreement within five years of requesting to enter into such an agreement). Significant items excluded from FAPI include income from an active business, income from property that is directly or indirectly attributable to the active business operations of another FA of the Canadian taxpayer (in which the taxpayer has a "qualifying interest") that is deemed to be income from an active business under certain recharacterization rules, and gains and losses related to the acquisition and disposition of "excluded property".

ITA 91, 95, ITR 5900–5910

¶3530 — Foreign Investment and Income Information Reporting

In addition to reporting foreign investment income on the T1 return, taxpayers may be required to file the following foreign reporting forms in respect of a taxation year:

1. Form T1135: *Foreign Income Verification Statement* (see ¶3531)

2. Form T1134: *Information Return Relating to Controlled and Not-Controlled Foreign Affiliates* (see ¶3532)

3. Form T1141: *Information Return in Respect of Transfers or Loans to a Non-Resident Trust* (see ¶3533)

4. Form T1142: *Information Return in Respect of Distributions From and Indebtedness to a Non-Resident Trust* (see ¶3534)

Substantial penalties may be levied in respect of a failure to file foreign reporting forms by the filing-due date or for knowingly or under circumstances amounting to gross negligence making false statements or omissions in any of the information returns.

¶3531 — *Foreign Income Verification Statement (Form T1135)*

Individuals who own, or hold a beneficial interest in, "specified foreign property" with an aggregate "cost amount" (ITA 248(1)) of at least CAD$100,000 at any time in the taxation year must report and provide details of these holdings annually by filing Form T1135, *Foreign Income Verification Statement*. Note that if the total cost of all specified foreign properties owned at any time during the year exceeds $100,000, then Form T1135 must be filed, reporting all specified foreign properties held during the year, even if some or all of the property was sold before the end of the year. Form T1135 is due for filing at the same time as the taxpayer's T1 return for the year. Individual taxpayers can file Form T1135 electronically for the 2014 and subsequent taxation years.

The CRA implemented changes to Form T1135 for 2015 and later taxation years (see canada.ca/en/revenue-agency under "Form T1135 — Reporting for 2015 and later tax years"). The changes allow individuals who hold specified foreign property with a total cost amount of less than $250,000 throughout the year to report under a simplified reporting method, rather than providing the detail of each property. Accordingly, taxpayers with an interest in specified foreign property with a total cost in excess of $100,000 but less than $250,000 are only required to complete the simplified information reporting in Form T1135 Part A, while taxpayers who own specified foreign property with a total cost of $250,000 and above are required to complete the detailed reporting in Form T1135 Part B.

Individuals can electronically file Form T1135 for the 2014 and later taxation years. Form T1135 can also be paper-filed with the CRA, either attached to the paper-filed tax return, or separately by the filing due date of the T1 return, and mailed to: Ottawa Technology Centre, Data Assessment and Evaluations Program, Validation and Verification Section, Foreign Reporting Returns, 875 Heron Road, Ottawa ON K1A 1A2. See also the Filing Requirements Quick Reference Table at ¶1410.

For purposes of Form T1135, "specified foreign property" includes:

- Funds and intangible property held outside Canada (e.g.; foreign bank accounts)

- Shares of Canadian corporations on deposit with a foreign broker

- Shares of non-resident corporations held with a Canadian or foreign broker

- Indebtedness owed by non-residents

- Real property located outside Canada, other than personal use property and real property used in an active business, including the cost of any improvements made to the property (e.g., foreign rental property)

- Interests in mutual funds that are organized in a foreign jurisdiction

- Interests in non-resident trusts that were acquired for consideration

- Precious metals, gold certificates, and futures held outside Canada

- Patents, copyrights or trademarks held outside Canada

- An interest in, or a right with respect to, an entity that is non-resident

For purposes of Form T1135, "specified foreign property" does not include:

- Property used or held exclusively in the course of carrying on an active business

- Personal-use property (e.g., vacation property used primarily as a personal residence)

- An interest in a U.S. Individual Retirement Account

- An interest in a non-resident trust that was not acquired for consideration

- An interest in a tax-exempt non-resident trust providing pension, retirement or employee benefits primarily to non-resident beneficiaries

- An interest in a partnership that is a specified Canadian entity

- A right with respect to, or indebtedness of, an authorized foreign bank enforceable at a Canadian branch

- An interest in, or right to acquire, excluded property

The CRA considers the following types of property to be specified foreign property: a debt owed to a partner by a partnership that includes non-resident partners (VD 2013-0484461I7), digital currency held outside Canada (VD 2014-0561061E5), an interest in a foreign partnership that holds digital currency (VD 2014-0561061E5), an interest in a foreign pension fund which operates as a trust (VD 2015-0595461E5), a vacant rental apartment building (VD 2015-0614371E5), and a mineral right situated outside Canada (VD 2016-0631181I7).

Note that, generally, taxpayers who are joint owners of specified foreign property will determine if the $100,000 cost limit has been exceeded based on their share of the cost amount of the property. At the 2015 CTF Conference CRA Roundtable, the CRA provided guidance regarding Form T1135 reporting requirements where specified foreign property is jointly held by spouses (VD 2015-0610641C6). In the first situation, A and B (who are spouses) intend to purchase a specified foreign property with a cost of $150,000 as joint property. First, A gifts $75,000 to B, and then each of A and B pays $75,000 to jointly acquire the property. Neither A nor B has any other specified foreign property. In this situation, the CRA stated that neither spouse would be required to file Form T1135, as each spouses share of the specified foreign property should be compared to the reporting threshold. In the second situation, A and B intend to increase their joint investment in the specified foreign property from $150,000 to $400,000. To effect this, A gifts another $125,000 to B, and then each of A and B pays $125,000 to jointly acquire the additional property. In this example, the CRA stated that both spouses would be required to file Form T1135.

In VD 2015-0595461E5, the CRA states that "where it is not possible to determine the cost amount of a specified foreign property, taxpayers should use their best efforts to reasonably estimate the cost amount of the property".

It is the CRA's view that the specified foreign property reporting rules are independent of any reporting requirements with respect to the attribution rules. Accordingly, individuals should report their ownership and share of income and/or gains/losses with respect to specified foreign property on Form T1135 based on their ownership interest in the underlying property and without consideration given to the attribution rules (VD 2016-0669081E5). Where an individual becomes a resident of Canada during a taxation year and must file Form T1135, the reporting period is the individual's entire taxation year, not just the period when the individual is a Canadian resident. However, when determining whether an individual must file a Form T1135 for a taxation year, the period in the year during which the individual is not a resident of Canada is excluded from the analysis (see VD 2015-0611141E5).

There are certain penalties that are applicable for failure to file Form T1135 by the reporting deadline, or for making a false statement or omission with respect to the required information (see the Penalties Quick Reference Table at ¶1420). A T1135 late-filing penalty assessed under ITA 162(7) was cancelled in *Douglas*, 2012 CarswellNat 479 (TCC) based on a judge-made due diligence defence. The case involved a low-income individual who did not owe tax for the year. However, the penalty was upheld in *Seabrook*, 2009 CarswellNat 3310 (TCC), *Leclerc*, 2010 CarswellNat 1627 (TCC), *Sandler*, [2010] 5 C.T.C. 1 (FC), and *Canwest Communications*, [2012] 1 C.T.C. 207 (FCA). The CRA must apply the penalty under ITA 162(7) automatically; ITA 220(3.1) does not allow the Minister to waive the penalty for taxation years ending more than 10 years before a voluntary disclosure is made (VD 2017-0708511C6).

ITA 162(10) imposes a penalty on a person or partnership that is required to file Form T1135 for a taxation year or a fiscal period and, knowingly or under circumstances amounting to gross negligence, fails to file that return as and when required. ITA 162(10.1) imposes an additional penalty on the person or partnership if the return is more than 24 months late. With respect to the penalty formula contained in ITA 162(10.1), in VD 2015-0590681I7, the CRA takes the position the penalty should be computed based on the highest of the total costs of all specified foreign property during the year, rather than on the total of the highest cost of each specified foreign property during the year.

The filing deadline for Form T1135 is the same as for the filing of the Part I return, and any assessment for failure to file on time pursuant to ITA 162(7) must be made within the normal reassessment period for Part I tax, unless one of the exceptions in ITA 152(4) applies (e.g.; the taxpayer has made a misrepresentation that is attributable to neglect, carelessness or wilful default) (VDs 2015-057277I7, 2016-0641511C6). In the CRA's view, the failure to file Form T1135 constitutes a misrepresentation for the purposes of ITA 152(4)(a)(i); however, whether such misrepresentation is attributable to neglect, carelessness, wilful default or fraud is a question of fact. Generally, the Minister would have to prove that the taxpayer made an error in failing to file the Form T1135 and, although that error may have been made in good faith, it was an error that a prudent and conscientious person would not have made (VD 2016-0645001C6).

ITA 233.3, canada.ca/en/revenue-agency under "Questions and answers about Form T1135", VDs 2016-0639481E5 (a co-owner of a specified foreign property has a reporting obligation regardless of whether the co-owner made any financial contribution towards the acquisition of the property), 2015-0610641C6 (reporting in respect of jointly held property), 2015-0611141E5 (the reporting period under ITA 233.3(3) applies with respect to the reporting entity's taxation year), 2016-0645001C6 & 2015-057277I7 (penalty for failure to file T1135), 2014-0529371E5 (emigration year), May 2016 Alberta CPA/CRA Roundtable, Q.17 (T1135 VDP submissions), 2015-0588971C6 (ITA 220(3.1) does not allow the CRA to waive a late filing penalty under ITA 162(7) for taxation years that end more than 10 years before the VD)

¶3532 — Information Return Relating to Controlled and Not-Controlled Foreign Affiliates (Form T1134)

Applicable for 2011 and later taxation years, Forms T1134A and T1134B were combined into one form, T1134, *Information Return Relating to Controlled and Not-Controlled Foreign Affiliates*. Form T1134 is required to be filed for each foreign affiliate (i.e., a non-resident corporation or non-resident trust) of the taxpayer that is either a controlled foreign affiliate or non-controlled foreign affiliate at any time in the year. Form T1134 is in supplement/summary format. Individuals must complete the summary sheet and a separate supplement for each foreign affiliate.

Individuals are not required to file Form T1134 where the individual's total cost amount at any time in year of the interest in all foreign affiliates was less than $100,000 and the foreign affiliate is "dormant" or "inactive" for the affiliate's taxation year ending in the individual's taxation year. For purposes of completing Form T1134, a dormant or inactive foreign affiliate means one that had gross receipts (including proceeds from the disposition of property) of less than $25,000 in the year; and at no time in the year had assets with a total fair market value of more than $1,000,000. For the purpose of completing Form T1134, the definition of gross receipts refers to any receipt received in the year, and not just income amounts. This would include all non-revenue receipts, such as loans, etc. The purpose of the test is meant to indicate the level of activity in the foreign affiliate.

For filings related to taxation years before 2020, Form T1134 is due within 15 months of the end of the individual's tax year. The filing deadline is being shortened to 12 months for filings related to the 2020 taxation year, and to 10 months for filings related to taxation years after 2020. Form T1134 cannot be electronically filed; it must be paper-filed to the address provided on the back of the form. For more information on filing Form T1134, see the Filing Requirements Quick Reference Table at ¶1410. For information on penalties that are applicable for failure to file Form T1134 by the reporting deadline, or for making a false statement or omission with respect to the required information, see the Penalties Quick Reference Table at ¶1420.

> The Form T1134 filing deadline is being shortened to 12 months (from 15 months) for filings related to the 2020 taxation year, and to 10 months for filings related to taxation years after 2020. These changes are contained in Bill C-86.

Frequently asked questions and answers about Form T1134 are posted on the CRA's web site at: canada.ca/en/revenue-agency/services/tax/international-non-residents/information-been-moved/foreign-reporting/questions-answers-about-form-t1134.html.

ITA 233.4

¶3533 — Information Return in Respect of Transfers or Loans to a Non-Resident Trust (Form T1141)

Form T1141, *Information Return in Respect of Transfers or Loans to a Non-resident Trust*, is required to be filed by Canadian residents who have transferred or loaned property to a non-resident trust that has a Canadian beneficiary (referred to as a "specified foreign trust") or a non-resident corporation controlled by the trust. Note that individuals are still required to report on Form T1141 transfers or loans to foreign trusts that are deemed to be resident in Canada under ITA 94.

A trust is a "specified foreign trust" if it is non-resident and either has "specified beneficiaries" or, under the terms of the trust or any arrangement relating to the trust, a person could become beneficially interested in the trust. A "specified beneficiary" is any person who is beneficially interested in the trust unless they fall within the exceptions set out in subparagraphs (i)–(x) of the definition in ITA 233.2(1). Specified foreign trusts do not include exempt trusts as defined in ITA 233.2(1). The main filing exclusions are in respect of information from specified foreign pension plans and specified foreign mutual fund trusts.

The foreign reporting rules apply with respect to a specified foreign trust only where a non-arm's length indicator applies with respect to a transfer or loan of property made at an earlier time to a trust or corporation. These non-arm's length indicators are set out in ITA 233.2(2).

Generally, Form T1141 requires taxpayers to provide information on the trust's settlors, trustees, and beneficiaries; the amount of transfers or loans to or distributions from the trust occurring after 1990; and the amount of indebtedness owed to and by the trust. Filers are required to attach the trust documents (if filing for the first time), as well as any later changes to the documents or new documents created since the last reporting period; and the financial statements of the trust (if the trust prepares financial statements).

The reference on Form T1141 to "person with whom the trustee must consult before exercising discretionary powers" and "persons who have any powers relating to the trust" includes a protector.

Form T1141 is due on the same date as the individual's income tax return for the tax year that includes the trust's year-end. For information on filing Form T1141, see the Filing Requirements Quick Reference Table at ¶1410. For information on penalties that are applicable for failure to file Form T1141 by the reporting deadline, or for making a false statement or omission with respect to the required information, see the Penalties Quick Reference Table at ¶1420.

After filing an initial Form T1141 to disclose a transfer or loan with a related non-resident trust, there still exists a requirement to annually file the form even if no new transfers or loans take place. On the other hand, Form T1142 is only required for years that a Canadian resident receives a distribution from or becomes indebted to a nonresident trust (i.e., the Form is not required to be filed in taxation years in which transactions do not occur).

Frequently asked questions and answers about Form T1141 are posted on the CRA's web site at: canada.ca/en/revenue-agency/services/tax/international-non-residents/information-been-moved/foreign-reporting/questions-answers-about-form-t1141.html.

ITA 233.2, ITR 4801.1, VD 2006-0185642C6

¶3534 — *Information Return in Respect of Distributions From and Indebtedness to a Non-Resident Trust (Form T1142)*

Form T1142, *Information Return in Respect of Distributions from and Indebtedness to a Non-resident Trust*, is required to be filed where a taxpayer is beneficially interested in a non-resident trust (excluding a non-resident estate) at any time in the taxation year and has received a distribution from, or was indebted to, that non-resident trust. Distributions received from, and indebtedness owed to, foreign trusts that are deemed to be resident in Canada under ITA 94 must still be reported on Form T1142 by Canadian resident beneficiaries.

Form T1142 is still required to be filed even if the distribution is a capital distribution that is not taxable to the recipient beneficiary. There are exceptions to the reporting requirement for distributions from an estate that arose on the consequence of the death of an individual, for distributions or loans made from foreign testamentary trusts, and for first-year Canadian residents.

Generally, Form T1142 requires taxpayers to provide the name of the trust and the trustees, and the amount of distributions received from the trust and the amount of indebtedness owed to the trust.

Form T1142 is due on the same date as the individual's income tax return for the tax year that includes the trust's year-end. For information on filing Form T1142, see the Filing Requirements Quick Reference Table at ¶1410. For information on penalties that are applicable for failure to file Form T1141 by the reporting deadline, see the Penalties Quick Reference Table at ¶1420.

Frequently asked questions and answers about Form T1142 are posted on the CRA's web site at: canada.ca/en/revenue-agency/services/tax/international-non-residents/information-been-moved/foreign-reporting/information-return-respect-distributions-indebtedness-a-non-resident-trust.html.

ITA 233.6

¶3600 — Net Partnership Income: Limited or Non-Active Partners Only (T1: Line 122)

A partnership is not defined in the ITA. The relevant provincial partnership law should generally be referred to when determining whether a partnership exists for tax purposes. The traditional common law definition of a partnership, which is reflected in the modern partnership Acts, contains three elements: 1) there must be a "business", 2) carried on for profit, 3) by, or on behalf of, the alleged partners. In determining whether a partnership exists, regard must be paid to the intention of the parties considering the whole facts of the case. This requires an inquiry into whether the objective, documentary evidence, and the surrounding facts, including what the parties actually did, are consistent with a subjective intention to carry on business in common with a view to profit. Whether the existence of a partnership has been established in a particular case depends on an analysis and weighing of the relevant factors in the context of all the surrounding circumstances. See also Folio S4-F16-C1: *What is a Partnership?*. Although co-ownership of property does not, of itself, constitute a partnership, the manner in which parties treat items of property used by them in common may, in the presence of other indicators, indicate the existence of a partnership.

Partnerships are not taxed as separate entities under the ITA. Rather, the taxable income or loss of a partnership is computed at the partnership level for tax purposes as though the partnership were a person under the ITA and the taxable income or loss is then allocated to the partners in the manner agreed upon by them (i.e., the appropriate share of partnership income and losses is included in the calculation of each member's income, net capital loss, non-capital loss, restricted farm loss, and taxable income). Because the partnership is a flow-through entity, sources of income retain their character (e.g., capital gains, dividends, interest, foreign income) when flowed out from the partnership to the partners. Each partnership computes its income for tax purposes in accordance with the general rules·under the ITA, as well as certain specific rules applicable to partnerships.

Subject to certain exceptions, each partnership is required to file a T5013 Summary: *Information Return of Partnership Income* and T5013 slips for each fiscal period. Where an individual is a member of a partnership, enter the partnership taxable income or loss allocation (per Form T5013) on Line 122. If the partnership does not provide a T5013 slip, the taxable income (loss) of the partnership must nonetheless be computed in the normal manner and the allocation to each partner determined. The partner(s) responsible for the preparation of tax reporting information should be specified in the partnership agreement. The income of a partnership for tax purposes can be assessed by the CRA by virtue of ITA 152(1.4)–(1.8).

Each province in Canada has statutory rules setting out the criteria for the creation, use, and termination of limited partnerships. Typically, a limited partnership must consist of at least one general partner and at least one limited partner. A general partner controls or takes part in the control of the business of the partnership and has unlimited liability in respect of the liabilities and obligations of the partnership. A limited partner does not control or take part in the control of the business of the partnership and has liability in respect of the liabilities and obligations of the partnership only to the extent of the limited partner's contribution of capital to the partnership. This is called the "at risk amount" (see ¶3620). A limited partner who actively manages the business of the partnership will generally lose limited liability status, although each province has its own variation on this principle. A limited partnership must register with a provincial authority.

Subject to certain exceptions, each partnership is required to file a T5013 Summary, *Information Return of Partnership Income*, and T5013 slips, *Statement of Partnership Income*, for each fiscal period. The information an individual partner needs to complete Line 122 will generally be provided on the T5013 slip. Where the investment is a tax shelter, the tax shelter identification number must be reported with the return. In addition, the individual must complete Form T5004, *Claim for Tax Shelter Loss or Deduction*, if claiming a loss, deduction, or credit in respect of a tax shelter investment. For more information on claims for tax shelter losses or deductions, see ¶1330 and Guide T4068, *Guide for the T5013 Partnership Information Return*.

Only limited partners or individuals not actively involved in the partnership and not otherwise involved in a business or profession similar to that carried on by the partnership report their net income or loss from a partnership on Line 122. Rental income from a partnership is reported on Line 126 (see ¶5300). Partnership income for an individual who is not a limited partner or who is actively involved in the partnership is reported as self-employment income on Lines 135 to 143 (see Chapter 6). Carrying charges and interest expenses in relation to a limited partner's investment in a partnership are reported in Part IV of Schedule 4, *Statement of Investment Income*, and deducted on Line 221 (see ¶3700).

ITA 96, ITR 229, *Continental Bank of Canada*, [1998] 4 C.T.C. 77 (SCC), *Strauss*, [1960] C.T.C. 86 (Exch); *Cole*, [1964] C.T.C. 219; *Northern Sales (1963) Ltd.*, [1973] C.T.C. 239 (FCTD); *Backman*, [2001] 2 C.T.C. 11 (SCC), Folio S4-F16-C1: *What is a Partnership?*

¶3610 — Limited Partner Definition

A partner is considered to be a limited partner if the partnership interest is not an "exempt interest", and if at the particular time or within three years after that time:

- By operation of law governing the partnership arrangement, the partner's liability exposure as a member of the partnership is limited except where such liability is limited by a law that limits liability for debts, obligations, and liability of a limited liability partnership by reason of negligent acts or omissions of another member of the partnership or of an employee, representative or agent of the partnership;

- The liability exposure of the partner or person with whom the partner does not deal at arm's length is limited either immediately or in the future, or either contingently or absolutely, by virtue of contract as particularly described;

- The existence of the partner who owns the interest is for the purpose of providing limited liability to another person and may not reasonably be considered to permit the partner to carry on the partner's ordinary business in the most effective manner (for example, where a corporation is formed for the sole purpose of holding the partnership interest, thereby affording the ultimate shareholder limited liability in respect of the partnership interest); or

- There is an agreement or other arrangement for the disposition of the partnership interest, one of the main reasons for which can reasonably be considered to avoid the application of the definition of a limited partner to the particular partner.

An exempt interest means an interest in a partnership that was carrying on business or earning income from the rental or leasing of property on a regular and continuous basis on February 25, 1986 and continuously thereafter until that particular time. However, a partnership interest can lose exempt status where, after February 25, 1986, there has been a substantial contribution of capital to the partnership or substantial partnership borrowings.

In *Docherty*, [2005] 2 C.T.C. 97 (FCA), two "general partners" were held to be limited partners, such that the at-risk rules applied, on the basis that the partnership agreement essentially provided that the partners did not have to suffer losses arising from the development costs from the project over a 15-year period. In *Foley*, [2004] 1 C.T.C. 2795 (TCC), two limited partners tried unsuccessfully to argue that they were general partners so that the at-risk rules applied.

ITA 96(2.4), (2.5), *Raby*, [2007] 2 C.T.C. 2146 (TCC), *Central Supply Co (1972) Ltd*, [1995] 2 C.T.C. 2320 (TCC), *Goren*, [1997] 3 C.T.C. 2025 (TCC)

¶3620 — At-Risk Amount

A limited partner is liable for the obligations of the limited partnership only to the extent of the partner's contribution to the capital of the partnership. Special income tax rules limit the losses that may be claimed by a limited partner to the amount of the actual capital at risk. A partner's at-risk amount is required to be entered in Box 22-1 of the T5013 or T5013A information slips when the partnership completes a T5013 return.

Generally, a limited partner's at-risk amount is defined as: the adjusted cost base of the limited partner's interest in the partnership (see ¶4123), plus any partnership income allocated to the limited partner for the fiscal period, less any amounts the limited partner owes to the partnership, and less any amount or benefit the limited partner (or a person non-arm's length with the limited partner) is entitled to receive in any form or manner, immediately or in the future and absolutely or contingently, to reduce the impact of any loss to the partnership interest.

The amount of a partner's indebtedness to a partnership that reduces the at-risk amount of the partner includes not only amounts that are contingently owed, but also amounts in respect of which the obligation to pay is absolute. ITA 96(2.2)(c) generally ensures that the at-risk amount is not increased until the amounts owed are actually paid by the limited partner to the partnership and risked in the partnership's business.

A limited partner's at-risk amount is reduced where the partner is entitled to receive any benefit granted for the purpose of reducing the impact of any loss that the partner may sustain in respect of the partnership interest. This rule applies regardless of whether the entitlement to the benefit is immediate or in the future, or whether it is absolute or contingent. Furthermore, the amount received or benefit may be by way of reimbursement, compensation, revenue guarantee, proceeds of disposition or loan, or any other form of indebtedness in any form or manner whatever. The at-risk amount is not reduced by the entitlement to, or receipt of, assistance which reduces the taxpayer's cumulative Canadian exploration expense, cumulative Canadian development expense, or cumulative Canadian oil and gas property expense. Also, certain other amounts or benefits to which the limited partner is or may become entitled are excluded for the purposes of the reduction in the at-risk amount pursuant to ITA 96(2.2)(e)-(f).

If the limited partner purchased the interest on the secondary market, see CRA Guide T4068 under "Cost of a limited partner's interest when the limited partner is not the first owner of the interest." Generally, where the individual has not acquired the partnership interest from the partnership, the individual's ACB is limited to the vendor's ACB, thereby ensuring that the at-risk amount is not increased unless additional capital is contributed to the partnership. More specifically, ITA 96(2.3) provides that the ACB is to be computed as if the cost to the acquiring partner were the lesser of: 1) the partner's cost otherwise determined, and 2) the greater of: a) the ACB of that interest to the transferor immediately before the time the interest was acquired by the limited partner, and b) nil.

Limited and certain other partners are required to report, as a capital gain, any negative ACB in their partnership interest at the end of a fiscal period of the partnership. Because of this rule, limited partners are generally not able to extract, tax-free, more than the ACB of their interest in the partnership.

Calculating the at-risk amount of a partnership interest can be complex; for example calculations, see CRA Guide T4068.

The ITA includes a rule intended to prevent a taxpayer from making a contribution of capital to a partnership in order to artificially increase the taxpayer's ACB and at-risk amount. The rule provides that a contribution of capital made by the limited partner to the partnership is deemed not to have been made to the extent of a loan or repayment by the partnership to the limited partner if it is established, by subsequent events or otherwise, that the loan or repayment was made as part of a series of loans or other transactions and repayments.

ITA 96(2.2), (2.7), *Goren*, [1997] 3 C.T.C. 2025 (TCC), *Hazelwood*, [1990] 1 C.T.C. 5 (FCTD), *Central Supply Company (1972) v. R.*, [1997] 3 C.T.C. 102 (FCA), Guide T4068

¶3700 — Deductions in Computing Investment Income (Sch. 4: Part III, Line 221)

Generally, expenses an individual incurs to earn investment income are deductible where the following requirements are met:

- the expense is reasonable in the circumstances;

- the expense is made or incurred for the purpose of earning the investment income;

- the expense is not a capital outlay or loss (except for amounts specifically allowed, such as interest expenses);

- the expense is not a personal or living expense;

- the expense is not made or incurred for the purpose of earning exempt income; and

- there are no specific provisions in the ITA that deny the deduction.

Carrying charges and interest expenses incurred to earn investment income and which meet the above requirements should be reported in Part III of Schedule 4, and deducted on Line 221 of the T1 return.

Carrying charges and interest expenses incurred in respect of rental income or self-employment income are deducted in the computation of net rental income (Line 126) (see Chapter 5) and net self-employment income (Lines 135–143) (see Chapter 6).

ITA 18(1)(a)–(c), 18(1)(h), 18(11), 20(1)(c)-(d), 67

¶3710 — Carrying Charges

Taxpayers can claim as a deduction the following carrying charges to earn investment income:

- Investment counsel fees and custodial fees

- Fees paid for investment record-keeping

- Fees paid for investment advice on buying or selling investments

- Fees to have someone complete the taxpayer's income tax return, but only if the taxpayer has income from a business or property, accounting is a usual part of the operations of his or her business or property, and the amounts are not claimed to reduce the business or property income reported

Taxpayers cannot deduct the following amounts as carrying charges:

- Safety deposit box charges (for 2014 and later taxation years)

- Fees paid for investment advice, investment management, investment record-keeping, etc., relating to registered investment accounts (i.e., RRSPs, RPPs, TFSAs, etc.)

- Subscription fees paid for financial newspapers, magazines, or newsletters

- Brokerage fees or commissions paid when buying or selling securities (use these costs when calculating the capital gain or capital loss) (see ¶4111)

Effective for 2014 and later taxation years, individuals can no longer deduct the cost of renting a safety deposit box for income tax purposes.

ITA 20(1)(bb), IT-238R2: *Fees Paid to Investment Counsel*

¶3711 — *Investment Counsel Fees*

The full amount of a fee (other than a commission) paid by the taxpayer in the year for investment counselling or for the administration or management of securities is deductible in computing income. In order to be deductible, the payee's principal business must be either to provide advice as to the advisability of buying or selling specific securities or else include managing or administering securities. Fees paid to a stockbroker would not be eligible, nor would subscription fees to financial journals. However, fees paid to executors and trustees for administering or managing an investment portfolio will generally qualify. Fees paid for investment counselling or administrative services relating to a registered retirement savings plan, a registered retirement income fund, or a tax-free savings account are not deductible, regardless of whether such fees are paid within or outside of the plan.

In late 2016, the CRA announced a change in its position with respect to the tax consequences of investment management fees for RRSPs, RRIFs and TFSAs that are paid outside of a registered plan. In the CRA's view, investment management fees represent a liability of the registered plan, and thus would be expected to be paid by the trustee using funds from within the plan. If paid outside of the plan, it is the CRA's view that the resulting indirect increase in value of the plan assets would likely constitute an "advantage" under ITA 207.01(1). However, in October 2018, the CRA announced that it will be deferring implementation of this administrative policy, pending completion of a review of the issue by the Department of Finance. Accordingly, paragraph 3.35 of Folio S3-F10-C3, *Advantages — RRSPs, RESPs, RRIFs, RDSPs and TFSAs*, provides that comments on the tax treatment of fees and expenses incurred in connection with a registered plan and its investments will be included in a future update to the Folio (see VDs 2016-0670801C6, 2017-0722391E5 and 2018-0779261E5).

With respect to the deductibility of trustee fees, in VD 2010-0381561E5, the CRA states:

> [W]here the principal business of a trustee is advising others, or includes the provision of services in respect of the administration or management of shares or securities, the portion of the trustee fees paid for advising others or for services in respect of the administration or management of shares or securities held by the trust generally would be deductible under paragraph 20(1)(bb) of the Act to the trust.

> Where the trustee pays, on behalf of the trust, fees for advice as to the advisability of purchasing or selling shares or securities or for services in respect of the administration or management of the shares or securities held by a trust, to another person described in paragraph 20(1)(bb) of the Act, any reimbursement by the trust to the trustee for such fees may be deductible to the trust under paragraph 20(1)(bb) of the Act provided the requirements in paragraph 20(1)(bb) of the Act are otherwise fully satisfied.

In VD 2010-0381561E5, the CRA states "[paragraph 20(1)(bb)] contains several restrictions including an ownership requirement (the shares or securities to which the advice or services pertain to must be shares or securities of the taxpayer), and a requirement that the payment for the advice or services must be to a person whose principal business is advising others as to the advisability of purchasing or selling specific shares or securities ("advising others") or includes the provision of services in respect of the administration or management of shares or securities". With respect to the "ownership requirement", the CRA has stated in the past that for eligible fees to be deductible, a share does not have to be purchased (see, for example, VD 9607657).

Commissions paid to stockbrokers or investment advisors on the purchase or sale of shares, bonds or similar securities are not deductible expenses for tax purposes unless the taxpayer is a trader in securities whose gains are taxed as ordinary income and losses are deductible as non-capital losses. Instead, these charges are considered to be capital outlays and are included in the computation of taxable capital gains and allowable capital losses (see ¶4111).

ITA 18(1)(u), 20(1)(bb), *Hume*, [1980] C.T.C. 2645 (TRB), *Beadle*, [1979] C.T.C. 2917 (TRB), *Vatcha*, [1991] 1 C.T.C. 2413 (TCC), IT-238R2: *Fees Paid to Investment Counsel*, VDs 2006-0207071E5, 2006-017087117

¶3720 — Interest Expense

Subject to special rules discussed below, by virtue of ITA 20(1)(c), interest of a reasonable amount may be deducted in computing income for tax purposes where borrowed money is used for the purpose of earning income from a business or property (other than borrowed money used to acquire property the income from which would be exempt or to acquire a life insurance policy), and is paid pursuant to a legal obligation to pay interest. Interest is also deductible if it is payable in respect of property acquired for the purpose of gaining or producing income.

ITA 20(1)(c)(i) effectively includes both a purpose and a use test. The leading case regarding the purpose test (i.e., that the interest be incurred to earn income from a business or property) is *Ludco Enterprises Ltd*, [2002] 1 C.T.C. 95 (SCC), in which the Court stated (paras. 50 and 51):

> [I]t is perfectly consistent with the language of s. 20(1)(c)(i) that a taxpayer who uses borrowed money to make an investment for more than one purpose may be entitled to deduct interest charges provided that one of those purposes is to earn income.

> In this connection, the adjectives that have been heretofore used by courts to characterize the requisite purpose in s. 20(1)(c)(i), such as "bona fide", "actual", "real" or "true", are to my mind ultimately useful only when describing whether the transaction at issue was a mere sham or window-dressing designed to obtain the benefit of interest deductibility. Absent a sham or window dressing or other vitiating circumstances, a taxpayer's ancillary purpose may be nonetheless a bona fide, actual, real and true objective of his or her investment, equally capable of providing the requisite purpose for interest deductibility in comparison with any more important or significant primary purpose.

The Court went on to summarize that "the requisite test to determine the purpose for interest deductibility under ITA 20(1)(c)(i) is whether, considering all the circumstances, the taxpayer had a reasonable expectation of income at the time the investment is made". The Court noted that the concept of "income" for this purpose was income generally (i.e., an amount that could come into income for tax purposes) and not just net income. CRA views on the *Ludco* decision are provided in paragraphs 1.26, 1.27, 1.38 and 1.69 of Folio S3-F6-C1 and in VD 2003-0018115.

The leading decision on the interest deductibility use test is *Singleton*, [2002] 1 C.T.C. 121 (SCC), in which the Court set forth the following principles: the relevant test is "to what use were the borrowed funds put?"; the "direct" use of funds is the relevant use, subject to an "indirect" use exception (commonly referred to as the "exceptional circumstances" test); the purpose of the borrowing or arrangement is irrelevant for purposes of the use test; the legal effect of transactions as opposed to "economic realities" are relevant when applying the use test; and transactions must be viewed independently and not as one simultaneous transaction. With respect to the use test, the current use, as opposed to the original use, of borrowed funds is relevant in determining whether interest payments are deductible (see Folio S3-F6-C1: para. 1.35, VDs 2009-0329781C6, 2009-0344721E5, 2007-0230341E5, 2004-0069941C6).

As mentioned above, in addition to interest that clearly relates to amounts borrowed to earn income from a business or property (i.e., where the direct use of the borrowed funds is to earn income), money borrowed for the purpose of redeeming shares, returning capital, or paying dividends is also considered a deductible expense where the so-called indirect/exceptional circumstances test is met. See paragraphs 1.48–1.52, 1.54–1.57, and 1.65 of Folio S3-F6-C1 for the CRA's position on the indirect use test.

Other considerations with respect to the interest deductibility rules include:

- *Construction Soft Costs*: Certain interest expenses incurred during the construction of a building are not deductible from income for tax purposes (see ¶5255)

- *Vacant Land*: Interest in respect of funds used to purchase vacant land is generally not deductible from income (see ¶5256)

- *Non-Deductible Interest*: Interest charged under the ITA or *Excise Tax Act* is specifically not deductible from income for tax purposes

- *Guarantees*: Interest on funds borrowed to honour a guarantee may or may not be deductible (see paras. 1.76–1.80 of Folio S3-F6-C1)

- *Financing Fees*: Fees incurred in the course of borrowing funds are generally deductible over a period of 5 years on a straight-line basis for tax purposes

- *Loss of Income Source*: All or a portion of interest may continue to be deductible where property acquired with borrowed funds declines in value or is disposed of

- *Wind-up of Corporation*: Interest on money borrowed to purchase shares of a corporation will continue to be deductible if the corporation is wound-up, provided the assets received on the winding-up continue to be used for the purpose of earning income (see paras. 1.44, 1.63.1 and 1.63.2 of Folio S3-F6-C1, VD 2014-0555291I7)

ITA 18(1)(t), 20(1)(c), (d), 20(2)-(3), 248(1)"borrowed money", ITR 201, *McLarty*, 2014 CarswellNat 2332 (TCC), *Crown Forest Industries Ltd v R*, [2006] 2 C.T.C. 2332 (TCC), *Penn Ventilator Canada Ltd v R*, [2002] 2 C.T.C. 2636 (TCC), *Canadian Helicopters Ltd.*, [2002] 2 C.T.C. 83 (FCA), *The Queen v Bronfman Trust*, [1987] 1 C.T.C. 117 (SCC), *Meredith v R*, [1975] C.T.C. 570 (FCTD), *Trans-Prairie Pipelines Ltd*, [1970] C.T.C. 537 (Exct), Folio S3-F6-C1, ITTN-3, ITTN-16, ITTN-18, ITTN-34, ITTN-41, VDs 2016-0666411E5, 2014-0563351E5, 2012-0443771E5, 2010-0379341C6, 2009-0331651E5, 2007-0243181C6, 2007-0236351E5, 2008-030484I7, 2010-0378661R3, 2009-0344721E5, 2004-0103721E5, Gosselin et al. "A Review of Interest Deductibility Since Ludco," *Report of the Proceedings of the Sixty-Seventh Tax Conference*, 2015 Conference Report (Toronto: Canadian Tax Foundation, 2016), 7: 1-23

¶3721 — *Personal Loans*

Interest on personal loans, such as a mortgage on a principal residence, is not deductible. Where a taxpayer has personal and investment debt, it is generally advisable to separate investment borrowings from personal borrowings. Where a line of credit is used for both personal and investment purposes, the CRA's view is that it is necessary to use a pro-rata approach to determine the deductibility of interest on amounts borrowed on a line of credit for personal and non-personal purposes. For example, if an individual has a line of credit of $100,000 of which $60,000 was used for personal purposes and $40,000 to acquire property which produces income, 40% of the line of credit is used to earn income and it is necessary to use this fraction on the remaining balance of the line of credit to calculate the interest which is deductible. In another example, if a taxpayer purchased a rental property for $300,000 by way of two separate loans of $200,000 and $100,000, lived in 1/3 of the space with the remainder being rented to third parties, and over the years repaid the $100,000 loan (in priority, with the intention of minimizing non-deductible interest), because the two loans were used to acquire the same property, the CRA's position is that only the 2/3 of the portion of the outstanding loan balance of $200,000 would be considered used to produce income from property.

Typically, an individual, desiring to acquire, for example, a new home, boat, or recreational property, will borrow funds by mortgaging rental property or by pledging securities as collateral for a loan. By adopting this method of financing, the individual is able to retain the income-producing property; however, where taxpayers have attempted to deduct the interest expense from the income so earned, the CRA has had consistent success in treating the interest as a personal and living expense because of the use to which the borrowed money is put (ITA 18(1)(h)).

Despite the above comments, based on paragraphs 1.29 to 1.31 of Folio S3-F6-C1, it is the CRA's view that taxpayers are generally entitled to restructure their borrowings and the ownership of assets to meet the direct use test. In *Singleton*, [2002] 1 C.T.C. 121 (SCC), interest was found to be deductible by a taxpayer who used capital from his partnership to pay off a mortgage on his personal residence and then borrowed funds to refinance his partnership. In other words, the taxpayer was effectively permitted to deduct his home mortgage interest under ITA 20(1)(c) because the direct use of the funds was to acquire an income-producing asset rather than a personal residence. In particular, the use of the borrowed funds could be traced to an income earning use (even though the funds had indirectly been used to purchase a personal residence). The significant decision of the Supreme Court of Canada was that the economic realities of a transaction could not be used to recharacterize a taxpayer's *bona fide* legal transactions.

The general anti-avoidance regime (GAAR) was held to apply in the case of *Lipson v. R.*, [2009] 1 C.T.C. 314 (SCC), in which the overall purpose of a series of transactions was to make interest on money borrowed to buy a personal residence deductible. It is important to note that although GAAR was not at issue in *Singleton*, the decision in *Lipson* confirmed that the principles set forth in *Singleton* continue to apply. In *Lipson*, the Court distinguished *Singleton* and reaffirmed that an overall purpose analysis was not appropriate in analyzing the interest deductibility test.

¶3722 — *Share Investments*

Interest on funds borrowed to invest in common shares is normally deductible, regardless of whether the investor anticipates dividends to be paid on the shares. Also, interest on funds borrowed to invest in preferred shares is normally deductible, even if the interest rate in respect of the debt exceeds the stated dividend rate of the shares. In paragraphs 1.69 and 1.70 of S3-F6-C1, the CRA states:

> Based on *Ludco*, where an investment carries a stated interest or dividend rate, the income-earning test will be met "absent a sham or window dressing or similar vitiating circumstances". Further, given the meaning of the term income as discussed in ¶1.27, and assuming all of the other tests are met, interest will neither be denied in full nor restricted to the amount of income from the investment where the income does not exceed the interest expense.

> Where an investment does not carry a stated interest or dividend rate, such as some common shares, it is necessary to consider whether the purpose test is met. Generally, the CRA considers interest costs in respect of funds borrowed to purchase common shares to be deductible on the basis that at the time the shares are acquired there is a reasonable expectation that the common shareholder will receive dividends. However, it is conceivable that in certain fact situations, such reasonable expectation would not be present. If a corporation has asserted that it does not pay dividends and that dividends are not expected to be paid in the foreseeable future such that shareholders are required to sell their shares in order to realize their value, the purpose test will not be met. However, if a corporation is silent with respect to its dividend policy, or its policy is that dividends will be paid when operational circumstances permit, the purpose test will likely be met. Each situation must be dealt with on the basis of the particular facts involved. These comments are also generally applicable to investments in mutual fund trusts and mutual funds.

Furthermore, in ITTN-41 (December 23, 2009) the CRA states:

> With respect to determining whether a common share investor has a reasonable expectation of income at the time the investment is made, in our view, it is not essential that dividends be received. This is merely one of many facts that would be considered. The dividend policy, if any, of the invested-in corporation would be another of the facts considered in such a determination, as well as evidence, if any, from corporate officials indicating whether dividends are expected to be paid, or whether shareholders are required to sell their shares in order to realize their value.

> Each situation involving the investment of borrowed money in common shares must be dealt with on the basis of the particular facts involved, and the requisite test to be met for interest deductibility is whether the taxpayer had a reasonable expectation of income at the time the investment was made. The requisite test will not be met in all situations. Where the taxpayer, based on a review of the particular facts, did not have a reasonable expectation of income at the time the investment in common shares was made, the requirements of paragraph 20(1)(c) of the Act will not be met.

Generally, interest on money borrowed to purchase shares in the capital stock of a corporation will continue to be deductible if the corporation is wound up provided the assets received on the winding-up continue to be used for the purpose of earning or producing income (see paras. 1.44, 1.63.1 and 1.63 of Folio S3-F6-C1, VD 2014-0555291I7).

In *Swirsky*, [2013] 3 C.T.C. 2104 (TCC); aff'd in [2014] 3 C.T.C. 79 (FCA), an interest deduction was denied in respect of funds borrowed to purchase shares in a family company that had no history of paying dividends in a series of tax planning transactions the principal purpose of which was creditor proofing. The Court indicated that the GAAR was not applicable since the primary purpose of the transactions in question was found to be creditor proofing rather than tax avoidance. In the case, Mr. Swirsky testified that the usual practice of the corporation was to declare a bonus or management fee sufficient to pay down an annual shareholder loan balance to nil. At paragraph 35, the Court concluded that "the income that the Swirskys claim the share transfer was intended to protect was not income from the Torgan shares" but rather was future income payable as a bonus. In denying the interest deduction, at paragraph 48, the Court stated:

> According to the test laid down by the Supreme Court in *Ludco*, there must be a reasonable expectation of income at the time the investment was made. The appellant has not shown that this test was met in this case. After considering all of the circumstances surrounding the transactions, including Ms. Swirsky's subjective intention in acquiring the shares, I find that she did not have a reasonable expectation of income when she acquired them.

Swirsky was a fact-specific decision and instances in which an interest deduction is denied in respect of an investment in common shares should remain uncommon. With respect to the facts that supported a denial of the interest deduction, at paragraphs 38, 39, 42 and the Court stated:

> [T]here is no evidence that the income producing potential of the Torgan shares was ever considered before the transactions took place. The plan to sell the shares to Ms. Swirsky and all of the steps in the transaction were devised by the

accountant, Mr. Steinberg. Those steps were set out in a letter dated February 18, 1991 addressed to Mr. Swirsky. Nowhere in the letter is there any discussion or consideration of an income earning purpose to the proposed acquisition of the shares by Ms. Swirsky. In cross-examination, Mr. Swirsky testified that he made no representations or promises to Ms. Swirsky that dividends would be paid on the Torgan shares he was selling her. In fact, there was no evidence that dividends were discussed at all ... The evidence also shows that Ms. Swirsky expected to return the shares to Mr. Swirsky at some point after the financial problems relating to the Yonge Street project passed ... In fact, Ms. Swirsky did transfer the shares back to Mr. Swirsky in 2008 as part of their divorce settlement.

Note that various objective indications of an income earning purpose were seemingly ignored by the Court in *Swirsky*, and the decision has been scrutinized by the tax community (for example: there was no policy against the payment of dividends; the corporation was profitable; dividends were, in fact, eventually paid; and the family business context of the case was seemingly not taken into appropriate consideration).

From a planning perspective, in respect of funds borrowed to purchase common shares, documentation should be in place that clearly supports the income-earning purpose of an investment. Preferably, there should be a history of dividends being paid on the shares, and a future dividend paying policy should be in place. In the case of closely-held companies, creating a dividend-paying history before and after a leveraged share acquisition would be beneficial to support the deductibility of interest.

TDL Group Co. v. The Queen, 2016 FCA 67, *Stewart*, [2002] 3 C.T.C. 439 (SCC), *Walls*, [2002] 3 C.T.C. 421 (SCC), *The Queen v Bronfman Trust*, [1987] 1 C.T.C. 117 (SCC), Folio S3-F6-C1, VDs 2010-0376711I7, 2008-0275171E5, 2006-0188071M4, 2006-0177371M4, 2004-0065481C6

¶3723 — *Loss of Source of Income*

Interest may be deducted on borrowed funds or on amounts payable for income-producing property provided the borrowings are used for the purpose of earning income from a business or property. As a general rule, when the borrowings can no longer be traced to an income-producing source, the interest paid on those borrowed funds is no longer deductible. However, provided certain conditions are satisfied, some portion of the interest expense may continue to be deducted even though the source may have disappeared.

In order to continue to be deductible, the following conditions must be satisfied: the money borrowed must be used for the purposes of earning income from capital property, except for real property or depreciable property; the property ceases to be used for that purpose after 1993; and part of the borrowed money has been lost because of the decrease in the value of the property. In those circumstances, the part of the money that has been lost will be deemed for tax purposes to continue to be used for income-producing purposes. Consequently, the interest expense relating to that part will continue to be deductible regardless of whether the taxpayer has disposed of the property. Similarly, where money is borrowed, for example, to acquire shares of a corporation which subsequently goes bankrupt, interest may still continue to be deductible even though the taxpayer did not dispose of the shares.

The permitted deduction by virtue of ITA 20.1 only applies to the part of the money considered to be lost. Accordingly, if property is disposed of at its fair market value, the amount deemed to be lost would be the difference between the amount of borrowed funds owing immediately before the disposition and the fair market value consideration for the disposition. For example, if the outstanding borrowed funds were $30,000 and the fair market value consideration for the sale was $20,000, $10,000 would be considered the amount lost. This would be the amount in respect of which interest would continue to be deductible. If the property is not disposed of for fair market value consideration, this amount is determined as if the taxpayer had disposed of the property for an amount equal to the fair market value of the property. If the property is disposed of to a creditor to reduce the amount owed, the amount of the reduction reduces the amount of borrowed money for the purposes of determining the amount considered to be lost.

Where there is more than one debt obligation, the amount of borrowed money includes the total of those obligations where the funds were used to earn income from property.

Once ITA 20.1 applies to deem borrowed money to continue to be used to earn income from property, the interest on any subsequent refinancing will similarly be deductible.

In those circumstances in which ITA 20.1 does not apply (such as when the money was borrowed for the purposes of earning income from real property or depreciable property), the implications of the Supreme Court of Canada decision in *Tennant*, [1996] 1 C.T.C. 290 are of particular importance. The decision in *Tennant* may provide relief in situations outside the scope of ITA 20.1, at least in certain limited instances involving the disposition at a loss of property acquired with borrowed money and the use of the diminished proceeds to acquire a replacement property.

In *Tennant*, the taxpayer used $1 million of borrowed money to purchase common shares and later sold the shares for $1,000 and received as consideration shares of a holding corporation with an equivalent value. The Supreme Court of Canada overturned the decisions of the lower courts and permitted the deduction of interest on the full amount of the $1 million borrowing. This result followed from the establishment of a link between the borrowed money, the originally acquired shares, and the shares of the holding corporation received by the taxpayer as proceeds and a replacement property. The Court expressly rejected the CRA's contention that the amount of the interest deduction should be limited by the value of the replacement shares. According to the Court, the continuing use of the borrowed money was an eligible income-earning use irrespective of the relative costs and values of the different shares compared with the principal amount of the borrowed money.

By virtue of ITA 20.1(4), interest may also continue to be deductible where it relates to an amount payable for property that was acquired to earn income from property or a business. The amount payable is deemed to be on account of borrowed money.

In VD 2015-0588951C6, the CRA takes the position that interest would generally continue to be deductible under ITA 20(1)(c)(i), without relying on ITA 20.1(1), by the sole shareholder of a company who uses borrowed money to fund an interest-free loan to the company where the loan is subsequently forgiven by the shareholder, provided that there is a reasonable expectation of deriving dividends from the shares.

ITA 20.1, 20(3), Folio S3-F6-C1 (paras. 1.41, 1.63), VDs 2009-0335101E5, 2009-0329171E5

Chapter 4 — Capital Gains and Losses

Contents

¶4000 Dispositions of Capital Property

   ¶4005 Capital Gains and Losses (Sch. 3)

   ¶4010 Capital Gains versus Income

   ¶4015 Adventure or Concern in the Nature of Trade

¶4100 Computation of Capital Gains and Losses

   ¶4110 Proceeds of Disposition (Sch. 3: Col. 2)

   ¶4120 Adjusted Cost Base (ACB) of Capital Property (Sch. 3: Col. 3)

   ¶4130 Total Capital Gains (Sch. 3: Line 191)

   ¶4140 Capital Gains Reserves (Sch. 3: Line 192)

¶4200 Qualified Dispositions (Sch. 3: Parts 1 and 2)

   ¶4210 Lifetime Capital Gains Exemption

   ¶4220 Qualified Small Business Corporation Shares (Sch. 3: Part 1)

   ¶4230 Qualified Farm or Fishing Property (Sch. 3: Part 2)

   ¶4240 Cumulative Net Investment Loss (CNIL)

   ¶4250 Surplus Stripping

¶4300 Disposition of Publicly Traded Shares, Mutual Fund Units, Deferral of Eligible Small Business Corporation Shares and Other Shares (Sch. 3: Part 3)

   ¶4310 Disposition of Mutual Fund Units or Shares

   ¶4315 Disposition of Digital Currencies

   ¶4320 Employee Security Options

   ¶4330 Donations of Capital Property

   ¶4340 Capital Gains Deferral for Eligible Small Business Corporation Shares

   ¶4350 Proceeds of Disposition of Securities: Special Rules

   ¶4360 Investments in a Bankrupt Corporation: Deemed Disposition of Shares

   ¶4370 Convertible Shares or Debt

¶4400 Disposition of Real Estate, Depreciable Property and Other Properties (Sch. 3: Part 4)

   ¶4410 Disposition of Land and Building

   ¶4420 Disposition of Depreciable Property

¶4430 Principal Residence Exemption

¶4500 Disposition of Bonds, Debentures, Promissory Notes and Other Properties (Sch. 3: Parts 5–8)

¶4510 Bonds, Debentures, Treasury Bills, Promissory Notes and Similar Properties (Sch. 3: Part 5)

¶4520 Debts Held on Capital Account (Bad Debts) (Sch. 3: Part 5)

¶4530 Foreign Exchange Gains and Losses on Capital Account (Sch. 3: Part 5)

¶4540 Options to Buy or Sell Property (Sch. 3: Part 5)

¶4550 Other Capital Properties (Sch. 3: Part 5)

¶4560 Other Mortgage Foreclosures and Conditional Sales Repossessions (Sch.3 Part 6)

¶4570 Personal-Use Property (Sch.3: Parts 7 and 8)

¶4600 Allowable Business Investment Losses (ABILs)

¶4610 Deductibility of ABILs (T1: Lines 217 and 228; Sch. 3: Line 178)

¶4620 Small Business Corporation Definition

¶4630 Guarantees of Debt

¶4700 Replacement Property Rules

¶4710 Former Business Property

¶4720 Replacement Property (Involuntary Dispositions)

¶4730 Applicable Rollover Rules Where Election is Filed

¶4740 Disposition of Land and Building: Reallocation of Proceeds

¶4800 Miscellaneous Loss Denial and Limitation Rules

¶4810 Losses on Transfers between Affiliated Persons

¶4820 Dividend Stop-Loss Rules

¶4000 — Dispositions of Capital Property

¶4005 — Capital Gains and Losses (Sch. 3)

An individual who realized a capital gain or incurred a capital loss in the year is required to complete Schedule 3 of the T1 return. Generally, individuals are required to report dispositions in the taxation year of the following types of property on Schedule 3:

- Qualified small business corporation (QSBC) shares (Schedule 3: Part 1)

- Qualified farm or fishing property (Schedule 3: Part 2)

- Publicly traded shares, mutual fund units, and other shares (Schedule 3: Part 3)

- Real estate, depreciable property and other properties (Schedule 3: Part 4)

- Bonds, debentures, promissory notes, and other similar properties (Schedule 3: Part 5)

- Mortgage foreclosures and conditional sales repossessions (Schedule 3: Part 6)

- Personal-use property (Schedule 3: Part 7)

178

- Listed personal property (Schedule 3: Part 8)

A capital gain arises when an individual sells (or is deemed to sell) a capital property for net proceeds of disposition (see ¶4110) in excess of the adjusted cost base (ACB) (see ¶4120). A capital loss arises when an individual sells (or is deemed to sell) a capital property for less than its ACB. A capital property is one that is acquired for the purposes of earning investment income. A capital property that is acquired for the purposes of resale in the course of business would generally be considered business income. It is a question of fact whether or not a gain or loss on the disposition of a property is on account of income or capital. To determine whether a gain is income or capital in nature, it generally must be determined whether an investment is being sold or a trade is being carried on. The distinction between profits on account of income (i.e., business income) and capital is discussed at ¶4010.

One-half of a capital gain is included in income for tax purposes. Also, only one-half of a capital loss may be deducted from income, and only to the extent that the loss can offset taxable capital gains (the inclusion rate was 3/4 from 1990 to February 27, 2000, 2/3 from February 28 to October 17, 2000, and has been 1/2 since October 18, 2000). Capital losses may be carried back three years and applied to offset taxable capital gains realized in those years. Capital losses may be carried forward indefinitely for use in future taxation years.

Gains and losses are not calculated as part of the taxpayer's business income, but are determined separately for each taxation year in accordance with their own set of rules, as discussed in this chapter. A capital gain or loss from the disposition of capital property used in a business is determined on a calendar year basis, regardless of the fiscal period of the business in which the property was sold. For example, assume that the fiscal year end for a taxpayer's business is June 30, 2017. In August 2017, the taxpayer incurred a capital gain on the sale of capital property used in the taxpayer's business. The taxpayer has to report the capital gain in the 2017 T1 return even though the sale took place after the business's fiscal year end date of June 30.

Lottery prizes and gambling winnings are not considered capital gains (or income under any other provision of the ITA). However, betting or gambling proceeds are taxable where such amounts are considered income from a business. Also excluded as capital gains are proceeds that are taxable as income under some other provision of the ITA, including proceeds arising from the sale of inventory, insurance policies, disposition of resource properties including timber resource properties and an interest under a qualifying environmental trust, disposition of goodwill or other eligible capital property (before 2017), or a disposition of an interest of a beneficiary under a mining reclamation trust. A capital gain on the disposition of certified Canadian cultural property to a designated institution is also excluded from being a capital gain and is exempt from tax under the ITA (see ¶10214.1). Likewise, certain dispositions do not give rise to a capital loss. These include dispositions of depreciable property, eligible capital property (before 2017), Canadian resource property, a foreign resource property, an insurance policy, and dispositions of an interest of a beneficiary under a mining reclamation trust.

Where an individual gifts shares, debt obligations, or rights listed on a designated stock exchange, a share of a mutual fund, a unit of a mutual fund trust, an interest in a related segregated fund trust, or a prescribed debt obligation to a qualified donee (generally, a charitable organization, public or private foundation, government body, etc.), no part of the capital gain is included in income (see ¶10214.6). This rule also applies to qualifying ecological gifts (see ¶10214.2).

A gain realized on the sale of the taxpayer's principal residence, as defined, is exempt from tax if it has always been used as a principal residence since the time it was acquired, or since January 1, 1972, whichever is later (see under ¶4430). For Canadian resident individuals, a lifetime capital gains exemption is available for property disposed of that qualifies as shares of a qualified small business corporation (see ¶4220) or qualified farm or fishing property (see ¶4230).

By virtue of various deeming rules in the ITA, in addition to regular sales of capital property, an individual may also realize a capital gain or loss where the individual exchanges one property for another (see ¶4370); donates a capital property as a gift (see ¶4330); settles a debt denominated in a foreign currency (see ¶4530); owns property that was expropriated, stolen or destroyed (see ¶4700); has an option to buy or sell property that expires (see ¶4540); owns securities that a corporation redeems or cancels; or changes all or part of a property's use (see ¶4434).

A capital loss resulting from the disposition of a share or debt obligation of a Canadian-controlled private corporation (CCPC) that is a small business corporation (SBC) is referred to as a business investment loss, the deductible portion of which is called an allowable business investment loss (ABIL). Under special tax rules, ABILs are deductible from any source of income in the year, not just from taxable capital gains (see ¶4600).

ITA 3(a), (b), 38, 39, 40, 54, 248(1)"disposition", "small business corporation", "taxable Canadian property", CRA Guide: T4037: *Capital Gains*, S3-F9-C1: *Lottery Winnings, Miscellaneous Receipts and Income (and Losses) From Crime*, IT-218R: *Profit, Capital Gains and Losses from the Sale of Real Estate, Including Farmland and Inherited Land and Conversion of Real Estate from Capital Property to Inventory and Vice Versa*, IT-407R4(C): *Dispositions of Cultural Property to Designated Canadian Institutions*

¶4010 — Capital Gains versus Income

A disposition of a capital property giving rise to a gain or a loss may be treated as either a capital gain or loss (i.e., a capital transaction, which is 50% taxable) or as an income gain or loss (i.e., an income transaction, which is 100% taxable) under the ITA. Thus, when an individual disposes of property, it must be determined whether the transaction is a capital transaction or an income transaction. For example, if an investor who derives income from the receipt of real estate rentals and interest and dividends from stocks and bonds were to sell the real estate or dispose of the stocks and bonds, the taxpayer would be disposing of capital assets and any profit would be taxed as a capital gain. If, however, the taxpayer was in the business of buying and selling real estate or was a broker buying and selling shares or bonds, the taxpayer would be disposing of inventory or stock in trade rather than capital assets and any profits would be taxable as business income.

The distinction between "income" and "capital gains" is primarily derived from case law. It is a question of fact whether or not a gain or a loss on the disposition of any property is on account of income or capital. To determine whether a gain is income or capital in nature, it must be determined whether an investment is being sold or a trade is being carried on. Where it is not clear whether the activity is in the nature of an investment or a trade, the courts have generally looked at the intention of the taxpayer at the time of acquiring the asset, the taxpayer's whole course of conduct in dealing with the asset, and the taxpayer's intention at the time of disposition of the asset. It is possible to have an investment intention at the time of acquisition but to have altered that intention and to have become a trader at the time of disposition. Intention is generally determined by the facts. Taxpayers should consider documenting any facts supporting an investment intention from the purchase to the disposition stages of a capital property where there is likely to be a doubt as to the characterization of a potential gain.

The taxpayer's intention is not the only factor that the courts have considered when determining whether a gain or loss is on account of income or capital. For example, in *Bowyer-Boag Ltd*, 2 Tax A.B.C. 202, the court stated that the following factors should be taken into consideration, in addition to the intention of the recipient at the time that the asset was received: the manner in which the asset came into the hands of the recipient, the manner in which the asset was dealt with by the recipient in the period during which it was held, the economic factors present during the period that the asset was held, and the surrounding circumstances and economic factors present when the asset was disposed of.

Following is a summary of the general case law principles applicable to individuals for distinguishing between business income and property income:

- The determination in each specific situation is a question of fact;

- The fact that property is used to earn income is not determinative;

- Property income may be derived either from a business or from the property, depending on the level of activity associated with acquiring the property income;

- Where funds are employed and risked by a business and the investment of these funds is necessary for the individual to conduct the business, the income from this investment activity will likely be considered income from a business;

- Income from property does not require active and extensive business-like intervention to produce it; it is passive income resulting from the mere ownership of property, without a significant commitment of time, labour, or attention; and

- Income from business requires organization, systematic effort, and a certain degree of activity.

ITA 39, IT-218R: *Profit, Capital Gains and Losses from the Sale of Real Estate*, IT-479R: *Transactions in Securities*, VDs 2001-0107655, 2005-0127861E5, 2006-0185041E5, 2008-0269481E5, 2009-0321871E5, Roskos, et al., "The Impact of Recent Supreme Court of Canada and Other Decisions on Real Estate Transactions," *Report of Proceedings of Fifty-Fourth Tax Conference*, 2002 Conference Report (Toronto: Canadian Tax Foundation, 2003), 30:1–29

¶4011 — *Security Gains or Losses*

The principles that apply for determining the characterization of a gain or loss on shares as income or capital are the same as those discussed above. Normally, ordinary stock market trading gives rise to capital gains and losses. However, if a taxpayer is a trader or dealer in securities, the gains and losses will not be capital gains and losses but will be considered a business income or loss. A similar result occurs if the disposition is considered an adventure or concern in the nature of trade, even if the taxpayer is not otherwise a trader or dealer (see ¶4015). Gains or losses on account of income are fully taxable or deductible and should not be reported on Schedule 3.

Generally, rather extensive trading in stocks and bonds is required for a taxpayer to be considered to be carrying on a securities trading business. In paragraphs 11–15 of IT-479R, the CRA states that some of the factors to be considered in ascertaining whether the taxpayer's course of conduct indicates the carrying on of a business are as follows:

- frequency of transactions — a history of extensive buying and selling of securities or of a quick turnover of properties,

- period of ownership — securities are usually owned only for a short period of time,

- knowledge of securities markets — the taxpayer has some knowledge of or experience in the securities markets,

- security transactions form a part of a taxpayer's ordinary business,

- time spent — a substantial part of the taxpayer's time is spent studying the securities markets and investigating potential purchases,

- financing — security purchases are financed primarily on margin or by some other form of debt,

- advertising — the taxpayer has advertised or otherwise made it known that he is willing to purchase securities, and

- in the case of shares, their nature — normally speculative in nature or of a non-dividend type.

Although none of the individual factors above may be sufficient to characterize the activities of a taxpayer as a business, the combination of a number of those factors may be sufficient for that purpose. Further, ITA 248(1) defines the term "business" to include "an adventure or concern in the nature of trade" and the courts have held that "an adventure or concern in the nature of trade" can include an isolated transaction in shares where the "course of conduct" and "intention" clearly indicate it to be such.

A taxpayer's intention to sell at a gain is not sufficient, by itself, to establish that the taxpayer was involved in an adventure or concern in the nature of trade. That intention is almost always present, even when a true investment has been acquired if circumstances should arise that would make it financially more beneficial to sell the investment than to continue to hold it. Where, however, one or other of the above tests clearly suggests an adventure or concern in the nature of trade and, in addition, it can be established or inferred that the taxpayer's intention was to sell the property at the first suitable opportunity, intention will be viewed as corroborative evidence. On the other hand, inability to establish an intention to sell does not preclude a transaction from being regarded as an adventure or concern in the nature of trade if it can otherwise be so regarded pursuant to one or more of the above tests.

With regard to a taxpayer who holds himself out to the public as a dealer in securities, there is a presumption that all gains or losses on security transactions are part of the normal operations of such a business and thus are on income account. In paragraph 17 of IT-479R, the CRA states that the presumption that gains and losses from security transactions are on income account will also be taken in any situation where it is apparent that the taxpayer has used special information not available to the public to realize a quick profit.

ITA 39(4) permits certain taxpayers to treat all of their Canadian securities as capital property such that any gains or losses would be on capital account. A taxpayer may elect to declare all profits and losses from the sale of Canadian securities to be on account of capital, both for the taxation year in respect of which the election is first made and for all subsequent years. This election does not apply to traders or dealers in securities. For the purposes of the election, a Canadian security is defined as a share of a corporation resident in Canada; a unit of a mutual fund trust; or a bond, debenture, bill, note, mortgage, hypothec, or similar obligation issued by a Canadian resident. Taxpayers make this election by completing Form T123, *Election on Disposition of Canadian Securities*, and attaching it to their paper-filed T1 return. If the return is being filed electronically, the election should be sent to the taxpayer's CRA Tax Centre by the filing-due date of the T1 return for the taxation year.

ITA 9, *Commercial Investments Corporation*, 32 Tax A.B.C. 1, *Foote*, 2017 CarswellNat 1729 (active trading by the co-head of institutional trading at an investment firm was held to be a business), *Gairdner Securities Ltd*, [1954] C.T.C. 24 (SCC), *Placements Bourget Inc*, [1988] 2 C.T.C. 8 (FCTD), *Donata Investments Ltd*, [1976] C.T.C. 2288 (TRB), VD 2010-0381231E5, 2005-0127861E5, 2001-0087365, 2001-0107655, 2001-0092085, 2004-006514117, Woolley, "Corporate Business Income Revisited — Where Are We? Part Two", *Canadian Tax Foundation's 66th Tax Conference*, 2014, Tennant, "The Taxation of Derivatives: The Basic Rules," *Report of Proceedings of Fifty-Seventh Tax Conference*, 2005 Tax Conference (Toronto: Canadian Tax Foundation, 2006), 41:1–15; Lefebvre, "Holding Companies: Selected Issues," in "Personal Tax Planning" (2004), vol. 52, no. 2 *Canadian Tax Journal*, 602–632

¶4015 — Adventure or Concern in the Nature of Trade

Special rules apply with respect to profits from "an adventure of concern in the nature of trade". Such profits are considered fully taxable business income rather than a capital gain, and should not be reported on Schedule 3. Essentially, an adventure or concern in the nature of trade involves the purchase of a property with a primary or secondary intention of reselling the property for profit.

In IT-459: *Adventure or Concern in the Nature of Trade*, the CRA provides the following general principles to assist in determining when an activity will be regarded as an "adventure or concern in the nature of trade":

1. It is a general principle that when a person habitually does a thing that is capable of producing a profit, then he is carrying on a trade or business notwithstanding that these activities may be quite separate and apart from his ordinary occupation. An example is that of a dentist who habitually buys and sells real estate.

2. Where such a thing is done only infrequently, or possibly only once, rather than habitually, it still is possible to hold that the person has engaged in a business transaction if, in accordance with the definition of "business" in ITA 248(1), it can be shown that he has engaged in "an adventure or concern in the nature of trade". That phrase has been interpreted in numerous decisions of the Courts and some of those decisions, where the transactions involved real estate, are reflected in IT-218 entitled "Profit from the Sale of Real Estate".

3. Although an adventure or concern in the nature of trade is included in the definition of the term "business" in ITA 248, it does not necessarily mean that a taxpayer who is engaged in an adventure or concern in the nature of trade is "carrying on" a business or has "carried on" a business. Where these phrases are used in the Act, a determination is made based on the degree of activity and each situation must be considered in the light of its own particular facts.

4. In determining whether a particular transaction is an adventure or concern in the nature of trade the Courts have emphasized that all the circumstances of the transaction must be considered and that no single criterion can be formulated. Generally, however, the principal tests that have been applied are as follows:

(a) whether the taxpayer dealt with the property acquired by him in the same way as a dealer in such property ordinarily would deal with it;

(b) whether the nature and quantity of the property excludes the possibility that its sale was the realization of an investment or was otherwise of a capital nature, or that it could have disposed of other than in a transaction of a trading nature; and

(c) whether the taxpayer's intention, as established or deduced, is consistent with other evidence pointing to a trading motivation.

Comments on the significance of the above tests appear below under the headings "Taxpayer's Conduct", "Nature of the Property" and "Taxpayer's Intention".

Taxpayer's Conduct

5. The primary consideration is whether the taxpayer's actions in regard to the property in question were essentially what would be expected of a dealer in such a property. What is required, therefore, is to compare what dealers in the same kind of property ordinarily do with what the taxpayer did when he purchased the property, when he sold it and during the time when it was in his possession. Where the property is real estate, some relevant factors are set out in IT-218.

6. Evidence that efforts were soon made to find or attract purchasers or that a sale took place within a short period of time after the acquisition of the property by the taxpayer points to a trading intention.

7. During the time the taxpayer owned the property it is significant whether steps were taken with the intended result of improving its marketability. Where the property consisted of an operating business, such steps might involve various changes in the way the business was operated so as to improve the profit potential. The listing of the business for sale when the improved marketability was achieved would suggest that the business had not been acquired as an investment but had been acquired, improved and offered for sale in a manner similar to procedures followed by a dealer in businesses.

8. The fact that the taxpayer has a commercial background in similar areas or has had previous experience of a similar commercial nature has been held to be a pertinent consideration in some circumstances.

Nature of the Property

9. Where property acquired by a taxpayer is of such a nature or of such a magnitude that it could not produce income or personal enjoyment to its owner by virtue of its ownership and the only purpose of the acquisition was a subsequent sale of the property, the presumption is that the purchase and sale was an adventure or concern in the nature of trade. This was a finding of the courts, for instance, where the property acquired was a large quantity of one kind of goods.

10. The property acquired may be capable of producing income but only if the taxpayer is in a position to operate or lease it, as for example, a cargo ship. If the taxpayer is not in a position to operate it and could make use of it only by selling it, the presumption again would be that the purchase and subsequent sale was an adventure or concern in the nature of trade.

11. Some kinds of property (e.g. a business, a security) are prima facie of an investment nature in that they are normally used to produce income through their operation or mere possession. Where property is of this kind and the taxpayer was in a position, if he so wished, to have operated or held it but he chose to sell it, then the manner in which he dealt with it and the intention when he acquired it must be the governing factors in deciding whether the transaction was an adventure or concern in the nature of trade.

Taxpayer's Intention

12. A taxpayer's intention to sell at a profit is not sufficient, by itself, to establish that he was involved in an adventure or concern in the nature of trade. That intention is almost invariably present even when a true investment has been acquired, if circumstances should arise that would make it financially more beneficial to sell the investment than to continue to hold it. Where, however, one or other of the above tests clearly suggests an adventure or concern in the nature of trade, and, in addition, it can be established or inferred that the taxpayer's intention was to sell the property at the first suitable opportunity, intention will be viewed as corroborative evidence. On the other hand, inability to establish an intention to sell does not preclude a transaction from being regarded as an adventure or concern in the nature of trade if it can otherwise be so regarded pursuant to one of the above tests.

13. It must be recognized that a taxpayer may have more than one intention when a property is acquired. If the primary intention is said to be the holding of the property as an investment, regard must be had to whether, at the time of the acquisition, there was a secondary intention to sell the property if the primary intention could not be fulfilled. Secondary intention is particularly significant when the circumstances suggest that there was little likelihood of the property being retained by the taxpayer because of a lack of financial resources or for some other reason. Further, a taxpayer's intentions are not limited to the purposes for acquiring the property but extend to the time at which the disposition was made. A taxpayer's intention, if any, at the time of acquisition of the property may change at any time during ownership and up to disposition because the taxpayer may form an intention or otherwise change or abandon the primary, dominant or secondary intention with respect to the property.

Isolated Transactions

14. The following factors, in and of themselves, are not sufficient to prevent a finding that a transaction was an adventure or concern in the nature of trade:

   (a) the transaction was a single or isolated one;

   (b) the taxpayer did not create any organization to carry out the transaction;

   (c) the transaction is totally different from any of the other activities of the taxpayer and he never entered into such a transaction either before or since.

Particular considerations with respect to the characterization of real estate transactions are discussed in IT-218R: *Profit, Capital Gains and Losses from the Sale of Real Estate, Including Farmland and Inherited Land and Conversion of Real Estate from Capital Property to Inventory and Vice Versa*. In paragraph 3 of IT-218R, the CRA states:

> 3. There is no provision in the *Income Tax Act* which describes the circumstances in which gains from the sale of real estate are to be determined as being either income or capital. However, in making such determinations, the courts have considered factors such as those listed below: (The list is not intended to be exclusive of any other factor.)
>
> > (a) the taxpayer's intention with respect to the real estate at the time of its purchase;
> >
> > (b) feasibility of the taxpayer's intention;
> >
> > (c) geographical location and zoned use of the real estate acquired;
> >
> > (d) extent to which intention carried out by the taxpayer;
> >
> > (e) evidence that the taxpayer's intention changed after purchase of the real estate;
> >
> > (f) the nature of the business, profession, calling or trade of the taxpayer and associates;
> >
> > (g) the extent to which borrowed money was used to finance the real estate acquisition and the terms of the financing, if any, arranged;
> >
> > (h) the length of time throughout which the real estate was held by the taxpayer;
> >
> > (i) the existence of persons other than the taxpayer who share interests in the real estate;
> >
> > (j) the nature of the occupation of the other persons referred to in (i) above as well as their stated intentions and courses of conduct;
> >
> > (k) factors which motivated the sale of the real estate;
> >
> > (l) evidence that the taxpayer and/or associates had dealt extensively in real estate.

> None of the above factors is conclusive in itself. Whether real estate owned by an individual is a capital property at a particular time is a question of fact that can only be determined on the basis of all the relevant information at that time. If the property was used in the business of the taxpayer, a gain on disposal will normally be a capital gain. In other cases, for capital gains treatment to apply, generally a taxpayer has to establish, on a balance of probabilities, that when the property was acquired, the individual did not have either a primary or secondary intention of selling it at a profit.

Intention at the time of purchase is the most significant factor in determining whether a transaction is an adventure or concern in the nature of trade. For example, in *Canada Safeway Ltd.*, 2008 FCA 24 (FCA), the Court stated (para. 43):

> I agree entirely with the authors of *Principles of Canadian Income Tax Law*, supra, when they say, at page 334, that although the courts have used various factors to determine whether a transaction constituted an adventure in the nature of trade or a capital transaction, namely, those found in IT-218R, the most determinative factor is the intention of the taxpayer at the time of acquiring the property. If that intention reveals a scheme for profit-making, then the Court will conclude that the transaction is an adventure in the nature of trade.

Nonetheless, as noted in IT-459, intention to resell a property at a profit when the property is acquired is only one factor (albeit the most important) in determining whether a transaction is an adventure or concern in the nature of trade and other factors must be considered. In *Minister of National Revenue v. Taylor*, [1956] C.T.C. 189 (Ex Ct), the Court stated (at p. 211):

> And a transaction may be an adventure in the nature of trade although the person entering upon it did so without any intention to sell its subject matter at a profit. The intention to sell the purchased [property] at a profit is not of itself a test of whether the profit is subject to tax for the intention to make a profit may be just as much the purpose of an investment transaction as of a trading one. Such intention may well be an important factor in determining that a transaction was an

adventure in the nature of trade but its presence is not an essential prerequisite to such a determination and its absence does not negative the idea of an adventure in the nature of trade. The considerations prompting the transaction may be of such a business nature as to invest it with the character of an adventure in the nature of trade even without any intention of making a profit on [the] sale of the purchased commodity. And the taxpayer's declaration that he entered upon the transaction without any intention of making a profit on the sale of the purchased property should be scrutinized with care. It is what he did that must be considered and his declaration that he did not intend to make a profit may be overborne by other considerations of a business or trading nature motivating the transaction.

A secondary intention of a taxpayer is also an important consideration in determining the character of gain or loss. Generally, a profit on the disposition of a property might be held to be taxable even though, had the taxpayer's original intention been carried out, that property would have become a capital asset. In cases involving secondary intention, the court may find that a taxpayer had, or can be deemed to have had, from the beginning, an alternative intention to turn the asset to account in whatever way seemed best if the dominant intention was frustrated. To be successful under the principle of secondary intention, the Minister must successfully argue that a secondary intention to sell the property in question for a profit was a significant motivating factor in the purchase.

In *Canada Safeway Ltd.*, [2008] 2 C.T.C. 149 (FCA), after considering various jurisprudence on the matter of secondary intention, the Court stated (para. 61):

A number of principles emerge from these decisions which I believe can be summarized as follows. First, the boundary between income and capital gains cannot easily be drawn and, as a consequence, consideration of various factors, including the taxpayer's intent at the time of acquiring the property at issue, becomes necessary for a proper determination. Second, for the transaction to constitute an adventure in the nature of trade, the possibility of resale, as an operating motivation for the purchase, must have been in the mind of the taxpayer. In order to make that determination, inferences will have to be drawn from all of the circumstances. In other words, the taxpayer's whole course of conduct has to be assessed. Third, with respect to "secondary intention", it also must also have existed at the time of acquisition of the property and it must have been an operating motivation in the acquisition of the property. Fourth, the fact that the taxpayer contemplated the possibility of resale of his or her property is not, in itself, sufficient to conclude in the existence of an adventure in the nature of trade. In *Principles of Canadian Income Tax Law*, *supra*, the learned authors, in discussing the applicable test in relation to the existence of a "secondary intention", opine that "the secondary intention doctrine will not be satisfied unless the prospect of resale at a profit was an important consideration in the decision to acquire the property" (see page 337). I agree entirely with that proposition. Fifth, the *viva voce* evidence of the taxpayer with respect to his or her intention is not conclusive and has to be tested in the light of all the surrounding circumstances.

As discussed above, there are many other factors to be considered in determining whether a transaction is an adventure or concern in the nature of trade beyond initial and secondary intention. In distinguishing between trading profits and capital gains, in *Cragg v. Minister of National Revenue*, [1951] C.T.C. 322 (Exch), the Court noted:

Such a decision cannot depend solely on the number of transactions in the series, or the period of time in which they occurred, or the amount of profit made, or the kind of property involved. Nor can it rest on statements of intention on the part of the taxpayer. The question in each case is what is the proper deduction to be drawn from the taxpayer's whole course of conduct in the light of all the circumstances. The conclusion in each case must be one of fact.

In paragraph 14 of IT-459, the CRA notes that an isolated transaction may be considered an adventure or concern in the nature of trade. A single or isolated transaction that has no purpose except to earn a trading profit is normally considered an adventure of concern in the nature of trade where the badges of trade are present. For example, in *Chutter v. Minister of National Revenue*, [1955] C.T.C. 377 (Exch), the appellant, whose sole occupation was that of managing director of a company making wire rope, purchased four used diesel engines and sold them for a substantial profit; the Court concluded:

The purchase and re-sale of the four engines by the appellant bear the badges of trade. The purchase cannot be regarded as an ordinary investment. The engines were purchased for the purpose of re-sale at a profit and not with any thought of deriving any income through the leasing or rental of them. The transaction was a deal in machinery.

In *Taylor*, [1956] C.T.C. 189 (Exch), the taxpayer purchased lead in Europe for resale to his own company because it was unable to purchase the lead itself. When the lead was delivered the taxpayer sold it immediately, realizing a substantial profit. The taxpayer had never been in the business of buying and selling lead or other metals on his own account and this was the first and only occasion on which a purchase and sale of this nature had taken place. The Court found that the taxpayer's profit arose from an adventure or concern in the nature of trade.

Once a taxpayer has established that a certain type of activity is part of the taxpayer's business, it would be difficult to argue that a subsequent transaction is capital in nature as opposed to income in nature. Also, frequency of transactions is a factor that suggests a business is being carried on. Duration of ownership or property is not a prime indication of investment intent; however, it creates a presumption of investment intention when the asset has been producing income for a period of time and the motivation for the eventual sale is with investment realizations as opposed to trading incentives. See also paragraphs 5–9 of IT-459 above.

ITA 248(1)"business", *Staltari*, 2015 CarswellNat 1788 (TCC), *Regal Heights Ltd.*, [1960] C.T.C. 384 (SCC), *Kit-Win Holdings (1973) Ltd.*, [1981] C.T.C. 43 (FCTD), *Regina Shoppers Mall Ltd.*, [1986] 1 C.T.C. 261; aff'd [1989] 2 C.T.C. 278 (FCA), *Crystal Glass Canada Ltd.*, [1989] 1 C.T.C. 330, *Gairdner Securities Ltd.*, [1954] C.T.C. 24 (SCC), *Greater Sarnia Investment Corp.*, [1987] 1 C.T.C. 2158 (TCC), *Dubé*, [2007] 2 C.T.C. 2437 (TCC); *Zaenker*, [2008] 1 C.T.C. 2128 (TCC); *Schwartz*, [2009] 1 C.T.C. 2576 (TCC); *Dalron Construction Ltd.*, [2009] 1 C.T.C. 2499 (TCC), *Smitlener*, 2009 CarswellNat 1315 (TCC)

¶4100 — Computation of Capital Gains and Losses

¶4110 — Proceeds of Disposition (Sch. 3: Col. 2)

In Column 2 in each Part of Schedule 3, enter the proceeds of disposition for the capital property disposed of. The expression "proceeds of disposition", which is relevant for the purposes of determining a taxpayer's capital gain or loss from the disposition of property, is contained in ITA 54. The proceeds of disposition (POD) of any property that has been sold is its sale price, in money or money's worth, whether paid or still owing. The POD of a property is normally the selling price. In cases where proceeds of disposition are still owing after the end of the taxation year in which the disposition took place, taxpayers are permitted to claim a capital gains reserve (see ¶4140).

Where a taxpayer owes money under a mortgage or agreement for sale and the property is either sold or seized by the creditor for nonpayment, the amount by which the taxpayer's indebtedness is reduced (plus any part of the sale proceeds received) is considered proceeds of disposition of the property. Mortgage foreclosures and conditional sales repossessions are reported in Part 6 of Schedule 3 (see ¶4560).

Any compensation received or receivable as insurance proceeds, an award for damages, or otherwise, for property that has been destroyed, as well as any amount payable under a policy of insurance in respect of property that has been lost, is included in proceeds of disposition. However, as discussed below under ¶4700, the ITA permits a taxpayer to defer recognition of the gain resulting from the receipt of proceeds of such disposition to the extent that an amount is spent to acquire replacement property before the end of the second taxation year following that in which the proceeds of disposition were received.

Proceeds of disposition of a property include any compensation received or receivable for property damaged including any amount payable under a policy of insurance in respect of damage to property.

However, if the compensation or amount of insurance proceeds is used within a reasonable time to repair the damage, it may to that extent be excluded from the proceeds of disposition of the property. In such a case, the cost of the repairs may not be added in computing the property's ACB. Where depreciable property is damaged and the insurance proceeds are used to repair the damage, the part so used is specifically excluded from being treated as proceeds of disposition and is instead required to be included in computing the taxpayer's income for the year. The cost of the repairs will be deductible under the general law such that there is normally no net effect on the taxpayer's income.

Proceeds of disposition also include any compensation received or receivable for property that has been unlawfully taken, whether by theft or otherwise. Such compensation could take the form of insurance proceeds or an award for damages. The taxpayer cannot defer recognition of the gain on the receipt of such compensation as can be done in the case of receiving insurance proceeds for lost property. Proceeds of disposition also include any compensation received or receivable for property taken under statutory authority, such as by expropriation, as well as the sale price of any property sold to a person by whom notice of an intention to take it under statutory authority has been given.

The assumption of a vendor's liability by a purchaser normally constitutes part of the sale price and therefore part of the proceeds of disposition; however, this may not be the case where the liability directly reduces the inherent value of the property (i.e., if the liability is embedded in the asset). For example, if land with a fair market value of $1M is sold for consideration consisting of the assumption of a $500K mortgage and $500K in cash, the proceeds of disposition would be $1M. In this case, the mortgage does not reduce the inherent value of the land. If, for example, the land had been purchased with cash and there was no mortgage, the land would still be worth $1M. However, assume instead the land is worth $500K because of a related $500K site restoration liability. In this case, if the land were purchased in exchange for the assumption of the $500K mortgage, the proceeds of disposition would be $500K, not $1M (i.e., since the value of the land is $500K when the site restoration liability is considered).

ITA 68 applies where an amount received or receivable can reasonably be regarded as being in part consideration for the disposition of a particular property of a taxpayer or as being in part consideration for the provision of particular services. If the amount is in part consideration for the disposition of property, that part of the consideration that can reasonably be regarded as being for the disposition of property is deemed to be the proceeds of disposition of that property and, reciprocally, the cost of the property for the acquirer. In order to determine if an amount can reasonably be regarded as the consideration for the disposition of a particular property, ITA 68 requires considering whether a reasonable business person, with business considerations in mind, would have allocated that amount to that particular property. In applying this rule, long-standing industry practices, auditing, and valuation standards and practices are relevant.

In *Transalta Corp.*, 2010 CarswellNat 2297 (TCC), the court varied a purchase price allocation agreement in accordance with ITA 68, even though the allocation had been arrived at between parties dealing with each other at arm's length. Significantly, the decision of the Tax Court was overturned by the Federal Court of Appeal, which stated (2012 CarswellNat 124 (FCA), paras. 77-78, 80–82):

> An allocation agreed between the parties to an arm's length transaction is an important factor to consider for the purpose of section 68 of the Act. However, the weight to be given to such an agreement will vary according to the circumstances. An agreement where the parties have strong divergent interests concerning the allocation will be given considerable weight, while an agreement where one of the parties is indifferent, or where both parties' interests are aligned as regards the allocation, will be given less weight: *R.L. Petersen v. The Minister of National Revenue* (1987), 88 D.T.C. 1040 at pp. 1046-1047. The fact that the parties have agreed to an allocation does not trump the reasonableness test under section 68 of the Act. As I have already noted, that test is whether a reasonable business person, with business considerations in mind, would have made the allocation. That the parties to an arm's length transaction have agreed on an allocation is an important factor to consider, but an agreed allocation which does not meet the reasonableness test may still be challenged under section 68 . . .

In *Golden*, [1986] 1 C.T.C. 274 (SCC), the Court upheld the allocation between land and buildings under an agreement of sale in an arm's length transaction. In reaching this conclusion, the Court stated that although ITA 68 (as it then read) was applicable to the transaction, the allocation agreed to by the arm's length parties was reasonable in the circumstances. At paragraph 15 of the Federal Court of Appeal decision (1983 CarswellNat 741), the Court stated:

> It is my opinion that the correct approach to a section 68 determination would be, as suggested by the above authorities, to consider the matter from the viewpoint of both the vendor and the purchaser and to consider all of the relevant circumstances surrounding the transaction. Where, as in this case, as found by the Trial Judge, the transaction is at arm's length and is not a mere sham or subterfuge, the apportionment made by the parties in the applicable agreement is certainly an important circumstance and one which is entitled to considerable weight.

In VD 9204895, the CRA states:

> The second issue in [*Golden*] was whether the allocation of the sale price by the parties to the particular transaction was reasonable within the meaning of section 68 of the Act. This part of the decision involved a question of fact, and not a principle of law. In such cases, it is of course a matter of considering all the facts, deciding on how much weight should be given to each and making a decision. The decision in *Golden* suggested that the Department should, among other things, consider the relationship of the parties and how they arrived at their apportionment. It does not, however, change the basic principle that each such case must be decided on the basis of its own facts and one of these facts is the reasonableness of the allocation. Thus, without reference to the figures used in your hypothetical example, the Department may very well challenge the values assigned to depreciable, non-depreciable and other assets such as goodwill, quotas, inventory, etc. where those figures or allocations appear to be unreasonable in the circumstances. The Department might also assign a value where one was not assigned to such assets.

ITA 12(1)(f), 13(21)"proceeds of disposition"(f), 40(1)(a)(iii), 44(1), 54"proceeds of disposition", 79, IT-259R4: *Exchange of Property*, IT-271R (cancelled), VD 2008-0297051E5, *Canadian Propane*, [1972] C.T.C. 566 (FCTD), *Robert Glegg Investments*, 2008 CarswellNat 4148 (FCA), *Wagner*, 2013 CarswellNat 120 (FCA), *Golden*, [1986] 1 C.T.C. 274 (SCC), *Sunrise Realty*, 2013 CarswellNat 29 (TCC), McCue, "The Section 68 Reasonableness Standard After TransAlta", 62(1) Canadian Tax Journal 43–67 (2014)

¶4111 — *Outlays and Expenses (Sch.3: Col. 4)*

> Outlays and expenses incurred for the purpose of making a disposition of capital property or in putting the property into saleable condition are deductible for purposes of calculating a capital gain or loss on the property. These include certain repair expenses, finder's fees, real estate or other commissions, surveyor's fees, transfer taxes, and other reasonable expenses incurred to dispose of the property. In each Part of Schedule 3, in Column 4, enter the amount of outlays and expenses deducted from proceeds of disposition when calculating the capital gain or loss.

Whether or not an outlay or expense is incurred for the purpose of making a disposition is a question of fact. Generally, expenses relating to the continued ownership by a taxpayer of a capital property, although perhaps relevant in computing the adjusted cost base of the property, are not deductible from the proceeds of disposition. Expenses which are otherwise deductible under the ITA in computing income from a business or property are also not deductible in computing a capital gain. It is generally more beneficial to deduct an expense from income for tax purposes than to offset proceeds of disposition, as only 50% of capital gains are included in income for tax purposes. Under the ITA, the proceeds of disposition of a property are required to be offset by "any outlays and expenses to the extent that they were made or incurred by the taxpayer for the purpose of making the disposition".

In Guide T4037, the CRA states:

> Outlays and expenses — are amounts that you incurred to sell a capital property. You can deduct outlays and expenses from your "proceeds of disposition" when calculating your capital gain or loss. You cannot reduce your other income by claiming a deduction for these outlays and expenses. These types of expenses include fixing-up expenses, finders' fees, commissions, brokers' fees, surveyors' fees, legal fees, transfer taxes, and advertising costs.

The CRA provides the following comments in paragraph 14 of IT-99R5 *(Consolidated): Legal Fees*:

> Legal and accounting fees incurred on the acquisition of capital property are normally included as part of the cost of the property. In the case of depreciable property, the claim for capital cost allowance is based on the total capital cost including such fees. Pursuant to subsection 40(1), any outlay or expense (including legal or accounting fees) incurred for the purpose of making the disposition of a property is added to the adjusted cost base of the property in calculating the amount of the capital gain, capital loss, terminal loss or business investment loss, as the case may be, arising from the disposition.

In *Deschênes*, 2015 FCA 147, the Court ruled that that legal fees incurred by the taxpayer to increase the value of an estate being inherited were neither a business expense, nor an expense for the purpose of earning income from a property, and were therefore on capital account.

ITA 40(1)(a), IT-99R5(C): *Legal fees*

¶4112 — *Seizure of Property by a Creditor*

ITA 79 and 79.1 respectively govern the tax consequences to a debtor and creditor where property is acquired by a creditor from a debtor as a consequence of the debtor's failure to pay a debt. In very general terms, ITA 79 deems the debtor to have proceeds of disposition of the property equal to the aggregate of the unpaid principal amount and the unpaid accrued interest on such debt.

A debtor is considered to have surrendered property to a creditor when the creditor acquires or reacquires the beneficial ownership of the property from the debtor as a result of the failure of the debtor to pay part or all of the debt. A creditor is defined to include a person (including by definition a partnership) to whom the person in question is obliged to pay an amount under a mortgage, hypothecary claim, or similar obligation. Where the property is sold under a conditional sales agreement, the vendor of the property or an assignee of the agreement is deemed to be a creditor in respect of the property. A debt is defined to include an obligation to pay an amount under a mortgage, hypothecary claim, or similar obligation or conditional sales agreement. Property is defined not to include money or indebtedness owed by or guaranteed by the government of a country, or a province, state, or other political subdivision of the country. ITA 79 does not apply where, for example, the debtor has transferred the property to a third party and the creditor acquires the property from that person unless the third party is liable to the creditor and the property is acquired on the default of the third party.

The amount included in the debtor's income as proceeds of disposition of the property surrendered is determined by the formula set out in ITA 79(3) as follows:

$$(A + B + C + D + E + F) \times G/H$$

where

A   equals the total of all specified amounts (defined in ITA 79(1) to include unpaid interest) of debts owing by the debtor to the creditor including unpaid interest, in respect of which the property is surrendered;

B   equals the total specified amount of debts owing to persons other than the creditor to the extent those amounts are no longer owing by reason of the surrender of the property to the creditor;

C   equals the total specified amount of other debts owing where the property was security for the debt as well as a subordinate debt owing to the creditor to whom the property was surrendered;

D   equals a specified amount of a debt owing to a creditor other than the one to whom the property is surrendered where the debt is no longer secured by all of the debtor's properties as adjusted;

E   equals the excess of the fair market value of the property surrendered over the total amount of debts owing in circumstances where the parties do not deal at arm's length;

F   equals the amount in respect of obligations otherwise taken into account under other provisions of the ITA; and

G & H   equal the proration factor of the fair market value of the relevant part of the surrendered property over the total fair market value of the total surrendered property where the surrendered property consists of more than one type of property.

A debtor is not considered to have paid or repaid any amount as a consequence of the acquisition or reacquisition of surrendered property. In the case of debts denominated in foreign currency, the proceeds of disposition for the property surrendered are determined based on the historical foreign exchange rate when the debt was issued.

Generally, the cost of the property to the creditor is the cost of the debt to the creditor, less the inclusions in such cost base that are reversed as a consequence of the acquisition of the property. The latter adjustment applies to the extent of a reserve claimed in the immediate prior year under ITA 20(1)(n) for inventory sales, under ITA 40(1)(a)(iii) for sales of capital properties, or 44(1)(e)(iii) for replacement properties. By eliminating these reserves without an income inclusion, ITA 79.1 reverses the income or gain recognized on the original sale that gave rise to the debt in question, and to this extent it is appropriate to reduce the creditor's cost of the debt and, ultimately, the acquired property. A comparable rule applies to reverse the consequences of the sale of capital property that is now being seized and that was sold earlier in the same taxation year. In general terms, the creditor is deemed to have disposed of the debt at the time of the seizure for an amount equal to its ACB or cost amount, as the case may be.

ITA 79, 79.1, IT-170R: *Sale of property — When included in income computation*, VD 2009-0305751E5, *Pigeau*, 2009 CarswellNat 4076 (TCC) (transfer to someone other than creditor), *Waltz*, [2001] 2 C.T.C. 2627 (TCC) (time for calculation of foreign exchange gain or loss is date of foreclosure); *Jones*, [1999] 1 C.T.C. 2644 (TCC) (surrender and subrogation gave rise to new creditor; provision applicable), *Hallbauer*, [1998] 3 C.T.C. 115 (FCA); aff'd [1997] 1 C.T.C. 2428 (TCC) (non-contingent, irreversible transfers were dispositions), *Corbett*, [1997] 1 C.T.C. 2 (FCA) (section intended to apply where no fixed price of sale), *Peters (D.L.)*, [1993] 1 C.T.C. 2628 (TCC) (ITA 80 applies to unpaid interest on obligation to which ITA 79 applied), Shillinger et al., "Advanced Topics in Real Estate Tax Planning," *Report of Proceedings of Sixty-First Tax Conference*, 2009 Tax Conference (Toronto: Canadian Tax Foundation, 2010), 33:1–34

¶4120 — Adjusted Cost Base (ACB) of Capital Property (Sch. 3: Col. 3)

A capital gain or loss is computed by subtracting the ACB of the capital property disposed of by the net proceeds of disposition received. The ACB of a capital property is the original cost of the property (in Canadian dollars) that has been adjusted to reflect certain transactions or occurrences that took place after acquiring the property. "Capital property" is defined as including both depreciable property and any other property the gain or loss from the disposition of which would give rise to a capital gain or loss. In Column 3 of the various Parts of Schedule 3, enter the ACB of the capital property disposed of that is used to calculate any capital gain or loss.

Normally, the ACB of a property is the actual cost of acquiring it, including the purchase price plus any related costs, such as commissions, legal fees, and other reasonable expenses. It also includes the cost of additions and improvements to the property that are capital in nature (see ¶5210). Current expenses that are deducted in computing income for tax purposes, such as maintenance and repair costs, are not included in the ACB of a property.

In the absence of a specific provision in the ITA, by definition the adjusted cost base of a property can never be less than nil. Where the adjusted cost base would otherwise be a negative amount, this amount is considered to be a capital gain to the taxpayer.

ITA 53, which determines the adjustments that must be made to the cost base of a capital property, does not apply to depreciable property (defined in ITA 13(21)). However, it is important to highlight that the capital cost of depreciable property is not necessarily its historical cost. For example, ITA 13(7.1) provides that the capital cost of a property in respect of which a taxpayer has either claimed an investment tax credit (ITC) for a preceding taxation year or received a municipal or other public grant or subsidy is its actual cost to the taxpayer minus the amount of the ITC or grant or subsidy. It is also important to highlight that a capital loss cannot be incurred on a disposition of depreciable capital property; a fully deductible terminal loss may, however, arise (see ¶7150).

The ACB of any property other than depreciable property is defined as the cost to the taxpayer of the property adjusted in accordance with ITA 53.

Amounts added to the ACB of all capital properties include:

- Deemed gains resulting from negative ACBs (see ¶4128);

- Superficial losses where substituted property is acquired (see ¶4821); and

- Losses on dispositions of debt to related persons that are deemed to be nil (see ¶4522).

Amounts deducted from ACB of all capital properties include:

- In respect of partial disposals, the ACB of the part disposed of (where a taxpayer has disposed of part of a property and retained the other part, the ACB of the part disposed of is determined to be such portion of the ACB to the taxpayer at that time of the whole property as may reasonably be regarded as attributable to that part);

- Amounts required to be applied against the ACB of a property as a result of the application of the debt forgiveness rules;

- The amount of assistance (including subsidies, forgivable loans, deductions from tax, and investment allowances) received from a government, municipality, or other public authority in respect of, or for the acquisition of, capital property. Similarly, where the taxpayer has claimed an ITC in respect of a capital property, the ITC reduces the ACB of the property;

- Any amounts in respect of the cost to the taxpayer of a capital property that was deducted in computing the taxpayer's income for tax purposes for any taxation year.

ITA 43, 53(1)(a), (f), (f.1), (2)(b.2), (d), (g), (g.1), (k), (m), 87(2)(e), 88(1)(a)(iii), IT-264R and IT-264R(SR): *Part Dispositions*, *Gaynor*, [1987] 1 C.T.C. 2359 (TCC); aff'd [1988] 2 C.T.C. 163 (FCTD) and [1991] 1 C.T.C. 470 (FCA)

¶4121 — *Identical Properties*

Properties of a group are considered to be identical if each property in the group is the same as all the others. The most common examples of identical properties are shares of the same class of the capital stock of a corporation or units of a mutual fund trust. A taxpayer may buy and sell several identical properties at different prices over a period of time. In such a case, the average cost of each property in the group at the time of each purchase must be calculated to determine the ACB of a property in the group. The average cost of identical properties is calculated by dividing the total cost of the identical properties purchased (normally the cost of the property plus any expenses involved in acquiring it) by the total number of identical properties owned.

A bond, debenture, or similar debt obligation that a debtor issues is considered to be identical to another if the same debtor issues both and all the attached rights are the same. The principal amount of individual debt obligations is not relevant. For example, assume a corporation purchases 10 bonds ("the old bonds") having a face value of $500 each and an aggregate ACB of $2,400. Subsequently, the corporation acquires 10 more bonds for $9,600 ("the new bonds") which are identical to the old bonds except that their face value is $1,000 each. At the time of the second purchase, the ACB to the corporation of the bonds is determined as follows: each bond of $500 principal value = ($2,400 + $9,600)/(15,000/500) = $400; each bond of $1,000 principal value = ($9,600 + $2,400)/(15,000/1,000) = $800.

The CRA discussed identical properties in IT-387R2 (cancelled): *Meaning of Identical Properties*. The CRA takes the position that stripped bonds are not to be regarded as identical to bonds of the same issue from which interest coupons have not been detached.

Although identical properties may be difficult to separately identify in the event of a partial sale, the CRA has stated it is possible to have separate pools of properties having their own distinct tax attributes within a pool of identical properties. Such a distinction may be relevant, for example, where certain tax elections are being made involving identical properties acquired at different times.

ITA 47, IT-387R2 (cancelled): *Meaning of Identical Properties*, Info Sheet RC4169: *Tax Treatment of Mutual Funds for Individuals*, VDs 2011-0394231E5, 2011-0426531E5, 2006-0197401E5, 2000-0028665, *Gervais*, 2016 CarswellNat 22 (FCA)

¶4122 — *Shares*

Where shares are held as capital property, in addition to amounts described under ¶4120, amounts added to the ACB of the shares include:

- Dividends deemed to be received by a shareholder of a Canadian resident corporation where the corporation increases its paid-up capital otherwise than by payment of a stock dividend, a transaction increasing net assets or decreasing net liabilities by an amount at least equal to the increase in paid-up capital, or a reduction of paid-up capital in respect of some classes of shares at least equal to the increase in paid-up capital in respect of other classes of shares

- Deemed dividends received by a shareholder of an immigrating corporation

- Contributions to the capital of the corporation

- FAPI imputed to the shareholder from a foreign affiliate

Regarding a capital contribution to the corporation, the ACB of the shares held does not increase where the contribution is made by way of loan or to the extent that the contribution can reasonably be regarded as a "benefit conferred" by the corporation on a person (other than the corporation) who was related to the corporation. Many court decisions have considered what might constitute the conferring of a "benefit"; see, for example, *Dufresne*, [1967] C.T.C. 153 (Exch) and *Immobiliare*, [1977] C.T.C. 481 (FCTD). The expression "contribution of capital" is not defined in the ITA. Presumably, it includes any amount contributed by a taxpayer to the capital of a corporation in excess of amounts allocated by the corporation to its share capital on the issue of shares, including both premiums and outright contributions of property. Forgiveness of a loan, waiving rights to dividends, etc., may also constitute contributions of capital as well.

Amounts deducted from the ACB of shares, in addition to amounts described under ¶4120, include:

- In the case of a share of a Canadian corporation: (1) any amount received as a tax-free dividend (other than a capital dividend); (2) any amount received as a reduction of capital (other than any part included in income pursuant to ITA 84(4) or (4.1) as a deemed dividend); (3) any amount which is treated under ITA 84(8) as a return of capital rather than a dividend; and (4) any amount required by ITA 44.1(2)(b) to be deducted in respect of a replacement share;

- In respect of shares of a foreign affiliate, foreign tax credits available against imputed FAPI, dividends paid out of previously taxed FAPI and deductible under ITA 91(5), and dividends deductible by virtue of ITA 113(1)(d) as having been paid out of pre-acquisition surplus;

- In the case of property acquired through a payment made to a joint exploration corporation, such part of the payment as related to the relevant exploration and development expenses; and

- In the case of property received by a shareholder in consideration for a loan or payment made to a joint exploration corporation where the corporation has agreed to renounce certain expenses in favour of the shareholder, an amount equal to the amount of the renounced expenses.

> The ACB of shares must also be recalculated to reflect stock splits and consolidations. Generally, a stock split takes place if a company's outstanding shares are divided into a larger number of shares, without changing the total market value of the company's holdings. The total market value of each investor's holdings and their proportionate equity in the company are not affected by a stock split.

ITA 53(1)(b), (1)(b.1), (1)(c), (1)(d), (1)(d.3), 53(2)(a), (b), (e), (f.1), (f.2), 66(10.4)(a), 66(15), 80.1(4)(d), 92, IT-456R: *Capital property — Some adjustments to cost base*, IT-65: *Stock splits and consolidations*, VD 2015-060967I7 (earnout payments — see also He, "Earnouts Not Eligible Capital Expenditures", Canadian Tax Focus, Vol. 7-2, May 2017)

¶4123 — *Partnership Interests*

Membership in a partnership generally carries with it a right to share in partnership income and in any distributions of property upon termination of the partnership. The rules governing the taxation of members of partnerships are set forth in ITA 96–103. Partnership income for tax purposes is computed at the partnership level and allocated to partners.

The rights that a taxpayer has by virtue of membership in a partnership are, for income tax purposes, referred to as an "interest in a partnership". This interest itself is an item of "property" within the broad meaning given that term in the ITA. In most cases, a partnership interest is "capital property" and a taxpayer who disposes of an interest in a partnership must compute a capital gain or loss. Generally, the ACB of a partnership interest includes the original investment plus the partner's share of the profits and contributions of capital, minus the partner's share of partnership losses and partnership drawings. However, a variety of special adjustments may also be required, as outlined below.

The first step in determining the ACB of an interest in a partnership is the determination of the cost of the interest, which depends on how the interest was acquired. Where the interest was acquired by contributing cash to the partnership, the cost of the interest is equal to the monetary amount contributed. Where the interest was acquired by contributing property to the partnership, the cost is the fair market value of the property contributed (unless an election is made under ITA 97, in which case the cost base will be determined by reference to the elected values). If the interest was acquired from an existing partner, the cost of the interest is the amount paid for the interest.

After determining the initial cost, special adjustments must be made to the cost base of a partnership interest in order to compute the appropriate gain or loss on its disposition. Amounts added to the ACB of a partnership interest generally reflect amounts that have already been taxed to a partner or that could have been received tax-free by the partner were it not for the interposition of the partnership.

The following amounts may be added to the ACB of a partnership interest:

- The taxpayer's share of partnership profits for each prior fiscal period ending after 1971, including the full amount of partnership capital gains (i.e., not just the taxable portion) and amounts included in income in respect of eligible capital property (before 2017). The amount added to the ACB is based on the income of the partnership for tax purposes. Thus, for example, the non-deductible portion of meals and entertainment expenses that is added to the partnership's income computed for tax purposes is included in the ACB of the partnership interest;

- The taxpayer's share of any capital dividends and any life insurance capital dividends received by the partnership (such amounts are not taxable when flowed through to the partner);

- The taxpayer's share of any net life insurance proceeds after 1971 (such amounts are not taxable in the hands of the partner) (see VDs 2011-0398421C6, 2008-0275471E5, 2005-0125401E5);

- Royalty amounts paid by the partner to the partnership but not deductible by the partner under former ITA 18(1)(m). This adjustment covers reimbursement payments (see ITA 80.2(1)) in respect of a Crown charge described in former ITA 12(1)(o) or 18(1)(m) made by a partner to a partnership in a taxation year ending after 2002 where the reimbursed Crown charge is paid or payable in a taxation year or fiscal period of the recipient that begins before 2007. An addition should be made in respect of the part of the reimbursement payment that is not deductible in computing the partner's income;

- Capital contributed after 1971 to the partnership that cannot reasonably be regarded as a benefit conferred on any other member of the partnership who was related to the partner. The benefit conferral rule is intended to prevent the effective transfer of property by contribution to a partnership in which a related taxpayer has a share. An amount added to the ACB under this provision does not include loans that the partner made to the partnership;

- Amounts required to be reported as a gain under ITA 40(3.1) in connection with a negative ACB of a limited partnership interest. ITA 40(3.1) provides that a passive member of a partnership is deemed to realize a gain from the disposition, at the end of a fiscal period of the partnership, of the member's interest in the partnership where the member is a "limited partner" or was a "specified member" of the partnership at all times since becoming a partner and the member's ACB of the interest is negative at that time. The CRA has stated a non-resident partner would not be considered to have disposed of taxable Canadian property when a gain is triggered under ITA 40(3.1)(a) (negative ACB) on a partnership interest that is taxable Canadian property (VD 2011-0417491E5);

- Any amount deemed by ITA 98(1)(c) or 98.1(1)(c) to be a gain. The latter provisions apply to deem a member of a partnership to have a capital gain equal to the "negative" ACB in the member's partnership interest where the partnership ceases to carry on business and where the member has a residual interest in a partnership. While a partnership is active, the rules regarding taxation of a negative cost base under ITA 40(3) are not applicable (ITA 40(3)(a));

- The taxpayer's share of CDE or COGPE expenses incurred by the partnership where an election is made by the partner. A taxpayer can elect to have a share of a partnership's CDE or COGPE expenses in a fiscal period excluded in determining the taxpayer's own CDE or COGPE. If the taxpayer makes the election, the taxpayer is not allowed to deduct any amount in respect of its share of such expenses in computing income. However, ITA 53(1)(e)(vii.1) provides an addition in computing the ACB to the taxpayer of the taxpayer's interest in the partnership. This addition offsets the subtraction under ITA 53(2)(c) (see below) of the same amount in computing the ACB to the taxpayer of the partnership interest. To make this election, file Form T1086: *Election by a partner waiving Canadian development expenses or oil and gas property expenses*, within 6 months after the end of the taxpayer's taxation year in which the fiscal period of the partnership ends;

- Income deemed by ITA 66.1(7), 66.2(6), or 66.4(6) to have been received on the sale or "recovery" of certain resource expenses (see also ITTN-12). Resource expenses, assistance, expense recoveries, and proceeds are recognized for computing income only at the partner level and are included in calculating the partner's CEE, CDE, COGPE, or FRE cumulative pools. On the sale of a Canadian resource property or on the recovery of a CEE, CDE, or COGPE, the partner's cumulative accounts are reduced by their share and if a negative balance results, the balance is included in the partner's income. ITA 53(1)(e)(viii) and (viii.1) serve to prevent such amounts from being taxed again as capital gains by providing for their addition to the cost base of the partnership interest;

- The partner's share of any tax-free exploration and development grant and assistance received by the partnership from a government, municipality, or other public authority, for a Canadian resource property or a CEE or CDE in Canada, net of any amount repaid. Similar to resource expenses, assistance funds for resource expenses are recognized for computing income only at the partner level and are included in calculating the partner's CEE, CDE, or COGPE pools;

- Any amount required by ITA 97 to be included in the ACB of the partnership interest in respect of a contribution of property to the partnership in exchange for partnership units. Generally, where property is contributed to a partnership on a rollover basis under ITA 97(2), if the proceeds of disposition are less than the fair market value of the consideration received (not including a partnership interest), the shortfall is to be added to the ACB of the partnership interest immediately after the disposition;

- Where the partner's share of income or loss is 10% or more, any soft costs (such as interest and property tax expenses) denied to the partner by virtue of ITA 18(2) or (3.1) in connection with vacant land or construction of a building by a third party (ITA 53(1)(e)(xi)); and

- Amounts added to a partner's tax payable in respect of ITC recapture income pursuant to ITA 127(30) (generally speaking, where the ITC recapture rules result in a "negative" partnership ITC, each member of the partnership is required to add to Part I tax payable for the year the member's share of the excess as described in ITA 127(30). This rule offsets ACB reductions described below in respect of ITC amounts previously allocated to the corporate partner.

The following amounts are deducted from the ACB of a partnership interest:

- The taxpayer's share of partnership losses after 1971 (other than limited partnership losses — see directly below) including the full amount of any capital losses (i.e., not just the 50% portion) or losses in respect of eligible capital property (before 2017). Consistent with the rules referred to above, the loss deducted from the ACB of the partnership interest is based on the partnership loss computed for tax purposes (i.e., the loss is adjusted for items such as the non-deductible portion of meals and entertainment expenses);

- The taxpayer's limited partnership loss to the extent deducted by the taxpayer (the reduction in the ACB is effective immediately after the beginning of the taxation year in which the deduction for the limited partnership loss is claimed by the limited partner). Limited partnership losses can only be applied against income from the same limited partnership. If the partnership ceases to exist, any unused loss cannot be applied against income from any other source or partnership;

- In respect of passive partners (i.e., a limited partner or a specified member of the partnership at all times since becoming a partner), the amount of any capital loss reported under ITA 40(3.12), which generally enables a taxpayer that is a member of a partnership at the end of a fiscal period of the partnership to elect to treat a positive ACB as a capital loss from the disposition of the partnership interest at that time. The elected loss may not exceed the amount by which previous gains required to be included in income in respect of a negative ACB by virtue of ITA 40(3.1) exceeds previous losses claimed under ITA 40(3.12). If an election under ITA 40(3.12) is made within 3 taxation years following the taxation year in which the taxpayer realized a gain under ITA 40(3.1), the capital loss under ITA 40(3.12) can be carried back to offset the gain;

- In respect of passive partners (i.e., a limited partner or a specified member of the partnership at all times since becoming a partner), the amount of any limited-recourse debt (which is also excluded in computing a limited partners at-risk amount) that can reasonably be considered to have been used to acquire the partnership interest other than an interest which is a tax shelter investment. A limited-recourse debt generally includes the unpaid principal of any indebtedness for which recourse is limited (even if that limitation applies only in the future or contingently);

- The taxpayer's share of the partnership's Canadian and foreign resource pool expenses. Resource expenses are recognized for computing income only at the partner level and are included in calculating the partner's CEE, CDE, COGPE, or FRE pools. As a result, the cost base of a partnership interest is reduced by the partner's share of the resource deductions;

- The taxpayer's share of the eligible amount of the partnership's charitable donations and political contributions by reason of the taxpayer's membership in the partnership. Donations made by a partnership are added to the partnership's income for tax purposes (computed using T5013 Sch. 1) and may only be deducted at the partner level. An adjustment is required even if the partner has not been able to claim any of these amounts;

- Any amount required by ITA 97 (rules regarding contributions of property to a partnership) to be deducted from the ACB of the partnership interest. Generally, where property is contributed to a partnership on a rollover basis under ITA 97(2), if the fair market value of the consideration received from the partnership (not including a partnership interest) is more than the fair market value of the property contributed, the excess amount is to be deducted from the ACB of the partnership interest immediately after the disposition;

- Profits withdrawn from the partnership by the taxpayer after 1971. In addition to standard withdrawals, examples include income tax instalments remitted to the CRA on behalf of a partner, the cost of products available for sale that the partner consumed, the partner's expenses that the partnership paid, and a return of capital;

- The part of any ITC claimed by the taxpayer that represents the taxpayer's share of the partnership's ITC. ITA 127(5) and (8) enable a partner to deduct from Part I tax otherwise payable the partner's share of the ITCs that a partnership, if it were a taxpayer, would otherwise be entitled to under ITA 127(5) (i.e., the ITC flows to the partner for computing income at the partner level). The ACB adjustment is required for ITC amounts only when the partner claims the ITC;

- The amount of government assistance received by the partner that has resulted in a reduction of the capital cost of depreciable property of the partnership. ITA 13(7.2) effectively provides for a reduction in the capital cost of depreciable property owned by a partnership where a partner has received government assistance (for example, a grant, subsidy, forgivable loan, deduction from tax, or investment allowance) in respect of the acquisition of such property by the partnership;

- Where the partnership has ceased to exist, the taxpayer's share of certain undeducted issue expenses and borrowing costs that the partnership would otherwise have deducted but, by virtue of the dissolution, are deductible to the partner. The ACB adjustment is required even if the partner has not claimed the amounts;

- An amount payable by the partnership under a private health services plan to the extent deductible under ITA 20.01(1) (an ACB adjustment is required even if the partner has not claimed any of these amounts); and

- An amount by which a deemed dividend under ITA 247(12) (transfer pricing secondary adjustments) in respect of a transaction or series of transactions in which the partnership was a participant is reduced under ITA 247(13) as the result of a repatriation of funds to the taxpayer. This ACB reduction, which is applicable to transactions after March 28, 2012, effectively results from a distribution of funds from the partnership to the taxpayer that is made through the repatriation mechanism in ITA 247(13). ITA 53(2)(c)(xiii) was added consequential to the introduction of the secondary transfer pricing adjustment rules found in ITA 247(12)–(15).

ITA 53(1)(e), (2)(o), 143.2(1), *Tesainer*, [2009] 3 C.T.C. 109 (FCA) (settlement payments), IT-338R2 (cancelled), IT-353R2 (cancelled), VDs 2011-0416611E5, 2011-0421491I7

¶4124 — Bonds

Pursuant to ITA 16(2) and (3), owners of certain debt obligations are required to include in income the excess of the principal amount of the obligation over the amount for which the obligation was issued. Any amount required by ITA 16(2) or (3) to be included in computing the income of the taxpayer is added to the taxpayer's ACB of the debt obligation (see also ¶3227).

In addition, owners of indexed debt obligations can add to the ACB of the obligation any interest in respect of the obligation required to be included in income under ITA 16(6). This addition ensures that an indexed amount is taxed to the holder of an indexed debt obligation only as interest and not as a capital gain on a disposition of the obligation. Similarly, amounts allowed as a deduction in computing income for tax purposes in respect of an indexed debt obligation are subtracted from the ACB of the obligation (see also ¶3226).

Where a debt obligation (other than an income bond, an income debenture, a small business development bond, or a small business bond) is transferred or assigned to a taxpayer, ITA 20(14) permits the taxpayer to deduct in computing income for the year interest paid to the taxpayer in respect of the obligation to the extent that it accrued before the day on which it was acquired. ITA 53(2)(l) requires that the amount so deducted from income be deducted from the ACB to the taxpayer of the obligation.

ITA 53(1)(g), (g.1), (2)(l), (l.1)

¶4125 — Land

Where a taxpayer disposes of farm land and has unclaimed restricted farm losses that were not deductible in prior years, the taxpayer may add the unclaimed losses to the ACB of the land. Thus, the taxpayer can reduce any capital gain on the eventual disposition of the land by the amount of the unclaimed losses. Once the farming land has been disposed of, the taxpayer's farming losses, to the extent that they have been added in computing the ACB of the land immediately before the disposition, may no longer be carried forward for the purposes of computing the taxpayer's taxable income in subsequent years.

Non-deductible interest and taxes in respect of vacant land (see ¶5256) are added to the ACB of the land.

ITA 31, 53(1)(h), (i), 111(6)

¶4126 — Property for Which Form T664 Was Filed

Special rules apply to determine the adjusted cost base (ACB) of a property for which a taxpayer filed Form T664, *Election to Report a Capital Gain on Property Owned at the End of February 22, 1994*. Taxpayers who filed Form T664 were considered to have sold their capital property at the end of February 22, 1994 and to have immediately reacquired it on February 23, 1994. The ACB of the taxpayer's property on February 23, 1994 depends on the type of property for which an election was filed. Generally, for elections filed for capital property, other than a flow-through entity, the taxpayer's ACB is the amount designated as proceeds of disposition on Form T664. If the property is a cottage, rental property, or other non-qualifying real property, the taxpayer's ACB is the designated proceeds of disposition less the reduction for non-qualifying real property.

If the taxpayer's designated proceeds of disposition were more than the fair market value of the property at the end of February 22, 1994, the taxpayer's ACB on February 23, 1994 may be reduced. In this case, taxpayers should complete Chart 2 or 3 in Guide T4037 to determine their ACB on February 23, 1994.

¶4127 — V-Day Value

Special rules apply when determining the cost of capital property owned on December 31, 1971. Generally, tax is not assessed and losses are not allowed for any gain or loss that arose before that date.

The "V-Day value" of a property is its fair market value on Valuation Day, which was December 22, 1971, for publicly-traded shares or securities and December 31, 1971 for all other capital property. Schedule VII of the ITR lists the values of publicly-traded shares on Valuation Day (V-Day), December 22, 1971.

Sec. 26 of the *Income Tax Application Rules*, Form T1105: *Supplementary Schedule for Dispositions of Capital Property Acquired Before 1972*, IT-132R2 (cancelled), VD 2009-0319501I7

¶4128 — Negative ACB

When deductions from the cost base of a property (other than a partnership interest) reduce the balance to a negative amount at any time in the taxation year, a capital gain is considered to arise equal to the amount of the negative balance and the ACB becomes nil (i.e., as the deemed gain is added to the ACB of the property).

Whenever a partnership is terminated without all of the partnership property having been distributed to the partners, the provisions of ITA 40(3) become applicable and any negative balance in the adjusted cost base becomes a deemed gain. Interests in a partnership that a limited partner or an inactive partner holds are subject to the negative ACB rule. ITA 40(3.14) provides an extended definition of "limited partner" for the purpose of determining whether a member's interest in a partnership is subject to the negative adjusted cost base rule in ITA 40(3.1).

ITA 53, 54, 40(3)–(3.2), VD 2013-0482081E5, Bonanno et al., "Limited Liability Partnerships" (2017) 25:2 CTH 7-8

¶4129 — Inheritance or Gifts

The acquisition of capital property by gift or inheritance does not result in a capital gain to the recipient. For tax purposes, the recipient of a gift is deemed to have acquired the property at a cost equal to its fair market value on the date received. Similarly, when a taxpayer inherits property from a deceased, the cost of the property is equal to the deemed proceeds of disposition to the deceased, which is usually the fair market value of the property immediately before death (some exceptions apply where property is inherited as a result of the death of a spouse or common-law partner, or the property is a farm property or a woodlot transferred on the death of a child).

The cost of property won in a lottery is its fair market value at the time the property is won.

ITA 69(1)(b), Guide T4011: *Preparing Returns for Deceased Persons*

¶4130 — Total Capital Gains (Sch. 3: Line 191)

The total capital gains or losses from Column 5 (before reserves) are aggregated and reported on Line 191 of Schedule 3. Specifically, Line 191 of Schedule 3 will include:

- Capital gains and losses calculated in Parts 1–8 of Schedule 3 (Sch. 3: Lines 107, 110, 124, 132, 138, 153, 155, 158, 159)

- Capital gains or losses reported on T5, T5013, T5013A, and T4PS information slips (Sch. 3: Line 174)

- Capital gains or losses reported on T3 slips (Sch. 3: Line 176)

Less:

- Capital gains deferral from qualifying dispositions of eligible small business corporation shares (Sch. 3: Line 161)

- Capital loss from a reduction in the taxpayer's business investment loss (Sch. 3: Line 178)

ITA 38, 39, 54, IT-170R: *Sale of property — When included in income computation*, IT-448(SR): *Dispositions — Changes in terms of securities*, IT-460: *Dispositions — Absence of consideration*

¶4140 — Capital Gains Reserve (Sch. 3: Line 192)

Where all or part of the proceeds of disposition of a capital property are not received until after the end of the taxation year, a taxpayer can claim a reserve to defer part of the capital gain. By claiming a capital gains reserve, a capital gain can generally be spread over a maximum of five years. However, a 10-year reserve is provided for transfers of family farm property, family fishing property, and small business corporation shares to a child, as well as gifts of non-qualifying securities made to a qualified donee.

Where a capital gains reserve is claimed, the taxpayer is still required to calculate and report the capital gain in Schedule 3 in the normal manner. The taxpayer is then allowed to calculate and deduct a reserve for the year. To calculate the reserve, the taxpayer should complete Form T2017: *Summary of Reserves on Dispositions of Capital Property*. In the first year the reserve is claimed, it should be deducted from total capital gains for the year on Line 192 of Schedule 3. In subsequent years, the reserve deducted in the prior year is required to be added to total capital gains for the year and a new reserve balance can be calculated on Form T2017 and claimed on Line 192.

A capital gain from a reserve brought into income qualifies for the capital gains deduction only if the original capital gain was from a property eligible for the capital gains deduction.

Generally, the capital gains reserve a taxpayer can claim in a taxation year cannot be more than the lesser of the following two amounts:

1. (Capital gain / Proceeds of disposition) × Amount not due until after the end of the year, and

2. For the year of disposition, 4/5 of the capital gain, for the second year, 3/5 of the capital gain, for the third year 2/5 of the capital gain, and for the fourth year, 1/5 of the capital gain.

As such, one-fifth of a gain as determined before any reserve is taken must be recognized in the year of disposition and in each of the four subsequent taxation years. In the year of disposition, the reserve cannot be greater than four-fifths of the gain otherwise determined; in the taxation year immediately following the year of disposition, the maximum reserve available is, in effect, three-fifths of such gain; and so on. A taxpayer is not required to claim the maximum reserve available in a taxation year.

A 10-year reserve is provided for transfers of family farm property, family fishing property, and small business corporation shares to a child, as well as gifts of non-qualifying securities made to a qualified donee. For these types of transfers, the capital gains reserve a taxpayer can claim in a taxation year cannot be more than the lesser of the following two amounts:

1. (Capital gain / Proceeds of disposition) × Amount not due until after the end of the year,

and

2. For the year of disposition, 9/10 of the capital gain, for the second year, 8/10 of the capital gain, for the third year 7/10 of the capital gain, for the fourth year, 6/10 of the capital gain, etc.

As such, one-tenth of a gain as determined before any reserve is taken must be recognized in the year of disposition and in each of the nine subsequent taxation years. In the year of disposition, the reserve cannot be greater than nine-tenths of the gain otherwise determined; in the taxation year immediately following the year of disposition, the maximum reserve available is, in effect, eight-tenths of such a gain; and so on. A taxpayer is not required to claim the maximum reserve available in a taxation year.

Taxpayers who realize a capital gain on a donation of a non-qualifying security (other than an excepted gift) to a qualified donee may be able to claim a reserve in order to postpone the inclusion of the capital gain in income over a maximum of five years (for gifts of non-qualifying securities made after December 20, 2002, the reserve claimed cannot be greater than the eligible amount of the gift). The reserve is not available if the charity disposes of the security, or if the security ceases to be a non-qualifying security before the end of the tax year. If this happens, the taxpayer will be considered to have made a charitable donation in that year and can claim the charitable donation tax credit.

However, applicable to dispositions of non-qualifying securities made by qualified donees after March 21, 2011, where a qualified donee has received a gift of a non-qualifying security, no tax receipt may be issued for the gift and, therefore, no charitable donation tax credit may be claimed by the donor, unless, within the 5-year reserve period, the non-qualifying security ceases to be a non-qualifying security or has been disposed of in exchange for property that is not another non-qualifying security. If the security is not disposed of within the 5-year reserve period, the taxpayer will not be required to bring the reserve back into income in the year following the end of that period. Taxpayers should complete Form T2017 to calculate the reserve. See also ¶4330 for a discussion of the rules for gifts of capital property.

A taxpayer cannot claim a capital gains reserve in any of the following circumstances: the taxpayer was not a resident of Canada at the end of the year or at any time in the following year; the taxpayer was exempt from tax at the end of the year or any time in the following year; or the taxpayer sold the capital property to a corporation that the taxpayer controlled in any way.

ITA 40(1)(a), (1.01), 40(2)(a), 79.1(3), (4), (6), 87(2)(m), 248(1)"majority interest partner", 251.1, *The Queen v Derbecker*, [1984] C.T.C. 606 (FCA), *Pineo*, [1986] 2 C.T.C. 71 (FCTD), CRA Guide T4037, IT-236R4 (cancelled), VDs 2013-0505391E5, 2013-0492721E5, 2005-0116081E5, 2004-0090461E5, 2002-0133797

¶4200 — Qualified Dispositions (Sch. 3: Parts 1 and 2)

¶4210 — Lifetime Capital Gains Exemption

Under ITA 110.6, Canadian resident individuals can claim a lifetime capital gains exemption against taxable capital gains on the disposition of qualified small business corporation shares, qualified farm or fishing property, or a reserve brought into income from any of these types of qualified property (see ¶4140).

The amount of the capital gains exemption is $800,000 for dispositions of qualified small business corporation shares. The exemption amount was also $800,000 for dispositions of qualified farm or fishing property before April 21, 2015, and increased to $1,000,000 for dispositions of qualified farm or fishing property on or after April 21, 2015. The $800,000 lifetime capital gains exemption amount is indexed to inflation for 2015 and later taxation years; the indexed amount is $848,252 for 2018. This is a cumulative limit that includes the former $100,000 general capital gains exemption. A capital gains exemption claimed in respect of qualified farm or fishing property would reduce the amount of exemption otherwise available on the disposition of qualified small business corporation shares by a corresponding amount, and vice versa. In determining the amount of available exemption, the amount of deduction previously claimed is adjusted to restate the amount claimed in current terms based on the inclusion rate of capital gains for the particular year.

Form T657: *Calculation of Capital Gains Deduction*, provides guidance concerning calculating the capital gains deduction. Also, if an individual has investment income or investment expenses in any years after 1988, the individual should complete Form T936: *Calculation of Cumulative Net Investment Loss (CNIL)* (See ¶4240).

Where a taxpayer either becomes a Canadian resident or ceases to be a Canadian resident at any time during a taxation year, the taxpayer will be considered resident throughout the year for the purposes of the capital gains exemption if the taxpayer was resident in Canada throughout either the immediately preceding year or the following year. As a result, the taxpayer may claim the capital gains exemption to the extent otherwise available in respect of a year when residency status changes. Any gains or losses realized by an individual while not a Canadian resident do not affect the individual's entitlement to claim the capital gains exemption. Further, no capital gains exemption may be claimed in respect of an individual for a period throughout which the individual is a non-resident of Canada.

In order to monitor the utilization of the capital gains exemption, every individual is required to file an income tax return for any year in which the individual disposes of property or realizes a taxable capital gain regardless of whether any tax is payable. Where a taxpayer has realized a capital gain in a particular taxation year and knowingly or under circumstances amounting to gross negligence either fails to report the disposition on a tax return for that year, or fails to file a tax return within one year following the date on which the return for the particular year was due, the exemption is denied for the unreported gain. For example, if the taxpayer realized a gain in 2016, the taxpayer's return for that year would normally be required by April 30, 2017. In order to maintain eligibility for the exemption in respect of the capital gain, the taxpayer would have to file a return no later than April 30, 2018. The burden of proof is on the CRA to establish the facts upon which the denial of the exemption is based.

ITA 110.6(2)(9), 110.6(13), 110.6(19), 150(1), Form T657, Form T936

¶4220 — Qualified Small Business Corporation (QSBC) Shares (Sch. 3: Part 1)

Capital gains of up to $800,000 (indexed for 2015 and subsequent taxation years; $848,252 for 2018) realized on the disposition of qualifying small business corporation shares are eligible for the capital gains exemption. Capital gains from the disposition of qualified small business corporation shares are reported in Part 1 of Schedule 3. Losses on the disposition of small business corporation shares (to arm's length persons) are not reported in Part 1; an allowable business investment loss may be claimed (see ¶4600). If the taxpayer is electing to defer the capital gain resulting from the disposition of qualified small business corporation shares, see ¶4340.

¶4221 — *Definition of Qualified Small Business Corporation (QSBC) Shares*

A "qualified small business corporation share" is defined in ITA 110.6(1) as a share in the capital stock of a corporation that meets the following three tests contained in paragraphs (a), (b), and (c) of the definition:

Test 1

At the time of determination, the share is a share of a small business corporation owned by an individual, the individual's spouse, common-law partner, or a partnership related to the individual.

A small business corporation is a Canadian-controlled private corporation (CCPC), all or substantially all of the fair market value of the assets of which at that time were attributable to assets that were either used principally in an active business carried on primarily (i.e., more than 50%) in Canada by the corporation or a related corporation; shares or indebtedness of one or more small business corporations that are connected with the particular corporation within the meaning of ITA 186(4), or a combination of the two.

By virtue of the "small business corporation" definition, a holding company or an operating company can qualify as a small business corporation. The CRA considers the "particular time" referred to in the "small business corporation" definition and the "determination time" referred to in the "qualified small business corporation share" definition to be the time when the share is actually disposed of. To determine the date a transaction takes place, reliance is generally placed on the legal documents and the legal rights they create; however, there are situations in which the courts have issued rectification orders to reflect the true intention of parties versus the legal effect created by the original documentation.

Test 2

Throughout the 24-month period immediately preceding the determination time, the share was not owned by anyone other than the individual, spouse, common-law partner, or related partnership.

This test is commonly referred to as the "holding period test". The test does not necessarily require the individual to hold the shares for 24 months, but merely that no unrelated person holds the shares during the holding period. Shares issued by a corporation from treasury must be held for 24 months before disposition in order to qualify for the small business capital gains exemption, since they are deemed to have been owned by an unrelated person immediately before their issue. However, this deeming rule does not apply to shares issued as consideration for other shares; to shares issued as part of a transaction in which a person or partnership disposes of substantially all active business assets to a corporation; or to an interest in a partnership whose assets are used in an active business.

When relying on the holding period test, a shelf company should generally not be utilized as the conditions of the provision may not be satisfied. A shelf company is a company in which a small number of shares have been initially issued for a nominal amount to someone unrelated to the proprietor (typically, a lawyer). Such shares would generally not qualify under the holding period test as they would not have been issued as a direct result of the transfer of the business to the company.

The holding period test would not apply if assets disposed of to a corporation did not represent all or substantially all of the assets of a separate active business of the transferor. No statutory guidelines are available to assist in determining what distinguishes one business from another. In *Dupont*, [2001] 2 C.T.C. 315 (FCA), the Court found that the fact that an explosives plant was physically separate from other operations was not sufficient to overcome indicators that the taxpayer was operating a single integrated business. In general, a business is defined to include a profession, calling, trade, manufacture, or undertaking of any kind whatever and an adventure or concern in the nature of trade. However, for the purposes of ITA 110.6(14)(f) and 54.2 (and certain other provisions), an adventure or concern in the nature of trade is excluded. This exclusion is designed to prevent the conversion of an isolated income transaction into a capital gain transaction.

The CRA's position is that the holding period test "would ordinarily be satisfied where a joint venturer, whose contribution to the undertaking of the joint venture is such that he can be said to be carrying on an active business, transfers to a corporation all of his interests in the assets used in such business" (VD 1990-207). Also, the CRA's general position is that the limited partners of a partnership would be regarded as carrying on an active business for the purposes of the holding period test provided the partnership itself is carrying on an active business (VDs July 1990-264 and 2004-0101761E5).

An individual does not have to be resident in Canada throughout the 24 months immediately preceding the time of the disposition in order to meet the holding period test (VD 2010-0359781E5).

See ITA 110.6(14) when determining who is a related person for purposes of the definition of a qualified small business corporation share.

Test 3

Throughout that part of the 24-month period while owned by the individual, spouse, common-law partner, or related partnership, the share was a share of a CCPC, where more than 50% of the fair market value of the assets were attributable to:

- assets used principally in an active business carried on primarily in Canada by the corporation or by a related corporation (see below under "Active Business Assets");

- shares or indebtedness issued by one or more connected corporations, where throughout that part of the 24 months immediately preceding, the shares or indebtedness were not owned by anyone but the corporation, a person or partnership related to the corporation, or a person or partnership related to such person or partnership;

- shares or indebtedness of one or more connected corporations, where throughout that period while owned by the corporation or related person they were shares or indebtedness of a Canadian controlled private corporation, where more than 50% of the fair market value of its assets were either assets used in carrying on an active business carried on by that person in Canada or shares or indebtedness of connected corporations which otherwise qualified, or were a combination of assets and qualifying shares or indebtedness.

Paragraphs (d) to (f) of the "qualified small business corporation share" definition provide certain exceptions to the general tests contained in paragraphs (a) to (c) discussed above. If, for any particular period of time in the 24-month period ending at the determination time, a particular corporation's assets or those of another corporation with which it is connected do not substantially (i.e., 90% or more) consist of either: i) assets used principally in an active business carried on primarily in Canada by it or a related company, or ii) shares or indebtedness of connected corporations that meet the 50% active business asset test during the relevant period, then paragraph (d) requires that each of the connected corporations meet the definition of a small business corporation (i.e., 90% or more test) throughout the period that the particular corporation did not so qualify. For this purpose, for a corporation to be "connected" with another, (i) the corporation must be connected within the meaning of ITA 186(4) with the other corporation, and (ii) the other corporation must own shares of the capital stock of the corporation (for this purpose, shares owned indirectly by the particular corporation through other tiers of corporations are deemed to be owned by the particular corporation).

The purpose of this rule is to prevent abuses which may result from the use of tiers of companies. For example, assume that Corporation A has $100 of "bad" assets and that its wholly-owned subsidiary, Corporation B, has $180 of "good" assets and $150 of "bad" assets. Corporation B meets the 50% test. Corporation A also meets the 50% test because the shares of Corporation B comprise more than 50% of its assets. However, on a consolidated basis there are $250 of bad assets and only $180 of good assets. Absent paragraph (d), Corporation A would meet the paragraph (c) test.

Where at any time in the 24-month period ending at the determination time the relevant share was substituted for another share, the other share must have met the holding period test throughout the period beginning 24 months before the determination time and ending at the time of substitution, and must have satisfied the 50% active business asset requirements. As well, where a share of a connected corporation has been substituted for another share during the 24-month holding period, the other share must have met the two conditions required in respect of shareholdings or indebtedness of connected CCPCs throughout the 24-month period preceding the determination time and ending at the time of substitution. The purpose of these rules is to ensure that the holding period requirement and the 50% active business asset test are satisfied in the situation where there is a substitution of shares.

ITA 110.6(14), 248(1)"small business corporation", VDs 2003-0012695, 2006-0208691E5, 2010-0381961E5

¶4222 — *Active Business Assets*

In determining whether an asset is "used" in a particular active business, in *Ensite Limited*, [1986] 2 C.T.C. 459 (SCC), it was established that the asset must be "employed" or "risked" in the business. The Court held that the term "risked" meant more than a remote risk and that the withdrawal of the property would have a destabilizing effect on the business operations themselves.

In *McCutcheon Farms Ltd.*, [1991] 1 C.T.C. 50 (FCTD), a farming operation which processed and sold seed and chemicals attempted to claim the small business deduction in respect of interest income on short-term deposits, arguing that such interest constituted income from property used or held principally for the purpose of gaining or producing income from its farm business. The Tax Court found that the test in *Ensite* had not been met, since it could not be said that the property in issue was employed or risked in the farm business. The Court held that the term deposits were neither an integral part of the taxpayer's financing nor necessary to the overall operation but rather surplus and collateral to the active business and not used regularly in the course of the business. Alternative arguments that the income was incident to or pertaining to an active business were rejected by the Court.

The CRA's general position is that cash and cash equivalents are not an active business asset unless the cash is held "to fulfill a mandatory condition precedent to trade" or its withdrawal would "have a decidedly destabilizing effect on the corporate operations themselves" (see paras. 14 and 15 of *Ensite Limited*).

The CRA considers cash held to satisfy employee bonuses or stock option requirements to qualify as active business assets (VD 2009-0330071C6). Also, the CRA has stated that marketable securities held as security under a financing arrangement are a qualifying asset where the arrangement is fundamental to the business operations and there is a real expectation that the security will be resorted to; however, the employment of marketable securities merely as collateral is not generally sufficient to enable it to be considered to be used in a business (VD 9514695).

In paragraph 6 of IT-73R6, the CRA takes the following position:

> [A]lthough a mortgage receivable is an asset whose existence may be relevant to the equity of a corporation, it is not generally an asset used in an active business because the funds tied up in the mortgage are not available for the active business use of a corporation. However, if the corporation could establish that the mortgages are employed and risked in the business such that the mortgages are inextricably tied to or vitally connected with the business, they could be considered to be used in an active business carried on by the corporation.

In VD 2012-0435351I7, in applying the small business corporation tests to a corporation resident in Quebec, the CRA stated that the cash balance of the corporation should not be reduced by outstanding cheques since according to Quebec civil law, the issuance of a cheque does not constitute payment. With respect to the principal use of a building, in VD 2009-0307931E5, the CRA states:

> Although there are no set guidelines as to which factors to use in different situations, there are two aspects to be considered in determining the nature of use of a building — quantitative factors (e.g., the total square footage occupancy in the building) and qualitative factors (e.g., the original intent for purchasing the building, actual use to which the building is put in the course of the business, the nature of the business involved and the practice in the particular industry). The square footage use of a building is generally accepted as a factor to be given significant weight in the determination of the particular use to which the building is put. However, qualitative factors need also be considered. If the fair rental value of the space rented to tenants is greater than the fair rental value of the space used in an active business, this may indicate that a building is not used principally in an active business. Whether such a factor would be decisive in relation

to the square footage test would have to be determined on a case by case basis. We are unable to provide a definitive comment without the opportunity to review all the relevant facts.

In *Belzile*, [2006] 5 C.T.C. 2011 (TCC), a corporation that rented out homes that were originally purchased with the intention to sell was found to be a small business corporation (the homes could not be sold as planned). However, in *Venneri*, [2007] 3 C.T.C. 155 (FCA), the Court found that a corporation holding land for speculation was not a small business corporation. In *Glaxo Wellcome Inc.*, [1999] 4 C.T.C. 371 (FCA), the Court found that the word "use" connotes actual utilization for some purpose and not holding for future use.

The term "principally" in respect of the use of an asset has been interpreted by the CRA as requiring a greater than 50% proportion of time to be used in the qualifying activity (Folio S4-F15-C1 (para. 1.21), VDs 2010-0381321E5, 2010-0381361E5).

Assets not reflected on the balance sheet of a corporation for financial reporting purposes, such as internally generated goodwill, may assist in meeting the determination time test where such assets are used in the active business.

Income tax refunds receivable by a corporation are generally considered an active business asset by the CRA. The CRA has also stated a tax receivable in respect of corporate tax instalments paid by a corporation carrying on an active business is an asset used principally in an active business carried on by the corporation. A tax receivable related to a loss carryback from an active business carried on by a corporation also constitutes an asset used principally in an active business carried on by the corporation (see *Munich Reinsurance Co.*, [2002] 1 C.T.C. 199 (FCA), and VDs 2002-0169565, and 2008-0285291C6).

The CRA does not consider a deferred income tax asset recognized for accounting purposes to be an active business asset. Also, the CRA does not take into consideration the portion of a corporation's refundable dividend tax on hand for which no dividend refund is made when applying the asset-use test (VDs 2008-0285301C6, 2006-0174131C6).

Land inventory of a real estate developer that is used to carry on the business of land development is considered an asset used in an active business (VD 9619985).

The CRA generally considers a partnership interest to be an asset used in an active business if the underlying assets of the partnership are used in an active business. The CRA does not, however, consider a retired partner's right to partnership income to be an active business asset.

When determining whether assets meet the principal-use test, the CRA's general position is that the test must be applied on a property-by-property basis. For example, if a corporation owns several parcels of land and certain of the parcels do not meet the principal-use test, but 57% of total acreage is used in an active business, the CRA would not consider all the land parcels to be used principally in an active business (VD 9716155).

Refundable deposits made as a requirement to operate a particular business would generally be considered an active business asset based on VD 9226045.

For the purposes of the definition of a qualified small business corporation share (and the share of the capital stock of a family farm corporation), the fair market value of a life insurance policy owned by the corporation before the shareholder's death is considered to be its cash surrender value. In the absence of this provision, the value of life insurance held by a corporation could fluctuate based on the health of the insured with the result that the corporation could fail to meet the asset test. For these purposes, insurance proceeds received by a corporation on the death of a shareholder would not generally be considered a qualifying asset if the insurance proceeds are intended to fund a redemption or acquisition of shares. Consequently, the corporation may not meet the asset test. However, until the redemption, acquisition or purchase for cancellation, the fair market value of the proceeds will be considered not to exceed the cash surrender value of the policy immediately before death *provided* the proceeds are actually used either directly or indirectly to redeem or acquire the shares owned by the deceased shareholder. In order for this provision to apply, the redemption or acquisition must occur within 24 months after the death of the life insured person. This period may be extended upon written application to the CRA within the 24-month period.

The rule in ITA 129(6) that deems income of a recipient corporation from a source in Canada that is a property to be income from an active business does not apply for purposes of determining whether a corporation is a small business corporation. Thus, the deeming provision is of no assistance in meeting the asset-use test in the small business corporation definition (VD 2012-0435101E5).

ITA 110.6(15), VDs 9132835, 9310115, 9636835, 9636835, 9706965, 1999-0006485, 2008-0299741I7, Glenn Stephens, LLB, "Planning Ideas for Corporate-Owned Life Insurance," 2004 Ontario Tax Conference (Toronto: Canadian Tax Foundation, 2004) 11B:1–26, May 2005 Alberta CAs CRA Tax Roundtable, Q.10

¶4223 — *Purification of a Small Business Corporation*

To claim the capital gains exemption in respect of the disposition of QSBC shares, at the determination time, "all or substantially all" of the fair market value of the corporation's assets must be used principally in an active business carried on primarily in Canada. Where this test is not met, steps may be taken to "purify" the corporation (i.e., remove assets from the corporation that are not used in an active business being carried on in Canada). Common assets that may prevent the determination time test from being met include cash and cash equivalents in excess of operating needs, investments in foreign subsidiaries, unused land, buildings that generate rental income, and loans receivable (unless the company is in the business of lending money).

In respect of non-qualifying assets other than cash, a "purification" may be accomplished via a reorganization by which the non-qualifying assets are transferred on a tax-free basis to a newly formed corporation (i.e., a "butterfly" transaction under ITA 55), provided that a sale to an arm's length party of the shares of the small business corporation is not contemplated at the time of the reorganization. If an arm's length sale is contemplated, such a reorganization may still take place but generally not on a tax-free basis. Non-qualifying assets can also be removed from a small business corporation by distributing the assets through a dividend in kind. The shareholders would be subject to tax on the dividend and the tax costs would have to be weighed against the benefit of the capital gains exemption. Other purification transactions may include the sale of non-qualifying assets and the purchase of qualifying assets; borrowing funds to purchase qualifying assets to increase the ratio of qualifying versus non-qualifying assets; the use of non-qualifying assets to settle liabilities of the corporation; paying a taxable dividend (preferably an eligible dividend) which triggers an RDTOH refund; the payment of an RRSP eligible retiring allowance; and returns of capital or payments of capital dividends to reduce cash reserves.

A small business corporation may also adopt long-term purification strategies. When implementing such strategies, the removal of non-qualifying assets in a tax-efficient manner may not be limited to safe income attributable to shares held by a holding corporation as ITA 55(2) should not apply provided the strategy is not considered part of a series of transactions that includes an eventual sale of shares to a non-arm's length party. A long-term strategy may include, for example, annually paying dividends to a holding corporation in excess of non-qualifying assets and lending required funds back to the small business corporation. Alternatively, after an estate freeze transaction, a holding corporation could hold preferred shares of the small business corporation which could be redeemed as necessary to distribute excess cash.

The CRA stated in the Round Table at the 1988 Canadian Tax Foundation Conference that the GAAR would generally not apply to the "purification" of a corporation to meet the small business corporation tests, although ITA 55(2) or 110.6(7) could potentially apply (see also example 15 in IC 88-2). The ITA contains an important anti-avoidance rule related to the capital gains exemption that is intended to prevent the tax-free removal of taxable corporate surplus as a return of capital through a non-arm's length transfer of shares of a Canadian resident corporation by a Canadian resident individual to a corporation (see ¶4250).

In VD 2011-0415161E5, the CRA states that since the active business asset test only contemplates looking to the fair market value of the particular corporation's total assets (including intangibles), there is no legislative basis for netting the amount or value of the corporation's liabilities against its assets for this purpose. As such, it is not possible to "purify" a corporation by netting the particular corporation's liabilities against its non-active business assets. The CRA also states:

> [I]t is our view that it is also not possible to "purify" a corporation simply by making one or more accounting journal entries (that are intended to remove or eliminate non-active business assets). Any purification transactions entered into by the particular corporation, such as the transfer of property to another person or the payment or settlement of inter-company indebtedness (by way of a dividend or other method) must be bona fide and legally effective. Please refer to the comments in Income Tax Technical News #14, paragraph 15(b) of Interpretation Bulletin IT-109R2; paragraphs 25 and 26 of Interpretation Bulletin IT-119R4; and paragraph 10 of Interpretation Bulletin IT-362R for some general guidance on this issue.

VDs 2009-0330071C6F, 2009-0307931E5, 2007-0243241C6, 2009-0330071C6, 9705823, 9605165, 9301993, Len Vandenberg, "The Capital Gains Deduction — A Checklist Approach," 2000 B.C. Tax Conference (Vancouver: Canadian Tax Foundation, 2000), 8:1–64

¶4224 — *Special Rules*

Where a taxpayer disposes of all or substantially all of the assets used in an active business carried on by the taxpayer to a corporation, and at least part of the consideration for the assets includes shares of the corporation, the shares are considered to be capital property to the taxpayer. Accordingly, a subsequent disposition of the shares will give rise to a capital gain. The assets must be active business assets and there must be a sale of all or substantially all active business assets if this provision is to apply. For the purposes of this section, a business is defined to exclude an adventure in the nature of trade.

> Where the shares disposed of are identical properties, the taxpayer is deemed to dispose of them in the order of acquisition. Accordingly, if only some of the shares met the 24-month holding period, the taxpayer could dispose of those shares and claim the qualified small business corporation share exemption, retaining the balance in respect of which the exemption would not be available.

In determining whether a corporation is a small business corporation or a Canadian-controlled private corporation, its status will not be affected by a right to purchase the shares of the corporation pursuant to an agreement of purchase and sale which relates to the shares. In the absence of this provision, if, for example, an individual were to enter into an agreement of purchase and sale to sell otherwise qualified small business corporation shares (representing control of the corporation) to a non-resident, at the time of disposition being the date of closing, the corporation would not technically meet the definition of a Canadian-controlled private corporation and the exemption would be lost.

If shares are held by a personal trust, the period of holding by the trust will be included for the holding period of the individual. In addition, a personal trust is always deemed to be related to any person from whom it acquired shares in a corporation where, at the time the trust disposes of the shares, all beneficiaries are related to the person from whom the shares were acquired.

Where a holder of qualified small business corporation shares transfers shares to a holding corporation and substantially all of the consideration for the transfer is common shares, the holding corporation is considered related to its shareholders and the enhanced exemption continues to be available. As well, a capital gains deferral is available when proceeds from the sale of a small business corporation are reinvested in a new eligible small business corporation.

Where a taxpayer dies owning shares which would otherwise be qualified small business corporation shares but for the accumulation of non-qualifying assets in the corporation, special rules apply. In these circumstances, the enhanced capital gains exemption is available provided the shares satisfied the qualified small business corporation share definition at any time within the 12-month period before death and did not otherwise qualify at death only by reason of not being a small business corporation at the time of death.

Where a corporation ceases to be a small business corporation because a class of its shares or shares of another corporation are listed on a designated stock exchange, an individual shareholder may elect to be deemed to have disposed of the shares immediately before the corporation ceases to qualify as a small business corporation for proceeds of disposition stipulated in the election. The election is made using Form T2101: *Election for gains on shares of a corporation becoming public* (for Quebec residents, see also Form TP-247.2-V). In order to ensure that a gain just sufficient to use the available capital gains exemption is triggered, the elected amount may be any amount between the adjusted cost base and the fair market value of the shares, assuming that the fair market value is greater than the adjusted cost base. The amount elected becomes the new cost for the shares immediately after the deemed disposition and any gain in excess of the elected amount is deferred. This election applies only to shares which are capital property. The election must be filed with the individual's tax return for the year in which the corporation becomes public and must be filed by the individual's "balance due" date, generally April 30 of the following taxation year. Late-filed elections may be made for up to two years after the balance due date, subject to a penalty of 1/4 of 1% per month of the capital gain resulting from the elected disposition, to a maximum of $100 per month. The penalty payment must accompany the late-filed election.

ITA 44.1, 48.1, 54.2, 110.6(1), 110.6(14), 110.6(16), Form T2101: *Election for gains on shares of a corporation becoming public*, Form TP-247.2-V

¶4230 — Qualified Farm or Fishing Property (Sch. 3: Part 2)

Canadian resident individuals can claim a lifetime capital gains exemption against capital gains realized on the disposition of qualified small business corporation shares, qualified farm or fishing property, or a reserve brought into income from any of these types of qualified property (see ¶4140). The amount of the lifetime capital gains exemption was increased to $1,000,000 (from $800,000) for dispositions of qualified farm or fishing property (or a reserve brought into income from these types of qualified property) made on or after April 21, 2015.

Applicable to transfers and dispositions that occur in 2014 and subsequent taxation years, in order to better accommodate taxpayers involved in a combination of farming and fishing, the eligibility of the intergenerational rollover and capital gains exemption was extended to: 1) property of an individual used principally in a combination of farming and fishing; and 2) to an individual's shares in a corporation, or interest in a partnership, where the corporation or partnership carries on both a farming and fishing business.

> The lifetime capital gains exemption limit was increased to $1,000,000 (from $800,000) for dispositions of qualified farm or fishing property made on or after April 21, 2015.

¶4231 — *Definition of Qualified Farm or Fishing Property*

For 2014 and later taxation years, the following types of property owned by an individual (including a personal trust), the spouse or common-law partner of the individual, or a partnership an interest in which is an "interest in a family farm or fishing partnership" of an individual or the individual's spouse or common-law partner, constitute "qualified farm or fishing property":

1. Real or immovable property or a fishing vessel that was used in the course of carrying on a farming or fishing business in Canada by any of the following eligible users:

   (i) the individual;

   (ii) if the individual is a personal trust, a beneficiary of the trust that is entitled to receive directly from the trust any income or capital of the trust;

   (iii) a spouse, common-law partner, child or parent of an individual referred to in (i) or (ii);

   (iv) a corporation, a share of the capital stock of which is a share of the capital stock of a family farm or fishing corporation of an individual referred to in any of (i), (ii) or (iii); or

   (v) a partnership, an interest in which is a family farm or fishing partnership of an individual referred to in any of (i), (ii) or (iii);

2. An eligible capital property (or a Class 14.1 property after 2016) used by a person or partnership referred to in any of (i) to (v) above, or by a personal trust from which the individual acquired the property, in the course of carrying on a farming or fishing business in Canada;

3. A share of the capital stock of a family farm or fishing corporation of the individual or the individual's spouse or common-law partner; or

206

4. An interest in a family farm or fishing partnership of the individual or the individual's spouse or common-law partner.

"Farming" is defined in ITA 248(1) to include tillage of the soil, livestock raising or exhibiting, maintaining of horses for racing, raising of poultry, fur farming, dairy farming, fruit growing, and the keeping of bees. See Folio S4-F11-C1, *Meaning of Farming and Farming Business*, for the CRA views on the meaning of farming and farming business. See also *Tinhorn Creek Vineyards Ltd*, [2006] 1 C.T.C. 2096 (TCC) (wine business was farming) and *Levy*, [1990] 2 C.T.C. 83 (FCTD) (member of syndicate that bred and raced horses held to be in the farming business despite not actively participating).

In VD 2010-0385151E5, the CRA states the following when asked whether income from a rental activity is considered farming income or income from property:

> The CRA will generally consider income from a certain activity that, by itself would be a non-farming activity, to be income from a farming business if the activity is incidental to the taxpayer's farming operations and the income generated by the activity is not substantial in relation to the taxpayer's farming revenue. The expression "incidental" implies a subordinate relationship or "having a minor role in relation to". Factors that may be relevant in the determination of whether a particular activity is incidental to another would include the income generated and the capital or labour invested in the activity.

> Farming income does not normally include rental income, unless the rental activity is incidental to other activities that qualify as farming. In determining whether the revenue from the rental of real property gives rise to income from a business of farming or from property, other factors may have to be considered such as whether the rental is on an ongoing basis and whether the farming operation to which the rental relates is discontinued, or simply temporarily suspended. For example, an individual may rent out, for one crop season, a barn previously used by the individual in farming pending the resumption of farming operations by the individual. If the individual subsequently uses the barn in farming, it would not necessarily be correct in all cases to conclude that the rental revenue is not farming income, without further investigation of the circumstances leading to the temporary rental of the barn.

A "child" is defined for purposes of the ITA as including a child born within or outside marriage; a wholly dependent person who either is, or was immediately before attaining the age of 19, under the custody and control of the taxpayer; a spouse or a common-law partner of a child of the taxpayer; a child of the taxpayer's spouse or common-law partner; and an adopted child of the taxpayer. For the purposes of the capital gains exemption, a "child" also includes the child of a child, and a child of a child's child, as well as a person who, at any time before attaining the age of 19, was wholly dependent on the taxpayer for support and of whom the taxpayer had at that time, in law or in fact, the custody and control.

"Fishing" is defined in ITA 248(1) to include "fishing for or catching shell fish, crustaceans and marine animals but does not include an office or employment under a person engaged in the business of fishing".

As the definition in ITA 248(1) is not exhaustive, the normal meaning of the term "fishing" is also applicable.

ITA 70(10)"child", 110.6(1)"qualified farm or fishing property", 252(1)"child", Guide T4003, Folio S4-F11-C1, *Meaning of Farming and Farming Business*

¶4232 — *Property Used in a Farming or Fishing Business*

Property will be considered to have been used in the course of carrying on a farming or fishing business in Canada if the following conditions in ITA 110.6(1.3)(a) are met:

Test 1

The property (or property for which the property was substituted) was owned by an eligible user (other than a family farm or fishing corporation), or by a personal trust from which the individual acquired the property, throughout the period of at least 24 months immediately preceding the time of disposition.

Test 2

In at least two years while the property was owned by an eligible user, depending on who the user of the property is, either a gross revenue test or a principal use period test (described below) must be satisfied. This test must be met throughout a period of at least 24 months while the property was owned; the test does not necessarily have to be met in the 24-month period immediately preceding the disposition. An eligible user, must, however, own the property throughout the period of at least 24 months immediately preceding the determination time (i.e., Test 1).

ITA 110.6(1.3), Guide T4003, IT-268R4: *Inter vivos transfer of farm property to child*

¶4232.1 — *Gross Revenue Test*

To meet the gross revenue test, *while the property was owned* (not necessarily immediately before the determination time) by an eligible user (other than a family farm or fishing corporation), or by a personal trust from which the individual or a child or parent of the individual acquired the property, the gross revenue of the eligible user (or the personal trust) from the farming or fishing business in which the property was principally used must have exceeded the income of the user from all other sources for the year. Further, an eligible user (or the beneficiary of the personal trust) must have been actively engaged on a regular and continuous basis in the farming or fishing business in which the property principally was used. The gross revenue test and the actively engaged test do not need to be met by the same individual.

The term "principally" in respect of the use of an asset has been construed by the CRA as requiring a greater than 50% proportion of time to be used in the qualifying activity. Gross revenue relates to the farming or fishing business in which the *particular property was used* and does not relate specifically to the particular property.

The gross revenue test applies to the person using the property in the business of farming or fishing whether or not such person is also the person realizing the gain or claiming the exemption (i.e., the operator meeting the gross revenue test does not have to be the individual who disposes of the property). For example, if, while the operator owned the property, the property was used by the operator principally in a farming or fishing business in which the operator was actively engaged on a regular and continuous basis and the operator met the gross-revenue test, the property would be qualified farm or fishing property in the hands of the operator and as well as in the hands of a child of the operator to whom the property may have been transferred. The application of the gross revenue test is discussed further in VDs 2010-0380951E5, 2007-0257221E5, 2006-0181771E5 and 2005-0144881E5.

The requirement that the individual be "actively engaged on a regular and continuous basis", although not defined in the ITA, is presumably intended to limit the availability of the capital gains exemption for qualified farm or fishing property to *bona fide* farmers and fishers. See paragraph 27 of IT-268R4 concerning the meaning of active engagement on a regular and continuous basis in the business of farming. In VD 2003-0024401E5, the CRA states that "the person would be expected to contribute time, labour and attention to the business to a sufficient extent that such contributions would be determinant in the successful operations of the business". Also, the CRA states "[w]hen farming is not the chief source of income of a taxpayer, it may be more difficult to demonstrate that the taxpayer was actively engaged on a regular and continuous basis in the farm business".

¶4232.2 — *Principal Use Test*

The principal use test referred to in ITA 110.6(1.3)(a)(ii) must be satisfied if the property was used by a family farm or fishing corporation or a family farm or fishing partnership. In such a case, the property must have been used principally in the course of carrying on a farming or fishing business throughout at least a 24-month period during which time an eligible individual was actively engaged on a regular and continuous basis in the farming or fishing business in which the property was used. The 24-month period for use is not required to be the period immediately preceding the disposition. The principal use test is discussed further in VD 2001-0068987.

¶4232.3 — *Property Acquired on or before June 17, 1987*

Where property is last acquired before June 18, 1987, a less stringent test applies. In particular, property last acquired on or before June 17, 1987, or after that date pursuant to an agreement in writing entered into on or before that date, will be considered to have been used in the course of carrying on the business of farming or fishing in Canada if the property (or property for which the property was substituted) was used by an eligible user referred to in (i) to (v) under ¶4231, or by a personal trust from which the individual acquired the property, principally in the course of carrying on the business of farming or fishing in Canada in the year the property was disposed of by the individual or in at least five years during which the property was owned by an eligible user referred to in (i) to (iii) and (v) under ¶4231 or by a personal trust from which the individual acquired the property (see, for example, VD 2010-0380951E5).

¶4233 — *Share of the Capital Stock of a Family Farm or Fishing Corporation*

A share owned by an individual (including a personal trust) will qualify as a "share of the capital stock of a family farm or fishing corporation" where the following two tests are met:

Test 1

Throughout *any* 24-month period ending before the particular time (not necessarily the 24-months immediately before the disposition), more than 50% of the fair market value of the corporation's property must be attributable to property that was used principally in the course of carrying on a farming or fishing business in Canada in which the individual, a beneficiary (where the individual is a personal trust), or a spouse or common-law partner, child or parent of the individual or beneficiary was actively engaged on a regular and continuous basis by:

(a) the corporation,

(b) the individual,

(c) a beneficiary where the individual is a personal trust,

(d) a spouse, common-law partner, child, or parent of the individual or beneficiary,

(e) a partnership, an interest in which was an interest in a family farm or fishing partnership of the individual or the beneficiary (where the individual is a personal trust), or the spouse, common-law partner, child, or parent of the individual or the beneficiary, or

(f) another corporation that is related to the corporation and of which a share of the capital stock was a share of the capital stock of a family farm or fishing corporation of the individual, of a beneficiary of the personal trust (where the individual is a personal trust) or of a spouse or common-law partner, child, or parent of the individual or the beneficiary.

The individual, beneficiary (where the individual is a personal trust) or a spouse, common-law partner, child, or parent of the individual or the beneficiary must have been actively engaged on a regular and continuous basis in the particular business of farming or fishing in Canada during the applicable 24-month period. See paragraph 27 of IT-268R4 and VD 2003-0024401E5 concerning the meaning of active engagement on a regular and continuous basis.

A share will also qualify as a family farm or fishing corporation share where throughout *any* 24-month period more than 50% of the fair market value of the corporation's property was attributable to shares or indebtedness of one or more other corporations all or substantially all of the fair market value of the property of which was attributable to property described above. Also, a share will further qualify where throughout any 24-month period more than 50 percent of the fair market value of the corporation's property was attributable to a partnership interest in or indebtedness of one or more partnerships all or substantially all of the fair market value of the property of which was attributable to properties described above. Finally, either or all of these types of property described above may be owned by the corporation so long as the total holding meets the "more than 50%" test during any 24-month period.

For the purpose of the definition of a "share of the capital stock of a family farm or fishing corporation", ITA 110.6(1.1) provides that the fair market value of a net income stabilization account shall be deemed to be nil.

The phrase "all or substantially all" is not defined in the ITA but has been interpreted for administrative purposes generally to mean 90% or more. This rule of thumb has been generally accepted; however, in any given case the courts will generally determine the meaning of such a phrase on the basis of the particular facts and circumstances of that case. In *Wood*, [1987] 1 C.T.C. 2391 (TCC), the term was considered in the context of a non-resident individual trying to claim a personal exemption under the ITA. In *Wood*, Taylor J stated that there could be no simple mathematical formula and commented that the "90 percent rule" is merely an arbitrary assessing policy. While such a mechanism is useful and functional, Taylor J stated that "the Minister might be hard pressed to refuse a claim where the percentage was 89%, maybe even 85% or 80% or lower . . .".

Test 2

At the determination time, all or substantially all of the fair market value of the corporation's property must be attributable to property described in Test 1 above. This test only applies at the time of disposition. This rule was added to prevent qualification long after the disposition of the farming or fishing assets. See VD 2004-0063481E5 regarding the application of this test.

ITA 110.6(1)"share of the capital stock of a family farm or fishing corporation", Guide T4003, VDs 2010-0380951E5, 2008-029974117, 2003-0052991E5, 2001-0088115

¶4234 — Interest in a Family Farm or Fishing Partnership

The definition of an "interest in a family farm or fishing partnership" is generally parallel to the definition of a "share of the capital stock of a family farm or fishing corporation". The CRA has stated that the 24-month period referred to in paragraph (a) of the definition cannot be met by a partnership that has not been in existence for at least 24 months (VD 2004-0075041E5). See VD 2012-0443421E5 for an example of a surplus stripping transaction that utilizes a partnership structure to avoid the application of ITA 84.1 (the CRA stated GAAR may apply to the transactions in question).

ITA 70(10)"child", 110.6(1.1), 110.6(1.3), 252(1)"child", Folio S4-F15-C1: *Manufacturing and Processing*, 2004-0063481E5, 2007-0257221E5, 2008-029974117, 2009-033287117, 2010-0356961E5, 2010-0380951E5, 2010-0381321E5, 2010-0381361E5, Zuhair Ladha, "Capital Gains Deduction Planning for Family Farm Partnerships", 1(2) *Canadian Tax Focus* (ctf.ca) 2-3 (Aug. 2011)

¶4235 — Inter Vivos Transfer of Farming or Fishing Property to Child

ITA 73(3) provides a tax-deferral for an *inter vivos* transfer of farming or fishing property by a taxpayer to a child of the taxpayer. In particular, the rollover rules in ITA 73(3.1) apply in respect of property that has been transferred by a taxpayer to a child of the taxpayer where the following conditions are met: 1) immediately before the transfer, the property was land in Canada, depreciable property in Canada of a prescribed class, or, before 2017, eligible capital property in respect of a fishing or farming business carried on in Canada by the taxpayer; 2) the child of the taxpayer was resident in Canada immediately before the transfer; and 3) the property transferred has been used principally (i.e., more than 50%) in a fishing or farming business in which the taxpayer, the taxpayer's spouse or common-law partner, a child of the taxpayer or a parent of the taxpayer was actively engaged on a regular and continuous basis.

With respect to the principal-use test in (3) above, see paragraphs 21 to 27 of IT-268R4. ITA 73(3) does not require the taxpayer transferring the property to be the individual undertaking the business of farming or fishing. Also, the requirement is that the property "has been used principally" in a fishing or farming business, and it is not solely the current use of the property that is relevant (there is no requirement that the property be used immediately before the transfer in the business of farming; VD 2007-0240321E5). Additionally, the person that used the eligible farming or fishing property principally in the business of farming or fishing does not have to be alive at the time of the transfer of the property (VD 2008-029405117).

Provided that the consideration, if any, for the transfer is between the property's fair market value and its adjusted cost base (or undepreciated capital cost, as the case may be), the sale price will be both the transferor's proceeds of disposition and the recipient's cost for tax purposes. To the extent that proceeds of disposition are not due and payable until after the end of the year, the transferor may claim a capital gains reserve (see ¶4140). Where, however, the price is greater than both the fair market value and the adjusted cost base (or undepreciated capital cost), the proceeds of disposition and the recipient's cost will be deemed to be equal to the greater of fair market value and adjusted cost base. If the price is less than both those amounts, the proceeds and the recipient's cost will be deemed to be the lesser of the two amounts. This rollover is also available where farm or fishing property is transferred on the death of a child to a parent where the child received the property from a parent either *inter vivos* or on death.

For all purposes of the ITA, a child of the taxpayer is defined to include an adopted child, step-child, a child of whom the taxpayer is the natural parent, son-in-law, daughter-in-law, step son-in-law, step daughter-in-law, and any person who is wholly dependent on the taxpayer and who, immediately before age 19, was in the taxpayer's custody and control. For these purposes, a child of the taxpayer is further defined to include a grandchild and great-grandchild, as well as a person who at any time before attaining the age of 19 was wholly dependent on the taxpayer for support and who in fact or in law was in the custody and control of the taxpayer. These definitions are equally valid in respect of the transfer to a child of a family farm or fishing corporation or small business corporation. These rules do not apply unless the transferee is resident in Canada at the time of the transfer.

If the recipient of the property later disposes of it and realizes a capital gain or loss, the gain or loss will be attributed to the transferor unless the transfer was made for a price at least equal to fair market value or the recipient has attained the age of 18 before the end of the year in which the disposition takes place, or at the time of the disposition the transferor has died or is no longer resident in Canada. This applies to both shares in a family farm or fishing corporation and interests in family farm or fishing partnerships.

ITA 73(3) could apply to an intergenerational transfer of a life interest in farm property (VD 2006-0216421E5). Also, a transfer of farm property from a father to a corporation as bare trustee for his children can qualify as a transfer of farm property pursuant to ITA 73(3) (VD 2006-0167011I7). See VD 2005-0152241E5 regarding a transfer of farm property from a parent to a trust for the sole benefit of a minor child where the minor child is mentally disabled.

The CRA's general position is that farm land that is owned or held in a partnership cannot be transferred to a child under ITA 73(3) (VD 2010-0383601E5); see, however, ITA 73(4.1).

ITA 70(9.6), 70(10)"child", 73(3), 73(3.1), 73(4.1), 75.1, 252(1)"child", CRA Guide T4003

¶4235.1 — *Inter Vivos Transfer of Family Farm or Fishing Corporations, etc., to Child*

The principle governing the transfer of family farm or fishing property to children is further extended to apply to transfers of shares in a family farm or fishing corporation or of an interest in a family farm or fishing partnership. In particular, ITA 73(4) provides a tax-deferral for an *inter vivos* transfer of shares of a family farm or fishing corporation or an interest in a family farm or fishing partnership by a taxpayer to a child of the taxpayer. Also included are shares in a holding corporation, all or substantially all the property of which is shares or debt of a farm or fishing corporation involving the same family.

The terms "share of the capital stock of a family farm or fishing corporation" and "interest in a family farm or fishing partnership" are defined in ITA 70(10). The definitions are generally parallel with the definitions of the same terms in ITA 110.6 discussed under ¶4233 and ¶4234. As an exception, the ability to claim the capital gains deduction is limited unless property of the corporation or partnership was held and used for qualified purposes for 24 months; the rollover provisions under ITA 73(3) and (4) do not impose such a restriction.

Rules similar to those applying to the transfer of farm or fishing property, set out above, provide that the deemed proceeds to the vendor (and the deemed cost to the transferee) are determined as follows:

- if the transfer price (if any) falls between fair market value and the adjusted cost base of the shares or partnership interest, that price will be considered as the proceeds of disposition;

- if the transfer price exceeds both those amounts, the proceeds will be deemed to be equal to the greater;

- if the transfer price is less than both amounts, the proceeds will be deemed to be the lesser of them;

- in the case of an interest in a family farm or fishing partnership, the taxpayer or qualifying trust for the benefit of a spouse or common-law partner is considered not to have disposed of the interest and the recipient is considered to have acquired the interest at its cost to the taxpayer or trust; and

- the partnership interest is subject to the same adjustments under ITA 53(1) and 53(2) as applied to the transferor of the interest.

To the extent that proceeds of disposition are not due and payable until after the end of the year, the transferor may claim a capital gains reserve pursuant to ITA 40(1.1) (see ¶4140).

As in the case of a transfer of farm or fishing property, if the shares of the family farm or fishing corporation or interest in the family farm or fishing partnership are later disposed of and a capital gain or loss arises, that gain or loss will be attributed to the transferor unless the transfer was made at fair market value, the recipient has attained the age of 18 before the end of the year in which the disposition takes place, or at the time of the disposition the transferor has died or has become a non-resident of Canada.

Although a partnership must be in existence for 24 months for a partnership interest to qualify as an interest in a family farm or fishing partnership, the CRA has stated that a partner does not need to hold the partnership interest for 24 months in order for the interest to qualify (VDs 2004-0075041E5 and 2006-0217861E5). However, any opportunity to quickly utilize the capital gains exemption, for example, by transferring a qualifying interest to a child on a tax-deferred basis under ITA 73 which the child shortly thereafter disposes of, is limited by ITA 69(11). ITA 69(11) is an anti-avoidance provision directed at transfers of property for proceeds less than fair market value where the transfer is part of a series of transactions designed to obtain the benefit on a subsequent disposition of any deduction (including the capital gains deduction), credit or exemption available to a person who is unaffiliated with the transferor (parents and children are not affiliated under ITA 251.1). If this anti-avoidance provision applies to a transfer of property, the transferor is deemed to have disposed of the relevant property at its fair market value notwithstanding any other provisions of the ITA.

In VD 2002-0143635, the CRA stated that where the "one of the main purposes" test has been met, ITA 69(11) will apply where ITA 73(3) or (4) are first used to transfer farm property to an adult child and the farm property is then sold within a three year period (the CRA makes similar comments in VDs 2010-0383601E5, 2009-0344851E5, 2008-0294051I7, 2005-0154271E5, and 2000-0042945). Where ITA 69(11) applies, the CRA's position is that the child's adjusted cost base would reflect the parent's deemed proceeds of disposition as computed under ITA 69(11).

To multiply access to the capital gains exemption while avoiding the application of ITA 69(11), spouses may, for example, sell a portion of their interest in a qualifying farming or fishing partnership to their child and his or her spouse at an amount greater than cost but less than fair market value, utilizing their capital gains deduction on the transfer. After three years, the child and his or her spouse could then crystallize their capital gains exemption by transferring their partnership interests to a corporation under ITA 85. The CRA has stated that GAAR would normally not apply if an individual gave shares of a family farm corporation to his children under ITA 73(4) and immediately thereafter the children sold the shares to an unrelated party and claimed the enhanced capital gain exemption (VDs 9208955, October 1990-249 and August 1990-185; the latter views documents do not consider the potential application of ITA 69(11)).

Where shares of a qualifying farm or fishing corporation are transferred to a child, a parent may retain voting control of the corporation by holding non-participating voting shares. In such a case, the CRA has stated that they would not consider such voting non-participating shares to have more than a nominal value where they are issued as part of an estate freeze transaction and are held to protect that taxpayer's economic interest in the corporation (VDs 2008-0285241C6 and 2009-0330211C6, May 2009 Alberta CAs Roundtable question 20).

In VD 9702425, the CRA states that where a corporation holds an interest in a partnership that carries on the business of farming, the fair market value of that partnership interest will likely be attributable to the use by the partnership of its assets in the business of farming.

ITA 69(11), 70(10), 73(3), 73(4), 75.1, Jeff Henkelman, "Farm Succession Planning," *2010 Prairie Provinces Tax Conference*, (Toronto: Canadian Tax Foundation, 2010), 13:1–22, John F Oakey, CA, "Tax Developments in the Fishing and Farming Industry," *2007 Atlantic Provinces Tax Conference*, (Halifax: Canadian Tax Foundation, 2007), 3A:1–23. May 2009 Alberta CAs roundtable question 20

¶4240 — Cumulative Net Investment Loss (CNIL)

The extent to which an individual may claim the lifetime capital gains exemption is limited by the individual's cumulative net investment loss ("CNIL"). Under the formula, the cumulative gains limit at the end of the year is reduced by the individual's CNIL. As a result, the use of the capital gains exemption will be deferred, at least in part, to the extent of the taxpayer's CNIL. The CNIL is defined as the amount by which total "investment expenses" for all years ending after 1987 exceed total "investment income" for those years. The CNIL is based on total amounts and is not traced to any particular investment. So, for example, if a taxpayer borrowed funds to purchase a rental property and, in an unrelated transaction, sold shares for a capital gain, the amount of capital gains deduction available on the sale of the shares would be decreased to the extent of the CNIL arising by virtue of the interest expense on the rental property.

¶4241 — *Investment Expenses*

A taxpayer's CNIL balance is increased by the taxpayer's "investment expenses", which include interest paid on money borrowed for investment purposes, investment counsel fees, one-half of most resource deductions, and property or rental losses where the taxpayer is not actively involved in the property owned. Specifically, "investment expenses" are defined in ITA 110.6(1) as:

- amounts deducted for the year in computing income from property, except to the extent that the amount was otherwise taken into account in computing the taxpayer's investment expense or investment income for the year. Also excluded are expenses related to debt incurred (generally before November 13, 1981) for the purpose of acquiring an income-averaging annuity contract, an RRSP, or an RPP, as well as any amount deducted pursuant to ITA 20(1)(j) relating to the repayment of a shareholder loan previously included in income together with amounts deducted pursuant to ITA 65(1), 66(4), 66.1(3), 66.2(2), 66.21(4), or 66.4(2);

- interest and other specified expenses deducted in computing income from a partnership of which the individual was a specified member (defined in ITA 248(1) as a limited partner or a non-active partner), including expenses relating to financing costs incurred by a partnership that has ceased to exist;

- amounts deducted as the individual's share of losses (other than allowable capital losses) of a partnership of which the individual was a specified member;

- 50% of amounts deducted under ITA 66(4), 66.1(3), 66.2(2), or 66.21(4) by the individual attributable to certain resource and exploration expenses renounced under ITA 66(12.6), (12.601), (12.62), or (12.64);

- all losses from property or from renting or leasing rental property or a multiple unit residential building; and

- net capital losses of other taxation years deducted pursuant to the loss carry-over rules in ITA 111(1)(b) subject to specific limitations.

¶4242 — *Investment Income*

A CNIL balance is reduced by a taxpayer's "investment income", which includes interest and dividend income, property income, or rental income where the taxpayer is not actively involved in the property owned, and net taxable capital gains that are ineligible for the capital gains exemption.

Specifically, "investment income" is defined in ITA 110.6(1) as:

- income from property including recaptured depreciation with respect to income-producing property pursuant to ITA 13(1), except income amounts otherwise included in investment income or deducted in computing investment expense (also excluded are shareholder loans included in income pursuant to 15(2) and annuity payments included in income under ITA 56(1)(d) and former ITA 56(1)(d.1));

- income from all partnerships of which the individual was a specified member in the year;

- 50% of all amounts included in income under ITA 59(3.2) with respect to the recovery of exploration and development expenses;

- amounts included in income from property or from renting or leasing rental property;

- amounts received as an annuity, other than an income-averaging annuity contract or one purchased pursuant to a deferred profit sharing plan as provided in ITA 56(1)(d) and former ITA 56(1)(d.1), net of the capital portion deducted pursuant to ITA 60(a); and

- net capital gains which are not otherwise eligible for the capital gains exemption.

ITA 110.6(1)"cumulative net investment loss", 110.6(1)"investment expenses", 110.6(1)"investment income"

¶4250 — Surplus Stripping

An important anti-avoidance rule in ITA 84.1(1) requires a paid-up capital reduction and may also require an immediate recognition of a deemed dividend in respect of certain non-arm's length transfers of shares to a corporation. The general purpose of the rule is to prevent an individual from using the capital gains exemption to receive non-share consideration or shares with high paid-up capital from a non-arm's length corporation (i.e., the purpose of the provision is to prevent surplus stripping). Generally, the maximum amount that can be received by the transferor of the shares from the transferee corporation in the form of non-share consideration and paid-up capital is restricted to the greater of the paid-up capital of the transferred shares and the transferor's adjusted cost base of the shares (as adjusted by ITA 84.1(2)(a) and (a.1)). The taxpayer's adjusted cost base in the transferred shares is reduced by the lesser of the capital gain realized by the taxpayer or a non-arm's length person in respect of a previous disposition and the portion of the whole gain in respect of which a capital gains exemption was claimed by the taxpayer or the non-arm's length person. The intent of the reduction is to allow the adjusted cost base of a share to be increased on a non-arm's length transfer only to the extent that any related capital gain has been subject to tax.

ITA 84.1 only applies where the following conditions are met:

- There is a disposition of shares (the "subject shares") of a Canadian resident corporation (the "subject corporation") by a Canadian resident taxpayer other than a corporation;

- The shares are capital property of the disposing taxpayer;

- The taxpayer transfers the subject shares to a corporation with which the taxpayer does not deal at arm's length (the "purchaser corporation"). Note that there is no restriction regarding the purchaser corporation and ITA 84.1(1) could apply where shares are transferred to a non-resident corporation; and

- The subject corporation is "connected" with the purchaser corporation immediately after the disposition (see ITA 186(4) for the meaning of "connected").

ITA 84.1 may apply, for example, when family members buy a business from other family members and to facilitate the transaction, a new corporation is formed to borrow the required funds to finance the acquisition. It is also important to highlight that ITA 84.1 contains rules which deem certain persons that would normally be considered to be dealing at arm's length not to be dealing at arm's length. The deeming rules significantly expand the potential applicability of ITA 84.1 and can result in a tax trap. ITA 84.1 can also apply when taxpayers are not dealing at arm's length on a factual basis. The CRA's view is that such a situation may arise, for example, when a transaction is structured to accommodate a vendor. It should also be noted that when transactions are structured to avoid the application of ITA 84.1, GAAR has applied in several court cases. ITA 84.1 does not apply to arm's length transactions.

For an example of a transaction which successfully circumvented the application of ITA 84.1, see *Evans v. R.*, [2006] 2 C.T.C. 2009 (TCC). GAAR was found not to apply in *McMullen v. R.*, [2007] 2 C.T.C. 2463 (TCC); however, GAAR applied in *McNichol v The Queen*, [1997] 2 C.T.C. 2088 (TCC), *RMM Canadian Enterprises Inc v The Queen*, [1998] 1 C.T.C. 2300 (TCC) and *Desmarais v. R.*, [2006] 3 C.T.C. 2304 (TCC). Despite the decision in *McMullen*, the CRA has stated that they will continue to apply ITA 84.1 or GAAR in those situations where the purchaser corporation acts as an accommodator or facilitator for the taxpayer in order to avoid the application of ITA 84.1.

IT-489R: *Non Arm's Length Sale of Shares to a Corporation*, VDs 2005-0141061C6, 2005-0134831I7

¶4300 — Disposition of Publicly Traded Shares, Mutual Fund Units, Deferral of Eligible Small Business Corporation Shares, and Other Shares (Sch. 3: Part 3)

Taxpayers should report in Section 3 of Schedule 3 the dispositions of shares that are not described in any other section of Schedule 3, including the disposition of mutual fund trust units; publicly traded shares; Canadian securities that are not qualified small business corporation shares or qualified family farm or fishing corporation shares; shares issued by foreign corporations and digital currencies. Taxpayers should also report in Section 3 the donation of the following types of capital property to a qualified donee: shares listed on a designated stock exchange; shares of the capital stock of a mutual fund corporation; units in a mutual fund trust; or an interest in a related segregated fund trust (see ¶4330).

Capital gains (or losses) realized on the redemption of shares or units of a mutual fund should also be reported in Section 3 of Schedule 3. Generally, taxpayers will receive a T5008 slip, *Statement of Securities Transactions*, or an account statement from the mutual fund reporting the gains or losses on redemption. Capital gains realized by the mutual fund from its investment portfolio which are then flowed out to the taxpayer will generally be reported on an information slip and should be reported on Line 174 or Line 176 of Schedule 3, as applicable.

The deferral of capital gains incurred on the disposition of small business investments should also be reported in Part 3 of Schedule 3 (see ¶4340).

¶4310 — Disposition of Mutual Fund Units or Shares

When a taxpayer redeems (or cashes in) mutual fund units or shares, the taxpayer may realize a capital gain or loss on the redemption. Generally, taxpayers will receive a T5008 slip, *Statement of Securities Transactions*, or an account statement from the mutual fund reporting the gains or losses on redemption. Capital gains and losses from a taxpayer's mutual fund units and shares should be reported on Lines 131 and 132 of Schedule 3. List the information for each mutual fund separately. Multiple redemptions from the same fund in the same year should be grouped together. Where a taxpayer has bought and sold the same mutual fund units or shares (i.e., identical properties) over a period of time, see the discussion of the cost averaging rules in ¶4121.

To calculate the taxpayer's capital gain from the mutual fund units or shares redeemed, calculate the ACB of the units or shares redeemed, and multiply the average cost per unit of all units or shares held immediately before the redemption by the number of units or shares redeemed. The average cost per unit or share of the total investment will increase or decrease when the taxpayer purchases new units or shares, or reinvests distributions, depending on the price when the transaction occurred. Every time additional units or shares are purchased, or distributions are reinvested, the average cost per unit or share must be recalculated for each mutual fund the taxpayer owns.

Where the taxpayer receives a T3 slip with an amount in Box 42 — Amount resulting in a cost base adjustment, the ACB of that mutual fund trust identified on the slip will change. If Box 42 contains a negative amount, the amount is added to the ACB of the units of the trust. If Box 42 contains a positive amount, the amount is subtracted from the ACB of the units of the trust. If the ACB of the trust units is reduced below zero during the tax year, the negative amount is deemed to be a capital gain in the year. Enter the amount of the capital gain on Line 132 of Schedule 3. Place a zero on Line 131 since there is no actual sale of units. The new ACB of the trust units is deemed to be zero.

See Information Sheet RC4169, *Tax Treatment of Mutual Funds for Individuals*, for a detailed example that provides instructions for calculating capital gains or losses and completing Schedule 3 on a redemption of mutual fund units or shares.

¶4315 — Disposition of Digital Currencies

For Canadian tax purposes, digital currencies are considered to be a commodity, and not a currency. Cryptocurrencies are a type of digital currency created using computer algorithms. The most popular cryptocurrency is Bitcoin. The CRA considers the buying and selling of digital currencies to be similar to the buying and selling of regular securities, such as mutual funds or shares. Accordingly, an investor in a digital currency must pay tax on the disposition of the digital currency in the form of a capital gain when it is converted into another currency (e.g. the Canadian dollar). Generally, the capital gain (or loss, as the case may be) is calculated based on the market value of the digital currency when it is exchanged for currency, less the amount originally paid for the digital currency. The capital gain (or loss, as applicable) is reported in Part 3 of Schedule 3.

Note that if the sale of digital currency is on account of income, the taxpayer must record the proceeds of disposition as business income (see Chapter 6 for the discussion of business income). The following factors are considered when determining whether a disposition of a security is on account of income or capital (see IT-479R, *Transactions in Securities*):

1. Frequency of transactions — Is the investor trading a few times a year or a few times a day?

2. Period of ownership — Is the investor holding the cryptocurrency for a few years or a few weeks?

3. Knowledge of securities markets — Is the investor knowledgeable and familiar with the cryptocurrency (or other securities) market or are they just dabbling?

4. Time spent — Does the investor spend hours a day on trading and keeping up to date with the market or just a few hours a month?

A capital gain may also be realized where an individual uses digital currency to pay for goods or services. The exchange of digital currency for a good or service is considered to be a barter transaction for Canadian tax purposes, which the CRA defines as a transaction between two persons in which one commodity is exchanged for another without the use of money (see IT-490, *Barter Transactions*). In this case, the purchaser of the good or service has disposed of a commodity (i.e., the digital currency) in exchange for a good or service, and must pay tax in the form of a capital gain. Generally, the capital gain (or loss, as the case may be) is calculated based on the fair market value of the good or service purchased less the amount originally paid for the digital currency. Again, the capital gain (or loss, as applicable) is reported in Part 3 of Schedule 3.

For the CRA's views on digital currency, see VD 2014-0525191E5 and the CRA's website at: canada.ca/en/revenue-agency/news/newsroom/fact-sheets/fact-sheets-2015/what-you-should-know-about-digital-currency.html.

ITA 9(1), IT-479R, *Transactions in Securities*, IT-490, *Barter Transactions*, Alatopulo et al., "Bitcoins and Blockchains: The Taxation and Caselaw of Cryptocurrencies in the US and Canada", *Tax Disputes and Resolution Centre* (Taxnet Pro), Nov. 2017, Fournier et al, "Rebooting Money: The Canadian Tax Treatment of Bitcoin and Other Cryptocurrencies," *Report of the Proceedings of the Sixty-Sixth Tax Conference*, 2014 Conference Report (Toronto: Canadian Tax Foundation, 2015), 11:1–27, Pinto, "Options To Address the Direct Tax Challenges Raised by the Digital Economy — A Critical Analysis" (2016) 63:2 *Canadian Tax Journal* 291–331, bennettjones.com/en/Blogs-Section/Getting-In-on-Bitcoin-Canadian-Income-Tax-Implications-of-Cryptocurrencies, collinsbarrow.com/en/cbn/publications/taxalert-bitcoin-mining-cra-inter-pretation-under-fire

¶4320 — Employee Security Options

When an employee receives an option to buy eligible securities (i.e., a common share listed on a designated stock exchange inside or outside Canada, or a unit of a mutual fund trust) at a certain price through their employer, it does not immediately affect the employee's tax situation. However, when the employee exercises their option and purchases the securities at less than the fair market value, the employee will have a taxable employment benefit equal to the difference between what the employee paid for the securities and the fair market value of the securities at the time the option was exercised, reduced by the amount, if any, that the employee paid to acquire the option. The amount paid to acquire the security, including any amount paid to acquire the rights under the option agreement, cannot be less than the fair market value of the security at the time the option is granted. In addition, the security must be a security in respect of which a security option deduction may be claimed on Line 249 of the taxpayer's T1 return (see ¶2510 and ¶9330).

Where an employee security option is granted to an employee by a Canadian-controlled private corporation (CCPC) with which the employee deals at arm's length, the taxable benefit can be deferred until the year the employee sells the securities. To qualify for the deferral, immediately before the option was granted, the employee must have been dealing at arm's length with the employer and the employee cannot be a specified shareholder of the employer (a specified shareholder is generally one who owns 10% or more of any class of a corporation's shares). The employee must also be a resident of Canada at the time the option is exercised to qualify for the deferral. Similarly, for public securities under option agreements exercised before 4:00 p.m. EST on March 4, 2010, an income deferral of the taxable benefit may have been allowed subject to an annual limit of $100,000 on the fair market value of the securities. In this situation, the taxable benefit is deferred until the year in which the first of the following events occurs: the employee disposes of the eligible security, the employee dies, or the employee becomes a non-resident. The election to defer the security option benefit is no longer available for public security options exercised after 4:00 p.m. EST on March 4, 2010.

¶4321 — *Employee Security Option Cash-Out Rights*

Employees who acquire eligible securities under a security option agreement and meet certain conditions may be entitled to a deduction equal to one-half of the security option benefit ("security option deduction"). In this case, the employer cannot claim a deduction for the issuance of the share. Employee security option agreements can also be structured in such a way that the employee can dispose of his or her security option rights to the employer for a cash payment or other in-kind benefit ("cash-out payment"). For such transactions occurring after 4:00 p.m. EST on March 4, 2010, the security option deduction can only be claimed in situations where either:

- the employee exercises his or her options by acquiring shares of their employer; or

- the employer has elected (as indicated by completing Box 86, Security option election, of the employee's T4 slip) for all security options issued or to be issued after 4:00 p.m. EST on March 4, 2010, under the agreement and files such election with the Minister of Revenue, that neither the employer nor any person not dealing at arm's length with the employer will claim a deduction for the cash-out payment in respect of the employee's disposition of rights under the agreement.

Regardless of when a security option was exercised, the adjusted cost base of a security purchased through an employee security option agreement is not the actual price paid by the employee. To calculate the adjusted cost base of the employee's securities, add the following two amounts: the actual purchase price; and any amount included in income as a taxable employment benefit for the securities (even if the employee claimed a security option deduction for them).

The capital gain (or loss) should be reported in the year the employee exchanges or sells the eligible securities purchased through an employee security option agreement. If the securities are qualified small business corporation shares, report the transaction in Part 1 of Schedule 3. In all other cases, report the transaction in Part 3 of Schedule 3.

¶4330 — Donations of Capital Property

Where a taxpayer donates capital property, the taxpayer is considered to have disposed of the property for proceeds equal to the fair market value of the property. As such, a capital gain or loss may arise as a result of the donation. However, where a taxpayer donates a qualifying security to a qualified donee, the capital gains inclusion rate is nil, and thus, no capital gain will be realized as a result of the disposition by way of donation. For these purposes, a qualifying security includes shares, debt obligations or rights listed on a designated stock exchange; a share of the capital stock of a mutual fund corporation; a unit of a mutual fund trust; an interest in a related segregated fund trust; and a prescribed debt obligation. A qualified donee includes registered charities (including public and private foundations); registered Canadian amateur athletic associations; the government of Canada, a province, or a territory; and Canadian municipalities. Where the taxpayer has died, and a gift which would otherwise qualify for this preferential treatment is made by will, no capital gain will be realized on death.

Gifts of ecologically sensitive land made to a qualified donee (other than to a private foundation) are also eligible for a capital gains inclusion rate of zero.

Applicable in respect of gifts made after February 25, 2008, the zero inclusion rate also applies to capital gains realized on the exchange of unlisted securities for publicly traded securities, and to capital gains realized on the exchanges of an unlisted interest in a partnership, provided certain conditions are met. Special rules apply to the exchange of unlisted interest in a partnership which are intended to ensure that only capital gains that reflect economic appreciation of the partnership interest are exempted, while gains that arise because of various reductions to the adjusted cost base of a partnership interest are not exempted.

By virtue of ITA 40(12), where a taxpayer donates shares acquired under a flow-through share agreement entered into after March 21, 2011, the taxpayer is generally only entitled to a capital gains exemption to the extent that the capital gain exceeds the original cost of the flow-through shares. ITA 40(12) also applies where the flow-through shares were acquired by the taxpayer in certain rollover transactions where the property received in return is publicly-listed shares.

Applicable to gifts made after December 20, 2002, where a taxpayer is entitled to an advantage or benefit in respect of a gift, only part of the taxpayer's capital gain will be entitled to the special inclusion rate (i.e., the part of the gain that the eligible amount of the gift is of the taxpayer's total proceeds of disposition in respect of the property). ITA 248(30) to (33) provide rules for determining the eligible amount of a gift and for determining the amount of an "advantage" received.

Taxpayers who realize a capital gain on a donation of a non-qualifying security to a qualified donee may be able to claim a reserve in order to postpone the inclusion of the capital gain in income over a maximum of five years (see ¶4140). For gifts of non-qualifying securities made after December 20, 2002, the reserve claimed cannot be greater than the eligible amount of the gift. The reserve is not available if the donee disposes of the security, or if the security ceases to be a non-qualifying security before the end of the tax year. If this happens, the taxpayer will be considered to have made a charitable donation in that year and can claim the charitable donation tax credit. Generally, non-qualifying securities include shares of a private corporation with which the taxpayer does not deal with at arm's length after the donation was made (see: canada.ca/en/revenue-agency/services/charities-giving/charities/policies-guidance/non-qualifying-security.html).

Applicable to dispositions of non-qualifying securities by qualified donees after March 21, 2011, where a qualified donee has received a gift of a non-qualifying security, no tax receipt may be issued and no charitable donation tax credit may be claimed by the donor unless, within the 5-year reserve period, the non-qualifying security ceases to be a non-qualifying security or has been disposed of in exchange for property that is not a non-qualifying security. If the security is not disposed of within the 5-year period, the taxpayer will not be required to bring the reserve back into income in the year following the end of that period.

Capital gains on charitable donations are required to be reported and deducted in calculating capital gains, even though the inclusion rate may be nil. Taxpayers should report the disposition on Line 132 and/or Line 153 of Schedule 3, as applicable. Complete Form T1170: *Capital Gains on Gifts of Certain Capital Property*, to calculate the capital gain to report on Schedule 3. Even though, in most cases, the inclusion rate of 1/2 is reduced to zero for gifts of qualifying securities, Form T1170 should still be completed to report these gifts. Complete Schedule 9, *Donations and Gifts*, to claim a tax credit for the donation (see ¶10210).

ITA 38(a.1), 38(a.3), 38.1, 38.2, 40(12), 149.1(1)"qualified donee", 248(30)–(33), Form T1170: *Capital Gains on Gifts of Certain Capital Property*, CRA Pamphlet P113: *Gifts and Income Tax*, CRA Guidance CG-012: *Non-qualifying security*

¶4340 — Capital Gains Deferral for Eligible Small Business Corporation Shares

A capital gains deferral is available when proceeds from the disposition of eligible small business corporation shares are reinvested in a new eligible small business corporation. The adjusted cost base of the new investment is reduced by the capital gain deferred from the initial investment. The capital gains deferral applies only to eligible small business corporation shares. See under ¶4220 for a discussion of the definition of eligible small business corporation shares.

To qualify for the deferral, the taxpayer must have held the eligible small business corporation shares for more than 185 days from the date the taxpayer acquired them and the replacement shares have to be acquired at any time in the year in which the disposition is made or within 120 days after the end of that year. For example, where a taxpayer acquires eligible small business corporation shares in October 2006 and disposes of them on June 9, 2012, the taxpayer may acquire the replacement shares on or before April 30, 2013, which is within 120 days after the end of the tax year of the original disposition.

The permitted deferral of the capital gain from the disposition of eligible small business corporation shares is determined by the following formula:

$$B \times (D \div E)$$

where

B = the total capital gain from the original sale

E = the proceeds of disposition

D = the lesser of E and the total cost of all replacement shares

The total capital gain should be reported in Part 3 of Schedule 3 (on Lines 131 and 132) and the capital gains deferral on Line 161 of Schedule 3. Generally, the capital gain reported in the year of disposition will be determined by subtracting the capital gain deferral (Line 161) from the total capital gain realized from the disposition.

Capital gains that are deferred on the disposition of qualified small business corporation shares do not qualify for the $800,000 capital gains exemption/deduction (discussed under ¶4210). Therefore, do not report the disposition of qualified small business corporation shares in Part 1 of Schedule 3 where the taxpayer elects to defer the capital gains on the disposition of the shares. Instead, such dispositions should be reported on Lines 131 and 132 of Schedule 3.

The capital gains deferral will reduce the ACB of each of the eligible replacement shares by the amount determined by the following formula:

$$F \times (G \div H)$$

where

F = capital gains deferral

G = the cost of replacement shares

H = the total cost of all the replacement shares

¶4350 — Proceeds of Disposition of Securities: Special Rules

In addition to a normal disposition of shares or bonds in exchange for cash, a "disposition" is defined in the ITA as including any transaction or event by which:

1) A share, bond, debenture, note, certificate, mortgage, agreement of sale or similar property, or an interest therein, is in whole or in part redeemed, acquired, or cancelled;

2) A debt (or any other right to receive an amount) is settled or cancelled; or

3) A share is converted because of an amalgamation or merger (where shares of the predecessor company are exchanged for shares of the new or amalgamated company, ITA 87 normally permits a tax-free rollover).

The proceeds of disposition of a share do not include any part that is deemed to be received as a dividend by ITA 84(2), 84(3) or 84.1(1).

On the winding-up of a Canadian corporation, a distribution to shareholders out of its pre-1972 capital surplus is in some circumstances deemed by ITA 88(2)(b)(ii) not to be received as a dividend. The amount so deemed not to be a dividend is, however, required to be treated as proceeds of disposition of the relevant shares.

If a share is converted because of a merger or an amalgamation, ITA 248(1) deems a disposition to have occurred.

The existence of an "earnout agreement" attached to the sale price of shares makes the computation of the capital gain or loss difficult because the quantum of the proceeds of disposition is determined by reference to future earnings. In certain circumstances, the CRA is prepared to accept the practice of applying the proceeds of disposition against the ACB of the shares first, and to determine a capital gain only when the cumulative proceeds exceed that base; see IT-426R: *Shares Sold Subject to an Earnout Agreement* and VD 2013-0505391E5.

A change in the terms or attributes of shares may constitute a disposition. In IT-448, the following examples of changes that are normally considered by the CRA to be sufficient to be regarded as dispositions of shares are provided: a change in voting rights attached to shares that effects a change in the voting control of the corporation; a change in a defined entitlement to share in the assets of a corporation upon dissolution (preferred shares only); the giving up or the addition of a priority right to shares in the distribution of assets of the corporation upon dissolution; the addition or deletion of a right attaching to a class of shares that provides for participation in dividend entitlements beyond a fixed preferential rate or amount; or a change from a cumulative to a non-cumulative right to dividends or *vice versa*.

The CRA generally does not consider the following changes in the terms or attributes of shares to be dispositions: the addition of the right to elect a majority of the directors of the corporation if, at that time, the shareholders of that class are already in a position to control the election of directors; a change in the number of votes per share if the ability of any one shareholder to influence the day-to-day affairs of the corporation is neither enhanced nor impaired thereby; the giving up of contingent voting rights which, in the event they were exercised, would not be of sufficient number to control the affairs of the corporation; restrictions added or removed concerning transfer of shares; the addition of a right of redemption in favour of the corporation; stock splits or consolidations (see IT-65); a change of shares with par value to shares without par value or *vice versa*, provided that there is no change in any pre-set entitlements to dividends and/or distribution of assets upon dissolution; a change in ranking concerning preference features (e.g., 1st preference to 2nd preference); and, an increase or decrease in the amount or rate of a fixed dividend entitlement.

The CRA considers the settlement date, which is typically two to three days subsequent to the trade date, to be the date of disposition of shares for tax purposes. Where proceeds are received in a foreign currency, they should be converted to Canadian dollars on the settlement date using the noon exchange rate (VD 2015-0588981C6).

With respect to securities, events which the CRA has stated do not constitute a "disposition" for tax purposes include the following: a change in the stock exchange on which a security is listed (VD 2012-0455431C6); a corporate share split (VD 2010-0376681R3); an off-market swap of shares traded on one exchange to the same shares traded on another exchange (VD 2012-0455431C6); an exchange of shares for another class with same rights and conditions (VDs 2004-0092561E5, 2013-0495821C6); an automatic renewal of a foreign currency loan (VDs 2011-0422481R3, 2013-0507661I7); and an addition of an exchange right to a note (VD 2013-0514191R3).

54"proceeds of disposition"(i), (j), (k), 248(1)"disposition", *Deragon, C.*, 2015 TCC 294, IT-448: *Dispositions — Changes in Terms of Securities*, TEI/CRA Commentary 2012-12-04B (q.5), VD 2013-0505391E5

¶4360 — Investments in a Bankrupt Corporation: Deemed Disposition of Shares

The ITA provides that a share in a company that becomes a bankrupt during the shareholder's taxation year, or a share in a company that is insolvent and subject to a winding-up order under the *Winding-up and Restructuring Act* is deemed, on election, to be disposed of by the shareholder at the end of that year for no proceeds, and to be reacquired immediately after the end of the year at a cost of nil. The deemed disposition and reacquisition may also apply, via an election, pursuant to ITA 50(1)(b)(iii) where, at the end of the taxation year, the corporation is insolvent and neither it nor any corporation controlled by it carries on business, provided that the fair market value of the share is nil and it is reasonable to expect that the corporation will be dissolved or wound up and will not continue carrying on business. Any subsequent realization on the debt or shares in question will result in a capital gain.

A taxpayer is required to file an election with the taxpayer's T1 return for a deemed disposition to arise under ITA 50(1)(b)(iii). To file the election, the taxpayer should write and sign a letter stating that the taxpayer wants subsection 50(1) of the ITA to apply to the shares. This letter should be attached to a paper-filed return. If the return is being filed electronically, the letter should be sent to the taxpayer's CRA Tax Centre by the filing-due date of the T1 return for the taxation year.

The "superficial loss" rule does not apply to a deemed disposition under ITA 50. Also, capital losses arising from a disposition of shares deemed to have been made under ITA 50(1) are not subject to the loss deferral or denial rules under ITA 40(3.4) or 40(3.6) (see ¶4821).

ITA 50(1.1) provides rules where, following a deemed disposition by reason of ITA 50(1)(b)(iii), the taxpayer or a person with whom the taxpayer does not deal at arm's length owns shares of the insolvent corporation and the insolvent corporation or a corporation controlled by it carries on business within the 24-month period immediately following the deemed disposition. In this case, the taxpayer (or non-arm's length person) is deemed to have disposed of the shares at the earliest time the business is resumed for proceeds of disposition equal to the ACB of the shares as determined immediately before the previous deemed disposition by reason of ITA 50(1)(b)(iii) and to have reacquired them immediately after the resumption of business for that same amount. This forces the taxpayer to realize a capital gain that effectively offsets any previously claimed capital loss. See example 5 in Folio S4-F8-C1.

ITA 50, 54"superficial loss", *Jacques St-Onge Inc.*, [2004] 1 C.T.C. 2094, Folio S4-F8-C1: *Business Investment Losses*, VDs 2003-0046167, 2005-0150271E5, 2008-0274451E5

¶4370 — Convertible Shares or Debt

Generally, shares of the same corporation can be exchanged without resulting in a disposition for capital gains purposes, and bonds, debentures, or notes can be exchanged for shares if the convertible security has a term that gives the owner the right to make the exchange (shares can be exchanged even if the terms of the exchanged shares do not provide a right of exchange or conversion). The rollover is not elective and it applies automatically where the appropriate conditions are met. With respect to a bond, the bond is required to include a conversion term.

For the rollover to be available, the shares or debt must be held as capital property. The rollover is permitted where a taxpayer receives shares of more than one class upon the exchange. It is also necessary that no consideration be received on the exchange of the convertible property other than the share. The final condition would appear to preclude, for example, the possibility of receiving cash with a view to eliminating fractional interests. However, the CRA has administratively relaxed this rule, providing in effect that cash in lieu of a fraction of a share may be received, up to a maximum of $200, without disqualifying the exchange from the rollover provisions.

The cost to the taxpayer of the shares received in exchange for the convertible property is basically deemed to be the ACB to the taxpayer of the exchanged property immediately before the exchange. Where the taxpayer acquires shares of more than one class on the exchange, the ACB of the convertible property is allocated among the different classes in accordance with the relative fair market value of the shares of each class.

A special rule applies in certain circumstances where the excess in the fair market value of the convertible property over the fair market value of the share or shares received in exchange may reasonably be regarded as constituting a benefit in favour of persons related to the taxpayer effecting the conversion. In such a case, the rollover is limited to the extent that a gain has been decreased as a result of the indirect gift. To the extent that such capital gain has been so decreased, it will be recognized in the hands of the transferor at the time of the conversion. This rule is intended to prevent such an indirect gift from being accomplished through a tax-deferred conversion.

Where the convertible property is taxable Canadian property of the taxpayer, the share acquired on the exchange is also deemed to be, at any time that is within 60 months after the disposition, taxable Canadian property of the taxpayer. Thus, the rules in ITA 115 and 116 could apply to a non-resident converter who disposes of shares received on an exchange under ITA 51(1).

Where the taxpayer exchanging the shares is a non-resident of Canada, withholding tax may apply.

ITA 51, 53(2)(g.1), 89(1)"paid-up capital"(b), 116(5), 212(1), VDs 2014-052465117 (ITA 51(1) does not apply where conversion is not executed under the terms of the debenture), 2005-0150411E5, 2004-0093851E5, 2008-0300391C6, 2008-0293401E5, IT-146R4: *Shares entitling shareholders to choose taxable or capital dividends*, IT-115R2 (para. 3): *Fractional interests in shares*, IT-291R3: *Transfer of property to a corporation under subsection 85(1)*

¶4400 — Disposition of Real Estate and Depreciable Property (Sch. 3: Pt. 4)

In Part 4 of Schedule 3, list all real estate disposed of during the taxation year. Provide the municipal address of each property. Enter the total amount of gain or loss realized on Line 138. Real estate includes commercial and industrial land and buildings, vacant land, rental property (both land and buildings), and farm property.

Taxpayers should not report the sale of personal-use property (such as a cottage) or mortgages and other similar debt obligations on real property in Part 4. These transactions should be reported in Part 7 (Personal-use Property) and Part 5 (Bonds, debentures, promissory notes, and other similar properties) of Schedule 3, respectively. The disposition of a principal residence should be reported on page 2 of Schedule 3.

For each real property sold that includes land and a building, as discussed under ¶4410, the allocation of the net proceeds of disposition to the land and building is required to be determined in accordance with special rules contained in the ITA. The sale of land and a building should be reported separately on Schedule 3.

Dispositions of non-depreciable real property (i.e., land) give rise to a capital gain or loss (unless the property is inventory). Dispositions of depreciable property (i.e. a building or machinery) may result in a capital gain, a recapture of CCA included in income for tax purposes (see ¶7145), or a terminal loss deductible from income for tax purposes (see ¶7150).

Where real estate is converted from capital property into inventory or trading property, the ultimate disposition of the real estate may give rise to a gain or loss that is on capital account, a gain or loss on income account, or a gain or loss that is partly capital and partly income. For instance, on a conversion of capital property to inventory or trading property, the increase, if any, in value of the property between the date of conversion to the date of sale will be reported in full as income while the increase, if any, in value of the property between the date the property was acquired and the date of conversion would be treated as a capital gain. Where land is converted from capital property to a trading property, the taxpayer will have a notional capital gain on the date of conversion. However, this notional capital gain will not be considered to give rise to taxable capital gains until the taxation year during which the ultimate sale of the property occurs.

ITA 13(1), 20(16)–(16.3), 38, 39, IT-218R (paras. 23, 24): *Profits, capital gains and losses from the sale of real estate, including farmland and inherited land and conversion of real estate from capital property to inventory and vice versa*, VD 2008-027545117

¶4410 — Disposition of Land and Building

When a taxpayer disposes of a building and the land on which it stands, and the building is disposed of for less than its undepreciated capital cost, the taxpayer may have to reduce the gain on the sale of the land by the terminal loss (see ¶7150) on the sale of the building. The purpose of these rules is to restrict the amount of a loss otherwise arising on the sale of a land and building as there is an inherent motivation to overstate the allocation of the proceeds to the land (i.e., as a capital gain is 50% taxable and a terminal loss is 100% deductible).

The reduction of a terminal loss on the sale of the building is accomplished by reallocating the total proceeds of disposition for the land and the building from the land to the building to deem the proceeds of disposition for the building generally to be an amount not exceeding the greater of: i) the fair market value of the building, and ii) the UCC attributed to it immediately before the disposition. ITA 13(21.1) will only apply where the proceeds of disposition of a building are less than both its cost amount and its undepreciated capital cost.

ITA 13(21.1), Folio S3-F4-C1: *General Discussion of Capital Cost Allowance*, CRA Guide T4036 under "Disposing of a building"

¶4411 — *Disposition of Land and Building in Same Year*

Where a taxpayer disposes of a building, and in the same taxation year, the taxpayer or a non-arm's length person disposes of the subjacent land, and the amount of the proceeds of disposition allocated to the building is less than the lesser of: i) the "capital cost" of the building, and ii) its cost amount (being the proportion of the UCC of the CCA Class in which the building belongs), the allocation of proceeds of disposition between the building and the land must be adjusted.

An adjustment may arise in circumstances in which there would otherwise be a gain, a loss, or no gain or loss otherwise occurring in respect of the disposition of the land.

The amount of proceeds of disposition deemed to be allocated to the building is the lesser of:

1) the amount, if any, by which: A) the aggregate of the fair market value of the building at the particular time the building is disposed of and the fair market value of the land immediately before its disposition exceeds B) the lesser of: i) the fair market value of the land immediately before its disposition, and ii) the cost amount of the land otherwise determined less capital gains arising upon dispositions of the land within the three preceding years between the taxpayer and non-arm's length parties, and

2) the greater of: A) the fair market value of the building at the particular time, and B) the lesser of: i) the cost amount of the building, and (ii) the capital cost to the corporation of the building immediately before its disposition.

Normally, by virtue of the above rules, any loss on the sale of the building is reduced to the extent of any gain on the sale of the land. This is generally achieved by increasing the proceeds of disposition of the building by the lesser of the amount of the loss on the building and the gain on the sale of the land. The capital gain on the sale of the land is then reduced by a corresponding amount.

The reallocation rules will reduce the amount of a terminal loss or the UCC of depreciable property in the relevant class in circumstances where the allocated proceeds of disposition in respect of a building are less than the UCC attributable to it. It is not possible to have a situation where the terminal loss arising on the disposition is increased as a result of the allocation rules in ITA 13(21.1).

In applying the reallocation rules, the amount of proceeds of disposition for a building is determined without reference to the stop-loss rule in ITA 13(21.2). Effectively, the provisions of ITA 13(21.1) must be applied before the stop-loss rule in ITA 13(21.2) in determining the proceeds of disposition for a building. If a terminal loss remains after the adjustment under ITA 13(21.1), the stop-loss rule in ITA 13(21.2) can apply to defer recognition of the loss in the circumstances described in that provision.

See also paragraphs 1.87 to 1.93 of Folio S3-F4-C1, which discuss the rules governing the disposal of land and a building in the same year, and Example 8 in Folio S3-F4-C1, which illustrates the application of the rules in ITA 13(21.1)(a).

ITA 13(21.1)(a), VD 2004-0072411E5

¶4412 — *Separate Disposition of Building and Land*

If the land subjacent to the building sold by the taxpayer (and owned by the taxpayer or a person not dealing at arm's length with the taxpayer at any time before the disposition of the building) is not sold in the same taxation year, the reallocation rule is modified by adding to the actual proceeds of disposition of the building half of the amount by which the actual proceeds of disposition are exceeded by the greater of: i) the fair market value of the building and ii) the buildings cost amount (being the proportion of the UCC of the class to which the building belongs). The proceeds of disposition of the land are not reduced under this rule.

See also paragraph 1.94 of Folio S3-F4-C1, which discusses the rules governing the disposal of land and a building in different years, and Example 9 in Folio S3-F4-C1, which illustrates the application of the rules in ITA 13(21.1)(b).

ITA 13(21.1)(b)

¶4420 — Disposition of Depreciable Property

Where a taxpayer disposes of a depreciable property (i.e., a building or machinery) for more than its ACB plus the outlays and expenses incurred to sell the property, the taxpayer may realize a capital gain. Where a taxpayer sells a depreciable property for less than its original capital cost, but more than the UCC in its class, the taxpayer will not realize a capital gain.

Generally, the UCC of a class is the total capital cost of all the properties of the class less the CCA claimed in previous years. Where a taxpayer sells a depreciable property in a year, the taxpayer is required to subtract from the UCC the lesser of the following two amounts: (1) the proceeds of disposition of the property minus the related outlays and expenses; or (2) the capital cost of the property. Where the UCC of a class has a negative balance at the end of the year, this amount is considered to be a recapture of CCA and is included in the taxpayer's income for the year of sale (see ¶7145).

If the UCC of a class has a positive balance at the end of the year, and there are no properties left in the class, this amount is a terminal loss. Unlike a capital loss, the full amount of the terminal loss can be deducted from income in that year (see ¶7150).

If the balance for the UCC of a class is zero at the end of the year, there is no recapture of CCA or a terminal loss.

See Guide T4037 for a comprehensive example illustrating the tax consequences on the disposition of a depreciable property.

ITA 13, 40

¶4430 — Principal Residence Exemption

Personal residences are generally exempt from tax as a result of the "principal residence exemption". The principal residence exemption is a set of rules in the ITA that permit an individual (and certain trusts) to escape taxation on a gain realized on a home that is considered to be a principal residence. Certain conditions must be met to qualify for the exemption and there are certain limitations to the exemption. As well, calculations may be required in order to determine whether the gain on the disposition of a home is exempt, in whole or in part, and the amount of the exemption.

Individuals who dispose of property in 2016 or later taxation years for which they are claiming the principal residence exemption must complete page two of Schedule 3 to designate the property as a principal residence and report the details of the disposition. See ¶4432 below.

¶4431 — Qualifying as a Principal Residence

¶4431.1 — *Capital Property*

The term "principal residence" is defined in ITA 54. Since the principal residence definition in ITA 54 applies for purposes of computing taxable capital gains and allowable capital losses, the principal residence exemption only applies to a home that is a capital property. This means that a residence must be a capital property that would produce a capital gain on disposition to be eligible for the principal residence exemption. Where a gain on property is not a capital gain, the definition of a principal residence does not apply, even if the taxpayer has occupied the property. In that case, the related gain would be taxed as ordinary income. For example, a person who builds a house intending to sell it will be fully taxed on the gain as a business profit, even if they live in the home.

Per paragraph 2.7 of Folio S1-F3-C2, where a property is a capital property, following are the types of properties that can qualify as a principal residence:

- a housing unit, which includes a house, an apartment or unit in a duplex, apartment building, or condominium, a cottage, a mobile home, a trailer, or a houseboat;

- a leasehold interest in a housing unit; or

- a share of the capital stock of a co-operative housing corporation, if the sole purpose of acquiring the share was to obtain the right to inhabit a housing unit owned by the corporation.

¶4431.2 — Related Land

A principal residence is deemed to include the land subjacent to the housing unit and the immediately contiguous land that can reasonably be considered to be contributing to the use and enjoyment of the housing unit as a residence (except for property that consists of a share of the capital stock of a cooperative housing corporation). Essentially, this means that when the housing unit is located on land of less than half a hectare, the land will generally qualify as part of the principal residence. There is an exception to the half hectare rule where a portion of the land is used to earn business or property income — in this case, even though the total area of the property may be less than half a hectare, the income-producing portion is not considered to contribute to the use and enjoyment of the housing unit.

Where the total area of the subjacent land is greater than half a hectare, the excess is deemed not to have contributed to the use and enjoyment of the housing unit as a residence unless the taxpayer can provide evidence that the excess land is necessary to such use and enjoyment. Generally, land over one-half hectare is considered necessary for the residence "where the size or character of a housing unit together with its location on the lot make such excess land essential to its use and enjoyment as a residence, or where the location of a housing unit requires such excess land in order to provide its occupants with access to and from public roads" (Folio S1-F3-C2, paragraph 2.34).

In certain locations, a taxpayer who is purchasing a property to use as a principal residence may be subject to minimum lot size requirements and/or severance or subdivision restrictions imposed by local or municipal by-laws. In these circumstances, if a taxpayer is required to acquire land that exceeds half a hectare, the CRA will generally consider the land in excess of half a hectare that must be acquired necessary for the use and enjoyment of the housing unit as a residence throughout the time that the property is continuously owned by the taxpayer after the date of purchase. However, where the restrictions are imposed on agricultural land or where they preserve land for farming, the CRA has indicated that minimum lot size will not be a determinative factor. Also, the existence of such restrictive laws at the time the property is purchased does not necessarily mean that the excess land must be purchased; if it is likely that an application for severance of the excess land would be approved, the excess land would likely not be considered to form part of the principal residence.

The relevant time for determining whether the land in excess of half a hectare was necessary for the use and enjoyment of the property is the time of disposition or immediately before the disposition (*Cassidy v. R.*, [2012] 1 C.T.C. 105 (FCA)). There should be an annual consideration of whether the excess land qualifies as a principal residence for purposes of calculating the principal residence exemption. Where a question exists as to the qualification of the excess land, the proceeds of disposition should be allocated among (a) the home and surrounding half hectare (the Principal Portion), and (b) the excess land (the Excess Portion). Once allocated, the following two-stage approach should be adopted: (1) apply the formula to the Principal Portion, and (2) apply the formula to the Excess Portion.

¶4431.3 — Ordinarily Inhabited

To qualify as a principal residence, a housing unit must be "ordinarily inhabited" by the taxpayer, or by the taxpayer's spouse or common-law partner, former spouse or common-law partner or child. The term "ordinarily inhabited" is not defined in the ITA. The CRA provides the following comments on the meaning of ordinarily inhabited in paragraph 2.11 of Folio S1-F3-C2:

> The question of whether a housing unit is ordinarily inhabited in the year by a person (that is, the taxpayer, the taxpayer's spouse, common-law partner, former spouse, former common-law partner or child) must be resolved on the basis

of the facts in each particular case. Even if a person inhabits a housing unit only for a short period of time in the year, this is sufficient for the housing unit to be considered ordinarily inhabited in the year by that person. For example, even if a person disposes of his or her residence early in the year or acquires it late in the year, the housing unit can be considered to be ordinarily inhabited in the year by that person by virtue of his or her living in it in the year before such sale or after such acquisition, as the case may be. If the main reason for owning a housing unit is to gain or produce income then that housing unit will not generally be considered to be ordinarily inhabited in the year by the taxpayer where it is only inhabited for a short period of time in the year. With regard to whether the main reason for owning a housing unit is to earn income, a person receiving only incidental rental income from a housing unit is not considered to own the property mainly for the purpose of gaining or producing income. However, if the main reason for owning a housing unit is to earn income but the housing unit is rented to the taxpayer's child who also ordinarily inhabits the housing unit in that year, the taxpayer could still designate that housing unit as the taxpayer's principal residence provided the other conditions are met.

Since "ordinarily inhabited" is not a defined term, there have been several court cases that have considered its meaning. In *Ennist et al. v. MNR*, 85 D.T.C. 669 (TCC), the court concluded that a taxpayer's 24-hour stay in a condominium did not amount to ordinarily inhabiting it, reasoning that ordinarily inhabited means "in most cases, usually or commonly occupied as an abode." In *Flanagan v. MNR*, 89 D.T.C. 615 (TCC), the court considered the term ordinarily inhabited in the context of "ordinarily resident." It was the court's opinion that a person may ordinarily inhabit more than one housing unit in a year if he does so "in the course of the customary mode of his life" because the word ordinarily does not restrict a person to residence in one country.

An exception to the "ordinarily inhabited" test is where an election has been made under either ITA 45(2) or (3) in respect of a change in use of a property (see ¶4434).

¶4431.4 — Ownership

In order for a taxpayer to designate a property as a principal residence, the taxpayer must own the property. Like the "ordinarily inhabited" test, this condition must be satisfied during each year for which the home is being designated. The ownership can be "jointly with another person or otherwise", including sole ownership, joint tenancy, tenancy-in-common, and co-ownership (Folio S1-F3-C2, para. 2.9).

The most common cases of co-ownership involve spouses or common-law partners. Where spouses are joint tenants in respect of a home, they are each deemed to own 50% of the property for tax purposes. On the sale of a jointly owned home, both spouses must claim the principal residence exemption in relation to their share of the total gain in order to fully shelter the gain from tax. This will be the case even if only one spouse contributed to the purchase of the property, and attribution of any gain on disposition will result. Attribution applies to the taxable capital gain, which is determined after the transferee spouse has claimed the principal residence exemption.

Individuals who are not spouses or common-law partners can also jointly own a principal residence; however, in order for all co-owners to utilize the principal residence exemption to shelter any gain based on the percentage of ownership, each of the co-owners (or their eligible family members) must "ordinarily inhabit" the residence, as discussed above.

For taxation years beginning before 2017, a personal trust, including a spouse trust, which owns a home, could claim the principal residence exemption to reduce or eliminate a gain on disposition where the housing unit was inhabited by a specified beneficiary and no corporation or partnership was beneficially interested in the trust (an exception may apply if the corporation is a registered charity).

For taxation years beginning after 2016, the only types of trusts that can designate a property as a principal residence are the following:

- An alter ego, spousal or common-law partner, joint spousal or common-law partner trust, or certain trusts for the exclusive benefit of the settlor during the settlor's lifetime, where one of the beneficiaries: (i) is resident in Canada, (ii) occupies the property in the year, and (iii) is the trust's settlor, or the spouse or common-law partner or former spouse or common-law partner of the settlor (depending on the type of trust);

- A testamentary trust that is a qualified disability trust, where one of the beneficiaries: (i) is resident in Canada, (ii) occupies the property in the year, and (iii) is a spouse or common-law partner, former spouse or common-law partner or a child of the trust's settlor, or

226

- An inter vivos or testamentary trust, the settlor of which died before the start of the year, where one of the beneficiaries: (i) is resident in Canada, (ii) occupies the property in the year, (iii) is a minor child of the settlor, and (iv) has no other living parent at the start of the year.

If the trust acquires the property after October 2, 2016, the trust's terms must provide the beneficiary referred to above with a right to use and enjoy the property as a residence throughout the period in the year that the trust owns the property.

These rules apply when determining whether a trust that disposes of property in (or after) its first taxation year that begins after 2016 can designate the property as its principal residence for years after 2016. A transitional rule ensures that a trust that owns a principal residence property at the end of 2016, but no longer qualifies to designate the property as a principal residence because the trust does not fall into one of the three categories outlined above, can continue to benefit from the principal residence designation on its gain accrued to the end of 2016.

ITA 54"principal residence", 248(25)"beneficially interested", S1-F3-C2: *Principal Residence*, S6-F1-C1: *Residence of a Trust or Estate, R. v. Yates*, [1986] 2 C.T.C. 46 (FCA), *Joyner v. MNR*, [1988] 2 C.T.C. 280 (Fed. T.D.), *Augart v. The Queen*, [1993] 2 C.T.C. 34 (FCA), *Carlile v. Canada*, [1995] 2 C.T.C. 273 (FCA), *Lacina v. R*, [1997] G.S.T.C. 69 (FCA), *Stuart Estate v. R.*, [2004] 2 C.T.C. 332 (FCA), *Cayer*, [2007] 3 C.T.C. 2286 (TCC) (taxpayer's appeal to FCA discontinued), *Cassidy v. R.*, [2012] 1 C.T.C. 105 (FCA), VDs 9528405, 2005-0125521E5, 2006-0204111M4, 2008-0263781E5

¶4432 — *Principal Residence Designation*

The principal residence rules limit the annual designation for a specified family group. This means that where an individual designates a property as a principal residence for a year, no other property may be designated by either the individual or certain family members for that same year, including the individual's spouse or common-law partner and unmarried minor children. As a result, each family unit may designate only one home per year as a principal residence. For years before 1982, each individual could designate a property as a principal residence regardless of a designation made by another family member. As well, same-sex common-law partners can each designate different homes for years before 2001 and opposite-sex common-law partners can each designate separate homes for years before 1993.

The principal residence designation in respect of a home is made in the year in which the home is sold or is deemed to have been disposed of, in whole or in part. As with other capital property owned at death, a deceased is deemed to have disposed of his or her principal residence for proceeds equal to the fair market value of the property immediately before death. The gain, if any, arising on the deemed disposition is generally eligible for a full exemption from tax pursuant to the normal rules for principal residences.

For individuals, the prescribed form used to compute the principal residence exemption is Form T2091(IND), *Designation of a Property as a Principal Residence by an Individual (Other than a Personal Trust)*. For deceased individuals, the legal representative (executor, administrator, or a liquidator in Quebec) of a deceased person should use Form T1255, *Designation of a Property as a Principal Residence by the Legal Representative of a Deceased Individual*, to designate a property as a principal residence for the deceased.

Where an individual disposed of a principal residence before 2016, CRA did not require the individual to report the disposition on Schedule 3 or File Form T2091(IND) unless either: (1) a taxable capital gain remained on the disposition of the property after applying the principal residence exemption formula, or (2) the capital gains exemption was previously claimed in respect of the property. However, the CRA revised its requirements for reporting the disposition of a principal residence for 2016 and later taxation years.

Under CRA's revised administrative position, individuals who dispose of property in 2016 or later taxation years for which they are claiming the principal residence exemption must complete page two of Schedule 3 to designate the property as a principal residence and report the details of the disposition. Where the individual is designating the property as a principal residence for only some, but not all, years owned, Form T2091(IND) must also be completed to calculate the capital gain for the years that the property was not designated to be the individual's principal residence.

Below is an excerpt of CRA questions and answers regarding the revised reporting requirements for the sale of a principal residence (see: canada.ca/en/revenue-agency/programs/about-canada-revenue-agency-cra/federal-government-budgets/budget-2016-growing-middle-class/reporting-sale-your-principal-residence-individuals.html):

6. How will I report the sale of my principal residence on Schedule 3?

You will complete Schedule 3 and file it with your T1 Income Tax and Benefit Return for the year you sell the property. If the property was your principal residence for every year that you owned it, you will make the principal residence designation in your Schedule 3. In this case, the year of acquisition, proceeds of disposition and the description of the property are the information that will have to be reported. Schedule 3 will be modified accordingly. Form T2091 (or Form T1255) will still be required for the designation in the case the property was not your principal residence for all of the years that you owned it.

For dispositions in 2017 and later years, in addition to reporting the sale and designating the property as your principal residence on Schedule 3, you also have to complete Form T2091 (or Form T1255). Complete only page 1 of Form T2091 (or Form T1255) if the property you sold was your principal residence for all the years, or for all but one year, that you owned it.

If you were not a resident of Canada for the entire time you owned the designated property, contact the CRA. Your period of non-residence may reduce the amount of the principal residence exemption or eliminate it.

7. What should I do if I sold a property and want to claim the principal residence exemption but I forget to report the designation of principal residence on my income tax return for the year of sale?

For the sale of a principal residence in 2016 or later tax years, CRA will only allow the principal residence exemption if you report the sale and designation of principal residence in your income tax return. If you forget to make a designation of principal residence in the year of the sale, it is very important to ask the CRA to amend your income tax and benefit return for that year. Under proposed changes, the CRA will be able to accept a late designation in certain circumstances, but a penalty may apply.

The penalty is the lesser of the following amounts: $8,000; or $100 for each complete month from the original due date to the date your request was made in a form satisfactory to the CRA.

The CRA will focus efforts on communicating to taxpayers and the tax community the requirement to report the sale and designation of a principal residence in the income tax return. For dispositions occurring during this communication period, including those that occur in the 2016 taxation year (generally for which the designation would be required to be made in tax filings due by late April 2017) the penalty for late-filing a principal residence designation will only be assessed in the most excessive cases.

The CRA will accept a late designation in certain circumstances, but a penalty may apply.

The CRA will continue to focus efforts on communicating to taxpayers and the tax community the requirement to report the sale and designation of a principal residence in the income tax return. The CRA will extend its relief of imposing a penalty for late-filing a principal residence designation, except in the most excessive cases, for dispositions that occur in the 2017 taxation year.

8. What do I report when I actually sell my principal residence, if I used part of it as my principal residence and another part for my business or to earn rental income?

If only a part of your home qualifies as your principal residence and you used the other part to earn or produce income, you may have to split the selling price and the adjusted cost base between the part you used for your principal residence and the part you used for other purposes (for example, rental or business). You can do this by using square metres or the number of rooms, as long as the split is reasonable. Instructions will be provided in the guide T4037, Capital Gains 2016, on how to report the sale of your principal residence in this situation.

9. Does the new rule apply for deemed dispositions of property?

Yes. The new rules apply for deemed dispositions. A deemed disposition occurs when you are considered to have disposed of property, even though you did not actually sell it. For example, a deemed disposition will occur if there is a change in use of the property:

- You change all or part of your principal residence to a rental or business operation.

- You change your rental or business operation to a principal residence.

When you change the use of a property, you are generally considered to have sold the property at its fair market value and to have immediately reacquired the property for the same amount. You have to report the disposition (and designation) of your principal residence and/or the resulting capital gain or loss (in certain situations) in the year the change of use occurs.

For taxation years ending after October 2, 2016, the CRA is permitted to assess taxpayers beyond the normal reassessment period (i.e., three years from the date of the initial notice of assessment), for a taxation year in which the taxpayer does not report the disposition of property in the year in their tax return or does not file a tax return for the year in which the property was disposed of (see ITA 152(4)(b.3)). This also applies when the taxpayer owned the property indirectly through a partnership and the partnership did not report the disposition of the property in the partnership return.

ITA 40(2)(b), 54"principal residence", S1-F3-C2: *Principal Residence*, Info Sheet T1-101, Form T2091(IND): *Designation of a Property as a Principal Residence by an Individual (Other than a Personal Trust)*, Form T1255: *Designation of a Property as a Principal Residence by the Legal Representative of a Deceased Individual*, 2017-0709011C6

¶4433 — *Calculating the Principal Residence Exemption*

The formula for calculating the capital gain on the sale or disposition of a principal residence is contained in ITA 40(2)(b) and (c). Essentially, the principal residence exemption is a direct reduction of the capital gain that would otherwise be determined for property that is a principal residence. However, since a home is considered to be personal-use property, any loss realized on the disposition is specifically denied.

If more than one property was owned by members of a family unit at the end of 1981, and continuously thereafter until disposed of, the exempt portion of the gain is determined in accordance with transitional rules in ITA 40(6). Generally, if the property qualified as a principal residence before 1982, but did not qualify in the years subsequent because of another property that so qualified, only a portion of the gain that had accrued prior to 1982 will qualify for the exemption.

The computation can be done for a property that was a principal residence at any time. This means that at least one year of designation is required in order for the taxpayer to use the computation, which is possible where the property meets the principal residence criteria for even part of a year, as discussed above.

¶4433.1 — *Gain on a Principal Residence*

Generally, the capital gain on the disposition of a principal residence is reduced by the principal residence exemption portion of the gain and the 1994 capital gain on the property for which a 1994 capital gains exemption election was made.

The formula to compute the gain for a principal residence in ITA 40(2)(b) is $A - (A \times B/C) - D$, where:

- A is the gain that would otherwise be determined, without taking into account any prior capital gains exemption claim or reduction resulting from a principal residence exemption claim,

- B is one plus the number of taxation years that end after the acquisition date for which the property was the taxpayer's principal residence and during which the taxpayer was resident in Canada,

- C is the number of taxation years that end after the acquisition date during which the taxpayer owned the property, whether jointly with another person or otherwise, and

- D is an adjustment that may be required in computing the gain on the disposition of a principal residence where the capital gains exemption election was made in the individual's 1994 return in respect of the property.

On the elimination of the $100,000 capital gains exemption in 1994, taxpayers were allowed to use any remaining unused capital gains exemption for any accrued gains on property owned at that date (ITA 110.6(19)). Many individuals made the election in respect of a home to shelter gains that would not otherwise be eligible for exemption under the principal residence rules (e.g., where a family owned more than one home after 1981 or where a property was not occupied during the entire period of ownership). When a capital gains exemption election was made in respect of a property, the property was considered to have been disposed of at the end of February 22, 1994 for proceeds equal to the amount designated in the election. If the 1994 election was made in respect of a principal residence, an adjustment may be required under "D".

The inclusion of the "one-plus" in the formula under B contemplates the possible ownership of two homes in a year where one principal residence is sold and a replacement home is purchased. As a result of this formula, where a home qualifies as a principal residence for the entire period of ownership (except for one year), as would be the case for families that own only one home, the full gain will be exempt from tax. Accordingly, an individual who disposes of a home and acquires a replacement residence in the same year is not precluded from designating both properties as a principal residence.

For dispositions of property after October 2, 2016, the "one-plus" in variable "B" in the formula in ITA 40(2)(b) to compute the gain for a principal residence is eliminated if the purchaser was not resident in Canada during the year the property was purchased. This means that, for dispositions after October 2, 2016, a taxpayer who was a nonresident throughout the year that includes the acquisition of the property, will no longer have an extra year of exemption room when computing the reduction in the gain on the taxpayer's principal residence. The extra year of taxation room now applies only to taxpayers who were resident during the year that includes the date of acquisition of the property.

¶4433.2 — Properties Owned Before 1982

For years before 1982, each individual was allowed to designate a property as a principal residence, provided that the other conditions of ownership and occupancy are met. As a result, where a family unit has continuously owned more than one home since the pre-1982 period, it is possible to shelter a gain on more than just one property, at least in part, using the principal residence exemption.

The principal residence exemption formula in ITA 40(2)(b) assumes that gains have accrued evenly over the period of ownership. However, to ensure that gains that accrued before 1982 receive full principal residence exemption protection (assuming that all years of ownership up to 1981 are designated), an alternative calculation is available for properties owned before 1982 (ITA 40(6)). Under the alternative calculation, there is a notional disposition of the property at December 31, 1981 at fair market value and a reacquisition at January 1, 1982 for the same amount. The gain is then computed separately for the two periods using the basic principal residence exemption formula separately for each period, except that the "one plus" year does not apply for the post-1981 period.

The alternative formula is used only when it results in a gain that is less than the gain that would be determined using the standard formula. This could be the case where a property has declined in value since 1982, or where the gain per year in the pre-1982 ownership period is higher than the gain per year in the post-1981 period.

ITA 40(2)(b), (c), 40(6), 110.6(19)

¶4434 — *Partial Use and Change in Use*

A partial use of a taxpayer's principal residence arises where a portion of the residence is used on a regular basis for an income-producing purpose. A change in use results from a change in the proportion of the residence used for an income-producing purpose or a complete change in the use of the property from a principal residence to an income-producing purpose and *vice versa*. The rules relating to partial use and change in use are used to determine the cost and proceeds for purposes of computing a capital gain or loss on a deemed disposition or actual disposition of the property. They are also used to determine the capital cost for capital cost allowance (CCA) purposes and the proceeds for purposes of computing any recapture or terminal loss on the deemed disposition or actual disposition of depreciable property where the property has more than one use or where there has been a change in use.

¶4434.1 — *Partial Use*

It is common for individuals to use a portion of their principal residence for an income-producing or other purpose (e.g., working out of a home office or renting out a cottage for part of the year). For the purposes of calculating a capital gain or loss on a property that is only partially used as a principal residence, ITA 45(1)(b) contains a deemed acquisition rule. Specifically, where a principal residence has been used, in part, for the purpose of gaining or producing income since the date of acquisition, the taxpayer is deemed to have acquired the portion of the property used as the principal residence for a cost equal to the proportion of the total cost that the principal residence use is of the whole use of the property. Similarly, where the property is later disposed of, the proceeds of disposition of the principal residence portion of the property will be determined according to the same proportion. The ratio used to determine the allocation would likely be determined on the basis of area used (such as square footage), the number of days used for each purpose (in the case of a seasonal residence), or some other reasonable and factual basis. Accordingly, where there is a capital gain on the subsequent sale of the property, the principal residence exemption is available only to offset the portion of the gain attributable to the principal residence use of the property.

Where CCA is claimed on the income-producing portion of property that is depreciable property, ITA 13(7)(c) provides a similar rule for purposes of allocating the total capital cost of the property between the portion that is acquired for income-producing purposes and the portion that is not. The capital cost determined under this provision is used for purposes of claiming CCA and for determining any recapture or terminal loss on a subsequent disposition.

In certain circumstances, the partial use of a principal residence for an income-producing purpose may not require an allocation between income-producing and personal use. Specifically, the CRA allows a property to retain its principal residence status where all of the following conditions are met:

- the partial use for income-producing purposes is ancillary to the main use as a principal residence,

- there is no structural change to the property, and

- CCA has not been claimed on the property.

Where all three of these conditions are met, a taxpayer can maintain an office or workspace in his or her home that is used to earn business or employment income without affecting the home's principal residence status. Whether or not the partial use of a principal residence for an income-producing purpose satisfies all three administrative conditions noted above is a question of fact; however, the first two conditions will generally not be met where the partial use is substantial and of a more permanent nature.

¶4434.2 — *Complete and Partial Change of Use*

Where a property is initially used as a principal residence, but later converted to an income-producing property, wholly or in part, a change in use occurs. For example, a taxpayer might purchase a property to use as a principal residence and later decide to convert it into a rental property. Or an income-producing property could be converted into a principal residence. In general, a change in use, whether complete or partial, will result in the application of the deemed disposition rules (ITA 45(1) and 13(7)).

Where there is a complete change in use, the taxpayer will be deemed to have disposed of the property and to have reacquired it for an amount equal to its fair market value at the time of the change in use (ITA 45(1)(a)). Similarly, where there is a partial change in use, there will be a deemed disposition and reacquisition of the portion of the property that has been converted, for an amount equal to the proportion of the total fair market value that the portion converted is of the whole property at the time of the partial change in use (ITA 45(1)(c)).

As discussed above, where the change in use of a portion of a taxpayer's principal residence to an income-producing purpose is ancillary to its main use as a residence, there is no structural change to the property, and no CCA is being claimed, the entire property will keep its principal residence status and the change-in-use rules will not apply.

The CRA has recently issued several interpretations on the application of the change in use rules in various situations, including the implications of an owner moving from one unit of a duplex to another (VD 2015-0589821E5, 2016-0674831C6), modifications made to the units of a duplex (VD 2016-0625141C6, 2016-0652841C6), and having a secondary suite in a home (VD 2016-0673231E5).

¶4434.3 — *Elections Available on a Complete Change in Use*

The deemed disposition of a taxpayer's principal residence, resulting from a change in the use of the property to an income-producing purpose, may result in a capital gain, which may be eliminated or reduced by the principal residence exemption. Alternatively, recognition of the gain can be deferred to a later taxation year by filing a no-change-in-use election under ITA 45(2). The election is available only where there has been a complete change from the use of a property as a principal residence to an income-producing use. The election is filed by way of a signed letter attached to the taxpayer's tax return for the year in which the change in use occurs.

In general, where a taxpayer elects under ITA 45(2), the change in use of the property is deemed not to have occurred and the property can continue to qualify as the taxpayer's principal residence for a period of up to four taxation years (as long as the election is not rescinded). When the taxpayer later disposes of the property, any capital gains that may have accrued over the four years can be sheltered by the principal residence exemption. The taxpayer must be resident in Canada or deemed to be resident in Canada in order for the property to retain its principal residence status over the four-year period.

An election is also available under ITA 45(3) where an income-producing property is converted to a principal residence. This election also defers any gain that would otherwise be recognized on the deemed disposition under ITA 45(1); however, it does not defer any recapture that may arise from the deemed disposition. In general, where a taxpayer elects under ITA 45(3), the change in use of the property is deemed not to have occurred, and recognition of any capital gain accrued while the property was rented out can be deferred to a later year. Note that a ITA 45(3) election cannot be made if CCA has been allowed in respect of the property to the taxpayer, the taxpayer's spouse or common-law partner, and that during the period in which the election is in effect, the taxpayer must continue to report any net income earned from the property, since it is still considered to be an income-producing property.

ITA 13(7), 45(1)–(3), S1-F3-C2: *Principal Residence* (paras. 2.48–2.64)

¶4435 — *Principal Residence Exemption: Miscellaneous Issues*

¶4435.1 — Vacant Land

Since the definition of a principal residence includes only land subjacent and immediately contiguous to a housing unit, vacant land on its own cannot be a principal residence. However, a vacant lot acquired in conjunction with an adjacent property that includes a housing unit can be eligible for the principal residence exemption if it contributes to the use and enjoyment of the housing unit and if the total area of the properties does not exceed half a hectare (*Fourt v. The Queen*, 91 D.T.C. 5631 (FCTD)).

The CRA has provided some guidance relating to the acquisition of an adjacent vacant lot (where the total area is less than half a hectare). Where both the lot on which the home is situated and the adjacent vacant lot were acquired at the same time, no proof would normally be required with respect to the "use and enjoyment" requirement. However, if the adjacent lot was acquired after the acquisition of the original lot containing the housing unit, the taxpayer would be required to demonstrate that the vacant lot contributed to the use and enjoyment of the housing unit. If the adjacent lot is used to earn income from a business or property, it will not form part of the principal residence even if the total area is less than half a hectare (VD 9509607).

A vacant lot of less than half a hectare that is acquired for the purpose of constructing a housing unit on it in a subsequent year may not be designated as a taxpayer's principal residence for the year(s) before the year in which the taxpayer or another qualified family member commences to ordinarily inhabit the housing unit (Folio S1-F3-C2, para. 2.29). However, the period during which the land is vacant will be included in the "number of years of ownership" component in the computation of the principal residence exemption.

¶4435.2 — Farm Property

ITA 40(2)(c) sets out specific rules applicable to a disposition of land used in a farming business where the taxpayer's principal residence is situated on that land. One of two methods may be used to calculate the gain on the disposition. Under the first method (ITA 40(2)(c)(i)), the land is considered to be divided into two portions: the principal residence portion and the portion used in the farming business. The gain on the principal residence portion is calculated in the same manner as described above. To allocate the cost and the proceeds to the principal residence portion, taxpayers can either use the value of one-half hectare of land using comparable sales of similar farm properties in the area or use the value of a typical residential lot in the area (see Folio S1-F3-C2, paras. 2.40–2.42).

The second method (ITA 40(2)(c)(ii)) does not require the use of the principal residence exemption calculation or the allocation between the principal residence and the land used in the farming business. Under this method, the gain is first computed on the entire property, and then it is reduced by $1,000, plus $1,000 for each taxation year that the taxpayer used the property as a principal residence (see Folio S1-F3-C2, paras. 2.43–2.46). If a taxpayer chooses this method, the taxpayer is required to attach a letter to his or her income tax return for the taxation year of disposition describing the property and stating the number of years in which the property was the taxpayer's principal residence.

¶4435.3 — Property Held Outside Canada

There is no requirement for a home to be located in Canada in order for it to be considered a principal residence and eligible for the principal residence exemption, although the taxpayer claiming the exemption must be resident in Canada during the years in which the property is being designated a principal residence (ITA 40(2)(b)(B)). Therefore, a foreign vacation property owned by a Canadian resident could be designated as a principal residence if it made sense to do so. As well, an individual who immigrates to Canada and owns a foreign home can shelter any gains that accrue on the foreign home from the time the individual begins Canadian residency (provided that an eligible family member continues to "ordinarily inhabit" the home). When deciding whether it makes sense to designate a foreign property as a principal residence, taxpayers need to consider the income tax implications in the country in which the home is located and the effect of any tax treaty that that country may have with Canada.

¶4435.4 — Moving Within Canada

Individuals commonly move within Canada as a result of employment relocation or for other reasons. Where the relocation is expected to be temporary, an individual might decide not to sell his or her home but instead to rent it out. Although a taxpayer in these circumstances may file a no-change-in-use election to maintain the principal residence status of the property for a period of up to four years after the date of the move, the four-year limitation period can be extended indefinitely when certain conditions are met. Specifically, ITA 54.1 allows a housing unit to continue to qualify as a principal residence indefinitely, provided that the property is not ordinarily inhabited by the taxpayer as a consequence of an employment relocation. As long as the individual moves back into the home that was vacated as a result of the employment relocation, all of the years of absence qualify as principal residence years, even though the home was not inhabited by a member of the family unit for that period. However, the CRA may not apply this extended period treatment where an individual, while employed with the same employer, resumes habitation of a home for only a few days before moving into a new home, or where the individual returns to a different home in the same neighborhood (VD 9715875).

¶4435.5 — Moving To and From Canada

Where a taxpayer sells their home before departing Canada, the residence can qualify as a principal residence for the years of ownership. In this case, the principal residence exemption would be available to offset any gain on the disposition, to the extent that the taxpayer was a resident of Canada for each of the years in which the property is designated. Where a taxpayer emigrates from Canada and does not sell their Canadian home, some issues to consider are whether the individual has ceased Canadian residency for tax purposes, whether there has been a change in use of the individual's property during his or her absence, and whether the property continues to satisfy the conditions of a principal residence.

When an individual ceases Canadian residency, he or she is deemed to have disposed of each capital property owned, subject to certain exceptions, immediately before that time for proceeds equal to its fair market value (ITA 128.1(4)(b)). There is an exception to the deemed disposition on emigration for real estate situated in Canada (ITA 128.1(4)(b)(i)). Accordingly, there will be no deemed disposition of an individual's Canadian principal residence at the time the individual becomes a non-resident.

Where the individual rents out his or her Canadian home while non-resident, the property will be subject to a deemed disposition under the change-in-use rules, unless the individual files a no-change-in-use election (see ¶4434.3). If this election is filed, the home can continue to be considered a principal residence for up to four years following the move (or for an indefinite period if the move results from an employment relocation, subject to the conditions outlined in ¶4435.4). However, even though the property is considered to be the individual's principal residence for years of non-occupancy, it cannot be designated for those years in computing the principal residence exemption on a disposition because the individual was not resident in Canada in those years. Consequently, in contrast to moving within Canada, the no-change-in-use election under ITA 45(2) does not shelter the gain accruing during the period of non-occupancy from taxation.

ITA 40(2), 40(7), 45(2), 54.1, 69(1), 107(2), 107(2.01), Form T1079, Designation of a Property as a Principal Residence by a Personal Trust; Form T1079-WS, Principal Residence Worksheet; Form T2091(IND), Designation of a Property as a Principal Residence by an Individual (Other than a Personal Trust); S1-F3-C2, *Principal Residence*

¶4500 — Dispositions of Bonds, Debentures, Promissory Notes, and Other Similar Properties (Sch. 3: Parts 5–8)

Report capital gains or losses from the disposition of bonds, debentures, Treasury bills, promissory notes, and other properties in Part 5 of Schedule 3 on Lines 151 and 153. Other properties include bad debts, foreign exchange gains and losses, and options, as well as discounts, premiums, and bonuses on debt obligations. Generally, taxpayers will receive a T5008 slip, *Statement of Securities Transactions*, or an account statement from their financial institution reporting the dispositions.

¶4510 — Bonds, Debentures, and Promissory Notes (Sch. 3: Part 5)

In Part 5 of Schedule 3, list all bonds, debentures, and promissory notes disposed of during the taxation year. Provide the face value, the maturity date, and the issuer's name for each type of bond, debenture, or promissory note. Enter the total amount of gain or loss realized on dispositions of bonds, debentures, and promissory notes on Line 153. Where a taxpayer has bought and sold the same bonds or debentures (i.e., identical properties) over a period of time, see the discussion of the cost averaging rules in ¶4121. Also see ¶4124.

When a taxpayer disposes of a bond, debenture, or promissory note that is held as a capital investment, the amount of any realized discount is normally considered a capital gain. Similarly, a premium is normally considered a capital loss, either when the obligation matures or on the date the taxpayer disposes of the obligation.

A change in the terms or attributes of a bond may constitute a disposition of the bond. In ITTN-14, the CRA states:

> Interpretation Bulletin IT-448: *Disposition — Changes in Terms of Securities*, comments on whether or not there has been a disposition of a debt obligation and the creation of a new debt when there are changes in its terms. Paragraph 7 particularly provides examples of changes that are considered to be so fundamental to the holder's economic interest in the property that they almost invariably precipitate a disposition. This position has created some controversy and confusion. The Department has indicated at various tax conferences that the settlement, extinguishment or disposition of a debt obligation was primarily a matter of law and that the Department was reviewing its position expressed in paragraph 7 of IT-448.
>
> As a result of the review, it is now our position that if a debt obligation is renegotiated otherwise than as provided for in its original terms, the determination of whether a change in its terms is a substitution of a debt obligation for another should be made in accordance with the law of the relevant jurisdiction.
>
> If, in accordance with the relevant contract law in Quebec, the changes in the terms of the original debt obligation have resulted in a novation (where the original debt obligation is discharged and substituted by a new obligation), it is appropriate to view the original obligation as having been disposed of for income tax purposes.
>
> In the other provinces, a rescission of a debt obligation will be implied when the parties have effected such an alteration of its terms as to substitute a new obligation in its place, which is entirely inconsistent with the old, or, if not entirely inconsistent with it, inconsistent with it to an extent that goes to the very root of it. In such a case, it is appropriate to view the original obligation as having been disposed of for income tax purposes.
>
> This position applies for the purposes of the Act and will be reflected in the next revision of IT-448.

In *Quincaillerie Laberge Inc*, [1995] 2 C.T.C. 2975 (headnote only) (TCC), the Court held that the extension of a debt term was not a disposition for tax purposes. Also, in *Wigmar Holdings Ltd*, [1997] 2 C.T.C. 263 (FCA), it was held that removal of security in the form of a mortgage did not create a new debt.

In *General Electric Capital Equipment Finance*, [2002] 1 C.T.C. 217 (FCA), the Court found that changes in the maturity date, principal amount, and interest rate were substantial changes to the fundamental terms of the obligations in question and therefore created new obligations.

IT-479R(SR): *Transactions in securities*, Biringer, "When Is an Obligation New?", IX(4) *Corporate Finance* (Federated Press) 906-10 (2001)

¶4511 — *Treasury Bills (T-Bills) and Stripped Bonds*

When a T-bill or a stripped bond is issued at a discount and a taxpayer holds it until it matures, the difference between the issue price and the amount received when it is cashed in is considered to be accrued interest. However, if a taxpayer sells a T-bill or stripped bond before it matures, the taxpayer may also have a capital gain or loss in addition to the accrued interest.

Before calculating the capital gain or loss, the taxpayer must first determine the amount of interest accumulated to the date of disposition, subtract the interest from the proceeds of disposition, and calculate the capital gain or loss in the usual way. Following is an example from Guide T4037:

Example

Jesse bought a T-bill on May 1, 2017, for $49,500. The T-bill's term is 91 days and its maturity value on August 1, 2017, is $50,000. However, he sold it on June 13, 2017, for $49,750. The effective yield rate was 4.05%.

Jesse calculates interest on the T-bill as follows:

	Purchase price		Effective yield rate		Number of days T-bill held/Number of days in the year sold		Interest to be included in income
=	Purchase price	×	Effective yield rate	×	Number of days T-bill held/Number of days in the year sold	=	Interest to be included in income
=	$49,500	×	4.05%	×	44/365	=	$241.67

Jesse calculates his capital gain as follows:

Proceeds of disposition	$	49,750.00
Minus: Interest	-	241.67
Net proceeds of disposition	$	49,508.33
Minus: Adjusted cost base	-	49,500.00
Capital gain	$	8.33

¶4512 — Conversion of Debt Obligation

Where certain conditions are met, a tax-free rollover is available on the exchange of one debt obligation that is capital property for another obligation of the same debtor. For the rollover to apply, the following conditions must be met:

1) The acquired (new) obligation is a bond, debenture, or note of the same debtor as the exchanged (convertible) obligation;

2) The convertible obligation is capital property, the gain or loss from the disposition of which, would be a capital gain or a capital loss of the holder;

3) The right to make the exchange is conferred on the holder by the terms of the (convertible) obligation; and

4) The "principal amount" of the new obligation is equal to the principal amount of the convertible obligation (generally, the principal amount is defined to mean the amount that under the terms of the obligation or any related agreement is the maximum amount or maximum total amount payable on account of the obligation by its issuer, otherwise than as or on account of interest or any premium payable by the issuer conditional on the exercise by the issuer of a right to redeem the obligation before maturity).

Where the above conditions are met, the ITA provides for a rollover by deeming the cost of the new obligation and the proceeds of disposition of the convertible obligation to equal the ACB of the convertible obligation immediately before the exchange.

ITA 51.1, 248(1)"principal amount", VDs 2008-0300161R3, 9721405

¶4513 — Disposition of Debt of Related Person

By virtue of ITA 40(2)(e.1), a taxpayer's loss from a disposition to a person or partnership of a debt that was payable by another person or partnership is nil where the taxpayer, the transferee, and the debtor are related to each other at the time of the disposition, or would be related at that time if the assumptions set out in ITA 80(2)(j) for the purposes of determining whether two persons are related were applied. This stop-loss rule generally attempts to achieve consistency between the stop-loss rules and the debt-parking rules. A loss denied under this rule is added in computing the ACB to the transferee of the property. Where a loss is denied, the transferee is generally entitled to increase its ACB under ITA 53(1)(f.1) or (f.11).

ITA 40(2)(e.1), 53(1)(f.1), (f.11), 80(2)(j), VDs 2014-0522501E5, 2013-0479701R3, 2009-0350711R3, 2009-0343201R3, 2009-0347271R3, 2008-0300161R3, 2008-0266441R3, 2004-0081691R3

¶4514 — *Exchange of Commercial Obligations*

Generally, ITA 40(2)(e.2) reduces the loss a creditor may claim where a "commercial obligation" issued by a debtor is exchanged by the creditor for one or more other (new) commercial obligations issued by the same debtor. The amount of reduction in the loss is added in computing the ACB of the new obligations.

ITA 40(2)(e.2), 53(1)(f.12), 80(1)"commercial obligation"

¶4520 — **Debts Held on Capital Account (Bad Debts) (Sch. 3: Part 5)**

When a debt held on capital account (i.e., a loan or advance) becomes uncollectible, the taxpayer can elect under ITA 50(1) for the debt to be deemed to be disposed of at the end of the year for no consideration and to have been reacquired immediately at a cost of nil. The election allows the taxpayer to claim a bad debt as a capital loss equal to the ACB of the debt. Any later recovery of that debt will result in a capital gain.

In Guide T4037, the CRA states that "to claim a capital loss on a bad debt, you have to file an election with your return. To make this election, write and sign a letter stating that you want subsection 50(1) of the *Income Tax Act* to apply to the bad debt. Attach this letter to your return." If the T1 return is being filed electronically, the letter should be sent to the taxpayer's CRA Tax Centre by the filing-due date of the return for the taxation year. The CRA is permitted to accept a late-filed election. The CRA discusses situations in which it may allow an ITA 50(1) election to be revoked in paragraphs 1.26–1.28 of Folio S4-F8-C1.

In *Dhaliwal*, [2012] 4 C.T.C. 2169 (TCC), the court allowed a taxpayer to claim a bad debt in accordance with ITA 50(1) despite the fact that an election was not filed. The taxpayer recorded the capital loss in his tax return, but did not specify that a subsection 50(1) election was being made. The court was critical of the CRA, pointing out that the CRA does not have a recommended form available for electing under subsection 50(1) and that tax returns developed by the CRA do not have a space to expressly indicate an election is being made.

The "superficial loss" rules in ITA 54 do not apply to a deemed disposition under ITA 50.

A "business investment loss" (BIL) for a taxation year includes a taxpayer's capital loss for the year from a disposition of a debt due from a small business corporation to which ITA 50(1) applies.

ITA 50(1), 20(1)(p), 54"superficial loss", 220(3.2), (3.5), ITR 600, Folio S4-F8-C1, IT-442R: *Bad debts and reserves for doubtful debts*, Guide T4037, VDs 2014-0524951E5 (interaction with debt parking rules), 2008-0274451E5 (loss denial rules), 2006-0172111E5 (ABILs), 2005-0113051E5 (debt parking and shareholder loans), 2003-0029377 (life insurance collateral assignment), *St-Hilaire*, 2014 CarswellNat 5303 (TCC) (waived debt was not owned at year-end), *Gaumond*, 2014 CarswellNat 4870 (TCC) (waived debt was not disposed of at arm's length), *Mellieur*, 2016 CarswellNat 7011 (TCC) (debts were determined to be held on capital account), *Hopmeyer*, [2007] 2 C.T.C. 218 (FCA) (no deemed disposition where company continued to carry on business and might have survived); *Jodoin*, [2007] 1 C.T.C. 2211 (TCC) (key component in claim for ABIL is taxpayer election); *Super West Homes Inc.*, [2004] 5 C.T.C. 2103 (TCC) (where conduct indicated advances not made for purpose of producing income, loss denied); *Jacques St-Onge Inc*, [2004] 1 C.T.C. 2094 (TCC) (actual dissolution by year-end not required; reasonable expectation sufficient); *Gordon*, [1996] 3 C.T.C. 2229 (TCC) (payment directly to creditors instead of to company whose debt was guaranteed was acceptable); *Monaghan*, [1996] 2 C.T.C. 2169 (TCC) (significant events occurring well after year-end do not affect determination of bad debt)

¶4521 — *Time at which Debt Becomes Bad*

A taxpayer is required to determine whether or not a particular debt has become bad and the time at which it became bad. In paragraphs 1.34 and 1.39 of Folio S4-F8-C1, the CRA states its position that:

> The time at which a debt becomes a bad debt is a question of fact. Generally, a debt owing to a taxpayer will be a bad debt at the end of the year if: the taxpayer has exhausted all legal means of collecting on it; or the debtor has become insolvent and has no means of repaying it. While there is no legal requirement that in all cases a taxpayer must exhaust all legal means of collecting on a debt before determining that during the year it had become a bad debt, such a determination will generally fall short if it is evident that collection on the debt is reasonably possible but no proactive steps were taken to collect on it ... In some circumstances, accounting practice may require a write-down of a debt to net

realizable value; however such write-downs are not recognized for purposes of section 50. *A debt is considered bad for the purpose of section 50 when the whole amount is uncollectible.* Where a portion of a debt has been settled, the remaining portion of the debt is considered bad for purpose of section 50 if it is uncollectible. [*Emphasis added*; the CRA's position may not be correct as discussed further below.]

In *Rich*, [2004] 1 C.T.C. 308, the Federal Court of Appeal set out the following factors to be considered in determining whether a debt had become bad:

- the history and age of the debt;

- the financial position of the debtor, its revenues and expenses, whether it was earning income or incurring losses, its cash flow and its assets, liabilities and liquidity;

- changes in total sales compared with prior years;

- the debtor's cash, accounts receivable and other current assets at the relevant time and compared with prior years;

- the debtor's accounts payable and other current liabilities at the relevant time and compared with prior years;

- the general business conditions in the country, community of the debtor and in the debtor's line of business; and

- the taxpayer's past experience with writing off bad debts.

This list is not exhaustive and, in different circumstances, one factor or another may be more important.

While future prospects of the debtor company may be relevant in some cases, the predominant considerations would normally be past and present. If there is some evidence of an event that will probably occur in the future that would suggest that the debt is collectible on the happening of the event, the future event should be considered. If future considerations are only speculative, they would not be material in an assessment of whether a past due debt is collectible.

Nor is it necessary for a creditor to exhaust all possible recourses of collection. All that is required is an honest and reasonable assessment. Indeed, should a bad debt subsequently be collected in whole or in part, the amount collected is taken into income in the year it is received.

Whether the creditor has a non-arm's length relationship with the debtor may also be relevant in some cases. However, the predominant consideration will be the ability of the debtor to repay the debt in whole or in part. The non-arm's length relationship may justify closer scrutiny than in non-arm's length situations. But a non-arm's length relationship alone, without more, cannot lead to a finding that the creditor did not honestly and reasonably determine the debt to be bad . . .

[T]here is no legal requirement that proactive steps be taken in all cases. The obligation to take such steps will only arise where there is some evidence to show that collection on the loan is reasonably possible. This, of course, would include cases in which the Minister has assumed that collection was reasonably possible and the taxpayer has failed to address or has inadequately addressed that assumption . . .

Here, the question is whether it was honest and reasonable for the appellant to consider the debt to be bad on December 31, 1995. If there was some evidence to suggest that a workout or refinancing might have been available to enable collection of some or all of the loan, I would agree that the appellant, being intimately involved with the company, would have to show that he had at least attempted some proactive steps before declaring the loan bad . . .

The test the appellant had to meet was that he made an honest and reasonable determination that the loan was bad. It follows that, in the absence of any evidence to suggest that proactive steps could reasonably result in collection of all or part of the loan, such proactive steps were not rationally connected to the determination of whether the assessment made by the appellant was honest and reasonable.

Of course, the onus is on a taxpayer to demolish the assumptions made by the Minister in his reply to the notice of appeal. Here, there was no express assumption that the loan could be recovered through the taking of proactive steps. However, even if there had been, there is no obligation on the taxpayer to try to think of every conceivable proactive step and show that none would be productive. It is sufficient that the taxpayer provides evidence as to the condition of the debtor and its inability at the relevant time to repay the loan in whole or in part. That was the evidence in this case.

A taxpayer's continued support of a business through additional loans or contributions typically is considered by the Courts to be a strong indication that a debt has not become bad. For example, in *Sunatori*, [2010] 6 C.T.C. 2269

(TCC), the Court considered whether a taxpayer can assert that a company cannot repay its debt when the taxpayer is still lending the company money. The Court stated (paras. 54 and 55):

> Making advances implicitly suggests something positive in the future which contradicts a bad debt determination at the time of the advance. Following that rationale, a loan not due for some time cannot reasonably be found to be bad today, where the prospects of collection when due are promising as shown by recent advances and by the commitment and drive and ongoing work of the debtor whose actions reflect no sign of an imminent failure of the business.
>
> All this is to say that just because the Appellant was satisfied that the loans could not be repaid at the end of the years in question, does not mean it was reasonable to consider that they were bad. If it was, then all temporary, short term, insolvency situations would lead to an explosion of bad debt claims. Nothing in the language of the subject provisions warrants such an explosion.

Rich, [2004] 1 C.T.C. 308 (FCA), *Hogan* (1965), 15 Tax A.B.C. 1, *Coveley*, 2013 CarswellNat 4823 (TCC), *Kyriazakos*, [2007] 3 C.T.C. 2038 (TCC), *Fisher*, [2014] 1 C.T.C. 2049 (TCC), *Cosentino*, [2003] 2 C.T.C. 2447 (TCC), VDs 2010-0380821E5, 2010-0379201E5, 2006-0175701M4

¶4522 — *Loss Denial Rule*

If a debt that is capital in nature is disposed of for proceeds less than its ACB, including where the debt is deemed to have been disposed of under ITA 50(1), the resulting loss is deemed to be nil unless the debt or right to receive an amount was acquired by the taxpayer: 1) for the purpose of gaining or producing income from a business or property (other than exempt income); or 2) as consideration for the disposition of capital property to a person with whom the taxpayer was dealing at arm's length. This loss denial rule typically applies to loans between private corporations and their shareholders. In paragraph 1.47 of Folio S4-F8-C1, the CRA states its position that:

> [T]he potential to earn income from business or property must not be too remote. For example, instead of owning shares directly in the debtor, a taxpayer might be a shareholder of a parent company or other shareholder of the debtor. The burden of demonstrating a sufficient connection between the taxpayer's loan to (or the taxpayer's guarantee of the debts of) the debtor and the potential for income will be much higher in situations where the taxpayer is not a direct shareholder of the debtor.

In *MacCallum*, 2011 CarswellNat 2132 (TCC), the court found that the taxpayer was entitled to deduct an ABIL in respect of a guarantee payment made to a bank in connection with a line of credit owed by the corporation (Mitchco) of the taxpayer's son. The Court found that the taxpayer provided the guarantee to support Mitchco and to thereby protect and collect an amount owed by Mitchco to the taxpayer's subsidiary corporation. At paragraphs 40 and 41, the Court stated:

> I do find that one of the reasons the Appellant signed the guarantee on behalf of Mitchco was to help his son. It may even have been his primary reason. However, that does not prevent the Appellant from meeting the requirements of subparagraph 40(2)(g)(ii) of the Act. In *Rich v R*, Rothstein J.A., as he then was, stated:
>
> > The Minister agrees that, though gaining or producing income need not be the exclusive or even the primary purpose of the loan, as long as it was one of its purposes, that is sufficient to meet the requirements of subparagraph 40(2)(g)(ii) (see [*Ludco Enterprises Ltd. v. Canada*], [2001] 2 S.C.R. 1082 (S.C.C.) at para. 50).
>
> There does not have to be a direct link between the debt incurred by a taxpayer and the income he intends to earn. In *Byram v. R*, McDonald J.A. noted:
>
> > While subparagraph 40(2)(g)(ii) requires a linkage between the taxpayer (i.e. the lender) and the income, there is no need for the income to flow directly to the taxpayer from the loan . . .
>
> > It is equally clear that the anticipation of dividend income cannot be too remote. It is trite law that sections 3 and 4 of the Act, in conjunction with the rules set out in subdivisions (a) through (d) of division B, establish that the income of a taxpayer is to be determined on a source by source basis. Furthermore, the availability of certain deductions under the Act, including subparagraph 40(2)(g)(ii), require that some regard be given to the source of income that is relevant to the deduction. Accordingly, a deduction cannot be so far removed from its corresponding income stream as to render its connection to the anticipated income tenuous at best. This does not preclude a deduction for a capital loss incurred by a taxpayer on an interest-free loan given to a related corporation where it had a legitimate expectation of receiving income through increased dividends resulting from the infusion of capital.

In the similar case of *Scott*, 2010 CarswellNat 2490, in allowing a taxpayer to claim an ABIL in respect of loans made to a corporation controlled by the taxpayer's son, the Court stated (paras. 15 and 20):

> The requirement is not that the lender's purpose be earning the most amount of income he can; it is sufficient if he has an income producing purpose. The Court should continue to look at all of the lender's actions, arrangements and activities with respect to a loan in order to be satisfied of the lender's income earning purpose. This should include whether a reasonable return in the form of interest, premiums, discounts and fees, et cetera, was legally payable on the loan and was intended to be collected ...

> I see no reason to interpret subparagraph 40(2)(g)(ii) more stringently than Parliament wrote it. It is sufficient if one of the purposes of lending the money was to earn income from the loan. The enhanced deductibility of allowable business investment losses are intended to apply to non-arm's length and related party loans, provided the conditions set out in the Act are met. Mr. Scott has been able to demonstrably satisfy the Court with clear, unequivocal written evidence that such was the case when he entered into the financing agreement and advanced the first $115,000.

ITA 40(2)(g)(ii), *Byram*, [1999] 2 C.T.C. 149 (FCA), Folio S4-F8-C1, VDs 2003-0038755, 2005-0117541I7

¶4530 — Foreign Exchange Gains and Losses on Capital Account (Sch. 3: Part 5)

Foreign exchange gains and losses from capital transactions in foreign currencies are considered to be capital gains or losses and should be reported in Part 5 of Schedule 3. The net gain or loss should be reported in Canadian dollars.

The tax treatment of a foreign exchange gain or loss depends on whether the gain or loss is on income or capital account. Normally, foreign exchange gains and losses on income account are included in computing income on an accrual basis. On the other hand, foreign exchange gains and losses on capital account are only recognized for tax purposes when the gain or loss is realized. Generally, where it can be determined that a foreign exchange gain or loss arose as a direct consequence of the purchase or sale of goods abroad or the rendering of services abroad, and such goods or services are used in the business operations of the taxpayer, such gain or loss is a business income or expense that would not be reported on Schedule 3.

The principles under case law with respect to distinguishing whether a foreign exchange gain or loss is on income or capital account are summarized in *Ethicon Sutures*, [1985] 2 C.T.C. 6 (FCTD), as follows:

- To determine whether a foreign exchange gain is to be treated as income or capital, it is necessary to look at the underlying transaction that gave rise to the gain or loss.

- If the foreign currency was acquired as a result of the taxpayer's trading operations or for the purpose of carrying on trading operations, any gains will be treated as occurring in the course of the taxpayer's trade and will be on income account.

- If the transaction is speculation made in the hope of profit, it will be treated as an adventure in the nature of trade and the gain will be taxed as income [In IT-459, the CRA attempts to distil the jurisprudence concerning an "adventure in the nature of trade" into some general principles. See also IT-479R: *Transactions in Securities*, and VDs 2009-0321871E5, 2008-0269481E5, 2005-0127861E5, 2006-0185041E5, and 2001-0107655].

- If the gain arises out of the investment of idle funds or the appreciation of a temporary investment, the gain will be treated as a capital gain.

- To be considered capital in nature, the funds must be surplus and must be exclusively for dividend or capital expenditures (i.e., "earmarked primarily" is not enough).

In paragraph 2 of IT-95R: *Foreign Exchange Gains and Losses*, the CRA states:

> Where it can be determined that a gain or loss on foreign exchange arose as a direct consequence of the purchase or sale of goods abroad, or the rendering of services abroad, and such goods or services are used in the business operations of the taxpayer, such gain or loss is brought into income account. If, on the other hand, it can be determined that a gain or loss on foreign exchange arose as a direct consequence of the purchase or sale of capital assets, this gain or loss is either a capital gain or capital loss, as the case may be.

In VD 2012-0436921I7, the CRA states its long standing position that ITA 40 will determine whether or not a taxpayer has "made a gain" or "sustained a loss" as a result of the disposition of a property and it is only after a gain or loss has been determined under the provisions of ITA 40 that one looks to ITA 39 to compute the capital gain or capital loss. In the situation considered, the CRA concludes that a taxpayer's foreign exchange loss upon a redemption of shares is deemed to be nil by virtue of ITA 40(3.6) and that neither of ITA 39(1) nor 39(2) would apply; it is unclear whether the CRA's conclusion is correct (see Barnicke et al., "Currency Losses on FA Share Redemption", *Canadian Tax Highlights*, Vol. 20, No. 10, October 2012).

Bank of Canada foreign exchange rates are available on the Bank of Canada's website at: bankofcanada.ca/en/rates/exchange-look.html.

ITA 9(1), 39(2), *Imperial Tobacco Co. (of Great Britain & Ireland) Ltd. v. Kelly*, [1943] 2 All E.R. 119, *Eli Lilly & Co. (Canada) Ltd*, [1955] C.T.C. 198 (SCC), *Salada Foods Ltd.*, [1974] C.T.C. 201 (FCTD), *Canadian General Electric Co.*, [1961] C.T.C. 512 (SCC), *MNR v. Tip Top Tailors Ltd.*, [1957] C.T.C. 309 (SCC), *No. 278* (1955), 13 Tax A.B.C. 324, *Alberta Natural Gas Co.*, [1969] C.T.C. 316 (Exch), IT-95R: *Foreign exchange gains and losses*, IT-459: *Adventure or concern in the nature of trade*, IT-479R(SR): *Transactions in securities*, ITTN-38, *Shell Canada Ltd.*, [1999] 4 C.T.C. 313 (SCC), VDs 2010-0386881E5, 2009-034592117, 2008-029708117, 2006-0215491C6, 2009-035206117, 2009-034896117, 2008-030465117, 2005-011775117, 2004-0104431R3

¶4540 — Options to Buy or Sell Property (Sch. 3: Part 5)

An option granted by a taxpayer is deemed to be a disposition of property the ACB of which is nil. Subject to the comments below, this means that a capital gain equal to the option price will be realized. However, if the option is exercised, the grantor is no longer required to treat the consideration received for granting the option as a capital gain and, if necessary, may file an amended tax return for the relevant taxation year. If the option is to acquire property, the consideration received by the vendor for the option is included in the proceeds of disposition of the property and the cost of the option to the purchaser is added to the cost of the property. If the option is to sell property, the vendor may deduct the ACB of the option from the proceeds of disposition and the purchaser must reduce the cost of the property to the purchaser by the consideration received for the option to sell it.

Where the option is exercised in a year later than that in which the option is granted, the amended return must be filed before the last day allowed for the filing of the return for the year in which the option was exercised and will not be accepted unless the return for the initial year was filed by the due date. The entitlement to a reassessment consequent upon the exercise of an option is discussed by the CRA in IT-384R: *Reassessment Where Option Exercised in Subsequent Year*.

The holder of an option which expires is deemed to have disposed of it and will accordingly have a capital loss equal to the ACB of the option. If the holder of an option sells the option, any gain or loss realized on the disposition will be the difference between the proceeds of disposition and the ACB of the option.

For example, John owns a tract of land. In consideration for $5,000 he grants a six-month option to buy the land for $300,000. In the year in which the option is granted, John is deemed to have disposed of a capital property for a gain of $5,000 and the grantee is considered to have acquired the option for a cost of $5,000. If, in the following year the option expires, the grantee is deemed to have disposed of the option in that year for no proceeds of disposition, and accordingly has sustained a capital loss of $5,000. If, on the other hand, the option is exercised in the following year, John is no longer deemed to have realized a gain of $5,000 upon granting the option, and may file an amended return for the previous year to exclude the taxable capital gain from the calculation of his income. In the year in which the option is exercised, assuming that the ACB of the land is $250,000, John's gain is determined as follows:

Proceeds of disposition	$	300,000
Consideration received for the option		5,000
	$	305,000
ACB of land		(250,000)
John's gain on the disposition of the land	$	55,000

The cost to the purchaser of the land is computed as follows:

Amount paid for the land	$	300,000
Amount paid for the option		5,000
Cost base of the land to purchaser	$	305,000

ITA 49, 248(1)"disposition", *Salt et al*, [1984] C.T.C. 414 (FCTD), IT-479R: *Transactions in Securities*, VDs 2004-0100771E5, 2003-0028033

¶4550 — Other Capital Properties (Sch. 3: Part 5)

In Part 5 of Schedule 3, describe any other capital property disposed of during the taxation year that the taxpayer has not already reported in Parts 1, 2, 3, or 4. Some of the types of gains and losses to report in Part 5 of Schedule 3, such as those in respect of bad debts on capital account and foreign exchange gains and losses on capital account, are discussed above.

Generally, certain capital gains and capital losses realized by a taxpayer will be reported on information slips received by the taxpayer, such as a Form T3 (Box 21 related to capital gains allocated from a trust). Such capital gains and losses should not be reported in Part 5. Instead, capital gains or losses from T5, T5013, T5013A, and T4PS information slips should be reported on Line 174 and capital gains or losses from T3 information slips should be reported on Line 176.

Gains and losses allocated from a partnership should be reported in the appropriate Part of Schedule 3 to which the gain or loss relates. Even if the taxpayer is a member of a partnership that does not file a T5013 Summary, the partner is still required to report his or her share of any capital gain or loss from each disposition of capital property of the partnership in the appropriate area of Schedule 3.

¶4560 — Other Mortgage Foreclosures and Conditional Sales Repossessions (Sch.3 Part 6)

Where a taxpayer owes money under a mortgage or agreement for sale and the property is either sold or seized by the creditor for nonpayment, the amount by which the taxpayer's indebtedness is reduced (plus any part of the sale proceeds received) is considered proceeds of disposition of the property. Mortgage foreclosures and conditional sales repossessions are reported in Part 6 of Schedule 3.

If the taxpayer is the mortgagee (i.e., the lender) who repossesses a property because the mortgagor failed to pay the taxpayer money owed under the mortgage, the taxpayer is considered to have purchased the property. However, there is no capital gain or loss at the time of repossession. Any gain or loss will be postponed until the taxpayer sells the property.

If the taxpayer is the mortgagor (i.e., the borrower) whose property is repossessed because the taxpayer did not pay money owed under the mortgage, the taxpayer is considered to have sold the property. Depending on the amount owed at the time of repossession, the taxpayer may have a capital gain, a capital loss, or, in the case of depreciable property, a terminal loss. However, if the property is personal-use property, the taxpayer cannot deduct the loss. For details on the tax consequences of mortgage foreclosures and conditional sales repossessions, see ¶4112.

If the capital gain or loss is from the disposition of qualified farm or fishing property, report the capital gain or loss on Line 124 in Part 2 of Schedule 3.

Any capital gains from a mortgage foreclosure or a conditional sales repossession should be excluded from net income when calculating the taxpayer's claim for the GST/HST credit, the Canada Child Benefit, credits allowed under certain related provincial or territorial programs, the age amount, and the taxpayer's social benefits repayment.

ITA 79, 79.1, IT-170R: *Sale of property — When included in income computation*, VD 2009-0305751E5, *Pigeau*, 2009 CarswellNat 4076 (TCC) (transfer to someone other than creditor), *Waltz*, [2001] 2 C.T.C. 2627 (TCC) (time for calculation of foreign exchange gain or loss is date of foreclosure); *Jones*, [1999] 1 C.T.C. 2644 (TCC) (Surrender and subrogation gave rise to new creditor; provision applicable), *Hallbauer*, [1998] 3 C.T.C. 115 (FCA); aff'd [1997] 1 C.T.C. 2428 (TCC) (non-contingent, irreversible transfers were dispositions), *Corbett*, [1997] 1 C.T.C. 2 (FCA) (section intended to apply where no fixed price of sale), *Peters (D.L.)*, [1993] 1 C.T.C. 2628 (TCC) (ITA 80 applies to unpaid interest on obligation to which ITA 79 applied), C. Stocco et al., ""Insolvency 101" and Related Income Tax Issues," *2009 British Columbia Tax Conference*, (Vancouver: Canadian Tax Foundation, 2009), 8:1–35, L. Shillinger et al., "Advanced Topics in Real Estate Tax Planning," *Report of Proceedings of Sixty-First Tax Conference*, 2009 Tax Conference (Toronto: Canadian Tax Foundation, 2010), 33:1–34

¶4570 — Personal-Use Property (Sch. 3: Parts 7 and 8)

Personal-use property is property owned by a taxpayer that is used primarily for the personal use and enjoyment of the taxpayer and related persons. Personal-use property includes such property as residences, cars, boats, cottages, etc. Personal-use property also includes a debt owing to the taxpayer in respect of the disposition of personal-use property, as well as an option to acquire personal-use property.

Personal-use property of a taxpayer is treated differently from other capital property for the purpose of computing capital gains and losses. Most personal-use property decreases in value with the passage of time, and losses incurred in respect of it are not deductible for tax purposes (except for personal-use property which is listed personal property; see ¶4571 below). Individuals should report the disposition of personal-use property (other than listed personal property), including a full description of the property, in Part 7 of Schedule 3. Enter the total amount of the capital gain realized on the disposition on Line 158 of Schedule 3.

If the ACB of personal-use property disposed of is less than $1,000, it is considered to be $1,000. As well, when the proceeds of disposition are less than $1,000, they are considered to be $1,000. If both ACB and proceeds are $1,000 or less, the taxpayer will not have a capital gain or a capital loss. The $1,000 rules does not apply when donors acquire personal-use property as part of an arrangement in which the property is gifted to a qualified donee, such as a registered charity.

The following example is provided in Guide T4037:

Example

Jane sold the following personal-use properties in 2017.

Property sold	Proceeds of disposition	Adjusted cost base	Outlays and expenses
China cabinet	$ 900	$ 500	$ 0
Boat	$ 1,200	$ 850	$ 50
Personal computer	$ 1,500	$ 3,200	$ 30

Jane calculates the capital gain or loss for each transaction as follows:

Calculation of capital gain (or loss)		China cabinet ($)		Boat ($)		Personal computer ($)
Proceeds of disposition (greater of selling price and $1,000)		1,000		1,200		1,500
Minus: ACB (greater of cost and $1,000) plus outlays and expenses	-	1,000	-	1,050	-	3,230
Capital gain (loss)	=	0	=	150	=	(1,730)

China cabinet — For the proceeds of disposition and the ACB, Jane uses $1,000, as both were less than that amount. As a result, there is no capital gain or loss for this transaction and Jane does not have to report it on Schedule 3.

Boat — Because the cost of the boat is less than $1,000, the ACB is considered to be $1,000. Jane reports $150 as a capital gain.

Personal computer — Jane's capital loss is not deductible. She also cannot use the loss to decrease any other capital gains realized in the year.

ITA 46, 54"personal-use property"

¶4571 — *Listed Personal Property*

Listed personal property is a special category of personal-use property that usually increases in value. Listed personal property includes: prints, etchings, drawings, paintings, sculptures, or other similar works of art; jewellery; rare folios, rare manuscripts, or rare books; stamps; and coins.

Losses from disposing of listed personal property can only be deducted from capital gains realized from disposing of listed personal property. A listed personal property loss is not deductible from capital gains from any other source, either in the same year or in any other year. However, listed personal property losses may be carried back three years to offset capital gains from listed personal property in those years and may be carried forward for up to seven years to offset capital gains from listed personal property in those years. Any portion of listed personal property losses may be deducted against such gains in any taxation year in the carryover period with no requirement to apply the losses to the earliest years first.

A taxpayer's net gain in any year from the disposition of listed personal property is the amount by which capital gains for the year from such property exceed capital losses for the year from such property, reduced by the carryover of listed personal property losses of other years.

Individuals should report the disposition of listed personal property, including a full description of the property, in Part 8 of Schedule 3. Enter the total amount of gains or losses realized on the disposition of listed personal property, subtract any unapplied listed personal property losses from previous years, and report the net gain only on the disposition of listed personal property on Line 159 of Schedule 3. To carry back any listed personal property losses to reduce listed personal property net gains from the previous three years, complete Form T1A, *Request for Loss Carryback* (see Line 253 at ¶9370).

The following example is from Guide T4037:

Example

Nathan bought some jewellery in 1997 for $5,800. In 2017, he sold it for $6,000. He ended up with a gain of $200. He also sold a coin collection for $2,000 in 2017. Nathan had originally bought this collection in 1999 for $1,700. He ended up with a gain of $300 when he sold the coin collection. In addition, he sold a painting in 2017 for $8,000. However, Nathan bought the painting in 2000 for $12,000. Therefore, he had a loss of $4,000. He had no outlays and expenses for these three transactions.

Nathan's loss from selling listed personal property in 2017 was more than his gain: his loss was $4,000; his total gain was $500 ($200 + $300). As a result, his net loss was $3,500 ($4,000 - $500). Nathan cannot use the difference to offset his capital gain on the sale of a property other than on listed personal property in the year. In addition, he cannot offset any income he had from other sources. However, he can apply his listed personal property loss against his gains from dispositions of listed personal property in any of the three preceding years or the seven years following 2017. Nathan should not complete Schedule 3 for 2017. However, he should keep a record of his listed personal property loss in case he wants to apply the loss against listed personal property gains in another year.

The following points summarize the tax rules relating to personal-use property:

- A capital loss from the disposition of personal-use property that is not listed personal property may not be used to offset capital gains from the disposition of other such property or any other property.

- A capital loss from the disposition of listed personal property may be used to offset capital gains from the disposition of other such property in the same year. To the extent not so used, they may be offset against capital gains from listed personal property in the preceding three years or following seven years.

- A special $1,000 rule relieves most taxpayers from maintaining detailed cost records and from reporting small gains and losses from minor dispositions of personal-use property since, for tax purposes, such property is deemed to have an adjusted cost base of at least $1,000. Generally, by reason of the $1,000 rule, the adjusted cost base of personal use property will never be less than $1,000 and the proceeds of disposition are deemed to be never less than $1,000. Where a taxpayer disposes of only part of a personal-use property (e.g., a half-interest), the adjusted cost base is determined on a proportionate basis and the $1,000 must be reduced in the same proportion. If the items constitute a set, the $1,000 minimum cost is to be allocated across the set.

The CRA provided the following guidance on listed personal property and the meaning of a "set" at the CRA Roundtable at the 2013 STEP Canada National Conference (VD 2013-0481001C6):

Question 8. — Listed Personal Property

Personal use property, including listed personal property, is deemed to have a cost of $1,000 per item, unless the items constitute a set, in which case the $1,000 minimum cost is to be allocated across the set.

In certain cases, it is easy to understand what is meant by a set. For example, one would speak of a set of dishes or cutlery, as constituting a set. However, in other cases, it is not clear as to what constitutes a set. Accordingly, we would ask clarification in the following hypothetical circumstances: The taxpayer has a series of paintings produced by the same artist, which were sold as a "set," but would not have any particular value as a set, and have an equal value independently. A person has a stamp collection consisting of a multitude of different stamps from different countries.

One can think of other examples which might constitute or not constitute a set. Can CRA please provide some guidance here?

CRA Response

The term "set" is not defined in the Act and therefore carries its ordinary meaning in the context in which it is used. The CRA considers that a set for these purposes is a number of properties belonging together and relating to each other. For example, in the case of the hobby of philately, in the past, the CRA considered that a set is a number of stamps which were produced and issued by one country simultaneously or over a short period of time. The fact that the value of a number of properties, if sold together, exceeds the aggregate of their values, if sold individually, may indicate the existence of a set. However, this is not in itself a decisive factor.

Regarding your question concerning what is a "set" insofar as paintings are concerned; it is our opinion that simply because they were painted by one artist would not in and by itself, mean that they are a set. Nor would all landscapes, waterscapes, figures, etc. necessarily be a "set." The criterion in the case of paintings would seem to be whether or not a group of paintings were painted as a set and would ordinarily be disposed of as a set. For instance, a painter might be commissioned to paint, as a set, all former premiers of a province or a family tree. These would ordinarily be inserted in identical frames. These facts would seem to conclusively establish that such a group of paintings were indeed a "set" for purposes of the Act.

The determination of whether a set exists is therefore a question of fact, and we have not been provided with sufficient information on the paintings and stamps, in order to establish whether they form part of a set or not.

ITA 41(1), 41(2), 46(1), 46(2), 54"listed personal property"

¶4572 — *Excluded Property*

Personal-use property does not include "excluded property". Excluded property is defined as property acquired by the taxpayer where it is reasonable to consider that its acquisition relates to an arrangement, scheme or plan promoted by a third party whereby the property will be donated to a charity and a charitable donation receipt issued. Such transactions have been used, for example, in "art flip" circumstances where a promoter would purchase a piece of art, for example, for $50, sell it to a taxpayer for $200 and arrange for the taxpayer to donate the art to a charity based on an appraised value of $1,000.

The taxpayer would be issued a charitable donation receipt for $1,000, but since the property was listed personal property, would pay no tax on the difference between the $200 cost and the $1,000 appraised value. By defining this property as excluded property, the difference will not be eligible for the $1,000 rule and will therefore be taxable. Further, such transactions have been successfully attacked by the CRA resulting in a reduction in the amount considered to be a charitable donation on the basis that the appraised value was inflated in view of the significantly lower acquisition cost shortly before the donation.

ITA 46(1)"excluded property", 46(5)

¶4573 — *Bad Debts*

Personal-use property is defined to include a debt owing to the taxpayer in respect of the disposition of personal-use property. However, listed personal property is not defined as including a debt in respect of the disposition of listed personal property. As a result, regardless of whether the property disposed of was listed personal property, the debt is personal-use property and not listed personal property. A loss from the disposition of personal-use property, other than listed personal property, or a debt relating to the disposition of personal use property which is owing to the taxpayer by an arm's length person and which is established to be bad, is deemed to be nil. A loss arising from failure to collect all the proceeds of disposition of a personal-use property is also nil. However, if the taxpayer had realized a capital gain on the disposition of the personal-use property, the loss from the uncollectable portion of the resulting debt will be treated as a capital loss up to the amount of the capital gain realized.

If, in a taxation year, a debt is established to be bad, a taxpayer who elects to have ITA 50(1) apply is deemed to have disposed of the debt at the end of that taxation year and to have reacquired it at the beginning of the subsequent taxation year at a cost equal to nil. ITA 50 also provides that a share in a company that becomes a bankrupt during the shareholder's taxation year, or a share in a company that is insolvent and subject to a winding-up order under the *Winding-up and Restructuring Act* is deemed (on election) to be disposed of by the shareholder at the end of that year for no proceeds and to be reacquired immediately after the end of the year at a cost of nil. In Guide T4037, the CRA states that "[t]o claim a capital loss on a bad debt, you have to file an election with your income tax and benefit return. To make this election, write and sign a letter stating that you want subsection 50(1) of the *Income Tax Act* to apply to the bad debt. Attach this letter to your return." See also ¶4360 and ¶4520.

ITA 40(2)(g)(iii), 50(1), 50(2), 54"personal-use property", Folio S4-F8-C1

¶4600 — Allowable Business Investment Losses (ABILs)

¶4610 — Deductibility of ABILs (T1: Lines 217 and 228; Sch. 3: Line 178)

A capital loss arising from the arm's length disposition or deemed disposition of shares or debt of a "small business corporation" (see ¶4620) is referred to as a business investment loss. One-half of a business investment loss, referred to as an allowable business investment loss (ABIL), can be deducted from any source of income (unlike a regular capital loss that can only be applied to reduce capital gains).

Two people (or entities) are dealing at arm's length with each other if they are independent, and one does not have undue influence over the other. The ITA also deems certain people not to be at arm's length with each other (non-arm's length). This is the case with "related persons," who are "individuals connected by blood relationship, marriage or common-law partnership or adoption" (see also Folio S1-F5-C1: *Related persons and dealing at arm's length*).

If the taxpayer incurred a business investment loss in the taxation year, complete Chart 6 in Guide T4037 to determine the ABIL and, if applicable, the business investment loss reduction. Claim the deduction for the ABIL on Line 217 of the T1 return and enter the gross business investment loss on Line 228 of the T1 return. Enter the business investment loss reduction, if any, calculated on Chart 6 on Line 178 of Schedule 3.

If the taxpayer's income is not sufficient to absorb the entire loss, the remainder is eligible for carryover as a non-capital loss and may be carried back to the three previous taxation years or carried forward ten years. If the taxpayer is unable to deduct an ABIL as a non-capital loss within the carry-over period, the unused portion of the ABIL becomes a net capital loss which can be carried forward indefinitely to reduce taxable capital gains. Although taxpayers can generally carry a non-capital loss back three years and forward 20 years, this extension does not apply to a non-capital loss resulting from an ABIL. Instead, an ABIL that has not been used within ten tax years will become a net capital loss in the eleventh year. To illustrate this, the following example is contained in paragraph 1.7 of Folio S4-F8-C1:

> Mr. K incurs an ABIL in the amount of $60,000 in the 2005 tax year. Ten years later, at the end of 2015, only $56,000 of the ABIL has been used as a non-capital loss. The remaining $4,000 becomes a net capital loss. Mr. K can carry this net capital loss forward indefinitely to be deducted against any taxable capital gains he realizes in the 2016 and subsequent tax years.

Business investment losses of an individual are reduced by the taxpayer's net capital gains for which the lifetime capital gains deduction was previously claimed (see ¶4210). In such circumstances, the amount of the reduction is considered a capital loss for the year in which the loss arose. Similarly, claiming an ABIL will reduce the capital gains deduction that a taxpayer can claim in future years.

For a deemed disposition of a debt or share to occur, as discussed under ¶4360 and ¶4520, an election, in the form of a letter, must be filed. An ABIL may be denied if the appropriate election was not filed. ITA 50 should be read in conjunction with ITA 40(2)(g)(ii), which deems to be nil all losses arising from the disposition of debts other than debts acquired for the purpose of gaining or producing income from a business or property or as consideration for the disposition, at arm's length, of a capital property. Gaining or producing income does need not to be the exclusive or even the primary purpose of a loan for the requirements of ITA 40(2)(g)(ii) to be met — provided gaining or producing income is one of the purposes of the loans, that fact is sufficient to meet the requirements of ITA 40(2)(g)(ii) (see *Rich*, [2004] 1 C.T.C. 308 (FCA), *MacCallum*, [2011] 6 C.T.C. 2172 (TCC), *Scott*, 2010 CarswellNat 2490 (TCC)).

ABIL claims are frequently audited by the CRA. Typically, a taxpayer that claims an ABIL will receive a standard information request letter with respect to the claim. When making a claim, a thorough supporting file should be prepared documenting the eligibility of the ABIL, including the qualification of the particular corporation as a small business corporation. With respect to a bad debt, supporting documentation should include a list of the steps taken (with supporting evidence) to recover the debt. At the 2012 CTF Ontario Tax Conference, the CRA was asked whether all ABIL claims are reviewed by the CRA's audit group and whether "[t]he CRA's audit policy of aggressively denying ABILs (hence the large number of cases on this issue that reach the TCC) [was] at odds with the underlying fiscal policy of encouraging investment in small business". The CRA responded as follows:

> As you may know, CRA is moving more and more toward intelligence based risk assessment and risk-based audit. That dictates that not all returns with any claims, including those containing [ABILs] are selected for Audit. During the processing of a return where an ABIL is claimed, a pre-assessment review (to assess risk of non-compliance) may be undertaken and a determination made as to whether additional verification is required. As for the underlying fiscal policy, our goal in reviewing claims for ABILs is not to discourage investment in small business, on the contrary, it is to support that policy's intention by preventing bogus claims from compromising the regime that's meant to encourage legitimate investment.

For the CRA's administrative comments on determining a taxpayer's ABIL and the deductibility of such a loss, see Folio S4-F8-C1: *Business Investment Losses*.

For examples of cases in which an ABIL claim was denied, see *Venneri*, [2007] 3 C.T.C. 155 (FCA) (holding land for speculation was not found to constitute an active business such that the corporation was not an SBC); *Singh*, [2006] 5 C.T.C. 80 (FCA) (inadequate documentation); *Hopmeyer*, [2007] 2 C.T.C. 218 (FCA) (company continued to carry on business after taxation year in respect of which claim was made); *MacKay*, [2007] 1 C.T.C. 2226 (spousal loan did not have income earning purpose); *Soja*, [2007] 3 C.T.C. 2263 (TCC) (ITA 50(1) election not filed with tax return); *Glynn*, [2007] 3 C.T.C. 2172 (TCC) (corporation was carrying on a specified investment business and did not qualify as an SBC); *Wilkins*, [2007] 3 C.T.C. 2414 (TCC) (ITA 50(1) found not to apply); *Gilbert*, 2009 CarswellNat 1471 (TCC) (failure to prove debt was bad); *Sunatori*, [2012] 1 C.T.C. 71 (FCA) (bad debt claim denied); *Grist*, 2011 CarswellNat 2127 (TCC) (insufficient evidence to verify corporation was an SBC); *MacCallum*, [2011] 6 C.T.C. 2172 (ITA 40(2)(g)(ii) did not apply); *Audet*, [2012] 6 C.T.C. 2001 (TCC) (taxpayer was not a shareholder of company in respect of which a guarantee was provided); *McDowell*, [2012] 6 C.T.C. 2156 (TCC) (corporation ceased business more than 12 months before loan written off); *Stinson*, [2013] 3 C.T.C. 2060 (TCC) (insufficient credible evidence); *Coveley*, 2014 CarswellNat 4904 (FCA) (loans were at nil interest and lacked income earning purpose and the debts were not considered to be bad in the year ABIL claim was made); *Barnwell*, 2016 CarswellNat 1561 (FCA) (loans were made to individual rather than his corporation); *D'Amour*, 2016 CarswellNat 2008 (TCC) (company was not dissolved until 2006 such that taxpayer could not qualify for ABIL in 2005); and *Di Cienzo*, 2016 CarswellNat 4063 (TCC).

For examples of cases in which an ABIL claim was allowed, see *Brand*, [2005] 4 C.T.C. 2411 (TCC) (loan through son found to be made "in trust" to be loaned on to corporation); *Litowitz*, [2005] 5 C.T.C. 2255 (TCC) (debt bad in year of ABIL claim although debt was recovered 5 years later); *Netolitzky*, [2006] 3 C.T.C. 2526 (TCC) (taxpayer conclusion that debts were bad was considered reasonable); Jodoin, [2007] 1 C.T.C. 2211 (TCC) (ABIL allowed for 2004 taxation year even though ITA 50(1) election could have been made in 2003 year); *Spillman*, [2007] 1 C.T.C. 2313 (taxpayer considered to have acquired debt by assuming a guarantee); *Kyriazakos*, [2007] 3 C.T.C. 2038 (TCC)

(ITA 50(1) applied); *Giasson*, 2009 CarswellNat 3053 (TCC) (losses claimed on guarantees); *Scott*, 2010 CarswellNat 2490 (TCC) (ABIL allowed in respect of loss on loan to son's company); *Dhaliwal*, 2012 CarswellNat 769 (TCC) (ABIL allowed despite fact that corporation did not file a tax return).

ITA 3(d), 38, 39(1)(c), 50(1), 111(1)(a), (8), ITA 248(1)"allowable business investment loss", *Abrametz*, [2009] 4 C.T.C. 173 (FCA), *Jodoin*, [2007] 1 C.T.C. 2211 (TCC), *Tipster Investments Ltd*, [1998] 2 C.T.C. 3005 (TCC), Folio S4-F8-C1, S1-F5-C1: *Meaning of Arm's Length*, S4-F8-C1: *Business investment losses*, VDs 2010-0382361E5, 2010-0380821E5, 9514515, Donnelly et al., "Substantiating an ABIL Deduction: An Analysis of the Key Elements," (2010), vol. 58, no. 2 *Canadian Tax Journal*, 229-276, Weder *et al*, "Allowable Business Investment Losses: What to do when the CRA calls," *2009 British Columbia Tax Conference*, (Vancouver: Canadian Tax Foundation, 2009), 7:1–21; Posthumus, CA, "Tax Loss Planning for the Owner Manager — An Update on Claiming Allowable Business Investment Losses," *2008 Prairie Provinces Tax Conference*, (Toronto: Canadian Tax Foundation, 2008), 12:1–24, Kakkar, "Practical Considerations of Claiming an ABIL and the Capital Gains Exemption" *2012 CTF Ontario Tax Conference*, Bangs, "TCC Denies Taxpayers' ABIL Claims", *Tax for the Owner-Manager*, Vol. 14 — 2, April 2014.

¶4620 — Small Business Corporation Definition

An ABIL can be realized on a loss incurred on shares or debt of a small business corporation. A small business corporation is a Canadian-controlled private corporation (CCPC), all or substantially all of the fair market value of the assets of which at that time were attributable to assets that were either used principally in an active business carried on primarily (i.e., more than 50%) in Canada by the corporation or a related corporation; shares or indebtedness of one or more small business corporations that are connected with the particular corporation within the meaning of ITA 186(4); or a combination of the two.

To qualify as a "small business corporation", the corporation must be a CCPC. Generally, a "private corporation" resident in Canada that qualifies as a "Canadian corporation" and is controlled by Canadian resident individuals either directly or through other private corporations is a CCPC, provided its shares and those of any corporation controlling it are not listed on a designated stock exchange (domestic or foreign). In determining whether a corporation is a CCPC, ITA 251(5)(b) deems the corporation to be controlled by a person who has a right under contract, in equity or otherwise, to acquire shares or voting control of the corporation. This rule has the effect of deeming the corporation not to be a CCPC if the person is, for example, a public corporation or a non-resident.

A holding company or an operating company can qualify as a small business corporation.

The definition "small business corporation" requires that all or substantially all of the fair market value of the corporation's property be attributable to property described in paragraphs (a) to (c) of the definition. The phrase "all or substantially all" is not defined in the ITA but has generally been interpreted by the CRA to mean at least 90%. This rule of thumb has been generally accepted; however, in any given case the courts will generally determine the meaning of such a phrase on the basis of the particular facts and circumstances of that case. For example, in *Wood v MNR*, [1987] 1 C.T.C. 2391 (TCC), the term was considered in the context of a non-resident individual trying to claim a personal exemption under the ITA. The exemption was disallowed by the CRA on the basis that not "all or substantially all" of the individual's income was included in computing his taxable income earned in Canada. The Court stated that there could be no simple mathematical formula and commented that the 90% rule is merely an arbitrary assessing policy. While such a mechanism is useful and functional, the Court noted that the CRA might be hard pressed to refuse a claim where the percentage was 89%, 80%, or possibly even lower. The CRA has acknowledged that that in certain cases, the "substantially all" test could, depending on the circumstances and context, be satisfied even if a 90% level were not reached (see, for example, VD 2013-0495631C6).

For purposes of claiming an ABIL, a small business corporation includes a corporation that was a small business corporation at any time during the 12 months before the disposition.

Regarding paragraph (b) of the definition, a "connected" corporation is defined as a corporation either controlled (otherwise than by virtue of ITA 251(5)(b)) by the particular corporation, or in which the particular corporation owns shares carrying more than 10% of the voting rights of the corporation and having a fair market value of more than 10% of the fair market value of all the issued shares of the corporation.

The definition of a "business" is discussed in ¶6112. A business is generally defined to include a profession, calling, trade, manufacture, or undertaking of any kind whatever and also includes an adventure or concern in the nature of trade. An active business is defined generally as any business other than a "specified investment business" or a "personal services business".

The concept of an "active business" has its ordinary meaning developed generally in the case law considering the meaning of a business carried on by a corporation. In *Ollenberger*, [2012] 3 C.T.C. 2090, a company that bought distressed oil and gas properties was found not to be carrying on "active" business. However, in overturning the decision of the TCC and allowing an ABIL to be claimed, the FCA held that the Tax Court judge erred when she held that more was required than carrying on a business (other than specified investment business or a personal services business) in order to conclude that a corporation was carrying on an "active" business (*Ollenberger*, 2013 CarswellNat 546 (FCA)). In other words, the Court found that an "active business" as defined in ITA 248(1) is not required to be "active".

As to the circumstances in which the principal purpose of a business will be regarded as one which is to derive income from property and as to the distinction between income from a business and income from a property, see under ¶4010.

With respect to the requirement that the active business be "carried on primarily in Canada", in VD 2011-0423951E5, the CRA states:

> Whether or not any business is being carried on in whole or in part in Canada (or some other jurisdiction) is a question of fact. As a general rule, in a traditional business (i.e., non e-commerce), such as the sale of goods, the most determinative factor is usually the place of the contract. Another factor to consider may be the country where the corporation is resident. Similarly, where a corporation's business involves the rendering of services, that business is generally considered to be carried on at the place or places where the services are rendered or performed. For the CRA's general views on determining where a particular business is carried on please refer to the comments in paragraph 23 of IT-270R3: *Foreign Tax Credit*. [Now in paras. 1.53 and 1.54 of Folio S5-F2-C1]

> In an e-commerce environment the above determination can be more complex than with more traditional forms of business. Notwithstanding this complexity, where a corporation operates a service business via a website from a server that is based and operated in Canada and where any related manual activity takes place in Canada, generally speaking, it would be our view that the corporation is carrying on business primarily in Canada.

The rule in ITA 129(6) that deems property income of a recipient corporation from a source in Canada to be income from an active business where such property income has been received from an associated corporation is of no assistance in meeting the asset-use test in paragraph (a) of the small business corporation definition; see VD 2012-0435101E5.

ITA 186(2), (4), (7), 251(5), 110.6(14)(b), 248(1)"active business", "business", "small business corporation", IT-73R6: *The small business deduction*, VD 9301993, Hickey, "Active Business Defined: ABIL Allowed", *CTH*, Vol. 21-4, April 2013, Friedlan, "A Question of Meaning: The Definition of Active Business in Subsection 248(1)", *Tax for the Owner-Manager*, Vol 13-3, July 2013

¶4621 — *Assets used Principally in an Active Business*

In determining whether an asset was "used" in a particular active business, in *Ensite Limited*, [1986] 2 C.T.C. 459 (SCC), it was established that the asset must be "employed" or "risked" in the business. Furthermore, the Court held that the term "risked" meant more than a remote risk and that the withdrawal of the property would have a destabilizing effect on the business operations themselves.

In *McCutcheon Farms Ltd*, [1991] 1 C.T.C. 50 (FCTD), a farming operation which processed and sold seed and chemicals attempted to claim the small business deduction in respect of interest income on short-term deposits, contending that such interest constituted income from property used or held principally for the purpose of gaining or producing income from its farm business. The Tax Court concluded that the test in *Ensite* had not been met, since it could not be said that the property in issue was employed or risked in the farm business. The Court considered that the term deposits were neither an integral part of the taxpayer's financing nor necessary to the overall operation but rather surplus and collateral to the active business and not used regularly in the course of the business. Alternative arguments that the income was incident to or pertaining to an active business were rejected.

Generally, the CRA's view is that cash and cash equivalents are not an active business asset unless the cash is held "to fulfill a mandatory condition precedent to trade" or its withdrawal would "have a decidedly destabilizing effect on the corporate operations themselves" (see paras. 14 and 15 of *Ensite Limited*). The CRA considers cash held to satisfy employee bonuses or stock option requirements to qualify as active business assets. Also, the CRA has stated marketable securities held as security under a financing arrangement are a qualifying asset where the arrangement is fundamental to the business operations and there is a real expectation that the security will be resorted to (however, the employment of marketable securities merely as collateral is not generally sufficient to enable it to be considered to be used in a business).

In paragraph 6 of IT-73R6, the CRA states:

> [A]lthough a mortgage receivable is an asset whose existence may be relevant to the equity of a corporation, it is not generally an asset used in an active business because the funds tied up in the mortgage are not available for the active business use of a corporation. However, if the corporation could establish that the mortgages are employed and risked in the business such that the mortgages are inextricably tied to or vitally connected with the business, they could be considered to be used in an active business carried on by the corporation.

In VD 2012-0435351I7, in applying the small business corporation tests to a corporation resident in Quebec, the CRA stated that the cash balance of the corporation should not be reduced by outstanding cheques since, according to Quebec civil law, the issuance of a cheque does not constitute payment.

With respect to the principal use of a building, in VD 2009-0307931E5, the CRA states:

> Although there are no set guidelines as to which factors to use in different situations, there are two aspects to be considered in determining the nature of use of a building — quantitative factors (e.g., the total square footage occupancy in the building) and qualitative factors (e.g., the original intent for purchasing the building, actual use to which the building is put in the course of the business, the nature of the business involved and the practice in the particular industry). The square footage use of a building is generally accepted as a factor to be given significant weight in the determination of the particular use to which the building is put. However, qualitative factors need also be considered. If the fair rental value of the space rented to tenants is greater than the fair rental value of the space used in an active business, this may indicate that a building is not used principally in an active business. Whether such a factor would be decisive in relation to the square footage test would have to be determined on a case by case basis. We are unable to provide a definitive comment without the opportunity to review all the relevant facts.

In VD 2008-0299741I7, the CRA considered a situation in which a corporation had an undivided one-half interest in a building and used half of the building as its business premises. Notwithstanding the fact that the corporation was using all of the space that it occupied in the building in its active business, the CRA's opinion was that the asset was not principally used in an active business by the corporation "because only 50% of its value in the building was being used in an active business". It is unclear whether the CRA's position was correct.

In *Belzile*, [2006] 5 C.T.C. 2011 (TCC), a corporation was found to be a small business corporation where the corporation rented out homes which were originally purchased with the intention to sell (the homes could not be sold as planned). However, in *Venneri*, [2007] 3 C.T.C. 155 (FCA), the Court found that a corporation holding land for speculation was not a small business corporation.

In *Glaxo Wellcome Inc*, [1999] 4 C.T.C. 371 (FCA), the Court found that the word "use" connotes actual utilization for some purpose, not holding for future use.

Additional considerations with respect to the small business corporation definition include:

- The term "principally" in respect of the use of an asset has been construed by the CRA as requiring a greater than 50% proportion of time to be used in the qualifying activity (Folio S4-F15-C1 (para. 1.21), VDs 2010-0381321E5, 2010-0381361E5);

- Assets not reflected on the accounting balance sheet of a corporation, including internally generated goodwill, may assist in meeting the determination time test where such assets are used in the active business;

- Income tax refunds receivable by a corporation are generally considered an active business asset. Also the CRA has stated a tax receivable in respect of corporate tax instalments paid by a corporation carrying on an active business is an asset used principally in an active business carried on by the corporation, as is tax receivable following a loss carryback from an active business carried on by a corporation constitutes an asset used principally in an active business carried on by the corporation (*Munich Reinsurance Co*, [2002] 1 C.T.C. 199 (FCA), VDs 2002-0169565, 2008-0285291C6);

- The CRA does not consider a future/deferred income tax asset recognized for accounting purposes to be an active business asset (i.e., the CRA's position is that deferred tax assets should be ignored for purposes of applying the SBC tests). Also, in applying the asset-use test, the CRA does not take into consideration the portion of a corporation's refundable dividend tax on hand for which no dividend refund is made (VDs 2014-0537611C6, 2013-0499671C6, 2012-0473261E5, 2008-0285301C6, 2006-0174131C6);

- Land inventory of a real estate developer which is used to carry on the business of land development is an asset used in an active business (VD 9619985);

- The CRA generally considers a partnership interest to be used in an active business if the underlying assets of the partnership are used in an active business. The CRA does not, however, consider a retired partner's right to partnership income to be an active business asset (VDs 2008-029974117, 9706965, 9636835, 9132835, 9636835);

- When determining whether assets meet the principal-use test, the CRA's position is that the test has to be applied on a property-by-property basis. For example, if a corporation owns several parcels of land and certain of the parcels do not meet the principal-use test, but 57% of total acreage is used in an active business, the CRA would not consider all the land parcels to be used principally in an active business (VD 9716155);

- Refundable deposits made as a requirement to operate a particular business would generally be considered an active business asset (VD 9226045).

Ensite Limited, [1986] 2 C.T.C. 459 (SCC), *Skidmore*, [2000] 2 C.T.C. 325 (FCA), *Reilly Estate*, [2007] 5 C.T.C. 2288 (TCC), VD 2009-0330071C6F, 2009-0330071C6, 9514695, Drouin, "Purification Strategies in Quebec", *Canadian Tax Focus*, Vol. 2, No. 4, Nov. 2012

¶4630 — Guarantees of Debt

A loss incurred by a guarantor in making good upon a guarantee is normally not deductible in computing income for tax purposes unless the guarantor is in the business of guaranteeing or securing loans. The guarantor may, however, be able to claim a capital loss or an ABIL if the guarantee was made for the purposes of earning income.

In *Steer* (1966), 66 D.T.C. 5481 (SCC), an investor in an oil drilling concern guaranteed a bank loan to provide working capital for the drilling operations. When the business failed and the company defaulted on the loan, the investor was required to honour the guarantee; the Court described the transaction as a deferred loan to the company, and held that the loss was a capital loss. For other examples of the same principle, see *H. Griffiths Co.* (1976), 76 D.T.C. 6261 (FCTD), and of *Morflot Freightliners Ltd.* (1989), 89 D.T.C. 5182 (FCTD).

In *Easton*, [1997] F.C.J. No. 1282 (FCA), the Court stated (paras. 16–18):

> As a general proposition, it is safe to conclude that an advance or outlay made by a shareholder to or on behalf of the corporation will be treated as a loan extended for the purpose of providing that corporation with working capital. In the event the loan is not repaid the loss is deemed to be of a capital nature for one of two reasons. Either the loan was given to generate a stream of income for the taxpayer, as is characteristic of an investment, or it was given to enable the corporation to carry on its business such that the shareholder would secure an enduring benefit in the form of dividends or an increase in share value. As the law presumes that shares are acquired for investment purposes it seems only too reasonable to presume that a loss arising from an advance or outlay made by a shareholder is also on capital account. The same considerations apply to shareholder guarantees for loans made to corporations . . .

> There are two recognized exceptions to the general proposition that losses of the nature described above are on capital account. First, the taxpayer may be able to establish that the loan was made in the ordinary course of the taxpayer's business. The classic example is the taxpayer/shareholder who is in the business of lending money or granting guarantees. The exception, however, also extends to cases where the advance or outlay was made for income-producing purposes related to the taxpayer's own business and not that of the corporation in which he or she holds shares. For example, in *Berman, L., & Co. Ltd. v. M.N.R.*, [1961] C.T.C. 237 (Ex. Ct.) the corporate taxpayer made voluntary payments to the suppliers of its subsidiary for the purpose of protecting its own goodwill. The subsidiary had defaulted on its obligations and as the taxpayer had been doing business with the suppliers it wished to continue doing so in future. (*Berman* was cited with apparent approval in the Supreme Court decision in *Stewart & Morrison Ltd. v. M.N.R.*, [1974] S.C.R. 477, at page 479.)

> The second exception is found in *Freud*. Where a taxpayer holds shares in a corporation as a trading asset and not as an investment then any loss arising from an incidental outlay, including payment on a guarantee, will be on income account. This exception is applicable in the case of those who are held to be traders in shares. For those who do not fall within this category, it will be necessary to establish that the shares were acquired as an adventure in the nature of trade. I do not

perceive this "exceptional circumstance" as constituting a window of opportunity for taxpayers seeking to deduct losses. I say this because there is a rebuttable presumption that shares are acquired as capital assets: see *Mandryk (O.) v. Canada*, [1992] 1 C.T.C. 317 (F.C.A.), at pages 323-324.

As mentioned above, a small business corporation includes a corporation that was at any time in the 12 months preceding that time a small business corporation. This rule was added so that a taxpayer would not be precluded from claiming an ABIL on the disposition of shares or debt of a small business corporation where it ceases to carry on an active business because it has become bankrupt or is being wound up prior to the disposition.

Where a taxpayer is required to honour a guarantee of the debt of a small business corporation, time may be required to enable the creditor to dispose of the debt or establish that it has become a bad debt within the provisions of ITA 50(1). In the case of a payment made by a taxpayer under a guarantee in respect of a corporation's liabilities, a debt does not arise between the corporation and the taxpayer until the payment is made. In some cases, this payment may be made subsequent to the time the corporation was a small business corporation and this may otherwise preclude any resulting capital loss from being a business investment loss. However, by virtue of ITA 39(12), a payment made by a taxpayer under a guarantee of the debts of a corporation is deemed to be a debt owing to the taxpayer by a small business corporation if the payment was made to an arm's length person and the corporation was a small business corporation both at the time the corporation's debt in respect of which the payment was made was incurred and at any time in the 12 months before the time any amount first became payable under the guarantee. When these conditions are met, a taxpayer may be eligible to claim a business investment loss on any amounts owing to the taxpayer for payments made under the guarantee, even if the small business corporation has ceased to carry on an active business.

ITA 39(12), *Aylward Estate v. R.*, [2001] 3 C.T.C. 2437 (TCC), *Becker*, [1983] C.T.C. 11 (FCA); rev'g [1981] C.T.C. 184 (FCTD), S3-F6-C1: *Interest Deductibility*, VDs 2011-0411151R11 (tax treatment of payment under a guarantee), 2011-039872117, 2005-0122544E5

¶4700 — Replacement Property Rules

Ordinarily, any insurance recovery or other compensation received for property that has been lost, stolen, or expropriated must be taken into account as proceeds of disposition and might therefore cause an income inclusion for tax purposes for the year in which such loss or destruction occurred. However, where property is stolen, lost, destroyed, or taken under statutory authority, or when a "former business property" is disposed of, a taxpayer can elect to defer the capital gain, recapture of CCA (see ¶7145), or business income in respect of a gain on eligible capital property (applicable before 2017) (see ¶7315) to the extent that the taxpayer reinvests the proceeds of disposition in a replacement property within a certain period of time.

In addition to other requirements, for the rollover election to be available, the replacement property must be acquired:

1) Where it replaces property that was stolen, lost, destroyed, or expropriated before the end of the second taxation year following the initial year, or

2) Where it replaces a "former business property", before the end of the first taxation year following the initial year.

The replacement property rules are elective; it is not sufficient to acquire similar property intended as a replacement property (and which would otherwise qualify as such) if no election is made. The election is due on or before the taxpayer's filing-due date for the taxation year in which the taxpayer acquires a replacement property. A separate election is required in respect of depreciable property, eligible capital property, (applicable before 2017), and non-depreciable capital property. The CRA is permitted to accept a late-filed election.

The CRA provides instructions for making the election in paragraph 7 of IT-259R4.

If the election is filed in the form of a letter, the letter should be attached to a paper-filed return. If the tax return is being filed electronically, the letter should be sent to the CRA Tax Centre that serves the taxpayer by the filing-due date of the T1 return for the taxation year.

Regarding the timing of filing an election where a tax return is filed in the year of disposition and the replacement property is acquired in the following year, in paragraph 3 of IT-259R4, the CRA states:

> A taxpayer is required to report any recaptured capital cost allowance, taxable capital gain or amount determined under subsection 14(1) arising from the disposition of a former property in the year of disposition where the replacement property is acquired in a subsequent taxation year. However, provided a replacement property is acquired within the specified time limits, the taxpayer may request that the income tax return for the year of disposition of the former property be reassessed to generate a refund in respect of the income taxes paid on income arising on that disposition. In order to alleviate the financial burden that might ensue from this situation, acceptable security may be provided in lieu of payment of taxes owing until the time for the final determination of taxes is made or the time period for acquiring the replacement property has expired. Where this practice is followed, the full cost of providing such security is borne by the taxpayer and the interest on the unpaid taxes will continue to accrue at the appropriate prescribed rates subject to being reduced by interest credited on any subsequent reassessment giving effect to the deferral.

The arrangements to provide security as discussed above are the responsibility of the local CRA Tax Services Office.

In computing the amount received as compensation for an expropriated property, interest paid between the time of the expropriation (i.e., the date on which the expropriating authorities took possession of the property and undertook legal action) and the time a settlement respecting the compensation for the expropriation was held to be taxable as interest income in *Elliott*, [1996] 1 C.T.C. 391 (FCTD).

The time at which a taxpayer has disposed of a property for purposes of the replacement property rules is deemed to be the earliest of (see ITA 44(2)):

1) The day the taxpayer has agreed to an amount as full compensation to the taxpayer for the property lost, destroyed, taken or sold (in VD 2012-0461511E5, the CRA states that the fact that some insurance proceeds may have already been received does not, in and of itself, affect the application of ITA 44(2) provided that the parties have not otherwise reached a final settlement in respect of the total proceeds);

2) Where a claim, suit, appeal or other proceeding has been taken before one or more tribunals or courts of competent jurisdiction, the day on which the taxpayer's compensation for the property is finally determined by those tribunals or courts; and

3) Where a claim, suit, appeal or other proceeding has not been taken before a tribunal or court of competent jurisdiction within two years of the loss, destruction, or taking of the property, the day that is two years following the day of the loss, destruction, or taking.

ITA 44(4) provides that if a taxpayer elects under either ITA 13(4) or 44(1), the taxpayer will be deemed to have elected under the other provision as well.

ITA 13(4)–(4.3), former 14(1), (6), (7), 44(1), (2), (4), (6), 220(3.2), (3.5), 248(1)"former business property", ITR 600, *Hawkins*, [1991] 2 C.T.C. 148 (FCTD), *Howatt*, [1989] 1 C.T.C. 2325 (TCC), *Elliott*, [1984] C.T.C. 2373, ITTN-25, IT-259R4: *Exchanges of property*, IT-491(SR): *Former business property*, VD 2010-0391061E5

¶4710 — Former Business Property

The replacement property rules in ITA 13(4) and 44(1) permit a taxpayer to elect to defer the recognition of income or capital gains where a "former business property" is voluntarily disposed of and a "replacement property" is acquired. A "former business property" is defined as a capital property of the taxpayer that is real property (or an interest therein) that is used by the taxpayer or a person related to the taxpayer primarily for the purpose of gaining or producing income from a business.

For a discussion of the meaning of "used...primarily for the purpose of gaining or producing income from a business", see *McKervey*, [1992] 2 C.T.C. 2015 (TCC), and paragraph 2 of IT-491. Also, see *Grove Acceptance Ltd*, [2003] 1 C.T.C. 2377 (TCC), where the Court held that a quantitative analysis of the proportion of the property used to earn business income is the principal test to be applied in determining whether the "primarily" condition has been satisfied. In *Glaxo Wellcome Inc*, [1999] 4 C.T.C. 371 (FCA), the Court found that the word "use" connotes actual utilization for some purpose, not holding for future use. Vacant land, for example, cannot meet the use requirement since it is not "used" by the taxpayer (VD 2004-0088421E5).

In VD 2003-0012135, the CRA states that, in addition to the particular time requirement that the taxpayer has to acquire a replacement property under ITA 44(1) and 13(4), the taxpayer or a person related to the taxpayer must also commence using the particular property for a use that is the same as or similar to the use to which the taxpayer or a person related to the taxpayer put the former property, within such time periods.

Excluded from being "former business property" are: a rental property, the land beneath rental property, land contiguous to a rental property used as a parking area, driveway, yard or garden or that is otherwise necessary for the use of such rental property, and a leasehold interest in any such rental property or relevant land. For this purpose, rental property means real property owned by the taxpayer, jointly or otherwise, and used by the taxpayer principally for the purpose of gaining or producing gross revenue that is rent, except for property leased to a related person and used by that person principally for some purpose other than that of gaining or producing gross revenue that is rent. Accordingly, a property would be disqualified as a "former business property" if it was used in the taxation year in which it was disposed of principally for the purpose of producing rent (even if the property was used to earn active business income, it would be disqualified as a former business property if it was used in the taxation year in which it was disposed of principally for the purpose of producing rent).

Since depreciable property does not include land, and since a "former business property" must be real property or an interest in real property (such as a leasehold interest), the replacement property rules applicable to the deferral of CCA recapture in respect of a "former business property" is of relatively narrow application and would generally apply only to certain leasehold interests.

In paragraphs 4–7 of IT-491: *Former Business Property*, the CRA states:

> Where property is used in part to earn gross revenue that is rental income and in part to earn income from a business other than rental income, the principal use of the property is determined on the basis of the facts in the particular case. The word "principally" is considered to mean "mainly" or "chiefly" and, accordingly, one should look to the main or chief purpose or intent for which the property is used by the owner. Although a pure quantum measurement, in and by itself, may not necessarily be conclusive in every case, one of the prime factors to consider is the actual or physical proportion of the property used in the two income-earning processes. In addition it may be necessary to consider other factors that are both relative and subjective. These may include: (a) income or gross revenue from each operation; (b) profits realized from each operation; (c) capital employed in and rate of return from each operation; (d) time, attention and effort expended in each operation; (e) the motivation or intent of the taxpayer in making the investment together with the ultimate utilization of the property.

> It is the Department's view that the operation of a hotel or motel is a business that provides services and that the revenue generated is not gross revenue that is rent.

> If a property that would otherwise qualify as a former business property is rented for a short period prior to its disposition, it is a question of fact as to whether or not the renting was simply an interim measure while bona fide attempts were being made to sell the property. If such is the case, the Department may accept that the status of the property as a former business property was maintained, subject to the rule in 3 above.

> Likewise, if the property remained idle for a period of time while attempts were made to sell it, the Department would consider paragraph 44(1)(b) applicable provided the property otherwise qualifies as a former business property.

An "interest" in real property is defined as including a leasehold interest in real property (except as referred to below) but as not including an interest held merely as security for a mortgage, agreement for sale, or similar obligation.

ITA 248(1)"former business property", 248(4), ITR 1102(2), IT-491(SR): *Former business property*, VDs 2014-0523551R3, 2014-0517491E5, 2011-0427411E5, 2010-0388881E5, 2004-0088421E5

¶4720 — Replacement Property (Involuntary Dispositions)

In respect of depreciable property, to qualify as a "replacement property", the depreciable property acquired must meet the following tests:

- it must be reasonable to conclude that the property was acquired by the taxpayer to replace the former property;

- it must be acquired by the taxpayer and used by the taxpayer or a person related to the taxpayer for the same or a similar use as that to which the former property was put by the taxpayer or a related person(see VD 2013-0495681C6);

- where the former property was a business asset, the replacement property must be acquired for the purpose of gaining or producing income from the same or a similar business, or for use by a related person for such a purpose;

- where the former property was a "taxable Canadian property" of the taxpayer, the replacement property must also be a "taxable Canadian property" of the taxpayer.

The description of replacement property in respect of depreciable property is parallel to that for the purposes of the replacement property rules applicable to capital property and capital gains. A "depreciable property" is defined generally as a property that was acquired by the taxpayer and in respect of which the taxpayer has been allowed (or would have been allowed if the taxpayer owned the property at the end of the year and the available-for-use rules were not applicable) a CCA deduction. Thus, for example, leasehold improvements acquired to replace a former business property can be considered replacement property.

In VD 2016-0648971E5, when asked whether a commercial rental property (land and building) could be considered replacement property in respect of expropriated farmland that was used to earn rental income, the CRA took the following position: ". . . it is our view that in order to comply with the conditions set out in paragraph 44(5)(a.1), the replacement property should have the same physical characteristics as the former property. Since the commercial rental property (which includes land and a building) does not have the same physical characteristics of the farmland (land only), the commercial rental property would not be considered replacement property within the meaning of subsection 44(5) regardless of the fact that the use of both the farmland and the commercial rental property may be used to earn rental income."

The CRA's position is that the replacement property rules require a causal relationship between the acquisition and disposition of the properties under consideration (ITTN-25, VDs 2014-0517491E5, 2010-0374241E5, 2010-0378261E5, 2008-028834117, 2002-0156414, 2003-0006993). Relevant facts the CRA will consider in determining whether a causal relationship exists include purchase financing, the date the offer to purchase is made, and the date the sale opportunity is identified. The fact that a property is purchased under a business expansion would not, in and of itself, mean that the property could not be considered a replacement property eligible for the rollover rules (VD 2008-028834117).

In VD 2014-0561101E5, the CRA stated "the fact that a rental property, such as an industrial warehouse, is replaced with another rental property, such as an office building, would not, in and by itself, preclude the office building from being considered as a replacement property for the industrial warehouse for purposes of the replacement property rules". The CRA accepts that two or more capital properties of a taxpayer may be replaced by one replacement property (IT-259R4, para. 28, VD 2016-0632001R3).

The CRA's views on satisfying the replacement property requirements are discussed in paragraph 15 of IT-259R4:

> [I]t must be reasonable to conclude that the property was acquired to replace the former property. In this regard, there must be some correlation or direct substitution, that is, a causal relationship between the disposition of a former property and the acquisition of the new property or properties. Where it cannot readily be determined whether one property is actually being replaced by another, the newly acquired property will not be considered a replacement property for the former property. For example, consider the situation where a taxpayer has a number of retail locations some of which are in the process of commencing operations while others are scheduled for closing. A new location probably would not be considered a replacement property for an old location if the business operations at the two locations are carried on simultaneously (other than for a brief transitional period, for example, while the inventory at the old location is liquidated). Generally, the geographical location of the "replacement property" is not determinative when considering whether one property is a replacement for another.

The CRA has indicated that the replacement property rollover rules in ITA 13(4)–(4.3) will generally not apply to Class 14.1 property given such property will generally not meet the definition of "former business property" in ITA 248(1) ("former business property" must be "real or immovable property") (VD 2016-0666901E5).

ITA 13(4.1)–(4.3), (21), 44(5), ITR 1101(1ag), ITTN-25, IT-259R4: *Exchanges of property*, VDs 2008-0288341I7, 2003-0012135, 2004-0088421E5, 2004-0099311E5, 2006-0213921E5, 2005-0156171E5, 2008-0288341I7, 2002-0156414, 2003-0006993

¶4730 — Applicable Rollover Rules Where Election is Filed

In respect of depreciable property, where a valid election is made, part of the proceeds of disposition of the former property is in effect transferred from the year in which the disposition occurred to the year in which the replacement property is acquired. The amount so transferred is the lesser of:

1) The amount (if any) by which the net proceeds of the former property exceeds the UCC of the class to which the former property belonged immediately before the time of its disposition (not the amount that would be the undepreciated cost, if any, at the end of the year), and

2) The amount of the taxpayer's outlay to acquire the replacement property.

The part of the proceeds of disposition, so determined, of the former property is deemed to be proceeds of disposition of property of the class in which the replacement property belongs and is deemed to arise from a disposition made either at the time the replacement property is acquired or, if later, at the time the former property is disposed of. Presumably, the proceeds of disposition relevant for the election under ITA 13(4) would be the proceeds of disposition as adjusted (if applicable) by ITA 13(21.1) (see under ¶4410).

In respect of capital gains, where a valid election is filed, special rules apply in determining the cost or capital cost of the relevant properties (the rules deal with both the replacement of depreciable property and with the replacement of capital property other than depreciable property). In the year in which an amount becomes receivable as proceeds of disposition of the capital property (the "initial year"), the gain of the taxpayer on the disposition of the taxpayer's former property is deemed to be the lesser of:

1) The proceeds of disposition of the former property less the total of the ACB of the property and any outlays and expenses incurred in making the disposition, or, where the property is depreciable property, the proceeds of disposition minus the lesser of i) the proceeds of disposition of the former property determined before any reallocation of the proceeds of disposition under ITA 44(6), and ii) the total of the ACB of the property and any outlays and expenses incurred in making the disposition; and

2) The proceeds of disposition of the former property minus the total of the cost of the replacement property or, if the property is depreciable property, the capital cost of such property, and any outlays and expenses incurred in making the disposition.

The gain on the disposition of the former property will therefore be less than the gain normally arising on such a disposition where the cost of the replacement property exceeds the ACB of the former property.

The cost to the taxpayer of the new property acquired to replace the former property is deemed to be:

a) The cost to the taxpayer or, in the case of depreciable property, the capital cost to the taxpayer, of the replacement property otherwise determined; less

b) The amount, if any, by which,

(i) the amount by which the proceeds of disposition of the former property exceed the total of its ACB and any outlays and expenses made or incurred in making the disposition, or, where the property is depreciable property and is disposed of after February 15, 1984, the amount by which the proceeds of disposition exceed the lesser of: 1) the proceeds of disposition of the former property determined before any reallocation of the proceeds of disposition under ITA 44(6); and 2) the total of the ACB of the property and any outlays and expenses incurred in making the disposition, exceeds

> (ii) the amount by which the proceeds of disposition of the former property exceed the total of the cost to the taxpayer, or in the case of depreciable property, the capital cost to the taxpayer, of the replacement property and any outlays and expenses made or incurred in making the disposition.

¶4740 — Disposition of Land and Building: Reallocation of Proceeds

Where the property disposed of is a former business property that was in part a building and in part land (or an interest therein) subjacent to or immediately contiguous to and necessary for the use of the building and the proceeds of disposition of one such part exceed the ACB of that part, the taxpayer may elect to reallocate any part of such difference to the proceeds of disposition of the other part of the property in question. The amount eligible for reallocation is limited to the excess of proceeds of disposition otherwise determined of one or the other of the components over its ACB.

If, for example, the proceeds of disposition of land determined without reference to ITA 44(6) exceed its ACB, a taxpayer can elect to treat all or a portion of the excess as being proceeds of disposition of the building component of the former business property and thereby defer recognition of all or a portion of the accrued capital gain with respect to the land. See paragraph 29 of IT-259R4 for an example of the operation of ITA 44(6).

The election is due by the filing-due date of the taxpayer's T1 return for the year that the replacement property is acquired. If the tax return is filed electronically, the letter should be sent to the CRA Tax Centre that serves the taxpayer by the filing-due date of the T1 return for the taxation year. The CRA is permitted to accept a late-filed election.

ITA 44(6), 220(3.2), (3.5), ITR 600, VD 2002-0173815

¶4800 — Miscellaneous Loss Denial and Limitation Rules

¶4810 — Losses on Transfers between Affiliated Persons

By virtue of the many stop-loss rules contained in the ITA, losses on transfers between a taxpayer and an "affiliated person" are normally suspended for tax purposes until the property is sold to a non-affiliated party. The concept of "persons" for tax purposes includes both natural persons and corporations. For some purposes, including the affiliation rules, partnerships are also treated as persons.

ITA 13(21.2), 18(15), 40(3.3), 40(3.6), 40(2)(g)(i), 251.1

¶4811 — *Definition of Affiliated Persons*

¶4811.1 — Individuals

Persons are considered to be affiliated with themselves. Also, an individual and a spouse or common-law partner of the individual are affiliated with each other. A corporation is affiliated with:

> 1) An individual by whom the corporation is controlled, and if applicable, their spouse or common-law partner, and

> 2) Each member of an affiliated group of individuals by which the corporation is controlled, and, if applicable, the spouse or common-law partner of a member of the group.

An affiliated group of persons is defined in ITA 251.1(2) as a group of persons each member of which is affiliated with every other member.

For example, F, an individual, controls one corporation ("F Ltd") alone, and controls a second corporation ("FG Ltd") as a member of a group that consists of F and G, and another individual. F is a spouse of a third individual, M, but not of G. F and M are affiliated persons under ITA 251.1(1)(a). F Ltd is affiliated with F under ITA 251.1(1)(b)(i) and with M under 251.1(1)(b)(iii). Since F and G are not affiliated with one another (and are thus not an affiliated group), FG Ltd is not affiliated with either F or G.

ITA 251.1(1)(b)

¶4811.2 — Partnerships

A partnership is affiliated with a majority interest partner of the partnership. A majority interest partner of a partnership is defined as any member of a partnership whose share of income of the partnership for the most recently completed fiscal period (or for the current fiscal period if it is the first fiscal period of the partnership) is greater than 50%. A majority interest partner could also be a partner who, in combination with other partners whom they are affiliated with, would be entitled to more than 50% of the total amount that would be paid out to partners on the windup of the partnership.

Effectively, any person affiliated with a person who holds a majority interest in a partnership is also a majority-interest partner, and thus is affiliated with the partnership under ITA 251.1(1)(e).

Two partnerships are affiliated with each other if: i) the same person is a majority-interest partner of both partnerships, ii) a majority-interest partner of one partnership is affiliated with each member of a majority-interest group of partners of the other partnership, or iii) each member of a majority-interest group of partners of each partnership is affiliated with at least one member of a majority-interest group of partners of the other partnership.

The possibility that a partnership may have more than one "majority-interest group of partners" means that the interests of all partners, and of all persons affiliated with a partner, should be carefully considered in determining whether two partnerships (or a partnership and a corporation) are affiliated.

In VD 2013-0515651E5, the CRA considers a situation in which a corporation is controlled by a single person who is the majority interest partner of a partnership. The CRA concluded that although the corporation and the partnership would not be affiliated with each other under ITA 251.1(1)(d), the corporation and the partnership could be affiliated with each other under ITA 251.1(1)(e) "based on the definition of majority interest partner [in subsection 248(1)] which is broadened by the use of the concept of affiliated persons". The CRA was also of the view that if the partnership had *de facto* control over the corporation, the corporation and the partnership would be affiliated with each other under ITA 251.1(1)(b)(i).

ITA 251.1(1)(e), (f), 248(1)"majority interest partner"

¶4811.3 — Trusts

When considering questions of affiliation involving trusts, the general rule in the ITA is that any reference to a trust is also a reference to the trustee is not applicable. ITA 251.1(4)(c) provides that two trusts are not affiliated simply because they share the same trustee. Also, a person is not affiliated with a trust simply because that person is affiliated with the trustee of the trust.

A trust and a majority interest beneficiary of the trust are affiliated with each other pursuant to ITA 251.1(1)(g). A majority interest beneficiary of a trust is defined as a beneficiary whose interest in the income of the trust, either alone or in combination with that of all persons with whom they are affiliated, has a fair market value of more than 50% of all income interests in the trust. It can also be a person that passes the same test in respect of a capital interest in the trust. A trust is also affiliated with a person that is affiliated with a majority interest beneficiary of the trust if ITA 251.1 were read without reference to ITA 251.1(1)(g). Thus, two trusts are not affiliated under ITA 251.1(1)(g) simply because they share a majority interest beneficiary.

A sole beneficiary of a trust is, by virtue of being a majority interest beneficiary of the trust, affiliated with the trust.

Two trusts are affiliated with each other if a contributor to one trust is affiliated with a contributor to the other trust, and i) a majority interest beneficiary of one of the trusts is affiliated with a majority interest beneficiary of the other trust, ii) a majority interest beneficiary of one of the trusts is affiliated with each member of a majority interest group of beneficiaries of another trust, or iii) each member of the majority interest group of beneficiaries of each trust is affiliated with a least one member of a majority interest group of beneficiaries of the other trust. A contributor to a trust is defined as a person who has transferred or loaned property to the trust in any manner whatever; however, if the person deals at arm's length with the trust and is not immediately after that time a majority interest beneficiary in the trust, there are two exceptions to being considered a "contributor" to the trust. These exceptions are made if a loan is made at a reasonable rate of interest or if property is transferred for fair market value consideration.

Two trusts are affiliated where a corporation that is a majority interest beneficiary of one trust is controlled by the other trust. For example, Trust B owns all of the shares of Canco, a corporation. Canco is a majority interest beneficiary of Trust C. Trust B controls Canco, and thus is affiliated with it. Trust C is also affiliated with Canco, because Canco is a majority interest beneficiary of Trust C. Since Trust B and Canco are affiliated otherwise than solely because of ITA 251.1(1)(g), their affiliation means that Trust B is affiliated with Trust C.

ITA 251.1(4)(d) provides rules that apply in determining whether a person is affiliated with a trust. ITA 251.1(d)(i) maximizes the amount of income or capital of the trust a person may receive as a result of a discretionary power when determining whether a person is affiliated with a trust. ITA 251.1(4)(d)(ii) ensures that a beneficiary under a trust may transfer funds or property to the trust for fair market value consideration and not be considered in all cases to be a contributor to the trust. Pursuant to ITA 251.1(4)(d)(iii), a trust is not a majority interest beneficiary of another trust unless the first trust has an interest as a beneficiary in the income or capital of the other trust. Finally, ITA 251.1(4)(d)(iv) expands the categories of individuals who are considered to be affiliated with one another.

As a result, individuals who are connected by a blood relationship, common-law partnership, or adoption will also be considered to be affiliated with one another for these purposes. By virtue of these rules, a trust that shares a majority interest beneficiary with another trust is not a majority interest beneficiary of the other trust unless the person has an interest as a beneficiary in either the income or capital of the other trust.

A deceased person is not affiliated with his or her estate. Additionally, after the death of a taxpayer, the deceased person is not affiliated with his or her spouse or common-law partner (VD 2004-0105471E5). If a testamentary trust acquires shares of a corporation from a deceased's estate and the remaining shares are redeemed by the corporation, the CRA has stated the estate and the corporation would not be affiliated after the redemption even if the estate and the trust have the same trustees (VD 2002-0151025).

ITA 251.1(1)(g), (h), 251.1(4), 2004 Technical Notes, VDs 2009-0330501E5 (whether an individual's spouse is affiliated with the individual's corporation that is controlled by a trust), 2006-0185581C6 and 2004-0105471E5 (determining the majority-interest beneficiary of an unadministered estate)

¶4812 — *Transfers between Affiliated Persons*

¶4812.1 — Superficial Losses

ITA 40(2)(g)(i) provides that where a taxpayer incurs a "superficial loss" as defined in ITA 54, the loss is denied. A superficial loss is sustained by a taxpayer in the following circumstances:

1. capital property has been disposed of by the taxpayer at a loss;

2. the same or identical property is acquired during the period beginning 30 days before the disposition and ending 30 days after the disposition;

3. the substituted property must have been acquired by the taxpayer or a person affiliated with the taxpayer (note that an affiliated person does not include a child of an individual); and

4. at the end of the period ending 30 days after the disposition, the substituted property, or a right to acquire such property, was owned by the taxpayer or a person affiliated with the taxpayer.

ITA 40(2)(g)(i) deems the amount of a superficial loss to be nil, thereby precluding its deduction by the taxpayer. The amount of the denied loss is added to the cost of the substituted property under ITA 53(1)(f). A superficial loss is generally only applicable to individuals, and specifically excludes a loss to which the stop-loss rule contained in ITA 40(3.4) applies.

A loss on foreign currency is not a superficial loss (see VDs 2008-0280111I7 and 2017-0705201C6).

ITA 40(2)(g)(i), ITA 53(1)(f), 54"superficial loss", VDs 2009-0327081C6, 2003-0017075, 2001-0106905, 2003-0017075, 2009-0327081C6

¶4812.2 — Transfers of Depreciable Property between Affiliated Persons

Stop-loss rules apply to transfers of depreciable property between affiliated persons by virtue of ITA 13(21.2). The stop-loss rule in ITA 13(21.2) only applies if there is an accrued loss on the transferred property. In particular, ITA 13(21.2) applies when a person disposes of depreciable property, and:

1) The proceeds of disposition, as otherwise determined, are less than the lesser of: i) the capital cost of the property, and ii) the proportion of the UCC of the class to which the transferred property belonged immediately before the transfer that the FMV of the property is of the total value of all properties of the class, and

2) The transferor, or an affiliated person, holds or has a right to acquire, the transferred property on the 30th day after the disposition.

Specifically excepted are various deemed dispositions that are excluded from the category of transactions otherwise within the definition of a "superficial loss" in ITA 54. The proceeds of disposition for the transferred property would be determined after applying ITA 13(21.1), which reallocates the proceeds as between a building and the underlying land in certain circumstances.

When the above conditions are met:

1) The rollover rules in ITA 85 and 97 do not apply to the disposition;

2) The proceeds of disposition of the property for the transferor are deemed to be the lesser the two amounts listed in (1) above;

3) Where more than one depreciable property of the same class is disposed of at the same time, the transferor is required to indicate the order in which the dispositions occurred (otherwise, the CRA will designate the order of disposition);

4) The excess of the lesser of the capital cost of the transferred property and the proportional amount of UCC of that class over the proceeds of disposition of the transferred property as otherwise determined (e.g. fair market value of the property) constitutes the capital cost of a notional property, included in the *same class* as that from which the transferred property came, acquired by the transferor immediately before the taxation year in which the transfer took place. The transferor is permitted to claim CCA after the transfer on the amount of the deferred loss. Because the notional property is in the same class as the property disposed of, any accrued terminal loss can be realized only when one of the loss triggering events in ITA 13(21.2)(e)(iii) arises (see below); and

5) For purposes of the "available-for-use" rule, the "new" property is considered to be available for use by the transferor at the time the transferred property becomes available for use by the acquirer.

The acquirer is deemed to have acquired the property at the capital cost of the transferor and to have claimed, as CCA, the difference between that capital cost and the fair market value of the property (this rule is relevant in computing recapture on a future disposition of the property).

The "new" property (i.e., the deferred loss) is deemed to belong to the transferor until the earliest of the following events: i) a subsequent disposition of the transferred property to a person who is neither the transferor nor an affiliated person (provided that neither the transferor nor an affiliated person acquires the property, or has a right to acquire the property, within 30 days following the subsequent disposition); ii) a change in the property's use from income-earning to a non-income-earning purpose; or, iii) a deemed disposition of the transferred property due to ceasing to be resident in Canada or due to commencing or ceasing to be exempt from tax. When any of the latter events arise, any portion of the notional property (i.e., the deferred loss) not claimed as CCA may be eligible for recognition as a terminal loss provided the transferor has no other properties of the same class.

ITA 13(21.2), IT-291R3 (para. 23): *Transfer of property to a corporation under subsection 85(1)*, VDs 2005-0125501E5

¶4812.3 — Transfer of Shares of a Corporation to the Issuing Corporation

Pursuant to ITA 40(3.6), a loss is generally denied on a disposition of shares to the issuer of the shares where the shareholder is affiliated with the issuer immediately after the disposition (a special rule is required in this case because on a share repurchase by the issuer, the relevant shares are typically cancelled and the transferee does not own the transferred property at the end of the relevant 30-day period). This rule may apply, for example, in the case of the redemption or purchase for cancellation of a share by the corporation.

ITA 40(3.6) preserves the amount of any denied loss by adding it to the cost of any shares of the transferee owned by the transferor after the disposition of shares to the transferee corporation. This rule applies equally to individuals, corporations, and trusts. The ACB addition is spread among all shares of the issuer owned by the taxpayer based on their relative fair market values immediately after the disposition. If the transferor does not hold any shares of the affiliated issuer after the transfer, there is no cost base adjustment and recognition of the loss is not only deferred but is eliminated.

An important exception to ITA 40(3.6) applies when the legal representative of a deceased taxpayer has disposed of property at a loss and has made an election in respect of the loss under ITA 164(6) to have the loss applied in the terminal return of the deceased taxpayer.

ITA 40(3.6)

¶4812.4 — Transfers of Inventory between Affiliated Persons

The recognition of superficial losses sustained by a taxpayer in respect of non-capital property held as an adventure or concern in the nature of trade (i.e., held as inventory and taxed on income account, such as speculative land; see ¶4015) is denied.

A superficial loss under these provisions is a loss realized by a taxpayer on the sale or transfer of a property (other than a capital property) where the same or identical property (referred to as "substituted property") is acquired by the taxpayer or a non-arm's length person or partnership during the period beginning 30 days before and ending 30 days after the disposition, and is held by the taxpayer or the person or partnership at the end of that period. ITA 18(14) sets out the conditions under which certain losses of adventurers in trade are deferred, and ITA 18(15) describes the loss deferral. Any loss that would otherwise be deductible with respect to a property that is preserved in the transferor's hands is deductible by the transferor upon the first occurrence of any of the following events:

1) A subsequent disposition of the property to a person that is neither the transferor nor a person affiliated with the transferor (provided that for 30 days after that subsequent disposition neither the transferor nor an affiliated person owns either the substituted property or an identical property acquired after the beginning of the period described above); or

2) A "deemed disposition" of the property under ITA 128.1 (change of residence) or ITA 149(10) (change of taxable status).

ITA 18(13)–(15)

¶4820 — Dividend Stop-Loss Rules

¶4821 — *Capital Loss on Shares held by an Individual*

A capital loss incurred on the disposition of shares held by an individual may be reduced where capital dividends have been received on the shares. Generally, the amount by which the capital loss is reduced is the lesser of: 1) the total amount of capital dividends received by the individual on the shares; and 2) the excess of the loss otherwise determined over the total of all taxable dividends received by the individual on the shares. As a result, the dividend stop-loss rules only apply to a capital loss realized by an individual on the disposition of shares if the individual has previously received capital dividends on the shares.

Generally, portfolio investment dividends on shares that have been owned for more than a year are excluded for purposes of determining the amount of the capital loss reduction under the dividend stop-loss rules. For a dividend received on shares held by an individual to be excluded for these purposes, it must meet the following requirements: the dividend was received by the individual at a time when the individual and persons with whom the individual did not deal at arm's length held no more than 5% of any class of the dividend payer's shares; and the dividend was paid on a share owned by the individual throughout the 365-day period that ended immediately before the disposition.

ITA 112(3), (3.01), (6.1)

¶4822 — *Capital Loss on Shares held by an Estate*

Generally, a capital loss incurred by an estate in the year following an individual's death may be carried back to offset any capital gains reported on the deceased's final T1 return arising from the deemed disposition of capital property at the deceased's death. However, the dividend stop-loss rules limit the capital loss arising on a redemption of shares by an estate where the estate has received a capital dividend on the shares that results in the elimination of tax on the deemed dividend. If the capital dividend account is used to fully eliminate the tax on the deemed dividend, the capital loss on the disposition is reduced, such that it cannot fully offset the related capital gain on the deemed disposition of the shares in the deceased's final return.

Generally, the reduction in the capital loss is equal to the capital dividends received on the shares minus 50% of the lesser of: 1) the deemed capital gain on the shares included in the deceased's final return, and 2) the capital loss realized by the estate on the disposition of the shares within the first taxation year of the estate.

There is an exception to this stop-loss rule if the shares are "grandfathered", which may permit the full loss to be carried back to the deceased's final return. To qualify as "grandfathered shares", the share disposition must occur in accordance with a written agreement (generally, a shareholder or buy-sell agreement) made before April 27, 1995, or the corporation must have been a beneficiary of a life insurance policy that insured the life of the individual on April 26, 1995, where a main purpose of the life insurance policy was to fund, in whole or in part, a redemption, acquisition, or cancellation of the shares by the corporation that issued the shares.

Generally, portfolio investment dividends on shares that have been owned for more than a year are excluded for purposes of determining the amount of the capital loss reduction under the dividend stop-loss rules. For a dividend received on shares held by an individual's estate to be excluded for these purposes, it must meet the following requirements: the dividend was received by the estate at a time when the estate and persons with whom the estate did not deal at arm's length held no more than 5% of any class of the dividend payer's shares and the dividend was paid on shares owned by the estate throughout the 365-day period that ended immediately before the disposition.

ITA 164(6), 112(3.2), (3.31), (6.1)

Chapter 5 — Rental Income

Contents

¶5000 Rental Income (T1 Lines 126 and 160)

    ¶5005 U.S. Rental Income

¶5100 Real Property Rental: Business or Property Income?

    ¶5110 Nature of Rental Income

    ¶5120 Income Tax Consequences

¶5200 Rental Expenses

    ¶5210 Current vs. Capital Expense

    ¶5220 Deductible Rental Expenses

    ¶5230 Non-Deductible Expenses

    ¶5240 Capital Cost Allowance (CCA) (Form T776: Lines 9936, 9947, 9948, Charts A–F)

    ¶5250 Rental Expenses: Special Situations

¶5300 Rental Losses

¶5400 Principal Residence: Change-in-Use Rules

    ¶5410 Change in Use from Personal to Income Producing

    ¶5420 Change in Use from Income-Producing to Personal

    ¶5430 Partial Changes in Use

¶5500 Non-Residents Electing under Section 216

    ¶5510 Alternative re Rents

    ¶5520 Meaning of "Timber Royalty"

    ¶5530 Optional Method of Payment

    ¶5540 Subsequent Sale of Canadian Property

    ¶5550 Rental or Other Business

¶5600 Completing Form T776, *Statement of Real Estate Rentals*

    ¶5610 Identification and Details of Other Co-Owners

    ¶5620 Rental Income (Form T776: Lines 8141, 8230, 8299)

    ¶5630 Rental Expenses

ental Income (T1: Lines 126 and 160)

income (or loss) that is not business income is reported on Line 126 (net rental income) and Line 160 (gross l income) of the T1 return. Form T776, *Statement of Real Estate Rentals* (or a similar statement) showing rental income and expenses for the year should be included with a taxpayer's paper-filed return. If the taxpayer was a member of a partnership, include amounts shown in Boxes 23 and 26 of the taxpayer's T5013 or T5013A slip, or amounts the partnership allocated to the taxpayer in its financial statements.

Generally, an individual is required to use the accrual method of calculating income from business or property, in accordance with generally accepted accounting principles and business practices. Therefore, rental income is included into income in the year in which it is earned or due (not when it is received), and expenses are deducted from income in the year in which they are incurred (not when they are paid). For example, if an owner receives rental income in advance that relates to future years, it may be excluded from rental income in the year received and included in income in the later year or years to which it relates. The cash method is permitted only if the result would be virtually the same as the income (or loss) calculated using the accrual method. If the accrual and cash methods would produce a different income or loss amount, the accrual method must be used.

¶5005 — U.S. Rental Income

Canadian residents who rent out a residence located in the United States are subject to tax in Canada on any net rental income earned on the rental, just as they would be for a rental property located in Canada. In addition, the Canadian owner will be subject to a 30% withholding tax in the U.S. on their gross rental revenue, which is required to be deducted by the tenant or property manager and remitted to the U.S. Internal Revenue Service (IRS).

Taxpayers can avoid the 30% withholding tax in the U.S. by electing to pay tax on net rental income at the U.S. graduated tax rates, which allows the taxpayer to report their net rental income, after claiming deductions related to owning and operating the rental property during the rental period. The taxpayer makes the "net rental income" election by filing a statement with his or her timely filed U.S. tax return (Form 1040NR) for the year. A taxpayer who makes a "net rental income" election is also required to provide the tenant or property manager a completed copy of Form W-8ECI, *Certificate of Foreign Person's Claim That Income Is Effectively Connected With the Conduct of a Trade or Business in the United States*.

Taxpayers who make this election are required to file a U.S. tax return to report and pay U.S. tax on net rental income. Rental income earned from U.S. rental properties must also be included in rental income on the taxpayer's Canadian T1 return. Generally, the income is calculated in the same way as for a Canadian rental property, and the rules and limitations discussed below regarding Canadian rental property also apply to U.S. rental properties (e.g., deductible and non-deductible expenses, limitations on rental losses, etc.). Amounts are required to be reported in Canadian dollars. Dollar amounts for income transactions should be converted into Canadian dollars using the Bank of Canada exchange rate on the day of the transaction (www.bankofcanada.ca). The taxpayer may be able to claim a foreign tax credit for U.S. taxes paid (see ¶11010, Line 405, federal foreign tax credit).

ITA 9, 20, IT-95R, Form W-8ECI, IRS Publication 515: *Withholding of Tax on Non-resident Aliens and Foreign Entities*, IRS Publication 527: *Residential Rental Property*, www.irs.gov

¶5100 — Real Property Rental: Business or Property Income?

¶5110 — Nature of Rental Income

Depending on the size of the operation and the extent of additional services provided to the occupants by the owner or landlord, rental income derived from renting real estate may be considered either income from property or income from a business. "Business" is defined very broadly in the ITA and includes a profession, calling, trade, manufacture, or undertaking of any kind whatever, as well as "an adventure or concern in the nature of trade". In *Dansereau v. R.*, [2002] 1 C.T.C. 19 (FCA); rev'g [2000] 1 C.T.C. 2582 (TCC), the Court held that the expansive definition of "business" in ITA 248(1) is not exhaustive and "extends to any endeavour that occupies time, labour and attention with a view to profit."

Income from property typically includes interest, dividends, rents, royalties, etc. "Property" is defined in the ITA as "property of any kind whatever whether real or personal, immovable or movable, tangible or intangible, or corporeal or incorporeal and, without restricting the generality of the foregoing, includes: (a) a right of any kind whatever, a share or a chose in action, (b) unless a contrary intention is evident, money, (c) a timber resource property, (d) the work in progress of a business that is a profession and (e) the goodwill of a business, as referred to in subsection 13(34)".

Essentially, it is a question of fact whether income from real property is considered property income or business income. In general, the number and kinds of services provided in relation to the rental of the property will determine whether the income is property or business income. If only basic services are provided to rental occupants, the rental income is likely to be property income. Basic services include things such as heat, light, parking, and laundry facilities. Where an individual rents various apartments in a building, the CRA considers the following to be basic services: heat, water, elevator service, lobby telephone, parking, laundry facilities, general building maintenance, maintenance of adjacent areas, and maintenance of appliances and furnishings provided with the rental units.

If services are provided over and above those usually provided by a landlord (for example, cleaning of areas that are not common areas, security, or meals), rental income earned is more likely to be business income. In addition, providing the following services may be a significant factor in determining whether the owner operates a business: meals and drinks for tenants, on-site restaurant or lounge, cleaning services for the rental accommodation, maid services, fresh linens and washroom supplies, security services, or mail and parcel pickup and delivery. Generally, the more services provided, the more likely that the income will be considered business income. The number of rental properties being managed does not affect the classification of the income, nor does the amount of time the individual spends managing the property.

The CRA discusses the criteria for determining whether a rental operation carried on by an individual is a source of business income or property income in paragraphs 2 to 8 of IT-434R (archived): *Rental of Real Property by Individual*:

> 2. The delegation by the owner of real property of its management and supervision to an agent will not, in itself, alter the nature of the rental income. If the renting of the property would have constituted a business when carried on by the owner himself, it will still be a business when undertaken by an agent on the owner's behalf.

> 3. Where the renting of real property to others by an individual is incidental to, or is part of the fabric of, his business, the renting will be regarded as a business operation and any rental income or loss will form part of the individual's business income or loss; examples are the renting of temporarily unused space in the taxpayer's factory or warehouse and the renting of land held for future expansion.

> 4. Where it is not part of, or incidental to, an existing business, the renting of real property by an individual is not, in itself, indicative of a business operation. It will be regarded as a business operation only when the landlord supplies or makes available to tenants services of one kind or another to such an extent that the rental operation has gone beyond the mere rental of real property. Accordingly, where the nature of a particular rental operation must be determined, it is the number and kinds of services supplied that will have to be ascertained. The size or number of properties being rented, the extent to which their management or supervision occupies the owner's time, whether the accommodation is rented bare or provided with appliances or even partly or completely furnished — none of these are factors to be taken into account in determining if the operation is a business.

> 5. Where a building is rented *en bloc* (e.g., an office building), with the landlord providing (in addition, of course, to the accommodation) only maintenance of the building as such and perhaps heat and air conditioning, the rental clearly is one

of property and does not constitute the carrying on of a business. The same situation is considered to exist where a building is rented piecemeal (e.g. an apartment block) and the tenants are provided with only those basic services which, by custom, have come to be regarded as an inherent part of that kind of property rental, e.g.: heat, water, elevator service, telephone in lobby, indoor or outdoor parking spaces, laundry room with equipment for tenants, maintenance of the building itself (including janitor and window washing service, repainting of apartments), maintenance of adjacent areas (including snow and garbage removal service) and maintenance of any appliances and furnishings provided in the rented accommodation.

6. If, however, services additional to those mentioned above are provided, it is possible that the landlord may be carrying on a business rather than merely renting real property, and the more services he provides the more it becomes arguable that this is so. At this point, both the basic services and the number and kinds of additional services provided for, or made available to, tenants must be considered. For example, the landlord of an office building may not only supply the services basic to its operation but, in addition, office cleaning and protective services in respect of the rented accommodation; these latter could be the decisive factors in a determination that a business is being carried on. In the case of an apartment block, it is the extent to which basic and additional services are supplied to tenants that will determine if its operation is a business. These latter may include, but are not necessarily limited to, the supplying of meals and drinks to tenants, a restaurant or lounge on the premises, cleaning service for the rented accommodation (as distinct from the building itself), maid service for tenants, a constant supply of fresh linens, and washroom supplies, commissionaire or other protective service, a mail and parcel pick-up and delivery service, etc.

7. The operation of a rooming or lodging house that does no more than rent rooms is likely to be a rental business because of the supplying of cleaning and maid services, linens, washroom supplies and so on. The operation of a trailer court or campground where all services are provided, e.g., laundromat, cafeteria, swimming pool, showers, playgrounds, etc. and the operation of a hotel, motel or boarding house of any size would be a business, but not a rental business due to the magnitude of services provided.

8. Where two or more individuals participate in a rental operation, the question of whether it is a business still must be determined according to the principles outlined above. The fact that a rental operation is carried on by what appears, or purports, to be a partnership does not, in itself, justify an assumption that the operation therefore must be a business. Where, however, the application of those principles indicates that a rental operation is a business, the fact that the relationship of its owners appears, or is claimed, to be that of partners rather than merely co-owners tends to confirm the other indications that it is indeed a business (see the comments in IT-90, *What is a Partnership?*).

ITA 9(1), 9(2), 248(1)(b), IT-434R: *Rental of Real Property by Individual*, IT-459: *Adventure or Concern in the Nature of Trade*, Guide T4002, Guide T4036, John Durnford, "The Distinction Between Income from Business and Income from Property, and the Concept of Carrying on Business," (1991), vol. 39, no. 5 *Canadian Tax Journal* 1131–1205

¶5120 — Income Tax Consequences

It is important to properly classify a taxpayer's rental income because there may be different income tax consequences depending on whether rental income is determined to be income from business or income from property. Outlined below are some of the income tax consequences which flow from that determination.

¶5121 — *Capital Cost Allowance*

Special rules limit the amount of capital cost allowance that may be claimed on rental property and leasing property. For the purposes of calculating rental income, capital cost allowance cannot exceed the net rental income available, such that that a rental loss cannot be created or increased by claiming capital cost allowance. There is no similar limitation for capital cost allowance in calculating business income. For more information, see ¶5240, ¶7165 and IT-195R4: *Rental Property — Capital Cost Allowance Restrictions*.

ITR 1100(11)–(14.2), IT-195R4: *Rental Property — Capital Cost Allowance Restrictions*, CRA Guide T4036

¶5122 — *Earned Income*

Rental income from real property, whether business or property income, constitutes "earned income" for the purposes of calculating a taxpayer's allowable RRSP deduction. However, for purposes of calculating the child care expense deduction, "earned income" includes "income from all businesses carried on either alone or as a partner actively engaged in the business", but does not include income from property. Thus, rental income can be included in "earned income" only where it constitutes income from a business that is carried on either as a sole proprietor or by a partner actively engaged in the business.

ITA 63,146(1)"earned income", Folio S1-F3-C1: *Child Care Expense Deduction*

¶5123 — *Income Attribution Rules*

The attribution rules in ITA 74.1(1) and (2) provide that any income or loss arising from property transferred either to the transferor's spouse, common-law partner, or to a child under 18 years is attributed back to, and deemed to be the income or a loss of, the transferor. These attribution rules only apply when transferred property produces income from "property", such as rentals. They do not apply to attribute income from a business, even if the business operates with some or all of the property obtained originally from the transferor. See ¶14220 for a discussion of the attribution rules in ITA 74.1.

¶5124 — *Non-Resident Taxpayer*

Where the rental of real property by a non-resident individual is a business carried on in Canada, the taxable income will be computed pursuant to ITA 115(1). The individual will be taxable under Part I of the ITA and pay provincial income tax on the rental income earned in a province. In calculating taxable income, the individual will be eligible for Part I deductions. Where the non-resident's rental operation is found not to be a business or part of a business, the individual will be subject to Part XIII tax on the gross amount of rent received (subject to alternative treatment pursuant to ITA 216, discussed at ¶5500).

IT-420R3: *Non-Residents — Income Earned in Canada*

¶5125 — *Travel Expenses*

Travel expenses are deductible only in limited circumstances for the purposes of calculating rental income from property. See below under ¶5220.11 (Travel Costs) and ¶5220.13 (Motor Vehicle Expenses).

ITA 6(1)(e), 18(1)(h), Guide T4002, Guide T4036, IT-521R: *Motor Vehicle Expenses Claimed by Self-Employed Individuals*

¶5126 — *Allocation of Rental Income to a Province*

Where an individual earns or receives rental income from real property in a province or territory, all rental income, wherever earned or received, is deemed to be income earned in the province or territory in which the individual resides on the last day of the taxation year, if the rental income constitutes income from property. On the other hand, if the rental income constitutes business income, the rental income must be allocated to the permanent establishment in the province through which it was earned in accordance with Part XXVI of the Regulations.

ITA 120(4), ITR 2600–2607, IT-434R: *Rental of Real Property by Individual*

¶5200 — Rental Expenses

Both current and capital expenses may be deducted against rental income. Current expenses are recurring expenses that provide short-term benefits and are deductible in the year incurred. Current expenses include mortgage interest (but not principal), property taxes, utility costs, house insurance, maintenance costs, advertising, and property management fees. In contrast, capital expenses are expenses which provide an enduring benefit. Capital expenses include the purchase price of the rental property (excluding land), furniture and fixtures and enduring repairs. Generally, capital expenses are depreciated over a period of several years as capital cost allowance (CCA). See ¶5240 for more information on calculating and claiming capital cost allowance for rental property.

ITA 18, 20, Guide T4036

¶5210 — Current vs. Capital Expense

Renovations and expenses that extend the useful life of a property or improve it beyond its original condition are usually capital expenses. However, an increase in a property's market value because of an expense is not an important factor in deciding whether the expenses are capital or current. To decide whether an amount is a current or a capital expense, ask the following questions (reproduced from Guide T4036, *Rental Income*):

Criteria	Capital expenses	Current expenses
Does the expense provide a lasting benefit?	A capital expense generally gives a lasting benefit or advantage. For example, the cost of putting vinyl siding on the exterior walls of a wooden house is a capital expense.	A current expense is one that usually recurs after a short period. For example, the cost of painting the exterior of a wooden house is a current expense.
Does the expense maintain or improve the property?	The cost of a repair that improves a property beyond its original condition is probably a capital expense. If you replace wooden steps with concrete steps, the cost is a capital expense.	An expense that simply restores a property to its original condition is usually a current expense. For example, the cost of repairing wooden steps is a current expense.
Is the expense for a part of a property or for a separate asset?	The cost of replacing a separate asset within a property is a capital expense. For example, the cost of buying a refrigerator to use in your rental operation is a capital expense. This is the case because a refrigerator is a separate asset and is not a part of the building.	The cost of repairing a property by replacing one of its parts is usually a current expense. For instance, electrical wiring is part of a building. Therefore, an amount you spend to rewire is usually a current expense, as long as the rewiring does not improve the property beyond its original condition.
What is the value of the expense? (Use this test only if you cannot determine whether an expense is capital or current by considering the three previous tests)	Compare the cost of the expense to the value of the property. Generally, if the cost is considerable in relation to the value of the property, it is a capital expense.	This test is not a determining factor by itself. You might spend a large amount of money for maintenance and repairs to your property all at once. If this cost was for ordinary maintenance that was not done when it was necessary, it is a maintenance expense, and you deduct it as a current expense.

Criteria	Capital expenses	Current expenses
Is the expense for repairs to the used property that you acquired made to put it in a suitable condition for use?	The cost of repairing used property that you acquired to put it in a suitable condition to use in your business is considered a capital expense even though in other circumstances it would be treated as a current operating expense.	Where the repairs were for ordinary maintenance of a property you already had in your business, the expense is usually current.
Is the expense for repairs made to an asset in order to sell it?	The cost of repairs made in anticipation of selling a property or as a condition of sale is regarded as a capital expense.	Where the repairs would have been made anyway, but a sale was negotiated during the course of the repairs or after their completion, the expense is considered current.

¶5220 — Deductible Rental Expenses

Below is a listing of expenses incurred to earn rental income and a discussion of the treatment of the expense for tax purposes. Generally, the expenses are listed in the order that they appear on Form T776.

¶5220.1 — *Prepaid Expenses*

ITA 18(9) requires taxpayers to deduct certain prepaid expenses in the taxation year to which they can reasonably be considered to relate, and not in any earlier taxation year in which they may in fact have been made or incurred. The CRA provides the meaning of a prepaid expense in IT-417R2: *Prepaid Expenses and Deferred Charges*, as follows:

> A prepaid expense occurs where an outlay or expense has been made or incurred by a taxpayer in a particular taxation year and it represents, for example, all or part of the cost of services which will be provided to the taxpayer after the fiscal year end. For example, a premium paid in advance to obtain a fire insurance policy, which provides protection for a period extending beyond the year in which the expenditure was made, is one type of prepaid expense.

Specifically, an expense deduction is denied in respect of an outlay or expense to the extent that it can reasonably be regarded as having been made or incurred as consideration for services to be rendered after the end of the year (i.e., future services), or on account of interest, taxes, rent, or insurance in respect of a future period. Only the portion of the outlay or expense that relates to one of the specific expenses for a future period is denied. In this way, there is an effective proration of the outlay or expense.

The reference to "services" would not appear to be limited to the services of an independent contractor, but would normally include the services of an employee as well. It is generally the CRA's view that a substantial lease payment made at the beginning of a lease resulting in lower monthly payments throughout the lease term represents consideration for services to be rendered after the end of the year such that this provision would apply to limit the deductibility of the outlay or expense (see VD 2003-0015675).

The effect of ITA 18(9) is to defer the deduction of outlays or expenses made or incurred for future services or in respect of one of the specific types of periodic payments referred to until such time as the services are rendered or until the period arrives to which the periodic payment may reasonably be considered to relate.

The following example is provided in Guide T4036:

> Maria paid $2,100 for insurance on her rental property. The insurance was for the current tax year and the two following years. Although she paid the insurance for three years, she can deduct only the part that applies to the current tax year from her gross rental income. Therefore, Maria can deduct $700 in the current tax year and $700 in each of the following two years.

ITA 18(9), IT-261R, *Prepayment of Rents*, IT-417R2, *Prepaid Expenses and Deferred Charges*

¶5220.2 — *Advertising (Form T776: Line 8521)*

Costs incurred to advertise that a rental property is available for rent are deductible.

¶5220.3 — *Insurance (Form T776: Line 8690)*

Premiums paid for insurance coverage on a rental property that relate to the current year are deductible in the year. Premiums that relate to a future year are deductible in that future year (see ¶5220.1).

¶5220.4 — *Interest and Bank Charges (Form T776: Line 8710)*

The rules governing the deduction of interest payments and bank charges for purposes of calculating net rental income are as follows:

- Interest paid on money borrowed to buy or make improvements to a rental property are deductible; however, there are restrictions on the deductibility of certain "soft costs", such as interest for the period during the construction, renovation, or alteration of a building (see the rules for "soft costs" under ¶5255).

- Interest paid in a lump sum, such as fees paid to reduce the interest rate on a mortgage, are not fully deductible in the year, but are pro-rated over the original remaining term of the mortgage or loan.

- A penalty or bonus incurred to pay off a mortgage or loan before it is due is not fully deductible in the year, but is pro-rated over the original remaining term of the mortgage or loan.

- The following financing fees relating to a mortgage or loan to buy or improve rental property are deductible in equal amounts over five years (i.e., 20% in the first year and in each of the following four years): fees for mortgage applications, appraisals, processing, and insurance; mortgage guarantee fees; mortgage brokerage and finder's fees; and legal fees relating to mortgage financing. If the mortgage or loan is repaid before the end of the five years, the remaining financing fees can be deducted at that time.

- Where a rental property is refinanced to obtain funds for a purpose other than buying or improving the property, the associated interest is deductible as a business expense or as a carrying charge if the additional funds are for business or investment purposes.

- Standby charges, guarantee fees, registrar fees, filing fees, service fees, and similar fees are deductible in the year incurred, provided that the fees relate to that taxation year and that they are incurred for borrowing money to be used in earning income from a business or property, incurring debt for property acquired to produce income, or restructuring the borrowed funds or indebtedness.

- Interest paid to tenants on rental deposits is deductible.

ITA 20(1)(c), (d), (e), (e.1)

¶5220.5 — *Office Expenses (Form T776: Line 8810)*

The cost of miscellaneous office supplies is deductible (e.g., pens, pencils, paper, paper clips, etc.).

¶5220.6 — *Professional Fees (Form T776: Line 8860)*

Fees paid for legal services to prepare leases or collect overdue rents; for accounting, bookkeeping, audits of records, and the preparation of financial statements; and for advice and assistance to prepare tax and information returns relating to rental operations are deductible for purposes of calculating net rental income.

Legal fees related to the purchase or sale of a rental property are capital expenses that should be allocated proportionately between the cost base of the land and the building. For example, assume an individual buys a property worth $200,000 ($50,000 for the land and $150,000 for the building) and incurs legal fees of $10,000. The $10,000 of fees should be split proportionately between the land and building as follows: $2,500 is added to the cost of the land (for a total of $52,500) and $7,500 is added to the cost of the building (for a total of $157,500). The legal fees an individual incurs when selling a rental property are deducted from the proceeds of disposition for purposes of calculating the capital gain or loss on the property (see also ¶4111 and under ¶4410).

IT-99R5(C): *Legal and Accounting Fees*

¶5220.7 — *Management and Administration Fees (Form T776: Line 8871)*

Management and administration fees incurred to manage and supervise a rental property, and commissions paid to an agent for collecting rents or finding tenants are deductible for purposes of calculating net rental income. Commissions paid on the sale of a rental property are a cost of sale and reduce the gain on the disposition of the property (see also ¶4111 and under ¶4410).

¶5220.8 — *Repairs and Maintenance (Form T776: Line 8960)*

Current expenses for repairs and maintenance on a rental property are deductible (e.g., cost for labour and materials). Capital expenses are deducted over a period of years as capital cost allowance (see ¶5240). Where the individual owner completes the repairs and maintenance on the rental property, the value of the owner's labour is not deductible.

¶5220.9 — *Salaries, Wages, and Benefits (Form T776: Line 9060)*

The following salaries, wages, and benefits are deductible for purposes of calculating net rental income: 1) salaries, wages, and benefits paid or payable to superintendents, maintenance workers, and other operational staff to care for a rental property; 2) the employer portion of Canada or Quebec pension plan contributions, employment insurance premiums, and workers' compensation; and 3) premiums paid to an employee sickness, accident, disability, or income insurance plan.

¶5220.10 — *Property Taxes (Form T776: Line 9180)*

Property taxes paid on a rental property that were assessed by a province, territory, or Canadian municipality and relate to the period when the property was available for rent are deductible. Property taxes cannot be deducted during a construction or renovation period (see ¶5255), and the deduction for property taxes cannot create or increase a rental loss.

¶5220.11 — *Travel (Form T776: Line 9200)*

Generally, travel expenses are not deductible from rental income. However, in certain circumstances, CRA administratively allows taxpayers to deduct costs to travel between the owner's residence and the rental property that are incurred to collect rents, supervise repairs, or manage properties. Costs for board and lodging are not deductible. In order to claim travel costs as an expense, the same requirements as discussed under ¶5220.13 (Motor Vehicle Expenses) must be met.

¶5220.12 — *Utilities (Form T776: Line 9220)*

The cost of utilities (e.g., gas, hydro, water, cable) is deductible when paid by the owner.

¶5220.13 — *Motor Vehicle Expenses (Form T776: Line 9281)*

> Generally, travel expenses are not deductible from rental income; however, CRA administratively allows automobile expenses to be deducted in certain circumstances.

In CRA Guide T4036, the CRA sets forth its policy on deducting expenses in respect of travel to different rental properties as follows:

> You might travel to collect rents, supervise repairs, and manage your properties . . . Travelling expenses include the cost of getting to your rental property. Travelling expenses do not include board and lodging, which we consider to be personal expenses . . .
>
> You can deduct motor vehicle expenses in the following circumstances:
>
> • *If you own one rental property*: You can deduct reasonable motor vehicle expenses if you meet all the following conditions: you receive income from only one rental property that is in the general area where you live; you personally do part, or all, of the necessary repairs and maintenance on the property; and you have motor vehicle expenses to transport tools and materials to the rental property. You cannot deduct motor vehicle expenses you incur to collect rents. These are personal expenses.
>
> • *If you own two or more rental properties*: In addition to the expenses listed above, you can deduct reasonable motor vehicle expenses you incur to do any of the following: collect rents; supervise repairs; and manage the properties. This applies whether your rental properties are located in or outside the general area where you live. Your rental properties have to be located in at least two different sites, away from your principal residence. The motor vehicle expenses that we consider to be reasonable depend on the circumstances of your situation.
>
> For information on how to calculate the motor vehicle expenses, see Guide T4002, *Business and Professional Income*.

Despite the CRA's policy on rental properties, the CRA's general position is that travel expenses are not deductible in computing investment income (VD 2009-0324901E5).

In *Benjamin v MNR*, 5 Tax A.B.C. 85, expenses incurred for visiting out-of-town properties to collect rents were held to not be deductible. In *Bernard v MNR*, [1985] 2 C.T.C. 2144 (TCC), the services of a taxpayer consisted mainly in providing rooms in a building with a janitor; since income was generated by the property itself and not by special services rendered by the landlord, cost of travelling to supervise work and collect rents held not to be expenses incurred to earn income from property. In *Clairoux v MNR*, 28 Tax A.B.C. 385, an individual who derived rental revenue from an apartment building containing four suites was held not entitled to any deduction for automobile expenses incurred in almost daily inspections. Similarly, a rooming house owner sought to deduct 50% of his automobile expenses, but these were determined to be personal and living expenses and disallowed (*Peters v MNR*, 34 Tax A.B.C. 85).

> Individuals who claim automobile expenses should keep proper and continuous records as to the total kilometres covered and the expenses incurred. The CRA recommends keeping an automobile log for this purpose. For more information, see: canada.ca/en/revenue-agency/services/what-s-new/documenting-use-a-vehicle.html.

ITA 6(1)(e), 18(1)(h), Guide T4002, Guide T4036, IT-521R: *Motor Vehicle Expenses Claimed by Self-Employed Individuals*

¶5220.14 — Other Expenses (Form T776: Line 9270)

Other expenses should be deducted on Line 9270. These may include expenses such as landscaping costs and lease cancellation payments.

¶5230 — Non-Deductible Expenses

The following expenses are generally not deductible from rental income: the cost of land, land transfer taxes paid on the purchase of rental property, mortgage or loan principal repayments on rental property, penalties imposed on a Notice of Assessment or Reassessment, the personal portion of expenses, and the value of the owner's labour or services. Note that land transfer taxes can be added to the cost of the property.

The personal portion of a rental expense should be reported in the "Personal portion" column on Form T776. The total personal portion of rental expenses on Line 9949 should be deducted from total expenses to calculate total deductible expenses to report on Line 7 on Form T776.

ITA 18(1)(b), Guide T4036

¶5240 — Capital Cost Allowance (Form T776: Lines 9936, 9947, 9948, Charts A–F)

Taxpayers filing Form T776 should calculate their capital cost allowance (CCA) using Charts A to F on page 3 of the form. The total CCA claim calculated using Chart A is entered on Line 9936 on page 1 of Form T776, while any recaptured CCA or terminal losses are entered on Line 9947 or 9948, respectively.

The CCA rules relating specifically to rental property are discussed below. See ¶7100 for a more detailed discussion of the CCA rules generally. See also ¶7006 for a discussion of the accelerated investment incentive for CCA that was announced in the 2018 Fall Economic Statement, which allows Canadian businesses to claim an enhanced first-year CCA on qualifying property acquired after November 20, 2018 that becomes available for use before 2028.

The amount of CCA a taxpayer can claim depends on the type of rental property owned and the date it was acquired. Depreciable property owned by a taxpayer is grouped into classes. A different rate of CCA applies to each class. The main classes of depreciable rental property and the rates that apply to each class are outlined below.

In most cases, taxpayers use the declining balance method to calculate CCA. This means that CCA is claimed on the capital cost of the property minus the CCA, if any, claimed in previous years. The remaining balance declines over the years as CCA is claimed.

> Taxpayers do not have to claim the maximum amount of CCA in any given year. For example, where a taxpayer does not have to pay income tax for the year, the taxpayer may not want to claim CCA. Claiming CCA reduces the amount of CCA available for future years.

For taxpayers who are partners of a partnership, the amount of CCA has already been determined by the partnership. The CCA amount will be reported in Box 26 of the T5013 slip, *Statement of Partnership Income*, or T5013A slip, *Statement of Partnership Income for Tax Shelters and Renounced Resource Expenses* that the taxpayer receives from the partnership. For partners who do not receive this slip, the total partnership CCA will be shown on the financial statements received from the partnership.

ITA 13(21), 18(1)(b), 20(1)(a), ITR 1100–1103, Folio S3-F4-C1: *General Discussion of Capital Cost Allowance*

¶5241 — *CCA Limitations*

In the year a taxpayer acquires rental property, the taxpayer can usually claim CCA only on one-half of the net additions to a class. This is called the half-year rule (also known as the 50% rule). The available-for-use rules may also affect the amount of CCA a taxpayer can claim. These rules provide that CCA can only be claimed on rental property when it becomes available for use. For more information on the half-year rule and the available for use rules, see ¶7140 and ¶7125 respectively. See also ¶7006 for information on the accelerated investment incentive for CCA that was announced in the 2018 Fall Economic Statement, which suspends the application of the half-year rule and allows Canadian businesses to claim an enhanced first-year CCA on qualifying property acquired after November 20, 2018 that becomes available for use before 2028.

In the year that a taxpayer disposes of rental property, the taxpayer may have to add an amount to income as a recapture of CCA. A recapture of CCA can occur when the proceeds from the sale of depreciable rental property are more than the total of the undepreciated capital cost (UCC) of the class at the start of the year and the capital cost of any additions during the year. Conversely, a taxpayer may be able to deduct an amount from income as a terminal loss. A terminal loss occurs when there is no more property in the class at the end of a year, but there is undeducted CCA remaining. In the year a taxpayer disposes of rental property, the taxpayer can subtract the terminal loss from rental income and, if the loss is more than the taxpayer's rental income, the taxpayer will have a rental loss. For more information on terminal losses and recapture of CCA, see ¶7145, ¶7150 and Folio S3-F4-C1: *General Discussion of Capital Cost Allowance*.

If a taxpayer owns more than one rental property, the taxpayer must calculate the overall net income or loss for the year from all of the taxpayer's rental properties before the taxpayer can claim CCA. Partners should include the net rental income or loss from their T5013 or T5013A slip in the calculation. Taxpayers should combine the rental incomes and losses from all of their properties, even if they belong to different classes. This also applies to furniture, fixtures, and appliances used in the rental building. Taxpayers can claim CCA for these properties, the building, or both. However, taxpayers cannot use CCA to create or increase a rental loss. See ¶5300, ¶7165 and IT-195R4, *Rental Property — Capital Cost Allowance Restrictions*.

ITA 13(26)–(32), 20(28), (29), ITR 1100(2), (2.2), Folio S3-F4-C1: *General Discussion of Capital Cost Allowance*

¶5242 — CCA Classes

Below is a discussion of the most common classes of depreciable rental property and the rates that apply to each class. Following the discussion is a listing of depreciable property for rental purposes illustrated in table format, for quick reference. For a more detailed discussion of capital cost allowance, see ¶7100. See also ¶7006 for a discussion of the accelerated investment incentive for CCA that was announced in the 2018 Fall Economic Statement, which allows Canadian businesses to claim an enhanced first-year CCA on qualifying property acquired after November 20, 2018 that becomes available for use before 2028.

¶5242.1 — Land & Buildings

Most land is not depreciable property. Therefore, when a taxpayer acquires property, only include the cost that relates to the building for depreciation purposes. Generally, a rental building may belong to class 1, 3, 6, 31, or 32, depending on what the building is made of and the date it was acquired. Also include in these classes the parts that make up the building, such as electric wiring, lighting fixtures, plumbing, sprinkler systems, heating equipment, air-conditioning equipment (other than window units), elevators and escalators.

A condominium unit in a building belongs to the same class as the building. For example, if a taxpayer owns a condominium in a Class 3 building, the unit in the building is Class 3 rental property.

¶5242.2 — Leasehold Interest in Real Property that is a Rental Property

A leasehold interest is the interest of a tenant in any leased tangible property. Taxpayers who own a leasehold interest in a real property that is a rental property should include the leasehold interest in Class 1, 3, 6, or 13. For more information on leasehold interests, see ¶7210.

¶5242.3 — Class 1 (4%)

Class 1 includes most buildings acquired after 1987, unless they specifically belong in another class. Class 1 also includes the cost of certain additions or alterations made after 1987 to a Class 1 building.

¶5242.4 — *Class 8 (20%)*

Class 8 includes certain property not included in other classes such as furniture, household appliances, tools costing $500 or more, some fixtures, machinery, outdoor advertising signs, refrigeration equipment, and other equipment used in the rental operation. Photocopiers and electronic communications equipment, such as fax machines and electronic telephone equipment, are also included in Class 8.

¶5242.5 — *Class 10 (30%)*

Class 10 includes general-purpose electronic data-processing equipment (i.e., computer hardware) and systems software for that equipment, including ancillary data-processing equipment, if acquired before March 23, 2004, or after March 22, 2004, and before 2005, and the taxpayer made an election.

Also included in Class 10 are motor vehicles, automobiles, and some passenger vehicles. Include a passenger vehicle in Class 10 unless it meets a Class 10.1 condition.

¶5242.6 — *Class 10.1 (30%)*

Passenger vehicles can belong to either Class 10 or Class 10.1. To determine the class to which a vehicle belongs, use the cost of the vehicle before GST/HST or PST. Include a vehicle in Class 10.1 if the taxpayer bought it during the current year and it cost more than $30,000. List each Class 10.1 vehicle separately. The capital cost of a Class 10.1 vehicle is $30,000 plus the related GST/HST or PST. Use the GST rate of 5% and the appropriate PST rate for the taxpayer's province or territory. For more information on the rules for Class 10.1 vehicles, see ¶7160.

¶5242.7 — *Class 13 (straight line)*

The capital cost of a leasehold interest of Class 13 property includes:

- an amount that a tenant expends in respect of improvements or alterations to a leased property that are capital in nature, other than improvements or alterations that are included as a building or structure; and

- an amount that a tenant expends to obtain or extend a lease or sublease or pays to the landlord to permit the sublease of the property.

The maximum CCA rate depends on the type of leasehold interest and the terms of the lease. Certain amounts are not included in the capital cost of a leasehold interest. These include an amount paid by a tenant to cancel a lease and an amount paid by a tenant in lieu of rent or as a prepayment of rent. See ¶7210 and IT-464R, *Capital Cost Allowance — Leasehold Interests*, for more information on leasehold interests.

¶5242.8 — *Class 45 (45%)*

Include general-purpose electronic data-processing equipment (i.e., computer hardware) and systems software for that equipment, including ancillary data-processing equipment, in Class 45 if the taxpayer acquired them after March 22, 2004, and before March 19, 2007.

¶5242.9 — *Class 50 (55%)*

Include in Class 50 property acquired after March 18, 2007, that is general-purpose electronic data-processing equipment (i.e., computer hardware) and systems software for that equipment, including ancillary data-processing equipment (not included in Class 52).

¶5242.10 — *Class 52 (100%)*

Include in Class 52 (with no half-year rule) general-purpose electronic data-processing equipment (i.e., computer hardware) and systems software for that equipment, including ancillary data-processing equipment, if acquired after January 27, 2009, and before February 2011.

ITR 1100, 1101

¶5243 — *Capital Cost Allowance Table*

The following table lists and describes the most common classes of depreciable rental property and the rates that apply to each class. For a complete listing of depreciable property alphabetically listed by property type, see ¶7000.

Class	Description	Rate
1	Most buildings made of brick, stone, or cement acquired after 1987, including their component parts such as electric wiring, lighting fixtures, plumbing, heating and cooling equipment, elevators, and escalators; also includes the cost of certain additions or alterations made after 1987. The rate for eligible non-residential buildings acquired after March 18, 2007, used for M&P in Canada of goods for sale or lease includes an additional allowance of 6% (total 10%). For all other eligible non-residential buildings in this class, the rate includes an additional allowance of 2% (total 6%). To be eligible for the additional allowances, elections have to be filed.	4%–10%
3	Most buildings made of brick, stone, or cement acquired before 1988, including their component parts as listed in Class 1	5%
6	Buildings made of frame, log, stucco on frame, galvanized iron, or corrugated metal that are used in the business of farming or fishing or that have no footings below-ground; fences; most greenhouses	10%
8	Depreciable property not included in any other class, such as furniture and fixtures, cash registers, refrigeration equipment not used for a qualifying M&P purpose and fax machines, printers, scanners, photocopiers and other office equipment that does not qualify as "general-purpose electronic data processing equipment" (i.e., computer hardware) or as ancillary data processing equipment; tools costing $500 or more; outdoor advertising billboards and neon signs; greenhouses with rigid frames and plastic covers	20%
10	Automobiles (except taxis and others used for lease or rent or "luxury" passenger vehicles), vans, wagons, trucks, buses, tractors (except certain long-haul tractors included in Class 16), trailers; contractor's movable equipment; timber-cutting and removing equipment	30%
10.1	"Luxury" passenger vehicles costing more than $30,000 and acquired after 2000 (each such vehicle is included in a separate Class 10.1, the recapture and terminal loss rules do not apply, and a special 15% CCA claim may be made in the year of disposition)	30%
13	Property that is leasehold interest (the maximum CCA which may be claimed on a straight-line basis in a taxation year depends on the type of leasehold and the terms of the lease; however, no matter how short the unexpired period of the lease, no more than one-fifth of the capital cost of an addition may be deducted in a taxation year)	SL
45	Computer equipment that is "general-purpose electronic data processing equipment" (i.e., computer hardware) and systems software (i.e., operating systems), including ancillary data processing equipment (such as a printer attached to a desktop computer) acquired after March 22, 2004 and before March 19, 2007 (see now classes 50 and 52)	45%

Class	Description	Rate
50	Property described in Class 45 (i.e., computer equipment) acquired after March 18, 2007, other than such equipment included in Class 52	55%
52	Property described in Class 45 (i.e., computer equipment) acquired after January 27, 2009 and before February 2011 that is new and that is situated in Canada for use in a business carried on in Canada or for the purpose of earning income from property situated in Canada	100%

¶5244 — Completing the CCA Charts

Use Part A on page 3 of Form T776 to calculate the taxpayer's CCA claim. If the taxpayer acquired or disposed of rental buildings or equipment during the year, complete Parts B, C, D, or E (whichever applies) before completing Part A. Even if the taxpayer is not claiming a deduction for CCA, complete these areas to show any additions or dispositions during the year. For more details on CCA and completing the CCA charts, see ¶7100.

¶5244.1 — Column 1 — Class Number

If this is the first year the taxpayer is claiming CCA, determine the classes to which the property belongs. If the taxpayer claimed CCA in the previous tax year, get the class numbers from that year's form.

Generally, if a taxpayer owns several properties in the same CCA class, the capital cost of all the properties is combined into one class and the total is entered in Part A.

As an exception to combining properties into the same CCA class, where a taxpayer acquired a rental property after 1971 that had a capital cost of $50,000 or more, the property must be placed into a separate class and CCA is calculated separately for each rental property that is in a separate class by listing the rental property on a separate line in Part A. For more information about CCA for rental properties with a capital cost of over $50,000, see ¶7165 and IT-274R, *Rental Properties — Capital Cost of $50,000 or More.*

For CCA purposes, the capital cost is the part of the purchase price that relates to the building only. When the taxpayer disposes of a rental property that is in a separate class in Part A, base any CCA recapture or terminal loss on the disposition of that rental property only. When calculating these amounts, do not consider any other rental property the taxpayer owns that has the same class number as the rental property disposed of. For more information on recapture of CCA and terminal losses, see ¶5244.5, ¶7145 and ¶7150.

¶5244.2 — Column 2 — Undepreciated Capital Cost (UCC) at the Start of the Year

If this is the first year the taxpayer is claiming CCA, skip this column. Otherwise, enter in this column the UCC for each class at the end of the previous year. If the taxpayer completed Part A on Form T776 for the previous year, use the amounts in Column 10 of that year's form.

¶5244.3 — Column 3 — Cost of Additions in the Year

If the taxpayer acquired or made improvements to depreciable property in the year, they are generally considered to be additions to the class in which the rental property belongs. Enter the details of current-year additions on Form T776 by completing Parts B and C, if applicable; and for each class, enter in Column 3 of Part A the amounts from Column 5 for each class in Parts B and C. When completing Parts B and C, enter the part of the property that the taxpayer personally uses (separate from the part rented) in the column called "Personal portion". For example, if a taxpayer rents 25% of their personal residence, the personal use portion is the other 75% (see ¶5400).

List in Part B the details of all equipment or other property the taxpayer acquired or improved in the current tax year. Group the equipment or other property into the applicable classes and put each class on a separate line. Equipment includes appliances, maintenance equipment and other property (such as furniture and some fixtures) the taxpayer acquired to use in the rental operation. Enter on Line 9925 the total rental portion of the cost of the equipment or other property.

List in Part C the details of all buildings and leasehold interests the taxpayer acquired or improved in the current tax year. Group the buildings and leasehold interests into the applicable classes, and put each class on a separate line. Enter on Line 9927 the total rental portion of the cost of the buildings and leasehold interests. The cost includes the purchase price of the building or leasehold interest, plus any related expenses that should be added to the capital cost of the building, such as legal fees, land transfer taxes, and mortgage fees (see ¶4111).

If the taxpayer acquired a rental property that includes both land and a building, enter in Column 3 of Part C only the cost of the building. To determine the building's capital cost, split any fees that relate to the purchase of the rental property, such as legal and accounting fees, between the cost of the land and the building. Calculate the part of the related fees to include in the capital cost of the building as follows: Building value/Total purchase price × Legal, accounting or other fees. Do not split a fee if it relates specifically to the land or the building. Instead, add the amount of the fee to the cost to which it relates.

Enter in Part F the total cost of acquiring land in the current tax year. The capital cost of the land includes the actual purchase price of the land plus any related expenses, such as legal fees, land transfer taxes, and mortgage fees (see ¶4111). Enter on Line 9923 the total cost of all land additions in the year. CCA cannot be claimed on land. Do not enter this amount in Column 3 of Part A.

¶5244.4 — Column 4 — Proceeds of Dispositions in the Year

If the taxpayer disposed of depreciable property in the current tax year, complete, for each class, Parts D and E on Form T776, if applicable; and enter in Column 4 of Part A the amounts for each class from Column 5 of Parts D and E. When completing Parts D and E, enter in Column 3 the lesser of the proceeds of disposition minus any related expenses, or the capital cost of the rental property.

List in Part D the details of all equipment and other property the taxpayer disposed of in the current tax year. Group the equipment and other property into the applicable classes, and put each class on a separate line. Enter on Line 9926 the total rental portion of the proceeds of disposition of the equipment and other property.

List in Part E the details of all buildings and leasehold interests the taxpayer disposed of in the current tax year. Group the buildings and leasehold interests into the applicable classes, and put each class on a separate line. Enter on Line 9928 the total rental portion of the proceeds of disposition of the buildings and leasehold interests. When completing Parts D and E, enter the part of the property that the taxpayer personally uses, separate from the part rented, in the column called "Personal portion".

Enter on Line 9924 the total of all amounts the taxpayer has received or will receive for disposing of land in the year.

¶5244.5 — Column 5 — UCC after Additions and Dispositions

CCA cannot be claimed when the amount in Column 5 is negative (recapture of CCA), or when the amount is positive and there is no property left in that class at the end of the current tax year (a terminal loss). In either case, enter zero in Column 10.

If the amount in Column 5 is negative, the taxpayer has a recapture of CCA. Enter the amount of recapture on Line 9947 of Form T776. A recapture of CCA occurs when the proceeds from the sale of depreciable rental property are more than the total of the UCC of the class at the start of the year and the capital cost of any additions during the year.

If the amount in Column 5 is positive and the taxpayer no longer owns any property in that class, the taxpayer has a terminal loss. A terminal loss occurs when the taxpayer has no more property in the class at the end of a year, but still has an amount not deducted as CCA. In the year the taxpayer disposes of the rental property, the terminal loss can be subtracted from rental income and, if the loss is more than the rental income, a rental loss is created. Enter the terminal loss on Line 9948 of Form T776.

For more information on terminal losses and recapture of CCA, see ¶7145, ¶7150, and Folio S3-F4-C1, *General Discussion of Capital Cost Allowance.*

¶5244.6 — Column 6 — Adjustment for Current-Year Additions

In the year the taxpayer acquires or makes additions to a rental property, CCA can generally be claimed only on one-half of net additions (Column 3 minus Column 4). Calculate the CCA claim only on the net adjusted amount. Do not reduce the cost of the additions in Column 3 or the CCA rate in Column 8. For example, if the taxpayer acquired a rental property for $50,000, the CCA claim is calculated on $25,000 ($50,000 × 50%) in the year the property is acquired.

If the taxpayer acquired and disposed of depreciable rental property of the same class in the current tax year, the calculation in Column 6 restricts the taxpayer's CCA claim. In this case, calculate the CCA claim as follows:

- Determine which of the following amounts is less: the proceeds of disposition of the rental property minus any related costs or expenses, or the capital cost of the acquired property.

- Subtract the above result from the capital cost of the addition.

- In Column 6, enter 50% of the result. If the result is negative, enter zero.

Do not make an adjustment in Column 6 if the property is not subject to the half-year rule. For example, Class 13 (leasehold interests), Class 52 (computer equipment and systems software) and some Class 12 properties (most small tools that cost less than $500) are not subject to the half-year rule. For more information on the half-year rule, see ¶7140 and Folio S3-F4-C1, *General Discussion of Capital Cost Allowance.*

¶5244.7 — Column 7 — Base Amount for Capital Cost Allowance

This is the amount in Column 5 minus the amount in Column 6. Base the CCA claim on this amount.

¶5244.8 — Column 8 — Rate (%)

Enter the rate (percentage) for each class of property listed in Part A. See ¶7000 and ¶7005 to determine the CCA rate.

¶5244.9 — Column 9 — CCA for the Year

Enter the CCA deduction for the current tax year. The CCA deducted cannot be more than the amount in Column 7 multiplied by the rate in Column 8. Taxpayers are not required to deduct the maximum amount of available CCA. Any amount up to the maximum can be claimed. Add up all the amounts in Column 9 for all the classes of depreciable property. Enter the total CCA being claimed on Line 9936 of Form T776. Co-owners should enter only their share of the CCA.

¶5244.10 — Column 10 — UCC at the End of the Year

This is the undepreciated capital cost (UCC) at the end of the current tax year. This will be the amount entered in Column 2 of next year's CCA claim. If the taxpayer has a terminal loss or a recapture of CCA, enter zero in Column 10.

ITA 13, 20(1)(a), 20(16), 20(16.1), 20(28)–(29), ITR 1100–1103, Folio S3-F4-C1: *General Discussion of Capital Cost Allowance*, IT-195R4: *Rental Property — Capital Cost Allowance Restrictions*

¶5250 — Rental Expenses: Special Situations

Certain types of expenditures made to earn rental income are subject to special rules. These expenditures are discussed below.

¶5251 — Condominiums

Generally, an individual who rents a condominium unit may deduct all expenses that are normally deductible from rental income, as discussed above. An owner of a condominium is required to pay condominium fees, proportionately, based on ownership. The condominium fees may be made up of both current expenses (e.g., utilities, repairs and maintenance of common areas) and capital expenses (e.g., contribution to the reserve fund for future repairs, special assessments for capital repairs). Generally, the CRA's views with respect to the deductibility of condominium fees is that fees relating to current expenses incurred in the current year are deductible in the current year, fees relating to capital expenses incurred in the current year are capitalized in the current year, and fees relating to future years should be deducted or capitalized in the year that the related expense is incurred.

The following CRA comments in paragraph 8 of IT-304R2: *Condominiums*, discuss the deductibility of condominium fees when a condominium unit is rented by a taxpayer:

> 8. Usually, a part of the condominium fee paid by the unit owner goes into the condominium corporation's reserve fund for maintenance, repairs, improvements or additions to the common elements. Furthermore, a unit owner may be charged an extraordinary levy by the condominium corporation for a portion of the costs relating to repairs or renovations required to be made to the common elements. In either case, no deduction or capitalization of the expense is permitted until the amount is laid out to earn income by the condominium corporation. This is because prepaid expenses, or expenses which are paid before they are actually incurred, are not deductible as explained in the current version of IT-417, *Prepaid Expenses and Deferred Charges*. Whether the unit owner deducts the amount as a current expense or capitalizes it depends on the nature of the work done. Refer to the current version of IT-128, *Capital Cost Allowance — Depreciable Property* for further details on how such costs are classified. Certain capital expenditures incurred for disability-related devices or modifications to a building to accommodate disabled individuals are deductible under paragraph 20(1)(qq) or 20(1)(rr) in the year the expense is paid. The devices and modifications which qualify under these provisions are listed in sections 8800 and 8801 of the Regulations. Capital expenditures incurred in respect of the land do not form part of the capital cost of the building portion of the unit and are not deductible in computing income except as specifically provided for in the Act. The cost of landscaping, for example, may be deductible under paragraph 20(1)(aa).

¶5252 — Disability-Related Modifications

Where an owner renovates their rental property to accommodate persons with disabilities, the outlays and expenses made for eligible disability-related modifications may be deducted in the year paid, instead of having to add them to the capital cost of the building. Eligible disability-related modifications include installing hand-activated electric door openers, installing interior and exterior ramps, and modifying a bathroom, elevator, or doorway so a person in a wheelchair can use it. Expenses paid to install or acquire disability-related devices and equipment may also be deducted.

ITA 20(1)(qq), (rr), ITR 8800, 8801

¶5253 — *Landscaping Costs*

By virtue of ITA 20(1)(aa), the cost of landscaping the grounds around a building or other structure owned by the taxpayer and used primarily to earn income either from the property or from a business is deductible in the taxation year in which it is paid. ITA 20(1)(aa) is required to permit a deduction because landscaping is normally considered a capital expenditure in respect of the land. IT-296 (cancelled): *Landscaping of Grounds*, discusses what the CRA considers to constitute landscaping.

The expenses are deductible only in the year they are paid, regardless of the year to which they relate. To claim the deduction, the individual must own the building (i.e., the deduction cannot be claimed by a tenant). However, the individual does not need to own the land that is landscaped, provided the individual owns the building adjacent to the land.

The CRA's view is that landscaping costs incurred by a land developer constitute a component of the cost of the inventory of land for the purposes of ITA 10(1); the CRA does not consider such costs deductible under ITA 20(1)(aa). The CRA's position is supported by the decision in *Qualico Developments Ltd*, [1984] C.T.C. 122 (FCA).

ITA 20(1)(aa), IT-153R3: *Land Developers — Subdivision and Development Costs and Carrying Charges on Land*, ITTN-20, VDs 2013-0479421E5 (cranberry farm), 2013-0476561E5 (a land drainage system would include plastic pipes), 2007-0231881I7, 2005-0111301E5, 2003-0024037, 2008-0300731E5, 2001-0068425

¶5254 — *Lease Payments*

Regular operating lease payments in respect of leased property used to earn income are deductible in the year incurred for tax purposes provided the amount paid is reasonable. The treatment of special lease payments is discussed below. For more information on leasehold interests, see ¶7210.

¶5254.1 — *Lease Cancellation Payments*

Where a landlord makes a payment to a tenant in respect of the cancellation of a lease, the deduction of the payment for tax purposes is generally treated as a prepaid expense deductible over what would have been the remaining term of the lease (but not exceeding 40 years). If the payment is made in connection with the disposition, or the deemed disposition as a change of use property, it is considered to be an outlay or expense made or incurred for the purpose of making the disposition or deemed disposition and forms part of the calculation of the capital gain or loss, provided the payment is reasonable in the circumstances.

With respect to the treatment of a cancelation payment received by a lessee, in paragraph 7 of IT-359R2, the CRA states a premium or other amount received by a tenant as consideration for assigning a lease, granting or extending a sublease, or in the case of an amount received from a landlord, permitting the cancellation of a lease is a capital rather than an income receipt to the recipient. It should, however, be noted that in VD 2014-0519401E5, in considering the treatment of a lease cancelation payment, the CRA did not refer to IT-359R2 and instead stated the character of the receipt should be determined by reference to the surrogatum principle (i.e., by reference to the amount it is intended to replace, which should typically lead to the conclusion that the payment is capital in nature).

Lease cancellation payments paid by a tenant to a landlord are normally fully deductible by the lessee. Generally, any amount received by a landlord from a tenant for cancelling a lease is considered income from a business or property. However, in certain cases, such payments have been found to be capital receipts. In particular, compensation received by a landlord for the cancellation of a lease is in principle a capital receipt rather than an income receipt unless it is received from the tenant and can be equated to the loss of rent otherwise payable under the lease.

ITA 18(1)(q), 20(1)(z)-(z.1), 40(1), 45(1), *Canderel and Toronto College Park Limited v The Queen*, [1998] 2 C.T.C. 78 (SCC), *Monart Corp.*, [1967] C.T.C. 263 (Ex. Ct.); *R. Reusse Construction Co.*, [1999] 2 C.T.C. 2928 (TCC); *Bueti and Spezzano*, [2006] 4 C.T.C. 2266 (TCC); aff'd [2008] 1 C.T.C. 18 (FCA), IT-359R2, VD 2000-0056045

¶5254.2 — *Lease Inducements and Premium Payments*

Paid by Lessor

The treatment of an amount paid by a landlord to a tenant as an inducement to enter into a lease depends on the facts of the case. If the payment is a contribution towards the cost of leasehold improvements to be made by the tenant, the amount contributed by the landlord to improve the leased property would generally be added to the landlord's capital cost of the leased property. Otherwise, the courts have generally found that such payments are deductible for tax purposes in the year incurred.

It is the CRA's position that a taxpayer may be entitled to fully deduct lease inducement payments in the year incurred where the following three conditions are met: the payments cannot be viewed as having been principally incurred for the specific purpose of earning a discrete and identifiable item of future revenue; current deductibility of the payments is permissible under GAAP or any other well-accepted business principle, and this gives the most accurate picture of the profit; and no portion of the payments is on capital account.

By virtue of ITA 12(1)(x), leasehold inducement payments received by a tenant renting property for business or rental purposes are included in computing taxable income.

Paid by Lessee

Where a landlord receives a premium for granting or extending a lease, if the rent charged is less than fair market value, the premium is included in income to the extent that it can reasonably be regarded as being in the nature of rent. A lease sometimes provides for the payment of a premium but its terms indicate that it is actually a prepayment of rent. Where a premium or other amount received by a lessor for granting or extending a lease or permitting a sublease cannot be regarded as income, it represents proceeds of disposition of rights which are capital property. Based on paragraph 5 of IT-359R2: *Premiums and Other Amounts with Respect to Leases*, the CRA will normally agree to treat an amount equal to the proceeds from such disposition as the reasonable portion of the adjusted cost base of the whole property attributable to the part disposed of, resulting in the adjusted cost base of the property to the lessor being reduced by the amount of proceeds. A capital loss cannot be claimed on the granting or extending of a lease or the permitting of a sublease.

In paragraph 17 of IT-359R2, the CRA states that where the tenant pays an amount to obtain or extend a lease, and the amount is not merely in lieu of rent or a prepayment of rent, the amount is a capital expenditure to acquire a leasehold interest which, if acquired for the purpose of gaining or producing income, is depreciable as Class 13 property (see ¶7210).

ITA 12(1)(x), *Canderel Ltd.*, [1998] 2 C.T.C. 35 (SCC), *Spezzano*, [2008] 1 C.T.C. 18 (FCA), *St-Germain*, [1968] C.T.C. 148 (Exch), IT-359R2, VDs 2011-043090E5, 2000-0056405

¶5255 — *Soft Costs on Construction and Renovation of a Building*

Soft costs (such as interest, legal and accounting fees, and property taxes) that can reasonably be regarded as attributable to the period of the construction, renovation or alteration of a building are required to be capitalized to the capital cost of the building for tax purposes pursuant to ITA 18(3.1). Soft costs include those pertaining to the ownership of the related land, which consists of the land that is under the building and the land that is immediately adjacent to the land under the building, used or intended for use for a parking area, driveway, yard, garden, or any other similar use, and necessary for the use or intended use of the building.

The terms "soft costs" is not used in the ITA. In *Kuhlmann*, 1995 CarswellNat 307 (TCC), Bowman J. defined "soft costs" as follows (para. 11): "It is sought here to deduct what are somewhat ambiguously called "soft costs" — a term of some elasticity comprising, I gather, costs not directly attributable to the bricks and mortar and labour involved in creating the building, such as financing costs, legal fees, commissions, carrying costs, municipal taxes, landscaping and similar expenses". Other examples of soft costs include expenses of representation, site investigation costs, utility service connection costs, municipal fees (e.g. lot levies), legal and accounting fees, architectural and engineering fees, insurance charges, guarantee, standby and mortgage commitment fees, structure inspection fees, building permit costs, cost of plans and drawings, property taxes, sewer, water and hydro charges and clean-up costs. Soft costs do not include repairs and maintenance.

The soft cost capitalization rules do not apply to CCA (see ¶5240), landscaping costs (see ¶5253), or costs for disability-related modifications to buildings (see ¶5252). However, representation expenses, site investigation expenses, and utility connection expenses cannot be deducted during the construction period even though ITA 20(1)(cc), 20(1)(dd) and 20(1)(ee) would normally permit the deduction of those items. If possible, such costs should be incurred before the commencement of the construction period or after its completion.

> The CRA considers the period of construction, renovation, or alteration to be completed on whichever date is earlier: the date the work is completed or the date the owner rents 90% or more of the building. It is not clear whether ITA 18(3.1) permits some latitude to recognize the completion of parts of a building capable of independent use. It is possible that a reasonable interpretation of ITA 18(3.1) and (3.3) would recognize the possibility of several completion dates in respect of components of a single building project.

With respect to the starting period of a construction project, in VD 2010-0386121E5, the CRA states:

> While subsection 18(3.3) of the Act provides for the determination of the date on which the construction, renovation or alteration is completed, the Act does not define when construction is considered to commence for purposes of subsection 18(3.1). In our view, this is a question of fact that can only be determined on a case-by-case basis. Paragraph 8 of Interpretation Bulletin IT-153R3, entitled "Land Developers — Subdivision and Development Costs and Carrying Charges on Land", states that "site development is considered to begin with the installation of services" and further states "where serviced lots are acquired site development is considered to begin at the earlier of the date the taxpayer starts to install further services to the lots or the date he starts to pour footings".

It is a question of fact as to whether an expense "can reasonably be regarded as a cost attributable to the period of the construction, renovation or alteration of a building". In *Preiss*, [2010] 1 C.T.C. 2164 (TCC), the Court states (paras. 30, 31):

> Subsection 18(3.1) is not intended to apply to periods during which general repairs are being undertaken. Rather, subsection 18(3.1) requires more extensive work that constitutes construction, renovation or alteration.

> It would be unreasonable to suggest that every time a repair is undertaken the deduction of the related soft costs will be denied under subsection 18(3.1). The issue is one of degree, with general repairs and cosmetic touch-ups at one end of the spectrum and construction, renovation or alteration falling at the other end.

The CRA's position is that ITA 18(3.1) is not an enabling provision with respect to the deductibility of expenses; rather, the provision simply precludes a deduction for certain outlays and expenses that would have been otherwise deductible (the CRA's position is consistent with the findings in *Mikhail*, [2002] 2 C.T.C. 2612 (TCC)). In VD 2001-0069497, the CRA states:

> From a tax policy perspective, it would appear that subsection 18(3.1) of the Act is intended to allow for the capitalization of only those soft costs that, if not for that provision, would otherwise be deductible. For example, subsection 18(3.1) of the Act should not apply to those "soft costs" that would otherwise be non-deductible pursuant to paragraphs 18(1)(a), (b) and (h) of the Act. We also assume, from a tax policy perspective, that a provision that is intended to permanently deny a deduction of a particular amount (e.g. subsection 18(4)) would override a provision that would operate to capitalize that amount (e.g. subsection 18(3.1)).Financing costs incurred in the course of a borrowing of money used to fund the construction costs of a building may be capitalized in equal portions over a five year period in accordance with ITA 20(1)(e)(iii); such costs cannot be fully capitalized in the year incurred by virtue of ITA 18(3.1). In VD 2004-0056861E5, the CRA states until an amount that is a financing expense described in ITA 20(1)(e)(ii) is deductible pursuant to ITA 20(1)(e), ITA 18(3.1) will not have any application.

It is unclear from ITA 18(3.1) and (3.2) what, if any, application the provisions should have to the costs of securing permanent financing. The "relating to" tests which apply both to the building and to the associated land may be sufficiently broad to require the capitalization of such costs during the period of construction, renovation or alteration. However, the principal purpose of a permanent financing arrangement, which extends beyond the completion of a building project, may be regarded as different from that of interim financing, which is more directly related to the construction, renovation or alteration of a building. Generally, it would appear ITA 18(3.1) should not apply to the costs of securing permanent financing, particularly where such fees are not due until after the construction phase of the building project when substantial reliance on the permanent financing commences. Similarly, interest in respect of the portion of a mortgage used for the original purchase of a property should not be captured by ITA 18(3.1). However, it should be noted that in VD 2005-0141071C6, which deals with financing fees incurred during the construction period, the CRA states it "considers an expense to be attributable to the period of construction of a building when that expense is related to the construction period, irrespective of whether it is incurred during the pre-construction period or during or after construction of the building". The expense is related to the construction of the building if it is incurred as a result of the construction. The CRA takes the position that ITA 18(3.1) would apply to financing fees related to the period of construction that are deductible under ITA 20(1)(e) in taxation years after the period of construction.

In VD 2009-0329971C6, in respect of a real estate construction project that is in progress and from which no income has been generated, the CRA is asked to consider the treatment of the following expenses: the current insurance expenses of the building; the accounting and bookkeeping expenses; the advertising expenses incurred in order to sell or to rent the buildings; and the general and administrative expenses directly relating to the rental or the sale of the apartments. The CRA states:

Whether or not a specific expense, like those mentioned in this question, is described in subsection 18(3.1) of the ITA is a question of fact which must be resolved by considering the period for which the expense is incurred and by establishing if it is or is not incurred for construction purposes. Therefore, the insurance expenses incurred during the construction should be added to the cost of the building but only to the extent of the portion relating to the construction. For example, this would be the case for the additional insurance expenses that the taxpayer must assume to cover the risk relating to the construction.

The accounting and bookkeeping expenses, the general and administrative expenses and the advertising expenses are normally not considered as costs relating to the construction of a building. However, if one of these expenses can clearly be related to the construction, subsection 18(3.1) of the ITA will apply to this expense for the period described by this subsection. This expense must therefore be included in computing the cost or capital cost of the building in question.

In CRA Guide T4036: *Rental Income*, the CRA states:

Construction soft costs

You may have certain costs relating to the period you were constructing, renovating, or altering your rental building to make it more suitable to rent. These expenses are sometimes called soft costs. They include: interest; legal fees; accounting fees; and property taxes.

Soft costs for the period of construction, renovation, or alteration of a building are made up of the soft costs related to the building and ownership of the related land. The building's related land consists of the land: that is under the building; or that is just beside the land under the building; used or intended for use for a parking area, driveway, yard, garden, or any other similar use; and necessary for the use or intended use of the building.

Depending on your situation, soft costs may be deductible as a current expense or added to the cost of the building.

Soft costs related to the building may be deductible as a current expense if they relate to: only the construction, renovation, or alteration of the building; and the time period it took place in.

We consider the period of construction, renovation, or alteration to be completed on whichever date is earlier: the date the work is completed; or the date you rent 90% or more of the building.

When these conditions are met, the amount of soft costs related to the building that you can deduct is limited to the amount of rental income earned from the building.

Soft costs that do not meet the above conditions can be added to the capital cost of the building and not the land.

ITA 18(3.1)–(3.3), 53(1)(d.3), (e)(xi), *Morris*, 2014 CarswellNat 1753 (TCC) (repairs and minor renovations did not trigger ITA 18(3.1)), *Firth*, [2009] 5 C.T.C. 2027 (TCC), *Lee*, 2008 CarswellNat 1902 (TCC), *Janota*, 2010 CarswellNat 2476 (TCC), *Preiss*, [2010] 1 C.T.C. 2164 (TCC), CRA Guide T4036, Folio S3-F4-C1, IT-79R3, VDs 2010-0386121E5, 2004-0056861E5, 2007-0231881I7, 2002-0147295, 2002-0141627, 2001-0069497, 9426975, December 1990-259, Quebec Bulletin IMP. 157-4/R1: *Utility service connections*

¶5256 — *Undeveloped or Vacant Land*

Income taxes, profit taxes, or land transfer taxes related to vacant land are not deductible. Expenses for interest on debt relating to the purchase of the land and property taxes payable on the land are deductible, limited to the net rental income before the interest and property tax deductions. The deduction cannot create or increase a rental loss or reduce other sources of income; however, the cost of the land may be increased by the non-deductible portion of interest and property taxes. If no rental income is earned, the mortgage interest and property taxes are not deductible, and the non-deductible interest and property taxes are not added to the cost of the land.

ITA 18(2) places a limit on the deduction of interest and property taxes incurred in connection with vacant land unless the land is held primarily for the purpose of producing income or is used in the course of a business carried on in the year. "Business" for this purpose does not include an "adventure or concern in the nature of trade" (see ¶4015). As such, the deduction of carrying charges is restricted in respect of land held for speculation even if it could be successfully argued that such land was "used" in the undertaking.

Interest on debt relating to the acquisition of land includes interest paid or payable by the taxpayer in a year in respect of borrowed money that cannot be identified with particular land if it may reasonably be considered that borrowed money has been used in respect of, or for the acquisition of, land.

Where ITA 18(2) applies, the deduction of carrying charges is limited to the net revenue, if any, from the land for the year.

ITA 10(1.1) permits a taxpayer to include in the cost of land that is held as inventory, amounts for which a deduction is denied by reason of ITA 18(2) to the taxpayer. Where the relevant carrying charges were disallowed to another taxpayer, the addition to the cost of the land can only be made if such charges have not been added to the cost of any property of the other taxpayer (except as an addition to the adjusted cost base of a specified shareholder's shares by virtue of ITA 53(1)(d.3) or as an addition to the adjusted cost base of a taxpayer's partnership interest under ITA 53(1)(e)(xi)).

In the case of land that is held as capital property, compensation for the loss of current deductibility is provided by ITA 53(1)(h), which allows the carrying charges to be added to the adjusted cost base of the land to the taxpayer.

For the purpose of computing disallowed interest and property taxes relevant to vacant land, land is defined as excluding a building or other fixed structure on the land, as well as the land underneath such building or immediately adjoining it that is a parking area, driveway, yard, or garden that is necessary for the use of such building.

The CRA regards a taxpayer as having acquired a building or other structure when site development has begun on land unequivocally committed to use as a building site provided that completion of construction proceeds in an orderly and continuous fashion without undue delay (IT-153R3, paras. 7 and 8). Site development is considered to begin with the installation of services.

Land is defined in ITA 18(3) as including a parking lot for which fees are charged. However, such lots would qualify for exclusion from the expense restriction rules in ITA 18(2) if held primarily for the purpose of gaining or producing income of the taxpayer therefrom for the year.

As mentioned above, the restriction imposed under ITA 18(2) does not apply if the land can reasonably be considered to have been, in the year, used in the course of a business carried on in the particular year by the taxpayer, other than a business in the ordinary course of which land is held primarily for the purpose of resale or development, or held primarily for the purpose of gaining or producing income of the taxpayer from the land for the particular year. In VD 9638817, the CRA stated the exception would not apply in a situation in which an adjacent parcel of land was acquired by a motel to prevent others from developing it to the detriment of the motel business where the land acquired was left vacant. The CRA's position was that vacant land is not generally considered to be "used" in the course of carrying on business. If the land had been used for additional parking or some other use (such as a picnic area, etc), the CRA's position may have changed. Also, in VD 2001-0081607, the CRA stated that the fact that a taxpayer generates rental income would not, in and of itself, satisfy the purpose test in ITA 18(2)(d). The CRA's position is that the main question that must be addressed is the taxpayer's main reason for holding the land.

ITA 10(1.1), 18(2)-(3), 53(1)(d.3), 53(1)(h), 53(1)(e)(xi), *Heinze*, [1985] 1 C.T.C. 2046 (TCC); aff'd by FCTD 1997 CarswellNat 365, *Anstel Holdings Ltd*, [1991] 2 C.T.C. 2515 (TCC), IT-153R3, Form T2005, 2010-0386121E5, 2007-0262121E5, 2008-0280971E5, 2004-0061651E5, 2002-0141627, 9606735, Lorne Shillinger, "Developments in the Taxation of Real Estate Investments," *Report of Proceedings of Fifty-Ninth*

Tax Conference, 2007 Tax Conference (Toronto: Canadian Tax Foundation, 2008), 13:1–61, Quebec Bulletin IMP. 164-1/R1: *Tax Treatment of Certain Expenses (Interest and Property Taxes) in Relation to Land*

¶5300 — Rental Losses

Taxpayers will have a rental loss if the taxpayer's rental expenses are greater than the taxpayer's gross rental income. Rental losses are non-capital losses that can be applied against other sources of income. Generally, rental losses may be carried back three years or forward 20 years and deducted against taxable income in those years. For more information on the deduction of non-capital losses of other years, see Line 252 at ¶9360.

Prior to the decision of the Supreme Court of Canada in *Stewart v R*, [2002] 3 C.T.C. 439, taxpayers claiming losses attributable to expenses involved in renting out property were denied the deduction where there was no "reasonable expectation of profit" (REOP) from the property in question. Instead, the expenses were held to be personal or living expenses. However, in *Stewart*, the Supreme Court concluded that "reasonable expectation of profit" should not be accepted as the test to determine whether a taxpayer's activities constitute a source of income, and therefore, severely restricted the application of the REOP test.

In *Stewart*, an experienced real estate investor acquired four condominium units from which he earned rental income. The units were highly leveraged. For the 1990 to 1992 taxation years the taxpayer claimed losses resulting mainly from the interest expenses on the money borrowed to acquire the units. The Minister disallowed the losses on the basis that the taxpayer had no reasonable expectation of profit for the years in question. The Supreme Court of Canada applied the source test and concluded that the taxpayer's rental activities constituted a source of income. In allowing the taxpayer's appeal, the Court stated that a property rental activity lacking any element of personal use or benefit is clearly a commercial activity. While there was no personal element in this case, the Court stated that even if the appellant had made use of one or more of the properties for his personal benefit, the Minister would not be entitled to conclude that no business existed without further analysis. At pg. 464 of the judgment, the Court noted:

> A taxpayer in such circumstances would have the opportunity to establish that his or her predominant intention was to make a profit from the activity and that the activity was carried out in accordance with objective standards of business-like behaviour. Whether a reasonable expectation of profit existed may be a factor that is taken into consideration in that analysis.

In place of the REOP test, the Supreme Court established a two-stage "pursuit of profit" test to determine whether a taxpayer's activities constituted a source of income. First, one asks whether the activity of the taxpayer is undertaken in pursuit of profit or whether it is a personal endeavour. This requires the taxpayer to establish that his or her predominant intention is to make a profit from the activity and that the activity has been carried out in accordance with objective standards of businesslike behaviour. While the reasonable expectation of profit is a factor to be considered at this stage of the test, it is not the only factor, nor is it conclusive.

Second, if it is not a personal endeavour, one asks whether the source of the income is a business or property. To the Supreme Court, the "pursuit of profit" source test only requires analysis in situations where there is some personal or hobby element to the activity in question. Where the nature of an activity is clearly commercial, there is no need to analyze the taxpayer's business decisions, as such endeavours necessarily involve the pursuit of profit. Moreover, where the nature of a taxpayer's venture contains elements suggesting that it could be considered a hobby or other personal pursuit, but the venture is undertaken in a sufficiently commercial manner, the venture is to be considered a source of income for purposes of the ITA.

The Supreme Court also stated in this case that the motivation of capital gains accords with the ordinary business person's understanding of "pursuit of profit", and may be taken into account in determining whether the taxpayer's activity is commercial in nature. In applying its source test to the *Stewart* case, the Supreme Court concluded that the taxpayer's rental activities constituted a source of income from which he was entitled to deduct losses.

In *Preiss v R*, [2010] 1 C.T.C. 2164 (TCC), expenses of a rental property were disallowed where the property was rented to the taxpayer's mother (the Court found there was no expectation of profit). In *Lessard v R*, 2010 CarswellNat 4823 (TCC), expenses to renovate a rental property shortly before it was converted to personal use were held to be personal expenses (the taxpayer was unable to prove on balance of probabilities that expenses made for his rental property were commercial in nature).

The CRA provides the following comments in Guide T4036 regarding rental losses and renting below fair market value:

> You have a rental loss if your rental expenses are more than your gross rental income. If you incur the expenses to earn income, you can deduct your rental loss against your other sources of income.

Renting below fair market value

> You can deduct your expenses only if you incur them to earn income. In certain cases, you may ask your son or daughter, or anyone else living with you, to pay a small amount for the upkeep of your house or to cover the cost of groceries. You do not report this amount in your income, and you cannot claim rental expenses. This is a cost-sharing arrangement, so you cannot claim a rental loss.

> If you lose money because you rent a property to a person you know for less money than you would to a person you do not know, you cannot claim a rental loss. When your rental expenses are consistently more than your rental income, you may not be allowed to claim a rental loss because your rental operation is not considered to be a source of income. You can claim a rental loss if you are renting the property to a relative for the same rate as you would charge other tenants and you expect to make a profit.

VD 2011-0393551E5, ITTN-25, Elaine S Sibson, FCA, "Reasonable Expectation of Profit: A Return to Sanity?" *Report of Proceedings of Fifty-Fourth Tax Conference, 2002 Tax Conference* (Toronto: Canadian Tax Foundation, 2003), 6:1–10, Gordon Williamson and Larry Chapman, "The Evolution of the Reasonable Expectation of Profit Test," (2010), vol. 58, *Special Supplement Canadian Tax Journal*, 175–190.

¶5400 — Principal Residence: Change-In-Use Rules

Generally, a taxpayer's personal residence is exempt from tax as a result of the "principal residence exemption" (see ¶4430). Essentially, the principal residence exemption permits individuals to escape taxation on a gain realized on a home that is considered to be the taxpayer's principal residence. However, special "change in use" rules apply where a taxpayer rents out all or a portion of their principal residence for the purposes of earning income.

¶5410 — Change in Use from Personal to Income Producing

Where a taxpayer completely converts their principal residence to an income-producing use, the taxpayer is deemed to have disposed of the property at fair market value, and reacquired it immediately thereafter at the same amount. Any gain on the deemed disposition may be eliminated or reduced by the principal residence exemption. Individuals who dispose of property in 2016 or later taxation years for which they are claiming the principal residence exemption must complete page two of Schedule 3 to designate the property as a principal residence and report the details of the disposition. This reporting requirement also applies to deemed dispositions arising from a change in use (see ¶4432).

The taxpayer may defer recognition of any gain that is not eliminated by the principal residence exemption for up to four taxations years by electing under ITA 45(2) to be deemed not to have made the change in use of the property. The election is made by means of a letter signed by the taxpayer and filed with the income tax return for the year in which the change in use occurred. The taxpayer is not required to live in the property during the four years; however, the taxpayer must be resident in Canada during those years for the full benefit of the principal residence exemption to apply. Any net rental income earned in respect of the property must be reported for tax purposes; however, for taxation years covered by the election, CCA cannot be claimed on the property.

The following example is provided in paragraph 2.50 of Folio S1-F3-C2, *Principal Residence*:

> Mr. A and his family lived in a house for a number of years until September 30, 2003. From October 1, 2003 until March 31, 2008 they lived elsewhere and Mr. A rented the house to a third party. On April 1, 2008, they moved back into the house and lived in it until it was sold in 2011. When he filed his 2011 income tax return, Mr. A designated the house as his principal residence for the 2004 to 2007 taxation years inclusive (i.e., the maximum four years) by virtue of a subsection 45(2) election (which he had already filed with his 2003 income tax return) having been in force for those years. (He was able to make this designation because no other property had been designated as a principal residence by him or a member of his family unit for those years.) He designated the house as his principal residence for all the other years in which he owned it by virtue of his having ordinarily inhabited it during those years, including the 2003 and 2008 years. Having been resident in Canada at all times, Mr. A's gain otherwise determined on the disposition of the house in 2011 was, therefore, completely eliminated by the principal residence exemption.

If the reason for the change in use is that the taxpayer or his or her spouse or common-law partner has been relocated for employment purposes, the property may qualify as the taxpayer's principal residence for more than four taxation years, subject to the following conditions: 1) the employer must not be related to the taxpayer or the taxpayer's spouse or common-law partner; 2) the property must be at least 40 kilometers farther from the new place of employment than the subsequent residence; and 3) either the taxpayer resumes inhabitation of the property during the term of employment with the same employer, or by the end of the taxation year following the year in which the employment terminates.

¶5420 — Change in Use from Income-Producing to Personal

Where a taxpayer has completely changed the use of a property from income-producing to personal, the taxpayer is deemed to have disposed of the property, and reacquired it immediately thereafter at fair market value. Individuals who dispose of property in 2016 or later taxation years for which they are claiming the principal residence exemption must complete page two of Schedule 3 to designate the property as a principal residence and report the details of the disposition. This reporting requirement also applies to deemed dispositions arising from a change in use (see ¶4432).

If the deemed disposition results in a taxable capital gain, the taxpayer may defer recognition of the gain for up to four taxation years by electing under ITA 45(3) to be deemed not to have made the change in use of the property. The election is made by means of a letter signed by the taxpayer and filed with the income tax return for the year in which the property is ultimately disposed of.

Where an election is made under ITA 45(3), the net income from the property for the period before the change in use must still be reported. Note that this election is not allowed to be made if the taxpayer has claimed capital cost allowance on the property. As in the case of an election under ITA 45(2) (see ¶5410), the taxpayer must be resident in Canada for the full benefit of the principal residence exemption to apply.

The following example is provided in paragraph 2.56 of Folio S1-F3-C2, *Principal Residence*:

> Mr. X bought a house in 2003 and rented it to a third party until mid-2009. Mr. X and his family then lived in the house until it was sold in 2011. Mr. X has been resident in Canada at all times. When he filed his 2011 income tax return, Mr. X designated the house as his principal residence for the 2009 to 2011 taxation years inclusive, by virtue of his having ordinarily inhabited it during those years. He also designated the house as his principal residence for the 2005 to 2008 years inclusive (i.e., the maximum 4 years) by virtue of a subsection 45(3) election, which he filed with his 2011 income tax return (he was able to make this designation because (i) no other property had been designated by him or a member of his family unit for those years, and (ii) he did not claim any CCA when reporting the net income from the property before the change in use). However, his gain otherwise determined on the disposition of the house in 2011 could not be fully eliminated by the principal residence exemption formula in ¶8 because he could not designate the house as his principal residence for the 2003 and 2004 years.

¶5430 — Partial Changes in Use

Where a taxpayer has partially converted a principal residence to an income-producing use, there is a deemed disposition of the portion of the property so converted (such portion is usually calculated on the basis of the area involved) for proceeds equal to its proportionate share of the property's fair market value, and a deemed reacquisition immediately thereafter of the same portion at the same value. Any gain on the deemed disposition is usually eliminated or reduced by the principal residence exemption. Individuals who dispose of property in 2016 or later taxation years for which they are claiming the principal residence exemption must complete page two of Schedule 3 to designate the property as a principal residence and report the details of the disposition. This reporting requirement also applies to deemed dispositions arising from a change in use (see ¶4432).

Where the portion of the property so changed is later converted back to use as part of the principal residence, there is a second deemed disposition (and reacquisition) thereof at fair market value. A taxable capital gain attributable to the period of use of such portion of the property for income-producing purposes can arise from such a second deemed disposition or from an actual sale of the whole property subsequent to the original partial change in use. An election under ITA 45(2) or (3) (see ¶5410 and ¶5420) cannot be made where there is a partial change in use of a property.

The deemed disposition on a partial change in use of a property only applies where the partial change in use is substantial and of a more permanent nature (i.e., where there is a structural change). An example would be where a taxpayer converts a portion of a house into a self-contained domestic establishment for purposes of earning rental income (i.e., into a duplex, triplex, etc.). In this case, the taxpayer reports the income and may claim the expenses pertaining to the altered portion of the property (i.e., a reasonable portion of the expenses relating to the whole property).

It is the CRA's practice not to apply the deemed disposition rule, but rather to consider that the entire property retains its nature as a principal residence, where all of the following conditions are met: (a) the income-producing use is ancillary to the main use of the property as a residence, (b) there is no structural change to the property, and (c) no CCA is claimed on the property. These conditions can be met, for example, where a taxpayer rents one or more rooms in their home. In this case, the taxpayer reports the income and may claim the expenses (other than CCA) pertaining to the portion of the property used for income-producing purposes. In the event that the taxpayer commences to claim CCA on the portion of the property used for producing income, the deemed disposition rule is applied as of the time at which the income-producing use commenced.

ITA 13(7), 45(1)–(3), 54.1, S1-F3-C2, *Principal Residence*, paras. 2.48–2.64

¶5500 — Non-Residents Electing under Section 216

The purpose of ITA 216 is to extend to non-resident persons the privilege of paying tax on their net income derived from the rental of real property in Canada or from timber royalties instead of being subject to the flat rate of withholding tax normally required by ITA 212 to be deducted at the source from the gross amount.

¶5510 — Alternative re Rents

A non-resident recipient of real property rentals or timber royalties from a Canadian source is normally subject to a 25% flat rate of withholding tax on the gross amount of rent or royalties that the non-resident is entitled to, without any deduction for expenses or depreciation. By virtue of ITA 216(1), however, the non-resident may choose to file a T1 return (Form T1159, *Income Tax Return for Electing under Section 216*) as if the non-resident had been a resident of Canada in the taxation year in which the rent or royalties were received and as if that income were the only income the recipient had that was taxable under Part I of the ITA. If this alternative method is chosen, the following conditions apply:

1. The non-resident must file the required return (i.e., Form T1159) within two years after the end of the year in which the income in question was received (the alternative method will be forfeited if the return is not filed within that two-year period);

2. Where the non-resident has made an undertaking under ITA 216(4) on Form NR6, *Undertaking to File an Income Tax Return by a Non-Resident Receiving Rent from Real Property or Receiving a Timber Royalty*, to file a T1 return (i.e., Form T1159) within 6 months after the end of the taxation year, the return must be filed within that 6-month period;

3. The special return required by ITA 216 must reflect all rental income derived from real property in Canada in the year and all timber royalties (i.e., only one such return may be filed for a given taxation year) and such a return in no way affects a regular return which the non-resident may also be required to file for the same year by reason of being employed in Canada in the year or carrying on business in Canada;

4. There may be claimed as deductions from the income in question capital cost allowance under ITA 20(1)(a) and all other expenses incurred for the purpose of earning that income within the conditions imposed by ITA 18(1)(a), (b), (h) and 60 (see Form T1159 and paragraph 4 of IT-393R2);

5. None of the deductions normally allowable in determining taxable income may be claimed (i.e., those contained in Division C of Part I of the ITA);

6. No tax credits under ITA 118 to 118.9 (e.g., personal tax credits, medical expense credit, etc.) may be claimed;

7. Amounts of tax that had been deducted at the source and remitted under Part XIII of the ITA in respect of the income in question will be treated as payments on account of the non-resident's tax under ITA 216, and any surplus will be refunded to the non-resident; and

8. The regular provisions regarding payment of tax will apply (i.e., relating to assessments and appeals).

¶5520 — Meaning of "Timber Royalty"

For the purposes of Part XIII, a timber royalty includes any consideration for a right under or pursuant to which a right to cut or take timber from a timber resource property or a timber limit in Canada is obtained or derived, computed by reference to the amount of timber cut or taken.

¶5530 — Optional Method of Payment

If the non-resident person files an "undertaking" with the Minister on Form NR6 by January 1 of the taxation year in question (or by the due date of the first rental payment for the year) under which the non-resident undertakes to file a return under ITA 216 within 6 months after the end of the taxation year, the Canadian payer will be authorized to not remit the normal withholding tax on the gross income as otherwise required, but instead pay to the Receiver General in the course of the year only tax at the normal withholding rate computed on whatever net amounts become available for remittance to the non-resident. Tax so paid will be applied directly to the non-resident's tax for the year under ITA 216.

If, however, the non-resident person later fails to file the return in accordance with the undertaking, or fails to pay the tax in respect thereof on time, the Canadian resident or agent must pay the full tax which would be payable on the gross amount, minus the tax already remitted in the year under the alternative arrangement.

¶5540 — Subsequent Sale of Canadian Property

Where a non-resident individual chooses to file a return under ITA 216 for a taxation year and claims a deduction for capital cost allowance in respect of the Canadian property or timber limit, then in any subsequent year in which that property is disposed of for an amount in excess of its undepreciated capital cost, the non-resident is required to file a T1 return for that subsequent year and report therein the amount of capital cost allowance subject to recapture. Such a return is not required if the proceeds of disposition are not sufficient to make the recapture provisions applicable (see also para. 7 of IT-393R2).

Capital cost allowance recapturable under these circumstances is not restricted to capital cost allowance claimed by the taxpayer under ITA 216 while resident outside Canada but, if the taxpayer was formerly resident in Canada, may extend to capital cost allowance claimed during such period (*Deitcher v. R.*, [1978] C.T.C. 2002; aff'd by FCTD [1979] C.T.C. 500.

Where a return is required due to a recapture of capital cost allowance, it must also reflect any rental income or timber royalties received in the year. The same conditions as described in 1–8 above apply in respect of this return.

At the 2010 CTF Annual Tax Conference CRA Roundtable (November 30, 2010), the CRA stated that effective after 2010, where a non-resident taxpayer files a section 216 return in respect of a Canadian rental property and elects to capitalize interest on funds borrowed to purchase the property under ITA 21, the CRA's position is that the computation of a capital gain on a subsequent disposition of the property should not take into account the capitalized interest. In respect of interest capitalized before 2011, the CRA will not automatically deny the amount added to the cost base of the rental property; however, the CRA stated that it will review the reasonableness of the interest rate, particularly in respect of interest that is payable to a non-arm's length person.

ITA 216, Guide T4144, IT-393R2: *Election Re: Tax on Rents and Timber Royalties Non-Residents*

¶5550 — Rental or Other Business

Where a non-resident individual's rental activities in Canada are such as to constitute "carrying on business in Canada", the non-resident is taxable under Part I of the ITA and must file a T1 return to report the net income from the Canadian business. The non-resident is permitted to deduct expenses incurred to carry on the business just as a Canadian resident would. Because the latter deductions are not allowed in a return filed under ITA 216 in respect of rental income, it may be to the non-resident's advantage to be found to be "carrying on business" in respect of Canadian rentals.

ITA 253 extends the common law concept of "carrying on business" in Canada by deeming a non-resident person to have been carrying on business in Canada if the person engages in certain specified activities in Canada or disposes of certain property, interests or options. These are summarized in paragraph 8 of IT-420R3, *Non-Residents — Income Earned in Canada*:

Income earned in Canada by a non-resident includes, by virtue of subparagraph 115(1)(a)(ii), income from carrying on business in Canada. Supplementing the normal meaning of the term, ITA 253 deems a non-resident to be "carrying on business in Canada" if

(a) the non-resident solicits orders or offers anything for sale in Canada through an agent or servant, whether the contract or transaction is to be completed inside or outside Canada or partly inside and partly outside Canada;

(b) the non-resident (or an agent acting on behalf of the non-resident) produces, grows, mines, creates, manufactures, fabricates, improves, packs, preserves or constructs, in whole or in part, anything in Canada, whether or not it is exported from Canada prior to its sale; or

(c) the non-resident disposes of: (i) Canadian resource property, except where the disposition results in an amount being included under paragraph 66.2(1)(a) or 66.4(1)(a); (ii) property (other than depreciable property) that is a timber resource property or an interest in or option on timber resource property; or (iii) real property (other than capital property) situated in Canada, including an interest in or option on such real property, whether or not the property exists;

ITA 253, *Backman*, [2001] 2 C.T.C. 11, *Maya Forestales*, 2005 CarswellNat 724 (TCC), IT-420R3

¶5600 — Completing Form T776, Statement of Real Estate Rentals

¶5610 — Identification and Details of Other Co-Owners

¶5611 — *Identification & Period*

If this is the first year of operation, enter the year, month, and day the taxpayer's rental operation began. Otherwise, enter January 1 of the current year. Enter the current tax year in the area after "to:".

¶5612 — *Are You a Co-Owner or a Partner of a Partnership?*

Generally, if a taxpayer owns the rental property with one or more persons (including a spouse or common-law partner), the taxpayer is a co-owner, unless a partnership exists. A partnership is a relationship between two or more people carrying on a business, with or without a written agreement, to make a profit. If there is no business in common, there is no partnership. Co-ownership of a rental property as an investment does not constitute a partnership (for more information, see Folio S4-F16-C1, *What is a Partnership?*).

Partnerships that meet certain financial thresholds or that have another partnership, corporation, or trust as a partner are required to file a T5013 Summary, *Information Return of Partnership Income*. If the taxpayer is a partner of either of these types of partnerships, the taxpayer should receive two copies of a T5013 or T5013A slip from the partnership. If the taxpayer is a partner of a partnership and received a T5013 or T5013A slip, do not complete all of Form T776. Enter the taxpayer's 9 digit Partnership Business Number and percentage of ownership in the Identification area. Enter on Line 9369 the amount from Box 26 — Canadian and foreign net rental income (loss) (or Box 23 — Limited partnership rental income (loss) if a limited partnership) of the T5013 or T5013A slip.

The taxpayer's share of the net partnership income (loss) on Line 9369 may need to be adjusted if the taxpayer received a GST/HST rebate for partners (see Line 9974 — GST/HST rebate for partners received in the year) or if the taxpayer is claiming deductible expenses as a partner that were not deducted elsewhere on Form T776 (see Line 9943 — other expenses of the partner). Then enter on Line 9946 the net income (loss).

If the taxpayer is a partner in a partnership and did not receive a T5013 or T5013A slip, or if the taxpayer is a co-owner, complete all of the areas of Form T776 that apply. Also complete the "Details of other co-owners and partners" area of the form.

¶5613 — *Tax Shelter Identification Number*

Enter the taxpayer's tax shelter identification number, if applicable, from Box 3 of the T5013 or T5013A slip. To claim deductions or losses from tax shelter investments, attach to the income tax return information slips T5003, *Statement of Tax Shelter Information*, and T5013A, *Statement of Partnership Income for Tax Shelters and Renounced Resource Expenses*, if applicable. Also attach a completed Form T5004, *Claim for Tax Shelter Loss or Deduction, Gift and Donation Tax Credit, or Political Donation Tax Credit*. Make sure the form shows the tax shelter identification number. If this is the first year the taxpayer is making a claim for a tax shelter, include a copy of Form T5003 with the income tax return. If the tax shelter is a partnership, include the T5013A slip with the return.

¶5620 — Rental Income (Form T776: Lines 8141, 8230, 8299)

¶5621 — *Total Gross Rents (Form T776: Line 8141)*

List the address of the taxpayer's rental property and the number of units rented and report the rental income earned in the calendar year (from January 1 to December 31). Include rents in income for the year in which they are due, whether or not the taxpayer received them in that year, and deduct expenses in the year incurred, no matter when the expense was actually paid. Do not change the percentage of the rental income or loss reported each year unless the percentage of the taxpayer's ownership in the property changes.

Rental income earned from rental properties located outside of Canada must also be included in rental income (see ¶5005). Generally, the income is calculated in the same way as for a Canadian rental property. Amounts are required to be reported in Canadian dollars. Dollar amounts for income transactions should be converted into Canadian dollars using the Bank of Canada exchange rate on the day of the transaction (www.bankofcanada.ca). The taxpayer may be able to claim a foreign tax credit for foreign taxes paid (see ¶11010).

¶5622 — *Other Related Income (Form T776: Line 8230)*

Enter on Line 8230 any other income related to rental income. For example, where an individual rents farmland in exchange for a share of a tenant's crop (i.e., "sharecropping"), the fair market value of the crop share must be included in rental income as other related income. Also include on this line amounts of lease payments received, such as payments for granting or extending a lease or sublease; permitting a sublease; and cancelling a lease or sublease.

¶5623 — *Gross Rental Income (Form T776: Line 8299)*

The taxpayer's gross rental income is the total "Gross rents" on Form T776. Enter this amount on Line 160 of the income tax return. If the taxpayer is a co-owner of the rental property or a partner of a partnership that is not required to provide a T5013 or T5013A slip, enter the gross rental income for the entire property on Line 160. Do not split the gross income according to the taxpayer's ownership share.

¶5630 — Rental Expenses

Enter the taxpayer's expenses from the rental property on Form T776. In the first column, "Total expense", enter the full amount of each expense. In the second column, "Personal portion", enter the part of each expense that was for personal use. Enter the totals of each column on the appropriate lines to calculate the taxpayer's deductible expenses. Then subtract them from gross rental income (Line 8299). If the taxpayer is a co-owner or partner of a partnership, show the personal portion of the expenses for all co-owners or partners.

As discussed earlier in this chapter, expenses include the allowable portion of advertising costs (see ¶5220.2), insurance (see ¶5220.3), interest (see ¶5220.4), office expenses (see ¶5220.5), professional fees (see ¶5220.6), management and administration fees (see ¶5220.7), maintenance and repairs (see ¶5220.8), salaries, wages, and benefits (see ¶5220.9), property taxes (¶see ¶5220.10), travel (see ¶5220.11), utilities (see ¶5220.12), motor vehicle expenses (see ¶5220.13) and other expenses (see ¶5220.14). Taxpayers cannot deduct land transfer taxes, mortgage principal, penalties, or the value of the taxpayer's own services or labour.

¶5631 — *Net Income (Loss) before Adjustments (Form T776: Line 9369)*

Enter the gross income minus deductible expenses. This amount is the net rental income of all co-owners or partners before any claim for capital cost allowance. If the taxpayer is a co-owner, enter the share of the amount from Line 9369 on Line 9. This amount is based on the taxpayer's share of ownership of the rental property. If the taxpayer is a co-owner or partner, complete the area called "Details of other co-owners and partners" on page 1 of Form T776.

¶5632 — *Other Expenses of the Co-owner (Form T776: Line 9945)*

Enter the amount of deductible expenses as a co-owner that was not deducted elsewhere on Form T776.

¶5633 — *Recaptured Capital Cost Allowance & Terminal Loss (Form T776: Lines 9947, 9948)*

Enter any recapture of CCA on Line 9947 and any terminal loss on Line 9948 (see ¶5240, ¶7145, and ¶7150). If the taxpayer is a co-owner, enter the taxpayer's share of the amount of the recapture or the terminal loss.

¶5634 — *Capital Cost Allowance (Form T776: Line 9936)*

Enter the amount of the taxpayer's CCA as calculated in Part A on Form T776 (see under ¶5240). If the taxpayer is a partner of a partnership that does not need to issue a T5013 or T5013A slip, enter the total CCA allocated on the financial statements of the partnership. Do not use this line if the taxpayer is a member of a partnership that has to file Form T5013. The CCA amount is already included in Box 26 of the T5013 or T5013A slip.

¶5635 — *Net Income (Loss)(Form T776: Line 17)*

Enter on Line 17 the taxpayer's net income (or loss) after subtracting the claim for CCA on Line 9936.

¶5636 — *Partnerships (Form T776: Line 18)*

If the taxpayer is a member of a partnership, enter the taxpayer's share of Line 17 or the amount from Box 26 or 23 from theT5013 or T5013A slip.

¶5637 — *GST/HST Rebate for Partners Received in the Year (Form T776: Line 9974)*

If the taxpayer received a GST/HST rebate for partners, report the amount of the rebate that relates to eligible expenses other than CCA on Line 9974 of Form T776 in the year received.

¶5638 — *Other Expenses of the Partner (Form T776: Line 9943)*

Enter the amount of deductible expenses as a partner that was not deducted elsewhere on Form T776.

¶5639 — *Your Net income (Loss) (Form T776: Line 9946)*

Enter this amount on Line 126 of the taxpayer's income tax return. If the taxpayer has a rental loss, show the loss in brackets. A rental loss occurs when the taxpayer's rental expenses are more than the taxpayer's gross rental income. If the taxpayer incurred the expenses to earn income, the rental loss can be deducted against the taxpayer's other sources of income (see ¶5300).

Chapter 6 — Business and Professional Income

Contents

¶6100 Business Income (T1: Lines 135, 162)

    ¶6110 Determining Business Income

    ¶6120 Limitations on Deductibility of Expenses

    ¶6130 Allowable Deductions for Expenses

    ¶6140 Non-Allowable Deductions for Expenses

    ¶6150 Capital Cost Allowance (CCA)

    ¶6160 Eligible Capital Expenditures

    ¶6170 Special Situations

¶6200 Professional Income (T1: Lines 137, 164)

    ¶6210 Determining Professional Income

    ¶6220 Election to Exclude Work in Progress (WIP)

    ¶6230 Professional Expenses

    ¶6240 Incorporation of a Professional Practice

    ¶6250 Service and Management Corporations

¶6300 Farming and Fishing Income (T1: Lines 141, 143, 168, 170)

    ¶6310 Computing Farming and Fishing Income

    ¶6320 Definition of Farming and Fishing

    ¶6330 Other Considerations

    ¶6340 Net Income Stabilization Account (NISA)

    ¶6350 Farming Losses

This Chapter discusses the calculation of self-employment income, including business and professional income, which are calculated on Form T2125, *Statement of Business or Professional Activities*. Business income calculated on Form T2125 is reported on Line 135 (net business income) and Line 162 (gross business income). Professional income calculated on Form T2125 is reported on Line 137 (net professional income) and Line 164 (gross professional income).

This Chapter also discusses the calculation of farming and fishing income. Farming income is calculated on Form T2042, *Statement of Farming Activities*, and the farming income information from Form T2042 is reported on Line 141 (net farming income) and Line 163 (gross farming income). Fishing income is calculated on Form T2121, *Statement of Fishing Activities*, and the fishing income information from Form T2121 is reported on Line 143 (net fishing income) and Line 165 (gross fishing income).

¶6100 — Business Income (T1: Lines 135, 162)

¶6110 — Determining Business Income

¶6111 — *Distinguishing Business Income from Other Types of Income*

It may not always be clear whether an individual's income should be classified as business income, property income, or employment income. Distinguishing business income from other types of income is important because it may affect the rate of income inclusion, the nature and allowable amount of deductible expenses, the timing of income recognition, and the method of tax payments, among other things.

¶6111.1 — *Business Income vs. Property Income*

The distinction between profits on account of income or capital is often very difficult. The taxpayer must distinguish between assets that are of a purely capital nature with which income is earned and those that are of an inventory or stock nature that are turned over, consumed, or sold in the ordinary course of earning income from a business. For example, if an investor deriving income from the receipt of real estate rentals and interest and dividends from bonds and stocks were to sell the real estate or to dispose of the stocks and bonds, the taxpayer would be disposing of capital assets and not inventory. Profit, if any, would be taxed as a capital gain. If, however, the taxpayer were in the business of buying and selling real estate or was a broker buying and selling shares or bonds, the taxpayer would be disposing of inventory or stock in trade rather than capital assets. Consequently, any profits would be taxable as business income.

The distinction between "income" and "capital gains" is primarily derived from case law. It is a question of fact whether or not a gain or a loss on the disposition of any property is on account of income or capital. The basic question to consider when distinguishing between income and capital gains is generally: is an investment being sold or is a trade being carried on? Where the issue is in doubt, there are two main tests: the intention of the taxpayer, and the taxpayer's whole course of conduct in dealing with the item in question. The intention test embraces the taxpayer's intention at the time of acquiring the object of the transaction as well as at the time of its disposition. It is possible to have an investment intention at the time of acquisition, but to have altered that intention and to have become a trader at the time of disposition. Intention is generally determined by the facts.

Following is a summary of the general case law principles applicable to individuals for distinguishing between business income and property income:

- The determination in each specific situation is a question of fact;

- The fact that property is used to earn income is not determinative;

- Property income may be derived either from a business or from the property, depending on the level of activity associated with acquiring the property income;

- Where funds are employed and risked by a business and the investment of these funds is necessary for the individual to conduct the business, the income from this investment activity will likely be considered income from a business;

- Income from property does not require active and extensive business-like intervention to produce it; it is passive income resulting from the mere ownership of property, without a significant commitment of time, labour, or attention; and

- Income from business requires organization, systematic effort, and a certain degree of activity.

For CRA comments on distinguishing between income and capital gains, see IT-218R: *Profit, Capital Gains and Losses from the Sale of Real Estate, Including Farmland and Inherited Land and Conversion of Real Estate from Capital Property to Inventory and Vice Versa*; IT-479R: *Transactions in Securities*; and VDs 2009-0321871E5, 2008-0269481E5, 2005-0127861E5, 2006-0185041E5, and 2001-0107655. See also IT-159R3: *Capital Debts Established to be Bad Debts*; IT-359R2: *Premiums and Other Amounts re Leases*; IT-346R: *Commodity Futures and*

Certain Commodities; IT-426R: *Shares Sold Subject to an Earnout Agreement*; IT-444R: *Corporations — Involuntary Dissolutions*; Folio S3-F4-C1: *General Discussion of Capital Cost Allowance*; Folio S4-F8-C1: *Business Investment Losses*; ITTN-34; and CRA Guide T4037: Capital Gains.

¶6111.2 — *Business Income vs. Employment Income*

Generally, the classification of an individual's income as either employment income or self-employment income is a question of fact, determined by looking at the following factors in the individual's specific situation: control, ownership of tools, chance of profit, and risk of loss. Distinguishing between employment income and business income is important because it affects the nature and allowable amount of deductible expenses, the timing of income recognition, and the method of tax payments. See CRA Guide RC4110, *Employee or Self-Employed?*, for more information. The taxation of employment income, benefits, and allowances are discussed in 2017 Chapter 2.

¶6112 — *Definition of Business and Carrying on Business*

"Business" is defined in ITA 248(1) to include the following: a profession, calling, trade, manufacture, or undertaking of any kind whatever, and an adventure or concern in the nature of trade. It does not, however, include an office or employment. Generally, case law has suggested asking the following two-part question to determine whether an individual's income is business income: (1) is the activity of the individual undertaken in pursuit of profit, or is it a personal endeavour?; and (2) if it is not a personal endeavour, is the source of the income business or property? The first question distinguishes between an individual's commercial and personal activities and the second question determines whether income from the activity is business income or income from property.

The concept of carrying on business in Canada is not defined in the ITA. Based on the current jurisprudence, the principal *indicia* of carrying on business are as follows:

- Habitual activity with a potential of profit or gain. The fact that profit may never result does not change the nature of the activity if the operations carried on are such that a gain is possible.

- In the absence of such habitual activity, a single purchase followed by a number of sales, or a number of purchases followed by a single comprehensive sale.

- A single isolated transaction (sometimes referred to as an adventure in the nature of trade) for the purpose of profit which, if repeated, would be a transaction in a business undertaking, and which is undertaken with the intent that it should be the first of several such transactions. In IT-459, the CRA attempts to distil the jurisprudence concerning an "adventure in the nature of trade" into some general principles. See also IT-479R: *Transactions in Securities*, and VDs 2009-0321871E5, 2008-0269481E5, 2005-0127861E5, 2006-0185041E5, and 2001-0107655.

- A single isolated transaction by a corporation that is authorized by the corporation's articles of incorporation or charter or by corporate law and that fits the pattern of the corporation's business history.

- A single purchase and transformation of the item purchased by manufacturing or industrial process followed by resale for the purpose of profit, provided the transaction is of such magnitude that it might be the whole business for the time being if the person were regularly engaged in a trade.

- The realization of property which based on the facts relating to its acquisition and retention could not reasonably be considered to have been acquired for the purposes of investment.

¶6113 — *Calculating Business Income*

The gross revenue of a business may be either the total amounts received in cash during the year (the cash method) or the total amounts billed to customers for goods sold or services rendered during the year, whether or not received in cash during the year (the accrual method). The accrual method is required to be used for all businesses, except where business income is derived from farming or fishing.

Income for a taxation year from a business is the profit therefrom for the year. Profit is determined by deducting from gross revenue the costs of carrying on business, established in accordance with provisions of the ITA. Where the ITA is silent, and the general law is not in conflict, the basis for acceptance or rejection of an expense will depend upon the generally accepted business and accounting principles applicable to the particular trade or business. Jurisprudence will also affect the interpretation of certain provisions in the ITA, with the result that, in some cases, recognized accounting principles will be rejected as a test of what is a deductible expenditure. The Supreme Court of Canada (*Canderel Limited v The Queen*, [1998] 2 C.T.C. 35) set out the following principles for calculating profit under the ITA:

1. The determination of profit is a question of law;

2. Profit is determined by setting against the revenues from the business for that year the expenses incurred in earning said income;

3. In seeking to ascertain profit, the goal is to obtain an accurate picture of the taxpayer's profit for the given year;

4. The taxpayer is free to adopt any method which is not inconsistent with the provisions of the *Income Tax Act*, established case law principles or "rules of law" and well-accepted business principles;

5. Well-accepted business principles, which include but are not limited to the formal codification found in GAAP, are not rules of law but interpretative aids on a case-by-case basis, depending on the facts of the taxpayer's financial situation; and

6. On reassessment, once the taxpayer has shown that he has provided an accurate picture of income for the year, which is consistent with the Act, the case law, and well-accepted business principles, the onus shifts to the Minister to show either that the figure provided does not represent an accurate picture, or that another method of computation would provide a more accurate picture.

From a practical perspective, where a provision of the ITA does not have the effect of altering the concept of "profit" under Generally Accepted Accounting Principles (GAAP), the CRA will normally accept a computation of "profit" in the ordinary accounting sense (CRA VDs 2008-0288691E5 and 2003-0051241E5).

¶6120 — Limitations on Deductibility of Expenses

ITA paragraph 18(1)(a) imposes a general restriction against the deduction of expenses, providing that, in computing the income of a taxpayer from a business or property, no deduction shall be made in respect of . . . "an outlay or expense except to the extent that it was made or incurred by the taxpayer for the purpose of gaining or producing income from the business or property." ITA 18(1)((h) further clarifies paragraph 18(1)(a) by specifically prohibiting personal or living expenses of the taxpayer as business expenses.

Accordingly, while employees are restricted with respect to expenses that are deductible against employment income, self-employed individuals may deduct any expense incurred to earn business income, subject to the following conditions: (1) the expense is made or incurred for the purpose of earning business income; (2) the expense is not a capital outlay or loss (unless specifically allowed, such as capital cost allowance); (3) the expense is not a personal or living expense; (4) the expense is reasonable in the circumstances; and (5) there are no specific provisions in the ITA that deny the deduction. These limitations are discussed below.

¶6121 — *Incurred to Earn Business Income*

In computing business income for tax purposes, an expense is deductible only to the extent it was incurred by the individual for the purpose of producing income from that business. This determination must be made on a case-by-case basis and there are no specific criteria that can be examined to determine whether an expense is deductible.

¶6122 — *Not a Capital Expense*

Capital expenses are generally not deductible in computing an individual's taxable income, except for the deduction of capital cost allowance for depreciable property. These rules limit the deduction of capital expenditures to an amount specifically permitted under the capital cost allowance regime, with the cost being deducted over a number of years.

Capital expenses in respect of depreciable property are deductible over a period of time for tax purposes under the capital cost allowance system. Whether a certain outlay is a capital expenditure or a deductible expense is often difficult to determine and will be based on the particular facts. Generally, a one-time expenditure or one that produces an enduring benefit will be capital in nature. Expenditures of a recurring nature relating to the business are generally deductible as current expenses. Questions to consider when determining whether an expense is current or capital in nature include the following:

- Does the expenditure recur in day to day operations?
- Are the costs a constant part of the daily and annual cost of doing business?
- Are similar expenditures required in the future?
- Can the operations continue in the future without this expenditure?
- Did the expenditure produce anything permanent?
- What is the relative value of the expenditure compared to previous expenditures?
- Would the expenditure produce an asset that would be eligible for a capital cost allowance claim?
- Were expenditures incurred in anticipation of a sale?

For a list of factors the CRA considers, see CRA Guide T4002, *Self-Employed Business, Professional, Commission, Farming and Fishing Income*, under "Current or capital expenses?"

¶6123 — *Not a Personal or Living Expense*

Personal or living expenses incurred by an individual are not deductible unless the expenses are incurred by the taxpayer while travelling away from home in the course of carrying on business (ITA 18(1)(h)). The deductibility of business meals and entertainment is subject to the 50% rule such that an amount equal to only one-half of the expense can be deducted (ITA 67.1). It is a question of fact whether certain expenditures are personal in nature; however, according to case law, three key questions must be considered when it is unclear whether an expense should be classified as business or personal:

- What need (personal or business) is being met by incurring the particular expenditure?
- Would the expense have been incurred if the individual was not engaged in the particular business?
- Is the need being met intrinsic to the carrying on of the individual's business?

¶6124 — *Reasonable in the Circumstances*

All expenses are subject to the test of reasonableness in ITA 67 which provides as follows: "[i]n computing income, no deduction shall be made in respect of an outlay or expense in respect of which any amount is otherwise deductible under this Act, except to the extent that the outlay or expense was reasonable in the circumstances." Even if an expense is otherwise deductible under one of the provisions discussed above, a deduction will not be allowed for any portion of the expense that is unreasonable. When determining whether an expense is reasonable, one must consider the nature and value of the expenditure. Reasonableness may be examined at both the individual expense and total expense level. In determining whether an individual expense is reasonable "in the circumstances" one would look to the amount sought to be deducted, the purpose of the expenditure, the nature of the expenditure, the similarity to and amount of other such expenses claimed, expenses of other employees or officers employed in a similar capacity, and so on (VD 9520875).

In *Mohammad v. The Queen*, 1997 CarswellNat 1025, the Federal Court of Appeal concluded that ITA 67 does not tie the reasonableness of a particular expense to revenues (i.e., it should not apply simply because the particular expense is excessive or disproportionate in relation to revenues).

Generally, the issue of reasonableness arises when dealing with payments between non-arm's length parties (such as management fees, salaries paid to family members, etc.). In non-arm's length transactions, there may be an issue of whether or not the expenditure is reasonable when compared with the services provided, and a disproportionate amount will be disallowed.

¶6125 — No Specific Provision Denying the Deduction

¶6125.1 — Political Contributions

An individual is not allowed to deduct political contributions in computing income from a business. However, individuals may be entitled to a tax credit for federal political contributions in calculating their income tax payable for the year (see ¶11020).

¶6125.2 — Prepaid Expenses

Certain prepaid expenses are not deductible in the year to which they relate (ITA 18(9)). If an individual incurs a cost in the year but does not expect to realize a benefit from it until after the end of the year, the cost is a prepaid expense. An example is a rental charge paid in the current year for a rental period after the end of the year. Generally, in computing an individual's business income, no amount may be deducted for outlays and expenses incurred in the year for services to be rendered in a subsequent year; taxes, interest, rent, and royalties relating to a subsequent year; or insurance for a period after the end of the year. If a prepaid expense or outlay cannot be deducted in a taxation year because of this limitation, the expense may be deducted in the next taxation year to which it can reasonably be considered to relate. For more information, see IT-417R2, *Prepaid Expenses and Deferred Charges*.

¶6125.3 — Recreational Facilities and Club Dues

An individual is not allowed to deduct amounts incurred for the use or maintenance of a property that is a yacht, camp, lodge, or golf course or facility, unless the expense is incurred in the ordinary course of the individual's business of providing that property for hire or reward (ITA 18(1)(l)). In addition, club membership dues (including initiation fees) are not deductible if the main purpose of the club is to provide dining, recreational, or sporting facilities for its members.

¶6125.4 — General Anti-Avoidance Rule (GAAR)

The deduction of an expense in relation to a transaction (or series of transactions) will be disallowed if the transaction is subject to the GAAR. In general, GAAR applies to transactions that are avoidance transactions (defined as a transaction that would, if not for GAAR, result in a tax benefit of any kind, and that is not undertaken or arranged primarily for *bona fide* purposes other than to obtain that benefit) which result in a misuse of the provisions of the ITA, ITR, Income Tax Application Rules, a tax treaty, or any other relevant legislation; or an abuse of any of these provisions, read as a whole. For further discussion of the GAAR, see ¶14400.

¶6130 — Allowable Deductions for Expenses

The following are some of the more common expenses that are generally allowed as deductions for the purposes of calculating an individual's business or professional income, along with a brief discussion for each expense.

¶6130.1 — *Advertising Expenses*

Expenses for advertising merchandise or products of a business are ordinary business expenses and deductible in computing income, provided the amount is reasonable in relation to the type and volume of business transacted (ITA 18(1)(a), 67)). In certain circumstances, advertising placed in a non-Canadian newspaper or periodical or broadcast by a foreign broadcasting undertaking may not be a deductible expense by a Canadian business (ITA 19, 19.01, 19.1) (see ¶6140.1 below). However, it is the CRA's position that the limitations in ITA 19, 19.01 and 19.1 do not apply to the deductibility of advertising expenses on foreign internet websites (VDs 2017-0691771M4, 2017-0700121M4). If substantial advertising expenses are deferred and amortized for book purposes, for tax purposes, a deduction can normally be claimed either in the year the expense was incurred, or the book treatment of the expense can be followed based on the argument that such treatment reflects an accurate picture of profit. See also paragraph 4 of IT-417R2: *Prepaid Expenses and Deferred Charges*.

Advertising can be done in a variety of ways including via various media outlets, sponsoring or owning sports teams, sponsoring tournaments, community events, etc. The courts have sided favourably with the taxpayer in the following cases, and allowed advertising and promotion expenses with respect to various forms of advertising and sponsorships, even though the expenses were somewhat remote from the business: *Matt Harris & Son Ltd.*, [2001] 1 C.T.C. 2513 (TCC) (stock car and snowmobile racing, for a wood and gravel business); *Otterbrook Percherons*, [2004] 5 C.T.C. 2010 (TCC) (exhibiting horses, for a wood supply business); *Ross*, [2005] 3 C.T.C. 2281 (TCC; Crown's appeal to FCA discontinued) (maintaining thoroughbred horses, for a stockbroker earning commission income); *Bilous*, [2011] 3 C.T.C. 2277 (TCC) (snowmobile museum, for a farm chemicals business). It seems that the key to proving advertising or sponsorships as deductible expenses is being able to evidence a clear relationship between the expenditures and the possible production of income from those expenditures. The costs also need to be reasonable in the circumstances.

In VD 2012-0432621E5, the CRA stated that incentives paid by a real estate agent for marketing purposes are normally deductible.

¶6130.2 — *Alterations, Repairs and Maintenance*

The cost of minor alterations that do not materially increase the capacity or value of a building beyond its capacity or value when acquired by the taxpayer are allowable as an expense in the year in which incurred (or when paid for, if the taxpayer reports income according to the cash method). They may not be deferred and spread over a period of years. Extensive alterations may be capital expenditures which are not deductible as a current expense but are subject to capital cost allowance and are deductible over a period of years (ITA 20(1)(a)) (see ¶6150, Capital Cost Allowance).

¶6130.3 — *Annual Membership Fees*

Membership fees paid by taxpayers to trade or commercial associations formed for the purpose of advancing the collective interest of the members of any particular branch of a trade or commercial enterprise may be deducted. Examples of this would be Boards of Trade and Chambers of Commerce, Commercial Travellers' Association, Canadian Creditmen's Association, etc.

¶6130.4 — *Appeals*

The cost of preparing, instituting, and prosecuting an appeal from an assessment of tax, interest, or penalties under the ITA or any provincial income tax statute is deductible in the year in which incurred (ITA 60(o)(i)). This provision also applies to allow the deduction of similar expenses incurred in objecting to or appealing from an assessment of any foreign tax claimed as a tax credit under ITA 126 or any related interest or penalty, a decision of the Canada Employment and Immigration Commission, the Canada Employment and Insurance Commission or board of referees or umpire under the *Unemployment Insurance Act* or the *Employment Insurance Act*, or an assessment or decision under the Canada Pension Plan or a provincial pension plan (for example the Quebec Pension Plan). Such costs are deductible from any source of income (ITA 60(o)).

In paragraph 6 of IT-99R5: *Legal and Accounting Fees*, the CRA states that a taxpayer may deduct amounts expended in connection with legal and accounting fees incurred for advice and assistance in making representations after having been informed that the taxpayer's income or tax for a taxation year is to be reviewed, whether or not a formal Notice of Objection or Appeal is subsequently filed. Expenses incurred to contest a GST assessment would normally be deductible under ordinary profit computation principles. Expenses to contest another person's assessment are generally deductible if the corporation has a pecuniary or other interest in the outcome that is not overly remote (*Flood*, [2006] 3 C.T.C. 2345 (TCC)).

Professional fees paid to advisors for filing a voluntary disclosure are not deductible, even if the income voluntarily disclosed arises from a business or property, because a voluntary disclosure is not an objection or an appeal. However, a deduction is available for professional fees incurred to defend a taxpayer's position once the taxpayer's voluntary disclosure is accepted. As well, a deduction may be available for professional fees incurred in the preparation of tax returns resulting from a voluntary disclosure (VDs 2014-0532121E5, 2016-0625731C6).

¶6130.5 — *Auditing and Accounting Fees*

The cost of auditing the records of a business is a deductible business expense. The cost of special services rendered by an accountant or auditor is also normally deductible. These would include the work involved in preparing income tax returns, preparing and conducting any of the appeals referred to above under "Appeals" and work relating to an issue of bonds, shares, or another financial instrument (see ¶6130.10).

¶6130.6 — *Automobile Expenses*

Automobile expenses relating to vehicles used in the business, such as gas, oil, and repairs and maintenance are allowed as deductions. When an automobile is used by the owner partly for business and partly for non-business purposes, an appropriate portion of the expense and capital cost allowance may be deducted in computing the income from the business. For example, if a taxpayer's total automobile expenses (including licences, insurance, ordinary repairs, gasoline, oil, service charges, rental, capital cost allowance and, if applicable, interest expense) were $7,000 and the total mileage for the year is 20,000 kilometres, of which 12,000 kilometres represents business use, the taxpayer will normally be entitled to deduct 12,000/20,000 of $7,000 or $4,200. Major accident repair expenses (both to the automobile and to property of others) are deductible only if the automobile was being used for business purposes at the time of the accident.

There are restrictions on the total amount of automobile expenses that may be deducted (ITA 67.2–67.4). These restrictions are intended to deny a portion of the automobile deduction with respect to "luxury cars". For tax purposes, "automobile" includes motor vehicles designed primarily to carry individuals and their personal luggage, which would generally include cars, mini-vans, station wagons, and pick-up trucks (ITA 248(1)). For these purposes, an "automobile" does not include an ambulance, a bus, a taxi, or vehicles acquired to be sold, rented, or leased in the course of carrying on such a business.

Where an automobile is leased and it is worth more than a prescribed amount, the amount that may be deducted is limited by a formula (ITA 67.3; adjusted by ITR 7307(3)). Generally, the amount that may be deducted is restricted to the least of the following amounts: (1) the actual lease cost; (2) $800 per month; and (3) the (actual least cost) × ($30,000/85% of manufacturer's suggested list price). Currently, the prescribed amount is $30,000 plus related federal and provincial sales tax. That is, the deductible amount is the lesser of two calculations. For more information and to see examples of the calculations, see paragraphs 10–12 of IT-521R: *Motor Vehicle Expenses Claimed by Self-Employed Individuals*, and in paragraphs 8–10 of IT-522R: *Vehicle, Travel and Sales Expenses of Employees*.

Where funds are borrowed to purchase an automobile, the amount of interest that is deductible may not exceed a prescribed amount per month (ITA 67.2; adjusted by ITR 7307(2)), which is currently $300 per month. The cost of an automobile that exceeds $30,000 (before GST and PST) is required to be included in a separate class (Class 10.1) for capital cost allowance purposes. See ¶6150Capital Cost Allowance below.

When two or more persons jointly own or lease an automobile, the maximum amount deductible by each person for capital cost allowance interest or leasing fees is based on the proportionate interest in the fair market value of the vehicle. The result is that the restrictions on the deductibility of these amounts is based on the vehicle rather than on the person (ITA 67.4). Also see the table "Automobiles — Deductions and Benefits" in Appendix B.

¶6130.7 — *Bad Debts*

Taxpayers are permitted to write off any bad debts that have been established by the taxpayer to have become worthless during the taxation year and that have been included in computing the income of the year or a previous year (ITA 20(1)(o)(i)). Bad debts recovered must be included as income in the year in which they are recovered (ITA 12(1)(i)). However, where a debt that is capital in nature for tax purposes (such as an advance to a related party or an investment loan) is written off for accounting purposes, the loss should be added back to compute taxable income. For tax purposes, if a debt held on capital account is established to be bad in a taxation year, a taxpayer may elect under ITA 50(1) to have disposed of the debt at the end of that taxation year and to have reacquired it at the beginning of the subsequent taxation year at a cost equal to nil, thereby realizing a capital loss. Generally, 50% of capital losses incurred in a taxation year may be applied to offset taxable capital gains realized in the year or in any of the three preceding taxation years. A debt that is capital in nature is considered to be a bad debt for tax purposes when the taxpayer has exhausted all legal means of collection or the debtor has become insolvent.

¶6130.8 — *Bank Charges*

Bank and other financial institution charges that relate to money used in the business may be deducted in the year in which incurred. See also under "Interest on Borrowed Capital".

¶6130.9 — *Bonuses*

Reasonable bonuses paid to employees are allowable as deductions. See also under "Salaries and Wages".

¶6130.10 — *Expenses of Borrowing Money*

Expenses such as legal, accounting, and other fees in the course of borrowing money used for the purpose of earning income from a business or property are deductible in equal annual instalments over a five-year period (ITA 20(1)(e)(ii)), (see IT-341R4, *Expenses of Issuing or Selling Shares, Units in a Trust, Interests in a Partnership or Syndicate and Expenses of Borrowing Money*).

Also deductible are expenses incurred in the course of incurring indebtedness where an amount is payable to acquire income earning property. Similarly, expenses incurred in restructuring or rescheduling debt or in assuming debt, either where the borrowings are used to earn business income or to pay for income earning property, are also deductible (ITA 20(1)(e)(ii.2)). This would include any commission, fee, or other amount on account of sales, agency, or dealer commissions. For these purposes, the restructuring or rescheduling must either be a change in the terms and conditions of the debt, or a conversion or substitution of debt to shares or to another debt obligation (ITA 20(1)(e)(ii.2)). If the borrowings are repaid, any balance of borrowing expenses not yet deducted are deductible in the year of repayment unless the repayment was made in the course of a refinancing.

Expenses subject to this provision include legal, accounting and other fees, printing, registration, amounts paid to guarantors, and other costs normally payable, including standby interest. Also included are amounts payable as commissions or otherwise to a salesperson, agent or dealer in securities for services rendered in the course of borrowing the money. Certification fees and other expenses incurred in connection with the sale of acceptances are also deductible for tax purposes. See paragraphs 16 and 17 of IT-341R4 for additional examples.

Where the expense incurred is a standby charge, guarantee fee, registrar fee, transfer agent fee, filing fee, service fee, or any similar fee, the expense is fully deductible in the year paid or payable as consideration for the undertaking provided it is reasonably related solely to the year when incurred (ITA 20(1)(e.1)). This applies equally to such expenses which relate to amounts payable for property acquired to earn business income or to expenses related to debt rescheduling, restructuring, or assumption.

¶6130.11 — *Business Taxes*

Business, water, and property taxes and similar expenses in respect of premises used for business operations are allowable deductions.

¶6130.12 — *Catalogues*

The costs of compiling and distributing catalogues to promote the sale of merchandise by a taxpayer are allowable deductions. Generally, the expenditure for catalogues should be deducted in the year of issue although the cost of unissued but usable catalogues must be deferred as an inventory of advertising material.

¶6130.13 — *Commissions*

Commissions paid to salespersons by an employer in the course of the business are deductible. Commissions paid to obtain or dispose of capital assets are not deductible in computing income from business but may be an adjustment in computing the capital gain or loss from the disposition of the property. Commissions paid on the purchase of a building to be used in the business may be added to the cost of the building for purposes of claiming capital cost allowance (ITA 20(1)(a)).

¶6130.14 — *Convention Expenses*

ITA 20(10) provided that, in computing a taxpayer's income for a taxation year for a business, reasonable expenses may be deducted that are incurred by a taxpayer in attending, in connection with the business, not more than two conventions held during the year by a business or professional organization *at a location that may reasonably be regarded as consistent with the territorial scope of that organization*. That is, a convention held outside the province by a provincial organization or a convention held outside Canada by a Canadian organization will normally not qualify under this provision. However, Canada-U.S. Tax Treaty:Art. XXV.8 would allow a deduction of such fees for a convention held in the U.S. if such fees would otherwise be deductible in Canada. Where convention expenses have been incurred to earn income in connection with the taxpayer's business and are not on account of capital, they should be deductible even if they do not meet the restrictions in ITA 20(10) (VD 2017-0709111C6).

A taxpayer who combines attendance at a convention, regardless of location, with a vacation trip is expected to allocate expenses on some reasonable basis and to eliminate those that are essentially for vacation purposes. A reasonable basis is considered to be one that allows the taxpayer to deduct the full cost of travel (i.e., transportation and necessary meals and accommodation *en route*) from the place of business to the convention and back by the most direct route available, and the costs and accommodation while participating in the convention.

Where an employer requires an employee to attend a convention, no taxable benefit would generally apply except to the extent of any personal benefit. Expenses incurred by or for an employee's spouse or common-law partner and children while accompanying the employee to a convention or on a combined convention and vacation trip are generally considered to be personal. As such, they would be considered a taxable employee benefit unless the employer requires the spouse or common law partner to attend in order to satisfy business objectives.

Where the convention fee entitles the participant to food, beverages, or entertainment and a reasonable part of the fee, based on the cost of providing the food, beverages, or entertainment is not identified in the fee, the amount deemed to be paid for meals and entertainment is $50 per day (unless otherwise prescribed by regulation) (ITA 67.1(3)). Since this amount is subject to the 50% rule in subsection 67.1(1), the amount of the deduction would be $25 per day. The amount deductible as the convention fee is net of the amount deemed by subsection 67.1(3) to relate to meals and entertainment.

¶6130.15 — *Damages*

Damages paid as a result of a judgment or a court order arising in connection with an accident or other event or occurrence which is a normal and expected risk of the business are deductible (ITA 18(1)(a)). In paragraph 6 of IT-467R2: *Damages, Settlements and Similar Receipts*, the CRA states for purposes of establishing whether damages have been incurred for the purpose of gaining or producing income, "the taxpayer need not have attempted to prevent the act or omission that resulted in the damages and the taxpayer need only establish that there was an income-earning purpose for the act or omission, regardless of whether that purpose was actually achieved".

Damages paid out: In *Canadian Imperial Bank of Commerce*, 2013 CarswellNat 1306 (FCA), a $3 billion settlement paid by CIBC in the Enron debacle could not be non-deductible by virtue of being "egregious and repulsive": the "morality" of the taxpayer's conduct is not relevant (paras. 1, 21). Damages were deductible in: *McNeill*, [2000] 2 C.T.C. 304 (FCA) (paid for violating a restrictive covenant); *ZR*, [2008] 3 C.T.C. 2051 (TCC) (paid to settle a US lawsuit against the taxpayer to collect a judgment against her spouse, relating to hotels they operated). Damages were not deductible in: *St-Georges*, 2006 CarswellNat 5378 (FCA); leave to appeal denied 2007 CarswellNat 345 (SCC) (paid by director to company's creditors for wrongfully causing company to pay a dividend); *Nisker*, [2008] 2 C.T.C. 256 (FCA, reversing the TCC) (; leave to appeal denied 2008 CarswellNat 2559 (SCC)) (paid by corporation's officer to settle tort claim for acting in bad faith on a real estate deal); *Hanmar Motor Corp.*, [2008] 2 C.T.C. 2118 (TCC) (payments to subsidiary's employees for unpaid wages, under a Court order).

¶6130.16 — *Discounts*

Discounts to customers to encourage the prompt payment of accounts are considered to be a normal business expense and deductible. The CRA will allow the deduction of a reserve for cash discounts expected to be taken by customers after the end of the year in respect of goods sold to them before the end of the year.

¶6130.17 — *Foreign Exchange Losses*

Premiums paid or losses sustained in respect of foreign exchange transactions of a revenue or income nature are considered normal expenses of doing business. Similarly, discounts earned or premiums received on transactions of this nature must be included in income or claimed as a reduction in expenses.

Premiums or discounts in connection with capital transactions or items not related to the usual business of the taxpayer are not deductible in computing business income, but rather give rise to a capital gain or loss. Generally, whether a foreign exchange gain or loss is on income or capital account depends upon whether the gain or loss arose as a consequence of a capital transaction (such as the purchase of a capital asset) or an income transaction (such as the purchase and sale of inventory). Normally, foreign exchange gains and losses on income account are included in computing income on an accrual basis. On the other hand, foreign exchange gains and losses on capital account should be recognized for tax purposes when realized. For example, a foreign exchange gain or loss related to a debt obligation that is capital in nature (i.e., a debt incurred to purchase or invest in depreciable or non-depreciable capital property or to finance a capital project) should be recognized for tax purposes when payments are made against the principal portion of the debt and a portion of the gain or loss is realized. For further information on distinguishing between profits and losses on income account and those on capital account, see IT-95R: *Foreign Exchange Gains and Losses*.

¶6130.18 — *Gifts to Employees*

No monetary gift is deductible when made to an employee unless made to the employee as part of the employee's remuneration and taxed as such to the employee.

¶6130.19 — *Guarantees and Warranties*

Any outlay required to fulfill the conditions of a guarantee will be allowed as an expense in the year in which the expenditure is incurred. A guarantee fee paid to a third party for guaranteeing a loan obtained by a taxpayer for business purposes would be deductible as an expense incurred in the course of borrowing money. Taxpayers engaged in the contracting or construction business may be obliged by law or by contract to guarantee against defective work, possibly for several years after the completion of the contract. No reserve may be claimed for a potential future liability since this would be a contingent reserve which is expressly prohibited by ITA 20(7)(a). However, any actual outlay required to fulfill the conditions of a guarantee will be allowed as an expense in the year in which the expenditure is incurred.

¶6130.20 — *Home Office*

ITA 18(12) provides that a self-employed individual, in computing income from a business for a taxation year, is not entitled to any deduction for expenses otherwise deductible under the ITA related to any part of a self-contained domestic establishment in which the individual resides, except where the work space is either:

(a) the principal place of the business of the individual, or

(b) used exclusively to earn business income and on a regular and continuous basis for meeting clients, customers or patients of the individual in respect of the business.

A "self-contained domestic establishment" is defined as a dwelling house, apartment, or other similar place of residence in which a person as a general rule sleeps and eats.

The phrase "principal place of business" is not defined in the ITA. A home-office work space should qualify as an individual's principal place of business if the particular work space is the only "office" used in the business, even if many of the business activities are carried on outside of the "office" (VD 2000-0008905E). If the first test is not met, the work space must be used exclusively to earn business income, and it must be used for meeting clients, customers, or patients "on a regular and continuous basis". One should consider the definition of "meetings" when applying the second test, specifically phone calls, web based meetings, etc. Informal procedure courts indicate that physical presence of the client, customer, or patient may not be necessary (see *Vanka v. R.*, 2001 CarswellNat 2118 (TCC)). See paragraphs 2.11 to 2.16 of Folio S4-F2-C2, *Business Use of Home Expenses*, for the CRA's interpretation of "principal place of business" and "regular and continuous basis".

An individual who carries on a business in a work space, and has met the test in either 1(a) or (b) above, will be able to deduct only the expenses related to the work space to the extent they are otherwise deductible and do not exceed the income from the business for the taxation year, carried on in the home or elsewhere, determined prior to deducting the expenses related to the work space. Thus, such expenses for a taxation year cannot create or increase a loss for income tax purposes from the business for which the work space is used.

The expenses related to the work space could include, for example, the prorated portion of rent, capital cost allowance, property insurance, property taxes, mortgage interest, or operating costs such as heating and lighting, and maintenance and repairs. The principal residence protection from capital gains does not apply to a work space for which CCA has been claimed. The capital gain and recapture rules apply if a taxpayer deducts CCA on the business-use part of the home and later sells the home (see ¶4434 and ¶7145).

The expenses should be apportioned between business and non-business use on a reasonable basis, such as, square metres of floor space used. If a taxpayer uses part of the home for both business and personal living, calculate how many hours in the day the rooms are used for business, divide that amount by 24 hours, and multiply the result by the business part of the total home expenses. If a taxpayer runs the business for only part of the week or year, reduce the claim accordingly. See Guide T4002 and Folio S4-F2-C2 for examples of how to calculate business-use-of-home expenses.

The amount otherwise deductible in respect of the work space cannot exceed the taxpayer's income from the business for the year. Any expenses not deductible in the year may be carried forward indefinitely, and deducted for the work space in respect of the business income in later years as long as the requirements discussed above continue to be met.

ITA 18(12), 248(1)"self-contained domestic establishment", Guide T4002, Folio S4-F2-C2: *Business Use of Home Expenses*

¶6130.21 — *Inducement Payments*

A deduction is allowed for amounts in respect of inducement payments that are repaid, where such amounts were previously included in income. ITA 48(16) provides that an amount claimed by a taxpayer as a GST input tax credit or a rebate in respect of a property or service is deemed to be assistance from a government. However, such credit would normally not be included in income as it would reduce the cost or capital cost of the property or the amount of the related expenditure or expenditure pool. In VD 2009-0309291I7, the CRA states the payment of GST by a purchaser of goods or services is deductible in computing income if it has been made for the purpose of gaining or producing income from a business or property pursuant to the general rules of ITA 9.

ITA 20(1)(hh)

¶6130.22 — *Insurance*

The following types of insurance payments are deductible in computing income:

- *Life insurance*: Premiums paid by a taxpayer on a life insurance policy, where the policy has been assigned as collateral to secure a loan required by the taxpayer for business purposes (see IT-309R2, *Premium on Life Insurance Used as Collateral*).

- *Accident insurance*: When the proceeds of accident insurance policies are payable to an employee, or to beneficiaries of the employee, premiums paid on the employee's behalf by an employer. For sickness and accident insurance plans to which both employer and employee contribute, the employer's contributions are deductible as a general expense.

- *Business Overhead Expense Insurance*: Overhead expense insurance purchased by professional individuals to defray specific overhead expenses of their practice in the event of illness or incapacity is a normal business practice. The premiums are deductible and the proceeds are taxable.

- *Collateral insurance*: Where an insurance policy is assigned as collateral for a loan, premiums payable in respect of that policy are deductible provided that the lender requires the assignment of the policy as collateral for the loan; the lender is a restricted financial institution and the interest on the borrowed money must otherwise be deductible (ITA 20(1)(e.2)). The amount which may be deducted is the lesser of the premiums payable under the policy and the net cost of pure insurance for the year. If the taxation year of the taxpayer is different from the policy year, the premiums payable and the net cost of pure insurance must be prorated accordingly. In addition, the portion which is deductible must be determined based on what is owing on the loan. For example, if the life insurance coverage is greater than the principal amount of the loan, the deductible amount of the premium will be determined based on the percentage that the amount of the loan is to the coverage under the policy. Where the insurance policy has some savings element, the amount of premium which is deductible will be reduced to reflect only the net cost of pure insurance based on standard mortality assumptions. For more information, see IT-309R2.

- *Credit insurance*: Premiums paid in respect of credit insurance to protect against incurring excessive losses on bad debts are deductible in computing income from a business. Any claims recovered are included in income as an offset against bad debts.

- *Fire and casualty insurance*: These items are considered to be normal business expenses and are deductible provided they relate to the insurance of property actively used for purposes of earning income.

- *Group life insurance*: Premiums paid by a business on group insurance policies on the lives of its employees are deductible as expenses necessarily incurred to ensure the efficient conduct of the business.

- *Employment insurance*: The employer's portion of contributions under the *Employment Insurance Act* are deductible for tax purposes.

¶6130.23 — *Interest on Borrowed Money*

Interest expense incurred as a result of a legal obligation to pay interest on money borrowed for the purpose of earning income from a business or property, or indebtedness to the vendor of property purchased for the purpose of earning income therefrom or acquired for business purposes is deductible. However, a deduction is not allowed for an interest expense relating to property if the income from that property is, or would be, exempt from tax, or to property that is an interest in a life insurance policy (as defined in ITA 20(2.2)). Note that dividends received on shares are not exempt income (ss. 248(1)"exempt income"). Interest expense incurred for any of the following purposes is specifically prohibited as a deduction: making a contribution to an RRSP, RESP, RDSP, TFSA, or prescribed provincial pension plan; making an employee contribution to an RCA; and making a payment for an annuity on the transfer of a refund of premiums under an RRSP (see ITA 18(11)).

Policy loans on insurance policies are not borrowed money (ITA 20(2.1)). That is, they are not subject to any obligation for repayment but are advances on account of the proceeds of the policy. However, the CRA is prepared to consider the interest paid on policy loans as deductible under ITA 20(1)(c) if the proceeds are used to earn income from a business or property. The deduction is set out in ITA 20(2.1), which provides that interest paid on a policy loan will not be deductible except to the extent that it is verified by the insurer, on Form T2210, to be interest paid in the year on the loan, and not added to the adjusted cost basis to the taxpayer of the interest in the policy. Form T2210 is required to be filed by the taxpayer no later than the last day for filing the return for the year in respect of which the interest was paid.

ITA 20(1)(d) provides that compound interest on borrowed money which would otherwise qualify may be deducted if paid or payable in the year. Further, interest on the full face value of borrowed money is deductible even though the full face value was not received by the borrower. This may arise where, for example, a bond was issued at a discount, provided the borrowed funds are used for the purpose of earning income from a business or property (ITA 20(2)).The deduction for interest may be claimed either in the year in which it is paid or in the year to which it relates, on an accrual basis, whichever method is regularly followed by the taxpayer (ITA 20(1)(c)).

Where a taxpayer uses borrowed money to repay money borrowed previously, the money is deemed to have been used for the purpose for which the first borrowed money was being used (ITA 20(3)). Money borrowed for the purpose of redeeming shares or paying dividends is ordinarily considered to be a deductible expense. In paragraphs 1.48 to 1.52 of Folio S3-F6-C1, *Interest Deductibility*, the CRA states:

Redeem shares or return capital

1.48 Interest expense on borrowed money used to redeem shares or return capital can be an exception to the direct use test. In connection with this use, the purpose test will be met if the borrowed money replaces capital (contributed capital or accumulated profits) that was being used for eligible purposes that would have qualified for interest deductibility had the capital been borrowed money.

1.49 Contributed capital generally refers to funds provided by a corporation's shareholders to commence, or otherwise further, the carrying on of its business. While in most situations the legal or stated capital for corporate law purposes would be the best measurement of contributed capital, other measurements may be more appropriate depending on the circumstances. In situations where some proportion of shares is being replaced with borrowed money, only the capital of those shares, computed on a pro-rata basis, would be considered to be replaced with the borrowed money. A corporation's deficit does not reduce contributed capital for purposes of this exception to the direct use test.

Pay dividends

1.50 Similarly, interest expense on borrowed money used to pay dividends (including deemed dividends), can be an exception to the direct use test. In connection with this use, the purpose test will be met if the borrowed money replaces accumulated profits of a corporation that have been retained and used for eligible purposes. Accumulated profits would generally be the retained earnings of the corporation computed on an unconsolidated basis with investments accounted for on a cost basis. The accumulated profits of a corporation do not track any particular shareholdings.

1.51 Generally, accumulated profits can reflect transactions arising in the ordinary course of business between non-arm's length parties. The impact on accumulated profits of other non-arm's length transactions must be examined on the basis of the particular facts involved.

1.52 The key concept in this context remains that of filling the hole of capital withdrawn from the business.

The CRA will also normally allow interest paid on notes or debentures issued to the shareholders themselves, representing the re-borrowing of the proceeds of the dividend paid, to be deducted provided it is clear that the arrangement did not facilitate the acquisition of property the income from which would be exempt.

In appropriate circumstances, the interest on money borrowed to purchase shares of a corporation will be considered to be deductible even after the corporation is wound up, provided the assets received on the winding-up continue to be used for the purpose of earning or producing income (para. 1.44 of Folio S3-F6-C1 and CRA VD's 2006-0196291C6, 2004-0070981R3, 2004-0087001C6, and 2004-0061951R3).

A taxpayer may elect to capitalize interest (including compound interest) incurred in respect of borrowed money used to acquire depreciable property, or in respect of an amount payable for depreciable property acquired by the taxpayer (ITA 21(1)). Similarly, financing expenses and annual financing fees may also be capitalized rather than expensed. An example would be interest incurred during construction. An election to capitalize interest must be made when filing the tax return for the year in which the depreciable property is acquired (ITA 21(1)). A taxpayer may elect to capitalize all or part of the interest (and other costs incurred in borrowing money) not only for the taxation year, but also (retroactively) for the three preceding years. Once an election is made, the taxpayer may make further elections with each successive annual return such that the taxpayer may continue to capitalize interest and other expenses incurred in borrowing money in relation to the depreciable property acquired (ITA 21(3)). The election may be restricted to a portion of the interest expense. If the taxpayer fails to make an election in a subsequent year in respect of interest and borrowing expenses, the taxpayer may not elect to capitalize expenses relevant to the same borrowed money in a later year (ITA 21(3)(a)(i)). Amounts in respect of which an election is made pursuant to this provision are added to the capital cost of the depreciable property (ITA 21(1)(b)). The election to capitalize interest and other costs is optional. Under a similar provision in ITA 18(3.1), the capitalization of interest and soft costs attributable to the period of construction, renovation, or alteration of a building is mandatory. Nevertheless, the taxpayer may include the latter costs when making an election under ITA 21. This will enable the taxpayer to make an election under ITA 21(3) in subsequent years in respect of borrowing costs after the completion of the building which are not affected by ITA 18(3.1). An election under ITA 21 to capitalize interest or to add it to exploration and development costs is to be made by including a statement making the election in the income tax return for the year (ITA 21(1), (2)).

ITA 20(1)(c), (d)

¶6130.24 — *Legal Fees*

Generally, the following fees are deductible:

- Legal expenses of a recurring nature incurred in connection with a taxpayer's business,

- Legal expenses incurred in connection with borrowing money for use in a business or with the issuance of shares of a corporation are deductible over five years (ITA 20(1)(e)),

- Legal or other expenses incurred in the preparation, filing and prosecution of an income tax or other objection or appeal under the ITA or provincial income tax legislation, or objecting to or appealing from an assessment of foreign income tax claimed as a tax credit (ITA 60(o), ITA 126),

- Legal expenses incurred in appealing an adverse decision under the *Unemployment Insurance Act, Employment Insurance Act*, Canada Pension Plan or Quebec Pension Plan (ITA 60(o.1), and

- Fees paid in connection with the presentation of briefs or the making of representations to government departments and officials.

For more information on the deductibility of legal and accounting fees, see IT-99R5(C), *Legal and Accounting Fees*.

¶6130.25 — *Licences*

Annual licence fees paid to municipalities and provinces are generally deductible in the year to which they relate. If the taxpayer's fiscal period does not correspond to the period covered by the licence, the cost should be prorated to the relevant fiscal periods. With some exceptions, a licence for a limited period constitutes depreciable property of Class 14 and is written off over the period covered by the licence (ITR 1100(1)(c)).

¶6130.26 — *Meals and Entertainment*

ITA 67.1 restricts the deduction for most meals and entertainment expenses to 50 percent of the lesser of the actual expenditure and a reasonable amount that would otherwise have been deductible under the ITA. For the purposes of the 50 percent limitation, the cost of food or beverages includes expenses such as taxes and tips thereon. The cost of a restaurant gift certificate is also considered to be an expense for food or beverages and is subject to this limitation.

The ITA does not define the term "entertainment". ITA 67.1(4)(b) includes amusement and recreation as "entertainment" and ITA 67.1 mentions the "enjoyment of entertainment". The courts and CRA have commented that the expression "enjoyment of entertainment" refers to the entertainment itself (involving some activity) and not to the gift of some tangible properties that could be used for entertainment purposes. Some examples of entertainment provided by the courts and CRA, and subject to the 50 percent limitation include the cost of the following:

- Tickets for a theatre, concert, athletic event, or other performance;

- Private boxes at sports facilities;

- Room rentals to provide entertainment, such as a hospitality suite;

- A cruise;

- Admission to a fashion show; and

- Entertaining guests at night clubs, athletic, social and sporting clubs, and on vacation and other similar trips.

A deduction for entertainment expenses is permitted only where it can be conclusively shown that the outlay was made for the purpose of gaining or producing income from the business. Also, ITA 18(1)(l) denies the deductibility of expenses incurred for the entertainment of clients (or employees) if the expense relates to the use of a yacht, camp, lodge, golf course or facility. As well, club dues are not deductible when their main purpose is to provide dining, recreational, or sporting facilities. The CRA has stated that a facility will not include the dining room, banquet halls, conference rooms, beverage rooms, or lounges of a golf club and, thus, the deduction of the cost of meals and beverages incurred at a golf club will not be fully denied; however, such costs are subject to the 50 percent deduction limit applicable to meals and entertainment.

Following are exceptions to the general 50 percent limitation in ITA 67.1(2):

- The amount is paid for food, beverages, or entertainment provided in the ordinary course of business for compensation (e.g., restaurants, hotels, airlines, etc.);

- The taxpayer's product or service is food, beverage or entertainment (this also includes promotional samples);

- The expenses for food, beverages, or entertainment are for a fund-raising event, the primary purpose of which is to benefit a registered charity;

- The person is compensated for the amount, the amount is reasonable, and it is specifically identified to the person reimbursing the expense (i.e., the amounts are billed to clients). In this case, the person reimbursing the expense would be subject to the 50% limitation (see VD 2004-0094761E5);

- Allowances or reimbursements for meals or entertainment that are included in an employee's income;

- In respect of one of six or fewer special events if an employer incurs the amount for food, beverages or entertainment that is generally available to all its employees. This exempts costs incurred for a Christmas party or similar events to which all employees at a particular place of business have access;

- The amount is paid or payable for travel on an airplane, train, or bus.

Advisors and taxpayers should also be aware of the deeming rule in ITA 67.1(3) which applies for food, beverages, or entertainment at conferences, conventions, and seminar's, etc. Where the organizer of the event has not allocated or identified a reasonable portion for food, beverages, or entertainment, $50 per day (or such other amount as may be prescribed) is deemed to be paid or payable in respect of food, beverages, and entertainment, and the fee for the event will be deemed to be the actual fee paid minus the deemed amount for these benefits. No other amount than $50 has been prescribed to date.

ITA 67.1, IT-131R2: *Convention Expenses*, IT-518R: *Food, Beverages and Entertainment Expenses*, VD 2017-0714381E5

¶6130.27 — *Membership Dues*

Membership fees in professional associations, trade or commercial associations, societies, service clubs, and cultural organizations are allowable deductions if they reasonably relate to earning income from business or property. An exception is any expense incurred for membership dues that entitle the taxpayer, the taxpayer's employees, or anyone else to use the facilities of any club, the main purpose of which is to provide dining, recreational, or sporting facilities for its members. Lump-sum life-membership fees paid in lieu of future annual fees or dues are considered deductible if they replace annual fees that would be deductible. Lump-sum fees may be deducted in the year paid. Initiation or admission fees which a taxpayer pays only once to obtain an enduring benefit, such as admission fees to a Law Society, are not deductible since they are considered a capital outlay. However, such fees generally qualify as capital expenditures where it can be shown that the annual membership fees of the organization are allowable deductions in computing income of a business.

Folio S2-F3-C2: *Benefits and Allowances Received from Employment*, IT-211R: *Membership Dues — Associations and Societies*

¶6130.28 — *Moving Expenses*

Expenses of moving a business from one location to another and expenses of an employer incurred for moving an employee, the employee's family and household effects from one city or post to another in the course of the employer's business are deductible from income. Expenses incurred by an individual in connection with an eligible relocation, defined in ITA 248(1) as a relocation to enable the taxpayer to carry on a business, are deductible pursuant to ITA 62 (see ¶9200). For information on the meaning of an "eligible relocation", the conditions for deducting moving expenses, the eligibility of various moving expenses, and the timing of the deduction, see Folio S1-F3-C4: *Moving Expenses*.

Form T1-M, Folio S1-F3-C4: *Moving Expenses*

¶6130.29 — *Rent*

The annual rental paid for the occupation of an office, warehouse or other property used in a business may be deducted.

¶6130.30 — *Representation Expenses*

Expenses incurred by a taxpayer in making representations to a government authority in connection with a business, including representations for the purpose of obtaining a licence, permit, franchise, or trademark may be deducted in the year in which paid. Alternatively, they may be deducted in equal annual amounts over a 10-year period, beginning with the year of payment (ITA 20(9)). In this case, a taxpayer must elect to do so by submitting a letter to the Minister specifying the amount in respect of which the election is being made (ITR 4100(a)). To the extent that representation expenses are considered a payment on account of the capital cost of depreciable property the deduction is deemed to be allowed as capital cost allowance. This prevents a double deduction and ensures the possibility of recapture on disposition (ITA 13(12)).

¶6130.31 — *Reserves*

Reserves for Doubtful Debts

A reserve may be claimed for doubtful debts that have been included in income for that year or a previous year (ITA 20(1)(l)(i)). This reserve is calculated annually at the end of each fiscal period, with the reserve claimed in one year being added back to income in the next year. Accordingly, a new reserve is claimed for each year, which the taxpayer must be able to justify as reasonable (ITA 201(i)(l)(i)). The amount of the reserve should be in a relation to the amount of doubtful or overdue debts included in the accounts receivable. Accordingly, a reserve provided on a fixed percentage basis of the accounts receivable would only be accepted if it is justified by the actual condition of the accounts at the date of closing the books or within a reasonable time thereafter. See IT-442R, *Bad Debts and Reserves for Doubtful Debts*.

Reserve for Amount not yet Due

When a taxpayer sells merchandise on an instalment plan where all or part of the amount at the time of the sale was not due until at least two years after the time of the sale, the profit on the sale can be deferred and taken into income on a pro rata basis (in proportion to instalments received) over the life of the contract (ITA 201(1)(n)). The taxpayer may deduct a reserve at the end of each taxation year equal to the profit not yet received in respect of the sale. The reserve (which is required by ITA 20(1)(e) to be included income in the following year) would be calculated as follows: (gross profit)/(gross selling price) × amount receivable at year-end = reserve.

Special Reserve

Where real or immovable property sold in the course of a taxpayer's business is subject to instalment payments of the purchase price that extend beyond the end of the taxation year, the taxpayer may claim a reserve in respect of that part of the profit on the sale that can reasonably be regarded as not yet due (ITA 20(1)(n)).The CRA considers it reasonable to assume that the profit element in the transaction is realized proportionately as the proceeds are received. The maximum reserve at the end of any year would be computed by the following formula: (gross profit)/(gross selling price) × amount due after the end of the taxation year = reserve. Where part of the sale price is secured by a mortgage given by the purchaser, the vendor may claim a reserve in respect of the part of the mortgage not due until after the end of the year. For more information, see IT-152R3.

IT-442R: *Bad Debts and Reserves for Doubtful Debts*, IT-152R3: *Special Reserves — Sale of Land*

¶6130.32 — *Salaries and Wages*

Salaries and wages paid to officers and employees, and commissions paid to salespersons or agents based on the volume of business procured by them are deductible expenses if reasonable. To the extent that a salary (or any other expense) is in excess of a reasonable amount, considering all the circumstances, it may be disallowed as a deduction (ITA 67). Amounts of salary or bonus payable to an owner-manager are normally deductible on the basis that the owner's expertise, know-how, managerial skills, and effort are responsible for the company's profits (VDs 2004-0092931R3, 2004-0072741R3). Bonuses and salary paid to an owner-manager's minor children or spouse must be reasonable to be deductible (*Mépalex Inc.*, 2002 CarswellNat 4727 (TCC), *Costigane*, [2003] 3 C.T.C. 2087 (TCC)). In *Ambulances B.G.R. Inc.*, 2004 CarswellNat 1054 (TCC), relatively large bonuses paid to adult children were held to be deductible on the basis that they represented reasonable compensation for exceptional services performed by the individuals. Under ITA 78(4), salary or wages that remain unpaid 180 days after the end of the taxation year in which accrued are deemed not to have been incurred as an expense in the year and are deductible only in the year in which paid (the latter rule does not apply to reasonable vacation or holiday pay). There is no provision for an agreement to be filed to deem the unpaid amount to have been paid. Where the employer remits the applicable payroll withholdings, issues a T4 information return and the employee includes the accrued wages in income, the CRA's administrative position is not to apply ITA 78(4).

¶6130.33 — *Scientific Research Expenditures (SR&ED)*

Certain expenditures made on scientific research related to the business being carried on are deductible (ITA 37). Expenditures on scientific research may also qualify the taxpayer for an investment tax credit (see Line 412 at ¶11030). The definition of "scientific research and experimental development" (SR&ED) refers to systematic investigation or research carried out in a field of science or technology by means of experiment or analysis. This definition includes basic research, applied research, and development.

Five criteria have been used by the Courts to assist in determining whether a particular activity constitutes SR&ED:

1. Was there a technological risk or uncertainty which could not be removed by routine engineering or standard procedures?

2. Did the person claiming to be doing SR&ED formulate hypotheses specifically aimed at reducing or eliminating that technological uncertainty?

3. Did the procedure adopted accord with the total discipline of the scientific method including the formulation testing and modification of hypotheses?

4. Did the process result in a technological advancement?

5. Was a detailed record of the hypotheses tested and results kept as the work progressed?

Expenditures that are normal operating expenses of a taxpayer, such as the cost of market research or surveys of customer acceptance, are not scientific research within the definition in ITA 248(1), but would be deductible as ordinary expenses. If an expenditure for scientific research falls within both ITA 37 and under ITA 110.1 or 118.1 (as a charitable donation), a deduction may be claimed only under ITA 37. Expenditures that qualify as scientific research may be either current or capital in nature.

Scientific research expenditures are generally allowable only to the extent that they are related to a business carried on by the taxpayer. Scientific research and experimental development is not considered to be a business of the taxpayer to which scientific research may be related unless all or substantially all of the taxpayer's revenue is derived from the prosecution of scientific research, including the sale of rights arising out of such research.

ITA 37, IC 86-4R3, Guide T4088, canada.ca/en/revenue-agency/services/scientific-research-experimental-development-tax-incentive-program/program-policies.html

¶6130.34 — *Split Income*

A taxpayer who is a "specified individual" (as defined ITA 120.4(1)) may deduct an amount equal to the taxpayer's split income for the year. Split income generally consists of dividends derived from certain dividend-sprinkling structures, business income derived through a partnership or trust used in a management-services structure and certain capital gains. The deduction available in respect of split income ensures that the types of passive income subject to the special tax under ITA 120.4 are not also subject to tax under Part I of the ITA as ordinary income (ITA 20(1)(ww)). For a full discussion of tax on split income, see ¶11070 and ¶14210.

¶6130.35 — *Taxes*

Real estate and business taxes on real property used in the business to earn income are deductible. GST/HST paid in respect of an expense that is deductible for income tax purposes is deductible in computing taxable income where an input tax credit is not claimed (CRA VD 2004-0076561E5). However, amounts payable as interest under the GST portion of the *Excise Tax Act* are not deductible for tax purposes.

¶6140 — Non-Allowable Deductions for Expenses

Following are some of the more common outlays that cannot be deducted as current expenses for the purposes of calculating an individual's business or professional income.

¶6140.1 — *Advertising in Non-Canadian Media*

Expenses for advertising directed primarily at the Canadian market in foreign radio and television broadcasts (ITA 19.1) or in non-Canadian newspapers (ITA 19) are generally non-deductible for tax purposes. Also, 50% of advertising in periodicals with less than 80% original Canadian content is non-deductible. However, ITA 19.01 generally permits full deductibility of expenses or outlays for advertising space in an issue of a periodical where the advertisement is directed at the Canadian market, provided the issue contains at least 80% non-advertising Canadian editorial content. It is the CRA's position that the limitations in ITA 19, 19.01 and 19.1 do not apply to the deductibility of advertising expenses on foreign internet websites (VDs 2017-0691771M4, 2017-0700121M4).

¶6140.2 — *Appraisal Costs*

The cost of an appraisal of the assets of a business in order to establish the price at which they are to be sold is not a deductible expense. However, the expense of an appraisal to determine the adequacy of insurance coverage is generally allowed as a deduction. Also, it is arguable that an appraisal in the course of borrowing money or raising of capital by the issuance of additional shares of capital stock should be considered a deductible expense under paragraph 20(1)(e).

¶6140.3 — *Contingent Liabilities*

Unless specifically permitted under a provision of the ITA, for tax purposes, no amount as or on account of a reserve or contingent liability (i.e., an obligation that may arise out of present circumstances providing certain developments occur) is deductible in computing taxable income simply on the ground that it may be dictated by good accounting practice governing the determination of a taxpayer's profit. Examples of contingent liabilities or reserves may include a liability accrued for the expected settlement of a legal suit.

¶6140.4 — *Charitable Donations*

Charitable donations are not deductible in computing the income of the donor; however, if they are made to a registered charitable, religious, or educational institution in Canada, they are creditable in computing the donor's tax payable (see Line 330 at ¶10190).

¶6140.5 — *Club Dues*

The deduction of membership fees or dues in any club the main purpose of which is to provide dining, recreational, or sporting facilities for its members is prohibited under ITA 18(1)(l). Also non-deductible is the cost of maintaining a yacht, camper, lodge, or a golf course or facility, or rent paid for the use of such facilities (except in the case of a taxpayer whose business it is to operate such a property for profit).

The CRA considers a facility to be a golf course, and the term is intended also to include any amenities provided by a golf club, such as a health club, swimming pool, or a tennis court. However, the CRA will permit a deduction for the meals and beverages consumed at a golf course provided that there is a genuine business purpose for the meals and beverages. In paragraph 4 of IT-148R3: *Recreational Properties and Club Dues*, the CRA states "[e]xpenses incurred for food and beverages at a restaurant, dining room, banquet hall or conference room of a golf club are not subject to paragraph 18(1)(l), provided there is a genuine business purpose to the use of the facilities and the expenses are not incurred in conjunction with a game of golf or other recreational activity at the golf club". As well, in VD 2012-0442681M4, the CRA states that it "considers that the restriction on deducting expenses relating to the maintenance or use of a golf club applies only to the recreational amenities provided by the golf club. Accordingly, this will not include the golf club's dining room, banquet hall, conference room, beverage room, or lounge. Consequently, the tax treatment of meals and beverages consumed at a golf club is the same as that of meals and beverages consumed at a restaurant." This means that the costs would be subject to the regular 50 percent deduction limit applicable to meals and entertainment under ITA 67.1.

The Tax Court of Canada considered the meaning of "lodge" for the purposes of ITA 18(1)(l)(i) in *Hewlett-Packard (Canada) Co. v. R.*, 2005 CarswellNat 1765 (TCC). In this case, the taxpayer's deductions for weekend vacation trips provided to employees were disallowed as expenses relating to "lodge" fees. The taxpayer appealed and the court allowed the deductions, concluding that "lodge" and "hotel" could not be used interchangeably and that a "lodge" does not include large, full service resort-like hotels such as Deerhurst, Chateau Whistler, and others that were used by the taxpayer. As well, it is the CRA's position that, even if the resort meets the definition of a "lodge", and if the company uses the resort primarily for business purposes, then the cost of the resort accommodations and the related expenditures would be deductible, subject to the 50 percent limitation.

Annual membership fees in professional associations and societies (such as medical, legal, accounting, architectural, and engineering professional associations) are deductible in the computation of income from the professional practice. For more information, see IT-148R3, *Recreational Properties and Club Dues*.

¶6140.6 — *Entertainment Expenses*

A deduction for entertainment expenses is permitted only where it can be conclusively shown that the outlay was made for the purpose of gaining or producing income from the business. Also, ITA 18(1)(l) denies the deductibility of expenses incurred for the entertainment of clients (or employees) if the expense relates to the use of a yacht, camp, lodge, golf course, or facility. As well, club dues are not deductible when their main purpose is to provide dining, recreational, or sporting facilities. Unlike meals and entertainment expenses, 100 percent of the deduction for the latter expenses is denied. The CRA has stated that a facility will not include the dining room, banquet halls, conference rooms, beverage rooms, or lounges of a golf club and, thus, the deduction of the cost of meals and beverages incurred at a golf club will not be fully denied; however, such costs are subject to the 50 percent deduction limit applicable to meals and entertainment.

¶6140.7 — *Expenses Prior to Start of Business*

Expenditures leading up to, but incurred prior to the commencement of business operations, are not deductible. See IT-364, *Commencement of Business Operations*.

¶6140.8 — *Expenses Incurred to Earn Exempt Income*

Expenses incurred in connection with income that is exempt from tax are not deductible and should not be allowed to reduce the taxpayer's income from other sources. Where an expense is incurred to earn both taxable and exempt income, it is necessary to apportion the expense.

¶6140.9 — *Fines and Penalties*

No deduction may be claimed in respect of an amount paid as a fine or penalty, except for a prescribed fine or penalty as set out in ITR 7309 (which includes fines imposed under specified provisions of the *Excise Tax Act*, *Excise Act* and *Air Travellers Security Charge Act*). Penalties and interest on unremitted source deductions are deductible in computing income for tax purposes (ITA 67.6). See Folio S4-F2-C1, *Deductibility of Fines and Penalties*, for the CRA's administrative views on the deductibility of fines and penalties for business purposes.

¶6140.10 — *Goodwill*

Before January 1, 2017, three-quarters of the taxpayer's outlay for goodwill was an eligible capital expenditure that could be written off for tax purposes at the rate of 7% per year and one-half of the proceeds from the disposition of an eligible capital property was included in income.

As of January 1, 2017, the eligible capital property regime was replaced with a new capital cost allowance (CCA) class available to businesses, and taxpayers' existing cumulative eligible capital pools are transferred to the new CCA class. The new CCA class is Class 14.1, and has a rate of 5 percent. Goodwill is deemed to constitute "property" for purposes of the ITA, and a taxpayer is deemed to own a single "goodwill property" in respect of a business for as long as it carries on that business. The cost of the taxpayer's goodwill property in respect of a business generally includes the cost of any goodwill acquired in respect of the business and any capital expenditures incurred in respect of the business that do not relate to any specific property. For further discussion, see under "Eligible Capital Expenditures" below.

¶6140.11 — *Guarantees and Warranties*

Although a taxpayer's product may be sold subject to a guarantee, no amount may be deducted as a reserve to meet the expense of repairing or replacing defective merchandise. The expense is deductible only when it is actually incurred.

¶6140.12 — *Illegal Payments*

No deduction is allowed in respect of an outlay or expense which is incurred for the purpose of committing a criminal offence or bribery of a foreign official.

¶6140.13 — *Insurance (Accident and Sickness)*

Premiums paid for insurance to cover personal injury or disability are not expenses laid out for the purpose of gaining or producing income and are not deductible.

¶6140.14 — *Interest and Penalties on Income Taxes*

Interest and penalties paid on income taxes owing are not deductible from income.

¶6140.15 — *Legal Expenses*

Legal and accounting fees incurred on the acquisition of a capital property are normally capitalized to the cost of the property. Prior to 2017, legal and accounting fees that are capital in nature may qualify as eligible capital expenditures for tax purposes (e.g., expenses incurred in protecting a business franchise or expenses in defending an action for slander). As of January 1, 2017, the eligible capital property regime was replaced with a new capital cost allowance (CCA) class available to businesses, and taxpayers' existing cumulative eligible capital pools are transferred to the new CCA class. The new CCA class is Class 14.1, and has a rate of 5 percent. For further discussion, see under "Eligible Capital Expenditures" below.

Legal costs involved in the purchase of another company's assets may be permanently denied as a non-deductible expense for tax purposes. For more information, see IT-99R5(C), *Legal and Accounting Fees*.

¶6140.16 — *Lease Fees — Vehicles*

ITA 67.3 limits the amount of lease costs of a "passenger vehicle" (ITA 248(1)) that is otherwise deductible in computing taxable income in the case of so-called luxury vehicles. ITA 67.3 is complementary to ITA 13(7)(g) under which a passenger vehicle owned by a taxpayer will be deemed to have a capital cost not exceeding a prescribed amount (currently $30,000 plus applicable taxes; see CCA Class 10.1 and ITR 7307(1)). In general terms, the maximum deductible lease charges are computed as the lesser of: 1) the actual lease payments paid or incurred in the year; 2) the prescribed monthly rate (currently $800 plus applicable taxes) multiplied by the number of months in the year the vehicle was leased; and 3) the annual lease limit, which is equal to the monthly pre-tax lease cost multiplied by the ratio of CCA cost limit (currently $30,000 plus applicable taxes) divided by 85% times the greater of the prescribed limit ($30,000 plus applicable taxes) and the manufacturer's suggested list price. See the example calculations provided in paragraphs 10 to 12 of IT-521R, *Motor Vehicle Expenses Claimed by Self-Employed Individuals*.

¶6140.17 — *Lists of Customers*

An outlay made to acquire a list of potential customers may or may not be deductible, depending on the circumstances. Where the list of customers and related information is of temporary value, the outlay is considered a deductible expense. Prior to 2017, where the transaction represents the acquisition of the vendor's business, the cost attributable to customers' lists was an eligible capital expenditure, ¾ of which was included in the taxpayer's cumulative eligible capital, amortized at a rate of 7 percent per year.

As of January 1, 2017, the eligible capital property regime was replaced with a new capital cost allowance (CCA) class available to businesses, and taxpayers' existing cumulative eligible capital pools are transferred to the new CCA class. The new CCA class is Class 14.1, and has a rate of 5 percent. For further discussion, see under "Eligible Capital Expenditures" below.

¶6140.18 — *Organization Expenses*

Before 2017, expenditures incurred for the initial organization of a business, including expenses of registering a business, were generally eligible capital expenditures, 3/4 of which was included in the taxpayer's cumulative eligible capital and subject to amortization at a rate of 7% per year.

As of January 1, 2017, the eligible capital property regime was replaced with a new capital cost allowance (CCA) class available to businesses, and taxpayers' existing cumulative eligible capital pools are transferred to the new CCA class. The new CCA class is Class 14.1, and has a rate of 5 percent. For further discussion, see under "Eligible Capital Expenditures" below.

IT-364: *Commencement of Business Operations*

¶6140.19 — *Personal or Living Expenses*

Personal or living expenses are not deductible, except for travelling expenses incurred by the taxpayer while away from home in the course of carrying on business (ITA 18(1)(h)). Personal or living expenses are defined in ITA 248(1). ITA 67.1 provides a general restriction on the deduction for business-related meal and entertainment expenses to 50% of the lesser of the amount actually paid or payable, or an amount that would be reasonable in the circumstances. An expense, such as an automobile expense or travelling expense, may be incurred for a dual purpose. In that case only the proportion that can be attributed to the business is deductible. See also "Automobile Expenses" under "Items Allowed as Deductions".

¶6140.20 — *Political Contributions*

Political contributions are expressly prohibited as deductions in computing income from a business or property (ITA 18(1)(n)). However, a tax credit is allowed for certain political contributions made by a taxpayer (ITA 127(3); see Lines 409 and 410 at ¶11020).

¶6140.21 — *Private Health Services Plan Premiums*

Where an individual carries on business either directly or as a member of a partnership, the individual may deduct premiums paid in respect of a private health services plan for coverage of the individual, their spouse or members of the individual's household (ITA 20.01). In order for premiums to be deductible, self-employed workers must carry on an active business, either alone or in partnership, the individual's total business income (excluding losses) must represent more than 50 percent of the individual's income for the year or the individual's income from other sources cannot exceed $10,000.

In addition, the premiums must be payable to (i) a person licensed to carry on the insurance business or trustee business, or to (ii) a person which is in the business of offering services as a private health services plan administrator, or to (iii) a tax-exempt entity that is a business or professional organization or a trade union of which the individual or a majority of the individual's employees are members (ITA 20.01(1)(b)).

A deduction for such premiums may be claimed only to the extent that they are not otherwise claimed as a medical expense or deducted by any other person (ITA 20.01(2)(a)). If the individual or partnership has one or more full-time employees with more than three months service, the deduction is based on the lowest cost of equivalent coverage which is made available to any arm's length employee (ITA 20.01(2)(b)). If there are no employees or if arm's length employees who could be covered represent less than 50 percent of the persons in the business and who could be covered, then the maximum amount which can be claimed is $1,500 for the individual, their spouse or common-law partner, and members of the household who are 18 or over, and $750 for other members of the household (ITA 20.01(2)(c)).

ITA 20.01(3) sets out the provisions for the purposes of determining equivalent coverage as provided in subsection 20.01(2).

IT-339R2: *Meanings of Private Health Services Plan*

¶6140.22 — *Salary Paid to Spouse or Common-Law Partner*

Remuneration paid by the taxpayer to the taxpayer's spouse or common-law partner is deductible provided the amounts paid are reasonable in the circumstances.

There is no restriction on the deduction of remuneration paid by the taxpayer (or by a partnership of which the taxpayer is a partner) to the taxpayer's spouse or common-law partner as long as it is reasonable in the circumstances (ITA 67). Amounts of salary or bonuses paid or payable to an owner-manager are normally deductible on the basis that the owner's expertise, know-how, managerial skills and effort are responsible for the company's profits. The CRA will generally not question the reasonableness of owner-manager salaries and bonuses paid to Canadian residents who are actively involved in the day-to-day operations of the company. This position does not, however, extend to remuneration paid to spouses or other family members of the principal shareholder.

The CRA is more likely to question the reasonableness of bonuses and salary paid to a business owner's minor children or spouse, particularly when the bonuses and salaries are perceived by the CRA to merely be an income-splitting measure designed to take advantage of the lower personal tax brackets of the spouse and children. Nonetheless, salaries and bonuses paid to the spouse and children of a business owner are deductible provided the compensation is reasonable in relation to the services provided. The Courts have allowed bonuses paid to family members to be deducted in certain cases; however, in certain other cases, the courts have denied a deduction.

In *Ambulances B.G.R. Inc.*, 2004 CarswellNat 1054 (TCC), relatively large bonuses paid to adult children were held to be deductible on the basis that they represented reasonable compensation for exceptional services performed. In *Costigane*, [2003] 3 C.T.C. 2087 (TCC), amounts paid for bookkeeping services by a dentist to a financial services company owned by a family trust (of which the dentist's minor children were the beneficiaries) were found to be unreasonable when compared to the cost of the dental staff doing the work directly. However, the Court accepted a reduced mark-up of 15 percent on such services.

¶6140.23 — *Taxes*

Neither federal nor provincial income taxes are deductible in computing business income.

ITA 18(1)(t), 20(1)(v)

¶6150 — Capital Cost Allowance (CCA)

Generally, where a taxpayer acquires a depreciable property, such as a building, furniture, or equipment, to use in the taxpayer's business or rental operation, the cost of the property cannot be deducted when calculating net business or rental income for the year. However, since these properties wear out or become obsolete over time, taxpayers can deduct their cost over a period of several years; the deduction is referred to as capital cost allowance (CCA).

The principal characteristics of the CCA system are summarized below:

- A taxpayer can claim CCA based on the depreciation percentages set forth in the Regulations. A taxpayer can deduct all or a portion of the prescribed CCA available or choose to claim none at all in a particular year, thus postponing the deduction until a subsequent year. The CRA permits a taxpayer to make retroactive CCA claims in certain circumstances (generally when the tax year is not statute-barred and the claim does not create a loss).

- Eligible assets are grouped into prescribed CCA classes to each of which is allotted a maximum percentage rate of CCA. The dollar amount of the balance outstanding in each class (the UCC) is adjusted upward when additional assets of the class are acquired and downward when assets of the class are disposed of. Thus, the UCC of the class is increased by the capital cost of eligible assets that fall within the class and are acquired during the year and decreased by the proceeds of disposition of eligible assets (to the extent of the capital cost of such assets) that fall within the class and are disposed of during the year.

- A taxpayer may not include an asset in a CCA class until the time at which the property is considered to have become "available for use" by the taxpayer.

- CCA is claimed as of the end of the year. The diminishing-balance method rather than the straight-line method is normally used. Any CCA claimed is deducted from the UCC at the end of the year. If no new assets of the class are acquired and if CCA is claimed, the UCC will diminish from year to year.

- For most depreciable property acquired, the amount of CCA that may be claimed in the year of acquisition is limited to one-half of the amount that would otherwise be calculated by applying the maximum percentage rate of CCA prescribed for the particular class to which the property belongs (this rule is commonly referred to as the half-year rule). However, the application of the half-year rule is suspended for qualifying property acquired after November 20, 2018 that becomes available for use before 2028; see ¶7006 for more information.

- On disposal of assets, depreciation already allowed is "recaptured" and included in income to the extent that the proceeds exceed the UCC of the group of assets in the particular class. In general terms, recaptured CCA is attributable to CCA that has been claimed in preceding taxation years in excess of the "actual" depreciation in the value of a group of assets of a particular class. For recapture to arise, the proceeds of disposition of a property of a class must exceed the UCC of the class as determined in accordance with the rules discussed above. Proceeds of disposition in excess of the original capital cost of an asset would normally result in a capital gain.

- On disposal of an asset, if the proceeds exceed its original capital cost, the excess is normally considered a capital gain and is not subject to recapture. Additionally, the excess is not deducted from the depreciable base of other assets in the same class. Whereas the entire amount of recapture is included in computing income, only 50% of a capital gain is included in computing taxable income.

- On disposal of all of the assets in a particular class, if there still remains a balance of UCC, the amount is deductible in the year from income as a "terminal loss." Essentially, a terminal loss is attributable to unrecognized depreciation (i.e., depreciation in which a CCA claim has not yet been made). It should be highlighted that a taxpayer cannot realize a capital loss on a disposition of depreciable property (see ITA 39(1)(b)(i)).

- The accelerated investment incentive for CCA (accelerated CCA or ACCA) allows Canadian businesses to claim enhanced first-year CCA on qualified assets acquired after November 20, 2018 that are available for use before 2028; see ¶7006 for more information.

¶6151 — CCA Classes

Below is a discussion of the more common classes of depreciable business property for business purposes and the rates that apply to each class. Following the discussion is a listing of depreciable property for business purposes illustrated in table format, for quick reference. For more details, see 2017 Chapter 7.

Class 1 (4%)

A building may belong to class 1, 3, or 6, depending on what the building is made of and the date of acquisition. Also include the parts that make up the building, such as electrical wiring, lighting fixtures, plumbing, sprinkler systems, heating equipment, air-conditioning equipment (other than window units), elevators and escalators. Most land is not depreciable property. Therefore, when you acquire property, only claim CCA on the cost that relates to the building. For more information, see IT-79R3, Capital Cost Allowance — Buildings or Other Structures.

Class 3 (5%)

Most buildings acquired before 1988 were included in Class 3 or Class 6. If you acquired a building before 1990 that does not fall into Class 6, you can include it in Class 3 with a CCA rate of 5% if you acquired the building under the terms of a written agreement entered into before June 18, 1987, or the building was under construction on June 18, 1987. Include in Class 3 the cost of any additions or alterations made after 1987 to a Class 3 building that does not exceed the lesser of $500,000 or 25% of the building's capital cost (including the cost of additions or alterations to the building included in class 3, 6, or 20 before 1988). Any amount that exceeds the lesser amount above is included in Class 1.

Class 6 (10%)

Include in Class 6 a building if it is made of frame, log, stucco on frame, galvanized iron, or corrugated metal. In addition, one of the following conditions has to apply: you acquired the building before 1979; the building must have no footings or other base supports below ground level; or the building must be used to gain or produce income from farming or fishing (farming and fishing income is not rental income).

If any of the above conditions applies, also add to Class 6 the full cost of all additions and alterations to the building. If neither of the above conditions applies, include the building in Class 6 if one of the following situations applies: you entered into a written agreement before 1979 to acquire the building, and the footings or other base supports of the building were started before 1979; or you started construction of the building before 1979 (or it was started under the terms of a written agreement you entered into before 1979), and the footings or other base supports of the building were started before 1979.

For additions or alterations to such a building:

- add to Class 6 the first $100,000 of additions or alterations made after 1978;

- add to Class 3 the part of the cost of additions or alterations above $100,000 made after 1978 and before 1988; and the part of the cost of additions or alterations above $100,000 made after 1987, but only up to $500,000 or 25% of the building's capital cost, whichever is less; and

- add to Class 1 any additions or alterations that are more than these limits.

Also include in Class 6, certain greenhouses and fences.

Class 8 (20%)

Class 8 includes certain property not included in other classes such as furniture, household appliances, tools costing $500 or more, some fixtures, machinery, outdoor advertising signs, refrigeration equipment, and other equipment you use in your business. Photocopiers and electronic communications equipment, such as fax machines and electronic telephone equipment, are also be included in Class 8. If this equipment cost $1,000 or more, you can elect to have it included in a separate class. The CCA rate will not change but a separate CCA deduction can now be calculated for a five year period. When all the property in the class is disposed of, the UCC is fully deductible as a terminal loss. Any UCC balance remaining in the separate class at the end of the fifth year has to be transferred back to the general class in which it would otherwise belong. To make an election, attach a letter to your income tax return for the tax year in which you acquired the property.

Class 10 (30%)

Include in Class 10 computer equipment that is general-purpose electronic data-processing equipment (i.e., computer hardware) and systems software (i.e., operating systems), including ancillary data-processing equipment, if acquired before March 23, 2004, or after March 22, 2004, and before 2005, and you made an election. Also include in Class 10 motor vehicles, automobiles, and some passenger vehicles. Include a passenger vehicle in Class 10 unless it meets a Class 10.1 condition. For more information on Class 10 and Class 10.1 and definitions of motor vehicle and passenger vehicle, see Guide T4002, Self-employed Business, Professional, Commission, Farming and Fishing Income.

Class 10.1 (30%)

Your passenger vehicle can belong to either Class 10 or Class 10.1. To determine the class to which your passenger vehicle belongs, use the cost of the vehicle before you add GST/HST or PST. Include your passenger vehicle in Class 10.1 if you bought it in the current fiscal period and it cost more than $30,000. List each Class 10.1 vehicle separately. The capital cost of a Class 10.1 vehicle is $30,000 plus the related GST/HST or PST. Use the GST rate of 5% and the appropriate PST rate for your province or territory. If your province is a participating province, use the HST.

Class 12 (100%)

Class 12 includes china, cutlery, linen, uniforms, dies, jigs, moulds, cutting or shaping parts of a machine, tools, and computer software (except systems software). Also included are video cassettes, video laser discs, or digital video disks that you rent and do not expect to rent to any person for more than seven days in a 30-day period. Tools eligible under this class specifically exclude electronic communication devices and electronic data processing equipment.

Class 14.1 (5%)

Starting January 1, 2017, include in Class 14.1 property that:

- is goodwill;

- was eligible capital property (ECP) immediately before January 1, 2017 and is owned at the beginning of that day;

- is acquired after 2016, other than:

  - property that is tangible or corporeal property;

  - property that is not acquired for the purpose of gaining or producing income from business;

  - property in respect of which any amount is deductible (otherwise than as a result of being included in class 14.1) in computing the income from the business;

  - an interest in a trust;

  - an interest in a partnership;

  - a share, bond, debenture, mortgage, hypothecary claim, note, bill or other similar property; or

  - property that is an interest in, or for civil law a right in, or a right to acquire, a property described in any of the above sub-bullets.

For tax years that end prior to 2027, properties included in class 14.1 that were acquired before January 1, 2017 will be allowed an additional CCA. Transitional rules will apply. Properties that are included in Class 14.1 and acquired after 2016 will be included in this class at a 100% inclusion rate with a 5% CCA rate on a declining-balance basis and the existing CCA rules will normally apply.

Class 29 (straight line)

Include in Class 29 eligible machinery and equipment used in Canada primarily for the manufacture and process of goods for sale or lease acquired after March 18, 2007 and before 2016 that would otherwise be included in Class 43. Calculate CCA using the straight line method as follows: claim up to 25% in the first year, 50% in the second year, and the remaining 25% in the third year. Any amount not claimed in a year can be claimed in a later year.

Class 43 (30%)

Include in Class 43 eligible machinery and equipment used in Canada for the manufacture and process of goods for sale or lease that are not included in Class 29 or 53. You may put this property in a separate class if you file an election by attaching a letter to your income tax return for the year in which you acquired the property.

Class 45 (45%)

Include in Class 45 computer equipment that is general-purpose electronic data processing equipment (i.e., computer hardware) and systems software (i.e., operating systems), including ancillary data processing equipment, if acquired after March 22, 2004, and before March 19, 2007.

Class 46 (30%)

Include in Class 46 data network infrastructure equipment and systems software for that equipment if acquired after March 22, 2004. If acquired before March 23, 2004, include it in Class 8.

Class 50 (55%)

Include in Class 50 computer equipment that is general-purpose electronic data-processing equipment (i.e., computer hardware) and systems software (i.e., operating systems), including ancillary data-processing equipment, if acquired after March 18, 2007, but not including property that is included in Class 29 or Class 52 or that is principally or is used principally as: (a) electronic process control or monitor equipment; (b) electronic communications control equipment; (c) systems software for equipment referred to in (a) or (b); or (d) data handling equipment (other than data handling equipment that is ancillary to general-purpose electronic data processing equipment).

Class 52 (100%)

Include in Class 52 computer equipment that is general-purpose electronic data processing equipment (i.e., computer hardware) and systems software (i.e., operating systems), including ancillary data processing equipment, if acquired after January 27, 2009 and before February 2011, but not including property that is principally or is used principally as: (a) electronic process control or monitor equipment; (b) electronic communications control equipment; (c) systems software for equipment referred to in (a) or (b); or (d) data handling equipment (other than data handling equipment that is ancillary to general purpose electronic data processing equipment). The equipment must be new and situated in Canada for use in a business carried on in Canada or for the purpose of earning income from property situated in Canada.

Class 53 (50%)

Include in Class 53 eligible machinery and equipment that is acquired after 2015 and before 2026 (that would generally otherwise be included in Class 29) to be used in Canada primarily in the manufacturing or processing of goods for sale or lease. The rate for qualifying property acquired after November 20, 2018 and before 2024 is 100% (see under ¶7006).

¶6152 — CCA Class Summary Table

The following table lists and describes most common classes of depreciable business property and the rates that apply to each class. For a complete listing of depreciable property alphabetically listed by property type, see ¶7000. For more information on claiming CCA, see 2017 Chapter 7.

CCA classes for commonly used business assets		
Class	**Description**	**Rate**
1	Most buildings made of brick, stone, or cement acquired after 1987, including their component parts such as electric wiring, lighting fixtures, plumbing, heating and cooling equipment, elevators, and escalators (an additional allowance of 6% (for a total of 10%) may be claimed in respect of an "eligible non-residential building" which is used for the M&P in Canada of goods for sale or lease)	4%–10%
3	Most buildings made of brick, stone, or cement acquired before 1988, including their component parts as listed in Class 1	5%
6	Buildings made of frame, log, stucco on frame, galvanized iron, or corrugated metal that are used in the business of farming or fishing or that have no footings below-ground; fences; most greenhouses	10%

CCA classes for commonly used business assets		
Class	**Description**	**Rate**
8	Depreciable property not included in any other class, such as furniture and fixtures, cash registers, refrigeration equipment not used for a qualifying M&P purpose and fax machines, printers, scanners, photocopiers and other office equipment that does not qualify as "general-purpose electronic data processing equipment" (i.e., computer hardware) or as ancillary data processing equipment thereto; tools costing $500 or more; outdoor advertising billboards and neon signs; greenhouses with rigid frames and plastic covers	20%
10	Automobiles (except taxis and others used for lease or rent or "luxury" passenger vehicles), vans, wagons, trucks, buses, tractors (except certain long-haul tractors included in Class 16), trailers; contractor's movable equipment; timber-cutting and removing equipment	30%
10.1	"Luxury" passenger vehicles costing more than $30,000 and acquired after 2000 (each such vehicle is included in a separate Class 10.1, the recapture and terminal loss rules do not apply, and a special 15% CCA claim may be made in the year of disposition)	30%
12	Chinaware; cutlery; linen; uniforms; dies; jigs; moulds or lasts; computer software, except "systems software" (i.e., operating systems); cutting or shaping parts of a machine; certain property used for earning rental income such as apparel or costumes; videotape cassettes; certain property costing less than $500 such as kitchen utensils, tools, and medical or dental instruments	100%
14.1	Goodwill, property that was eligible capital property (ECP) before 2017, and property acquired on or after January 1, 2017, the cost of which would be treated as an eligible capital expenditure under the former ECP rules. For taxation years that end before 2027, the depreciation rate is 7% in respect of expenditures incurred before January 1, 2017	5%–7%
29	Machinery and equipment that is used in Canada primarily to manufacture and process goods for sale or lease acquired after March 18, 2007 and before 2016 that would otherwise be included in Class 43 (now see Class 53)	50% SL
43	Eligible machinery and equipment used for the M&P in Canada of goods for sale or lease that are not included in Class 29 or 53	30%
45	Computer equipment that is "general-purpose electronic data processing equipment" (i.e., computer hardware) and "systems software" (i.e., operating systems) therefore, including ancillary data processing equipment (such as a printer attached to a desktop computer) acquired after March 22, 2004 and before March 19, 2007 (now see Classes 50 and 52)	45%
46	Data network infrastructure equipment, which generally includes network infrastructure equipment and "systems software" that controls, transfers, modulates or directs data and that operates in support of telecommunications applications such as e-mail or Web browsing	30%
50	Property described in Class 45 (i.e., computer equipment) acquired after March 18, 2007, other than such equipment included in Class 52	55%
52	Property described in Class 45 (i.e., computer equipment) acquired after January 27, 2009 and before February 2011 that is new and that is situated in Canada for use in a business carried on in Canada or for the purpose of earning income from property situated in Canada	100%

CCA classes for commonly used business assets		
Class	Description	Rate
53	Machinery and equipment acquired by a taxpayer after 2015 and before 2026 primarily for use in Canada for the manufacturing and processing of goods for sale or lease. The rate for qualifying property acquired after November 20, 2018 and before 2024 is 100% (see under ¶7006).	50%

¶6160 — Eligible Capital Expenditures

Eligible capital expenditures are generally expenditures made before 2017 for intangible property, including the following:

- goodwill

- customers lists and ledger accounts (unless deductible as an expense)

- trademarks

- patents, franchises and licences (unless depreciable as Class 14 property)

- incorporation, reorganization or amalgamation expenses

- milk quotas and other governmental right or licences

- expenditures for research and business expansion

IT-143R3: *Meaning of Eligible Capital Expenditure*, IT-187: *Customer Lists and Ledger Accounts*, IT-386R: *Eligible Capital Amounts*, IT-475: *Expenditures on Research and for Business Expansion*

¶6161 — *Cumulative Eligible Capital Account*

For taxation years before 2017, the cumulative eligible capital (CEC) account operated similarly to the UCC account of a class of depreciable property (as discussed above). Essentially, where an individual purchased eligible capital property (called an eligible capital expenditure (ECE)), 3/4 of the expense was included as cumulative eligible capital. A deduction was allowed of up to 7% of the balance in the CEC account for each business at the end of a taxation year and the balance in the CEC was reduced by the amount of the deduction claimed (former ITA 20(1)(b)). For short taxation years, the deduction was pro-rated by the number of days in the year over 365 days. If no additions or dispositions occurred in a year, the maximum 7% was applied to the declining balance and is deductible. The half-year rule did not apply to eligible capital expenditures.

Where an individual disposed of eligible capital property, the CEC account was reduced by 3/4 of the net proceeds of disposition of eligible capital property (i.e., net of any expenses incurred in bringing about the disposition). The maximum annual deduction was 7% of the balance at the end of each year. If the disposition did not create a negative balance, the taxpayer could still deduct a maximum of 7% of the remaining balance annually.

Where a disposition caused the CEC balance to fall to a negative amount at the end of the taxation year, the amount of the negative balance was required to be included in income, similar to a recapture of capital cost allowance (ITA 14(1)). This required the taxpayer to include in income deductions previously allowed under former ITA 20(1)(b)). Where a taxpayer ceased to carry on business and had a positive balance in their CEC account after disposing of all eligible capital property, the total amount could be deducted from income as a "terminal deduction" (ITA 24(1); see IT-313R2). A separate cumulative eligible capital pool was required for each separate business of the taxpayer (see IT-206R, *Separate Businesses*). A recapture and terminal allowance each caused the cumulative eligible capital account to be reset to zero.

¶6162 — *Repeal of Eligible Capital Property Regime*

As of January 1, 2017, the eligible capital property regime was replaced with a new capital cost allowance (CCA) class available to businesses, and taxpayers' existing cumulative eligible capital pools were transferred to the new CCA class. The new CCA class is Class 14.1, and has a rate of 5%. Expenditures that would have been added to cumulative eligible capital (CEC) at a 75% inclusion rate under the previous rules are now included in Class 14.1 at a 100% inclusion rate. Because of this increased expenditure recognition, Class 14.1 has a 5% annual depreciation rate (instead of 7% of 75% of eligible capital expenditures). All of the existing rules regarding CCA generally apply to Class 14.1 property, including rules relating to recapture, capital gains and depreciation (e.g., the "half-year rule").

The existing "cumulative eligible capital" pool of a taxpayer's business will be calculated and transferred to Class 14.1 as of January 1, 2017. The opening balance of Class 14.1 in respect of a business is equal to the balance at that time of the existing CEC pool for that business. For the first 10 years, the depreciation rate for Class 14.1 is 7% in respect of expenditures incurred before January 1, 2017.

Under the new rules, eligible capital expenditures that relate to acquisitions or dispositions of specific properties other than goodwill are treated in the same way as depreciable property falling within an existing CCA class. However, eligible capital expenditures that relate to acquisitions or dispositions of goodwill (or to no particular property at all) are accounted for in a different manner. Goodwill is now deemed to constitute "property" for purposes of the ITA, and a taxpayer is deemed to own a single "goodwill property" in respect of a business for as long as it carries on that business. The cost of the taxpayer's "goodwill property" in respect of a business generally includes the cost of any goodwill acquired in respect of the business and any capital expenditures incurred in respect of the business that do not relate to any specific property. When a taxpayer disposes of goodwill, it is treated as having carried out a partial disposition of its goodwill property in respect of the business, and the portion of the goodwill property disposed of is deemed to have a cost equal to the lesser of the full cost of the taxpayer's goodwill property and the proceeds received by the taxpayer. A capital gain will be realized to the extent that the proceeds exceed the deemed cost of the portion of the taxpayer's goodwill property disposed of, and recapture will be realized in the event that the reduction to the UCC of the taxpayer's Class 14.1 property causes the UCC in respect of the class to go negative. On a go-forward basis, the cost of the remaining portion of the taxpayer's goodwill property is deemed to be the full cost of the taxpayer's goodwill property less the deemed cost of the portion of the goodwill property disposed of. When a taxpayer receives an amount on account of capital in respect of the business that does not relate to a specific property, the taxpayer is deemed to have disposed of a portion of its goodwill property for proceeds equal to the amount received, leading to the application of the above rules.

Under transitional rules for receipts received after January 1, 2017 that relate to property acquired, or expenditures otherwise made, before January 1, 2017, certain qualifying receipts will reduce the balance of Class 14.1 at a 75% rate. Receipts that qualify for the reduced rate will generally be those from the disposition of property, the cost of which was included in the taxpayer's CEC and receipts that do not represent the proceeds of disposition of property. The total amount of such qualifying receipts, for which only 75% of the receipt will reduce Class 14.1, will generally equal the amount that could have been received under the eligible capital property regime before triggering an eligible capital property gain.

There are also special rules to simplify the transition for small businesses. To allow small initial balances to be eliminated quickly, taxpayers are permitted to deduct as CCA, in respect of expenditures incurred before 2017 and for taxation years that end prior to 2027, the greater of $500 per year and the amount otherwise deductible for that year. As well, in order to reduce compliance burdens associated with the depreciation of incorporation expenses under the CCA system, a lump sum deduction is provided for in respect of the first $3,000 of such expenditures.

The repeal of the eligible capital property regime and the implementation of new Class 14.1, including the associated transitional rules, are contained in Bill C-29, and apply as of January 1, 2017.

IT-143R3: *Meaning of Eligible Capital Expenditure*, IT-123R6: *Transactions Involving Eligible Capital Property*, IT-386R: *Eligible Capital Amounts*, IT-313R2: *Eligible Capital Property — Rules Where a Taxpayer has Ceased Carrying on a Business of has Died*

¶6170 — Special Situations

¶6171 — *Foreign Exchange Gains and Losses*

Generally, whether a foreign exchange gain or loss is on income or capital account depends upon whether the gain or loss arose as a consequence of a capital transaction (such as the purchase of a capital asset or long-term borrowings) or an income transaction (such as the purchase and sale of inventory). Normally, foreign exchange gains and losses on income account are included in computing income on an accrual basis. On the other hand, foreign exchange gains and losses on capital account should be recognized for tax purposes when realized (foreign exchange gains and losses on income account for tax purposes can also be recognized on a realized basis provided the income computation method used is consistent year-over-year). For example, a foreign exchange gain or loss related to a debt that is capital in nature (i.e., a debt incurred to purchase or invest in depreciable or non-depreciable capital property or to finance a capital project) should be recognized for tax purposes when payments are made against the principal portion of the debt and a portion of the gain or loss is realized.

¶6172 — *Contractors Completed Method*

In respect of contractors, generally, where a construction project may reasonably be expected to be completed within two years from the date of commencement, under the CRA's administrative policies, revenue (including holdbacks) may be deferred and included in taxable income in the year in which the work is physically completed. Normally, the CRA will accept the date the final engineer's or architect's certificate is issued as the date of physical completion. Additions to a job requiring extra work to be performed that will postpone completion of the job from one taxation year to a later one should be treated as a separate contract. In IT-92R2, *Income of Contractors*, the CRA states that a contractor who chooses to adopt the completion method is required to do so in respect of all short-term contracts and is required to use the same method consistently from year to year. Also, where the completed contract method is used, a contractor must defer to the year in which a short-term contract is completed all the direct costs of that contract incurred in a previous year. Furthermore, under the completion method, a loss on a short-term contract is taken into account only in computing the income of the year in which the contract is physically completed.

¶6200 — Professional Income (T1: Lines 137, 164)

Professional income (and losses) are reported on Form T2125, *Statement of Business or Professional Activities*. The information reported on Form T2125 is in turn reported on Line 137 (net professional income) and Line 164 (gross professional income).

¶6210 — Determining Professional Income

Professional income is required to be computed according to the accrual method with some modifications (ITA 34).

Fees received in advance of services rendered must be included in income, but a reasonable reserve may be deducted in respect of services reasonably anticipated to be rendered after the end of the year (ITA 20(1)(m)(ii)). Accordingly, every amount which becomes receivable during the fiscal year of the professional's business is included in income, regardless of whether such amounts are realized that year (subject to a reserve for doubtful debts), and all expenses incurred during the year must be deducted, regardless of whether actually paid within the year. To prevent deliberate deferral of income, the ITA requires fee income to be accounted for on the date the account for services would have been rendered if there had been no undue delay in presenting it (ITA 12(1)(b)). Professionals are required to maintain an accurate record of income received, including both fees received from the professional practice and other income, such as interest and dividends.

¶6220 — Election to Exclude Work in Progress (WIP)

For taxation years ending on or before March 21, 2017, in computing income from a business that is a profession, taxpayers with income from the professional practice of an accountant, dentist, lawyer, medical doctor, veterinarian, or chiropractor had the choice of excluding work in progress (WIP) at the end of each year (ITA 34). All other professional persons are required to treat WIP as inventory. The fair market value of inventory at the end of the year is defined as the amount that can reasonably be expected to become receivable after the end of the year; however, under the general rule, inventory is valued at the lesser of cost or fair market value. An election to exclude WIP was made in the tax return and applied for all subsequent years until the taxpayer revoked the election.

Applicable to taxation years ending after March 21, 2017, taxpayers with income from the professional practice of an accountant, dentist, lawyer, medical doctor, veterinarian, or chiropractor can no longer elect to exclude WIP at the end of each year. However, there is a 5-year phase-in period for the new rules, which will allow these professionals to reduce some of the upfront impact of the changes. Under the transitional rules, for the purposes of computing the income from one of these designated professions, the cost and fair market value of the taxpayer's WIP from the business is deemed to be:

- 20% of the lower of cost and fair market value of unbilled WIP at the end of the first taxation year that begins after March 21, 2017;
- 40% of the cost and fair market value of the taxpayer's unbilled WIP at the end of the second taxation year that begins after March 21, 2017;
- 60% of the cost and fair market value of the taxpayer's unbilled WIP at the end of the third taxation year that begins after March 21, 2017; and
- 80% of the cost and fair market value of the taxpayer's WIP at the end of the fourth taxation year that begins after March 21, 2017.

For the fifth taxation year that begins after March 21, 2017, the full amount in respect of WIP must be included in computing income. This transitional relief is only available to a taxpayer who elected to exclude WIP in computing income in respect of the last taxation year that begins before March 22, 2017, and only applies to income of a business that is a professional practice of an accountant, dentist, lawyer, medical doctor, veterinarian or chiropractor.

These changes were announced in the 2017 Federal budget and are contained in Bill C-63, which received Royal Assent on December 14, 2017.

The CRA provides guidance on questions of valuation with respect to including WIP into income under the transitional rules in VDs 2017-0709101E5 and 2018-0743031E5. In determining the cost or fair market value of a professional's WIP, the CRA states that taxpayers must consider the principles in *Canderel Ltd.*, 1998 CarswellNat 80, which sets out general principles in relation to the concept of profit, including that the taxpayer is free to adopt a method to determine profit which provides an accurate picture which is consistent with the ITA, case law, and well-accepted business principles. The CRA's position in paragraph 12 of IT-473R, *Inventory Valuation*, has not changed, which provides that the CRA accepts the use of either the direct costing method or the absorption method for costing inventory or WIP. The following additional comments are provided on costs: (1) the total cost of professional labour, including employee benefits, should form part of the cost of WIP; (2) for purposes of direct costing, fixed overheads (such as rental of premises) do not have to be included in the cost of WIP; and (3) when a partner or owner contributes to WIP, no amount representing the owner's time is required to be included in the cost of WIP.

With respect to fair market value, ITA 10(4)(a) defines the fair market value of WIP at the end of a taxation year to be "the amount that can reasonably be expected to become receivable in respect thereof after the end of the year". In contingency fee agreements, the fair market value of such WIP would be nil at the end of the taxation year, except that when it is possible to "establish an amount that can reasonably be expected to become receivable in respect of this WIP after the end of the taxation year", the fair market value should correspond to such amount. The CRA also provides the following guidance on its website with respect to contingency fee arrangements:

> Under the terms of a contingency fee arrangement, all or a portion of a designated professional's fees may only become known and billable at some time after the taxation year in which the professional provided services under the arrangement (e.g., where, under the terms of a written contingency fee agreement between a personal injury lawyer and a client, legal fees are only billable by the lawyer on a periodic basis as amounts are received by the client under a negotiated settlement or a court judgment). Until such time, there is often no liability on the professional's client to pay any fee; consequently, no amount is receivable by the professional until the right to collect the amount is established. Under these circumstances, for purposes of determining the value of the professional's work in progress at the end of the year, no amount would normally be recognized. As a result, the proposed change to eliminate the ability of designated professionals to elect to use billed-basis accounting is not expected to have any impact on these types of contingency fee arrangements where the terms and conditions of such arrangements are *bona fide*.

> Where a designated professional incurs expenses to earn income under a contingency fee arrangement, and the terms of the arrangement provide that the client has no risk or obligation to the professional in respect of those expenses unless and until some successful outcome is obtained in the future, the expenses would be deductible by the professional in computing business income for the taxation year in which they were incurred, assuming no other provision of the *Income Tax Act* would prohibit the deduction.

10(14.1), 34, IT-457R: *Election by Professionals to Exclude Work in Progress from Income*, Infanti, "CRA Confirms Partner Time Not Part of Professional's WIP Cost", Tax for the Owner-Manager, Vol. 18-3, July 2018.

¶6230 — Professional Expenses

Generally, the above discussion of current and capital expenses under ¶6140 also applies to professional income. The common expenses of maintaining a professional office will include some or all of the following items:

- Salaries of clerical and administrative staff, salaries of para-professionals and other assistants, and salaried professionals.

- Rent paid for business premises — where a practice is conducted from a property that is owned or rented and resided in, a proportion of the household expenses may be claimed in respect of the study, laboratory, office and waiting room space, in the proportion that this space bears to the total space of the residence. Eligible expenses include property taxes or rent, light, heat, insurance, repairs, depreciation (capital cost allowance) and mortgage interest. Certain conditions must be satisfied in order to claim a deduction for a home office. First, the part of the domestic establishment, referred to in the ITA as a work space, must be either the individual's principal place of business or used exclusively for the purpose of earning business income and used on a regular and continuous basis for meeting clients, customers or patients of the business. Secondly, provided these conditions are satisfied, the deductions allowed cannot exceed the income from the business for the year. Finally, any amounts not otherwise deductible by virtue of these restrictions are eligible for indefinite carry-forward and may be deducted as workspace expenses in following years (see Folio S1-F3-C2, *Principal Residence*, and Folio S4-F2-C2, *Business Use of Home Expenses*).

- Telephone, including business related long distance charges.

- Business insurance, including malpractice insurance and overhead expense insurance (also see above under Business Income).

- Property and business taxes.

- Licences, any annual fee paid to a governing body, membership in which is a prerequisite to practicing the profession

- Electricity and gas, postage, stationery, and related courier expenses.

- Office supplies, including related laundry, etc., and in the case of the medical and dental professions, medical, surgical and similar supplies, including instruments which cost less than $500.

- Capital cost allowance — office furniture and fixtures may be depreciated on the declining balance basis at a rate of 20% per year subject to the one-half rule in the year of acquisition. Medical instruments costing less than

$500 per item are in effect depreciated 100 percent in the first year as Class 12(e) property, so that the recapture provisions would apply in respect of any subsequent proceeds of disposition. See the discussion of capital cost allowance in ¶6150 and in 2017 Chapter 7.

- Books (except in the case of the purchase of a library, where 20 percent CCA should be claimed).

- Automobile expenses, where it can be shown that the use of an automobile is required to carry on the professional practice. Proper books and records should be maintained and data should be kept to indicate the extent to which the car is operated for business or personal use. Costs related to personal use will not be deductible for tax purposes.

- Entertainment expenses incurred for the promotion of the taxpayer's business are normally allowed subject to the general restriction on the deduction for meal expenses to 50 percent of their cost. The taxpayer should keep a record of the date, the amount of the expenditure and an indication that the outlay was made in the normal course of business, as it is necessary to establish that entertainment expenses are a normal requirement of the particular profession concerned. Annual membership fees paid to social, recreational, or sporting clubs are not deductible, nor is the expense of using or maintaining a yacht, camp, lodge, or golf course.

- Convention Expenses — A taxpayer may deduct from professional or business income the cost of attending not more than two conventions per year in connection with a profession or business (ITA 201(10)); however, such conventions are restricted to locations that are consistent with the territorial scope of the relevant professional organization.

¶6240 — Incorporation of a Professional Practice

Professional individuals sometimes arrange their affairs so that they are employed by a corporation that they own or control and the corporation carries on the business of the professional practice. Alternatively, the professional might have services provided by a service or management corporation owned or controlled by the professional or their relatives. The advantages of such arrangements would include access to the low rate of tax for a small business corporation (pursuant to ITA 125), access to the capital gains deduction for qualifying shares in a small business corporation (pursuant to ITA 110.6), and, in some cases, the ability to split income among family members and creditor proofing.

If the relevant provincial law allows the incorporation of a professional practice, it is essential to comply with the provisions of the relevant legislation, which would generally include obtaining approval from the requisite governing body. For the purposes of the ITA, a professional corporation is defined as a corporation that carries on the professional practice of an accountant, dentist, lawyer, medical doctor, veterinarian or chiropractor (ITA 248(1)). However, CRA recognizes that a corporation is carrying on a professional practice if its activities and its relationships to its employees and clients are similar to those ordinarily associated with a corporation carrying on any business. Such an arrangement would ordinarily be accepted as bona fide in the case of a corporation:

- owning or renting the premises of the business;

- owning or leasing the furniture, fixtures and major equipment of the business;

- operating a bank account in its own name through properly authorized signing officers;

- purchasing necessary supplies;

- providing clerical services;

- billing clients for services in its own name;

- depositing the collections in the bank;

- paying salaries to individuals performing services offered by the corporation;

- making the clients aware that they are dealing with the corporation; and

- maintaining an employer-employee relationship between the corporation and the individual, with the services to be performed clearly set out in a written agreement wherein specific provisions determine a reasonable salary for the services performed.

However, a corporation will not be considered to be carrying on the profession if it merely collects amounts that were billed in the name of the individual practitioner or partnership, pays the practitioner a salary, and pays the rent and other overhead expenses. The professional income will be taxed in the hands of the individual, although the corporation may be allowed to have a reasonable profit for the services it performs. The fiscal period of a professional corporation which is a member of a partnership is based on the calendar year (ITA 249.1(1)(b)).

¶6250 — Service and Management Corporations

Professional individuals or other persons may be provided with premises or management and administrative services by a corporation controlled by one or more particular professionals or their relatives. The corporation will be expected to remunerate its employees and to charge its customers an appropriate amount for the premises and services provided, which would include a reasonable profit to the corporation. The deduction of the amount paid to the corporation by the professionals will be allowed, provided the charges for the premises and services are reasonable in relation to the amount that an arm's length person would pay in a free market for the same facilities. The corporation is taxable on its income earned from the performance of its functions.

¶6300 — Farming and Fishing Income (T1: Lines 141, 143, 168, 170)

Farming income is calculated on Form T2042, *Statement of Farming Activities*, and the farming income information from Form T2042 is reported on Line 141 (net farming income) and Line 163 (gross farming income). Fishing income is calculated on Form T2121, *Statement of Fishing Activities*, and the fishing income information from Form T2121 is reported on Line 143 (net fishing income) and Line 165 (gross fishing income).

The ITA allows for a rollover of capital gains on certain intergenerational transfers of farming and fishing property. Also, the lifetime capital gains exemption is available in respect of the disposition of certain farming or fishing property, shares or interests. For dispositions and transfers in 2014 and subsequent taxation years, the availability of the intergenerational rollover and the lifetime capital gains exemption has been extended to: 1) property of an individual used principally in a combination of farming and fishing; and 2) to an individual's shares in a corporation, or interest in a partnership, where the corporation or partnership carries on both a farming business and a fishing business. For further discussion of the rollover and capital gains exemption on transfers and dispositions of farming and fishing property, see under ¶4230.

¶6310 — Computing Farming and Fishing Income

As an exception to normal rules, farmers and fishermen (other than fish packers or canners, or manufacturers of fish products) are permitted to compute their income for tax purposes according to the "cash method". When the cash method is used, income is computed without taking into account uncollected sales invoices, unpaid amounts owing for supplies, unsold inventories of farm products or livestock, etc. The ability to file on the cash method permits farmers and fishermen to postpone their tax until their product is converted into cash and also provides relief from the necessity to maintain more complex accounting records.

In the case of a farming or fishing business carried on by two or more persons jointly, or in partnership, all parties must use the same method for computing farm income (i.e., all must adopt the cash method or all the accrual method). Once the cash method is adopted, it must be used every subsequent year and may only be changed by approval of the Minister.

In order to reduce the impact of the deferred taxation of inventory, a farmer or fisherman is permitted to value farm or fishing inventory for tax purposes while retaining the cash method in all other respects. This means that each year (other than the year of death), farm or fishing inventory on hand at the end of the year may be valued at any amount between zero and fair market value. Like any inventory, the value assigned at the end of one year, and included in determining profits, is deductible in computing the profit of the following year. If this procedure is followed every year, the ultimate benefit will be realized in the year when a final disposal is made when it is likely that the farmer or fisherman will benefit the most from this deduction. In a loss year (other than the year of death), there is a mandatory inventory adjustment which requires the taxpayer to add to income an amount equal to the lesser of the loss and the value of purchased inventory on hand at the end of the year. The amount included in income is allowed as a deduction to reduce tax liability in a future year. Generally, inventory is defined to include property which would otherwise be considered inventory had the business income not been computed on a cash basis, including all livestock held in the course of carrying on the business. For the purposes of the mandatory inventory adjustments, inventory is valued at the lower of either original purchase price or fair market value.

ITA 28, Folio S4-F11-C1: *Meaning of Farming and Farming Business*, IT-433R: *Farming or Fishing — Use of Cash Method*, IT-373R2: *Woodlots*, IT-200: *Surface Rentals and Farming Operations*, IT-425R: *Miscellaneous Farm Income*, CRA Guide T4002, *Self-employed Business, Professional, Commission, Farming, and Fishing Income*

¶6320 — Definition of Farming and Fishing

Farming is defined in the ITA as *including* tillage of the soil, livestock raising or exhibiting, maintaining of horses for racing, raising of poultry, fur farming, dairy farming, fruit growing, and the keeping of bees, but specifically excludes an office or employment under a person engaged in the business of farming (ITA 248(1)"farming"). Fishing is defined as *including* fishing for or catching shell fish, crustaceans, and marine animals but does not include an office or employment under a person engaged in the business of fishing (ITA 248(1)"fishing").

The definition of both farming and fishing in the ITA are non-exhaustive. The meaning of "farming" from the perspective of the CRA is discussed in Folio S4-F11-C1: *Meaning of Farming and Farming Business* and VDs 2014-0527651E5 (zoo keeping is not a farming activity), 2014-0523871E5, 2013-0491141E5, 2014-0528251I7 (incidental farming income), 2004-0086271E5 and 2011-0403761I7, among others. See also the list of activities the CRA considers to constitute farming income in CRA Guide T4002, *Self-employed Business, Professional, Commission, Farming, and Fishing Income* (see under "Farming Income"). Examples of activities the CRA states may constitute farming includes: tree farming, cultivating crops in water or hydroponics, Christmas tree growing, operating a wild game reserve, operating a chicken hatchery, or operating a feedlot. In certain circumstances, the CRA states farming would also include raising fish, (see also VD 2014-0522091I7), market gardening, operating a nursery or greenhouse, and operating a maple sugar bush (includes maple sap transformation into maple products if this activity is considered incidental to the basic activities of a maple sugar bush, such as the extraction and collection of maple sap).

In VD 2012-0440061E5, the CRA took the position that the use of grazing lands owned by a co-operative corporation by some or all of its shareholders/members in their respective farming businesses would not result in that co-operative corporation being considered to be carrying on a farming business.

VDs 2011-0396431E5, 2005-0155851E5, *Tinhorn Creek Vineyards Ltd.*, [2006] 1 C.T.C. 2096 (TCC) (wine business was farming), *Levy*, [1990] 2 C.T.C. 83 (FCTD) (member of syndicate that bred and raced horses held to be in farming business despite not actively participating); John F Oakey, CA, "Tax Developments in the Fishing and Farming Industry," *2007 Atlantic Provinces Tax Conference*, (Halifax: Canadian Tax Foundation, 2007), 3A:1–23

¶6330 — Other Considerations

Other considerations with respect to farming businesses include:

- The CRA will generally consider income from a certain activity (such as rental income) that, by itself would be a non-farming activity, to be income from a farming business if the activity is incidental to the taxpayer's farming operations and the income generated by the activity is not substantial in relation to the taxpayer's farming revenue (VD 2010-0385151E5, 2007-0254211E5);

- The granting of an easement or right of way by a landowner is considered to be a disposition of a part of the property in respect of which it is granted (VD 2009-0312701E5);

- Generally, sales of agricultural land on a share crop basis extending over a period of years are not considered to give rise to taxable income in the hands of the seller unless the selling of agricultural lands is part of the business of the taxpayer. The CRA generally gives a restrictive meaning to "agricultural land" by excluding therefrom farm buildings, equipment, livestock and crops (ITA 12(1)(g), IT-462);

- A deduction is allowed for expenditures made for clearing or levelling farm land, or for installing a land drainage system, in computing income for tax purposes from a farming business (ITA 30, VD 2013-0479421E5);

- Generally, payments received by a landowner as compensation for damage to crops and compensation for additional costs and losses of a property owner who carries on farming operations around structures situated on the owner's property should be included in computing the property owner's income from farming operations (VD 2008-0297051E5);

- All small tools such as forks, spades, picks, shovels, etc. costing less than $500 may be deducted as an expense and need not be included with depreciable assets (see ¶7000, Class 12);

- An individual taxpayer can claim the $1,000,000 capital gains exemption in respect of a disposition of qualifying farming or fishing property (see ¶4230);

- ITA 80.3(4) provides for a deferral of up to 90% of the sale proceeds from sales of "breeding animals" by a taxpayer carrying on a farming business in a prescribed drought or flood region where the taxpayer's "breeding herd" is reduced by at least 15% in the taxation year. The deferral allows farmers to use the sale proceeds to fund the acquisition of replacement livestock (the inclusion in taxable income in the year of replacement will generally be offset by the cost of the replacement livestock). "Breeding animals" are defined as deer, elk and other similar grazing ungulates, bovine cattle, bison, goats, sheep, and horses, that are over 12 months of age and are kept for breeding (a deferral is also available in respect of "breeding bees"). For an up-to-date list of prescribed regions (see ITR 7305–7305.02), visit agr.gc.ca (see under "Programs and Services", "Drought Watch", "Livestock Tax Deferral Provision"; and

- The value of goods produced by a farm and consumed by the farmer or a member of the farmer's family should be added to the income derived from the farm if the costs of producing such items were deducted as expenses. The value placed on these goods should represent the farmer's cost of raising or producing them.

¶6340 — Net Income Stabilization Account (NISA)

A net income stabilization account (NISA) is an AgriInvest account set up under the *Farm Income Protection Act* for the stabilization of the net income of a farmer. A NISA consists of two separate funds: Fund No. 1, which includes all after-tax contributions by the taxpayer to the NISA, and Fund No. 2, which includes contributions made to the NISA in respect of the farmer other than contributions made by the farmer, including government contributions, interest earned on NISA contributions, bonuses, and any other contributions by third parties.

ITA 12(10.2) brings into a farmer's income all amounts paid in the year out of the farmer's NISA Fund No. 2. Within certain limits, farmers can make a deposit into an AgriInvest account (such contributions are neither taxable nor tax deductible and are held in a NISA Fund No. 1 account) and receive a matching contribution from federal and provincial governments (government contributions are held in a NISA Fund No. 2 account). ITA 12(10.2) generally permits a farmer to defer income tax on government contributions to the NISA Fund 2, by providing that funds withdrawn from a NISA Fund No 2 are taxable only when received or deemed received. Also, income may be earned on government contributions on a tax-deferred basis by virtue of ITA 12(10.3). Funds contributed by a farmer to an AgriInvest account are not deductible, and earnings on such funds are taxable annually.

A farmer can choose to participate in either or both of the AgriInvest and AgriStability programs. AgriStability provides support when a farmer experiences a large margin decline. Individuals, co-operatives, and corporations can participate in AgriStability. Generally, an AgriStability payment may be received when current year "program margins" fall below 85% of a producer's "reference margin". The CRA views payments from AgriStability as being farming income (to be reported on Box 14 of Form AGR-1).

The CRA is not involved in administering the AgriStability and AgriInvest programs. For information on these programs, visit: agr.gc.ca (Agriculture and Agri-Food Canada). Also, refer to CRA Guides RC4060: *Farming Income and the AgriStability and AgriInvest Programs Guide* (PE, ON, SK, AB) and RC4408: *Farming Income and the AgriStability and AgriInvest Programs Harmonized Guide* (BC, MB, NB, NS, NL, YK). AgriInvest is delivered by the federal government in all provinces except Quebec. In Quebec, AgriInvest is delivered provincially by La Financière agricole.

¶6350 — Farming Losses

¶6351 — *Unrestricted Farm Losses*

Where farm losses are incurred by full-time farmers for whom farming is normally their chief source of income or is part of their chief source of income (i.e., if the taxpayer's chief source of income can be regarded as a combination of farming and something else, even if farming income is subordinate to another source), the farming loss is an "unrestricted" farm loss that is fully deductible from the taxpayer's income from any source. Any remainder is available for carryover to other years as a non-capital loss on Line 252. Unrestricted farm losses may be carried forward 20 years and carried back three years.

¶6352 — *Restricted Farm Losses*

ITA 31(1) restricts the farming losses deductible by a taxpayer against income from other sources in a taxation year unless the taxpayer's chief source of income for the year is farming or a combination of farming and some other source of income. This restriction ensures that taxpayers for whom farming is not the principal occupation are limited in their ability to deduct from their non-farm income losses from farming.

The restricted farm loss rules in ITA 31(1) have been amended to codify the interpretation set out in the Supreme Court of Canada's decision in *Moldowan v. The Queen*, [1978] 1 SCR 480. Specifically, the amendment clarifies that a taxpayer will be limited to the deduction in respect of farm losses set out in ITA 31(1) if the taxpayer does not look to farming, or to farming and some subordinate source of income, for their livelihood. This amendment replaces the interpretation placed on ITA 31 by the Supreme Court of Canada in its decision in *The Queen v. Craig*, 2012 SCC 43, and applies to taxation years that end after March 20, 2013.

For taxation years that end on or before March 20, 2013, the unrestricted portion of such farm losses is limited to $2,500 plus ½ of the next $12,500 of losses (i.e., $8,750). For taxation years that end after March 20, 2013, the unrestricted portion of losses from farming for a taxpayer that is limited by ITA 31(1) is increased to $2,500 plus ½ of the next $30,000 of losses (i.e., $17,500). The remainder of such a loss is defined as a "restricted farm loss". A restricted farm loss is not included in a taxpayer's farm losses or non-capital losses. A restricted farm loss for a taxation year is deductible under ITA 111(1)(c) in computing taxable income for the three preceding taxation years or the 20 following taxation years, only to the extent of the taxpayer's income from farming in those years. The loss expires after the carry-forward period.

Where a taxpayer disposés of land used in a farming business, and in respect of which there remains any unabsorbed "restricted farm losses", ITA 53(1)(i) provides that part of that amount may be added in computing the ACB of the land for the purpose of computing any taxable capital gain. A similar rule in ITA 101 applies where the farming business was carried on by a partnership. The latter rule gives credit for unabsorbed restricted farm losses in computing a partner's taxable income for the year in which the land is sold.

An individual's notice of assessment should set out any loss carryover amounts and the cumulative amount of available losses. If the loss is being carried back to a prior year, calculate the non-capital loss carryback amount on Form T1A, *Request for Loss Carryback*, for the loss taxation year. See ¶9360 for more information on applying non-capital losses of other years.

31(1.1), 96(2.1)-(2.2), 111(1), 111(3), 111(8)"non-capital loss", IT-232R3: *Losses — Their Deductibility in the Loss Year of in Other Years*, IT-262R2: *Losses of Non-Residents and Part-Year Residents*; IT-322R: *Farm Losses*, CRA Guides T4002, RC4060, *Gunn*, [2006] 5 C.T.C. 191 (FCA), *Stackhouse*, [2007] 3 C.T.C. 2402 (TCC), *Loyens*, [2009] 1 C.T.C. 2547 (TCC), *Johnson*, 2009 CarswellNat 2253 (TCC), Robert McMechan, "Restricted Farm Losses: SCC Reverses Itself", *Canadian Tax Highlights*, Vol. 20, No. 9, September 2012, Bruce Russel, "*Craig* — Restricting Restricted Farm Losses", *Tax Hyperion*, Vol. 9, No. 9 September 2012

Chapter 7 — Depreciation, Amortization, and Resource Deductions

Contents

¶7000 Depreciable Property Quick Reference Table

¶7005 CCA Class Summary Table

¶7006 Accelerated Investment Initiative for Capital Cost Allowance (ACCA)

¶7100 Capital Cost Allowance (CCA)

¶7105 General Rules Applicable to Depreciable Property

¶7110 CCA Claim for the Year (Form T776 or T2125: Part A)

¶7115 Depreciable Property Additions (Form T776 or T2125: Part A, Column 3)

¶7120 Adjustment for Current-Year Additions (Form T776 or T2125: Part A, Column 6)

¶7125 Available-For-Use Rules

¶7130 Depreciable Property — Special Situations

¶7135 Dispositions of Depreciable Property (Form T776 or T2125: Part A, Column 4)

¶7140 Half-Year Rule (Form T776 or T2125 Part A: Column 6)

¶7145 CCA Recapture (Form T776: Line 9947, Form T2125: Line 8230)

¶7150 Terminal Losses (Form T776: Line 9948, Form T2125: Line 9270)

¶7155 Property included in a Separate Class

¶7160 "Luxury" Passenger Vehicles (Class 10.1)

¶7165 Rental Properties

¶7170 Revising CCA Claims

¶7200 Special Depreciable Property Rules

¶7205 Patents, Franchises, Concessions, and Licences

¶7210 Leasehold Interests (Class 13)

¶7215 Specified Leasing Property

¶7220 Lease Transactions

¶7225 Mining Projects (Classes 41, 41.2)

¶7230 Oil Sands Projects (Classes 41, 41.1)

¶7235 Clean Energy Equipment (Classes 43.1, 43.2)

¶7300 Eligible Capital Property

¶7305 Eligible Capital Property Additions (Applicable before 2017)

¶7310 Eligible Capital Amounts (Applicable before 2017)

¶7315 Gain on Dispositions of Eligible Capital Property (Applicable before 2017)

¶7320 Restrictive Covenants

¶7325 Class 14.1

¶7400 Resource Pools

¶7405 Canadian Exploration Expenses (CEE) (Form T1229: Parts II and III)

¶7410 Canadian Development Expenses (CDE) (Form T1229: Parts II and III)

¶7415 Canadian Oil and Gas Property Expenses (COGPE) (Form T1229: Parts II and III)

¶7000 — Depreciable Property Quick Reference Table

For tax purposes, depreciable properties are divided into separate classes. Properties falling into the various classes lose their identities and are pooled. Schedule II of the ITR contains a complete list of these prescribed classes. Below, several hundred assets are listed in alphabetical order with a reference to the CCA class to which the asset belongs (where applicable). The table can be used to determine CCA asset class allocations in respect of fixed assets acquired by a taxpayer during the taxation year. In addition to property included in a CCA class, the table also references eligible capital expenditures (ECE, which are included in CCA Class 14.1 after 2016) (see ¶7300), and resource related expenditures (see ¶7400). Special CCA rules applicable to different asset classes are also highlighted. These rules are discussed in more detail in the commentary in this chapter.

Certain properties may be described in more than one CCA class. In such a case, it is important to note that certain classes refer to property "that would otherwise be included in another class" or to property "not included in any other class".

Where a depreciable property is not described in any particular class, Class 8(i) (20%) acts as a final catch-all class applicable to depreciable property that is not otherwise excluded from CCA treatment.

The rates in the table below do not reflect the temporary special first-year accelerated investment incentive deduction rules that were introduced in the federal November 2018 Economic Statement (except in the case of M&P and clean energy equipment, which is subject to a 100% write-off rate for a temporary period). These rules, which affect all depreciable property, apply to "accelerated investment incentive property" (AIIP) acquired after November 20, 2018. For most property, the new rules allow for a first-year CCA deduction that is three times higher than the normally available deduction. The new rules do not change the allocation of assets between classes or the prescribed rates that apply to each class. The new rules and the mechanism that provides for the accelerated first-year deduction are discussed under ¶7006.

The table below is a guideline only; the ITRs should always be consulted for precise wording, exceptions and restrictions.

Asset	Class	Rate	Comments
Advertising billboards or poster panels			
Outdoor and acquired after 1987	Sch. II:Cl. 8(l)	20%	See also ITR 1101(5l) (separate class election available).
Attached to the exterior of rented premises (including a removable store front door, doorway or show window)	Sch. II:Cl. 13, Sch. III	SL	Generally included in Class 13 when the sign was purchased by a tenant and must be left behind upon expiration of the lease (para. 8 of IT-472). See under "Leasehold interests". Half-year rule inapplicable (see ITR 1100(2)(a)(iv)).
Other than those described above	Sch. II:Cl. 8(i)	20%	See paragraph 8 of IT-472.
Air-conditioning equipment			
Component of a building	Depends on class of building	—	May be included in Class 1(q), 3(a), or 6(a); see under "Buildings".
Portable (i.e., window units)	Sch. II:Cl. 8(i)	20%	VD 2004-0070211E5.
Aircraft			
Acquired after May 25, 1976	Sch. II:Cl. 9(g), (h) or (i)	25%	Includes spare parts (e.g., spare engine or other expensive replacement parts — see VD 2012-0461421E5) and furniture and fixtures attached to the aircraft. See also ITA 8(1)(j) (CCA deductions from employment income) and IT-160R3 (archived). The CRA considers an aircraft to include a hot air balloon; VD 2001-0083827.
Animals	N/A	N/A	Treated as inventory. Farmers who report on the accrual method must make an inventory valuation of their livestock annually as required by ITA 10 and Part XVIII of the ITRs; this task may be simplified by the adoption of a fixed unit price under ITR 1802.
Apparel or costumes			
For rental	Sch. II:Cl. 12(k)	100%	Half-year rule does not apply. See ITR 1100(2)(a)(iii).
Wearing apparel and accessories used by models employed by a fashion expert in the course of lectures and demonstrations	Sch. II:Cl. 8(i)	20%	See *No 428*, 17 Tax A.B.C. 236.
See also "Dresses for rental"			
Appliances	Sch. II:Cl. 8(i)	20%	Includes, for example, clothes washers and dryers and dishwashers. See also Chapter 4 of CRA Guide T4002
Application software (generally acquired after May 25, 1976)	Sch. II:Cl. 12(o)	100%	Half-year rule applies. See ITR 1100(2)(a)(iii). See under "Computer software".

Asset		Class	Rate	Comments
Artwork and antiques				
	Acquired after November 12, 1981 and not described in ITR 1102(1)(e) (see below)	Sch. II:Cl. 8(i)	20%	Generally, applies to artwork created by a Canadian and or artwork that costs under $200. See also ITR 1104(10)(a) and VD 2015-0580391E5.
	Certain non-Canadian works of art acquired after November 12, 1981	N/A	N/A	Per ITR 1102(1)(e), CCA cannot be claimed in respect of a) a print, etching, drawing, painting, sculpture or other similar work of art costing at least $200 and created by a non-Canadian; b) a hand-woven tapestry or carpet or a handmade appliqué costing at least $215 per square metre and created by a non-Canadian; c) an engraving, etching, lithograph, woodcut, map or chart made before 1900; or d) any antique object (including furniture) produced more than 100 years before the date of its acquisition by the taxpayer and costing at least $1,000.
Audio books		Sch. II:Cl. 8(i)	20%	CRA's view is that an audio book is not a "book"; VD 2008-0268131E5.
Automobiles				
	Other than those described below	Sch. II:Cl. 10(a)	30%	See also ITA 8(1)(j) (CCA deductions from employment income) and CRA Guide T4044. Also, see the definitions "automobile" and "motor vehicle" in ITA 248(1).
	Taxi cabs acquired after May 25, 1976	Sch. II:Cl. 16(d)	40%	
	Used in a daily car-rental business (i.e., used for short-term leasing)	Sch. II:Cl. 16(e)	40%	

Asset	Class	Rate	Comments
"Passenger vehicle" (defined in ITA 248(1) — note that certain vans, pick-up trucks or similar vehicles are excluded from the definition "passenger vehicle" depending on their use in transporting goods, equipment or passengers in the course of gaining or producing income) acquired after 2000 that cost more than $30,000 (in determining the class to which a passenger vehicle belongs (i.e., Class 10 or 10.1), the cost of the vehicle before applicable GST and PST or HST is relevant)	Sch. II:Cl. 10.1	30%	Each such vehicle is included in a separate Class 10.1 and the maximum amount included in Class 10.1 cannot exceed the prescribed amount plus applicable GST and PST or HST (see under ¶7160). For example, if a passenger vehicle cost $33,000 before GST and PST or HST, the amount included in Class 10.1 would be $30,000 + the applicable amount of GST and PST or HST that would have been payable in the particular province or territory. The recapture and terminal loss rules do not apply to Class 10.1. See also ITA 13(2) and (7), 20(4) and (16.1), ITA 67.2–67.4, ITA 85(1)(e.4) and ITRs 1101(1af) and 7307(1). Also, see VDs 2007-0238631E5 and 2004-0064901I7 and Chapter 8 of CRA Guide T4044 under the heading "Vehicle definitions chart".
Passenger vehicles acquired in 2000 that cost more than $27,000	Sch. II:Cl. 10.1	30%	Amount included in Class 10.1 includes applicable GST and PST or HST on cost limit.
Passenger vehicles acquired in 1998 or 1999 that cost more than $26,000	Sch. II:Cl. 10.1	30%	Amount included in Class 10.1 includes applicable GST and PST or HST on cost limit.
Passenger vehicles acquired in 1997 that cost more than $25,000	Sch. II:Cl. 10.1	30%	Amount included in Class 10.1 includes applicable GST and PST or HST on cost limit.
Passenger vehicles acquired after 1991 and before 1997 that cost more than $24,000	Sch. II:Cl. 10.1	30%	Amount included in Class 10.1 includes applicable GST and PST or HST on cost limit.
Automotive equipment	Sch. II:Cl. 10(a)	30%	Includes a trolley bus and excludes an automotive railway car acquired after May 25, 1976, a railway locomotive, or a tramcar. Includes outboard motors, hovercrafts, all-terrain vehicles, motor homes, and self-propelled sprayers (VDs 2002-0141367, 2003-0045525, 2011-0402501E5).
Bakery equipment (ovens, proofers, mixers, etc)	Sch. II:Cl. 8(i)	20%	
Bar code scanners	Sch. II:Cl. 8(i)	20%	See also ITRs 1101(5p) and (5q) (separate class election available; see under ¶ 7157.50). See under "Cash registers". Certain scanners capable of calculating and recording multi-jurisdictional sales taxes acquired after August 8, 1989 and before 1993 are included in Class 12(s).
Bed linens and blankets			

Asset	Class	Rate	Comments
General	Sch. II:Cl. 12(g)	100%	Half-year rule does not apply. See ITR 1100(2)(a)(iii).
Mattresses, pillows, eiderdowns, electric sheets, electric blankets and other bedding used by hotels and motels	Sch. II:Cl. 8(i)	20%	See paragraph 8 of IT-472.
Blackberry	Depends on acquisition date	—	See iPhone under "Computer equipment & systems software".
Boats	Depends on type and acquisition date	—	See under "Vessels". Also, see ATR-52 and IT-267R2.
Boilers	Depends on class of building	—	May be included in Class 1(q), 3(a), or 6(a); See under "Buildings".
Books			
Part of a lending library	Sch. II:Cl. 12(a)	100%	Half-year rule does not apply. See ITR 1100(2)(a)(iii).
Audio books	Sch. II:Cl. 8(i)	20%	CRA's view is that an audio book is not a "book"; VD 2008-0268131E5.
Libraries of practicing professionals	Sch. II:Cl. 8(i)	20%	Such libraries, including reference libraries, data banks, land surveyor's field notes, credit bureau dockets, archives of a notary public or reference material purchased by a taxpayer are Class 8(i) assets; paragraph 8(a) of IT-472.
Buildings (including component parts)			Component parts include electric wiring, lighting fixtures, plumbing, sprinkler systems, non-portable heating and cooling equipment, elevators and escalators. May also includes parking lots in an underground parking garage of the building (VD 2008-026753117) and movable/removable walls (VD 2012-0441991E5). A building includes a hockey arena (VD 2014-0560281E5).
Most buildings made of brick, stone, or cement acquired after 1987	Sch. II:Cl. 1(q)	4%	See also IT-79R3 (Buildings), IT-304R2 (Condominiums) and IT-367R3 (archived) (Multiple-Unit Residential Buildings).
Most buildings made of brick, stone, or cement acquired before 1988 (subject to certain grandfathering provisions)	Sch. II:Cl. 3(a)	5%	For additions/alterations, see ITR 1102(19) and Classes 3(g) and 3(k). Generally, Class 1 includes the cost of any additions or alterations made after 1987 to a Class 3 building that exceeds the lesser of: 1) $500,000 and 2) 25% of the building's capital cost (including the cost of additions or alterations to the building included in Class 3, 6, or 20 before 1988).

Asset		Class	Rate	Comments
	Made of frame, log, stucco on frame, galvanized iron, or corrugated metal and either: 1) used in the business of farming or fishing or 2) has no footings below-ground	Sch. II:Cl. 6(a)	10%	For additions/alterations, see ITR 1102(19) and Classes 6(i) and (k).
Buses (including trolley buses)		Sch. II:Cl. 10(a)	30%	
Camera		Sch. II:Cl. 8(i)	20%	VD 2011-0392831M4.
Canoes		Sch. II:Cl. 7(a)	15%	
Cars (motor vehicles)		Depends on type of vehicle and cost	—	See under "Automobiles".
Cash registers				
	Other than those described below	Sch. II:Cl. 8(i)	20%	
	Certain registrars capable of calculating and recording multi-jurisdictional sales taxes acquired after August 8, 1989 and before 1993	Sch. II:Cl. 12(s)	100%	For the applicable period, Class 12(s) applies to certain electronic point-of-sale equipment (including electronic bar code scanning equipment, certain cash registers and similar sales recording devices) and computer software acquired to be used in a retail business carried on in Canada. Half-year rule does not apply. See ITR 1100(2)(a)(iii).
Cement mixers				
	Not designed for the direct placing of concrete	Sch. II:Cl. 10(h)	20%	Paragraph 15 of IT-469R.
	Truck-mounted cement mixer not designed for the direct placing of concrete	Sch. II:Cl. 38	30%	See paragraph 15 of IT-469R and "Power-operated movable equipment". Also may be included in Class 22.
	Designed for the direct placing of concrete	Sch. II:Cl. 38	30%	See paragraph 15 of IT-469R and "Power-operated movable equipment". Also may be included in Class 22.
	Used by a contractor in a construction business	Sch. II:Cl. 10(h)	30%	See under "Contractor's movable equipment".
Clothing for rental		Sch. II:Cl. 12(k)	100%	Half-year rule does not apply. See under "Apparel or costumes". See ITR 1100(2)(a)(iii).
Cold storage warehouses		Sch. II:Cl. 8(i)	20%	See paragraph 8 of IT-472.

Asset	Class	Rate	Comments
Computer equipment & systems software			Classes 10, 45, 50 and 52 refer to "general-purpose electronic data processing equipment", which is defined in ITR 1104(2) as electronic equipment that, in its operation, requires an internally stored computer program that a) is executed by the equipment, b) can be altered by the user of the equipment, c) instructs the equipment to read and select, alter or store data from an external medium such as a card, disk or tape, and d) depends upon the characteristics of the data being processed to determine the sequence of its execution (in other words, computer hardware). The definition is discussed in *Funtronix Amusements Ltd*, [1989] 2 C.T.C. 2296 (TCC).
Acquired after March 18, 2007 (other than after March 18, 2007 and before February 2011 and included in Class 29 or 52)	Sch. II:Cl. 50	55%	
New and acquired after January 27, 2009 and before February 2011	Sch. II:Cl. 52	100%	Half-year rule does not apply (ITR 1100(2)(a)(iv)). Class 52 only applies to computer equipment situated in Canada that is acquired for use in a business carried on in Canada. A refurbished computer is not a new computer; VD 2011-0392831M4.
Acquired after March 22, 2004 and before March 19, 2007	Sch. II:Cl. 45	45%	Class 10(f) can apply to property acquired after March 22, 2004 and before 2005 where an election is filed.
Acquired before March 23, 2004	Sch. II:Cl. 10(f)	30%	Class 10(f) also applies to such property acquired after March 22, 2004 and before 2005 if an election is made under ITR 1101(5q) to include the property in a separate class (see under ¶ 7157.50).
That is principally or is used principally as electronic process control or monitor equipment, electronic communications control equipment, or data handling equipment (other than data handling equipment that is ancillary to general-purpose electronic data processing equipment)	Sch. II:Cl. 8(i)	20%	Such property is specifically excluded from Classes 10(f), 45, 50 and 52 and the CRA's position is that the property should be included in Class 8(i) (VD 2004-0070211E5). See also ITR 1104(2) "computer software". Also, see ITRs 1101(5p) and (5q) (separate class election available; see under ¶ 7157.50) and under "Telephone equipment".

Asset	Class	Rate	Comments
Printers, scanners, and other ancillary equipment	Depends on type, use, and acquisition date	—	Classes 10(f), 45, 50 and 52 include "ancillary data processing equipment" to "general-purpose electronic data processing equipment". The CRA generally considers that, for example, printers connected to a general-purpose computer (such as a desktop or laptop) qualify as ancillary data processing equipment (see VDs 2009-0325861M4 and 2007-0243381C6). It is also possible for a modern multi-functioning printer, scanner or photocopier to qualify as "general purpose electronic data processing equipment" itself; See under "Printers and scanners" and "Photocopiers".
iPhone	Depends on acquisition date	—	The CRA's view is that an iPhone is "general-purpose electronic data processing equipment"; VD 2009-0344551I7.
Personal digital assistant	Depends on acquisition date		Generally qualifies as general electronic data processing equipment; VD 2009-0347471E5.
Point-of-sales systems	Depends on acquisition date	—	Point-of-sales systems or computer hardware and systems for taking customer orders, transmitting orders to kitchens, and producing restaurant cheques generally qualifies as general electronic data processing equipment; see VD 2009-0311501E5.
Computer software (defined in ITR 1104(2))			
Application software acquired after May 25, 1976	Sch. II:Cl. 12(o)	100%	"Computer software" includes a right or licence to use computer software. Application software generally refers to programs that instruct a computer to carry out specific applications related to managing and processing data (such as accounting programs and spreadsheet tables). See VD 2004-0070211E5. For software tax shelter investment rules, see ITR 1100(20.1). Note that although "computer software" is defined as including "systems software", Class 12(o) specifically excludes "systems software". The half-year rule applies. See ITR 1100(2)(a)(iii).
"Systems software" (defined in ITR 1104(2)) for "general purpose data processing equipment" (i.e., for computer hardware)	Depends on acquisition date	—	See under "Computer equipment & systems software". "Systems software" essentially comprises the general operating system that enables application software to be run and that directs and coordinates the different operations of a computer. The definition "systems software" also includes a right or licence to use systems software.

Asset	Class	Rate	Comments
Concessions and other rights			
For an unlimited period and acquired after 2016	Sch. II:Cl. 14.1	5%	Acquired before 2017, will normally qualify as an ECE; see IT-143R3 and under ¶7300. See also "Rights of way and Easements". See also under ¶7205.
For a limited period	Sch. II:Cl. 14	SL	CCA may be claimed over useful life (half-year rule does not apply). See ITR 1100(2)(a)(iv).
Contractor's immovable equipment	Sch. II:Cl. 8(i)	20%	Paragraph 5 of IT-306R2.
Contractor's movable equipment			Applies to property acquired for use in a construction business or for lease to another taxpayer for use in that other taxpayer's construction business.
Other than equipment described below	Sch. II:Cl. 10(h)	30%	Refers to the kind of equipment that normally is moved from place to place in the course of a contractor's business activities; see IT-306R2. Examples may include pile drivers and related equipment, truck weigh scales, and equipment transporters. See also paragraphs 15 and 16 of IT-469R.
Power-operated movable equipment designed for the purpose of excavating, moving, placing or compacting earth, rock, concrete or asphalt (may include, for example, a rock drill, tractor or certain compressed air drills)	Sch. II:Cl. 38	30%	See also ITRs 1100(1)(zd) and 1101(5l) (separate class election available; discussed under ¶7155), IT-306R2 and IT-469R. Can include front-end loaders used in sand or gravel pit operations (see *Nomad Sand & Gravel Ltd.*, [1991] 1 C.T.C. 60 (FCA)) or a portable feeder used in the asphalt batching process (see *L & R Asphalt Ltd*, [1989] 1 C.T.C. 2370). For this type of power-operated movable equipment acquired before 1988, refer to Class 22 (CCA rate of 50%).
Copyright or trademark costs incurred after 2016	Sch. II:Cl. 14.1	5%	Acquired before 2017, will normally qualify as an ECE. Alternatively, the costs may be deductible under ITA 20(1)(cc); see, for example, *Services Farmico Inc.*, [1979] C.T.C. 3012 (TRB). See also IT-143R3 and under ¶7300.
Costumes or apparel for rent	Sch. II:Cl. 12(k)	100%	Half-year rule does not apply. See under "Apparel or costumes".
Cranes or hoists			
Other than those described below	Sch. II:Cl. 8(i)	20%	Paragraph 14 of IT-469R.

Asset	Class	Rate	Comments
Designed, modified or acquired with special accessories to enable it to be used for the purposes of excavating, moving, placing or compacting earth, rock, concrete or asphalt	Sch. II:Cl. 38	30%	Paragraph 14 IT-469R. Also may be included in Class 22. See also under "Power-operated movable equipment", *Armand Guay Inc*, [1974] C.T.C. 168 (FCTD), *Nomad Sand & Gravel Ltd*, [1987] 2 C.T.C. 112 & *Paju et al*, [1974] C.T.C. 2121.
Used by a contractor in a construction business	Sch. II:Cl. 10(h)	30%	See under "Contractor's movable equipment".
Customer lists acquired after 2016	Sch.II:Cl.14.1	5%	Acquired before 2017, will normally qualify as an ECE; see paragraph 5 of IT-143R3, IT-187, and under ¶7300. See also *Aliments CA-MO Foods Inc.*, [1980] C.T.C. 75 (FCTD).
Cutlery	Sch. II:Cl. 12(b)	100%	Half-year rule does not apply. See ITR 1100(2)(a)(iii).
Cutting or shaping part in a machine	Sch. II:Cl. 12(j)	100%	Half-year rule applies. See ITR 1100(2)(a)(iii).
Data communication equipment			
Telephone, telegraph or data communication equipment that is a wire or cable acquired after February 22, 2005	Sch. II:Cl. 42(b)	12%	See also VD 2002-0127845. Acquired before February 23, 2005, included in Class 3(j).
Property that is ancillary to a wire or cable referred to in Class 42 and that is supporting equipment such as a pole, mast, tower, conduit, brace, crossarm, guy or insulator	Sch. II:Cl. 3(l)	5%	Can also include an underground conduit which carries wire or cable; VD 2004-0064781E5.
Switching equipment	Sch. II:Cl. 17(b)	8%	Applies to telephone, telegraph or data communication switching equipment other than equipment installed on customers' premises or property that is principally electronic equipment or systems software therefor.

Asset	Class	Rate	Comments
Data network infrastructure equipment (defined in ITR 1104(2))			Subject to certain exceptions, generally includes network infrastructure equipment and systems software therefor that controls, transfers, modulates or directs data, and that operates in support of telecommunications applications such as e-mail or Web browsing, including data switches, multiplexers, routers, remote access servers, hubs, domain name servers, and modems. Does not include office equipment included in Class 8 (such as telephone equipment; see under "Office equipment" and "Telephone equipment"), computer hardware (See under "Computer equipment & systems software"), wires or cables or similar property or structures (see under "Data communication equipment"). See also VDs 2003-0015997 and 2009-0331861E5.
Acquired after March 22, 2004	Sch. II:Cl. 46	30%	
Acquired before March 23, 2004	Sch. II:Cl. 8(i)	20%	
Network equipment that operates in support of telecommunications applications if the bandwidth made available by that equipment to single end-users is equivalent to the amount of bandwidth made available by a single voice channel of the Public Switched Telephone Network (PSTN)	Sch. II:Cl. 8(i)	20%	See ITR 1104(2) "data network infrastructure equipment"(a) and VDs 2003-0015997 and 2009-0331861E5.
Radio network equipment that operates in support of wireless telecommunications applications unless the equipment supports digital transmission over a radio channel, in which case Class 46 applies	Sch. II:Cl. 8(i)	20%	See ITR 1104(2) "data network infrastructure equipment"(b). For example, Advanced Mobile Phone Service (AMPS) radio network equipment which provides analog speech modulation is excluded from "data network infrastructure equipment". See also VD 2003-0015997.
Network equipment that operates in support of broadcast telecommunications applications and that is unidirectional	Sch. II:Cl. 8(i)	20%	See ITR 1104(2) "data network infrastructure equipment"(c). Also, see VD 2003-001599.7
Network equipment that is end-user equipment	Sch. II:Cl. 8(i)	20%	See ITR 1104(2) "data network infrastructure equipment"(d). See also VD 2003-0015997 and "Office equipment".

Asset	Class	Rate	Comments
Data processing equipment	Depends on type, use, and acquisition date	—	See under "Computer equipment & systems software".
Dental instruments			
Costing under $500	Sch. II:Cl. 12(e)	100%	Half-year rule does not apply. See ITR 1100(2)(a)(iii). See also IT-422.
Costing $500 or more	Sch. II:Cl. 8(i)	20%	See comments above and paragraph 8 of IT-472.
Dishes	Sch. II:Cl. 12(b)	100%	Half-year rule does not apply. See ITR 1100(2)(a)(iii).
Dresses for rental	Sch. II:Cl. 12(k)	100%	Half-year rule does not apply. See ITR 1100(2)(a)(iii). See under "Apparel or costumes".
Drones	Sch. II:Cl. 9(g)	25%	VD 2016-0633111E5
Dummies or mannequins for merchandise displays	Sch. II:Cl. 8(i)	20%	See paragraph 8 of IT-472.
Electrical advertising signs			
Acquired after May 25, 1976	Sch. II:Cl. 8(i)	20%	Includes neon signs; See paragraph 8 of IT-472.
See also "Advertising billboard or poster panel"			
Electrical wiring	Depends on class of building	—	May be included in Class 1(q), 3(a), or 6(a); See under "Buildings".
Electronic bar code scanners	Sch. II:Cl. 8(i)	20%	See also ITRs 1101(5p) and (5q) (separate class election available; see under ¶ 7157.50). Also, see under "Cash registers"; certain scanners capable of calculating and recording multi-jurisdictional sales taxes acquired after August 8, 1989 and before 1993 are included in Class 12(s).
Electronic communication equipment	Sch. II:Cl. 8(i)	20%	Note that Classes 10(f), 45, 50 and 52 exclude "electronic communications control equipment", which is not defined in the ITA. Class 8 includes property such as telephone equipment. See also VDs 2007-0243381C6, 2003-0015997 and 2000-0038025 and CRA Guide T4003.
Electronic data processing equipment	Depends on acquisition date	—	See under "Computer equipment & systems software".
Electronic point-of-sale equipment	Depends on acquisition date	—	See under "Computer equipment & systems software".
Electronic video game equipment	Depends on type and acquisition date	—	See under "Computer equipment & systems software" and "Video games (coin-operated)". Such equipment will often qualify as "general purpose electronic data processing equipment". See also *Funtronix Amusements Ltd*, [1989] 2 C.T.C. 2296 (TCC).

Asset	Class	Rate	Comments
Energy conservation equipment	Sch. II:Cl. 43.1	30%	Generally, qualifies for Class 43.2 (50%) when acquired after February 22, 2005 and before 2025. The rate for qualifying property acquired after Nov. 20, 2018 and before 2024 is effectively 100% (see under ¶7006).
Engines (spare parts)			
Spare boat engines	Depends on type of Vessel	—	See under "Vessels".
Spare aircraft engines	Depends on acquisition date	—	See under "Aircraft".
Equipment (not included in any other class)	Sch. II:Cl. 8(i)	20%	Class 8(i) acts as a catch-all class for depreciable property governed by Sch. II of the ITRs that is not included in any other class. See IT-472.
Facsimile transmission devices (fax machines)	Sch. II:Cl. 8(i)	20%	CRA's view is that an internet fax (FoIP) or fax modem would also be included in Class 8(i); VD 2007-0243381C6. See also ITRs 1101(5p) and (5q) (a separate class election is available for rapidly depreciating electronic equipment that has a cost of at least $1,000 and is a photocopier or office equipment that is electronic communications equipment; see under ¶ 7157.50).
Farm quota (unlimited life and acquired after 2016)	Sch.II: Cl.14.1	5%	Acquired before 2017, qualifies as an ECE; VD 2010-0369801E5. See also VD 2016-0660861E5 (CRA typically considers farm quota units to be identical properties) and under ¶7300.
Farming equipment (general)	Sch. II:Cl. 8(i)	20%	Including bee equipment; brooders; buildings and component parts: fruit and vegetable storage; casing, cribwork for water wells; cleaners — grain or seed; coolers (milk); cream separators; cultivators; diggers (all types); drills (all types); electric motors; electric-generating equipment (portable); elevators; engines — stationary; graders — fruit or vegetable; grain loaders; grain separators; grain-drying equipment; greenhouses of rigid frames covered with replaceable flexible plastic; grinder; harrows; hay loaders; ice machines; incubators; irrigation equipment (overhead); manure spreaders; milking machines; mixers; mowers; nets; planters (all types); ploughs; pumps; rakes; silo fillers; silos; sprayers; stable cleaners; stalk cutters; threshers; tillers (all types); traps (fishing); welders; weirs (fish); welding equipment; well equipment; wind chargers (CRA Guide RC4060).

Asset	Class	Rate	Comments
Farming equipment (automotive, mechanical, or otherwise described in Class 10)	Sch. II:Cl. 10(a), (c), (n), (d), (o)	30%	Including chain-saws; harness; outboard motors; sleighs; tractors; trailers; trucks; wagons (CRA Guide RC4060).
Farming equipment (self-propelled)	Sch. II:Cl. 10(a)	30%	Including a sprayer, combines, swathers, balers, forage harvesters, stookers, etc.; VD 2011-0402501E5 and CRA Guide RC4060. If the latter equipment were drawn rather than self-propelled, it would be included in Class 8(i).
Farming equipment (drawn)	Sch. II:Cl. 8(i)	20%	Equipment described directly above that is drawn rather than self-propelled.
Fences	Sch. II:Cl. 6(c)	10%	For use in an amusement park, included in Class 37(b)(iv).
Fibre-optic cables	Sch. II:Cl. 42(a)	12%	See Class 3(l) for ancillary equipment. Also, See under "Telephone wire or cable".
Franchises for a limited period	Sch. II:Cl. 14	SL	CCA claimed over useful life of property (half-year rule does not apply). See ITRs 1100(2)(a)(iv) and 1100(1)(c). See also VD 2010-0365771E5 and IT-477. See also under ¶7205.
Franchises for an unlimited period acquired after 2016	Sch.II: Cl.14.1	5%	Acquired before 2017, will normally qualify as an ECE; see IT-143R3 and under ¶7205 and ¶7300.
Furniture and fixtures			
Office, window display fixtures, water coolers, and general	Sch. II:Cl. 8(i)	20%	CRA Guide T4002.
Of an aircraft or vessel	Depends on type and acquisition date	—	Included in same class as vessel or aircraft; see under "Aircraft" and "Vessels".
General-purpose electronic data processing equipment	Depends on acquisition date and use	—	See under "Computer equipment & systems software".
Glass tableware	Sch. II:Cl. 12(b)	100%	Half-year rule does not apply. See ITR 1100(2)(a)(iii).
Global Positioning System (GPS) Device	Sch. II:Cl. 8(i)	20%	An electronic device with an internal GPS and global system for mobile communication modem enabling real time tracking and remote communication between an office and haul trucks is not general purpose electronic data processing equipment; VD 2009-0331861E5. Class 8(i) would also include an advanced Global Navigation Satellite System receiver and GPS equipment used in the construction, engineering and land surveying industry; VD 2011-0425111E5.

Asset	Class	Rate	Comments
Goodwill acquired after 2016	Sch.II: Cl.14.1	5%	Acquired before 2017, will normally qualify as an ECE; see IT-143R3 and under ¶7300.
Grain handling equipment (line & grain elevators)	Sch. II:Cl. 8(i)	20%	Includes driers and related heating equipment, scales, cleaning equipment, elevator legs, conveyors and spouting, car dumpers and shovels, and dust control systems; See paragraph 8 of IT-472 and VD 2001-0070895.
Grain storage silos			
Other than those described below	Sch. II:Cl. 8(i)	20%	VD 2005-0112831E5.
Grain-storage building (other than wood or galvanized steel which are included in Class 6)	Sch. II:Cl. 1(q)	4%	See under "Buildings" and see also CRA Guide RC4060.
Greenhouses			
Other than those described below	Sch. II:Cl. 6(d)	10%	
With rigid frames and plastic covers and acquired after 1987	Sch. II:Cl. 8(m)	20%	
Greenhouse steam plant	Sch. II:Cl. 8(i)	20%	Class 6 rather than Class 8 applies where the steam plant is located in or immediately adjacent to the greenhouse (or a combined greenhouse and storage or shipping building) and its steam output is used primarily to heat only that one greenhouse (or combined building); See paragraph 8 of IT-472.
Helicopters	Depends on acquisition date	—	See under "Aircraft".
Hoppers	Sch. II:Cl. 8(b)	20%	Paragraph 4 of IT-472 and paragraph 17 of IT-79R3.
Incorporation expenses incurred after 2016 in excess of $3,000	Sch.II:Cl.14.1	5%	Acquired before 2017, such expenses will normally qualify as an ECE; see paragraphs 13 and 14 of IT-143R3 and under ¶7300. After 2016, incorporation expenses of up to $3K per corporation are deductible under ITA 20(1)(b).
Inventory	N/A	N/A	Property that forms part of the inventory of a business is not eligible for CCA (ITR 1102(1)(b)). See also VDs 2007-0257121I7 and 2005-0156181I7, and IT-102R2 (conversion of inventory to a depreciable capital property).
iPhone	Depends on acquisition date	—	See under "Computer equipment and systems software".
Kitchen utensils			

Asset	Class	Rate	Comments
Costing under $500	Sch. II:Cl. 12(c)	100%	Half-year rule does not apply. See ITR 1100(2)(a)(iii).
Costing $500 or more	Sch. II:Cl. 8(i)	20%	See comments above and see paragraph 8 of IT-472.
Land			
General	N/A	N/A	Land is a non-depreciable property; see ITR 1102(2). Note the clearing and levelling costs are generally deductible if incurred in a farming business; otherwise, such costs are generally capitalized to the cost of the land. See also IT-485, VDs 2012-0442571E5 and 2013-0476561E5 and Guide T4012 under "Line 9796 — Clearing, levelling, and draining land".
Reclamation and clean-up costs	N/A	N/A	Generally, costs incurred to remediate a parcel of land are considered part of the capital cost of the land rather than a Class 8(i) property; VD 2007-0228881E5.
Acquired in circumstances under which the taxpayer has paid rent for a building or land and later acquires the property	Sch. II:Cl. 36	Nil	In these circumstances, subject to certain limitations, the rent is "recaptured" if the property is subsequently sold for a profit generally by treating the rental payments as depreciation; see ITA 13(5.2) and ITRs 1100(14) and 1101(5g).
Soft costs incurred by land developers (i.e., carrying charges directly attributable to the development of land (e.g., legal, consulting, mortgage, and survey fees) and costs in respect of installations within the subdivision (e.g., costs of roads, sewers, watermains, street lighting, sidewalks, landscaping, and recreational facilities))	N/A	N/A	Generally, land held by a developer is treated as inventory rather than a capital property and costs incurred by a land developer are considered to constitute a component of the cost of the inventory for the purposes of ITA 10(1); see IT-153R3 and ITA 10(1.1). Note that certain costs incurred on vacant land can be deducted on a current basis via a taxpayer's base level deduction (see 18(2)(f) and 18(2.2)). See also VDs 2004-0061651E5, 2007-0262121E5, 2003-0024037, and 2001-0081607.
Land surveyor's field notes	Sch. II:Cl. 8(i)	20%	See paragraph 8 of IT-472.
Laptop computers	Depends on acquisition date	—	See under "Computer equipment & systems software".
Leased properties (rules applicable to lessees)			

Asset	Class	Rate	Comments
Other than leases described below in respect of which an election is filed under ITA 16.1	N/A	N/A	Generally, if property (such as computers, cell phones, fax machines, or other equipment) is leased to earn income, a taxpayer can deduct the full amount of the lease payments. For restrictions on the amount deductible in respect of a leased "passenger vehicles", see ITA 67.3 and ITR 7307 (generally, the limit on deductible leasing costs is $800 per month (which is the current prescribed amount), plus applicable federal and provincial sales taxes); see under "Automobiles".
Where a joint election is filed under ITA 16.1 by the lessee and the lessor	Depends on property	—	Under ITA 16.1, a lessor and lessee may jointly elect (see Form T2145) with the effect that from the lessee's perspective the lease will be treated as a borrowing and purchase. The election is available in respect of an arm's length lease of tangible depreciable property (other than prescribed property; see ITRs 1100(1.13) and 8200 and VDs 2015-0566011E5 and 2014-0548041E5) for a term of more than one year. See also ITRs 1100(1.1) and 4302. Where an ITA 16.1 election is filed, the lessor may continue to claim CCA in respect of the leased property.
Specified leasing properties (defined in ITR 1100(1.11) generally as depreciable property with a value of at least $25,000, other than "exempt property" (defined in ITR 1100(1.13)), used principally for the purpose of gaining or producing rent or leasing revenue and that is the subject of an arm's length lease)	Depends on property	—	Generally, ITR 1100(1.1) restricts the amount of CCA that may be deducted in respect of such property to the amount of notional repayments of principal by the lessee. "Specified leasing properties" do not include intangible property. Also, there are many types of "exempt property" which are not subject to the rules, including general purpose office furniture or office equipment and certain computer equipment other than an individual piece of such property that has a capital cost in excess of $1 million. Subject to certain exceptions, a building or part thereof included in Class 1, 3, 6, 20, 31, or 32 is also "exempt property". See under ¶7215.

Asset	Class	Rate	Comments
Leasing properties (rules applicable to lessors)	Depends on type and use of property	—	In respect of "leasing properties" (defined ITR 1100(17)), CCA generally cannot be deducted in excess of net rental income from all the leasing properties owned by a taxpayer in a taxation year (see ITRs 1100(15)–(20)). Subject to certain exceptions, "leasing property" includes all depreciable property that is used principally for the purpose of gaining or producing gross rental, royalty, or leasing revenue. See also IT-443 and IT-195R4. Note that the CRA views furniture, fixtures and appliances acquired for a rental building as being "leasing properties"; see also "Rental properties".
Leasehold interests			
Minor improvements or alterations (note that the capital cost of a leasehold interest, referred to in ITR 1100(1)(b), includes both the cost of acquiring the interest and any amount expended by the taxpayer for or in respect of an improvement or alteration to the leased property)	Sch. II:Cl. 13	SL	Class 13 property is generally depreciated over the term of the lease (see Sch. III of the ITRs and paragraphs 12–19 of IT-464R). However, no matter how short the unexpired period of the lease, no more than one-fifth of the capital cost of an addition to Class 13 may be deducted in a taxation year (2(a) of Sch. III). Subject to certain exceptions, a rule that is congruent with the half-year rule applies to Class 13 additions (see ITR 1100(1)(b)(i)). Leasehold interests in real property described in ITR 1100(13) are required to be included in a separate class by virtue of ITR 1101(5h) (see ¶7155. See also ITRs 1100(1)(b) and 1102(4)–(6) and VDs 2006-0175611E5 and 2006-0199451E5. See also under ¶7210.
Leasehold interest acquired by reason of the fact that the taxpayer erected a building or structure on leased land, made an addition to a leased building or structure, or made alterations to a leased building or structure that substantially changed the nature of the property (see ITR 1102(5))	Depends on acquisition date	—	Such assets are excluded from amortization as improvements or alterations under Class 13. Instead, they may be written off at the appropriate rate applicable to the particular building to which they pertain (ITR 1102(5)); See under "Buildings". See also ITR 1102(5.1), paragraph 20 of IT-464R and VD 2012-0455081I7.

Asset	Class	Rate	Comments
An interest in minerals, petroleum, natural gas, other related hydrocarbons or timber and property relating thereto or in respect of a right to explore for, drill for, take or remove minerals, petroleum, natural gas, other related hydrocarbons or timber	Depends on interest	—	Class 13 does not apply to such properties; see Class 13(a).
Libraries of practicing professionals	Sch. II:Cl. 8(i)	20%	Includes reference libraries, data banks, land surveyor's field notes, credit bureau dockets, archives of a notary public or reference material purchased by a taxpayer; paragraph 8(a) of IT-472.
Licences (for a limited period)			
Other than those described below	Sch. II:Cl. 14	SL	CCA claimed over useful life (half-year rule does not apply). See ITR 1100(2)(a)(iii). In VD 2006-0199451E5, the CRA states that a particular licence agreement for a childcare facility should be included in Class 14 rather than Class 13 and that in contrast to a lease, which creates an interest in the property for the lessee, a licence does not create an interest in the property but simply gives a right to use a property. See also VDs 2006-0218781R3, 2006-0175611E5 and 2003-0000637. See also under ¶7205.
To use application software	Sch. II:Cl. 12(o)	100%	See under "Computer software". Half-year rule applies. See ITR 1100(2)(a)(iii).
In respect of minerals, petroleum, natural gas, other related hydrocarbons or timber and property relating thereto or in respect of a right to explore for, drill for, take or remove minerals, petroleum, natural gas, other related hydrocarbons	Depends on licence	—	Class 14 does not apply (see Class 14(a)).
Where the bulk of the payment is made in respect of a reasonable expectation that licenses will be renewed	Depends on facts	N/A	The CRA may view the bulk of the expenditure as being an ECE before 2017 or a Class 14.1 property after 2016; see VD 2000-0038827, 2014-0552041E5, IT-143R3 and under ¶7300.
Licence (for an unlimited period) and acquired after 2016	Sch.II:Cl.14.1	5%	Acquired before 2017, will normally qualify as an ECE; see IT-143R3 (para 11) and under ¶7300. See also *R. c. Léopold Lague Inc.*, [1981] C.T.C. 348 (FCTD) where school bus routes were held to be ECP.

Asset	Class	Rate	Comments
Lighting fixtures	Depends on class of building	—	May be included in Class 1(q), 3(a), or 6(a); see under "Buildings".
Linens	Sch. II:Cl. 12(g)	100%	See also "Bed linens and blankets". Half-year rule does not apply. See ITR 1100(2)(a)(iii).
Logging equipment			
Mechanical equipment acquired for use in logging operations (other than property included in Class 7 (vessels))	Sch. II:Cl. 10(o)	30%	Examples include yarders, sulkies, logging arches, slashers, barkers, loaders, unloaders, hoists, winches, garage equipment, machine shop equipment, blacksmith shop equipment, railway locomotives and rolling stock and power-operated movable, road-building equipment acquired to construct roads to or within a timber limit; paragraph 9 of IT-501.
Automotive equipment acquired for use in logging operations	Sch. II:Cl. 10(a)	30%	Per paragraph 9 of IT-501, examples of Class 10(a) property applicable to logging operations include trucks, tractors, skidders, "tree harvesters" and self-propelled cranes.
Mannequins or dummies for merchandise display	Sch. II:Cl. 8(i)	20%	See paragraph 8 of IT-472.
Mattresses and bedding for hotels or motels	Sch. II:Cl. 8(i)	20%	See under "Bed linen/blankets".
Medical instruments			
Costing under $500	Sch. II:Cl. 12(e)	100%	Half-year rule does not apply. See ITR 1100(2)(a)(iii). See also IT-422.
Costing $500 or more	Sch. II:Cl. 8(i)	20%	See comments above and paragraph 8 of IT-472.
Mobile homes			
Not attached to a permanent foundation	Sch. II:Cl. 10(e)	30%	See *Lansdowne Equity Ventures Ltd. V. R.*, [2007] 1 C.T.C. 2362 (TCC). See also VD 2009-0332411M4.
Permanently attached to a foundation with utility services installed	Sch. II:Cl. 1(q)	4%	VD 2008-029653117. Acquired before 1988, see Class 3(a). See also VD 2009-0332411M4.
Motor homes	Sch. II:Cl. 10(a)	30%	VD 2003-0045525. See also "Automobiles" and "Mobile homes".
Motor vehicles	Depends on type and cost	—	See under "Automobiles".
Multiple-unit residential buildings	Depends on type and acquisition date	—	See under "Buildings".
Musical scores, sheet music and transcriptions	Sch. II:Cl. 8(i)	20%	Applies when acquired by a self-employed professional musician or an orchestra; See paragraph 8 of IT-472.
MRI machine	Sch. II:Cl. 8(i)	20%	VD 2012-0434821E5.

Asset	Class	Rate	Comments
Notary public archives or purchased reference material	Sch. II:Cl. 8(i)	20%	See paragraph 8 of IT-472.
Office equipment (electronic communications equipment)	Sch. II:Cl. 8(i)	20%	See VD 2004-0070211E5. Also see ITRs 1101(5p) and (5q) (separate class election available for rapidly depreciating electronic equipment that has a cost of at least $1,000 and is a photocopier or office equipment that is electronic communications equipment (such as telephone equipment); discussed under ¶ 7157.50), "General-purpose electronic data processing equipment", "Facsimile transmission devices (fax machines)", and "Photocopiers".
Parking areas			
Acquired after May 25, 1976 and not described below	Sch. II:Cl. 17(c)	8%	
Parking lots in an underground parking garage considered to be part of (i.e., a component of) a building	Depends on class of building	—	VD 2008-026753117. Also, see Class 1(g) and *No 64*, 7 Tax A.B.C. 35, *McManus Motors Limited*, 8 Tax A.B.C. 390, *Laurentide Motels Ltd*, 25 Tax A.B.C. 104, *Thibodeau Express Ltd* (1966), 40 Tax A.B.C. 419, *Windsor Raceway Holdings Ltd*, [1973] C.T.C. 2137 (TRB) and *Chantecler Hotel Ltd*, 4 Tax A.B.C. 126.
Passenger vehicle (defined in ITA 248(1))	Depends on cost and acquisition date	—	See under "Automobiles". See also ¶7160.
Patents			
Acquired after April 26, 1993 (including a right to use patented information for a limited or unlimited period)	Sch. II:Cl. 44	25%	See also ITRs 1100(1)(c), (9) and (9.1) (accelerated rate) and ITR 1103(2h) (election not to include in Class 44). See also under ¶7205.
Limited life and ITR 1103(2)(h) election filed not to include in Class 44	Sch. II:Cl. 14	SL	CCA apportioned over useful life of property. Half-year rule does not apply. See ITR 1100(2)(a)(iv).
Unlimited life, election filed under ITR 1103(2)(h), and acquired after 2016	Sch.II:Cl.14.1	5%	Acquired before 2017, will normally qualify as an ECE; see IT-143R3 and under ¶7300.
Deferred costs in respect of an abandoned patent incurred after 2016	Sch.II:Cl.14.1	5%	Acquired before 2017, will normally qualify as an ECE; see VD 2010-0365861R3 and under ¶7300.
Personal computers	Depends on acquisition date	=	See under "Computer equipment & systems software".

Asset	Class	Rate	Comments
Personal digital assistant	Depends on acquisition date		Generally qualifies as general electronic data processing equipment; VD 2009-0347471E5. See under "Computer equipment & systems software".
Phonograph records	Sch. II:Cl. 8(i)	20%	Class 8(i) applies to sheet music, scores, transcriptions, phonograph records and the like acquired by a self-employed professional musician or an orchestra; see paragraph 8 of IT-472. See also ITA 8(1)(p).
Photocopiers			
Other than those described below	Sch. II:Cl. 8(i)	20%	See ITRs 1101(5p) and (5q) (separate class election available for rapidly depreciating electronic equipment that has a cost of at least $1,000 and is a photocopier or office equipment that is electronic communications equipment (such as telephone equipment); discussed under ¶ 7157.50). CRA's view is generally that if the bulk of the value of the equipment lies in its technological components (for example, the processor) as opposed to its mechanical components, the property does not qualify as "general-purpose electronic data processing equipment"; VD 2007-0243381C6.
Multi-functioning photocopiers that qualify as "general-purpose electronic data processing equipment" or that are "ancillary data processing equipment" to "general-purpose electronic data processing equipment"	Depends on acquisition date	—	See under "Computer equipment & systems software", "Printers and scanners", VDs 2009-0325861M4, 2005-0163331I7 and 2007-0243381C6, and *Funtronix Amusements Ltd*, [1989] 2 C.T.C. 2296 (TCC).
Pillows for motels or hotels	Sch. II:Cl. 8(i)	20%	See paragraph 8 of IT-472. See also "Bed linens and blankets".
Platforms (used solely to provide access to machinery)	Sch. II:Cl. 8(b)	20%	See paragraph 4 of IT-472.
Plumbing	Depends on class of building	—	May be included in Class 1(q), 3(a), or 6(a); See under "Buildings".
Porcelain dishes	Sch. II:Cl. 12(b)	100%	Half-year rule does not apply (see ITR 1100(2)(a)(iii)). See under "Tableware (chinaware, cutlery, glassware, etc.)".
Portable air conditioning equipment (window units)	Sch. II:Cl. 8(i)	20%	VD 2004-0070211E5. Generally, air conditioning equipment other than portable air conditioners is included in the same class as the related building; see under "Buildings".

Asset	Class	Rate	Comments
Power saws acquired by employees	N/A	N/A	Employees required by a contract of employment to supply a power saw may deduct the cost of the saw in the year of purchase from employment income (see IT-501 at paragraph 12, VD 2002-0145415, and Chapter 5 of CRA Guide T4044). See also "Tools".
Power-operated immovable equipment	Sch. II:Cl. 8(i)	20%	May include, for example, a machine for manufacturing cement blocks which is used for the purpose of compacting concrete that is not movable; see IT-469R.
Power-operated movable equipment			
Acquired after 1987 and designed for the purpose of excavating, moving, placing or compacting earth, rock, concrete or asphalt (may include, for example, a rock drill, tractor or certain compressed air drills)	Sch. II:Cl. 38	30%	See ITRs 1100(1)(zd) and 1101(5l) (separate class election available; see under ¶7155). See also IT-306R2 and IT-469R. Can include front-end loaders used in sand or gravel pit operations (see *Nomad Sand & Gravel Ltd.*, [1991] 1 C.T.C. 60 (FCA)) and a portable feeder used in the asphalt batching process (*L & R Asphalt Ltd*, [1989] 1 C.T.C. 2370).
Designed for purposes other than those described in Class 38	Sch. II:Cl. 8(i)	20%	May include, for example, pile drivers and related equipment, truck weigh scales, equipment transporters and crushing, washing and screening equipment; see IT-469R.
Printers and scanners			
That are ancillary data processing equipment for "general-purpose electronic data processing equipment"	Depends on acquisition date	—	Included in same class as related computer equipment; see under "Computer equipment & systems software". The CRA generally considers printers connected to a general-purpose computer such as a desktop or laptop to be ancillary data processing equipment for "general-purpose electronic data processing equipment"; VDs 2009-0325861M4 and 2007-0243381C6.
That qualify as "general-purpose electronic data processing equipment" (may include, for example, a modern multi-functioning printer that is not ancillary equipment of a personal computer)	Depends on acquisition date	—	See under "Computer equipment & systems software". Also, see VDs 2005-0163331I7 and 2007-0243381C6 (CRA's view is generally that if the bulk of the value of equipment lies in its technological components (for example, the processor) as opposed to its mechanical components, it may qualify as "general-purpose electronic data processing equipment") and *Funtronix Amusements Ltd*, [1989] 2 C.T.C. 2296 (TCC).

Asset	Class	Rate	Comments
That are neither "general-purpose electronic data processing equipment" nor ancillary equipment to such equipment (may include, for example, a large printing press)	Sch. II:Cl. 8(i)	20%	See comments above.
Radar equipment			
Acquired after May 25, 1976	Sch. II:Cl. 8(i)	20%	
Reference libraries	Sch. II:Cl. 8(i)	20%	See under "Books" and see also IT-472.
Refrigeration equipment, machinery and lockers	Sch. II:Cl. 8(i)	20%	Includes a frozen food locker plant, refrigerating units used in walk-in refrigeration rooms and cold storage warehouses; See paragraph 8 of IT-472.
Rental properties (defined in ITR 1100(14))	Depends on acquisition date	—	See under "Buildings" for class allocation. Subject to certain exceptions, a "rental property" is generally defined as a building or "leasehold interest" in real property used principally for the purpose of gaining or producing gross rental revenue. Per ITR 1100(11), CCA deductible in respect of "rental properties" is limited to the taxpayer's net income from all such properties before deducting CCA. See also ITRs 1100(11)–(14.2) and 1101(1ac)–(1ae) (separate class for rental properties costing not less than $50,000; see ¶7165), IT-195R4, IT-274R, IT-371, Chapter 3 of CRA Guide T4036, and VD 2008-0267531I7 (CRA's view is that an underground parking lot is a "rental property" where the lot can be considered a component of a building).
Rights of way and easements acquired after 2016	Sch.II:Cl.14.1	5%	Acquired before 2017, will normally qualify as an ECE; see para 29 of IT-143R3, VDs 2009-0312701E5 and 2008-0297051E5, and ¶7300. Also, see ITR 1102(14.3) and ITA 13(7.5)(b), (c) and (d).
Rowboats	Sch. II:Cl. 7(a)	15%	
Rugs and carpets	Sch. II:Cl. 8(i)	20%	Per paragraph 8 of IT-472, Class 8(i) includes rugs and carpets initially installed to furnish a new or renovated hotel, theatre, store or similar establishment (see also VD 9923675). Note that where the property is rented, rugs or carpets acquired could constitute a leasehold interest.
Satellite set-top boxes			
New and acquired after March 4, 2010	[Sch. II:Cl. 30]	40%	See also under "Systems interface equipment".

Asset	Class	Rate	Comments
Acquired before March 5, 2010	Sch. II:Cl. 8(i)	20%	
Scales (metric, for retail use)			
Other than those described below	Sch. II:Cl. 8(i)	20%	
Acquired after March 31, 1977 and before 1984 having a maximum weighing capacity of 100 kilograms	Sch. II:Cl. 12(p)	100%	Half-year rule does not apply (see ITR 1100(2)(a)(iii)).
Sheet music, musical scores and transcriptions	Sch. II:Cl. 8(i)	20%	Per paragraph 8 of IT-472, Class 8(i) applies when such property is acquired by a self-employed professional musician or an orchestra.
Ships	Depends on type	—	See under "Vessels".
Sleighs	Sch. II:Cl. 10(d)	30%	
Software	Depends on type and acquisition date	—	See under "Computer software" and "Computer equipment & systems software".
Sprinkler systems	Depends on class of building	—	May be included in Class 1(q), 3(a), or 6(a); see under "Buildings".
Stable equipment	Sch. II:Cl. 10(c)	30%	
Swimming pools			
Other than ancillary properties described below	Sch. II:Cl. 6(e)	10%	See also *Podhorn v MNR* (1966), 40 Tax A.B.C. 366.
Underwater lights and the wiring therefor, ladders, diving boards, slides, etc	Sch. II:Cl. 8(i)	20%	Per paragraph 8 of IT-472, Class 8(i) includes such property unless the taxpayer includes the property in Class 6 as component parts of the pool.
Systems interface equipment			
New and acquired after March 4, 2010	[Sch. II:Cl. 30]	40%	New cable set-top boxes that are acquired after March 4, 2010 are included in Class 30.
Acquired after August 31, 1984 and before March 5, 2010	Sch. II:Cl. 10(v)	30%	Applies to equipment used for the purpose of effecting an interface between a cable distribution system and electronic products used by consumers of that system and that is designed primarily to augment the channel capacity of a television receiver or radio, to decode pay television or other signals provided on a discretionary basis, or to achieve any combination of the latter functions.
Systems software	Depends on type and acquisition date	—	See under "Computer software" and "Computer equipment & systems software".
Tableware (chinaware, cutlery, glassware, etc.)	Sch. II:Cl. 12(b)	100%	Half-year rule does not apply (see ITR 1100(2)(a)(iii)).

Asset	Class	Rate	Comments
Tangible depreciable property (not included in any other class)	Sch. II:Cl. 8(i)	20%	Class 8(i) acts as a catch-all class for depreciable property not included in any other class. See also IT-472.
Taxicabs (acquired after May 25, 1976)	Sch. II:Cl. 16(d)	40%	See under "Automobiles".
Telephone and telegraph systems			
Acquired after May 25, 1976	Depends on property	—	See under "Buildings", "Data communication equipment", "Telephone equipment", "Telephone wire or cable", and "Telephone or telegraph switching equipment". As defined in ITR 1104(2) "telephone system" and "telegraph system" include the buildings, structures, general plant and communication and other equipment pertaining thereto.
Telephone or telegraph switching equipment			
Acquired after May 25, 1976	Sch. II:Cl. 17(b)	8%	Class 17(b) does not include equipment installed on customers' premises or property that is principally electronic equipment or systems software therefor; such property would normally be included in Class 8(i). See under "Telephone and telegraph systems".
Telephone wire or cable			
New and acquired after February 22, 2005	Sch. II:Cl. 42(b)	12%	
Acquired after May 25, 1976 and before February 23, 2005	Sch. II:Cl. 3(j)	5%	
Ancillary supporting equipment	Sch. II:Cl. 3(l)	5%	Includes a pole, mast, tower, conduit, brace, crossarm, guy, or insulator.
Telephone equipment	Sch. II:Cl. 8(i)	20%	See also ITRs 1101(5p) and (5q) (separate class election available for rapidly depreciating electronic equipment that has a cost of at least $1,000 and is a photocopier or office equipment that is electronic communications equipment such as telephone equipment). CRA's view is that an IP(VoIP) telephone or other computerized telephone equipment (i.e., an IP telephone and its related hardware) would be included in Class 8(i); VDs 2007-0243381C6 and 2010-0362061E5. To the extent that Skype telephone software constitutes an application software as opposed to system software, it would be included in Class 12(o); VD 2007-0243381C6.
Television equipment			
Acquired after May 25, 1976	Sch. II:Cl. 8(i)	20%	Included in Class 9(d) (25%) if acquired before May 26, 1976.

Asset		Class	Rate	Comments
Tools				CRA's view is that a tool is an instrument of manual operation to be used and managed by hand instead of being moved and controlled by machinery; IT-422.
	Small and costing less than $500	Sch. II:Cl. 12(h)	100%	Half-year rule does not apply. See ITR 1100(2)(a)(iii). In paragraph 3 of IT-422, the CRA states "the fact that an object can be moved or set up by hand does not, in itself, make it a tool for Class 12 purposes" and that "pallets that are moved by lift trucks when loaded with goods, or scaffolding, which is assembled by hand and moved by hand but not "manually used" are not Class 12 items". On the other hand, the CRA considers shopping carts, metal trays used for carrying bread by hand, milk crates and returnable soft drink cases as being Class 12 assets when they are capitalized.
	Large and costing $500 or more	Sch. II:Cl. 8(i)	20%	See paragraph 8 of IT-472. See also comments above.
	Large, portable and acquired to earn income from rent acquired after May 25, 1976	Sch. II:Cl. 10(b)	30%	
Tractors				
	Other than those described below	Sch. II:Cl. 10(a)	30%	
	Designed for hauling freight and acquired after December 6, 1991	Sch. II:Cl. 16(g)	40%	Class 16 applies to a truck or tractor that is principally used in a business that includes hauling freight and that weighs more than 11,788 kilograms. There may also be situations where a taxpayer hauls its own freight (i.e., rather than on a for-hire basis with third parties) and the truck or tractor qualifies for Class 16 treatment; VD 2003-0019495.
Trailers (including bimodal transport trailers)		Sch. II:Cl. 10(e)	30%	Includes a trailer designed to be hauled on both highways and railway tracks, and portable wellsite trailers that are that are moved around frequently from site to site (units are generally fitted with a washroom, full kitchen, washer and dryer, satellite bed and furniture — VD 2017-0733971I7).
Trees, shrubs, or similar growing things		N/A	N/A	Excluded from CCA treatment; see Class 8(i)(iii).
Trucks				
	General	Sch. II:Cl. 10(a)	30%	

Asset	Class	Rate	Comments
Designed for hauling freight and acquired after December 6, 1991	Sch. II:Cl. 16(g)	40%	See under "Tractors" for additional comments on requirements for Class 16 inclusion.
Uniforms	Sch. II:Cl. 12(i)	100%	Half-year rule does not apply. See ITR 1100(2)(a)(iii). See under "Apparel or costumes".
Vans	Sch. II:Cl. 10(a)	30%	See under "Automobiles".
Vehicles	Depends on type and cost	30%	See under "Automobiles".
Vessels			Per section 2 of the *Canada Shipping Act, 2001*, a "vessel" means a boat, ship or craft designed, used or capable of being used solely or partly for navigation in, on, through or immediately above water, without regard to method or lack of propulsion, and includes such a vessel that is under construction. It does not include a floating object of a prescribed class." See ITA 13(21) "vessel".
Other than those described below	Sch. II:Cl. 7(c)	15%	Includes furniture, fittings and equipment attached to the vessel (but not including radiocommunication and radar equipment) and a spare engine for the vessel; see Classes 7(d) and (e). See VD 2010-0377841E5 (a vessel with its motor removed and used for another purpose is still a Class 7 property).
Canadian vessels (defined in ITR 1101(2a)) acquired, or their "conversion cost" (defined in ITA 13(21)) incurred, after November 12, 1981	N/A	33.33% SL	Includes the furniture, fittings, radiocommunication equipment and other equipment attached thereto. See also ITA 13(14)–(17) and IT-267R2. As per ITR 1100(1)(v), 16 2/3% allowance allowed in the year of acquisition, 33 1/3% in each of the second and third years, and 16 2/3% in the fourth year. For Canadian vessels acquired, or conversion costs incurred, before November 13, 1981, 33 1/3% allowance allowed each year on a SL basis.
Video games (coin-operated)			
Acquired after February 15, 1984	Sch. II:Cl. 16(f)	40%	See under "Computer equipment & systems software", *Funtronix Amusements Ltd v MNR*, [1989] 2 C.T.C. 2296 (TCC), and VD 2005-0163331I7.
Video equipment	Sch. II:Cl. 8(i)	20%	VD 2011-0392831M4.
Video tapes			
Acquired after May 25, 1976	Sch. II:Cl. 10(s)	30%	
Wagons	Sch. II:Cl. 10(d)	30%	
Water coolers	Sch. II:Cl. 8(i)	20%	

Asset	Class	Rate	Comments
Web pages (software and labour)	Sch. II:Cl. 12(o)	100%	Where a web page will have "a relatively short useful life", the related costs may be treated as a current expense; otherwise, the cost of application software purchased from third parties used to develop the page and labour costs incurred to design and develop software to carry out the page functions and/or to create a page to be displayed should be included in Class 12(o) (VD 2010-0380521E5). Half-year rule applies (ITR 1100(2)(a)(iii)). See also "Computer software".
Welding equipment			
General	Sch. II:Cl. 8(i)	20%	
Used by a contractor in a construction business	Sch. II:Cl. 10(h)	30%	See paragraph 4 of IT-306R2 and "Contractor's movable equipment".

¶7005 — CCA Class Summary Table

A summary of the types of property included in the most common CCA classes is provided below for quick reference purposes.

Class	Description	Rate
1	Most buildings made of brick, stone, or cement acquired after 1987, including their component parts such as electric wiring, lighting fixtures, plumbing, heating and cooling equipment, elevators, and escalators (an additional 6% allowance may be claimed in respect of an "eligible non-residential building" at least 90% of the floor space of which is used at the end of the taxation year for the manufacturing or processing in Canada of goods for sale or lease — an additional 2% allowance may be claimed in respect of other "eligible non-residential buildings")	4%–10%
3	Most buildings made of brick, stone, or cement acquired before 1988, including their component parts as listed in Class 1	5%
6	Buildings made of frame, log, stucco on frame, galvanized iron, or corrugated metal that are used in the business of farming or fishing or that have no footings below-ground; fences; most greenhouses	10%
7	Canoes, boats, and most other vessels, including their furniture, fittings, or spare parts (Canadian vessels (defined in ITR 1101(2a)) are generally subject to a CCA rate of 33.33% (ITR 1100(1)(v))	15%

Class	Description	Rate
8	Depreciable property not included in any other class, such as furniture and fixtures, cash registers, refrigeration equipment not used for a qualifying M&P purpose and fax machines, printers, scanners, photocopiers and other office equipment that does not qualify as "general-purpose electronic data processing equipment" (i.e., computer hardware) or as ancillary data processing equipment thereto; tools costing $500 or more; outdoor advertising billboards and neon signs; greenhouses with rigid frames and plastic covers	20%
9	Aircraft, including furniture, fittings, or equipment attached thereto, and their spare parts	25%
10	Automobiles (except taxis and others used for lease or rent or "luxury" passenger vehicles), vans, wagons, trucks, buses, tractors (except certain long-haul tractors included in Class 16), trailers; contractor's movable equipment; timber-cutting and removing equipment	30%
10.1	"Luxury" passenger vehicles costing more than $30,000 and acquired after 2000 (each such vehicle is included in a separate Class 10.1, the recapture and terminal loss rules do not apply, and a special 15% CCA claim may be made in the year of disposition) — see ¶7160	30%
12	Chinaware; cutlery; linen; uniforms; dies; jigs; moulds or lasts; computer software, except "systems software" (i.e., operating systems); cutting or shaping parts of a machine; certain property used for earning rental income such as apparel or costumes; videotape cassettes; certain property costing less than $500 such as kitchen utensils, tools, and medical or dental instruments	100%
13	Property that is leasehold interest (the maximum CCA which may be claimed on a straight-line basis in a taxation year depends on the type of leasehold and the terms of the lease; however, no matter how short the unexpired period of the lease, no more than one-fifth of the capital cost of an addition may be deducted in a taxation year) — see ¶7210	SL
14	Franchises, concessions, and licences for a limited period and patents for a limited period that a taxpayer elects not to include in Class 44 (CCA may be claimed on a straight-line basis over the useful life of the property) — see ¶7205	SL
14.1	Goodwill, property that was ECP before 2017, and property acquired on or after January 1, 2017, the cost of which would be treated as an ECE under the former ECP rules. ITR 1100(1)(c.1)(i) provides that, for taxation years that end before 2027, the depreciation rate is 7% in respect of expenditures incurred before January 1, 2017 — see ¶7325 and ¶7355	5%–7%
16	Automobiles for lease or rent acquired after November 12, 1981; taxicabs acquired after May 25, 1976; coin-operated video games or pinball machines acquired after February 15, 1984; certain tractors and large trucks acquired after December 6, 1991 that are used to haul freight and that weigh more than 11,788 kilograms	40%

Class	Description	Rate
17	Roads and similar surface constructions; sidewalks; parking areas; storage areas; telephone, telegraph, or non-electronic data communication switching equipment	8%
29	Machinery and equipment that is used in Canada primarily to manufacture and process goods for sale or lease acquired after March 18, 2007 and before 2016 or acquired after November 12, 1981 and before 1988 (see paragraphs 1100(1)(t) and (ta)) (see now Class 53)	50% SL
33	Timber resource property	15%
38	Most power-operated movable equipment acquired after 1987 used for moving, excavating, placing, or compacting earth, rock, concrete, or asphalt	40%-30%
42	Fibre-optic cable; telephone, telegraph or data communication equipment that is a wire or cable acquired after February 22, 2005	12%
43	M&P machinery and equipment acquired after February 25, 1992 that is used in Canada primarily to manufacture and process goods for sale or lease other than such assets included in Class 29 or Class 53; property to be used directly or indirectly in Canada primarily in "Canadian field processing" (gas processing activities)	30%
43.1	Clean (i.e., renewable or efficient) energy equipment used in Canada in an industrial process or to generate electricity — see ¶7235. The rate for qualifying property acquired after November 20, 2018 and before 2024 is 100% — see under ¶7006.	30%
43.2	Clean energy equipment described in Class 43.1 (with some modifications) acquired after February 22, 2005 and before 2025 — see ¶7235. The rate for qualifying property acquired after November 20, 2018 and before 2024 is 100% — see under ¶7006.	50%
44	Patents or licences to use patented information for a limited or unlimited period acquired after April 26, 1993 (a taxpayer can elect not to include such property in Class 44, in which case the property will generally either be included in Class 14 (where the property as a limited life) or Class 14.1 (where the property has an unlimited life, see ¶7300 and ¶7205)	25%
45	Computer equipment that is "general-purpose electronic data processing equipment" (i.e., computer hardware) and "systems software" (i.e., operating systems) therefore, including ancillary data processing equipment (such as a printer attached to a desktop computer) acquired after March 22, 2004 and before March 19, 2007 (see now classes 50 and 52 and see former Class 10(f))	45%

Class	Description	Rate
46	Data network infrastructure equipment, which subject to certain exceptions generally includes network infrastructure equipment and "systems software" therefor that controls, transfers, modulates or directs data and that operates in support of telecommunications applications such as e-mail or Web browsing, including data switches, multiplexers, routers, remote access servers, hubs, domain name servers, and modems	30%
50	Property described in Class 45 above (i.e., computer equipment) acquired after March 18, 2007, other than such equipment included in Class 52	55%
52	Property described in Class 45 above (i.e., computer equipment) acquired after January 27, 2009 and before February 2011 that is new and that is situated in Canada for use in a business carried on in Canada or for the purpose of earning income from property situated in Canada	100%
53	Machinery and equipment acquired by a taxpayer after 2015 and before 2026 primarily for use in Canada for the manufacturing and processing of goods for sale or lease. The rate for qualifying property acquired after November 20, 2018 and before 2024 is 100% — see under ¶7006.	50%

ITR 1100

¶7006 — Accelerated Investment Incentive for Capital Cost Allowance (ACCA)

In the November 21, 2018 Fall Economic Statement, the federal Government introduced amendments to allow for the accelerated deduction of depreciable property. The new accelerated investment incentive (accelerated CCA or ACCA) generally allows Canadian businesses to claim an enhanced first-year tax depreciation on "accelerated investment incentive property" (AIIP) acquired after November 20, 2018. AIIP generally includes both tangible and intangible capital assets (e.g., vehicles, equipment, buildings, patents, intellectual property, etc.) subject to the capital cost allowance (CCA) rules that are acquired by a taxpayer after November 20, 2018 and become available for use before 2028 (ITR 1104(4)). AIIP excludes property acquired by the taxpayer on a tax-deferred "rollover basis" and any property that was previously owned by the taxpayer or by a non-arm's length person or partnership. Accordingly, AIIP generally includes all depreciably property except for these limited exceptions.

Under the accelerated CCA rules, taxpayers can deduct up to three times the amount of tax depreciation that would normally be deductible in the year that an AIIP becomes available for use. This is achieved by allowing taxpayers to apply the regular prescribed CCA rate to 1.5 times (i.e., 150%) the net qualifying additions to the relevant class for the year, and by suspending the application of the regular half-year rule (ITR 1100(2)). Property that is not AIIP continues to be subject to the normal half-year rule. Note that the total amount of CCA available over the life of an AIIP does not change as a result of the accelerated CCA rules — the increased deduction in the year of acquisition is effectively offset by reductions to CCA allowed in future years. The accelerated investment incentive will be gradually phased out starting in 2024, where the maximum enhanced depreciation will be up to two times the normal amount, and will not apply to capital property available for use after 2027.

If a CCA deduction is not claimed in the year an AIIP becomes available for use (i.e., as the deduction of CCA is discretionary), an enhanced deduction may not be claimed in a subsequent taxation year. Also, the normal restrictions that can apply to limit the amount of CCA deductible in a particular year will still apply to property that qualifies for the accelerated investment initiative.

The table below illustrates the application of the accelerated CCA deduction in respect of a Class 10 property:

First year acquired AIIP becomes available for use	Pre-2018 Economic Statement Rules	Accelerated CCA Rules
Cost of property acquired	$10,000	$10,000
Half-year rule	(5,000)	N/A
Depreciable amount	$5,000	$10,000
CCA rate	30%	30%
Regular CCA	$1,500	$3,000
Accelerated CCA	N/A	$1,500
Total CCA deduction in Year 1	$1,500	$4,500

The accelerated CCA rules also apply to property that is depreciated on a straight-line basis (i.e., Class 13 property) and property that is depreciated on the basis of use (i.e., Class 14 property). Class 13 allows a taxpayer to deduct CCA with respect to the cost of improvements or alterations to leased tangible property. Generally, the CCA deduction for Class 13 is the lesser of: (a) 1/5 of the capital cost, and (b) the amount equal to the capital cost divided by the number of years in the lease. Where a leasehold interest is an AIIP, an enhanced first-year CCA deduction will be allowed of 1.5 times (i.e., 150%) the amount that would otherwise be allowed, and the half-year rule will not apply (ITR 1100(1)(b)(i)). This provision only applies to AIIP that is acquired before 2024; the regular CCA rate and half-year rule apply for property acquired after 2023. Class 14 includes patents, franchises, concessions, and licenses that exist for a limited time-period. Generally, the CCA deduction for Class 14 property is a straight-line depreciation of the property's capital cost over its life. Where the Class 14 property is AIIP, the first-year CCA deduction otherwise determined for the year the property is acquired will increase by: 1.5 times in the case of AIIP acquired before 2024, and 1.25 times in the case of AIIP acquired after 2023 (ITR 1100(1)(c)).

The accelerated CCA rules also allow a taxpayer to immediately expense the entire cost of AIIP acquired after November 20, 2018 that is specified clean energy property or machinery and equipment used to manufacture and process goods in Canada. The rules effectively increase the CCA rate for specified clean energy property included in Class 43.1 or 43.2 or M&P property included in Class 53 (or Class 43, if acquired after 2025) to 100% in the year the property becomes available for use (ITR 1100(2)). The 100% CCA rate is reduced to 75% for investments that become available for use after 2023 and before 2026, and to 55% for investments that become available for use after 2025 and before 2028. An accelerated CCA deduction is not available for property that becomes available for use after 2027.

Under the accelerated CCA rules, eligible Canadian development expenses (CDE) and Canadian oil and gas property expenses (COGPE) are also generally eligible for a first-year deduction equal to 1.5 times the deduction that would otherwise be available.

ITR 1100, 1104

¶7100 — Capital Cost Allowance (CCA)

¶7105 — General Rules Applicable to Depreciable Property

For tax purposes, ITA 18(1)(b) denies the deduction of any outlay, loss or replacement of capital, a payment on account of capital, or an allowance in respect of depreciation, obsolescence or depletion, except as expressly permitted by another provision of the ITA. ITA 20(1)(a), which allows for the deduction of CCA, is an exception from the general rule in ITA 18(1)(b). Other exceptions provided for in the ITA allow for the partial amortization of ECP in respect of intangible capital property expenditures (i.e., ECEs) incurred before 2017 (see ¶7300 — after 2016, expenditures formerly treated as ECEs are included in Class 14.1) and for deductions from various pools in respect of resource expenditures (see ¶7400). CCA, which is an allowance in respect of the capital cost of depreciable property, is essentially the tax equivalent of the accounting concept of depreciation.

CCA may be deducted as an expense in computing an individual's business or professional net income on Form T2125, *Statement of Business or Professional Activities* (see ¶6150) or net rental income on Form T776, *Statement of Real Estate Rentals* (see ¶5240). In limited circumstances, CCA in respect of a musical instrument, motor vehicle, or aircraft may also be claimed as an employment-related expense on Form T777, *Statement of Employment Expenses* (see ¶2456 and ¶2460).

"Depreciable property" is defined, in essence, to mean property that is included in a prescribed class and in respect of which CCA may be claimed. The term "depreciable property" is defined in ITA 13(21) as follows:

> "depreciable property" of a taxpayer as of any time in a taxation year means property acquired by the taxpayer in respect of which the taxpayer has been allowed, or would, if the taxpayer owned the property at the end of the year and this Act were read without reference to subsection (26) [see ¶7125], be entitled to, a deduction under paragraph 20(1)(a) in computing income for that year or a preceding taxation year;

Further discussion on the meaning of "depreciable property" is provided in Folio S3-F4-C1, *General Discussion of Capital Cost Allowance*.

Depreciable property is grouped into prescribed classes and CCA is calculated on the undepreciated capital cost (UCC) of all the property in that class. The application of the CCA rules does not apply to individual properties (except in special circumstances); rather, the rules apply to the combined totals, or balances, in the various classes. For most assets, CCA is claimed using the diminishing-balance method (rather than the straight-line method). A separate line should be maintained for each class of property (on occasion, multiple lines should be maintained in respect of certain assets included in the same class; see below under ¶7155).

The amount to which the prescribed rate of allowance is directly applied is the UCC of property in each of the prescribed classes. Generally, the UCC is the balance of the capital cost of assets of a prescribed class which remains after deducting the aggregate of past CCA claimed (see ¶7110) in respect of that class and after deducting proceeds of disposition (up to the capital cost of the asset disposal of) in respect of previous disposals of that class (see ¶7135). In other words, UCC represents the as yet unamortized cost of the relevant assets in the class. Any CCA claimed in a taxation year is deducted from the UCC of property at the end of the year. Under the diminishing-balance method, annual deductions become progressively smaller. If no new assets of the class are acquired and if CCA is claimed, the UCC will diminish from year to year.

CCA cannot be claimed under the ITA in respect of the following properties/expenditures:

- Property the cost of which is deductible in computing the taxpayer's income as an ordinary expense (see ¶5210);

- Costs that form part of the taxpayer's inventory;

- Property not acquired for the purpose of gaining or producing income;

- Property the cost of which is included in a deductible resource pool (see ¶7400);

- Intangible assets acquired before 2017 (see ¶7300 — Eligible Capital Property — such expenditures are included in CCA Class 14.1 after 2016); or

- Land, animals, trees, or plants.

As mentioned above, resource expenditures included in a deductible resource pool under the ITA are not governed by the CCA system. A separate set of rules allow for the deduction of expenditures incurred in exploring for and developing or producing oil, gas, or minerals and the cost of acquiring resource properties (see ¶7400). The allowable deduction available in respect of resource pools is computed on Form T1229, *Statement of Resource Expenses and Depletion Allowance*. Resource expenditures include "Canadian development expenses", "Canadian exploration expenses", "Canadian oil and gas property expenses", "foreign resource expenses", and "foreign exploration or development expenses". Where an expense could either be a cost of depreciable property or a resource expense, the expense is considered a cost of depreciable property.

ITA 13(21), 18(1)(b), 20(1)(a), (b), 13(34), 66–66.8, ITR 1100(3), 1101, 1102, Parts XI, XII, XVII, Class 8, Folio S3-F4-C1, *General Discussion of Capital Cost Allowance*

¶7110 — CCA Claim for the Year (Form T776 or T2125: Part A)

In column 1 of Part A ("Calculation of CCA Claim") on Form T776 or T2125 (as applicable), identify each applicable class of property with the assigned class number (see ¶7000 and ¶7005 to determine Class numbers applicable to a particulate asset). Enter the amount of the UCC at the end of the previous taxation year in column 2 of Part A. This is generally the amount from column 10 of the prior taxation year's Part A. To determine the UCC balance in respect of which CCA may be claimed for the year (column 7), additions (see ¶7115), adjustments (see ¶7120), and dispositions (see ¶7135) in the taxation year must be considered. In particular, the amount reported in column 7 is computed by adding the amounts in columns 2 (opening balance) and 3 (assets acquired in the year), and subtracting the amounts in column 6 (adjustment for current-year additions) and 4 (proceeds of disposition for the year of property of a prescribed class, but only up to the cost of the asset included in the class).

As outlined in the Depreciable Property Reference Table (¶7000), a maximum CCA rate is prescribed for each CCA class. Apply the prescribed rate to the UCC of the class as reported in column 7 to determine the maximum CCA that may be claimed for the year in respect of the class. CCA cannot be claimed when the amount in column 7 is positive but no property is left in that class at the end of the taxation year; in such a case, see ¶7150 (Terminal Losses). Also, CCA cannot be claimed if the amount in column 7 is negative; in such a case, see ¶7145 (CCA Recapture).

In column 8 of Part A, enter the prescribed CCA rate that applies, as provided for under Part XI of the ITR and summarized under ¶7005. If a specific rate has not been provided for a particular class of property, enter N/A in the column. To claim the maximum CCA for each class, multiply the amount in column 7 by the rate in column 8 and enter the result in column 9. The total of all amounts in column 9 is the CCA claim for the taxation year. Deduct this amount on Line 9936 of Form T776 or Form T2125, as applicable. In column 10, enter the UCC at the end of the year. To compute the balance, subtract the amount in column 9 from the amount in column 5 and enter the difference.

> The maximum amount of CCA available for deduction in a taxation year is not required to be claimed; any amount up to the maximum may be claimed.

If the taxation year is less than 365 days, pursuant to ITR 1100(3), the maximum CCA claim available should be prorated for all property except for Class 14 and 15 assets, timber limits and cutting rights, industrial mineral mines, certified productions, Canadian film or video productions, and certain mining equipment included in Class 41.

ITA 20(1)(a), ITA 1100–1107

¶7111 — *UCC at the Start of the Year (Form T776 or T2125: Part A, Column 2)*

In most cases, the UCC at the start of the year ("Opening UCC") will be the amount from column 10 of the prior taxation year's Part A. However, in certain cases, the Opening UCC must be adjusted in accordance with various rules under the ITA.

Adjustments that reduce Opening UCC include ITCs claimed by the taxpayer or refunded to the taxpayer in the previous taxation year in respect of the acquisition of depreciable property; ITCs that were carried back to a year before the previous taxation year in respect of the acquisition of depreciable property; and GST/HST input tax credits received in the previous taxation year in respect of depreciable property. The Opening UCC should be adjusted by subtracting these amounts.

Adjustments that increase the Opening UCC include the repayment of GST/HST input tax credit previously claimed, and government assistance repaid in the year that previously reduced the capital cost.

ITA 13(7.1), (7.4), 13(21), 12(1)(x), *Prince Albert Pulp Co.*, [1992] 1 C.T.C. 262 (FCA) (reduction in capital cost occurs in year ITC used), Folio S3-F4-C1, IT-273R2, May 2010 Alberta/Saskatchewan CAs CRA roundtable (Member Advisory, Oct 2010, albertacas.ca, question 13), Quebec Bulletin IMP. 101-1/R2: *Government assistance in respect of depreciable property*

¶7115 — Depreciable Property Additions (Form T776 or T2125: Part A, Column 3)

If the taxpayer acquired (or made improvements to) depreciable property in the taxation year, complete Part B ("Details of Equipment Additions in the Year") and Part C ("Details of Building Additions in the Year") of Form T776 or T2125 (as applicable).

In Part B, list the details of all equipment acquired (or improved) by the taxpayer in the taxation year. Group the equipment into the applicable classes and put each class on a separate line. Equipment includes items acquired to use in the taxpayer's business or professional activities to earn income or for maintenance (e.g., motor vehicles, cement mixer, office equipment, etc.). Enter on Line 9925 the total business part of the cost of the equipment.

In Part C, list the details of all buildings acquired (or improved) by the taxpayer in the taxation year. Group the buildings into the applicable classes, and put each class on a separate line. Enter on Line 9927 the total business part of the cost of the buildings. The cost includes the purchase price of the building and any related expenses, such as legal fees, land transfer taxes, mortgage fees, etc. (see ¶4120). Where the chart asks for the "personal part" of a property, this refers to the portion that the taxpayer uses personally, separately from the portion used for business. For example, if the taxpayer uses 25% of a building in which the taxpayer lives for business, the personal part is the other 75%. Note that land is generally not depreciable property. Therefore, where a taxpayer acquires a property that includes both land and a building, enter in column 3 of Part C only the cost that relates to the building. To calculate the building's capital cost, any fees that relate to buying the property (e.g., legal and accounting fees) must be split between the land and the building. Calculate the part of the related fees to include in the capital cost of the building as follows: Building value/Total purchase price × Legal, accounting, or other fees. Do not split a fee if it relates specifically to the land or the building. Instead, add the amount of the fee to the cost to which it relates.

For each CCA class, enter in column 3 of Part A the cost of depreciable property acquired during the taxation year from column 5 of each class in Part B and Part C. For example, if a taxpayer acquired three motor vehicles during the taxation year at a cost of $15,000 per vehicle, $45,000 would be entered in column 3 of Part A in the Class 10 row.

In Part F ("Details of Land Additions and Dispositions in the Year"), enter the total cost of acquiring land in the year on Line 9923, including the purchase price of the land plus any related expenses, such as legal fees, land transfer taxes, and mortgage fees. CCA cannot be claimed on land. Do not enter this amount in column 3 of Part A.

The "capital cost" of a depreciable property added to a CCA class should be calculated in accordance with generally accepted commercial and accounting practices. "Capital cost" is the base from which a taxpayer determines the amount of CCA that may be claimed. "Capital cost" is not a defined term and, in general, means the actual cost of assets to the taxpayer, including legal, accounting and other fees. Special rules apply in certain circumstances, such as when assets are acquired from a non-arm's length vendor (see ¶7133). The original cost of the asset (plus any capitalized additions in respect of the asset added to the applicable UCC class) is the only value that needs to be tracked in respect of particular items of depreciable property. The capital cost must be tracked since, on a disposition, the lower of the proceeds of disposition and the capital cost of the asset must be subtracted from the applicable CCA class.

Where brokerage fees, commissions, or valuation costs are incurred in connection with the acquisition of an asset, they are considered as part of the actual cost of that asset (see ¶4120).

The cost of a property that is acquired for consideration other than money is determined with reference to the fair market value of the consideration given in exchange. The CRA's general position is that the cost of a property does not include any amount in respect of profits forgone. For example, if a taxpayer manufactures an asset for his or her own use, the cost of such asset would include material and labor costs and reasonable allocations of overhead and administrative expenses but would not include any amount in respect of the profit which might have been earned if the asset had been sold.

The date of acquisition of depreciable property may be significant in determining the taxation year in which the taxpayer may first be entitled to claim CCA in respect of the property. The CRA discusses the date at which it considers a taxpayer to have acquired a property in Folio S3-F4-C1, *General Discussion of Capital Cost Allowance*. Generally, property is "acquired" when title passes or when the purchaser has all incidents of title such as possession, use, and risk (for example, a property may be considered to have been acquired even if legal title remains with the vendor as security for a purchase price in a conditional sales agreement).

Generally, ITR 1102(19) applies to an addition or alteration made to a property that would have been in a different class if the property had been acquired at the time the addition or alteration was made. For example, an addition or alteration made after 1987 to a Class 3 building is included in Class 1 where the building would have been included in Class 1 if it had been acquired at the time of the addition or alteration. For an additional example of the application of ITR 1102(19), see VD 2001-0103795. Certain exceptions apply to this rule (see, for example, Class 6(i)).

In respect of a trade-in, where a taxpayer acquires a depreciable property for consideration that can reasonably be considered to include a transfer of property, the portion of the cost to the person of the depreciable property attributable to the transfer may not exceed the fair market value of the property so transferred.

Generally, the ITA requires that costs incurred during a period of construction, renovation, or alteration of a building, which relate to such construction, renovation or alteration, be added to the capital cost of the building rather than deducted by the taxpayer as current expenses; see ¶5255. Such costs would include interest on borrowed money used by the taxpayer in respect of the construction, renovation, or alteration of the building. As discussed under ¶7220, special rules deal with the acquisition by a lessee of property in respect of which a leasehold interest is held.

ITA 13(5.1)–(7.4), (33), 18(3.1)–(3.7), ITR 1100(2), (2.2), *Terexcavation Antoine Grant Inc.*, 2002 CarswellNat 5183 (TCC), Folio S3-F4-C1, IT-464R: *Capital Cost Allowance — Leasehold Interests*

¶7120 — Adjustment for Current-Year Additions (Form T776 or T2125: Part A, Column 6)

In the year a taxpayer acquires or makes additions to a property, CCA can generally be claimed only on one-half of the net additions (i.e., the amount in column 3 minus the amount in column 4). This is called the half-year rule (see ¶7140). The CCA claim should only be calculated on the net adjusted amount. Generally, where a taxpayer acquired and disposed of depreciable property of the same class in the taxation year, the calculation in column 6 restricts the CCA claim. In column 6 in Part A, subtract the amount in column 4 from the amount in column 3 and multiply it by 50% to reflect the half-year rule. If the result is negative, enter zero.

An adjustment to reflect the half-year rule is not required in the following circumstances: the taxpayer acquires property in a non-arm's length transaction (see ¶7141), the property is in a class that is not subject to the half-year rule (see ¶7142), or the available-for-use rules apply (see ¶7125).

¶7125 — Available-For-Use Rules

The capital cost to a taxpayer of a property may not be added to the UCC of the prescribed class to which the property belongs until the time at which the property is considered to have become "available-for-use" by the taxpayer (i.e., the available-for-use rule determines the earliest taxation year in which a taxpayer can claim CCA in respect of a depreciable property).

Generally, by virtue of a two-year rolling start rule, a property is deemed to be available-for-use (i.e., if it has not yet otherwise become available-for-use) in the second taxation year after the year in which the property is acquired. Where the "two-year rolling start" rule applies, the "half-year rule" (see ¶7140) does not apply (except in respect of certain straight-line accelerated depreciable classes, such as Class 29, that have a separately prescribed half-year rule and are excluded from the general half-year rule; see ¶7142).

Property other than a building is considered available-for-use at the earliest of the following dates:

- when the taxpayer first uses the property to earn income;

- the beginning of the first taxation year that starts at least 358 days after the taxation year during which the taxpayer acquired the property (referred to as the two-year rolling start rule);

- immediately before the taxpayer disposes of the property; or

- when the taxpayer can use the property to either produce a saleable product or perform a saleable service.

A building is considered available-for-use on the earliest of the following dates:

- when the taxpayer uses all or substantially all of the building for its intended purpose;

- when construction of the building is completed;

- the beginning of the first taxation year that starts at least 358 days after the taxation year during which the taxpayer acquired the property (referred to as the two-year rolling start rule);

- immediately before the taxpayer disposes of the property; or

- when the taxpayer acquires a replacement property, if it is replacing one it involuntarily disposed of (for example, expropriation) that it either acquired before 1990 or had already become available-for-use

As an exception to above rules, CCA may be claimed to the extent of the rental income from a building before the building becomes available-for-use.

Although a property may not be considered to have become available-for-use by a taxpayer in accordance with the rules contained in ITA 13(27)–(32) such that CCA cannot be claimed in respect of the property, the application of other provisions of the ITA that apply generally to depreciable property continue to apply.

The available-for-use rules do not apply where the property is acquired from a person with whom the taxpayer was not dealing at "arm's length" where the property was considered available-for-use by the transferee (generally speaking, the transferee steps into the shoes of the transferor and the property that had become available-for-use by the transferor is considered to have become available-for-use by the transferee).

ITA 13(26)–(32), 20(28), (29), ITR 1104(2), CRA Guide T4036, VD 2003-0051741R3

¶7130 — Depreciable Property — Special Situations

¶7131 — *Personal Use of Property*

Where a taxpayer purchases depreciable property for both business and personal use, the business part of the property can be reported in Part B or Part C (as applicable) in one of the following two ways:

- If the taxpayer's business use stays the same from year to year, enter in Part B or Part C the total cost of the property in column 3, the personal part in column 4, and the business part in column 5. To calculate the CCA, enter in column 3 of Part A the amount from column 5 of Part B or Part C.

- If the taxpayer's business use changes from year to year, enter in Part B or Part C the total cost of the property in column 3 and column 5, and enter zero in column 4. Enter in column 3 of Part A the amount from column 5 of Part B or Part C and calculate the CCA amount (both business and personal) in column 9. The amount in column 10 (UCC at the end of the year) is equal to the amount in column 5 minus the amount in column 9. The taxpayer then calculates the allowable part of the column 9 amount based on the business use in the year.

See the example provided in CRA Guide T4002.

Taxpayers are required to report the CCA calculated for the business use of a work space in the taxpayer's home in Area A of Form T2125 in the "Calculation of business-use-of-home expenses" chart on page 3 of the form. Subtract the CCA from the total amount of the CCA for the year calculated in Area A and do not include it on Line 9936 (Capital cost allowance).

¶7131.1 — *Changing from Personal to Business Use*

Where a taxpayer purchased a depreciable property for personal use and started using the property in the taxpayer's business in the taxation year, there is a change in use of the property, and the taxpayer must determine the capital cost for business purposes (see ¶5400). At the time of the change in use, if the fair market value of a depreciable property is less than its original cost, the amount entered into column 3 of Part B or Part C is the fair market value of the property (excluding the land value if the property is land and a building). If the fair market value is more than the original cost of the property at the time of the change in use, use the "Capital Cost Calculation" chart under "Changing from personal to business use" in Guide T4002 to determine the amount to enter in column 3 of Part B or Part C.

When a taxpayer begins using personal property for business use, there is a deemed disposition of the property. If the fair market value is more than its capital cost, the taxpayer may have a capital gain.

ITA 13(7), 45(1)–(3), Guide T4036

¶7132 — *Grant, Subsidies and Rebates*

Under the provisions of ITA 13(7.1), certain types of assistance from a government (including federal ITCs), municipality or other public authority serve to reduce the capital costs of depreciable property. Such assistance will not be included in income under ITA 12(1)(x) and an election is not required to be filed when the capital cost of a depreciable property is automatically offset by the application of ITA 13(7.1). Paragraph 2 of IT-273R2 describes the tax treatment of government assistance as follows:

¶2. When assistance is received in the course of earning income from a business or property, the application of well-accepted business principles for the purpose of calculating profit or loss under section 9 commonly requires the cost of an asset or the amount of an expense to be reduced by any reimbursement or similar payment that relates to the acquisition of the asset or the expense incurred.

. . .

If the application of well-accepted business principles relating to the calculation of profit or loss for the purpose of section 9 does not require the government assistance to be included in income, or to reduce the cost or capital cost of a property or the amount deductible as an expense, a specific provision of the *Income Tax Act*, such as paragraph 12(1)(t), 12(1)(x), 12(1)(x.1) or 28(1)(d) (which refers to amounts deferred under section 80.3), or subparagraph 56(1)(a)(vi), may apply to require the amount to be included in income.

Generally, where a taxpayer receives a grant or subsidy from a government or government agency to buy depreciable property, the amount of the grant, subsidy, or rebate should be deducted from the property's capital cost before the amount is entered in column 3 of Part B or Part C (as applicable). GST/HST input tax credits are considered to be government assistance and should also be subtracted from the property's capital cost before the amount is entered into column 3 of Part B or Part C (as applicable).

¶7132.1 — *Inducements or Other Assistance*

A taxpayer that receives inducements or other assistance to purchase depreciable property has the option of either reducing the capital cost of the property by this amount, or including the assistance in income. An election must be filed to reduce the capital cost of the property under ITA 13(7.4). The election is due on or before the taxpayer's T1 filing-deadline for the year of receipt of the inducement or other assistance or, where the depreciable property is acquired in the immediately following taxation year, for such subsequent taxation year.

When the property is acquired in the following year and the taxpayer makes an election, the T1 return for the previous year will be reassessed to remove the amount included in income to the extent of the elected amount. If the property is acquired on or before the date on which the T1 return is filed, the election can be filed with that return and the amount of the assistance that is subject to the election need not be included in income for that previous year.

In paragraph 12 of IT-273R2, the CRA states the election should be made by means of a signed letter accompanying the T1 return. The letter should state: a) the subsection under which the election is being made (i.e., ITA 13(7.4)); b) the elected amount; c) the amount of assistance and the date it was received; d) the date the property was acquired; and e) the capital cost of the property as determined before it is reduced by the elected amount. If the T1 return is filed electronically, the letter should be sent to the CRA Tax Centre that serves the taxpayer by the filing-due date of the return for the taxation year. The CRA is permitted to accept a late-filed election.

If the rebate is more than the remaining UCC in the particular class, report the excess amount on Line 8230 (Other income) of Form T2125.

ITA 12(1)(t), (x), 13(7.1), (7.4), 220(3.2), (3.5), ITR 600, IT-273R2, Folio S3-F4-C1, Quebec Bulletin IMP. 101.6-1/R1: *Election concerning an amount of assistance or an inducement received by a taxpayer in respect of depreciable property*

¶7133 — *Non-Arm's Length Transactions*

When a taxpayer acquires a depreciable property from a non-arm's length person, if the cost to the taxpayer as otherwise determined exceeds the transferor's capital cost of the property immediately before the disposition, the capital cost of the property to the taxpayer is deemed to be the total of the transferor's capital cost plus one-half of the excess of the transferor's proceeds of disposition over that capital cost.

The above rule is generally intended to prevent taxpayers from increasing the depreciable base of property through the use of a non-arm's length transfer in respect of which the transferor benefits from the 50 percent capital gains inclusion rate.

If the acquirer's capital cost of the property, as otherwise determined, is less than the transferor's capital cost, the acquirer's capital cost is deemed to be the same as the transferor's capital cost, with the excess deemed to have been claimed as a CCA deduction (i.e., the potential for recapture of the transferor's CCA is carried through to the non-arm's length acquirer).

> Where the transferor is a Canadian resident individual, the transferee can only deduct CCA in respect of that portion of any capital gain of the transferor to the extent that an exemption (such as the capital gains exemption under ITA 110.6) was not claimed.

In the case of a non-arm's length acquisition of a passenger vehicle, the capital cost of the vehicle to the taxpayer is deemed to be the least of: 1) the fair market value of the vehicle at the time of acquisition, 2) the "cost amount" of the vehicle to the transferor (i.e., the pro rata share of the UCC of the relevant class determined with reference to the capital cost of the assets in that class), and 3) the prescribed amount (i.e., $30,000 plus applicable sales taxes; see ¶7160). This rule effectively prevents a taxpayer from increasing the capital cost of a passenger vehicle in excess of the prescribed limit. This rule is not limited to Class 10.1 passenger vehicles.

ITA 13(7)(e), (h), 85(1)(e.4)), VD 2003-0014995

¶7134 — *Transferred or Misclassified Property*

Special rules apply under ITA 13(5) when one or more depreciable properties of a prescribed class become included in another prescribed class or have been transferred from one class to another.

A transfer of property between classes can arise when a new class of depreciable property is prescribed for property previously in an existing class, when property is transferred from one class to another existing class by an amendment to the ITA or ITRs, when property in the wrong class has been transferred to the correct class by the CRA under ITA 13(6), or when the taxpayer elects to transfer a former property to a new class to avoid recapture (see under ¶7146). Under the transfer rules, recapture should not arise in respect of the old class where there is an individual or a simultaneous transfer of more than one of a taxpayer's depreciable properties from one prescribed class to a new class; see Folio S3-F4-C1: *General Discussion of Capital Cost Allowance*.

ITA 13(5), (6), 152(4), IT-327 (archived), Folio S3-F4-C1, IC 84-1, VD 2010-0365171M4

¶7135 — Dispositions of Depreciable Property (Form T776 or T2125: Part A, Column 4)

Where a depreciable property is disposed of, the amount subtracted from the UCC of the class to which the property belongs is limited to the lesser of: i) the net proceeds of disposition received, and ii) the capital cost of the property disposed of (generally the amount added to the class when the property was acquired). Any proceeds in excess of the cost of the asset disposed of are not deducted from the asset class. If the proceeds of disposition exceed the capital cost of the property, the excess is normally taxable as a capital gain, 50% of which is included in computing taxable income; capital gains are reported on Schedule 3 (see ¶4000). Normally, the unamortized cost of a depreciable asset disposed of remains part of the balance in the UCC class and is subject to future CCA claims.

If the taxpayer disposed of depreciable property in the current tax year, complete, for each class, Parts D and E on Form T776 or Form T2125, as applicable, and enter in column 4 of Part A the amounts for each class from column 5 of Part D and Part E. When completing Parts D and E, enter in column 3 the lesser of the proceeds of disposition minus any related expenses, or the capital cost of the property. Therefore, as discussed above, if the property is disposed of for more than its capital cost, the capital cost, not the actual proceeds of disposition, should be entered into column 3.

In Part D, list the details of all equipment and other property the taxpayer disposed of in the current tax year. Group the equipment and other property into the applicable classes, and put each class on a separate line. Enter on Line 9926 the total rental portion (Form T776) or business portion (Form T2125) of the proceeds of disposition of the equipment and other property.

In Part E, list the details of all buildings and leasehold interests the taxpayer disposed of in the current tax year. Group the buildings and leasehold interests into the applicable classes, and put each class on a separate line. Enter on Line 9928 the total rental portion (Form T776) or business portion (Form T2125) of the proceeds of disposition of the buildings and leasehold interests. When completing Parts D and E, enter the part of the property that the taxpayer personally uses, separate from the part rented, in the column called "Personal portion".

In Part F, enter the total of all amounts the taxpayer has received or will receive for disposing of land in the year on Line 9924. CCA cannot be claimed on land. Do not enter this amount in column 4 of Part A.

On a disposal of assets, depreciation already allowed is "recaptured" to the extent that the proceeds exceed the UCC of the group of assets in the particular class (see ¶7145). On the other hand, on a disposal of all of the assets in a particular class, if there still remains a positive UCC balance, the balance is deductible in the year from income for tax purposes as a "terminal loss" (see ¶7150). A capital loss cannot be realized on a disposition of depreciable property.

Example

In 2010, John bought a piece of machinery to use in his business, at a cost of $10,000. It is the only property in its class at the beginning of 2017. The class has a UCC of $6,000. John disposes of the machinery in 2017 and did not buy any other property included in the same class. The following chart illustrates the tax results based on three different selling prices:

Description	A ($)	B ($)	C ($)
Calculation of capital gain			
Proceeds of disposition	4,000	8,000	12,000
Minus: Capital cost	- 10,000	- 10,000	- 10,000
Capital gain	= 0	= 0	= 2,000
Calculation of terminal loss or (recapture of CCA)			
Capital cost	10,000	10,000	10,000
Minus: CCA 2010–2016	- 4,000	- 4,000	- 4,000
UCC at the beginning of 2017	= 6,000	= 6,000	= 6,000
Minus the lesser of:			
The capital cost of $10,000 and the proceeds of disposition	- 4,000	- 8,000	- 10,000
Terminal loss or (recapture of CCA)	= 2,000	= (2,000)	= (4,00)

In situation A, John does not have a capital loss; however, he has a terminal loss of $2,000 that can be deducted from business income on Form T2125.

In situation B, John does not have a capital gain; however, he has recapture of CCA of $2,000 that is included in income for tax purposes on Form T2125.

In situation C, John has a capital gain of $2,000. The capital gain is reported in Schedule 3 and the taxable capital gain (i.e., 50% of the capital gain) is included in income for tax purposes. John also has a recapture of CCA of $4,000 that is included in income for tax purposes on Form T2125.

ITA 13(1), 20(16), 39(1)(b)(i)

¶7136 — *Net Proceeds of Disposition of Depreciable Property*

Proceeds of disposition include the sale price of depreciable property when it is sold, damages or compensation received in respect of damage to or destruction or expropriation of depreciable property, insurance proceeds in respect of the loss or destruction of or damage to depreciable property (except such proceeds that are expended to repair such damage), and any amount by which the taxpayer's indebtedness to a mortgagee is reduced upon the foreclosure or sale under a power of sale of depreciable property. Special considerations with respect to determining the proceeds of disposition of a property are discussed under ¶4110.

ITA 13(21.1) contains special rules for determining proceeds of disposition in respect of a building where the taxpayer disposes of a building and the land subjacent or immediately contiguous thereto in the same taxation year or disposes of a building and, at any time prior to such disposition, owned the land subjacent or immediately contiguous thereto; see ¶4410.

A taxpayer must credit a class with the full amount of proceeds receivable (if less than the original cost) of an asset in the year of disposition even if only a portion of proceeds are actually received in the year. Unlike in the case of a capital gain, a deferral of CCA recapture income cannot be claimed in respect of outstanding proceeds of disposition. If proceeds of disposition of a depreciable property become uncollectible, a deduction can be claimed (see ¶4510).

An ITC received under ITA 127(5) (see Line 412 at ¶11030) in respect of the acquisition of depreciable property in a taxation year ending before that time is normally deducted under ITA 13(7.1)(e) in computing the capital cost of that property in a taxation year following that in which the credit is deducted. If, however, such a tax credit is claimed after the relevant property has been disposed of by the taxpayer, the credit is instead deducted in computing the UCC of the class to which the property belonged. A similar rule applies in respect of government assistance received subsequent to the disposition of the relevant property.

Folio S3-F4-C1, *General Discussion of Capital Cost Allowance* reviews the implications of a disposition of depreciable property and the possible application of various sections of the ITA in relation thereto.

ITA 13(21)"proceeds of disposition", "undepreciated capital cost", 20(4), (5), *Avril Holdings Ltd*, [1970] C.T.C. 572 (SCC), IT-481, VD 2008-0302631I7

¶7140 — Half-Year Rule (Form T776 or T2125 Part A: Column 6)

In the year a taxpayer acquires depreciable property, the maximum CCA claim is limited to half of the allowable rate for net acquisitions of property in that class by what is commonly referred to as the "half-year rule". The taxpayer can claim the full CCA for that property starting in the next taxation year.

The half-year rule applies to both the cost of depreciable property acquired during the year and the increase in UCC from the repayment of any government assistance after the disposition of a depreciable property. To apply the half-year rule, the UCC of the property has to be adjusted by one-half of the net amount of additions to the class (the net cost of acquisitions minus the proceeds of dispositions) during the taxation year; enter this amount in column 6 of Part A. In column 7 of Part A, enter the amount obtained by subtracting the amount in column 6 from the amount in column 5.

If the capital cost of acquisitions were less than the proceeds of disposition (up to capital cost) of property disposed of in the taxation year, there would be no restriction on the CCA that could be claimed as a result of the half-year rule.

ITA 1100(2), Folio S3-F4-C1

¶7141 — *Half-Year Rule Exceptions*

Properties acquired from a non-arm's-length vendor are exempt from the half-year rule where the transferor owned the property from a day that was at least 364 days before the end of the taxation year of the transferee.

The basic intent of the exception in respect of non-arm's length transfers is that the half-year rule should not have application provided that the property has been held by the non-arm's length vendor for at least one year before the end of the taxation year of the taxpayer acquiring the property.

For purposes of the exception from the half-year rule, a relationship that is not at arm's length because of the existence of certain rights and options does not qualify as a non-arm's length relationship.

ITR 1100(2.2)

¶7142 — *Properties Excluded from the Half-Year Rule*

If a depreciable property addition is not subject to the half-year rule, this fact is highlighted in the Depreciable Property Reference Table (¶7000); almost all properties acquired during the year are subject to the half-year rule and exceptions are limited.

The half-year rule does not apply to Class 14 patents, franchises, concessions, or licences (CCA in respect of such property is apportioned over its useful life), or Class 15 woodland assets (CCA in respect of a woodland asset is apportioned by the number of cords, board feet, or cubic metres of timber taken). Also, several types of Class 12 property are exempt from the half-year rule, including: apparel for rent, bed linens and blankets, books that are part of a library, chinaware, cutlery, dishes, glass tableware, scales, uniforms and kitchen utensils, tools, and medical or dental instruments costing less than $500. The half-year rule applies to application software included in Class 12.

ITR 1100(1)(b), (c), (f), (2)(a)(iii), (2.2), (16), Classes 10(w) and 12(a) to (c), (e) to (i), (k), (l) and (p) to (s), Folio S3-F4-C1, VD 2010-0384021E5

¶7145 — CCA Recapture (Form T776: Line 9947, Form T2125: Line 8230)

If the amount recorded in column 5 of Part A is negative, "recaptured" CCA must be included in income for tax purposes. A recapture of CCA occurs when the lower of cost or proceeds of disposition reported in column 4 of Part A is more than the total of columns 2 (opening UCC) and 3 (additions), minus the amount in column 6 (adjustments) of that class. The total amount of recapture from Part A column 5 in respect of all CCA classes should be added to income for tax purposes on Line 9947 of Form T776 or Line 8230 on Form T2125 (as applicable).

Recaptured CCA is attributable to CCA that has been claimed in preceding taxation years in excess of the "actual" depreciation in the value of a group of assets of a particular class (recapture may also be thought of as a negative balance of UCC at year-end which is added to income for tax purposes to reset the UCC balance of the class to nil). For recapture to arise, the proceeds of disposition of a property of a class must exceed the UCC of the class. Unlike a capital gain which is 50% taxable, 100% of recapture is included in income for tax purposes.

The recapture and terminal loss rules do not apply to passenger vehicles included in Class 10.1 (see ¶7160).

A rollover election is available when compensation is received for depreciable property that has been lost, stolen, or expropriated to the extent that the taxpayer reinvests the proceeds in a replacement property within a certain period of time; see ¶4730.

Where proceeds of disposition that triggered recapture income are outstanding at the end of the taxation year, a reserve cannot be claimed (i.e., there is no equivalent to the capital gains reserve (see ¶4140) that is applicable to recapture income).

> The capital cost of a depreciable property acquired during the year that is not yet available-for-use is not included in the UCC of a class and cannot offset recapture.

Accelerating the purchase of a property just prior to a year-end may allow a taxpayer to reduce or eliminate recapture that would otherwise arise in a particular class to which the property belongs, provided the property is available-for-use by the end of the taxation year. Also, when a taxpayer disposes of a property of a class in a taxation year and before the end of that year acquires another property of another class, the taxpayer may be able to elect to transfer the former property from the former class to the new class if certain requirements are met; see ¶7146.

ITA 13(1), 13(21)"undepreciated capital cost"

¶7146 — *Transfer of Former Property to a New Class*

When a taxpayer disposes of a property (the "former property") of a prescribed class (the "former class") in a taxation year and before the end of that year acquires another property (the "new property") of another prescribed class (the "new class"), the taxpayer is able to elect under ITR 1103(2d) to transfer the former property from the former class to the new class in which the new property is included if certain requirements are met. By virtue of the election, a taxpayer can avoid a recapture of CCA on the disposition of the former property where the taxpayer acquires new property before the end of the taxation year (i.e., the taxation year in which the former property was disposed of) that would have been included in the former class if the new property had been acquired at the same time as the former property and from the same person.

For the election to be available, the new property must be included in a class (i.e., the new class) that is neither: i) the former class, nor ii) a separate class described in ITR 1101. Where the election is made, the former property is deemed to have been transferred to the new class immediately before the disposition of the former property such that the proceeds of disposition from the property fall into the new class.

The election is made by attaching a letter to the taxpayer's T1 return for the applicable taxation year on or before the filing-due date for the return. If the T1 return is filed electronically, the letter should be sent to the CRA Tax Centre that serves the taxpayer by the filing-due date of the return for the taxation year. The CRA is permitted to accept a late-filed election.

When a taxpayer acquires a property, in certain circumstances, ITR 1102(14) requires that the taxpayer place the property in the same prescribed class or separate prescribed class as that of the vendor of the property. The CRA has stated a taxpayer may elect under ITR 1103(2d) in respect of properties that were acquired in a transaction to which ITR 1102(14) applies.

ITR 1103(2d), ITA 13(5)-(6), 220(3.2), (3.5), ITR 600, VDs 2002-0136163, 2000-0012565, 2000-0002885, 2000-0001473, and 9528985

¶7147 — *Election to Include Property in Class 1*

A taxpayer can elect to place all of the taxpayer's depreciable property otherwise falling into Classes 2–10, 11 and 12 into Class 1. Such an election applies to all properties on hand at the beginning of the year or acquired during the year the election is filed (the election does not apply to properties acquired thereafter unless other elections are made in respect thereof). The election only applies to properties used in the same business.

> An advantage of electing to include various properties in Class 1 may be to defer recapture that would otherwise arise in one of the other classes from which the properties are transferred (i.e., by aggregating the UCC of properties in one class, proceeds of disposition from properties sold can be offset by the aggregate UCC of all the properties in the class).

The election is made by attaching a letter to the T1 return. The election is due on or before the taxpayer's T1 return filing-due date for the applicable taxation year in respect of which the election is being made. If the T1 return is filed electronically, the letter should be sent to the CRA Tax Centre that serves the taxpayer by the filing-due date of the return for the taxation year. The CRA is permitted to accept a late-filed election.

The CRA has stated that an election can be made notwithstanding that ITA 13(21.1) may be applicable (ITA 13(21.1) sets out rules that in certain cases adjust a taxpayer's proceeds of disposition in respect of land and buildings disposed of by the taxpayer).

ITA 220(3.2), (3.5), ITR 1103(1), 600, VDs 2006-0171111E5, 2004-0072411E5, 2000-0033755

¶7150 — Terminal Losses (Form T776: Line 9948, Form T2125: Line 9270)

A terminal loss results when a taxpayer disposes of all the property in a particular class and there is an amount of UCC remaining in column 5 in Part A of Form T776 or T2125 (as applicable). A terminal loss is fully deductible in computing income for tax purposes. Enter any terminal loss from column 5 in Part A onto Line 9948 of Form T776 or Line 9270 of Form T2125 (as applicable). A terminal loss must be deducted in the taxation year in which it arises (if the loss cannot be utilized in the year, it would be added to the non-capital loss carryforward balance; see ¶9360). A terminal loss is attributable to unrecognized depreciation (i.e., depreciation in which a CCA claim has not yet been made). A terminal loss may also be thought of as an adjustment required to reset a positive UCC balance to nil where no assets remain in the CCA class at the end of the year, yet the class has a positive UCC balance.

> It may be beneficial to defer a purchase of a property to immediately after a taxation year-end where the property will be included in a class in which a terminal loss may be claimed (a terminal loss cannot be claimed if a property remains in the UCC class at the end of the year).

The CRA's position is that a terminal loss may not be claimed simply as a result of the fact that a business has ceased operations; rather, all of the property of the relevant class must be disposed of. When a terminal loss is realized, it is automatically triggered for tax purposes (i.e., unlike CCA, it is not a discretionary deduction); failing to claim the loss does not prevent it from being carried forward as a non-capital loss (*Benedict*, 2012 CarswellNat 1589 (TCC), para. 9).

CCA may not be claimed in respect of a particular class for the year a terminal loss is claimed in respect of the class (an exception applies in the case of Class 10.1 passenger vehicles; see ¶7160).

There is no requirement to reduce a terminal loss incurred on the disposition of a rental property by accumulated losses from a rental operation in taxation years prior to the disposition. Special CCA rules applicable to rental properties are discussed under ¶7165. A terminal loss incurred on the disposition of depreciable capital property to a non-arm's length person is generally deferred if, on the 30th day after the transfer, the transferor or a person affiliated with the transferor owns or has a right to acquire the transferred property. Recognition of a deferred loss is preserved with the transferor and the transferor is able to deduct the deferred loss on an amortized basis; see ¶4822.

The amount of a terminal loss otherwise arising on the sale of a building is restricted when a taxpayer (or a person with whom the taxpayer was not dealing at arm's length) also sells the land subjacent to (or contiguous to and necessary for the use of) that building in the same taxation year and the proceeds of disposition of the building are less than the lesser of the capital cost and the UCC of the building; see ¶4410.

ITA 20(16)–(16.3), Folio S3-F4-C1, VDs 2008-0277681E5, 2004-0073141E5, Amanda Stacey et al., "Current Cases," (2008), vol. 56, no. 4 *Canadian Tax Journal*, 923–956

¶7155 — Property included in a Separate Class

Normally, as discussed above, depreciable property of the same class is grouped together (i.e., each CCA class normally represents a pool of assets) and CCA is computed based on the UCC of all of the property in that class.

Properties of a taxpayer that would otherwise fall into the same class are required to be included in separate classes, unless they are related to each other through business use. Whether a taxpayer is carrying on two or more separate businesses simultaneously or whether all of a taxpayer's activities constitute one business can be a complex question. In IT-206R: *Separate Businesses*, the CRA sets out its views in the matter. Taxpayers should complete a separate Form T2125, and thus a separate CCA calculation, for each business that is carried on by the taxpayer.

ITR 1101(1), (1a)

¶7156 — *Property Required to be Included in a Separate Class*

Under special rules, certain properties are required to be included in a separate class. The following properties should be entered on a separate line in Part A (for example, Part A may include multiple Class 10.1 rows applicable to each passenger vehicle acquired at a cost in excess of the prescribed limit):

- *Passenger Vehicles*: As discussed under ¶7160, Class 10.1 passenger vehicles are also required to be included in a separate class;

- *Rental Properties*: As discussed under ¶7165, rental properties with a capital cost in excess of $50,000 are required to be included in a separate class;

- *Canadian Film or Video Production*: Where certain conditions are met, ITR 1101(5k.1) prescribes a separate class for property included in Class 10(x), which includes a "Canadian film or video production" (see ITR 1106(4)). ITR 1100(1)(m) provides for an additional allowance in respect of property for which a separate class is prescribed by ITR 1101(5k.1);

- *Computer Tax Shelter Property:* A separate class is prescribed for "computer tax shelter property", which is generally computer software or property described in Class 50 or 52 where: (1) the person's or partnership's interest in the property is a tax shelter investment, or (2) an interest in the person or partnership is a tax shelter investment (1101(5r), 1100(20.1), (20.2));

- *Certain Leasehold Interests*: Properties that are leasehold interests in real property described in ITR 1100(13) are required to be included in a separate class (¶7210, ITR 1101(5h));

- *Leasing Properties*: CCA on "leasing properties" is restricted to the amount of revenue derived therefrom. Where a taxpayer owns more than one such property, each is placed in a separate class (¶7211, ITR 1101(5c), 1100(15) to (20));

- *Timber Limits and Mines*: Each of a taxpayer's timber limits, or rights to cut timber, falls into a separate class. Similar treatment is accorded to industrial mineral mines (ITR 1101(3)-(4), Sch. IV–VI);

- *Vessels*: A separate class applies to each new vessel constructed and registered in Canada (33.33% straight-line depreciation rate). However, the separate class rule does not apply in cases where the Minister of Industry has agreed to a structured financing facility (ITR 1101(2a), (2c)).

¶7157 — *Separate Class Elections*

Certain properties can be included in a separate class when an election is filed. Where a property is included in a separate class, the recapture provisions and the terminal loss provisions become immediately operative upon the sale or disposition of the property. In other words, by virtue of a separate class election, upon a sale of the applicable property, immediate effect is given to the CCA adjustments normally only required when all of the properties in a class are disposed of or when proceeds of disposition exceed the UCC of a group of properties in a particular class. A separate class election may be beneficial where it allows for the acceleration of a terminal loss claim. Also, a separate class election is required to be filed in the case of a non-residential building in order to be eligible to claim an enhanced CCA rate. Available separate class elections are discussed under separate subheadings below.

ITA 13(1), 20(16)

¶7157.25 — *Eligible Non-Residential Buildings*

An additional allowance may be claimed in respect of an "eligible non-residential building" if the taxpayer elects to include the building in a separate class. The amount of this additional allowance is 6% where at least 90% of the floor space of the building is used at the end of the taxation year for manufacturing, or 2% otherwise. To qualify for an additional allowance, the qualifying-use test must be met at the end of each taxation year. The half-year rule applies to the additional CCA allowance.

An "eligible non-residential housing building" is defined to include a building (other than a building used, or acquired for use, by any person or partnership before March 19, 2007) that is located in Canada, is included in Class 1 and is acquired by the taxpayer on or after March 19, 2007 for a non-residential use.

The capital cost of an addition to, or alteration of, a taxpayer's building (other than an eligible non-residential building included in a separate class) is deemed to be the capital cost of a separate building for purposes of making this election (i.e., such that a taxpayer who incurs an expenditure that is an addition to, or alteration of, a building that itself is not an eligible non-residential building (for example, where the building was acquired before March 19, 2007) may qualify for an additional allowance).

The election to include the building (or additions to a building) in a separate class is due on or before the taxpayer's filing-due date for the taxation year in which the building (or addition or alteration) is acquired. The election is made by attaching a letter to the T1 return. The CRA has stated that a taxpayer would not be considered to have elected under ITR 1101(5b.1) without a letter attached to the T1 return even if the taxpayer entered a separate Class 1 in Schedule 8 and claimed CCA at the enhanced rate. The CRA has also stated that they will not accept a late-filed election under ITR 1101(5b.1). If the T1 return is filed electronically, the letter should be sent to the CRA Tax Centre that serves the taxpayer by the filing-due date of the return for the taxation year.

At the 2012 CTF Ontario Tax Conference, the CRA confirmed it would not deny an election under ITR 1101(5b.1) on the basis that it was mailed separately and not attached to an electronic return when the election is sent in the form of a letter.

Other considerations with respect to eligible non-residential buildings include:

- A partnership can make an election under ITR 1101(5b.1);

- It is the intended use of the building, not its actual use, which is relevant in determining whether a building is an eligible non-residential building;

- For the CRA's interpretation of the term "non-residential", see VD 2010-0361081E5;

- ITR 1102(25) ensures that the capital cost of an eligible non-residential building that was under construction on March 19, 2007 and that is eligible for a separate class election under ITR 1101(5b.1) includes the capital cost of the building that was incurred before March 19, 2007;

- Where an election is not filed in respect of an eligible non-residential building, the applicable CCA rate would be 4% (Class 1).

ITA 1105(5b.1), 1100(1)(a.1) and (a.2), 1104(2), 1101(22) and (23), VDs 2010-0381311E5, 2008-0271891E5, 2010-0379751E5, 2009-0332581E5, 2010-0361081E5

¶7157.50 — *Rapidly Depreciating Electronic Equipment (Class 8) and M&P Property (Class 43) Separate Class Elections*

An election can be made pursuant to ITR 1101(5q) to include Class 43 manufacturing and processing property with a cost of at least $1,000 or Class 8 photocopiers or electronic communications equipment (such as facsimile transmission devices or telephone equipment) with a cost of at least $1,000 in a separate class. The election rules allow for an individual property to be included in a separate class or for several qualifying properties to be included in one or more than one separate class. There is no limit to the number of separate classes that may be created.

The election is made by attaching a letter to the taxpayer's T1 return. The election is due on or before the taxpayer's filing-due date for the taxation year in which the property or properties are acquired. If the T1 return is filed electronically, the letter should be sent to the CRA Tax Centre that serves the individual by the filing-due date of the return for the taxation year. The CRA is permitted to accept a late-filed election.

Generally, where an election under ITR 1101(5q) has been made, all property remaining in such a separate class at the beginning of the fifth taxation year following the first taxation year in which a property of the class became available-for-use is required, at that time, to be transferred into a general multiple asset class (either Class 8 or 43, depending on the property).

ITR 1101(5p), (5q), (5s), 1103(2)(g)

¶7160 — "Luxury" Passenger Vehicles (Class 10.1)

> If the cost of a passenger vehicle exceeds $30,000 plus applicable federal and provincial sales taxes, the vehicle is required to be included in a separate Class 10.1 (30% CCA rate). As a special rule, neither recapture nor a terminal loss will arise upon a disposition of a Class 10.1 vehicle. Also, a taxpayer who owns such a vehicle at the beginning of a year and disposes of it before the end of the year is entitled to a deduction equal to 50% of the CCA deduction that would have been available for that year if the vehicle had not been disposed of.

A "passenger vehicle" is defined as an "automobile" and an "automobile" is in turn defined as a motor vehicle designed or adapted primarily to carry individuals on highways and streets, having a seating capacity for not more than a driver and 8 passengers. However, the following are excluded from the definition of an "automobile" and therefore are excluded from Class 10.1:

- an ambulance,

- a clearly marked police or fire emergency-response vehicle,

- a clearly marked emergency medical response vehicle,

- a motor vehicle acquired primarily for use as a taxi,

- a bus used in a business of transporting passengers or a hearse used in a business of arranging or managing funerals,

- a motor vehicle acquired to be sold, rented, or leased in the course of carrying on a business of selling, renting, or leasing motor vehicles,

- a motor vehicle used to transport passengers in the course of carrying on a funeral business,

- a van, pick-up truck, or similar vehicle either:

    i) having a seating capacity for not more than a driver and two passengers and used in the taxation year of its acquisition or leasing primarily for the transportation of goods or equipment in the course of gaining or producing income, or

ii) "all or substantially all" (considered by the CRA to mean 90%) of the use of which in the taxation year of its acquisition or leasing is for the transportation of goods, equipment, or passengers in the course of gaining or producing income, and

- a pick-up truck used in the taxation year of its acquisition or leasing primarily for the transportation of goods, equipment, or passengers in the course of earning or producing income at one or more remote or special work sites in Canada that are at least 30 kilometres from the nearest urban area having a population of at least 40,000.

A "motor vehicle" is defined as an automotive vehicle designed or adapted to be used on highways and streets but not including a trolley bus, or a vehicle designed or adapted to be operated exclusively on rails.

See also Chapter 8 of CRA Guide T4044 under "Vehicle definitions chart".

When determining whether a vehicle belongs in Class 10 or Class 10.1, GST and PST, or HST, are not considered (i.e., the test is whether the vehicle cost more than $30,000 before taxes). For example, on July 1, 2017, John purchased two passenger vehicles to use in his business. The applicable PST rate was 8%.

	Cost	GST	PST	Total
Vehicle 1	$33,000	$1,650	$2,640	$37,290
Vehicle 2	$28,000	$1,400	$2,240	$31,640

Vehicle 1 is included in a separate Class 10.1. The amount added to the class in column 3 of Schedule 8 is $30,000 × 1.05 (GST) × 1.08 (PST) = $33,900 ($30,000 + $1,500 + $2,400). Vehicle 2 is included in Class 10, with a capital cost of $31,640 ($28,000 + $1,400 + $2,240).

Where a "passenger vehicle" is acquired in a non-arm's length transaction, the capital cost of the vehicle to the acquiring taxpayer is deemed to be the least of: a) the fair market value of the vehicle at the time of acquisition, b) the "cost amount" of the vehicle to the transferor (generally the pro rata share of the UCC of the relevant class determined with reference to the capital cost of the assets in that class), and c) the prescribed amount (currently $30,000 plus applicable sales taxes). This rule is not limited to Class 10.1 vehicles and also applies to passenger vehicles included in Class 10.

ITA 13(2), (7)(g), (h), 20(16.1), 248(1)"automobile", "motor vehicle", "passenger vehicle", ITR 1100(2.5), 1101(1af), 7307(1), IT-63R5 (paras. 6, 12, 23), CRA Guide T4044 under "Vehicle definitions chart", VDs 2007-0238631E5, 2004-0064901I7, 2004-0057251E5, 2006-0168551E5

¶7165 — Rental Properties

A separate class is prescribed for each rental property acquired at a capital cost of $50,000 or more. The term "rental property" includes both buildings and leasehold interests in buildings. Additionally, a rental loss cannot be increased by claiming CCA. The amount of CCA deductible by a taxpayer in respect of "rental properties" is limited to the taxpayer's net income from all such properties before deducting CCA.

The rental property CCA restriction rules do not apply to property owned by, and used in a business carried on in the year by, a taxpayer. Also, the restriction imposed does not apply in the case of a taxpayer whose principal business is the leasing, rental, development, or sale (or any combination of such activities) of real property.

For the CRA's views concerning the meaning of the terms "rental property" and "rent", see paragraphs 3, 4 and 6 of IT-195R4: *Rental Property — Capital Cost Allowance Restrictions*. Generally, a building falls within the rental property rules where it is used principally for the purpose of earning gross revenue that is rent, which is a question of fact. A property would normally be considered to be used principally for producing rental revenue if the property was used more than 50% of the time for earning rent or if more than 50% of the total area of the property was used for rental purposes.

In VD 2008-0267531I7, the CRA states that an underground parking lot may qualify as being a "rental property" subject to the CCA restriction rules.

In *The Canada Trust Company*, [1979] C.T.C. 2199 (TRB), an office building in which the appellant, as owner, occupied only 25% of the rental space was held to be used principally for the purpose of the appellant's business operations and not "principally for the purpose of gaining or producing gross revenue that is "rent". However, an appeal on similar facts was dismissed by the Tax Court of Canada on the basis of percentage of occupancy in *The Canada Trust Company*, [1985] 1 C.T.C. 2367.

ITR 1100(2.21), (14), (11)–(14.2), 1101(1), (1a), (1ac), (1ad), (1ae), 1102(20), *Elwood Smith Limited*, [1981] C.T.C. 2208, *Combined Appraisers and Consultants Co Ltd*, [1979] C.T.C. 2970, *Hady Construction (1971) Ltd*, [1980] C.T.C. 2135 (TRB), IT-195R4, IT-274R, IT-371, CRA Guide T4036

¶7170 — Revising CCA Claims

A taxpayer may choose to defer CCA claims to manage the balance of carryforward non-capital losses which expire after 20 taxation years (see ¶9360). However, if taxable income in future years is higher than was originally expected when prior year T1 returns were filed, the taxpayer may wish to retroactively increase CCA claims (i.e., to increase the balance of non-capital losses carried forward). The CRA will allow such requests where the conditions described in IC 84-1: *Revision of Capital Cost Allowance Claims and Other Permissive Deductions*, are met. Generally, the CRA will accept the request if there is no change in the taxes payable by the taxpayer for any previous taxation year as a result of the request. However, the CRA is under no obligation to recognize retroactive CCA claims made after a taxpayer's T1 return for a particular taxation year has been assessed and the period within which a notice of objection may be filed has expired.

¶7200 — Special Depreciable Property Rules

¶7205 — Patents, Franchises, Concessions, and Licences

Special accelerated first-year CCA rules apply in respect of qualifying property acquired after November 20, 2018; see under ¶7006.

CCA in respect of patents, franchises, concessions, and licenses included in Class 14 is prorated by apportioning the capital cost of the property over its remaining life at the time the cost is incurred. As Class 14 CCA is apportioned based on useful life, assets in this class are exempted from the general half-year rule. IT-477 (Consolidated): *Capital Cost Allowance — Patents, Franchises, Concessions and Licences* discusses the depreciation of patents, franchises and licences under Class 14.

For Class 14 to apply, the patent, franchise, concession, or licence must have a limited life. A licence, concession, franchise, or other right for an unlimited period that is a capital expenditure incurred to earn income from a business will normally qualify as an ECE before 2017, and be included in Class 14.1 if incurred after 2016 (see ¶7300). In paragraphs 15 and 16 of IT-477, the CRA states (see also VD 2014-0552041E5):

> 15. The provisions of a franchise, concession or licence concerning renewals or extensions following the original term are relevant in determining the life of the property and whether or not the property is for a limited period. Where such renewals or extensions are automatic or within the control of the taxpayer, that is they do not require any further negotiation with or the concurrence or consent of the grantor, the life of the property includes such additional periods. For instance, where a franchise with an initial term of 5 years can be renewed at the option of the franchise for one further 3-

year period, the life of the franchise is 8 years. On the other hand, where the concurrence of the franchisor is required, the life of the property does not include any renewal period. Where the taxpayer has an option to renew or extend the term only if certain conditions are met, for instance meeting certain performance or sales criteria, the circumstances of the particular case must be examined to determine whether or not, when he acquired the property, it was reasonably certain that these conditions would be met. If so, the additional periods are included in the life of the property.

16. Where renewal or extension periods are considered part of the life of the property under the criteria set out in ¶15 above, and where the number of such renewals or extensions is indefinite, the property is not for a limited period and does not qualify as a class 14 property. Where the number of such renewals or extensions is definite, for example, where a licence is for an initial term of 5 years and the licensee has options to renew the licence for two further 3-year periods, the property is for a limited term, in this example 11 years. The number of renewals or extensions may, in fact, be limited in certain circumstances even if the relevant agreement does not expressly provide such limits. For instance, a licence under a Canadian patent under which the licensee has unlimited rights of renewal has a limited life because the life of the patent is itself limited to 17 years.

Costs incurred in an attempt to acquire a patent, franchise, or license may qualify as eligible capital expenditures if a property is not acquired. In paragraph 11 of IT-143R3, the CRA states:

An outlay or expense made or incurred to acquire, or in an attempt to acquire, a patent, franchise, concession or licence for use in a business qualifies as an eligible capital expenditure provided that the outlay or expense did not result in the acquisition of a depreciable property of class 14 of Schedule II of the *Income Tax Regulations* or a property that is described as an exception in paragraphs (a), (b), (c), (d) or (e) of class 14. See the current version of IT-477, *Capital Cost Allowance — Patents, Franchises, Concessions and Licences*, for comments regarding properties that qualify as class 14. An amount paid by a taxpayer, either separately or as part of the purchase price paid for the acquisition of the assets or business of another person, for the right to stand in the place of that other person in making an application for a patent, franchise, concession or licence or a renewal thereof, may also qualify as an eligible capital expenditure.

Certain representation expenses are deductible in computing income for tax purposes pursuant to ITA 20(1)(cc). In paragraphs 19–22 of IT-477, the CRA states:

19. The capital cost of a class 14 property includes the purchase price, if any, and any legal fees and disbursements, registration fees and representation expenses laid out to acquire the property. Expenses paid in a year in making a representation, relating to a business being carried on by a taxpayer, to a government, government agency or other body referred to in paragraph 20(1)(cc), including any representation for the purpose of obtaining a licence, permit, franchise or patent, are deductible under paragraph 20(1)(cc) (or, if an election is made, under subsection 20(9)). However, if the representation expense was laid out to acquire a class 14 property, it will also form part of the capital cost thereof. To avoid a further deduction under paragraph 20(1)(a) in respect of the same amount and to permit recapture of the expenditure, subsection 13(12) deems the amount deducted under paragraph 20(1)(cc) (or in respect of which an election has been made under subsection 20(9)), to the extent that it forms part of the capital cost of the property, to have been allowed as capital cost allowance.

20. Where expenses related to the acquisition of a class 14 property are incurred in a year prior to the year in which the property is acquired, they will be added to the capital cost of the property in the year of its acquisition. No claim for capital cost allowance may be made in a year prior to the year of the actual acquisition of the relevant property.

21. The capital cost to the original owner of a patent or industrial design includes research and development expenses incurred in discovering, designing or developing the property to the extent that such expenses have not already been deducted as scientific research expenditures or ordinary operating expenses in the computation of income.

22. Once the invention or design has been developed to the point where a patent or an industrial design registration can be obtained, subsequent expenses for the purpose of turning the property to account would not form part of its capital cost.

Certain properties are excluded from Class 14, including any franchise, concession, licence, or other right in respect of: minerals, oil and gas, timber, or computer software. An allowance for the cost of an industrial mineral mine or of a right to remove minerals therefrom is provided by ITR 1100(1)(g) and Schedule V. Oil and gas concessions in respect of the cost of acquiring interests in oil or gas property or of a right to explore for and remove such products are provided by ITA 60–66.8 (see ¶7400). An allowance for the cost of timber limits or of the right to remove timber therefrom (other than a timber resource property) is prescribed by ITR 1100(1)(e) and Schedule VI. A "timber resource property", as defined in ITA 13(21), is included in Class 33. A licence or right to use computer software is accorded the same treatment as computer software that is purchased. Also excluded from Class 14 are leasehold interests (see ¶7210) and property included in Class 44 (see ¶7206).

Applicable in respect of dispositions and terminations that occur after December 20, 2002, the replacement property rollover rules apply in respect of the disposition or termination of a franchise, concession or licence for a limited period; see ¶4720.

ITA 1100(1)(c), VDs 2013-0506641E5, 2012-0461021E5, 2000-0006067, IT-143R3, IT-492

¶7206 — *Patents (Class 44)*

Class 44 (25% CCA rate) applies to a patent or a right to use patented information for a limited or unlimited period. However, a taxpayer can elect in the year in which the taxpayer acquires a patent not to include the property in Class 44. Where such an election is made, a patent with a limited lifespan would normally be included in Class 14 (see ¶7205), while a patent acquired for an unlimited period would normally be treated as an ECE (included in Class 14.1 after 2016) (see ¶7300).

The election is made by attaching a letter to the taxpayer's return for the taxation year in which the patent is acquired on or before the filing-due date for the return. If the T1 return is filed electronically, the letter should be sent to the CRA Tax Centre that serves the taxpayer by the filing-due date of the return for the taxation year. The CRA is not permitted to accept a late-filed election.

A payment made to purchase a patent while still pending is not depreciable as Class 14 property until after the actual issuance of the patent.

ITR 1103(2)(h), 1100(1)(c), (9) IT-143R3: *Meaning of Eligible Capital Expenditure*, *Weinberger*, [1964] C.T.C. 103, *No 244*, 12 Tax A.B.C. 371, VD 2010-0365861R3

¶7207 — *Licences*

Where technology is licensed and there are also related costs to be incurred (such as training costs), if the related costs are not agreed to in a separate contract with a separately identified cost determined by the parties involved, the CRA may take the view that the entire licence cost (including related costs such as training costs) are a Class 14 asset.

A licence to construct and operate a facility can be a Class 14 asset, as can a licence for the use of real property interests for the purpose of building and operating a project.

The CRA has stated that a licence agreement for a childcare facility should be included in Class 14 rather than Class 13. In VD 2006-0199451E5, the CRA states "in contrast to a lease, which creates an interest in the property for the lessee, a licence does not create an interest in the property for the licensee but simply gives such person the right to use a property, the use of which without the said right would result in trespassing".

In VD 2000-0038827, the CRA states that where it is probable that a licence will be renewed each time it is up for renewal, the bulk of the cost of the licence may be an ECE (included in Class 14.1 after 2016) rather than a Class 14 asset.

VDs 2006-0218781R3, 2005-0133281R3, 2003-0000637, 2002-0140537, 2000-0038827

¶7210 — Leasehold Interests (Class 13)

Special accelerated first-year CCA rules apply in respect of qualifying property acquired after November 20, 2018; see under ¶7006.

Leasehold interests, which are interests of a lessee in depreciable property which is held under a lease for a term upon the termination of which the rights of the lessee will come to an end and the property will automatically revert to the lessor, are included in Class 13. A leasehold interest is generally evidenced by four factors: i) exclusive possession is conveyed to the lessee; ii) the conveyance is for a definite period, having a certain beginning and a certain end; iii) provision is made for the payment of rent; and iv) the parties intend to create a lease.

Generally speaking, the capital cost of a leasehold interest may be deducted in equal annual amounts over a period of five years or over the term of the lease (including one renewal period), whichever is longer. Class 13 property is excluded from the half-year rule. However, in the year of acquisition, CCA is generally available in respect of a leasehold interest only to the extent of 50% of the amount calculated in accordance with Schedule III of the ITR.

All capital expenditures made in a taxation year in respect of a particular "leasehold interest" are deemed, in effect, to have been made on the first day of that taxation year and their aggregate may be amortized over the number of whole 12-month intervals contained in the period beginning on that day and ending on the date on which the lease is to expire. Where the taxpayer (the tenant) has the right to renew the lease for one or more additional terms after the term that includes the end of the particular taxation year in which the capital cost was incurred, the lease is deemed to terminate at the end of the first such renewal period.

If the unexpired period of the lease exceeds 40 twelve-month periods, the period over which the capital cost may be amortized is reduced to 40 periods.

The capital cost of a leasehold interest includes both the cost of acquiring the interest and any amount expended by the taxpayer for, or in respect of, an improvement or alteration to the leased property, but it does not include the cost of erecting a building or structure on leased land, the cost of making an addition to a leased building or structure or the cost of alterations to a leased building or structure that substantially change the nature of the property. The costs of the latter amounts can be written off at the appropriate rate applicable to the building to which they pertain. In VD 2006-0175611E5, the CRA states:

> It is generally understood that when a chattel becomes affixed to a building and becomes a fixture, that fixture becomes part of the building and is therefore owned by the owner of the building. The person leasing the building, or part thereof, would only have a leasehold interest in such fixtures or chattels. If modifications were made and chattels were affixed to the building, they would be considered to be leasehold improvements and would be included in Class 13. Subsection 1102(4) of the Regulations provides that the "capital cost" of a leasehold interest includes any amount expended for an improvement or alternation to a leased property.

> Whether or not a particular property remains a chattel or becomes a fixture must be determined on a case-by-case basis. Relevant factors include the degree of affixation . . .; whether the affixation was done for the better enjoyment of the chattel as a chattel and not with the intent in improving the freehold; . . . and the intention of the parties.

For purposes of Class 13, a leasehold interest does not include: an interest in minerals and property relating thereto; an interest in petroleum, natural gas, other related hydrocarbons, and property relating thereto; an interest in timber and property relating thereto; a right to explore for, drill for, take, or remove minerals; a right to explore for, drill for, take, or remove petroleum, natural gas, and other related hydrocarbons; a right to explore for, take, or remove timber, the cost of erecting a building or structure on leased land; the cost of an addition to a leased building or structure; the cost of alterations to a leased building or structure which substantially change the nature or character of the property; or a property that is included in Class 23.

If the leasehold expires, is cancelled, or is otherwise disposed of (and not by the acquisition of the freehold interest by the lessee) before the total cost thereof has been claimed by the taxpayer, the unamortized cost of that leasehold interest must be deducted from income as a terminal loss if there are no other assets left in the class. If there are other assets left in Class 13, the CRA's policy is that the balance of the unamortized cost of the property disposed of can only be written off at the rate applicable to that property. The CRA has also stated where a tenant cancels a lease and continues to occupy the premises on a periodic tenancy or other continuing basis, the tenant will not be considered to have disposed of the leasehold interest.

Although the pool or class concept persists so long as any assets of Class 13 are in the lessee's possession, different rates of amortization may be applicable in respect of each leasehold interest, or there may be different rates applicable with respect to costs incurred at different times with reference to the same leasehold interest. As a practical matter, it is often useful to track each separate Class 13 addition in a separate row in Part A. Fundamental changes which substantially affect the basic elements of an agreement may result in the acquisition of a new leasehold interest.

For CRA comments on the treatment of bargain purchase options under a lease agreement, see VDs 2004-0100771E5 and 2003-0028033.

Where a taxpayer, having a leasehold interest in a property included in Class 13, acquires ownership of the underlying property, the leasehold interest is deemed to be disposed of for proceeds equal to its capital cost less CCA deducted in respect thereof. The underlying property so acquired is deemed to comprise property of a prescribed class and to have been acquired at a capital cost equal to its actual capital cost plus the capital cost of the leasehold interest. The amount of CCA deducted in respect of the leasehold interest is deemed to have been allowed in respect of the new class (thus allowing for the recapture rules to apply to the CCA previously claimed under Class 13 if the property acquired is disposed of). Even if the underlying property is land, it may be deemed to be depreciable property of a prescribed class so as to ensure that the CCA deducted in respect of the leasehold interest will be subject to recapture if the property is sold at a profit. Any terminal loss incurred would also be deductible.

For an illustration of the application of Schedule III of the ITR, see Appendix I of IT-464R. Also, see the examples provided in VD 2004-0071821E5.

ITA 13(5.1), 20(16), ITR 1100(1)(b), 1102(4), (5), (5.1), Class 36, IT-464R, VDs 2006-0199451E5, 2008-0300731E5, 2004-0071821E5, 2001-0063737, 9128265

¶7211 — *Leasing Properties*

A taxpayer is not entitled to deduct CCA in excess of the net rental income in respect of "leasing properties". Excluded from these restrictions are taxpayers whose principal business consists of leasing or renting leasing properties (or of both renting or leasing such properties and also of selling or servicing property of the same general description) provided that at least 90% of the taxpayer's gross revenue is derived from such principal business.

Leasing property is defined in ITR 1100(17) as a depreciable property that is used principally for the purpose of gaining or producing gross revenue that is rent, royalty or leasing revenue. In VD 2004-0090591E5, the CRA states:

> The word "principally" in the definition of leasing property in subsection 1100(17) of the Regulations means "primarily" or "chiefly." In establishing whether a depreciable property is used principally for a given purpose, the determining factor is the proportion of time that the property is used for that purpose. Property used more than 50% of the time for the purpose of gaining or producing gross revenue that is rent, royalty or leasing revenue is considered to be used principally for that purpose.

Specifically excluded from the "leasing property" definition is: rental property referred to in ITR 1100(11)–(14) (see ¶7165); a computer tax shelter property; a certified feature film referred to in Class 10(w) or 12(n); and depreciable property acquired via a rollover in various circumstances where the property was not a leasing property of the vendor.

The amount of CCA that may be deducted in respect of a taxpayer's leasing property is limited to the total net rental income from such leasing property and from any other property that would be leasing property if not excluded from that category by ITR 1100(18)–(20). Where leasing properties would fall into the same class as other non-leasing properties of a taxpayer, they are required to be segregated in a separate class.

ITR 1100(15)–(20), 1101(5c), IT-443: Leasing Property, VDs 2011-0395221E5, 2005-0141551E5, 2002-0156515, 2002-0156515, VD 2003-0030597

¶7215 — Specified Leasing Property

Restrictions apply on the deduction of CCA by certain lessors in respect of "specified leasing property". The restrictions relate to a series of rules intended to curtail the use of leasing transactions as a source of tax-assisted financing. Generally, where the rules apply, the lessor is treated as having loaned the lessee an amount equal to the purchase price of the property and lease payments received by the lessor are treated as blended payments of interest and principal on the loan. The rules restrict a lessor's claim for CCA on the leased property to the lesser of the amount of CCA that would otherwise be deductible and the amount of lease payments received, less a calculation of notional interest amount for the year. Effectively, the rules put lessors in the same position as lenders who receive blended payments of principal (non-taxable) and interest (taxable).

ITR 1101(5n) prescribes a separate class in respect of each specified leasing property of the taxpayer, including any additions or alterations included in the same class. Where the restricted CCA deductions do not fully reflect the decline in the economic value of the specified leasing property, the separate class provision will permit a lessor to recognize a terminal loss on the sale of the property.

ITR 1100(1.1)(a)(i)(B) governs the calculation of the notional interest payments. Interest is calculated on the amount of the notional loan outstanding from time to time, compounded semi-annually and not in advance, at the prescribed interest rate in effect at the earlier of the time the property last became a specified leasing property and the time the taxpayer last entered into an agreement to lease the property. Where, however, the lease provides that the rental payments vary according to the prevailing interest rates in effect from time to time, the lessor may elect for the prescribed rate in effect at the beginning of the period for which the interest is being calculated to apply. The lessor must make the election in respect of all of the property subject to that lease in the lessor's return for the taxation year in which the lease was entered into. There is no prescribed election form. ITR 1100(1.1)(a)(i)(B) states the election should be made in the taxpayer's return of income.

"Specified leasing property" is defined as tangible, depreciable property, other than "exempt property", used by the taxpayer, or by a non-arm's length person, principally (i.e., more than 50%) for the purpose of gaining or producing gross revenue that is rent or leasing revenue, and that is the subject of an arm's length lease. However, property excluded from being "specified leasing property" if it is the subject of a lease for a term of one year or less, or where the tangible property that is the subject of the lease has an aggregate fair market value (calculated as of the time the lease was entered into) of $25,000 or less.

Intangible property is excluded from the definition of "specified leasing property" in ITR 1100(1.11). Intangible property includes systems software, certain certified productions or feature films, and certain computer software.

"Exempt property, which is excluded from the specified leasing rules is, for the most part, property in respect of which the applicable CCA rate is approximately equal to the economic depreciation rate and, accordingly, is not normally leased as a means of tax-assisted financing. Specifically, "exempt property" includes:

- General-purpose office furniture and equipment (including mobile office equipment such as cell phones and pagers) other than any individual asset having a capital cost in excess of $1 million;

- General-purpose electronic data-processing equipment and ancillary data-processing equipment other than any individual asset having a capital cost in excess of $1 million;

- Furniture, appliances, television or radio receivers, telephones, furnaces, hot water heaters, and other similar properties designed for residential use;

- Automobiles of all kinds, including station wagons, vans, pickup trucks, ambulances, funeral vehicles, taxis, and rental vehicles;

- Trucks or tractors designed for hauling freight on highways, and trailers designed to be hauled under normal operating conditions by the truck or tractor;

- Buildings and component parts (such as electric wiring, plumbing, sprinkler systems, air-conditioning equipment, heating equipment, lighting fixtures, elevators, and escalators) other than, under certain conditions, a building leased to a tax-exempt person;

- Vessel mooring space; and

- Railway cars or a rail suspension device designed to carry trailers that are designed for both highway and railway tracks.

Where general-purpose office furniture and equipment is owned by two or more persons or partnerships, the capital cost of the property to each person or partnership is deemed to equal the total capital cost of the property to all the owners of the property for purposes of the $1-million threshold referred to above.

Applicable to leases entered into after March 4, 2010, the specified leasing rules apply to otherwise exempt property that is the subject of a lease to a government or other tax-exempt entity or to a non-resident (see ITR 1100(1.13)(a.1)). Such a lease, however, continues to be exempt if the total value of the property that is the subject of the lease is less than $1 million. An anti-avoidance rule in ITR 1100(1.13)(a.2) applies if it may reasonably be considered that one of the purposes of dividing property (or a class of property) among separate leases is to meet the $1 million exception. Based on the October 2012 Technical Notes, these rules were apparently added because Finance had concerns that some taxpayers were "exploiting" the exemptions from the specified leasing rules by leasing exempt property (and claiming CCA in respect of that property) to a lessee who was not subject to Canadian income tax and could not make use of CCA claims either because the lessee was tax-exempt or non-resident.

ITA 16.1(1) provides special rules which may apply in computing the income of a lessee of property, other than prescribed property, leased for a term of more than one year from an arm's length person who is resident in Canada or who carries on business in Canada through a permanent establishment. These special rules apply only where the lessor and lessee jointly elect in a prescribed form that is filed by the lessee with the T1 return for the year in which the lease was entered into. Where an election is made, a lessee is deemed to have purchased the leased property and to have borrowed the purchase price from the lessor, entitling the lessee to deduct both the notional interest payments and CCA.

A lessee would normally not elect under ITA 16.1(1) unless it anticipates other income against which to deduct the increased losses.

ITR 4302 prescribes the interest rate in effect for the particular month for the purposes of ITA 16.1(1)(d). The CRA posts the rate on its website at: canada.ca/en/revenue-agency/services/tax/rates.html.

Special rules apply to breakdowns, replacements, additions, alterations, and renegotiations of leases where the specified leasing rules apply. ITR 1100(1.17) provides a continuity rule applicable when a lessor replaces leased property, for example, in the event of the destruction or breakdown of the property.

The provision applies where the substituted property is property similar to the originally leased property, the property is provided for the remaining term of the lease, and the amounts payable by the lessee for the use of, or the right to use, the replacement property are the same as the rental payments in respect of the original property. In these circumstances, the original property is deemed to have ceased to be the subject of the lease at the time of the replacement, the replacement property is deemed to have been leased to the lessee at the same time and for the same term as the original property, the original principal amount of the notional loan is deemed to be unchanged, the CCA available to the lessor in respect of the original property prior to its becoming a specified leasing property is unchanged, and the amounts received as rent from leasing the original property are considered to have been rent received from leasing the replacement property.

ITR 1100(1.19) applies when the lessor makes an addition or alteration to specified leasing property and, in consequence, the aggregate amount of rental income receivable by the lessor is increased. In effect, the provision creates a separate class of specified leasing property constituting the fair market value of improvements or alterations.

Where a lease is renegotiated otherwise than by reason of an addition or alteration to the leased property by the lessor and, in consequence, the rental payments by the lessee are altered, ITA 1100(1.2) provides that the original lease is deemed to have expired and the renegotiated lease is deemed to be a new lease of the property entered into at that time. The lease period before the renegotiation does not cause the property to be deemed to be the subject of a lease of more than one year.

An anti-avoidance rule deems property to be the subject of a lease with a term of more than one year if the property is actually leased for a period of more than one year by the lessee, a non-arm's length person, or a combination of such persons, or if it is reasonable, having regard to all the circumstances, to conclude that the lessor knew or ought to have known that the lessee and/or non-arm's length persons would lease the property for more than one year. Another anti-avoidance rule is intended to ensure that lessors cannot avoid the limitation on the deduction of CCA by entering into multiple leases to meet the $25,000 threshold.

ITA 16.1, ITR 1100(1.1)–(1.3), 1100(2)(v), 1101(5n), IT-443, VDs 2013-0516251E5, 2013-0478091E5, 2010-0384021E5, 2010-0379411E5, 2008-0284691E5, 9323875, Wong et al., "Tax Implications of Asset Securitizations," *Report of the Proceedings of the Sixty-Seventh Tax Conference*, 2015 Conference Report (Toronto: Canadian Tax Foundation, 2016), 12:1-29

¶7220 — Lease Transactions

The determination of whether a contract between two parties is a lease agreement or a sales contract for tax purposes is determined based on the legal relationship created by the terms of the agreement. Formerly, the CRA's administrative position regarding the distinction between a lease and a sale was set out in IT-233R, which was cancelled by ITTN-21.

The CRA has indicated it may apply the GAAR to leasing transactions it considers to be abusive. For example, in ITTN-21, the CRA states:

> [T]he determination of whether a contract is a lease or sale is based on the legal relationship created by the terms of the agreement, rather than on any attempt to ascertain the underlying economic reality. Therefore, in the absence of sham, it is our view that a lease is a lease and a sale is a sale. However, notwithstanding the legal relationship, GAAR may be used to assess cases in which there is an avoidance transaction that results in a misuse or an abuse of provisions of the Act.

Shell Canada Limited, [1999] 4 C.T.C. 313, 1999 D.T.C. 5682 (SCC), *Construction Bérou Inc*, [2000] 2 C.T.C. 174 (FCA), *Terexcavation Antoine Grant Inc*, 2002 CarswellNat 5183 (TCC), *Chibougamau Lumber Limitée*, [1973] C.T.C. 2174 (TRB), VDs 2004-0100771E5, 2002-0138875, 2001-0115657, 2001-0067665, 2000-EM20425.

¶7221 — Lease Options

A special rule deals with an acquisition by a taxpayer where the taxpayer or a non-arm's length person was previously entitled to a deduction in computing income in respect of any amount paid or payable (normally rent) for the use of or the right to use the property. In such a case, the amount paid (i.e., the rent) may be "recaptured" if the property is subsequently sold for a profit.

This rule would normally apply upon the acquisition by a taxpayer of property in respect of which the taxpayer previously paid rent. Under these rules, the ITA deems land to be a depreciable property, included in Class 36. Each Class 36 property is deemed to be included in a separate class. CCA may not be claimed in respect of Class 36 property.

For example, equipment is leased for a three-year term for $250 per month with an option to purchase at the end of the term for $4,000. At the end of the term of the lease, the property is worth $21,000. The lessee purchases the equipment for the $4,000 option price and immediately sells it for $21,000. Total rent of $9,000 has been paid and deducted in respect of the lease. The cost to the purchaser is deemed by ITA 13(5.2)(a) to be the lesser of: i) fair market value ($21,000), and ii) actual cost plus rent paid ($13,000). Pursuant to ITA 13(5.2)(b), the excess of $13,000 over the actual cost of the property ($4,000) is added to the "total depreciation" allowed in respect of property of the class. Assuming there is no other property in that class, $9,000 is subject to recapture when the property is sold for $21,000, and there is also a capital gain of $8,000 ($21,000 - $13,000). But for the enactment of ITA 13(5.2), the capital gain would have been $17,000 ($21,000 - $4,000).

ITA 13(5.2), 1101(5g), IT-233R (cancelled), VD 5-8003, D. Gilbert, "Principles of Leasing," *2000 Prairie Provinces Tax Conference*, (Toronto: Canadian Tax Foundation, 2000), 7:1–51

¶7222 — *Lease-Leasebacks and Similar Arrangements*

ITA 13(5.4) ensures similar treatment to that imposed described under ¶7221 where a taxpayer acquires property and subsequently incurs an expense (such as rent) for the use of the property. This may occur on a lease-leaseback transaction (for example, where land owned by a taxpayer is leased to a developer who constructs a building thereon and leases it back to the taxpayer). The taxpayer would pay rent for the use of the property throughout the term of the lease. Pursuant to ITA 13(5.4), the rental payments are, within certain limits, added to the capital cost of the property and deemed to have been claimed previously as depreciation. Therefore, on subsequent disposition of the property at a profit, the rental payments would be included in income as CCA recapture. ITA 13(5.4) does not apply where the taxpayer disposed of the property to a person with whom the taxpayer was not dealing at arm's length and that person was subject to the provisions of ITA 13(5.2) with respect to the acquisition by that person of the property.

ITA 13(5.4)

¶7225 — **Mining Projects (Classes 41, 41.2)**

Most machinery, equipment and structures used in mining projects acquired before March 21, 2013 are included in Class 41. Such property acquired after that date is generally included in either Class 41 or Class 41.2. The CCA rate applicable to Class 41 and Class 41.2 property is 25%; however, in addition to regular CCA, an accelerated CCA deduction is available in respect of assets acquired for new mines (Class 41(a), 41.2(a)), as well as in respect of assets acquired for major mine expansions (i.e., those that increase the capacity of a mine by at least 25%).

Additionally, accelerated CCA applies to eligible assets acquired in a taxation year for use in a project to the extent that the cost of those assets exceeds 5% of the gross revenue for the year from the mine or project (i.e., minor mine expansion projects; Class 41(a.1), 41.2(a)). The additional allowances allow a taxpayer to claim up to 100% of the remaining cost of eligible assets, not exceeding the taxpayer's income for the year from the project (calculated after deducting regular CCA but before making any deduction under paragraph 1100(1)(y) or (ya) or ITA 65, 66, 66.1, 66.2 or 66.7). Separate classes are required to be maintained for each mine; however, where a property is used in two or more mines, that property must be included in a separate Class. The separate class provisions do not apply where the additional allowance provisions are not applicable. As announced in Budget 2013, the additional CCA provided in relation to certain properties acquired for use in a new mine or as part of an eligible mine expansion is being phased out. To facilitate these measures, Class 41.2 was added.

Class 41.2 includes property that would otherwise be included in Class 41(a) or (a.1) (related to new mines or qualifying expansions) if the property was acquired before March 21, 2013. Property that is generally not eligible for accelerated CCA (i.e., property described in Class 41(a.3)–(d)) continues to be included in Class 41. ITR 1101(4h) prescribes a separate class for multiple mine properties that are included in Class 41.2(a) and ITR 1101(4g) provides for a separate class for single mine properties that are included in Class 41.2(a). These separate classes of properties remain eligible for the full accelerated CCA until 2016. Beginning in the 2017 taxation year, only 90% of the additional CCA amount is deductible; this percentage decreases to 80% in 2018, 60% in 2019, 30% in 2020, and 0% for 2021 and subsequent years (see ITR 1100(1)(y.2) (single mines) and (ya.2) (multiple mines)).

As a transitional measure, 100% of the additional amount of accelerated CCA continues to be deductible in respect of the cost of property, referred to as "eligible mine development property" (ITR 1104(2)), acquired after March 20, 2013 and before 2018 for the purpose of gaining or producing income: 1) from a new mine or an expansion of a mine, if the property was acquired under a written agreement entered into by the taxpayer before March 21, 2013, 2) from a new mine, if either the construction of the new mine or the engineering and design work for the construction of the new mine was started by, or on behalf of, the taxpayer before March 21, 2013, or 3) from an expansion of a mine, if either the construction for the expansion of the mine or the engineering and design work for the construction of the expansion of the mine was started by, or on behalf of, the taxpayer before March 21, 2013. For this purpose, obtaining permits or regulatory approvals, conducting environmental assessments, community consultations or impact benefit studies, and similar activities are not considered construction or engineering and design work. Eligible mine development property is included in Class 41 rather than in the Class 41.2. Accelerated CCA may continue to be claimed in respect of property included in Class 41(a) or (a.1).

For the purpose of determining the maximum additional CCA that may be claimed, the income of the particular mine or group of mines includes income reasonably attributable to the processing of ore from a resource owned by the taxpayer to a stage not beyond the prime metal stage, processing iron ore to any stage not beyond the pellet stage or equivalent, and to any income from the transportation, by use of property falling into Class 10(m) (i.e., railway track and grading and ancillary machinery and equipment including conveying, loading, unloading or storage machinery or equipment), of the output from a mineral resource or iron ore of the taxpayer that has been processed by the taxpayer to any stage not beyond that of the prime metal.

For inclusion in Class 41(a), the new mine or major expansion criterion must be satisfied. Otherwise, such property is included in Class 41(b) (except to the extent included in Class 41(a.1) where the minor expansion criterion is met). Generally, a mine is regarded as having been "the subject of a major expansion" where the greatest designed capacity (measured in weight of input of ore) of the mill processing the ore from the mine increases by at least 25% as a result of the mine expansion. Applicable to expansions of mines commencing after June 18, 1987, a mine may also be regarded as having been subject to a major expansion where the Minister of National Revenue, in consultation with the Minister of Energy, Mines and Resources, determines that the greatest designed capacity of the mine (measured in weight of output of ore) immediately after the expansion was not less than 25% greater than its greatest capacity immediately before the expansion.

Class 41(a.1) provides a formula for calculating the percentage of the capital cost of each of the taxpayer's properties described in Classes 41(a.1)(i)–(iv) that qualify for the accelerated CCA.

The meaning of a "new mine" is considered in: *North Bay Mica Co*, [1958] C.T.C. 208 (SCC) (new mine exemption held applicable in respect of new operations commenced on an abandoned mining property), *Bermah Mines Ltd* (1966), 41 Tax A.B.C. 359 (new mine status recognized re ore pocket discovered on worked out gold and silver property); *MacLean Mining Co Ltd*, [1970] C.T.C. 264 (SCC) (new ore body, worked by extension of shafts from existing mine, held not a new mine, though it might conceivably have been developed as such); *Marbridge Mines Ltd*, [1971] C.T.C. 442 (Exch) (appellant's No 2 mine, all the physical workings for which were separate and distinct from those of its No 1 mine, held a new mine despite common management and staff); and *Bethlehem Copper Corp Ltd*, [1973] C.T.C. 345 (FCA) (new mine status recognized for second ore body requiring different techniques and separate facilities though serviced by same labour force and crushing plant (; aff'd [1974] C.T.C. 707 (SCC)).

ITR 1100(1)(y), (y.2), (ya), (ya.2), 1101(4c), (4d), (4g), (4h), 1104(1)–(8), VD 2010-0362481R3, *Extractive Sector Transparency Measures Act* (nrcan.gc.ca/mining-materials/cstma/18180), PWC, *"Canadian Mining Taxation"*, pwc.com/ca/, kpmg.com/ca/en/home.html (industries, mining), Gowling WLG, "Guide to Doing Business in Canada: Mining", gowlingwlg.com/en/canada/

¶7230 — Oil Sands Projects (Classes 41, 41.1)

As mentioned above, accelerated CCA claims are available for mines including, before 2014, oil sands mines (such benefits are not available in respect of conventional oil and gas wells). Most machinery, equipment and structures used in oil sands projects are included in Class 41.1. Formerly, such properties were included in Class 41. Class 41.1(a) applies to property acquired after March 18, 2007 and before 2016 where the property would have been included in Class 41(a), (a.1) or (a.2) had it been acquired before March 19, 2007 (other than property acquired before 2012 and included in Class 41(a), (a.1) or (a.2) that is required to complete a "specified development phase" of an "oil sands project").

As in the case of mining properties discussed above, properties included in Class 41.1(a) are eligible for accelerated CCA rates; however, for properties used in oil sands projects (both mining and in-situ), the accelerated rates only apply until 2014. More specifically, the percentage allowed as accelerated CCA in each calendar year is 90% in 2011, 80% in 2012, 60% in 2013, and 30% in 2014 of the amount otherwise allowable as accelerated CCA.

No accelerated CCA is allowed after 2014. ITR 1101(4e) prescribes a separate class for single mine properties that are included in Class 41.1(a) and ITR 1101(4f) prescribes a separate class for multiple mine properties that are included in Class 41.1(a). Most property used in an oil sands project acquired after March 18, 2007 that is not included in Class 41.1(a) is included in Class 41.1(b). An accelerated CCA deduction is not available in respect of property included in Class 41.1(b).

Access to accelerated CCA continues to apply for oil sands assets acquired before March 19, 2007. Additionally, accelerated CCA is available without any phase-out in respect of "specified oil sands property" acquired before 2012 that is included in Class 41(a), (a.1), or (a.2) and is required to complete a "specified development phase" of a taxpayer's "oil sands project." A "specified development phase" is defined with reference to a threshold level of activity involving a "designated asset" that must have been acquired or under construction before March 19, 2007. In determining whether an oil sands property is required for a "specified development phase" to reach completion, reference is made to the planned level of average daily output from the phase of the "oil sands project".

Oil sands projects typically take more than three years; however, CCA can be claimed before assets are fully constructed by virtue of available-for-use rolling start rules discussed under ¶7125 (an election must be made in the third year of the project to benefit from this rule).

ITR 1101(4c)–(4f), 1100(1)(y)-(ya.1), 1104(5)–(8.1), IT-476R (paras. 10–14), VDs 2004-0105021R3, 2004-0106281R3, 2006-0188921R3, kpmg.com/ca/(industries, energy), pwc.com/ca (industries, energy)

¶7235 — Clean Energy Equipment (Classes 43.1, 43.2)

The accelerated CCA rules introduced in the 2018 Fall Economic Statement effectively increase the CCA rate for specified clean energy property included in Class 43.1 or 43.2 to 100% in the year the property becomes available for use, for qualifying property acquired after November 20, 2018 and before 2024. The 100% CCA rate is reduced to 75% for property that become available for use after 2023 and before 2026, and to 55% for property that become available for use after 2025 and before 2028. An accelerated CCA deduction is not available for property that becomes available for use after 2027 (see also ¶7006).

Class 43.1 provides a detailed list of eligible clean energy equipment that generates energy in the form of electricity or heat by using a renewable energy source (e.g., wind, solar, small hydro), using waste fuel (e.g., landfill gas, wood waste, manure), or making efficient use of fossil fuels (e.g., high efficiency cogeneration systems that produce electricity and heat simultaneously). An accelerated CCA rate of 50% is provided under Class 43.2 generally in respect of assets described in Class 43.1 that are acquired after February 22, 2005 and before 2025. To qualify for inclusion in Class 43.2, the equipment must: 1) be situated in Canada; 2) be acquired by a taxpayer for use by the taxpayer (or to be leased by the taxpayer to a lessee for use by the lessee) for the purpose of earning income from a business carried on in Canada or from property situated in Canada; and 3) must not have been used for any purpose whatever before it was acquired by the taxpayer unless certain exceptions are met.

Eligibility for inclusion in Class 43.2 must generally be determined annually based on the use of the property in the taxation year. In a particular taxation year, if a property included in Class 43.2 no longer satisfies the conditions for inclusion, ITA 13(5) requires that the UCC of the property be transferred to the class in which the property would otherwise have been included. Similarly, if in a subsequent year, the property again satisfies the requirements for inclusion in Class 43.2, ITA 13(5) would apply to reclassify the property into the particular class as of the commencement of that year.

Folio S3-F8-C2: *Tax Incentives for Clean Energy Equipment*, discusses the tax measures intended to encourage investments in qualifying clean energy generation and conservation projects.

ITA 13(18.1), 241(4)(d)(vi.1), ITR 1100(2), 1100(24)–(29), 1104(13)–(15), 1101(5m), 1219, ITR 8200.1, VDs 2016-0670661E5, 2016-0635031E5, 2015-0568271E5, 2015-0565761E5, 2014-0521261I7, 2013-0478091E5, 2013-0486441E5, 2012-0469941E5, Sinclair, "Resource Taxation Update," *2007 British Columbia Tax Conference*, (Vancouver: Canadian Tax Foundation, 2007), 13C:1-2

¶7300 — Eligible Capital Property

Some business-related expenditures to acquire intangible property, referred to before 2017 as "eligible capital property" (ECP), were capital in nature but did not qualify as depreciable property. Such expenditures were referred to as "eligible capital expenditures" (ECEs). To qualify as an ECE, the expenditure had to be incurred on account of capital and for the purpose of gaining or producing income from the taxpayer's business. Common examples of ECP included purchased goodwill and customer lists. The cost of eligible capital property was recognized in a pool system similar to the CCA system. However, only three-quarters of ECEs were included in the pool and only three-quarters of proceeds of disposition of property included in the pool was subtracted from the pool upon a disposition of ECP (see ¶7310). Also, only 50% of gains on dispositions of ECP were included in income.

Former ITA 14, IT-123R6: *Transactions Involving Eligible Capital Property*, IT-386R: *Eligible Capital Amounts*, VD 2016-0637031E5 (ECP is not "capital property")

¶7305 — Eligible Capital Property Additions (Applicable before 2017)

Before 2017, on Line 2 of the chart provided in Chapter 5 of Guide T4002, taxpayers entered the total cost of ECP acquired during the year multiplied by 75%. For examples of former eligible capital expenditures, see under ¶7335.

Former ITA 14, 20(1)(hh.1), 80(7), 87(2)(f), 88(1)(e.2), *Brooke Bond Foods Ltd.*, [1984] C.T.C. 115 (FCTD), *International Nickel Co.*, [1969] C.T.C. 106 (Exch), *Léopold Lague Inc.*, [1981] C.T.C. 348 (FCTD), *Services Farmico Inc.*, [1979] C.T.C. 3012 (TRB), IT-143R3, IT-467R2 (para. 18), IT-350R, IT-477, IT-187, VDs 2010-0369801E5, 2009-0345121E5, 2002-0151405

¶7310 — Eligible Capital Amounts (Applicable before 2017)

Before 2017, three-quarters of all net proceeds of disposition in respect of the sale of ECP in the taxation year was subtracted from the ECE pool. Proceeds of disposition in respect of an ECP were referred to as an eligible capital amount.

Examples of situations in which an eligible capital amount may have been received included: sale of a franchise or licence for an unlimited period; sale of a business (except in the case of a sale of shares) to the extent the proceeds are attributable to goodwill (goodwill may include reputation, services of employees, favourable commercial contracts, trademarks or trade names, favourable financial relationships, and managements performance record); and amounts received for disclosure of and right to use a secret process.

Former ITA 14, VDs 2010-0366321I7, 2011-0429691I7, 2013-0510371E5

¶7315 — Gain on Dispositions of Eligible Capital Property (Applicable before 2017)

Before 2017, any excess of the negative amount over recaptured CEC deductions was treated as appreciation in the value of the assets in the pool and included in income for tax purposes at the capital gains inclusion rate (i.e., 50% of the gain is taxable) on Line 8230 of Form T2125. This was achieved by multiplying the excess of the negative amount in the CEC account in excess of recaptured CEC deductions by two-thirds. In this way, the excess was converted from a three-quarters recognition rate to a one-half recognition rate consistent with that for gains on capital property generally (i.e., 75% × 2/3 = 50%).

Former ITA 14, ITR 600, IT-259R4 (paras. 7, 15), IT-442R, VD 2002-0133797, Bauer et al., "Eligible Capital Expenditures: Some Practical Issues," *2013 Conference Report*, (Toronto: Canadian Tax Foundation, 2014), 11: 1–30

¶7320 — Restrictive Covenants

In *Fortino*, [2000] 1 C.T.C. 349 (FCA), and *Manrell*, [2003] 3 C.T.C. 50 (FCA), the Court characterized payments received by the taxpayers for entering into a non-competition agreement on the sale of a business as giving rise to a non-taxable gain. Characterization as eligible capital amounts was precluded by the fact that the taxpayers were only shareholders of the corporation and did not carry on the business themselves. In response to the latter decisions, subject to certain transitional rules, ITA 56.4 was generally added applicable to amounts received or receivable after October 7, 2003 to provide for a series of technical rules that apply to amounts that are received or receivable in respect of a "restrictive covenant". A "restrictive covenant" is broadly defined in ITA 56.4(1) and includes more than what would typically be considered non-competition payments in practice. For example, the CRA has taken the position that definition is broad enough to potentially include signing bonuses, exclusivity clauses, and break fees.

Subject to three narrow exceptions in ITA 56.4(3), ITA 56.4(2) provides that amounts receivable by a taxpayer in respect of a "restrictive covenant" granted by the taxpayer must be included in computing income. A full amount must be included in the grantor's income whether the amount is received or receivable by the grantor or by a taxpayer with whom the grantor does not deal at arm's length. Also, the full amount received or receivable in the taxation year in which the covenant is granted must be included in income regardless of whether a portion of the amount will be received in a subsequent taxation year.

The three exceptions available under ITA 56.4(3) are only applicable if the covenant is given to a person with whom the grantor deals at arm's length, the grantor of the covenant is the person who is entitled to receive the payment, and consideration has been allocated by the parties to the restrictive covenant.

First, ITA 56.4(3)(a) provides that ITA 56.4(2) does not apply to an amount if ITA 5 or 6 applies to include the amount in computing a taxpayer's employment income for the year (see ITA 6(3.1) and VDs 2015-0599581E5 and 2014-0526931E5).

Second, ITA 56.4(3)(b) provides that ITA 56.4(2) does not apply to a restrictive covenant granted by a non-arm's length taxpayer (determined without reference to ITA 251(5)(b)) if the amount would (if the ITA were read without reference to ITA 56.4) be required to be included in the pod of a property included in Class 14.1, or an amount to which ITA 13(38) (ECP elimination transitional rules) applies, in respect of the business to which the restrictive covenant relates, and the taxpayer and the purchaser elect in prescribed form to apply ITA 56.4(3)(b) in respect of the amount (regarding the manner in which the election is to be filed, see ITA 56.4(13)). The latter exception generally applies to an asset sale of a business (see also para. 5 of IT-330R). It is important to highlight than an exception is not available if a shareholder receives an amount as a grantor of a covenant as, in such a case, the grantor would not be the person selling the business. Where this exception is available, the signing of the election by the purchaser may create significant tax savings for the vendor and the purchaser may, therefore, be able to negotiate a reduced sale price.

Third, ITA 56.4(3)(c) provides that ITA 56.4(2) does not apply to an amount to the extent that the amount is additional proceeds of disposition from the disposition of an "eligible interest" (i.e., a capital property of a taxpayer that is a partnership interest in a partnership that carries on a business, a share of the capital stock of a corporation that carries on a business, or a share of the capital stock of a corporation 90% of the fair market value of which is attributable to eligible interests in one other corporation) if the following conditions are met: the amount must directly relate to the taxpayer's disposition of an eligible interest in the partnership or corporation that carries on the business to which the restrictive covenant relates (or that is an eligible interest by virtue of paragraph (c) of the definition where the other corporation referred to in that paragraph carries on the business to which the restrictive covenant relates); the disposition of the eligible interest must be to the purchaser of the restrictive covenant (or to a person related to that purchaser); the amount received or receivable must be consideration for an undertaking by the taxpayer not to provide property or services in competition with the property or services provided by the purchaser (or by a person related to the purchaser); the restrictive covenant must be reasonably considered to have been granted to maintain or preserve the value of the eligible interest disposed of to the purchaser; to add the restrictive covenant amount to the proceeds of disposition of an eligible interest that is a share, there cannot be a redemption, acquisition or cancellation of the share to which ITA 84(3) applies. Subsection 84(3) provides that on the redemption, acquisition or cancellation of its shares, a corporation is treated as having paid a dividend); and the taxpayer and the purchaser of the restrictive covenant are required to jointly elect in prescribed form to apply this exception (see ITA 56.4(13) regarding the manner in which the election is to be filed).

As ITA 56.4(2) is generally punitive in nature (i.e., as a full income inclusion is required), it would normally be beneficial for a vendor and purchaser not to allocate any amount to a restrictive covenant in a purchase and sale agreement. However, ITA 68(c) allows the CRA to revise the allocation of proceeds between assets, services, and restrictive covenants when such allocation is regarded as unreasonable. This reallocation affects both the grantor of the restrictive covenant and the grantee, and can apply even in situations where the parties have not allocated any consideration for the restrictive covenant. It should be noted that historically, it has been common for parties to allocate nil consideration to a restrictive covenant and business purchase and sale agreements.

In *Wagner*, 2013 CarswellNat 120 (FCA); aff'd 2012 CarswellNat 2823 (TCC), the Court held that the value of certain non-competition agreements with respect to a share sale was nil rather than $4M as argued by the taxpayer. ITA 56.4 did not apply to the taxation years in question and the taxpayer argued that the restrictive covenant receipts were non-taxable. At paragraph 45 of the TCC decision, the Court stated that the value attributed to the non-competition covenants appeared to be "clearly unreasonable in the circumstances".

If ITA 56.4(5) applies in respect of a restrictive covenant granted by a taxpayer, ITA 68 cannot apply to deem consideration to have been received or be receivable by the taxpayer for the restrictive covenant. However, ITA 56.4(5) only applies if the conditions set forth in ITA 56.4(6) or (7) are met.

Where the conditions in ITA 56.4(6) are met, the provision effectively prevents ITA 68 from applying where an arm's length employee grants a restrictive covenant without receiving any consideration in order to allow the sale of a business. ITA 56.4(12) provides that if ITA 56.4(5) applies in respect of restrictive covenant granted by a taxpayer such that ITA 68 does not apply to allocate consideration to the taxpayer's grant of a restrictive covenant, "for greater certainty", the amount referred to in ITA 56.4(6)(f) (i.e., the amount received by vendors other than the taxpayer) is to be added in computing the amount received or receivable by those vendors as consideration for the disposition of the interest referred to in ITA 56.4(6)(b) and the amount that can reasonably be regarded as being in part consideration received or receivable for shares of a target corporation or family corporation (as referred to in ITA 56.4(7)(c)) is to be added in computing the consideration received or receivable for disposing of the shares.

ITA 56.4(7) generally applies where a vendor grants a restrictive covenant that is a non-compete agreement in conjunction with a realization of a goodwill amount or the disposition of property. If, for example, ITA 56.4(7) applies to the grant of a non-competition covenant that directly relates to a transfer of goodwill by the vendor, no amount is required to be allocated to the restrictive covenant under ITA 68 provided the amount is included in the vendor's goodwill amount. There are various conditions in ITA 56.4(7) that must be satisfied for ITA 68 to be made inapplicable. The conditions that must be met depend on whether the grant is made on an arm's length basis or to an eligible individual.

Regarding the tax treatment of the purchaser of a restrictive covenant, pursuant to ITA 56.4(4), an amount paid for a restrictive covenant is:

1) Considered to be wages paid or payable by the purchaser to an employee if the amount is required because of ITA 5 or 6 to be included in computing the income of an employee of the purchaser;

2) Before 2017, considered to be incurred by the purchaser on account of capital for the purpose of the "eligible capital expenditure" definition and not to be an amount paid for all other purposes of the ITA if an election has been made under ITA 56.4(3)(b) in respect of the amount. After 2016, ITA 56.4(4)(b) provides that if an election has been made under ITA 56.4(3)(b) in respect of the amount, the amount is to be considered to be an outlay incurred by the purchaser on account of capital for the purpose of determining the cost of the property or for the purposes of ITA 13(35) (deemed acquisition of goodwill), as the case may be, and not to be an amount paid or payable for all other purposes of the ITA; or

3) Included in computing the cost to the purchaser of an "eligible interest" and not considered an amount paid or payable for all other purposes of the ITA if: i) an election has been made under ITA 56.4(3)(c) in respect of the amount, and ii) the amount relates to the purchaser's acquisition of property that is (immediately after the acquisition) an "eligible interest" of the purchaser.

ITA 56.4 does not deal with the tax treatment applicable to the purchaser of a restrictive covenant when such payment is included in computing the income of the recipient under ITA 56.4(2). In any case in respect of which ITA 56.4(4) does not apply, the general rules of the ITA are applicable to the treatment of the purchaser of the covenant.

> A vendor should consider including a provision in a purchase and sale agreement that requires the purchaser to file a joint election under ITA 56.4 if requested to do so (such an election should not have adverse tax consequences for the purchaser but may be beneficial to the vendor).

VDs 2015-0618601E5, 2013-0495691C6, 2010-0366321I7, Joint Committee Submission 2006-01-30, TEI Submission 2006-02-10 — *TEI: Legislative Proposals Relating to the Treatment of Restrictive Covenants*, Coburn, "Practical Strategies for Dealing with the Restrictive Covenant Provisions," *Report of the Proceedings of the Sixty-Sixth Tax Conference*, 2014 Conference Report (Toronto: Canadian Tax Foundation, 2015), 8:1-29, Peters et al., "Deal Points: Restrictive Covenants and the Assumption of Liabilities", *2013 Ontario Tax Conference*, (Toronto: Canadian Tax Foundation, 2013)

¶7325 — Class 14.1

¶7330 — *Overview*

Effective January 1, 2017, the eligible capital property regime, including ITA 14 and 20(1)(b), were repealed and replaced with CCA Class 14.1. Each CEC pool balance of a taxpayer was transferred to a new Class 14.1 on January 1, 2017. After 2016, ECEs that would normally be added to the CEC pool are instead included in CCA Class 14.1 at a 100% inclusion rate. A 5% CCA rate on a declining-balance basis applies to Class 14.1 assets; however, as a transitional measure, for the first 10 years of the new regime, the depreciation rate is 7% in respect of ECEs incurred before 2017. Under the new regime, every business is considered to have goodwill associated with it, even if there has been no purchased goodwill (ITA 13(34), (35)). Expenditures and receipts that would have been ECEs or eligible capital receipts under the former regime that do not relate to a specific property are accounted for under the new regime by adjusting the capital cost of the goodwill of the business. Otherwise, the regular CCA rules apply to Class 14.1, including the rules relating to recapture, terminal losses, capital gains, depreciation, and the half-year rule. Upon a disposition of a Class 14.1 property for more than its original cost, the excess is treated as a regular capital gain.

New ITA 20(1)(b) allows for the deduction of incorporation expenses of up to $3,000 per corporation in respect of incorporation expenses incurred after 2016. Incorporation expenses in excess of $3,000 are included in Class 14.1.

The CRA has indicated that the replacement property rollover rules will generally not apply to Class 14.1 property given such property will generally not be "former business property" as defined in ITA 248(1) ("former business property" must be "real or immovable property") (VD 2016-0666901E5). The former ECP replacement property rules were repealed effective January 1, 2017.

There are various transitional rules dealing with issues related to the adoption of the new regime, including rules governing the future sale of former ECP so that excess recapture will not result, dispositions of ECP before 2017 during a taxation year that straddles January 1, 2017, and non-arm's length dispositions of former ECP which will prevent the use of such transfers to increase the UCC of new Class 14.1.

Paproski, "Effectively Dealing with Eligible Capital Property Under the New Regime," *2017 Prairie Provinces Tax Conference* (Toronto: Canadian Tax Foundation, 2017), 9B:1-25.

¶7335 — *Class 14.1 Properties*

Class 14.1 generally includes goodwill, property that was ECP before 2017, and property acquired after 2016 the cost of which would have been treated as an ECE under the former ECP rules. Specifically, in respect of a business of a corporation, Class 14.1 includes "property" that:

(1) is goodwill;

(2) was ECP of the corporation immediately before 2017 and is owned by the corporation on January 1, 2017; or

(3) is acquired after 2016, other than: (a) property that is tangible or, for civil law, corporeal property; (b) property that is not acquired for the purpose of gaining or producing income from business; (c) property in respect of which any amount is deductible (otherwise than as a result of being included in Class 14.1) in computing the taxpayer's income from the business; (d) property in respect of which any amount is not deductible in computing the taxpayer's income from the business because of any provision of the ITA, other than ITA 18(1)(b), or the ITRs; (e) an interest in a trust; (f) an interest in a partnership; (g) a share, bond, debenture, mortgage, hypothecary claim, note, bill or other similar property; or (h) property that is an interest in or a right to acquire a property described in any of (a) to (h).

In accordance with (3) above, Class 14.1 generally includes intangible properties that would otherwise not be included in any other CCA class (i.e., property that would have been ECP before 2017). The description of property in Class 14.1 is generally consistent with the ECE definition in former ITA 14(5). Property that was formerly included in the ECE pool and that would now be included in Class 14.1 includes:

- purchased goodwill

- customers lists and ledger accounts (unless trade in nature and deductible as a running expense)

- patents, franchises, concessions, and licences for an unlimited life

- PCV trucking licences, radio and television broadcasting licences, taxi cab licences, etc.

- incorporation, reorganization, or amalgamation expenses

- training expenses that are considered to be on capital account

- commission or bonus paid related to the issuance of shares or borrowing of money that are excluded from being deducted as financing fees

- appraisal for the purpose of a purchase or sale of capital property where the property is not acquired or sold

- trademark and copyright costs, etc., where used in a business, except where the costs are deductible under ITA 20(1)(cc)

- milk quotas or other governmental rights or licences

- costs incurred with respect to property where the corporation does not obtain title to the property

- rights of way and easements

- covenants not to compete in situations in which ITA 56.4(4) is not applicable

- damages that are not deductible as a current expense

- transaction costs incurred by purchaser in respect of an aborted share or asset acquisition

- expenditures incurred to put in place a tax-efficient income earning structure

- a farm quota with an unlimited life

As a result of the introduction of Class 14.1, the definition of "property" in ITA 248(1) was amended to provide that the "goodwill" of a business is property for the purposes of the ITA. Goodwill that is acquired when the assets of a business are acquired is a property that is included in Class 14.1(a). This is distinguishable from the deemed acquisition of goodwill under ITA 13(35), which relates to capital expenditures that are not incurred to acquire an identifiable property. The cost of goodwill deemed to have been acquired under ITA 13(35) is added to the cost of the single goodwill property of a business by virtue of ITA 13(34), and to the UCC of the class in respect of the business as a result of ITA 13(21) "undepreciated capital cost" A. Consistent with the former ECE rules, ITA 13(35) does not apply to an outlay or expense that is made for the purpose of gaining or producing income from property.

"Goodwill" is not defined in the ITA. Goodwill included in Class 14.1 includes both goodwill within the normal commercial meaning of the term as developed by jurisprudence, as well as certain outlays not related to property deemed to be acquisitions of goodwill by ITA 13(35). With respect to the meaning of "goodwill" as developed by the Courts, see paragraphs 51 to 58 of *Transalta Corp*, 2012 CarswellNat 124 (FCA). For the CRA's views, see paragraphs 5–7 of IT-143R3. If the shares of a corporation are acquired (i.e., rather than directly acquiring all of the assets of the corporation's business), the price paid for the shares may include an element of consideration for the goodwill of the business; however, goodwill purchased in this way is not a Class 14.1 property in respect of the purchaser (nor are the proceeds taxable to the vendor as proceeds from the sale of Class 14.1 property). If shares are acquired, the cost of goodwill and all other assets acquired are reflected in the ACB of the shares.

ITA 13(34) to (37) provide special rules for dealing with expenditures and receipts of a business that would have adjusted the CEC pool under the former regime. After 2016, such expenditures or receipts are accounted for by adjusting the capital cost of the goodwill of the business. Generally, by virtue of the application of ITA 13(34) to (37) in conjunction with the regular CCA rules:

(1) each identifiable property included in Class 14.1 has a cost that is identifiable, as is the case with other depreciable property;

(2) capital expenditures that do not relate to an identifiable property (or that are to acquire goodwill) are pooled into the cost of a single goodwill property of the business (ITA 13(34), (35)); and,

(3) if a business receives a capital receipt that does not relate to an identifiable property, the receipt is deemed to be the proceeds of disposition of a portion of the goodwill property of the business, the cost of the property disposed of is the cost in the pool (not exceeding the amount of the proceeds), and where the taxpayer continues to carry on the business, the taxpayer is deemed to still have a goodwill property in respect of the business, but the new cost of that property (if any) is the old cost less the proceeds just received.

See the October 2016 Technical Notes for examples illustrating the application of the above rules.

¶7340 — *Opening Class 14.1 Balance*

The opening UCC of Class 14.1 in respect of a business at January 1, 2017 is equal to the amount that would have been the CEC balance in respect of the business at that date (ITA 13(38)). More specifically, ITA 13(38)(a) provides for the total capital cost (at the beginning of January 1, 2017) of all property included in Class 14.1 in respect of the business, each of which was an ECP immediately before January 1, 2017 or is the goodwill property in respect of the business. The total capital cost is relevant for determining the amount of gains or recapture, but is not required to be calculated in order to determine the amount of CCA that may be claimed under Class 14.1, since the UCC on January 1, 2017 is equal the amount that would be the CEC balance on January 1, 2017 (by virtue of the application of ITA 13(38)(a) and (c)).

Pursuant to ITA 13(38)(a), at the beginning of January 1, 2017, the total capital cost of Class 14.1 is deemed to be the amount determined by the formula 4/3 (A + B - C), where:

A   is equal to the positive balance, if any, of the CEC in respect of the business at the beginning of January 1, 2017,

B   is equal to the amount determined for F in the CEC definition in former ITA 14(5) at the beginning of January 1, 2017 (i.e., the amount of deductions taken from the CEC pool that have not been recaptured), and

C   is equal to the negative balance, if any, of the CEC in respect of the business at the beginning of January 1, 2017.

ITA 13(38)(b) provides various rules for allocating that total capital cost as between goodwill property and each identifiable property in Class 14.1 that was an ECP. Although the determination of the total capital cost of Class 14.1 under ITA 13(38)(a) and the capital cost of a particular property under ITA 13(38)(b) applies as of January 1, 2017, these determinations are generally not required to be calculated until property of Class 14.1 is disposed of (i.e., since the total capital cost and individual capital costs are not required to be known in order to calculate the UCC of Class 14.1).

ITA 13(38)(c) ensures that the UCC of Class 14.1 at the beginning of January 1, 2017 is equal to the amount that would be the CEC balance in respect of the business at the beginning of January 1, 2017. ITA 13(38)(c) also ensures that any negative CEC balance is reflected in the calculation of the opening UCC balance of Class 14.1.

See the October 2016 Technical Notes for examples illustrating the application of the above rules.

¶7400 — Resource Pools

ITA 66 to 66.8 are part of an incentive program designed to encourage the search for oil, gas, and minerals in Canada (and, to a somewhat less generous extent, outside Canada) by allowing expenditures incurred in exploring for, developing or producing oil, gas or minerals, and the cost of acquiring resource properties to be deducted in computing income, subject to certain limitations. Special rules are necessary because expenditures of the kind permitted might otherwise be regarded as non-deductible capital expenditures or expenditures laid out prior to the income-earning process rather than in the course of it. The provisions have also been expanded to allow certain expenditures in relation to renewable energy projects to be deducted in computing income.

> Effectively, the determination of whether property is depreciable property is made before the determination of whether the cost of the property is eligible for inclusion in any of the resource pools. Properties included in a depreciable property class are listed in the Depreciable Property Quick Reference Table at the beginning of this Chapter (see ¶7000).

ITA 66.8 restricts the ability of a limited partner to deduct the limited partner's share of resource expenses incurred by the partnership to the limited partner's "at-risk-amount" in respect of the partnership. The rules are similar to those limiting the deduction of limited partnership losses in ITA 96(2.1)–(2.7) (see ¶3620 and ¶9350). Since resource expenses are not deductible at the partnership level, the restrictions in ITA 96(2.1)–(2.7) to limited partnership losses do not apply.

Where a taxpayer invested in an oil, gas, or mining venture in the year but did not actively participate, the taxpayer's exploration and development expenses are deducted on Line 224 (Exploration and development expenses). If the taxpayer actively participated in the venture, the expenses are deducted in the calculation of the taxpayer's net business income on Line 135 (see Chapter 6).

Taxpayers who were passive investors in an oil, gas, or mining venture in the year should complete Form T1229, *Statement of Resource Expenses and Depletion Allowance*. Taxpayers should enter the renounced Canadian exploration and development expenses reported on the taxpayer's T101 and T5013 slips in Part 1 of Form T1229. The amounts calculated on Form T1229 should be transferred to the taxpayer's T1 return as follows:

- A negative CEE or CDE balance from Line A in Part II should be entered on Line 130 (Other income) of the T1 return

- Total exploration and development expenses from Part III should be entered on Line 224 (Exploration and development expenses) of the T1 return

- Eligible resource expenditures qualifying for an ITC as calculated in Part IV should be entered on Line 6717 of Form T2038(IND), *Investment Tax Credit (Individuals)* (see Line 412 at ¶11030)

- Depletion allowances from Part V should be entered on Line 232 (Other deductions) of the T1 return

ITA 65, 66, 66.8, ITR Part XII, 1102(1)(a), PWC, "Oil and Gas Taxation in Canada", pwc.com/ca, KPMG, "Guide to oil and gas taxation in Canada", kpmg.com/ca

¶7405 — Canadian Exploration Expenses (CEE) (Form T1229: Parts II and III)

CEE are defined in ITA 66.1(6) and generally are costs incurred to locate petroleum or mineral deposits or to bring mines into production. CEEs exclude drilling and related costs other than costs incurred in respect of an oil or gas well drilled in an area where a commercial accumulation of oil or gas was not previously known to exist, in which case the costs will be included in CEE only if the well is abandoned within 12 months of its completion or if it is the first well in the area capable of production in commercial quantities (costs incurred in drilling other wells qualify as CDE).

The treatment of pre-production mine development expenses transitioned from being Canadian exploration expenses to being Canadian development expenses over five years as follows:

Year	2013	2014	2015	2106	2017	After 2017
CEE proportion	100%	100%	80%	60%	30%	—
CDE proportion	—	—	20%	40%	70%	100%

Generally, a taxpayer may deduct up to 100% of the taxpayer's cumulative CEE at the end of the taxation year. To the extent that a CEE is not deducted in computing a taxpayer's income, it may be accumulated from year to year in the cumulative CEE account.

Where a taxpayer's cumulative CEE account (Form T1229: Part II, Line A) becomes a negative balance, that balance is included in income on Line 130 (Other income). Among the amounts that reduce cumulative CEE are government incentives that reimburse or otherwise reduce the cost of expenses treated as CEE for tax purposes; amounts receivable as a result of transactions for property or services the original cost of which may reasonably be regarded as having been primarily expenses treated as CEE for tax purposes; and amounts receivable under the terms of a unit agreement which represent a reimbursement of expenses previously incurred by the recipient which were CEE.

ITA 59(3.2), 66(12.1)(a), 66.1, VDs 2012-0472311E5, 2012-0462511E5, 2005-0143221R3, 2005-0119731E5, Carr et al., "What is Depreciable Property?", *Resource Sector Taxation* (Federated Press), Vol. X, No.1, 2017

¶7410 — Canadian Development Expenses (CDE) (Form T1229: Parts II and III)

The general rules relevant to CDE are similar to those applicable to CEE. Eligible expenses are largely restricted to expenses made or incurred for drilling an oil or gas well (unless the expenses qualify as CEE) and the cost of a Canadian resource property (other than any such cost which would constitute a COGPE).

Generally, a taxpayer may deduct up to 30% of the taxpayer's cumulative Canadian development expense pool at the end of a taxation year. In addition, the accelerated investment incentive announced in the 2018 Fall Economic Statement allows an additional first-year deduction for Canadian development expenses that are incurred after November 20, 2018 and before 2028. The additional deduction rates are 15% for taxation years that end before 2024, and 7.5% for taxation years that begin after 2023. The rates are pro-rated for taxation years that straddle the end of 2023. See ¶7006 for more information.

Where a taxpayer's cumulative CDE account (Form T1229: Part II, Line A) becomes a negative balance, that balance is included in income on Line 130 (Other income). The cumulative CDE account is reduced by, among other things, any negative balance in the taxpayer's cumulative COGPE account. The COGPE account is in turn reduced by proceeds of disposition of certain oil and gas resource properties, as well as by equalization payments received under unit agreements in respect of costs that were COGPE for tax purposes and government incentives that reimburse or otherwise reduce the cost of expenses treated as COGPE. The cumulative CDE account is similarly reduced by such government incentives in respect of CDE; by amounts receivable for property or services the original cost of which may reasonably be regarded as having been primarily expenses treated as CDE for tax purposes; and by amounts receivable under the terms of a unit agreement that represent a reimbursement of expenses previously incurred by the recipient and which were CDE for tax purposes.

ITA 66(12.5)(a), 66.2, 59(3.2), VD 2013-0505431R3 (transfer of royalty), Diep, "Expanding Farm-Outs to Royalties", *Resource Sector Taxation* (Federated Press), Vol. X, No.1, 2017

¶7415 — Canadian Oil and Gas Property Expenses (COGPE) (Form T1229: Parts II and III)

The general rules relevant to COGPE are similar to those applicable to CDE. The following outlays or expenses qualify as COGPE: the cost of any right (including any payment for the preservation of a taxpayer's rights in respect of), licence, or privilege to explore for, drill or take petroleum, natural gas, or related hydrocarbons in Canada; the cost of any oil or gas well in Canada; the cost of any rental or royalty computed by reference to the amount or value of production from an oil or gas well in Canada; the cost of any right to, or interest in, any of the latter properties; and an amount receivable under an agreement to unitize an oil or gas field in Canada in respect of Canadian oil and gas property expense incurred by the other party to the agreement.

A partner's share in a COGPE is also included in the partner's COGPE if the person was a member of the partnership at the end of the fiscal period. Special "at-risk" rules apply to limited partners as set forth in ITA 66.8.

Generally, a taxpayer may deduct up to 10% of the cumulative COGPE at the end of a taxation year. In addition, the accelerated investment incentive announced in the 2018 Fall Economic Statement allows an additional first-year deduction for Canadian oil and gas property expenses that are incurred after November 20, 2018 and before 2028. The additional deduction rates are 5% for taxation years that end before 2024, and 2.5% for taxation years that begin after 2023. The rates are pro-rated for taxation years that straddle the end of 2023. See ¶7006 for more information.

Recovery of COGPE is brought back into income by first applying any credit (i.e., negative) balance in cumulative COGPE against cumulative CDE. Where a taxpayer's COGPE account (Form T1229: Part II, Line A) becomes a negative balance, that balance is included in income on Line 130 (Other income). Amounts that reduce COGPE include amounts receivable in respect of the disposition of Canadian oil and gas properties, amounts receivable under an agreement to unitize an oil or gas well in Canada in respect of COGPE, and any amount of assistance or benefit received.

ITA 59(3.2), 66.4, VD 2007-0227981E5

Chapter 8 — Pensions and Other Income

Contents

¶8000 Pensions and Other Income

¶8100 Pension Income (T1: Lines 113–116)

    ¶8110 Old Age Security Pension (T1: Line 113)

    ¶8120 CPP/QPP Benefits (T1: Line 114)

    ¶8130 Other Pensions or Superannuation (T1: Line 115)

    ¶8140 Elected Split-Pension Amount (T1: Line 116)

¶8200 Other Income (T1: Lines 117–130)

    ¶8210 Universal Child Care Benefit (T1: Line 117)

    ¶8220 Employment Insurance & Other Benefits (T1: Line 119)

    ¶8230 Registered Disability Savings Plan Income (T1: Line 125)

    ¶8240 Support Payments Received (T1: Line 128)

    ¶8250 RRSP Income (T1: Line 129)

    ¶8260 Other Income (T1: Line 130)

¶8300 Workers' Compensation and Other Benefits (T1: Lines 144, 145, 146)

    ¶8310 Workers' Compensation Benefits (T1: Line 144)

    ¶8320 Social Assistance Payments (T1: Line 145)

    ¶8330 Net Federal Supplements (T1: Line 146)

¶8000 — Pensions and Other Income

The sources of income that have been discussed so far in this Guide include employment income, investment income, capital gains, rental income, and business and professional income. This chapter discusses the remaining sources of income, including pension income and all other miscellaneous sources of income, which are generally included in income pursuant to ITA 56. These include the following types of income: Old Age Security pension benefits (¶8110), CPP/QPP benefits (¶8120), other pension or superannuation benefits (¶8130), elected split-pension income (¶8140), employment insurance benefits (¶8220), registered disability saving plan income (¶8230), support payments (¶8240), RRSP income (¶8250), workers' compensation benefits (¶8310), social assistance payments (¶8320), net federal supplements (¶8330), and other income such as scholarships and bursaries (¶8261), apprenticeship grants (¶8262), lump-sum payments from certain deferred income plans (¶8263), retiring allowances and severance pay (¶8264), death benefits (¶8265), certain RESP payments (¶8266), distributions from a retirement compensation arrangement, and certain annuity payments.

¶8100 — Pension Income (T1: Lines 113–116)

Any amount received as a superannuation or pension income is included in income and taxable when received by the recipient. A pension is defined to include any "superannuation or pension benefit", whether or not the plan is one that has been accepted by the Minister for registration. A "superannuation or pension benefit" is defined to include any amount received out of or under a superannuation or pension fund or plan, whether by the beneficiary (i.e., employee or his/her heirs) or by the employer (or former employer), and whether made in accordance with the fund or plan or resulting from an amendment to or the termination of the fund or plan. This includes regular pensions paid periodically as retirement income, as well as lump sum withdrawal payments upon cessation of employment. Pensions received under the *Old Age Security Act* after age 65, under the Canada Pension Plan (CPP), or the Quebec Pension Plan (QPP), and under a prescribed provincial pension plan constitute superannuation or pension income of the recipient, as does any supplement or spouse or common-law partner's allowance, whether paid under the federal *Old Age Security Act* or under similar provincial legislation. Also included are payments received in respect of a foreign retirement arrangement (as prescribed by the Regulations) established under the laws of a foreign jurisdiction. Individual Retirement Accounts (IRAs) under the U.S. *Internal Revenue Code* would be considered foreign retirement arrangements. If the payments would not be taxable in the foreign jurisdiction if the recipient were a resident of that country, they would generally not be taxable in Canada. This might be the case, for example, where funds could be transferred on a rollover basis from one foreign plan to another or where the receipt represented a refund of non-deductible contributions.

The *Canada Pension Plan Act* allows a portion of the taxpayer's Canada Pension Plan to be paid to a spouse or common-law partner. Where a direction is made by the taxpayer pursuant to section 65.1 of the *Canada Pension Plan Act* or any similar provision of a provincial pension plan, the pension will be included in the income of the recipient spouse or common-law partner rather than in the income of the spouse or common-law partner who earned the income. ITA 56(2), which would otherwise require such amounts to be included in the income of the taxpayer making the direction, contains a specific exception in the case of pension amounts that are assigned in accordance with the provisions of the *Canada Pension Plan Act* or similar provincial pension legislation.

Any death benefit received under the Canada Pension Plan or under a similar provision of a provincial pension plan that arises as a consequence of the death of an individual is included in the income of the individual's estate rather than in the individual's income for the year of death. Where an individual receives income that qualifies for the pension income credit, up to one-half of that income may be allocated to a spouse or common-law partner, provided that both spouses are Canadian residents. In such circumstances, the transferee spouse or common-law partner must include the transferred pension income in computing their income (see Line 116 at ¶8140).

Note that the following types of pensions are not required to be included in the recipient's income for tax purposes:

- A pension or allowance received under the *Pension Act*, the *Civilian War-related Benefits Act* or the *War Veteran's Allowance Act*, an amount received under the Gallantry Awards Order, or compensation received under section 9 of the *Aeronautics Act* (ITA 81(1)(d));

- A pension received on account of disability or death arising out of war service and paid by one of Canada's wartime allies if that other country reciprocates the deductibility privilege (ITA 81(1)(e));

- A Halifax disaster pension, grant or allowance (ITA 81(1)(f));

- Compensation paid by the Federal Republic of Germany to victims of Nazi persecution, provided such compensation would be exempt under German tax law if received by a resident of Germany (ITA 81(1)(g));

- A pension or compensation received under section 5, 31, or 45 of the *Royal Canadian Mounted Police Pension Continuation Act* or section 32 or 33 of the *Royal Canadian Mounted Police Superannuation Act* (ITA 81(1)(i));

Also excluded are benefits received under an employee benefit plan that are included in income under ITA 6(1)(g) (see ¶2180), amounts received under a retirement compensation arrangement that are included in income under ITA 56(1)(x) and (z) (see ¶2305), amounts received under a salary deferral arrangement that are included in income under ITA 56(1)(w) (see ¶2020), and death benefits paid to an estate under the Canada Pension Plan or similar provincial legislation as discussed above.

ITA 110(1)(f) permits a deduction in computing taxable income of amounts that represent a social assistance payment, including a supplement or spouse or common law partner allowance under the federal *Old Age Security Act* or any similar payment under a law of a province. The net effect of these provisions is to relieve the recipient of any tax liability in respect of that amount. However, by including the amount in the income of the recipient, another taxpayer in respect of whom the recipient would otherwise qualify as a dependant for tax purposes may be denied a personal tax credit in respect of the recipient.

56(1)(a), IT-499R: *Superannuation or Pension Benefits*, IT-508R: *Death Benefits*, ITTN-31R2

¶8110 — Old Age Security Pension (T1: Line 113)

The Canadian Old Age Security (OAS) pension is available to Canadian citizens age 65 or older, who have lived in Canada for at least 10 years after age 18. For Canadians living outside Canada, the OAS is still available for those who were Canadian citizens or legal residents at the time they left the country, as long as they lived at least 20 years in Canada after age 18. Seniors who have lived in Canada for 40 years after age 18 should be eligible to receive the maximum pension. OAS benefits are reported on Form T4A(OAS), *Statement of Old Age Security*, for Canadian residents, and Form NR4-OAS, *Statement of Old Age Security Pension Paid or Credited to Non-Residents of Canada*, for non-residents.

In 2013, Service Canada implemented a process to automatically enroll individuals who are eligible to receive the OAS pension. Generally, Service Canada will send a notification letter the month after an eligible individual turn 64. If no letter is received, taxpayers must apply in writing for the OAS pension on Form ISP-3000. OAS monthly payments are adjusted quarterly, based on changes in the Consumer Price Index. See: canada.ca/en/services/benefits/publicpensions/cpp/old-age-security.html for more information on OAS.

¶8111 — *OAS Voluntary Deferral*

As of July 1, 2013, the federal government allows for the voluntary deferral of the OAS pension, for up to five years, to receive a higher, actuarially adjusted, annual pension. The annual OAS pension will be increased by 7.2 percent for each full year that it is deferred. For more information, see: canada.ca/en/services/benefits/publicpensions/cpp/old-age-security/eligibility.html.

¶8112 — *OAS Recovery Tax*

OAS payments are considered taxable income. Seniors whose income exceeds the threshold will be required to pay back all or a portion of their OAS if their net income exceeds a certain threshold. For 2018, seniors with net income before adjustments greater than $75,910 will have to repay 15 percent of the excess over this amount, to a maximum of the total amount of OAS received. For 2018, the annual OAS benefit is fully clawed back at about $123,000 of income. For more information on the OAS "clawback", see: canada.ca/en/services/benefits/publicpensions/cpp/old-age-security/repayment.htm.

Seniors should be aware that capital gains income can increase the amount of their OAS clawback, even if the senior has capital loss carryforwards that will eliminate the capital gains. Since the OAS clawback is calculated based on the taxpayer's net income before adjustments on Line 234 of the T1 return, and capital losses (and non-capital losses) carried forward are deducted on line 253, capital gains income can increase the OAS clawback. Accordingly, seniors who have current year capital losses, and also have unrealized gains should realize some of those capital gains to offset the losses in the same year.

¶8113 — *Claiming and Filing*

Only the OAS pension reported in Box 18 of Form T4A(OAS) or Box 16 of Form NR4-OAS should be included on Line 113. The GIS and the Allowance are reported on Line 146 as net federal supplements (see ¶8330).

Enter on Line 113 the amount shown in Box 18 of the T4A(OAS) slip or Box 16 of the NR4-OAS slip. If, at any time in the year, an individual was a non-resident of Canada receiving OAS pension, see Form T1136, *Old Age Security Return of Income*. If the individual's net income on Line 234 (with certain adjustments) exceeds $75,910, the individual may be required to repay all or part of the OAS benefits received (see ¶8112 above).

ITA 56(1)(a)(i)(A)

¶8120 — CPP/QPP Benefits (T1: Line 114)

The Canada Pension Plan (CPP) pays benefits for retirement pension, disability benefits (including benefits for disabled contributors and their dependent children), and survivor benefits (including the death benefit, survivor's pension, and children's benefit). The province of Quebec has its own program, the Quebec Pension Plan (QPP), which provides similar benefits. The CPP/QPP retirement pension is available to individuals who have made contributions to the CPP or QPP and who are at least 65 years of age (or between 60 and 64 years of age if they meet certain requirements). These retirement benefits are reported in Boxes 14 and 20 of Form T4A(P).

CPP/QPP disability benefits are reported in Boxes 16 and 20 of Form T4A(P) and are available to individuals who have contributed to the CPP/QPP and who have a severe and prolonged disability that prevents them from working. The amount in Box 16 must also be reported on Line 152 of the T1 return. Benefits paid for dependent children of disabled contributors are reported in Boxes 17 and 20 of Form T4A(P) and must be included in the children's income even if they are received by the disabled contributor.

CPP/QPP survivor benefits are paid to a deceased contributor's estate, surviving spouse or common-law partner, and dependent children. These amounts are reported in Boxes 15, 17, or 18 and 20 of Form T4A(P). These benefits include a death benefit (a one-time payment made to the estate of the deceased contributor); a survivor pension (a monthly pension paid to the surviving spouse or common-law partner); and a children's benefit (a monthly benefit paid to children of a deceased contributor).

¶8121 — *Claiming and Filing*

Enter on Line 114 the total CPP or QPP benefits shown in Box 20 of the T4A(P) slip. The amount in Box 20 is the total of the amounts shown in Boxes 14 to 18. If the T4A(P) slip has an amount shown in Box 16, 17, or 18:

- CPP or QPP disability benefit (Box 16) — enter the CPP or QPP disability benefits from Box 16 on Line 152. This amount is already included in income on Line 114, so do not add it again when calculating total income on Line 150.

- CPP or QPP child benefit (Box 17) — include a child benefit only if it was received because the taxpayer was the child of a deceased or disabled contributor. Any benefits paid for a taxpayer's children are their income, even if the taxpayer received the payment.

- CPP or QPP death benefit (Box 18) — if the taxpayer received this amount and is a beneficiary of the deceased person's estate, either include it on Line 114 of the taxpayer's return, or on a T3 Trust Income Tax and Information Return for the estate. Do not report it on the deceased individual's return. The taxes payable may be different, depending on which return is chosen. For more information, see Guide T4013, *T3 Trust Guide*.

Taxpayers may receive a lump-sum CPP/QPP payment that represents payments in respect of a number of previous years, as well as the current year. The full amount of the payment must be reported on T1 Line 114 in the year of receipt. If the amount that relates to prior years exceeds $300, CRA computes the tax on the prior-year amounts as though they have been received in the prior years to which they relate. If this tax is less than the tax payable using current-year income and rates, the lower tax amount applies, and CRA will assess accordingly.

ITA 56(1)(a)(i), 56(1)(a.1), 56(8), 120.3

¶8130 — Other Pensions or Superannuation (T1: Line 115)

Various other types of superannuation or pension benefits, annuities and registered retirement income fund (RRIF) payments are included in income on Line 115.

¶8131 — *Superannuation or Pension Benefits*

A superannuation or pension benefit includes any amount received out of or under a superannuation or pension fund or plan. The following amounts are considered superannuation or pension benefits: pension income received from registered pension plans (RPPs); benefits paid under the old age security (OAS) program; benefits paid under the Canada Pension Plan (CPP) or Quebec Pension Plan (QPP); benefits paid out of or under the Saskatchewan Pension Plan (SPP); and payments out of or under certain foreign retirement arrangements.

Not all superannuation and pension benefits are included on Line 115. Generally, if a superannuation or pension benefit received by an individual is not reported on another line of the T1 return, it is reported on Line 115. For example, the following amounts are reported elsewhere on an individual's T1 return:

- OAS pension benefits (other than net federal supplements) — see ¶8110;

- CPP/QPP benefits — see ¶8120;

- Workers' compensation and social assistance payments — see ¶8310 and ¶8320;

- Net federal supplements — see ¶8330;

- Certain pension benefits received under an employee benefit plan — see ¶2180; and

- RCA distributions, RRIF or RPP benefits rolled into a RDSP, death benefits (other than CPP or QPP death benefits) and certain annuity and RRIF payments received by individuals under the age of 65 — see Line 130 at ¶8260.

Following is a discussion of some of the types of income that are included in income on Line 115.

¶8132 — *Registered Pension Plans*

On Line 115, an individual must report pension income from RPPs to which the individual or his or her employer or former employer has contributed over the years. These amounts are generally reported in Form T4A Box 016 or Form T3 Box 31.

¶8133 — *Registered Retirement Income Funds and Annuities*

The following payments and annuities must be reported on Line 115 if the individual is 65 or older or receives the payments or annuities as a consequence of the death of a spouse or common-law partner: annuity payments reported in Form T4A Box 024 or Form T5 Box 19, and RRIF payments reported in Form T4RIF Boxes 16 and 20.

Generally, lump-sum payments (Form T4A Box 018 and Form T3 Box 22) and annuity and RRIF payments for individuals under age 65 must be included on Line 130 (see ¶8260, Other Income). However, annuity payments reported in Form T5 Box 19 for these individuals should be included on Line 121 (see ¶3300). For more information on the tax treatment of payments received from a RRIF (including when tax is withheld), see Guide T4040, *RRSPs and Other Registered Plans for Retirement*.

¶8134 — *Foreign Pensions*

Most benefits from a foreign pension plan received by a Canadian resident individual must be included in income for Canadian tax purposes. The benefits may be reported on an information slip from the foreign country (e.g., U.S.

pension benefits are reported on IRS Form 1099). Where a foreign plan is a superannuation or pension plan for Canadian tax purposes, any benefits received out of or under the plan should be included on Line 115 (in Canadian dollars) unless the foreign plan qualifies as a retirement compensation arrangement, a salary deferral arrangement, or an employee benefit plan. Where a foreign plan is considered a retirement compensation arrangement, the benefits received are generally included in other income on Line 130 (see ¶8260). Benefits received from a foreign plan that is a salary deferral arrangement or an employee benefit plan are generally included in employment income on Line 101 (except for payments that are considered to be superannuation or pension benefits for a period before the individual became a Canadian resident, which are included on Line 115). For more information, see ¶2020, ¶2180, IT-502: *Employee Benefit Plans and Employee Trusts*, and Guide T4041, *Retirement Compensation Arrangements Guide*.

If an individual paid foreign tax on benefits received under a foreign pension plan, the individual may claim the foreign tax when computing the foreign tax credit. This credit is calculated on Form T2209, *Federal Foreign Tax Credits*, and reported on Line 405 (see ¶11010). Thus, when the benefits received are net of foreign taxes withheld, the amounts reported as income should be the gross amount of foreign pension in Canadian dollars.

If the pension income is not taxable in Canada under a tax treaty between Canada and the country from which the foreign pension is paid, a deduction may be claimed on Line 256 (see under ¶9400).

For the CRA's views on the taxation of benefits received from a foreign pension plan, see the following VDs: 2012-0458481E5 (Foreign Pension Receipt), 2012-0468271E5 (UK pension transfer to Canada), 2011-0409121E5 (Australian Pension Fund), 2012-0438671E5 (Treatment of German Social Security Pension), 2011-0398691E5 (Conversion of U.S. Traditional IRA into Roth IRA), 2011-0404071E5 (Election to defer income in U.S. traditional IRA), 2011-0407461E5 (Tax on 401(k) Transfer to IRA and IRA Withdrawal), 2012-0442561E5 (German reparation pension), 2012-0432281E5 (Foreign pension plan), 2011-0416841E5 (Singapore Pension), 2011-0405551E5 (Swiss disability and retirement pension payments), 2011-0400781E5 (German pension received by Canadian resident), 2010-0385371E5 (Foreign Retirement Income), 2010-0371131E5 (Payment from U.K. government pension plan), 2009-0342951E5 (U.K. war widows pension), 2006-0186661M4 (Taxation of Roth IRA), 2005-0140101E5 (Survivor Benefits Received From a U.S. Employer), 2005-0144501E5 (Division of a Foreign Pension), 2006-0168091E5 (Hong Kong Pension Payments), and 2005-0156471E5 (U.K. Pension not "Foreign Retirement Arrangement").

¶8135 — *U.S. Social Security*

An individual's U.S. social security benefits and any U.S. Medicare premiums paid on the individual's behalf are included in income on Line 115. However, a deduction may be claimed for part of this income on Line 256 (see under ¶9400).

VD 2011-0392071E5

¶8136 — *Claiming and Filing*

Include on Line 115 any other pensions or superannuation received in the year as discussed above, including the following amounts:

- T3 Box 31, qualifying pension income;

- T4A Box 016, pension or superannuation;

- T4A Box 024, 133 or 194 and T4RIF Box 16 or 20 — if the taxpayer was 65 years or older on the last day of the taxation year or received it because his or her spouse or common-law partner died; otherwise report on Line 130;

- T5 Box 19 — if the taxpayer was 65 years or older on the last day of the taxation year or received it because his or her spouse or common-law partner died; otherwise report on Line 121; and

- Gross foreign pension income, including any U.S. Social Security benefits and U.S. Medicare premiums paid on the taxpayer's behalf (a deduction can be claimed on Line 256 for the part of the taxpayer's foreign pension income that is tax free in Canada because of a tax treaty; see ¶9400).

See ¶8263 for amounts reported in T4A Box 018 (lump-sum payments) or T3 Box 22 (lump-sum pension income).

ITA 56(1)(a), 56(1)(d), 56(1)(h), 56(12), Guide T4040, Guide T4041, IT-499R: *Superannuation or Pension Benefits*, IT-508R: *Death Benefits*, ITTN-31R2

¶8140 — Elected Split-Pension Amount (T1: Line 116)

An individual taxpayer may be able to jointly elect with his or her spouse or common-law partner to split pension, annuity, and RRIF (including life income fund) payments reported on Line 115 if both of the following apply:

- Both the taxpayer and his or her spouse or common-law partner were residents of Canada on the last day of the tax year; and

- The taxpayer and his or her spouse or common-law partner were not, because of a breakdown in marriage or common-law relationship, living separate and apart from each other at the end of the year and for a period of 90 days commencing in the year.

> Pension income splitting can produce significant tax savings for married spouses and common-law partners. For example, it can allow a doubling up of the pension income credit, increases in OAS retention and the age credit because of reduced income to the transferor, and the use of lower marginal tax rates on the split income diverted to the transferee spouse or common-law partner.

¶8141 — *Eligible Pension Income*

For individuals 65 years or over, "eligible pension income" includes life annuity payments from a superannuation or pension plan, annuity payments from an RRSP, RCA, and deferred profit-sharing plan, and RRIF payments. For individuals under age 65, "eligible pension income" is the qualified pension income received by the individual in the year, which includes life annuity payments from a superannuation or pension plan and certain payments received as a result of the death of a spouse or common-law partner (e.g., a survivor pension annuity). A taxpayer under age 65 receiving RRSP or RRIF payments, other than as a result of the death of the taxpayer's spouse or common-law partner, is not eligible for the pension tax credit for these payments and is not eligible to split these payments with his or her spouse or common-law partner.

> Effective for 2013 and subsequent taxation years, amounts received out of an RCA are eligible pension income for pension income splitting, where the taxpayer is at least 65 years of age, the RCA payments are in the form of life annuity payments and supplemental to a pension received out of a RPP, and the RCA payments cannot exceed a certain specified limit less the taxpayer's other eligible pension income (see VD 2013-0497761E5).

For all taxpayers, regardless of age, eligible pension income does not include OAS, CPP/QPP benefits, death benefits, retiring allowances, RRSP withdrawals (other than annuity payments), or payments out of a salary deferral arrangement or employee benefit plan. A foreign pension annuity may qualify for income splitting; however, neither the portion that is tax-exempt due to a tax treaty with the foreign country, nor income from a U.S. individual retirement account qualifies.

Although CPP is not eligible pension income for the purposes of the pension income-splitting rules, spouses or common-law partners can apply to split CPP benefits if they are both at least 60 years of age and are either receiving or applying for CPP benefits. Taxpayers cannot choose how to split the income; the benefits are split equally. See www.servicecanada.gc.ca for information on splitting CPP income.

The pension income amount transferred cannot be greater than 50 per cent of the transferor's "eligible pension income" for the year, multiplied by the number of months in the year that the transferor was married to or in a common-law partnership with the transferee, divided by the number of months in the transferor's taxation year.

Where a pensioner and his or her spouse or common-law partner make a joint election in respect of a split-pension amount for a taxation year, the portion of the amount of taxes deducted or withheld under ITA 153(1) that may be reasonably considered to be in respect of the split-pension amount is deemed to have been deducted or withheld on account of the spouse or common-law partner's tax for the taxation year, and not on account of the pensioner's tax for the taxation year.

Splitting pension income with a deceased spouse is permitted for pension income that the deceased spouse received before death (VD 2008-0275731E5).

¶8142 — *Making the Election*

To make the election, a taxpayer and his or her spouse or common-law partner must complete Form T1032, *Joint Election to Split Pension Income*. Only one joint election can be made for a tax year; therefore, if both spouses have eligible pension income, they must decide whose pension income will be split. Most commercially-available tax preparation programs will automatically calculate the optimal split of pension income for tax purposes. Form T1032 must be completed and attached to both the individual's and the spouse or common-law partner's paper returns. The information provided on the forms must be the same. If the return is being filed electronically, the election form must be completed and kept on file in case the CRA asks for it.

When a joint election is filed to split pension income, for the purpose of determining the pensioner's pension income credit, the pensioner is deemed not to have received the pension income that is allocated to the spouse or common-law partner. Instead, the spouse or common-law partner is deemed to have received the pension income for the purposes of claiming the pension income credit. Accordingly, depending on the age of the spouse or common-law partner and the nature of the split-pension amount, the pension income credit may or may not be available to them.

¶8143 — *Claiming and Filing*

If an individual elects to split his or her eligible pension income with his or her spouse or common-law partner, the pensioner must still report the full amount of pension income on Line 115, but will claim a deduction for the elected split pension amount on Line 210 (see ¶9140). Form T1032 must be completed and attached to both the individual's and the spouse or common-law partner's paper returns. If the return is being filed electronically, Form T1032 must be completed and kept on file in case the CRA asks for it.

ITA 56(1)(a), 56(1)(a.2), 60(c), 60.03(1)–(4), 118(3), 118(7), 160(1.3); Form T1032; IT-499R: *Superannuation or Pension Benefits*, VDs 2012-0439791E5, 2011-042992117, 2011-0425871E5, 2010-0371161E5, 2010-0375511E5, 2009-0337451E5, 2008-0281261M4, 2008-0284411C6, 2008-0275731E5, 2007-0257001E5, 2006-0214951M4, 2006-0204981M4, 2006-0203581M4, 2005-0144501E5

¶8200 — Other Income (T1: Lines 117–130)

¶8210 — Universal Child Care Benefit (T1: Line 117)

For taxation years before 2017, allowances paid under section 4 of the *Universal Child Care Benefit Act* were included in the income of the spouse or common-law partner with the lower income. If the individual and his or her spouse or common-law partner's incomes were equal, then the allowance was included in the income of the taxpayer who received the allowance. If the individual had no spouse or common-law partner, the individual has the choice of including the Universal Child Care Benefit (UCCB) in their own income or in the income of a dependant for whom an eligible dependant credit (see ¶10040) was claimed.

For 2015 and 2016, the UCCB was increased from $100 to $160 per month ($1,920/year) for each child under the age of 6, and a new benefit of $60 per month ($720/year) was introduced for children aged 6 to 17. However, effective July 1, 2016, the UCCB was eliminated and replaced by the Canada child benefit.

ITA 56(6), 56(8), 60(y), 122.6, ITR 6301, 6302, *UCCB Act*, Form RC62, Form RC66, Guide T4114

¶8220 — Employment Insurance and Other Benefits (T1: Line 119)

Employment insurance (EI) provides temporary financial assistance for unemployed Canadians while they look for work or upgrade their skills. Canadians who are sick, pregnant, or caring for a newborn or adopted child, as well as those who must care for a family member who is seriously ill with a significant risk of death, may also receive employment insurance.

Any employment insurance benefits received under the federal *Unemployment Insurance Act* and benefits under Part I, VIII, or VIII.1 of the *Employment Insurance Act* are included as income for tax purposes except, in the case of the *Unemployment Insurance Act*, a payment relating to the cost of a course or program to facilitate the re-entry into the labour market of an unemployed person. Annual employment insurance premiums paid by an employee may be claimed as a tax credit.

An individual whose net income (Line 234) is too high may be required to repay some of the regular benefits received, except for special benefits such as maternity, parental, sickness, or compassionate care benefits; see Line 235 at ¶9280 (Social benefits repayment).

Self-employed individuals can choose to opt in to the EI program and receive special benefits similar to those available to salaried employees under the EI program, including maternity benefits, parental and adoption benefits, sickness benefits, and compassionate care benefits. A self-employed individual must earn a minimum of $6,000 in self-employment earnings during the preceding year to qualify for EI special benefits. An individual who has opted in to the EI program may opt out at the end of any taxation year, but only if the individual has never claimed any benefits. An individual who has claimed benefits must continue to pay premiums on self-employed earnings for as long as the individual is self-employed. Self-employed individuals who choose to participate in the EI program must do so for at least one year before claiming any benefits. Therefore, a self-employed individual who opted into the program in January 2016, for example, could make a special benefit claim beginning on January 1, 2017.

¶8221 — *Lump-Sum Payments*

If an individual receives a lump-sum payment of EI benefits in the year, part or all of which were for previous years, the entire payment must be reported on Line 119. However, the individual can request that the CRA tax the amounts relating to previous years as if they were received in those years, provided that the total of all parts of that lump-sum payment and any other lump-sum payments of other eligible income received in the year is $3,000 or more (excluding interest). Other types of income that are eligible for this treatment include support payments; superannuation or pension benefits otherwise payable on a periodic basis (except for CPP and QPP benefits); benefits from a wage-loss replacement plan; and employment income or damages for loss of employment received under the terms of a court order or judgment, as an arbitration award, or in settlement of a lawsuit. Form T1198, *Statement of Qualifying Retroactive Lump-Sum Payment*, must be completed for the CRA to apply this rule. See Form T1198 and its instructions for more information.

¶8222 — *Claiming and Filing*

Employment insurance benefits are reported in Box 14 of Form T4E, *Statement of Employment Insurance and Other Benefits* (or, for non-residents, in Box 16 or 26 of Form NR4, *Statement of Amounts Paid or Credited to Non-*

Residents of Canada). Enter the amount shown in T4E Box 14 less any amount in Box 18. If the individual repaid any excess benefits directly to the payer, see Line 232 at ¶9272 to claim a deduction.

ITA 56(1)(a)(iv), 110.2, 120.31, Form T4E, Form T1198

¶8230 — Registered Disability Savings Plan Income (T1: Line 125)

Individuals who have a prolonged and severe physical or mental impairment, their family members, and other authorized contributors are entitled to establish registered disability savings plans (RDSPs), which are designed to help parents and others save and provide for the long-term financial security of a disabled beneficiary. Contributions to an RDSP are not tax deductible; however, investment income accrues on a tax-deferred basis in an RDSP. Beneficiaries must include in income the taxable portion of a disability payment made from an RDSP. RDSP income is not included in the calculation of the individual's GST/HST credit, Canada Child Benefits payments, social benefits repayment, refundable medical expense supplement, or the Working Income Tax Benefit.

¶8231 — *Claiming and Filing*

RDSP income received by an individual in the year is reported in T4A Box 131. Taxpayers should enter this amount on Line 125.

ITA 56(1)(q.1), 146.4, *Canada Disability Savings Act*, Guide RC4460

¶8240 — Support Payments Received (T1: Line 128)

For tax purposes, a support payment is an amount payable or receivable as an allowance on a periodic basis for the maintenance of the recipient, children of the recipient, or both. Generally, a payment will be considered a support payment if the following five conditions are met:

1. The payment must be made under the terms of a court order or written agreement;

2. If the recipient is the payer's current or former spouse or common-law partner, the payer must be living separate and apart from the recipient at the time the payment was made because of a breakdown in the relationship. Otherwise, the payer must be the legal parent of a child of the recipient;

3. The payment is made for the maintenance of the recipient, the child of the recipient, or both, and the recipient has discretion as to the use of the amount;

4. The allowance must be payable on a periodic basis (the term "periodic" does not necessarily mean frequent, although there has to be a series of payments; for example, monthly, quarterly, semi-annually, or annually). The court order or written agreement has to set out the timing of the payments and only a new order or agreement can change the payment schedule; and

5. The payments must be made directly to the recipient (under certain conditions, payments can be made to a third-party (see ¶8242 below).

There are generally two types of support payments for tax purposes: spousal support and child support. Spousal support means support payments made under a court order or written agreement that are solely for the maintenance of the recipient (i.e., the spouse, former spouse, common-law partner, or former common-law partner, or parent of the child of whom the payer is a legal parent). Child support means any support payment that is not identified in the court order or written agreement as solely for the maintenance of the recipient. As a result, where an order or agreement only provides for a total amount of support to be paid for the recipient and a child, the full amount is considered child support. The tax rules are different depending on the type of support payment.

¶8241 — *Taxation of Support Payments*

The tax rules for support payments generally depend on type of support payment and the date that the taxpayer's court order or written agreement was made.

¶8241.1 — *Pre-May 1997 Order or Agreement*

Generally, support payments for a child or spouse or common-law partner, under a court order or written agreement made before May 1997, are taxable to the recipient and deductible by the payer. However, child support payments will become non-deductible to the payer and non-taxable to the recipient (i.e., essentially ignored for tax purposes) where any of the following four situations applies:

- The pre-May 1997 court order or written agreement is modified after April 1997 to change the amount of child support payable to the recipient. In this case, the child support payments are no longer taxable or deductible beginning on the day that the payer pays the revised amount to the recipient for the first time.

- A new court order or written agreement is entered into with the same person after April 1997, and the result of the new order or agreement is to change the total amount of child support payable. In this case, the child support payments made under both orders/agreements are no longer taxable or deductible as of the commencement day of the new order or agreement.

- The court order or written agreement specifies that child support payments made after a certain date (not earlier than May 1, 1997) will no longer be taxable and deductible.

- The payer and recipient of child support payments made under a pre-May 1997 court order or written agreement jointly elect that child support payable after a specific date will not be deductible and taxable. Both parties must complete and sign Form T1157, *Election for Child Support Payments*, and send it to the CRA. Once the election has been accepted, the order or agreement is subject to the post-April 1997 tax rules. The election cannot be revoked. A separate form must be completed for each order or agreement.

¶8241.2 — *Post-April 1997 Order or Agreement*

Child support payments made under a post-April 1997 court order or written agreement (or pre-May 1997 if any of the above situations apply) are not deductible by the payer and do not have to be included in income by the recipient; they are essentially ignored for tax purposes. Spousal support payments continue to be deductible to the payer and must be included in the recipient's income.

Where the taxpayer's court order or written agreement only provides for a total amount of support to be paid for the recipient and a child, and does not identify or carve out a spousal support amount, the full amount is considered to be child support for tax purposes, and is non-deductible and non-taxable. Accordingly, where it is intended that some portion of support is for the specific benefit or support of the recipient, that portion must be carved out and specifically identified in order for the amount to be included in the income of the recipient and deductible to the payer. Similar rules apply in respect of third party payments — in order for payments to third parties to be deductible, the order or agreement must provide that both ITA 56.1(2) and 60.1(2) apply to such payments.

Note that where the taxpayer's court order or written agreement does separately identify child support payments and spousal support payments, priority is given to the child support. This means that all payments made are first considered to have been made toward child support, and any amount paid over and above the child support amount is considered to be spousal support. All child support payable to a recipient must be fully paid before any amounts paid as spousal support can be claimed as a deduction.

Any arrears in the amount of child support is carried forward and added to the next year's support payable. However, the priority of child support does not apply when the child support and spousal support are payable under different court orders or written agreements and the recipients are different people. The following example is provided in Guide P102:

> Beginning January 2015, Mark had to make monthly support payments of $400 ($150 for his former spouse, and $250 for their children). Mark paid $400 from January to March for a total of $1,200. He made no other payment for the remainder of the year. Mark is in arrears for $1,800 in child support. When he filed his 2015 return, Mark could not deduct the spousal support payments because he did not fully pay his child support. In 2016, Mark must fully pay all child support owing for 2015 and 2016 before he can deduct anything he pays for spousal support.

¶8242 — *Prior, Specific-Purpose, Third-Party and Lump-Sum Payments*

The following types of payments may still be considered to be support payments for tax purposes even if they do not meet the five conditions outlined above: payments made before the date of the court order or written agreement, specific-purpose or third-party payments, and lump-sum payments.

¶8242.1 — *Prior Payments*

An amount paid before a court order or written agreement takes place or comes into effect is recognized if the order or agreement states that any amount previously paid is deemed paid under the order or agreement. However, the payments must be made in the year the order or agreement was made, or in the preceding year. The following example is provided in Guide P102:

> Since the couple separated in January 2014, Brendan has been paying $500 monthly to Sarah in spousal support. On January 8, 2016, a written agreement was established confirming that Brendan is required to pay $500 monthly in support. The written agreement also indicates that the amounts paid before January 2016 are considered paid and received under this agreement.
>
> The payments made in 2015 and 2016 are considered support payments because they were paid in the year of the written agreement and the previous year. Brendan may deduct the payments for 2015 and 2016 in the year the amounts were paid and Sarah will include the amounts received for 2015 and 2016 in the year the amounts were received. The 2014 payments are not considered support payments because they were not paid in the year of the written agreement or in the previous year, so they cannot be deducted by the payer and are not included in the recipient's income.

¶8242.2 — *Specific-Purpose and Third-Party Payments*

Third-party payments are support payments made under a court order or written agreement to someone other than the recipient (i.e., a third-party). Third-party payments that the recipient can use as he or she sees fit are considered support payments only if they meet all of the other conditions outlined above.

Specific-purpose payments are amounts made under a court order or written agreement for specific expenses for the maintenance of the recipient. These amounts may be paid directly to the recipient or to a third-party. Specific-purpose payments include rent, property taxes, insurance premiums; educational or medical expenses (such as prescription drugs or eye glasses); maintenance costs for the home in which the recipient lives; and up to 20% of the original principal amount of any debt from buying or improving the home in which the recipient lives. If the recipient can use the specific-purpose payments as he or she sees fit, they are considered support payments if they meet the conditions outlined above. However, if the recipient cannot use the specific-purpose payments as he or she sees fit, they are not considered support payments, unless the court order or written agreement states that the recipient will include the payments in income, and that the payer can deduct them. The following example is contained in Guide P102:

> Under a written agreement, Melissa has to pay $900 per month to her former spouse, Alex, as an allowance for maintenance. This written agreement provides that Melissa will pay an amount of $300 directly to Alex and $600 directly to his landlord for the rent of his apartment. The agreement also provides that Alex may, at any time, change the arrangement and require that the entire $900 be paid directly to him. The monthly amount of $600 paid directly to the landlord and the monthly amount of $300 payable to Alex are considered support payments because he can use the money as he sees fit.

¶8242.3 — *Lump-Sum Payments*

An amount paid as one lump-sum will generally not be considered a support payment because it is not paid on a periodic basis. However, if periodic payments required by a court order or written agreement have fallen into arrears and one payment is made to bring these requirements up to date, that payment would be considered a support payment. The following are generally not support payments:

- a lump-sum payment made in place of several periodic payments that were imposed under a court order or written agreement, but were not yet due to be paid (a prepayment). However, if a prepayment was made for the sole purpose of securing funds to the recipient, it may be considered a support payment;

- a lump-sum payment made under a court order or written agreement for a period before the date of the order or agreement;

- instalment payments of a lump-sum; and

- payments that release the payer from any obligation to pay arrears, future maintenance, or both.

The following example is provided in Guide P102:

Jason and Tracy have been living separate and apart since August 2013. Their court order requires Jason to pay $500 per month for Tracy's maintenance. In June 2014, Jason lost his job and was unable to make the spousal support payments. In February 2015, he got a new job. He is in arrears of $4,000. Jason and Tracy returned to court and reached a settlement where it was agreed that Jason will pay $3,500 of the $4,000 he owes. The other $500 will not be paid. The $3,500 lump-sum payment is considered a settlement amount paid by Jason to release him from his liability for the arrears and therefore, does not qualify as a support payment because it was not made in accordance with the original agreement.

Where periodic support payments fall into arrears, and the taxpayer makes one lump-sum payment (of at least $3,000 that is deductible to the payer and includable to the recipient) to bring support requirements for previous years up to date, the portion of the payment relating to previous years can be taxed as if it was received in those years. For more information, see Form T1198, *Statement of Qualifying Retroactive Lump-Sum Payment.*

¶8243 — *Support Payments Received from a Non-Resident*

Canadian residents who receive support payments from a non-resident payer must include the payments in income if the payments are otherwise includable for tax purposes, as discussed above. However, where the support payments are tax-free in Canada because of an income tax treaty between Canada and the foreign country, the taxpayer can claim a deduction for them (see Line 256 at ¶9400). If the foreign country withheld tax from support payments that the Canadian resident recipient is including in income and required to pay tax on, the recipient may be able to claim a foreign tax credit (see Line 405 at ¶11010). The following example is provided in Guide P102:

Carol and Doug divorced on December 9, 2015. Doug resides in Australia. Carol is a Canadian resident. Under a court order, Doug paid Carol $500 a month in spousal support beginning January 1, 2016. Under the terms of the Canada-Australia Income Tax Treaty, alimony and other maintenance payments are only taxable in the source country. The payment is taxable only in Australia. Carol must report $6,000 on lines 128 and 156 of her return. Carol also claims $6,000 as a deduction on line 256 because of the provisions of the Canada-Australia income tax treaty.

¶8244 — *Deductibility of Legal Fees*

A support recipient can deduct, on Line 221, legal fees paid to collect late support payments; establish the amount of support payments from their current or former spouse or common-law partner; establish the amount of support payments from the legal parent of their child (who is not their current or former spouse or common-law partner) where the support is payable under the terms of a court order; or try to get an increase in support payments (see under ¶3600). A support recipient can also deduct, on Line 232, legal fees paid to try to make child support payments non-taxable (see ¶9271). However, a support recipient cannot deduct legal fees incurred to obtain a separation or divorce, or to establish child custody or visitation rights for a child. Legal fees paid to collect a lump-sum payment, which does not qualify as a support payment, are also not deductible.

Income Tax Folio S1-F3-C3, *Support Payments*, provides the following comments regarding the deductibility of legal and accounting fees incurred with respect to support payments:

Non-deductible legal and accounting fees

3.78 Neither the payer nor the recipient may deduct legal and accounting fees incurred to:

- get a separation or divorce;

- establish custody or visitation rights to a child; or

- equalize family assets.

3.79 A recipient cannot deduct legal and accounting fees incurred to collect:

- a lump-sum payment which cannot be identified as being a payment in respect of a number of periodic payments of support amounts that were in arrears;

- an amount which does not qualify as a support amount; or

- an amount from the estate or succession of a deceased person.

See ¶3.44–3.46 for a discussion of lump-sum payments and ¶3.67 for a discussion of payments from an estate.

3.80 A payer cannot deduct legal and accounting fees incurred to establish, negotiate, contest, reduce or terminate the amount of support payments.

Deductible legal and accounting fees

3.81 A recipient can deduct legal and accounting fees incurred to:

- establish the amount of support payments from their current or former spouse or common-law partner;

- establish the amount of support payments from the legal parent of their child (who is not their current or former spouse or common-law partner) where the support is payable under the terms of a court order;

- seek an increase in support payments;

- defend against a reduction in support payments;

- collect late support payments; or

- request that child support payments be non-taxable.

3.82 Generally, pursuant to paragraph 18(1)(c), expenses incurred to earn exempt income are not deductible. However, the legal and accounting fees described in ¶3.81 are deductible even when the child support amount to which the fees relate is not included in the recipient's income because a support amount is excluded from the definition of exempt income in subsection 248(1). Therefore, the deduction of costs incurred in respect of support amounts is not denied by paragraph 18(1)(c) as being in respect of exempt income.

3.83 Legal and accounting fees are deductible by the recipient even where the claim for support was unsuccessful as long as the claim was bona fide and not frivolous, with a reasonable chance of success.

3.84 Qualifying legal and accounting fees may be deducted on an accrual basis. Where the recipient is awarded costs which include legal and accounting fees, only the net amount of legal fees may be deducted by the recipient. If the recipient had deducted the legal and accounting fees in a prior tax year, the award is included in income in the year of receipt.

For common law spouses in Quebec, the legal costs of negotiating support amounts are not deductible because there is no legal right to support (VD 2010-0373641C6).

¶8245 — *Claiming and Filing*

Support recipients reporting taxable support payments should enter on Line 156 the total amount of both taxable and non-taxable child and spousal support payments received in the year. Enter on Line 128 only the taxable portion of support payments received. The following example is provided in Guide P102:

> Diane and Gene recently divorced. In their court order made in December 2015, Gene was ordered to pay Diane $1,000 per month for their two children, and $500 per month for spousal support. Gene started making monthly support payments of $1,500 in January, and paid a total of $18,000 for 2016. Gene enters the total support payments amount of $18,000 on line 230 of his 2016 return. On line 220, he enters the deductible part of his support payments, which is the spousal support amount of $6,000.

Support recipients who repaid support payments because of a court order may be able to claim a deduction on Line 220 for the year of repayment or in either of the two following years if the recipient reported the original support payments received as income on that return or a previous year's return and has not already claimed a deduction for the repayment (see under ¶9210).

ITA 56.1, 60(b), 60(c.2), 60.1, 118(5), 118(5.1); *Donald*, [1999] 1 C.T.C. 2025 (TCC); *Nissim*, [1998] 4 C.T.C. 2496 (TCC); *Gallien*, [2001] 2 C.T.C. 2676 (TCC); *Nadeau*, [2004] 1 C.T.C. 293 (FCA); *Rabb*, [2006] 3 C.T.C. 2266 (TCC); *Gal*, [2006] 3 C.T.C. 2356 (TCC); *Loewig*, [2007] 1 C.T.C. 2062 (TCC); *Beauchamp*, [2008] 3 C.T.C. 2169 (TCC) *Dalfort*, 2009 CarswellNat 2518 (TCC); *McLaren*, 2009 CarswellNat 3155 (TCC); *Trignani*, 2010 CarswellNat 922 (TCC); *Persaud*, [2011] 3 C.T.C. 2377 (TCC); *Sarophim*, 2012 CarswellNat 845 (TCC); Guide P102, Form T1157, Form T1158, IT-99R5(C): *Legal Fees*, S1-F3-C3: *Support Payments*, ITTN-24, VDs 2012-0465511E5, 2011-0430161E5, 2011-0420971E5, 2011-0415191E5, 2011-0405131E5, 2011-0406701E5, 2011-0426211E5, 2011-0417661E5, 2011-0399111E5, 2010-0391461E5, 2010-0390451E5, 2010-0381601E5, 2010-0376821E5, 2010-037556117, 2010-0373061E5, 2010-0358951E5, 2009-0342281M4, 2008-0294511E5, 2006-0208471E5, 2006-0199271E5, 2006-0177891E5, canada.ca/en/revenue-agency/services/tax/individuals/topics/about-your-tax-return/support-payments.html

¶8250 — **RRSP Income (T1: Line 129)**

An RRSP is an arrangement under which an individual (or the individual's spouse or common-law partner) makes payments to an RRSP issuer and the issuer agrees to provide the individual with a retirement income. The contributions made to an RRSP are generally deductible in calculating net income (see Line 208 at ¶9130) and the income earned in the RRSP is not taxed until funds are withdrawn from the plan. Amounts received from an RRSP, such as withdrawals, annuity payments, and other payments, are reported on Line 129.

RRSP annuity payments reported in Box 16 of the taxpayer's T4RSP slip qualify for the pension income amount if the taxpayer is 65 years of age or older on the last day of the tax year or if the taxpayer received the payments because of the death of his or her spouse or common-law partner (see Line 314 at ¶10100).

The taxpayer may be able to jointly elect with his or her spouse or common-law partner to split the RRSP annuity payments reported on Line 129 where all of the following conditions are met: 1) the taxpayer is 65 years of age or older on the last day of the taxation year, or received the payments because of the death of his or her spouse or common-law partner; 2) the taxpayer and his or her spouse or common-law partner are both residents of Canada on the last day of the tax year; and 3) the taxpayer and his or her spouse or common-law partner were not, because of a breakdown in their marriage or common-law relationship, living separate and apart from each other at the end of the year and for a period of 90 days commencing in the year. To make this election, complete Form T1032, *Joint Election to Split Pension Income*.

Individuals who elect to split their RRSP annuity payments with a spouse or common-law partner must still report the full amount on Line 129, but can claim a deduction for the elected split-pension amount on Line 210. For more information, see ¶8140 (Line 116) and ¶9140 (Line 210).

¶8251 — *Home Buyers' Plan (HBP) and Lifelong Learning Plan (LLP)*

If, in previous years, an individual withdrew funds on a tax-free basis from his or her RRSP under the Home Buyers' Plan or the Lifelong Learning Plan, the individual may have to make a repayment for the year if he or she has repaid less than the minimum amount required for the year under the plan. The minimum repayment is shown on the individual's prior year Notice of Assessment or Notice of Reassessment. To make a repayment, the individual must contribute to his or her RRSP during the current taxation year or within 90 days after the end of the taxation year, and designate the contribution as a repayment on Schedule 7. For more information, see Guide RC4112, *Lifelong Learning Plan*, Guide RC4135, *Home Buyers' Plan*, and Guide T4040, *RRSPs and Other Registered Plans for Retirement*. Also see Line 208 at ¶9130.

¶8252 — *RRSPs for Spouse or Common-Law Partner*

Where an individual contributed to a spousal or common-law partner's RRSP in 2016, 2017 or 2018, the individual may need to include an amount on Line 129, up to the total of the individual's contributions during the three-year period, in the following circumstances:

- the spouse or common-law partner received amounts in 2018 from an unmatured spousal or common-law partner RRSP;

- the spouse or common-law partner is deemed to have received amounts in 2018 from a de-registered spousal or common-law partner RRSP; or

- the spouse or common-law partner has received commutation payments in 2018 from a matured spousal or common-law partner RRSP.

The amount of the withdrawal must also be included in the spouse or common-law partner's income, with a deduction for the amount included in the contributing individual's income. The net amount, if any, is included in the spouse or common-law partner's income on Line 129.

To ensure that a contributing spouse does not have an income inclusion when the annuitant spouse or common-law partner withdraws funds from a spousal or common-law partner RRSP, the contributing spouse should not contribute to a spousal or common-law partner RRSP in the year the spouse or common-law partner withdraws funds from the RRSP, or in either of the two preceding years. Otherwise, the contributor may have to include in income the funds that the spouse or common-law partner withdraws.

The rule that requires the contributing spouse to include certain amounts from a spousal or common-law partner RRSP into income does not apply in the following situations:

- At the time of payment, the contributing individual and his or her spouse or common-law partner were living separate and apart because of the breakdown of their relationship;

- At the time of payment, the contributing individual or his or her spouse or common-law partner were non-residents of Canada;

- The amount is a commutation payment that is transferred directly for the spouse or common-law partner to another RRSP, to a RRIF, or to an issuer to buy an eligible annuity that cannot be commuted for at least three years;

- The contributing spouse dies in the year of payment; or

- The deceased annuitant spouse received the amount because of death.

In the above situations, the annuitant spouse or common-law partner includes the payment in income for the year he or she receives it or is considered to have received it.

¶8253 — *Claiming and Filing*

Enter on Line 129 the total amount of withdrawals and payments from an RRSP as reported in the individual's T4RSP boxes 16, 18, 28, and 34. Amounts shown in Box 20 (refund of excess contributions), Box 22 (withdrawal and commutation payments), and Box 26 (amounts deemed received on deregistration) are also included in income unless the individual's spouse or common-law partner made a contribution to the individual's RRSP. Therefore, also include amounts shown in T4RSP Boxes 20, 22, and 26, unless the individual's spouse or common-law partner made a contribution to the individual's RRSP.

ITA 56(1)(h)–(h.2), 146.01, 146.02, 146(8), 146(8.3), Form T2205, Guide RC4112, Guide RC4135, Guide T4040, IT-307R4: *Spousal or Common-law Partner Registered Retirement Savings Plans*, IT-500R: *Registered Retirement Savings Plans — Death of Annuitant*, T1 Schedule 7

¶8260 — **Other Income (T1: Line 130)**

Taxable income that is not reported anywhere else on the T1 return should be reported on Line 130. Ensure that the amounts reported on Line 130 are not a type of income that should have been properly reported on Lines 101 to 129.

The following are some of the types of income that should be reported on Line 130 and the tax slip that it may be reported on:

- Scholarships, fellowships, bursaries, artists' project grants, and prizes (T4A Box 105); see ¶8261;

- Apprenticeship incentive grants and apprenticeship completion grants (T4A Box 130); see ¶8262;

- Lump-sum payments from an RPP, DPSP, or unregistered pension plan (T4A Box 018 or T3 Box 22); see ¶8263;

- Retiring allowances and severance pay (T4 Boxes 66 and 67); see ¶8264;

- Death benefits, other than CPP or QPP death benefits (T4A Box 106); see ¶8265;

- RESP accumulated income payments (T4A Box 040) and RESP educational assistance payments (T4A Box 042); see ¶8266;

- Amounts distributed from a retirement compensation arrangement (RCA) (T4A-RCA Box 14);

- Training allowances or other amounts reported in T4A Box 028 (other than amounts already reported on lines 104, 115 or 125);

- Payments of "other income" from a trust (T3 Box 26);

- Certain annuity payments (see ¶8130);

- Taxable amounts paid from a tax-free savings account (TFSA) (T4A Box 134);

- Designated benefits from a RRIF (T4RIF Box 22) or the registered pension plan amount (T4A Box 018) if the taxpayer rolled over an amount to an RDSP. See Line 232 under ¶9273 for information about the corresponding deduction; and

- Other amounts reported on the taxpayer's T4A slip that are not already reported anywhere else on the T1 return.

¶8261 — *Scholarships, Fellowships, Bursaries, Artists' Project Grants, and Prizes*

¶8261.1 — *Scholarships, Fellowships, and Bursaries*

Generally, the following scholarships and bursaries are not taxable: (1) elementary and secondary school scholarships and bursaries; (2) post-secondary school scholarships, fellowships and bursaries for enrolment in a program that entitled the individual to claim the education credit, or if the individual is considered to be a full-time qualifying student; and (3) as of January 1, 2017, scholarships or bursaries received by students aged 16 and over at the end of the year who are enrolled at a post-secondary educational institution in Canada for a program that is not at the post-secondary level but provides the student with skills for, or improves a student's skills in, an occupation. Generally, individuals are eligible for the education amount or considered to be a qualifying student in the year if the individual received Form T2202A, TL11A, TL11B or TL11C and the educational institution completed either column B or C of the form.

The value of all other scholarships, fellowships, and bursaries the individual received in the year in excess of the individual's "scholarship exemption" for the year should be included in income on Line 130 pursuant to ITA 56(1)(n). Generally, the scholarship exemption for the year is $500. If the individual received a research grant, report the amount on Line 104 (see ¶2301). Artists' project grants are discussed in Pamphlet P105, *Students and Income Tax*.

In *Jones v. R.*, [2002] 3 C.T.C. 2483 (TCC), the taxpayer received a scholarship from a private school in the form of a credit towards tuition. The Tax Court of Canada held that the amount of the benefit received by the taxpayer met the definition of "scholarship" in ITA 56(1)(n), notwithstanding the fact that the amount was deposited into his account with the school instead of being received in cash.

In *Simser v. R.*, [2005] 1 C.T.C. 229 (FCA), the court found that financial assistance in the form of a "Special Opportunities Grant for Disabled Students with Permanent Disabilities" (SOGD) constituted a bursary for purposes of ITA 56(1)(n). The court found that there was no distinction between recipients of an SOGD and recipients of other special opportunity grants. In VD 2006-0187471E5, the CRA states that "what constitutes a bursary is not defined in the Act and the Agency takes the general view that its meaning is broad enough to encompass almost any form of financial assistance paid to a student to enable the student to pursue his or her education".

The CRA discusses scholarships and bursaries in paragraphs 3.7 to 3.16 of Folio S1-F2-C3, *Scholarships, Research Grants and Other Education Assistance*:

3.7 Scholarships and bursaries are amounts paid or benefits given to students to enable them to pursue their education. The term bursary is not defined in the Act; however, its meaning is broad enough to encompass almost any form of financial assistance paid to enable a student to pursue his or her education. Bursaries can include amounts paid to defray living expenses, as well as amounts that are directly related to the cost of the education. The extent to which a student has discretion over the use of funds received will not affect its categorization as a bursary (see *Simser v. The Queen*, 2004 FCA 414, 2005 DTC 5001).

3.8 Scholarships and bursaries usually apply to education at a post-secondary level or beyond, such as at a university, college, technical institute or other educational institution. However, there are circumstances where scholarships or bursaries are awarded for education below the post-secondary school level.

Scholarships and bursaries normally assist the student in proceeding towards a degree, diploma, or other certificate of graduation. Scholarships and bursaries may apply to any field of study, including an academic discipline (such as the arts or sciences), a professional program (such as law or medicine), a trade (such as plumbing or carpentry) or skill (such as certified first aid and truck driver training courses). Normally, a student is not expected to do specific work for the payer in exchange for a scholarship or bursary.

Allowances or reimbursements

3.9 If a scholarship or bursary program provides allowances or reimbursements to pay for specific educational costs, such as those for lodging, personal travel, tools, books, equipment, technical aids, tutoring, note-taking, interpreting, specialized transportation, attendant care or dependent care, those amounts would generally fall within the scope of subparagraph 56(1)(n)(i) (see ¶3.68). Subparagraph 56(1)(n)(i) can also apply to the value of benefits in kind, such as free accommodation or equipment.

Scholarships or bursaries provided in employment situations

3.10 As a matter of good employee relations, an employer may pay tuition fees for, or give a grant or award to, its employees or its employees' family members (such as school-age or university-age children). The tax implications arising upon the award for the employee and/or the family member depends on the particular facts and circumstances in each case. A discussion of the most common types of arrangements is below.

Scholarship or bursary awarded to a current or former employee

3.11 During or immediately after a period of employment, employees and employers sometimes make agreements under which an employer agrees to pay all or a portion of an employee's education costs on the condition that the employee returns to work for the employer when the education is completed. In such cases, the education-related expenses paid by the employer will be considered to have been received in respect of, in the course of or by virtue of an office or employment and will not be included in computing the student's income under subparagraph 56(1)(n)(i).

3.12 The education-related expenses paid by the employer will be taxable to the student as employment income under section 6, subject to the exception where the course or training is determined to be primarily for the benefit of the employer (see ¶3.23 for further information). This will be the case notwithstanding any commitment of the student to repay all or a portion of the expenses paid by the employer in the event that they do not satisfy the terms and conditions of an employment agreement (for example, the student does not work for the employer for the requisite period after graduation).

3.13 Where a student is required to repay an employer for education expenses the employer previously incurred on their behalf, the student will be entitled to deduct the repayment under paragraph 8(1)(n) where the repayment is made by or on behalf of the student in the year pursuant to an arrangement requiring the reimbursement of any amounts received for a period throughout which the student did not perform the duties of the office or employment. However, the deduction under paragraph 8(1)(n) will be limited to the extent that:

- the amounts received were included in computing the student's employment income; and

- the total reimbursements do not exceed the total of the amounts received by the student for the period throughout which the student did not perform the employment duties.

Scholarship or bursary awarded prior to employment relationship

3.14 If an employer-employee relationship has not yet been established and a student receives a scholarship or bursary in return for undertaking to commence employment with the person granting the award after completion of the studies or course of training, the payments received would normally be considered to be scholarship or bursary income under paragraph 56(1)(n).

3.15 The determination of whether an employer-employee relationship exists at the time an award is granted is a question of fact. Payments received by the student after an employer-employee relationship has been established, should generally be treated in accordance with the comments in ¶3.11.

3.16 Where the student is committed to return all or a portion of the scholarship or bursary in the future under certain circumstances (e.g., as a result of a breach of an employment agreement), the amount received will be considered a repayable award. This is discussed in more detail at ¶3.49.

¶8261.2 — *Scholarships Paid to Family Members of Employees*

In *Bartley*, [2008] 5 C.T.C. 2403 (TCC), and *DiMaria*, 2008 CarswellNat 595 (TCC); both affirmed by [2009] 2 C.T.C. 73 (FCA), the taxpayers' children received payments from the taxpayer's employer under a Higher Education Award Program. The Court concluded that the scholarships paid by the employers to the taxpayers' children did not constitute employment benefits in the hands of taxpayers under ITA 6(1)(a). The Court's reasons included that the payment of the award was made directly to the taxpayer's child, the taxpayer had no legal obligation to support his adult son or to pay for his post-secondary education, the taxpayer had no legal right to receive any money from the award or to compel his employer to pay the amount to him, and the taxpayer did not negotiate with his employer to have the award included as an employment benefit or forego other benefits in order for his son to receive the award.

The Court also found that the amounts qualified as scholarships to the children within the meaning of ITA 56(1)(n). In *DiMaria*, the Court noted that:

> The base purpose, spirit and intent of a scholarship should be to enable a student to pursue his studies college or university — that is the basic premise behind any scholarship. It would appear that this is the basic premise behind the scholarship established by Dow. The fact that it may be tied into some scholastic achievement or some athletic ability is an add-on to the basic premise behind any scholarship, which is to enable a student to pursue his studies. This seems to have been lost on CRA as they became focused upon a threshold level which they thought was not realistic. It is not for CRA

to impose their view upon those who establish scholarships. The Act does not state that there is a certain academic threshold.

Furthermore, the Court concluded that:

> Parliament has given favorable treatment to scholarships in its recent amendment to section 56(3). If Parliament decides that an employer-provided scholarship ought to be taxed in the hands of the parent, it can amend the Act accordingly. If it does do so, I would expect they would consider including provisions so that lower-income parents do not see their tax burden increased. Absent of such an amendment, employer-provided scholarships should be taxed in the hands of the true recipient and beneficiary, which is the student. This decision is in keeping with sections 6 and 56 of the Act and also gives rise to a more consistent and certain result than that advocated by the Respondent. Now, contrary to the position of CRA, regardless of whether the parent's employment is ongoing or has been severed by reason of retirement or death, the scholarship will be taxed in the hands of the student.

See also *Okonski v. R.*, [2008] 5 C.T.C. 2515 (TCC), in which the Court concluded that a scholarship program open to the children of employees was not taxable in the hands of the parent.

The above decisions directly contradicted the CRA's policy that a scholarship paid to an employee's child by an employer was a taxable employee benefit to the employee, unless it was given to a limited number of students selected for significant scholastic achievement. In response, the CRA revised their views on scholarships and bursaries paid to the family members of employees. In VD 2009-0312451E5, the CRA states that:

> . . . [T]he CRA now accepts that where an arm's length employer provides a post-secondary scholarship, bursary or free tuition to family members of an employee under a scholarship program, the amount will be included in the particular student's income under paragraph 56(1)(n) of the *Income Tax Act* (the "Act") and not the employee's income as a taxable benefit under paragraph 6(1)(a) of the Act, regardless of the criteria used to award the particular amount. If the particular student is eligible to claim the education tax credit under subsection 118.6(2) of the Act, the entire amount may be exempt from tax pursuant to subsection 56(3) of the Act. The employer is still required to report the amount on a T4A slip.

> We would like to point out that the above-described position does not apply to an employer-provided scholarship program for attendance at an elementary or secondary school (private or otherwise). These amounts will continue to be treated as a taxable benefit to the particular employee.

In VD 2010-0364111E5, the CRA states that for ITA 56(1)(n) to apply to a dependent's scholarship, there must be objective selection criteria that focuses on the accomplishments of the dependent. In particular, to be a genuine scholarship, the CRA states that the scholarship program would need to be available to the children of all employees, not just the children of key employees/shareholders. Also, the CRA states there could not be a decrease in the employee's salary to fund or partially fund the scholarship.

The CRA's current administrative position with respect to scholarship or bursaries awarded to family members of employees is provided in paragraphs 3.17 to 3.20 of Folio S1-F2-C3 as follows:

Employer and employee dealing at arm's length

3.17 Where an arm's length employer provides a post-secondary scholarship, bursary or free tuition to the family member of an employee under a scholarship program, the amount will be included in computing the particular student's income under subparagraph 56(1)(n)(i) provided the employee's salary was not decreased to fund or partially fund the amount. If the student is eligible to claim the education tax credit under subsection 118.6(2) in respect of the program, the entire amount may be exempt from tax pursuant to the scholarship exemption provided in subsection 56(3) (this is discussed further in ¶3.90). The employee will not be considered to have received a taxable employment benefit under paragraph 6(1)(a) with respect to the award, regardless of the criteria used to award the particular amount. This income tax treatment has been adopted as a result of the Federal Court of Appeal decisions in *R v. DiMaria* and *R. v. Bartley*, 2008 FCA 390, 2009 DTC 5019. For information on what constitutes arm's length, see Income Tax Folio S1-F5-C1, *Related persons and dealing at arm's length*.

3.18 Under subparagraph 6(1)(a)(vi), any benefit received or enjoyed on or after October 31, 2011 by the family member of a taxpayer under a program offered by the taxpayer's employer that is designed to assist the family member in furthering his or her education, will not be included in the taxpayer's income as an employment benefit, where:

- the employer and the taxpayer deal with each other at arm's length; and

- it is reasonable to conclude that the benefit is not a substitute for salary, wages or other remuneration of the taxpayer.

Subparagraph 6(1)(a)(vi) applies to benefits received or enjoyed by the family member with respect to the family member's attendance at an elementary, secondary or post-secondary school (private or otherwise), including tuition discounts provided by educational institutions to the family members of its employees. The amount of the benefit received or enjoyed by the family member under these programs will be included in computing the family member's income under subparagraph 56(1)(n)(i). Subsection 56(3) may permit an exemption from the family member's income for some or all of the benefit amount. The exemption is discussed at ¶3.90.

Where the family member of an employee is provided with a scholarship, bursary or free tuition by an arm's length employer for attendance at an elementary or secondary school (private or otherwise) before October 31, 2011, the amount will be included in the employee's income as a taxable benefit under paragraph 6(1)(a), regardless of the criteria used to award the particular amount. As such, no amount will be included in the family member's income pursuant to paragraph 56(1)(n).

Employer and employee not dealing at arm's length

3.19 Where an employer provides an elementary, secondary or post-secondary school scholarship or bursary, or free tuition, to the family member of an employee under a scholarship program and the employer and employee are not dealing at arm's length, the income tax treatment will generally be as follows:

- if the employee is not a shareholder of the employer, or the benefit is not considered to be provided to the family member in the employee's capacity as a shareholder of the employer, the value of the benefit should be included in the employee's income pursuant to paragraph 6(1)(a). The employer will not be precluded from deducting the scholarship or bursary in computing its taxable income by virtue of paragraph 18(1)(a). Subject to satisfying the necessary requirements, the family member may also be eligible to claim the education tax credit under subsection 118.6(2) in respect of the program.

- if the employee is a shareholder of the employer (i.e., the Corporation) and it is determined that the benefit provided to the family member is by virtue of the employee's interest in the Corporation as a shareholder (or in contemplation of the employee becoming a shareholder), the value of the benefit must be included in the employee-shareholder's income under subsection 15(1). In addition, the amount of any scholarship or bursary provided will not be deductible by the Corporation for income tax purposes pursuant to paragraph 18(1)(a). Subject to satisfying the necessary requirements, the family member may also be eligible to claim the education tax credit under subsection 118.6(2) in respect of the program.

3.20 The determination of whether an employer and employee are dealing at arm's length, or whether a benefit is received by an employee-shareholder in his or her capacity as an employee or as a shareholder, involves findings of fact. There is a general presumption that an individual receives a benefit by virtue of his or her shareholdings in those situations where the shareholder, or shareholders, can significantly influence business policy, except where the individual is able to establish otherwise. Exceptions to this presumption would be a situation where the benefit is available to all employees of the Corporation under the same or similar circumstances, or a situation where the benefit is comparable in nature and quantum to benefits generally offered to employees who perform similar services and have similar responsibilities for other employers of a similar size.

Applicable to benefits received on or after October 31, 2011, ITA 6(1)(a)(vi) provides that any benefit received or enjoyed by the family member of a taxpayer under a program offered by the taxpayer's employer that is designed to assist the family member in furthering his or her education will not be included in the taxpayer's income as an employment benefit, where the employer and the taxpayer deal with each other at arm's length; and it is reasonable to conclude that the benefit is not a substitute for salary, wages, or other remuneration of the taxpayer.

These rules apply to benefits received or enjoyed by the family member with respect to the family member's attendance at an elementary, secondary, or post-secondary school (private or otherwise). It also applies to tuition discounts provided by such educational institutions to the family members of its employees. The amount of the benefit received or enjoyed by the family member under the program will be included in computing the family member's income under ITA 56(1)(n)(i). If the family member is eligible to claim the education tax credit under ITA 118.6(2) in connection with his or her enrolment in the educational program, or the benefit is received in connection with the family member's enrolment in an elementary or secondary school educational program, the entire amount may be exempt from tax pursuant to the scholarship exemption.

¶8261.3 — *Post-Doctoral Fellowships*

The scholarship exemption in respect of enrolment in a post-secondary program consisting principally of research is only available if it leads to a college or CEGEP diploma or a bachelor, masters, doctoral, or equivalent degree. The Supplementary Information in Annex 5 to the 2010 federal budget specifically states that post-doctoral fellowships will not qualify for the education tax credit (available before 2017) or the scholarship exemption. This is consistent with the CRA's historical policy that a post-doctoral fellowship is not exempt from tax. For example, in VD 2009-0310891M4, the CRA states that:

> [The CRA has] consistently viewed post-doctoral fellows as being similar to other individuals who are required to undertake a period of paid training after completing their studies but prior to pursuing an independent professional career. As with the compensation received by these other professionals (for example, doctors, lawyers, and accountants), the compensation received by post-doctoral fellows is generally taxable. The amendments announced in the 2010 federal budget regarding the scholarship exemption clarified the intent of the legislation and confirmed the CRA's existing position. Whether a post-doctoral fellow is an employee, an independent contractor, or a student for income tax purposes will depend on his or her particular situation.

In *Chabaud v. The Queen*, 2011 TCC 438, the court determined that the amounts paid from a research centre associated with Laval University to the taxpayer to conduct research as a post-doctoral fellow constituted income from employment; and thus, the taxpayer was not entitled to the education tax credit or the scholarship exemption.

The CRA provides the following comments in paragraphs 3.36 to 3.38 of Folio S1-F2-C3 regarding the meaning and taxation of post-doctoral fellowships:

> 3.36 The term fellow is generally understood and commonly used in at least two distinct circumstances for post-doctoral work:
>
> - The term is used (as in post-doctoral fellow or PDF) to indicate an individual who has recently obtained his or her Ph.D. (usually within the past five years or possibly longer) who is engaged in advanced research activities at a university or at a facility or laboratory connected with a university. The aim of the individual is often to obtain sufficient experience and published research as a PDF to be considered for a position as a professor at a university (an Academic PDF); and
>
> - The term is used, usually on its own, to refer to an individual who has completed both the required academic and professional training in a particular field (for example, a medical doctor), and who has been given a special grant to enable him or her to engage in specialized training or research. In the field of medicine, such fellows often receive the grant to work in a highly specialized area requiring clinical duties as a medical doctor within a hospital setting (a Clinical Fellow).
>
> 3.37 Post-doctoral fellows, such as Academic PDFs and Clinical Fellows, are primarily considered to receive employment income for purposes of subsection 5(1). In certain limited circumstances, however, amounts received by a post-doctoral fellow may be considered a research grant for purposes of paragraph 56(1)(o) (discussed further at ¶3.58).
>
> 3.38 Generally, post-doctoral fellows are not considered to be students as that term is used in the Act. For income tax purposes, post-doctoral fellows are viewed and treated like other taxpayers who are required to undertake a period of paid training after the completion of their studies prior to pursuing an independent professional career. Post-doctoral fellows are most similar to apprentices, articling students (for accounting and law, for example) and medical residents. As with the compensation received by these professionals, the compensation received by post-doctoral fellows is generally taxable. The nature and characterization of an amount received by a post-doctoral fellow should be determined on a

case-by-case basis, taking into account all of the relevant facts and circumstances. For information concerning the scholarship exemption as it relates to post-doctoral fellowships, see ¶3.102.

¶8261.4 — *Prizes, Including Prescribed Prizes*

Prizes received for achievement in a field of endeavour and any business- or work-related prizes or awards are specifically excluded as being scholarship income; and thus, these types of prizes and awards are not eligible for the $500 scholarship exemption. Rather, the full amount is generally treated as a taxable employee benefit, subject to the exception for prescribed prizes, discussed below. Also see the discussion of Prizes and Awards at ¶2280.

CRA provides the following comments regarding the taxation of prizes in paragraphs 3.53 to 3.55 of Folio S1-F2-C3:

3.53 Subparagraph 56(1)(n)(i) includes in computing a taxpayer's income, the amount of a prize for achievement in a field of endeavour ordinarily carried on by the taxpayer (other than a prescribed prize). Where the prize is included in income, subsection 56(3) may permit an exemption from income for some or the entire prize amount. The exemption is discussed at ¶3.90. A prize can be considered to be an award to a particular person selected from a group of potential recipients and given for something that is accomplished, attained or carried out successfully. However, the type of prize contemplated in subparagraph 56(1)(n)(i) is restricted. The criteria for awarding the prize must be such that a recipient is rewarded for success in an area in which the recipient regularly applies effort. Therefore, an amount generally qualifies as a prize for purposes of subparagraph 56(1)(n)(i) if it is paid in recognition of a genuine accomplishment in a challenging area, whether it be of an academic, vocational or technical nature. A prize that is not described by subparagraph 56(1)(n)(i) is considered to be a windfall and is not required to be included in income unless it is also a business receipt (see ¶3.55) or income from employment (see ¶3.54). The following points indicate how subparagraph 56(1)(n)(i) applies to certain situations.

- An award of damages to an injured party. This is not considered to be a prize.

- Lottery winnings. Although this is a prize, the recipient is not being recognized for an accomplishment nor are the winnings likely to relate to a field of endeavour ordinarily carried on by the recipient. As a result, subparagraph 56(1)(n)(i) does not apply.

- An award by a professional institution to the candidate obtaining the highest marks in examinations set by the institution. This is a prize subject to the provisions of subparagraph 56(1)(n)(i).

3.54 If an employee receives, from his or her employer, a prize or other award related to sales or other work performance (such as exceeding sales targets, success in examinations, suggestion awards or exceptional service), the fair market value of such an incentive is regarded as remuneration for services that must be included in the individual's employment income under subsection 5(1). Similarly, the fair market value of a prize or award that is not regarded as remuneration, but is considered to have been received by an employee in respect of, in the course of, or by virtue of the employee's office or employment, is included in income from an office or employment under paragraph 6(1)(a), subject to certain exceptions for small non-cash gifts and awards. A prize or other award that is considered to be income from an office or employment for purposes of subsection 5(1) or paragraph 6(1)(a), will be excluded from paragraph 56(1)(n).

3.55 If there is no employer-employee relationship between the payer and the recipient of an amount and it can be established that the amount is a business receipt, it should be included in the recipient's business income under subsection 9(1). However, if the amount received is a prize for achievement in a field of endeavour ordinarily carried on by the taxpayer and it cannot be regarded as a business receipt (and is not a prescribed prize), the amount should be used in computing the recipient's income under subparagraph 56(1)(n)(i).

A prize that meets all of the criteria of a prescribed prize is wholly exempt from tax, and thus, is not included in computing the income of the recipient, even if the prize relates to accomplishments in the recipient's ordinary field of endeavour. ITR 7700 defines a prescribed prize as any prize that is recognized by the general public and awarded for meritorious achievement in the arts, the sciences or service to the public, but not including any amount that can reasonably be regarded as having been received as compensation for services rendered or to be rendered. It is a question of fact whether a prize is considered to have been recognized by the general public for purposes of ITR

7700. In making such a determination, one should consider whether there is evidence suggesting a high level of public awareness of the prize and the extent to which the announcement or receipt of the prize is widely publicized by the media.

Examples of prescribed prizes include the Nobel Prize given to a scientist, the Governor General's Literary Award given to a professional writer, and various community service awards. Scholarships and bursaries awarded to students would not qualify as prescribed prizes. Furthermore, any amount that can reasonably be regarded as having been received as compensation for services rendered, or to be rendered, is not a prescribed prize.

In a recent case (*Knapik-Sztramko v. The Queen*, 2013 CarswellNat 3665, [2014]), the taxpayer was an opera singer who won a vocal competition, and received payments of about $80,000 over 10 years for singing coaches, stage presence training, physical training, accommodation, and travel expenses. The CRA reassessed the taxpayer to include these amounts into her income. The Tax Court held that the payments were a prize within meaning of ITA 56(1)(n), and were a prescribed prize within meaning of ITR 7700, and therefore exempt from income tax.

It is the CRA's administrative position that the following qualify as prescribed prizes: the Governor General's Performing Arts Awards (VD 9300075); certain Canada Council awards (IT-257R para. 9; VDs 933395, 2000-0002565, 2001-0077455, 2004-0076661E5); the Prime Minister's Award for Teaching Excellence in Science, Technology and Math (VD 9514155); the National Gallery of Canada Millenium Prize (VD 2001-0072015); the Carnegie Hero Fund Commission Prize (VD 2002-0142187); certain prizes for achievement in the sciences (2005-0145751E5); the Kobzar Literary Award (2006-0179911E5); Agri-Food Innovation Excellence awards (VD 2006-0202931E5); the Hnatyshyn Foundation Visual Arts Award (2007-0224981E5); the Leadership in Faculty Teaching Award (2007-0245311I7); INDEX Award (2008-0265731E5); certain prizes administered by a university (2010-0374461E5); and a prize awarded in competition to present sustainable business practice (2012-0438891E5).

It is the CRA's administrative position that the following do not qualify as prescribed prizes, and thus are taxable: university awards for scholastic achievement (VD 9911565); prizes for an essay contest awarded to high school students (2004-0084611E5); Olympic medals and Canadian Olympic Committee prize money (VDs 2004-0098691E5, 2008-0300071M4, 2012-0458181M4, 2012-0460111M4, 2013-0477251M4); awards akin to a fellowship (2005-0127741E5); a charitable foundation award related to the recipient's business or employment (2009-0313051E5); research grants; and certain Canada Council awards.

ITA 56(1)(n), 56(3), Pamphlet P105, Folio S1-F2-C3, VDs 2008-0300441E5, 2008-0303451M4, 2009-0307471M4, 2010-0364651M4, canada.ca/en/revenue-agency/services/tax/businesses/topics/payroll/benefits-allowances/scholarships-bursaries-tuition-training.html

¶8262 — *Apprenticeship Incentive Grants and Apprenticeship Completion Grants*

A registered apprentice who successfully completes the first or second year/level of an apprenticeship program in a designated Red Seal trade (see: red-seal.ca/trades/tr.1d.2s_l.3st-eng.html for a list of eligible trades) is eligible for an Apprenticeship Incentive Grant of $1,000 per year to a maximum of $2,000. Amounts received by a taxpayer under the Apprenticeship Incentive Grant program are required to be included in computing income on Line 130. Note that repayments under the Apprenticeship Incentive Grant program in respect of amounts included in computing a taxpayer's income in the year of repayment or in a prior taxation year are deductible in the year of repayment; see Line 232 under ¶9272.

A registered apprentice who successfully completes apprenticeship training is also eligible for an Apprenticeship Completion Grant of $2,000. This grant helps registered apprentices who have completed their training become certified journeypersons in designated Red Seal trades. Amounts received by a taxpayer under the Apprenticeship Completion Grant program are also required to be included in computing income on Line 130.

The apprenticeship incentive and completion grants are administered by Human Resources and Skills Development Canada. The amount received by an individual during the year is reported on Form T4A, *Statement of Pension, Retirement, Annuity, and Other Income*.

ITA 56(1)(n.1), 2009-0307391I7

¶8263 — *Lump-Sum Payments*

Lump-sum payments from pensions and deferred profit-sharing plans are included in income upon receipt when leaving a plan (T4A slip Box 18 and T3 slip Box 22). If, in the year, an individual received a lump-sum payment that included amounts earned in previous years, the whole payment is required to be reported on Line 130 of the individual's return. However, a request can be made for the CRA to apply a reduced tax rate to the part that relates to amounts earned before 1972 by attaching a note to the paper return. The CRA will report the results on the individual's notice of assessment or reassessment.

ITA 60(j) permits a deduction in respect of certain transfers of superannuation benefits to RPPs and RRSPs in respect of amounts paid in a year or within 60 days after the end of the year. The deduction is generally limited to lump sum payments received by a taxpayer from a pension plan (other than an RPP) attributable to services rendered while the taxpayer (or the taxpayer's spouse) was not resident in Canada and included in the taxpayer's income.

ITA 60(j), Guide RC4157, Guide T4001, Guide T4040

¶8264 — *Retiring Allowances*

A "retiring allowance" in respect of the termination of a taxpayer's employment includes two types of payments: (1) an amount received on or after retirement of the taxpayer from an office or employment in recognition of the taxpayer's long service, and (2) an amount received in respect of the loss of office or employment of the taxpayer, whether or not received as, on account of or in lieu of payment of, damages or pursuant to an order or judgment of a competent tribunal. Any amount received by the taxpayer or, after the taxpayer's death, by a dependant or relation of a taxpayer or by the legal representative of the taxpayer may also fall within the definition of a "retiring allowance" required to be included in the recipient's income. A retiring allowance includes severance pay, payment for unused sick leave and other amounts received for loss of office or employment, whether the individual was dismissed or resigned, and whether as payment of damages or a payment under an order or judgment of a tribunal. A retiring allowance may be made in lump-sum payments, but the payments must be included in income when received. A retiring allowance does not include the following types of payments: a superannuation or pension benefit; an amount received as a consequence of the death of an employee; accumulated vacation leave credit; or amounts received out of or under an employee benefit plan, retirement compensation arrangement or a salary deferral arrangement. When a "retiring allowance" is paid to a non-resident, a withholding tax of 25 per cent is payable, except where the rate is reduced by an applicable income tax treaty.

A loss of office or employment usually refers to the elimination or expiration of a particular office or employment (for example, the abolition of a job or position for economic reasons or as the consequence of an employer's withdrawal from a particular business). However, a loss of office or employment may also refer to the loss of an income source of an employee who is released from an office or employment whether unilaterally or not.

The CRA's views on the meaning of retirement and loss of office or employment for purposes of the definition of a retiring allowance are contained in paragraphs 2.6 to 2.13 of Folio S2-F1-C2:

> 2.6 A retiring allowance includes an amount received on or after retirement in recognition of long service. The term long service is usually considered to refer to the total number of years in an employee's career with a particular employer or affiliated employers.

> 2.7 Whether an individual has retired is a question of fact. The fact that an individual continues to participate in a health or dental plan of a former employer would not, on its own, indicate that the individual has not retired as it is relatively common for such plans to provide coverage to retirees. However, if the individual continues to accrue pension benefits, this would indicate a continued employment relationship as pension benefits only accrue to employees. The fact that an employer does not require an individual to report to work is not determinative of whether the individual has retired. For example, an individual who has been given a leave of absence for educational purposes is still an employee.

Loss of employment

> 2.8 A retiring allowance includes an amount received in respect of a loss of employment of an individual. In this context, the words in respect of have been held by the courts to imply a connection between the loss of employment and the subsequent receipt, where the primary purpose of the payment is to compensate for the loss of employment. Two ques-

tions set out by the courts to determine whether such a connection exists for purposes of a retiring allowance are as follows:

Question 1 — But for the loss of employment would the amount have been received?

Question 2 — Was the purpose of the payment to compensate a loss of employment?

Only if the answer to the first question is no and the answer to the second question is yes, will the amount received be considered a retiring allowance.

2.9 A loss of employment usually involves the elimination or expiration of particular employment. For example, a job or position might be abolished for economic reasons or as a consequence of the employer exiting a particular business. A loss of employment may also refer to the loss of an income source of an employee who is released from employment whether unilaterally or not. Since early retirement incentive plans are basically designed to eliminate a number of employment positions (even if it is on an elective basis), payments made upon such terminations are generally considered as being for a loss of employment.

Timing

2.10 If an individual continues to earn salary and benefits until a date after the date they cease to report to work, the retirement or loss of employment, as the case may be, is considered to take place only at the later date. Retiring allowance payments in recognition of long service must be made on or after retirement. However, there is no similar requirement for payments in respect of a loss of employment. A payment made in advance of loss of employment will be considered a retiring allowance if: it can be shown that the payment is in respect of the loss; there is evidence that the loss is not speculative or contingent; and the severing of the employment relationship, including the termination of all employment benefits, will occur on a specific date and within a reasonable time frame.

Exceptions

2.11 Retirement or loss of employment does not include situations where an employee is transferred from one work location or position to another with the same employer or an affiliate. For example, this could refer to a transfer: to a position in a different capacity; to a position with diminished responsibilities; or from a full-time position to a part-time position as part of a reorganization of an employer's business.

2.12 In addition, retirement or loss of employment does not include a termination of employment where arrangements have been made for the individual to obtain employment with an affiliate of the employer or to be re-hired by the employer. If there is no assurance or offer of new employment or re-employment at the time the individual terminates the employment, then the CRA will consider a retirement or loss of employment to have occurred, regardless of any subsequent events.

2.13 A termination of employment described in ¶2.11 or 2.12 will not be excluded solely because: prior to retirement from a full-time position in a government department, the individual obtains, through their own initiative, part-time employment with another department where the duties and responsibilities of the new position are unrelated to those of the former position; the individual continues as a corporate director (other than as a director of a public company) at nominal compensation; or after the sale of the employer's active business, the individual agrees to carry on certain administrative duties for which no remuneration or director fees are received.

¶8264.1 — Transfers to an RRSP or RPP

Part or all of an individual's retiring allowance may be contributed to the individual's RRSP or RPP, either by a direct or indirect transfer. Tax is not required to be withheld from the part of a retiring allowance that an employer transfers directly to an individual's RRSP or RPP. Tax will be withheld from the portion of a retiring allowance that is not transferred directly to an RRSP or RPP. Generally, the tax-free transfer is limited to $2,000 for each year of service before 1996, and $1,500 for each year of service in respect of which no employer contribution to an RPP or a DPSP had vested in the year (ITA 60(j.1)). Years of service after 1995 are not taken into account. A retiring allowance cannot be transferred to a spousal RRSP or RPP.

See paragraphs 2.30 and 2.31 of Folio S2-F1-C2, *Retiring Allowances*, for further details regarding transferring a retiring allowance to an RRSP. Also, the following example is contained in Folio S2-F1-C2:

> Jacques began working at ABC Company in October 1984 and retired in June 2016. In June 2016, Jacques received a $45,000 retiring allowance in recognition of his long service and includes this amount in income. Jacques has been a member of ABC's pension plan since October 1986. Jacques' regular RRSP deduction limit for 2016 is $8,000.
>
> The maximum that Jacques can contribute to his RRSP and claim a deduction under paragraph 60(j.1) is $27,000:
>
> | | | |
> |---|---|---|
> | $2,000 × 12 full or partial years before 1996 | $ | 24,000 |
> | plus | | |
> | $1,500 × 2 years before 1989 with no vested benefits | $ | 3,000 |
> | | | |
> | *Maximum deduction* | $ | *27,000* |
>
> During 2016, Jacques contributes $35,000 to his RRSP. Jacques is entitled to claim a deduction of $27,000 under paragraph 60(j.1). The remaining $8,000 can be deducted using Jacques' regular RRSP deduction limit.

¶8265 — *Death Benefits*

A death benefit is an amount received after a person's death for that person's employment service. It is reported in T4A Box 028 or T3 Box 26. An individual may not have to pay tax on up to $10,000 of the benefit received. If the individual is the only person to receive a death benefit for the same person, report the amount received that is more than $10,000. Even if all of the death benefit is not received in one year, the total tax-free amount for all years cannot be more than $10,000. To find out what to report if anyone else also received a death benefit for the same person, see IT-508R: *Death Benefits*. Attach to the paper return a note stating the amount of death benefits received but not included in income. See VD 2006-0178501E5 for CRA considerations in determining whether a particular amount is a death benefit or a retiring allowance.

When a Canadian resident pays a death benefit to a non-resident, a 25 per cent withholding tax must be withheld under ITA 212(1)(j) (subject to a tax treaty).

¶8266 — *RESP Accumulated Income and Educational Assistance Payments*

Pursuant to ITA 146.1, a registered education savings plan (RESP) is an arrangement whereby funds are held in trust, and managed by a person or an organization (promoter) to accumulate income to be paid for the higher education of a beneficiary. The funds may consist of amounts paid by an individual (subscriber) and government grants, namely, the Canada Education Savings Grant (CESG), the Canadian Learning Bond, or any designated provincial education savings program. The funds are available to the beneficiary on enrollment at a post-secondary educational institution.

Contributions to an RESP are not deductible for income tax purposes and are not taxed upon withdrawal. The investment income that accrues in an RESP is taxable only when an amount is withdrawn from the plan. For taxation years after 2006, there is no annual contribution limit for contributions made to an RESP; however, the maximum lifetime contribution limit is $50,000. In determining whether the lifetime contribution limit has been exceeded, all contributions for the beneficiary are considered, even if they have been withdrawn.

The following types of withdrawals may be made from an RESP: payments to a designated educational institution in Canada, refunds of contributions to the subscriber or beneficiary, educational assistance payments, and accumulated income payments. For a further discussion of RESPs, see ¶16220.

¶8266.1 — *Educational Assistance Payments (EAPs)*

Generally, an EAP is a payment (other than a refund of contributions) made to a designated beneficiary under an RESP to assist the beneficiary to further his or her post-secondary education. EAPs are included in computing the student's income. EAPs generally include RESP accumulated investment earnings, CESG payments, and investment earnings accumulated on those funds. The CESG program provides a basic grant of 20 per cent on contributions made to an RESP (up to and including the year in which the beneficiary turns 17) to a maximum of $500 per beneficiary per year (or $1,000 if there is unused grant room because contributions of less than the CESG annual contribution limit were made for previous years; i.e., less than $2,000 for years before 2007, and less than $2,500 for years after 2006). An additional CESG of up to $100 per year may be provided, depending on the family income of the beneficiary child. The maximum lifetime grant for the basic and additional CESG is $7,200. Grants are paid directly to the trustee of the RESP and are paid out to the beneficiary as part of his/her EAPs.

An EAP is reported in Form T4A Box 042. It is taxable to the beneficiary and must be included on Line 130. A refund of contributions to the subscriber or, at his or her direction, to the beneficiary is not taxable to the recipient.

¶8266.2 — Accumulated Income Payments (AIPs)

If an RESP beneficiary does not enroll in a qualifying educational program, the subscriber can withdraw the investment income from the RESP provided certain conditions are met. Such withdrawals are referred to as an "accumulated income payment" (AIP), and are taxable as ordinary income in the subscriber's hands. The amount is reported in Form T4A Box 040 and should be reported on Line 130.

The recipient of an AIP may also be subject to an additional tax under ITA 204.94(2) (see Line 418, Special Taxes, at ¶11060). The amount subject to this tax may be reduced or eliminated where certain conditions are met and a deductible RRSP contribution is made for the year in which the accumulated income payment was received. Beginning in 2014, accumulated income payments may be made from an RESP into an RDSP, where the plans both have the same beneficiary and certain conditions are met.

ITA 146.1, 204.94, *Canada Education Savings Act, Quinn*, [1973] C.T.C. 258, PwC, "RESPs: A user's guide", Tax Memo, Jan 7, 2013, Friedlan, "Tax Deferral: Old and New," 2009 Prairie Provinces Tax Conference, (Toronto: Canadian Tax Foundation, 2009), 13:1–44, Provenzano and Ross, "RESP Withdrawals Part 1" (2009) vol 17, no 4 Canadian Tax Highlights, 8-9 and "RESP Withdrawals Part 2" (2009) vol 17, no 5 Canadian Tax Highlights, 5-6

¶8300 — Workers' Compensation and Other Benefits (T1: Lines 144, 145, 146)

Amounts included in income on Line 144 (workers' compensation benefits), Line 145 (social assistance payments), and Line 146 (net federal supplements) are generally not taxable, as they benefit from an offsetting deduction on Line 250 in the calculation of taxable income (see ¶9340). Nevertheless, individuals must report the total of these benefits on Line 147 for purposes of calculating various credits or benefits, such as the Canada Child Benefit and the GST/HST credit and to reduce the amount of other deductions or credits that may be available to others, such as the non-refundable tax credit for a spouse or common-law partner on Line 303. These payments are generally reported on Form T5007, *Statement of Benefits*, or Form T4A(OAS), *Statement of Old Age Security*.

ITA 56(1)(a)(i)(A), 56(1)(u), 56(1)(v), 56(9), 81(1)(h), 110(1)(f), Guide T4001, Guide T4115, Guide T5007, ITTN-31R2, IT-202R2: *Employees' or workers' compensation*

¶8310 — Workers' Compensation Benefits (T1: Line 144)

Workers' compensation benefits are payments under federal, provincial, or territorial employees' or workers' compensation law for injury, disability, or death. Workers' compensation payments are required to be included in income on Line 144; however, a corresponding deduction is allowed on Line 250 in computing taxable income, with the result that the workers' compensation payments are not subject to tax.

The inclusion of workers' compensation benefits in the recipient's net income may affect certain credit and benefit amounts such as the age credit, Canada Child Benefit, GST/HST credit and medical expense credit, as well as the extent to which another taxpayer can claim a spousal or common-law partner credit or eligible dependant credit in respect of the recipient (see *Nicholson*, [2006] 5 C.T.C. 2359 (TCC), *Farah*, 2013 CarswellNat 61 (TCC), *Dakiri*, 2013 CarswellNat 63 (TCC), VD 2009-0324731I7 and VD 2011-0411231M4). It also affects OAS under the *Old Age Security Act* (*Dupuis*, 2011 CarswellNat 4936 (TCC)).

Workers' compensation benefits are discussed in IT-202R2: *Employees' or Workers' Compensation*, which provides as follows:

1. In this bulletin

> (a) "compensation board" includes any employees' or workers' compensation board or commission in any province or territory of Canada, and

> (b) "compensation" refers to the amount of an award, as adjudicated by a compensation board, which a worker or his or her dependants will receive as a result of the worker having suffered illness, injury or death in the performance of his or her duties of employment and includes any such compensation to which entitlement is provided under the *Government Employees Compensation Act* or any employees' or workers' compensation Act or Ordinance of a province or territory of Canada.

2. Prior to 1982, the amount of compensation that was received in a taxation year by any person (other than as the employer or former employer of the person in respect of whom the amount was paid) was excluded from income by virtue of paragraph 81(1)(h), which paragraph was repealed applicable to the 1982 and subsequent taxation years. The main income tax effect of the repeal of paragraph 81(1)(h), and other amendments to the Act, is that compensation received, while continuing to be non-taxable, is now included in the income of the person who receives it. The amount of compensation received in a taxation year is therefore relevant in determining

> (a) the extent to which the recipient thereof may be claimed as a dependant by another taxpayer, and

> (b) the amount that is the aggregate of the family net income and the other supporting person's net income for purposes of the child tax credit.

Inclusion in income

3. For 1982 and subsequent taxation years, the amount of compensation received in a taxation year by any person is, by virtue of paragraph 56(1)(v), required to be included in computing that person's income for the year.

4. For the purpose of paragraph 56(1)(v) the amount of compensation may be received either from a compensation board or from the employer or former employer of the person entitled thereto. An employee may, under the terms of an employment contract or collective agreement, or by reason of being granted injury leave with pay under the *Financial Administration Act*, be entitled to receive salary or wages during a period in which the employee is also entitled to compensation. Where, in these circumstances, the employee receives no payment from a compensation board, the amount received from his or her employer, to the extent that it does not exceed the compensation amount, will be included in the employee's income for the year, as compensation, under paragraph 56(1)(v). The excess, if any, will be included in the employee's income under subsection 5(1).

Deduction in Computing Taxable Income

5. For 1982 and subsequent taxation years, any compensation received by a taxpayer in a taxation year, that was included in the taxpayer's income under paragraph 56(1)(v), may, by virtue of subparagraph 110(1)(f)(ii), be deducted in computing the taxpayer's taxable income for the year, except any such compensation received by the taxpayer as the employer of former employer of the person in respect of whom the compensation was paid.

Payments received by Employers

6. Any amount received by an employer from a compensation board, or remitted by the employee to the employer, or any other amount paid to an employer in reimbursement of salary or wages paid by the employer is included, without exception, in computing the employer's income.

Loans or Advances

7. Where it can be established that an employee received a loan or advance from his or her employer which is to be repaid from future payments of compensation, the loan or advance constitutes neither income to the employee nor deductible expense to the employer. However, when the compensation is paid and is received by the employee, it will be

treated in accordance with 3 and 5 above. The amount received by the employer from or on behalf of the employee in repayment of the loan or advance will not constitute income to the employer.

Where workers' compensation amounts received are for payments in arrears, the benefits are included in income in the year they are received, not in the years for which they were paid (*Franklin*, [2004] 1 C.T.C. 2062 (TCC)).

In *Whitney*, [2002] 3 C.T.C. 476 (FCA), amounts paid by an employer under a collective agreement which used the provincial Workers' Compensation Board approval process were considered not to be taxable as workers' compensation benefits. As well, in *Suchon*, [2002] 3 C.T.C. 547 (FCA), disability payments made by an employer who was outside the Workers' Compensation Board system were taxable as employment income under ITA 6(1)(a) and did not fall under ITA 56(1)(v) (see also VD 2003-01828285, VD 2007-0239601E5 and *Gingras*, [1998] 2 C.T.C. 2557 (TCC)).

¶8311 — *Claiming and Filing*

Workers' compensation benefits are reported in Box 10 of Form T5007. Enter on Line 144 the amount shown in Box 10 of the individual's T5007 slip. Claim a deduction on Line 250 (see ¶9340) for the benefits entered on Line 144. If the individual repaid salary or wages in the year that were originally paid to the individual by his or her employer in a previous year in anticipation of workers' compensation benefits to be received by the individual in a future year, the amount should be shown in T4 Box 77 and the individual may be able to claim a deduction on Line 229 (see ¶9250).

ITA 56(1)(v), 110(1)(f)(ii), ITR 232, *Fraser*, [1996] 2 C.T.C. 2631 (TCC), *Coulter*, [2004] 4 C.T.C. 2374 (TCC), *Quebec (Ville)*, 2007 CarswellNat 5250 (TCC), *Simone Sherman*, [2009] 1 C.T.C. 2581 (TCC), Guide T4001, IT-202R2: *Employees' or workers' compensation*, VDs 2006-0189531I7, 2006-0191501I7, 2006-0208611I7, 2006-0211061I7, 2006-0213961E5, 2006-0215791E5, 2006-0217681E5, 2011-0421671E5

¶8320 — Social Assistance Payments (T1: Line 145)

Social assistance payments determined on the basis of a means, needs, or income test are included in income for tax purposes pursuant to ITA 56(1)(u). Assistance payments that are not based on a means, needs or income test are not included in income under ITA 56(1)(u), and may be non-taxable (for example, see VD 2003-0054611E5). Social assistance payments include welfare payments from government and municipalities, as well as payments by charities to needy persons (VDs 9825265 and 2011-0418701E5). In the case of a married or common-law couple living together, such payments should be included in the income of the spouse or common-law partner who has the higher income. If the spouses or common-law partners have the same income, the person named on the slip should include the payment into income.

A corresponding deduction is allowed on Line 250 (see ¶9340) for purposes of computing taxable income, with the result that social assistance payments are not taxed. As a result, the only effect is on net income, which affects certain credit and benefit amounts such as the age credit, Canada Child Benefit, GST/HST credit, medical expense credit and Old Age Security. It may also reduce the amount of other deductions or credits that may be available to others, such as the spouse or common-law partner credit or eligible dependant credit.

Social assistance payments for foster care are exempt under ITA 81(1)(h), but not if the cared-for person is related to the caregiver (VD 2010-0384491E5). As well, amounts received for in-home care may be exempt from tax under ITA 81(1)(h), rather than as social assistance under ITA 56(1)(u), or the amounts may be considered business income (VD 2011-0407071E5).

In the CRA's view, the following type of payments are considered to be social assistance payments includable under ITA 56(1)(u) and deductible under ITA 110(1)(f): charities' Individual Development Accounts (2006-0180281E5); a program providing medical devices to disabled persons (2009-0305961E5); financial assistance from a program providing employment assistance services (2009-0338621E5); an off-reserve Aboriginal housing program (2010-0357911E5); assistance with child-care costs to students in financial difficulty (2010-0389161E5); payments to a taxpayer as a caregiver for own child (2010-0359971M4, 2011-0414651E5); financial assistance by charity to needy persons (2011-0418701E5); and assistance under the B.C. Young Adult Program (2009-0345561I7).

Social assistance payments are required to be reported on a T5007 slip. It is the CRA's view that amounts that are excluded from T5007 reporting by ITR 233(2) are not required to be included in the recipient's net income (VDs 2003-0053511E5, 2010-0384571R3).

¶8321 — *Claiming and Filing*

Enter the amount from T5007 Box 11 on Line 145 of the return of the spouse or common-law partner with the higher net income on Line 236 (not including these payments or the deductions on Line 214 for child care expenses or Line 235 for social benefits repayment). If Line 236 is the same amount for both spouses, the person whose name is on the slip should report them. Claim a deduction on Line 250 for the social assistance payments entered on Line 145 (see ¶9340).

ITA 56(1)(u), 110(i)(f), ITR 233, *Nicholson*, [2006] 5 C.T.C. 2359 (TCC), *Gefter*, [2007] 2 C.T.C. 2198 (TCC), VDs 2003-0054611E5, 2003-0053511E5, 2010-0384571R3, 2011-0419111I7

¶8330 — Net Federal Supplements (T1: Line 146)

Net federal supplements include the federal Guaranteed Income Supplement (GIS), the Allowance, and the Allowance for the Survivor.

¶8331 — *Guaranteed Income Supplement (GIS)*

The Guaranteed Income Supplement (GIS) is available to low-income Canadian resident seniors who are receiving (or eligible to receive) the OAS pension. An application must be filed to receive this supplement; it is not done automatically when you file a tax return. Once a person is receiving the GIS, it will be automatically adjusted each year after the income tax return is filed.

Income from GIS is tax-free. However, it is reported on Line 146 of the T1 return, and included in total income (Line 150) and net income (Line 236) for tax purposes. It is later deducted on Line 250 of the tax return, so it is not included in taxable income (see ¶9340).

The amount of GIS payable depends on marital status and total income for the prior year. Total income for GIS purposes is income from Line 236 of the T1 return, less:

- OAS and GIS income; and

- The lesser of: (1) $3,500, and (2) employment income less allowable deductions, including CPP/QPP contributions and EI premiums

Although the GIS is normally determined based on the previous year's income, if an OAS pensioner or spouse retires or has a reduction in income for some other reason, Service Canada may use an income estimate for the current year to determine eligibility. However, if the actual income is later determined to be different from the estimated income, there will be an adjustment of the GIS paid. This could result in additional GIS being paid, or excess GIS being deducted from future payments.

See: canada.ca/en/services/benefits/publicpensions/cpp/old-age-security.html for more information on the GIS.

¶8332 — *Allowance and Allowance for the Survivor*

The Allowance is available to 60 to 64 year-old spouses or common-law partners of OAS pensioners who receive the GIS. The Allowance is available when the previous year's combined annual income of both spouses (excluding OAS and GIS) is less than $33,696. The Allowance must be applied for.

The Allowance for the Survivor may be available if the taxpayer's spouse or common-law partner has died, the taxpayer is 60 to 64 years old, and the taxpayer's previous year's annual income (excluding OAS and GIS, etc.) is less than $24,552.

See: canada.ca/en/services/benefits/publicpensions/cpp/old-age-security.html for more information.

¶8333 — *Claiming and Filing*

Enter the amount shown in T4A(OAS) Box 21 on Line 146 and claim a deduction on Line 250 for the benefits entered on Line 146 (see ¶9340).

Chapter 9 — Other Deductions

Contents

¶9000 Other Deductions

¶9010 Personal Tax Deductions Quick Reference Table

¶9100 Deductions from Total Income (T1: Lines 205–235)

¶9105 PRPP Employer Contributions (T1: Line 205)

¶9110 Pension Adjustment (T1: Line 206)

¶9120 Registered Pension Plan Deduction (T1: Line 207)

¶9130 RRSP and PRPP Deduction (T1: Line 208)

¶9140 Deduction for Elected Split-Pension Amount (T1: Line 210)

¶9150 Annual Union, Professional or Like Dues (T1: Line 212)

¶9160 Universal Child Care Benefit Repayment (T1: Line 213)

¶9170 Child Care Expenses (T1: Line 214)

¶9180 Disability Supports Deduction (T1: Line 215)

¶9190 Business Investment Loss (T1: Line 217)

¶9200 Moving Expenses (T1: Line 219)

¶9210 Support Payments Made (T1: Line 220)

¶9220 Carrying Charges & Interest Expenses (T1 Line 221)

¶9230 Deduction for CPP or QPP Contributions on Self-Employment and Other Earnings (T1: Line 222)

¶9240 Exploration & Development Expenses (T1: Line 224)

¶9250 Other Employment Expenses (T1: Line 229)

¶9260 Clergy Residence Deduction (T1: Line 231)

¶9270 Other Deductions (T1: Line 232)

¶9280 Social Benefits Repayment (T1: Line 235)

¶9300 Deductions from Net Income (T1: Lines 244–256)

¶9310 Canadian Forces Personnel and Police Deduction (T1: Line 244)

¶9320 Employee Home Relocation Loan Deduction (T1: Line 248)

¶9330 Security Options Deductions (T1: Line 249)

¶9340 Other Payments Deduction (T1: Line 250)

¶9350 Limited Partnership Losses of Other Years (T1: Line 251)

¶9360 Non-Capital Losses of Other Years (T1: Line 252)

¶9370 Net Capital Losses of Other Years (T1: Line 253)

¶9380 Capital Gains Deduction (T1: Line 254)

¶9390 Northern Residents Deduction (T1: Line 255)

¶9400 Additional Deductions (T1: Line 256)

¶9000 — Other Deductions

Chapter 2 discussed the deductions allowed in computing a taxpayer's income for a taxation year from an office or employment. This chapter discusses the other additional deductions that can be claimed, regardless of the taxpayer's source of income. These additional deductions are contained on Lines 205 to 256 of the T1 return, and include contributions to a registered pension plan or registered retirement savings plan, child care expenses, moving expenses, certain support payments, losses of other years, and other various deductions. These amounts are deducted from total income on Line 150, and from net income on Line 236, to calculate the taxable income of an individual on Line 260. Net income consists of the individual's total earnings, net of related expenses and current year deductible losses. Net income is used in the calculation of several non-refundable tax credits, such as the spouse or common-law partner amount and the age credit. Various additional deductions from net income are allowed to arrive at an individual's taxable income, which is used to calculate an individual's taxes payable.

¶9010 — Personal Tax Deductions Quick Reference Table

The 2018 Personal Tax Deductions Quick Reference Table lists the majority of the federal personal tax deductions that individuals can deduct from income on their 2018 T1 return. The deductions are generally claimed on Lines 205 to 232 and 244 to 256 of the T1 return. The table includes references to the relevant paragraphs of this Guide, line of the T1 return, T1 schedules, tax forms, CRA publications and guides, CRA Interpretation Bulletins and Information Circulars, sections of the *Income Tax Act*, and other relevant authority.

Deduction	References	Explanation
RPP deduction	¶9120 T1 Line 207 T4 slip Box 20 T4A slip Box 32 Guide T4040 IT-167R6 ITA 8(1)(m), 147.2(4)	Individuals can claim a deduction for contributions made to a registered pension plan (RPP) in the taxation year. RPPs are plans registered under the *Income Tax Act* in which funds are set aside by an employer to provide a pension to employees on retirement. RPP contributions are generally reported in T4 Box 20, T4A Box 32, or on union or RPP receipts. Special rules apply if an individual's total RPP deduction is more than $3,500 and the individual's slips show a past-service amount for service before 1990; if an individual contributed in a previous year and could not deduct part of the contributions; or if an individual made contributions to a foreign pension plan.
RRSP/PRPP deduction	¶9130 T1 Line 208 Schedule 7 Form T1-OVP Guide T4040, T4041, T4079, RC4112, RC4135 IT-124R6, IT-307R4 ITA 60(i)–(l), 146, 146.01, 146.02	Individuals can claim an RRSP/PRPP deduction for the least of the following amounts: (1) the individual's unused RRSP/PRPP contributions from prior years and total RRSP/PRPP contributions made in 2018, including contributions made in the first 60 days of the 2019, but not including amounts designated as Home Buyers' Plan (HBP) or Lifelong Learning Plan (LLP) repayments; and (2) the individual's 2018 RRSP/PRPP deduction limit (max $26,230 for 2018). RRSP/PRPP contributions will generally be reported on an RRSP or PRPP contribution slip received from the financial institution. Individuals should complete Schedule 7 if the individual is not deducting all of his or her unused RRSP/PRPP contributions; is not deducting all of the RRSP/PRPP contributions made in 2018 on his or her tax return; transferred certain amounts to his or her RRSP or PRPP that are included in income; withdrew funds from his or her RRSP or PRPP in 2018 under the HBP or LLP; or is designating contributions made to his or her RRSP or PRPP in 2018 as a repayment under the HBP or LLP.
Elected split-pension deduction	¶9140 T1 Line 210 Form T1032 IT-499R ITA 56(1)(a), 56(1)(a.2), 60(c), 60.03, 160(1.3)	An individual taxpayer may be able to jointly elect with his or her spouse or common-law partner to split "eligible pension income" reported on Line 115 if both individuals are Canadian residents and are not living separate and apart at the end of 2018. For individuals age 65 or over, eligible pension income includes life annuity payments from a superannuation or pension plan, annuity payments from an RRSP or DPSP, and RRIF payments. For individuals under age 65, eligible pension income includes life annuity payments from a superannuation or pension plan and a survivor pension annuity. For all individuals, eligible pension income does not include OAS, CPP/QPP benefits, death benefits, retiring allowances, RRSP withdrawals (other than annuity payments), or payments out of an SDA or employee benefit plan. Form T1032, *Joint Election to Split Pension Income*, should be completed to make the election. If an individual pensioner elects to split eligible pension income with their spouse or common-law partner, the pensioner must still report the full amount of pension income on Line 115, but will claim a deduction for the elected split pension amount on Line 210.

Deduction	References	Explanation
Union, professional or like dues	¶9150 T1 Line 212 T4 Box 44 Guide T4044 IT-103R, IT-158R2 ITA 8(1)(i), 8(5)	Individuals can claim a deduction for the following amounts that the individual paid related to employment (or that were paid for the individual and included in income): annual dues for membership in a trade union or an association of public servants; professions board dues required under provincial or territorial law; professional or malpractice liability insurance premiums or professional membership dues required to keep a professional status recognized by law; and parity or advisory committee dues required under provincial or territorial law. Annual membership dues do not include initiation fees, licences, special assessments, charges for anything other than the organization's ordinary operating costs, or charges for pension plans.
Child care expenses	¶9170 T1 Line 214 Form T778 IT Folio S1-F3-C1 ITA 63(1)–(4)	Individuals who paid for someone to look after their child so that the individual or his or her spouse or common-law partner could earn income, go to school, or conduct research can claim a deduction for the child care expenses. To qualify, the child must be under 16 years of age or have a mental or physical impairment at any time in 2018. Child care expenses may include babysitting, day nursery services, and services provided at a boarding school or camp. The annual child care expense amount deductible cannot exceed the least of: $11,000 for each child in respect of whom the taxpayer may claim the disability tax credit; $8,000 for each child under age 7 at the end of the year; $5,000 for each child ages 7–16 or who has a mental or physical infirmity but does not otherwise qualify for the disability tax credit; and 2/3 of the taxpayer's earned income for the year. Generally, the spouse or common-law partner with the lower net income must claim the child care expenses. To calculate the child care deduction, complete Form T778, *Child Care Expenses Deduction*.
Disability supports deduction	¶9180 T1 Line 215 Form T929 Guide RC4064 Folio S1-F1-C3 ITA 64	Individuals who have an impairment can claim a deduction for expenses (that have not been claimed as medical expenses) paid for personal attendant care and other disability support expenses that allowed the individual to be employed or carry on a business, do research, or go to school. For a complete list of expenses that qualify for the disability supports deduction, see Form T929, *Disability Supports Deduction*.
Allowable business investment losses	¶9190 T1 Line 217 Form T5003, T5004, T5013, T5013A Guide T4037 Folio S4-F8-C1	A business investment loss is a special type of capital loss that results from the disposition or deemed disposition of a share of, or a debt owed by, a small business corporation (SBC). A business investment loss may also arise on the deemed disposition of a bad debt of, or on a share of, a bankrupt or insolvent SBC. An allowable business investment loss (ABIL) is the allowable portion (i.e., 50%) of the actual or deemed capital loss. An ABIL may reduce income from any source, not just capital gains income. Use Chart 6, How to claim an allowable business investment loss, in Guide T4037, *Capital Gains*, to calculate an ABIL, including the business investment loss reduction from claiming the capital gains exemption in previous years.

Deduction	References	Explanation
Moving expenses	¶9200 T1 Line 219 Form T1-M Folio S1-F3-C4 ITA 62	Individuals who moved in 2018 may be able to deduct moving expenses where the following conditions are met: 1) the move is in respect of an eligible relocation; 2) the individual moves from a Canadian residence in order to earn salary or wages or business income at a new work location in Canada; and 3) the new residence is at least 40 kilometers closer than the former residence to the new place of employment or business. Costs that are deductible as moving expenses include transportation and storage costs for household items; travel expenses; costs of canceling a lease for the old residence; real estate commission, advertising, legal and other costs related to selling the old residence; legal fees related to the purchase of a new home, and certain taxes or fees paid on the transfer or registration of title to the new residence; certain costs related to maintaining the old residence; and change of address costs.
Alimony, maintenance, or support payments	¶9210 T1 Line 220 Form T1157, T1158 Guide P102, Folio S1-F3-C3, ITA 56.1, 60(b), 60(c.2), 60.1, 118(5), 118(5.1)	In certain circumstances, individuals who make child support payments may be able to claim a deduction for the payments made. Child support payments made under a pre-May 1997 order or agreement are deductible by the payer and taxable to the recipient, provided no subsequent variations have been made to the order or agreement. Child support payments made under a post-April 1997 order or agreement are not deductible to the payer or taxable to the recipient. Agreements or orders made prior to May, 1997 may be considered to have a post-April, 1997 commencement date (and thus cause child support payments to become non-deductible to the payer and non-taxable to the recipient) if the payer and recipient file a joint election with the Minister in which they specify a commencement day; the child support is varied by agreement or order after April, 1997; there is another order or agreement to change child support; or a commencement date is specified in the order, agreement or variation of the order or agreement.
Carrying charges and interest expense	¶9220 T1 Line 221 Schedule 4 Form T2210 Guide T4037 IT-238R2 ITA 9(1), 20(1)(c), (e.1), (bb)	Individuals can deduct the following carrying charges and interest expenses: bank service charges; investment management fees (except for RRSP/RRIF fees); investment counsel and financial advisory fees; certain accounting and record keeping fees; interest paid on money borrowed for investment purposes; legal fees relating to support payments; certain interest paid on a life insurance policy loan; and carrying charges for foreign income. Individuals are not allowed to deduct the following amounts: interest paid on money borrowed to contribute to a RRSP, RESP, RDSP or TFSA; subscription fees paid for financial newspapers, magazines, or newsletters; and safety deposit box fees.
CPP/QPP deduction	¶9230 T1 Line 222 Schedule 8 ITA 60(e)	Self-employed individuals must contribute both the employer and employee portions of CPP/QPP. Half of the total CPP/QPP contributions on self-employment are deductible on Line 222 and the other half is used to calculate the non-refundable tax credit for CPP/QPP contributions on Line 310. Complete Schedule 8 to calculate CPP or QPP contributions.

Deduction	References	Explanation
Exploration and development expenses	¶9240 T1 Line 224 Form T101, T1229, T5003, T5004, T5013, T5013A ITA 66, 66.1, 66.2, 66.4, 66.21	Individuals who invest in an oil, gas, mining, or renewable energy venture but did not actively participate, may be able to claim a deduction for exploration and development expenses (including renounced resource expenses). Complete Form T1229, *Statement of Exploration and Development Expenses and Depletion Allowance*, to calculate the exploration and development expenses that can be deducted using the tax slips or information statement received from the venture. Depletion allowances are claimed on Line 232.
Other employment expenses	¶9250 T1 Line 229 Form T777, T2200, TL2, Guide T4044 IC 73-21R9 IT-352R2, IT-525R ITA 4(3), 8(1), 8(2), 8(4), 8(6)–(6.1), 8(7), 8(9)–(11), 8(13), 67.1, 67.2; Reg. 7307	Individuals may claim certain other employment expenses on Line 229. The expenses that may be deducted on Line 229 are restricted to any specifically allowed employment expenses not already reported on another Line. To calculate and claim employment expenses, complete Form T777, *Statement of Employment Expenses*, Form T2200, *Declaration of Conditions of Employment*, or Form TL2, *Claim for Meals and Lodging Expenses*, as applicable. Employment expenses that can be deducted on Line 229 include the following: • Certain expenses of artists and musicians • Certain expenses of railway employees • Various sales expenses of commission employees • Certain meals and lodging expenses for transport employees • Legal fees paid to collect or establish a right to salary or wages owed • Professional membership dues • Office rent or salary for an assistant or substitute • The cost of supplies used directly in performing employment duties provided the employee was required to provide and pay for the supplies under the employment contract • Home office expenses • Union dues and association dues for public servants • Cost of tools for apprentice mechanics and tradespersons See Guide T4044, *Employment Expenses*, for the specific rules for employment expenses that can be claimed on Line 229.
Clergy residence deduction	¶9260 T1 Line 231 Form T1223 IT-141R(C) ITA 8(1)(c), 8(10)	An individual who is a member of a religious order and has taken a vow of perpetual poverty may deduct the total of their earned income and superannuation or pension benefits, provided that the individual has contributed at least that amount to the order. To claim the clergy residence deduction, the individual's employer must complete Form T1223, *Clergy Residence Deduction*.
Other deductions	¶9270 T1 Line 232 Form T746, T1043, T1229, T3012A Guide T4011, T4040, T4079	Amounts that can be claimed by an individual as "other deductions" on Line 232 include the following: • Split income (see Form T1206, *Tax on Split Income*) • Foreign non-business-income tax & foreign taxes on property income • Professional fees paid for responding to a CRA review or audit and objecting or appealing an assessment; to collect or establish a right to a retiring allowance or a pension benefit; and to make child support payments non-taxable

Deduction	References	Explanation
	RC4460 IT-99R5(C), IT-506, IT-528, Folio S5-F2-C1 ITA 20(11)-(12), 60, 146(8.2), 147.3(13.1)	• Certain amounts an individual repaid in 2018 that were included in income in a previous year, including OAS, EI, CPP or QPP benefits; scholarships, bursaries or research grants; retiring allowances and severance pay; shareholder loan repayment; life insurance policy loan repayment; and RDSP income • Depletion allowances (see Form T1229, *Statement of Exploration andDevelopment Expenses and Depletion Allowance*) • A refund of undeducted registered plan contributions (see Form T3012A, *Tax Deduction Waiver on the Refund of your Unused RRSP, PRPP or SPP Contributions from your RRSP*, and Form T746, *Calculating Your Deduction for Refund of Unused RRSP, PRPP and SPP Contributions*) • The excess portion of a direct lump-sum transfer from an RPP that the individual withdrew and is including in income on Line 129 or 130 (see Form T1043, *Deduction for Excess RPP Transfers You Withdrew Froman RRSP, PRPP, SPP or RRIF*, to calculate the deductible amount) • Designated benefits from a RRIF (T4RIF Box 22), a refund of RRSP premiums (T4RSP Box 28) or RPP amounts rolled to an RDSP (T4A Box 018)
Canadian forces personnel and police deduction	¶9310 T1 Line 244 Form T4 Box 43 ITA 6(1)(b)(ii), 6(1)(b)(iii), 110(1)(f)(v)	Employment income earned by members of the Canadian Forces or a police force serving on a deployed international operational mission is deductible in computing taxable income.
Employee home relocation loan deduction	¶9320 T1 Line 248 Form T4 Box 37 Guide T4130 IT-421R2 ITA 80.4, 110(1)(j), 110(1.4), 248(1)"home relocation loan" Reg. 4301(c)	An individual employee or shareholder who receives a low-interest or non-interest-bearing loan by virtue of his or her employment or shareholdings must include an imputed interest benefit into income. However, if the benefit results from a home relocation arising from an employment relocation, the employee can claim a deduction on Line 248 equal to the benefit that would be received if the loan were $25,000, and were extinguished on the earlier of 5 years after the day it was made and the day it was extinguished. A "home relocation loan" is a loan received by an individual employee or shareholder where the individual relocates within Canada, either to maintain existing employment or to begin a new job. The individual's new residence must be at least 40 kilometers closer than to the new work location than the old residence and must be the individual's ordinary place of residence. The employee home relocation deduction is eliminated after 2018.
Security options deductions	¶9330 T1 Line 249 T4 Box 39, 41 Form T1212, RC310 Guide T4037 IT-113R4 ITA 7(1), 110(1)(d), (d.1)	Individuals who acquire shares of their employer under a stock option agreement are required to include a taxable employment benefit in income equal to the difference between the fair market value of the share at the time the option is exercised and the amount paid to acquire the share. If the shares are CCPC shares, the taxable benefit is deferred until the employee sells the shares. For options granted on the purchase of publicly listed shares, employees can claim a deduction on Line 249 for 50% of the taxable employment benefit, as long as the exercise price is not less than the fair market value of the share at the time the option is granted. For options granted on the purchase of CCPC shares, employees can claim a deduction on Line 249, provided a two-year holding test is met.

Deduction	References	Explanation
Other payments deduction	¶9340 T1 Line 250 IT-202R2 ITA 110(1)(f)	The deduction for other payments allows a taxpayer to deduct from income workers' compensation payments, social assistance payments, and net federal supplements that were included in income on lines 144, 145, and 146 for purposes of determining other deductions or credits.
Limited partnership losses of other years	¶9350 T1 Line 251 IT-232R3, IT-262R2 ITA 96(2.1), 96(2.2), 111(1)(e), 111(3)	Individual partners can deduct limited partnership losses which are allocated to them as a limited partner to the extent of the amount which the partner has at risk as at the end of the partnership year-end ending in the partner's taxation year. The at risk amount is the partner's ACB of the partnership interest plus the partner's share of the current year's income of the partnership less amounts owing by the partner to the partnership and any amount or benefit to which the partner is entitled where the intention is to protect the partner from any loss of investment. Limited partnership losses which cannot be deducted in a year may be carried forward indefinitely and claimed against income generated by the limited partnership in respect of which the losses arose.
Non-capital losses of other years	¶9360 T1 Line 252 Form T1A IT-232R3, IT-262R2, S4-F8-C1, ITA 111	Individuals can deduct the amount of allowable non-capital losses of other years on Line 252. Available losses are usually reported on the individual's previous years' notice of assessment or reassessment. A non-capital loss arises when losses from employment, business, or property in a year exceed income from those sources and other income net of various deductions. Non-capital losses also include ABILs, which are capital losses resulting from the disposition of a share or debt obligation of a CCPC that is a SBC. Non-capital losses incurred in taxation years ending after 2005 may be carried back 3 years and carried forward 20 years, and deducted in calculating taxable income for that year. However, an ABIL has a carryforward period of only 10 years as a non-capital loss; after that, it reverts to a capital loss. Non-capital losses being carried back to a previous year are claimed by completing Form T1A, *Request for Loss Carryback*.
Net capital losses of other years	¶9370 T1 Line 253 Form T1A Guide T4037 IT-232R3, IT-262R2 ITA 111	Individuals can deduct the amount of allowable net-capital losses of other years on Line 253. Available losses are usually reported on the individual's previous years' notice of assessment or reassessment. An individual's net capital loss for a taxation year is the total of the excess of the individual's allowable capital losses over taxable capital gains for the year. Net capital losses may be carried back 3 years or carried forward indefinitely to be applied against net taxable capital gains in other taxation years. Net capital losses also include unused ABILs if the carryforward period as a non — capital loss has expired. ABILs may be carried back 3 years or forward 10 years as a non-capital loss; if ABILs are not used in the carryover period, they revert to a capital loss. Net capital losses being carried back to a previous year are claimed by completing Form T1A, *Request for LossCarryback*.

Deduction	References	Explanation
Lifetime capital gains deduction	¶9380 T1 Line 254, Schedule 3, Guide T4037, T4003, T4004, Form T657, T396 ITA 110.6	Individuals who are resident in Canada throughout the year are entitled to a lifetime capital gains exemption against taxable capital gains on the disposition of qualified small business corporation shares, qualified farm property or qualified fishing property. The capital gains deduction is calculated on Form T657 and reported on Schedule 3 of the T1 return. The capital gains deduction is reduced by the taxpayer's Cumulative Net Investment Loss (CNIL) balance, which is the amount by which the total of all investment expenses exceeds the total of all investment income for all tax years after 1987. The CNIL balance is calculated on Form T936.
Northern residents deduction	¶9390 T1 Line 255 T4 boxes 31–33 Form T2222 Guide RC4054, T4039 IT-91R4 ITA 6(6), 110.7	Individuals who reside in a prescribed northern or intermediate zone may claim a special deduction for a specified percentage of employee travel and housing benefits provided they resided in the area for at least a 6-month period beginning or ending in 2018. Examples of prescribed northern zones are Yukon, Nunavut, NWT, Labrador, and the northern parts of Manitoba, Ontario, and Quebec. Examples of prescribed intermediate zones are the Queen Charlotte Islands, Magdalen and Anticosti Islands, Sable Island, the northern parts of BC, Alberta, and Saskatchewan, and designated areas of Manitoba, Ontario, and Quebec.
Additional deductions	¶9400 T1 Line 256 T4E Box 21 IT-86R, IT-141R(C), IT-397R, IT-506, Folios S1-F2-C3, S5-F2-C1 ITA 8(1)(c), 110(1)(f), 110(1)(g), 110(2), Reg. 8900(1), (2)	Individuals can claim various additional deductions on Line 256, including the following: • Certain foreign income that is exempt from Canadian income tax because of a tax treaty (e.g.; U.S. social security benefits). • Individuals who have taken a vow of perpetual poverty as a member of a religious order can deduct the amount of earned income and pension benefits they have given to the order. • Individuals can deduct the amount of tuition assistance reported in T4E Box 21 if it is included in the individual's income, the individual has not claimed it as a tuition credit, and it is not otherwise deductible. • Employees of the UN and certain UN agencies may claim a deduction for employment income reported from that organization.

¶9100 — Deductions from Total Income (T1: Lines 205–235)

This section discusses the deductions on Lines 205 that may be claimed from total income on Line 150 to calculate the net income of an individual on Line 236. Net income is used to calculate an individual's taxable income (see ¶9300).

¶9105 — PRPP Employer Contributions (T1: Line 205)

A pooled registered pension plan (PRPP) is a deferred income plan for employees and self-employed individuals who do not have access to a workplace pension. ITA 147.5, ITR 213 and the *Pooled Registered Pension Plans Act* (PRPP Act) codify the rules applicable to PRPPs. Generally, the PRPP Act allows plan administrators to offer PRPPs to employees in federally regulated industries (such as banking) and the employed or self-employed in Yukon, the Northwest Territories and Nunavut. In order for PRPPs to be available to other taxpayers, provincial PRPP legislation is required.

A pooled pension plan is a plan that is registered under the PRPP Act or a similar law of a province or territory. A PRPP is a pooled pension plan that has been accepted for registration by the CRA for the purposes of the ITA. PRPP contributions are made to members' accounts and are invested in order to provide retirement income to the plan members. Only the PRPP member and the plan member's employer or former employer can contribute to the member's account under the plan. Contributions in a calendar year can be made up to a taxpayer's RRSP dollar limit for that year (see ¶9131) and are deductible as deemed RRSP contributions. Similar to an RRSP, investment income in a PRPP accumulates on a tax-free basis until benefits begin to be paid out of the plan. The only distributions that can be made from a PRPP are the payment of benefits or, in certain circumstances, a return of contributions. Similar to RRSPs and RPPs, amounts paid out of a PRPP are included in the member's income

ITA 147.5(10) provides a tax deduction to an employer for its contributions to a PRPP in respect of its employees (or former employees). Specifically, an employer contribution to a PRPP is deductible for tax purposes in computing the employer's income for a taxation year if the contribution is made in the year or within 120 days after the end of the year in respect of periods before the end of the year, is made in accordance with PRPP as registered, and was not deducted by the employer in computing its income for a previous year. An employer's annual contribution in respect of each plan member is limited to the "RRSP dollar limit" for the year, except as otherwise directed by a member.

¶9106 — *Claiming and Filing*

On line 205, individuals should report the total of all amounts shown in the designated "employer contribution amount" box of their PRPP receipts. This amount should not be reported as income or deducted on the individual's income tax return. The CRA will use it to calculate the individual's RRSP/PRPP deduction limit.

ITA 147.5, ITR 213, *PRPP Act*

¶9110 — Pension Adjustment (T1: Line 206)

The pension adjustment is the total of all of an individual's pension credits for the year. It measures the level of retirement savings accrued in a year by an individual or on the individual's behalf in his or her employer's registered pension plan and deferred profit-sharing plan. The pension adjustment is not used as a deduction in calculating net income, but it reduces the amount that the individual may otherwise deduct for RRSP contributions made in respect of the following year. The CRA will use the 2018 pension adjustment to calculate an individual's 2018 RRSP deduction limit. For 2018, the maximum pension adjustment is the lesser of $26,500 and 18% of the individual's 2018 earned income.

If an individual contributed to a foreign employer-sponsored pension plan or to a social security arrangement (other than a U.S. arrangement), see Form RC269, *Contributions to a Foreign Employer-Sponsored Pension Plan or to a Social Security Arrangement (other than a United States Arrangement)*. For U.S. residents working in Canada, who contributed to a U.S. employer-sponsored retirement plan, see Form RC267, *Contributions to a United States Employer-Sponsored Retirement Plan*. For commuters from Canada who contributed to a U.S. retirement plan, see Form RC268, *Contributions to a United States Retirement Plan by a Commuter from Canada*.

¶9111 — *Claiming and Filing*

Enter on Line 206 the total of all amounts shown in T4 Box 52 or T4A Box 34. Note that even if an individual had more than one employer during the year, the individual cannot have more than one pension adjustment for the year.

ITR 8301, Guide T4040, Guide T4084

¶9120 — Registered Pension Plan Deduction (T1: Line 207)

A registered pension plan (RPP) is a plan, registered under the ITA, in which funds are set aside by an employer, or by an employer and employees, to provide a pension to employees on retirement. Registered pension plans can be divided into two types: money purchase plans and defined benefit plans. A money purchase plan is a pension plan under which a member's pension benefits are based on the amounts contributed to the plan by the member and employer, plus the earnings on the contributions. A defined benefit plan is a pension plan which provides a certain level of benefits to a member, based on a formula which takes into account employment earnings and years of service.

Where an employee makes a contribution to a registered pension plan, the employer is required to report the amount in a T4 slip (in Box 20) and the individual claims this amount on Line 207. For money purchase plans, an individual may deduct on Line 207 all contributions the individual makes under the terms of the plan. For 2018, the combined employer and employee contribution limit is the lesser of: $26,500 and 18% of the employee's 2018 compensation. For a defined benefit plan, an individual can deduct on Line 207 all current service contributions; past service contributions for 1990 and later years; and past service contributions for 1989 or earlier years (either while or while not a contributor). The amount of past service contributions for 1989 or earlier years that can be deducted may be limited; see Guide T4040 (Chapter 1) for calculation instructions for these purposes. See also IT-167R6: *Registered Pension Plans — Employee's Contributions*.

If the individual contributed to a foreign employer-sponsored pension plan or to a social security arrangement (other than a U.S. arrangement), see Form RC269, *Contributions to a Foreign Employer-Sponsored Pension Plan or to a Social Security Arrangement (other than a United States Arrangement)*. For U.S. residents working in Canada, who contributed to a U.S. employer-sponsored retirement plan, see Form RC267, *Contributions to a United States Employer-Sponsored Retirement Plan*. For commuters from Canada who contributed to a U.S. retirement plan, see Form RC268, *Contributions to a United States Retirement Plan by a Commuter from Canada*.

¶9121 — *Claiming and Filing*

If an individual made an RPP contribution in the year, it will generally be reported in T4 Box 20 or T4A Box 32. Enter on Line 207 the total of the amounts shown in T4 Box 20, T4A Box 32, or from the individual's union or RPP receipts.

See Guide T4040, *RRSPs and Other Registered Plans for Retirement*, to find out how much to deduct if any of the following apply: 1) the individual's total RPP deduction is more than $3,500 and the individual's slips show a past-service amount for service before 1990, 2) the individual contributed in a previous year and could not deduct part of the contributions, or 3) the individual made contributions to a pension plan in a foreign country.

ITA 8(1)(m), 147.2(4), Guide T4040, IT-167R6: *Registered Pension Plans — Employee's Contributions*, VDs 2008-0284471C6, 2005-0161401I7, 2007-0243611E5

¶9130 — RRSP and PRPP Deduction (T1: Line 208)

The registered retirement savings plan (RRSP) rules are designed to assist self-employed and other individuals to defer tax on a limited part of their income if set aside in trust for the purpose of retirement income savings. Generally, a deduction is allowed for contributions that are dedicated to the purchase of an annuity for life, or an annuity for a fixed term terminating at age 90. As in the case of pension income for retired employees, the entire amount of the annuity income later received must be brought into income when received, without regard for capital accretions.

RRSP withdrawals made during the lifetime of an annuitant out of an RRSP are generally subject to tax (note that taxes are withheld on the withdrawal of funds from an RRSP). Exceptions apply in respect of withdrawals made under the Home Buyers' Plan or the Lifelong Learning Plan. See ¶8250 for more information.

Generally, an RRSP must be converted to an annuity or an RRIF by the end of the year in which the taxpayer turns 71.

¶9131 — *RRSP/PRPP Deduction Limit*

Generally, the maximum RRSP/PRPP contribution amount that an individual can deduct on Line 208 is the least of the following:

- The unused RRSP/PRPP contributions shown on Line B of the individual's 2017 Notice of Assessment or Reassessment or on Form T1028, *Your RRSP/PRPP Information for 2018*, plus the individual's total RRSP/PRPP contributions made from March 2, 2018 to March 1, 2019 (not including amounts designated as HBP or LLP repayments); and

- The individual's "RRSP deduction limit" for 2018.

The "RRSP deduction limit" may also be called "RRSP contribution room" or "RRSP deduction room." An individual's 2018 RRSP deduction limit is calculated on the individual's 2017 Notice of Assessment or Reassessment. Generally, the deduction limit is calculated as:

- 18% of "earned income" for the preceding year, to an annual maximum (called the RRSP dollar limit, see below)

- less the "pension adjustment" amount for participants in a Registered Pension Plan or Deferred Profit Sharing Plan (see ¶9110)

  - less any "past service pension adjustment" for participants in a RPP or DPSP

  - plus any "past service pension adjustment" reversals

  - plus unused deduction room carried forward from the previous year.

The RRSP dollar limit for a year is the maximum amount of new RRSP deduction room that can become available to an individual in that year. The RRSP dollar limit is $26,230 for 2018 and $26,500 for 2019. Also see the Retirement Plan Contribution Limits table in Appendix B.

The modifications to the RRSP deduction limit for the pension adjustment, the past service pension adjustment, and the pension adjustment reversal are meant to ensure that pension plan members in different types of retirement plans (i.e., RRSPs, RPPs, and DPSPs) receive equal tax assistance for retirement income purposes. Essentially, the adjustments are meant to take into account the portion of the RRSP deduction limit used by virtue of retirement benefits that accumulate in RPPs and DPSPs. The pension adjustment for a taxation year is used to determine the RRSP deduction limit for the following year.

Unlike TFSA withdrawals, which generally may be recontributed to a TFSA without creating an excess TFSA contribution, there is no provision, other than in respect of the Home Buyers' Plan (HBP) and the Lifelong Learning Plan (LLP), that allows for the re-contribution of amounts previously withdrawn from an RRSP.

¶9132 — *Earned Income*

Each year, 18% of a taxpayer's "earned income" for the preceding taxation year is added to the taxpayer's RRSP contribution room limit. "Earned income" is defined in ITA 146(1) and generally includes a taxpayer's income, earned while the taxpayer was resident in Canada, from the following:

- Income from salary or wages and other income from an office or employment;

- Net income from a business carried on by the taxpayer, either alone or as a partner actively engaged in the business;

- Net income from the rental of real property;

- Royalty income from a work or invention of which the taxpayer was the author or inventor; and

- Other amounts, including taxable support payments received, CPP or provincial disability pension income, supplementary unemployment insurance payments, and research grants.

Earned income also includes a taxpayer's employment income for a period in the year throughout which the taxpayer was not resident in Canada, or business income from carrying on business in Canada, either alone or as a partner actively engaged in the business, except to the extent that the income is exempt from income tax in Canada by reason of a tax treaty. Earned income does not include capital gains. Also, earned income is reduced by a taxpayer's loss for a period in the year throughout which the taxpayer was resident in Canada from carrying on a business or from the rental of real property, deductible support, maintenance and other payments, and the taxpayer's loss for a period in the year throughout which he or she was not resident in Canada from a business carried on in Canada.

Applicable to 2014 and subsequent taxation years, the definition of "earned income" in ITA 146(1) is amended to allow "qualifying performance income" (as defined in ITA 143.1(1)) of an individual that is contributed to an amateur athlete trust of the individual to be treated as earned income of the individual.

¶9133 — *Contribution to a Spousal or Common-Law Partner RRSP*

An individual can deduct RRSP contributions made to an RRSP of which the taxpayer's spouse or common-law partner is the annuitant. The maximum amount that can be deducted is the same as discussed above, less any contributions that the individual made to his or her own RRSP and deducted in the year. IT-307R4 discusses the rules for determining the maximum amount a taxpayer may deduct for contributions to a spousal or common-law partner RRSP.

To ensure that the contributing spouse does not have an income inclusion when the annuitant spouse or common-law partner withdraws funds from a spousal or common-law partner RRSP, the contributing spouse should not contribute to a spousal or common-law partner RRSP in the year the spouse or common-law partner withdraws the funds, or in either of the two preceding years. Otherwise, the contributor may have to include in income the funds that the spouse or common-law partner withdraws. See ¶8252 for more information.

¶9134 — *Qualified and Prohibited Investments*

The ITA imposes various investment restrictions on RRSPs (and other registered plans). In particular, RRSPs may only invest only in property that is a "qualified investment", cannot invest in property that is a "prohibited investment", and must avoid investments or transactions that are structured to artificially shift value into or out of the plan or result in certain other supplementary advantages. These rules are discussed at ¶16250.

¶9135 — *Overcontributions*

If an individual contributes more to an RRSP than his or her allowable RRSP deduction limit, the individual's RRSP will have a "cumulative excess" on which the individual may have to pay a tax of 1% per month (Part X.1 tax). The tax is payable within 90 days after the end of the calendar year. To pay the tax, the individual should file T1-OVP, *Individual Tax Return for RRSP Excess Contributions*. Under certain conditions, ITA 146(8.2) allows individuals to avoid the tax by requesting a refund of the "cumulative excess". This provision allows RRSP overcontributions to be withdrawn on a tax-free basis where the amounts are received during the year the contributions are made or in the following year. However, this relief is subject to an anti-avoidance rule that denies relief in cases where individuals are making the excess contributions intentionally.

A taxpayer is entitled to a deduction under ITA 146(8.2) upon withdrawing undeducted RRSP contributions, even where there is no cumulative excess amount for Part X.1 tax purposes at the time of the withdrawal (VD 2017-

0707781C6). As well, where an RRSP annuitant dies without having withdrawn over-contributions made in the preceding year, the deceased's legal representative may claim a deduction under ITA 146(8.2) against the amount included in income, provided all other conditions are met (VDs 2017-0685001E5 and 2017 -0710681C6).

For more information, see Guide T1040, *RRSPs and Other Registered Plans for Retirement*.

¶9136 — *RRSP Planning Points*

- *Rollover of refund of premiums* — A spouse or common-law partner of a deceased annuitant under an RRSP is permitted to avoid paying immediate tax on a refund of premiums received from that RRSP by rolling it over into an RRSP of his or her own. Also, financially-dependent children with mental or physical impairments are eligible to receive, on a tax-deferred basis, a deceased parent's (or in the case of a child that is financially dependent on a grandparent, the deceased grandparent's) proceeds from an RRSP or an RRIF if the funds are transferred to the child's RRSP or are used to purchase a life annuity.

- *In-kind contributions* — A payment of an RRSP premium can be made via a contribution or transfer of property (such as shares or other securities) other than cash. Where an in-kind contribution is made, the transfer constitutes a disposition for tax purposes. The proceeds of disposition and the amount of the contribution considered to be made are equal to the fair market value of the property transferred. The contribution-in-kind may give rise to a capital gain or loss. If a capital loss arises on the contribution, the loss is denied (ITA 40(2)(g)(iv)). Thus, if a property has an accrued loss, a taxpayer may first sell the property to realize the capital loss and then transfer the proceeds to an RRSP; however, if the RRSP repurchases the same property within 30 days, the loss incurred is denied as a "superficial loss." Similar rules apply in respect of contributions to an RESP, RDSP, or a TFSA.

- *Borrowing funds to contribute* — Taxpayers who do not have the funds to contribute the maximum amount to their RRSP should consider borrowing the funds to make the investment. Although the interest will not be deductible, this strategy is usually beneficial, provided the loan is repaid in a relatively short period of time. The additional tax refund from the contribution should be used to repay a portion of the loan.

- *Employer-provided RRSPs* — Where an employer offers an RRSP contribution matching program, employees should ensure they fully participate in the program. Also, many employers offer to cover RRSP investment advisor fees for employees who invest in a company sponsored RRSP. Normally, such employer sponsored programs are beneficial. In addition to saving costs on management fees, an employer does not have to withhold tax from an employee on taxable remuneration that is contributed to an RRSP where the employer has reasonable grounds to believe that the contributions are deductible by the employee.

- *Retiring allowances* — An individual is allowed a deduction for the portion of a retiring allowance received that is contributed to a registered pension plan or an RRSP (see ¶8264.1).

- *Allocating investments* — Taxpayers should consider putting funds that generate interest income inside their RRSP (e.g., Guaranteed Investment Certificates), and investments that generate tax-preferred sources of income such as capital gains or dividends in their non-registered portfolio.

- *Interest deductibility* — Interest on funds borrowed to make an RRSP contribution is not deductible (see under ¶3620).

- *Withdrawing funds before retirement* — Taxpayers who withdraw RRSP funds prior to retirement should withdrawal $5,000 or less each year to minimize withholding taxes (note that the gross amount withdrawn will be included in income regardless of any amount withheld).

¶9137 — *Schedule 7: RRSP and PRPP Unused Contributions, Transfers, and HBP or LLP Activities*

Schedule 7 should be completed if any one or more applies to an individual's 2018 tax return:

- The individual is not deducting all of his or her unused RRSP/PRPP contributions (Line B of the individual's 2016 Notice of Assessment or Reassessment or on Form T1028, *Your RRSP/PRPP Information for 2018*),

- The individual is not deducting all of the RRSP and PRPP contributions made from March 2, 2018 to March 1, 2019,

- The individual transferred certain amounts to his or her RRSP or PRPP that are included in income (see ¶8250),

- The individual is designating contributions made to his or her RRSP, PRPP or SPP as a 2018 repayment under the HBP or LLP,

- The individual withdrew funds from his or her RRSP in 2018 under the HBP or the LLP, or

- The individual will be the beneficiary of income that was contributed to an amateur athlete trust in 2018 and wants that income to be used in calculating their RRSP/PRPP contribution limit.

Part A — Contributions

Line 1 — Unused RRSP/PRPP contributions

Enter amounts the individual contributed to his or her own RRSP or PRPP or to a spousal or common-law partner RRSP or PRPP, but did not deduct on a previous return or designate as an HBP or an LLP repayment. The total of these amounts is shown on Line B of the 2017 Notice of Assessment or Reassessment or on Form T1028 (if included on a previous year's Schedule 7).

Lines 2 and 3 — Total RRSP/PRPP contributions

Include amounts the individual contributed to his or her own RRSP/PRPP or to a spousal or common-law partner RRSP/PRPP from March 2, 2018 to March 1, 2019, amounts transferred to the individual's RRSP/PRPP, and amounts the individual designated as HBP or LLP repayments. Include all RRSP or PRPP contributions made from January 1, 2019 to March 1, 2019, even if they are not being deducted on the 2018 return.

Do not include any of the following amounts as RRSP/PRPP contributions:

- Any unused RRSP/PRPP contributions made after March 2, 2018 that were refunded to the individual or the individual's spouse or common law partner in 2018. Report the refund on Line 129 (see ¶8250) and determine whether a deduction can be claimed on Line 232 (see ¶9273).

- Contributions the individual made to his or her RRSP or a spousal or common-law partner RRSP less than 90 days before either of them withdrew funds from that RRSP under the HBP or the LLP (see Guide RC4135, *Home Buyers' Plan* and Guide RC4112, *Lifelong Learning Plan*).

- An employer's contributions to the individual's PRPP (see ¶9105).

- A payment that was directly transferred to the individual's RRSP/PRPP if the individual did not receive an information slip for it or if it is shown in Box 35 of a T4RSP or T4RIF slip.

- The part of an RRSP withdrawal that the individual re-contributed to his or her RRSP and deducted on Line 232 (see ¶9273).

- The excess part of a direct transfer of a lump-sum payment from the individual's RPP to an RRSP/PRPP or RRIF that was withdrawn and included on Line 129 or 130 and deducted on Line 232 (see ¶9273).

Part B — Repayments under the HBP and the LLP

If an individual withdrew funds from his or her RRSP under the HBP before 2017, a repayment must be made for 2018. If an individual withdrew funds from his or her RRSP under the LLP before 2017, a repayment may be required for 2018. The amount of the 2018 minimum required repayment should be provided on the individual's 2017 Notice of Assessment or Reassessment or on Form T1028.

To make a repayment for 2018, an individual must make an RRSP/PRPP contribution from January 1, 2018 to March 1, 2019 and designate it as a repayment on Line 6 or 7, as applicable. An amount that was designated as a repayment on the individual's 2017 return or an amount that was refunded to the individual cannot be designated as a repayment amount on the individual's 2018 return. The RRSP/PRPP contribution amount that is designated as a HBP or LLP repayment cannot be deducted as an RRSP/PRPP contribution on Schedule 7. If less than the minimum amount is repaid for 2018, the difference must be included in income on Line 129 (see ¶8250).

Generally, the designated repayment under the HBP may not exceed the lesser of: 1) the total of all amounts paid by the individual in the year or within 60 days after the end of the year under an RRSP/PRPP under which the individual is the annuitant (i.e., only the individual who withdrew an amount under the HBP can make repayments to their RRSP/PRPP under which he/she is the annuitant and have these amounts designated as repayments under the HBP), and 2) the total of all eligible amounts withdrawn from all RRSPs under the HBP before the end of the year less the total of (i) repayments previously designated, and (ii) amounts already included in computing the individual's income under ITA 146.01(4) or (5) in respect of late repayments.

Note that the repayment contributions do not have to be made to the same RRSP from which the amounts were withdrawn (nor do they have to be made to an RRSP of the same issuer). As well, taxpayers cannot withdraw funds from their SPP or a PRPP under the LLP or the HBP, but an SPP or a PRPP contribution can be designated as an LLP or an HBP repayment.

If an individual's RRSP deduction limit for a repayment year is nil, the individual can still contribute to RRSPs/PRPPs and designate the amount contributed as a repayment under the HBP. Also, early repayments are permitted. If a repayment is more than the amount required to be repaid for the year, the individual's HBP balance for later years will be reduced; however, the individual will be required to make a payment for the following year (the CRA provides individuals with an annual HBP Statement of Account that will take into account any additional payments made).

If an individual did not buy or build a qualifying home or replacement property or became a non-resident before buying or building a qualifying home or a replacement property, see CRA Guide RC4135 under "Cancelling your participation."

Part C — RRSP/PRPP deduction

Lines 10–14 — RRSP/PRPP contributions you are deducting for 2018

An individual's 2018 RRSP/PRPP deduction limit is reported on Line A of the Notice of Assessment or Reassessment or on Form T1028, less any employer contributions made in 2018 to the individual's PRPP. Unused RRSP/PRPP deduction room can be carried forward indefinitely.

Line 15 — Transfers

An individual can deduct certain income transferred to his or her RRSP before March 1, 2019 (for example, the eligible amount of a retiring allowance received in 2018; see ¶8264.1). In addition to reporting the transfer amounts on Line 15, include the transferred amounts in total RRSP contributions on Line 2 or 3. For more information about amounts that can be transferred, see Guide T4040, *RRSPs and Other Registered Plans for Retirement*.

Part E — 2018 withdrawals under the HBP and the LLP

On Line 19, enter any 2018 HBP withdrawals (T4RSP Box 27). On Line 21, enter any 2018 LLP withdrawals (T4RSP Box 25). Tick the boxes on Lines 20 and 22, as applicable.

If an individual has made deductible RRSP contributions for 2018 (other than transfers) from March 2, 2018 to March 1, 2019, the full amount of those contributions does not have to be claimed in 2018. Instead, it may be more beneficial to carry forward and claim the contributions in future years, depending on the individual's 2018 income and expected future tax rates. An individual may want to carry forward 2018 contributions and claim them in future years if the individual's tax rates will be higher. However, even if not all contributions are being claimed as a deduction in 2018, the total contributions made from March 2, 2018 to March 1, 2019 must still be reported on Schedule 7 and Line 245.

ITA 4(3), 60(i), 60(j), 60(j.1), 60(j.2), 60(l), 146, 146.01, 146.02, 147.3(13.1), Part X.1, ITR Part LXIX, Form T1-OVP, Guide RC4112, Guide RC4135, Guide T4040, Guide T4041, Guide T4079, Folio S2-F1-C2, Folio S3-F10-C1, Folio S3-F10-C2, Folio S3-F10-C3, IT-124R6: *Contributions to RRSPs*, IT-307R4: *Spousal or Common-Law Partner RRSPs*, IC 72-22R9: *Registered Retirement Savings Plans*, IC 78-18R6: *Registered Retirement Income Funds*

¶9140 — Deduction for Elected Split-Pension Amount (T1: Line 210)

If the individual jointly elected with his or her spouse or common-law partner to split eligible pension income on Form T1032, *Joint Election to Split Pension Income*, report the deduction here for the elected amount. See ¶8140 for a complete discussion of the election to split eligible pension income.

ITA 56(1)(a), 56(1)(a.2), 60(c), 60.03(1)–(4), 118(3), 118(7), 160(1.3); Form T1032; IT-499R: *Superannuation or Pension Benefits*, VDs 2012-0439791E5, 2011-042992117, 2011-0425871E5, 2010-0371161E5, 2010-0375511E5, 2009-0337451E5, 2008-0281261M4, 2008-0284411C6, 2008-0275731E5, 2007-0257001E5

¶9150 — Annual Union, Professional, or Like Dues (T1: Line 212)

See ¶2405 for a complete discussion of the allowable and non-allowable deductions for annual union, professional, or like dues.

¶9160 — Universal Child Care Benefit Repayment (T1: Line 213)

If an individual or his or her spouse or common-law partner repays an amount in 2018 that was included in the individual's or spouse or common-law partner's income in a previous year under the *Universal Child Care Benefit Act*, the person who reported the UCCB income in the previous year may deduct the related repayment amount reported in Box 12 of the RC62 slip on Line 213.

¶9170 — Child Care Expenses (T1: Line 214)

Subject to certain prescribed qualifications and limitations, child care expenses may be deductible in computing a taxpayer's net income. The expenses must be incurred in the same year in respect of which they are deducted. In addition, the taxpayer may claim less than the maximum amount allowed where it is advantageous for the taxpayer to do so.

ITA 63(3) defines a "child care expense" as an expense incurred for the purpose of providing, in Canada, for an "eligible child" of a taxpayer, child care services, including babysitting services, day nursery services or services provided at a boarding school or camp, if the services were provided:

(a) to enable the taxpayer or the supporting person of the child who resided with the child at the time the expense was incurred, to: (i) perform the duties of an office or employment, (ii) carry on a business either alone or in partnership, (iii) carry on research or similar work for which the taxpayer or supporting person received a grant, or (iv) attend a designated educational institution or a secondary school, where the taxpayer is enrolled in a program of at least three consecutive weeks, that requires the taxpayer to spend at least 10 hours per week on courses or work in the program or 12 hours per month on courses in the program;

(b) by a resident of Canada *other than* a person: (i) who is the father or the mother of the child, (ii) who is a supporting person of the child or is under 18 years of age and related to the taxpayer, or (iii) in respect of whom an amount is deducted under ITA 118 (i.e., personal credits) by the taxpayer or by a supporting person of the child.

Based on the definition, child care expenses must relate to an "eligible child" of a taxpayer, which is defined in ITA 63(3) as:

- a child of the taxpayer or of the taxpayer's spouse or common-law partner, or

- any child in respect of whom the taxpayer claimed a dependants' credit pursuant to ITA 118 and whose income for the year does not exceed the amount that can be received on a tax free basis, if at any time during the year the child is either under age 16 or is dependent on the taxpayer or the taxpayer's spouse or common-law partner and has a mental or physical infirmity.

For these purposes, the definition of a "child" includes a person of whom the taxpayer is the natural parent regardless of whether born within or outside marriage; a child of whom the taxpayer has, or immediately before the child attained age 19 had, the custody and control and who is wholly dependent on the taxpayer for support; a spouse or common-law partner of a child of a taxpayer; a child of the taxpayer's spouse or common-law partner; and an adopted child of the taxpayer. A "supporting person" of an eligible child of a taxpayer includes the parent of the child, the spouse or common-law partner of the taxpayer, or a taxpayer who claimed a dependant credit for the child pursuant to ITA 118. However, the supporting person must have resided with the taxpayer at any time during the taxation year and within the 60-day period following the end of the year (ITA 63(3)).

Child care expenses may include babysitting, day nursery services, and child care services provided at a boarding school or camp, and must be provided in Canada by a resident of Canada. By way of exception, amounts paid for child care in the U.S. may be deductible by a Canadian resident who resides near the Canada-U.S. border. In order to qualify, the services must be provided at a place that is closer to the taxpayer's principal place of residence by a reasonably accessible route than to any place in Canada where child care expenses are available (ITA 63(4)). As well, for taxpayers living abroad who are deemed to be residents of Canada for tax purposes throughout all or part of the taxation year, the child care services need not be performed in Canada, nor by a resident of Canada (ITA 64.1).

Based on the definition of "child care expense", the following payments are not eligible for the child care deduction:

- Payments made to a person who is the father or mother of the child, to a dependant of the taxpayer or of the taxpayer's spouse or common-law partner if a tax credit for the dependant is being claimed for tax purposes, or to a person under 18 who is related to the taxpayer or the taxpayer's spouse or common-law partner by blood, marriage, or adoption;

- Boarding school or camp costs in excess of the periodic child care expense per child (defined as 1/40 of the annual child care expense amount in respect of the child) multiplied by the number of weeks in the year during which the child attended the school or camp. This translates to a weekly limit of $125 for children ages 7 to 16, $200 for children under age 7, and $275 for children eligible for the disability tax credit; and

- Medical expenses described in ITA 118(2) and any other expenses paid for medical or hospital care, clothing, transportation or education, or for board and lodging, except as otherwise specifically provided.

Generally, the courts have adopted either a restrictive or purposive interpretation with respect to the meaning of child care expenses. A purposive interpretation of the meaning of a child care expense looks at the purpose for which the expense was incurred; however, a restrictive interpretation excludes recreational or educational activities that are not explicitly listed in the definition of "child care expense". The Tax Court of Canada recently adopted a purposive interpretation of child care expenses, allowing the taxpayer to claim amounts paid for a chess program, math tutoring classes, Chinese language classes, a ski class and a summer camp, as eligible child care expenses. The court concluded that, even though the activities were educational and recreational in nature, they were eligible to be claimed as child care expenses since the purpose of the activities was to enable the parents to work (*Kwan*, 2018 CarswellNat 5170 (TCC)).

¶9171 — *Maximum Amount Deductible*

The annual child care expense amount deductible is limited to the amount paid in the year and cannot exceed the least of:

1. $11,000 for each eligible child in respect of whom the taxpayer may claim the disability tax credit pursuant to ITA 118.3;

2. $8,000 for each eligible child under age 7 at the end of the year;

3. $5,000 for each eligible child aged 7 to 16 or who has a mental or physical infirmity but does not otherwise qualify under subsection 118.3; and

4. 2/3 of the taxpayer's "earned income" for the year.

"Earned income" is defined in ITA 63(3) as the aggregate of salaries, wages and other remuneration including gratuities, taxable amounts in respect of adult training allowances, scholarships, fellowships, awards, apprenticeship incentive grants, research grants, income from any business of the taxpayer, and disability pension under the Canada Pension Plan or provincial pension plan. Also included in earned income are amounts that would have otherwise been included but for the specific exemption allowed under ITA 81.

Note that the total child care expenses claimed by a taxpayer are not required to be for each eligible child. For example, if a taxpayer has a 5-year old child for whom child care expenses are incurred, and a 14-year old for whom no child care expenses are incurred, the taxpayer may still claim up to $13,000 in child care expenses (i.e., $8,000 + $5,000) on account of the 5-year old child.

¶9172 — *Who May Claim the Child Care Expenses*

Generally, only the spouse or common-law partner with the lower net income (even if the net income is zero) can claim the child care expenses. Income for these purposes is determined before deducting any child care expenses, unemployment or employment insurance repayment or old age security repayment. Also, for purposes of determining which spouse or partner has the lower income for the year, it is the CRA's view that income that is exempt from tax under ITA 81 is not to be considered.

Where the individual has no spouse or common-law partner, the individual claiming the child care expenses must have paid the expenses. However, where the individual does have a spouse or common-law partner, the child care expenses to be claimed by either party can be paid by either party, except where the spouse or common-law partner has the lower income and is living separate and apart from the taxpayer at the end of the year and for a period of at least 90 days beginning in that year due to a breakdown in their marriage or common-law partnership. In this case, any child care expenses claimed by the taxpayer must have been paid by the taxpayer.

No deduction may be claimed for child care expenses for which any taxpayer is or was entitled to a reimbursement or any other form of assistance, unless the reimbursement or assistance is included in a taxpayer's income and is not deductible in computing that taxpayer's taxable income (ITA 63(1)(d)). An example of such assistance is the Hiring Credit for Small Business under the *Employment Insurance Act*, which may be received by a taxpayer who directly employs a person to care for their child. Employer-provided or employer-paid child care that is included in income as a taxable benefit to the employee can be claimed as a child care expense, assuming the other conditions are met (VD 2010-0390931E5).

The amount of the deduction claimed by a taxpayer in respect of a child must be reduced by child care expenses claimed by any other person providing support for that child. Where two or more taxpayers contributed to the support of a child, generally the taxpayer with the lower income must claim the child care deduction. Income for these purposes is determined before deducting any child care expenses, unemployment or employment insurance repayment, or old age security repayment.

The taxpayer with the higher income can claim the child care deduction only where the supporting person with the lower income is:

- by reason of breakdown of the marriage or domestic relationship living separate and apart from the taxpayer for a period of at least 90 days commencing in the year;

- in attendance at a designated educational institution or secondary school, and enrolled in a program of not less than three consecutive weeks, requiring the taxpayer to spend not less than 10 hours per week on courses or work in the program;

- certified in writing by a medical doctor as being incapable of caring for children by reason of being confined to a bed or a wheelchair, or being a patient in a hospital, institution, or asylum for at least a two week period;

- certified in writing by a medical doctor to be incapable of caring for children by reason of mental or physical infirmity for a long-continued period of indefinite duration; or

- confined to prison for a period of at least two weeks.

In such circumstances, the claim of the taxpayer with the higher income is based on the number of weeks throughout the year when the person with the lower income was separated, attending school, certified, confined, etc. as noted above. The amount deductible is subject to the normal limitations.

If the incomes of two spouses are equal, the child care deduction may be deducted only if they make a joint election as to which of them may make the claim. The election can be made by having either the taxpayer or the spouse, but not both, claim the deduction by filing Form T778.

¶9172.1 — *Separation and Shared Custody Situations*

The CRA provides the following comments in Folio S1-F3-C1: *Child Care Expense Deduction*, regarding claiming child care expenses in separation and shared custody situations:

> 1.33 The situations in which a higher income spouse or common-law partner may be able to claim child care expenses in the year of separation, where there has been a breakdown in the marriage or common-law partnership and there has been a reconciliation within 60 days after the end of the year, are discussed at ¶1.31. If, in the year of separation, reconciliation does not occur within 60 days after the end of the year, there will not be a supporting person for the year. In this case, child care expenses will be allowed only to the individual who resided with the eligible child and only to the extent that the expenses were paid by that individual to enable the individual to engage in one of the activities listed in ¶1.9.

> 1.34 In situations where there is no supporting person of the eligible child for the year, and the child lived with each parent at different times in a year (for example, in shared custody situations), both parents may claim a deduction for the year as provided in ¶1.38–1.42. Each parent may only claim child care expenses incurred for a period during the year that the eligible child resided with the parent and only to the extent that the expenses were paid by that parent to enable that parent to engage in the activities listed in ¶1.9. In these cases, the CRA will generally consider each parent to reside with a child while the child is in their custody.

> 1.35 In shared custody situations, one parent (the first parent) may pay the child care provider and be reimbursed for a portion of the child care costs by the other parent (the second parent). In these cases, the child care provider should issue a receipt to the first parent for the full amount of the payment for child care expenses. The first parent should issue a receipt to the second parent for the amount of the reimbursement. The first parent is generally considered to have paid child care expenses in the amount they paid the child care provider, net of the reimbursement received from the second parent. The second parent is generally considered to have paid child care expenses in the amount of the reimbursement they paid to the first parent. This will not be the case however, where the reimbursement is a support payment that must

be included in the income of the first parent and that is deductible in computing the taxable income of the second parent. A reimbursement that must be included in the first parent's income will not reduce the amount of the child care expenses that can be claimed by that parent. Where the amount of the payment made by the second parent to the first parent is a support payment that is deductible in computing the second parent's income, the payment would not be considered a child care expense paid by the second parent. For assistance in determining whether a payment is considered a support payment and whether it is taxable to the recipient and deductible to payer, please refer to Income Tax Folio S1-F3-C3.

1.36 The comments in ¶1.33–1.35 assume that neither parent is residing with a new supporting person during the year. If a parent remarries or enters into a new common-law relationship with another person in circumstances such that the other person is a supporting person, the new supporting person may be the one entitled to deduct child care expenses.

¶9173 — Eligible and Non-Eligible Child Care Expenses

¶9173.1 — Eligible Expenses

Folio S1-F3-C1 provides the following comments with respect to eligible child care expenses in paragraph 1.13 to 1.18:

1.13 Under the definition of child care expense in subsection 63(3), the expense must be incurred for the purpose of providing child care services in Canada (see ¶1.19 for exceptions), for an eligible child of the taxpayer. This includes payments to:

- an eligible child care provider;

- a day nursery school or day-care centre;

- a day camp or day sports school;

- a boarding school or camp (including a sports school where lodging is involved); and

- an educational institution for the purpose of providing child care services.

1.14 The above is not an exhaustive list of deductible child care expenses. For example, advertising expenses and placement agency fees incurred to locate a child care provider and mandatory registration fees may also qualify as child care expenses. In each case, the requirements in the definition of child care expense in subsection 63(3), as explained in ¶1.1 and ¶1.2 must also be met.

1.15 The term eligible child care provider refers to an individual or organization providing child care services. Where the child care services are provided by an individual, the individual must be a person other than:

- the father or mother of the eligible child;

- a supporting person of the eligible child;

- a person in respect of whom the taxpayer or a supporting person of the eligible child has deducted a tax credit under section 118 for the year; or

- a person who is under 18 years of age and related to the taxpayer.

1.16 Paragraph 251(2)(a) provides that individuals are related if they are connected by blood relationship, marriage, common-law partnership or adoption. Subsection 251(6) defines a connection by blood relationship, marriage, common-law partnership or adoption for the purposes of the Act. For example, a brother-in-law or sister-in-law of the taxpayer is related to the taxpayer under subsection 251(6). However, a niece, nephew, aunt, or uncle is generally not considered to be related to the taxpayer. For further information on the criteria used to determine whether persons deal with each other at arm's length under the Act see Income Tax Folio S1-F5-C1, *Related persons and dealing at arm's length*.

1.17 The term day sports school is intended to cover those day camps providing a sufficient degree of child care services. Where a child participates in a particular program that includes sports, there can be an element of education and perhaps training as well as an element of child care. However, in any particular case, it is a question of fact as to whether child care services can be regarded as having been provided or whether a program of training and/or education is essentially involved. With respect to any particular program, a degree of basic protection and safety (child care services) is normally involved although the program may also provide activities and instruction which enrich the program. In determining whether a particular sports program involves a sufficient degree of child care, some factors that would be considered are the age of the participating children, the instructors' qualifications, the extent that progress is measured and goal-orientation is involved, the time devoted to the program, the duration of the program and the training and educational facilities used. For example, sports day camps for young children are generally not of an ongoing nature and it is generally recognized that there is a sufficient degree of child care even though the program is enriched by sporting activities with instruction. On the other hand, children, particularly those who are older, may participate in a sports program that is ongoing for a lengthy period of time, the instructors have degrees or certificates in respect of physical education, progress is regularly monitored and is goal-oriented, and sophisticated training methods and facilities are used. In this type of scenario, it is our general view that education and training are essentially involved as opposed to child care.

1.18 An educational institution may offer child care as well as an educational program. An educational program is considered to be more goal-oriented than child care, with the child being expected to learn skills and progress through a planned program of instruction, whereas a child in a typical child care setting is not expected to achieve any specific educational goals. Where an educational institution provides both child care and an educational program, only the portion of the fees paid to the institution relating to child care (that is, supervision before and after classes or during the lunch period) may qualify as child care expenses. When payments are made to an educational institution for a child under the compulsory school age, the services being provided are generally considered child care rather than education unless the facts indicate otherwise.

As well, it is the CRA's administrative position that the following payments are generally eligible for the child care expense deduction:

- Daycare fees, including payments to hold a daycare space open during parental leave (VDs 2010-0365202E5, 2011-0402001E5, 2011-0404311E5);

- Extended day fees for care at school outside school hours (VDs 2010-0366941E5, 2012-0439601M4);

- Pre-school fees (VDs 2010-0360281E5, 2012-0439101E5);

- Babysitting fees, where the expense is incurred to enable the taxpayer to work or attend school (see *Allott*, 2010 CarswellNat 4008 (TCC));

- Nanny fees, including the employer's portion of CPP and EI contributions, travel and transportation costs, medical insurance, and workers' compensation premiums (VDs 2009-0317671E5, 2011-0430351E5);

- The portion of private school or boarding school fees that relate to child care services (VDs 2004-0104911E5, 2005-0114421E5, 2007-0232351E5);

- The portion of the fees that relate to child care where an educational institution offers a separate program of child care in addition to a half-day or alternate-day kindergarten (2007-0232351E5);

- The portion of overnight camp fees that relate to child care (VDs 2004-0086251E5); and

- Payments to certain family members and related entities for child care services, including the taxpayer's sister (VD 2010-0357341E5), the child's grandparents (VD 2011-0400631E5), and the taxpayer's company (2011-0417371E5).

¶9173.2 — *Non-Eligible Expenses*

Folio S1-F3-C1 provides the following comments with respect to excluded child care expenses in paragraphs 1.20 and 1.21:

1.20 Specifically excluded from the definition of child care expense in subsection 63(3) are:

- medical expenses described in subsection 118.2(2) (see Folio S1-F1-C1) and any other expenses for medical or hospital care;

- clothing, transportation or education costs; and

- board and lodging expenses, except to the extent they are included in the total charges for attendance at an overnight sports school or a boarding school or camp and those total charges do not exceed the product obtained when multiplying the periodic child care expense amount in respect of the child for the year by the number of weeks during which the child attended the school or camp.

The cost of meals is not disqualified when it is included in the cost of babysitting, day nursery or day camp services.

1.21 The term periodic child care expense amount is defined in subsection 63(3) as 1/40 of the annual child care expense amount in respect of an eligible child of the taxpayer for the year. The total periodic child care expense amounts of a taxpayer for a tax year is 1/40 of the sum of the annual child care expense amounts in respect of all eligible children of the taxpayer for the year.

As well, it is the CRA's administrative position that the following payments are generally not eligible for the child care deduction:

- Fees for day camps (VD 2006-0198991E5);

- Fees for after-school activities such as gymnastics, dance lessons, riding lessons, hockey, and music (see *Levine*, [1996] 2 C.T.C. 2147; *Keefer*, [2000] 2 C.T.C. 2622; *Bell*, [2001] 1 C.T.C. 2308; *Sykes*, [2005] 3 C.T.C. 2054; *Malecek*, [2007] 4 C.T.C. 2391); and

- Fees for education, including full-day kindergarten (VD 2012-0439601M4).

There is a refundable tax credit system for child care expenses in Quebec (see ¶12605).

¶9174 — *Claiming and Filing*

A claim for child care expenses is made by filing a completed Form T778, *Child Care Expenses Deduction*, with the individual's T1 return. Receipts for child care expenses are not required to be sent with the return. However, these documents should be retained as the CRA has the authority to request them as proof of the claims being made or in support of the information being reported.

ITA 4(3), 63, 64.1, *Kwan*, 2018 CarswellNat 5170 (TCC), Folio S1-F3-C1: *Child Care Expense Deduction*, Guide RC4064, VDs 2005-0147101E5, 2011-0409661E5, 2011-0405961E5

¶9180 — Disability Supports Deduction (T1: Line 215)

The disability supports deduction provides tax relief for individuals who have paid for certain medical expenses to enable them to perform employment duties, to carry on a business, or to attend a designated educational institution or a secondary school at which the taxpayer is enrolled in an education program, or to carry on research in respect of which they have received a grant. Note that an individual may not claim a disability supports deduction in respect of amounts paid for another person.

Taxpayers may deduct the total cost of their eligible disability supports expenses, net of reimbursements or other assistance, up to a maximum limit. Generally, the maximum limit is the total of the following three amounts:

(a) the taxpayer's employment income, scholarships, research grants and financial assistance;

(b) the taxpayer's income for the year from a business carried on, either alone or as a partner actively engaged in the business; and

(c) where the taxpayer attended a designated educational institution or secondary school during the year, the least of the following three amounts: (1) $15,000; (2) $375 times the number of weeks in the year during which the taxpayer attended the institution or school; and (3) the amount, if any, by which the taxpayer's income for the year exceeds the total income determined under (a) and (b).

Expenses cannot be claimed on this line if the individual or someone else will be claiming them as medical expenses on Line 330 or Line 331 (see ¶10190 and ¶10200). Where a taxpayer incurs an expense that can be claimed as either a disability supports deduction or a medical expense, the taxpayer will have to determine whether it is more beneficial for the amount to be claimed as a disability supports deduction or a medical expense tax credit.

Paragraphs 3.5 and 3.6 of Folio S1-F1-C3 provide the following information regarding the nature of expenses that are eligible for the disability supports deduction:

3.5 Section 64 provides a list of the specific types of expenditures that will qualify for the disability supports deduction. In many cases, a medical practitioner must prescribe the particular device, equipment or service, or must certify that the individual requires the device, equipment or service because of their impairment. Subsection 118.4(2) describes the requirements for a person to be considered a medical practitioner for purposes of sections 63, 64, 118.2, 118.3 and 118.6. A discussion of subsection 118.4(2) is found in ¶1.20–1.23 of Folio S1-F1-C1.

3.6 The expenditures that are eligible for the disability supports deduction and the conditions under which the expenses are eligible are described below:

a) Where the taxpayer has a speech or hearing impairment, the cost of sign-language interpretation services or real time captioning services is an eligible expense provided that the amount was paid to a person engaged in the business of providing such services.

b) Where the taxpayer is deaf or mute, the cost of a teletypewriter or similar device (including a telephone ringing indicator), to enable the taxpayer to make and receive telephone calls, is an eligible expense provided that the device is prescribed by a medical practitioner.

c) Where the taxpayer is blind, the cost of a device or equipment, including synthetic speech systems, Braille printers, and large-print on-screen devices, designed to be used by blind individuals in the operation of a computer, is an eligible expense provided that the device or equipment is prescribed by a medical practitioner.

d) Where the taxpayer is blind, the cost of an optical scanner or similar device, designed to be used by blind individuals to enable them to read print, is an eligible expense provided that the device is prescribed by a medical practitioner.

e) Where the taxpayer is mute, the cost of an electronic speech synthesizer, designed to be used by mute individuals to enable them to communicate by use of a portable keyboard, is an eligible expense provided that the synthesizer is prescribed by a medical practitioner.

f) Where the taxpayer has an impairment in physical or mental functions, the amount paid to a person engaged in the business of providing note-taking services, for the cost of such services, is an eligible expense. A medical practitioner must have certified in writing, that the taxpayer is a person who, because of that impairment, requires such services.

g) Where the taxpayer has an impairment in physical functions, the cost of voice recognition software is an eligible expense provided that a medical practitioner has certified in writing, that the taxpayer is a person who, because of that impairment, requires that software.

h) Where the taxpayer has a learning disability or an impairment in mental functions, the cost of tutoring services that are rendered to, and supplementary to the primary education of, the taxpayer may be eligible expenses. For the fees to be eligible, the tutor must be a person ordinarily engaged in the business of providing such services to individuals who are not related to the tutor and, the taxpayer must be certified in writing by a medical practitioner to be a person who, because of the disability or impairment in mental functions, requires those services.

i) Where the taxpayer has a perceptual disability, the cost of talking textbooks used by the taxpayer in connection with the taxpayer's enrolment at a secondary school in Canada or at a designated educational institution is an eligible expense, provided that a medical practitioner has certified in writing, that the taxpayer is a person who, because of that disability, requires those textbooks.

j) Where the taxpayer has an impairment in physical or mental functions, the cost of attendant care services provided in Canada may be an eligible expense (see paragraph 1.32 of Folio S1-F1-C1 for a discussion of the meaning of attendant care). For the fees to be eligible, the taxpayer must be a person who qualifies for the disability tax credit (see Folio S1-F1-C2), or a medical practitioner must have certified in writing, that the person is one who, because of that impairment is, and is likely to be indefinitely, dependent on others for their personal needs and care and who as a result requires a full-time attendant. Section 64 also requires that the amount paid for the attendant care services be paid to a person who is neither the taxpayer's spouse or common-law partner nor under 18 years of age.

k) Where the taxpayer has a severe and prolonged impairment in physical or mental functions, the cost of job coaching services (not including job placement or career counselling services) that was paid to a person engaged in the business of providing such services is an eligible expense provided that a medical practitioner has certified in writing, that the taxpayer is a person who, because of the impairment, requires such services.

l) Where the taxpayer is blind or has a severe learning disability, the cost of reading services that was paid to a person engaged in the business of providing such services is an eligible expense provided that a medical practitioner has certified in writing that the taxpayer is a person who, because of blindness or a severe learning disability, requires those services.

m) Where the taxpayer is blind and profoundly deaf, the cost of deaf-blind intervening services is an eligible expense provided that it was paid to a person engaged in the business of providing such services.

n) Where the taxpayer has a speech impairment, the cost of a device that is a Bliss symbol board or a similar device is an eligible expense provided that the device is prescribed by a medical practitioner to help the taxpayer communicate by selecting the symbols or spelling out words.

o) Where the taxpayer is blind, the cost of a device that is a Braille note-taker and that has been prescribed by a medical practitioner, to allow the taxpayer to take notes (that can, by the device, be read back to them, printed or displayed in Braille) with the help of a keyboard, is an eligible expense.

p) Where the taxpayer has a severe and prolonged impairment in physical functions that restricts their ability to use their arms or hands, the cost of a device that is a page turner prescribed by a medical practitioner to help the taxpayer to turn the pages of a book or other bound document is an eligible expense.

q) Where the taxpayer is blind or has a severe learning disability, the cost of a device or software that is designed to enable the taxpayer to read print is an eligible expense provided that the device or software is prescribed by a medical practitioner for use by the taxpayer.

Note that where a taxpayer is absent from Canada for all or part of the year but still resident in Canada for tax purposes (either because of residential ties to Canada or because he or she is deemed resident in Canada) for the period of the taxpayer's absence, for purposes of the disability supports deduction, the secondary school is not required to be located in Canada and the attendant care is not required to be provided in Canada.

¶9181 — *Claiming and Filing*

Taxpayers claiming the disability supports deduction should complete Form T929, *Disability Supports Deduction*, for each year in which such a deduction is claimed. The receipts and Form T929 do not need to be filed with the taxpayer's return but should be retained by the taxpayer so that they can be provided to CRA if requested.

ITA 4(3), 64, 64.1, 118.6(1)"designated educational institution", Form T929, Guide RC4064, Folio S1-F1-C3

¶9190 — Business Investment Loss (T1: Line 217)

A business investment loss is a special type of capital loss that results from the disposition or deemed disposition of a share of, or a debt owed by, a small business corporation (SBC). A business investment loss may also arise on the deemed disposition of a bad debt of, or on a share of, a bankrupt or insolvent SBC. An allowable business investment loss (ABIL) is the allowable portion (i.e., 50%) of the actual or deemed capital loss. See ¶4610 for a complete discussion of the deductibility of ABILs.

An SBC is defined as a Canadian-controlled private corporation, all or substantially all of the fair market value of the assets of which can be attributed to assets used in an active business carried on primarily in Canada by the corporation or by a corporation controlled by it, shares in one or more SBCs connected with the corporation (as defined in ITA 186(4)), or a combination of the two. For the purposes of determining a taxpayer's business investment loss, a special rule applies such that a corporation will be considered an SBC if it was an SBC at any time in the immediately preceding 12 months prior to the disposition of shares of, or debt in, the corporation. See ¶4620 for a complete discussion of the definition of a small business corporation.

An ABIL may reduce income from any source, not just capital gains income. If the taxpayer's income is not sufficient to absorb the entire loss, the remainder is eligible for carryover as a non-capital loss and may be carried back three years or forward ten years. If not used by the end of the ten years, it may be carried forward indefinitely and used as a capital loss. The amount of ABIL that may be deducted is reduced by any previous capital gains exemption, to the extent that such gains have not otherwise reduced other business investment losses. In such circumstances, the amount of the reduction is considered a capital loss for the year in which the loss arose. See under ¶4200 for a complete discussion of the lifetime capital gains exemption (¶4210) and the definition of qualified small business corporation shares (¶4220).

¶9191 — *Claiming and Filing*

Use Chart 6, "How to claim an allowable business investment loss", in Guide T4037, *Capital Gains*, to calculate an ABIL, including the business investment loss reduction from claiming the capital gains exemption in previous years.

ITA 39(1)(c), 39(9), 50(1), 186(4), 248(1)"small business corporation", Form T5003, Form T5004, Form T5013, Form T5013A, Guide T4037, Folio S4-F8-C1: *Business Investment Losses*, IT-262R2: *Losses of Non-Residents and Part-Year Residents*

¶9200 — Moving Expenses (T1: Line 219)

The moving expense deduction in ITA 62 is designed to allow taxpayers to deduct, in computing their income, moving expenses incurred by them in relocating closer to an employment site, place of business, or post-secondary educational institution. Important conditions attached to this deduction are that the move must bring the individual at least 40 kilometres closer to the site of the endeavour and that the expenses are deductible only from income earned at the site or, in the case of post-secondary students, from amounts received as grants or scholarships and included in computing income.

Folio S1-F3-C4: *Moving Expenses*, discusses the CRA's views on the meaning of an eligible relocation, the conditions for deducting moving expenses, the timing of the deduction, the eligibility of moving expenses, and multiple moves. See also Form T1-M, *Moving Expenses Deduction*, and the CRA's webpage regarding moving expenses at: canada.ca/en/revenue-agency/services/tax/individuals/topics/about-your-tax-return/tax-return/completing-a-tax-return/deductions-credits-expenses/line-219-moving-expenses.html.

¶9201 — *General Eligibility*

ITA 62(1) enables a taxpayer to deduct certain amounts paid as or on account of moving expenses incurred in respect of an eligible relocation. An "eligible relocation" means a relocation of a taxpayer to enable the taxpayer to carry on a business or to be employed at a location in Canada (referred to as "the new work location" in ITA 62 and the definition of "eligible relocation" in ITA 248(1)), or to be a student in full-time attendance in a program at a post-secondary level at a university, college, or other educational institution, provided: (1) both the old residence and new residence at which the taxpayer ordinarily resided are in Canada, and (2) the distance between the old residence and the new work location is not less than 40 kilometres greater than the distance between the new residence and the new work location (i.e., the new residence is at least 40 kilometres closer to the new work location than is the old residence).

There are conflicting court decisions regarding whether the interpretation of "eligible relocation" requires a taxpayer to commence work at a "new" location or in a "new" job in order to deduct moving expenses. In some recent decisions, the court concluded that the reference to a "new work location" in the "eligible relocation" definition does not require that the employee commence work at a "new" location or in a "new" job (for example, see *Wunderlich v. R.*, 2011 CarswellNat 5876 (TCC)). Similarly, in *Gelinas v. R.*, [2009] 4 C.T.C. 2232 (TCC), the court found that the term "new work location" in the definition "eligible relocation" did not introduce a requirement for an old work location; however, the court suggested that it may require the move be necessitated by a change in work circumstances. However, in other cases, the court found it necessary for the taxpayer to commence employment at a new location for moving expenses to be deductible under section 62 (for example, see *Zhao v. R.*, 2015 CarswellNat 1787 and *Moreland v. R.*, [2011] 2 C.T.C. 2068 (TCC)). As well, see VDs 2006-0176061E5, 2009-0308461E5, 2011-

0398301E5, and 2011-0394741E5. The courts have also found there is no time limit in respect of which the moving expenses must be incurred to be eligible for deduction (see *Beyette v MNR*, [1990] 1 C.T.C. 2001). As well, the CRA and the courts have consistently accepted that ITA 62 does not require a taxpayer to be employed prior to a move for the moving expenses to be deductible from income from an employment commenced after the move.

Where there has been an eligible relocation, amounts paid by the taxpayer as or on account of "moving expenses" are deductible in computing the taxpayer's income for a taxation year to the extent that the following conditions are met:

- they must not have been paid on a taxpayer's behalf in respect of the taxpayer's office or employment (ITA 62(1)(a));

- they were not deductible under ITA 62 in the preceding taxation year (ITA 62(1)(b)) (expenses that could not be deducted in the year of the relocation may be deducted in the following taxation year, subject to the income limitations in ITA 62(1)(c));

- where the relocation occurs to enable the taxpayer to carry on a business or to be employed at the work location in Canada, the total amount claimed may not exceed the taxpayer's employment (or business) income for the year at the work location (ITA 62(1)(b));

- where the relocation occurs to enable the taxpayer to be a student in full-time attendance at a post-secondary educational institution, the total amount claimed may not exceed the total of amounts included in computing the student's income for the year because of ITA 56(1)(n) (scholarships, bursaries, etc., in excess of a specified dollar amount) or ITA 56(1)(o) (research grants in excess of research expenses incurred) (ITA 62(1)(c)); and

- all related reimbursements and allowances received by the taxpayer must be included in computing the taxpayer's income (ITA 62(1)(d)).

The deduction of moving expenses is not restricted to the taxation year of the move and the immediately following year; if the taxpayer does not have sufficient income to utilize the deduction, the expenses can be carried forward and deducted against income (see *Evangelist v. R.*, 2013 CarswellNat 833 (TCC); *Mazurkewich v. R.*, [2008] 2 C.T.C. 2132 (TCC); *Abrahamsen v. R.*, [2007] 3 C.T.C. 2001 (TCC); *Beaudoin v. R.*, [2005] 1 C.T.C. 2821 (TCC) and *Moodie v. R.*, [2004] 4 C.T.C. 2329 (TCC)). ITA 62(1)(c)(i) allows for the amount paid in respect of eligible moving expenses that were not deductible in the year incurred to be carried forward and deducted in any future year when employment income is earned at the new work location.

Where a taxpayer moves from Canada, provided all other conditions are met, the taxpayer can claim eligible moving expenses if the taxpayer is a full-time student (including a co-operative student) or a factual or deemed resident, and the taxpayer moved from their place of ordinary residence to another place of ordinarily residence. Moving expenses cannot be claimed where a taxpayer rents an apartment in another country where they are working temporarily and maintains residential ties in Canada (for example, a spouse and children remain home in Canada), because CRA considers the Canadian home to be the taxpayer's ordinary residence. As well, where a taxpayer moves to Canada, or between locations outside of Canada, provided all other conditions are met, the taxpayer can claim eligible moving expenses if the taxpayer is a full-time student (including a co-operative student) or a factual or deemed resident.

¶9202 — *Students*

Full-time university or college students can deduct moving expenses on taking up employment or commencing a business or profession somewhere in Canada or when relocating to be a student at an institution either inside or outside Canada, provided that the move brings the student at least 40 kilometers closer to the place of employment or to the institution, as applicable. An individual is considered to be a full-time student if they satisfy the full-time enrolment requirement for purposes of the education tax credit. A discussion on this requirement can be found in paragraphs 1.25 to 1.27 of Folio S1-F2-C1, *Education and Textbook Tax Credits*. For students, moving expenses may be deducted either in the year of the move or the next year. A student who is moving solely for studies can claim a deduction for eligible moving expenses only from amounts included in the student's income in respect of scholarships, fellowships, other awards, and research grants (VD 2011-0421901E5). However, a full-time university or college student who moves home for summer employment may be able to deduct the moving expenses against that employment income (2012-0440251E5). A student cannot deduct eligible moving expenses against RESP income (VD 2011-0405491E5), training allowances (VD 2010-0388601E5), or employment income earned after completing their school studies (VD 2007-0242721E5).

¶9203 — *Eligible Expenses*

Paragraphs 4.20 to 4.22 of Folio S1-F3-C4 provide the following regarding eligible moving expenses:

4.20 To be eligible for the moving expense deduction, expenses must be paid in respect of an eligible relocation, as defined in ¶4.3 or 4.4.

4.21 In accordance with section 67, an expense that is otherwise deductible under section 62 can only be deducted up to an amount that is reasonable in the circumstances.

4.22 Under subsection 62(3), moving expenses that are eligible include expenses incurred as, or on account of:

a) travel costs, including reasonable amounts spent for meals, lodging and the use of a vehicle (see ¶4.25) incurred in the process of moving the individual and members of the individual's household from the old residence to the new residence. The members of an individual's household include individuals with close connections to the individual who live together as a family with the individual in the same self-contained domestic establishment, as well as their pets. Under subsection 248(1), a self-contained domestic establishment is a dwelling-house, apartment or other similar place of residence in which a person as a general rule sleeps and eats. A residence is considered to be a self-contained domestic establishment if it is a residential unit with restricted access and it is equipped with a kitchen, a bathroom, and a sleeping area.

b) the cost of transporting and storing household effects (including items such as boats and trailers) in the process of moving from the old residence to the new residence;

c) the cost of meals and lodging incurred near the old residence or the new residence for a period not exceeding 15 days;

d) the cost of cancelling a lease for the old residence. This may include penalties or administrative fees charged by the landlord for cancelling the lease agreement and forfeiture of the last month's deposit. It is the CRA's view that a lease would generally be cancelled when the terms of the lease allowing for the cancellation are satisfied or the lease is assigned (that is, another person takes over the lease with the permission of the landlord). A lease would generally not be cancelled where the individual sublets to another person because the lease between the individual and the landlord is not terminated.

e) costs related to the sale of the old residence (see ¶4.26 - ¶4.27). These include advertising, notary or legal fees, and real estate commissions. If a loan was used to finance the old residence, selling costs also include mortgage or hypothec prepayment penalties and costs to extinguish the hypothec or discharge the mortgage. Costs for the sale of the old residence do not include expenses for improvements or repairs done to make the property more saleable or any loss incurred on the sale. They also do not include travel costs to the old residence to undertake or finalize its sale or for any other reason while it is for sale.

f) legal fees related to the purchase of the new residence as well as taxes, fees, and duties (other than any goods and services tax or value-added tax) on the transfer or registration of title to the new residence. However, such costs are only eligible if: the individual or the individual's spouse or common-law partner is the owner of the old residence, alone or jointly; (see ¶4.27) and the old residence is sold because of the move. No costs incurred to acquire a new residence, other than those described above, are eligible as moving expenses.

g) interest, property taxes, insurance premiums and the cost of heating and utilities in respect of the old residence. These expenses are limited to those incurred for the period in which reasonable efforts are made to sell the old residence, to a maximum of $5,000. Furthermore, during this period, the old residence cannot be ordinarily occupied by the individual or by any other person who ordinarily resided there with the individual immediately before the move, nor can it be rented to any other person. In general, if each spouse or common-law partner has undertaken an eligible relocation, each can claim up to $5,000 in respect of the old residence, provided the same expense is not claimed twice.

h) the cost of changing legal documents to reflect the address of the individual's new residence, replacing drivers' licences and non-commercial vehicle permits (excluding any cost for vehicle insurance) as well as connecting or disconnecting utilities. Utilities can include telecommunication services, such as cable, satellite television, and Internet connection. However, the cost of equipment and installation for such services (for example the purchase of an antenna) and the cost of forwarding mail are not eligible as moving expenses.

Costs incurred to acquire a new residence (other than those noted in (f) above) are specifically excluded as eligible moving expenses. Also, based on the instructions to Form T1-M, *Moving Expenses Deduction*, the following expenses are also ineligible:

- Expenses for work done to make your home more saleable;

- Any loss from the sale of your home;

- Travel expenses for house-hunting trips before you move;

- Travel expenses for job hunting in another city;

- The value of items movers refused to take, such as plants, frozen food, ammunition, paint, and cleaning products;

- Expenses to clean or repair a rented home to meet the landlord's standards;

- Expenses to replace personal-use items such as tool sheds, firewood, drapes, and carpets;

- Mail-forwarding costs (such as with Canada Post);

- Costs of transformers or adaptors for household appliances;

- Costs incurred in the sale of your old home if you delayed selling for investment purposes or until the real estate market improved; and

- Mortgage default insurance.

¶9204 — *Claiming and Filing*

Taxpayers claiming a deduction for moving expenses should complete Form T1-M, *Moving Expenses Deduction*, to calculate the allowable moving expense deduction on Line 219. The receipts and Form T1-M are not required to be filed with the taxpayer's return, but should be retained by the taxpayer so that they can be provided to CRA if requested. For more information, see the instructions to Form T1-M.

ITA 62(1), Form T1-M, Guide P105, Folio S1-F3-C4, *Moving Expenses*, *Grill v. R.*, [2009] 4 C.T.C. 2013 (TCC); *Dierckens v. R.*, [2011] 3 C.T.C. 2328 (TCC); VDs 2013-0476171E5, 2012-0443211E5, 2012-0440241E5, 2012-0440251E5, 2012-0446601E5, 2012-0458801E5, 2011-0427911E5, 2011-0423201E5, 2011-0406871E5, 2011-0421901E5, 2010-0388601E5, 2010-0379001E5, 2010-0383551E5, 2009-0339721E5, 2010-037114117, 2010-0365151E5, 2009-0331701E5, 2010-0354531E5, 2009-0322651E5, 2009-0341571E5, 2009-0324641E5

¶9210 — Support Payments Made (T1: Line 220)

For tax purposes, a support payment is an amount payable or receivable as an allowance on a periodic basis for the maintenance of the recipient, children of the recipient, or both. Generally, a payment will be considered a support payment if the following five conditions are met:

1. The payment must be made under the terms of a court order or written agreement;

2. If the recipient is the payer's current or former spouse or common-law partner, the payer must be living separate and apart from the recipient at the time the payment was made because of a breakdown in the relationship. Otherwise, the payer must be the legal parent of a child of the recipient;

3. The payment is made for the maintenance of the recipient, the child of the recipient, or both, and the recipient has discretion as to the use of the amount;

4. The allowance must be payable on a periodic basis (the term "periodic" does not necessarily mean frequent, although there has to be a series of payments; for example, monthly, quarterly, semi-annually, or annually). The

court order or written agreement has to set out the timing of the payments and only a new order or agreement can change the payment schedule; and

5. The payments must be made directly to the recipient (under certain conditions, payments can be made to a third-party; see ¶9212 below).

There are generally two types of support payments for tax purposes: spousal support and child support. Spousal support means support payments made under a court order or written agreement that are solely for the maintenance of the recipient (i.e., the spouse, former spouse, common-law partner, or former common-law partner, or parent of the child of whom the payer is a legal parent). Child support means any support payment that is not identified in the court order or written agreement as solely for the maintenance of the recipient. As a result, where an order or agreement only provides for a total amount of support to be paid for the recipient and a child, the full amount is considered child support. The tax rules are different depending on the type of support payment.

¶9211 — *Taxation of Support Payments*

The tax rules for support payments generally depend on type of support payment and the date that the taxpayer's court order or written agreement was made.

¶9211.1 — *Pre-May 1997 Order or Agreement*

Generally, support payments for a child or current or former spouse or common-law partner, under a court order or written agreement made before May 1997, are taxable to the recipient and deductible by the payer. However, child support payments will become non-deductible to the payer and non-taxable to the recipient (i.e., essentially ignored for tax purposes) where any of the following four situations applies:

* The pre-May 1997 court order or written agreement is modified after April 1997 to change the amount of child support payable to the recipient. In this case, the child support payments are no longer taxable or deductible beginning on the day that the payer pays the revised amount to the recipient for the first time.

* A new court order or written agreement is entered into with the same person after April 1997, and the result of the new order or agreement is to change the total amount of child support payable. In this case, the child support payments made under both orders/agreements are no longer taxable or deductible as of the commencement day of the new order or agreement.

* The court order or written agreement specifies that child support payments made after a certain date (not earlier than May 1, 1997) will no longer be taxable and deductible.

* The payer and recipient of child support payments made under a pre-May 1997 court order or written agreement jointly elect that child support payable after a specific date will not be deductible and taxable. Both parties must complete and sign Form T1157, *Election for Child Support Payments*, and send it to the CRA. Once the election has been accepted, the order or agreement is subject to the post-April 1997 tax rules. The election cannot be revoked. A separate form must be completed for each order or agreement.

¶9211.2 — *Post-April 1997 Order or Agreement*

Child support payments made under a post-April 1997 court order or written agreement (or pre-May 1997 if any of the above situations apply) are not deductible by the payer and do not have to be included in income by the recipient; they are essentially ignored for tax purposes. Spousal support payments continue to be deductible to the payer and must be included in the recipient's income.

Where the taxpayer's court order or written agreement only provides for a total amount of support to be paid for the recipient and a child, and does not identify or carve out a spousal support amount, the full amount is considered to be child support for tax purposes, and is non-deductible and non-taxable. For example, in *Berty v. R.*, 2013 CarswellNat 2095, 2013 TCC 202 (Tax Court of Canada [Informal Procedure]), the taxpayer's separation agreement provided that he was obligated to pay his wife one-half of any bonuses he received from his employer as "lump sum child and spousal support", but since the agreement did not have any allocation of the bonus payments between child and spousal support, the entire amount had to be treated as child support, and was not deductible for tax purposes. Accordingly, where it is intended that some portion of support is for the specific benefit or support of the recipient, that portion must be carved out and specifically identified in order for the amount to be included in the income of the recipient and deductible to the payer. Similar rules apply in respect of third party payments — in order for payments to third parties to be deductible, the order or agreement must provide that both ITA 56.1(2) and 60.1(2) apply to such payments.

Note that where the taxpayer's court order or written agreement does separately identify child support payments and spousal support payments, priority is given to the child support. This means that all payments made are first considered to have been made toward child support, and any amount paid over and above the child support amount is considered to be spousal support. All child support payable to a recipient must be fully paid before any amounts paid as spousal support can be claimed as a deduction. Any arrears in the amount of child support is carried forward and added to the next year's support payable. However, the priority of child support does not apply when the child support and spousal support are payable under different court orders or written agreements and the recipients are different people. The following example is provided in Guide P102:

> Beginning January 2015, Mark had to make monthly support payments of $400 ($150 for his former spouse, and $250 for their children). Mark paid $400 from January to March for a total of $1,200. He made no other payment for the remainder of the year. Mark is in arrears for $1,800 in child support. When he filed his 2015 income tax and benefit return, Mark could not deduct the spousal support payments because he did not fully pay his child support. In 2016, Mark must fully pay all child support owing for 2015 and 2016 before he can deduct anything he pays for support.

¶9212 — *Prior, Specific-Purpose, Third-Party, and Lump-Sum Payments*

The following types of payments may still be considered to be support payments for tax purposes even if they do not meet the five conditions outlined above: payments made before the date of the court order or written agreement, specific-purpose or third-party payments, and lump-sum payments.

¶9212.1 — *Prior Payments*

An amount paid before a court order or written agreement takes place or comes into effect is recognized if the order or agreement states that any amount previously paid is deemed paid under the order or agreement. However, the payments must be made in the year the order or agreement was made, or in the preceding year. The following example is provided in Guide P102:

> Since the couple separated in January 2014, Brendan has been paying $500 monthly to Sarah in spousal support. On January 8, 2016, a written agreement was established confirming that Brendan is required to pay $500 monthly in support. The written agreement also indicates that the amounts paid before January 2016 are considered paid and received under this agreement.
>
> The payments made in 2015 and 2016 are considered support payments because they were paid in the year of the written agreement and the previous year. Brendan may deduct the payments for 2015 and 2016 in the year the amounts were paid and Sarah will include the amounts received for 2015 and 2016 in the year the amounts were received. The 2014 payments are not considered support payments because they were not paid in the year of the written agreement or in the previous year, so they cannot be deducted by the payer and are not included in the recipient's income.

¶9212.2 — *Specific-Purpose and Third-Party Payments*

Third-party payments are support payments made under a court order or written agreement to someone other than the recipient (i.e., a third-party). Third-party payments that the recipient can use as he or she sees fit are considered support payments only if they meet all of the other conditions outlined above.

Specific-purpose payments are amounts made under a court order or written agreement for specific expenses for the maintenance of the recipient. These amounts may be paid directly to the recipient or to a third-party. Specific-purpose payments include rent, property taxes, insurance premiums; educational or medical expenses (such as pre-scription drugs or eyeglasses); maintenance costs for the home in which the recipient lives; and up to 20% of the original principal amount of any debt from buying or improving the home in which the recipient lives. If the recipi-ent can use the specific-purpose payments as he or she sees fit, they are considered support payments if they meet the conditions outlined above. However, if the recipient cannot use the specific-purpose payments as he or she sees fit, they are not considered support payments, unless the court order or written agreement states that the recipient will include the payments in income, and that the payer can deduct them. The following example is contained in Guide P102:

> Under a written agreement, Melissa has to pay $900 per month to her former spouse, Alex, as an allowance for mainte-nance. This written agreement provides that Melissa will pay an amount of $300 directly to Alex and $600 directly to his landlord for the rent of his apartment. The agreement also provides that Alex may, at any time, change the arrangement and require that the entire $900 be paid directly to him. The monthly amount of $600 paid directly to the landlord and the monthly amount of $300 payable to Alex are considered support payments because he can use the money as he sees fit.

¶9212.3 — *Lump-Sum Payments*

An amount paid as one lump-sum will generally not be considered a support payment because it is not paid on a periodic basis. However, if periodic payments required by a court order or written agreement have fallen into arrears and one payment is made to bring these requirements up to date, that payment would be considered a support payment. The following are generally notsupport payments:

- a lump-sum payment made in place of several periodic payments that were imposed under a court order or written agreement, but were not yet due to be paid (a prepayment). However, if a prepayment was made for the sole purpose of securing funds to the recipient, it may be considered a support payment;

- a lump-sum payment made under a court order or written agreement for a period before the date of the order or agreement;

- instalment payments of a lump-sum; and

- payments that release the payer from any obligation to pay arrears, future maintenance, or both.

The following example is provided in Guide P102:

> Jason and Tracy have been living separate and apart since August 2013. Their court order requires Jason to pay $500 per month for Tracy's maintenance. In June 2014, Jason lost his job and was unable to make the spousal support payments. In February 2015, he got a new job. He is in arrears of $4,000. Jason and Tracy returned to court and reached a settle-ment where it was agreed that Jason will pay $3,500 of the $4,000 he owes. The other $500 will not be paid. The $3,500 lump-sum payment is considered a settlement amount paid by Jason to release him from his liability for the arrears and therefore, does not qualify as a support payment because it was not made in accordance with the original agreement.

Where periodic support payments fall into arrears, and the taxpayer makes one lump-sum payment (of at least $3,000 that is deductible to the payer and includable to the recipient) to bring support requirements for previous years up to date, the portion of the payment relating to previous years can be taxed as if it was received in those years. For more information, see Form T1198, *Statement of Qualifying Retroactive Lump-Sum Payment*.

¶9213 — *Deductibility of Legal Fees*

A support payer cannot deduct legal fees incurred to obtain a separation or divorce; to establish custody of or visitation arrangements for a child; or to establish, negotiate, or contest the amount of support payments. A support payer also cannot deduct legal fees to defend a claim for support, to recover overpayments of support, or to terminate child support once the child is independent.

Paragraph 21 of IT-99R5(C) provides as follows: "From the payer's standpoint, legal costs incurred in negotiating or contesting an application for support payments are not deductible since these costs are personal or living expenses. Similarly, legal costs incurred for the purpose of terminating or reducing the amount of support payments are not deductible since success in such an action does not produce income from a business or property. Legal expenses relating to obtaining custody of or visitation rights to children are also non-deductible." Also see *Lauber*, [2005] 2 C.T.C. 2490 (TCC) and *McIntyre*, [2008] 3 C.T.C. 2429 (TCC); appeal dismissed for delay 2009 CarswellNat 4869 (FCA); leave to appeal denied 2010 CarswellNat 536 (SCC).

For common law spouses in Quebec, the legal costs of negotiating support amounts are not deductible because there is no legal right to support (VD 2010-0373641C6).

See ¶8244 for the tax deductibility rules for legal fees incurred by a support recipient.

¶9214 — *Shared Custody and Tax Credits*

If the taxpayer and another person are both required to make support payments for a child and, as a result, no one would be entitled to claim the eligible dependant credit for the child (see Line 305 at ¶10040), the taxpayer can still claim the eligible dependent credit for the child as long as the taxpayer and the other person paying support agree that the taxpayer will make the claim. If the taxpayers cannot agree who will claim the eligible dependant credit, neither can make the claim. The following examples are provided in Guide P102:

> Ryan and Chloe share the custody of their child Faith. Faith spends 50% of her time with Ryan and 50% of her time with Chloe. The court order states that Ryan has to pay Chloe $200 a month and that Chloe has to pay Ryan $100 a month. For convenience, Ryan agrees that Chloe does not have to write him a monthly cheque and that he will simply pay her $100 a month, which will fulfill both their support obligations. Ryan and Chloe agree that Ryan will claim the amount for an eligible dependant on Line 305 of his income tax and benefit return. If they did not agree, neither of them could claim the amount on Line 305 for Faith.

> Nicholas and Christine share the custody of their children Sam and Amy. Sam and Amy spend 50% of their time with Nicholas and 50% of their time with Christine. The written agreement states that Nicholas has to pay Christine $300 a month and that Christine has to pay Nicholas $400 a month. For convenience, Christine agrees that Nicholas does not have to write her a monthly cheque and that she will simply pay him $100 a month, which will fulfill both their support obligations. Nicholas will claim the amount for an eligible dependant on Line 305 of his income tax and benefit return for Sam. Christine will claim the amount for an eligible dependant on Line 305 of her income tax and benefit return for Amy.

A payment based on a court order or written agreement that calculates child support obligations with reference to a statutory scheme (such as *The Federal Child Support Guidelines*), but does not obligate both parents to pay child support, is not considered a support amount for the recipient, since there is no legal obligation for the recipient to pay an amount. However, the payer may be considered to have made support payments. The following example is provided in Guide P102:

> William and Julie share custody of their children, Emily and Eric. Emily and Eric spend 50% of their time with William and 50% of their time with Julie. Based on William's and Julie's incomes, the court order states that William has to pay Julie $250 a month according to The Federal Child Support Guidelines. The amount William pays is considered a support payment because he has a legal obligation to pay the amount to Julie. Therefore, William is not entitled to a claim on Line 305 for either Emily or Eric. However, Julie can claim an amount for an eligible dependant on Line 305 of her return for Emily or Eric, as Julie has no legal obligation to pay an amount to William for Emily or Eric.

¶9215 — *Claiming and Filing*

Support payers claiming deductible support payments should enter on Line 230 the total of all deductible and non-deductible support payments paid under a court order or written agreement and enter on Line 220 only the deductible portion of the support payments paid. The following example is provided in Guide P102:

> Diane and Gene recently divorced. In their court order made in December 2015, Gene was ordered to pay Diane $1,000 per month for their two children, and $500 per month for spousal support. Gene started making monthly support payments of $1,500 in January, and paid a total of $18,000 for 2016. Gene enters the total support payments amount of $18,000 on line 230 of his 2016 return. On line 220, he enters the deductible part of his support payments, which is the spousal support amount of $6,000.

Canadian residents who make support payments to a non-resident do not have to withhold tax on the payments. The requirements for deductibility for tax purposes are the same as those discussed above for support payments made to a Canadian resident.

For support payers, a reimbursement of support payments received under a court order must be included in income on Lines 128 and 156 in the year it is received if the amount was deducted in the current year or in a previous year; see ¶8240 for more information.

¶9215.1 — *Change of Marital Status in the Year*

Generally, taxpayers who claim a support deduction in the year cannot also make a claim for a personal tax credit for the child, or current or former spouse or common-law partner in respect of whom the payments were made (except in cases of shared custody, as discussed above). As an exception, taxpayers who became separated from their spouse or common-law partner during the year and made support payments in the year can claim either the deductible child or spousal support paid for the year, or the applicable child or spousal tax credits, whichever is more beneficial to the taxpayer. Taxpayers who are claiming the non-refundable tax credits instead of the support payments should enter the total support paid on Line 230 and zero on Line 220. The following example is provided in Guide P102:

> Roger and Mary separated on September 1, 2016. Under the terms of the written agreement, beginning on that date Roger pays $300 monthly in spousal support. Mary had no other income in 2016. When filing his 2016 return, Roger could deduct either: the support he paid = $1,200 ($300 × 4 months); or the spouse or common-law partner amount for Mary (Line 303 of the return). Since Mary had no other income, Roger would be entitled to the full spouse or common-law partner amount. Therefore, Roger decides to claim the spouse or common-law partner amount at Line 303 since it is the most beneficial. He should enter the amount of support he paid on Line 230 and enter zero on Line 220. Mary has to report the $1,200 she received in support payments on her 2016 return.

ITA 56.1, 60(b), 60(c.2), 60.1, 118(5), 118(5.1); *Donald,* [1999] 1 C.T.C. 2025 (TCC); *Nissim,* [1998] 4 C.T.C. 2496 (TCC); *Gallien,* [2001] 2 C.T.C. 2676 (TCC); *Nadeau,* [2004] 1 C.T.C. 293 (FCA); *Rabb,* [2006] 3 C.T.C. 2266 (TCC); *Gal,* [2006] 3 C.T.C. 2356 (TCC); *Loewig,* [2007] 1 C.T.C. 2062 (TCC); *Beauchamp,* [2008] 3 C.T.C. 2169 (TCC) *Dalfort,* 2009 CarswellNat 2518 (TCC); *McLaren,* 2009 CarswellNat 3155 (TCC); *Trignani,* 2010 CarswellNat 922 (TCC); *Persaud,* [2011] 3 C.T.C. 2377 (TCC); *Sarophim,* 2012 CarswellNat 845 (TCC); Guide P102: Support Payments, Form T1157, Form T1158, IT-99R5(C): *Legal Fees,* Folio S1-F3-C3, *Support Payments,* ITTN-24, VDs 2012-0465511E5, 2011-0430161E5, 2011-0420971E5, 2011-0415191E5, 2011-0405131E5, 2011-0406701E5, 2011-0426211E5, 2011-0417661E5, 2011-0399111E5, 2010-0391461E5, 2010-0390451E5, 2010-0381601E5, 2010-0376821E5, 2010-0375561I7, 2010-0373061E5, 2010-0358951E5, 2009-0342281M4, 2008-0294511E5, 2006-0208471E5, 2006-0199271E5, 2006-0177891E5, canada.ca/en/revenue-agency/services/tax/individuals/topics/about-your-tax-return/support-payments.html

¶9220 — Carrying Charges & Interest Expenses (T1: Line 221)

See under ¶3700 for a complete discussion of the carrying charges and interest expense that taxpayers can claim as a deduction from investment income.

¶9230 — Deduction for CPP or QPP Contributions on Self-Employment and Other Earnings (T1: Line 222)

Generally, self-employed individuals are required to make contributions to the Canada Pension Plan (CPP) or the Quebec Pension Plan (QPP). The amount of CPP contributions payable on self-employment and other earnings is calculated on Schedule 8, CPP Contributions and Overpayments for 2018. The amount of QPP payable is calculated on Schedule 8, *QPP Contributions for 2018*. The maximum amount of CPP payable in 2018 is $5,187.60. The maximum amount of QPP payable in 2018 is $5,659.20.

Self-employed individuals must contribute both the employer and employee portions of CPP/QPP. Half of the total CPP/QPP contributions on self-employment are deductible on line 222 and the other half is used to calculate the non-refundable tax credit for CPP/QPP contributions on line 310 (see ¶10070). For 2018, a maximum of $2,593.80 ($2,829.60 in Quebec) can be deducted on Line 222. Essentially, this is equivalent to the CPP/QPP employer contributions made for an employee.

¶9231 — *Claiming and Filing*

Complete Schedule 8 to calculate CPP or QPP contributions. On Line 222, enter the amount from Line 24 of Schedule 8 (Line 23 of Schedule 8 for Quebec).

ITA 60(e); Part III of CPP Regulations; Schedule 8

¶9240 — Exploration & Development Expenses (T1: Line 224)

If a taxpayer invested in an oil, gas, mining, or renewable energy venture in 2018 but did not actively participate in it, exploration and development expenses can be claimed on Line 224 (see Chapter 6 if the taxpayer actively participated in the venture). Complete Form T1229, *Statement of Exploration and Development Expenses and Depletion Allowance*, to claim exploration and development expenses that can be deducted on Line 224. Complete Form T1229 using the information from the taxpayer's T5, T101, T5013, or T5013A slips or other information statement received from the venture. Claim exploration and development expenses (including renounced resource expenses) on Line 224. Claim depletion allowances on Line 232 (other deductions).

See under ¶7400 for more information on deducting Canadian exploration and development expenses and depletion allowances.

ITA 66(12.6)–(12.63), 66(15)"flow-through share", 66.1, 66.2, 66.21, 66.4, ITR Part XII, Form T101, Form T1229, Form T5003, Form T5004, Form T5013, Form T5013A

¶9250 — Other Employment Expenses (T1: Line 229)

No deductions are allowed in computing income from an office or employment except as provided in ITA 8. Even where an item is specified as being deductible, the expense must be reasonable in the circumstances and the amount deducted must be wholly applicable to the taxpayer's income from an office or employment. As well, the contract of employment must require the employee to pay the expenses and the employee cannot receive an allowance for the expenses (or the allowance received is included in income). The expenses that may be deducted on Line 229 are restricted to any specifically allowed employment expenses not already reported on lines 207, 212, or 231. To calculate and claim employment expenses, complete Form T777, *Statement of Employment Expenses*, Form T2200, *Declaration of Conditions of Employment*, or Form TL2, *Claim for Meals and Lodging Expenses*, as applicable.

Expenses that can be deducted from employment income on Line 229 are discussed in Chapter 2 under the following paragraphs:

- ¶2405 Annual Union, Professional and Membership Dues

- ¶2410 Apprentice Mechanics' Tools Deduction

- ¶2420 Artists' Employment Expenses
- ¶2435 Commission Sales Employees
- ¶2450 Legal Fees
- ¶2455 Motor Vehicle (or Aircraft) Expenses
- ¶2460 Musical Instrument Expenses
- ¶2470 Office Rent and Home Office Expenses
- ¶2480 Power Saw Operators
- ¶2485 Railway Employees' Expenses
- ¶2505 Salary Paid to a Substitute or Assistant
- ¶2515 Supplies
- ¶2520 Tradesperson's Tools Deduction
- ¶2525 Transport Employees' Expenses
- ¶2530 Travelling Expenses

¶9260 — Clergy Residence Deduction (T1: Line 231)

Certain members of the clergy or of religious orders, as well as certain regular ministers of religious denominations, are permitted to deduct an amount in respect of their living accommodations from their remuneration (which would include taxable benefits) for the year from the office or employment. To be eligible, the individuals must be in charge of, or ministering to, a diocese, parish, or congregation, or engaged exclusively in full-time administrative service by a religious order or a religious denomination.

For a complete discussion of the clergy residence deduction, see ¶2430.

¶9270 — Other Deductions (T1: Line 232)

Report on Line 232 any other allowable expenses or deductions that are not reported on any other line. Deductions that should be reported on this line include certain legal fees, income amounts that were included in income but that the taxpayer repaid in the year, and other miscellaneous amounts that are deductible for tax purposes.

¶9271 — *Legal Fees*

Individuals can deduct the following legal and professional fees on Line 232:

- Fees (including any related accounting fees) for advice or assistance responding to the CRA as a result of the CRA's review of the individual's income, deductions, or credits for a year, or to object to or appeal an assessment or decision under the *Income Tax Act*, the *Unemployment Insurance Act*, the *Employment Insurance Act*, the *Canada Pension Plan*, or the *Quebec Pension Plan*;

- Fees to collect or establish a right to a retiring allowance or pension benefit up to the amount of retiring allowance or pension income received in the year, less any part of these amounts transferred to an RRSP or RPP. Legal fees that cannot be claimed in the year can be carried forward for up to seven years; and

- Fees to try to make child support payments non-taxable (see ¶8244).

Legal fees relating to support payments that the individual's current or former spouse or common-law partner, or the parent of the individual's child paid to the individual must be deducted as carrying charges on Line 221 (see under

¶3700). Legal fees incurred to obtain a separation or divorce, to establish custody of or visitation arrangements for a child, or to establish, negotiate, or contest the amount of support payments cannot be claimed as a deduction for tax purposes. Legal fees paid to collect (or establish a right to) salary or wages can be deducted on Line 229 (see ¶2450).

In *Ridout v. The Queen*, 2013 TCC 260, the taxpayer was not entitled to deduct fees incurred for consultation and preparation of a claim for a disability tax credit form and a supplemental personal credit in respect of her son because the fees were not incurred in connection with an objection or an appeal; they were incurred with respect to the taxpayer's T1 Adjustment Request.

Generally, professional fees paid to advisors for filing a voluntary disclosure are not deductible, even if the income voluntarily disclosed arises from a business or property, because a voluntary disclosure is not an objection or an appeal. However, in VD 2014-0528451C6, the CRA stated that "[w]here a taxpayer earns income from a business, the cost of making a voluntary disclosure relating to that business may be deductible as a cost of representation pursuant to paragraph 20(1)(cc)". As well, a deduction is available for professional fees incurred to defend a tax-payer's position once the taxpayer's voluntary disclosure is accepted, and a deduction may be available for professional fees incurred in the preparation of tax returns resulting from a voluntary disclosure (VDs 2014-0532121E5, 2016-0625731C6).

Individuals must reduce their claim for legal fees by any award or reimbursements the individual received for the expenses. If the taxpayer is awarded the cost of deductible legal fees in a future year, that amount is required to be included in income for that year.

ITA 8(1)(b), 60(o), Guide P102, Guide T4044 under "Accounting and legal fees", IT-99R5(C): *Legal and Accounting Fees*, VDs 2012-044267117, 2012-043320117, 2011-0408071E5, 2011-0405861M4, 2010-0361641E5, 2010-0354711E5, 2009-034554117, 2009-031039117, 2008-0302451E5, 2008-0289751E5, 2006-0179401E5

¶9272 — *Income Amounts Repaid*

Certain amounts that the individual repaid in the year can be deducted on Line 232 where the individual received and included the amounts in income in the current year or in a previous year. Note that repayments of support are deducted on Line 220 (see ¶9210) and repayments of income tax refund interest are deducted on Line 221 (see ¶9220).

Repaid amounts that can be deducted on Line 232 include the following:

- OAS benefits paid directly to Service Canada as reported in Box 20 of the individual's T4A(OAS) slip;

- Employment insurance (EI) benefits repaid to Service Canada or other benefit payor as reported in Box 30 of the individual's T4E slip;

- Repayment of CPP or QPP benefits;

- Repayment of scholarships, bursaries, or research grants;

- Repayment of retiring allowances and severance pay;

- Repayment of a shareholder's loan;

- Repayments made by the taxpayer in the year for a policy loan under a life insurance policy;

- Repayment of income from a registered disability savings plan;

- Repayment of an Apprenticeship Incentive Grant (see ¶2415);

- An amount paid by or on behalf of an employee to an employer or former employer as a reimbursement of a "top-up disability payment" (see ¶2490); and

- Salary received by an employee and later repaid/refunded to the employer pursuant to an arrangement to do so (see ¶2495).

¶9273 — Other Deductible Amounts

Other miscellaneous amounts that may be deducted on Line 232 are described briefly below.

¶9273.1 — Allocations Under an EPSP

Amounts allocated to an employee under an employee profit sharing plan and previously included in the employee's income, but which the employee has not received, nor is entitled to receive because the employee ceased to be a beneficiary under the plan, can be deducted on Line 232. For more information, see ¶2445.

¶9273.2 — Contributions to a Retirement Compensation Arrangement

Individuals may deduct qualifying contributions made to a Retirement Compensation Arrangement on Line 232. For more information, see ¶2500.

¶9273.3 — Depletion Allowances

Individuals may deduct depletion allowances on Line 232. Attach a completed Form T1229, *Statement of Resource Expenses and Depletion Allowance*, to paper-filed returns. For more information, see ¶7400 and ¶9250.

¶9273.4 — Excess Transfers from RPP to RRSP/RRIF

Where an individual transferred a lump-sum payment amount from the individual's RPP to an RRSP, PRPP, SPP or RRIF that was in excess of the allowable limit, the excess portion must be withdrawn and included in income on Line 129 or 130 of the T1 return. To avoid double tax, the individual should deduct a corresponding amount on Line 232.

Use Form T1043, *Deduction for Excess Registered Pension Plan Transfers You Withdrew from an RRSP, PRPP, SPP or RRIF*, to calculate the deductible amount.

¶9273.5 — Foreign Taxes Paid on Property Income

Individuals who paid a foreign income or profits tax on foreign property income (e.g., foreign interest and dividend income earned on portfolio investments) can claim a foreign tax credit on Line 405 for the foreign taxes paid (see ¶11010), subject to certain restrictions and limited to 15% of the income from that property. Where the foreign tax paid exceeds 15%, the individual can claim the excess amount as a deduction on Line 232.

ITA 20(11)-(12), Folio S5-F2-C1: *Foreign Tax Credit*, IT-506: *Foreign Income Taxes as a Deduction from Income*

¶9273.6 — Foreign Non-Business Income Tax Paid

Non-business-income tax (i.e., tax on income from employment, income from property, and taxable capital gains) is defined in ITA 126(7) to include income tax paid to a foreign government, subject to certain exclusions. Any tax that would not have been payable if the taxpayer were not a citizen of that other country and that cannot reasonably be regarded as attributable to income derived from a source outside Canada is not eligible as non-business-income tax.

Where an individual has non-business income from another country, and has paid foreign tax on that income, the individual can claim a foreign tax credit on Line 405 (see ¶11010) or a deduction on Line 232. Generally, the amount of foreign non-business income tax that qualifies for the deduction is calculated pursuant to ITA 126(1) as the lesser of the following:

(a) the foreign non-business-income tax paid, and

(b) the amount of Canadian income tax otherwise payable on the foreign income determined by the following formula: (foreign non-business income/income from all sources) × Canadian tax otherwise payable

The Canadian tax otherwise payable in the above formula is defined in ITA 126(7) as the tax otherwise payable before various adjustments, including adjustments for the dividend tax credit, the foreign tax credit, and the deduction for political contributions.

If an individual's foreign-source income is from a country with which Canada has a tax treaty, the amount of foreign tax the individual is required to pay may be limited under the treaty. Generally, if the individual pays more than the treaty rate, the CRA does not consider the excess amount to be foreign taxes paid, and will not allow the excess to be claimed as a credit on Line 405 or as a deduction on Line 232. There are special rules for U.S. income.

ITA 20(11)-(12), Folio S5-F2-C1: *Foreign Tax Credit*, IT-506: *Foreign Income Taxes as a Deduction from Income*

¶9273.7 — Tax on Split Income

There is a special tax payable under ITA 120.4 on "split income" received by a "designated individual" from a private corporation. Split income must be deducted in computing net income, since the tax is computed separately from income tax. For more information on the tax on split income, see ¶11070 and ¶14210.

ITA 120.4

¶9273.8 — Transfers to an RDSP

Certain types of payments may be transferred on a rollover basis to the RDSP of an eligible individual of a deceased annuitant. An eligible individual is generally a child or grandchild of the deceased annuitant who was financially dependent on the deceased for support at the time of the deceased's death, due to impairment in physical or mental functions. The types of payments that can be transferred to an RDSP on a rollover basis include proceeds from the deceased's RRSP or RRIF, and certain lump-sum payments from the deceased's RPP, SPP or PRPP. The payments must be included in the income of the recipient and a deduction can be claimed on Line 232 for the amount transferred to the RDSP.

Individuals should attach a completed Form RC4625, *Rollover to a Registered Disability Savings Plan (RDSP)*, or a letter from the RDSP issuer, to the T1 return. For more information, see Guide RC4460, *Registered Disability Savings Plan*; Guide T4040, *RRSPs and Other Registered Plans for Retirement*; Guide T4079, *T4RSP and T4RIF Guide*; and IT-528: *Transfers of Funds Between Registered Plans*.

¶9273.9 — Unused RRSP Contributions

Certain unused RRSP contributions that were refunded to the taxpayer or the taxpayer's spouse or common-law partner in the year can be claimed as a deduction on Line 232. Attach to the paper return an approved Form T3012A, *Tax Deduction Waiver on the Refund of Your Unused RRSP Contributions*, or Form T746, *Calculating Your Deduction for Refund of Unused RRSP Contributions*.

For the CRA's guidance regarding "Withdrawing unused RRSP contributions", see: canada.ca/en/revenue-agency/services/tax/individuals/topics/rrsps-related-plans/making-withdrawals/withdrawing-unused-contributions.html.

¶9280 — Social Benefits Repayment (T1: Line 235)

Employment insurance (EI) and old age security (OAS) benefits may need to be repaid if net income (Line 234), as adjusted, is above a certain threshold. The repayment is reported on Line 422 (social benefits repayment) and claimed as a deduction on Line 235.

¶9281 — *Employment Insurance (EI) Benefits*

An individual may have to repay a portion of EI benefits received in the year if:

- There is an amount shown in Box 15 of the individual's T4E slip;

- The rate shown in Box 7 of the individual's T4E slip is 30%; and

- The individual's Line 234 net income (less any UCCB and RDSP amounts included in income on lines 117 and 125, plus any UCCB and RDSP amounts repaid during the year and deducted on lines 213 and 232) is more than $64,625 (i.e., 1.25 the maximum insurable earnings for the year).

Complete the chart on the T4E slip to calculate the amount of EI benefit repayment.

¶9282 — *Old Age Security (OAS) Benefits*

An individual may have to repay all or a part of OAS pension received (Line 113) or net federal supplements (Line 146) received in the year if the individual's Line 234 net income (less any UCCB and RDSP amounts included in income on lines 117 and 125, plus any UCCB and RDSP amounts repaid during the year and deducted on lines 213 and 232) is more than $75,910 for 2018.

Complete the chart for Line 235 on the federal worksheet in the forms book to calculate the amount of OAS pension repayment, even if tax was withheld.

Individuals can choose to delay receipt of the OAS pension for up to 5 years after the normal age 65 start date and be compensated for the shorter payment period. Accordingly, individuals who are subject to a full clawback of OAS pension may want to consider deferring the receipt of OAS where the individual's income will continue to remain high for several years after age 65 (because they continue to work full-time, for example). For 2018, seniors with net income before adjustments greater than $75,910 will have to repay 15 percent of the excess over this amount, to a maximum of the total amount of OAS received, and the annual OAS benefit is fully eliminated at about $123,000 of income.

ITA 60(v.1), 60(w), Part I.2, Part VII, *Employment Insurance Act*; T4A(OAS) slip, NR4-OAS slip, Form T4E, Form T1136, Guide T4155

¶9300 — Deductions from Net Income (T1: Lines 244–256)

This section discusses the deductions on Lines 244 to 256 that may be claimed from net income on Line 236 to calculate the taxable income of an individual on Line 260. Taxable income is used to calculate an individual's taxes payable.

¶9310 — Canadian Forces Personnel and Police Deduction (T1: Line 244)

For 2017 and later taxation years, employment income earned by a member of the Canadian Armed Forces or a police officer while serving on an international operational mission is deductible in computing taxable income, regardless of the risk score associated with the mission. ITR 7500 prescribes missions for these purposes. The deduction is limited to the lesser of the employment income while serving on the mission and the income that would have been earned if the taxpayer was paid the maximum rate of pay that applied during the mission to a Lieutenant Colonel of the Canadian Armed Forces.

For taxation years before 2017, only employment income earned by a member of the Canadian Armed Forces or a police officer while serving on an international operational mission that was assessed for risk allowance at level 3 or higher, a prescribed mission assessed for risk allowance at level 2, or any other prescribed mission, was deductible in computing taxable income. The deduction was limited to the lesser of the employment income while serving on the mission and the income that would have been earned if the taxpayer was paid the maximum rate of pay that applied during the mission to a non-commissioned member of the Canadian Armed Forces.

Civilian members of the RCMP are not entitled to this deduction (VD 2006-0215221E5).

¶9311 — *Claiming and Filing*

The amount of the Canadian Forces personnel and police and personnel deduction will generally be reported in Box 43 of the individual's T4 slip and should be entered on Line 244 of the T1 return.

ITA 6(1)(b)(ii)-(iii), 110(1)(f)(v), ITR 102(6), 7500, VDs 2011-0411921E5, 2010-0379321E5, 2010-0375241E5

¶9320 — Employee Home Relocation Loan Deduction (T1: Line 248)

> The employee home relocation loan deduction is eliminated, effective for benefits arising in 2018 and later taxation years.

Generally, an individual employee or shareholder who, by virtue of employment or shareholdings, receives a low-interest or non-interest bearing loan, must include an imputed interest benefit into income, computed in relation to the prescribed rate of interest. However, for taxation years before 2018, if the loan qualified as a "home relocation loan", the employee could claim a deduction on Line 248 equal to the benefit that would be received if the loan were $25,000 and was extinguished on the earlier of five years after the day on which it was made and the day on which it was extinguished. This means that the taxpayer did not have to pay any tax in respect of an imputed interest benefit equal to the prescribed interest on $25,000 of an interest-free home relocation loan, during the first five years that the loan was outstanding. The deduction was limited not by the actual amount of the loan, but by the amount of the imputed interest or the prescribed interest on $25,000 of a home relocation loan, whichever was less. The employee home relocation loan deduction is eliminated, effective for benefits arising in 2018 and later taxation years.

See ¶2440 for a complete discussion of the employee home relocation loan deduction.

¶9330 — Security Options Deductions (T1: Line 249)

Pursuant to ITA 110(1)(d) and (d.1), in the year that an employee includes a stock option benefit in income, the employee can claim a security options deduction on Line 249 equal to one-half of the related employment benefit (reported on Line 101 or Line 104), provided that certain conditions are met.

See ¶2510 for a complete discussion of the security options deduction.

¶9340 — Other Payments Deduction (T1: Line 250)

The deduction for other payments allows a taxpayer to deduct from income workers' compensation payments, social assistance payments, and net federal supplements that were included in income on Lines 144, 145, and 146. These amounts are initially included in total income for purposes of determining other deductions or credits (e.g., the GST/HST credit, the spousal credit).

Workers' compensation benefits are payments received under a federal or provincial employees' or workers' compensation law for injury, disability, or death. Social assistance payments are payments in respect of an individual or his or her spouse from any provincial, territorial, or municipal agency (or similar body) that are based on a means, needs, or income test. They include payments for food, clothing, and shelter. Net federal supplements consist of the guaranteed income supplement (GIS) and the spouse's or common-law partner's allowance. These amounts are paid under the OAS pension plan and are intended for low-income individuals. They are paid in addition to the universal OAS benefits. The GIS is a monthly benefit provided to low-income OAS pensioners.

If an employee is entitled to a payment under employees' or workers' compensation law, and the employer advances funds to the employee during the period of disability so that the employee does not lose income (e.g., because of the time required to process a claim), the CRA will still allow the employee to claim a deduction for the workers' compensation. The employer cannot claim the deduction because it belongs to the individual who has suffered the injury or disability. If an employer pays an amount to the employee in excess of the workers' compensation entitlement, the excess amount is treated as employment income. If an employee suffers an injury or disability and is paid by his or her employer during a leave period for recovery, the amount received by the employee is taxable as employment income if the employee is not entitled to compensation under Canadian or provincial employees' or workers' compensation law.

Net federal supplements from the OAS pension plan are subject to a clawback if the individual's net income on Line 234 is more than $75,910 for the year. Where there is a clawback of OAS, the net federal supplements may not be entirely deductible on Line 250. See also Line 235 at ¶9280.

¶9341 — *Claiming and Filing*

Enter on Line 250 the amount from Line 147 of the individual's tax return. This is the total of workers' compensation payments, social assistance payments, and net federal supplements entered on Lines 144, 145, and 146.

ITA 110(1)(f); IT-202R2: *Employees' or workers' compensation*, VDs 2011-0414651E5, 2011-0418701E5, 2010-0359971M4, 2010-0389831E5, 2011-0411231M4, 2010-0384491E5, 2010-0357911E5, 2009-0338621E5, 2009-0305961E5, 2007-0239601E5, 2006-0215791E5, 2006-0189531I7

¶9350 — Limited Partnership Losses of Other Years (T1: Line 251)

Taxpayers who had limited partnership losses in previous years that they have not already deducted may be able to claim part of these losses in the current year. However, the amount of a partnership loss that a limited partner can deduct in computing taxable income for a taxation year may be restricted depending upon the partner's "at-risk amount" with respect to the partnership interest. Specifically, limited partnership losses of prior taxation years may only be deducted to the extent that the partner's at risk amount in respect of the partnership at the end of the last fiscal period of the partnership ending in the taxation year of the individual partner exceeds the total of: 1) any investment tax credit (ITC) in respect of the partnership allocated to the individual partner for that taxation year, 2) the individual partner's share of any losses of the partnership for that fiscal period from a business or property, and 3) the individual partner's share of foreign resource pool expenses, Canadian exploration expenses, Canadian development expenses, and Canadian oil and gas property expenses, incurred by the partnership in that fiscal period. For more information, see ¶3610 (limited partner definition) and ¶3620 (at risk amount).

Limited partnership losses which cannot be deducted in a particular year by reason of these restrictions may be carried forward indefinitely and claimed against income generated by the limited partnership in respect of which the losses arose if the partner has a positive at risk amount. Those losses may also be deducted in any future year against income from any source where the partner's at risk amount at the end of the fiscal year of the limited partnership, net of current year losses and tax credits, has increased.

> Although limited partnership losses may be carried forward indefinitely, the deduction in a taxation year of limited partnership losses of prior taxation years is limited by the individual's at-risk amount in respect of the particular partnership in the year in which the deduction is claimed. Therefore, the right to claim limited partnership losses of prior taxation years is lost if the partnership is dissolved or if the individual ceases to be a limited partner of the partnership.

As noted in VDs 2013-0477711E5 and 2010-0379901I7, if a limited partnership winds up, any limited partnership losses that could not be claimed before the wind-up would expire. In other words, if a limited partnership has ceased to exist, no amount may be claimed in a subsequent year under ITA 111(1)(e) for any unused limited partnership losses in respect of that partnership.

¶9351 — *Claiming and Filing*

Individuals claiming limited partnership losses of previous years are required to attach to a paper-filed return a statement showing a breakdown of total losses, the year of each loss, and the amounts deducted in previous years. Individuals who are filing their returns electronically should keep the schedule on file in case the CRA requests it.

ITA 96(2.1), (2.2), 111(1)(e), Guide T4068, VDs 2012-0436521E5, 2010-0379901I7, 2004-0107981E5, 2004-0062801E5, ITTN-5, ITTN-12, IT-232R3: *Losses — Their Deductibility in the Loss Year or in Other Years*

¶9360 — Non-Capital Losses of Other Years (T1: Line 252)

A non-capital loss arises when losses from employment, business, or property in a year exceed income from those sources and other income net of various deductions. Non-capital losses also include business investment losses, which are capital losses resulting from the disposition of a share or debt obligation of a Canadian-controlled private corporation that is a small business corporation. See under ¶4600 for a discussion of allowable business investment losses.

Non-capital losses incurred in taxation years ending after 2005 may be carried back three years and carried forward 20 years, and deducted in calculating taxable income for that year (the carry-forward period is ten years for losses arising in taxation years ending after March 22, 2004 and before 2006, and seven years for losses arising in taxation years ended before March 23, 2004). However, a business investment loss has a loss carryforward period of only ten years as a non-capital loss; after that, the business investment loss reverts to a capital loss. Taxpayers must apply losses in the order in which they occurred (i.e., older losses must be claimed first). So, for example, a taxpayer who incurred non-capital losses in both 2016 and 2017 and wishes to apply the losses against income realized in 2018, must first apply the losses from 2016 before those from 2017.

¶9361 — *Farm Losses*

Where farm losses are incurred by full-time farmers for whom farming is normally their chief source of income or is part of their chief source of income (i.e., if the taxpayer's chief source of income can be regarded as a combination of farming and something else, even if farming income is subordinate to another source), the farming loss is an "unrestricted" farm loss that is fully deductible from the taxpayer's income from any source. Any remainder is available for carryover to other years as a non-capital loss on Line 252. Unrestricted farm losses may be carried forward 20 years and carried back three years.

ITA 31(1) restricts the farming losses deductible by a taxpayer against income from other sources in a taxation year unless the taxpayer's chief source of income for the year is farming or a combination of farming and some other source of income. This restriction ensures that taxpayers for whom farming is not the principal occupation are limited in their ability to deduct from their non-farm income losses from farming.

The restricted farm loss rules in ITA 31(1) have been amended to codify the interpretation set out in the Supreme Court of Canada's decision in *Moldowan v. The Queen*, [1978] 1 S.C.R. 480. Specifically, the amendment clarifies that a taxpayer will be limited to the deduction in respect of farm losses set out in ITA 31(1) if the taxpayer does not look to farming, or to farming and some subordinate source of income, for their livelihood. This amendment replaces the interpretation placed on ITA 31 by the Supreme Court of Canada in its decision in *The Queen v. Craig*, 2012 S.C.R. 43, and applies to taxation years that end after March 20, 2013.

For taxation years that end on or before March 20, 2013, the unrestricted portion of such farm losses is limited to $2,500 plus ½ of the next $12,500 of losses (i.e., $8,750). For taxation years that end after March 20, 2013, the unrestricted portion of losses from farming for a taxpayer that is limited by ITA 31(1) is increased to $2,500 plus ½ of the next $30,000 of losses (i.e., $17,500). The remainder of such a loss is defined as a "restricted farm loss". A restricted farm loss is not included in a taxpayer's farm losses or non-capital losses. A restricted farm loss for a taxation year is deductible under ITA 111(1)(c) in computing taxable income for the three preceding taxation years or the 20 following taxation years, only to the extent of the taxpayer's income from farming in those years. The loss expires after the carry-forward period.

¶9362 — Claiming and Filing

An individual's Notice of Assessment should set out any loss carryover amounts and the cumulative amount of available losses. Non-capital loss carryforwards incurred in 2007 to 2017 and reported on a T1 return can be deducted in 2018 on Line 252. If the loss is being carried back to a prior year, calculate the non-capital loss carryback amount on Form T1A, *Request for Loss Carryback*, for the loss taxation year.

31(1.1), 96(2.1)-(2.2), 111(1), 111(3), 111(8)"non-capital loss", IT-232R3: *Losses — Their Deductibility in the Loss Year of in Other Years*, IT-262R2: *Losses of Non-Residents and Part-Year Residents*; IT-322R: *Farm Losses*

¶9370 — Net Capital Losses of Other Years (T1: Line 253)

An individual's net capital loss for a taxation year is the total of the excess of the individual's allowable capital losses over the individual's taxable capital gains for the year. Net capital losses may be carried back three years or carried forward indefinitely to be applied against net taxable capital gains in other taxation years. Net capital losses also include unutilized allowable business investment losses (ABILs) if the carryforward period for the ABIL as a non-capital loss has expired. Any ABILs not fully claimed as a deduction in a taxation year may be carried back three years or forward ten years as a non-capital loss; however if ABILs are not used in the carryover period, they revert to an allowable capital loss. See under ¶4600 for a complete discussion of ABILs.

¶9371 — Applying Net Capital Losses to Previous Years

Taxpayers can carry their current year's net capital loss back to any of the three immediately prior taxation years (i.e., a loss incurred in 2018 can be carried back to 2015, 2016 and/or 2017), and use it to reduce taxable capital gains in any of these years. Applying a net capital loss to a previous year's taxable capital gain reduces taxable income for that previous year; however, net income, which is used to calculate certain credits and benefits, does not change. Note that applying a net capital loss to a previous year can reduce any capital gains deduction claimed in that year or a following year. Taxpayers must complete Form T1A, *Request for Loss Carryback*, to carry back net capital losses realized in the year to previous years.

¶9372 — *Applying Net Capital Losses of Other Years*

Taxpayers can also apply net capital losses of other years to the current year's taxable capital gains; however, the amount claimed depends on when the loss was incurred. This is because the inclusion rate used to determine taxable capital gains and allowable capital losses has changed over the years. Specifically, when a taxpayer is applying a net capital loss from taxation years prior to 2001, an adjustment must be made to the amount of the net capital loss to match the inclusion rate for the current year by dividing the inclusion rate for the current year by the inclusion rate for the year in which the loss arose. For more information on how to complete this calculation and on applying net capital losses of other years to the current year, see Chapter 5 of Guide T4037, *Capital Gains*. When a net capital loss from a previous year is applied to the current year's taxable capital gain, it will reduce taxable income for the current year; however, net income, which is used to calculate certain credits and benefits, will not change.

Taxpayers must apply losses in the order in which they occurred (i.e., older losses must be claimed first). So, for example, a taxpayer who incurred net capital losses in both 2016 and 2017 and wishes to apply the losses against taxable capital gains realized in the current year, must first apply the losses from 2016 before those from 2017.

In determining whether to apply a net capital loss carryforward to net taxable capital gains realized in the year, consider the individual's marginal tax rate in the year. For example, if the individual's marginal tax rate is low in 2018, and the individual expects to realize capital gains in the next year and also expect a higher marginal tax rate, it may make sense to defer the application of the net capital loss carryforward. Also, if an individual has the option of either claiming the remaining capital gains exemption or applying net capital loss carryforwards, it may make sense to claim the capital gains exemption since net capital losses may be carried forward indefinitely.

¶9373 — *Summary of Loss Application Rules*

Below is a summary of the loss application rules, reproduced in part from CRA Guide T4037, Capital Gains:

Type of loss	Application Rules	Limit to Annual Deduction
Allowable Business Investment Loss (ABIL)	Any unapplied portion of an ABIL incurred in 2004 or future years becomes a non-capital loss that can be carried back three years and forward 10 years.	No limit
	The unapplied portion of the non-capital loss will become a net capital loss that can be used to reduce taxable capital gains in the eleventh year or any year after.	Limited to taxable capital gains in the year
Net capital loss	Carry back three years Carry forward indefinitely	Limited to taxable capital gains in the year
Farm loss	Carry back three years For a loss incurred after 2005, carry forward 20 years. For a loss incurred before 2006, carry forward 10 years	No limit
Listed personal property (LPP) loss	Carry back three years Carry forward seven years	Limited to net gains from LPP in the year

Type of loss	Application Rules	Limit to Annual Deduction
Personal-use property loss	No loss allowed	Not applicable
Restricted farm loss	Carry back three years For a loss incurred after 2005, carry forward 20 years. For a loss incurred before 2006, carry forward 10 years You can use part of any unapplied loss to reduce your capital gains from the sale of the farmland that was used in a farming business.	Limited to net farming income in the year. Cannot be more than the property taxes and the interest on money you borrowed to buy the farmland that you included in the calculation of the restricted farm losses for each year. You cannot use it to create or increase a capital loss.
Superficial loss	No loss allowed You can usually add the amount of the loss to the adjusted cost base of the substituted property.	Not applicable

¶9374 — *Claiming and Filing*

Generally, a taxpayer's Notice of Assessment will set out their loss carryforward amounts and the cumulative amount of available losses. Net capital losses may be carried back three years or carried forward indefinitely to be applied against net taxable capital gains in other taxation years. Net-capital loss carryforwards from a previous taxation year are deducted on Line 253. Net capital losses being carried back to a previous year are claimed by completing Form T1A, *Request for Loss Carryback*.

ITA 111(1)(b), 111(1.1), 111(3), 111(8)"net capital loss"; Form T1A; Guide T4037; IT-232R3: *Losses — Their Deductibility in the Loss Year of in Other Years*; IT-262R2: *Losses of Non-Residents and Part-Year Residents*

¶9380 — Capital Gains Deduction (T1: Line 254)

Individuals who are resident in Canada throughout the year are entitled to a lifetime cumulative deduction (also called exemption) of net capital gains realized on dispositions of qualified small business shares and qualified farm and fishing property.

The amount of the capital gains exemption is $800,000 (indexed for 2015 and later taxation years) for dispositions of qualified small business corporation shares. For dispositions of qualified farm or fishing property, the exemption amount is $800,000 for dispositions before April 21, 2015, and is increased to $1,000,000 for dispositions on or after April 21, 2015. The capital gains deduction is a discretionary deduction. This means that individuals may claim a capital gains deduction that is less than the maximum or no deduction at all in a particular year. This allows the individual to maximize the use of other non-discretionary deductions and to preserve his or her remaining capital gains exemption for future years.

See ¶4210 for a complete discussion of the capital gains deduction, ¶4220 for a discussion of the meaning of qualified small business shares, and ¶4230 for a discussion of the meaning of qualified farm and fishing property. See also CRA Guide T4037, *Capital Gains*.

¶9381 — *Claiming and Filing*

To claim the capital gains deduction, complete Form T657, *Calculation of Capital Gains Deduction*. Taxpayers calculate their Cumulative Net Investment Loss on Form T936, *Calculation of Cumulative Net Investment Loss (CNIL) to December 31, 2018*.

ITA 110.6; Form T657; Form T936; Guide T4037

¶9390 — Northern Residents' Deduction (T1: Line 255)

Under ITA 110.7, individuals who reside in a "prescribed northern zone" or a "prescribed intermediate zone" for at least six months beginning or ending in the year are entitled to claim special deductions in computing taxable income for a specified percentage of employee travel and housing benefits. Examples of prescribed northern zones are Yukon, Nunavut, the Northwest Territories, Labrador, and the northern parts of Manitoba, Ontario, and Quebec. Examples of prescribed intermediate zones are the Queen Charlotte Islands (BC), Magdalen and Anticosti Islands (QC), Sable Island (NS), the northern parts of British Columbia, Alberta, and Saskatchewan, and designated areas of Manitoba, Ontario, and Quebec. See Guide T4039, *Northern Residents Deductions — Places in Prescribed Zones*, for a detailed list of places in the prescribed northern and intermediate zones.

See ¶2465 for a complete discussion of the Northern Residents' Deduction.

¶9400 — Additional Deductions (T1: Line 256)

Various additional deductions can be made on Line 256, including the following:

¶9401 — *Income Exempt Under a Tax Treaty*

The deduction for treaty-exempt income generally applies to certain foreign income that is exempt or partially exempt from Canadian income tax because of a tax treaty (e.g., U.S. social security benefits, support payments received from a resident of another country), or Canadian-source income that is exempt under a tax treaty and received by a non-resident who is required to file a T1 return.

The most common type of income that will be deducted on this line will be social security benefits received from a foreign country and support payments received from a resident of another country. Generally, a Canadian resident who receives U.S. social security benefits can claim a 15% deduction of the amount of the benefits received in the year. In addition, for 2010 and subsequent years, Canadian residents in receipt of U.S. social security benefits since January 1, 1996 (and their spouses and common-law partners who are eligible to receive survivor benefits) can deduct an extra 35% of the benefits in addition to the existing 15% deduction allowed under the Canada-U.S. tax treaty. This allows for a total combined deduction of 50%.

Under the Canada-Germany Treaty, 50% of German social security is deductible (*Hahn*, 2011 CarswellNat 4197 (FCA); leave to appeal denied 2012 CarswellNat 1508 (SCC)). For the CRA's comments on the treatment of German pensions, see VDs 2012-0438671E5, 2012-0442561E5 and 2011-0400781E5. See also the following Views documents dealing with income exempt under a treaty: 2012-0432281E5 (foreign pension plan), 2011-0392071E5 (U.S. Social Security disability lump sum benefit), 2011-0416841E5 (Singapore pension), 2011-0418171E5 (Philippine pension transfer to RRSP), 2010-0389831E5 (U.S. workers' compensation), 2011-042256117 (treaty exemption for non-resident employees), 2009-034248117 (Canada-France Tax Treaty, Article XX), 2009-0313171E5 (inherited IRA or U.S. pension plan), and 2008-030442117 (inherited IRA or U.S. pension plan).

ITA 110(1)(f), 115

¶9402 — *Vow of Perpetual Poverty*

A member of a religious order who has taken a vow of perpetual poverty is entitled to deduct all earned income and superannuation or pension benefits received in the year, as long as the income and benefits have been given to the religious order. The term "religious order" is not defined in the Act, although it is also used in reference to the clergy residence deduction (see ¶9260). The term "member of a religious order" does not only include a member of a church, congregation, or religious following. A member of an order is bound by a set of religious, moral, and social rules and discipline (VD 9523525).

For purposes of this deduction, the earned income of an individual includes employment income; net self-employment income; taxable scholarships, bursaries, fellowships, and similar awards; net research grants; apprenticeship incentive grants; disability benefits under the Canada or Quebec pension plan; and certain financial assistance.

Generally, an individual claiming this deduction must support it with a letter from the religious order stating that the individual is a member of the order and, as such, has taken a vow of perpetual poverty. The letter must also indicate that the individual has given all earned income for the year, as well as superannuation or pension benefits received in the year, to the order.

An individual who has not given all earned income and superannuation or pension benefits received in the year to the religious order cannot claim this deduction, but may be able to claim a charitable donation for amounts given. For more information, see IT-86R, *Vow of Perpetual Poverty*.

ITA 8(1)(c), 110(2), IT-86R, IT-141R(C): *Clergy Residence Deduction*

¶9403 — *Adult Basic Education Tuition Assistance*

An individual who has received assistance for all or part of the tuition fees paid for specified courses at a primary or secondary school level can claim a deduction for the amount of qualifying assistance reported in T4E Box 21 if the amounts are included in the individual's income, the individual has not claimed the amounts as part of the tuition credit on Line 323, and the amounts are not otherwise deductible.

Taxable tuition assistance reported in T4E Box 20 for post-secondary level courses or courses that provide or improve skills in an occupation are not deductible on Line 256; however, they may be eligible for the tuition, education, and textbook amounts (see ¶10160).

The financial assistance must be provided by a program established under the authority of the *Department of Human Resources and Skills Development Act*; established by the Canada Employment Insurance Commission under Part II of the *Employment Insurance Act*; or established by a government or government agency in Canada on a similar basis to a program established under Part II of the *Employment Insurance Act*.

ITA 110(1)(g), Folio S1-F2-C3: *Scholarships, Research Grants and Other Education Assistance*

¶9404 — *Employees of Prescribed International Organizations*

An employee of a prescribed international organization may claim a deduction on Line 256 for the net employment income the employee reports from that organization. The only prescribed international organizations are the United Nations and certain United Nations agencies (ITR 8900(1)). Also see VDs 2007-0248321E5, 2007-0262311E5, 2005-0132721I7, 2002-0143015, and 2000-0054485 which discuss the meaning of a prescribed international organization.

An individual may also deduct certain income received from employment with a prescribed international non-governmental organization in Canada, if all of the following conditions are met:

- the individual is not a Canadian citizen at any time in the year;

- the individual was a non-resident before beginning employment with the prescribed international non-governmental organization; and

- if the individual is now a resident, he or she became a resident solely for the purpose of that employment.

¶9405 — *Claiming and Filing*

Claim the applicable additional deductions on Line 256. In the space to the left of Line 256, specify the deduction. If there is more than one amount or the deduction requires additional explanation, attach a note to the paper return.

ITR 8900(1), (2), VDs 2012-0461051E5, 2011-0410811E5, 2010-0362631M4, 2008-0303191E5

Chapter 10 — Federal Non-Refundable Tax Credits

Contents

¶10000 Federal Non-Refundable Tax Credits (T1 Schedule 1: Lines 300–398)

¶10005 Personal Tax Credits Quick Reference Table

¶10010 Basic Personal Amount (T1 Schedule 1: Line 300)

¶10020 Age Amount (T1 Schedule 1: Line 301)

¶10030 Spouse or Common-Law Partner Amount (T1 Schedule 1: Line 303)

¶10035 Canada Caregiver Amount for Spouse or Common-Law Partner, or Eligible Dependant Age 18 or Older (T1 Schedule 1: Line 304)

¶10040 Amount for an Eligible Dependent (T1 Schedule 1: Line 305)

¶10050 Amount for Infirm Dependants Age 18 or Older (T1 Schedule 1: Line 306)

¶10055 Canada Caregiver Amount for Other Infirm Dependants Age 18 or Older (T1 Schedule 1: Line 307)

¶10060 CPP/QPP Contributions through Employment (T1 Schedule 1: Line 308)

¶10070 CPP/QPP Contributions on Self-Employment and Other Earnings (T1 Schedule 1: Line 310)

¶10080 Employment Insurance Premiums through Employment (T1 Schedule 1: Line 312)

¶10090 Adoption Expenses (T1 Schedule 1: Line 313)

¶10100 Pension Income Amount (T1 Schedule 1: Line 314)

¶10110 Caregiver Amount (T1 Schedule 1: Line 315)

¶10120 Disability Amount (for self) (T1 Schedule 1: Line 316)

¶10130 Employment Insurance Premiums on Self-Employment (T1 Schedule 1: Line 317)

¶10140 Disability Amount Transferred from a Dependant (T1 Schedule 1: Line 318)

¶10150 Interest Paid on Your Student Loans (T1 Schedule 1: Line 319)

¶10160 Tuition, Education and Textbook Amounts (T1 Schedule 1: Line 323)

¶10170 Tuition Amounts Transferred from a Child (T1 Schedule 1: Line 324)

¶10180 Amounts Transferred from Spouse or Common-Law Partner (T1 Schedule 1: Line 326)

¶10190 Medical Expenses for Self, Spouse and Dependent Children (T1 Schedule 1: Line 330)

¶10200 Medical Expenses for Other Dependants (T1 Schedule 1: Line 331)

¶10210 Donations and Gifts (T1 Schedule 1: Line 349)

¶10220 Volunteer Firefighters' Amount (T1 Schedule 1: Line 362)

¶10230 Canada Employment Amount (T1 Schedule 1: Line 363)

¶10240 Public Transit Amount (T1 Schedule 1: Line 364)

¶10250 Children's Fitness Amount (T1 Schedule 1: Line 365)

¶10260 Canada Caregiver Amount for Infirm Children Under 18 Years of Age (T1 Schedule 1: Line 367)

¶10270 Home Buyers' Amount (T1 Schedule 1: Line 369)

¶10280 Children's Arts Amount (T1 Schedule 1: Line 370)

¶10290 Search and Rescue Volunteers Tax Credit (T1 Schedule 1: Line 395)

¶10300 Home Accessibility Tax Credit (T1 Schedule 1: Line 398)

¶10000 — Federal Non-Refundable Tax Credits (T1 Schedule 1: Lines 300–398)

Non-refundable tax credits reduce an individual's federal tax; however, if the total of an individual's non-refundable credits is more than the individual's federal tax, the individual does not get a refund for the difference. All federal personal credits are indexed to inflation, which is measured by changes in the consumer price index.

Some non-refundable tax credits are available for carryover to future years if they cannot be fully used in the year. These include unused tuition, education, and textbook amounts (Line 323), donations and gifts (Line 349), and interest paid on student loans (Line 319). However, an individual does not have the choice to use one credit over another; the credits must be claimed in a particular order. The ordering of credits will be automatically applied by the tax preparation program used to complete the tax return.

Most non-refundable tax credits are calculated by multiplying the eligible amount to be claimed by 15%, which is the applicable percentage for 2018. However, the medical expense tax credit (Line 330) and the donation tax credit (Line 349) are calculated somewhat differently.

The provinces and territories also provide non-refundable tax credits similar to the federal tax credits, and provide for full or partial indexing of the credits. The indexation rate varies by province or territory. See 2017 Chapters 12 and 13 for further discussion.

If an individual is only resident for part of the year because the individual immigrated to, or emigrated from, Canada during the year, the federal non-refundable tax credits are either pro-rated on the basis of the number of days in the taxation year during which the individual is resident in Canada, or fully available to the extent the credits relate to the period of residency (on the basis of costs incurred during that period). Amounts that are already pro-rated or that relate to the period of residency do not need to be pro-rated. A part-year resident may also be entitled to claim non-refundable tax credits for the part of the year he or she was a non-resident, subject to the rules for non-residents. However, the amount that may be claimed cannot exceed the amount that would have been deductible had the individual been resident in Canada throughout the year. For more information, see 2017 Chapter 15 and Pamphlet T4055, *Newcomers to Canada*, or Guide T4056, *Emigrants and Income Tax*, whichever is applicable.

¶10005 — Personal Tax Credits Quick Reference Table

The 2018 Personal Tax Credits Quick Reference Table lists the federal non-refundable tax credits, refundable tax credits, and other federal supplements that individuals can claim on their 2018 T1 return. Federal personal tax credits reduce an individual's federal tax payable. A non-refundable tax credit can only be used to reduce taxes payable to zero, while a refundable tax credit is not limited by an individual's tax liability. Federal non-refundable tax credits are reported on Schedule 1 of the T1 return, and are generally calculated by multiplying the eligible amount to be claimed by 15% (subject to a few exceptions, which are noted). The table includes references to the relevant paragraphs of this Guide, applicable line of the T1 return, T1 Schedules, tax forms, CRA Guides and Pamphlets,

CRA Interpretation Bulletins, Income Tax Folios, and Information Circulars, sections of the ITA and ITR, and other relevant authority.

Credit	References	Comments
Basic Non-Refundable Tax Credits		
Basic personal credit	¶10010 T1 Schedule 1 Line 300 Folio S1-F4-C1 ITA 118(1)	All Canadian resident individuals are entitled to claim the basic personal amount of $11,809 in 2018. A non-resident is not eligible to claim the basic personal amount unless more than 90% of the non-resident's net world income is reported on the T1 return (see Schedule B, Allowable Amount of Non-Refundable Tax Credits).
Age credit	¶10020 T1 Schedule 1 Line 301 Folio S1-F4-C1 ITA 118(2)	Individuals who are 65 or older on the last day of the taxation year and whose 2018 net income was less than $36,976 can claim the maximum age credit of $7,333. The age credit begins to phase out at net income over $36,976, and is completely phased out at net income of $85,863. If an individual does not have sufficient income to use the age credit, all or part of it can be transferred to the individual's spouse or common-law partner (see Line 326 at ¶10180).
Spouse or common-law partner credit	¶10030 T1 Schedule 1 Line 303 Schedule 5 Folio S1-F4-C1 ITA 118(1)(a)	The spouse or common-law partner credit can be claimed by individuals who supported a spouse or common-law partner at any time in 2018 whose net income was less than $11,809 ($13,991 if eligible for the Canada caregiver credit). To claim the spouse or common-law partner credit, an individual must have been married or in a common-law relationship at some time during 2018; it does not have to be for the entire year.
Canada caregiver credit for spouse or common-law partner, or eligible dependant age 18 or older	¶10035 T1 Schedule 1 Line 304 Guide RC4064 ITA 118(1)(d)	Individuals who are eligible for the Canada caregiver amount for a spouse or common-law partner, or for an eligible dependant 18 years of age or older may be able to claim an amount on line 304 up to a maximum of $6,986.
Eligible dependant credit	¶10040 T1 Schedule 1 Line 305 Schedule 5 Folio S1-F4-C1 ITA 118(1)(b)	The eligible dependant credit can be claimed by individuals who do not have a spouse or common-law partner and who supported a dependant relative who lived with them whose net income was less than $11,809 ($13,991 if eligible for the Canada caregiver credit). The dependant must be related to the individual, and must be either under 18 years old, dependant by reason of mental or physical infirmity, or the individual's parent or grandparent. The eligible dependent credit cannot be claimed by individuals who are claiming a spouse or common-law partner credit, or if someone else in the individual's household is claiming the credit (even if there is more than one dependant in the household).
Infirm dependant credit	¶10050 T1 Schedule 1 Line 306	For 2017 and later taxation years, the infirm dependant credit and the caregiver tax credit were consolidated and replaced by the Canada caregiver credit. See ¶10055 for a discussion of the Canada caregiver credit.

Credit	References	Comments
Canada caregiver credit for other infirm dependants age 18 or older	¶10055 T1 Schedule 1 Line 307 Guide RC4064 ITA 118(1)(d)	For 2017 and later taxation years, an individual can claim a Canada caregiver credit on line 307 for each person who, at any time in the year, (1) is dependent on the individual because of mental or physical infirmity, and (2) is either (i) the spouse or common-law partner of the individual, or (ii) has attained the age of 18 years of age before the end of the taxation year and is a dependant of the individual. Dependants can include parents, grandparents, siblings, aunts, uncles, nieces, nephews, and adult children of the individual or the individual's spouse or common law partner. For 2018, the credit is $6,986, reduced by the dependant's net income in excess of $16,405.
CPP/QPP contributions through employment	¶10060 T1 Schedule 1 Line 308 Schedule 8 T4 Box 16, 17 Form T2204, RC381 ITA 118.7	Individuals (other than Quebec residents) can claim a credit for the amount of CPP contributions made as shown in T4 Box 16 (to a maximum of $2,593.80 in 2018). Quebec residents can claim a credit for QPP contributions made as shown in T4 Box 17 (to a maximum of $2,829.60 for 2018). For 2018, individuals must have CPP/QPP pensionable earnings of at least $55,900 to make the maximum contribution.
CPP/QPP contributions on self-employment & other earnings	¶10070 T1 Schedule 1 Line 310, Schedule 8 Form RC381 ITA 118.7, 60(e)	Individuals can claim a credit for the amount of CPP/QPP contributions on self-employment and other earnings, as calculated on Schedule 8. The maximum amount of CPP/QPP payable on self-employment and other earnings in 2018 is $5,187.60. Half of the total CPP/QPP contributions made on self-employment and other earnings are used to calculate the credit.
Employment insurance premiums through employment	¶10080 T1 Schedule 1 Line 312, Schedule 10 T4 Box 18 Form T2204 ITA 118.7	Individuals can claim a credit for the amount of EI premiums paid as shown in T4 Box 18 (to a maximum of $858 for 2018). Individuals must have insurable earnings of at least $51,700 to pay the maximum amount of premiums in 2018. Any overpayment amounts are calculated on Form T2204, Employee Overpayment of CPP Contributions and EI Premiums, and claimed on Line 450.
Adoption expense credit	¶10090 T1 Schedule 1 Line 313 ITA 118.01	Individuals can claim a tax credit for unreimbursed "eligible adoption expenses," to a maximum of $15,905 per adoption for 2018. Eligible adoption expenses include fees paid to a licensed adoption agency; court, legal or administrative expenses relating to an adoption order; reasonable and necessary travelling expenses for the child and adoptive parents; document translation fees; mandatory fees paid to a foreign institution; and any other reasonable expenses related to the adoption required by a provincial or territorial government or licensed adoption agency.

Credit	References	Comments
Pension income credit	¶10100 T1 Schedule 1 Line 314 Form T1023 IT-517R ITA 118(3), 118(7) Reg. 7800	Individuals who receive pension income in 2018 can claim a pension credit equal to the lesser of $2,000 and the amount of eligible pension income reported in 2018. For individuals age 65 and over, eligible pension income includes annuity payments from a superannuation or pension plan; payments from an RRSP, RRIF or DPSP; and certain accumulating funds in respect of an interest in a life insurance policy. For individuals under age 65, pension income includes annuity payments from a superannuation or pension plan and survivor benefit payments. For purposes of the pension income credit, pension income does not include OAS pensions/supplements; CPP, QPP or SPP payments; death benefits; or payments received under a salary deferral arrangement, employee benefit plan or employee trust. An individual who cannot use the pension income credit may be allowed to transfer all or part of it to a spouse or common-law partner (see Line 326).
Caregiver credit	¶10110 T1 Schedule 1 Line 315	For 2017 and later taxation years, the infirm dependant credit and the caregiver tax credit were consolidated and replaced by the Canada caregiver credit. See ¶10055 for a discussion of the Canada caregiver credit.
Disability credit	¶10120 T1 Schedule 1 Line 316 Form T2201 Guide RC4064 S1-F1-C2 ITA 118.3, 118.4	An individual can claim a disability credit of $8,235 if the individual has been certified as suffering from a severe and prolonged mental or physical impairment which markedly restricts the individual's ability to perform the basic activities of daily living. For new applications, individuals are required to submit Form T2201, Disability Tax Credit Certificate, to certify the impairment. A prolonged impairment is one that lasts for at least 12 continuous months. An individual is considered markedly restricted if the individual is blind or is unable to perform basic day-to-day activities. An individual will have the equivalent of a marked restriction if his/her ability to perform more than one basic day-to-day activity is significantly restricted and the restrictions together have the same effect as a marked restriction in a single activity. Basic day-to-day activities include eating, dressing, speaking, hearing, bowel or bladder functions and walking. Mental functions necessary for everyday life include memory, problem-solving, goal-setting, judgment and adaptive functioning. The disability credit cannot be claimed where the individual is claiming a medical expense tax credit for nursing home care or a full-time attendant.
Employment insurance premiums on self-employment & other earnings	¶10130 T1 Schedule 1 Line 317 Schedule 13 EI Act Part VII.	Self-employed individuals can choose to pay EI premiums to be eligible to receive EI special benefits. Individuals who have entered into an agreement with the Canada EI Commission to participate in the EI program for access to EI special benefits have to complete Schedule 13 to calculate their premiums payable to enter on Lines 317 and 430.
Disability credit transferred from a dependant	¶10140 T1 Schedule 1 Line 318 Form T2201 Guide RC4064 S1-F1-C2 ITA 118.3	An individual may be able to claim all or part of a dependant's disability credit where one of the following applies: (1) the individual claimed the eligible dependant credit for the dependant (or could have if the individual did not have a spouse or common-law partner and the dependant had no income); or (2) the dependant was the individual's or his or her spouse or common-law partner's parent, grandparent, child, grandchild, brother, sister, aunt, uncle, niece or nephew, and the individual claimed the infirm dependant credit or caregiver credit for that dependant (or could have if the dependant had no income and was 18 or older in 2018). An individual cannot claim this credit if the disabled person's spouse or common-law partner is already claiming the disability credit or other non-refundable tax credit (other than medical expenses) for the disabled person.

Credit	References	Comments
Interest paid on student loans	¶10150 T1 Schedule 1 Line 319 Pamphlet P105 ITA 118.62	Individuals can claim amounts paid in the year in respect of interest on their loans (whether new or outstanding) under the Canada Student Loans Program or a provincial student loans program. The credit applies only to interest paid and does not apply to interest accrued or interest forgiven. Any unused credit may be carried forward for up to 5 years.
Tuition, education and textbook credits	¶10160 T1 Schedule 1 Line 323, Schedule 11 Form T2202A, TL11A, TL11B, TL11C, TL11D Pamphlet P105 RC192 IT Folios S1-F2-C1, S1-F2-C2 ITA 118.5, 118.6, 118.8	Individuals can claim a tax credit for the cost of tuition fees for attending university, college, or other post-secondary institution. For taxation years before 2017, students could also claim an education tax credit and textbook credit. The education and textbook tax credits have been repealed for 2017 and later taxation years. Unused education and textbook tax credits carried forward from years prior to 2017 can be claimed in 2017 and subsequent years.
Tuition credits transferred from a child	¶10170 T1 Schedule 1 Line 324, Schedule 11 Form T2202A, TL11A, TL11B, TL11C, TL11D Pamphlet P105 ITA 118.81, 118.9, 118.92	Students who cannot use all of their tuition credits in the current year to reduce their taxes to zero can transfer all or part of the amount to their parent or grandparent. The maximum amount that can be transferred is $5,000 less the amount the student uses (even if there is still an unclaimed part). Students should complete Schedule 11 to calculate the amount available for transfer, and complete the applicable portion of Form T2202A, TL11A, TL11B, TL11C or TL11D to designate the individual. Students cannot transfer an unused credit to more than one person in a year.
Credits transferred from your spouse or common-law partner	¶ 10180 T1 Schedule 1 Line 326, Schedule 2 Pamphlet P105 Guide RC4064 Folio S1-F2-C2, S1-F4-C1 ITA 118(1)(b.1), 118(2), 118(3), 118.8, 118.81	An individual may be able to claim all or part of the following credits for which the individual's spouse or common-law partner qualifies, and that the spouse or common-law partner designates: the age credit, the Canada caregiver credit for infirm children under 18, the pension income credit, the disability credit and the tuition credit. Taxpayers are required to complete Schedule 2 to calculate their claim for amounts transferred from a spouse or common-law partner.

Credit	References	Comments
Medical expense tax credit for self, spouse or common-law partner & dependent children under age 18	¶10190 T1 Schedule 1 Line 330 Form T2201 Guide RC4065 Folio S1-F1-C1 ITA 118.2, 118.4 Reg. 5700, 5701	Individuals can claim a medical expense tax credit for the total eligible medical expenses paid for themselves, their spouse or common-law partner, or their or their spouse or common-law partner's children age 17 or younger who depended on the individual for support. For 2018, to make a claim, total medical expenses must be more than either 3% of net income (Line 236) or $2,302, whichever is less. An individual can claim medical expenses paid in any consecutive 12-month period that ends in 2018 and that have not been claimed for 2017. Either spouse can claim the medical expenses. Generally, it's better for the spouse with the lower net income to claim the medical expenses. In order to claim the cost of full-time in-home attendant care or full-time care in a nursing home as an eligible medical expense, the cared-for person must meet the eligibility criteria for the disability tax credit, which requires an approved Form T2201 on file. See the Medical Expense Quick Reference Table in Appendix A for an itemized list and description of medical expenses, and whether they are eligible or not for the medical expense tax credit.
Medical expense tax credit for other dependants	¶10200 T1 Schedule 1 Line 331, Schedule 5 Guide RC4065 Folio S1-F1-C1 ITA 118.2 Reg. 5700, 5701	Individuals can claim a medical expense tax credit for the total eligible medical expenses that the individual or his or her spouse or common-law partner paid for the individual or the individual's spouse or common-law partner's children who are 18 years or older, grandchild, parent, grandparent, brother, sister, aunt, uncle, niece or nephew who were resident in Canada at any time in the year. The expenses must meet the same criteria as those claimed on Line 330 and the claim must be for the same 12-month period used for Line 330. Calculate the medical expenses claimed on this Line individually for each dependent. For 2018, to claim a dependent's medical expenses, the total of the dependent's expenses must exceed the lesser of $2,302 or 3% of the dependant's net income for the year. See the Medical Expense Quick Reference Table in Appendix A for an itemized list and description of medical expenses, and whether they are eligible or not for the medical expense tax credit.
Donations and gifts	¶10210 T1 Schedule 1 Line 349, Schedule 9 Pamphlet P113 IC 84-3R5 Folio S7-F1-C1, IT-226R, IT-244R3 ITA 118.1, 149.1(1)	A taxpayer is permitted a tax credit for charitable donations made to qualified donees. Individuals are entitled to a federal tax credit of 15% on the first $200 of charitable donations and 29% on donations over $200 (33% to the extent that an individual has income taxed at the 33% rate). Charitable donations which are not claimed in a taxation year may be carried forward for up to 5 immediately following years. Administratively, CRA permits individuals to claim donations made by the individual's spouse or common-law partner on the individual's return.
Volunteer firefighter tax credit	¶10220 T1 Schedule 1 Line 362 ITA 118.06	Volunteer firefighters can claim a tax credit for up to $3,000 of volunteer firefighting services provided to one or more fire departments or search and rescue volunteer services provided to one or more search and rescue organizations. To qualify, an individual must complete at least 200 hours of service in the year, each of which is an hour of eligible volunteer firefighting service for a fire department or eligible search and rescue volunteer service for an eligible search and rescue organization.
Canada employment credit	¶10230 T1 Schedule 1 Line 363 ITA 118(10)	Individuals who earn employment income can claim the lesser of $1,195, and the total of the employment income reported on the individual's tax return.

Credit	References	Comments
Public transit credit	¶10240 T1 Schedule 1 Line 364 ITA 118.02	The public transit pass credit was repealed effective July 1, 2017. For the 2017 taxation year, individuals could claim the cost of eligible transit passes that were for the use of public transit services for the period January 1 to June 30, 2017. The public transit credit is eliminated completely for 2018 and later taxation years.
Canada caregiver credit for infirm children under 18 years of age	¶10260 T1 Schedule 1 Line 367 ITA 118(1)(b.1)	Individuals can claim a Canada caregiver credit of $2,182 on line 367 for each eligible dependant under 18 years of age who has an impairment in mental or physical functions.
Home buyer's credit	¶10270 T1 Schedule 1 Line 369 Guide RC4135, RC4509 ITA 118.05	Individuals can claim $5,000 for the purchase of a "qualifying home" in 2018 if both of the following apply: the individual or his or her spouse or common-law partner acquired a qualifying home and the individual is a first-time home buyer (i.e., the individual did not live in another home owned by the individual or his or her spouse or common-law partner during 2018 or at any time from 2014 to 2017). The following are considered qualifying homes: single-family houses, semi-detached houses, townhouses, mobile homes, condominium units, and apartments in duplexes, triplexes, fourplexes, or apartment buildings. The home must be in Canada, must be purchased in the individual's and/or his or her spouse or common-law partner's name, and the individual must intend to live in the home as a principal residence no later than one year after it is acquired. Both existing homes and homes under construction will qualify for the credit.
Children's arts tax credit	¶10280	The children's arts credit has been repealed for 2017 and later taxation years.
Search and rescue volunteers tax credit	¶10290 T1 Schedule 1 Line 395 ITA 118.07	Search and rescue volunteers can claim a tax credit for up to $3,000 of search and rescue volunteer services provided to one or more search and rescue organizations or volunteer firefighting services provided to one or more fire departments. To qualify, an individual must complete at least 200 hours of service in the year, each of which is an hour of eligible search and rescue volunteer service for an eligible search and rescue organization or eligible volunteer firefighting service for a fire department. An individual may not claim this tax credit if the individual has claimed the volunteer firefighter tax credit in the year.
Home accessibility tax credit	¶10300 T1 Schedule 1 Line 398 Schedule 12 ITA 118.041	Seniors, persons with disabilities and other eligible individuals can claim a non-refundable tax credit for up to $10,000 per year of expenditures made for "qualifying renovations" to a principle residence. Generally, a "qualifying renovation" is a renovation or alteration that is: (1) of an enduring nature and integral to the residence, and (2) undertaken to enable the senior or disabled person to gain access to, or to be mobile or functional within, the residence, or to reduce the risk of harm to the individual within the residence or in gaining access to the residence.

Other Non-Refundable Credits

Credit	References	Comments
Federal foreign tax credit (FTC)	¶11010 T1 Schedule 1 Line 405 Form T220 IT Folio S5-F2-C1 ITA 20(11), 20(12), 126(1), 126(9)	Individuals can claim a foreign tax credit (FTC) for income or profits taxes paid to a foreign country on income received outside of Canada and reported on their Canadian tax return. Taxes paid to a state or province of a foreign country are also eligible for the FTC. Foreign business-income tax and foreign non-business-income tax are determined using separate calculations, and within each category, a separate calculation is performed for each foreign country to which taxes were paid. Individuals may also be able to claim a provincial or territorial FTC if the federal FTC is less than the foreign tax paid. In most cases, the FTC that can be claimed for each foreign country will be the lesser of the foreign income tax the individual paid or the tax otherwise due in Canada on the individual's net income from that country. Non-business foreign taxes which are not recovered as a FTC may be deducted from income on Line 232 of the T1 return as a section 20(12) deduction. The federal FTC is calculated on Form T2209, Federal Foreign Tax Credits, and the provincial/territorial FTC is calculated on Form T2036, Provincial Foreign Tax Credit. IT Folio S5-F2-C1, Foreign Tax Credit, contains a description of the FTC calculation.
Political donation tax credit	¶11020 T1 Schedule 1 Lines 409, 410 IC 75-2R7 ITA 127(3)	Individuals can claim a tax credit for political contributions to candidates for election to the House of Commons or to registered federal political parties, up to a maximum of $650 for 2018. The credit available is equal to 75% of the first $400 of contributions, plus 50% of the next $350 of contributions, plus 33 1/3% of the next $525 of contributions. The maximum credit is reached with contributions of $1,275.
Investment tax credit	¶11030 T1 Schedule 1 Line 412 Form T101, T661, T1145, T1146, T2038(IND) Guide T4088 IC 86-4R3 ITA 127(5)–(26)	Individuals may claim an investment tax credit (ITC) in the year they make a qualified expenditure or, in the case of property, when it is available for use. Expenditures or investments that qualify for an ITC fall into the following categories: capital cost of qualified property, apprenticeship expenditures, qualified expenditures in respect of scientific research and experimental development (SR&ED), and renounced eligible exploration expenses. ITCs are calculated by applying a specified percentage to the capital cost of the asset acquired or the expenditure incurred. Unused ITCs may be carried back 3 years or forward 20 years. Individuals should complete Form T2038(IND), Investment Tax Credit (Individuals), to calculate ITCs.
Labour-sponsored funds tax credit	¶11040 T1 Schedule 1 Lines 413, 414 Form T5006 ITA 127.4, Part X.3, Reg. 6701	The labour-sponsored funds tax credit provides a tax credit for individuals who purchase shares of a prescribed provincially-registered labour-sponsored venture capital corporation (LSVCC) in 2018 or the first 60 days of 2019. A 15% credit is available for share purchases of provincially-registered LSVCCs, to a maximum of $5,000 (a $750 credit).
Family tax cut credit	¶11065	The family tax cut credit was repealed for 2016 and later taxation years.
Federal dividend tax credit (DTC)	¶11080 T1 Schedule 1 Line 425 Schedule 4 ITA 121	Individuals who reported taxable dividends (eligible and other than eligible) from taxable Canadian corporations on Line 120 of their tax return should enter the total of the dividend tax credits for eligible dividends and for other than eligible dividends reported on their information slips (T3, T5, T5013, etc.). Foreign dividends do not qualify for the dividend tax credit. The amount of the dividend tax credit depends on the type of corporation paying the dividend. Most dividends received from Canadian public corporations are eligible for the enhanced dividend tax credit ("eligible dividends"), while most dividends received from Canadian-controlled private corporations (CCPCs) are eligible for the regular dividend tax credit ("non-eligible" dividends).

Credit	References	Comments
Overseas employment tax credit (OETC)	¶11090	The OETC was gradually phased out in stages from 2013 to 2015, and for all employees, the OETC is eliminated for taxation years after 2015.
Minimum tax carryover	¶11100 T1 Schedule 1 Line 427 Form T691 ITA 120.2, 127.5–127.55	A taxpayer is liable for alternative minimum tax (AMT) if AMT is more than the individual's federal tax. To calculate "adjusted taxable income" for AMT purposes, certain adjustments are made to taxable income. Individuals are allowed an exemption of $40,000 to reduce their adjusted taxable income for AMT purposes. After deducting the basic exemption, AMT is 15% of the adjusted taxable income. The amount by which AMT exceeds the tax otherwise payable may be carried forward for up to 7 years to reduce tax in a future year to the extent that AMT is less than the regular tax in that year.

Refundable Tax Credits & Supplements

Credit	References	Comments
Refundable medical expense supplement	¶11280 T1 Line 452 Worksheet 5000-D1 ITA 122.51(1)	The federal refundable medical expense supplement is available to low income individuals who have paid medical expenses or disability supports expenses. To be eligible for this supplement, individuals must be 18 or older and have employment or self-employment income greater than $3,566 in 2018. For 2018, the maximum supplement is the lesser of $1,222, or 25% of both medical expenses (Line 332) and disability supports expenses (Line 215), reduced by 5% of family net income greater than $27,044.
Working income tax benefit (WITB)	¶11290 T1 Line 453 Schedule 6 Form RC201, RC210 Guide RC4227 ITA 122.7	The working income tax benefit (WITB) is a refundable credit payable to certain low-income individuals and families with working income over $3,000. The WITB is calculated on Schedule 6 of the T1 return. Eligible individuals and families can apply to the CRA for a prepayment of up to 50% of their estimated WITB using Form RC201, Working Income Tax Benefit Advance Payments Application. For 2019 and later taxation years, the WITB is being replaced by the Canada Workers Benefit (CWB), which is an enhanced version of the WITB.
Children's fitness tax credit	¶11325	The children's fitness credit has been repealed for 2017 and later taxation years.
Eligible educator school supply tax credit	¶11330 T1 Lines 468, 469 ITA 122.9 Reg. 9600	Teachers and early childhood educators can claim a refundable tax credit for the cost of eligible teaching supplies paid in a taxation year. The maximum allowable eligible supplies expense in a year is $1,000, which equals a $150 refundable tax credit.
GST/HST credit	¶1153 T1 return, page 1 Guide RC4210 ITA 122.5	The GST/HST credit is a non-taxable amount paid quarterly to eligible individuals age 19 or older with low or modest income. Individuals apply for the GST/HST credit by filing the T1 return. For 2018, the adult maximum payment is $284, the child maximum is $149, and the single supplement is $149. The phase-in threshold for the single supplement is $9,209 and the family net income at which the GST/HST credit begins to phase out is $36,976.

Credit	References	Comments
Canada child benefit (CCB)	Guide T4114 Form RC66 ITA 122.6–122.64	The Canada Child Tax Benefit (CCTB) and the Universal Child Care Benefit (UCCB) were replaced by the Canada Child Benefit (CCB), effective July 1, 2016. Similar to the CCTB, the CCB is a monthly tax-free benefit that is determined on the basis of adjusted family net income, the number of children, and the age of the children. The basic CCB for July 2018 to June 2019 is $6,496/year for each eligible child under the age of six, and $5,481/year for each eligible child aged 6 to 17. Where adjusted income is over $30,450, the CCB is reduced by a specified phase-out percentage based on the number of eligible dependants. For more information on the CCB, see: canada.ca/en/revenue-agency/services/child-family-bene-fits/canada- child-benefit-overview.html.
Universal child care benefit (UCCB)	¶8210 T1 Line 117 Guide T4114 RC62 ITA 56(6), *UCCB Act*	Effective July 1, 2016, the UCCB was eliminated and replaced by the Canada Child Benefit.

¶10010 — Basic Personal Amount (T1 Schedule 1: Line 300)

Generally, every individual is entitled to claim the basic personal amount of $11,809 for 2018, which results in a tax credit of $1,771 ($11,809 × 15% tax credit rate).

A non-resident is not eligible to claim the basic personal amount unless all or substantially all (more than 90%) of the non-resident's net world income is reported on a T1 return (see Schedule B, Allowable Amount of Non-Refundable Tax Credits).

ITA 118(1), Folio S1-F4-C1: *Basic Personal and Dependant Tax Credits*

¶10020 — Age Amount (T1 Schedule 1: Line 301)

Individuals who are 65 or older on the last day of the taxation year, and whose 2018 net income was less than $85,863 are eligible to claim the age amount. If the individual's 2018 net income is less than $36,976, claim the maximum age amount of $7,333 on Line 301. If the individual's income is between $36,976 and $85,863, calculate the age amount on the federal worksheet for Line 301. Individuals who turned 65 in 2018 are not required to pro-rate this credit. If an individual does not have sufficient income to use this credit, all or part of it can be transferred to the individual's spouse or common-law partner (see Line 326 at ¶10180).

ITA 118(2), Folio S1-F4-C1: *Basic Personal and Dependant Tax Credits*

¶10030 — Spouse or Common-Law Partner Amount (T1 Schedule 1: Line 303)

The spouse or common-law partner amount is $11,809 for 2018. This amount can be claimed by a taxpayer who supported a spouse or common-law partner at any time in 2018 whose net income (Line 236) was less than $11,809. The credit will be reduced for a spouse or common-law partner who earns income up to $11,809.

To claim the spouse or common-law partner amount for 2018, an individual must have been married or in a common-law relationship at some time during 2018; it does not have to be for the entire year. For example, if an individual got married or became a common-law partner in September 2018, the same amount can be claimed as if the individual was married or living common law for all or 2018.

The concept of "support" generally entails the provision of a home, food, clothing, and the necessary amenities of life consistent with one's position and mode of living. The fact that the spouse or common-law partner who is "supported" has private means from which he or she contributes to the common household would not disqualify the other spouse or common-law partner from claiming the spouse or common-law partner amount.

The Canada caregiver credit (see ¶10055) allows an individual to claim an additional amount of $2,182 in respect of a spouse or common-law partner who is dependent on the individual by reason of mental or physical infirmity. As a result, the total spousal or common-law partner amount that can be claimed on Line 303 for an individual claiming the Canada caregiver credit is increased by $2,182 to $13,991. The meaning of mental or physical infirmity is described in paragraph 1.21 of Folio S1-F4-C1 as follows:

> The term mental or physical infirmity is not specifically defined for the purposes of subsection 118(1). Therefore, it takes its ordinary meaning. For a person to be dependent on an individual because of mental or physical infirmity, the dependency must be brought about solely by reason of the infirmity. The degree of the infirmity must be such that it requires the person to be dependent on the individual for a considerable period of time. Temporary illness or injury is not considered to be an infirmity for purposes of the personal tax credits.

¶10031 — *Spouse or Common-Law Partner Net Income*

Enter the taxpayer's spouse's or common-law partner's net income in the "Information about your spouse or common-law partner" area on page 1 of the return, even if it is nil. If the individual was living with his or her spouse or common-law partner on December 31, 2018, use the spouse's income for the whole year.

If a couple separated in 2018 because of a breakdown in the relationship and were not back together on December 31, 2018, only use the spouse's or common-law partner's net income amount that relates to the period before the separation to calculate the credit. Alternatively, if the individual was required to make support payments to a current or former spouse or common-law partner, and was separated from him or her for only part of 2018 because of a breakdown in the relationship, the individual can either choose to claim the deductible support amounts paid in 2018 to the spouse or common-law partner (see Line 220 at ¶9210) or the spouse or common-law partner amount, whichever is more beneficial. The following example is provided in Guide P102:

> Roger and Mary separated on September 1, 2016. Under the terms of the written agreement, beginning on that date Roger pays $300 monthly in spousal support. Mary had no other income in 2016. When filing his 2016 return, Roger could deduct either: the support he paid = $1,200 ($300 × 4 months); or the spouse or common-law partner amount for Mary (Line 303 of the return). Since Mary had no other income, Roger would be entitled to the full spouse or common-law partner amount. Therefore, Roger decides to claim the spouse or common-law partner amount at Line 303 since it is the most beneficial. He should enter the amount of support he paid on Line 230 and enter zero on Line 220. Mary has to report the $1,200 she received in support payments on her 2016 return.

If an individual reconciled with his or her spouse or common-law partner before the end of 2018, claim the spouse or common-law partner amount and any allowable amounts on Line 326 (amounts transferred from your spouse or common-law partner; see ¶10180).

¶10032 — *Definition of Spouse and Common-Law Partner*

A spouse is a person to whom an individual is legally married. A common-law partner is a person, who is not the individual's spouse, with whom an individual is living in a conjugal relationship, and to whom at least one of the following situations applies. He or she:

- has been living with the individual in a conjugal relationship for at least 12 continuous months;

- is the parent of the individual's child by birth or adoption; or

- has custody and control of the individual's child (or had custody and control immediately before the child turned 19 years of age) and the child is wholly dependent on that person for support.

ITA 118(1)(a), Folio S1-F4-C1: *Basic Personal and Dependant Tax Credits*

¶10035 — Canada Caregiver Amount for Spouse or Common-Law Partner, or Eligible Dependant Age 18 or Older (T1 Schedule 1: Line 304)

Individuals who are eligible for the Canada caregiver amount for a spouse or common-law partner, or for an eligible dependant 18 years of age or older may be able to claim an amount up to a maximum of $6,986. However, caregivers must first claim the amount of $2,182 in calculating the spouse or common-law partner amount on Line 303 or the amount on Line 305 for an eligible dependant 18 years of age or older. See ¶10030 and ¶10055 for information on claiming the Canada caregiver amount for a spouse or common law partner. See ¶10040 and ¶10055 for information on claiming the Canada caregiver amount for an eligible dependant age 18 or older.

¶10036 — *Claiming and Filing*

For 2018, the Canada caregiver credit is $6,986 less the amount, if any, by which the dependant's net income for the year exceeds $16,405. To claim the Canada caregiver credit for a spouse or common-law partner or for an eligible dependant age 18 or older, complete the details for Line 304 on Schedule 5, *Details of Dependant*.

ITA 118(1)(d), Schedule 5, Guide RC4064, Folio S1-F4-C1: *Basic Personal and Dependant Tax Credits*

¶10040 — Amount for an Eligible Dependent (T1 Schedule 1: Line 305)

An individual can claim an eligible dependant credit of $11,809 (for 2018) if the individual does not claim a spouse or common-law partner tax credit in the tax year and if, at any time in the year, the individual:

- is either: (1) unmarried and did not live in a common-law partnership; or (2) married or in a common-law partnership but did not support or live with their spouse or common-law partner and was not supported by their spouse or common-law partner; and

- alone, or jointly with one or more other persons, maintains a self-contained domestic establishment where the individual lives and actually supports an eligible dependant.

For the purposes of this credit, an eligible dependant is a person who:

- is resident in Canada (this residency requirement does not apply if the person is a child of the individual);

- is wholly dependent for support on the individual, or the individual and the other person or persons as the case may be; and

- is either: (1) the individual's parent or grandparent by blood, marriage, common-law partnership, or adoption; or (2) the individual's child, grandchild, brother, or sister, by blood, marriage, common-law partnership, or adoption, and is either under 18 years of age or dependent on the individual by reason of a mental or physical infirmity.

The Canada caregiver credit (see ¶10055) allows an individual to claim an additional amount of $2,182 in respect of an eligible dependant who is dependent on the individual by reason of mental or physical infirmity. As a result, the total eligible dependant amount that can be claimed on Line 305 for an individual claiming the Canada caregiver credit is increased by $2,182 to $13,991. The meaning of mental or physical infirmity is described in paragraph 1.21 of Folio S1-F4-C1 as follows:

> The term mental or physical infirmity is not specifically defined for the purposes of subsection 118(1). Therefore, it takes its ordinary meaning. For a person to be dependent on an individual because of mental or physical infirmity, the dependency must be brought about solely by reason of the infirmity. The degree of the infirmity must be such that it

requires the person to be dependent on the individual for a considerable period of time. Temporary illness or injury is not considered to be an infirmity for purposes of the personal tax credits.

See paragraphs 1.39 to 1.58 of Folio S1-F4-C1: *Basic Personal and Dependant Tax Credits*, for a discussion of the eligible dependant credit, as well as various examples.

¶10041 — *Support of an Eligible Dependant*

The CRA provides the following guidance regarding the support of an eligible dependant in paragraphs 1.46 to 1.49 of Folio S1-F4-C1:

1.46 For an individual to claim the eligible dependant tax credit, a person must be wholly dependent for support on the individual. As discussed in ¶1.18, support involves providing the basic necessities of life, such as food, shelter, and clothing. Wholly dependent for support on the individual generally means the person is financially dependent on the individual such that the individual provides almost entirely for the person's well-being. For example, in order for a child to be considered wholly dependent for support on a parent, the parent must be responsible for the usual day-to-day activities of raising the child, such as ensuring the child attends school, and providing necessities such as food, shelter and clothing.

1.47 Where an individual receives support payments from a government agency responsible for a person's care, in order to care for that person, the person is generally not considered to be wholly dependent for support on the individual. For example, a foster child is not considered to be wholly dependent for support on a foster parent who receives payments from an agency responsible for the child's care.

1.48 A child born alive (even if alive only briefly after birth) is considered to be dependent for support on an individual. An individual may claim the eligible dependant tax credit for a newborn child provided the other requirements to claim that credit are met.

1.49 An individual may support an eligible dependant who moves away to attend school. If the eligible dependant ordinarily lives with the individual during the year when not in school, and the other requirements to claim the eligible dependant tax credit are met, the individual may claim the eligible dependant tax credit for that person.

Further to the above, the taxpayer must maintain a self-contained domestic establishment, whether alone or jointly with one or more other persons, in which the taxpayer lives and actually support the dependant in that establishment. A self-contained domestic establishment is a house, apartment, or other similar place of residence where a person as a general rule sleeps and eats.

The eligible dependent credit may also be claimed where two or more taxpayers jointly support the dependant and maintain a self-contained domestic establishment in which the dependant lives (eg; two unmarried siblings might be living at home and supporting a parent). Only one of the taxpayers may claim the credit for a taxation year, but they may alternate from year to year. If they cannot agree who will claim the credit for a particular year, neither of them will be allowed to claim it. Again, the dependant must be wholly dependent, be related to each of the supporting taxpayers, and, except in the case of claiming the taxpayer's own child, must be resident in Canada.

A dependant who lives away from home while attending school, but ordinarily lives with the taxpayer when not in school, will be considered to live with the taxpayer for the purposes of the eligible dependant credit.

¶10042 — *Limitations*

The following limitations apply with respect to claiming the eligible dependant tax credit:

1. An individual cannot claim an eligible dependant tax credit in a tax year for more than one person (ITA 118(4)(a)).

2. An individual cannot claim the eligible dependant tax credit for the year if they claim a spouse or common-law partner tax credit in that year. The individual may choose to claim either the spouse or common-law partner

credit or the eligible dependant credit in a tax year if the requirements for both are met. The individual can choose whichever is more beneficial (ITA 118(1)B(b), 118(4)(a); see Examples 4 and 5 in Folio S1-F4-C1).

3. An individual cannot claim an eligible dependant tax credit in a tax year for a person if another individual is claiming the spouse or common-law partner credit for that same person, and that person and the other individual are married or in a common-law partnership throughout the year and are not living separate and apart because of a breakdown of their relationship (ITA 118(4)(a.1); see Example 6 in Folio S1-F4-C1).

4. Only one individual can claim the eligible dependant credit in respect of the same person or the same domestic establishment in the same year. The eligible dependant credit cannot be split with another person; if two individuals are entitled to the credit in respect of the same person, they must agree which one will claim it (ITA 118(4)(b); see paragraphs 1.53 to 1.55 and Example 7 in Folio S1-F4-C1).

5. An individual cannot claim an eligible dependant credit for a child if the individual is required to pay a support amount for that child to his or her former spouse or common-law partner, unless the individual was separated from the spouse or common-law partner for only part of the year and is not claiming support amounts paid to the spouse or common-law partner as a deduction on Line 220. For more information, see paragraphs 3.73 to 3.77 of Folio S1-F3-C3 and ¶9214 and ¶9215.1 (ITA 118(5)).

6. The amount of the eligible dependant credit is reduced on a dollar for dollar basis for each dollar of income of the dependant person, and is eliminated when the dependant person's net income exceeds $11,809 (for 2018).

¶10043 — *Claiming and Filing*

To claim the eligible dependant credit, complete the details for Line 305 on Schedule 5, *Details of Dependant*.

ITA 118(1)(b), 118(4)(b), 118(5), 118(5), 248(1)"self-contained domestic establishment", 252(1), Folio S1-F4-C1: *Basic Personal and Dependant Tax Credits*

¶10050 — Amount for Infirm Dependants Age 18 or Older (T1: Schedule 1: Line 306)

> For 2017 and later taxation years, the infirm dependants credit and the caregiver credit were consolidated and replaced by the Canada caregiver credit. See ¶10055 for a discussion of the Canada caregiver credit.

¶10055 — Canada Caregiver Amount for Other Infirm Dependants Age 18 or Older (T1 Schedule 1: Line 307)

For 2017 and later taxation years, the caregiver tax credit and infirm dependants credit were consolidated and replaced by the Canada caregiver credit in ITA 118(1)(d). The Canada caregiver credit can be claimed by individuals who are caregivers for dependants who have an infirmity and are dependent on the caregiver for support by reason of that infirmity. The credit is available in respect of infirm dependants who are parents/grandparents, brothers/sisters, aunts/uncles, nieces/nephews or adult children of the claimant. There is no requirement that the dependant live with the claimant. For the 2018 taxation year, the maximum Canada caregiver credit is $6,986, reduced dollar-for-dollar by the dependant's net income above $16,405.

Amendments were also made to the family caregiver tax credit, which provided an additional amount for the care of infirm dependants who meet the requirements for the spouse or common-law partner credit (Line 303), the eligible dependant credit (Line 305), or the caregiver credit for infirm dependants under 18 years of age (Line 367), to increase the additional amount that can be claimed under these credits.

The CRA provides detailed information on the consolidation of the caregiver credits at: canada.ca/en/revenue-agency/programs/about-canada-revenue-agency-cra/federal-government-budgets/budget-2017-building-a-strong-middle-class/consolidation-caregiver-credits.html.

¶10056 — *Meaning of Dependant & Mental or Physical Infirmity*

An individual can claim the Canada caregiver credit for each person who, at any time in the year, (1) is dependent on the individual because of mental or physical infirmity, and (2) is either the spouse or common-law partner of the individual, or is 18 years of age before the end of the taxation year and is a dependant of the individual.

For the purposes of the Canada caregiver credit, a "dependant" means a person who is, at any time in the year, dependent on the individual for support and is: (a) whether or not resident in Canada, the child or grandchild of the individual or of the individual's spouse or common-law partner; or (b) if resident in Canada at any time in the year, the parent, grandparent, brother, sister, uncle, aunt, nephew or niece of the individual or of the individual's spouse or common-law partner (ITA 118(6)).

For the purposes of the Canada caregiver credit, a "child" includes the following: (a) a person of whom the taxpayer is the legal parent; (b) a person who is wholly dependent on the taxpayer for support and of whom the taxpayer has, or immediately before the person attained the age of 19 years had, in law or in fact, the custody and control; (c) a child of the taxpayer's spouse or common-law partner; and (d) a spouse or common-law partner of a child of the taxpayer (ITA 252(1)). However, a "child" does not include a foster child in respect of whom the foster parents receive support payments from an agency responsible for the child's care (para. 1.47 of Folio S1-F4-C1). Extended meanings also apply for "parent", "grandparent", "brother", "sister", "aunt" and "uncle" so that such relatives of a spouse or common-law partner are included within the meanings of those terms (ITA 252(2)). See also paragraphs 1.4 to 1.15 of Folio S1-F4-C1.

The CRA commented on the meaning of a "dependant" in VD 2012-0436431E5, stating:

> A "dependant" is defined in subsection 118(6) of the Act and includes a child who "at any time in the year is dependent on the individual for support . . ." It is a question of fact in each case to determine whether or not the actions or contributions of a particular individual are of such a nature and degree that they could be said to constitute "support" of another person. Although consideration should be given to the availability and quantum of support provided, a person is generally considered to be dependent on an individual if the individual has actually supplied necessary maintenance, or the basic necessities of life (food, shelter and clothing) to the person on a regular and consistent basis.

Because of the broad definition of "dependant", more than one person may be entitled to claim a Canada caregiver credit in respect of the same infirm dependant (for example, in the case of an individual helping to support his brother or sister still living in their parent's home). Also, because a dependant is a person who meets the requirements "at any time in the year", where one parent supports an infirm dependant for part of the year and, following a divorce or separation, the other parent supports the same dependant for the rest of the year, both parents may claim the credit in respect of the dependant for that year, provided that no one claims the spousal or common-law partner credit in respect of the dependant. In such cases, the Canada caregiver credit claimed in respect of the dependant cannot exceed the maximum amount deductible if only one individual were entitled to the credit (ITA 118(4)(d); see paragraph 1.68 of Folio S1-F4-C1).

The meaning of mental or physical infirmity is described in paragraph 1.21 of Folio S1-F4-C1 as follows:

> 1.21 The term mental or physical infirmity is not specifically defined for the purposes of subsection 118(1). Therefore, it takes its ordinary meaning. For a person to be dependent on an individual because of mental or physical infirmity, the dependency must be brought about solely by reason of the infirmity. The degree of the infirmity must be such that it requires the person to be dependent on the individual for a considerable period of time. Temporary illness or injury is not considered to be an infirmity for purposes of the personal tax credits.

¶10057 — *Limitations*

Where an individual is entitled to the spouse/common-law partner credit or the eligible dependant credit in respect of a person for a taxation year, no amount may be deducted for the year by any individual as a Canada caregiver credit in respect of that person, although the additional amount of $2,182 may be claimed for an infirm spouse/common-law partner or infirm eligible dependant (ITA 118(4)(c)). However, where an individual is entitled to both the Canada caregiver credit and the spouse/common-law partner or eligible dependant credit in respect of the same person, the amount available for purposes of the spouse/common-law partner or eligible dependant credit, as the case may be, is increased by the amount that would otherwise be determined under the Canada caregiver credit in respect of the person (ITA 118(1)(e)). Essentially, this rule is intended to ensure that the individual is not penalized by having to claim a lesser credit than would be available under the Canada caregiver credit.

As noted above, more than one person may claim a Canada caregiver credit in respect of the same infirm dependant in the same year. However, the total of all amounts deductible for the year by all individuals cannot exceed the maximum amount deductible for that person, if only one individual were entitled to the credit. If the individuals cannot agree as to what portion of the amount each can deduct, the CRA may determine the apportionment (ITA 118(4)(d), (e)).

¶10058 — *Claiming and Filing*

For 2018, the Canada caregiver credit is $6,986 less the amount, if any, by which the dependant's net income for the year exceeds $16,405. To claim the Canada caregiver credit, complete the details for Line 307 on Schedule 5, *Details of Dependant*.

ITA 118(1)(d), Schedule 5, Guide RC4064, Folio S1-F4-C1: *Basic Personal and Dependant Tax Credits*

¶10060 — CPP/QPP Contributions through Employment (T1 Schedule 1: Line 308)

Individual taxpayers (other than Quebec residents) can claim a credit for CPP contributions on Line 308, up to a maximum of $2,593.80 for 2018. Quebec residents can claim a credit for QPP contributions on Line 308, up to a maximum of $2,829.60 for 2018. For 2018, individuals must have CPP/QPP pensionable earnings of at least $55,900 to make the maximum contribution.

Taxpayers who are 60 to 70 years old, employed or self-employed, and receiving a CPP or QPP retirement pension must make contributions to the CPP or the QPP. However, taxpayers who are at least 65 years of age but under 70 years of age can elect to stop contributing to the CPP in the following circumstances:

- The taxpayer is employed — complete Form CPT30, *Election to Stop Contributing to the Canada Pension Plan or Revocation of a Prior Election*

- The taxpayer is self-employed — complete the applicable part of Schedule 8, *CPP Contributions on Self-Employment and Other Earnings*

- The taxpayer is both employed and self-employed — complete Form CPT30. However, to elect on self-employment earnings on an earlier date in the year than the effective date of the CPT30, also complete Schedule 8

¶10061 — *CPP Overcontributions*

Taxpayers who contributed more than the maximum amount can claim the excess contribution on Line 448 (CPP overpayment; see ¶11260) to obtain a refund of the excess amount. A refund for a QPP overpayment is claimed on Line 452 of the Quebec TP-1 return. In certain situations, over-contributions can also occur where the individual contributes less than the maximum amount. For example, if a taxpayer turned 18 or 70 in the year or received a CPP retirement or disability pension during the year, or the total amount of employment income shown in Box 14 of all of the individual's T4 slips is more than the total amount of CPP/QPP pensionable earnings shown in Box 26. Calculate CPP overcontributions on Schedule 8 or Form RC381, *Inter-Provincial Calculation for CPP and QPP Contributions and Overpayments for 2018*, whichever applies.

¶10062 — *Making Additional CPP Contributions*

If a taxpayer did not contribute to the CPP for certain income earned through employment (e.g., tips), or contributed less than required, the taxpayer can contribute 9.9% on any part of the income on which the taxpayer has not already made contributions. The maximum income for 2018 for which an individual can contribute to the CPP is $55,900. To make additional CPP contributions for 2018, complete Schedule 8 and Form CPT20, *Election to Pay Canada*

Pension Plan Contributions, to calculate the amount of the additional contributions and claim the appropriate amounts at Lines 222 (see ¶9230) and 310 (see ¶10070).

¶10063 — *Claiming and Filing*

Enter on Line 308 the total of Canada pension plan (CPP) or Quebec pension plan (QPP) contributions shown in Boxes 16 and 17 of your T4 slips.

ITA 118.7, *Canada Pension Plan*, Form T2204, Form CPT30, Schedule 8

¶10070 — CPP/QPP Contributions on Self-Employment and Other Earnings (T1 Schedule 1: Line 310)

Generally, self-employed individuals are required to make contributions to the Canada pension plan (CPP) or the Quebec pension plan (QPP). The amount of CPP contributions payable on self-employment and other earnings is calculated on Schedule 8, *CPP Contributions and Overpayment for 2018*. The amount of QPP contributions payable is calculated on Schedule 8, *QPP Contributions for 2018*. The maximum amount of CPP payable in 2018 is $5,187.60. The maximum amount of QPP payable in 2018 is $5,659.20.

Self-employed individuals must contribute both the employer and employee portions of CPP/QPP. Half of the total CPP/QPP contributions on self-employment are deductible on Line 222 (see ¶9230) and the other half is used to calculate the non-refundable tax credit for CPP/QPP contributions on Line 310.

¶10071 — *Claiming and Filing*

Complete Schedule 8 to calculate CPP or QPP contributions. Enter the Schedule 8 Line 11 amount on Lines 222 and 310, and enter the Schedule 8 Line 10 amount on Line 421 (residents of Quebec on December 31, 2018 should enter the Schedule 8 Line 10 amount on Lines 222 and 310. Line 421 does not apply).

ITA 118.7, 60(e), Canada Pension Plan, Part III of CPP Regulations

¶10080 — Employment Insurance Premiums through Employment (T1 Schedule 1: Line 312)

All individuals, except for those resident in Quebec on December 31, 2018, claim EI premiums paid on Line 312 as shown in T4 Box 24 (to a maximum of $858 for 2018). The maximum amount of 2018 EI premiums are reached at $51,700 of insurable earnings. Insurable earnings are the total of all earnings on which EI premiums are paid. Calculate any overpayment amount on Form T2204, *Employee Overpayment of 2018 Employment Insurance Premiums*, and claim a refund for an overpayment (or for all premiums paid if insurable earnings are $2,000 or less) on Line 450.

Residents of Quebec on December 31, 2018 claim EI premiums paid as shown in T4 Box 18 (to a maximum of $672 for 2018). A Quebec resident must have insurable earnings of at least $51,700 to pay the maximum amount of premiums in 2018. Any excess overpayment can be claimed as a refund on Line 450 (see ¶11270).

ITA 118.7

¶10090 — Adoption Expenses (T1 Schedule 1: Line 313)

This tax credit is restricted to amounts paid in respect of the completed adoption of an eligible child. Specifically, individuals can claim a tax credit for unreimbursed "eligible adoption expenses," to a maximum of $15,905 for 2018.

Eligible adoption expense is defined as amounts paid for expenses incurred during the "adoption period" in respect of an "eligible child" including:

- fees paid to an adoption agency licensed by a provincial or territorial government;

- court, legal or administrative expenses relating to an adoption order;

- reasonable and necessary travelling expenses for the child and adoptive parents;

- document translation fees;

- mandatory fees paid to a foreign institution; and

- any other reasonable expenses related to the adoption required by a provincial or territorial government or licensed adoption agency.

An "eligible child" is a child who is under 18 years-old at the time the adoption order is issued or recognized by a government of Canada. The "adoption period" begins at the earlier of: (1) the time that an adoptive parent makes an application to register with a provincial ministry responsible for adoption or with an adoption agency licensed by a provincial government; and (2) the time that an adoption-related application is made to a Canadian court.

If more than one person is entitled to claim the credit in respect of the same child, the maximum credit claimed by the individuals cannot exceed the amount that would otherwise be available if only one individual was entitled to claim the credit.

The tax credit for adoption expenses can only be claimed in respect of a completed adoption; therefore, amounts paid for expenses that were incurred at an adoption agency that did not result in a child being adopted cannot be claimed for purposes of this credit (VD 2017-0692561E5).

ITA 118.01

¶10100 — Pension Income Amount (T1 Schedule 1: Line 314)

Individuals who receive eligible pension income in 2018 can claim a pension amount equal to the lesser of $2,000 and the amount of eligible pension income reported in the year. The $2,000 amount is not indexed for inflation. The type of pension income that is eligible for this amount depends upon the age of the taxpayer.

¶10101 — *Eligible Pension Income*

For individuals aged 65 and over, the amount of eligible pension income is equal to the amount of "pension income" received in the year, as defined in ITA 118(7). For these purposes, pension income includes:

- payments in respect of a life annuity out of or under a superannuation or pension plan;

- annuity payments under a registered retirement savings plan;

- payments out of or under a registered retirement income fund;

- annuity payments under a deferred profit-sharing plan;

- certain instalment payments out of a deferred profit-sharing plan;

- the non-capital portion of certain annuity payments; and

- certain accumulating funds in respect of interest in a life insurance policy.

For individuals under age 65, the amount of eligible pension income is restricted to "qualified pension income" as defined in ITA 118(7). Qualified pension income includes:

- payments in respect of a life annuity out of or under a superannuation or pension plan; and

- if the income is received by the individual because of the death of a spouse or common-law partner, all income listed above as pension income.

Pursuant to ITA 118(8), the following types of pension income do not qualify for the pension income credit:

- Old age security pension or supplement (or similar amounts received from a provincial government);

- Benefits under the Canada pension plan or Quebec pension plan;

- A death benefit;

- Payments from a salary deferral arrangement, a retirement compensation arrangement, an employee benefit plan, or employee trust; and

- Lifetime pensions payable under an unfunded supplemental employee retirement plan (other than payments made under the *Judges Act* or *Lieutenant Governor's Superannuation Act*).

¶10102 — *Elected Split Pension Income*

An individual can allocate eligible pension income to a spouse or common-law partner within the rules provided for in ITA 60.03. To make the election, a taxpayer and his or her spouse or common-law partner must complete Form T1032, *Joint Election to Split Pension Income*. Where the taxpayer and his or her spouse or common-law partner elected to split pension income in a taxation year, the elected split-pension amount for a taxation year is deductible in computing the pensioner's income on Line 210 (see ¶9140), and included in computing the pension transferee's income on Line 116 (see ¶8140). Where a pensioner and a pension transferee have made a joint election to split pension income in a taxation year, the pensioner is deemed not to have received the portion of the pensioner's pension income or qualified pension income (as the case may be) equal to the pensioner's split-pension amount for that taxation year. Further, the pension transferee is deemed to have received the split-pension amount as pension income or qualified pension income to the extent that the split-pension amount was pension income or qualified pension income to the pensioner. As such, pension income allocated to a spouse or common-law partner is considered allocated for purposes of pension income credit where a joint election is filed, and the allocated pension income retains its character (i.e., its character in relation to the transferor) as either pension income or qualified pension income in the hands of the pension transferee.

ITA 56(1)(a.2), 60(c), 60.03

¶10103 — *Foreign Pensions*

Amounts received from foreign pension plans may qualify for the pension credit if the foreign pension is considered a superannuation or pension plan for Canadian income tax purposes. However, neither the portion that is tax exempt under a tax treaty, nor income from a U.S. individual retirement account qualifies for the pension credit.

¶10104 — *Non-Residents*

A part-year resident may claim the pension income credit for the period of residence to the extent the pension income relates to that period. The amount of the credit is not pro-rated for the number of days in the year during which the individual is resident. A non-resident is not eligible to claim the pension income credit unless all or substantially all (more than 90%) of the non-resident's net world income is reported on a T1 return. This calculation is performed on Schedule B, *Allowable Amount of Non-Refundable Tax Credits*. For a non-resident to claim the pension income credit, the related pension income must be reported on a T1 return. Pension income may not be included in income if an individual is subject to a 25% Part XIII non-resident withholding tax (which may be reduced by a tax treaty). However, an individual may elect under ITA 217 to report this income on a T1 return (see ¶15412).

¶10105 — *Claiming and Filing*

Determine eligible pension income and calculate the pension income amount on the federal worksheet for Line 314. The calculation on the worksheet begins with pension, superannuation, and annuity income reported on Line 115 (see ¶8130) and Line 129 (see ¶8250). The following amounts are then deducted to arrive at eligible pension income: any portion of foreign pension income that is exempt from Canadian tax as a result of a tax treaty, income from a U.S. individual retirement account, and excess amounts from a RRIF included on Line 115 and transferred to an RRSP or to another RRIF or annuity. Unlike other personal tax credit thresholds, the $2,000 limit is not indexed.

If the individual and his or her spouse or common-law partner elected to split pension income, the amount of eligible pension income for purposes of the pension credit is determined under Step 4 on Form T1032, *Joint Election to Split Pension Income*, and reported on Line 314 (up to a maximum of $2,000).

An individual who cannot use the pension income amount may be allowed to transfer all or part of it to a spouse or common-law partner (see Line 326 at ¶10180).

118(3), 118(7), ITR 7800, Form T1023, IT-517R: *Pension Tax Credit*

¶10110 — Caregiver Amount (T1 Schedule 1: Line 315)

> For 2017 and later taxation years, the infirm dependants credit and the caregiver credit were consolidated and replaced by the Canada caregiver credit. See ¶10055 for a discussion of the Canada caregiver credit.

¶10120 — Disability Amount (for self) (T1 Schedule 1: Line 316)

The disability tax credit provides tax relief for individuals who have a severe and prolonged impairment in physical or mental functions. The disability credit is $8,235 for the 2018 taxation year. The disability credit also includes a supplement in the amount of $4,804 for a person with severe and prolonged impairment in physical or mental functions who was under 18 years of age at the end of the tax year.

¶10121 — *Requirements for Eligibility*

An individual is eligible for the disability credit for a tax year where the following requirements are met:

1. the individual has one or more severe and prolonged impairments in physical or mental functions;

2. the effects of the impairment or impairments are such that the individual is either:

   a. markedly restricted in the ability to perform a basic activity of daily living or would be markedly restricted but for life-sustaining therapy (the "markedly restricted requirement"); or

   b. significantly restricted in the ability to perform more than one basic activity of daily living and the cumulative effect of the significant restrictions is equivalent to being markedly restricted in the ability to perform a basic activity of daily living (the "equivalent to markedly restricted requirement"); and

3. a medical practitioner certifies that the individual meets the above requirements.

¶10121.1 — *Prolonged Impairment*

An impairment is prolonged when it has lasted, or may reasonably be expected to last, for a continuous period of at least 12 months. This expectation test is applied at the time the disability begins. However, a claim will not be denied solely because the person dies within the 12-month period.

¶10121.2 — *Markedly Restricted and Equivalent to Markedly Restricted*

An individual's ability to perform a basic activity of daily living is markedly restricted only when the individual is blind or is unable (or requires an inordinate amount of time) to perform such an activity, all or substantially all of the time, even with therapy and the use of appropriate devices and medication. An individual is viewed as being markedly restricted in performing a basic activity of daily living all or substantially all of the time when the individual's ability to perform such an activity is restricted at least 90% of the time. When the individual's ability to perform such an activity is not restricted for at least 90% of the time, the individual may be viewed as not being markedly restricted.

An individual is considered to have the equivalent of a marked restriction in a basic activity of daily living only where all or substantially all of the time (that is, at least 90% of the time), even with therapy and the use of appropriate devices and medication, the individual's ability to perform more than one basic activity of daily living (including the ability to see) is significantly restricted, and the cumulative effect of those restrictions is tantamount to the individual's ability to perform a basic activity of daily living being markedly restricted. In the Supplementary Information (Annex 8) to the 2005 Federal Budget (2005-3), an individual with multiple sclerosis who continually experiences fatigue, depressed mood, and balance problems is provided as an example of an individual who may become eligible for the disability credit as a result of the cumulative effects criteria. In the example, each of the restrictions on their own do not markedly restrict the individual's ability to perform a basic activity of daily living; however, the cumulative effects of the restrictions taken together are equivalent to a marked restriction in a single activity of daily living. Form T2201 provides examples from the CRA's perspective of the cumulative effects of significant restrictions that are equivalent to a marked restriction in the ability to perform a basic activity of daily living.

¶10121.3 — *Basic Activities of Daily Living*

There are six categories of basic activities of daily living that may be markedly restricted for purposes of meeting the eligibility criteria. A basic activity of daily living means:

- The mental functions necessary for everyday life, which includes memory, problem solving, goal-setting and judgment (taken together), and adaptive functioning;

- Feeding oneself or dressing oneself, where:

  - feeding oneself does not include any of the activities of identifying, finding, shopping for or otherwise procuring food, or the activity of preparing food to the extent that the time associated with the activity would not have been necessary in the absence of a dietary restriction or regime;

  - dressing oneself does not include any of the activities of identifying, finding, shopping for, or otherwise procuring clothing;

- Speaking so as to be understood, in a quiet setting, by another person familiar with the individual;

- Hearing so as to understand, in a quiet setting, another person familiar with the individual;

- Eliminating (bowel or bladder functions); or

- Walking.

No other activity, including working, housekeeping, or a social or recreational activity is considered a basic activity of daily living. To meet the requirement that an activity take an inordinate amount of time, the activity must take significantly more time than would be taken by an average person who does not have the impairment. It is a question of fact as to whether an individual takes an inordinate amount of time to perform an activity in any particular case.

It is the effect of one or more impairments in physical or mental functions on a person's ability to perform the basic activities of daily living, which effects differ from person to person, rather than a medical condition itself (except where the person is blind), that determines whether a person is eligible for the disability tax credit.

¶10121.4 — *Life-Sustaining Therapy*

For purposes of the disability tax credit, life-sustaining therapy is therapy that is essential to sustain a vital function of the individual (e.g.; breathing, blood circulation) is required to be administered at least three times each week for a total duration averaging not less than 14 hours a week, and cannot reasonably be expected to be of significant benefit to persons who are not so impaired. For the purposes of determining whether therapy is required to be administered at least three times per week for a total duration averaging not less than an average of 14 hours a week, time spent on administering therapy:

- only includes time spent on activities that require time to be taken away from the individual's normal everyday activities to administer the therapy,

- includes time spent on activities, other than time spent on activities related to dietary or exercise restrictions or regimes, directly related to determining the dosage of medication where the therapy requires a regular dosage of medication that is required to be adjusted on a daily basis,

- includes time spent by a child's primary caregivers performing or supervising the administration of therapy where the child is unable to perform the activities as a result of the child's age, and

- does not include time spent on activities related to travel time, medical appointments, shopping for medication, recuperation after therapy, or dietary or exercise restrictions or regimes, even if the restrictions or regimes are a factor in determining the daily dosages of medication.

Time spent on therapy that requires an interruption in an individual's normal everyday activities should be included for purposes of determining the total duration of time spent receiving life-sustaining therapy. Therapy activities that do not require an interruption in an individual's normal everyday activities to receive the therapy are excluded from constituting life-sustaining therapy.

Children with very severe cases of Type 1 diabetes may qualify for the disability credit by virtue of the life-sustaining therapy rules. For example, children who require many insulin injections (that require knowledge of current blood sugar levels at the time of each injection) and who also require several additional blood sugar tests to monitor their condition. Examples of life-sustaining therapy from the CRA's perspective include chest physiotherapy to facilitate breathing and kidney dialysis to filter blood. The CRA's view is that life-sustaining therapy does not include implanted devices, such as a pacemaker (see Form T2201 and CRA Fact Sheet 2003-07B)

¶10121.5 — *Definition of Disability for other Purposes*

An individual entitled to a disability pension under the Canada or Quebec pension plan, under workers' compensation legislation, or under a private insurance arrangement is not automatically eligible for the disability tax credit. There is no universal definition of disability. Each government department or agency has its own definition, based on applicable legislation and the purpose of a given program. For example, CPP disability benefits are paid through Service Canada, under an income replacement program, based on CPP contributions made during employment and are dependent upon the effect of a person's disability on their ability to pursue any substantially gainful occupation. By contrast, for purposes of the disability tax credit, whether an individual is eligible depends on a severe and prolonged impairment in a physical or mental function, and the impact it has on their ability to perform one or more basic activities of daily living. Therefore, qualifying for a CPP disability benefit does not guarantee that an individual will also be eligible for the disability tax credit. Under private insurance arrangements, the plan documents will set out the necessary conditions for an individual to be considered disabled for purposes of the arrangement. Those conditions may or may not be the same as the eligibility requirements for the disability tax credit for income tax purposes.

¶10122 — *Certification Requirements*

A medical practitioner must certify on Form T2201, *Disability Tax Credit Certificate*, that the individual has a severe and prolonged impairment in physical or mental functions and that the individual meets either the markedly restricted requirement or the equivalent to markedly restricted requirement. Generally, the medical practitioner certifying that an individual meets the markedly restricted requirement must be a medical doctor. As an exception to this general rule, the certification of specific impairments may also be provided by certain other medical practitioners. Specifically:

- a sight impairment may be certified by either a medical doctor or an optometrist;

- a speech impairment may be certified by either a medical doctor or a speech-language pathologist;

- a hearing impairment may be certified by either a medical doctor or an audiologist;

- an impairment with respect to an individual's ability in feeding or dressing themselves may be certified by either a medical doctor or an occupational therapist;

- an impairment with respect to an individual's ability in walking may be certified by either a medical doctor, an occupational therapist, or a physiotherapist; and

- an impairment with respect to an individual's ability in mental functions necessary for everyday life may be certified by either a medical doctor or a psychologist.

The medical doctor, optometrist, speech-language pathologist, audiologist, occupational therapist, physiotherapist, or psychologist, as the case may be, must be authorized to practice as such under the laws of the jurisdiction in which the individual being certified resides, or under the laws of a province.

When a certification is being completed after the death of the eligible person with a disability, the disability tax credit will be available provided the certification is based on a prognosis, made by an appropriate medical practitioner before the person died, which concluded that the person's severe and prolonged impairment was reasonably expected to last for a continuous period of at least 12 months.

> In respect of certifications made after March 21, 2017, nurse practitioners were added to the list of medical practitioners that can certify eligibility for the disability tax credit.

Following are the CRA's comments at the January/February 2013 ICABC/CRA Liaison Meetings in response to questions regarding proper certification for the disability tax credit:

Question 19: Disability Tax Credit Certification

In situations of permanent disability why does CRA require further periodic certification?

To be eligible for the Disability Tax Credit (DTC) the following criteria are required:

1. an individual's ability to perform a basic activity of daily living must be markedly restricted,

2. all or substantially all of the time (90% of the time),

3. even with therapy and the use of appropriate devices and medication,

4. for a continuous period of at least 12 months.

Even though an individual can be "permanently disabled", their ability to perform a basic activity of daily living may not remain markedly restricted all or substantially all of the time on a permanent basis. For some individuals who are "permanently disabled" the severity of their impairments in performing a basic activity of daily living can improve (due to new therapies, devices, medications, etc.) such that they no longer meet the specific eligibility criteria for the DTC. In other words, "permanently disabled" does not always equate to "permanently markedly restricted all or substantially all of the time (90% of the time) even with therapy and the use of appropriate devices and medication". For this reason, on a case-by-case basis, it may be indicated for CRA to periodically review individuals with a "permanent disability" designation, to determine whether or not the individual continues to meet the specific DTC criteria for eligibility.

The *Income Tax Act* provides the CRA the authority to request re-certification for the DTC.

Question 20: T2201s

Is there any way to fast track approval of T2201s to reduce the number of T1 Adjustments required to be filed?

There are a number of ways:

1) Ensure that the Form T2201 submitted is original — not photocopied — and signed in the appropriate areas.

2) Ensure that both part A and B of the T2201 are fully completed, and that Part B is only completed by a qualified practitioner as outlined in the T2201 as per Section 118.3(1)(a.2) and (a.3) of the *Income Tax Act*. Since eligibility for the DTC is based on the level of restriction of an individual's ability to perform a basic activity of daily living, the qualified practitioner must fully complete the Effects of Impairment section with enough detail to clearly describe the extent of the individual's specific functional limitations. CRA will delay the determination of eligibility for the DTC until enough information regarding the effects of impairment is received to make a determination.

3) Form T2201 can be submitted on its own at any time during the year The T2201 does not have to be submitted with a T1 return or a Request for T1 Adjustment. Since every T2201 is individually reviewed, a timeline of eight weeks should be expected before a client receives a notice of determination. This eight week timeline will vary, especially during peak tax season, so taxpayers should be aware and plan ahead.

4) Individuals can complete a self-assessment questionnaire to determine if they may be eligible for the DTC before starting the application process.

¶10123 — *Related Credits and Deductions*

In many cases, an individual will be in a position to choose between the medical expense credit and the disability credit. However, with one exception, the disability credit is not available if the eligible person with a disability or any other person includes the cost of an attendant or care in a nursing home in respect of the eligible person in calculating a medical expense credit. An exception is provided for medical expenses claimed in respect of attendant care, to the extent that the expenses do not exceed $10,000 ($20,000 where the individual died in the year), and are not otherwise deducted in computing a taxpayer's income or otherwise included in computing a medical expense credit. The attendant must not be the spouse or common-law partner of the individual eligible for the disability credit or under 18 years of age at the time the remuneration is paid. The CRA's view is that a medical expense credit claimed for attendant care expenses of less than $10,000 does not prevent a disability credit claim because attendant care is not nursing home care, regardless of whether the institution is a nursing home (similar views also apply to nursing home care provided in a hospital; see VDs 2008-0293121I7, 2005-0155731E5, 2001-0116207, and 9708237). Individuals will need to determine, based on their specific circumstances, whether it is more beneficial to claim the limited amount of attendant care expenses plus the disability tax credit in respect of an eligible person with a disability, or to claim the full amount of the cost of attendant care with no claim for the disability tax credit. See under ¶10195.2 for a full discussion of claiming costs paid for attendant care, or care in certain types of facilities, for purposes of the medical expense tax credit.

The deduction of certain disability support costs incurred to earn certain types of income or attend a designated educational institution or secondary school should also be considered. To claim attendant care expenses for purposes of the disability supports deduction, the individual must either be entitled to the disability credit, or a medical practitioner must certify in writing that the individual is likely to be indefinitely dependent on others for personal needs and care, and therefore requires a full-time attendant. As such, to claim amounts paid for part-time attendant care as a disability supports deduction, an individual must qualify for the disability credit. However, to claim a disability supports deduction for amounts paid for full-time attendant care, an individual does not have to qualify for the disability credit. The disability credit can be claimed in addition to a disability supports deduction; however, expenses claimed for the disability supports deduction must not be included in computing the medical expenses credit for the year in question or any subsequent taxation year. See ¶9180 for a full discussion of the disability supports deduction that can be claimed on Line 215.

A disability credit may not be claimed for a child for whom the taxpayer is required to pay support (see ITA 118(5) and *Scott v. R.*, [2009] 3 C.T.C. 2258 (TCC).

¶10124 — *Calculating the Disability Tax Credit*

The disability tax credit is equal to 15% multiplied by the sum of two amounts: the base amount and, where applicable, the supplemental amount. The base amount is available to an eligible person with a disability. For 2018, the base amount is $8,235, which means that the basic disability tax credit for 2018 is $1,235 (15% × $8,235).

The supplemental amount is available to an eligible person with a disability who is under 18 years of age at the end of the tax year. The maximum supplemental amount for 2018 is $4,804. Assuming there is no reduction to the supplemental amount for the tax year, the maximum tax credit available in respect of the supplemental amount for 2018 is $720 (15% × $4,804). The supplemental amount may be reduced where an amount paid in the year for the care or supervision of the eligible person with a disability is claimed by any person as a child care expense deduction under ITA 63 (see ¶9170), a disability supports deduction under ITA 64 (see ¶9180), or a medical expense tax credit under ITA 118.2 (see ¶10190) for the tax year.

¶10125 — *Transferring the Disability Tax Credit*

¶10125.1 — *Transfer to a Supporting Individual*

In certain circumstances, a supporting individual, or the spouse or common-law partner of the eligible person with a disability may be able to claim all or part of the eligible person's disability tax credit for the year.

A supporting individual is an individual, other than the spouse or common-law partner of the eligible person with a disability, who supports the eligible person with a disability. A person is generally considered to be dependent on someone if the individual has actually supplied necessary maintenance, or the basic necessities of life (food, shelter and clothing) on a regular and consistent basis. Where the eligible person with a disability was in receipt of social assistance or any other type of financial or non-financial support, the supporting individual must be able to show that the other assistance was insufficient to fully meet the basic needs of the eligible person with a disability and that the person had to rely on the additional support provided by the supporting individual.

A transfer of the unused disability tax credit to a supporting individual in a tax year may generally only be made where the supporting individual claimed (or could have claimed if the eligible person with a disability had no income and was at least 18 years of age, and in the case of the eligible dependent credit, the supporting individual was not married or in a common-law partnership) one of the following credits in respect of the eligible person with a disability for the tax year: the eligible dependent credit on Line 305 (see ¶10040), or the Canada caregiver credit on Line 304 or 307 (see ¶10035 and ¶10055) where the eligible person is the parent, grandparent, child, grandchild, brother, sister, aunt, uncle, nephew or niece of the supporting individual or the supporting individual's spouse or common-law partner.

When more than one individual is entitled to deduct a tax credit transferred from the same eligible person with a disability, the total deductions for the tax year are limited to the maximum amount that could be claimed by one individual for that year if that individual were the only one entitled to use the amount transferred. If the individuals fail to agree on the portions to be claimed, the Minister may fix the portions.

A supporting individual will not be able to claim a transfer of the disability tax credit where the eligible person with a disability has a spouse or common-law partner who claims any personal tax credit for the eligible person, or any tax credit transferred from the eligible person.

See ¶10140 for more information on when a supporting individual is eligible to claim a dependant's disability credit.

¶10125.2 — *Transfer to a Spouse or Common-Law Partner*

The disability credit is one of a number of credits that are subject to a special transfer rule which, in effect, enables the unused portion of certain credits of an individual to be transferred to the individual's spouse or common-law partner. See ¶10180 for a full discussion of these rules.

¶10126 — *Claiming and Filing*

Form T2201, *Disability Tax Credit Certificate*, must be completed and filed by the person claiming the disability credit on their tax return. The original certified copy of Form T2201 must be submitted in its entirety. The eligible person with a disability or their legal representative must complete Part A of Form T2201, and Part B must be completed by the appropriate medical practitioner. Generally, for the first tax year in which an individual is claiming the disability credit, Form T2201 must either be filed before the filing of the individual's T1 return for the year, or with the individual's T1 return for the year.

Form T2201 will be reviewed to determine if the person with a disability is an eligible person with a disability before the income tax return is assessed. Filing Form T2201 with the CRA prior to the filing of the T1 return for the year of the person claiming the credit will prevent a delay in assessing the return while a determination is made whether the person is an eligible person with a disability. If the impairment is permanent, it is not necessary to file another Form T2201 in later years unless the circumstances change or a new form is requested. If the impairment is temporary, a new Form T2201 must be submitted if the period of eligibility has ended.

As discussed, any unused portion of the disability credit can be transferred to a spouse or common-law partner (who claims it on Line 326) or to another supporting person (who claims it on Line 318). See Line 318 at ¶10140 and Line 326 at ¶10180. Where a spouse or other supporting person claims a disability credit in respect of a person with a disability, it is not required that the person with a disability file a T1 return for the year if they have no taxes payable for that year.

An individual may request that a prior year T1 return be reassessed for the disability tax credit where the Form T2201 was signed in one year certifying that the impairment started in an earlier year. Where an individual wishes to claim a tax credit for a previous year already assessed by the CRA, the individual should send a request for a T1 return adjustment to his or her Tax Centre using Form T1-ADJ, *T1 Adjustment Request*, or by providing a signed letter containing the details of the request, social insurance number, address, and a daytime telephone number. In addition, the request must include all relevant documents, including the Form T2201, to support the claim for the disability tax credit. Where the adjustment is being requested in respect of a prior year tax return of a supporting individual, documents such as receipts, copies of cashed cheques and bank statements should be provided as evidence that the individual supported the eligible person with a disability in the particular tax year.

ITA 118.3, 118.4, *Scott*, 2009 CarswellNat 120, *Biron*, 2004 CarswellNat 3297, 2004 TCC 154, *Girard*, 2006 CarswellNat 3124, 2006 D.T.C. 6129, *Beauchamp*, 2008 CarswellNat 1755, 2008 TCC 189, *Boisvert*, 2005 CarswellNat 6386, 2005 CCI 249, *Lawlor*, 1996 CarswellNat 2938, [1996] 2 C.T.C. 2005, *Radage*, 1996 CarswellNat 1628, 96 D.T.C. 1615, *Johnston*, 1998 CarswellNat 169, *Tanguay*, 1997 CarswellNat 2559, [1998] 2 C.T.C. 2963, Form T2201, Guide RC4064, Folio S1-F1-C1: *Medical Expense Tax Credit*, Folio S1-F1-C2: *Disability Tax Credit*, Folio S1-F1-C3: *Disability Supports Deduction*, VDs 2001-0116207, 2006-0198641I7, 2010-0363321E5, 2011-0418081E5, 2011-0415541M4, 2011-0395031E5

¶10130 — Employment Insurance Premiums on Self-Employment (T1 Schedule 1: Line 317)

Self-employed individuals can opt in to the employment insurance (EI) program for access to EI special benefits by entering into an agreement with the Canada Employment Insurance Commission through Service Canada. Individuals who choose to participate in the program will receive the same EI special benefits as those available to employees, including maternity, parental, sickness, and compassionate care benefits. Individuals who opt into the EI program must wait 12 months from the date of confirmed registration before applying for special benefits. The amount of EI premiums payable is entered on Line 430. The individual may also claim a non-refundable tax credit for this amount on Line 317.

EI premiums payable on self-employment income are calculated on Schedule 13, *Employment Insurance Premiums on Self-Employment and Other Eligible Earnings*. To calculate the EI premiums payable, an individual must determine his or her total EI insurable earnings for the year. Total EI insurable earnings for the year are the lesser of:

- The total of the individual's self-employment income, which includes the following amounts: total net partnership income on Line 122 and business and professional income on Lines 135 to 143; for individuals who are employed by a corporation but are ineligible for the EI program as an employee because they control over 40% of the voting shares of the corporation, the amount in Box 14 from all T4 slips received from that corporation (excluding amounts that are not insurable earnings); and for individuals who are registered under the *Indian Act*, the total tax-exempt self-employed income earned on a reserve in Canada; and

- The maximum insurable earnings for the year ($51,700 for 2018) less the individual's total EI insurable earnings reported in Box 24 from all T4 slips (if Box 24 is blank, Box 14 amounts from all T4 slips unless Box 28 states that the T4 earnings are EI exempt), as well as any employment income for which no T4 slips were received.

For Canadian residents who are not residents of Quebec on December 31, 2018, the maximum amount of EI premiums a self-employed individual is required to enter on Line 430 is $858. This amount is also entered on Line 317 and claimed as a non-refundable tax credit. Individuals whose total amount of EI premiums from Box 18 and Box 55 of all T4 slips is $858 or more are not required to pay any premiums on self-employment and other eligible earnings.

For Canadian residents who are residents of Quebec on December 31, 2018, the maximum amount of EI premiums a self-employed individual is required to enter on Line 430 is $672. This amount is also entered on Line 317 and claimed as a non-refundable tax credit. Individuals whose total amount of EI premiums from Box 18 and Box 55 of all T4 slips is $672 or more are not required to pay any premiums on self-employment and other eligible earnings.

¶10131 — *Claiming and Filing*

Complete Schedule 13 to calculate EI premiums. Enter the amount from Line 10 of Schedule 13 on Line 317 of Schedule 1 and on Line 430 of the T1 return (see ¶11230).

Schedule 13, canada.ca/en/services/benefits/ei/ei-self-employed-workers.html

¶10140 — Disability Amount Transferred from a Dependant (T1 Schedule 1: Line 318)

An individual may be able to claim all or part of a dependant's disability credit (see Line 316 at ¶10120) if the dependant was resident in Canada at any time in the year, and was dependent on the individual for all or some of the basic necessities of life. A person is generally considered to be dependent on someone if the individual has actually supplied necessary maintenance, or the basic necessities of life (food, shelter and clothing) on a regular and consistent basis. Where the dependent person was in receipt of social assistance or any other type of financial or non-financial support, the supporting individual must be able to show that the other assistance was insufficient to fully meet the basic needs of the dependant and that the person had to rely on the additional support provided by the supporting individual.

A transfer of the unused disability tax credit to a supporting individual in a tax year may generally only be made where the supporting individual claimed (or could have claimed if the eligible person with a disability had no income and was at least 18 years of age, and in the case of the eligible dependent credit, the supporting individual was not married or in a common-law partnership) one of the following credits in respect of the eligible person with a disability for the tax year: the eligible dependent credit on Line 305 (see ¶10040), or the Canada caregiver credit on Line 307 (see ¶10055) where the eligible person is the parent, grandparent, child, grandchild, brother, sister, aunt, uncle, nephew or niece of the supporting individual or the supporting individual's spouse or common-law partner.

When more than one individual is entitled to deduct a tax credit transferred from the same eligible person with a disability, the total deductions for the tax year are limited to the maximum amount that could be claimed by one individual for that year if that individual were the only one entitled to use the amount transferred. If the individuals fail to agree on the portions to be claimed, the Minister may fix the portions.

A supporting individual will not be able to claim a transfer of the disability tax credit where the eligible person with a disability has a spouse or common-law partner who claims any personal tax credit for the eligible person or any tax credit transferred from the eligible person.

¶10141 — *Claiming and Filing*

Form T2201, *Disability Tax Credit Certificate*, must be completed and filed by the person claiming the disability credit on their tax return. The original certified copy of Form T2201 must be submitted in its entirety. The eligible person with a disability or their legal representative must complete Part A of Form T2201, and Part B must be completed by the appropriate medical practitioner. Generally, for the first tax year in which an individual is claiming the disability credit, Form T2201 must either be filed before the filing of the individual's T1 return for the year, or with the individual's T1 return for the year.

Form T2201 will be reviewed to determine if the person with a disability is an eligible person with a disability before the income tax return is assessed. Filing Form T2201 with the CRA prior to the filing of the T1 return for the year of the person claiming the credit will prevent a delay in assessing the return while a determination is made whether the person is an eligible person with a disability. If Form T2201 is being filed with the T1 return, the return should be filed in paper format with the original certified copy of Form T2201 attached. If the impairment is permanent, it is not necessary to file another Form T2201 in later years unless the circumstances change or a new form is requested. If the impairment is temporary, a new Form T2201 must be submitted if the period of eligibility has ended.

ITA 118.3, 118.4, *Scott*, 2009 CarswellNat 120, *Biron*, 2004 CarswellNat 3297, 2004 TCC 154, *Girard*, 2006 CarswellNat 3124, 2006 D.T.C. 6129, *Beauchamp*, 2008 CarswellNat 1755, 2008 TCC 189, *Boisvert*, 2005 CarswellNat 6386, 2005 CCI 249, *Lawlor*, 1996 CarswellNat 2938, [1996] 2 C.T.C. 2005, *Radage*, 1996 CarswellNat 1628, 96 D.T.C. 1615, *Johnston*, 1998 CarswellNat 169, *Tanguay*, 1997 CarswellNat 2559, [1998] 2 C.T.C. 2963, Form T2201, Guide RC4064, Folio S1-F1-C1: *Medical Expense Tax Credit*, Folio S1-F1-C2: *Disability Tax Credit*, Folio S1-F1-C3: *Disability Supports Deduction*, VDs 2001-0116207, 2006-0198641I7, 2010-0363321E5, 2011-0418081E5, 2011-0415541M4, 2011-0395031E5

¶10150 — Interest Paid on Your Student Loans (T1 Schedule 1: Line 319)

Individuals can claim amounts paid in the year in respect of interest on their loans (whether new or outstanding) under the under the former *Canada Student Loans Act*, the *Canada Student Financial Assistance Act*, the *Apprentice Loans Act*, or similar provincial or territorial statute governing the granting of financial assistance to students at the post-secondary school level. The credit applies only to interest paid, and does not apply to interest accrued or interest forgiven. Any unused credit may be carried forward for up to five years, but the credit may not be transferred. If the individual has no tax payable for the year the interest is paid, the individual should not claim the interest in that year, but instead carry the interest forward and apply it in any of the next five years.

> Interest paid on any other kind of loan, or on a student loan that has been combined with another kind of loan, cannot be claimed as a tax credit. If an individual renegotiated their student loan or included it in an arrangement to consolidate their loans, the interest on the new loan will not qualify for this tax credit. In addition, interest paid in respect of a judgment obtained after an individual failed to pay back a student loan cannot be claimed.

In *Vilenski v. R.*, 2003 CarswellNat 1945 (TCC), the taxpayer had used the proceeds of a line of credit (at a better interest rate) to pay off the balance of a loan under the *Canada Student Loans Act*. The Tax Court of Canada upheld the Minister's disallowance of the taxpayer's claim for a credit for interest paid on the new loan on the basis that, although the new loan was in essence the "same money" as the original loan, the new loan was not a loan under the *Canada Student Loans Act* or any other statute providing financial assistance to students. In *Lazarescu-King v. R.*, [2004] 1 C.T.C. 3063 (TCC), the taxpayer attempted to claim a credit for interest she paid in respect of a student loan in her spouse's name. The Court held that only the student to whom the student loan was made could claim the tax credit, and that the words "a person related to the individual" did not allow the related person to claim the credit on their own tax return.

ITA 118.62, Pamphlet P105, 2010-0376461I7, 2008-0285311C6

¶10160 — Tuition, Education and Textbook Amounts (T1 Schedule 1: Line 323)

A student may be able to claim a non-refundable tuition tax credit for the amount of eligible tuition fees paid in respect of the year. The unused amount of a student's tuition tax credit may be carried forward to future years, or may be transferred to a spouse or common-law partner, or to a parent or grandparent of either the student or the student's spouse or common-law partner, subject to certain requirements and limitations. Specifically, a tuition tax credit can be claimed for eligible fees paid to certain educational institutions in Canada, universities outside of Canada, and certain educational institutions in the United States to which a student commutes when the student resides in Canada near the Canada-United States border. In addition, a tuition tax credit can be claimed for fees paid by an individual to certain bodies, in respect of an occupational, trade, or professional examination.

¶10161 — *Educational Institutions*

¶10161.1 — *Educational Institutions in Canada*

A student who is enrolled at an educational institution in Canada may be eligible to claim a tuition tax credit for eligible tuition fees paid in respect of the year to that educational institution, as long as the total of such fees exceeds $100. In order for tuition fees to be eligible for the tuition tax credit, the educational institution in Canada must be either: (1) a university, college, or other educational institution providing courses at a post secondary school level; or (2) certified by the Minister of Human Resources and Skills Development Canada (HRSDC) to be an educational institution providing courses (other than courses designed for university credit) that furnish a person with skills for, or improve a person's skills in, an occupation. There is no requirement regarding the length of a course taken by a student at an educational institution in Canada. Thus, fees paid for relatively short courses, such as those taken during the summer, may be eligible for the tuition tax credit. However, no tuition credit may be claimed where the total fees are less than $100.

There is no list of universities, colleges, or other educational institutions in Canada providing courses at a post secondary school level. Some assumptions and interpretations that are normally applied in determining eligibility of an institution are provided in Folio S1-F2-C2:

Determining eligibility of an institution

2.5 For purposes of subparagraph 118.5(1)(a)(i), there is no all inclusive list of universities, colleges or other educational institutions in Canada providing courses at a post secondary school level. Some assumptions and interpretations that are normally applied in determining eligibility of an institution for purposes of subparagraph 118.5(1)(a)(i) are as follows:

a) Unless there is specific information to the contrary, an educational institution is generally accepted to be a university or college if the applicable province or territory in which the institution is located considers it to be a university or college, as long as courses are given at a post secondary school level. This means that the institution should be recognized and authorized by the province or territory to grant academic credentials and should be complying with provincial legislation with respect to the courses it offers;

b) Another educational institution may include a professional organization that provides educational courses at a post-secondary school level to members, as long as one minimum qualification for membership is secondary school graduation. Generally, a professional organization is one that is empowered, under federal or provincial legislation, to make regulations governing certification and licences to practice the profession, examination of candidates for membership and the right to practice, and the institution of a professional code of conduct for its members. An organization, professional or otherwise, that provides evaluation, examination, or other such services, but does not provide educational courses, is not considered to be an educational institution for purposes of paragraph 118.5(1)(a);

c) An educational institution is not ineligible under subparagraph 118.5(1)(a)(i) solely by reason of the fact that it provides other courses in addition to post secondary school level courses; or

d) An institution in Canada that has been designated as a specified educational institution under the *Canada Student Loans Act* or that has been recognized for the purposes of the *Canada Student Financial Assistance Act* or *An Act respecting financial assistance for education expenses* of the Province of Quebec is presumed to satisfy the eligibility requirements.

It is the CRA's view that tuition fees paid to an entity registered as a private career college under the *Ontario Private Career Colleges Act, 2005* in respect of a vocational program qualify for the tuition tax credit (see VD 2012-0445391I7).

¶10161.2 — *Educational Institutions Outside Canada*

Students at educational institutions outside Canada may claim a tuition tax credit for the tuition fees paid to that institution, where the individual is in full-time attendance at a university outside Canada in a course leading to a degree at not lower than the bachelor or equivalent level, and the course is not less than three consecutive weeks (13 consecutive weeks for 2010 and earlier tax years).

An educational institution outside Canada is presumed to offer courses leading to a degree if it is recognized by an accrediting body that is nationally accepted in that country as being an educational institution which confers degrees at least at the bachelor or equivalent level. For example, an institution listed in the current edition of *Accredited Institutions of Postsecondary Education* published by the American Council on Education and indicated in that publication as being an institution granting degrees at the "B" level (bachelor's degree or equivalent), "M" level (master's degree or equivalent), "D" level (doctoral degree), or "P" level (first professional degree such as J.D., M.D. or M.Div.) will be regarded as a university that qualifies for these purposes.

Also, institutions listed in Schedule VIII of the ITR are recognized as satisfying the requirements, as are universities that are members of the Association of Commonwealth Universities, if they can grant degrees at the bachelor or higher level. It should be noted, however, that the list of institutions provided in Schedule VIII of the ITR is not exhaustive. For example, in *Shea v. R.*, 2008 CarswellNat 833 (TCC), the CRA attempted to deny a tuition tax credit in respect of tuition fees paid to the London School of Economics since the institution was not listed in Schedule VIII. The court allowed the taxpayer's appeal, stating as follows: "I must say again that these provisions do not require universities to be prescribed. Therefore, Schedule VIII of the *Income Tax Regulations* has no application in this matter." The Court further cited *Klassen v. R.*, 2007 CarswellNat 3594, in which the Federal Court of Appeal stated: "a university is an institution of higher learning which confers degrees attesting to some definite proficiency."

With respect to satisfying the three consecutive week requirement, the tuition tax credit would not be denied for the following reasons: (1) if the student dropped out of the course before completing three weeks of study under the course, provided they were in full-time attendance before leaving the course; (2) the course usually satisfies the necessary consecutive weeks requirement, but does not do so in a particular academic term because the term falls a little short of being a full three weeks (for example, because of a holiday); or (3) the academic term in which the course falls is interrupted, for example, by a holiday. The CRA provides the following information in Folio S1-F2-C2 with respect to the requirements for full-time attendance and enrolment at an educational institution outside Canada:

2.17 Paragraph 118.5(1)(b) specifies that a student must be in full-time attendance at a university outside Canada. Students are ordinarily accepted as being in full-time attendance if the university regards them as such. Accordingly, a certificate from a university stating that a student was in full-time attendance in a particular academic year or semester will normally be accepted.

2.18 A student is not considered to be in full-time attendance at a university outside Canada if: only a few subjects at evening classes are being taken; courses are taken only by correspondence (see ¶2.20); or although a day student, the student is carrying only a minor course load and at the same time is devoting so much time and energy to other activities (such as money-earning activities) that they are clearly the student's primary occupation. However, a student holding a full-time job while taking a major course load is considered to be in full-time attendance, provided that the educational institution being attended regards the student as a full-time student.

Online attendance and correspondence courses

2.19 For 2007 and subsequent years, the requirement in paragraph 118.5(1)(b) for full-time attendance at a university outside Canada in a course leading to a degree can be met through online attendance. However, the university must be able to establish that the enrolment of a student at the university constituted full-time attendance, such as through scheduled, interactive, course-related activities conducted over the internet (for example, the use of on-Line course rooms, live on-Line conferences, chat-lines and/or virtual libraries).

2.20 On the other hand, correspondence courses, either by mail or over the Internet, are generally courses that require little or no significant interactive, scheduled sessions with either the instructor or other students. Email is typically used to correspond with an instructor, to submit assignments, or to access an online database or class Web site. As such, the requirement for full-time attendance at a university outside Canada for a correspondence course will not generally be satisfied. Prior to 2007, the requirement for full-time attendance could only be met through physical attendance at the university. Tuition fees paid for correspondence courses may be eligible for the tuition tax credit if taken with an educational institution in Canada, but not if taken with a foreign educational institution, since paragraph 118.5(1)(b) requires full-time attendance (see ¶2.20) and paragraph 118.5(1)(c) requires physical commuting to the institution.

Researching, writing and laboratory time

2.21 A student who is participating in graduate studies (for example, to obtain a master's degree or doctoral degree) on a regular basis is ordinarily considered to be in full-time attendance if registered for the regular academic year, even though the requirements for attendance in class are minimal. Therefore, such a registered student who spends much of the time in a laboratory or a library engaged in research or writing a thesis or who spends part of the academic year engaged in research elsewhere than at the university would normally be regarded as being in full-time attendance. As in ¶2.18, a graduate student holding a full-time job is not necessarily precluded from being considered in full-time attendance at a university.

Meaning of enrolled

2.22 Paragraphs 118.5(1)(a) and (c) require a student to be enrolled at an educational institution described in these paragraphs. There is no requirement that the student be in full-time attendance, although paragraph 118.5(1)(c) does require that the student commute to the institution in the United States. The term enrolled is not defined in the Act, but it is to be given its ordinary meaning. In the context of enrolment of a student at an educational institution, a student must be registered with the registrar of the institution such that the student would be liable for any tuition fees required to be paid to the institution with respect to the courses within a program of study. Consequently, tuition fees paid for courses by a part-time student, such as night school courses, can qualify for the tuition tax credit under these provisions.

¶10161.3 — Canadian Students Commuting to the United States

Canadian students who commute to a university, college, or other educational institution in the United States which provides courses at a post-secondary school level may claim a tuition tax credit for tuition fees paid for the year to the U.S. educational institution if the student resided throughout the year in Canada "near" the boundary between Canada and the U.S., and the student commuted to the U.S. educational institution. The term "commute" is not defined in the ITA. In paragraph 2.15 of Folio S1-F2-C2, the CRA states its position that commute means regular, physical travel to and from the educational institution. Students who take courses only over the internet and do not physically travel to the institution in the United States are generally not considered to be commuting to the educational institution. Consistent with the CRA's interpretation, in *Wellington v. R.*, [2004] 3 C.T.C. 2402 (TCC), the Court held that the term "commute" requires the physical movement of the Canadian taxpayer to and from the educational institution in the United States on a regular basis, such that telecommuting by way of an internet course does not qualify.

The term "near" is also not defined in the ITA. In VD 9919315, the CRA states: In our view, "commute", for the purpose of subparagraph 118.5(1)(c)(ii), generally means that the distance between two locations should not be so great that a daily or regular return trip between the two locations would be considered unreasonable. In other words, generally, an individual would be considered to commute if he or she travels back and forth from his or her place of residence to an educational institution in the United States daily or on a regular basis. In *Van De Water v. MNR*, [1991] 1 C.T.C. 2200 (TCC), the Court found that a residence that was 80 kilometres away from a postsecondary institution was not "near" the institution. Similarly, in *Yankson v. R.*, [2005] 4 C.T.C. 2511 (TCC), the Court denied a credit claim under ITA 118.1(5)(c) where the student lived in Calgary and commuted to an institution in Seattle. However, in *Humphreys v. R.*, [2010] 3 C.T.C. 2286 (TCC), the Court held that the taxpayer resided "near" the border even when the student had to commute over four hours, partly by ferry, from B.C. to an institution in Seattle. In the latter case, the Court stated that by choosing to use the word "near" rather than specifying a particular distance, "Parliament intended to recognize the great diversity of Canada's geography and demographics". Consistent with the decision in *Humphreys*, it may be reasonable to consider other students that commute further than 80 kilometres to attend a university in the United States to be residing "near" the border.

There is no requirement regarding the length of a course taken by a student who commutes from Canada to an educational institution in the United States. Thus, fees paid for relatively short courses, such as those taken during the summer, may be eligible for the tuition tax credit.

The eligibility of a U.S. educational institution to which a student commutes from Canada is determined by the CRA on an individual basis by applying considerations similar to those used in determining the eligibility of Canadian educational institutions. Any educational institution in the United States which is within commuting distance of Canada, and which is listed in the current edition of *Accredited Institutions of Postsecondary Education* (published by the American Council on Education) is presumed to be an institution that qualifies for these purposes. Also, any institution in the United States within commuting distance of Canada that is designated as a specified educational institution under the *Canada Student Loans Act*, or recognized for the purposes of the *Canada Student Financial Assistance Act* or Quebec's *Act Respecting Financial Assistance for Education Expenses* is presumed to be an eligible institution for these purposes. Information regarding educational institutions outside Canada can be found in Information Sheet RC190, *Information for Educational Institutions Outside Canada*, and Information Sheet RC192, *Information for Students — Educational Institutions Outside Canada*.

¶10162 — *Tuition Fees*

The tuition tax credit for a particular tax year can be based only on tuition fees and occupational, trade, or professional examination fees paid in respect of that year. This means that the credit is based only on fees paid for courses and exams taken in that calendar year. For example, when the academic session covered by eligible tuition fees paid in a particular year extends from September of that year to April of the next year, the tuition tax credit for the fees is computed for each of those years as one-half of the fees multiplied by 15 percent.

¶10162.1 — *Eligible Tuition Fees*

The following fees are considered eligible tuition fees for purposes of the tuition tax credit: admission fees; charges for use of library or laboratory facilities; exemption fees; examination fees (including re-reading charges) that are integral to a program of study; application fees (only if the student subsequently enrolls in the institution); confirmation fees; charges for a certificate, diploma or degree; membership or seminar fees that are specifically related to an academic program and its administration; mandatory computer service fees; academic fees; and GST or HST on eligible fees. Certain ancillary fees and charges, including health services fees and athletic fees, are also eligible for the tuition tax credit; however, such ancillary fees and charges are limited to $250 unless the fees are required to be paid by all students.

¶10162.2 — *Non-Eligible Tuition Fees*

The following tuition fees are not considered eligible tuition fees for the tuition tax credit:

1. Fees paid on behalf of, or reimbursed to, the student by his or her employer, where the amount paid or reimbursed is not included in the student's income.

2. Fees that are part of an allowance received by the student's parent on the student's behalf from an employer and are excluded from the parent's income.

3. Fees for which the student is, or was, entitled to receive a reimbursement or any form of assistance under a program of the federal or a provincial government designed to facilitate the entry or re-entry of workers into the labour force, if the amount of the reimbursement or assistance is not included in the student's income.

4. Fees paid on the student's behalf, or fees for which the student is, or was, entitled to receive a reimbursement, under a federal government program designed to assist athletes, where the fees so paid or reimbursed are not included in the student's income.

5. For 2017 and later taxation years, fees paid to a university or college in respect of courses not at the post-secondary level, unless the student is 16 years of age or older before the end of the year, and the purpose of his

or her enrolment is to provide the student with skills, or to improve his or her skills, in an occupation (for taxation years before 2017, fees paid to a university or college in respect of courses not at the post-secondary school level were excluded altogether).

6. Fees paid to an educational institution certified by the Minister of HRSDC where the student is not at least 16 years of age at the end of the year, and enrolled in the educational institution to obtain skills for, or to improve the student's skills in, an occupation.

The phrase "to obtain skills for an occupation" means that there must be sufficient skills to be acquired in the course to enable the student to work at an occupation. The phrase "to improve the student's skills in an occupation" implies that the student already possesses sufficient skills to enable the student to work at an occupation and the course must be capable of improving those skills. An occupation is considered to be a profession, vocation, trade, or other particular employment. If a student takes a number of courses that are required in order to acquire the skills necessary to work at an occupation, each course will qualify. On the other hand, if a student takes only an initial or introductory course in a particular trade or profession, that course will normally not qualify because sufficient skills have not been obtained. However, if the student goes on and takes the necessary additional courses required for a person to carry on that trade or profession, both the initial course and the additional courses will qualify. Second language training (in particular, French or English) may be viewed as providing a student with skills in an occupation as long as the course is undertaken for the purpose of gaining or improving language skills required for an occupation.

Where a course is taken at an HRSDC-certified institution for personal or recreational purposes, no tuition tax credit is available. The fact that an educational institution is certified by the Minister of HRDSC does not mean that the student is automatically eligible for the tuition tax credit. Such a determination depends on each individual's particular situation.

7. Fees paid for student social activities.

8. Medical expenses (health services fees are eligible, but are limited to $250, unless the fees are required to be paid by all students).

9. Board, lodging, transportation, and parking.

10. Goods of enduring value that are to be retained by students (e.g., microscope, uniforms, gown, computer (see VD 2011-0394391E5), paramedic supplies, cooking school supplies (see 2010-0356101E5), etc.

11. Initiation fees or entrance fees to professional organizations, including examination fees or other fees (such as evaluation fees) that are not integral to a program of study at an eligible educational institution.

12. Administrative penalties incurred when a student withdraws from a program or an institution.

13. The cost of books (other than books, compact discs, or similar material included in the cost of a correspondence course when the student is enrolled in such a course given by an eligible educational institution in Canada).

14. Ancillary fees levied in respect of:

- a student association

- property to be acquired by students

- tax-exempt financial assistance

- the construction, renovation or maintenance of a building or facility (except to the extent that the building or facility is owned by the institution and used to provide courses at the post-secondary level, or the building or facility is used to provide services for which the fees would be eligible as ancillary fees and the fees for such services are required to be paid by all students).

¶10162.3 — *Fees for Flying Instruction*

Fees paid by or on behalf of students enrolled at flying training schools or clubs certified by the Minister of HRSDC are eligible tuition fees, only if the student is taking flying lessons in order to become a commercial pilot or a professional instructor. Fees are eligible only to the extent that they may be regarded as having been paid for tuition. Therefore, a student must be under instruction and direct supervision before the cost of flying time is eligible for the tuition tax credit. As a result, the cost of solo flying does not, generally, qualify as tuition. However, the Transport Canada flight training requirements for certain licences or ratings include, in part, a specified number of hours of flying time under instruction, including both dual and solo flights. There is also a total flight experience requirement of a certain number of hours. The CRA accepts that the student is under instruction and direct supervision while completing the required minimum hours of dual and solo flight training time. However, as the additional flying time required to meet the total hour requirement need not be under instruction and direct supervision, these costs would not qualify as eligible tuition. Accordingly, the cost of dual and solo flying hours required to obtain certain licences or ratings, to become a commercial pilot or a professional instructor, to the minimum flight training requirements of Transport Canada, is considered to be part of the student's tuition.

Fees for ground school and flight simulators are also eligible for the tuition tax credit, but costs incurred by a student in flying a personal aircraft while taking a course at a flying training school or club are not eligible.

¶10162.4 — *Fees for Occupational, Trade, or Professional Examinations*

For 2011 and subsequent taxation years, fees paid in respect of an occupational, trade, or professional examination are eligible for the tuition tax credit, subject to certain exceptions.

To be eligible, an occupational, trade, or professional examination must satisfy all of the following criteria: (1) it is an examination required in order for the individual to obtain a professional status recognized under a federal or provincial statute, or to be licensed or certified as a tradesperson; (2) the status, license or certification allows the individual to practice the profession or trade in Canada; and (3) the fees in respect of the examination are paid to an educational institution, a professional association, provincial ministry, or other similar institution. The GST/HST portion of the examination fee is also eligible for the tuition tax credit.

Fees paid in respect of an occupational, trade, or professional examination do not qualify for the tuition fee tax credit to the extent that they are paid on behalf of, or reimbursed to, the individual by the individual's employer and the amount paid or reimbursed is not included in the individual's income; or are fees for which the individual is entitled to receive a reimbursement or any form of assistance under a government program designed to facilitate the entry or re-entry of workers into the labour force, if the amount of the reimbursement or assistance is not included in calculating the individual's income.

Examinations taken in order to begin study in a profession or field, such as a medical college admission test, would not qualify as occupational, trade, or professional examination fees for these purposes. However, fees paid by a foreign-trained lawyer or law graduate to the National Committee on Accreditation (NCA) to undertake a challenge examination that is required to obtain a Certificate of Qualification to access the bar admission process of a Canadian law society would qualify as occupational, trade, or professional examination fees (although fees paid by an NCA candidate to enroll in a program to prepare the individual for the challenge examination would not generally qualify; see VD 2012-0439811E5).

Ancillary fees paid for the cost of examination materials used during the examination and certain prerequisite study materials qualify for the tuition tax credit; however, the total for the year of such ancillary fees is $250, unless the fees are required to be paid by all of the individuals taking the occupational, trade, or professional examination. The following ancillary fees are not eligible for the tuition tax credit: fees for travel and parking; fees in respect of property to be acquired by the individual (e.g., lab coats, calculators, computers or other items of enduring value); tax-exempt financial assistance; and the construction, renovation, or maintenance of any building or facility.

In VD 2013-0480991E5, the CRA stated that examination fees paid to the Society of Actuaries may qualify as eligible examination fees for the purposes of the tuition tax credit; however, the online seminar fees paid to a professor so that a candidate who wants to become an actuary may prepare for the examination would not qualify as ancillary fees.

¶10163 — *Scholarships, Fellowships, Bursaries, or Prizes*

The CRA provides the following comments in paragraphs 2.23 to 2.27 of Folio S1-F2-C2 regarding the tuition tax credit and scholarships, fellowships, bursaries, and prizes:

2.23 As long as the conditions outlined in subsection 118.5(1) are otherwise satisfied, a student will be eligible to claim the tuition tax credit for tuition fees paid to an educational institution, whether the student pays the tuition fees personally, the fees are paid on behalf of, or reimbursed to, the student by a third party (see exceptions described in ¶2.7 and 2.11), or the student receives free tuition or a reduction in tuition fees directly from an educational institution (see ¶2.24).

2.24 A student in receipt of a scholarship, fellowship, bursary, or prize described in paragraph 56(1)(n) can generally claim a tuition tax credit for the value of their tuition, even if the award is exempt from the student's income by virtue of the scholarship exemption under subsection 56(3), providing it otherwise qualifies as tuition according to subsection 118.5(1) (see ¶2.25).

2.25 Where a student receives free tuition or a reduction in tuition fees from an educational institution, the difference between the pre-determined tuition fee established by the educational institution for the course(s) and the amount paid by the student will generally be considered a scholarship or bursary for tax purposes and included in computing the student's income under subparagraph 56(1)(n)(i), unless the amount is included in the student's employment income or the employment income of the student's family member. Awards received by a student from the student's employer will be eligible for the tuition tax credit to the extent that such amounts are included in computing the student's income (see ¶2.7 and 2.11).

2.26 Where an arm's length employer pays for or reimburses, in whole or in part, the cost of a student's tuition, in connection with the employment of the student's family member, such tuition will be eligible for the tuition tax credit provided it otherwise qualifies under subsection 118.5(1). For information concerning the taxability of this amount to the student or family member, see Income Tax Folio S1-F2-C3, Scholarships, Research Grants and Other Education Assistance.

2.27 The amount of tuition fees reported on the tuition certificate (see ¶2.63) that will be eligible for the tuition tax credit will be the full pre-determined tuition fee established by the educational institution for the course(s), prior to any reduction as a result of the award, providing it otherwise qualifies as tuition according to subsection 118.5(1).

¶10164 — *Education and Textbook Credits*

> For 2017 and later taxation years, both the education tax credit and textbook tax credit have been repealed. Unused education and textbook credits carried forward from years prior to 2017 will remain available to be claimed in 2017 and subsequent years.

For taxation years before 2017, in addition to the tuition tax credit, a student could claim education and textbook tax credits for each month in the calendar year during which the student was enrolled at a designated educational institution.

For taxation years before 2017, the education and textbook tax credits were calculated as follows:

- For full-time students: $465 ($400 education + $65 textbook) multiplied by the number of months in the year in which the individual was a full-time student in a "qualifying educational program"; and

- For part-time students: $140 ($120 education + $20 textbook) multiplied by the number of months in the year in which the individual was a part-time student in a "specified educational program" where the student is required to spend not less than 12 hours per month on courses in the program.

¶10165 — *Carry-Forward of Unused Tuition, Education, and Textbook Credits*

Students can carry forward unused tuition, education, and textbook tax credits to future taxation years.

A student is not required to claim any or all of the available tuition, education, and textbook tax credits in a particular year. However, the amount that can be carried forward is determined by a formula, and does not depend on what the student chooses to claim. Therefore, if a student chooses not to claim all or such portion of the available tuition, education, and textbook tax credits required to reduce federal taxes payable to zero before claiming certain other tax credits (i.e., the medical tax credit, donation tax credit, interest on student loans, dividend tax credit, and the foreign tax credit), the tuition, education, and textbook tax credits not claimed cannot be carried forward and will be lost. See the example provided in paragraphs 2.51 and 2.52 of Folio S1-F2-C2 illustrating the calculation of the tuition fee carry-forward.

> The claiming of a tuition credit is discretionary; however, if an available credit is not claimed, the formula in ITA 118.61(1) will still act to reduce the unused credits available for carry-forward.

¶10166 — *Transfer of Unused Tuition Credits*

> Students are required to claim their tuition amounts first on their own return to reduce their own federal taxes payable to zero, even if the fees were paid by someone else. A student may then transfer any unused credits to his or her spouse or common-law partner, parents, or grandparents, or to the spouse's or common-law partner's parents or grandparents. The maximum that may be transferred for federal purposes is $5,000 (for a 15% tax credit of $750). Any unused credits may be carried forward to be claimed in a future year by the student.

Students can transfer their unused tuition credits to a parent or grandparent where the student does not have a spouse or common-law partner, or where the student has a spouse or common-law partner who is not claiming a spousal or common-law partner tax credit in respect of the student and the student is not transferring any of his or her unused tax credits to the spouse or common-law partner.

The amount of tuition tax credits that may be transferred to the student's parent or grandparent is calculated according to the formula in ITA 118.81. A student may transfer unused tuition tax credits to only one supporting individual in a year; however, a parent or grandparent may claim transferred tuition tax credits from more than one child or grandchild in a year.

For purposes of the tuition credit transfer, a parent of a student includes a natural parent, step-parent, or adoptive parent of the student; a natural parent, step-parent, or adoptive parent of the student's spouse or common-law partner; and an individual whom the student is wholly dependent on for support, and under whose custody and control the student is, or was, immediately before attaining age 19. However, such an individual would not include a student's foster parent who received support payments from an agency responsible for the student's care, since the student would not be considered wholly dependent on the foster parent in such a case. For purposes of the tuition credit transfer, a grandparent includes the grandfather or grandmother of the student, or the grandfather or grandmother of the student's spouse or common-law partner.

Where a student's unused tuition tax credits are transferred to, and claimed by, the student's spouse or common-law partner or the student's parent or grandparent, a copy of the appropriate tuition certificate or receipt issued by the educational institution or body should be obtained from the student and retained for verification purposes.

> Students who are transferring unused tuition credits to another person should not transfer more than the person can use.

¶10167 — *Certificates to Support Claims*

A student who makes a claim for tuition fees must obtain one of the following certificates issued by the educational institution to support the claim:

- Form T2202A, *Tuition and Enrolment Certificate*, or an official income tax receipt for tuition fees paid to an educational institution in Canada;

- Form TL11A, *Tuition and Enrolment Certificate — University Outside Canada*, for tuition fees paid to a university outside Canada;

- Form TL11B, *Tuition and Enrolment Certificate — Flying School or Club*, if the fees are paid to a flying training school or club;

- Form TL11C, *Tuition and Enrolment Certificate — Commuter to the United States*, for tuition fees for individuals commuting to an educational institution in the United States; and

- Form TL11D, *Tuition Fees Certificate — Educational Institutions Outside Canada for a Deemed Resident of Canada*, for fees paid to an educational institution outside Canada for a deemed resident of Canada.

It is not necessary to file the certificate with the T1 return, but the individual must be able to provide the document upon request.

¶10168 — *Claiming and Filing*

Taxpayers should complete Schedule 11, *Tuition, Education, and Textbook Amounts*, to report total eligible tuition amounts for the year and any unused amounts carried forward from previous years that are shown on the taxpayer's Notice of Assessment or Notice of Reassessment.

As discussed at ¶10166, students must claim their tuition amounts first on their own return to reduce their own taxes payable, and any unused portion can be transferred to a designated person. Complete Schedule 11 to calculate the amount of transfer and complete the applicable portion of Form T2202A, TL11A, TL11B, TL11C, or TL11D to designate the amount (see Line 324 at ¶10170). Attach Schedule 11 to the return even if all tuition amounts are being transferred to another person. The tuition amounts that cannot be used by the student (and that are not transferred) can be carried forward and claimed in a future year. However, amounts carried forward cannot be transferred to anyone else, and must be claimed in the first year that federal tax is owing. Calculate the carry-forward amount on Schedule 11.

Students filing a paper return should attach a completed Schedule 11 to the paper return, but do not attach certificates, receipts or other forms. Keep them in case the CRA requests them. Electronic filers should keep all of their documents.

> Even if a student has no tax to pay and is transferring part of his or her tuition amounts, the student should file a T1 return and attach a completed Schedule 11 so the CRA updates their records with the student's unused tuition amounts available for carry-forward to other years.

ITA 118.5, 118.6, 118.61, 118.8, 118.9, Pamphlet P105, Information Sheet RC192, Schedule 11, Form T2202A, Form TL11A, Form TL11B, Form TL11C, Form T11D, Folio S1-F2-C1: *Education and Textbook Tax Credits*, Folio S1-F2-C2: *Tuition Tax Credit*

¶10170 — Tuition Amounts Transferred from a Child (T1 Schedule 1: Line 324)

As discussed above at ¶10166, if a student cannot use his or her tuition credits in the current year to reduce their taxes payable to nil, the student can transfer up to a maximum of $5,000 to his or her parent or grandparent, which is equal to a maximum credit of $750 that can be claimed on Line 324. To calculate the amount available for transfer, the student must complete Schedule 11. Also, to designate the individual who may claim the amount, the student must complete the applicable portion of Form T2202A, TL11A, TL11B, TL11C or TL11D, as applicable.

Students cannot transfer an unused credit to more than one person. Therefore, if a student has been claimed as a dependant for purposes of the spousal or common-law partner credit (Line 303) or has transferred tuition amounts for the year to a spouse or common-law partner (Line 326), the student cannot transfer any unused tuition amounts to a parent or grandparent in the same year.

ITA 118.5, 118.6, 118.61, 118.8, 118.9, Pamphlet P105, Information Sheet RC192, Schedule 11, Form T2202A, Form TL11A, Form TL11B, Form TL11C, Form T11D, Folio S1-F2-C1: *Education and Textbook Tax Credits*, Folio S1-F2-C2: *Tuition Tax Credit*

¶10180 — Amounts Transferred from Spouse or Common-Law Partner (T1 Schedule 1: Line 326)

ITA 118.8 permits an individual who is married or in a common-law partnership at any time in the year to transfer the unused portion of certain of his or her credits to the spouse or common-law partner to reduce the latter's Part I tax for the year. Transferable credits include the following: the age credit (see ¶10020); the pension credit (see ¶10100); the disability credit (see ¶10120); the tuition tax credit (see ¶10160); and the caregiver credit for an infirm child (see ¶10260). While the age and pension credits are transferable only to a spouse or common-law partner, the tuition credit (to a maximum dollar amount) may be transferred to a parent or grandparent (see ¶10166 and ¶10170). Also, the disability tax credit may be transferred to a supporting parent or grandparent (see ¶10140).

The amount by which transferable credits may reduce tax of the transferee spouse is equal to the amount of the credit transferred multiplied by the lowest personal tax rate for the year. As such, there is generally no benefit in transferring the credits to a spouse or common-law partner where an individual is able to utilize the credits to reduce his or her own taxes in the year. Where an individual with a spouse or common-law partner does not require the full amount of the transferable credits to reduce taxes payable for the year to nil, transferring the credits to a spouse or common-law partner who can utilize the credits is generally beneficial since the transferable credits are non-refundable, and only the tuition credit can be carried-forward for deduction in a subsequent taxation year.

¶10181 — *Claiming and Filing*

Taxpayers are required to complete Schedule 2 to calculate their claim for amounts transferred from a spouse or common-law partner. Ensure that marital status and the information concerning the taxpayer's spouse or common-law partner (including his or her net income, even if it is zero) in the Identification section on page 1 of the return are completed.

If the transferred amount includes a new application for the disability amount, attach a completed and certified Form T2201, *Disability Tax Credit Certificate* (not required if the spouse or common-law partner qualified for the disability amount in the previous year and continues to be eligible, unless the previous approval period ends before the current year).

Include the completed Schedule 2 with a taxpayer's paper return. If the taxpayer's spouse or common-law partner is not filing a return, attach the information slips that show his or her income to the taxpayer's return. Do not include any receipts or forms for the spouse or common-law partner's tuition amounts, but keep them in case the CRA requests them. Taxpayers filing electronically should keep all of their documents on file.

118(1)(b.1), 118(2), 118(3), 118.8, 118.81, Schedule 2, Pamphlet P105, Guide RC4065, Folio S1-F4-C1: *Basic Personal and Dependant Tax Credits*, Folio S1-F1-C2: *Disability Tax Credit*, Folio S1-F2-C1: *Education and Textbook Tax Credits*, Folio S1-F2-C2: *Tuition Tax Credit*

¶10190 — Medical Expenses for Self, Spouse and Dependent Children (T1 Schedule 1: Line 330)

The medical expense tax credit is intended to provide relief to taxpayers who sustain extraordinary medical expenses for themselves or for certain dependants. The types of medical expenses that qualify for purposes of the medical expense tax credit are specified in ITA 118.2(2)(a) to (u). In addition, certain employee benefits in respect of medical services, and the costs of certain travel expenses may qualify as medical expenses by virtue of the deeming provisions in ITA 118.2(3) and (4).

See the Medical Expense Credit Quick Reference Table in Appendix A which has a listing of over 400 itemized medical expenses, stating whether they qualify for the medical expense tax credit, and identifying the relevant authority (i.e., the *Income Tax Act*, *Income Tax Regulations*, Interpretation Bulletins, Income Tax Folios, CRA Guides, CRA Views Documents, case law, etc.).

For the 2018 taxation year, the medical expense tax credit is available where a taxpayer's qualifying medical expenditures exceed the lesser of: three percent of the individual's net income, or $2,302. Specifically, once the total of an individual's qualifying medical expenses have been determined, that amount is reduced by the lesser of: (a) three percent of the individual's income for the year, or (b) $2,302. The medical expense credit is then calculated by multiplying the difference by 15 percent, which is the lowest personal tax rate for the year. This can be illustrated by way of the following example:

Mary's 2018 net income is $50,000. Mary incurred $2,500 of qualifying medical expenses in 2018. Mary's medical expense tax credit is calculated as follows:

Qualifying medical expenses	$ 2,500
Less the lesser of: • 3% of Mary's net income ($50,000 × 3% = $1,500) • $2,302	($ 1,500)
Medical expenses eligible for medical expense tax credit	$ 1,000
Tax credit rate	15%
Federal medical expense tax credit	$ 150

There are a number of conditions that must be satisfied for an individual to claim a medical expense tax credit for amounts paid in respect of a patient for a particular tax year:

- The medical expenses must be eligible medical expenses as described in ITA 118.2(2). Eligible medical expenses are discussed below at ¶10195. The Medical Expenses Credit Quick Reference Table in Appendix A lists and describes over 400 itemized expenses, stating if they do or do not qualify for the medical expense tax credit, and identifying the authority. Also see paragraphs 1.18 to 1.146 of Folio S1-F1-C1: *Medical Expense Tax Credit*;

- The medical expenses must have been paid or deemed to have been paid by either the individual, the individual's spouse or common-law partner, or the individual's legal representative, and must not have been reimbursed or be reimbursable unless the reimbursed amount is required to be included in computing income and is not deductible in computing taxable income (see *Payment and Reimbursement of Expenditures* at ¶10191);

- The medical expenses must have been paid within any 12-month period ending in the calendar year, except where the person in respect of whom the expenses were paid died in the year, in which case the medical expenses must have been paid within any 24-month period that includes the date of death (see *Time of Expenditures* at ¶10192);

- The medical expenses must not have been used in calculating the individual's medical expense tax credit, a disability supports deduction (see ¶9180), or the refundable medical expense supplement (see ¶11280) for a previous year. Note, however, that the individual may claim the refundable medical expense supplement in addition to the medical expense credit in respect of the same expenses for the same year;

- The medical expenses must not have been used in calculating a medical expense tax credit, a disability supports deduction (see ¶9180), or a refundable medical expense supplement (see ¶11280) for any other taxpayer for any tax year; and

- The medical expenses must be proven by filing supporting receipts (see *Receipts* at ¶10194).

It should be noted that since medical expenses are creditable when paid, not when incurred, a taxpayer may have a valid claim in respect of a person who is no longer his or her spouse or common-law partner, or a dependant who no longer meets the definition of a "dependant" in ITA 118(6). For example, if a medical expense was incurred in one year on behalf of a spouse, common-law partner, or dependant, but is not paid until the following year at a time when such person is no longer a spouse, common-law partner, or a dependant of the individual, the expense can nevertheless qualify in the year of payment since the person referred to is only required to have been a spouse, common-law partner, or a dependant at the time the expense was incurred. As well, an individual can claim the medical expenses incurred by their spouse or common-law partner, regardless of that person's income in the tax year. A receipt in the name of either spouse or common-law partner is considered acceptable evidence of a medical expense of either, and the amount of that expense may be used by either, as agreed between them.

It should also be noted that eligible medical expenses are not restricted to those paid in Canada, or for medical services provided in Canada. For example, eligible medical expenses can include expenses incurred in the United States or in another country. There are two exceptions: expenses for attendant care must be provided in Canada (ITA 118.2(2)(b.1)), and expenses for care in a group home must be located in Canada (ITA 118.2(2)(b.2)).

Other related credits and deductions that the individual may be able to claim in addition to the medical expense credit include the refundable medical expense supplement (Line 452; see ¶11280), which is available to certain low-income working individuals with high medical expenses. The supplement may be claimed in addition to the medical expense credit, and in respect of the same expenses. As well, the disability supports deduction (Line 215; see ¶9180) allows for the deduction of certain disability support costs (which generally qualify for the medical expense tax credit) incurred to earn certain types of income, or to attend a designated educational institution or secondary school. However, unlike the refundable medical expense supplement, expenses claimed for the disability supports deduction cannot be included in computing the medical expense tax credit.

A general review of the treatment of medical expenses is set out in CRA Guide RC4065: *Medical Expenses*, and Folio S1-F1-C1: *Medical Expense Tax Credit*.

ITA 118(6), 118.2(2), (3), (4), Guide RC4065, Folio S1-F1-C1, Folio S1-F1-C3

¶10191 — *Payment and Reimbursement of Expenditures*

Where eligible medical expenses are paid or provided for by an employer, and are included in computing the individual's income (i.e., as an employee benefit, for example), the amount so included in income will be deemed to be a medical expense paid by the individual. Thus, such amount is included in the computation of an individual's income, but may be deducted in computing tax payable. This rule generally applies to all medical expenses except private health plan premiums, since where such premiums are paid for by an employer on behalf of an employee, the value of the benefit derived therefrom is specifically excluded from inclusion in the employee's income as an employee benefit under ITA 6(1)(a). The CRA has stated that "the employee is deemed to have paid such expenses at the time the employer paid or provided them" (see paragraph 1.15 of Folio S1-F1-C1).

An expense may not be included in calculating an individual's medical expense tax credit where the individual seeking to claim the expense, the patient in respect of whom the expense is being claimed, any person related to either of them, or the legal representative of any of them, is entitled to a reimbursement for the expense, unless the reimbursed amount is required to be included in income and is not deductible.

ITA 20.01, 118.2(2)(q), 118.2(3)(a), (b), IT-339R2: *Meaning of Private Health Services Plan*, Folio S1-F1-C1 (paras. 1.15-1.16)

¶10192 — *Time of Expenditures*

A taxpayer is entitled to base a claim on medical expenses paid in the course of any 12-month period ending in the calendar year. Thus, for example, expenses paid in the period commencing on February 1, 2017 and ending January 31, 2018 would be eligible medical expenses for the individual's 2018 taxation year. By thus extending the 12-month period into the following taxation year, a taxpayer who suffered a loss or had little income in 2017 could ascribe any or most of his or her 2017 medical expenses to 2018, with a consequent greater tax saving. However, expenses claimed in one taxation year may not be claimed again in the following year. Whether an expense is deductible in a particular year depends on the date of payment, not on the date on which such expenses are incurred.

> A 12-month period, once chosen by the taxpayer, does not need to be retained for subsequent taxation years. Thus, a 2017 claim might consist of expenses paid between October 1, 2016 and September 30, 2017, and a 2018 claim by the same taxpayer might consist of expenses paid between April 1, 2017 and March 31, 2018, provided that no expense was claimed twice.

In recognition of potentially significant medical expenses often incurred in the final illness of an individual, some of which may not be paid until after the individual's death, the legal representative of a deceased taxpayer may claim, in the year of a taxpayer's death, medical expenses paid by the representative or the taxpayer within any 24-month period that includes the day of death. For example, if a taxpayer dies during the year, not all medical expenses may have been paid by the date of death. In that case, the personal representatives of the taxpayer may choose any 24-month period that includes the date of death and claim a credit in respect of the expenses paid in that period. The 24-month period also applies to medical expenses for a deceased person that are claimed by a supporting taxpayer.

Folio S1-F1-C1 (para. 1.9)

¶10193 — *Medical Expenditures for Dependants*

Individuals can claim eligible medical expenses on Line 330 for eligible medical expenditures paid in respect of themselves, their spouse or common-law partner, and dependent children who have not attained the age of 18 years before the end of the taxation year. The definitions of spouse and common-law partner are discussed at ¶10032.

In addition to claiming medical expenses on Line 330 for themselves, a spouse or common-law partner, and for dependent children under age 18, individuals may also claim eligible medical expenses on Line 331 in respect of other dependants, where the dependant is a person who at any time in the year is dependent upon the individual for support and is:

- a child (who has attained the age of 18 years before the end of the taxation year) or grandchild of the individual or his or her spouse or common-law partner; or

- a parent, grandparent, brother, sister, aunt, uncle, niece, or nephew of the individual or his or her spouse or common-law partner, and who is a resident of Canada at some time in the year.

Whether a person is dependent upon the individual for support is a question of fact. Generally, a person is considered to be dependent on someone for support if the individual has actually supplied necessary maintenance, or the basic necessities of life (food, shelter and clothing) on a regular and consistent basis. This support may be given voluntarily or pursuant to a legal commitment. Where the dependent person was in receipt of social assistance or any other type of financial or non-financial support, the supporting individual must be able to show that the other assistance was insufficient to fully meet the basic needs of the dependant, and that the person had to rely on the additional support provided by the supporting individual.

See Line 331 at ¶10200 for a complete discussion of the rules for claiming medical expenses for other dependants.

ITA 118(6), 252, Folio S1-F1-C1 (paras. 1.2–1.7)

¶10194 — *Receipts*

Unlike some other expenses a taxpayer might claim (such as child care expenses), which the taxpayer must be prepared to substantiate only if the Minister so requests, a claim for medical expenses must, except for certain vehicle and meal expenses, be "proven by filing receipts" with the Minister. The receipts should normally be attached to the taxpayer's income tax return when a paper return is filed, in the same way as receipts in support of the donation tax credit. CRA provides the following comments regarding receipts in paragraph 1.147 of Folio S1-F1-C1:

> 1.147 Generally, all expenses claimed as eligible medical expenses must be supported by proper receipts. A receipt should indicate the purpose of the payment, the date of the payment, the patient for whom the payment was made and, if applicable, the audiologist, dentist, medical doctor, medical practitioner, nurse, occupational therapist, optometrist, pharmacist, physiotherapist, psychologist, or speech-language pathologist who prescribed the purchase or gave the service. A cancelled cheque is not acceptable as a substitute for a proper receipt. In addition to receipts, proof of payment or proof of support may be required in situations where an individual claims the medical expenses tax credit for amounts paid in respect of a dependant who is 18 years of age or older at the end of the year. If required forms, receipts or other supporting documents are not filed with the income tax return, such as when the return is electronically filed (E filed), they should nevertheless be retained and readily available as they may subsequently be requested as proof of the claims being made or in support of the information being reported Receipts are not required for meal and vehicle expenses claimed as transportation and travel expenses under paragraph 118.2(2)(g) and (h), or in connection with bone marrow or organ transplants under paragraph 118.2(2)(l.1) where the simplified method of calculating meal and vehicle expenses is chosen.

Medical expenses are normally considered to have been paid out of the pooled family income. The amount of a receipted expense in the name of either spouse is considered acceptable and allowed to either spouse as agreed between them. As a result of the way that the medical expense credit is calculated, it is generally more advantageous for tax purposes for the spouse or common-law partner with the lower net income to claim the medical expenses of both taxpayers.

Doyle v The Queen, [1989] 1 C.T.C. 113 (FCTD), Folio S1-F1-C1 (para. 1.147), VD 2007-0230921M4

¶10195 — *Eligible Medical Expenses*

The types of expenditures that qualify as medical expenses for purposes of the tax credit are set out in ITA 118.2(2)(a) to (u) and 118.2(2.2). Each of these provisions is discussed in more detail below. Also see the Medical Expense Credit Quick Reference Table in Appendix A which lists and describes over 400 itemized expenses, stating if they do or do not qualify for the medical expense tax credit, and identifying the authority. In addition, see paragraphs 1.18 to 1.146 of Folio S1-F1-C1, and CRA's list of eligible medical expenses at: canada.ca/en/revenue-agency/services/tax/individuals/topics/about-your-tax-return/tax-return/completing-a-tax-return/deductions-credits-expenses/lines-330-331-eligible-medical-expenses-you-claim-on-your-tax-return.html#mdcl_xpns.

Applicable for 2017 and later taxation years, ITA 118.2(2.2) allows certain amounts paid for fertility treatments for the purpose of an individual conceiving a child to qualify as medical expenses for the medical expense tax credit where the individual does not have an existing illness or condition (such as the medical condition of infertility), but nonetheless requires medical intervention to conceive a child. For more information, see ¶ 10195.20.

¶10195.1 — *Fees Paid to Medical Professionals*

ITA 118.2(2)(a) defines eligible medical expenses as those amounts paid to a medical practitioner, dentist, nurse, or to a public or licensed private hospital, in respect of medical or dental services provided to the individual, the individual's spouse or common-law partner, or a dependant. Thus, payments in respect of an illness of, or operation on, the individual, his or her spouse or common-law partner, or an eligible dependant would qualify. For purposes of the medical expense tax credit, ITA 118.4(2) provides that a reference to an audiologist, dentist, medical doctor, medical practitioner, nurse, nurse practitioner, occupational therapist, optometrist, pharmacist, physiotherapist, psychologist, or speech-language pathologist is a reference to a person who is authorized to practice as such, according to the following laws: for a service rendered to an individual, the laws of the jurisdiction in which the service is rendered; for a certificate issued for an individual, the laws of the jurisdiction in which the individual resides; and for a prescription issued to an individual, the laws of the jurisdiction in which the individual resides or in which the prescription is filled.

In accordance with the decision of the Federal Court of Appeal in *Canada v Couture*, [2009] 2 C.T.C. 80 (FCA), it is the CRA's view that an individual is authorized by the laws of the jurisdiction to act as a medical practitioner if there is specific legislation that enables, permits or empowers that individual to perform medical services. Generally, such specific legislation would provide for the licensing or certification of the practitioner, as well as for the establishment of a governing body (for example, a college or board) with the authority to determine competency, enforce discipline, and set basic standards of conduct.

The CRA provides a table listing authorized medical practitioners by province or territory for the purposes of claiming the medical expense tax credit at: canada.ca/en/revenue-agency/services/tax/individuals/topics/about-your-tax-return/tax-return/completing-a-tax-return/deductions-credits-expenses/lines-330-331-eligible-medical-expenses-you-claim-on-your-tax-return/authorized-medical-practitioners-purposes-medical-expense-tax-credit.html. The table summarizes publicly available provincial and territorial information identifying those health care professionals authorized to practice as medical practitioners. The CRA highlights that the list is not an all inclusive list of every profession that is authorized by each province or territory.

ITA 118.4(2), Folio S1-F1-C1 (paras. 1.20–1.23)

¶10195.2 — *Cost of Attendant Care and Care in Certain Types of Facilities*

Under ITA 118.2(2)(b) to (e), eligible medical expenses may include costs paid for attendant care or care in certain types of facilities (for example, nursing homes, group homes, schools, and institutions). CRA provides the following comments in paragraphs 1.32 and 1.33 of Folio S1-F1-C1 with respect to the meaning of "attendant care" and "nursing home":

> 1.32 Attendant Care is care provided by an attendant who performs those personal tasks which a patient is unable to do for him or herself. Depending on the situation, such tasks could include meal preparation, maid and cleaning services, transportation, and personal services such as banking and shopping. Attendant care would also include providing companionship to a patient. However, if a person is employed as a single service provider, such as a provider of only maid and cleaning services, or a provider of only transportation services, the provision of such service would not be viewed as attendant care. Where the expression one-full time attendant is used, it is not intended to mean one attendant only looking after the patient on a continuous basis but rather several attendants could be utilized over a specific period of time so long as there is only one attendant for any given period of time.

> 1.33 A nursing home is generally considered to be an establishment that provides full-time maintenance or nursing home care for patients who are unable to care for themselves. While a particular place need not be a licensed nursing home, it must have the equivalent features and characteristics of a nursing home. For example, a nursing home is normally a facility of a public character which offers 24-hour nursing care to patients who are not related to the facility owner/operator. The use of the expression full-time care in a nursing home is not intended to place a requirement of a minimum time spent caring for a patient but rather implies the constant care and attendance required by the patient by reason of an injury, illness or disability of the patient. The CRA is generally of the view that a retirement home does not provide the care required to be classified as a nursing home.

ITA 118.2(2)(b), (b.1) and (b.2) only apply in respect of the costs of caring for a person with a disability. A person with a disability is a person in respect of whom a disability tax credit could be claimed (either by the person with the disability or by some other person for the tax year in which the medical expense was incurred), if the rule in ITA 118.3(1)(c) did not apply. Generally, under ITA 118.3(1)(c), where an amount in respect of attendant care or care in a nursing home is claimed in a taxation year as a medical expense in respect of a person with a disability, no taxpayer may claim the disability tax credit in respect of that person for that tax year, unless the attendant care is being claimed as a medical expense under ITA 118.2(2)(b.1), which limits the medical expense claim that can be made for attendant care in respect of a person with a disability to $10,000 ($20,000 where the individual died in the year).

> Individuals will need to determine, based on their specific circumstances, whether it is more beneficial to claim the limited amount of attendant care expenses provided in ITA 118.2(2)(b.1) (i.e., $10,000) plus the disability tax credit (see ¶ 10120), or to claim the full amount of the cost of attendant care with no claim for the disability tax credit. For more information and examples showing how to determine which claim is more beneficial, see Guide RC4065: *Medical Expenses.*

The disability tax credit is generally available to, or in respect of, an individual who is properly certified as having a severe and prolonged mental or physical impairment, the effects of which are such that the individual's ability to perform a basic activity of daily living is markedly restricted. Generally, to be entitled to the disability tax credit, the individual must be markedly restricted in a basic activity of daily living, and the impairment should last at least 12 continuous months. For more information on determining whether a person qualifies for the disability tax credit, see under ¶10120 and Folio S1-F1-C2.

ITA 118.2(2)(c), (d), and (e) apply in respect of the costs of caring for a patient, regardless of whether the patient is a person with a disability. Details regarding the specific requirements relating to claims for eligible medical expenses under ITA 118.2(2)(b) to (e) are provided in paragraphs 1.37 to 1.63 of Folio S1-F1-C1.

The following chart, contained in Guide RC4065: *Medical Expenses,* explains what certification is needed to claim attendant care as medical expenses (on line 330 or line 331), and whether an individual can also claim the disability amount (line 316 or line 318).

Type of expense	Certification required	Can you claim the disability amount?
Fees paid for full-time care in a nursing home [see ¶10195.2E]	Form T2201 *or* a medical practitioner must certify in writing that you are, and in the foreseeable future will continue to be, dependent on others for your personal needs and care because of a lack of normal mental capacity.	You can claim the disability amount, if eligible, *or* these expenses, but not both.
Salaries and wages for attendant care given in Canada. This can include the part of the nursing home fees paid for full-time care that relate only to salaries and wages. [see ¶ 10195.2B]	Form T2201	You can claim the disability amount *and* up to $10,000 for these expenses ($20,000 if the person died in the year).
Salaries and wages for one full-time attendant outside of a self-contained domestic establishment [see ¶10195.2A]	Form T2201	You can claim the disability amount *or* these expenses, but not both.
Full-time attendant at home [see ¶10195.2D]	Form T2201 *or* a medical practitioner must certify in writing that you are, and will likely to be for a long continuous period of indefinite duration, dependent on others for your personal needs and care because of an impairment in physical or mental functions and need a full-time attendant.	You can claim the disability amount, if eligible, *or* these expenses, but not both.

Type of expense	Certification required	Can you claim the disability amount?
Salaries and wages for care in a group home in Canada [see ¶10195.2C]	Form T2201	You can claim the disability amount *and* these expenses.
Care, or training and care, at a school, institution, or other place (such as a detoxification clinic) [see ¶ 10195.2F]	Form T2201 *or* an appropriately qualified person must certify in writing that because of a mental or physical impairment, you need the equipment, facilities or staff specially provided by that place for persons with the same type of impairments. *Note* An appropriately qualified person includes a medical practitioner, the principal of the school or the head of the institution or other place.	You can claim the disability amount, if eligible, *and* these expenses.

ITA 118.2(2)(b)–(e), Folio S1-C1-F1 (paras. 1.31–1.63)

¶10195.2A — *Full-Time Care of an Individual with Severe and Prolonged Impairment*

ITA 118.2(2)(b) permits the deduction of expenses incurred for the remuneration of one full-time attendant or the cost of full-time care in a nursing home, provided to an individual is respect of whom the disability tax credit may be claimed for the taxation year in which the expenses were incurred. The full-time attendant must not be the spouse or common-law partner of the disabled individual, nor under 18 years of age at the time the remuneration is paid. Where a claim for remuneration paid for attendant care, or for care in a nursing home, is made under ITA 118.2(2)(b), no disability tax credit may be claimed in respect of the person with a disability by any taxpayer for that tax year. Amounts that are actually paid to an attendant for salary or remuneration, as well as the employer's portion of employment insurance premiums, CPP/QPP contributions, and workers' compensation insurance premiums will also qualify. Imputed salary or remuneration will not qualify since no actual payment is made.

> If a claim for remuneration paid for attendant care, or for care in a nursing home, is made under ITA 118.2(2)(b), no disability tax credit may be claimed in respect of the person with a disability by any taxpayer for that tax year.

To make a claim under ITA 118.2(2)(b), the CRA states that either Form T2201, *Disability Tax Credit Certificate*, is required, or a letter from a medical practitioner has to certify that the person is, and is likely to continue to be for a long-continued period of indefinite duration, dependent on others for his or her personal needs and care, and needs a full-time attendant because of an impairment in mental or physical functions.

It is the CRA's view that a taxpayer's private home would not be considered a "nursing home" for purposes of ITA 118.2(2)(b); the CRA accepts that a particular place need not be a licensed nursing home but is of the view that it must have the equivalent features and characteristics of a nursing home (see VD 2007-0253621E5). As well, the term "nursing home" in ITA 118.2(2)(b) does not include a retirement residence, even if it provides 24-hour nursing care (see *Miles Estate v. R.*, [2000] 2 C.T.C. 2165).

ITA 118.2(2)(b), 118.3(1), 118.4(1), (2), Folio S1-F1-C1 (paras. 1.31 to 1.39), Guide RC4064, Guide RC4065, VDs 2008-0285321C6, 2008-0291121E5

¶10195.2B — *Care of an Individual with Severe and Prolonged Impairment*

ITA 118.2(2)(b.1) permits the deduction of expenses incurred to pay for attendant care provided in Canada to an individual in respect of whom the disability tax credit may be claimed for the taxation year in which the expenses were incurred. The amount that may be claimed under ITA 118.2(2)(b.1) is the lesser of: (1) the amount paid as remuneration for attendant care, and (2) $10,000 ($20,000 where the individual died in the year). The amounts cannot otherwise be deducted in computing a taxpayer's income (i.e., as child care expenses under ITA 63 or as disability supports expenses under ITA 64), or otherwise claimed as a medical expense credit for the year. The attendant must not be the spouse or common-law partner of the disabled individual, nor under 18 years of age at the time the remuneration is paid. Amounts that are actually paid to an attendant for salary or remuneration, as well as the employer's portion of employment insurance premiums, CPP/QPP contributions, and workers' compensation insurance premiums will also qualify. Imputed salary or remuneration will not qualify since no actual payment is made.

Generally, most claims under ITA 118.2(2)(b.1) will be made for part-time attendant care; however, the CRA acknowledges in paragraph 1.42 of Folio S1-F1-C1 that remuneration for a full-time attendant may also be claimed under this paragraph, subject to the dollar limit and provided all the requirements are otherwise met, so that a disability tax credit may also be claimed for the year in respect of the individual. The CRA also acknowledges in VD 2006-0172181I7 that each person entitled to claim a medical expense tax credit under ITA 118.2(2)(b.1) in respect of attendant care costs provided to an individual patient may claim up to $10,000 (i.e., the $10,000 limit for attendant care applies to each person paying for attendant care).

The CRA accepts that where a portion of retirement home costs is identified as being paid for attendant care, it will qualify under ITA 118.2(2)(b.1) (VDs 2005-0142361E5 and 2003-0030965).

ITA 118.2(2)(b.1), Folio S1-F1-C1 (paras. 1.40–1.43), Guide RC4064, Guide RC4065

¶10195.2C — *Care in a Group Home*

ITA 118.2(2)(b.2) permits an individual to claim remuneration for care or supervision of an individual provided in a group home in Canada that is maintained and operated exclusively for the benefit of individuals with severe and prolonged impairments, where the following conditions are met:

1. the patient is eligible for the disability tax credit for the taxation year in which the expense is incurred;

2. No part of the remuneration is claimed by any taxpayer as a as a child care expense (under ITA 63), a disability supports deduction (under ITA 64), or otherwise claimed as a medical expense credit for the year; and

3. Receipts for payments are issued by the payee, and include, in the case of an individual, his or her Social Insurance Number.

Amounts that are actually paid to a group home for remuneration for care or supervision of the patient, including the employer's portion of employment insurance premiums, CPP/QPP contributions, and workers' compensation insurance premiums, will also qualify. Imputed salary or remuneration will not qualify since no actual payment is made.

Where a patient has received care and supervision in a group home and all of the other conditions have otherwise been met, a disability tax credit may be claimed by an individual in respect of the patient for the year (provided the conditions for the disability tax credit are otherwise met), in addition to the medical expense credit claim under ITA 118.2(2)(b.2). However, if the medical expense credit claim was for an amount paid for care in a nursing home, no taxpayer may claim a disability tax credit in respect of that patient for that tax year.

ITA 118.2(2)(b.2), Folio S1-F1-C1 (paras. 1.44–1.46), Guide RC4064, Guide RC4065

¶10195.2D — *Care in a Self-Contained Domestic Establishment*

ITA 118.2(2)(c) permits an individual to claim the cost of providing one full-time attendant required by a "patient" living in a self-contained domestic establishment (not a nursing home) who is certified by a medical practitioner as being dependent on others for personal needs and care because of an impairment in mental or physical functions, and who will likely continue to be so dependent for a long-continued period of indefinite duration. A medical practitioner may certify the person's mental or physical infirmity in a letter or on Form T2201. The attendant must not be the spouse or common-law partner of the disabled individual, nor under 18 years of age at the time the remuneration is paid. In addition, receipts for payments must be issued by the payee, and include, in the case of an individual, his or her Social Insurance Number.

Amounts that are actually paid to an attendant for salary or remuneration, as well as the employer's portion of employment insurance premiums, CPP/QPP contributions, and workers' compensation insurance premiums, will also qualify. Imputed salary or remuneration will not qualify since no actual payment is made.

To be an eligible medical expense under ITA 118.2(2)(c), the cared-for person is not required to qualify for the disability tax credit; however, where a medical expense claim is made under ITA 118.2(2)(c) for attendant care for a person who does qualify for the disability tax credit, no disability tax credit may be claimed in respect of that person by any taxpayer for that tax year.

It is the CRA's view that several attendants can qualify as one full-time attendant under ITA 118.2(2)(c) as long as there is only one attendant for any given period of time (see VD 2007-0253621E5). As well, the requirement that the attendant be "full-time" has been interpreted in case law to mean that the attendant must be engaged for the full normal day while employed as an attendant. It does not require that the attendant be employed for the whole of the year. In *Wakelyn v. MNR*, [1970] Tax A.B.C. 1296, several part-time attendants were held to be the equivalent of one full-time attendant.

ITA 118.2(2)(c), Folio S1-F1-C1 (paras. 1.47–1.50), Guide RC4064, Guide RC4065

¶10195.2E — *Full-Time Nursing Home Care due to Lack of Normal Mental Capacity*

ITA 118.2(2)(d) permits an individual to claim the cost of full-time care in a nursing home as an eligible medical expense, provided that a medical practitioner certifies that the patient receiving care in the nursing home is, and in the foreseeable future will continue to be, dependent upon others for personal needs and care due to a lack of normal mental capacity. A medical practitioner may certify the person's mental or physical infirmity in a letter or on Form T2201. Receipts from the nursing home are also required.

To be an eligible medical expense under ITA 118.2(2)(d), the cared-for person is not required to qualify for the disability tax credit. Where the individual does qualify for the disability tax credit, the cost of the nursing home care would generally be claimed under ITA 118.2(2)(b) (see ¶10195.2A), or, the cost of the nursing home care that can reasonably be regarded as remuneration paid for attendant care, would be claimed under ITA 118.2(2)(b.1) (see ¶10195.2B).

Where a medical expense claim is made under ITA 118.2(2)(d) for the cost of care in a nursing home for a person who does qualify for the disability tax credit, no disability tax credit may be claimed in respect of that person by any taxpayer for that tax year.

ITA 118.2(2)(d), 118.4(2)(b), Folio S1-F1-C1 (paras. 1.51–1.55), Guide RC4064, Guide RC4065

¶10195.2F — *Care in an Institution and Care and Training in a School*

Where an individual has been appropriately certified as a person who, by reason of mental or physical impairment, requires equipment, facilities, or personnel specially provided by a school, institution, or other place for the care and training of individuals with the same impairments, the costs of such care and training qualify as medical expenses under ITA 118.2(2)(e). It should be noted that the care need not be full-time to qualify. The person's mental or physical impairment may be certified in a letter or on Form T2201. Where an individual has received care and training in a school, institution or other place, a disability tax credit may be claimed in respect of the individual for the year (provided the conditions for the disability tax credit are otherwise met), in addition to the medical expense credit claim.

It is the CRA's view that a private home adapted to the needs of its owner/occupant would not qualify as an "other place" for these purposes (see VD 2007-0253621E5).

In VD 2006-0213231E5, the CRA states that:

> The student must be suffering from a physical or mental handicap, the severity of which is such that the student "requires" the equipment, facilities or personnel specially provided by the school, and not merely that the student will "benefit from" such equipment, facilities or personnel. An "appropriately qualified person" must certify that the above conditions are met with respect to the individual receiving the care or the care and training at that school. A medical practitioner, as well as any other person who has been given the required certification powers under provincial or federal law, may carry out this certification. The CRA must be satisfied the equipment, facilities or personnel provided by a particular school, meet the requirements outlined by the person who certified the need for those facilities. If all these conditions are met, the amount paid for the individual to attend the school may qualify as a medical expense, notwithstanding that some part of the amount paid could be viewed as tuition fees . . .

> The certificate should provide details on the nature of the individual's handicap and should explain why the equipment, facilities or the trained professionals at the school (or other institution) are required to provide the care and training that the individual needs. Further, the certification must clearly indicate that an "appropriately qualified person", who is fully informed as to the nature of the particular person's handicap, issued it.

Tuition fees for a taxpayer's child to attend a school for gifted children generally do not qualify (VD 2005-0115011E5), nor would tuition fees for driver training (VD 2007-0244411E5).

To qualify under ITA 118.2(2)(e), the Courts have found that the certification must specify the mental or physical handicap from which the patient suffers, and the equipment, facilities, or personnel that the patient requires in order to obtain the care or training needed to deal with that handicap: see *Title Estate v. R.*, [2001] 2 C.T.C. 226 (FCA) and *Lang v. R.*, 2009 CarswellNat 770 (TCC).

In *Scott v. R.*, [2009] 1 C.T.C. 224 ((FCA, reversing the TCC), the Court stated that "the fact that some of the services offered to the general student body were beneficial to the respondent's son and other students with special needs is insufficient to bring Rothesay [Collegiate School] within the ambit of [paragraph 118.2(2)(e)]". The Court also noted that "the school's focus is not on the provision of medical services and it does not specially provide equipment, facilities or personnel for the care of students with particular needs such as those of the respondent's son". A similar decision was made in *Vita-Finzi v. R.*, [2009] 2 C.T.C. 2378 (TCC).

Private school fees incurred for a child with behaviorial problems were held to be ineligible in *Somers v. MNR*, [1979] C.T.C. 2001 (TRB), since there was no evidence of mental or physical handicap, and the school in question was not an institution of the type specified. Also see *Flower v. R.*, [2005] 2 C.T.C. 2730 (TCC), in which fees to an Academy for children with learning disabilities did not qualify under ITA 118.2(2)(e). However, in *Rannelli v. MNR*, [1991] 2 C.T.C. 2040, the Court adopted an "object and spirit" approach in interpreting the word "care" and concluded that tuition and other fees paid to a school for dyslexic children should qualify as medical expenses.

In *McKinley v. R.*, [2004] 2 C.T.C. 2672 (TCC), the Court held that assisted living in a retirement community qualified for deduction under ITA 118.2(2)(e) (the taxpayer in the case was 88 years of age, legally blind, suffered from diabetes and dementia and, was unable to walk). However, in *Lister v. R.*, [2007] 1 C.T.C. 137 (FCA); leave to appeal to SCC denied 2007 CarswellNat 1229, assisted living in the same retirement community was found not to qualify, since the Court found that ITA 118.2(2)(e) contemplates institutional care. Amounts paid to a retirement home were also found not to qualify for the medical expense credit in *Shultis v. R.*, [2007] 1 C.T.C. 2182 (TCC); however, the Court stated that the expenses may have qualified "had the Appellant required the "safe unit" care" offered at the home.

ITA 118.2(2)(e), *Kushnir v. MNR*, [1986] 1 C.T.C. 2514 (TCC), *Marshall v. R.*, [2003] 4 C.T.C. 2794 (TCC), Folio S1-F1-C1 (paras. 1.56–1.63), Guide RC4064, Guide RC4065, VD 2005-0113121E5

¶10195.3 — *Transportation and Travel Expenses*

The cost of an ambulance to and from the hospital for a patient qualifies as a medical expense pursuant to ITA 118.2(2)(f).

ITA 118.2(2)(g) and (h) allow for certain transportation and travel expenses where an individual must travel some distance from home to obtain medical attention not available in the individual's locality. Provided that the medical services to be obtained are located at least 40 kilometres from the locality where the patient lives, the cost of transporting the patient and, in certain circumstances, one accompanying individual, may be treated as a medical expense pursuant to ITA 118.2(2)(g). In addition, where the medical services are located at least 80 kilometres from the patient's locality, reasonable travel expenses (in addition to transportation expenses) incurred in respect of the patient and, in certain circumstances, in respect of one accompanying individual, qualify as a medical expense pursuant to ITA 118.2(2)(h). For either of these provisions to apply, the following requirements must be met: (1) substantially equivalent medical services cannot be available in the locality where the patient lives; (2) the route travelled by the patient must be reasonably direct; and (3) it must be reasonable, having regard to the circumstances, that the patient travel to such place to obtain the medical services in question. However, it was CRA's view in VD 2008-0285981E5 that the requirements in ITA 118.2(2)(h) may be met even if medical services are available nearer to the individual's locality if, in the circumstances, it is reasonable for the individual to have travelled to the place where the medical services were obtained.

Although ITA 118.2(2)(g) refers to transportation provided by a person engaged in the business of providing transportation services (e.g., taxi, bus, or train), this requirement is waived by ITA 118.2(4), which provides that, where such transportation is not readily available, reasonable motor vehicle expenses can be claimed instead. The amount of vehicle expenses that may be claimed can be calculated using either the detailed or simplified method.

For transportation or travel expenses to qualify with respect to an accompanying individual, a qualified medical practitioner must certify in writing that the patient is incapable of travelling without the assistance of such an attendant. For a case in which this requirement was considered to have been met, even though the certification was not made until after the patient's travel, see *Revusky v The Queen*, [1997] 2 C.T.C. 2443 (TCC).

Other reasonable travel expenses (including meals, accommodation, and parking) incurred in respect of the patient's travel to and from the location where the medical services are provided are also eligible to be claimed as medical expenses. In addition, if a patient is an outpatient at a medical facility and is staying at a hotel, the patient can claim the cost of meals, accommodation, and parking. If the patient's medical practitioner certifies that the patient is incapable of travelling alone, the patient can also claim the cost of meals, accommodation, and parking of an accompanying individual (VD 2010-0353251M4).

ITA 118.2(2)(g), (h), *Young v. R.*, 2009 CarswellNat 4364 (TCC), *Patton v. R.*, [2006] 1 C.T.C. 2293 (TCC), Folio S1-F1-C1 (paras. 1.64–1.72), VDs 2007-0253261E5, 2007-0255831E5, 2004-0092971E5

¶10195.4 — *Artificial limbs, Aids, and Other Devices and Equipment*

ITA 118.2(2)(i) provides that expenditures "for, or in respect of" the following devices are eligible for the medical expense tax credit: an artificial limb, an iron lung, a rocking bed for polio victims, a wheelchair, crutches, a spinal brace, a brace for a limb, an iliostomy or colostomy pad, a truss for hernia, an artificial eye, a laryngeal speaking aid, an aid to hearing, an artificial kidney machine, phototherapy equipment for the treatment of psoriasis or other skin disorders, or an oxygen concentrator.

In addition, ITA 118.2(2)(i.1) provides that expenditures "for, or in respect of" the following devices for incontinence are eligible for the medical expense tax credit: diapers, disposable briefs, catheters, catheter trays, tubing or other products required by the patient by reason of incontinence caused by illness, injury or affliction.

Since these provisions refer to payments "in respect of" such items, payments for their rental, batteries for hearing aids, etc. would also be included (see paragraph 1.74 of Folio S1-F1-C1 and VD 2007-0251291I7). It is the CRA's view that the cost of an extended warranty for a hearing aid would be an amount paid in respect of an aid to hearing and, therefore, would also qualify for the medical expense tax credit (VD 2007-0247031E5).

118.2(2)(i), (i.1), Folio S1-F1-C1 (paras. 1.73–1.88)

¶10195.5 — *Vision Care*

Under ITA 118.2(2)(j), amounts paid for "eye glasses or other devices for the treatment or correction of a defect of vision" of a patient, as prescribed by a medical practitioner or optometrist, are eligible medical expenses.

According to paragraph 1.89 of Folio S1-F1-C1, contact lenses are included within the meaning of other devices. Prescription sunglasses would also generally qualify. However, the CRA has expressed the view that sunglasses purchased from a retail store that were prescribed by an optometrist to treat photosensitivity, which causes an individual to suffer from headaches caused by the sun or bright lighting, would not qualify for the credit (VD 2003-0046081E5). The CRA's opinion was that the glasses were "not prescribed by [the taxpayer's] optometrist for the treatment or correction of a defect of vision". The sunglasses in the particular situation were purchased from a retail story and were not prescription sunglasses.

Fees paid to a medical practitioner for eye exams and treatments, such as laser eye surgery, are also generally considered eligible medical expenses under ITA 118.2(2)(a) (see ¶10195.1).

ITA 118.2(2)(j), Folio S1-F1-C1 (para. 1.89)

¶10195.6 — *Oxygen, Insulin, and Injections for Pernicious Anaemia*

Under ITA 118.2(2)(k), the cost of buying or renting an oxygen tent or other equipment necessary to administer oxygen for medical purposes (including, for example, oxygen face masks, or tanks containing oxygen under pressure) is an eligible medical expense if prescribed by a medical practitioner for use by the patient. In addition, the cost of insulin, oxygen, liver extract injectible for pernicious anaemia, or vitamin B12 for pernicious anaemia for use by a patient is an eligible medical expense if these treatments are prescribed by a medical practitioner.

Although insulin substitutes are not covered under ITA 118.2(2)(k), they are generally considered drugs, medicaments, and other preparations or substances, the cost of which is an eligible medical expense under ITA 118.2(2)(n), provided the requirements under that provision are otherwise met (see ¶10195.12). Furthermore, when a patient with diabetes has to take sugar content tests using test tapes or test tablets and a medical practitioner has prescribed this diagnostic procedure, the tapes or tablets qualify as devices or equipment under ITA 118.2(2)(m) and ITR 5700 (see ¶10195.11). An amount paid by patients with diabetes for a scale to weigh themselves or their food is not an eligible medical expense.

ITA 118.2(2)(k), Folio S1-F1-C1 (paras. 1.90-1.91)

¶10195.7 — *Guide and Hearing Ear Dogs and Other Animals*

The cost of acquiring a service animal on behalf of an individual who is blind or profoundly deaf or who has severe autism, severe diabetes, severe epilepsy or a severe and prolonged impairment that markedly restricts the use of the individual's arms or legs, may be an eligible medical expense under ITA 118.2(2)(l). The cost of caring for and maintaining the animal, including food and veterinary care, as well as reasonable travel, board and lodging expenses incurred for full-time attendance at a facility that trains the individual in the handling of the animal, may also qualify as a medical expense.

Applicable to expenses incurred after 2017, ITA 118.2(2)(l) is expanded so that it also applies to the costs associated with animals that are specially trained to perform specific tasks for a person with a severe mental impairment to assist them in coping with the impairment (e.g., a psychiatric service dog trained to assist with PTSD). Note that expenses will only be eligible if they are in respect of an animal that has been specially trained to perform tasks that assist a patient with a severe mental impairment in coping with their impairment. Providing comfort or emotional support (such as by providing physical affection on command) is not such a task. Examples of tasks psychiatric service dogs could perform include: guiding a disoriented patient, searching the home of a patient with severe anxiety before they enter, and applying compression to a patient experiencing night terrors.

ITA 118.2(2)(l), Folio S1-F1-C1 (para. 1.92), tinyurl.com/cra-animals

¶10195.8 — *Bone Marrow or Organ Transplants*

Reasonable expenses, including legal fees and insurance premiums, of arranging and having a bone marrow or organ transplant qualify for purposes of the medical expenses credit.

Reasonable travel, board, and lodging expenses paid for the donor and the patient, in respect of the transplant, also qualify. The same types of expenses paid in respect of the transplant, for a person who accompanies the donor and for a person who accompanies the patient, are also eligible medical expenses. For these purposes, the option of using either the detailed or simplified method is available for calculating meal and vehicle expenses. For information on using the detailed or simplified method of calculating meal and vehicle expenses, see Guide T4044, *Employment Expenses*.

In *Zieber v. R.*, 2008 CarswellNat 1716 (TCC), the Court found that an embryo transplant constituted an "organ transplant".

ITA 118.2(2)(l.1), Folio S1-F1-C1 (para. 1.93)

¶10195.9 — *Home Alterations or Construction Costs*

Reasonable expenses relating to the construction of, or renovations or alterations to, the dwelling of a patient who either lacks normal physical development or who has a severe and prolonged mobility impairment, to enable the patient to gain access to, or to be mobile or functional within, the dwelling, qualify as eligible medical expenses, provided that such expenses: (1) are not of a type that would typically be expected to increase the value of the dwelling, and (2) are of a type that would not normally be incurred by persons who have normal physical development or who do not have a severe and prolonged mobility impairment.

See paragraphs 1.95 to 1.100 of Folio S1-F1-C1 for CRA's comments with respect to claiming home alterations or construction costs as a medical expense.

The installation of hardwood floors recommended for a patient who suffered from severe asthma was denied as a medical expense by the Court in *Hendricks v. R.*, 2008 CarswellNat 3091 (TCC), and the installation of a swimming pool for use by a patient who suffered from hemiplegia associated with brain damage was denied in *Barnes v. R.*, [2010] 1 C.T.C. 2009 (TCC). As well, an amount paid to add a bathroom to a home is not a qualifying home renovation cost where the addition of the bathroom increases the value of the home, or the cost would normally be expected to be incurred by a person without a disability. In *Chobotar v. R.*, 2009 CarswellNat 1308 (TCC), the credit was denied in respect of a specially designed bathroom for a person in a wheel chair because the addition of the bathroom increased the value of the home. In *Totten v. R.*, [2005] 3 C.T.C. 2061 (TCC), the Court found that renovation expenses incurred for the most part to meet future requirements of a patient (i.e., as the patient's condition became more serious), rather than immediate requirements, could qualify under ITA 118.2(1)(l.2).

Reasonable expenses relating to renovations or alterations to an RV that is used as a place of residence to enable the patient to gain access to the RV can qualify as a medical expense under ITA 118.2(1)(l.2) (VD 2005-0133691I7).

ITA 118.2(2)(l.2), (l.21), *Hillier v. The Queen*, [2000] 3 C.T.C. 2367 (TCC), Folio S1-F1-C1 (paras. 1.94–1.100), VDs 2009-0342581E5, 2007-0251071E5, 2007-0223571E5, 2007-0251071E5, 2006-0198081E5, 2005-0163161E5

¶10195.10 — *Various Miscellaneous Medical Expenses*

The following are additional enumerated miscellaneous expenses provided for in ITA 118.2(2)(l.3) to (l.91):

- *Lip Reading and Sign-Language Training*: Reasonable expenses relating to rehabilitative therapy, including training in lip reading and sign language, incurred to adjust for the patient's hearing or speech loss (ITA 118.2(2)(l.3), Folio S1-F1-C1, para. 1.101)

- *Sign-Language Services*: Sign language interpretation services or real-time captioning services paid on behalf of a patient who has a speech or hearing impairment, provided the fees are paid to a person engaged in the business of providing such services (ITA 118.2(2)(l.4), Folio S1-F1-C1, para. 1.102)

- *Note-Taking Services*: Amounts paid for note-taking services on behalf of a patient who has a mental or physical impairment, provided the patient has been certified in writing by a medical practitioner to be a person who requires such services because of that impairment, and the payment is made to a person in the business of providing such services (ITA 118.2(2)(l.41); Folio S1-F1-C1, para. 1.103)

- *Voice Recognition Software*: The cost of voice recognition software acquired for use by a patient who has a physical impairment, provided the patient has been certified in writing by a medical practitioner to be a person who requires the software because of the impairment (ITA 118.2(2)(l.42), Folio S1-F1-C1, para. 1.104)

- *Reading Services*: An amount paid for reading services for a patient who is blind or who has a severe learning disability, provided the payment is made to a person in the business of providing such services, and the patient has been certified in writing by a medical practitioner to be a person who requires such services because of the impairment (ITA 118.2(2)(l.43), Folio S1-F1-C1, para. 1.105)

- *Deaf-Blind Intervening Services*: Amounts paid for blind-deaf intervening services for a patient who is blind and profoundly deaf are eligible medical expenses if the payment is made to a person in the business of providing such services (ITA 118.2(2)(l.44), Folio S1-F1-C1, para. 1.106)

- *Moving Expenses*: Reasonable moving expenses (excluding those already deducted as moving expenses in any taxation year), up to a maximum of $2,000, to move a patient who lacks normal physical development or has a severe and prolonged mobility impairment, to a dwelling that is more accessible by the patient, or in which the patient is more mobile or functional (ITA 118.2(2)(l.5), ITA 62(3)"moving expenses", Folio S1-F1-C1, para. 1.107)

- *Driveway Alterations*: Reasonable expenses relating to alterations to the driveway of the principal place of residence of a patient who has a severe and prolonged mobility impairment, provided the alterations are made to facilitate the individual's access to a bus. Paragraph 1.108 of Folio S1-F1-C1 indicates that reasonable expenses relating to the alteration of a driveway would also qualify under this provision if they facilitate access to whatever mode of transportation, bus or otherwise, that is ordinarily used by the patient (ITA 118.2(2)(l.6), Folio S1-F1-C1, para. 1.108)

- *Van for Wheelchair*: The amount equal to 20 percent of the cost of a van (up to a maximum of $5,000) that, at the time of its acquisition or within 6 months thereafter, has been adapted for the transportation of an individual who requires the use of a wheelchair. Expenses related to the operation of the van, rather than to costs incurred for the acquisition or adaptation of the van are not eligible (ITA 118.2(2)(l.7), Folio S1-F1-C1, paras. 1.109–1.112; *Scully v. R.*, [2009] 2 C.T.C. 2225 (TCC))

- *Caregiver Training*: Remuneration paid for therapy provided by a person other than a qualified therapist or medical practitioner, due to the patient's severe and prolonged impairment, can be claimed as an eligible medical expense, provided the following conditions are met: (1) the patient qualifies for the disability tax credit for the year; (2) the therapy is prescribed by, and administered under the general supervision of, a medical doctor, nurse practitioner or psychologist in the case of a mental impairment, or a medical doctor, nurse practitioner or occupational therapist in the case of a physical impairment; (3) the payee is neither the individual's spouse or common-law partner, nor an individual who is under 18 years of age; and (4) receipts must be issued proving payment of the remuneration, and contain the payee's social insurance number, where the payee is an individual (ITA 118.2(2)(l.8), Folio S1-F1-C1, paras. 1.113-1.114)

- *Therapy for Disabled Person*: Remuneration paid for therapy provided by a person other than a qualified therapist or medical practitioner, due to the patient's severe and prolonged impairment, can be claimed as an eligible medical expense, provided the following conditions are met: (1) the patient qualifies for the disability tax credit for the year; (2) the therapy is prescribed by, and administered under the general supervision of, a medical doctor or a psychologist in the case of a mental impairment, or a medical doctor or an occupational therapist in the case of a physical impairment; (3) the payee is neither the individual's spouse or common-law partner, nor an individual who is under 18 years of age; and (4) receipts must be issued proving payment of the remuneration, and contain the payee's social insurance number, where the payee is an individual (ITA 118.2(2)(l.9), Folio S1-F1-C1, paras. 1.115-1.116)

- *Tutoring Services*: Eligible medical expenses may include amounts paid as remuneration for tutoring services provided to a patient where the following conditions are satisfied: the tutoring is supplementary to the primary education of the patient; the patient has a learning disability or a mental impairment; a medical practitioner has certified in writing that the patient requires the tutoring services because of that disability or impairment; and the payment must be made to a person ordinarily engaged in the business of providing tutoring services to persons who are not related to the payee (ITA 118.2(2)(l.91), Folio S1-F1-C1, para. 1.117, *Hoare v. R.*, [2007] 4 C.T.C. 2283 (TCC))

- *Design of Therapy Plan*: Remuneration paid for the design of an individualized therapy plan can be claimed as a medical expense if: (1) the therapy set out in the plan is prescribed by and, if undertaken, administered under the general supervision of a medical doctor, nurse practitioner or occupational therapist (or, in the case of a mental impairment, a medical doctor, nurse practitioner or psychologist); (2) an individualized therapy plan is required to access public funding for specialized therapy, or a medical doctor, nurse practitioner or occupational therapist (or, in the case of a mental impairment, a medical doctor, nurse practitioner or psychologist) prescribes an individualized therapy plan; (3) the plan is designed for an individual with a severe and prolonged mental or physical impairment who is, because of the impairment, eligible for the disability tax credit; and (4) the amounts are paid to persons ordinarily engaged in the business of providing such services to unrelated individuals (ITA 118.2(2)(l.92), Folio S1-F1-C1, para. 1.117.1)

¶10195.11 — Prescribed Devices and Equipment

Under ITA 118.2(2)(m), eligible medical expenses include amounts paid for devices or equipment for use by a patient, where the device or equipment is prescribed by a medical practitioner, is specified by ITR 5700, meets the conditions set out in ITR 5700 applicable to its use or the reason for its acquisition, and is not described in any other paragraphs of ITA 118.2(2). The device or equipment does not need to be purchased new in order to be eligible for the credit. Whether purchased new or used, the amount that may be claimed is the amount actually paid to acquire the device, up to any maximum amount specified. Reasonable servicing and repair costs related to the devices and equipment are also generally considered to be eligible medical expenses.

Devices and equipment that are prescribed for these purposes of ITA 118.2(2)(m) are set out in ITR 5700 as follows:

(a) a wig made to order for an individual who has suffered abnormal hair loss owing to disease, medical treatment or accident;

(b) a needle or syringe designed to be used for the purpose of giving an injection;

(c) a device or equipment, including a replacement part, designed exclusively for use by an individual suffering from a severe chronic respiratory ailment or a severe chronic immune system disregulation, but not including an air conditioner, humidifier, dehumidifier, heat pump or heat or air exchanger;

(c.1) an air or water filter or purifier for use by an individual who is suffering from a severe chronic respiratory ailment or a severe chronic immune system disregulation to cope with or overcome that ailment or disregulation;

(c.2) an electric or sealed combustion furnace acquired to replace a furnace that is neither an electric furnace nor a sealed combustion furnace, where the replacement is necessary solely because of a severe chronic respiratory ailment or a severe chronic immune system disregulation;

(c.3) an air conditioner acquired for use by an individual to cope with the individual's severe chronic ailment, disease or disorder, to the extent of the lesser of $1,000 and 50% of the amount paid for the air conditioner;

(d) a device or equipment designed to pace or monitor the heart of an individual who suffers from heart disease;

(e) an orthopaedic shoe or boot or an insert for a shoe or boot made to order for an individual in accordance with a prescription to overcome a physical disability of the individual;

(f) a power-operated guided chair installation, for an individual, that is designed to be used solely in a stairway;

(g) a mechanical device or equipment designed to be used to assist an individual to enter or leave a bathtub or shower or to get on or off a toilet;

(h) a hospital bed including such attachments thereto as may have been included in a prescription therefor;

(i) a device that is exclusively designed to assist an individual in walking where the individual has a mobility impairment;

(j) an external breast prosthesis that is required because of a mastectomy;

(k) a teletypewriter or similar device, including a telephone ringing indicator, that enables a deaf or mute individual to make and receive telephone calls;

(l) an optical scanner or similar device designed to be used by a blind individual to enable him to read print;

(l.1) a device or software designed to be used by a blind individual, or an individual with a severe learning disability, to enable the individual to read print;

(m) a power-operated lift or transportation equipment designed exclusively for use by, or for, a disabled individual to allow the individual access to different areas of a building or to assist the individual to gain access to a vehicle or to place the individual's wheelchair in or on a vehicle;

(n) a device designed exclusively to enable an individual with a mobility impairment to operate a vehicle;

(o) a device or equipment, including a synthetic speech system, braille printer and large print-on-screen device, designed exclusively to be used by a blind individual in the operation of a computer;

(p) an electronic speech synthesizer that enables a mute individual to communicate by use of a portable keyboard;

(q) a device to decode special television signals to permit the script of a program to be visually displayed;

(q.1) a visual or vibratory signalling device, including a visual fire alarm indicator, for an individual with a hearing impairment;

(r) a device designed to be attached to infants diagnosed as being prone to sudden infant death syndrome in order to sound an alarm if the infant ceases to breathe;

(s) an infusion pump, including disposable peripherals, used in the treatment of diabetes or a device designed to enable a diabetic to measure the diabetic's blood sugar level;

(s.1) a blood coagulation monitor, including disposable peripherals, for use by an individual who requires anti-coagulation therapy;

(t) an electronic or computerized environmental control system designed exclusively for the use of an individual with a severe and prolonged mobility restriction;

(u) an extremity pump or elastic support hose designed exclusively to relieve swelling caused by chronic lymphedema;

(v) an inductive coupling osteogenesis stimulator for treating non-union of fractures or aiding in bone fusion;

(w) a talking textbook for use by an individual with a perceptual disability in connection with the individual's enrolment at an educational institution in Canada, or a designated educational institution;

(x) a Bliss symbol board, or similar device, designed to be used to help an individual who has a speech impairment communicate by selecting the symbols or spelling out words;

(y) a Braille note-taker designed to be used by a blind individual to allow them to take notes (that can be read back to them or printed or displayed in Braille) with the help of a keyboard;

(z) a page turner, designed to be used by an individual who has a severe and prolonged impairment that markedly restricts their ability to use their arms or hands to turn the pages of a book or other bound document;

(z.1) an altered auditory feedback device designed to be used by an individual who has a speech impairment;

(z.2) an electrotherapy device designed to be used by an individual with a medical condition or by an individual who has a severe mobility impairment;

(z.3) a standing device designed to be used by an individual who has a severe mobility impairment to undertake standing therapy; and

(z.4) a pressure pulse therapy device designed to be used by an individual who has a balance disorder.

The CRA has provided the following views with respect to prescribed devices and equipment (also see the Medical Expenses Credit Quick Reference Table in Appendix A): if an air exchanger and air purifier are separate units such that each may be purchased separately, only the cost of the air purifier may qualify under ITR 5700(c.1) (VD 2002-0140205); where a television contains a closed-caption decoder, the cost of the decoder chip may qualify (VD 2004-0068651I7); an electric breast pump does not qualify (VD 2007-0248701E5); the cost of electricity used to operate an air conditioner does not qualify (VD 2007-0251291I7); a water softener may be considered a water filter or purifier for purposes of ITR 5700(c.1) (VD 2007-0255191E5); an RIK Fluid Overlay mattress does not qualify (VD 2009-0318231E5); and a whole body vibration unit may qualify under ITR 5700(z.3) (VD 2010-0358821E5).

ITA 118.2(2)(m), ITR 5700, Folio S1-F1-C1 (paras. 1.118–1.122), *Mattinson v. R.*, [2008] 5 C.T.C. 2229 (TCC) ("lifeline" emergency response alarm does not qualify), *Reid*, 2008 CarswellNat 2069 (TCC) ("Ceragem massager bed" does not qualify), *Crockart v. R.*, [1999] 2 C.T.C. 2409 (TCC) (Slumberland adjustable bed qualifies); *Vucurevich v. R.*, [2000] 1 C.T.C. 3044 (TCC) (redesigning a bed to be a hospital bed qualifies); *T. Preugschas v. R.*, [2005] 5 C.T.C. 2315 (TCC)

¶10195.12 — *Drugs, Medicaments, and Other Preparations or Substances*

Generally, amounts paid for drugs, medicaments, or other preparations or substances are eligible medical expenses under ITA 118.2(2)(n)(i), provided that the drug is manufactured, sold, or represented for use in the diagnosis, treatment, or prevention of a disease, disorder or abnormal physical state, or its symptoms, or in restoring, correcting, or modifying an organic function. The drug can only be lawfully acquired if it is prescribed by a medical practitioner or dentist for use by the patient, and the purchase of the drug is recorded by a pharmacist. Generally, the costs of drugs that can be acquired without a prescription do not qualify as medical expenses, even if prescribed by a medical practitioner or dentist.

The cost of over-the-counter products such as vitamins, herbs, and low-dose aspirin will generally not qualify as a medical expense, even where a prescription has been obtained from a medical practitioner, as these products can be lawfully acquired without a prescription and do not require the intervention of a medical practitioner to be lawfully acquired.

The cost of insulin substitutes, prescribed by a medical practitioner for use by a patient, is an eligible medical expense under ITA 118.2(2)(n), provided the conditions are otherwise met. As well, the cost of insulin prescribed by a medical practitioner for use by a patient is an eligible medical expense under ITA 118.2(2)(k) (see ¶10195.6). Birth control pills prescribed by a medical practitioner for use by a patient are eligible medical expenses, provided the conditions are otherwise met.

In *Bentley v. R.*, 2009 CarswellNat 1518 (TCC), the Court found that while a patient appeared to benefit from naturopathic medicines, the requirements of ITA 118.2(2)(n) were not met, as the naturopathic medicines bought at a naturopath's office were not dispensed by a licensed pharmacist.

Amounts paid to a medical doctor, nurse practitioner or public or licensed private hospital for medical assistance to lawfully end an individual's life as outlined in the *Criminal Code*, including the cost of medicaments or other preparations or substances used to lawfully end an individual's life, are considered an eligible medical expense for purposes of the medical expense tax credit (VD 2017-0703891C6).

118.2(2)(n), ITR 5701, Folio S1-F1-C1 (paras. 1.123–1.127)

¶10195.13 — *Preventive, Diagnostic, and Other Treatments*

Eligible medical expenses under ITA 118.2(2)(o) include the cost of laboratory, radiological, and other diagnostic procedures or services, with necessary interpretations, for maintaining health, preventing disease, or assisting in the diagnosis or treatment of any injury, illness or disability of the patient. The procedures or services must be prescribed by a medical practitioner or dentist for their costs to qualify as medical expenses. The reference to other diagnostic procedures or services is generally limited to diagnostic services or procedures of the same class as laboratory or radiological services. That is, the procedures or services must assist a medical practitioner or dentist in making a diagnosis and formulating a course of treatment (where the medical practitioner or dentist determines it is appropriate to do so).

Examples of expenses that may fall under ITA 118.2(2)(o) include the following expenses involved with artificial insemination: the in-vitro fertilization procedure, daily ultrasound and blood tests once the in-vitro procedure has begun, anaesthetist fees, and cycle monitoring fees.

There are costs associated with a number of procedures or treatments that may be considered to be for maintaining health, preventing disease, or assisting in the diagnosis or treatment of any injury, illness or disability of a patient, but are not generally considered eligible medical expenses under ITA 118.2(2)(o) because they are not laboratory, radiological, or other diagnostic procedures or services; however, they may be eligible medical expenses under other paragraphs of ITA 118.2(2). For example, the cost of a hot tub or whirlpool treatment, prescribed by a medical practitioner and paid to a public or licensed private hospital or a medical practitioner is generally an eligible medical expense under ITA 118.2(2)(a); however, the cost of purchasing a hot tub or whirlpool bath is not an eligible medical expense as it is not prescribed in ITR 5700. The cost of acupuncture treatments may be eligible medical expenses under ITA 118.2(2)(a) where the acupuncture treatments are provided by, and paid to, a medical practitioner.

¶10195.14 — *Dentures*

Under ITA 118.2(2)(p), amounts paid to a dental mechanic, denturist, or denturologist, who is authorized under the laws of a province to make or repair dentures or to otherwise carry on the business of a dental mechanic, are eligible medical expenses. The provision covers amounts paid for the making or repairing of an upper or lower denture, or for the taking of impressions, bite registrations, and insertions in respect of the making, producing, constructing, and furnishing of an upper or lower denture for the patient. Where a denture is prescribed and fitted by a dentist, even though it may have been made in a dental laboratory, the payment is an eligible medical expense under ITA 118.2(2)(a) as an amount paid to a dentist.

¶10195.15 — *Premiums Paid to Private Health Services Plans (PHSP)*

Basic hospital care in Canada is generally available under the various provincial hospitalization plans and, to that extent, cannot enter into a claim for medical expenses. However, if extra services are provided (such as for a private room), which must be paid for by the taxpayer, such costs will qualify as medical expenses, unless the taxpayer is entitled to reimbursement under a private insurance plan. Hospital costs incurred outside Canada would also qualify, unless the taxpayer is entitled to reimbursement under either a provincial hospital plan or a private hospital insurance contract.

Premiums or other contributions paid by the individual under a private (i.e., non-governmental) hospital, medical, or dental insurance contract may be claimed as medical expenses. However, an otherwise eligible medical expense for which the taxpayer, the patient, any person related to either of them, or the legal representative of any of the above is entitled to receive a reimbursement under such an insurance scheme (or under a public medical insurance plan) will not normally qualify as an eligible medical expense (see, for example, VD 2007-0254811R3). Effective January 1, 2015, the CRA considers that a plan is a PHSP as long as all or substantially all (i.e., 90% or more) of the premiums paid under the plan relate to medical expenses that are eligible for the medical expense tax credit. The plan must also meet all other conditions as outlined in paragraph 3 of IT-339R2, *Meaning of private health services plan*. The CRA's position before 2015 was that all medical expenses covered under a plan had to be eligible for the medical expense tax credit for the plan to qualify as a PHSP.

For an insurance premium to be deductible, the contract must relate to the individual, or the spouse or common-law partner, or any members of the household with whom the individual is connected by blood relationship, marriage, common-law partnership, or adoption. A premium or other contribution may not be included as a medical expense to the extent that it is deducted in computing an individual's income from a business for any taxation year.

Specifically excluded from the definition of a "private health services plan" is a health care plan which is operated by a provincial government but which receives federal funding, and a federal hospital or medical care plan for the benefit of government employees outside Canada and their families. Thus, premiums paid by a taxpayer under any of the provincial hospital or medical care plans may not be claimed as a medical expense. However, to the extent that medical costs are not completely covered by a provincial hospital plan — for example, where a province allows hospital "user fees" to be charged to a patient covered by a plan, or allows physicians to bill patients amounts in excess of their fees for services covered by a provincial plan — such excess billing to a patient would generally qualify as a deductible medical expense.

> It is the CRA's view that the Ontario Health Premium does not qualify as an eligible medical expense under ITA 118.2(2)(q) as it is considered a tax imposed under Ontario's *Taxation Act, 2007.*

ITA 118.2(2)(q), 118.2(3)(b), IT-339R2, Folio S1-F1-C1 (paras. 1.133–1.135)

¶10195.16 — *Gluten-Free Food*

ITA 118.2(2)(r) includes as a qualifying medical expense an amount paid on behalf of a patient who has celiac disease for the incremental cost of acquiring gluten-free food products as compared to comparable non-gluten-free food products, provided the patient has been certified in writing by a medical practitioner to be a person who requires a gluten-free diet because of celiac disease.

ITA 118.2(2)(r), Folio S1-F1-C1 (para. 1.136)

¶10195.17 — *Drugs and Medical Devices Not Yet Approved for Sale*

ITA 118.2(2)(s) includes as a qualifying medical expense drugs purchased for use by a patient that are obtained under Health Canada's Special Access Programme in accordance with sections C.08.010 and C.08.011 of the *Food and Drug Regulations*. Additionally, ITA 118.2(2)(t) includes as a qualifying medical expense medical devices purchased for use by a patient that are obtained under Health Canada's Special Access Programme in accordance with Part 2 of the *Medical Devices Regulations*. According to the Supplementary Information (Annex 8) to the 2005 Federal Budget (2005-3), in certain circumstances Health Canada's Special Access Programme allows access to drugs and devices that have not yet been approved for sale in Canada.

ITA 118.2(2)(s), (t), Folio S1-F1-C1 (para. 1.138)

¶10195.18 — *Medical Marihuana*

If a patient is authorized to possess marihuana or cannabis for medical purposes under the *Access to Cannabis for Medical Purposes Regulations* or section 56 of the *Controlled Drugs and Substances Act*, the cost of the medical marihuana plants or seeds, cannabis or cannabis oil may qualify as a medical expense under ITA 118.2(2)(u). In order for its cost to qualify as a medical expense, the medical marihuana/cannabis must be purchased from either: Health Canada; or an individual who possesses, on behalf of that patient, a designated-person production license to produce marihuana/cannabis under the *Access to Cannabis for Medical Purposes Regulations* or an exemption for cultivation or production under section 56 of the *Controlled Drugs and Substances Act*.

The cost of marihuana seeds will only qualify as a medical expense if purchased from Health Canada. None of the costs related to growing the medical marihuana from seed (other than the cost of the seeds as discussed above) are included under ITA 118.2(2)(u).

ITA 118.2(2)(u), Folio S1-F1-C1 (paras. 1.139–1.142)

¶10195.19 — *Fees Paid for Cosmetic Procedures*

Pursuant to ITA 118.2(2.1), medical expenses do not include amounts paid for medical or dental services, nor any related expenses, provided purely for cosmetic purposes unless necessary for medical or reconstructive purposes.

The CRA provides the following comments in paragraphs 1.43 to 1.46 of Folio S1-F1-C1 regarding cosmetic procedures:

1.143 An amount that may otherwise be an eligible medical expense described under subsection 118.2(2) may be denied pursuant to subsection 118.2(2.1) if the service was provided purely for cosmetic purposes. In particular, subsection 118.2(2.1) excludes from eligible medical expenses, an amount paid for medical or dental services (including any related expenses), which are provided purely for cosmetic purposes. Cosmetic procedures that are necessary for medical or reconstructive purposes will not be denied under subsection 118.2(2.1).

1.144 It is a question of fact whether a particular service or procedure was provided purely for cosmetic purposes, and the onus is on the individual claiming the credit to substantiate that a particular expense is not subject to this provision. Thus, where a particular medical procedure or service is cosmetic in nature, taxpayers may wish to obtain a detailed description of the nature and purpose of the medical service from the authorized medical practitioner performing the service as a means of establishing that subsection 118.2(2.1) does not apply.

1.145 Procedures that would generally be considered to have a medical or reconstructive purpose include those that would ameliorate a deformity arising from, or directly related to, a congenital abnormality, a personal injury resulting from an accident or trauma, or a disfiguring disease. Some common procedures, which are not disallowed by subsection 118.2(2.1) are: breast implant and related procedures for reconstructive purposes after a mastectomy; hair removal, in limited circumstances, such as for persons with polycystic ovarian syndrome; and removal of excess skin after rapid weight loss due to a risk of infection.

1.146 Common procedures the costs of which are generally not considered to be eligible medical expenses because of the application of subsection 118.2(2.1) include: augmentations (such as chin, cheek, lips); filler injections (for removal of wrinkles); liposuction; and teeth whitening.

Cosmetic procedures generally include surgical and non-surgical procedures purely aimed at enhancing one's appearance (e.g., liposuction, hair replacement procedures, botox injections, and teeth whitening). The CRA has stated that corrective laser eye surgery and dental crowns will qualify as medical expenses (VD 2010-0362981M4).

118.2(2)(a), 118.2(2.1), VD 2010-0358421E5

¶10195.20 — *Fertility Expenses*

Applicable for 2017 and later taxation years, ITA 118.2(2.2) deems an amount to be a qualifying medical expense for the purposes of the medical expense tax credit if it:

- is paid for the purpose of an individual conceiving a child; and

- would be a medical expense, within the meaning of ITA 118.2(2), if the individual were incapable of conceiving a child because of a medical condition.

Generally, this new provision allows certain amounts paid for fertility treatments for the purpose of an individual conceiving a child to qualify as medical expenses for the medical expense tax credit where the individual does not have an existing illness or condition (such as the medical condition of infertility), but nonetheless requires medical intervention to conceive a child, and the amount would already qualify as a medical expense under ITA 118.2(2) in respect of a person with a medical condition.

CRA provides the following answers to frequently asked questions regarding this new provision:

1. What is the proposed change to the METC?

For 2017 and subsequent tax years, Budget 2017 proposes to clarify the application of the METC so that an amount will be considered a medical expense if the amount is paid for the purpose of conceiving a child and would be a medical expense if the person were incapable of conceiving a child because of a medical condition.

2. What eligible expenses can I include in the calculation of the METC as a result of the proposed change?

Generally the cost of medical services, drugs, and lab tests will be included in the calculation of the METC for an individual receiving treatment to conceive a child, such as in vitro fertilization. For more information refer to Lines 330 and 331-Eligible medical expenses you can claim on your tax return.

3. Will I be able to include the fees I paid for the services of a surrogate mother in the calculation of the METC?

No. The METC is generally not available to cover fees for the services of a surrogate mother.

4. If I am a surrogate mother, will I be able to include my eligible expenses incurred for the use of reproductive technologies in the calculation of the METC?

Yes. Refer to question 2.

5. I have already incurred expenses for the use of reproductive technologies but have not claimed them in my return. Will this proposed change allow me to claim these expenses?

Yes, under the proposed legislation, you will be able to make a request for an adjustment because of these eligible medical expenses for a prior year. The CRA will consider your request only if it relates to a tax return for any of the 10 calendar years before the year in which you make your request. For example, your request made in 2017 must relate to a tax return for 2007 or later. You can request an adjustment by filing a T1 Adjustment request or by requesting the change directly using My Account.

ITA 118.2(2.2)

¶10200 — Medical Expenses for Other Dependants (T1 Schedule 1: Line 331)

In addition to claiming medical expenses on Line 330 for themselves, a spouse or common-law partner, and for dependent children under age 18, individuals may also claim eligible medical expenses on Line 331 in respect of other dependants, where the dependant is a person who at any time in the year is dependent upon the individual for support, and is:

- a child (who has attained the age of 18 years before the end of the taxation year) or grandchild of the individual, or his or her spouse or common-law partner; or

- a parent, grandparent, brother, sister, aunt, uncle, niece, or nephew of the individual or his or her spouse or common-law partner, and who is a resident of Canada at some time in the year.

Whether a person is dependent upon the individual for support is a question of fact. Generally, a person is considered to be dependent on someone for support if the individual has actually supplied necessary maintenance, or the basic necessities of life (food, shelter and clothing) on a regular and consistent basis. This support may be given voluntarily or pursuant to a legal commitment. Where the dependent person was in receipt of social assistance or any other type of financial or non-financial support, the supporting individual must be able to show that the other assistance was insufficient to fully meet the basic needs of the dependant, and that the person had to rely on the additional support provided by the supporting individual.

The expenses must meet the same criteria as those claimed on Line 330, and the claim must be for the same 12-month period that was used for Line 330 (see under ¶10190). Calculate the medical expenses claimed on this line individually for each dependent. For the 2018 taxation year, the amount of the medical expense credit in respect of dependent relatives is reduced by the lesser of $2,302 and 3 percent of the dependant's income for the year (Line 236). This means that in order to claim a dependent's medical expenses for the 2018 taxation year, the total of the dependent's expenses must exceed the lesser of $2,302 or 3 percent of the dependant's net income for the year. There is no upper limit on the claim for a dependent person's medical expenses.

ITA 118(6), 252, Folio S1-F1-C1 (paras. 1.4–1.7)

¶10210 — Donations and Gifts (T1 Schedule 1: Line 349)

Individuals are entitled to a federal non-refundable tax credit of 15% on the first $200 of charitable donations. For donations over $200 made in 2016 and later taxation years, the rate is 33% to the extent that an individual has taxable income taxed at 33% (i.e., taxable income over $205,842 for 2018). If the individual has taxable income in 2018 of less than $205,842, the rate for donations over $200 is 29%. Donations made in taxation years before 2016 and carried forward and claimed in 2017 or a later year will not be eligible for the 33% tax rate.

The maximum annual claim for charitable donations is 75% of net income for the year. Donations that are made in the year of death may, to the extent that amounts in respect of such donations are not deducted in computing the individual's tax payable for that year, be carried back to the immediately preceding taxation year. In the year of death and in the immediately preceding year, the donation limit increases to 100% of net income.

Applicable for 2016 and later taxation years, donations made by will and donations made by designation under an RRSP, RRIF, TFSA or life insurance policy are no longer deemed to be made by an individual immediately before the individual's death. Instead, these donations are deemed to have been made by the individual's estate at the time at which the property that is the subject of the donation is transferred to a qualified donee, provided that the transfer occurs within 36 months after death. In addition, the trustee of the individual's estate is permitted to allocate the available donation among any of: (1) the taxation year of the estate in which the donation is made; (2) an earlier taxation year of the estate; or (3) the last two taxation years of the individual. An estate will still be able to claim a charitable donations tax credit in respect of other donations in the year in which the donation is made or in any of the five following years.

A taxpayer is permitted a donation tax credit for total charitable donations made during the year to a "qualified donee", which is defined in ITA 149.1(1) as a person that is:

- a registered Canadian charity (which includes charitable organizations and private and public foundations);

- a registered Canadian amateur athletic association;

- the Government of Canada or a province, the United Nations or an agency of the UN;

- registered by the Minister and that is:

  - a Canadian resident housing corporation that is exempt from tax under ITA 149(1)(i);

  - a municipality in Canada;

  - a municipal or public body performing a function of government in Canada that has applied for registration;

  - applicable before February 27, 2018, a university outside Canada that is prescribed to be a university, the student body of which ordinarily includes students from Canada (prescribed in ITR Schedule VIII);

  - applicable after February 26, 2018, a university outside Canada, the student body of which ordinarily includes students from Canada, that has applied for registration (note that any university listed in ITR Schedule VIII as of February 26, 2018 is deemed to have applied for registration); and

• a foreign charity to which the Government of Canada has made a gift in either 2017 or 2018.

For a current listing of universities outside Canada that are registered as qualified donees, see: tinyurl.com/cra-univs. Also see "Universities Outside Canada" at: tinyurl.com/cra-foreign-univs and CRA Information Sheet RC191, *Qualified Donee: Becoming a Prescribed University Outside Canada.*

¶10211 — *Calculation of Charitable Donation Tax Credit*

The credit available to an individual in determining tax payable in respect of total gifts made is computed by the following formula in ITA 118.1(3) for 2016 and later taxation years:

$$A \times B + C \times D + E \times F$$

where:

A = the "appropriate percentage" for the year (i.e., 15%)

B = the lesser of $200 and the individual's total gifts for the year

C = the "highest individual percentage" for the year (i.e., 33%)

D the lesser of (i) the amount, if any, by which the individual's total gifts for the year exceeds $200, and (ii) the amount, if any, by which the individual's taxable income for the year exceeds the first dollar amount for the year referred to in ITA 117(2)(e) ($205,842 for 2018)

E 29%; and

F the amount, if any, by which the individual's total gifts for the year exceeds the total of $200 and the amount determined for D.

For 2016 and later taxation years, the formula in ITA 118.1(3) was amended consequential to the introduction of a new top personal income tax rate ("the highest individual percentage") in ITA 117(2). The highest individual percentage is 33% for 2016 and later taxation years. ITA 118.1(3) applies a tax credit rate equal to the highest individual percentage of 33%, to the extent that the individual's total gifts for the year exceed $200, and to the extent that the individual has income that is subject to the top marginal tax rate.

Donations up to and including $200 will continue to receive the 15% credit rate. Donations in excess of $200 will qualify for the 29% credit rate, except to the extent that the 33% credit rate applies; and will receive the 33% credit rate on the lesser of the amount of those donations and the donor's taxable income in excess of $205,842. For example, if a taxpayer had $225,842 in taxable income and donations of $10,000, a 33% rate will be applied on the full amount of the donation above the first $200 (i.e., $9,800). However, if the individual donated $30,000, the 33% rate will be applied on $20,000 (15% applies to the first $200, and 29% applies to the remaining $9,800).

¶10211.1 — *First-Time Donor's Super Credit*

For donations made after March 20, 2013, qualifying first-time donors were eligible to receive an additional federal tax credit of 25 percent on the first $1,000 of monetary donations, over and above the normal donation tax credit as calculated above. The first-time donor's super credit could be claimed once from the 2013 to 2017 taxation years.

¶10211.2 — *Donation Carry-Forward*

The amount creditable in any year in respect of charitable donations is limited to the taxpayer's total gifts. However, charitable donations which are not claimed in a taxation year may be carried forward and claimed in the five immediately following years, as long as the sum of the amount carried forward to a subsequent year plus the amount of the taxpayer's charitable donations for that subsequent year does not exceed 75 percent of the taxpayer's income for that year. There is an ordering rule that requires tax credits in respect of gifts to be claimed in the order in which the gifts were made. This means that an individual may not claim the tax credit for a gift made in the current year until all credits in respect of gifts made in previous years have been claimed.

ITA 118.1(1), 118.1(3)

¶10212 — Meaning of a "Gift"

¶10212.1 — Common Law

The Courts have generally found that where consideration is received in respect of a transfer of property, the transfer does not constitute a gift even if there is a clear gift element and donative intent. In other words, to constitute a "gift", the property transferred must be transferred voluntarily and without consideration — i.e., the "donor" cannot by way of return receive any advantage of a material character (see *Woolner*, [2000] 1 C.T.C. 35 (FCA) and *Zandstra*, [1974] C.T.C. 503 (FCTD)).

In *Tite*, [1986] 2 C.T.C. 2343, the Tax Court found that it was not possible to make a "gift" for purposes of the donation tax credit if some valuable consideration such as goods or services was received in return. More recently, in *Maréchaux v. R.*, [2011] 2 C.T.C. 77 (FCA) (leave to appeal to SCC denied), the taxpayer participated in a "leveraged donation" program in which he received a charitable donation receipt for $100,000 based on a cash payment of $30,000. The Federal Court of Appeal upheld the Tax Court's ruling disallowing the taxpayer's donation tax credit on the basis that he had not made a "gift" within the meaning of ITA 118.1 because he made the payment to the foundation expecting to receive, and did receive, a significant benefit of an interest-free loan of $80,000 repayable in 20 years. The Court reached the same conclusion in *Kossow v. R.*, [2014] 2 C.T.C. 1 (FCA) (leave to appeal to SCC denied), which also dealt with a taxpayer being denied charitable donation credits in connection with her involvement in a leveraged donation program. In affirming the Tax Court's decision, the Court of Appeal stated that the TCC judge committed no error in finding that interest-free loans constitute a benefit to donors "whether the benefit comes from the donee or another person". Similarly, in *Berg v. R.*, 2014 CarswellNat 136 (FCA, reversing the TCC), the Court of Appeal denied the taxpayer a donation tax credit where the taxpayer purchased timeshare units for which 90% of the purchase price came from a promissory note, because it was the court's view that the taxpayer intended to profit from the deal and thus did not have the requisite donative intent required under ITA 118.1.

The CRA provides the following comments regarding the meaning of the term gift in Folio S7-F1-C1, *Split-receipting and Deemed Fair Market Value*:

> 1.2 Under the common law, "a gift is a voluntary transfer of property owned by a donor to a donee, in return for which no benefit or consideration flows to the donor" (*The Queen v Friedberg*, [1992] 1 C.T.C. 1, 92 D.T.C. 6031 (FCA)). Generally, for purposes of sections 110.1 and 118.1, a gift under common law is made if a taxpayer has donative intent, and all three of the following conditions are satisfied: there must be a voluntary transfer of property to a qualified donee; the property transferred must be owned by the donor; and no benefit or consideration must flow to the donor.

> 1.3 Under the civil law, Article 1806 of the *Civil Code of Québec* (C.C.Q.) provides that a gift is a contract by which the donor transfers ownership of property to the donee by gratuitous title. It is generally accepted that a transfer is made by gratuitous title when: the transfer impoverishes the donor to the benefit of the donee and is made without any corresponding consideration; and it is the donor's intention to enrich the donee without receiving any corresponding consideration. The donor's intention to enrich the donee does not need to involve the full value of the transferred property. Therefore, a transfer of property for partial consideration may result in a gift under the civil law. For example, under the civil law, it is possible to sell a property to a qualified donee at a price below fair market value, resulting in a gift of the difference, if all the other requirements of the civil law are met. Article 1810 of the C.C.Q. also formally recognizes the validity of gifts with partial consideration that are remunerative gifts or gifts with a charge.

The split-receipting rules, discussed below, may now apply in these situations if the requirements are met. The split-receipting rules deal with the tax implications of a transfer of property for partial consideration in the context of charitable giving.

¶10212.2 — *Split-Receipting Rules*

The split-receipting rules and deemed fair market value rule in ITA 248(30) to (41) were enacted on June 26, 2013 and are generally applicable to charitable gifts made after December 20, 2002. In effect, the meaning of a gift under the common law is modified for purposes of the split-receipting rules. The rules allow for the recognition of a gift for tax purposes in certain circumstances, even though some form of benefit or consideration flows back to the taxpayer. The split-receipting rules and deemed fair market value rule are discussed in Folio S7-F1-C1, *Split-receipting and Deemed Fair Market Value.*

Under the split-receipting rules, the existence of an amount of an "advantage" in respect of a transfer of property to a qualified donee does not in and of itself disqualify the transfer from being a gift for tax purposes. Specifically, a gift can be recognized if the amount of the advantage does not exceed 80% of the fair market value of the transferred property (ITA 248(30)(a)). If the amount of the advantage exceeds 80% of the fair market value of the transferred property, the transfer may still qualify as a gift for tax purposes if the taxpayer can establish that the transfer was made with the intention to make a gift (ITA 248(30)(b)). It is the CRA's view that even if the requirements in ITA 248(30)(a) or (b) are met, the other requirements with respect to whether a transfer of property qualifies as a gift at law must still be met.

Generally, the "eligible amount" of a gift is used to calculate a donor's donation tax credit. The "eligible amount" of a gift is generally the amount by which the fair market value of the gifted property exceeds the amount of an advantage, if any, received or receivable for the gift (ITA 248(31)). Generally, if there is no advantage, the eligible amount of a gift is the fair market value of the gifted property. For the purposes of determining the eligible amount of a gift, the fair market value of a property gifted by a taxpayer to a qualified donee might be deemed to be an amount that is less than its actual fair market value where the taxpayer acquired the property under a gifting arrangement that is a tax shelter (as defined in ITA 237.1(1)). See paragraphs 1.26 to 1.38 of Folio S7-F1-C1 and the examples contained therein for a discussion of the deemed fair market value rule.

An "advantage" is the total value, at the time the gift is made, of any property, service, compensation, use or other benefit that the taxpayer obtained, received or enjoyed as consideration for, in gratitude for or in any other way related to the gift (ITA 248(32)). An advantage may be contingent or receivable in the future either by the donor or by a person or partnership that does not deal at arm's length with the donor. An advantage also includes any limited-recourse debt in respect of the gift at the time it was made. A "limited-recourse debt" is defined as including the unpaid principal of any debt for which recourse is limited (even if that limitation applies only in the future or contingently), and any other indebtedness of the taxpayer related to the gift or contribution if there is a guarantee or similar indemnity in respect of that or any other indebtedness. The CRA uses the term "split-receipting" to describe the practice of issuing tax receipts for a portion (the "eligible amount") of a gift where the donor receives an "advantage" in return for a donation.

Where a taxpayer receives an advantage from a qualified donee as a token of gratitude for making a gift, the CRA administratively provides for a nominal threshold to simplify matters for taxpayers and qualified donees where such advantages are insignificant. Specifically, if the amount of an advantage received by the taxpayer does not exceed the lesser of 10% of the fair market value of the gifted property and $75, it will not be regarded as an advantage for the purposes of determining the eligible amount. However, the nominal threshold does not apply to cash or near-cash items (for example, gift certificates and gift cards). As well, an advantage will not be considered nominal if its fair market value cannot be ascertained.

ITA 248(30)–(41), Folio S7-F1-C1: *Split-receipting and Deemed Fair Market Value*, Pamphlet P113

¶10213 — *Donations to U.S. Charities*

Charitable donations eligible for donation tax credit are not restricted to those made to organizations in Canada. The universities outside Canada that are eligible to receive deductible donations are listed in ITR Schedule VIII. The CRA announces from time to time the names of foreign organizations to which the federal government has made gifts. A Canadian taxpayer who makes a donation to a specified organization during a defined period would qualify for a donation tax credit in respect of the donation. The organizations are identified in Information Circulars from time to time (see IC 84-3R6).

As well, certain donations made to U.S. charities by Canadian residents who commute to their principal place of employment or business in the United States may qualify as a charitable donation for the purposes of claiming a tax credit in Canada. To be eligible, the donation must be made to a religious, charitable, scientific, literary or educational organization which would qualify for deduction under the United States *Internal Revenue Code*. Donations are not eligible, however, unless the taxpayer resides in Canada near the Canada-U.S. border throughout the whole taxation year, commutes to the principal place of employment or business in the United States, and the income from such employment or business is the taxpayer's chief source of income for the year.

Other circumstances in which a credit may be claimed for donations made to U.S. organizations are provided by Canada-U.S. Tax Treaty: Article XXI, under which a Canadian taxpayer with income from U.S. sources may claim (subject to the relevant income limit) credits in respect of donations made to recognized U.S. charities.

ITA 118.1(1) "total charitable gifts" (e), (f), (g), 118.1(9), ITR Schedule VIII

¶10214 — *Donations of Property*

¶10214.1 — *Donations of Certified Cultural Property*

A donation tax credit may be claimed in respect of a gift to a designated institution or public authority in Canada of an object that has been identified by the Canadian Cultural Property Export Review Board to be cultural property for purposes of the *Cultural Property Export and Import Act*. The total eligible amount for a donation of cultural property is not limited to 75% of net income, but may be deducted against the full amount of the taxpayer's income. An amount not deducted for the year may be carried forward as a deduction in computing taxable income in the following five years, as described above. The intention of this provision is to encourage the accumulation of Canada's cultural treasures in public museums and art galleries in Canada.

Donations of Canadian cultural property are also exempt from capital gains. This means that a donor of a gift of Canadian cultural property may claim a donation tax credit based on the fair market value of the property donated, as determined by the Board, without incurring a capital gain, even though the property may have increased in value since its acquisition. A disposition of Canadian cultural property may give rise to a capital loss. Where the gift is a work of art which was created by the donor and is held in inventory, assuming the gift otherwise qualifies as cultural property, the credit is based on the value of the work of art, but the deemed proceeds of disposition is the cost amount of the property. Accordingly, the donor would not recognize any income on making the gift either during the donor's lifetime or by the donor's will.

ITA 118.1(7.1), 118.1(10), *Cultural Property Export and Import Act*, *Heffel Gallery Limited v. Attorney General of Canada*, 2018 FC 605 (meaning of "national importance" and "outstanding significance"), IT-407R4(C): Dispositions of Cultural Property to Designated Canadian Institutions, IT-504R2(C): Visual Artists and Writers

¶10214.2 — *Donations of Ecologically Sensitive Land*

In order to qualify as an ecological gift, the following conditions must be satisfied:

- The gift must be land (including a covenant, easement or servitude);

- The property must be certified by the Minister of the Environment as ecologically sensitive;

- The fair market value of the gift must be certified by the Minister of the Environment;

- In the opinion of the Minister of the Environment, the land must be important to the preservation of Canada's environmental heritage;

- The beneficiary must be a Canadian municipality or registered charity whose primary purpose is the conservation or protection of Canada's environmental heritage; and

- If the donee is a registered charity, it must be approved by the Minister of the Environment in respect of the gift.

In some cases, it may be difficult to determine the fair market value of the property rights given pursuant to this provision. However, the fair market value will not be considered less than the decrease in the value of the land that resulted from making the gift. The amount so determined is deemed to be the donor's proceeds in computing any gain or loss on the disposition.

The amount of ecological gifts which may be deducted in any particular year is not limited to 75% of net income, but may be deducted against the full amount of the taxpayer's income. As well, donations of ecologically sensitive land that meet the above requirements are also exempt from capital gains.

Applicable to donations made after February 10, 2014, the carry-forward period for unclaimed donations of qualifying certified ecologically sensitive land was extended to ten years (from five years). This measure is intended to permit donors to take greater advantage of tax assistance and thereby encourage larger donations.

Effective March 22, 2017, private foundations are no longer permitted to receive donations of ecologically sensitive land due to the government's concerns about potential conflicts of interest.

ITA 118.1(1), 118.1(12)

¶10214.3 — *Direct Beneficiary Designations*

A charitable donation credit may be claimed in respect of eligible transfers under a life insurance policy which result from the designation of proceeds to a charity in respect of insurance on the donor's life. In order for the credit to be available on the death of the taxpayer, the following conditions must be satisfied:

- the policy must be a life insurance policy and the individual's life must be insured under that policy immediately before death;

- the transfer by way of money or other negotiable instrument must be solely by reason of the insurer's obligation under the policy, as provided in the individual's will or by non-testamentary written designation;

- the individual's consent would have been required to change the recipient of the proceeds;

- the donee was neither the policyholder nor an assignee of the interest of the individual in the policy; and

- the transfer to the donee occurs within 36 months after death or such longer period as the Minister considers reasonable.

If the foregoing conditions are satisfied, the gift is deemed to have been made immediately before the death of the individual, and the fair market value of the gift is generally considered the money or proceeds transferred to the donee.

A charitable donation credit may also be claimed where money or other negotiable instrument transfer is made as a consequence of the individual's death from a RRSP or RRIF to a qualified donee where the donee is named as beneficiary under the plan. Provided the individual was the annuitant under the plan immediately before death and the transfer takes place within the 36 months that begins at the time of death, or, upon written application, such longer period as the Minister considers reasonable, the individual is considered to have made a gift immediately before death of a fair market value equal to that of the right to the transfer.

ITA 118.1(5.1), 118.1(5.2), ITA 118.1(5.3)

¶10214.4 — *Gifts In-Kind*

A gift includes a gift in-kind. A gift in-kind refers to a gift of property other than cash, such as gifts of capital property (including depreciable property), personal-use property, a leasehold interest, a residual interest, a right of any kind whatever, a licence, a share, a chose in action and inventory of a business. A gift of cryptocurrency units to a registered charity will also be treated as in-kind gift of capital property. A gift in-kind, however, does not include a gift of services. Furthermore, gifts of little value to the donor, such as used clothing, do not qualify as gifts in kind.

For more information, see Pamphlet P113 under "Gifts in Kind", IT-297R2, *Gifts in Kind to Charity and Others*, IT-288R2, *Gifts of Capital Properties to a Charity and Others*, and Guide T4037.

ITA 118.1(6), IT-226R: *Gift to a Charity of a Residual Interest in Real Property or an Equitable Interest in a Trust*

¶10214.5 — *Gift of Life Insurance Policy*

If a taxpayer assigns an insurance policy to a charitable organization, the taxpayer is treated as having made a charitable donation equal to the cash surrender value of the policy at the time of transfer. The subsequent payment of additional premiums, if paid to the insurance company, will not be treated as charitable donations, but the payment to the charity of sums intended for the payment of the premiums will be regarded as charitable donations.

IT-244R3: *Gifts by Individuals of Life Insurance Policies as Charitable Donations*, VDs 2008-0270391C6, 2008-0267091E5

¶10214.6 — *Gifts of Listed Securities*

Where a taxpayer makes a donation of an eligible security, the amount of the gain which must otherwise be included in income as a taxable capital gain is reduced to zero. This also applies to qualifying donations made by will. An eligible security includes a share, debt obligation or a right listed on a prescribed stock exchange, a share in a mutual fund corporation, a unit of a mutual fund trust, an interest in a related segregated fund trust, or a prescribed debt obligation.

In order for this provision to apply, the gift must be to a qualified donee other than a private foundation. A qualified donee is a person to whom gifts may be made that qualify for the charitable donation deduction or tax credit, including registered charities and public foundations.

The capital gains exemption on donations of flow-through shares acquired by a taxpayer on or after March 22, 2011 is only available to the extent that the capital gain exceeds a threshold amount (the "exemption threshold"). Generally, the threshold amount will be the original cost of the shares, but the threshold amount will be reduced by capital gains realized after March 22, 2011 on any shares of the same class. This rule is contained in ITA 40(12).

For more information on gifts of capital property, see ¶4330.

¶10215 — *Claiming and Filing*

Add up all eligible donations made in the year plus any donations made in any of the previous five years that have not yet been claimed. Individuals can claim donations that his or her spouse or common-law partner made. Generally, individuals can claim on Line 340 all or part of this amount, up to the limit of 75% of net income (or 100% of net income in the year of death or immediately preceding year).

Do not include contributions to political parties. If the individual contributed to a federal political party, see Line 410 at ¶11020. If the individual contributed to a provincial or territorial political party, see the applicable provincial or territorial form.

If the individual is filing a paper return, include a completed Schedule 9, as well as the official donation receipts. To be acceptable, a receipt must contain prescribed information. Detailed instructions as to what must appear on receipts issued by registered Canadian charitable organizations are contained in ITR Part XXXV. Donation receipts are not required for amounts shown on tax slips or on financial statements showing a donation amount a partnership allocated to the individual.

If the individual received a T5003 slip with an amount in Box 13, submit this slip, as well as the charitable donation receipt received from the registered charity. Also complete and attach Form T5004, *Claim for Tax Shelter Loss or Deduction*, to the return.

Note that the donation tax credit may only be claimed after most of the other credits in ITA 118 to 118.9. However, it is applied before the credit for interest on student loans (ITA 118.62) and the dividend tax credit (ITA 118.92). In VD 2011-0410641E5, the CRA confirmed that an individual can reduce the amount of charitable donations tax credit claimed in any particular year in order to maximize a tax credit claimed for interest on student loans or the dividend tax credit.

ITA 118.1, 149.1(1)"qualified donee", 248(30)–(41), ITR Part XXXV, ITR Schedule VIII, Folio S7-F1-C1, *Split-receipting and Deemed Fair Market Value*, Pamphlet P113, IC 84-3R6: *Gifts to Certain Organizations Outside Canada*

¶10220 — Volunteer Firefighters' Amount (T1 Schedule 1: Line 362)

The volunteer firefighter tax credit is a non-refundable tax credit for volunteer firefighting services provided to one or more fire departments or search and rescue volunteer services provided to one or more search and rescue organizations. The amount of the credit is $450 ($3,000 × 15%). To qualify for the credit, the individual must complete a minimum of 200 hours of service in the year, each of which is an hour of eligible volunteer firefighting service for a fire department or eligible search and rescue volunteer service for an eligible search and rescue organization.

"Eligible volunteer firefighting services" are defined as services, provided to a fire department by an individual in the individual's capacity as a volunteer firefighter, that consist primarily of responding to and being on call for firefighting and related emergency calls, attending meetings held by the fire department and participating in required training related to the prevention or suppression of fires. If an individual was also engaged by the same fire department (other than as a volunteer) for the same or similar duties, the individual cannot include any hours related to that department in determining if he or she has met the 200-hour threshold.

"Eligible search and rescue volunteer services" are defined as services, other than eligible volunteer firefighting services, provided by an individual in the individual's capacity as a volunteer to an eligible search and rescue organization that consist primarily of responding to and being on call for search and rescue and related emergency calls, attending meetings held by the organization and participating in required training related to search and rescue services. Eligible search and rescue services do not include services provided to an organization if the individual provides search and rescue services to the organization otherwise than as a volunteer. An "eligible search and rescue organization" is an organization that is a member of the Search and Rescue Volunteer Association of Canada, the Civil Air Search and Rescue Association or the Canadian Coast Guard Auxiliary; or whose status as a search and rescue organization is recognized by a provincial, municipal or public authority.

¶10221 — *Claiming and Filing*

Claim the volunteer firefighter tax credit on Line 362. Do not send any documents with the T1 return. Keep them in case the CRA requests to see them at a later date. The CRA may request certification from a fire chief or delegated official within the fire department to verify the number of hours of eligible volunteer firefighting services the individual performed for the department, or certification by the team president, or other individual who fulfils a similar role, to verify the number of hours of eligible search and rescue volunteer services the individual performed for the organization. Individuals who claim the $1,000 income exemption for payments for volunteer services (reported in Box 87 of the individual's T4 slip) are not eligible to claim the volunteer firefighter tax credit.

ITA 118.06, VDs 2013-0481951E5, 2012-0434951E5, 2012-0442321E5, 2012-0444461E5, 2012-0432221I7, 2012-0433181E5, 2012-0439071M4, 2012-0444191E5, 2012-0436941M4, 2012-0436861M4, 2011-0431921E5, 2011-0421551E5

¶10230 — Canada Employment Amount (T1 Schedule 1: Line 363)

The Canada employment credit allows individuals to claim a non-refundable credit where the individual earns employment income for the year. This credit is intended to recognize work-related expenses incurred by employees. The maximum Canada employment credit for 2018 is $1,195.

¶10231 — *Claiming and Filing*

On Line 363, claim the lesser of $1,195, and the total of the employment income reported on Lines 101 and 104 of the return.

ITA 118(10), VDs 2010-0373051E5, 2010-0365351E5, 2010-0361001E5, 2010-0356101E5, 2009-0306571E5, 2007-0222521E5

¶10240 — Public Transit Amount (T1 Schedule 1: Line 364)

As announced in the 2017 federal budget and implemented by SC 2017, c 20 (Bill C-44), the public transit pass credit was repealed effective July 1, 2017. For the 2017 taxation year, individuals could claim the cost of eligible transit passes that were for the use of public transit services for the period January 1 to June 30, 2017. The public transit credit is eliminated completely for 2018 and later taxation years.

¶10250 — Children's Fitness Amount (T1: Schedule 1: Line 365)

For taxation years before 2015, the children's fitness tax credit was non-refundable and claimed on line 365. For the 2015 and 2016 taxation years, the children's fitness tax credit was refundable and claimed on lines 458 and 459. The children's fitness tax credit has been repealed for 2017 and later taxation years.

¶10260 — Canada Caregiver Amount for Infirm Children Under 18 Years of Age (T1 Schedule 1: Line 367)

This credit provides parents with a tax credit for the care of an eligible dependent under 18 years of age who has a mental or physical infirmity. This credit can be claimed either on line 367 or in the calculation of line 305 — if the eligible dependant is not the individual's or the individual's spouse's or common-law partner's child, claim the amount of $2,182 in the calculation of line 305 (amount for an eligible dependant; see ¶10040).

The following requirements must be met to claim the caregiver amount of $2,182 for an infirm child on line 367:

- the child must be the individual's or the individual's spouse's or common-law partner's child;

- the child must be under 18 years of age at the end of the taxation year; and

- the child is, by reason of mental or physical infirmity, likely to be, for a long and continuous period of indefinite duration, dependent on others for significantly more assistance in attending to the child's personal needs and care, when compared to children of the same age.

The meaning of mental or physical infirmity is described in paragraph 1.21 of Folio S1-F4-C1 as follows:

> The term mental or physical infirmity is not specifically defined for the purposes of subsection 118(1). Therefore, it takes its ordinary meaning. For a person to be dependent on an individual because of mental or physical infirmity, the dependency must be brought about solely by reason of the infirmity. The degree of the infirmity must be such that it requires the person to be dependent on the individual for a considerable period of time. Temporary illness or injury is not considered to be an infirmity for purposes of the personal tax credits.

The full amount of the credit can be claimed in the year of the child's birth, death, or adoption. If the child did not live with both parents throughout the year, the parent or the spouse or common-law partner who claims the amount for an eligible dependant on line 305 (see ¶10040) for that child can make the claim on line 367. However, a caregiver amount can still be claimed on line 367 for the child if the parent or the spouse or common-law partner could not claim an amount for an eligible dependant on line 305.

¶10261 — *Claiming and Filing*

Enter the number of infirm children for whom the taxpayer is claiming the caregiver amount in box 352. Claim the result of the calculation on line 367. The CRA may ask for a signed statement from a medical practitioner showing when the impairment began; what the duration of the impairment is expected to be; and that, because of the impairment, the child is, and will continue to be, dependent on others for an indefinite duration. This dependence means they need much more assistance for their personal needs and care compared to children of the same age. However, a signed medical statement is not required if the CRA already has an approved Form T2201, *Disability Tax Credit Certificate*, for the child.

ITA 118(1)(b.1)

¶10270 — **Home Buyers' Amount (T1 Schedule 1: Line 369)**

Individuals can claim $5,000 ($\times$ 15% = $750 tax credit) for the purchase of a "qualifying home" in the year if both of the following apply:

- The individual or his or her spouse or common-law partner acquired a qualifying home (for these purposes, a home is only considered to have been acquired by an individual if the individual's interest in the home is registered in accordance with the applicable land registration system); and

- The individual is a first-time home buyer (i.e., the individual did not live in another home owned by the individual or his or her spouse or common-law partner during the year or at any time in the previous four taxation years).

An exception to the above requirements is that an individual does not have to be a first-time home buyer if the individual is eligible for the disability amount or purchased a home for the benefit of a related person who is eligible for the disability amount. However, the purchase must be made to allow the disabled person to live in a home that is more accessible or better suited to the needs of that person. Related persons include individuals connected by blood relationship, marriage or common-law partnership, or adoption. Examples of blood relatives include grandparents, parents, brothers, sisters, and children. Examples of persons related by spousal relationship include the grandparents of a spouse, the parents of a spouse, the brothers and sisters of a spouse, the spouse of a child, and the spouse of a grandchild. Generally, in determining arm's length relationships, common law partners are treated in the same way as legally married spouses, and adopted children are treated in the same way as blood-related children.

To be a qualifying home, the home must be purchased in the individual's and/or his or her spouse's or common-law partner's name, and must be in Canada. It includes existing homes and homes under construction. The following are considered qualifying homes: single-family houses, semi-detached houses, townhouses, mobile homes, condominium units, and apartments in duplexes, triplexes, fourplexes, or apartment buildings. A share in a co-operative housing corporation that entitles the individual to own, and gives an equity interest in, a home located in Canada also qualifies. However, a share in a co-operative housing corporation that gives only the right to tenancy in a home does not qualify.

As well, the individual must intend to occupy the home (or must intend that the related person with a disability occupy the home) as a principal place of residence no later than one year after it is acquired. The term "principal place of residence" is not a defined term. The CRA has stated in other contexts that it considers the terms "chief" and "main" to be synonymous with "principal". Accordingly, where an individual has more than one place of residence, it would appear that the individual must use or intend to use the home as his/her main residence for the home to be a "qualifying home". Where two individuals take title to a home in joint names, the credit must be split between the individuals but the combined total cannot exceed $5,000.

It is the CRA's view that the acquisition of a qualifying home by way of gift is valid for the purposes of the first-time homebuyers' credit. Consequently, provided that all the other conditions of ITA 118.05 are met, the acquisition of a home by way of gift does not prevent the individual from claiming the credit (VD 2016-0674851C6).

¶10271 — *Claiming and Filing*

The individual who acquired the home or the individual's spouse or common-law partner can claim the home buyers' credit on Line 369, up to a maximum of $750 ($5,000 × 15%). If two arm's length individuals purchased a home together, either one can claim the credit; however, the total of both claims cannot exceed $750 ($5,000 × 15%). If individuals cannot agree as to the apportionment of eligible costs, the Minister may fix the portions. Any unused portion of an available credit may not be carried-forward. Supporting documentation does not have to be filed with a paper return but must be available should it be requested by the CRA.

ITA 118.05, RC4135, RC4509, VDs 2011-0394311E5, 2010-0360131E5, 2010-0362841E5, 2010-0357201E5

¶10280 — Children's Arts Amount (T1 Schedule 1: Line 370)

The children's arts credit has been fully repealed for 2017 and later taxation years.

For taxation years before 2017, the children's arts tax credit was a non-refundable tax credit available for eligible amounts paid by parents who registered a qualifying child in an eligible program of artistic, cultural, recreational, or developmental activity. Parents could claim a maximum of $250 per year ($500 for taxation years before 2016) for eligible fees paid for registration or membership in an eligible program for each qualifying child.

This credit has been repealed for 2017 and later taxation years.

¶10290 — Search and Rescue Volunteers Tax Credit (T1 Schedule 1: Line 395)

The search and rescue volunteers tax credit is a non-refundable tax credit for search and rescue volunteer services provided to one or more search and rescue organizations or volunteer firefighting services provided to one or more fire departments. The amount of the credit is $450 ($3,000 × 15%). To qualify for the credit, the individual must complete a minimum of 200 hours of service in the year, each of which is an hour of eligible search and rescue volunteer service for an eligible search and rescue organization or eligible volunteer firefighting service for a fire department.

"Eligible search and rescue volunteer services" are defined as services, other than "eligible volunteer firefighting services" (see ¶10220), provided by an individual in the individual's capacity as a volunteer to an eligible search and rescue organization that consist primarily of responding to and being on call for search and rescue and related emergency calls, attending meetings held by the organization and participating in required training related to search and rescue services. Eligible search and rescue services do not include services provided to an organization if the individual provides search and rescue services to the organization otherwise than as a volunteer. An "eligible search and rescue organization" is an organization that is a member of the Search and Rescue Volunteer Association of Canada, the Civil Air Search and Rescue Association or the Canadian Coast Guard Auxiliary; or whose status as a search and rescue organization is recognized by a provincial, municipal or public authority.

¶10291 — *Claiming and Filing*

Claim the search and rescue volunteers tax credit on Line 395. Do not send any documents with the T1 return. Keep them in case the CRA requests to see them at a later date. The CRA may request certification by the team president, or other individual who fulfils a similar role, to verify the number of hours of eligible search and rescue volunteer services the individual performed for the organization, or certification from a fire chief or delegated official within the fire department to verify the number of hours of eligible volunteer firefighting services the individual performed for the department. An individual may not claim this credit for a taxation year if the individual has claimed the volunteer firefighters' tax credit for the year. As well, individuals who claim the $1,000 income exemption for payments for volunteer services (reported in Box 87 of the individual's T4 slip) are not eligible to claim the search and rescue volunteers tax credit.

ITA 118.07

¶10300 — Home Accessibility Tax Credit (T1 Schedule 1: Line 398)

The 2015 federal budget introduced a new tax credit to help seniors and persons with disabilities renovate their principal residence to make it more accessible. Specifically, the Home Accessibility Tax Credit (HATC) provides a non-refundable tax credit that may be claimed by seniors, persons with disabilities and other "eligible individuals" in respect of "qualifying expenditures" up to a maximum amount of $10,000 directly attributable to "qualifying renovations" made to an "eligible dwelling". The credit is available to be claimed in 2016 and later taxation years.

¶10301 — "Eligible Individual" and "Eligible Dwelling"

The following individuals are eligible to claim this credit ("eligible individual"):

- an individual who is 65 years of age or older by the end of a taxation year, or in respect of whom an amount is deductible under ITA 118.3(1) (i.e., the disability tax credit; see ¶10120) in computing tax payable for the year (called a "qualifying individual");

- the spouse or common-law partner of the qualifying individual;

- a parent, grandparent, child, grandchild, brother, sister, aunt, uncle, niece or nephew of the qualifying individual; and

- a parent, grandparent, child, grandchild, brother, sister, aunt, uncle, niece or nephew of the qualifying individual's spouse or common-law partner.

More specifically, an "eligible individual" is an individual who has claimed the spouse or common-law partner amount (see ¶10030), eligible dependant amount (see ¶10040), or the Canada caregiver amount (see ¶10055) for the qualifying individual for the taxation year. In addition, an eligible individual includes an individual who could have claimed such an amount for the taxation year if:

- in the case of the spouse or common-law partner amount, the qualifying individual had no income for the particular taxation year;

- in the case of the eligible dependent amount, the eligible individual was not married or in a common-law partnership and the qualifying individual had no income in the particular taxation year; and

- in the case of the Canada caregiver amount, the qualifying individual had been 18 years of age or older and had no income in the particular taxation year.

An "eligible dwelling" of an individual generally means a housing unit in Canada where the individual owns (either jointly with another person or otherwise) the housing unit; or a share of the capital stock of a co-operative housing corporation that was acquired for the sole purpose of acquiring the right to inhabit the housing unit, which is owned by the corporation. A trust under which the individual is a beneficiary may also own the housing unit (or the share of the capital stock of a co-operative housing corporation). An eligible dwelling includes the land subjacent to the housing unit and up to 1/2 hectare of contiguous land (or such greater area of land that the individual establishes is necessary for the use and enjoyment of the housing unit as a residence).

To qualify for the credit, the housing unit must be ordinarily inhabited, or be reasonably expected to be ordinarily inhabited, at any time during the taxation year by the qualifying individual (i.e., the senior or disabled person), or by both the qualifying individual and an eligible individual, if the qualifying individual does not own and ordinarily inhabit another housing unit in Canada (see under ¶4431 for a discussion of the meaning of "ordinarily inhabited").

For the purposes of this credit, a qualifying individual may have only one principal residence at any time, but may have more than one principal residence in a taxation year (for example, where an individual moves in the tax year). In situations where a qualifying individual has more than one principal residence in a tax year, the total qualifying expenses in respect of all such principal residences of the qualifying individual will be subject to the $10,000 limit. Rentals do not qualify as an eligible dwelling.

Where the housing unit is owned by a co-operative housing corporation, a condominium corporation or a trust, an outlay or expense incurred by the corporation or trust may qualify as a qualifying expenditure of a qualifying or eligible individual if it would have otherwise been a qualifying expenditure if the corporation or trust were an individual. The corporation or trust must notify the individual in writing of the individual's share of the outlay or expense.

Qualifying or eligible individuals who earn business or rental income from part of their principal residence will only be allowed to claim the credit for the amount of eligible expenditures made in respect of the qualifying individual's personal-use areas of the residence. For expenditures made in respect of common areas or that benefit the housing unit as a whole, the administrative practices ordinarily followed by the CRA to determine how business or rental income and expenditures are allocated between personal use and income-earning use will apply in establishing the amount that qualifies for the credit (see CRA Guide T4036, *Rental Income*).

¶10302 — *"Qualifying Expenditures" and "Qualifying Renovation"*

A "qualifying expenditure" is defined in ITA 118.041(1) as an outlay or expense that is made or incurred during the taxation year, that is directly attributable to a qualifying renovation of an eligible dwelling of a qualifying individual or an eligible individual (in respect of a qualifying individual).

A qualifying expenditure includes costs or expenditures for goods acquired during the year such as building materials and fixtures; labour and professional services hired for the qualifying renovation; permits required for the qualifying renovation; and the rental of equipment used in the course of the qualifying renovation. Annex 5 of the 2015 federal budget documents states that eligible expenditures for purposes of this credit could include costs associated with the purchase and installation of wheelchair ramps, walk-in bathtubs, wheel-in showers and grab bars.

However, the definition of a "qualifying expenditure" for purposes of the home accessibility tax credit specifically *excludes* an outlay or expense:

(a) to acquire a property that can be used independently of the qualifying renovation;

(b) for annual, recurring or routine repairs or maintenance;

(c) to acquire a household appliance (for purposes of this credit, household appliances do not include furnaces and other heating systems);

(d) to acquire an electronic home-entertainment device;

(e) for housekeeping, security monitoring, gardening, outdoor maintenance or similar services;

(f) for financing costs in respect of a qualifying renovation;

(g) made or incurred primarily for the purpose of increasing or maintaining the value of the eligible dwelling;

(h) made or incurred for the purpose of gaining or producing income from a business or property;

(i) in respect of goods or services provided by a person not dealing at arm's length with the qualifying individual or the eligible individual, unless that person is registered for the purposes of part IX of the *Excise Tax Act* (i.e., the GST); and

(j) that can reasonably be considered to have been reimbursed, otherwise than as assistance from the federal or provincial government, including a grant, subsidy, forgivable loan or a tax deduction.

In addition, the value of the individual's own labour or tools would not be considered a qualifying expenditure.

As mentioned above, expenses are not eligible if the goods or services are provided by a person not dealing at arm's length with the homeowner, unless that person is registered for GST/HST under the *Excise Tax Act*. If a related person is registered for the GST/HST and if all other conditions are met, the expenses are eligible. Individuals connected by blood relationship, marriage or common-law partnership, or adoption are defined to be "related persons" and are therefore deemed not to deal with each other at arm's length (see Folio S1-F5-C1). Related persons include individuals connected by blood relationship, marriage or common-law partnership, or adoption. Examples of blood relatives include grandparents, parents, brothers, sisters, and children. Examples of persons related by spousal relationship include the grandparents of a spouse, the parents of a spouse, the brothers and sisters of a spouse, the spouse of a child, and the spouse of a grandchild. Generally, in determining arm's length relationships, common-law partners are treated in the same way as legally married spouses. Adopted children are treated in the same way as blood-related children.

A "qualifying renovation" by a homeowner is defined in subsection 118.041(1) as a renovation or alteration of an eligible dwelling of a qualifying individual or an eligible individual in respect of a qualifying individual. The renovation or alteration must be: (a) of an enduring nature and integral to the eligible dwelling; and (b) undertaken to enable the qualifying individual to gain access to, or to be mobile or functional within, the eligible dwelling, or to reduce the risk of harm to the qualifying individual within the eligible dwelling or in gaining access to the dwelling.

Generally, it is a question of fact whether a renovation or alteration to a dwelling is of an enduring nature that is integral to the dwelling. Annex 5 of the 2015 federal budget documents provides that eligible expenditures will include the cost of labour and professional services, building materials, fixtures, equipment rentals and permits. However, items such as furniture, as well as items which retain a value independent of the renovation (such as construction equipment and tools), would not be integral to the dwelling, and expenditures for such items will therefore not qualify for the credit.

¶10303 — *Claiming and Filing*

Taxpayers should list their eligible expenses and calculate the amount that can be claimed for the home accessibility tax credit on Schedule 12, *Home Accessibility Expenses*. A separate Schedule 12 should be completed for each claimant with respect to each eligible dwelling. The amount calculated on Schedule 12 should be reported on line 398 of Schedule 1. Expenses claimed for the home accessibility tax credit must be supported by documentation, such as agreements, invoices, and receipts, that identify the type and quantity of goods purchased or services provided. Taxpayers who are filing paper returns should not include their receipts or documents supporting their claim, but keep them in case the CRA requests them.

If one or more individuals can make a claim in respect of an eligible dwelling, the total of all amounts claimed for the year in respect of the eligible dwelling cannot exceed $10,000. As well, where more than one qualifying individual ordinarily inhabits, or reasonably expects to ordinarily inhabit, an eligible dwelling, the total amount of qualifying expenditures that may be claimed by the qualifying individuals, or by eligible individuals in respect of those qualifying individuals, in respect of the eligible dwelling cannot exceed the maximum amount of $10,000.

Note that an outlay or expense may qualify for both the home accessibility tax credit and the medical expense tax credit (see ¶10190), if it would otherwise qualify for the purposes of those credits.

For more information on the home accessibility tax credit, see: canada.ca/en/revenue-agency/programs/about-canada-revenue-agency-cra/federal-government-budgets/budget-2015-strong-leadership/home-accessibility-tax-credit-hatc.html.

ITA 118.041

Chapter 11 — Calculation of Net Federal Tax

Contents

¶11000 Calculation of Net Federal Tax (T1 Schedule 1: Lines 405–427)

¶11010 Federal Foreign Tax Credit (T1 Schedule 1: Line 405)

¶11020 Federal Political Contribution Tax Credit (T1 Schedule 1: Line 410)

¶11030 Investment Tax Credit (T1 Schedule 1: Line 412)

¶11040 Labour-Sponsored Funds Tax Credit (T1 Schedule 1: Lines 413, 414)

¶11050 Working Income Tax Benefit Advance Payments (T1 Schedule 1: Line 415)

¶11060 Special Taxes (T1 Schedule 1: Line 418)

¶11065 Family Tax Cut Credit (T1 Schedule 1: Line 423)

¶11070 Federal Tax on Split Income (T1 Schedule 1: Line 424)

¶11080 Federal Dividend Tax Credit (T1 Schedule 1: Line 425)

¶11090 Overseas Employment Tax Credit (T1 Schedule 1: Line 426)

¶11100 Minimum Tax Carryover (T1 Schedule 1: Line 427)

¶11200 Calculation of Refund Due or Balance Owing (T1: Lines 420–486)

¶11210 CPP Contributions Payable on Self-Employment and Other Earnings (T1: Line 421)

¶11220 Social Benefits Repayment (T1: Line 422)

¶11230 EI Premiums Payable on Self-Employment and Other Earnings (T1: Line 430)

¶11240 Total Income Tax Deducted (T1: Line 437)

¶11250 Refundable Quebec Abatement (T1: Line 440)

¶11260 CPP Overpayment (T1: Line 448)

¶11270 Employment Insurance Overpayment (T1: Line 450)

¶11280 Refundable Medical Expense Supplement (T1: Line 452)

¶11290 Working Income Tax Benefit (T1: Line 453)

¶11300 Refund of Investment Tax Credit (T1: Line 454)

¶11310 Part XII.2 Trust Tax Credit (T1: Line 456)

¶11320 Employee and Partner GST/HST Rebate (T1: Line 457)

¶11325 Children's Fitness Tax Credit (T1: Lines 458, 459)

¶11330 Eligible Educator School Supply Tax Credit (T1: Lines 468, 469)

¶11340 Tax Paid by Instalments (T1: Line 476)

¶11350 Refund or Balance Owing (T1: Lines 484, 485)

This chapter discusses the calculation of an individual's federal tax owing or refundable on taxable income reported on Line 260. Specifically, ¶11000 covers the calculation of net federal tax reported on Line 420, which is determined on Schedule 1, *Federal Tax*, and includes a discussion of various amounts applied for purposes of calculating federal tax, including the foreign tax credit, political contribution tax credit, investment tax credit, labour-sponsored funds tax credit, tax on split income, dividend tax credit and alternative minimum tax. In addition, ¶11200 covers the calculation of an individual's refund due or balance owing, which includes a discussion of CPP contributions or EI premiums payable on self-employment earnings, social benefits repayment, refundable Quebec abatement, refundable medical expense supplement, working income tax benefit, investment tax credit refund, employee and partner GST/HST rebate, and the determination of whether a refund is due or a balance is owing. Federal non-refundable tax credits are discussed in Chapter 10. The calculation of provincial or territorial tax is discussed in Chapter 12 (provincial and territorial) and Chapter 13 (Quebec).

¶11000 — Calculation of Net Federal Tax (T1 Schedule 1: Lines 405–427)

This section discusses the calculation of net federal tax reported on Line 420, which is determined on Schedule 1, *Federal Tax*. To calculate federal tax, the individual's taxable income from Line 260 of the T1 return is entered on Line 36 of Schedule 1, and the calculations on Lines 37 to 43 of Schedule 1 are done to apply progressive tax rates to that income.

For 2016 and subsequent taxation years, the 22% tax rate for the middle income bracket was reduced to 20.5%, and a new higher tax bracket of 33% was introduced for taxable income over $200,000 (indexed to inflation). Therefore, for 2018, the federal tax brackets are as follows:

- 15.0% on taxable income up to $46,605

- 20.5% on taxable income over $46,605 to $93,208

- 26.0% on taxable income over $93,208 to $144,489

- 29.0% on taxable income over $144,489 to $205,842

- 33.0% on taxable income over $205,842

The following amounts are then applied against the federal tax calculated on Line 43 in order to calculate net federal tax: foreign tax credit (see Line 405 at ¶11010), political contribution tax credit (see Line 410 at ¶11020), investment tax credit (see Line 412 at ¶11030), labour-sponsored funds tax credit (see Line 414 at ¶11040), WITB advance payments received (see Line 415 at ¶11050), tax on split income (see Line 424 at ¶11070), dividend tax credit (see Line 425 at ¶11080), minimum tax carryover (see Line 427 at ¶11100), and special taxes such as Part X.5 tax on accumulated income payments from an RESP and tax on excess EPSP amounts (see Line 418 at ¶11060).

In certain circumstances, federal tax must also be calculated under the alternative minimum tax. This is a separate calculation from the calculation on Schedule 1, and is done on Form T691, *Alternative Minimum Tax*. See Minimum Tax Carryover at ¶11100 for more information.

The tax brackets on Schedule 1 are indexed on the basis of the annual increase in the consumer price index for the 12-month period ending on September 30 of the previous year.

Schedule 1 must be attached to a paper-filed or electronically filed T1 return.

¶11010 — Federal Foreign Tax Credit (T1 Schedule 1: Line 405)

The foreign tax credit (FTC) in ITA 126 is designed to provide relief from double taxation on income arising from a source outside Canada. Relief is granted by means of a deduction from the Canadian tax otherwise payable of all or part of the foreign tax (i.e., an FTC). In certain cases, when an FTC cannot be fully utilized, a deduction can be claimed in computing income for tax purposes in respect of foreign taxes (see ¶9273). Unused non-business foreign tax credits cannot be carried forward. Where a Canadian resident has income from more than one foreign jurisdiction, the amount of the tax credits in respect of each is required to be computed separately.

Canadian resident individuals should calculate their FTC on Form T2209 (IND), *Federal Foreign Tax Credits*, in Canadian dollars. Individuals should only submit one Form T2209. If the total of the foreign taxes paid to all foreign countries is more than $200, individuals should do separate calculations on a separate sheet for each foreign country to which the individual paid taxes, and enter the totals on Form T2209.

ITA 126, Folio S5-F2-C1: *Federal Foreign Tax Credit, Marchan*, [2008] 5 C.T.C. 2670 (TCC) (taxpayer must prove amounts paid were foreign taxes), *Meyer*, [2004] 2 C.T.C. 2934 (TCC) (payment of tax in excess of legal liability not available for credit), *Zhang*, [2008] 2 C.T.C. 2097 (TCC) (FTC based on foreign tax actually paid), *Icanda Ltd.*, [1972] C.T.C. 163 (FCTD) (taxpayer receiving U.S. tax refund not allowed foreign tax credit)

¶11011 — *Federal Non-Business Foreign Tax Credit (Form T2209: Lines 1–3)*

A federal non-business foreign tax credit is available to prevent double taxation of non-business income earned in a foreign country that was taxed by that foreign country. The credit reduces Canadian Part I tax that the individual would otherwise have to pay. To claim the credit, complete Form T2209, *Federal Foreign Tax Credits*. Calculate the federal non-business foreign tax credit for each country separately. Foreign non-business income includes dividends, interest, and capital gains. It does not include income from operating a business in a foreign country or any foreign tax paid on income that is exempt from tax in Canada under an income tax treaty.

After claiming the federal non-business foreign tax credit, if there is any non-business foreign tax credit left over, the credit can be claimed as a provincial or territorial FTC, which is calculated on Form T2036, *Provincial or Territorial Foreign Tax Credit*.

If an individual paid tax on income from foreign property (other than real property), the foreign tax credit for the income from that property cannot be more than 15% of the individual's net income from that property. However, the individual may be able to deduct the portion of the foreign taxes paid in excess of 15% on Line 232 (see under ¶9270).

ITA 126(1), Form T2209, Form T2036, Folio S5-F2-C1: *Federal Foreign Tax Credit*

¶11011.1 — *Foreign Non-Business Income Tax Paid (Form T2209: Line 1 or 431)*

In respect of each amount of foreign non-business income earned in the year, report the amount of foreign non-business income tax paid for the taxation year in respect of that income. Generally, this is the total of the non-business income or profits tax paid to the government of a state, province, or other political subdivision of a foreign country for the year, minus any part of this tax that is deductible under ITA 20(11) or deducted under ITA 20(12).

However, non-business income tax paid to a foreign country does not include tax that can reasonably be attributed to an amount that:

- Any other person or partnership has received, or is entitled to receive, from the foreign country;

- Any other person or partnership has received, or is entitled to receive, from the government;

- Relates to taxable capital gains from that country, and the taxpayer or the taxpayer's spouse or common-law partner claimed a capital gains deduction for that income;

- Was deductible as income exempt from tax in Canada under a tax treaty between Canada and the foreign country; or

- Was taxable in the foreign country because the taxpayer was a citizen of that country, and relates to income from a source within Canada.

Any amount of tax paid to a foreign government in excess of the amount that the taxpayer was required to pay under a tax treaty is considered a voluntary contribution, and does not qualify as foreign taxes paid.

Additional considerations with respect to the amount of foreign non-business income tax reported include the following:

- For the purpose of claiming a foreign tax credit, the income taxes payable to a foreign government in a foreign currency should be converted to Canadian dollars at the same rate at which the income itself was converted. For investment income that was subject only to a tax similar to that imposed by ITA Part XIII, the conversion rate should be the rate applicable on the date of receipt of the income, although use of the average rate for the month or the mid-month rate would usually be acceptable. For capital gains, the rate should approximate the rate applicable at the time the gain was realized. Taxpayers may also choose to use the relevant spot rates for the days on which the particular amounts of foreign income and foreign tax arose in accordance with ITA 261(2)(b). Whichever method the taxpayer chooses, it should be consistently applied year-over-year (ITA 261(2), Folio S5-F2-C1 para. 1.42);

- The taxpayer's contribution to a foreign public pension plan is considered a non-business income tax for foreign tax credit purposes where the following twoconditions apply: the taxpayer is required to make the contribution under the legislation of the foreign country; and it is reasonable to conclude that the taxpayer will not be eligible for any financial benefit from the contribution considering that the employment in the foreign country was temporary and for a short period of time (e.g., contributions made under the U.S. *Federal Insurance Contributions Act* (FICA), including social security and Medicare taxes may qualify); and

- Any foreign tax included in the taxpayer's business income tax paid in respect of a foreign country cannot also be reported as non-business income tax (the FTC available in respect of foreign business income tax is discussed below under ¶11012).

In addition to the requirements outlined above, to qualify for an FTC, the foreign tax must be in the nature of an income or profits tax. In *Kempe*, [2001] 1 C.T.C. 2060 (TCC), a German church tax was held to be a non-business income tax as it was calculated as a percentage of income tax and was collected by the German government in the same manner as an income tax. In *Lai*, [1980] C.T.C. 2073 (TRB), a so-called property tax imposed on owners of land and buildings at the rate of 15% of the net assessed value based on expected annual rent from the property was held to be an income or profits tax.

A tax levied by a U.S. state would, among other things, have to qualify as an "income or profits tax" to give rise to an FTC. In order for a foreign tax to qualify as an "income or profits tax", the CRA's position is that the basis of taxation must be substantially similar with that of the ITA. The CRA generally considers this requirement to be met if the foreign tax is levied on net income or profits. If a payment is not an "income or profits tax", it may be deductible from income for tax purposes if it is incurred for the purpose of gaining or producing income from the business.

The CRA provides the following guidance in paragraphs 1.5 to 1.12.1 of Folio S5-F2-C1 with respect to determining whether a foreign tax qualifies for a foreign tax credit:

1.5 In order to qualify for the purposes of a foreign tax credit, an amount paid to a foreign jurisdiction must be a tax, not any other type of payment that might be made to the foreign jurisdiction. In general terms, a tax is a levy of general application for public purposes enforceable by a governmental authority. A levy imposed by a governmental authority will not be considered a tax if it is a charge meant to recoup the costs for services directly rendered or to finance a specific regulatory scheme. Examples of payments to governmental authorities that do not qualify as payments of a tax include the following: user fees; regulatory charges payments made to acquire a specific right or privilege; and voluntary contributions to governmental authorities.

1.6 To qualify for foreign tax credit purposes, a payment of tax: must be made to the government of a foreign country or to the government of a state, province or other political subdivision of a foreign country; cannot be conditional on the availability of a foreign tax credit in Canada, or a deduction in respect of a dividend received from a foreign affiliate under section 113; and must be an income or profits tax.

1.7 In determining whether a particular foreign tax qualifies as an income or profits tax, the name given to the tax by the foreign jurisdiction is not the deciding factor. Rather, the basic scheme of application of the foreign tax is compared with the scheme of application of the income and profits taxes imposed under the Act. Generally, if the basis of taxation is substantially similar, the foreign tax is accepted as an income or profits tax. To be substantially similar, the foreign tax must be levied on net income or profits (but not necessarily as would be computed for Canadian tax purposes) unless it is a tax similar to that imposed under Part XIII of the Act. Since taxable capital gains are included in a taxpayer's income for Canadian income tax purposes, a foreign tax on what would be considered a capital gain under the Act is also considered to be an income or profits tax for the purposes of section 126.

1.8 If a particular tax imposed by a foreign country is specifically identified, in an elimination of double tax article of an income tax treaty between Canada and that country, as a tax for which Canada must grant a deduction from Canadian taxes on profits, income or gains which arose in that other country and which gave rise to the foreign tax in question, the foreign tax will qualify as an income or profits tax when applying section 126 in conjunction with that treaty article. (See, for example, the United States taxes referred to in paragraph 2(a) of Article XXIV of the Canada-United States Income Tax Convention, as amended by the protocols to that convention.)

1.9 Examples of taxes that are not levied on net income or profits, and therefore generally will not qualify for a foreign tax credit under section 126 include the following: resource royalties; sales, commodity, consumption, or turnover taxes; succession duties or inheritance taxes; property or real estate taxes; customs or import duties; excise taxes or duties; gift taxes; capital or wealth taxes; documentary or stamp taxes. Despite not qualifying as income or profits taxes, some treaties may specifically provide for a deduction in respect of such foreign taxes paid from Canadian taxes otherwise payable independently of section 126. (See, for example, paragraph 6 of Article XXIX B of the Canada-United States Income Tax Convention, which addresses certain taxes imposed by reason of death.)

1.10 A unitary tax of a state of the United States cannot be regarded as an income or profits tax if it is not computed on the basis of net business income. The following are instances where a unitary tax does not qualify as an income or profits tax:

- The tax represents an annual minimum franchise tax.

- The tax is applicable even when there is no income.

- The calculation of the tax does not attempt to allocate income to the particular state.

- The tax is in the nature of a capital tax.

1.11 A decision as to whether a particular state's unitary tax can be regarded as an income or profits tax for purposes of claiming a foreign tax credit can be made only after a review of the applicable state legislation. (See also the comments regarding a unitary tax in ¶1.18 and 1.38). A unitary tax that does not qualify as an income or profits tax for purposes of claiming a foreign tax credit would likely be deductible in computing the taxpayer's income pursuant to subsection 9(1) as an expense for the purpose of earning income.

1.12 Where it is clear that an amount of tax has been paid to a foreign governmental authority, a foreign tax levy based on net income as calculated under a prescribed formula is considered to be an income or profits tax if the following conditions are met: it can be considered that the formula produces a reasonable approximation of actual net income in typical situations; and an attempt to compute actual net income would be significantly affected by arbitrary or estimated expense allocations.

1.12.1 In addition, a foreign tax levied on gross revenue is considered to be an income or profits tax if, after a review of the applicable legislation, it is determined that the tax on gross revenue is part of a comprehensive income tax regime and is tightly linked and subordinate to what would otherwise be accepted as an income or profits tax.

The following factors would be considered when determining whether a particular foreign tax on gross revenue is part of a comprehensive income tax regime and is tightly linked and subordinate to what would otherwise be accepted as an income or profits tax:

- The contextual relationship of the taxes. For example, a single statute containing an option between a tax on gross revenue and a tax on net income may demonstrate that such a tax on gross revenue is part of a comprehensive income tax regime. Furthermore, the ability to elect annually, under a single statute, between a tax on gross revenue and a tax on net income may demonstrate that such a tax on gross revenue is tightly linked to what would otherwise be accepted as an income or profits tax.

- The interaction of their provisions. For example, the elective nature of an annual choice between a tax on gross revenue and a tax on net income, which effectively results in the tax on gross revenue option being capped at what would otherwise be the amount of tax had the taxpayer's tax liability been computed under the tax on net income option, may demonstrate that such a tax on gross revenue is subordinate to what would otherwise be accepted as an income or profits tax. However, if the rate of tax on the tax on net income option is so unreasonably high that it effectively removes the elective nature of a taxpayer's choice to be taxed on gross revenue, such a tax on gross revenue would not be considered to be subordinate to what would otherwise be accepted as an income or profits tax. Moreover, if the ability to elect out of a tax on gross revenue option is irrevocable, such a tax on gross revenue would not be considered to be subordinate to what would otherwise be accepted as an income or profits tax.

When, based on the factors noted above, a particular foreign tax levied on gross revenue is determined to be part of a comprehensive income tax regime and is tightly linked and subordinate to what would otherwise be accepted as an income or profits tax, it is the CRA's view that such a tax on gross revenue would be indirectly determined by reference to a taxpayer's income or profits and, therefore, qualifies as an income or profits tax for the purposes of the Act.

At the 2013 Annual CTF Tax Conference CRA Roundtable, the CRA stated for all purposes of the ITA, it will generally consider a tax on gross revenue to be an "income or profits tax" where: 1) the tax is levied under the same statute as the regular income tax, 2) the regular income tax rate is not unreasonably high, and 3) the taxpayer has the annual ability to elect which tax it will pay (see VD 2013-0508171C6).

At the 2018 STEP-CRA Roundtable, the CRA stated that the new US "transition tax" under section 965 of the *Internal Revenue Code* that is imposed on repatriated foreign earnings of certain foreign corporations should qualify as an "income or profits tax" for purposes of the Canadian FTC rules; however, a Canadian foreign tax credit would only be available for the year in question even if the US tax is paid over several annual installments (VD 2018-0748811C6).

ITA 126(4), (5), (7)"non-business-income tax", VDs 2011-0428791E5, 2010-038865117, 2010-0356621E5, 2009-0337531E5, 2003-0022651E5

¶11011.2 — *Net Foreign Non-Business Income (Form T2209: Line 433)*

In respect of each foreign country, enter the amount of net foreign non-business income earned in the taxation year on Line 433 of Form T2209.

Net foreign non-business income is the excess of non-business income earned in a foreign country over the non-business losses incurred in that country. Claim the allowable expenses and deductions relating to the foreign income or loss when calculating the non-business income and losses. Subtract the following from foreign non-business income:

- any income from that foreign country for which the taxpayer claimed a capital gains deduction;

- any income that was, under a tax treaty between Canada and that country, deductible as exempt from tax in Canada or in that country;

- any foreign resource and exploration and development deductions; and

- any deduction claimed under ITA 20(11), 20(12), or 4(3) (i.e., deductions for foreign taxes on income from property exceeding 15% and for foreign non-business income tax) relating to the foreign income, including any deduction claimed for foreign union dues; contributions to a foreign pension plan or a social security arrangement; and foreign carrying charges.

Generally, the exclusions from foreign non-business income listed above are intended to ensure that income eligible for an FTC is subject to Canadian and source-country tax.

Do not include foreign income earned in a Tax-Free Savings Account (TFSA) in "net foreign non-business income" on Line 433. Also, do not include any foreign tax withheld from it in "non-business income tax paid to a foreign country" on Line 431.

Do not reduce foreign non-business income by any deduction the taxpayer claimed for a dividend he or she received from a controlled foreign affiliate. If the taxpayer's net foreign non-business income is more than the taxpayer's net income, use the net income amount in the calculation. For more information on deductions claimed under ITA 20(11) and 20(12), see IT-506: *Foreign Income Taxes as a Deduction from Income*.

The reduction of foreign non-business income by the amount of losses ensures that the amount of foreign non-business income is determined on a net basis. Symmetry is maintained in the determination of such losses by providing that the losses must be computed without reference to income amounts exempt from Canadian tax and any losses that arise from sources that are otherwise exempt by treaty from taxation in the source country.

If any income from a source in a particular country would be tax-exempt income but for the fact that a portion of the income is subject to an income or profits tax imposed by the government of a foreign country, the portion is deemed to be income from a separate source in the particular country. This rule ensures that the portion of foreign non-business income that is not subject to any foreign tax is characterized as tax-exempt income for the purpose of the "qualifying incomes" and "qualifying losses" definitions such that foreign tax on taxable income sources cannot be used to reduce Canadian tax on the tax-exempt portion.

Part-year residents of Canada should only include foreign non-business income for the part of the year the individual was resident of Canada.

The treatment of foreign capital gains and losses for purposes of the computation of a non-business income FTC is discussed and illustrated by way of two detailed examples in paragraphs 1.89 to 1.92 of Folio S5-F2-C1.

ITA 126(1)(b), (6)–(9)

¶11011.3 — Net Income (Form T2209: Line 433)

To compute the available FTC for the year, the net income of the taxpayer must first be determined. Net income for purposes of calculating the foreign tax credit is defined as net income from Line 236 of the taxpayer's return plus the amount on Line 4 of Form T1206, *Tax on Split Income*, less the following amounts:

- amount deductible as a Canadian Forces personnel and police deduction (see Line 244 at ¶9310);

- amount deductible as security options deductions (see Line 249 at ¶9330);

- amount deductible as an other payments deduction (see Line 250 at ¶9340);

- net capital losses of other years claimed (see Line 253 at ¶9370);

- capital gains deduction claimed (see Line 254 at ¶9380); and

- amount deductible as net employment income from a prescribed international organization; as foreign income exempt under a tax treaty; or as adult basic education tuition assistance (included on Line 256; see ¶9400).

ITA 126(1)(b)(ii), (2.1)(a)(ii)

¶11011.4 — *Calculation of Non-Business Income FTC (Form T2209: Lines 1–3)*

Generally, a Canadian resident taxpayer can claim an FTC in respect of non-business income tax paid to a foreign jurisdiction to the extent that the FTC does not exceed that proportion of the Part I tax otherwise payable that the taxpayer's non-business income in that foreign country bears to the taxpayer's total income.

In particular, the deductible non-business FTC is limited to the lesser of:

1. The amount of foreign non-business income tax paid in the year (Form T2209: Line 1); and

2. The amount determined by the following formula:

(Net foreign non–business income/Net income) × Basic federal tax (Form T2209: Line 2)

Basic federal tax for these purposes is the tax on Line 429 of Schedule 1, plus the following amounts:

- Federal dividend tax credit (Line 425 of Schedule 1; see ¶11080); and

- Federal surtax on income earned outside Canada (Line 10 of Part 2 of Form T2203 or 48% of the amount from Line 429 of Schedule 1);

Less: any refundable Quebec abatement (Line 440 or Line 15 of Part 2 of Form T2203; see ¶11250).

For Quebec resident individuals, basic federal tax is the tax on Line 429 of Schedule 1 plus the federal dividend tax credit (Line 425 of Schedule 1; see ¶11080) less the refundable Quebec abatement (Line 440 or Line 15 of Part 2 of Form T2203; see ¶11250).

ITA 126(1), (4.2), (7)

¶11011.5 — *Foreign Tax Deduction (T1: Line 232)*

ITA 20(12) provides for a deduction in lieu of claiming an FTC under ITA 126 in certain limited cases. The deduction is claimed as an "other deduction" on Line 232 of the T1 return (see ¶9273). The deduction is only available with respect to foreign taxes paid in respect of income from property (i.e., in respect of non-business income tax). Also, an amount may only be deducted under ITA 20(12) from the source to which the tax relates. To the extent that a taxpayer claims a deduction under ITA 20(12), the right to claim an FTC in respect of that amount is lost.

Normally, it is more advantageous to claim an FTC rather than a deduction under ITA 20(12) in respect of foreign non-business income tax. A deduction under ITA 20(12) is normally only claimed if an FTC is not available because, for example, the foreign tax applies to income that is Canadian-source income under the ITA, the tax was not paid in the year, or the amount of the FTC is limited by virtue of the formula discussed under ¶11011.4.

Some considerations with respect to ITA 20(12) include the following:

- Foreign tax paid in respect of a capital gain cannot be deducted under ITA 20(12) because a capital gain is not income from business or property (VD 2003-0003095);

- An amount of foreign non-business income tax allocated by a partnership to a partner and in respect of which the partner claims a deduction under ITA 20(12) will not result in a reduction to the ACB of the partnership interest (VD 2004-0075931E5); and

- There is no restriction on the deductibility of foreign tax under ITA 20(12) to the actual amount of gross income received from property. Thus, for example, the CRA has stated that an ITA 20(12) deduction is available with respect to U.S. income tax paid for the year on a taxpayer's share of income of an S corporation where there is no distribution of income by the S corporation in the year (VD 2008-0284351I7).

ITA 20(12.1) provides a deduction in computing business income for foreign taxes that are ineligible for an FTC because they are paid in connection with certain property acquisitions that lack an economic profit.

ITA 20(12), (12.1), 126(7)"non-business-income tax"(e), *Roenisch*, [1928–34] C.T.C. 69 (Exch); *Hastings*, [1970] Tax A.B.C. 1175, *The Exolon Co* (1951), 4 Tax A.B.C. 175

¶11012 — *Federal Business Foreign Tax Credit (Form T2209: Lines 4–11)*

To prevent double taxation, a taxpayer who pays foreign tax on income or profits earned from operating a business in a foreign country can claim a federal business foreign tax credit. This FTC reduces the Part I tax that the taxpayer would otherwise have to pay. Compute the credit using Form T2209. Unlike foreign non-business income tax, excess foreign business income tax paid cannot be deducted as a provincial or territorial FTC.

ITA 126(2), Folio S5-F2-C1: *Federal Foreign Tax Credit*

¶11012.1 — *Foreign Business Income Tax Paid (Form T2209: Line 4 or 434)*

In respect of each amount of foreign net business income earned in the year, report the amount of foreign business income tax paid for the taxation year in respect of that income. Foreign business income tax is the total of business income or profits tax paid to a country or a political subdivision of a country for the year (residents of Quebec multiply this amount by 55%). Business income tax does not include a tax, or the portion of a tax, that can reasonably be regarded as relating to an amount that any other person or partnership has received, or is entitled to receive, from that government. Also, business income tax does not include a tax or the portion of a tax that can reasonably be regarded as relating to an amount exempt from Canadian income tax by virtue of a tax treaty.

Any amount of tax paid to a foreign government in excess of the amount that the taxpayer was required to pay under a tax treaty is considered a voluntary contribution and does not qualify as foreign taxes paid.

An adjustment to foreign tax payable may result in an adjustment to Canadian tax payable where an FTC has been claimed. While interest is payable on the adjustment to Canadian tax payable, ITA 161(6.1)(a) and (c) provide that such interest will not be exigible for the period ending 90 days after a taxpayer is first advised of the adjustment.

To be eligible for an FTC in a taxation year, the foreign tax must be paid for the year. A refund of foreign taxes in a subsequent year can reduce the Canadian FTC retroactively. The CRA provides the following comments in paragraph 1.45 of Folio S5-F2-C1 with respect to the evidence required for proof of payment of the foreign tax:

> 1.45 Evidence of the payment of foreign tax is to accompany each return in which a foreign tax credit is claimed. If a taxpayer's foreign tax liability is settled by an amount withheld by the payer of the related income (that is, in a way which is analogous to tax under Part XIII of the Act), a copy of the foreign tax information slip is usually satisfactory. In most other cases, a copy of the tax return filed with the foreign government is required together with copies of receipts or documents establishing payment. The CRA should be notified of any increase or decrease in the amount of foreign tax paid as a result of a subsequent assessment or reassessment by the foreign tax authority, and the rules discussed in ¶1.32, 1.35, and ¶1.42–1.44 should be followed to the extent they are applicable. If the foreign assessment or reassessment results in additional foreign tax paid, proof of payment should be provided.

ITA 126(1)(a), (4.1)–(4.4), (7)"business-income tax", Folio S5-F2-C1 (paras 1.32–1.45), VDs 2011-0411121I7, 2010-0388651I7

¶11012.2 — *Net Foreign Business Income (Form T2209: Line 439)*

In respect of each foreign country, enter the amount of net foreign business income earned in the taxation year on Line 210 of Schedule 21 (identify the source country on Line 200). For the purposes of determining the amount of qualifying foreign business income, "qualifying incomes", and "qualifying losses" are determined in the same manner described above under ¶10311 (see also paragraphs 1.80 to 1.88 of Folio S5-F2-C1).

For purposes of computing net foreign business income, the CRA's position is that the ITA requires that profits be allocated between Canada and the foreign jurisdiction in a manner that adequately reflects the business activities in each jurisdiction that gave rise to those profits (Folio S5-F2-C1, para. 1.83).

In VD 2003-0013335 and Folio S5-F2-C1, the CRA states that the starting point in the calculation of foreign business income is the net income amounts as calculated in accordance with the provisions of the ITA. Thus, for example, the amount of a capital gain to be included in foreign business income would be the 50% taxable portion of the gain. In paragraph 1.80 of Folio S5-F2-C1, the CRA also notes that all direct costs, as well as reasonable allocations of overhead expenses, must be deducted in calculating foreign net business income.

Net foreign business income and related FTCs must be computed in respect of each foreign country in which the corporation carries on business. As such, foreign business income must be allocated to each foreign country. With respect to this allocation, the CRA states the following in paragraphs 1.84 to 1.88 of Folio S5-F2-C1:

1.84 The rules provided by section 4 apply to the calculation of the net income (or loss) from a particular source of income, or from sources of income in a particular place, for the purpose of (among other things) calculating a foreign tax credit under section 126. Subject to the specific rules contained in subsection 4(3) (see ¶1.85), each type of allowable deduction (including an outlay or expense) in arriving at a taxpayer's total income under section 3 is, theoretically, allocable in whole or in part to a source of income in a particular country. Ordinarily such an allocation can be made on the basis of a factual relationship between the particular deduction and the gross income arising from a source in a particular country. This is not always the case, however, and some types of deductions that frequently present apportionment problems are discussed in ¶1.87–1.88.

1.85 For purposes of a foreign tax credit under section 126, subsection 4(3) generally provides that all deductions permitted in computing a taxpayer's income for the year under Part I of the Act apply, either wholly or in part, to a particular source of income or to sources in a particular place. The reference to a particular place would, of course, include a place in a foreign country. However, subsection 4(3) contains some exceptions to this general rule. Each deduction applied in calculating the taxpayer's total income under section 3 that is not specifically referred to in the exceptions in subsection 4(3) must be allocated on a reasonable basis among all sources of income to which they can reasonably be applied, including those in foreign countries. The deduction amounts allocated in this manner to income from a particular source in a particular foreign country must be deducted when calculating either FNBI or FBI in the foreign tax credit formulas, as the case may be, for that country.

1.86 An allocation of expenses to a source of gross income in a particular foreign country for financial statement purposes is normally accepted for the purpose of computing a foreign tax credit for that country, provided that the rules of subsection 4(3), as discussed above, are satisfied. Once a basis for allocation has been established, future allocations are expected to be made on a consistent basis.

1.87 Various methods of allocating interest expenses to sources of income are accepted in particular situations. For example, a specific tracing method is appropriate when funds are borrowed and used for an identifiable purpose related to the earning of income in a particular country. For interest on general purpose borrowing, an allocation based on relative net asset values in different countries may be appropriate in some cases. An allocation of interest expenses based on the relationship of gross incomes in different countries is accepted only when a less arbitrary method is not readily evident. The location of property assigned as security for an amount borrowed is not necessarily an indication that the funds obtained were for the purpose of earning income from a source in the same country in which the property is located.

1.88 The total amount of capital cost allowance claimed by a taxpayer for a tax year must be allocated among the countries to which it relates. The allocation cannot exceed the allowable maximums under Part XI of the Regulations in respect of property situated in a particular country. In particular, the limitation in the case of rental properties must be respected on a country-by-country basis. Subject to these conditions, capital cost allowance deductions may be arbitrarily allocated to income sources in various countries.

ITA 126(7)–(9), VDs 2010-038865I7, 2008-0280941E5 (French), 2006-018191117

¶11012.3 — *Calculation of Business Income FTC (Form T2209: Lines 4–11)*

Generally, a Canadian resident taxpayer can claim an FTC in respect of business income tax paid to a foreign jurisdiction to the extent that the FTC does not exceed that proportion of the Part I tax otherwise payable that the taxpayer's business income in that foreign country bears to the taxpayer's net income.

In particular, the deductible business FTC is limited to the least of the following three amounts (Form T2209: Lines 4, 7, or 10):

1. The amount of foreign business income tax paid in the year, plus any unused FTC for that country for the ten taxation years immediately preceding, and the three taxation years immediately following the year (Form T2209: Line 4);

2. The total of the following amounts (Form T2209: Line 7):

   a. The amount determined by the following formula: (Net foreign business income/Net income) × Basic federal tax (Form T2209: Line 5); and

   b. Federal surtax on income earned outside Canada (i.e., the amount from Line 10 of Part 2 of Form T2203 or 48% of the amount from Line 429 of Schedule 1) (Form T2209: Line 6); and

3. The basic federal tax otherwise payable for the year (including the federal surtax on income earned outside Canada) less any non-business foreign tax credit deductible under ITA 126(1) as calculated on Form T2209 Line 3 (Form T2209: Line 10)

Basic federal tax for these purposes is the tax on Line 429 of Schedule 1, plus the federal dividend tax credit (Line 425 of Schedule 1; see ¶11080).

Generally, non-business income foreign tax credits may be deducted before business income foreign tax credits. This rule is important because non-business FTCs cannot be carried forward.

ITA 126(1), (2), (2.1), (7)

¶11012.4 — *Application of Unused Foreign Business FTCs*

A taxpayer can carry back any unused foreign business income tax credits to the three previous taxation years, and can carry forward unused credits for ten taxation years. To carry back a FTC to previous years, a taxpayer should complete Form T1-ADJ, *T1 Adjustment Request*. Form T1-ADJ must be filed with the CRA no later than the day on which the taxpayer's T1 return for the current year is due (see ¶14010). Without the filing of a timely election, the benefits of the unused FTC carryback provisions are unavailable.

The amount of FTCs claimed in a taxation year is considered first to be in respect of foreign taxes paid for that year against tax payable under Part I, and any remaining balance is considered to be a deduction in respect of unused FTCs carried over from other years. Unused FTCs must be utilized in the order in which they arise. A taxpayer can only use the credit to reduce Part I tax on income originating from the same foreign country.

ITA 126(2), (2.3), (7)"unused foreign tax credit"

¶11013 — *Claiming and Filing*

Taxpayers should complete Form T2209 in Canadian dollars as discussed in the above sections. If the taxpayer was a member of a partnership and is entitled to claim a part of the foreign taxes the partnership paid, include in the calculations the amount shown in the partnership's financial statements or in Box 81 and Box 82 of the T5013 slip.

Enter the amount from Line 12 of Form T2209 on Line 405 of Schedule 1. The amount on Line 12 cannot be greater than the amount of basic federal tax on Line 429 of Schedule 1.

If a taxpayer's federal foreign tax credit on non-business income is less than the taxpayer's foreign taxes paid, taxpayers who are not Quebec residents may be able to claim a provincial or territorial foreign tax credit on Form T2036, *Provincial or Territorial Foreign Tax Credit*.

Taxpayers may be able to deduct the amount of net foreign taxes paid on Line 232 for which the taxpayer has not received a federal, provincial, or territorial foreign tax credit (see ¶11011.5) This does not include certain taxes, such as those on amounts the taxpayer could have deducted under a tax treaty on Line 256 (see ¶9400).

Taxpayers who are filing electronically should keep a copy of all relevant documents in case the CRA requests them at a later date. Taxpayers who are paper-filing should include a completed Form T2209, official receipts that show the foreign taxes paid, and a note showing the taxpayer's calculations. If the taxpayer paid taxes to the U.S., attach the W-2 information slip, U.S. 1040 return, and any other supporting documents that apply.

In 2015, the CRA changed the requirements for acceptable supporting documents related to foreign tax credit claims made by individuals with U.S. source income. The documents necessary to support a claim for U.S. taxes paid are noted on Form T2209, and include federal, state, and municipal tax returns and associated schedules and forms, a copy of the federal account transcript, and an account statement or similar document from the state and/or municipal tax authority. A breakdown by income type, country and recipient is also required if the taxpayer filed a joint return with their spouse or common-law partner. If the taxpayer is unable to provide a copy of a notice of assessment or other document from the U.S. tax authority indicating U.S. income and final tax liability, the CRA will accept proof of payment or refund (i.e., bank statements, cancelled cheques, or official receipts). The following information must be clearly indicated: that the payment was made to or received from the applicable U.S. tax authority; the amount of the payment or refund; the tax year to which the payment or refund applies; and the date that the amount was paid or received (see VD 2016-0634941C6).

¶11020 — Federal Political Contribution Tax Credit (T1 Schedule 1: Line 410)

A non-refundable federal tax credit is available for political contributions to candidates for election to the House of Commons or to registered federal political parties, up to a maximum of $650 for the year. The credit available is equal to 75% of the first $400 of contributions, plus 50% of the next $350 of contributions, plus 33 1/3% of the next $525 of contributions. The maximum credit is reached with contributions of $1,275. No tax credit in respect of political contributions is available where the taxpayer has received any other financial benefit by virtue of a contribution, including a grant, subsidy, other tax deduction, or provincial credit.

Some provinces and territories also allow a provincial or territorial tax credit for donations to a provincial or territorial party. See Chapters 12 and 13 for provincial and territorial information.

¶11021 — *Claiming and Filing*

Enter on Line 409 the total that the taxpayer and his or her spouse or common-law partner contributed during the year to a registered federal political party or a candidate for election to the House of Commons. Complete the chart for Line 410 on the federal worksheet in the forms book to calculate the credit. If the taxpayer's total political contributions are $1,275 or more, enter $650.

Official receipts must be filed with the taxpayer's paper-filed return in support of any political contributions claimed on the return. However, do not attach official receipts for amounts shown in T5003, T5013 or T5013A slips, or on financial statements showing an amount a partnership allocated to you. Taxpayers who are e-filing should keep all receipts in case the CRA requests them.

ITA 127(3), 143.2(6.1), 248(31), (32), ITR Part XX, ITR 2000, IC 75-2R7

¶11030 — Investment Tax Credit (T1 Schedule 1: Line 412)

The investment tax credit (ITC) provides taxpayers an incentive for the following types of investments and expenditures:

1. The cost of acquiring qualified property in Atlantic Canada (see ¶11031);

2. Qualified scientific research and experimental development (SR&ED) expenditures (see ¶11032);

3. Flow-through mining expenditures (see ¶11033);

4. Apprenticeship expenditures (see ¶11034); and

5. Eligible child care space expenditures (see ¶11035).

Generally, the amount of ITC available depends upon the nature of the property acquired or expenditure incurred, the date the property is acquired or the expenditure incurred, and the status of the taxpayer. ITCs are computed by multiplying a specified percentage by the cost of the property acquired or the expenditure incurred (net of any government or non-government assistance received, including any GST/HST input tax credit or rebate received). If a property in respect of which an ITC has been claimed is ultimately disposed of, the ITC recapture provisions in ITA 127(27) to (35) may be applicable.

Individuals calculate ITCs on Form T2038 (IND), *Investment Tax Credit (Individuals)*. An individual should complete Form T2038 (IND) if the individual: (1) earned an ITC during the current tax year; (2) is claiming a carryforward of unused ITCs from a previous tax year; (3) has a recapture of ITC on a SR&ED expenditure and/or a recapture of ITC on a child care spaces expenditure; (4) is requesting a carryback of ITCs to a prior taxation year; or (5) is claiming a refund for an ITC earned during the current tax year. Form T2038 (IND) is due for filing no later than 12 months after the filing due date of the individual's income tax return for the tax year in which the property was acquired or the expenditure was made.

An ITC normally reduces the cost of the related expenditure for tax purposes (e.g., the cost or capital cost of the property to which the ITC relates, or the UCC of the relevant class of depreciable property in which the property belongs). To the extent that such a reduction does not take place (for example, when the tax credit relates to non-depreciable property that was acquired and disposed of in taxation years preceding the year in which the credit is claimed), the amount of the ITC is included in income under ITA 12(1)(t) for the taxation year following the later of the year in which the credit is claimed and the year in which the related expenditure took place.

A taxpayer is not considered to have acquired a property or made capital expenditures for purposes of earning an ITC until the property becomes available-for-use. Generally, an asset becomes available-for-use at the earliest of: 1) the time at which the property is first used by the claimant for the purpose of earning income, and 2) the time the property is delivered or is made available to the claimant and is capable of producing a saleable product or service. The application of the available-for-use rule will, in certain cases, delay the time at which a taxpayer may claim an ITC. However, *eligibility* for an ITC is not affected by the available-for-use rules. The available-for-use rules are discussed in more detail at ¶7125.

ITA 13(7.1), 13(26)–(32), 37(1), 37(1.2), 127(5)–(36), 248(19), IT-273R2: *Government Assistance: General Comments*, CRA Guide T4088

¶11031 — *Qualified Property (Form T2038: Line 6714)*

Complete the calculations on Form T2038 (IND) to claim the 10% non-refundable ITC in respect of the acquisition of qualified property acquired after 1994 for use in prescribed Atlantic regions reported on Line 6714.

Qualified property includes *new* prescribed buildings, machinery, or equipment acquired during the year for use in designated activities in specific geographical areas. The geographical areas are Newfoundland and Labrador, Nova Scotia, Prince Edward Island, New Brunswick, the Gaspé Peninsula, and prescribed offshore regions. Designated activities include (among others): manufacturing or processing goods for sale or lease; prospecting, exploring, extracting, and developing minerals; exploring, drilling, operating an oil or gas well, and extracting oil or natural gas; processing ore, iron ore, or tar sands to the prime metal stage only; logging; farming, or fishing; and Canadian field processing.

The qualified property ITC was phased out in respect of qualified property primarily used in oil, gas and mining activities in Atlantic Canada (referred to as "qualified resource property"). Subject to grandfathering, the 10% ITC was reduced to 5% for qualified resource property acquired in 2014 and 2015 and was eliminated in respect of assets acquired after 2015. As an exception, qualified resource properties acquired before 2017 as part of a grandfathered phase of a project are eligible for the 10% ITC. Grandfathering applies if the expenditure is incurred under a written agreement entered into by the corporation before March 29, 2012, or as part of the development of a grandfathered mine.

127(9)"ITC"(a)

¶11032 — *Qualified SR&ED Expenditures (Form T2038: Line 6712)*

Qualified expenditures incurred by an individual in respect of SR&ED activities may be eligible for an ITC. Qualifying SR&ED expenditures may be current or capital in nature. Generally, to be a qualified expenditure, the amount must be incurred for the purpose of carrying out SR&ED activities in Canada.

SR&ED is defined in the ITA as systematic investigation or search carried out in a field of science or technology by means of experiment or analysis to advance scientific knowledge or to achieve technological advancement. Qualifying SR&ED work must either be:

1) *Experimental development*: work done to achieve technological advancement for the purpose of creating new, or improving existing, materials, devices, products, or processes;

2) *Applied research*: work done to advance scientific knowledge with a specific practical application in view;

3) *Basic research*: work done to advance scientific knowledge without a specific practical application in view; or

4) *Support work*: work done in direct support of one the three categories described above and that is engineering, design, operations research, mathematical analysis, computer programming, data collection, testing or psychological research (eligible support work must correspond to the needs of the experimental development, applied research or basic research performed).

> Most SR&ED claims are for experimental development work, which includes work undertaken for the purpose of achieving a technological advancement for the purpose of creating new, or improving existing materials, devices, products or processes, including incremental improvements. A project does not have to succeed to qualify for the SR&ED credit (i.e., it is the attempt that is applicable).

The following work does not qualify as SR&ED: market research or sales promotion; quality control or routine testing of materials, devices, products, or processes; research in social sciences or the humanities; prospecting, exploring or drilling for, or producing minerals, petroleum or natural gas; commercial production of a new or improved material, device or product, or the commercial use of a new or improved process; style changes; or routine data collection.

Eligible SR&ED claims generally must include detailed explanations, adequately supported arguments, and evidence supporting all aspects of the SR&ED project. With respect to making a claim, the CRA has issued many SR&ED publications, including guides, policy documents, forms, brochures, circulars, and bulletins. Detailed information about the SR&ED program, including how to claim SR&ED tax incentives and SR&ED forms and publications, is available at: canada.ca/en/revenue-agency/services/scientific-research-experimental-development-tax-incentive-program.html.

ITA 127(9) "ITC"(a.1)

¶11033 — *Flow-Through Mining Expenditures (Form T2038: Line 6717)*

Flow-through shares allow resource companies to renounce or "flow through" tax expenses associated with their Canadian exploration activities to investors, who can deduct the expenses in calculating their own taxable income. The mineral exploration tax credit provides an additional income tax benefit for individuals who invest in mining flow-through shares, which augments the tax benefits associated with the deductions that are flowed through. This credit is equal to 15% of specified mineral exploration expenses incurred in Canada and renounced to flow-through share investors.

The 2018 federal budget extended the eligibility for the mineral exploration tax credit for an additional year, to flow-through share agreements entered into on or before March 31, 2019, and the 2018 Fall Economic Statement further extended eligibility for the credit by an additional five years, until March 31, 2024. Under the "look-back" rule, funds raised in one calendar year with the benefit of the credit can be spent on eligible exploration up to the end of the following calendar year. Therefore, funds raised with the credit during the first three months of 2019 can support eligible exploration until the end of 2020.

Mineral exploration expenses eligible for ITCs are reported to an individual in Box 128 of Form T101, *Statement of Resource Expenses*, in the case of direct investment in flow-through shares, or in Box 128 of Form T5013A, *Statement of Partnership Income for Tax Shelters and Renounced Resource Expenses*, if the investment is made through a partnership.

ITA 127(9)"ITC"(a.2)

¶11034 — *Apprenticeship Expenditures (Form T2038: Line 6718)*

Enter the required information and complete the calculations on Form T2038 (IND) to claim the apprenticeship ITC reported on Line 6718.

A taxpayer can earn an ITC equal to 10% of eligible salaries and wages paid to eligible apprentices employed in the business in the taxation year to a maximum credit of $2,000, per year, per apprentice. An eligible apprentice is one who is working in a prescribed trade in the first 24 months of the apprenticeship contract registered with a province or Canada. The contract must be registered with Canada or a province or territory under an apprenticeship program designed to certify or license individuals in the trade. Prescribed trades include all of the trades listed as Red Seal Trades at red-seal.ca. The Red Seal allows a journeyperson to engage in their trade, without having to write further examinations, in any province or territory in Canada where the trade is recognized.

The amount of eligible salary and wages for a taxation year is deemed to be the amount of the eligible salary and wages for the year otherwise determined, less the amount of any government assistance or non-government assistance in respect of the eligible salary and wages for the year that, at the time of the filing of the taxpayer's return for the year, the taxpayer has received, is entitled to receive, or can reasonably be expected to receive.

Where an amount paid to an eligible apprentice is eligible for both the apprenticeship and the SR&ED ITCs, the taxpayer can only claim one credit in respect of the expenditure.

ITA 127(9)"ITC"(a.4), 127(11.1)(c.4), VDs 2009-0330311C6, 2008-0285401C6, 2009-033375117, 2009-0313821E5, 2007-024462117, 2009-030739117

¶11035 — *Eligible Child Care Space Expenditures (Form T2038: Line 6719)*

This credit has been eliminated for expenditures incurred after March 21, 2017 (other than those incurred before 2020 under a written agreement entered into by that date). Therefore, the information below is only applicable to expenditures incurred before March 22, 2017.

Complete the calculations on Form T2038 (IND) to claim the non-refundable eligible child care space ITC reported on Line 6719.

A taxpayer, carrying on business in Canada, other than a child care services business, can claim an ITC to create one or more new child care spaces in a new or existing licensed child care facility for the children of employees and for other children in the community. The ITC is computed as the lesser of: $10,000, and 25% of the eligible expenditures (per child care space created).

Expenditures incurred before March 22, 2017 for the cost of depreciable property and specified start-up costs acquired or incurred before March 22, 2017 to create the new child care space at a licensed child care facility are eligible to be claimed. The intention of the credit is to encourage businesses to create licensed child care spaces for the children of their employees. The provision of child care spaces must be ancillary to one or more businesses of the taxpayer that do not include the provision of child care spaces for the credit to be available. Eligible depreciable property includes the building or the part of the building in which the child care facility is located; furniture and appliances; computer and audio-visual equipment; and playground structures and equipment. Specified child care start-up costs include the initial costs for building permits and architect's fees; landscaping for the children's playground; regulatory inspections and licensing fees; and children's educational material. The ITC is not available for any of the ongoing expenses of the child care facility such as supplies, wages, salaries, or utilities.

ITA 127(9)"ITC"(a.5)

¶11040 — Labour-Sponsored Funds Tax Credit (T1 Schedule 1: Lines 413, 414)

A labour-sponsored venture capital corporation (LSVCC) is a venture capital corporation established by either federal or provincial legislation and sponsored by a trade union or other specified employee organization. LSVCCs are intended to provide venture capital to qualifying businesses by investing in small- and medium-sized business with less than $50 million in assets and 500 employees. The labour-sponsored funds tax credit provides a tax credit for individuals who purchase shares of a prescribed LSVCC, to a maximum of $5,000. There may also be a corresponding provincial or territorial tax credit.

The LSVCC tax credit was phased out as illustrated in the table below (see: fin.gc.ca/n13/data/13-072_1-eng.asp):

Year	2013	2014	2015	2016	after 2016
Tax Credit Rate	15%	15%	10%	5%	—

However, for 2016 and later taxation years, the 15% LSVCC tax credit was restored for share purchases of provincially-registered LSVCCs, up to a maximum investment of $5,000 (i.e., a $750 credit). Therefore, for 2016 and later taxation years, a 15% tax credit is available for share purchases of provincially-registered LSVCCs only, to a maximum investment of $5,000.

¶11041 — *Claiming and Filing*

The LSVCC will provide investors with Form T5006, *Statement of Registered Labour-Sponsored Venture Capital Corporation Class A Shares* (or a provincial or territorial information slip), which provides all the information required to complete the claim. Enter the net cost of shares on Line 413. Net cost is the amount paid for the shares, minus any government assistance (other than federal or provincial tax credits) received on the shares. Enter the amount of the allowable credit on Line 414.

ITA 127.4, ITR Part X.3, 6701, Form T5006, VD 2005-0153771E5

¶11050 — Working Income Tax Benefit Advance Payments (T1 Schedule 1: Line 415)

The working income tax benefit (WITB) is a refundable tax credit payable to certain low-income individuals and families who earn employment or business income. The WITB consists of a base amount and a disability supplement. Only one spouse can claim the basic WITB and two persons cannot both claim the basic WITB for the same eligible dependant.

Individuals who expect to be entitled to a WITB for a taxation year (on the basis of expected working income and adjusted net income) can apply to CRA for a prepayment of up to 50% of their estimated WITB, provided the prepayment is at least $100. Individuals apply for prepayment of the WITB on Form RC201, *Working Income Tax Benefit Advance Payments Application*. The application must be submitted each year to CRA by September 1 of the applicable taxation year (e.g., between January 1 and September 1, 2018 for the 2018 taxation year). The individual may receive WITB advance payments not exceeding one-half of the individual's estimated WITB (i.e., one-half of the Basic WITB and the WITB Supplement). The person who receives the WITB advance payments is the person who must claim the basic WITB for the year on Line 453 (see ¶11290).

In the case of a couple or common-law partners, a joint application is required designating which spouse or partner is to receive the advance payment. The designated individual must be either the person expected to have the higher working income or who can reasonably be expected to be entitled to the WITB Supplement. However, no advance payment will be made if the total WITB is estimated to be less than $100 or if the individual did not file a tax return for a preceding tax year in respect of which the individual received an advance payment.

Note that, for 2019 and later taxation years, the WITB is being replaced by the Canada Workers Benefit (CWB), which is an enhanced version of the WITB (see ¶11290 for more information).

¶11051 — *Claiming and Filing*

CRA will send Form RC210, *WITB Advance Payments Statement*, outlining the advance payments made. Individuals who received WITB advance payments for 2018 must file a T1 return and report the amounts received on Line 415. Any additional WITB an individual is entitled to receive is calculated by subtracting the advance payments (Line 415) against the full refundable WITB calculated (Line 453; see ¶11290). Individuals entitled to any additional WITB will receive it after the T1 return is filed. If the WITB advance payments are greater than the individual's total WITB entitlement, the individual may be required to repay the difference when filing the T1 return.

ITA 122.7–122.71, Schedule 6, Form RC201, Form RC210, Guide RC4227

¶11060 — Special Taxes (T1 Schedule 1: Line 418)

¶11061 — *RESP Accumulated Income Payments*

Individuals who received an accumulated income payment (AIP) from an RESP in the year may have to pay Part X.5 tax in addition to the regular Part I tax (see Line 130 at ¶8266) on all or part of the amount reported in Box 040 of the individual's T4A slips. An "accumulated income payment" means any amount paid out of an RESP other than a distribution that is an educational assistance payment, a refund of payments, the repayment of a CES grant to the government, a payment to a designated educational institution in Canada, or a transfer to another RESP.

¶11061.1 — *Calculating Part X.5 Tax*

Part X.5 tax is determined by the formula $(A + B - C) \times D$, where:

- "A" is defined as the total of all AIPs made at any time under an RESP under which the recipient is a subscriber; or, where there is no subscriber under the plan, the recipient is the surviving spouse or common-law partner of a deceased original subscriber, to the extent that the payments are included in computing the person's Part I income for the year; and

- "B" is defined as any other AIPs from an RESP or revoked plan that have been included in computing the recipient's Part I income for the year.

The tax payable for a taxation year is basically 20 per cent (12 per cent where a similar tax is payable by the recipient for the year under Quebec law) of the AIPs received in the year, as described in A and B, reduced by RRSP deductions as described in C for recipients of the payments included in A.

For recipients of AIPs included in A, the total of these amounts may be reduced by the total of all amounts deducted in computing the person's Part I income for the year (up to the value of A in respect of the person for the year), but this reduction may not exceed the lifetime limit of $50,000 minus the total amounts previously used to reduce the Part X.5 tax payable on AIPs in previous years. In order to take advantage of this reduction by making offsetting contributions to an RRSP or spousal RRSP, the AIP recipient must have sufficient RRSP deduction room available for the year. Note that the deduction must be claimed for the year in which the AIPs were made.

The following comments and example are provided in CRA Guide RC4092: *Registered Education Savings Plans*:

How AIPs are taxed

Promoters report AIPs in Box 040 of a T4A slip, *Statement of Pension, Retirement, Annuity and Other Income*, and send a copy to the recipient of the AIP. The recipient has to include the AIP as income on his or her income tax and benefit return for the year he or she receives it. An AIP is subject to two different taxes: the regular income tax and an additional tax of 20% (12% for residents of Quebec).

Regular tax — This is the tax you calculate when you fill out your income tax and benefit return. It is based on your total taxable income.

Additional tax — You calculate this tax separately, using Form T1172, *Additional Tax on Accumulated Income Payments from RESPs*. Include a filled out copy of Form T1172 with your income tax and benefit return for the year you receive the AIP. You have to pay the additional tax by the balance due date for your regular tax, usually April 30 of the year that follows the year in which you received the AIP.

Reducing the amount of AIPs subject to tax — You can reduce the amount of AIPs subject to tax if you are the original subscriber or, where there is no other subscriber, the spouse or common-law partner of a deceased original subscriber and you meet both of the following conditions:

- you contribute an amount not more than the amount of the AIPs (to a lifetime maximum of $50,000 worth of AIPs) to your registered retirement savings plan (RRSP), or your spouse's or common-law partner's RRSP, in the year the AIPs are received or in the first 60 days of the following year; and

- your RRSP deduction limit allows you to deduct the amount contributed to your or your spouse's or common-law partner's RRSP on Line 208 of your tax return. Claim the deduction for the year in which any payments are made.

You cannot reduce the AIPs subject to tax if you became a subscriber because of the death of the original subscriber.

By claiming a deduction for a contribution to your RRSP, PRPP or SPP, you reduce your taxable income, which reduces your regular tax. The deduction for the contribution also reduces the amount of additional tax payable by reducing the amount of AIPs subject to tax (see Form T1172). If the amount of the deduction for the contribution equals the amount of the AIPs, the taxes on the AIPs are zero.

Promoters usually have to withhold regular and additional taxes on AIPs. However, they do not have to withhold tax if both of the following apply:

- the AIPs are transferred directly to your RRSP, PRPP or SPP or your spouse's or common-law partner's RRSP or SPP; and

- your RRSP/PRPP deduction limit allows you to deduct the contribution in the year it is made.

Fill out Form T1171, *Tax Withholding Waiver on Accumulated Income Payments from RESPs*, to ask the promoter to transfer the payment directly to your or your spouse's or common-law partner's RRSP without withholding tax.

¶11061.2 — *Claiming and Filing*

Individuals who received an accumulated income payment from an RESP in the year and are liable for Part X.5 tax on all or part of the amount reported in Box 40 of the individual's T4A slips should complete Form T1172, *Additional Tax on Accumulated Income Payments from RESPs*. For more information, see RC4092, *Registered Education Savings Plans (RESPs)*.

ITA 146.1, 204.94, PwC, "RESPs: A user's guide", Tax Memo, Jan 7, 2013

¶11062 — *Tax on Excess Employee Profit-Sharing Plan (EPSP) Amounts*

Applicable after 2011, "specified employees" who receive an "excess EPSP amount" under an employee profit sharing plan may have to pay a special tax on the excessive allocations. A "specified employee" is a person who deals with an employer in a non-arm's length relationship or who owns, directly or indirectly, at any time in the year, not less than 10 per cent of the issued shares of any class of the capital stock of the employer corporation, or any other corporation that is related to the employer corporation. Generally, a taxpayer's "excess EPSP amount" for a taxation year is the portion of the employer's total contributions to an EPSP that is allocated to the taxpayer for the year that exceeds 20 per cent of the taxpayer's total other employment income received in the year from the employer.

To calculate the available deduction, see Form RC359: *Tax on Excess Employees Profit-Sharing Plan Amounts*. The special tax imposed in respect of excess EPSP amounts may be waived or cancelled by the CRA in certain circumstances.

Consequential to the addition of ITA 207.8, ITA 8(1)(o.2) was added to allow a taxpayer to deduct an "excess EPSP amount" in computing income for a taxation year (see ¶2445).

ITA 8(1)(o.2), 146.1, 207.8, Form T1172, Form RC359, Guide RC4092

¶11065 — *Family Tax Cut Credit (T1 Schedule 1: Line 423)*

> The family tax cut credit has been repealed for 2016 and subsequent taxation years. The commentary below discusses the former provision, as applicable to the 2014 and 2015 taxation years only.

The Family Tax Cut Credit was a non-refundable tax credit of up to $2,000 for couples with children under 18 years of age that was available in the 2014 and 2015 taxation years. Essentially, the family tax cut credit allowed a higher-income spouse or common-law partner to notionally transfer up to $50,000 of taxable income to an "eligible relation" in a lower income tax bracket for federal tax purposes, up to a maximum tax benefit of $2,000.

An "eligible relation" of a particular individual is an individual who is resident in Canada at the end of a taxation year; who is the spouse or common-law partner of the particular individual; and who is not, due to a breakdown in the marriage or common-law partnership, living separate and apart from the particular individual at the end of year and for a period of at least 90 days commencing the year.

¶11066 — *Calculating the Credit*

The family tax cut credit was calculated as the difference between:

- the combined taxes payable (after non-refundable tax credits are claimed) by an individual and the individual's eligible relation, and

- the combined taxes that would be payable (after non-refundable tax credits are claimed) by them if the higher-income individual notionally transferred taxable income (up to $50,000) to the lower-income individual.

However, if this difference exceeded $2,000, the credit was limited to this amount.

¶11070 — Federal Tax on Split Income (T1 Schedule 1: Line 424)

ITA 120.4 imposes a special tax on split income (TOSI) at the highest individual rate on certain passive income of a "specified individual" to limit the benefits of dividend sprinkling structures. Dividend sprinkling generally refers to the acquisition of shares of a private corporation by low-income members of the family of the high-income principal shareholder.

The scope of the TOSI has been significantly expanded for 2018 and later taxation years, and extended to adults in certain circumstances.

For a detailed discussion of the application of the TOSI for 2018 and later taxation years, see ¶14210.

¶11071 — *Claiming and Filing*

The tax on split income is calculated on Form T1206, *Tax on Split Income*, and reported on Line 424. The specified individual reports the split income on his or her T1 return and claims a deduction for the same amount on Line 232 (see ¶9273).

For a detailed discussion of the calculation of the TOSI for 2018 and later taxation years, see ¶14210.

ITA 120.4, 160(1.2), Form T1206

¶11080 — Federal Dividend Tax Credit (T1 Schedule 1: Line 425)

Individuals who receive an eligible dividend from a Canadian resident corporation in 2018 must gross up the amount of the dividend received by 38%. The grossed-up amount of the dividend is reported on Line 120 and the individual may claim a non-refundable dividend tax credit equal to 6/11 the amount of the gross up (or 15.02% of the amount of the grossed-up dividend) on Line 425.

Individuals who receive a taxable dividend other than an eligible dividend (i.e., a "non-eligible" or "small business" dividend) from a Canadian resident corporation in 2018 must gross up the amount of the dividend received by 16%. The grossed-up amount of the dividend is reported on Line 120 and the individual may claim a non-refundable dividend tax credit equal to 8/11 of the amount of the gross-up (or 10% of the amount of the grossed-up dividend) on Line 425.

As a result of the reduction in the small business tax rate for 2018 and subsequent taxation years, the gross-up factor for non-eligible dividends decreased to 16% for the 2018 taxation year, and to 15% for 2019 and subsequent taxation years. The dividend tax credit rate decreased to 10% for the 2018 taxation year, and to 9% of taxable dividends for 2019 and subsequent taxation years. These changes are illustrated in the following table:

Non-Eligible Dividends	2017	2018	2019+
Dividend gross-up	17%	16%	15%
Dividend tax credit	10.5%	10%	9%

The actual and taxable amount of the dividend, as well as the dividend tax credit, are generally reported on a T5 slip, but may also be reported on a T3 slip where the individual earns dividends through a trust, or a T5013 slip where the individual earns dividends through a partnership.

¶11081 — *Claiming and Filing*

Taxpayers who reported dividends on Line 120 of the T1 return should enter on Line 425 the total of the dividend tax credits from taxable Canadian corporations shown on their information slips as follows:

- Non-eligible dividends: Box 12 of the T5 slip, Box 39 of the T3 slip, or Box 51-2 of the T5013 slip
- Eligible dividends: Box 26 of the T5 slip, Box 51 of the T3 slip, or Box 52-2 of the T5013 slip.

ITA 82(1), 89(1), 89(14), 121(a), 212(b)

¶11090 — Overseas Employment Tax Credit (T1 Schedule 1: Line 426)

An employee who is abroad for a period of time in connection with a work project of an employer is generally considered a resident of Canada during the period of temporary absence and is liable to tax on income earned while abroad. However, for taxation years before 2016, employees could claim an Overseas Employment Tax Credit (OETC) against tax otherwise payable.

The OETC was gradually phased out in stages from 2013 to 2015, and *for all employees, the OETC is eliminated for taxation years after 2015*.

ITA 122.3, ITR Part XXXIV, LX, Form T626, IT-497R4: *Overseas Employment Tax Credit*

¶11100 — Minimum Tax Carryover (T1 Schedule 1: Line 427)

Minimum tax limits the tax advantage an individual can receive in a year from certain incentives. Essentially, minimum tax is intended to ensure that individuals who would otherwise pay little or no tax because they have a significant number of tax preference items (i.e., specific items that reduce taxable income, such as the capital gains exemption and tax shelters) pay higher tax instead. A taxpayer is liable for minimum tax if it is more than the federal tax calculated in the usual manner. A basic exemption amount of $40,000 is allowed for purposes of calculating taxable income for minimum tax purposes.

Minimum tax applies to individuals resident in Canada (including deemed residents) and also generally applies to trusts, as trusts are considered to be individuals for tax purposes. Minimum tax also applies on income earned in Canada by non-resident individuals; however, it does not apply in the year of a taxpayer's death, nor does it apply to any of the special returns that may be filed on behalf of bankrupt or deceased individuals.

Generally, in determining minimum tax payable, the lowest tax rate of 15 per cent is applied to an "adjusted taxable income" amount, as reduced by an individual's basic exemption of $40,000. This amount is then adjusted to take into account certain non-refundable personal tax credits.

Generally, a taxpayer must pay the higher of alternative minimum tax and regular federal tax. Where alternative minimum tax exceeds regular federal tax, the excess may be carried forward for 7 years and can offset regular federal tax in those years to the extent that regular federal tax exceeds alternative minimum tax. A provincial alternative minimum tax is imposed by the provinces.

Reproduced below is an excerpt from CRA's T1 Guide (5000-G):

> Minimum tax limits the tax advantage you can receive in a year from certain incentives. You have to pay minimum tax if it is more than the federal tax you calculate in the usual manner. When calculating your taxable income for this tax, which does not apply to a person who died in the year, you are allowed a basic exempt amount of $40,000.

> To find out if you have to pay this tax, add the amounts shown in B later in this section and 60% of the amount on Line 127 of your return. If the total is $40,000 or less, you probably do not have to pay minimum tax. If the total is more than $40,000, you may have to pay it.

> Use Form T691, *Alternative Minimum Tax*, to find out if you have to pay minimum tax. You also have to complete Form 428 to calculate additional provincial or territorial tax for minimum tax purposes.

> Here is a list of the most common situations where you may have to pay minimum tax:

> A. You reported a taxable capital gain on Line 127 of your return.

> B. You claimed any of the following on your return:

> • a loss (including your share of a partnership loss) resulting from, or increased by, claiming capital cost allowance on rental properties;

> • a loss from a limited partnership that is a tax shelter;

- most carrying charges (Line 221) on certain investments;

- a loss from resource properties resulting from, or increased by, claiming a depletion allowance, exploration expenses, development expenses, or Canadian oil and gas property expenses; or

- a deduction on Line 249 for security options.

C. You claimed any of the following tax credits on Schedule 1:

- a federal political contribution tax credit on lines 409 and 410;

- an investment tax credit on Line 412;

- a labour-sponsored funds tax credit on Line 414; or

- a federal dividend tax credit on Line 425.

ITA 120.2, 120.4, 127.5–127.55, Form T691, Form T1206

¶11101 — *Adjusted Taxable Income*

"Adjusted taxable income" represents a recalculation of taxable income otherwise determined under ITA Part I. Generally speaking, it is an individual's taxable income, recomputed in accordance with special rules in ITA 127.5 to 127.55. Pursuant to these rules, some amounts that are non-taxable for purposes of Part I tax are included in income for the purposes of minimum tax, while certain amounts allowed as deductions under Part I are not deductible for purposes of determining income subject to minimum tax. The result of this computation is an individual's "adjusted taxable income". In circumstances where an investment is made through a partnership, a member of the partnership who is an individual is treated as having claimed the partnership's deductible amounts in proportion to the individual's share of the partnership income. Accordingly, in computing the adjusted taxable income, the individual's restriction would be based on a proportionate partnership interest. Where the individual is a non-resident, it is the non-resident's taxable income earned in Canada that must be recalculated for minimum tax purposes.

See Form T691, *Alternative Minimum Tax*, for the various adjustments contained in ITA 127.52 that must be made for purposes of determining an individual's "adjusted taxable income" for minimum tax purposes.

¶11102 — *Basic Exemption and Basic Minimum Tax Credit*

Adjusted taxable income is reduced by a basic exemption of $40,000 to arrive at the amount in respect of which minimum tax is payable. The basic exemption is not subject to indexing and is available to all individual taxpayers.

Individuals are allowed a basic minimum tax credit for the following personal and other credits that the individual deducted in computing tax payable under Part I for the year: the personal credits in ITA 118(1), age credit in ITA 118(2), Canada employment credit in ITA 118(10), adoption expense credit in ITA 118.01, first-time home buyers' credit in ITA 118.05, volunteer firefighter tax credit in ITA 118.06, search and rescue volunteers credit in ITA 118.07, donation tax credit in ITA 118.1, medical expense tax credit in ITA 118.2, credit for mental or physical impairment in ITA 118.3(1), tuition credit in ITA 118.5, unused tuition, textbook and education credits in ITA 118.61, credit for student loan interest in ITA 118.62, credit for *Employment Insurance Act* premiums and CPP/QPP contributions in ITA 118.7, credit for former residents regarding certain dispositions of Canadian property in ITA 119, and logging tax credit in ITA 127(1).

The amount which is deductible for minimum tax purposes in respect of a particular tax credit is the amount that is deductible for regular tax purposes. For example, if the individual could have claimed $5,000 for charitable donations but chose to claim only $2,000 on their tax return, the deduction for minimum tax would be $2,000.

ITA 127.53, 127.531

¶11103 — *Special Foreign Tax Credit*

A special foreign tax credit is available in ITA 127.54 to individuals subject to minimum tax. The foreign tax credit provided in respect of the minimum tax liability is the greater of: (1) the amount otherwise deductible as a foreign tax credit under ITA 126; and (2) the lesser of: 15 per cent of the taxpayer's foreign income for the year, and the foreign tax paid on that income (the foreign tax paid is equal to the total foreign tax paid on foreign source business income plus two-thirds of the foreign tax paid on foreign source non-business income). Thus, for purposes of the minimum tax rules, an individual will be entitled to deduct from minimum tax an amount at least equal to the deduction available under ITA 126.

ITA 127.54

¶11104 — *Carryforward of Minimum Tax*

The amount by which the minimum tax exceeds the tax otherwise payable under Part I (excluding tax on split income under ITA 120.4) is called the "additional tax". "Additional tax" may be carried forward for up to seven years and deducted from a taxpayer's regular Part I tax liability. However, the deduction in respect of the carryover cannot reduce an individual's tax liability below the minimum that would otherwise be payable for that year. Generally speaking, the "additional tax" is the excess of the minimum tax over total regular tax plus the additional foreign tax credit allowed under ITA 127.54 in excess of the normal foreign tax credit under ITA 126. The carryover may not be used to reduce the tax otherwise payable in respect of the special returns filed on behalf of a deceased or in respect of the return of a bankrupt.

ITA 120.2

¶11105 — *Claiming and Filing*

Form T691, *Alternative Minimum Tax*, should be completed to calculate minimum tax. The applicable provincial or territorial Form 428 is used to calculate any additional provincial or territorial minimum tax.

Taxpayers who paid minimum tax in any of the previous seven years, and who are not subject to minimum tax in the current year may be able to claim a credit against their current year's taxes for all or part of the minimum tax paid in those years. Taxpayers applying a minimum tax carryover from those previous years against the current year's taxes should complete Parts 1, 2, and 8 of Form T691.

Attach Form T691 to paper-filed returns. Taxpayers filing electronically should keep Form T691 for their records.

¶11200 — Calculation of Refund Due or Balance Owing (T1: Lines 420–482)

This section discusses the calculation of an individual's tax refund due or balance owing, which includes a discussion of CPP contributions or EI premiums payable on self-employment earnings, social benefits repayment, refundable Quebec abatement, refundable medical expense supplement, working income tax benefit, investment tax credit refund, employee and partner GST/HST rebate, and the determination of whether a refund is due or a balance is owing.

¶11210 — CPP Contributions Payable on Self-Employment and Other Earnings (T1: Line 421)

As discussed at Line 222 (see ¶9230), most self-employed individuals are required to make contributions to the Canada pension plan (CPP). The amount of CPP contributions payable by an individual (half of which are reported on Line 222 as an income deduction) are calculated on Schedule 8, *CPP Contributions on Self-Employment and*

Other Earnings, and are reported on Line 421.The maximum amount of CPP payable by an individual in 2018 is $5,188.

¶11211 — *Claiming and Filing*

Complete Schedule 8 to calculate CPP contributions. Enter the amount from Line 10 of Schedule 8 on Line 421. This line does not apply to individuals who were resident in Quebec on the last day of the year. Residents of Quebec should enter the Quebec pension plan contributions required to be paid on the Quebec income tax return.

CPP 10, 11, 13–14.1, CPP Reg. Part III, Schedule 8, Form CPT20

¶11220 — Social Benefits Repayment (T1: Line 422)

As discussed at Line 235 (see ¶9280), all or some of an individual's employment insurance (EI) and old age security (OAS) benefits received in the year may need to be repaid if the individual's net income is above a certain threshold. The repayment is reported on Line 422 and claimed as a deduction on Line 235.

¶11221 — *Employment Insurance (EI) Benefits*

EI provides temporary financial assistance for individuals who are unemployed, sick, pregnant, caring for a newborn or adopted child, or caring for a family member who is seriously ill with a significant risk of death. EI benefits are reported on Form T4E, *Statement of Employment Insurance and Other Benefits*, and are included as income on Line 119.

The repayment of EI benefits is determined under Part VII of the *Employment Insurance Act*. An individual may have to repay a portion of EI benefits received in the year if:

- There is an amount shown in Box 15 of the individual's T4E slip;

- The rate shown in Box 7 of the individual's T4E slip is 30%; and

- The individual's Line 234 net income (less any UCCB and RDSP amounts included in income on Lines 117 and 125, plus any UCCB and RDSP amounts repaid during the year and deducted on Lines 213 and 232) is more than $64,625 (i.e., 1.25 the maximum insurable earnings for the year).

Special benefits such as maternity, parental, sickness, or compassionate care benefits do not need to be repaid.

¶11221.1 — *Claiming and Filing*

Complete the repayment chart on the back of Form T4E to calculate the amount of EI benefit repayment.

¶11222 — *Old Age Security (OAS) Benefits*

OAS benefits are monthly benefits available to individuals who are 65 years of age or older, and who lived in Canada for at least 10 years after reaching age 18. OAS benefits include the basic OAS pension, the guaranteed income supplement, and the spouse's or common-law partner's allowance. OAS benefits are reported on Form T4A(OAS), *Statement of Old Age Security*, and are included in income on Line 113 (OAS pension; see ¶8110) and Line 146 (net federal supplements; see ¶8330).

The repayment of OAS benefits is determined under Part I.2 of the ITA. An individual may have to repay all or a part of OAS pension received or net federal supplements received in the year if the individual's Line 234 net income (less any UCCB and RDSP amounts included in income on Lines 117 and 125, plus any UCCB and RDSP amounts repaid during the year and deducted on Lines 213 and 232) is more than $75,910 for 2018.

In *Coté c. R.*, [2002] 4 C.T.C. 2025 (TCC), the court ruled that a deduction under ITA 110.2 (lump-sum averaging) should not be taken into consideration in computing the taxpayer's income for purposes of Part I.2 tax. The CRA also takes the view that there is no relief from the application of Part I.2 tax in the case of retroactive lump sum payments (see VD 2004-0073081E5). As well, in *Swantje v. R.*, [1994] 2 C.T.C. 382 (FCA); aff'd [1996] 1 C.T.C. 355, the Court held that the taxpayer's German pension should be included in income for purposes of computing the taxpayer's Part I.2 tax, and in *Doswell v. R.*, [2003] 4 C.T.C. 2209 (TCC), the Court held that the taxpayer's income for purposes of determining Part I.2 tax included the gross-up on dividend income.

The Tax Court cannot modify a Part I.2 tax assessment for reasons based on equity (see *Dubois v. R.*, [2007] 5 C.T.C. 2460 (TCC). However, see the following Remission Orders (re: remission where a taxable lump sum paid all in one year due to government agency delay led to OAS clawback applying): *Dane Pocrnic Remission Order*, P.C. 2005-624; *Keith Kirby Remission Order*, P.C. 2005-1533; *Josephine Pastorious Remission Order*, P.C. 2005-1534; *Jacques Beauvais Remission Order*, P.C. 2006-406; *Wesley Kool Remission Order*, P.C. 2006-1277; and *Murray Chalmers Remission Order*, P.C. 2007-254.

Individuals can choose to delay receipt of the OAS pension for up to 5 years after the normal age 65 start date, and be compensated for the shorter payment period. Accordingly, individuals who are subject to a full clawback of OAS pension may want to consider deferring the receipt of OAS where the individual's income will continue to remain high for several years after age 65 (because they continue to work full-time, for example). For 2018, the annual OAS benefit is fully eliminated at about $123,000 of income.

¶11222.1 — *Withholding*

A system of withholding ensures that OAS benefits are reduced at source where incomes are above the threshold, rather than paying out the benefits and subsequently recovering them when the T1 return is filed. Part I.2 tax amounts are required to be withheld from each OAS monthly benefit payment throughout the year. An individual is required to calculate the OAS pension repayment for the year, even if tax has been withheld. Any amount withheld may be deducted on Line 437 of the T1 return.

However, where an individual's net income for a year exceeds the threshold (i.e., $75,910 in 2018) and it is expected that net income for the following year will be substantially lower, the individual may request a waiver from CRA to have Service Canada reduce income tax withheld at source, commencing in July of that following year. Such requests are made using Form T1213(OAS), *Request to Reduce Old Age Security Recovery Tax at Source*.

¶11222.2 — *Claiming and Filing*

Complete the chart for Line 235 on the federal worksheet in the forms book to calculate the amount of OAS pension repayment, even if tax was withheld.

ITA Part I.2, Form T4A(OAS), T1136

¶11230 — EI Premiums Payable on Self-Employment and Other Earnings (T1: Line 430)

Self-employed individuals can opt in to the employment insurance (EI) program for access to EI special benefits by entering into an agreement with the Canada Employment Insurance Commission through Service Canada. Individuals who choose to participate in the program will receive the same EI special benefits as those available to employees, including maternity, parental, sickness, and compassionate care benefits. Individuals who opt into the EI program must wait 12 months from the date of confirmed registration before applying for special benefits. The amount of EI premiums payable is entered on Line 430. The individual may also claim a non-refundable tax credit for this amount on Line 317 (see ¶10130).

EI premiums payable on self-employment income are calculated on Schedule 13, *Employment Insurance Premiums on Self-Employment and Other Eligible Earnings*. To calculate the EI premiums payable, an individual must determine his or her total EI insurable earnings for the year. Total EI insurable earnings for the year are the lesser of:

- The total of the individual's self-employment income, which includes the following amounts: total net partnership income on Line 122 and business and professional income on lines 135 to 143; for individuals who are employed by a corporation but are ineligible for the EI program as an employee because they control over 40% of the voting shares of the corporation, the amount in Box 14 from all T4 slips received from that corporation (excluding amounts that are not insurable earnings); and for individuals who are registered under the *Indian Act*, the total tax-exempt self-employed income earned on a reserve in Canada; and

- The maximum insurable earnings for the year less the individual's total EI insurable earnings reported in Box 24 from all T4 slips (if Box 24 is blank, Box 14 amounts from all T4 slips unless Box 28 states that the T4 earnings are EI exempt), as well as any employment income for which no T4 slips were received.

For Canadian residents who are not residents of Quebec on the last day of the year, the maximum amount of EI premiums a self-employed individual is required to enter on Line 430 is $858. This amount is also entered on Line 317 and claimed as a non-refundable tax credit. Individuals whose total amount of EI premiums from Box 18 and Box 55 of all T4 slips is $858 or more are not required to pay any premiums on self-employment and other eligible earnings.

For Canadian residents who are residents of Quebec on the last day of the year, the maximum amount of EI premiums a self-employed individual is required to enter on Line 430 is $672. This amount is also entered on Line 317 and claimed as a non-refundable tax credit. Individuals whose total amount of EI premiums from Box 18 and Box 55 of all T4 slips is $672 or more are not required to pay any premiums on self-employment and other eligible earnings.

¶11231 — *Claiming and Filing*

Complete Schedule 13 to calculate EI premiums. Enter the amount from Line 10 of Schedule 13 on Line 430. This is the amount of EI premiums the individual has to pay for the year.

Schedule 13, canada.ca/en/services/benefits/ei/ei-self-employed-workers.html

¶11240 — Total Income Tax Deducted (T1: Line 437)

An individual's total federal income tax withheld at source as indicated on all information slips is included on Line 437. The information slips include the following:

- Form T4, Statement of Remuneration Paid

- Form T4A, Statement of Pension, Retirement, Annuity and Other Income

- Form T4A(OAS), Statement of Old Age Security

- Form T4A-RCA, Statement of Distributions From a Retirement Compensation Arrangement

- Form T4E, Statement of Employment Insurance and Other Benefits

- Form T4RIF, Statement of Income From a Registered Retirement Income Fund

- Form T4RSP, Statement of RRSP Income

- Form T5013, Statement of Partnership Income

If an individual elects to split pension income with his or her spouse or common-law partner (see Line 116 at ¶8140 and Line 210 at ¶9140), both individuals must enter an amount on Line 437 of their respective T1 returns. For each individual, the amount is calculated in proportion to the amount of pension income reported on his or her return (see Form T1032, *Joint Election to Split Pension Income*).

Non-residents should include all Part I federal income tax withheld at source (e.g., on employment income) on Line 437. In addition, a non-resident electing under section 217 must include the amount of non-resident tax indicated in Box 17 of Form NR4-OAS, *Statement of Old Age Security Pension Paid or Credited to Non-residents of Canada*, and all non-resident taxes withheld on any other eligible section 217 income, as specified on the individual's information slips (such as tax on employment insurance benefits). See ¶15412 for a discussion of the section 217 election.

¶11241 — *Claiming and Filing*

Enter the total of all the amounts shown in the "Income tax deducted" Box from all Canadian information slips. If tax was paid by instalments in the year, claim it on Line 476 (see ¶11340). If an individual paid foreign taxes, do not claim these amounts on Line 437; however, a foreign tax credit may be claimed for the foreign taxes paid. For more information, see Line 405 at ¶11010.

¶11250 — Refundable Quebec Abatement (T1: Line 440)

An individual who is required to file a Quebec TP-1 return because the individual resided in Quebec at the end of the year or carried on business in Quebec during the year may claim the refundable Quebec abatement on Line 440 of the T1 return.

The refundable Quebec abatement is calculated as follows:

16.5% × Federal tax otherwise payable × (Income earned in Quebec/Total income for the year)

The federal tax otherwise payable used in the calculation of the refundable Quebec abatement is the basic federal tax calculated on Schedule 1 of the T1 return (for Quebec residents), unless the individual has federal tax payable on split income or is subject to the alternative minimum tax. In this case, the abatement is calculated with information from Form T1206, *Tax on Split Income*, (see Line 424 at ¶11070) or Form T691, *Alternative Minimum Tax* (see Line 427 at ¶11100). The basic federal tax reported on Schedule 1 is essentially federal tax calculated on taxable income, less the non-refundable tax credits, federal dividend tax credit, and credit for minimum tax carryover. It does not take into account the foreign tax credit or any other tax credits.

Where an individual reports income earned in Quebec on the T1 return in addition to income not earned in Quebec, the allocation of the two types of income is determined, and the refundable Quebec abatement is calculated, on Form T2203. An individual who is a resident of Quebec may have income earned outside Quebec only if the individual has a business with a permanent establishment outside Quebec. Where a resident of Quebec has business income earned outside Quebec, an allocation of business income must be performed. An allocation of income is required if an individual resided in a province other than Quebec on December 31 and had income from a business with a permanent establishment in Quebec; or resided in Quebec on December 31 and had income from a business with a permanent establishment in another province or country during the year.

¶11260 — CPP Overpayment (T1: Line 448)

Overpayments of Canada pension plan (CPP) contributions are claimed on Line 448. Overpayments of Quebec pension plan (QPP) contributions are claimed on Line 452 of the Quebec TP-1 return.

A CPP overpayment can occur where: (1) an individual contributes more than the maximum amount required, which is $2,594 for 2018; or (2) an individual contributes $2,594 or less, if CPP pensionable earnings are less than the total employment income reported on the individual's T4 slips.

The CPP overpayment is calculated on Schedule 8, *CPP Contributions and Overpayments for 2018.*

¶11270 — Employment Insurance Overpayment (T1: Line 450)

An employment insurance (EI) premium overpayment is claimed on Line 450. The calculation of the overpayment varies depending on whether the individual is a resident of Quebec at the end of the year. Because Quebec offers its own parental benefits to its residents under the Quebec parental insurance plan (QPIP), the federal EI premiums payable in Quebec are reduced.

¶11271 — *Individuals Not Resident in Quebec*

For an individual who is not resident in Quebec on the last day of the taxation year, an EI overpayment can occur where: (1) an individual contributes more than the maximum amount required, which is $858 for 2018; or (2) an individual contributes $858 or less, if insurable earnings are less than the total employment income reported on his or her T4 information slip(s).

The amount of EI premiums an individual is required to pay in a year is calculated as follows: individual's EI insurable earnings ($51,700 maximum) × 1.66%. This is the calculation that an individual should use to determine if there was any overpayment of EI premiums. If an individual's EI insurable earnings are $2,000 or less, no EI premiums are payable. The EI overpayment is calculated on Form T2204, *Employee Overpayment of 2018 Employment Insurance Premiums*.

¶11272 — *Individuals Resident in Quebec*

For an individual who is a resident of Quebec on the last day of the taxation year, an EI overpayment can occur where: (1) an individual contributes more than the maximum amount required, which is $672 for 2018; or (2) an individual contributes $672 or less, if insurable earnings are less than the total employment income reported on his or her T4 information slip(s).

The amount of EI premiums a Quebec resident individual is required to pay in a year is calculated as follows: individual's EI insurable earnings ($51,700 maximum) × 1.30%. This is the calculation that an individual should use to determine if there was any overpayment of EI premiums. If an individual's EI insurable earnings are $2,000 or less, no EI premiums are payable. The EI overpayment is calculated on Form T2204, *Employee Overpayment of 2018 Employment Insurance Premiums*.

The amount of EI overpayment determined on Line 450 may be reduced by QPIP premiums payable by employees who worked outside Quebec during the year. The QPIP premiums are determined in Part B of Schedule 10, *Employment Insurance (EI) and Provincial Parental Insurance Plan (PPIP) Premiums*. These employees may need to pay QPIP premiums to Revenu Quebec in respect of employment income earned outside Quebec. If these employees make an EI overpayment (calculated on Part C of Schedule 10), a net EI overpayment is reported on Line 451 of the T1 return for Quebec residents. The amount reported on Line 451 is determined by subtracting the QPIP premiums payable and claimed on Line 376 from the EI overpayment reported on Line 450. The QPIP premiums, up to the amount of EI overpayment reported on Line 450, are transferred directly to Revenu Quebec by the CRA, rather than being paid by the individual when filing the Quebec TP-1 return, and only the net EI overpayment is refunded.

¶11280 — Refundable Medical Expense Supplement (T1: Line 452)

In addition to being able to claim a medical expense tax credit (see ¶10190) and, where applicable, the disability supports deduction (see ¶9180), an individual who has high medical expenses and low income for a tax year may be able to claim a refundable medical expense supplement under ITA 122.51. When it applies, ITA 122.51 deems a portion of the individual's combined allowable medical expenses and disability supports deduction for the year, as taxes paid in respect of the year. To the extent an individual's amount under ITA 122.51 exceeds their taxes payable for the year before factoring in the ITA 122.51 amount, the excess will result in a tax refund.

The maximum amount that an individual may claim as a refundable medical expense supplement for the 2018 taxation year is equal to the lesser of: (1) $1,222; and (2) the total of: 25% of the individual's allowable medical expenses for the year and 25% of the amount of any disability supports deduction claimed by the individual for the year. Where the individual claiming the refundable medical expense supplement has adjusted income for the year that exceeds $27,044 (for 2018), the maximum supplement is reduced by 5% of the excess. Generally, adjusted income is the same amount as that used in computing an individual's child tax benefit.

An individual must meet the following requirements to make a claim for a refundable medical expense supplement for a particular tax year:

- the individual must have been resident in Canada throughout the year and at least 18 years of age at the end of the tax year;

- the individual must have earned at least $3,566 during the year, on a combined basis, from the following sources: office or employment (excluding employment insurance benefits), businesses carried on by the individual either alone or as a partner actively engaged in the business, and the program established under the *Wage Earner Protection Program Act*;

- the individual must have been entitled to claim a medical expense tax credit (see ¶10190) or a disability supports deduction (see ¶9180) for the year; and

- a tax return must be filed for the year in respect of the individual.

¶11281 — *Claiming and Filing*

Use the worksheet for Line 452 to calculate the refundable medical expense supplement that should be reported on Line 452.

ITA 122.51, Guide RC4064, Folio S1-F1-C1 (paras. 1.148–1.153), Folio S1-F1-C3

¶11290 — Working Income Tax Benefit (T1: Line 453)

For 2019 and later taxation years, the WITB is being replaced by the Canada Workers Benefit (CWB), which is an enhanced version of the WITB. The CWB will be equal to 26% of each dollar of earned income over $3,000, to a maximum credit of $1,355 for single individuals without children and $2,335 for families. The maximum credit will be reduced by 12% of adjusted net income over $12,820 for single individuals without children and $17,025 for families. For more information on the changes to the CWB applicable for taxation years after 2018, see: tinyurl.com/cra-cwb.

The working income tax benefit (WITB) is a refundable tax credit for certain low-income individuals and families who earn "working income" in a taxation year, within certain income thresholds. The WITB consists of a base amount and a disability supplement. The person who receives the WITB advance payments (see Line 415 at ¶11050) is the person who must claim the basic WITB for the year. Only one spouse can claim the basic WITB and two persons cannot both claim the basic WITB for the same eligible dependant.

Generally, to be eligible for the WITB, an individual must be resident in Canada throughout the taxation year and, *at the end of the taxation year*, the individual must be either: (1) 19 years of age or older, (2) residing with a spouse or common-law partner, or (3) the parent of a child with whom the individual resides. "Working income" includes the individual's total income from an office or employment (before any employment deductions allowed in computing income), business income, research grants, fellowships, scholarships, bursaries, and prizes.

An individual who is enrolled as a full-time student at a designated educational institution for more than 13 weeks in the year cannot claim the WITB credit, unless the individual has an eligible dependant at the end of the year. Generally, an eligible dependant is a child of the individual who lived with the individual, is under 19 years of age, and who is not eligible for the WITB credit. The WITB credit should not be claimed by both spouses. For these purposes, there are rules to ensure that only one spouse or partner may claim the WITB for a particular taxation year. When the WITB credit is available to an individual in a taxation year, an amount is deemed to have been paid by the individual for the taxation year in respect of the individual's tax liability for the year (i.e., the credit is deemed to be an instalment paid by the taxpayer).

There are two parts to the working income tax benefit. The first part is the Basic WITB, which is a refundable tax credit equal to 25% of each dollar of working income earned in excess of $3,000. The second part of the WITB credit is the WITB Supplement, which is available to individuals who are entitled to the disability tax credit. The WITB Supplement is equal to 25% of each dollar of working income in excess of $1,150. Both the Basic WITB and WITB Supplement are phased out within certain adjusted net income thresholds. Note that the computation of the WITB credit is subject to adjustments by provincial and territorial governments. For adjusted dollar amounts, see: canada.ca/en/revenue-agency/services/child-family-benefits/working-income-tax-benefit-witb.html.

As discussed at ¶11050, an application can be made by a taxpayer to receive advance WITB payments in respect of a taxation year. Generally, advance payments can be received on the same payment cycle as the GST/HST credit. If the application is submitted between January 1 and September 1 of the particular year, the individual may receive advance payments not exceeding one-half of the individual's estimated WITB (i.e., one-half of the Basic WITB and the WITB Supplement). In the case of a couple or common-law partners, a joint application is required designating which spouse or partner is to receive the advance payment. The designated individual must be either the person expected to have the higher working income or who can reasonably be expected to be entitled to the WITB Supplement. However, no advance payment will be made if the total WITB is estimated to be less than $100, or if the individual did not file a tax return for a preceding tax year in respect of which the individual received an advance payment. An individual who has applied for an advance payment must notify the Minister of certain events which might otherwise affect the individual's WITB entitlement.

¶11291 — *Claiming and Filing*

Complete Schedule 6, *Working Income Tax Benefit*, to calculate the Basic WITB and, if applicable, the WITB Supplement. Enter on Line 453 the amount calculated on Schedule 6, and attach a copy of the schedule to a paper-filed return.

ITA 122.7–122.71, Schedule 6, Form RC201, Form RC210, Guide RC4227

¶11300 — Refund of Investment Tax Credit (T1: Line 454)

Investment tax credits may be claimed by an individual with respect to the following expenditures or investments made in the year: qualified properties used in specific areas of Canada (see ¶11031); qualified expenditures on scientific research and experimental development (see ¶11032); certain renounced eligible mineral exploration expenditures (see ¶11033); eligible apprenticeship expenditures (see ¶11034); and eligible child care space expenditures incurred by an individual who carries on business (see ¶11035).

Individuals who are eligible for an investment tax credit (on Line 412, see ¶11030) based on expenditures or investments made in the year may be able to claim a refund of unused investment tax credits on Line 454. This refund will reduce the amount of credit available for other years.

The refundable part of the investment tax credit is calculated on Form T2038(IND), *Investment Tax Credit (Individuals)*, and is based on a percentage of the investment or expenditure. An individual is allowed to carry back a credit for up to three years or carry forward a credit for up to twenty years to reduce federal tax in those years.

ITA 127.1, Form T2038(IND), VD 2005-0143681I7

¶11310 — Part XII.2 Trust Tax Credit (T1: Line 456)

Part XII.2 of the ITA imposes a trust-level distribution tax on trusts that make certain Canadian source income payable to non-resident beneficiaries and other designated beneficiaries. One of the objectives of Part XII.2 tax is to prevent the minimization of tax on specified Canadian-source income that would otherwise arise where a Canadian trust's income is distributed to a non-resident and is subject only to Part XIII tax. Part XII.2 tax is also intended to discourage transactions between taxable and tax-exempt beneficiaries designed to allow taxable income earned by a trust to be flowed-through to tax exempt beneficiaries after the acquisition of a trust unit by a tax-exempt beneficiary from a taxable beneficiary.

Where a Canadian trust allocates "designated income" to a "designated beneficiary" of the trust, the trust is subject to Part XII.2 tax of 40% on the designated income. A "designated beneficiary" of a trust is a beneficiary who is a non-resident person; or a person exempt from Part I tax owning an interest in the trust acquired from a beneficiary under the trust, unless no taxable entity previously owned that interest. The "designated income" of a trust is net income from real property in Canada, timber resource property, Canadian resource property, businesses carried on in Canada, net taxable capital gains from the disposition of taxable Canadian property, and net taxable gains from the disposition of property (or property for which the disposed of property is a substitute) that was transferred to another trust in certain circumstances (e.g., where the transfer occurred in anticipation of the emigration of a person beneficially interested in the other trust, and a person beneficially interested in the other trust did subsequently cease to reside in Canada).

A pro-rated portion of the Part XII.2 tax payable by the trust is credited on Line 456 to taxable Canadian resident beneficiaries who are not designated beneficiaries, as well as to non-resident beneficiaries taxable under Part I of the ITA. Net income after tax is allocated to these beneficiaries and reported on Form T3, *Statement of Trust Income Allocations and Designations*, together with the allocable tax paid by the trust. The Part XII.2 trust tax credit is reported in Box 38 of Form T3.

Below is an excerpt from IT-342R: *Trusts — Income Payable to Beneficiaries*, which discusses Part XII.2 tax:

> 8. Part XII.2 of the Act was added applicable to the 1988 and subsequent taxation years and it assesses a special tax on the designated income, as defined in subsection 210.2(2), of certain trusts. Part XII.2 tax generally applies where designated income of a trust is payable during the year to designated beneficiaries (generally non-residents and exempt persons) as defined in section 210, but does not apply, where, throughout the year, the trust was (a) a testamentary trust, (b) a mutual fund trust, (c) a trust exempt from tax by reason of subsection 149(1), (d) a trust described in subparagraph 108(1)(j)(ii) or (iv), or (e) a non-resident trust.

> These provisions are intended to ensure that designated income earned by trusts for the benefit of non-residents and exempt persons will be subject to full tax rates rather than the lower non-resident tax rates under Part XIII or no rate at all in the case of exempt persons.

> When a trust is subject to Part XII.2 tax and has taxable resident beneficiaries, or non-resident beneficiaries whose tax liability is computed under Part I of the Act, or both, a pro-rata share of the Part XII.2 tax can be designated by the trust in respect of any of the aforementioned beneficiaries. Such share of tax is then deemed by subsection 210.2(3) to be an amount paid on account of the tax payable under Part I for the beneficiary's taxation year in which the taxation year of the trust ends. The amount deemed by subsection 210.2(3) is also deemed, by subsection 104(31), to be an amount in respect of the income of the trust for the year that has become payable by the trust to the beneficiary at the end of the year. That amount is included in the beneficiary's income under subsection 104(13). Subsection 104(31) applies to taxation years of trusts commencing after 1987. Part XII.2 tax may be calculated on Form T3 Trust Schedule 4.

¶11311 — *Claiming and Filing*

Individuals should include the amount of the Part XII.2 trust tax credit reported in Box 38 of Form T3 on Line 456.

ITA 104(31), Part XII.2, Form T3

¶11320 — Employee and Partner GST/HST Rebate (T1: Line 457)

Employees who deduct expenses from employment income on Line 212 (Annual union, professional or like dues; see ¶2405) or Line 229 (Other employment expenses; see ¶9250), and partners who deduct expenses from partnership income on lines 135 to 143 (see Chapter 6) may be eligible for a rebate of the GST/HST they paid on those expenses. See ¶2401 for a complete discussion of the employee and partner GST/HST rebate.

¶11325 — Children's Fitness Tax Credit (T1: Lines 458, 459)

The children's fitness tax credit has been fully repealed for 2017 and later taxation years.

For taxation years before 2017, the children's fitness tax credit allowed parents to claim a refundable tax credit (non-refundable and claimed on line 365 of Schedule 1 for taxation years before 2015) for eligible fees paid in the year for the registration or membership of a child under 16 years of age in a prescribed program of physical activity. Parents could claim a maximum of $500 per year ($1,000 for taxation years before 2016) for eligible fees paid for registration or membership in an eligible program for each qualifying child.

This credit has been fully repealed for 2017 and later taxation years; however, some provinces may provide a provincial children's fitness tax credit.

¶11330 — Eligible Educator School Supply Tax Credit (T1: Lines 468, 469)

For 2016 and later taxation years, teachers and early childhood educators ("eligible educators") can claim a refundable tax credit for the cost of teaching supplies ("eligible supplies expense") paid in a taxation year. The maximum allowable eligible supplies expense in a year is $1,000, which equals a $150 refundable credit.

This tax credit can only be claimed by an "eligible educator", which is an eligible teacher or early childhood educator employed at an elementary or secondary school or a regulated child care facility. Generally, an eligible teacher holds a teacher's certificate that is valid in the province or territory in which they are employed, and an eligible early childhood educator holds a certificate or diploma in early childhood education that is recognized in the province or territory in which the individual is employed.

¶11331 — *Eligible Expenditures*

An "eligible supplies expense" of an "eligible educator" for a taxation year, means an amount (other than any amount deducted in computing any person's income for any taxation year or any amount otherwise included in computing a deduction from any person's tax payable under the ITA for any taxation year) paid by the eligible educator in the taxation year for teaching supplies to the extent that:

- the teaching supplies were: (i) purchased by the eligible educator for the purpose of teaching or facilitating students' learning, and (ii) directly consumed or used in an elementary or secondary school or in a regulated child care facility in the performance of the duties of the eligible educator's employment; and

- the eligible educator is not entitled to receive a reimbursement, allowance or any other form of assistance (other than an amount that is included in computing the income for any taxation year of the eligible educator and that is not deductible in computing the taxable income of the eligible educator) in respect of the amount paid.

For the purposes of the definition of an "eligible supplies expense", ITA 122.9(1) defines "teaching supplies" as consumable supplies and prescribed durable goods.

The CRA provides the following examples of school supplies that would be considered consumable supplies for the purposes of this credit: construction paper for activities and flashcards for activity centres; items for science experiments, such as seeds, potting soil, vinegar, baking soda and stir sticks; art supplies such as paper, glue and paint; and various stationary items, such as pens, pencils, posters and charts.

For the purpose of the definition of teaching supplies, the following are prescribed durable goods: books; games and puzzles; containers (such as plastic boxes or banker boxes); and educational support software. Computers, tablets and rugs are not eligible expenses because they are durable goods (which can be used repeatedly or continuously for a relatively long time) that are not included in the list of durable goods that qualify as teaching supplies. As well, the cost or value of used goods (eg; used books, games and puzzles brought from home for children to use in the classroom) are not an eligible supplies expense because a teaching supply has to be purchased in the same year that it is included in calculating the tax credit, and must have been purchased for the purpose of teaching or facilitating students' learning.

¶11332 — *Calculation of the Credit*

Pursuant to the formula contained in ITA 122.9(2), the school supply tax credit available to an eligible educator in a taxation year is computed as: $A \times B$, where:

A   is the appropriate percentage for the year (i.e., 15% for taxation years after 2006); and

B   is the least of the following:

- $1,000,

- the total of all amounts each of which is an eligible supplies expense of the eligible educator for the year, and

- nil, if the eligible educator fails to provide the certificate referred to in ITA 122.9(3) when requested by the Minister.

Therefore, the maximum refundable tax credit that can be claimed in a taxation year by an eligible educator in respect of an eligible supplies expense is $150 (i.e., $15\% \times \$1,000$).

¶11333 — *Certification*

Generally, ITA 122.9(3) requires an eligible educator who is making a claim for the school supply tax credit to provide the Minister with a written certificate from their employer or a delegated official of the employer, attesting to the eligible supplies expenses of the eligible educator for the year, if the Minister so demands. A delegated official of the employer should be a person who would ordinarily have reasonable knowledge of the supplies purchased by the teacher or educator, what they are being used for and whether the teacher or educator would be entitled to any allowance, reimbursement or deduction.

The certification should be a statement signed by the individual's employer, or delegated official of the employer, that provides and attests (to the best of their knowledge) to the amount paid for eligible teaching supplies purchased in the year by the eligible teacher or early childhood educator; for the purpose of teaching or facilitating students' learning; directly consumed or used in an elementary or secondary school or in a regulated child care facility in the performance of the individual's employment duties; and not reimbursable, not subject to an allowance or other form of assistance (unless the reimbursement, allowance or assistance is included in the income of the teacher or educator and not deductible), and not deducted or used in calculating a deduction from any person's income for any taxation year.

The employer or delegated official should take a reasonable approach in respect of the requirement that the teacher or educator is not entitled to receive a reimbursement, allowance or any other form of assistance and that the amount is not otherwise deductible. For example, an employer should not be providing the certification of eligible teaching supplies when a Form T2200, *Declaration of Conditions of Employment*, which may allow the employee to deduct the amount from income, will also be completed by the employer (when the contract for employment requires the teacher or educator to provide and pay for the supplies); or when the teacher or educator is entitled to be reimbursed by their employer, the parents or students, or through fundraising activities, for the expense.

¶11334 — *Claiming and Filing*

Individuals should enter the total eligible supplies expense for the year on Line 468 (up to a maximum of $1,000), multiply it by 15%, and enter the result on Line 469. It is not necessary to include the eligible supplies' receipts with the tax return; however, individuals should retain all their receipts in case CRA requests supporting documentation in the future.

ITA 122.9, ITR 9600

¶11340 — Tax Paid by Instalments (T1: Line 476)

Taxes paid by instalments should be reported on Line 476 of the T1 return.

Individuals who earn income that is not subject to withholding at source may be required to pay tax by instalments. Instalments are periodic income tax payments that individuals have to pay to the CRA on certain dates, to cover tax that they would otherwise have to pay in a lump sum on April 30 of the following year. Instalments are not paid in advance; they are paid throughout the calendar year in which the taxable income is earned. If an individual still owes tax at the end of a taxation year, the remainder is due on or before the balance-due date, which is generally April 30 in the following year (see ¶1230).

Generally, individuals are required to pay income tax by instalments for the year if the individual's taxes payable are more than $3,000 ($1,800 for Quebec residents) in both the current year, and in either of the two preceding taxation years. Tax payable for a tax year for purposes of computing instalments is the total tax payable for the year before taking into consideration "specified future tax consequences" for the year. "Specified future tax consequences" are adjustments arising because of the carryback of losses, tax credits or similar amounts, or because of corrections of certain amounts renounced in connection with the issue of flow-through shares. Taxes payable includes both federal and provincial or territorial income taxes. Refundable and non-refundable federal, provincial, and territorial tax credits should be included in the calculation of instalment payments (use estimated credits for the current year to calculate instalment payments).

For individuals (other than farmers and fishers), quarterly instalments are due on March 15, June 15, September 15, and December 15. Where the instalment due date falls on a Saturday, Sunday, or a statutory holiday, the payment is considered to be made on time if it is received or postmarked on the next business day.

For more information on paying tax by instalments, see the following: ¶1210–¶1214 (instalment methods), ¶1215 (making tax instalment payments), ¶1220 (interest charges on late or deficient instalments), and ¶1420 (instalment penalties).

ITA 153, 155, 156, 156.1, 161(2), (11), 163.1, ITR 5300, Pamphlet P110

¶11350 — Refund or Balance Owing (T1: Lines 484, 485)

¶11351 — *Refund Due (T1: Line 484)*

The tax refund due to an individual is reported on Line 484. If the CRA reassesses the taxpayer's return, the amount of refund may increase or decrease. For individuals who overpaid their taxes and are due a refund, the CRA will pay compound daily interest on the individual's tax refund for the year, starting on the latest of May 31st of the following year, the 31st day after the return is filed, or the day after the taxes are overpaid.

The CRA may withhold a taxpayer's refund if the individual has an outstanding amount owing to the CRA, is subject to a garnishee order under the *Family Orders and Agreements Enforcement Assistance Act,* or has other outstanding debts owing to the federal, provincial or territorial government. An individual can request that a refund be transferred to the individual's instalment account for the next taxation year; however, an individual cannot apply his or her refund to a spouse or common-law-partner's taxes payable.

If the individual is claiming a refund, the refund can be received via direct deposit. To enroll for direct deposit at the individual's account at a financial institution, or to update information the individual previously provided the CRA, complete the "Direct deposit — Enrol or update" at the bottom of page 4 of the T1 return. This area does not have to be completed if the individual is already using the CRA's direct deposit service and the direct deposit information has not changed.

ITA 160.1, 164

¶11352 — *Balance Owing (T1: Line 485)*

On Line 485, enter the amount of taxes owing. If the CRA reassesses the taxpayer's return, the amount of refund may increase or decrease. Where an individual has a balance of tax owing for the year, the individual should consider whether instalment payments will be required for the next taxation year. Generally, where withholdings and income tax instalment payments are less than an individual's tax payable for the current and preceding taxation years, instalment payments may be required; see Line 476 at ¶11340.

Generally, the "balance-due day" for an individual's taxes owing for the year is April 30 of the following year. Where an individual or his or her spouse or common-law partner carried on a business in the year, the return must be filed on or before June 15 of the following year; however, the individual still must pay any balance owing for the year on or before April 30 of the following year. ITA 248(7) deems anything, other than a remittance of source deductions or an amount payable by a corporation, sent by first class mail or its equivalent (which includes lettermail, registered mail, or courier service), to have been received by the Receiver General on the day that it was sent. Therefore, a payment of tax owing from an individual, sent to the Receiver General by first class mail or its equivalent, is considered to have been received on the day that it was sent (VD 2013-0481351I7). Where the due date falls on a Saturday, Sunday, or a statutory holiday, the payment is considered to be made on time if it is received or postmarked on the next business day.

An individual may pay the balance of tax owing electronically, in person at a financial institution in Canada, or by cheque or money order made out to the Receiver General. For additional information about payments options, see: canada.ca/en/revenue-agency/services/make-a-payment-canada-revenue-agency.html. An individual can also make a payment online using the CRA's My Payment option, available at: canada.ca/en/revenue-agency/services/e-services/payment-save-time-pay-online.html. My Payment is an electronic payment service offered by the CRA that uses *Interac* Online to allow individuals (and businesses) to make payments directly to the CRA from their online banking account. Below is a summary of when payment is considered to be made for the various types of payment methods:

Method of payment	Date when payment considered to be made
In person at financial institution	Date stamped on remittance voucher
By mail	Date of mailing (CRA considers a tax payment made in respect of an individual to be received on the day it is mailed to the CRA, provided it is sent by first-class mail or equivalent)
Online banking	Date when financial institution credits CRA with payment
Post-dated cheque or pre-authorized debit	Date when payment is negotiable

The CRA charges compound daily interest on unpaid taxes according to the prescribed rate, beginning on the day after the return is due, on any unpaid amounts owing for the year, including any balance owing if the T1 return is reassessed by the CRA. For more information on interest charges on unpaid amounts, see ¶1230. The CRA also charges interest on any penalties, beginning the day after the return is due. Where the penalty is for failure to file a return when due or for filing an incomplete return or a return containing false statements, the penalty bears interest from the date when the return was required to be filed. A list of prescribed interest rates for current and previous years can be found at: canada.ca/en/revenue-agency/services/tax/prescribed-interest-rates.html. For more information on penalties, see the Penalties Quick Reference Table at ¶1420.

ITA 156.1, 161, 248(1)"balance-due day", 248(7), Form T7DR, Pamphlet P110

Chapter 12 — Provincial and Territorial Taxes and Credits

Contents

¶12010 Provincial Tax Overview

   ¶12020 Provincial Residence

   ¶12030 Provincial or Territorial Tax (Form T1: Line 428)

   ¶12040 Provincial or Territorial Credits (Form T1: Line 479)

   ¶12050 Administration and Enforcement

¶12100 Alberta

   ¶12110 Liability for Tax

   ¶12120 Tax Rate

   ¶12130 Tax on Split Income (Form AB428: Line 34)

   ¶12140 Additional Minimum Tax (Form AB428: Line 42)

   ¶12150 Non-Refundable Tax Credits

   ¶12160 Other Tax Credits, Benefits and Incentives

¶12200 British Columbia

   ¶12210 Liability for Tax

   ¶12220 Tax Rates

   ¶12230 Tax on Split Income (Form BC428: Line 42)

   ¶12240 Additional Minimum Tax (Form BC428: Line 50)

   ¶12250 Non-Refundable Tax Credits

   ¶12260 Other Tax Credits, Benefits and Incentives

¶12300 Manitoba

   ¶12310 Liability for Tax

   ¶12320 Tax Rates

   ¶12330 Tax on Split Income (Form MB428: Line 43)

   ¶12340 Additional Minimum Tax (Form MB428: Line 51)

   ¶12350 Non-Refundable Tax Credits

   ¶12360 Other Tax Credits, Benefits and Incentives

¶12400 New Brunswick

   ¶12410 Liability for Tax

¶12420 Tax Rates

¶12430 Tax on Split Income (Form NB428: Line 39)

¶12440 Additional Minimum Tax (Form NB428: Line 48)

¶12450 Non-Refundable Tax Credits

¶12460 Other Tax Credits, Benefits and Incentives

¶12500 Newfoundland and Labrador

¶12510 Liability for Tax

¶12520 Tax Rates

¶12530 Tax on Split Income (Form NL428: Line 42)

¶12540 Additional Minimum Tax (Form NL428: Line 50)

¶12550 Non-Refundable Tax Credits

¶12560 Other Tax Credits, Benefits and Incentives

¶12600 Northwest Territories

¶12610 Liability for Tax

¶12620 Tax Rates

¶12630 Tax on Split Income (Form NT428: Line 39)

¶12640 Additional Minimum Tax (Form NT428: Line 47)

¶12650 Non-Refundable Tax Credits

¶12660 Other Tax Credits, Benefits and Incentives

¶12700 Nova Scotia

¶12710 Liability for Tax

¶12720 Tax Rates

¶12730 Tax on Split Income (Form NS428: Line 41)

¶12740 Additional Minimum Tax (Form NS428: Line 49)

¶12750 Non-Refundable Tax Credits

¶12760 Other Tax Credits, Benefits and Incentives

¶12800 Nunavut

¶12810 Liability for Tax

¶12820 Tax Rates

¶12830 Tax on Split Income (Form NU428: Line 40)

¶12840 Additional Minimum Tax (Form NU428: Line 48)

¶12850 Non-Refundable Tax Credits

¶12860 Other Tax Credits, Benefits and Incentives

¶12900 Ontario

¶12910 Liability for Tax

¶12920 Tax Rates

¶12930 Tax on Split Income (Form ON428: Line 40)

¶12940 Additional Minimum Tax (Form ON428: Line 48)

¶12950 Non-Refundable Tax Credits

¶12960 Other Tax Credits, Benefits and Incentives

¶121000 Prince Edward Island

¶121010 Liability for Tax

¶121020 Tax Rates

¶121030 Tax on Split Income (Form PE428: Line 41)

¶121040 Additional Minimum Tax (Form PE428: Line 49)

¶121050 Non-Refundable Tax Credits

¶121060 Other Tax Credits, Benefits and Incentives

¶121100 Saskatchewan

¶121110 Liability for Tax

¶121120 Tax Rates

¶121130 Tax on Split Income (Form SK428: Line 45)

¶121140 Additional Minimum Tax (Form SK428: Line 53)

¶121150 Non-Refundable Tax Credits

¶121160 Other Tax Credits, Benefits and Incentives

¶121200 Yukon

¶121210 Liability for Tax

¶121220 Tax Rates

¶121230 Tax on Split Income (Form YT428: Line 45)

¶121240 Additional Minimum Tax (Form YT428: Line 53)

¶121250 Non-Refundable Tax Credits

¶121260 Other Tax Credits, Benefits and Incentives

¶12010 — Provincial Tax Overview

A provincial/territorial income tax is imposed in all ten provinces and in all three territories (in this Guide, references to a "province" include the territories). In the "agreeing provinces", provincial personal tax is collected by the CRA in conjunction with federal personal tax in accordance with tax collection agreements. Currently, all of the provinces other than Québec are agreeing provinces. Under the tax collection agreements, the Government of Canada and the government of a province agree that the CRA will collect and administer certain taxes imposed under provincial legislation and will pay the province its share of the taxes collected. The province also generally agrees to harmonize fundamental elements of provincial tax rules with federal tax rules under the Agreements. As a result, for the agreeing provinces, the personal tax rules are for the most part identical to those under the ITA and ITR.

Provincial personal tax is imposed under provincial legislation (each province has its own *Tax Act*). For example, the computation of personal taxable income for provincial personal tax purposes is equivalent to the computation for federal personal tax purposes (i.e., the agreeing provinces use the same tax base as the federal government). This means that in all of the Canadian provinces except Québec, income tax is expressed as a percentage of the federal income tax for the year. Québec has not entered into a tax collection agreement and administers its own *Tax Act*. However, despite not harmonizing its income tax act with the federal ITA, there is a high degree of similarity between the tax bases and tax rules in Québec with those in the other jurisdictions in Canada.

Generally, an individual is subject to provincial tax on his or her worldwide income from all sources if the individual is resident in a particular province on December 31 of the particular taxation year. A non-resident must also calculate provincial tax if he or she earned income from employment in a province or received income from a business with a permanent establishment in a province.

An individual's non-business income is deemed to be entirely earned in the province in which the individual resides on the last day of the year. In the case of an individual not resident in Canada, income from an office or employment is required to be imputed to the provinces in which the duties were performed.

An individual's business income is deemed to be earned in the provinces (and foreign jurisdictions) in which the individual has a "permanent establishment". Business income attributable to permanent establishments in more than one province must be allocated between those provinces on Form T2203, *Provincial and Territorial Taxes — Multiple Jurisdictions*.

See the personal tax reference tables in the Appendix for a complete listing of provincial and territorial income tax rates, brackets, and surtaxes for 2018, and for provincial and territorial non-refundable tax credit rates and amounts for 2018.

Form T2203

¶12020 — Provincial Residence

Provincial income tax must be calculated in the province where the individual is resident on the last day of the tax year. The ITA does not define what constitutes residence in Canada, but generally relies on the meaning attributed to residence in common law. There are, however, some circumstances in which an individual is deemed to be resident in Canada for Canadian tax purposes. In particular, pursuant to ITA 250(1), an individual is deemed to have been resident in Canada in any taxation year in which the individual:

- sojourned in Canada in the year for a period of, or periods the aggregate of which is, 183 days or more (ITA 250(1)(a));

- was, at any time in the year, a member of the Canadian Forces (ITA 250(1)(b));

- was, at any time in the year, an ambassador, minister, high commissioner, officer or servant of Canada, or an agent-general, officer or servant of a province, and was resident in Canada immediately prior to appointment or employment by Canada or the province or received representation allowances in respect of the year (ITA 250(1)(c));

- performed services, at any time in the year, in a country other than Canada under a prescribed international development assistance program of the government of Canada and was resident in Canada at any time in the 3 months' period preceding the day on which such services commenced (ITA 250(1)(d));

- was, at any time in the year, a member of the overseas Canadian Forces school staff who filed a return for the year on the basis that the individual was a person resident in Canada only throughout the period while a member (ITA 250(1)(d.1));

- was at any time in the year, a child of and dependent for support on a person described in ITA 250(1)(b), (c), (d) or (d.1), and had income not exceeding the basic personal amount in ITA 118(1) (ITA 250(1)(f)); or,

- was exempt from tax otherwise payable in another jurisdiction at any time during the year by reason of a tax agreement or convention between Canada and that country, or was entitled to such tax exemption by reason of being related to or a member of the family of an individual resident in Canada at that time (ITA 250(1)(g)).

In computing the length of a sojourn for the purpose of ITA 250(1)(a), each calendar year is considered separately. An individual who ceases to be a person described in ITA 250(1)(b)–(f) is deemed to be resident in Canada only throughout that part of the year in which the description applied (ITA 250(2)). An individual who is deemed to be a resident of Canada for tax purposes under any of these rules is not deemed to be a resident of a province. As a result, the individual will be exempt from provincial income tax, but will be liable for the federal surcharge under ITA 120(1) (currently 48%).

ITA 250(5) provides that a person is deemed not to be resident in Canada at any time at which the person would, but for ITA 250(5) and any tax treaty, be resident in Canada for the purposes of the ITA, but is, under a tax treaty with another country, resident in that other country and not in Canada (see, for example, Canada-U.S. Tax Treaty:Art.IV:2). The treaty tie-breaker rule in ITA 250(5) overrides all other provisions of the ITA except ITA 126(1.1)(a) (see, for example, CRA VDs 2011-0422561I7 (treaty exemption for non-resident employees); 2010-0382801E5 (Canadian employees working in USA); and 2005-0139501E5 (residency of international students)).

As mentioned above, where the deeming rule in ITA 250 or an applicable treaty does not apply, common law principles must be referred to in determining the residency status of an individual. In accordance with common law principles, the CRA's position is that an individual is resident in the province or territory where he or she has significant residential ties.

Folio S5-F1-C1 deals with determinations of residence status for provincial and federal tax purposes. CRA considers the following factors to almost always be significant residential ties:

- dwelling place

- spouse or common-law partner

- dependants

The CRA's opinion is that the following secondary residential ties should also be taken into account:

- personal property

- social ties

- economic ties

- hospitalization or medical insurance coverage

- driver's license

- vehicle registration

- seasonal dwelling place or leased dwelling place

- memberships in unions or professional organizations

The CRA's opinion is that secondary residential ties must be looked at collectively, and that it would be unusual for a single secondary residential tie to be determinative.

Finally, the CRA's view is that the following residential ties, which may be taken into account, will generally be of limited importance:

- mailing address

- post office box
- safety deposit box
- address on personal stationary such as business cards
- telephone listings
- local newspaper and magazine subscriptions

An individual who is resident in more than one province on the last day of the tax year is deemed to have resided on that day only in that province "which may reasonably be regarded as his principal place of residence." The term "principal place of residence" is not defined in the ITA or ITR. The CRA's position is that where an individual may be considered to be resident in more than one province on the last day of the tax year, the individual will be resident in the province where the individual has the most significant residential ties.

The CRA advises individuals that require clarification of their Canadian residency status for income tax purposes to complete Form NR73: *Determination of Residency Status (leaving Canada)*.

If an individual is resident in Canada for the entire year, worldwide income from all sources earned during that year is taxable in Canada. The individual is entitled to the benefits of Canada's extensive tax treaties and to a credit for foreign taxes paid on foreign source income which is taxed in Canada.

An individual may be resident in Canada for only part of the year. In that case, only worldwide income for the period in the year during which the individual resided in Canada, less the proportionate part of the applicable credits and deductions, is taxed.

ITA 2, 114, 115, 126, 250, ITR 2607, Folio S5-F1-C1, CRA Pamphlet T4055: *Newcomers to Canada*, CRA Fact Sheet T4133: *Are You a Newcomer to Canada*

¶12030 — Provincial or Territorial Tax (Form T1: Line 428)

Canadian resident individuals who were not resident in Quebec on the last day of the year should use the appropriate Form 428 for their province or territory of residence to calculate the provincial or territorial taxes to be entered on Line 428.

¶12040 — Provincial or Territorial Credits (Form T1: Line 479)

The provinces and territories all have their own non-refundable tax credits similar to federal non-refundable tax credits, although the amounts may differ. The rules for claiming these credits are generally the same as the rules for the federal non-refundable tax credits. To claim these tax credits, individuals complete the appropriate Form 428 or Form 479, as applicable, for their province or territory of residence.

The provinces and territories also have various province- and territory-specific tax credits, discussed below. Some of these tax credits are claimed on separate forms.

> See the personal tax reference tables in the Appendix for a complete listing of provincial and territorial income tax rates, brackets, and surtaxes for 2018, and for provincial and territorial non-refundable tax credit rates and amounts for 2018.

¶12050 — Administration and Enforcement

As mentioned, provincial personal tax is imposed under provincial income tax legislation (which provides that taxable income is harmonized with federal taxable income) and the CRA administers and collects the tax. With appropriate modifications, each of the provincial income tax statutes generally adopts the federal rules applicable in respect of tax returns, assessments, appeals, administration and enforcement.

The provincial personal income tax acts generally provide that the assessment provisions contained in section 152 of the federal ITA apply for provincial corporate tax purposes. Thus, the normal and extended reassessment periods for federal purposes also generally apply to each of the harmonized provinces. Furthermore, when applicable, a notice of objection need only be filed for federal purposes to also object to the provincial portion of the disputed taxes in question. With respect to assessment rules, it should be noted that certain special rules may apply under the provincial income tax statutes to provide for appropriate modifications. The harmonized provinces also adopt the federal rules with respect to personal tax refunds, and again, certain appropriate modifications may also be made.

Subject to certain exceptions, the Tax Court of Canada has jurisdiction over most personal income tax issues with respect to the agreeing provinces. Certain provincial specific rules do, however, apply where necessary.

¶12100 — Alberta

¶12110 — Liability for Tax

Alberta personal income tax is imposed under the *Alberta Personal Income Tax Act* (APITA). The CRA is responsible for administration of the APITA. Alberta income tax is payable by individuals resident in the province on the last day of the taxation year and non-residents of the province who have earned income in the province during the year.

An individual's Alberta tax is determined based on taxable income reported for federal income tax purposes, and allocated to the province under the federal allocation rules. For reporting purposes, Alberta tax is based on *federal taxable income* as shown on the T1 return, which is carried to Form AB428 where Alberta tax is calculated.

APITA 1(1)(v), 3(1), 5

¶12120 — Tax Rate

Effective January 1, 2017, Alberta began indexing its income tax brackets annually for inflation. Therefore, Alberta's tax rates and brackets for the 2017 and 2018 tax years are as follows:

2018 Taxable Income	2018 Tax Rates	2017 Taxable Income	2017 Tax Rates
first $128,145	10.0%	first $126,625	10.0%
over $128,145 up to $153,773	12.0%	over $126,625 up to $151,950	12.0%
over $153,773 up to $205,031	13.0%	over $151,950 up to $202,600	13.0%
over $205,031 up to $307,547	14.0%	over $202,600 up to $303,900	14.0%
over $307,547	15.0%	over $303,900	15.0%

APITA 4, 6, 6.1

¶12130 — Tax on Split Income (Form AB428: Line 40)

Where federal tax must be paid on split income, an additional Alberta tax must also be paid. Alberta's tax on split income is calculated as the amount of split income imposed under ITA 120.4 multiplied by the highest Alberta tax rate.

The tax on split income is calculated on federal Form T1206, and is reported on Form AB428. The dividend tax credit and the foreign tax credit are the only credits that may be deducted against tax on split income.

See ¶14210 for a detailed discussion of the tax on split income.

APITA 47, CRA Guide 5009-PC, Form AB428, Form T1206

¶12140 — Additional Minimum Tax (Form AB428: Line 47)

Individuals who are subject to federal minimum tax under ITA 127.5 will be subject to Alberta minimum tax at the rate of 35% of the federal minimum tax amount. Individuals who are entitled to a minimum tax carryover for federal purposes under ITA 120.2 may be eligible for a provincial minimum tax credit. The amount of the credit is calculated by multiplying the federal credit amount on Schedule 1 by 35%. Federal minimum tax is calculated on Form T691. Alberta minimum tax is reported on Alberta Form AB428.

APITA 27, 48, CRA Guide 5009-PC, Form AB428, Form T691

¶12150 — Non-Refundable Tax Credits

Alberta has adopted many of the personal non-refundable tax credits offered by the federal government, including the following:

- Basic personal amount
- Spouse or common-law partner amount
- Age amount
- Disability amount
- Caregiver amount
- Pension income amount
- Medical expenses
- Adoption expenses
- Donations and gifts
- Dividend tax credit

Although the eligibility rules for Alberta's non-refundable tax credits are generally the same as the corresponding federal tax credits, the amounts and method for calculation generally differ.

Alberta's non-refundable tax credit amounts are multiplied by its lowest tax rate of 10% to arrive at the amount of the deduction. There is an exception for donations and gifts, such that the amount of donations and gifts exceeding $200 will be multiplied by a credit rate of 21%. Most of Alberta's non-refundable tax credits and income thresholds are indexed annually for inflation.

See the tax reference tables in the Appendix for a complete listing of non-refundable tax credits available in Alberta.

APITA Part 1, CRA Guide 5009-PC, Form AB428, Form 5009-D

¶12151 — *Provincial Foreign Tax Credit (Form AB428: Line 49)*

If an individual's federal foreign tax credit for foreign non-business income is less than the tax paid to a foreign country related to that income, the individual may be entitled to an additional provincial foreign tax credit. An Alberta foreign tax credit may be claimed by an individual who resided in Alberta on the last day of the taxation year, and who paid non-business-income tax to a foreign country.

Generally, the Alberta foreign tax credit is equal to the lesser of:

- foreign taxes paid on foreign non-business income but not claimed for purposes of the federal foreign tax credit; and
- the proportion of Alberta income tax equal to the ratio of: net foreign non-business income/net income allocated to Alberta

For purposes of calculating the provincial foreign tax credit, net income is subject to the same adjustments as for federal purposes in claiming the federal non-business foreign tax credit.

The foreign tax credit is calculated on federal Form T2036 and claimed on Form AB428.

APITA 23, CRA Guide 5009-PC, Form AB428, Form T2036

¶12152 — *Political Contribution Tax Credit (Form AB428: Lines 51 to 55)*

This tax credit is available to individuals who have made contributions during the tax year to:

- a registered Alberta political party, a registered candidate, or a registered constituency association in an election held under the Alberta *Election Act*;

- a registered Alberta political party that has nominated a candidate or a registered candidate in an election held under the Alberta *Senatorial Selection Act*; or

- party leadership elections and candidate nomination races that meet the criteria established under the *Election Finances and Contributions Disclosure Act* (effective for contributions made on or after January 1, 2017).

A tax credit may be claimed for each of the above types of political contributions. In order to claim the tax credit, an individual must have an official receipt.

The maximum tax credit for each type of political contribution is $1,000. To calculate the tax credit, the first $200, or portion thereof, of contributions is multiplied by 75%, the next $900, or portion thereof, of contributions is multiplied by 50%, and the next $1,200, or portion thereof, of contributions is multiplied by 33.33%. The maximum tax credit will be reached when contributions total $2,300.

Application for the tax credit must be made with the individual's return for the taxation year or within 90 days from the date of mailing of the notice of assessment or reassessment.

APITA 24, CRA Guide 5009-PC, Form AB428, Form 5009-D

¶12153 — *Alberta Investor Tax Credit*

The 2016 Alberta budget announced a new Alberta Investment Tax Credit (AITC) for share investments made by eligible investors in certain eligible Alberta businesses. The AITC came into force on January 1, 2017 under the *Investing in a Diversified Alberta Economy Act*, and is intended to encourage investment in Alberta small businesses that are bringing new products and services to market and creating jobs in Alberta. For individuals, an investor must be an Alberta resident or have business income in the province, and own less than 50% of the equity in the companies in which they invest.

The AITC provides a 30% tax credit for share investments made after April 13, 2016 in Alberta small businesses that are substantially engaged (at least 50%) in the following activities:

- tourism activities such as resorts, skiing facilities, amusement and recreation industries, hunting and fishing camps, scenic and sightseeing transportation;

- research, development and commercialization of proprietary technology, products and processes;

- development of interactive digital media and game products; and

- post-production, visual effects and digital animation.

The maximum credit for an individual is $60,000 per year, up to $300,000 over five years. The AITC is refundable for individual investors and may be carried forward for up to four years. An individual who is claiming the AITC must file a copy of the investor tax credit certificate (provided by the corporation) with his or her income tax return for any taxation year in respect of which the AITC is being claimed.

For more information on the AITC, see www.alberta.ca/alberta-investor-tax-credit.aspx.

APITA 35.01, *Alberta Investor Tax Credit Regulations*

¶12160 — Other Tax Credits, Benefits and Incentives

¶12161 — *Alberta Family Employment Tax Credit (AFETC)*

This tax credit is intended to support children in low- and middle-income families in Alberta and to provide incentives for the parents of these children to continue to work. It is not necessary to apply for the AFETC. Eligibility is determined from information the federal government uses to calculate the federal Canada Child Benefit (CCB), and from the income tax returns filed by both spouses in the previous year. Eligible individuals will be notified each year near the end of July.

An individual must meet the following requirements to be eligible for the AFETC:

* file a tax return;

* be a parent of one or more children under 18;

* be a resident of Alberta for at least one month prior to receiving the credit; and

* earn a family working income of more than $2,760, and less than: $61,862 for families with 1 child, $79,662 for families with 2 children, $90,337 for families with 3 children, and $93,887 for families with 4 or more children.

A family's working income is the combined earned income of an individual and his or her spouse or common-law partner, including self-employment income, but does not include income from alimony or child maintenance.

AFETC payments are made to the same parent who receives the Canada Child Benefit payments. Generally, the payment is made to the parent who is primarily responsible for the care of the child. When both a male and female parent live in the same home as the child, the female parent is usually considered to be primarily responsible for the child. Individuals who are considered shared-custody parents for the purposes of the Canada Child Benefit will also be considered shared-custody parents for the AFETC.

The amount that a family receives depends on annual family working and net income, and how many children under the age of 18 are in the family. A family's working income is the combined earned income of an individual and his or her spouse or common-law partner, including self-employment income, but does not include income from alimony or child maintenance. Family net income is a family's total income minus registered pension plan and RRSP contributions, annual union dues, child care expenses and moving and other expenses.

Benefit amounts are phased in and out based on income level. The table below displays the maximum benefit amounts for the AFETC, effective July 1, 2018:

Number of children	AFETC (max.)
1 child	$783
2 children	$1,495
3 children	$1,922
4 or more children	$2,064

AFETC payments are made in January and July of each year. These are advance payments covering the six month period following the payment; if a recipient family leaves Alberta during the six month period, any payment received for the months the family is not living in Alberta must be repaid.

APITA 28–35, CRA Guide 5009-PC, CRA Guide T4114, www.alberta.ca/alberta-family-employment-tax-credit.aspx

¶12162 — *Alberta Centennial Education Savings Plan (ACES)*

On March 26, 2015, the Government of Alberta announced the closing of the Alberta Centennial Education Savings Plan.

¶12163 — *Alberta Child Benefit (ACB)*

The Alberta Child Benefit (ACB) provides an annual benefit for families of up to $1,128 for one child, and up to $564 for each of the next three children. Families with net income of up to $26,141 will receive the maximum benefit available. Benefits begin to phase out above $26,141, and are fully phased out once family net income reaches $42,255. The Alberta Child Benefit is refundable and is administered by the CRA on the province's behalf. Payments are made in as many as four installments (in August, November, February and May), depending on how much a family is eligible to receive. The table below displays the maximum benefit amounts, effective July 1, 2018:

Number of children	ACB (max.)
1 child	$1,128
2 children	$1,692
3 children	$2,256
4 or more children	$2,820

References: APITA 28-35, CRA Guide 5009-PC, CRA Guide T4114, www.alberta.ca/alberta-child-benefit.aspx

¶12200 — British Columbia

¶12210 — Liability for Tax

BC's personal income tax is imposed under the BC *Income Tax Act* (BCITA). The CRA is responsible for administration of the BCITA. BC income tax is payable by individuals resident in the province on the last day of the taxation year and non-residents of the province who have earned income in the province during the year.

An individual's BC tax is determined based on taxable income reported for federal income tax purposes, and allocated to the province under the federal allocation rules. For reporting purposes, BC tax is based on federal taxable income as shown on the T1 return, which is carried to Form BC428, where BC tax is calculated.

BCITA 1(1)"taxable income", 2(1), 4(1)

¶12220 — Tax Rates

The BC September 2017 Budget announced the introduction of a new top personal tax rate of 16.8% for taxable income that exceeds $150,000, effective January 1, 2018. Accordingly, BC's tax rates for the 2017 and 2018 tax years are as follows:

2018 Taxable Income	2018 Tax Rates	2017 Taxable Income	2017 Tax Rates
first $39,676	5.06%	first $38,898	5.06%
over $39,676 up to $79,353	7.70%	over $38,898 up to $77,797	7.70%
over $79,353 up to $91,107	10.50%	over $77,797 up to $89,320	10.50%
over $91,107 up to $110,630	12.29%	over $89,320 up to $108,460	12.29%
over $110,630 up to $150,000	14.70%	over $108,460	14.70%
over $150,000	16.80%	—	—

BC's tax brackets are indexed annually for inflation using the BC provincial inflation rate; however the $150,000 bracket is not indexed for inflation.

BCITA 4.1, 4.52, CRA Guide 5010-PC, Form BC428

¶12230 — Tax on Split Income (Form BC428: Line 47)

Where federal tax must be paid on split income, an additional British Columbia tax must also be paid.

BC's tax on split income is calculated as the amount of split income imposed under ITA 120.4 multiplied by the highest BC tax rate.

The tax on split income is calculated on federal Form T1206, and is reported on Form BC428. The dividend tax credit and the foreign tax credit are the only credits that may be deducted against tax on split income.

See ¶14210 for a detailed discussion of the tax on split income.

BCITA 4.84, CRA Guide 5010-PC, Form BC428, Form T1206

¶12240 — Additional Minimum Tax (Form BC428: Line 54)

Individuals who are subject to federal minimum tax under ITA 127.5 will be subject to BC minimum tax at the rate of 33.7% of the federal minimum tax amount. Individuals who are entitled to a minimum tax carryover for federal purposes under ITA 120.2 may be eligible for a provincial minimum tax credit. The amount of the credit is calculated by multiplying the federal credit amount on Schedule 1 by 33.7%.

Federal minimum tax is calculated on Form T691. BC minimum tax is reported on Form BC428.

BCITA 4.68, 4.8, CRA Guide 5010-PC, Form BC428, Form T691

¶12250 — Non-Refundable Tax Credits

> Effective, January 1, 2019, the BC education tax credit will be eliminated. Unused education amounts carried forward from prior years will remain available to be claimed in 2019 and subsequent taxation years.

British Columbia has adopted many of the personal non-refundable tax credits offered by the federal government, including the following:

- Basic personal amount
- Spouse or common-law partner amount
- Age amount
- Disability amount
- Caregiver amount
- Pension income amount
- Medical expenses
- Adoption expenses
- Donations and gifts
- Dividend tax credit

Although the eligibility rules for British Columbia's non-refundable tax credits are generally the same as the corresponding federal tax credits, the amounts and method for calculation generally differ.

British Columbia's non-refundable tax credit amounts are multiplied by its lowest tax rate to arrive at the amount of the deduction. There is an exception for donations and gifts, such that the amount of donations and gifts exceeding $200 are multiplied by British Columbia's highest tax rate.

See the tax reference tables in the Appendix for a complete listing of non-refundable tax credits available in British Columbia.

BCITA 4.3–4.78, CRA Guide 5010-PC, Form BC428

¶12251 — *Provincial Foreign Tax Credit (Form BC428: Line 56)*

If an individual's federal foreign tax credit for foreign non-business income is less than the tax paid to a foreign country related to that income, the individual may be entitled to an additional provincial foreign tax credit. A BC foreign tax credit may be claimed by an individual who resided in BC on the last day of the taxation year, and who paid non-business-income tax to a foreign country.

Generally, the BC foreign tax credit is equal to the lesser of:

* foreign taxes paid on foreign non-business income but not claimed for purposes of the federal foreign tax credit; and

* the proportion of BC income tax equal to the ratio of: net foreign non-business income/net income allocated to BC

For purposes of calculating the provincial foreign tax credit, net income is subject to the same adjustments as for federal purposes in claiming the federal non-business foreign tax credit.

The foreign tax credit is calculated on federal Form T2036 and claimed on Form BC428.

BCITA 4.71, CRA Guide 5010-PC, Form BC428, Form T2036

¶12252 — *British Columbia Tax Reduction Credit (Form BC428: Lines 58 to 64)*

This is a non-refundable tax credit available to reduce the British Columbia taxation of low-income individuals. The maximum tax reduction credit is available to individuals who have a net income below the threshold amount for the tax year, and is reduced by a percentage of an individual's net income over the threshold amount. The tax reduction credit will be zero once the maximum net income is reached.

For the 2018 taxation year, the maximum credit amount is $453. The maximum credit amount is available to individuals with a net income of $20,144 or less in 2018. The tax credit then phases out at a reduction rate of 3.56% of net income above $20,144, and is completely phased out when net income exceeds $32,869.

BCITA 4.301, CRA Guide 5010-PC, Form BC428, www2.gov.bc.ca/gov/content/taxes/income-taxes/personal/credits/basic

¶12253 — *British Columbia Logging Tax Credit (Form BC428: Line 66)*

This tax credit is available to individuals with income earned from logging operations in British Columbia on which British Columbia logging tax is payable.

The amount of the tax credit is one-third of the logging tax paid.

The credit is non-refundable and there are no carry-forward or carry-back provisions.

BCITA 19.1, CRA Guide 5010-PC, Form BC428, www2.gov.bc.ca/gov/content/taxes/income-taxes/corporate/credits/logging

¶12254 — *British Columbia Political Contribution Tax Credit (Form BC428: Lines 69, 70)*

This tax credit is available to individuals who have made contributions during the tax year to a registered British Columbia political party or constituency association; or a candidate for an election to the Legislative Assembly of British Columbia.

The maximum tax credit is $500. To calculate the tax credit, the first $100 of contributions or portion thereof is multiplied by 75%, the next $450 of contributions or portion thereof is multiplied by 50%, and contributions in excess of $550 are multiplied by 33 1/3%.

The tax credit is non-refundable and there are no carry-forward or carry-back provisions.

BCITA 20, CRA Guide 5010-PC, Form BC428, www2.gov.bc.ca/gov/content/taxes/income-taxes/personal/credits/political-contribution

¶12255 — *Employee Share Ownership Plan and Employee Venture Capital Tax Credits (Form BC428: Lines 72–74)*

Individuals may claim a tax credit if they acquired shares from a registered British Columbia employee share ownership plan (ESOP) or a registered British Columbia employee venture capital corporation (EVCC) during the tax year or in the first 60 days of the following tax year.

The ESOP credit amount is up to 20% of the individual's investment and the EVCC credit amount is up to 15% of the individual's investment. The maximum total ESOP and EVCC tax credits that an individual can claim in a tax year is $2,000.

Individuals entitled to an ESOP or EVCC credit will receive a Certificate ESOP 20 or a Certificate EVCC 30, respectively, confirming the amount of their investment and the amount of the credit to which they are entitled.

The ESOP and EVCC tax credits that are not claimed in a tax year are not refundable and cannot be carried forward to future years.

BCITA 13.1, *Employee Investment Act* Parts 1 and 2, CRA Guide 5010-PC, Form BC428, www2.gov.bc.ca/gov/content/taxes/income-taxes/personal/credits/employee-investment

¶12256 — *British Columbia Mining Flow-Through Share Tax Credit (Form BC428: Line 76)*

This tax credit allows individuals who invest in flow-through shares to claim a non-refundable tax credit equal to 20% of their British Columbia flow-through mining expenditures incurred after July 30, 2001.

Individuals entitled to the tax credit will receive a T101 Information Slip from the mining exploration corporation. If the individual is a member of a partnership with flow-through mining expenditures, the individual will receive a T5013A Information Slip instead. To claim the credit, individuals must complete Form T1231, *British Columbia Mining Flow-Through Share Tax Credit*.

The tax credit is non-refundable. Any unused credit amount may be carried back 3 years or carried forward 10 years.

The expiry date for the mining flow-through tax credit is December 31, 2018.

BCITA 4.721, CRA Guide 5010-PC, Bulletin PIT 001, Form BC428, Form T1231, www2.gov.bc.ca/gov/content/taxes/income-taxes/personal/credits/mining-flow-through

¶12257 — *BC Volunteer Firefighters' Credit and Search and Rescue Volunteers' Credit (Form BC428: Lines 5830, 5845)*

The volunteer firefighters' credit and search and rescue volunteers' credit are available for 2017 and later taxation years.

BC residents can claim a 5.06% non-refundable tax credit for up to $3,000 of volunteer firefighting services provided to one or more fire departments and/or search and rescue volunteer services provided to one or more search and rescue organizations. To qualify, an individual must complete at least 200 hours of service in the year, each of which is an hour of "eligible volunteer firefighting services" for a fire department or "eligible search and rescue volunteer services" for an eligible search and rescue organization.

The requirements and criteria that must be met to claim the BC volunteer firefighters' credit and the search and rescue volunteers' credit are the same as the criteria to claim the federal volunteer firefighter tax credit under ITA 118.06 (see ¶10220) and the federal search and rescue volunteer tax credit under ITA 118.07 (see ¶10290), as applicable.

BCITA 4.37

¶12258 — BC Caregiver Credit (Form BC428: Line 5840)

Effective for 2018 and subsequent tax years, the BC caregiver tax credit and the BC infirm dependent tax credit are replaced with a new BC caregiver credit that parallels the Canada caregiver credit. The BC caregiver credit is available to BC residents who care for an eligible adult relative who is dependent on the caregiver because of a mental or physical infirmity. The caregiver is not required to live with the dependent in order to claim the credit.

For 2018, the maximum BC caregiver credit amount is $4,556 per infirm dependent, providing a benefit of up to $231, and is indexed to inflation for future years.

Individuals caring for an infirm spouse or common-law partner are eligible for the greater of the BC caregiver credit or the spousal tax credit, and individuals who are single and caring for an infirm adult relative are eligible for the greater of the BC caregiver credit or the eligible dependent tax credit.

BCITA 4.3, BC428

¶12259 — BC Farmers' Food Donation Tax Credit (Form BC428: Line 5898)

This non-refundable tax credit is available to both individuals and corporations that carry on the business of farming and donate a qualifying agricultural product to a registered charity that provides food to those in need or helps to operate a school meal program.

All of the following conditions must be met to claim this credit:

- the taxpayer was a resident of BC at the end of the year, or was not a resident of BC on the last day of the year but earned farming income in BC in the year;

- the taxpayer or his or her spouse or common-law partner was a farmer in the year;

- the taxpayer made a qualifying gift to an eligible charity in the year; and

- the taxpayer has claimed the qualifying gift on line 340 of federal Schedule 9 and on line 34 of Form BC428 as a charitable donation or gift for the year.

A "qualifying gift" is a gift of one or more agricultural products that the taxpayer produced in BC, and donated to an eligible charity in BC after February 16, 2016. An agricultural product is any of the following: meat products, eggs or dairy products, fish, seafood, fruits, vegetables, grains, pulses, herbs, honey, maple syrup, mushrooms, nuts, or anything else that is grown, raised or harvested on a farm and can legally be sold, distributed, or offered for sale at a place other than the producer's premises as food or drink in British Columbia.

An eligible charity is a registered charity under the ITA that meets one of the following conditions: it distributes food to the public without charge in BC and does so to provide relief to the poor (eg; a food bank); or it is engaged in providing meals or snacks to students in a qualifying school.

The credit is equal to 25% of the eligible amount of the total qualifying gifts made to an eligible donee after February 16, 2016, and before January 1, 2020, and must be claimed in the same year that the charitable donation tax credit is claimed for the donation. The farmers' food donation credit was originally available for the 2016, 2017 and 2018 tax years only; however, the 2018 BC Budget extended this credit to December 31, 2019.

To claim the farmers' food donation credit, enter the amount of donations included on line 340 of federal Schedule 9 that are qualifying gifts for this credit. Then enter 25% of this amount in box 5898 and on line 36 of Form BC428.

BC ITA 20.1

¶12260 — Other Tax Credits, Benefits and Incentives

¶12261 — *Home Renovation Tax Credit for Seniors and Persons with Disabilities (Form BC479)*

This is a refundable tax credit to assist seniors aged 65 and over with the cost of certain home renovations. For eligible expenditures made after February 16, 2016, this tax credit is expanded to persons with disabilities who are eligible to claim the federal disability tax credit (see ¶10120).

To qualify, the home renovation must be permanent and must assist a senior or disabled person by improving the senior or disabled person's access to the home or land, improving the senior or disabled person's mobility and functions within the home or land, or reducing the risk of harm to the senior or disabled person within the home or land. The primary purpose of the renovation cannot be to increase the value of the home or land. Eligible expenses include handrails, grab bars, walk-in bathtubs, and wheel-in showers; wheelchair ramps, lifts, and elevators; and motion-activated lighting. Non-eligible expenses include general maintenance, including plumbing, electrical and roof repairs; appliances; equipment for medical monitoring and home security; and services, including home care, housekeeping, and gardening.

An individual is eligible to claim the tax credit if, on the last day of the tax year, the individual is a resident of British Columbia and is a senior or a person with a disability who is eligible for the federal disability tax credit, or a family member living with a senior or disabled person. Family member includes a parent, step-parent, grandparent, in-law, sibling, spouse, common-law partner, aunt, uncle, great-aunt, great-uncle, child, step-child, grandchild, niece, or nephew. The home renovation must be to the principal residence of the individual claiming the credit, whether the residence is owned or rented. If more than one resident of the home is eligible, the credit may be shared.

The maximum credit is $1,000 annually, calculated as 10% of eligible permanent home renovation expenses paid in the tax year. A renovation expense will be deemed paid on the earlier of the date it becomes payable and the date it is paid. The maximum credit will be reached when the renovation expenses total $10,000 or more in a tax year.

To claim this credit, complete Schedule BC(S12), *British Columbia Home Renovation Tax Credit for Seniors and Persons with Disabilities*. Enter beside box 6048 of Form BC479 the amount from line 5 of Schedule BC(S12) and enter 10% of this amount on line 14 of Form BC479. Supporting documentation, such as receipts, should be retained.

BCITA Part 11, CRA Guide 5010-PC, Form BC479, Schedule BC(S12), www2.gov.bc.ca/gov/content/taxes/income-taxes/personal/credits/seniors-renovation

¶12262 — *Venture Capital Tax Credit (Form BC479)*

This tax credit is available to individuals who acquired shares from a registered British Columbia venture capital corporation (VCC) or an eligible business corporation (EBC) during the tax year or in the first 60 days of the following tax year.

The maximum credit amount is 30% of the individual's investment. The maximum investment that can be claimed by an individual in a tax year is $60,000.

Individuals entitled to this tax credit will receive a Certificate SBVC 10 indicating the amount of the credit they are entitled to.

The tax credit is fully refundable but must first be applied against the individual's total income tax payable. If an individual's tax credit certificate is for an amount greater than $60,000, the excess may be carried forward for up to 4 years.

BCITA 21, *Small Business Venture Capital Act*, CRA Guide 5010-PC, Form BC479, www2.gov.bc.ca/gov/content/taxes/income-taxes/personal/credits/venture-capital

¶12263 — *Mining Exploration Tax Credit (Form BC479)*

This tax credit is available to individuals who incur qualified mining exploration expenses before January 1, 2020 for determining the existence, location, extent, or quality of a mineral resource in British Columbia. The credit applies to exploration for all base and precious metals, coal, and some industrial minerals.

The credit is calculated on Form T88 as 20% of qualified mining exploration expenses less the amount of any assistance received, including reimbursements, grants, subsidies, rebates, and forgivable loans.

An additional credit of 10% is available for qualified mineral exploration undertaken in prescribed Mountain Pine Beetle affected areas after February 20, 2007.

The credit is fully refundable but must first be applied against the individual's total income tax payable. There are no carry-forward or carry-back provisions.

BCITA 25.1, *Mining Exploration Tax Credit Regulation*, CRA Guide 5010-PC, BC Bulletin CIT 006 Form BC479, Form T88, www2.gov.bc.ca/gov/content/taxes/income-taxes/personal/credits/mining-exploration

¶12264 — *Training Tax Credit (Form BC479)*

A refundable tax credit is available to individuals resident in British Columbia at the end of the tax year whom are registered in eligible apprenticeship programs administered through the British Columbia Industry Training Authority and who have completed level requirements in the tax year.

The amount of the tax credit available to individuals varies based on the program and level completed. An enhanced tax credit is available for First Nations individuals and individuals with disabilities.

To claim the tax credit, individuals must complete Form T1014, *British Columbia Training Tax Credit (Individuals)*. The credit must be claimed within 36 months after the end of the relevant tax year.

A refundable tax credit in respect of salaries and wages paid is also available to employers resident in British Columbia at the end of the tax year that carried on business in British Columbia in the tax year and employed an individual in an eligible apprenticeship program administered through the British Columbia Industry Training Authority.

The amount of the credit available to employers varies based on the program and the level completed by the employee. An enhanced tax credit is available where the employee is a member of a First Nation or has a disability.

To claim the tax credit, employers must complete Form T1014-1, *British Columbia Training Tax Credit (Employers)*. The credit must be claimed within 36 months after the end of the relevant tax year.

The expiry date for the tax credit is December 31, 2020.

BCITA Part 9, CRA Guide 5010-PC, BC Bulletin CIT 013, BC Bulletin PIT 002, Form BC479, Form T1014, Form T1014-1, www2.gov.bc.ca/gov/content/taxes/income-taxes/corporate/credits/training

¶12265 — *Shipbuilding and Ship Repair Industry Tax Credit (Form BC479)*

This is a refundable tax credit in respect of salaries and wages paid by employers that employ apprentices in the shipbuilding and ship repair industry. For the purpose of the tax credit, the definition of ships does not include vessels ordinarily used for personal or recreational purposes.

Individuals resident in British Columbia whose principal business is constructing, repairing, or converting ships and who employ an apprentice registered with the British Columbia Industry Training Authority and enrolled in an eligible apprenticeship program are eligible for the tax credit.

The amount of the tax credit is based on the salary and wages paid and varies depending on the program and level of completion.

BCITA Part 9 Division 3.1, CRA Guide 5010-PC, Form BC479, www2.gov.bc.ca/gov/content/taxes/income-taxes/corporate/credits/ship-build-repair

¶12266 — *British Columbia Sales Tax Credit (Form BC479)*

The British Columbia Sales Tax Credit was reintroduced effective January 1, 2013 as part of the return to the provincial sales tax system.

Individuals are eligible to claim the sales tax credit for a tax year if they were a resident of British Columbia on the last day of the tax year and are 19 years of age or older, or have a spouse or common-law partner or were a parent.

The maximum amount of the credit is $75 for each of the claimant and his or her cohabiting spouse or common-law partner, if any. If an individual is single, the credit amount is reduced by 2% of the individual's net income over $15,000. If the individual has a cohabiting spouse or common-law partner, the credit is reduced by 2% of family net income over $18,000.

The tax credit is refundable.

BCITA 8, Form BC479, www2.gov.bc.ca/gov/content/taxes/income-taxes/personal/credits/sales-tax

¶12267 — *British Columbia Low Income Climate Action Tax Credit*

This tax credit is a tax-free payment to help low-income individuals and families with the carbon taxes they pay.

Individuals are eligible to claim the tax credit if they are resident in British Columbia and are 19 years of age or older, or have a spouse or common-law partner, or are a parent who resides with his or her child. Only one person can claim the credit on behalf of a family.

The amount of the tax credit depends on the size of the individual's family and his or her adjusted family net income. The maximum annual payment amount for the period July 2018 to June 2019 is $135 per each of the adult claimant and his or her spouse or common-law partner, and $40 per child ($135 for the first child in a single parent family). The maximum credit amount is reduced by 2% of family net income in excess of $33,993 for single individuals with no children and $39,658 for families.

Application for the tax credit is made by applying for the federal GST/HST credit. The credit is paid quarterly together with the federal GST/HST credit. To be eligible to receive a quarterly payment, the individual must be a resident of British Columbia on both the first day of that quarter and the first day of the previous quarter.

BCITA 8.1, CRA Guide 5010-PC, www2.gov.bc.ca/gov/content/taxes/income-taxes/personal/credits/climate-action

¶12268 — *British Columbia Training and Education Savings Grant*

Parents or guardians can apply at a participating financial institution for the British Columbia Training and Education Savings Grant, which is a one-time contribution of $1,200 to the RESP of children born in 2006 or later after the child turns 6 years of age.

To be eligible for the grant, the child must be resident in British Columbia and enrolled in an educational program when the child turns 6 years of age.

To receive the grant, an RESP must be opened for the child before the child turns 9 years of age. It is not necessary to make any contributions to the RESP in order to receive the grant.

www2.gov.bc.ca/gov/content/education-training/k-12/support/bc-training-and-education-savings-grant

¶12269 — British Columbia Early Childhood Tax Benefit

The British Columbia Early Childhood Tax Benefit is a tax-free monthly payment made to eligible families to help with the cost of raising young children under the age of six. Benefits from this program are combined with the federal Canada Child Benefit into a single monthly payment.

The BC early childhood tax benefit provides a benefit of up to $55 per month per child under age 6 ($660 per year). Benefits are based on the number of children in the family and the family's net income. The benefit starts to phase out when net family income exceeds $100,000, and is eliminated when net family income exceeds $150,000.

The CRA is administering the program for the province. Individuals do not have to apply separately for the BC early childhood tax benefit — the CRA uses the information from the taxpayer's federal Canada Child Benefit application to determine eligibility. For eligible individuals, the amount of any payments will be calculated automatically based on information from filed tax returns.

BCITA 13.07–13.09, www2.gov.bc.ca/gov/content/family-social-supports/caring-for-young-children/bc-early-childhood-tax-benefit

¶12300 — Manitoba

¶12310 — Liability for Tax

Manitoba personal income tax is imposed under Manitoba's *The Income Tax Act* (MITA). The CRA is responsible for administration of the MITA.

Manitoba income tax is payable by individuals resident in the province on the last day of the taxation year and non-residents of the province who have earned income in the province during the year.

An individual's Manitoba tax is determined based on taxable income reported for federal income tax purposes, and allocated to the province under the federal allocation rules. For reporting purposes, Manitoba tax is based on federal taxable income as shown on the T1 return, which is carried to Form MB428, where Manitoba tax is calculated.

MITA 1(1), 3(1), 4.1

¶12320 — Tax Rates

Manitoba began indexing its personal income tax brackets in 2017. After indexing, Manitoba's tax rates for the 2017 and 2018 tax years are as follows:

2018 Taxable Income	2018 Tax Rates	2017 Taxable Income	2017 Tax Rates
first $31,843	10.80%	first $31,465	10.80%
over $31,843 up to $68,821	12.75%	over $31,465 up to $68,005	12.75%
over $68,821	17.40%	over $68,005	17.40%

¶12330 — Tax on Split Income (Form MB428: Line 45)

Where federal tax must be paid on split income, an additional Manitoba tax must also be paid. Manitoba's tax on split income is calculated as the amount of split income imposed under ITA 120.4 multiplied by the highest Manitoba tax rate.

The tax on split income is calculated on federal Form T1206, and is reported on Form MB428. The dividend tax credit and the foreign tax credit are the only credits that may be deducted against tax on split income.

See ¶14210 for a detailed discussion of the tax on split income.

MITA 4.4, CRA Guide 5007-PC, Form MB428, Form T1206

¶12340 — Additional Minimum Tax (Form MB428: Line 52)

Individuals who are subject to federal minimum tax under ITA 127.5 will be subject to Manitoba minimum tax at the rate of 50% of the federal minimum tax amount. Individuals who are entitled to a minimum tax carryover for federal purposes under ITA 120.2 may be eligible for a provincial minimum tax credit. The amount of the credit is calculated by multiplying the federal credit amount on Schedule 1 by 50%.

Federal minimum tax is calculated on Form T691. Manitoba minimum tax is reported on Form MB428.

MITA 4.5, 4.9, CRA Guide 5007-PC, Form MB428, Form T691

¶12350 — Non-Refundable Tax Credits

Manitoba has adopted many of the personal non-refundable tax credits offered by the federal government, including the following:

- Basic personal amount
- Spouse or common-law partner amount
- Age amount
- Disability amount
- Caregiver amount
- Pension income amount
- Medical expenses
- Adoption expenses
- Donations and gifts
- Dividend tax credit

Although the eligibility rules for Manitoba's non-refundable tax credits are generally the same as the corresponding federal tax credits, the amounts and method for calculation generally differ.

Manitoba's non-refundable tax credit amounts are multiplied by its lowest tax rate to arrive at the amount of the deduction. There is an exception for donations and gifts such that the amount of donations and gifts exceeding $200 are multiplied by Manitoba's highest tax rate.

The 2018 Manitoba budget increased the basic personal tax credit to $10,392 (from $9,382), effective for the 2019 tax year, and to $11,402 (from $10,392) effective for the 2020 taxation year.

See the tax reference tables in the Appendix for a complete listing of non-refundable tax credits available in Manitoba.

MITA 4.6–4.91, CRA Guide 5007-PC, Form MB428, Form MB479

¶12351 — *Fitness Tax Credit (MB428: Line 5839)*

This non-refundable tax credit is for fees paid in the tax year on registration or membership for a prescribed program of physical activity. The credit differs from the corresponding federal credit as it is available for fees for programs for young adults under the age of 25, in addition to children.

To qualify, a program must be ongoing, supervised, suitable for children or young adults, and require significant physical activity. For a child or young adult who qualifies for the disability amount, the requirement for significant physical activity will be met if the activity is recreational and results in movement and an observable use of energy.

The tax credit may be claimed for:

- an individual, for himself or herself, if he or she is under the age of 25 at the end of the tax year;

- an individual or his or her spouse or common-law partner's children under the age of 18 at the end of the tax year; and

- an individual's spouse or common-law partner, if he or she is under the age of 25 at the end of the tax year.

Only one individual may claim the tax credit for each child or young adult.

The maximum amount of fees that can be claimed per child or young adult is $500. If a child or young adult qualifies for the disability amount, an additional $500 can be claimed for that child or young adult, provided that a minimum of $100 is spent on prescribed programs of physical activity.

The 2017 Manitoba budget announced that the province's fitness tax credit will be maintained, despite the elimination of the federal children's fitness tax credit.

MITA 4.6(10.2)–(10.6), CRA Guide 5007-PC, Form MB428, www.gov.mb.ca/finance/personal/pcredits.html#fitness

¶12352 — *Children's Arts Credit (Form MB428: Line 5841)*

This tax credit provides individuals with children less than 16 years of age with a non-refundable tax credit for children's participation in eligible non-fitness activities, including artistic, cultural, recreational, or developmental activities.

To qualify, a program must be ongoing, supervised, and suitable for children. The program must also meet at least one of the following criteria:

- it must contribute to the development of creative skills or expertise in an artistic or cultural activity;

- it must substantially focus on wilderness and the natural environment;

- it must contribute to the development and use of intellectual skills;

- it must include structured interaction between children, with supervision and assistance in developing such skills; or

- it must provide academic enrichment or tutoring.

Examples of eligible programs include organized and supervised activities outside of a school's regular programs in performing, graphic, or language arts; tutoring in academic subjects; leadership and personal effectiveness training; environmental stewardship; crafts; and safety (e.g., Girl Guides, Scouts, 4-H, Cadets, etc.). Camps and memberships may also qualify. Eligible expenses do not include costs for the purchase or rental of equipment for exclusive personal use, accommodation, travel, food, or beverages.

The maximum amount that can be claimed per child is $500. If a child has a disability, an additional $500 can be claimed for that child, provided that a minimum of $100 is spent on eligible programs.

The 2017 Manitoba budget announced that the province's children's arts tax credit will be maintained, despite the elimination of the federal children's arts tax credit.

MITA 4.6(10.7), (10.8), CRA Guide 5007-PC, Form MB428, www.gov.mb.ca/finance/personal/pcredits.html#cultural

¶12353 — *Manitoba Family Tax Benefit (Form MB428: Line 6147)*

This non-refundable tax credit is the sum of:

- $2,065 basic amount for the individual claiming the credit;

- $2,065 for a spouse, common-law partner or eligible dependent, if claimed;

- $2,065 if the individual is 65 years of age or older;

- $2,065 if the individual's spouse is 65 years of age or older, and spouse's age amount is claimed;

- $2,752 for each disability claim;

- $2,752 for each of the individual's disabled dependents 18 years of age or older, if claimed; and

- $2,752 for each of the individual's dependents 18 years of age or under,

less 9% of the individual's net income.

To claim this tax credit, individuals must complete Schedule MB428-A and attach a copy to their income tax return.

MITA 4.6(16.1), CRA Guide 5007-PC, Form MB428, Schedule MB428-A, www.gov.mb.ca/finance/personal/pcredits.html#mbftb

¶12354 — *Political Contributions Tax Credit (Form MB428: Lines 54, 55)*

This non-refundable tax credit is available to individuals who have made contributions during the tax year to a recognized Manitoba political party; or a candidate for election to the Manitoba Legislature.

For 2017 and 2018, the tax credit that may be claimed by a taxpayer is equal to the lesser of:

- $650, or

- the sum of:

  - 75% of the first $400 of contributions;

  - 50% of the next $350 of contributions; and

  - 33.33% of the next $1,575 of contributions

MITA 4.11, CRA Guide 5007-PC, Form MB428, www.gov.mb.ca/finance/personal/pcredits.html#pctc

¶12355 — *Labour-Sponsored Funds Tax Credit (Form MB428: Line 6080)*

> The 2018 Manitoba budget eliminated the Labour-Sponsored Funds Tax Credit, effective for shares acquired after 2018. Therefore, 2018 is the last year to claim this credit.

This tax credit is available to individuals who invest in registered labour-sponsored venture capital corporations during the 2018 tax year.

The amount of the tax credit is equal to 15% of the investment, to a maximum annual credit of $1,800 for investments in corporations registered after June 30, 2006, and $750 for investments in corporations registered before July 1, 2006.

Individuals with eligible investments should receive a Slip T2C (MAN) indicating the amount of the tax credit they are entitled to.

The Labour-Sponsored Venture Capital Corporations Act, CRA Guide 5007-PC, Form MB428

¶12356 — *Provincial Foreign Tax Credit (Form MB428: Line 59)*

If an individual's federal foreign tax credit for foreign non-business income is less than the tax paid to a foreign country related to that income, the individual may be entitled to an additional provincial foreign tax credit. A Manitoba foreign tax credit may be claimed by an individual who resided in Manitoba on the last day of the taxation year, and paid non-business-income tax to a foreign country.

Generally, the Manitoba foreign tax credit is equal to the lesser of:

- foreign taxes paid on foreign non-business income but not claimed for purposes of the federal foreign tax credit; and

- the proportion of Manitoba income tax equal to the ratio of: net foreign non-business income/net income allocated to Manitoba

The foreign tax credit is calculated on federal Form T2036 and claimed on Form MB428.

MITA 4.12, CRA Guide 5007-PC, Form MB428, Form T2036

¶12357 — *Community Enterprise Development Tax Credit (Form MB428: Line 6085 and Form MB479: Line 6135)*

The Community Enterprise Development Tax Credit is intended to encourage Manitoba-resident investors to invest in specific community enterprises or in community development investment pools in their communities. The aim is to assist community-based enterprise development projects in raising local equity capital. Individual investors have the option of acquiring eligible shares through their RRSP or TFSA.

With respect to eligible shares issued before June 12, 2014:

- The tax credit rate is 30%;

- The maximum credit that an individual investor can earn in a year is $9,000, based on a maximum $30,000 eligible investment;

- The maximum eligible shares an approved company can issue under the program is $1 million;

- The tax credit is non-refundable; and

- Any credits earned but unused in a given year are available to be carried forward for up to ten years and carried back up to three years.

The Community Enterprise Development Tax Credit has been extended to 2020. With respect to eligible shares issued on or after June 12, 2014:

- The tax credit rate is 45%;

- The maximum credit that an individual investor can earn in a year is $27,000, based on a maximum $60,000 eligible investment;

- The maximum eligible shares an approved company can issue under the program is $3 million;

- The tax credit is fully refundable (only with respect to shares issued after 2014); and

- Beginning on January 1, 2015, shares purchased in the first 60 days following the end of a given calendar year are eligible for the credit in that year (this allows a shareholder who makes an eligible investment through an RRSP to elect to retroactively claim the tax credit in the same taxation year as the RRSP deduction).

To claim the tax credit, individuals must complete Form T1256, *Manitoba Community Enterprise Development Tax Credit*.

MITA 11.8–11.12, Manitoba *Community Enterprise Development Tax Credit Regulation*, CRA Guide 5007-PC, Form MB428, Form T1256, www.gov.mb.ca/finance/personal/pcredits.html#cedtc

¶12358 — *Small Business Venture Capital Tax Credit (Form MB428: Line 6092)*

The Small Business Venture Capital Tax Credit encourages Manitoba-resident individuals and companies to acquire equity capital in emerging enterprises that require larger amounts of capital than community ownership can provide. The tax credit is non-refundable and offsets Manitoba income tax otherwise payable. Credits earned in a year but unused can be carried back three years or carried forward ten years to offset Manitoba income tax in any of those years.

Eligible shares must be acquired directly by the investor. The minimum investment by an investor is $20,000 prior to March 12, 2018 and $10,000 effective March 12, 2018. The maximum investment an investor can make in a qualifying corporation is $450,000. The minimum issuance by an approved qualifying corporation is $100,000. The maximum tax savings claimable under the tax credit in a year is $10 million.

With respect to eligible shares issued before June 12, 2014:

- The tax credit rate is 30%;

- The maximum annual tax credit claimable by an investor is $45,000;

- An existing shareholder who has less than 10% equity in a company is eligible to purchase tax-creditable shares; and

- The maximum tax credit earned by an investor when investing in a company is $135,000.

With respect to eligible shares issued on or after June 12, 2014:

- The tax credit rate is 45%;

- The maximum annual tax credit claimable by an investor is $67,500;

- The lifetime limit in tax creditable shares an approved corporation can issue is doubled from $5 million to $10 million;

- An existing shareholder who has less than 35% equity in a company is eligible to purchase tax creditable shares; and

- The maximum tax credit earned by an investor when investing in a company is $202,500.

To claim the tax credit, individuals must complete Form T1256-1, *Manitoba Small Business Venture Capital Tax Credit (Individuals)*.

CRA Guide 5007-PC, Form MB428, Form T1256-1, www.gov.mb.ca/finance/personal/pcredits.html#ceitc

¶12359 — *Mineral Exploration Tax Credit (Form MB428: Line 6083)*

Manitoba provides a 30% non-refundable mineral exploration tax credit for individuals on the purchase of flow-through shares of eligible mineral exploration companies. The Manitoba credit parallels the federal investment tax credit for flow-through mining expenditures, and follows the federal eligibility rules. However, the provincial credit is only available where substantially all of the exploration activity is undertaken in Manitoba.

This non-refundable tax credit is available to individuals who invest in flow-through shares of qualifying mineral exploration corporations before April 1, 2021.

Unused credits may be carried back three years or forward 10 years.

Individuals with eligible investments should receive an Information Slip T101 indicating their qualifying expenses. Individuals who are members of partnerships with eligible investments will receive an Information Slip T5013A. To claim the credit, individuals must complete Form T1241, *Manitoba Mineral Exploration Tax Credit*.

MITA 11.7, CRA Guide 5007-PC, Form MB428, Form T1241, www.gov.mb.ca/finance/personal/pcredits.html#mineral

¶12359.1 — *Manitoba Volunteer Firefighters' Amount and Search and Rescue Volunteers' Amount (Form MB428: Lines 5830, 5845)*

Individuals who are resident in Manitoba at the end of the year who perform a combination of at least 200 hours volunteer firefighting and volunteer search and rescue services in the year can claim a non-refundable credit on $3,000. Individuals may claim either the volunteer firefighter or the search and rescue volunteer tax credit, but not both. The maximum annual benefit is $324.

The requirements and criteria that must be met to claim the Manitoba volunteer firefighter or the search and rescue volunteer amounts are the same as the criteria to claim the federal volunteer firefighter tax credit under ITA 118.06 (see ¶10220) or the federal search and rescue volunteer tax credit under ITA 118.07 (see ¶10290), as applicable.

MITA 4.6(15.3), www.gov.mb.ca/finance/personal/pcredits.html#firefighters

¶12360 — Other Tax Credits, Benefits and Incentives

¶12361 — *Personal Tax Credit (Form MB479)*

This refundable tax credit is available to individuals who, at the end of the tax year, were a resident of Manitoba and were 19 years of age or older, and to those under age 19 who are parents or have a spouse or common-law partner..

The calculation of the personal tax credit starts with a basic credit that is available to all taxpayers, with further credits in prescribed amounts available for certain taxpayers based on factors such as age, family status, disability and number of dependants. The total of these amounts is reduced by 1% of family income to determine the personal tax credit. Family income is defined as the individual's income for the year plus the income of the individual's cohabiting spouse or common-law partner, if any.

The following amounts are used in the calculation of the personal tax credit:

- the basic credit and credits for spouse and equivalent-to-spouse are $195;
- the age credits for self and spouse are $113;
- the disability credit for self, spouse and dependents other than a spouse are $113;
- the credit for disabled dependants is $62; and
- the credit for dependent children is $26.

This tax credit cannot be claimed by individuals who:

- were claimed as a dependant by anyone on his or her Manitoba income tax return;
- were confined to a prison or similar institution at the end of the tax year and were there for 6 or more months during the tax year; or
- have a spouse or common-law partner who is claiming a transfer of part or all of their age amount, or a spouse, common-law partner, or anyone else who is claiming a transfer of all or part of their disability amount.

Only one of an individual and his or her spouse or common-law partner can claim the tax credit unless they were separated or divorced at the end of the tax year or lived apart for part or all of the tax year for medical reasons.

Individuals cannot claim the personal tax credit for dependants who received provincial or municipal social assistance payments in the tax year, other than their spouse or common-law partner. If an individual or his or her spouse or common-law partner received provincial or municipal social assistance payments in the tax year, the individual can only claim part of the personal tax credit.

The credit is claimed on Form MB479.

MITA 5(2), 5.7, CRA Guide 5007-PC, Form MB479, www.gov.mb.ca/finance/personal/pcredits.html#ptc

¶12362 — *Education Property Tax Credit (Form MB479)*

> The 2018 Manitoba budget announced that, effective for 2019, the calculation of the Education Property Tax Credit will be based on school taxes, with the $250 deductible being eliminated.

This tax credit is available to individuals who:

- were resident in Manitoba at the end of the tax year;
- paid rent or property tax on a principal residence in Manitoba in the tax year;
- have occupancy costs of more than $250; and
- were 16 years of age or older at the end of the tax year.

Individuals cannot claim the tax credit if they were living in the home of someone who, for the tax year:

- will claim them as a dependant;
- will claim a spouse or common-law partner amount for them, or to whom they will transfer part or all of their age or disability amount; or
- has received or will receive an education property tax credit.

Only one of an individual and his or her spouse or common-law partner may claim the tax credit, unless the individual and his or her spouse or common-law partner became spouses or common-law partners during the tax year, lived apart at the end of the tax year for medical reasons, or were separated or divorced at the end of the tax year, in which case, the tax credit can also be claimed for the separate residence occupied by the individual or his or her spouse or common-law partner during part of the tax year.

If an individual shares accommodation, only one tenant may claim the tax credit for the entire period during which accommodation was shared. If the individual rents and shares accommodation with the owner of the home, he or she cannot claim the credit.

A principal residence is a residential dwelling unit in Manitoba owned, rented, and usually lived in by the individual or the individual and his or her spouse or common-law partner. The tax credit can only be claimed on one principal residence at a time.

For individuals under age 65, the tax credit amount is equal to the individual's occupancy costs exceeding $250, up to the maximum credit amount of $700. For individuals age 65 and older, the tax credit amount is equal to the individual's occupancy costs exceeding $250, up to the maximum credit amount of $1,100 minus 1% of family income to a minimum of $700.

An individual's occupancy costs are net property taxes paid or 20% of total rental payments.

Only the portion of property taxes that applies to the principal residence, and not, for example, property taxes applicable to adjoining farmland, may be used to calculate the tax credit.

If an individual or his or her spouse or common-law partner received provincial or municipal social assistance payments in the tax year, the individual can only claim part of the tax credit.

For homeowners, the tax credit is usually received automatically as an offset to property taxes due on the local government property tax bill. Tenants and homeowners who did not receive the credit automatically may apply for the credit on their Manitoba income tax return.

MITA 5(2), 5.3, 5.4, Manitoba *Education Property Tax Regulation*, CRA Guide 5007-PC, Form MB479, www.gov.mb.ca/finance/personal/pcredits.html#eptc

¶12363 — *Homeowner's School Tax Assistance (Form MB479)*

This tax credit is available to individuals who:

- were 55 years of age or older at the end of the tax year;

- have family income of less than $23,800;

- own, are buying, or are a life tenant of a principal residence, or have a spouse or common-law partner who owns, is buying, or is a life tenant of a principal residence; and

- have assessed school tax for their principal residence of more than $160 for the tax year.

Only one tax credit may be claimed per dwelling.

The amount of the tax credit is equal to the lesser of:

- $175 minus 2% of family income in excess of $15,100;

- school taxes paid in excess of $160; or

- occupancy costs (i.e., net property taxes paid or 20 per cent of total rent payments, in excess of the property tax credit).

MITA 5.5, CRA Guide 5007-PC, Form MB479, www.gov.mb.ca/finance/personal/pcredits.html#hsta

¶12364 — *Primary Caregiver Tax Credit (Form MB479)*

The Primary Caregiver Tax Credit is a refundable tax credit that provides financial support to individuals who serve as primary caregivers for more than 90 days. The primary caregiver may be a spouse, other relative, neighbour, or friend who provides care without remuneration. The cared-for individual must be assessed as requiring Care Levels 2, 3, or 4 while living at home (e.g., those with a disability, people with life threatening illnesses and others needing care and supervision for periods of more than 90 days).

The cared-for individual must:

- be a resident of Manitoba in an area under the jurisdiction of a Regional Health Authority;

- reside in a private residence (i.e., not a group home, foster home, hospital, or personal care home, in supportive housing, or on a reserve);

- be assessed as having care level requirements equivalent to level 2 or higher; and

- designate only one primary caregiver to claim this credit.

The primary caregiver must:

- be a resident of Manitoba;

- provide caregiving for longer than 90 days;

- personally provide care or supervision to the care recipient without compensation of any kind; and

- not be the spouse or common-law partner of a person who receives compensation for providing care to a qualified care recipient.

For more information on this credit and to download the *Primary Caregiver Tax Credit — Registration Form*, see: gov.mb.ca/finance/tao/caregiver.html.

MITA 5.11, CRA Guide 5007-PC, Form MB479

¶12365 — *Fertility Treatment Tax Credit (Form MB479)*

This is a refundable tax credit available to individuals who were resident in Manitoba at the end of the tax year if they or their spouse or common-law partner paid eligible medical expenses for fertility treatment in the tax year.

Eligible medical expenses for fertility treatment are expenses an individual can claim as medical expenses on his or her federal income tax return. The expenses must be for infertility treatment services and must be paid to a fertility clinic or licensed physician in Manitoba. Medications prescribed in relation to infertility treatment are also eligible, including medications prescribed by a licensed physician in Manitoba in relation to fertility treatments received outside of Manitoba. Expenses for the reversal of previous elective sterilization procedures, such as vasectomies, are not eligible. The expenses that may be claimed are net of any reimbursements, such as private health care coverage.

Only one of an individual and his or her spouse or common-law partner can claim the tax credit; the credit cannot be split.

The amount of the tax credit is 40% of eligible medical expenses for fertility treatment, up to the maximum credit amount of $8,000.

MITA 5.13, CRA Guide 5007-PC, Form MB479, www.gov.mb.ca/finance/personal/pcredits.html#fertility

¶12366 — *Paid Work Experience Tax Credit (Form MB479)*

The Paid Work Experience Tax Credits (formerly named the Co-op Education and Apprenticeship Tax Credits) are refundable credits available to employers who paid salaries or wages in the tax year to individuals under the following hiring incentives:

1. Youth Work Experience Hiring Incentive — Employers that hire high school students and those recently out of high school who completed an approved youth work experience training program in high school can claim a tax credit equal to 25% of salary and wages paid to the student, to a maximum of $5,000.

2. Co-op Student Hiring Incentive — Employers that provide qualifying work placements for students enrolled in a recognized post-secondary co-operative education program can claim a tax credit equal to 15% of the salary or wages paid to the student, to a maximum of $5,000.

3. Co-op Graduate Hiring Incentive — Employers who hire graduates from a recognized post-secondary co-operative education program can claim a tax credit equal to 15% of wages and salaries paid to the graduate in each of the first two years of employment, to a maximum of $2,500 for each year.

4. Apprentice Hiring Incentive — Employers who hire apprentices can claim a tax credit equal to 15% of wages and salaries paid to the apprentice, to a maximum of $5,000 per apprentice per year (the tax credit rate is increased to 20% for employers of apprentices who work in rural and northern Manitoba and 25% for employers of high school apprentices).

5. Journeyperson Hiring Incentive — Employers who hire recent graduates of apprenticeship programs can claim a tax credit for up to two years for each full-time journeyperson they hire. The credit is equal to 15% of wages and salaries, to a maximum credit of $5,000 per year.

MITA 10.1, CRA Guide 5007-PC, Form MB479, gov.mb.ca/finance/personal/pcredits.html#ceatc-indiv

¶12367 — *Green Energy Equipment Tax Credit (Form MB479)*

Manitoba property owners who install a geothermal heat pump system can receive a 7.5% tax credit on the cost of the geothermal heat pump if it is manufactured in Manitoba, plus a 15% tax credit for the eligible capital installation costs for the geothermal system (excluding the heat pump) if the installer is certified by the Manitoba Geothermal Energy Alliance (see www.mgea.ca). As well, purchasers who install qualified solar heating equipment in Manitoba may qualify for a 10% credit on the eligible capital cost of the equipment.

For more information on the Green Energy Equipment Tax Credit, see: gov.mb.ca/finance/tao/green.html.

MITA 10.3, *Manitoba Green Energy Equipment Tax Credit Regulation*, CRA Guide 5007-PC, Form MB479

¶12368 — *Book Publishing Tax Credit (Form MB479)*

A refundable tax credit of 40% of eligible book publishing labour costs (to a maximum of $100,000) plus 15% of eligible printing costs is available to individuals resident in Manitoba at the end of the tax year:

- whose primary business activity is publishing books;

- who published at least two eligible books within the two-year period ending at the end of the tax year; and

- who paid at least 25% of the total salaries and wages paid by them in the tax year to employees who were residents in Manitoba at the end of the tax year.

Eligible books include Canadian-authored fiction, non-fiction, poetry, drama, biography, and children's books published before 2019. The book must be at least 48 pages in length (unless a children's book), and a minimum of 300 copies must be printed. The following types of books are not eligible: corporate and vanity publications, directories, agendas, catalogues, calendars, loose-leaf publications, colouring, sticker, and activity books, and those containing advertising other than the publisher's own promotional material.

To claim the tax credit, individuals must complete Form T1299. See Form T1299 for details on how to calculate this credit.

MITA 10.4, CRA Guide 5007-PC, Form MB 479, Form T1299

¶12369 — *Cultural Industries Printing Tax Credit (Form MB479)*

This refundable tax credit is available to individuals resident in Manitoba at the end of tax year who:

- print, assemble, and bind eligible books in the course of their business carried on in Manitoba; and

- received payments in the tax year from a publisher for printing, assembling, or binding copies of an eligible book. The publisher must be resident in Canada, must not be related to the individual, and must confirm that the book is eligible for the Manitoba book publishing tax credit.

The amount of the tax credit is 15% of eligible printing revenue for the tax year for printing, assembling, or binding an eligible book. The credit is capped at $30,000 per eligible book title.

Eligible books include those eligible for the Manitoba book publishing tax credit, with the exception that the books do not have to be first editions. This includes books, substantially all of which have been written, adapted, or translated by a Canadian author, in the categories of fiction, non-fiction, poetry, biography, or children's books. Additional criteria also apply, including prescriptions for minimum length and print run. Certain types of books are specifically excluded from eligibility including directories, agendas, catalogues, maps, loose leaf publications, colouring or activity books, periodical publications, and publications containing advertising other than the publisher's own promotional material. Additionally, for a book to be eligible, it must contain at least 90% new material that has not been previously published; it must be sold through an established distributor; and the ratio of text to pictures must be at least 65% (except in the case of a children's book).

MITA 10.4.1, CRA Guide 5007-PC, Form MB479, www.gov.mb.ca/finance/business/pubs/printer_forms.pdf

¶12370 — *Employee Share Purchase Tax Credit (Form MB479)*

This refundable tax credit is available to individuals who purchased shares in the capital stock of their employer in the tax year under a registered employee share ownership plan (ESOP).

The amount of the tax credit is 30% of the cost to the individual of the shares issued in the tax year. The maximum tax credit that can be claimed is $27,000.

To claim the credit, complete Form T1256-2, *Manitoba Employee Share Purchase Tax Credit*.

MITA 11.18, Form MB479

¶12371 — *Seniors' School Tax Rebate (Form MB479)*

The maximum Seniors' School Tax Rebate is $470.

To qualify for the tax rebate, an individual must: (1) be 65 years of age or older, or have a spouse or common-law partner 65 years of age or older by the end of the year; (2) own their principal residence in Manitoba, or occupy their principal residence and pay school taxes; and (3) qualify as a Manitoba resident in the property tax year.

The rebate is reduced by 2% of net family income over $40,000. Eligible seniors below the $40,000 income-tested threshold will receive the full rebate of $470 depending on net school taxes paid, but senior households with a family net income of $63,500 or higher are not eligible for the rebate. The rebate is claimable on the annual personal income tax return on Form MB479.

The rebate received must be reported on the taxpayer's personal income tax return. Seniors who receive this rebate will be required to reduce their school taxes paid by the value of the rebate when applying for the Seniors' Education Property Tax Credit (see ¶12362) and the Homeowner's School Tax Assistance (see ¶12363).

MITA 5.5.1, Form MB479, www.gov.mb.ca/finance/tao/sstrebate.html

¶12400 — New Brunswick

¶12410 — Liability for Tax

New Brunswick personal income tax is imposed under the *New Brunswick Income Tax Act* (NBITA). The CRA is responsible for administration of the NBITA.

New Brunswick income tax is payable by individuals resident in the province on the last day of the taxation year and non-residents of the province who have earned income in the province during the year.

An individual's New Brunswick tax is determined based on taxable income reported for federal income tax purposes, and allocated to the province under the federal allocation rules. For reporting purposes, New Brunswick tax is based on *federal taxable income* as shown on the T1 return, which is carried to Form NB428, where New Brunswick tax is calculated.

NBITA 1, 11, 13

¶12420 — Tax Rates

New Brunswick's tax rates for the 2017 and 2018 tax years are as follows:

2018 Taxable Income	2018 Tax Rates	2017 Taxable Income	2017 Tax Rates
first $41,675	9.68%	first $41,059	9.68%
over $41,675 up to $83,351	14.82%	over $41,059 up to $82,119	14.82%
over $83,351 up to 135,510	16.52%	over $82,119 up to 133,507	16.52%

2018 Taxable Income	2018 Tax Rates	2017 Taxable Income	2017 Tax Rates
over $135,510 up to 154,382	17.84%	over $133,507 up to 152,100	17.84%
over $154,382	20.30%	over $152,100	20.30%

New Brunswick's tax brackets are indexed annually for inflation using the federal inflation rate.

NBITA 14, CRA Guide 5004-PC, Form NB428

¶12430 — Tax on Split Income (Form NB428: Line 39)

Where federal tax must be paid on split income, an additional New Brunswick tax must also be paid. New Brunswick's tax on split income is calculated as the amount of split income imposed under ITA 120.4 multiplied by the highest New Brunswick tax rate.

The tax on split income is calculated on federal Form T1206, and is reported on Form NB428. The dividend tax credit and the foreign tax credit are the only credits that may be deducted against tax on split income.

See ¶14210 for a detailed discussion of the tax on split income.

NBITA 45, CRA Guide 5004-PC, Form NB428, Form T1206

¶12440 — Additional Minimum Tax (Form NB428: Line 47)

Individuals who are subject to federal minimum tax under ITA 127.5 will be subject to New Brunswick minimum tax at the rate of 57% of the federal minimum tax amount. Individuals who are entitled to a minimum tax carryover for federal purposes under ITA 120.2 may be eligible for a provincial minimum tax credit. The amount of the credit is calculated by multiplying the federal credit amount on Schedule 1 by 57%.

Federal minimum tax is calculated on Form T691. New Brunswick minimum tax is reported on Form NB428.

NBITA 34, 46, CRA Guide 5004-PC, Form NB428, Form T691

¶12450 — Non-Refundable Tax Credits

New Brunswick has adopted many of the personal non-refundable tax credits offered by the federal government, including the following:

- Basic personal amount

- Spouse or common-law partner amount

- Age amount

- Disability amount

- Caregiver amount

- Pension income amount

- Medical expenses

- Donations and gifts

- Dividend tax credit

Although the eligibility rules for New Brunswick's non-refundable tax credits are generally the same as the corresponding federal tax credits, the amounts and method for calculation generally differ.

New Brunswick's non-refundable tax credit amounts are multiplied by its lowest tax rate to arrive at the amount of the deduction. There is an exception for donations and gifts, such that the amount of donations and gifts exceeding $200 are multiplied by 17.95%.

Most of New Brunswick's non-refundable tax credits and the New Brunswick low-income tax reduction are indexed for inflation.

See the tax reference tables in the Appendix for a complete listing of non-refundable tax credits available in New Brunswick.

NBITA 17–36, CRA Guide 5004-PC, Form NB428

¶12451 — *Provincial Foreign Tax Credit (Form NB428: Line 49)*

If an individual's federal foreign tax credit for foreign non-business income is less than the tax paid to a foreign country related to that income, the individual may be entitled to an additional provincial foreign tax credit.

A New Brunswick foreign tax credit may be claimed by an individual who resided in New Brunswick on the last day of the taxation year, and paid non-business-income tax to a foreign country.

Generally, the New Brunswick foreign tax credit is equal to the lesser of:

- foreign taxes paid on foreign non-business income but not claimed for purposes of the federal foreign tax credit; and

- the proportion of New Brunswick income tax equal to the ratio of: net foreign non-business income/net income allocated to New Brunswick

For purposes of calculating the provincial foreign tax credit, net income is subject to the same adjustments as for federal purposes in claiming the federal non-business foreign tax credit.

The foreign tax credit is calculated on federal Form T2036 and claimed on Form NB428.

NBITA 49, CRA Guide 5004-PC, Form NB428, Form T2036

¶12452 — *Political Contribution Tax Credit (Form NB428: Lines 71, 72)*

This tax credit is available to individuals who have made contributions during the tax year to:

- a registered New Brunswick political party or riding association; or

- a candidate for an election to the New Brunswick legislature.

The maximum credit amount is $500. To calculate the credit amount, the first $200 of contributions or portion thereof is multiplied by 75%, the next $350 of contributions or portion thereof is multiplied by 50%, and contributions in excess of $550 are multiplied by 33 1/3%.

The tax credit is non-refundable and there are no carry-forward or carry-back provisions.

NBITA 61, CRA Guide 5004-PC, Form NB428, www2.gnb.ca/content/gnb/en/departments/finance/taxes/political_contributionstaxcredit.html

¶12453 — *Labour-Sponsored Venture Capital Fund Tax Credit (Form NB428: Line 74)*

This non-refundable tax credit is available to individuals who purchased approved shares in prescribed labour sponsored venture capital (LSVC) corporations in the tax year or within 60 days of the end of the tax year.

Individuals who purchased approved shares of LSVC corporations are eligible for a 20% tax credit up to a maximum credit of $2,000 per year.

If an RRSP for a spouse or common-law partner became the first registered holder of an LSVC share, either the RRSP contributor or the annuitant may claim the tax credit for the share.

If the LSVC shares are not held by the individual for at least 8 years, the tax credit must be repaid.

Individuals entitled to the tax credit should receive a NB-LSVC-1 tax certificate from the LSVC corporation indicating the amount of the credit.

NBITA 50, New Brunswick *Registered Labour-sponsored Venture Capital Corporations Regulation*, CRA Guide 5004-PC, Form NB428, www2.gnb.ca/content/gnb/en/departments/finance/taxes/capital.html

¶12454 — *Small Business Investor Tax Credit (Form NB428: Line 76)*

This tax credit is available to individuals who are at least 19 years of age and who invested $1,000 or more in eligible small businesses in New Brunswick in the tax year or within 60 days of the end of the tax year.

For investments made on or before March 31, 2015, the amount of the credit is 30% of the investment up to a maximum credit amount of $75,000 per year. For investments made after March 31, 2015, the amount of the credit is 50 per cent of the investment up to a maximum credit amount of $125,000. As a result, for investments made after March 31, 2015, this credit is available to taxpayers who invest up to $250,000 in eligible small businesses in the province (i.e., $250,000 investment × 50% credit rate).

The tax credit is non-refundable but unused amounts can be carried forward 7 years or back 3 years.

If the investment is not held by the individual for at least 4 years, the tax credit must be repaid with interest.

Individuals entitled to the tax credit should receive a NB-SBITC-1 tax certificate from the small business. To claim the credit, individuals must complete Form T1258.

NBITA 50.1, *Small Business Investor Tax Credit Act*, CRA Guide 5004-PC, Form NB428, www2.gnb.ca/content/gnb/en/departments/finance/taxes/credit.html

¶12455 — *New Brunswick Low-Income Tax Reduction (Form NB428: Lines 53–69)*

The purpose of the New Brunswick Low-Income Tax Reduction is to reduce the income tax payable by low- and middle-income taxpayers.

To claim the tax reduction, individuals must be resident in New Brunswick at the end of the tax year. Only one of an individual and his or her spouse or common-law partner can claim the reduction; however, if an individual's spouse or common-law partner claims the reduction and does not need the entire amount to reduce his or her New Brunswick income tax payable to zero, the individual can claim the unused amount.

For the 2018 tax year, the tax reduction will eliminate New Brunswick provincial income tax for individuals with incomes below $16,761. The reduction is phased out at a rate of 3% of income in excess of this amount.

This tax reduction is non-refundable.

NBITA 49.1, CRA Guide 5004-PC, Form NB428

¶12460 — Other Tax Credits, Benefits and Incentives

¶12461 — *New Brunswick Low-Income Seniors' Benefit*

This benefit is an annual tax-free payment to assist low-income seniors.

To be eligible for the benefit, individuals must have been resident in New Brunswick on the last day of the previous tax year, must be at least 60 years old, and must have received a benefit under Canada's *Old Age Security Act* in the previous tax year, namely, the Federal Guaranteed Income Supplement, the Federal Allowance for the Survivor, or the Federal Allowance.

Where both spouses reside in the same household, only one benefit will be paid.

The amount of the benefit is $400 per year.

NBITA 52, CRA Guide 5004-PC, Form NB428, www2.gnb.ca/content/gnb/en/departments/finance/promo/seniors.html

¶12462 — *Home Energy Assistance Program*

The New Brunswick Home Energy Assistance Program provides a $100 annual benefit payment for eligible low-income individuals and families.

To be eligible to receive the benefit, individuals must be resident in New Brunswick at the end of the year, with total family income of $28,000 or less for the benefit year. Individuals with expected income below this amount in the payment year may also be eligible for the credit. An individual's family income includes both the individual's income, plus that of his or her spouse or common-law partner. Only one individual per household may apply for the credit. As well, an individual must maintain a principal place of residence in the province at the time the benefit application is made, and must have filed a tax return for the benefit year. Only one individual may claim the benefit per household.

To obtain the benefit, individuals are required to make an annual application to the New Brunswick Department of Finance. A copy of the individual's most recent home electricity bill, or for renters, the name of an individual's landlord, must be filed with the application. Application forms are posted annually on the New Brunswick Department of Finance Web site, and must be filed by the end of June of the benefit payment year.

For more information, see: www2.gnb.ca/content/gnb/en/departments/finance/promo/heap/program.html

NBITA 52.1, Application for Home Energy Assistance Program

¶12463 — *New Brunswick Child Tax Benefit and Working Income Supplement*

The New Brunswick Child Tax Benefit is a non-taxable amount paid monthly to qualifying families with children under the age of 18.

The amount of the benefit is $250 annually for each dependent child less 2.5% of family net income in excess of $20,000 for families with one child, or 5% of family net income in excess of $20,000 for families with more than one child.

The New Brunswick Working Income Supplement is an additional non-taxable amount paid to qualifying families with children under the age of 18 who have more than $3,750 of earned income.

The amount of the supplement is 4% of family earned income in excess of $3,750 less 5% of family net income in excess of $20,921, up to the maximum amount of $250 annually per family. The maximum benefit is reached when family earned income is $10,000, and the benefit is completely phased out when family net income reaches $25,921.

The New Brunswick Child Tax Benefit and Working Income Supplement are administered through the federal Canada Child Benefit program and are combined in a single monthly payment.

NBITA 51, CRA Guide T4114, www2.gnb.ca/content/gnb/en/departments/finance/taxes/child_tax_benefit.html

¶12464 — *Seniors' Home Renovation Tax Credit*

Effective for 2015 and subsequent taxation years, this initiative provides a refundable personal tax credit of up to $1,000 per year to assist seniors and their relatives with eligible home renovation expenses worth up to $10,000. For the 2018 tax year, individuals can claim expenses related to work that was paid for, or was billed (whichever is earlier) between January 1 and December 31, 2018.

To be eligible for the credit, an individual must be a New Brunswick resident senior at the end of the taxation year (i.e., at least 65 years of age), or a "qualifying relation" of the senior at the end of the taxation year. For these purposes, a "qualifying relation" means a person who is related to the senior in any manner described in ITA 251(6) or 251(2) (i.e., an individual related to the senior by blood relationship, marriage, common-law partnership or adoption).

The renovation must be made to a "qualifying principal residence", which is a residence in New Brunswick that is:

- if the individual is a senior at the end of the taxation year, the principal residence of the senior at any time during the taxation year or a residence that is reasonably expected to become the principal residence of the senior within 24 months after the end of the taxation year, or

- if the individual is not a senior at the end of the taxation year, the principal residence of the senior at any time during the taxation year that is, at the same time, also the principal residence of a qualifying relation of the senior at the end of the taxation year, or a residence that is reasonably expected to become such a shared principal residence within 24 months after the end of the taxation year.

Qualifying Expenditures

For purposes of this credit, a "qualifying expenditure" means an outlay or expense made by, or on behalf of, the senior in the taxation year that is directly attributable to a qualifying renovation. This would include an expense for permits required for, or for the rental of equipment used in the course of, the qualifying renovation. A "qualifying renovation" means an improvement prescribed by Regulation or an improvement:

- that is part of a renovation or alteration of a qualifying principal residence of a senior or of the land on which the residence is situated, or that is part of the construction of the residence, that has been undertaken to enable the senior to gain access to, or to be mobile or functional within, the residence or land, or to reduce the risk of harm to the senior within the residence or land;

- that is of an enduring nature and that is integral to the residence or the land on which the residence is situated, or relates to the purchase and installation of a modular or removable version of an item of a type that can otherwise be installed as a permanent fixture to the residence or the land, including modular ramps and non-fixed bath lifts;

- whose primary purpose is not to increase the value of the residence or the land;

- that would ordinarily be undertaken by, or on behalf of, a person who has an impairment to enable the person to gain access to, or to be mobile or functional within, the person's residence or land, and;

- that is not an improvement excluded by Regulation.

Examples of expenses that are eligible expenses for purposes of this credit include:

- Renovations to permit a first-floor occupancy or secondary suite for a senior;

- Grab bars and related reinforcements around the toilet, tub and shower;

- Handrails in corridors, widening passage doors and swing clear hinges on doors to widen doorways;

- Wheelchair ramps, stair/wheelchair lifts and elevators;

- Walk-in bathtubs, wheel-in showers and comfort height toilets;
- Lowering existing counters/cupboards and installing adjustable counters/cupboards;
- Light switches and electrical outlets placed in accessible locations;
- Door locks that are easy to operate and lever handles on doors and taps, instead of knobs;
- Pull-out shelves under a counter to enable work from a seated position;
- Non-slip flooring and motion-activated lighting;
- Hand-held shower on an adjustable rod or high-low mounting brackets;
- Additional light fixtures throughout the home and exterior entrances;
- Creating knee space under a basin to enable use while seated (and insulating hot-water pipes);
- Hands-free taps and relocation of tap to front or side for easier access; and
- Touch-and-release drawers and cupboards.

Expenses that are not eligible for the credit include amounts paid for the following:

- Devices, including equipment for home medical monitoring, equipment for home security (anti-burglary), wheelchairs, walkers, vehicles adapted for people with mobility limitations, fire extinguishers, smoke alarms and carbon monoxide detectors;
- Services, including security or medical monitoring services, home care services, housekeeping services and outdoor maintenance and gardening services;
- Previously used or leased goods;
- Property acquired that can be used independently of the qualifying renovation;
- Annual, recurring or routine repairs, maintenance or service (e.g., plumbing or electrical repairs, roof repairs, etc.);
- Aesthetic enhancements such as landscaping or redecorating;
- Installing new windows and heating or air conditioning systems, replacing insulation;
- Household appliances and electronic home-entertainment devices;
- Financing costs in respect of the qualifying renovation;
- Outlays made for the purpose of producing income from a business or property; and
- Amounts paid in respect of goods or services provided by a non-arm's length person, unless the person is registered for the purposes of Part IX of the *Excise Tax Act* (Canada).

If more than one individual is entitled to claim the credit for a taxation year in respect of a single residence, the total amount of qualifying expenditures that may be claimed by all of the individuals in respect of the residence cannot exceed $10,000. As well, if an individual and the individual's spouse or common-law partner are both entitled to the credit, the total amount of qualifying expenditures that may be claimed by the two individuals for the taxation year cannot exceed $10,000 (unless, on December 31, the individual and his or her spouse or common-law partner have been living separate and apart for at least 90 days because of a breakdown of their marriage or common-law partnership, or are living separate and apart because of medical necessity). Note that the seniors' home renovation tax credit can be claimed for all eligible expenses during the tax year up to a maximum of $10,000, even if a portion or all of the expenses are also eligible expenses for the purpose of claiming the medical expense tax credit during the same year.

Taxpayers will be required to complete New Brunswick Schedule 12, *Seniors' Home Renovation Tax Credit*, to claim the credit. Receipts from retailers, suppliers and contractors do not have to be submitted with the income tax return. However, they should be kept in case the CRA asks for them.

References: NBITA 52.01, Schedule NB(S12), www2.gnb.ca/content/gnb/en/departments/finance/promo/renovation.html

¶12465 — Harmonized Sales Tax (HST) Credit

The 2016-17 New Brunswick budget introduced a refundable provincial HST credit to lessen the impact of the provincial HST, which increased from eight to 10% on July 1, 2016. The maximum HST credit is $300 for individuals, $300 for a spouse or equivalent, and $100 per child under the age of 19. Single parent families receive a $300 credit for their first child. The full HST credit is provided to New Brunswick residents with a family income of less than $35,000 per year, reduced by 2% for every dollar of income above $35,000 per year. Some amount of credit is provided to families with incomes up to $75,000 or more, depending on the number of children.

Eligible individuals do not have to apply for the HST credit. The CRA determines eligibility, and issues the credit to all eligible individuals. However, individuals must file their annual income tax return in order to receive the credit. The CRA distributes the HST credit on behalf of the government of New Brunswick by adding it to the GST/HST credit payments received by eligible New Brunswick residents.

References: NBITA 52.02

¶12500 — Newfoundland and Labrador

¶12510 — Liability for Tax

The 2016 Newfoundland and Labrador budget introduced a temporary "deficit reduction levy", applicable for the 2016 to 2019 taxation years, based on an individual's taxable income. Individuals with taxable income of $50,000 or less are exempt from the levy. The levy increases by 10% within each $100 increase in taxable income over $50,000. For individuals with taxable income greater than $50,000, see the table at: fin.gov.nl.ca/fin/tax_programs_incentives/personal/temp_drl.html to determine the amount of levy payable.

Newfoundland and Labrador personal income tax is imposed under the Newfoundland and Labrador *Income Tax Act, 2000* (NLITA). The CRA is responsible for administration of the NLITA.

Newfoundland and Labrador income tax is payable by individuals resident in the province on the last day of the taxation year and non-residents of the province who have earned income in the province during the year.

An individual's Newfoundland and Labrador tax is determined based on taxable income reported for federal income tax purposes, and allocated to the province under the federal allocation rules. For reporting purposes, Newfoundland and Labrador tax is based on *federal taxable income* as shown on the T1 return, which is carried to Form NL428, where Newfoundland and Labrador tax is calculated.

NLITA 2(1)(i), 5(c), 6, 7, 7.1

¶12520 — Tax Rates

Newfoundland and Labrador's tax rates for the 2017 and 2018 tax years are as follows:

2018 Taxable Income	2018 Tax Rates	2017 Taxable Income	2017 Tax Rates
first $36,926	8.7%	first $35,851	8.7%
over $36,926 up to $73,852	14.5%	over $35,851 up to $71,701	14.5%
over $73,852 up to $131,850	15.8%	over $71,701 up to $128,010	15.8%
over $131,850 up to $184,590	17.3%	over $128,010 up to $179,214	17.3%

2018 Taxable Income	2018 Tax Rates	2017 Taxable Income	2017 Tax Rates
over $184,590	18.3%	over $179,214	18.3%

Newfoundland and Labrador's tax brackets are indexed annually for inflation using the Newfoundland and Labrador provincial inflation rate.

NLITA 5(b), 6.1, 7, CRA Guide 5001-PC

¶12530 — Tax on Split Income (Form NL428: Line 42)

Where federal tax must be paid on split income, an additional Newfoundland and Labrador tax must also be paid. Newfoundland and Labrador tax must also be paid. Newfoundland and Labrador's tax on split income is calculated as the amount of split income imposed under ITA 120.4 multiplied by the highest Newfoundland and Labrador tax rate.

The tax on split income is calculated on federal Form T1206, and is reported on Form NL428. The dividend tax credit and the foreign tax credit are the only credits that may be deducted against tax on split income.

See ¶14210 for a detailed discussion of the tax on split income.

NLITA 49, CRA Guide 5001-PC, Form NL428, Form T1206

¶12540 — Additional Minimum Tax (Form NL428: Line 49)

Individuals who are subject to federal minimum tax under ITA 127.5 will be subject to Newfoundland and Labrador minimum tax at the rate of 54.7% of the federal minimum tax amount. Individuals who are entitled to a minimum tax carryover for federal purposes under ITA 120.2 may be eligible for a provincial minimum tax credit. The amount of the credit is calculated by multiplying the federal credit amount on Schedule 1 by 54.7%.

Federal minimum tax is calculated on Form T691. Newfoundland and Labrador minimum tax is reported on Form NL428.

NLITA 19, 30, CRA Guide 5001-PC, Form NL428, Form T691

¶12550 — Non-Refundable Tax Credits

Newfoundland and Labrador have adopted many of the personal non-refundable tax credits offered by the federal government, including the following:

- Basic personal amount
- Spouse or common-law partner amount
- Age amount
- Disability amount
- Caregiver amount
- Pension income amount
- Medical expenses
- Donations and gifts
- Volunteer firefighters' amount
- Child care amount

- Adoption expenses

Although the eligibility rules for Newfoundland and Labrador's non-refundable tax credits are generally the same as the corresponding federal tax credits, the amounts and method for calculation generally differ.

Newfoundland and Labrador's non-refundable tax credit amounts are multiplied by its lowest tax rate to arrive at the amount of the deduction. There is an exception for donations and gifts, such that the amount of donations and gifts exceeding $200 are multiplied by Newfoundland and Labrador's highest tax rate.

See the tax reference tables in the Appendix for a complete listing of non-refundable tax credits available in Newfoundland and Labrador.

NLITA 9–26, CRA Guide 5001-PC, Form NL428

¶12551 — *Newfoundland and Labrador Child Care Credit (Form NL428: Line 11)*

This non-refundable tax credit is in addition to the deduction allowed for child care expenses.

The maximum amount is $8,000 of child care expenses for each child under 7 years of age and $5,000 of child care expenses for each child 7 to 16 years of age, for a maximum credit of $696 for each child under 7 years of age and $435 for each child 7 to 16 years of age.

The tax credit must be claimed by the same individual claiming the child care expenses.

NLITA 17.2, Form NL428, Form T778

¶12552 — *Provincial Foreign Tax Credit (Form NL428: Line 51)*

If an individual's federal foreign tax credit for foreign non-business income is less than the tax paid to a foreign country related to that income, the individual may be entitled to an additional provincial foreign tax credit. A Newfoundland and Labrador foreign tax credit may be claimed by an individual who resided in Newfoundland and Labrador on the last day of the taxation year, and paid non-business-income tax to a foreign country.

Generally, the Newfoundland and Labrador foreign tax credit is equal to the lesser of:

- foreign taxes paid on foreign non-business income but not claimed for purposes of the federal foreign tax credit; and

- the proportion of Newfoundland and Labrador income tax equal to the ratio of: net foreign non-business income/net income allocated to Newfoundland and Labrador

For purposes of calculating the provincial foreign tax credit, net income is subject to the same adjustments as for federal purposes in claiming the federal non-business foreign tax credit.

The foreign tax credit is calculated on federal Form T2036 and claimed on Form NL428.

NLITA 33, CRA Guide 5001-PC, Form NL428, Form T2036

¶12553 — *Political Contribution Tax Credit (Form NL428: Lines 53, 54)*

This tax credit is available to individuals who have made contributions during the tax year to:

- a registered Newfoundland and Labrador political party or district association; or

- a registered Newfoundland and Labrador independent political candidate during an election period.

The maximum credit amount is $500. To calculate the credit amount, the first $100 of contributions or portion thereof is multiplied by 75%, the next $450 of contributions or portion thereof is multiplied by 50%, and contributions in excess of $550 are multiplied by 33.33%.

The tax credit is non-refundable and there are no carry-forward or carry-back provisions.

NLITA 47, CRA Guide 5001-PC, Form NL428

¶12554 — *Direct Equity Tax Credit (Form NL428: Line 56)*

This tax credit is available to individuals who are at least 19 years of age and who acquire eligible shares in an eligible corporation in the tax year or within 60 days of the end of the tax year.

The tax credit is intended to support small businesses in growing areas of the economy. To be eligible, a corporation must, among other requirements, be a Canadian controlled corporation with a permanent establishment in Newfoundland and Labrador and have less than $20 million in assets and not more than 50 full time positions. The corporation must be engaged in, and use the capital raised for, qualifying activities such as technology, research and development, aquacultue, forestry and agrifoods, manufacturing and processing, export and import replacement, tourism, or cultural industries.

The amount of the tax credit is equal to 20% of the investment made in eligible businesses located in the North East Avalon area and 35% of the investment made in eligible businesses located elsewhere in Newfoundland and Labrador, up to the maximum credit amount of $50,000.

The tax credit is non-refundable; however, unused amounts may be carried forward 7 years or back 3 years.

The credit is calculated on Form T1272, *Newfoundland and Labrador Direct Equity Tax Credit*, and is claimed on Form NL428.

For answers to frequently asked questions regarding the Direct Equity Tax Credit, see: www.fin.gov.nl.ca/fin/faq/tax_¶rogram.html.

NLITA 46, *Direct Equity Tax Credit Regulations, Reg.* N.L.R. 26/01, CRA Guide 5001-PC, CRA Guide 5001-PC, Form NL428, Form T1272

¶12555 — *Resort Property Investment Tax Credit (Form NL428: Line 58)*

This tax credit is available to individuals who invested in a registered resort development property in the tax year and were at least 19 years of age at the time of the investment.

The amount of the tax credit is equal to 45% of the purchase price of qualifying resort development property units outside of the North East Avalon area. The maximum credit amount is $50,000 per tax year. There is also a lifetime maximum credit amount of $150,000.

The tax credit is non-refundable; however, unused amounts can be carried forward 7 years and back 3 years.

For individual investors, the credit is calculated on Form T1297, *Newfoundland and Labrador Resort Property Investment Tax Credit (Individuals)*, and is claimed on Form NL428.

For answers to frequently asked questions regarding the Resort Property Investment Tax Credit, see: www.fin.gov.nl.ca/fin/faq/resort_¶roperty.html.

NLITA 46.1, *Resort Property Investment Tax Credit Regulations*, N.L.R. 85/07, CRA Guide 5001-PC, Form NL428, Form T1297

¶12556 — *Newfoundland and Labrador Venture Capital Tax Credit (Form NL428: Lines 60–62)*

The Venture Capital Tax Credit is available to individuals who make investments in a qualifying venture capital fund during the taxation year or within 60 days of the end of the taxation year. Under this initiative, the provincial government will invest in two venture capital funds, which will focus on strategic sectors, improve access to larger venture capital pools, and leverage private sector investment.

The maximum amount that can be claimed is $75,000.

Unused venture capital tax credits can be carried forward for seven years.

NLITA 46.2, NL VCTC Certificate

¶12557 — *Newfoundland and Labrador Low-Income Tax Reduction (Form NL428: Lines 64–83)*

This non-refundable tax credit is available to low-income individuals who were resident in Newfoundland and Labrador at the end of the tax year.

Only one of an individual and his or her spouse or common-law partner can claim the tax credit for the family; however, if the entire credit amount is not needed to reduce the claimant's Newfoundland and Labrador income tax to zero, unused amounts can be transferred to the claimant's spouse or common-law partner.

For 2018, the basic reduction for an individual is $812 plus $452 for a spouse, common-law partner, or eligible dependant. These amounts are reduced by 16% of income in excess of $19,994 until the reduction is eliminated. Consequently, the credit will eliminate provincial income tax for individuals with income up to $19,994.

NLITA 21.1, CRA Guide 5001-PC, Form NL428, www.fin.gov.nl.ca/fin/tax_programs_incentives/personal/lowincometaxreduction.html.

¶12558 — Newfoundland and Labrador Search and Rescue Volunteers' Tax Credit

The 2018 Newfoundland and Labrador budget introduced a non-refundable search and rescue volunteer tax credit for first responders, available for 2019 and subsequent taxation years.

Eligible Newfoundland and Labrador search and rescue volunteers can claim a non-refundable tax credit for up to $3,000 of search and rescue volunteer services provided to one or more search and rescue organizations. To qualify, an individual must complete at least 200 hours of service in the year, each of which is an hour of eligible search and rescue volunteer service for an eligible search and rescue organization.

The requirements and criteria that must be met to claim the provincial search and rescue volunteer credit are the same as the criteria to claim the federal search and rescue volunteer tax credit under ITA 118.07 (see ¶10290).

NLITA 17.4, CRA Guide 5001-PC, Form NL428

¶12560 — Other Tax Credits, Benefits and Incentives

¶12561 — *Newfoundland and Labrador Child Benefit and Mother Baby Nutrition Supplement*

The Newfoundland and Labrador child benefit it a non-taxable amount paid monthly to assist low-income families with the cost of raising children.

The child benefit is available to families whose income is less than $25,028 and have children under 18 years of age. Individuals with net family income below $17,397 will receive the full benefit; however, there will be a reduced amount if net family income is between $17,397 and $25,028. The amount of benefit is based on net family income from the previous year.

The maximum Newfoundland and Labrador child benefit amount from July 2018 to June 2019 is as follows:

Family Size	Monthly Total	Yearly Total
1 Child	$33.16	$398
2 Children	$68.32	$820
3 Children	$106.15	$1,274
4 Children	$146.65	$1,760

The mother baby nutrition supplement is an additional benefit for families with children under 1 year of age. The amount of the mother baby nutrition supplement is $60 per month for each child under 1 year of age, plus an additional $90 for the month each child is born.

It is not necessary to apply for these tax credits. Eligibility is determined on the basis of information provided on the taxpayer's Canada child benefit application and income tax return.

These tax credits are paid monthly together with the federal Canada Child Benefit.

NLITA 38, *Child and Parental Benefits Regulations*, N.L.R. 43/09, CRA Guide 5001-PC, CRA Guide T4114

¶12562 — *Newfoundland and Labrador Seniors' Benefit*

The Newfoundland and Labrador Seniors' Benefit is a refundable tax credit for low income seniors. The non-taxable annual seniors' benefit amount is $1,313 for a single senior (65 years of age or older at any time during the year) or a married or common-law couple with at least one senior whose adjusted family net income is $29,402 or less. Seniors will receive a partial payment if their adjusted family net income is between $29,402 and $40,663. The benefit is indexed annually using the Consumer Price Index.

Adjusted family net income includes the individual's income and the income of a cohabiting spouse or common-law partner, but does not include amounts received under the Universal Child Care Benefit or a registered disability savings plan.

In order to qualify for this benefit, the person must be 65 years of age by December 31st of the taxation year. This benefit is paid in October of each year and is included in the same cheque as the GST/HST credit. The amount of the credit is based on adjusted family net income from the previous year.

No application is required. However, individuals must ensure that their annual income tax return is filed.

NLITA 34, *Seniors' Benefit Regulations*, 2007, N.L.R. 119/07, CRA Guide 5001-PC, Booklet RC4210

¶12563 — *Research and Development Tax Credit*

Newfoundland and Labrador provides a 15% refundable tax credit for scientific research and experimental development expenditures by a business with a permanent establishment in the province. Unlike most provinces, which only allow corporations to claim R&D credits, Newfoundland and Labrador also allows the credit to be claimed by individuals. Expenditures flowed through partnerships and trusts also qualify.

Generally, eligible expenditures are "qualified expenditures" for purposes of the federal investment tax credit for scientific research.

Individuals can claim the Newfoundland and Labrador research and development tax credit by filing Form T1129, *Newfoundland and Labrador Research and Development Tax Credit (Individuals)*, with the T1 income tax return.

NLITA 42

¶12564 — *Newfoundland and Labrador Income Supplement*

The Newfoundland and Labrador Income Supplement (NLIS) was introduced to assist low income seniors, individuals and persons with disabilities. The NLIS replaced the provincial HST credit and the Home Heating Rebate.

The NLIS is based on family net income and paid directly to eligible individuals in quarterly instalments in January, April, July and October. The amount of the credit is based on adjusted family net income from the previous year. No application is required; however, individuals must ensure that their annual income tax return is filed.

The annual amounts for the NLIS are as follows:

	NLIS Amount
Amount for eligible individuals (1)	Basic credit — $220 Max credit — $450
Amount for spouse	$60
Amount for eligible children	$200
Amount for individuals claiming the disability tax credit	$200
Phase-in income threshold	$15,000
Lower phase-out income threshold (2)	$40,000

Notes:

(1) Additional amount of $230 to be phased in at a rate of 4.6% for family net income in excess of $15,000. Eligible individuals with family net income of $20,000 to $40,000 will receive the maximum benefit of $450.

(2) The phase-out of the benefit begins at family net income of $40,000 at a rate of 9%.

NLITA 34, www.fin.gov.nl.ca/fin/tax_programs_incentives/personal/income_supplement.html

¶12600 — Northwest Territories

¶12610 — Liability for Tax

Northwest Territories personal income tax is imposed under the Northwest Territories *Income Tax Act* (NTITA). The CRA is responsible for administration of the NTITA.

Northwest Territories income tax is payable by individuals resident in the province on the last day of the taxation year and non-residents of the province who have earned income in the province during the year.

An individual's Northwest Territories tax is determined based on taxable income reported for federal income tax purposes, and allocated to the province under the federal allocation rules. For reporting purposes, Northwest Territories tax is based on *federal taxable income* as shown on the T1 return, which is carried to Form NT428, where Northwest Territories tax is calculated.

NTITA 1(1), 2(1), 2.1, 2.11

¶12620 — Tax Rates

The Northwest Territories' tax rates for the 2017 and 2018 tax years are as follows:

2018 Taxable Income	2018 Tax Rates	2017 Taxable Income	2017 Tax Rates
first $42,209	5.90%	first $41,585	5.90%
over $42,209 up to $84,420	8.60%	over $41,585 up to $83,172	8.60%
over $84,420 up to 137,248	12.20%	over $83,172 up to 135,219	12.20%
over $137,248	14.05%	over $135,219	14.05%

The Northwest Territories' tax brackets are indexed annually for inflation using the federal inflation rate.

NYITA 2.11, CRA Guide 5012-PC

¶12630 — Tax on Split Income (Form NT428: Line 39)

Where federal tax must be paid on split income, an additional Northwest Territories tax must also be paid. The Northwest Territories' tax on split income is calculated as the amount of split income imposed under ITA 120.4 multiplied by the highest Northwest Territories tax rate.

The tax on split income is calculated on federal Form T1206, and is reported on Form NT428. The dividend tax credit and the foreign tax credit are the only credits that may be deducted against tax on split income.

See ¶14210 for a detailed discussion of the tax on split income.

NTITA 2.42, CRA Guide 5012-PC, Form NT428, Form T1206

¶12640 — Additional Minimum Tax (Form NT428: Line 46)

Individuals who are subject to federal minimum tax under ITA 127.5 will be subject to Northwest Territories' minimum tax at the rate of 45% of the federal minimum tax amount. Individuals who are entitled to a minimum tax carryover for federal purposes under ITA 120.2 may be eligible for a provincial minimum tax credit. The amount of the credit is calculated by multiplying the federal credit amount on Schedule 1 by 45%.

Federal minimum tax is calculated on Form T691. Northwest Territories' minimum tax is reported on Form NT428.

NTITA 2.31, 2.43, CRA Guide 5012-PC, Form NT428, Form T691

¶12650 — Non-Refundable Tax Credits

The Northwest Territories have adopted many of the personal non-refundable tax credits offered by the federal government, including the following:

- Basic personal amount
- Spouse or common-law partner amount
- Age amount
- Disability amount
- Caregiver amount
- Pension income amount
- Medical expenses
- Donations and gifts

Although the eligibility rules for the Northwest Territories' non-refundable tax credits are generally the same as the corresponding federal tax credits, the amounts and method for calculation generally differ.

The Northwest Territories' non-refundable tax credit amounts are multiplied by its lowest tax rate to arrive at the amount of the deduction. There is an exception for donations and gifts such that the amount of donations and gifts exceeding $200 are multiplied by the Northwest Territories' highest tax rate.

See the tax reference tables in the Appendix for a complete listing of non-refundable tax credits available in the Northwest Territories.

NTITA 2.14–2.41, CRA Guide 5012-PC, Form NT428

¶12651 — *Territorial Foreign Tax Credit (Form NT428: Line 48)*

If an individual's federal foreign tax credit for foreign non-business income is less than the tax paid to a foreign country related to that income, the individual may be entitled to an additional territorial foreign tax credit.

A Northwest Territories foreign tax credit may be claimed by an individual who resided in Northwest Territories on the last day of the taxation year, and paid non-business-income tax to a foreign country.

Generally, the Northwest Territories foreign tax credit is equal to the lesser of:

- foreign taxes paid on foreign non-business income but not claimed for purposes of the federal foreign tax credit; and

- the proportion of Northwest Territories income tax equal to the ratio of: net foreign non-business income/net income allocated to Northwest Territories

For purposes of calculating the provincial foreign tax credit, net income is subject to the same adjustments as for federal purposes in claiming the federal non-business foreign tax credit.

The foreign tax credit is calculated on federal Form T2036 and claimed on Form NT428.

NTITA 3, CRA Guide 5012-PC, Form NT428

¶12652 — *Political Contribution Tax Credit (Form NT428: Line 51)*

This tax credit is available to individuals who have made contributions during the tax year to a candidate seeking election to the Northwest Territories Legislative Assembly.

The amount of the tax credit is 100% of contributions of $100 or less, plus 50% of contributions of over $100, up to the maximum credit amount of $500. The maximum credit amount will be reached when contributions exceed $900.

The tax credit is non-refundable and there are no carry-forward or carry-back provisions.

NTITA 5, CRA Guide 5012-PC, Form NT428

¶12660 — Other Tax Credits, Benefits and Incentives

¶12661 — *Cost of Living Tax Credit and Supplement (Form NT479)*

The cost of living tax credit is a refundable tax credit available to individuals who were resident in the Northwest Territories at the end of the tax year.

The tax credit is calculated as a percentage of adjusted net income, where adjusted net income is net income less social assistance payments, workers' compensation payments, and foreign income. The amount of the tax credit is as follows:

- For individuals with adjusted net income below $12,000, 2.6% of adjusted net income;

- For individuals with adjusted net income between $12,000 and $48,000, $312 plus 1.25% of adjusted net income exceeding $12,000;

- For individuals with adjusted net income between $48,000 and $66,000, $762 plus 1% of adjusted net income exceeding $48,000; and

- For individuals with adjusted net income exceeding $66,000, $942.

The cost of living supplement is $350 per individual and $700 per couple, regardless of income. Unlike the cost of living tax credit, which is claimed by each individual, only one of an individual and his or her spouse or common-law partner can claim the supplement.

The supplement is reduced dollar-to-dollar by the amount of the claimant and his or her spouse or common-law partner's cost of living tax credits, such that there is no double payment, and a minimum total credit of $350 per individual and $700 per couple.

NTITA 4.1, CRA Guide 5012-PC, Form NT479

¶12662 — *Northwest Territories Child Benefit and Territorial Workers' Supplement*

The Northwest Territories Child Benefit is administered by the CRA and is included with monthly federal Canada Child Benefit payments. The benefit is based on number and age of children and family net income declared on the previous year's income tax return.

The child benefit has been enhanced for 2017 and later taxation years. Families with less than $30,000 in family income will be eligible for the full benefit amount. The benefit is gradually reduced as family income increases above $30,000, and is completely phased out at family income of $80,000 and above. The monthly benefit amount is as follows:

- For eligible children under the age of six: $67.92 for one child, $122.25 for two children, $166.42 for three children, and $203.75 for four children (plus $30.58 for each additional child); and

- For eligible children aged 6 to 17: $54.33 for one child, $97.83 for two children, $133.08 for three children, and $162.99 for four children (plus $24.41 for each additional child).

The Territorial Workers' Supplement (TWS) is also available to low-income working families. This annual benefit is phased in starting with working income of $3,750 and provides a maximum benefit of $275 for one child or $350 for two or more children when working income reaches $10,000.

NTITA 3.1–3.4, CRA Guide T4114, Form RC66

¶12700 — Nova Scotia

¶12710 — Liability for Tax

Nova Scotia personal income tax is imposed under the Nova Scotia *Income Tax Act* (NSITA). The CRA is responsible for administration of the NSITA.

Nova Scotia income tax is payable by individuals resident in the province on the last day of the taxation year and non-residents of the province who have earned income in the province during the year.

An individual's Nova Scotia tax is determined based on taxable income reported for federal income tax purposes, and allocated to the province under the federal allocation rules. For reporting purposes, Nova Scotia tax is based on *federal taxable income* as shown on the T1 return, which is carried to Form NS428, where Nova Scotia tax is calculated.

NSITA 5, 7(e)

¶12720 — Tax Rates

Nova Scotia's tax rates for the 2017 and 2018 tax years are as follows:

2017 & 2018 Taxable Income	2017 & 2018 Tax Rates
first $29,590	8.79%
over $29,590 up to $59,180	14.95%
over $59,180 up to $93,000	16.67%
over $93,000 up to $150,000	17.50%

2017 & 2018 Taxable Income	2017 & 2018 Tax Rates
over $150,000	21.00%

Nova Scotia does not index its income tax system for inflation.

NSITA 8, 33, CRA Guide 5003-PC

¶12730 — Tax on Split Income (Form NS428: Line 40)

Where federal tax must be paid on split income, a Nova Scotia tax must also be paid. The Nova Scotia tax on split income is calculated as the amount of split income imposed under ITA 120.4 multiplied by the highest Nova Scotia tax rate.

The tax on split income is calculated on federal Form T1206, and is reported on Form NS428. The dividend tax credit and the foreign tax credit are the only credits that may be deducted against tax on split income.

See ¶14210 for a detailed discussion of the tax on split income.

NSITA 30, CRA Guide 5003-PC, Form NS428, Form T1206

¶12740 — Additional Minimum Tax (Form NS428: Line 47)

Individuals who are subject to federal minimum tax under ITA 127.5 will be subject to Nova Scotia minimum tax at the rate of 57.5% of the federal minimum tax amount. Individuals who are entitled to a minimum tax carryover for federal purposes under ITA 120.2 may be eligible for a provincial minimum tax credit. The amount of the credit is calculated by multiplying the federal credit amount on Schedule 1 by 57.5%.

Federal minimum tax is calculated on Form T691. Nova Scotia's minimum tax is reported on Form NS428.

NSITA 31, CRA Guide 5003-PC, Form NS428, Form T691

¶12750 — Non-Refundable Tax Credits

Nova Scotia has adopted many of the personal non-refundable tax credits offered by the federal government, including the following:

- Basic personal amount

- Spouse or common-law partner amount

- Age amount

- Disability amount

- Caregiver amount

- Pension income amount

- Medical expenses

- Donations and gifts

Although the eligibility rules for Nova Scotia's non-refundable tax credits are generally the same as the corresponding federal tax credits, the amounts and method for calculation generally differ.

Nova Scotia's non-refundable tax credit amounts are multiplied by its lowest tax rate to arrive at the amount of the deduction. There is an exception for donations and gifts such that the amount of donations and gifts exceeding $200 are multiplied by Nova Scotia's highest tax rate.

See the tax reference tables in the Appendix for a complete listing of non-refundable tax credits available in Nova Scotia.

Effective January 1, 2018, for individuals with taxable income under $25,000, the basic personal amount, spousal amount and eligible dependent amount has increased to $11,481 (from $8,481), and the age amount has increased to $5,606 (from $4,141). These enhanced amounts will be phased out between taxable incomes of $25,000 and $75,000, and will be fully eliminated at $75,000 of taxable income.

NSITA 10–17, CRA Guide 5003-PC, Form NS428

¶12751 — *Amount for Young Children (Form NS428: Line 5823)*

This non-refundable credit is available to parents or guardians respecting children under six years of age. For a couple, the spouse or common-law partner with the lower net income must claim the credit.

Individuals can claim $1,200 per year (or $100 for each month the child is less than six years old). The credit is calculated by multiplying this amount by the lowest Nova Scotia personal income tax rate of 8.79%, resulting in a maximum tax credit of $105 per year.

NSITA 10(5)–(8), CRA Guide 5003-PC, Form NS428, novascotia.ca/finance/en/home/taxation/tax101/personalincometax/childcare.aspx

¶12752 — *Provincial Foreign Tax Credit (Form NS428: Line 49)*

If an individual's federal foreign tax credit for foreign non-business income is less than the tax paid to a foreign country related to that income, the individual may be entitled to an additional provincial foreign tax credit. A Nova Scotia foreign tax credit may be claimed by an individual who resided in Nova Scotia on the last day of the taxation year, and paid non-business-income tax to a foreign country.

Generally, the Nova Scotia foreign tax credit is equal to the lesser of:

- foreign taxes paid on foreign non-business income but not claimed for purposes of the federal foreign tax credit; and

- the proportion of Nova Scotia income tax equal to the ratio of: net foreign non-business income/net income allocated to Nova Scotia

For purposes of calculating the provincial foreign tax credit, net income is subject to the same adjustments as for federal purposes in claiming the federal non-business foreign tax credit.

The foreign tax credit is calculated on federal Form T2036 and claimed on Form NS428.

NSITA 34, CRA Guide 5003-PC, Form NS428, Form T2036

¶12753 — *Nova Scotia Low-Income Tax Reduction (NS428: Lines 58–69)*

The Nova Scotia Low-Income Tax Reduction provides low-income taxpayers a reduction of provincial tax otherwise payable.

The reduction is equal to $300 per taxpayer, plus $300 for the taxpayer's spouse, common-law partner, or eligible dependant, plus an additional $165 for each dependent child. The total of these amounts is then reduced by 5% of the taxpayer's family net income for the year in excess of $15,000.

If the taxpayer and his or her spouse or partner were divorced or separated for at least 90 days at the end of the taxation year, income for the taxpayer's spouse or common law partner does not need to be included in the calculation of family net income, and the reduction should not be claimed in respect of a spouse or partner.

To be eligible to claim the credit, a taxpayer must be resident in the province at the end of the taxation year, and must be 19 years of age or older or be a spouse or common-law partner or a parent. While either spouse or common-law partner may claim the reduction, only one claim may be made.

NSITA 35, CRA Guide 5003-PC, Form NS428

¶12754 — Nova Scotia Political Contribution Tax Credit (NS428: Line 71)

This non-refundable tax credit is available to individuals who made contributions in the tax year to:

- a recognized Nova Scotia political party; or
- a candidate seeking election in the Nova Scotia House of Assembly.

The amount of the tax credit is equal to 75% of the contributions, up to the maximum amount of $750.

NSITA 50, CRA Guide 5003-PC, Form NS428, www.novascotia.ca/finance/en/home/taxation/personalincometax/donationsandgifts.aspx

¶12755 — Food Bank Tax Credit for Farmers (NS428: Line 73)

This non-refundable tax credit is available to Nova Scotia resident farmers who donate a qualifying agricultural product to an eligible food bank during the year.

All of the following conditions must be met to claim this credit:

- the taxpayer was a resident of Nova Scotia at the end of the year;
- the taxpayer or his or her spouse or common-law partner was a farmer in the year;
- the taxpayer made a qualifying donation in the year; and
- the taxpayer has claimed the qualifying donation on line 340 of federal Schedule 9 and on line 29 of Form NS428 as a charitable donation or gift for the year.

A "qualifying donation" is a donation of one or more agricultural products produced in Nova Scotia and donated to an eligible food bank in Nova Scotia during the year. An eligible food bank is a registered charity under the ITA that distributes food to the public without charge in Nova Scotia and does so mainly to provide relief to the poor.

The amount of qualifying donations can be split between spouses or common-law partners; however, the total amount of qualifying donations that can be claimed by spouses or common-law partners cannot be more than the total qualifying donations made in the tax year.

The credit is equal to 25% of the eligible amount of the total qualifying donations made to an eligible food bank, and must be claimed in the same year that the charitable donation tax credit is claimed for the donation.

To claim this credit, enter the amount of donations included on line 340 of federal Schedule 9 that are qualifying donations for this credit. Then enter 25% of this amount on line 73 of Form NS428.

¶12756 — Labour-Sponsored Venture Capital Tax Credit (NS428: Line 75)

This tax credit is available to individuals who invested in eligible shares of a labour-sponsored venture capital corporation (LSVCC) in the tax year or within 60 days of the end of the tax year.

To be eligible, individuals must be residents of Nova Scotia who are over 19 years of age and who have valid reasons for making the investment, other than obtaining the tax credit.

If an RRSP for a spouse or common-law partner was the first registered holder of the share, either the RRSP contributor or the annuitant can claim the tax credit for the share.

The amount of the tax credit is equal to 20% of the investment, up to the maximum credit amount of $2,000.

The tax credit is non-refundable and there are no carry-forward or carry-back provisions.

If the individual does not hold the shares for at least 8 years, he or she may be required to repay the tax credit.

Eligible individuals should receive a Form NSLSV from the LSVCC.

NSITA 38, CRA Guide 5003-PC, Form NS428, www.novascotia.ca/finance/en/home/taxation/personalincometax/laboursponsoredventurecapitaltaxcredit.aspx

¶12757 — *Equity Tax Credit (NS428: Line 77)*

This tax credit is intended to assist small businesses, co-operatives, and community economic development initiatives in Nova Scotia to obtain equity financing.

The tax credit is available to individuals who acquired eligible shares in the tax year or within 60 days of the end of the tax year.

For investments before January 1, 2010, the amount of the tax credit is 30% of the investment, up to the maximum annual credit of $15,000. For investments made after December 31, 2009, the amount of the tax credit is 35% of the investment, up to the maximum annual credit of $17,500.

The tax credit is non-refundable; however, unused amounts may be carried forward 7 years or carried back 3 years.

To claim the tax credit, individuals must complete Form T1285.

NSITA 37, *Equity Tax Credit Act*, S.N.S. 1993, c.3, *Equity Tax Credit Regulations*, N.S. Reg. 18/94, CRA Guide 5003-PC, Form NS428, Form T1285, www.novascotia.ca/finance/en/home/taxation/personalincometax/equitytaxcredit/default.aspx

¶12758 — *Age Tax Credit (NS428: Line 79)*

Seniors who are eligible for the credit will receive a deduction of $1,000 from income tax otherwise payable.

To be eligible for the credit, individuals must be age 65 or older and resident in Nova Scotia on the last day of the taxation year, and have taxable income or taxable income earned in Canada of less than $24,000.

NSITA 36B

¶12760 — Other Tax Credits, Benefits and Incentives

¶12761 — *Nova Scotia Volunteer Firefighter and Ground Search and Rescue Tax Credit (NS428: Line 81)*

This refundable tax credit is available to individuals to whom all of the following conditions apply:

- resident of Nova Scotia at the end of the tax year;

- volunteer firefighter or ground search and rescue volunteer for at least 6 months during the tax year;

- did not receive salary, wages, or compensation, other than reasonable reimbursement or allowance for expenses; and

- if a volunteer firefighter, listed on a report filed by the fire chief and participated in at least 20% of each of the volunteer fire department's emergency calls, training sessions, and meetings, or, if a ground search and rescue volunteer, identified in a report filed by the ground search and rescue president.

The amount of the tax credit is $500. For more information on eligibility for the credit, see: www.novascotia.ca/finance/en/home/taxation/tax101/personalincometax/volunteerfirefighterstaxcredit.aspx.

NSITA 38A, *Volunteer Firefighter Tax Credit Regulations*, N.S. Reg. 63/2008, Sch. A, CRA Guide 5003-PC, Form NS428

¶12762 — *Affordable Living Tax Credit*

This tax credit is a non-taxable quarterly payment to make life more affordable for low- and modest-income individuals and families resident in Nova Scotia.

The program provides a maximum annual credit of $255 for individuals or couples, plus $60 per child. The credit is phased out at a rate of 5% of adjusted family net income over $30,000.

To apply for the tax credit, individuals must file an income tax return. The tax credit is paid quarterly, together with the federal GST/HST credit.

NSITA 80, *Nova Scotia Affordable Living Tax Credit Regulations*, N.S. Reg. 178/2013, CRA Guide 5003-PC, Form NS428, Booklet RC4210

¶12763 — *Poverty Reduction Tax Credit*

This tax credit is a non-taxable quarterly payment to individuals resident in Nova Scotia who are living in poverty.

To be eligible, an individual or married or common-law couple must:

- have received Income Assistance throughout the previous year;
- have filed income tax returns for the previous tax year;
- have had adjusted income of less than $12,000 in the previous tax year; and
- not have children.

Only one of an individual and his or her spouse or common-law partner can receive the tax credit.

The amount of the tax credit is $250.

There is no application process. Eligibility is determined by the Department of Community Services each June and the first payment is made to eligible individuals in July.

NSITA 80, CRA Guide 5003-PC, Form NS428, www.novascotia.ca/coms/noteworthy/PovertyReductionCredit.html

¶12764 — *Nova Scotia Child Benefit*

This tax credit is a non-taxable monthly payment to help low- and modest-income families with the cost of raising children under 18 years of age.

For July 2018 to June 2019, the maximum amount of the tax credit is:

- $52.08 per month for the first child;
- $68.75 per month for the second child; and
- $75.00 per month for each additional child.

The maximum credit amount is available to families with adjusted family net income of less than $18,000. Families with adjusted family net income between $18,000 and $26,000 will receive partial benefits.

It is not necessary to apply for the tax credit. Eligibility is determined based on the information in an individual's Canada child benefits application. The credit is paid together with the federal Canada Child Benefit.

NSITA 80, Nova Scotia *Child Benefit Regulations*, N.S. Reg. 62/98, CRA Guide 5003-PC, Form NS428, Booklet T4114

¶12765 — *Property Tax Rebate for Seniors*

This rebate is designed to assist seniors to remain in their homes.

An individual is eligible for the rebate if he or she meets all of the following conditions:

- receiving either the Guaranteed Income Supplement or The Allowance in January of this year;

- living in his or her home; and

- previous year's property taxes were paid in full.

The amount of the rebate is 50% of municipal property taxes paid in the previous year, up to the maximum amount of $800 per year.

Individuals must apply for the rebate to Service Nova Scotia and Municipal Relations. See: www.accessns.ca/seniors-rebate for applications, Municipal Property Tax Sheet and frequently asked questions.

NSITA 35A, Nova Scotia *Tax Refund for Seniors Receiving the Guaranteed Income Supplement Regulations*, N.S. Reg. 263/2011, www.novascotia.ca/sns/access/individuals/consumer-awareness/property-tax-rebate-for-seniors.asp

¶12766 — *First-Time Home Buyers' Rebate*

Nova Scotia's First-Time Home Buyers' Rebate is a rebate for first-time home buyer's equivalent to 18.75% of the provincial portion of the HST for the purchase or construction of a new home, up to a maximum amount of 3,000. This program is for newly constructed homes only and does not include renovations or conversions from rentals to condominiums.

An individual will qualify for the rebate if:

- the newly constructed home will be used as the individual's primary residence or, where applicable, the primary residence of a relation; and

- the individual home owner or relation who will occupy the newly constructed home:

  - are the first individual(s) to occupy the new home after it was substantially completed; and

  - have not owned and occupied a home in Canada in the last five years; or

  - the home they owned and were occupying at the time was involuntarily destroyed within the last five years

A relation is an individual related to the individual by blood, marriage, common law relationship or adoption. A common law relationship means a relationship between two individuals who have been cohabitating together in a conjugal relationship for a period of at least one year or a relationship that is registered as a domestic partnership under the *Vital Statistics Act*.

Only one owner of a newly constructed home may apply for the rebate. If there is more than one owner, the other owners are considered to have received rebate for the home under the program. There is only one rebate for each newly constructed home.

For more information on the first-time home buyers' rebate and answers to frequently asked questions, see: www.novascotia.ca/snsmr/access/land/first-home-buyers-rebate.asp

¶12800 — Nunavut

¶12810 — Liability for Tax

Nunavut personal income tax is imposed under the Nunavut *Income Tax Act* (NUITA). The NUITA was created by duplicating the provisions of the Northwest Territories *Income Tax Act* that were in effect on April 1, 1999. The CRA is responsible for administration of the NUITA.

Nunavut income tax is payable by individuals resident in the province on the last day of the taxation year and non-residents of the province who have earned income in the province during the year.

An individual's Nunavut tax is determined based on taxable income reported for federal income tax purposes, and allocated to the province under the federal allocation rules. For reporting purposes, Nunavut tax is based on federal taxable income as shown on the T1 return, which is carried to Form NU428, where Nunavut tax is calculated.

NUITA 2(1), 2.1, CRA Guide 5014-G, Form NU428

¶12820 — Tax Rates

Nunavut's tax rates for the 2017 and 2018 tax years are as follows:

2018 Taxable Income	2018 Tax Rates	2017 Taxable Income	2017 Tax Rates
first $44,437	4.0%	first $43,780	4.0%
over $44,437 up to $88,874	7.0%	over $43,780 up to $87,560	7.0%
over $88,874 up to 144,488	9.0%	over $87,560 up to 142,353	9.0%
over $144,488	11.5%	over $142,353	11.5%

Nunavut's tax brackets are indexed annually for inflation using the federal inflation rate.

NUITA 2.11, CRA Guide 5014-PC

¶12830 — Tax on Split Income (Form NU428: Line 40)

Where federal tax must be paid on split income, an additional Nunavut tax must also be paid. The Nunavut tax on split income is calculated as the amount of split income imposed under ITA 120.4 multiplied by the highest Nunavut tax rate.

The tax on split income is calculated on federal Form T1206, and is reported on Form NU428. The dividend tax credit and the foreign tax credit are the only credits that may be deducted against tax on split income.

See ¶14210 for a detailed discussion of the tax on split income.

NUITA 2.42, CRA Guide 5014-PC, Form NU428, Form T1206

¶12840 — Additional Minimum Tax (Form NU428: Line 47)

Individuals who are subject to federal minimum tax under ITA 127.5 will be subject to Nunavut minimum tax at the rate of 45% of the federal minimum tax amount. Individuals who are entitled to a minimum tax carryover for federal purposes under ITA 120.2 may be eligible for a provincial minimum tax credit. The amount of the credit is calculated by multiplying the federal credit amount on Schedule 1 by 45%.

Federal minimum tax is calculated on Form T691. Nunavut minimum tax is reported on Form NU428.

NUITA 2.31, 2.43, CRA Guide 5014-PC, Form NU428, Form T691

¶12850 — Non-Refundable Tax Credits

Nunavut has adopted many of the personal non-refundable tax credits offered by the federal government, including the following:

- Basic personal amount

- Spouse or common-law partner amount

- Age amount

- Disability amount

- Caregiver amount

- Pension income amount

- Medical expenses

- Donations and gifts

Although the eligibility rules for Nunavut's non-refundable tax credits are generally the same as the corresponding federal tax credits, the amounts and method for calculation generally differ.

Nunavut's non-refundable tax credit amounts are multiplied by its lowest tax rate to arrive at the amount of the deduction. There is an exception for donations and gifts, such that the amount of donations and gifts exceeding $200 are multiplied by Nunavut's highest tax rate.

See the tax reference tables in the Appendix for a complete listing of non-refundable tax credits available in Nunavut.

NUITA 2.14–2.41, CRA Guide 5014-PC, Form NU428

¶12851 — *Amount for Young Children Less than 6 Years of Age (Form NU428: Line 5823)*

This non-refundable tax credit is available to individuals who were resident in Nunavut at the end of the tax year and who had a young child to whom the following conditions apply:

- the child was less than 6 years of age at any time during the tax year;

- the child lived with the individual at the end of the tax year (or on the date of death, if the child died during the tax year);

- no one has received a special allowance under the *Children's Special Allowances Act* for the child; and

- no one has claimed the child as an eligible dependant.

Only one of an individual and his or her spouse or common-law partner can claim the tax credit. If both an individual and his or her spouse or common-law partner are eligible to make the claim, the individual with the lower net income must make the claim. Any amount not needed to reduce the claimant's Nunavut tax to zero can be transferred to the claimant's spouse or common-law partner.

The amount of the tax credit is $1,200 per eligible child. This amount is not indexed for inflation.

NUITA 2.211, CRA Guide 5014-PC, Form NU428

¶12852 — *Territorial Foreign Tax Credit (Form NU428: Line 49)*

If an individual's federal foreign tax credit for foreign non-business income is less than the tax paid to a foreign country related to that income, the individual may be entitled to an additional territorial foreign tax credit. A

Nunavut foreign tax credit may be claimed by an individual who resided in Nunavut on the last day of the taxation year, and paid non-business-income tax to a foreign country.

Generally, the Nunavut foreign tax credit is equal to the lesser of:

- foreign taxes paid on foreign non-business income but not claimed for purposes of the federal foreign tax credit; and

- the proportion of Nunavut income tax equal to the ratio of: net foreign non-business income/net income allocated to Nunavut

For purposes of calculating the provincial foreign tax credit, net income is subject to the same adjustments as for federal purposes in claiming the federal non-business foreign tax credit.

The foreign tax credit is calculated on federal Form T2036 and claimed on Form NU428.

NUITA 3, CRA Guide 5014-PC, Form NU428

¶12853 — *Volunteer Firefighters' Tax Credit (Form NU428: Line 51)*

This tax credit is available to volunteer firefighters to whom the following conditions apply:

- resident of Nunavut at the end of the tax year;
- volunteer firefighter for a minimum of 6 months in the tax year;
- completed a minimum of 200 hours of community service, including training, in the tax year;
- did not receive salary, wages, or compensation, other than reasonable reimbursement or allowance for expenses, in the tax year; and
- listed as a volunteer firefighter on the report filed by the fire chief.

The amount of the tax credit is $586 for the 2018 tax year and is adjusted for inflation.

NUITA 6.2, CRA Guide 5014-PC, Form NU428

¶12860 — Other Tax Credits, Benefits and Incentives

¶12861 — *Cost of Living Tax Credit and Supplement for Single Parents (Form NU479)*

The cost of living tax credit is a refundable tax credit available to individuals who were resident in Nunavut at the end of the tax year.

The amount of the cost of living tax credit is 2% of an individual's adjusted net income, up to the maximum credit amount of $1,200.

The cost of living supplement for single parents is a refundable tax credit available to individuals' resident in Nunavut at the end of the tax year to whom, at any time during the tax year, all of the following conditions applied:

- not married or living in a common-law partnership, or married or in a common-law partnership, but living apart due to a breakdown in the marriage or partnership; and
- have custody of a child under 18 years of age, or 18 years of age or older and dependant due to a mental or physical impairment, for at least 50% of the time.

The amount of the cost of living supplement for single parents is 2% of an individual's adjusted net income exceeding $60,000, up to the maximum credit amount of $255.12.

NUITA 4.1, CRA Guide 5014-PC, Form NU479

¶12862 — *Political Contribution Tax Credit (Form NU479)*

This refundable tax credit is available to individuals who have made contributions during the tax year to a candidate seeking election to the Nunavut Legislative Assembly.

The amount of the tax credit is 100% of contributions of $100 or less, plus 50% of contributions of over $100, up to the maximum credit amount of $500. The maximum credit amount will be reached when contributions exceed $900.

NUITA 5, CRA Guide 5014-PC, Form NU479

¶12863 — *Nunavut Child Benefit and Territorial Workers' Supplement*

The Nunavut child benefit is a non-taxable amount paid monthly to qualifying families with children under 18 years of age.

The amount of the Nunavut child benefit is based on the number of children and the family's net income. Families with net income of $20,921 or less will receive the maximum credit amount of $330 per year for each child under 18 years of age. The tax credit is phased out at a rate of 3% for families with one child, and 5% for families with two or more children.

Families with earned income of more than $3,750 may also receive the territorial workers' supplement of up to $275 per year for one child and $75 for the second child. The supplement is phased in such that the maximum credit amount is available when earned income reaches $10,000. The supplement is phased out at a rate of 3% for families with one child, and 5% for families with two or more children, of family net income exceeding $20,921.

Eligibility is determined on the basis of an individual's Canada child benefits application and previous year's income tax filings. Payments are made together with the federal Canada Child Benefit.

NUITA 3.1–3.4, CRA Guide 5014-PC, CRA Booklet T4114

¶12900 — Ontario

¶12910 — Liability for Tax

Ontario personal income tax is imposed under the Ontario *Taxation Act, 2007* (OTA). The CRA is responsible for administration of the OTA.

Ontario income tax is payable by individuals resident in the province on the last day of the taxation year and non-residents of the province who have earned income in the province during the year.

An individual's Ontario tax is determined based on taxable income reported for federal income tax purposes, and allocated to the province under the federal allocation rules. For reporting purposes, Ontario tax is based on federal taxable income as shown on the T1 return, which is carried to Form ON428, where Ontario tax is calculated.

OTA 3(1), 4(1), 6(1)

¶12920 — Tax Rates

Ontario's tax rates for the 2017 and 2018 tax years are as follows:

2018 Taxable Income	2018 Tax Rates	2017 Taxable Income	2017 Tax Rates
first $42,960	5.05%	first $42,201	5.05%
over $42,960 up to $85,923	9.15%	over $42,201 up to $84,404	9.15%
over $85,923 up to $150,000	11.16%	over $84,404 up to $150,000	11.16%
over $150,000 up to $220,000	12.16%	over $150,000 up to $220,000	12.16%

2018 Taxable Income	2018 Tax Rates	2017 Taxable Income	2017 Tax Rates
over $220,000	13.16%	over $220,000	13.16%

Ontario's tax brackets are indexed annually for inflation using the Ontario provincial inflation rate, except for the $150,000 and $220,000 brackets, which are not indexed for inflation.

Ontario also imposes surtax on Ontario tax payable above certain threshold amounts, which are indexed annually for inflation. For 2018, Ontario surtax is equal to the total of:

- 20% of the amount, if any, by which the gross tax amount of an individual for the taxation year exceeds $4,638, and

- 36% of the amount, if any, by which the gross tax amount of an individual for the taxation year exceeds $5,936.

Ontario surtax is calculated on an individual's "gross tax amount" for the taxation year, which is the individual's Ontario income tax payable for the year, before the addition of surtax, CPP adjustments, lump-sum payment adjustments, the Ontario Health Premium, and refundable tax credits.

Effective January 1, 2017, the surtax calculation is modified for Ontario residents who pay tax to another province and non-residents of Ontario who pay tax to Ontario, in order to ensure consistency between how the surtax is computed for multi jurisdictional filers and all other tax filers.

OTA 3(1), 6(1), 16, CRA Guide 5006-PC

¶12930 — Tax on Split Income (Form ON428: Line 40)

Where federal tax must be paid on split income, an Ontario tax must also be paid. The Ontario tax on split income is calculated as the amount of split income imposed under ITA 120.4 multiplied by the highest Ontario tax rate.

The tax on split income is calculated on federal Form T1206, and is reported on Form ON428. The dividend tax credit and the foreign tax credit are the only credits that may be deducted against tax on split income.

See ¶14210 for a detailed discussion of the tax on split income.

OTA 12, CRA Guide 5006-PC, Form ON428, Form T1206

¶12940 — Additional Minimum Tax (Form ON428: Line 47)

Individuals who are subject to federal minimum tax under ITA 127.5 will be subject to Ontario minimum tax at the rate of 33.67% of the federal minimum tax amount. Individuals who are entitled to a minimum tax carryover for federal purposes under ITA 120.2 may be eligible for a provincial minimum tax credit. The amount of the credit is calculated by multiplying the federal credit amount on Schedule 1 by 33.67%.

Federal minimum tax is calculated on Form T691. Ontario minimum tax is reported on Form ON428.

OTA 11, 15(1), CRA Guide 5006-PC, Form ON428, Form T691

¶12950 — Non-Refundable Tax Credits

Ontario has adopted many of the following personal non-refundable tax credits offered by the federal government, including the following:

- Basic personal amount

- Spouse or common-law partner amount

- Age amount

- Disability amount
- Caregiver amount
- Pension income amount
- Medical expenses
- Donations and gifts

Although the eligibility rules for Ontario's non-refundable tax credits are generally the same as the corresponding federal tax credits, the amounts and method for calculation generally differ.

Ontario's non-refundable tax credit amounts are multiplied by Ontario's lowest tax rate to arrive at the amount of the deduction. There is an exception for donations and gifts, such that the amount of donations and gifts exceeding $200 are multiplied by 11.16%.

See the tax reference tables in the Appendix for a complete listing of non-refundable tax credits available in Ontario.

OTA 8–23, CRA Guide 5006-PC, Form ON428

¶12951 — Ontario Tax Reduction (Form ON428: Lines 62 to 68)

This tax reduction is available to reduce the Ontario tax of low-to-moderate income individuals with income below a certain threshold who were resident in Ontario at the end of the tax year.

The tax reduction cannot be claimed by an individual who is subject to Ontario additional minimum tax.

For the 2018 tax year, the amount of the tax reduction is $239 for the individual claiming the tax credit, plus $442 for each dependent child 18 years of age or younger, and $442 for each dependent child with a mental or physical infirmity claimed by the individual or his or her spouse or common-law partner. If an individual has a dependent child under 18 years of age with a mental or physical infirmity, the individual may claim a total of $884 for that child.

The amount of $442 may also be claimed for a spouse or common-law partner with a mental or physical infirmity if the individual claiming the credit claimed a disability amount for the spouse or common-law partner.

Only one person can claim the tax reduction for a dependent child. If an individual had a spouse or common-law partner at the end of the tax year, the person with the higher net income must claim the reduction for dependants.

Effective January 1, 2017, the calculation of the Ontario tax reduction was modified for Ontario residents who pay tax to another province and non-residents of Ontario who pay tax to Ontario, in order to ensure consistency between how the tax reduction is computed for multijurisdictional filers and all other tax filers.

OTA 20, CRA Guide 5006-PC, Information Bulletin 6301, 6311, CRA Guide 5006-PC, Form ON428

¶12952 — Ontario Foreign Tax Credit (Form ON428: Lines 70)

If an individual's federal foreign tax credit for foreign non-business income is less than the tax paid to a foreign country related to that income, the individual may be entitled to an additional Ontario foreign tax credit. An Ontario foreign tax credit may be claimed by an individual who resided in Ontario on the last day of the taxation year, and paid non-business-income tax to a foreign country.

Generally, the Ontario foreign tax credit is equal to the lesser of:

- foreign taxes paid on foreign non-business income but not claimed for purposes of the federal foreign tax credit; and

- the proportion of Ontario income tax equal to the ratio of: net foreign non-business income/net income allocated to Ontario

For purposes of calculating the provincial foreign tax credit, net income is subject to the same adjustments as for federal purposes in claiming the federal non-business foreign tax credit.

The foreign tax credit is calculated on federal Form T2036 and claimed on Form ON428.

OTA 21, CRA Guide 5006-PC, Form ON428, Form T2036

¶12960 — Other Tax Credits, Benefits and Incentives

¶12961 — *Ontario Political Contribution Tax Credit (Form ON479)*

This refundable tax credit is available to individuals who were resident in Ontario at the end of the tax year, and who made contributions in the tax year to a registered Ontario political party or constituency association, or to a candidate in an Ontario provincial election.

The amount of the political contribution tax credit depends on how much you give. The rate is:

- 75% on the first $399 of donations;
- 50% on the portion of donation between $399 and $1,330; and
- 33.33% on the portion between $1,330 and $3,026

The maximum credit amount is $1,330.

OTA 102, CRA Guide 5006-PC, Form ON479, Information Bulletin 6304: *Political Contribution Tax Credit*

¶12962 — *Ontario Focused Flow-Through Share Tax Credit (Form ON479)*

This refundable tax credit is intended to stimulate mineral exploration in Ontario and improve access to capital for small mining exploration companies.

The tax credit is available to individuals who:

- were resident in Ontario at the end of the tax year;
- were subject to Ontario income tax for the tax year;
- purchased eligible flow-through shares; and
- have eligible Ontario exploration expenditures.

The amount of the tax credit is equal to 5% of eligible expenses.

To apply for the tax credit, individuals must obtain a Form T101, or a Form T5013 if claiming as a member of a partnership, from the mining exploration company that incurred eligible expenses, and complete Form T1221.

OTA 103, CRA Guide 5006-PC, Form ON479, Form T1221, Information Bulletin 6315, www.fin.gov.on.ca/en/credit/offts/

¶12963 — *Ontario Graduated Apprenticeship Grant for Employers (formerly Apprenticeship Training Tax Credit)*

Effective November 15, 2017, the Graduated Apprenticeship Grant for Employers (GAGE) replaced the Apprenticeship Training Tax Credit (ATTC). The ATTC is "grandfathered" for all eligible employers in respect of apprentices registered before November 15, 2017, so that these employers will continue to be eligible for the ATTC for up to 36 months.

Employers with apprentices who have registered their apprenticeship program with the Ontario College of Trade after November 14, 2017 are eligible for employer grants under the GAGE. Employers receive a payment each time the apprentice successfully completes a level of training, and when the apprentice receives their Certificate of Apprenticeship or Certificate of Qualification. Payments are broken down as follows: Level 1 — $2,500, Level 2 — $2,500, Level 3 — $3,500, Level 4 — $3,500, and Certificate of Apprenticeship/Certificate of Qualification — $4,700. To encourage increased apprenticeship opportunities for underrepresented groups, the GAGE also provides a $500 bonus at each level if the apprentice is from an underrepresented group. The GAGE is available to all 125 trades that are eligible for the ATTC, plus five additional Red Seal service sector trades: hairstylist, cook, horticultural/landscape technician, baker/patissier and appliance service technician.

For more information on the GAGE, see: ontario.ca/page/graduated-apprenticeship-grant-employers.

¶12964 — Ontario Co-Operative Education Tax Credit (Form ON479)

This refundable tax credit is available to individuals with unincorporated businesses that employ one or more co-op students enrolled in an Ontario university or college in a qualifying work placement at a permanent establishment in Ontario.

A qualifying work placement is 10 to 16 consecutive weeks of employment of a student under a qualifying co-operative educational program of an eligible education institution ending in the tax year.

The amount of the tax credit is a percentage of eligible expenditures. Eligible expenditures are reasonable salaries, wages and other remuneration paid or payable to a student in a qualifying work placement at a permanent establishment in Ontario, or a reasonable fee paid or payable to an employment agency for a qualifying work placement. An individual's eligible expenditures are reduced by any government assistance received or reasonably expected to be received for the expenditures, or to which the individual is entitled to.

The tax credit rate differs for small and large businesses, as determined on the basis of total payroll. If the business' total salaries and wages paid in the tax year are $600,000 or more, the amount of the credit is equal to 25% of eligible expenditures for each qualifying work placement. If total salaries and wages paid in the tax year are $400,000 or less, the amount of the credit is equal to 30% of eligible expenditures for each qualifying work placement. If total salaries and wages paid in the tax year are between $400,000 and $600,000, the amount of the credit is determined according to a formula set out in the Provincial Worksheet, which applies the higher rate on gradually reduced basis.

The maximum amount of the tax credit for the year is $3,000 per qualifying work placement.

OTA 88, CRA Guide 5006-PC, Information Bulletin 4014, Form ON479, VD 2011-0396271E5, www.fin.gov.on.ca/en/credit/cetc/

¶12965 — Ontario Trillium Benefit (Form ON-BEN)

This non-taxable payment is comprised of the Ontario sales tax credit, the Ontario energy and property tax credit, and the Northern Ontario energy credit, discussed below.

To apply for the benefit, individuals and their spouses or common-law partners must file their income tax returns and complete Form-ON-BEN.

Individuals are not eligible for the benefit if they died in the tax year, and may not be eligible if they were confined to a prison or similar institution for a period of 90 days or more that includes the first day of a payment month.

OTA 103.2–103.12, Ontario Reg. 468/11, CRA Guide 5006-PC, Form ON-BEN, fin.gov.on.ca/en/credit/otb/index.html

Ontario Sales Tax Credit

This tax credit is intended to help low- to moderate-income individuals and families resident in Ontario with the sales tax they pay.

Individuals claiming the credit must be at least 19 years of age.

For the 2018 benefit year (which is based on an individual's 2017 income), the maximum annual Ontario sales tax credit is $301 for each adult and each child in a family. For single individuals with no children, the credit is reduced by 4 per cent of the individual's adjusted net income over $23,156. For single parents, or individuals who are married or living in a common-law relationship, the credit is reduced by 4 per cent of adjusted family net income over $28,944.

Individuals apply for the credit by completing the ON-BEN form, which is part of the personal income tax return.

OTA 103.2–103.12, Ontario Reg. 468/11, CRA Guide 5006-PC, Form ON-BEN, www.fin.gov.on.ca/en/credit/stc/

Ontario Energy and Property Tax Credit

This tax credit is intended to help low- to moderate-income families and individuals resident in Ontario with property taxes and the sales tax on energy costs.

To be eligible for the energy component, an individual must:

- have been resident in Ontario at the end of the tax year;

- be 18 years of age or older, have had a spouse or common-law partner at the end of the tax year, or be a parent who lives with or previously lived with his or her child; and

- have paid, or had paid on his or her behalf, rent or property tax for his or her principal residence in the tax year, lived in a public-long-term care home in Ontario and paid, or had paid on his or her behalf, an amount for accommodation in the tax year, or lived on a reserve in Ontario and paid, or had paid on his or her behalf, home energy costs for his or her principal residence in the tax year.

To be eligible for the property component, an individual must:

- have been resident in Ontario at the end of the tax year;

- be 18 years of age or older, have had a spouse or common-law partner at the end of the tax year, or be a parent who lives with or previously lived with his or her child; and

- have paid, or had paid on his or her behalf, rent or property tax for his or her principal residence in the tax year, or lived in a designated Ontario university, college, or private school residence in the tax year.

The maximum credit amounts for the 2018 benefit year are as follows:

- $1,043 for taxpayers between 18 and 64 years of age;

- $1,187 for taxpayers over 65 years of age;

- $232 for taxpayers who live on a reserve or in a public long-term care home; and

- $25 for the time the taxpayer lived in a designated college, university or private school residence.

OTA 103.2–103.12, Ontario Reg. 468/11, CRA Guide 5006-PC, Form ON-BEN, www.fin.gov.on.ca/en/credit/oeptc/

Northern Ontario Energy Credit

This credit is designed to help low- to middle-income families and individuals resident in Northern Ontario with their energy costs.

To be eligible individuals must:

- have been resident in Northern Ontario at the end of the tax year;

- be 18 years of age or older, have had a spouse or common-law partner at the end of the tax year, or be a parent who lives with or previously lived with his or her child; and

- have paid, or had paid on his or her behalf, rent or property tax for his or her principal residence in the tax year, lived in a public-long-term care home in Northern Ontario and paid, or had paid on his or her behalf, an amount for accommodation in the tax year, or lived on a reserve in Northern Ontario and paid, or had paid on his or her behalf, home energy costs for his or her principal residence in the tax year.

Northern Ontario includes the districts of Algoma, Cochrane, Kenora, Manitoulin, Nipissing, Parry Sound, Rainy River, Sudbury, Thunder Bay, and Timiskaming.

For the 2018 benefit year, the maximum amount of the Northern Ontario energy credit is $151 for single individuals and $232 for families.

OTA 103.2–103.12, Ontario Reg. 468/11, CRA Guide 5006-PC, Form ON-BEN, www.fin.gov.on.ca/en/credit/noec/

¶12966 — *Ontario Senior Homeowners' Property Tax Grant (Form ON-BEN)*

To be eligible for this non-taxable payment, individuals must meet the following conditions at the end of the tax year:

- resident in Ontario;

- 64 years of age or older;

- owned and occupied a principal residence in Ontario for which the individual, or someone on the individual's behalf, paid property tax in the tax year.

If an individual has a spouse or common-law partner, only one person can apply for the tax credit for the couple.

The maximum amount of the tax credit per senior individual or couple is $500. The credit is phased out at a rate of 3.33% of income over $35,000 for single seniors, and $45,000 for senior couples.

OTA 104.1, CRA Guide 5006-PC, Form ON-BEN, www.fin.gov.on.ca/en/credit/shptg/index.html

¶12967 — *Ontario Child Benefit*

The Ontario child benefit is a non-taxable payment to help low- to moderate-income families to provide for their children.

For the 2018 benefit year, the maximum annual benefit amount is $1,378 per child, reduced by 8% of adjusted net family income over $21,037. The calculation of adjusted net family income for purposes of the Ontario child benefit is based on the calculation of adjusted income for the federal Canada Child Benefit. The maximum annual child benefit and the income threshold at which the child benefit begins to be reduced is subject to indexation, based on annual increases in the Ontario Consumer Price Index.

Benefit entitlement is determined by the Minister, without application by the taxpayer. Where it is determined that a taxpayer is eligible to receive the benefit, the Ministry will send a notice to the taxpayer of the benefit amount, together with payment.

Benefits payments are issued monthly to eligible individuals. To be eligible to receive a payment in a given month, an individual must be resident in the province of the first day of that month, and must be eligible to receive the federal Canada Child Benefit for that month.

OTA 104, CRA Guide 5006-PC, CRA Guide T4114

¶12968 — *Ontario Student Grant*

The Ontario Student Grant (OSG) is effective for the 2017-2018 school year. As a result of the introduction of the Ontario student grant program, Ontario eliminated its provincial tuition and education tax credits. Ontario students can claim the tuition tax credit for eligible tuition fees paid in respect of studies up to and including September 4, 2017, and the education tax credit for months of study before September 2017. The eligible portion of 2017 tuition and education tax credits can be transferred to a qualifying family member.

Tax filers who are resident in Ontario on December 31, 2017, and have unused tuition and education tax credits available for carryforward, can claim them in future years. Tax filers who move to Ontario from other provinces after December 31, 2017 can no longer claim their accumulated tuition and education tax credits in Ontario.

References: OTA 9(14)–(16)

¶12969 — *Ontario Seniors' Public Transit Tax Credit*

The seniors' public transit tax credit is available to Ontario resident seniors who are aged 65 as of January 1 of the relevant taxation year. Generally, the credit is a refundable tax credit equal to 15% of eligible public transit costs incurred on or after July 1, 2017. For 2017, seniors can claim up to $1,500 in transit expenses for a maximum credit of $225 (i.e., $1,500 × 15%). For 2018 and later taxation years, seniors can claim up to $3,000 in transit expenses for a maximum credit of $450.

Seniors can claim the fare paid for eligible Ontario or municipally-operated public transit services, (including transit services offered by Metrolinx). To qualify for the credit, the transit service must be: a short-haul service that individuals would commonly use for a return trip in a single day, offered to the general public, and operated by a bus, subway, train or tram. This includes public transit services that run from within Ontario to a destination outside Ontario (e.g., from Windsor to Detroit or Ottawa to Gatineau). Expenses for specialized public transit services that are designed to transport persons with disabilities also qualify as long as they meet the same conditions as conventional public transit services. Services that do not qualify for the transit credit include long-haul and private-sector services, such as Via Rail or Greyhound.

Generally, the following types of payments are eligible for the public transit credit: a single-use ticket or token, a public transit pass, an electronic payment card (e.g., PRESTO), a payment for specialized transit services (for persons with disabilities), and any other prescribed method of payment for transit access. For single-use tickets or tokens, limited or unlimited-use passes, and cash fare for specialized transit services, the receipt can serve as proof of payment. For electronic payment cards, a receipt is not required if the electronic payment card provides a usage report and shows the senior's name. Note that a cash fare paid in a fare box for a single ride is eligible for the tax credit only if it was used to pay for a specialized transit service.

OTA 103.0.1

¶121000 — Prince Edward Island

¶121010 — Liability for Tax

PEI personal income tax is imposed under the PEI *Income Tax Act* (PEITA). The CRA is responsible for administration of the PEITA.

PEI income tax is payable by individuals resident in the province on the last day of the taxation year and non-residents of the province who have earned income in the province during the year.

An individual's PEI tax is determined based on taxable income reported for federal income tax purposes, and allocated to the province under the federal allocation rules. For reporting purposes, PEI tax is based on federal taxable income as shown on the T1 return, which is carried to Form PE428, where PEI tax is calculated.

PEITA 1(6), 3, 6(e)

¶121020 — Tax Rates

PEI's tax rates for the 2017 and 2018 tax years are as follows:

2017 & 2018 Taxable Income	2017 & 2018 Tax Rates
first $31,984	9.80%
over $31,984 up to $63,969	13.80%
over $63,969	16.70%

For high-income earners, a surtax is imposed equal to 10% of the amount of provincial tax payable by an individual that exceeds $12,500. At this threshold and under the current tax rates, the surtax applies to individuals with income over approximately $98,000, depending on personal tax credits.

PEI does not index its income tax system for inflation.

PEITA 7, 27, 31, CRA Guide 5002-PC

¶121030 — Tax on Split Income (Form PE428: Line 41)

Where federal tax must be paid on split income, a PEI tax must also be paid. The PEI tax on split income is calculated as the amount of split income imposed under ITA 120.4 multiplied by the highest PEI tax rate.

The tax on split income is calculated on federal Form T1206, and is reported on Form PE428. The dividend tax credit and the foreign tax credit are the only credits that may be deducted against tax on split income.

See ¶14210 for a detailed discussion of the tax on split income.

PEITA 29, CRA Guide 5002-PC, Form PE428, Form T1206

¶121040 — Additional Minimum Tax (Form PE428: Line 48)

Individuals who are subject to federal minimum tax under ITA 127.5 will be subject to PEI minimum tax at the rate of 57.5% of the federal minimum tax amount. Individuals who are entitled to a minimum tax carryover for federal purposes under ITA 120.2 may be eligible for a provincial minimum tax credit. The amount of the credit is calculated by multiplying the federal credit amount on Schedule 1 by 57.5%.

Federal minimum tax is calculated on Form T691. PEI minimum tax is reported on Form PE428.

PEITA 19, 30, CRA Guide 5002-PC, Form PE428, Form T691

¶121050 — Non-Refundable Tax Credits

PEI has adopted many of the personal non-refundable tax credits offered by the federal government, including the following:

- Basic personal amount

- Spouse or common-law partner amount

- Age amount

- Disability amount

- Caregiver amount

- Pension income amount

- Medical expenses

- Donations and gifts

Although the eligibility rules for PEI's non-refundable tax credits are generally the same as the corresponding federal tax credits, the amounts and method for calculation generally differ.

PEI's non-refundable tax credit amounts are multiplied by PEI's lowest tax rate to arrive at the amount of the deduction. There is an exception for donations and gifts, such that the amount of donations and gifts exceeding $200 are multiplied by PEI's highest tax rate.

The 2018 PEI budget announced an increase in the province's basic personal credit by $500 for 2018 and a further $500 for 2019, as well as an increase in the spousal and eligible dependent credits by a proportionate amount.

See the tax reference tables in the Appendix for a complete listing of non-refundable tax credits available in PEI.

PEITA 9–21, CRA Guide 5002-PC, Form PE428

¶121051 — *Amount for Young Children (Form PE428: Line 5823)*

This non-refundable tax credit is available on a monthly basis to individuals who were resident in PEI at the end of the tax year and who had a dependent child to whom all of the following conditions applied in the relevant month:

- the child was living with the claimant on the first day of the month;

- the child was less than 6 years of age on the first day of the month;

- no one else claimed the tax credit for the child for the month; and

- no one received a special allowance under the *Children's Special Allowances Act* for the child for the month.

The amount of the tax credit is $100 per month for each child.

If an individual had a spouse or common-law partner at the end of the tax year, only one spouse or common-law partner can claim the tax credit. If one spouse or common-law partner had a lower net income, that spouse or common-law partner must claim the credit.

PEITA 9(5), CRA Guide 5002-PC, Form PE428

¶121052 — *Teacher School Supply Amount (Form PE428: Line 5850)*

This non-refundable tax credit is available to teachers who are resident in the province, and to staff members and supervisors of a child care facility. The credit is available for eligible expenditures on school supplies to a maximum of $500 per year.

Supplies must fit within the guidelines established by the Department of Education and be approved by the school principal using a prescribed form. The procedure for approval is set out in the Regulations.

PEITA 15.1, PEI *School Act*, R.S.P.E.I. 1988, c. S-2.1, PEI *Child Care Facilities Act*, R.S.P.E.I. 1988, c. C-5, PEI *Income Tax Regulations*, EC2001-505, CRA Guide 5002-PC, Form PE428

¶121053 — *Prince Edward Island Low-Income Tax Reduction (Form PE428: Lines 52–73)*

This tax credit is available to individuals who were resident in PEI at the end of the tax year and who were 19 years of age or older, had a spouse or common-law partner, or were a parent.

If an individual had a spouse or common-law partner at the end of the tax year, only one spouse or common-law partner may claim the tax credit; however, amounts not needed to reduce the claimant's PEI tax to zero may be claimed by the other spouse or common-law partner.

The tax reduction cannot be claimed by individuals who were confined to a prison or similar institution at the end of the tax year and for more than 6 months during the tax year.

The tax credit cannot be claimed for an individual who died in the tax year.

The amount of the tax credit is as follows:

- $350 for the claimant;

- $350 for the claimant's spouse or common-law partner at the end of the tax year, or for an eligible dependant, if claimed;

- $300 for each dependent child 18 years of age or younger, other than a child the tax credit has been claimed for as an eligible dependant; and,

- $250 for each senior aged 65 and older.

Taxpayers earning up to $17,000 of taxable income will receive the full value of the credits. The value of each credit decreases by 5 per cent for every dollar of income earned above $17,000.

A dependent child is an individual who, at the end of the tax year, was 18 years of age or younger, did not have a spouse or common-law partner, was not a parent, and lived with the claimant or was claimed as a dependant only by the claimant or his or her spouse or common-law partner. Only one person can claim the tax credit for a dependent child.

PEITA 32, CRA Guide 5002-PC, Form PE428

¶121054 — *Provincial Foreign Tax Credit (Form PE428: Line 75)*

If an individual's federal foreign tax credit for foreign non-business income is less than the tax paid to a foreign country related to that income, the individual may be entitled to an additional provincial foreign tax credit. A PEI foreign tax credit may be claimed by an individual who resided in PEI on the last day of the taxation year, and paid non-business-income tax to a foreign country.

Generally, the PEI foreign tax credit is equal to the lesser of:

- foreign taxes paid on foreign non-business income but not claimed for purposes of the federal foreign tax credit; and

- the proportion of PEI income tax equal to the ratio of: net foreign non-business income/net income allocated to PEI

For purposes of calculating the provincial foreign tax credit, net income is subject to the same adjustments as for federal purposes in claiming the federal non-business foreign tax credit.

The foreign tax credit is calculated on federal Form T2036 and claimed on Form PE428.

CRA Guide 5002-PC, Form PE428, Form T2036

¶121055 — *Prince Edward Island Political Contribution Tax Credit (Form PE428: Lines 77, 78)*

This non-refundable tax credit is available to individuals who made contributions in the tax year to:

- a recognized political party of PEI; or

- a candidate seeking election to the PEI Legislative Assembly.

The maximum amount of the tax credit is $500. To calculate the tax credit, the first $100, or portion thereof, of contributions is multiplied by 75%, the next $450, or portion thereof, of contributions is multiplied by 50%, and the next $600, or portion thereof, of contributions is multiplied by 33.33%. The maximum tax credit will be reached when contributions total $1,150.

PEITA 42, CRA Guide 5002-PC, Form PE428

¶121056 — *Equity Tax Credit (Form PE428: Lines 80–82)*

This tax credit is available to individuals who are resident in PEI and who invested in approved Community Economic Development Businesses in the tax year or within 60 days of the end of the tax year.

Individuals must be over 19 years of age to claim the tax credit.

The amount of the tax credit is 35% of eligible investments, up to the maximum annual credit amount of $7,000. The maximum annual credit amount will be reached when investments exceed $20,000.

If an investment is not held by the individual for at least 5 years, the amount of the tax credit will be reduced pro-rata.

The tax credit is non-refundable; however, unused amounts can be carried forward 7 years or back 3 years.

PEITA 36.1, *Community Development Equity Tax Credit Act*, CRA Guide 5002-PC, Form PE428, www.gov.pe.ca/cedb/index.php3?number=1038173&lang=E

¶121060 — Other Tax Credits, Benefits and Incentives

¶121061 — *Prince Edward Island Volunteer Firefighter Tax Credit (Form PE428: Line 84)*

Prince Edward Island offers a $500 refundable tax credit for volunteer firefighters.

The credit is available to individuals, resident in the province at the end of the year, who are entitled to claim the federal volunteer firefighter tax credit under ITA 118.06 (see ¶10220). This includes individuals who have completed at least 200 hours of eligible volunteer services within the year. To claim the credit, any payments received in respect of the services must have been included in the calculation of the taxpayer's income.

The credit is claimed on Form PE428 filed with an individual's tax return.

PEITA 36.2, CRA Guide 5002-PC, Form PE428

¶121062 — *Specialized Labour Tax Credit*

This tax rebate is designed to provide an incentive for workers with specialized expertise or skills not yet available in the PEI labour market to accept employment in PEI.

To be eligible, an individual must move to PEI to fill a specific, identified position the employer could not fill from the existing PEI labour pool. The employer must be active in a strategic sector such as aerospace, bio-science, export-focused manufacturing and processing, financial services, interactive information and communications technology, or renewable energy.

The amount of the tax rebate is 17% of personal income tax on eligible income earned by the individual.

The employer must apply to Innovation PEI in advance, and if approved, a certificate will be issued. To claim the tax rebate, the individual must submit the certificate and a copy of his or her notice of assessment to the CRA.

CRA Guide 5002-PC, *Specialized Labour Tax Credit Application for Certificate*, princeedwardisland.ca/en/service/apply-specialized-labour-tax-credit

¶121063 — *Share Purchase Tax Credit*

This tax rebate is available to individuals who make an eligible investment in an eligible PEI corporation and who are 19 years of age or older and resident in PEI when the investment is made.

To be eligible, the corporation must have a permanent establishment in PEI, pay 75% or more of its salary payroll to employees resident in PEI, and be active in a strategic sector such as export-focused manufacturing and processing, interactive, information and communications technology, aerospace, the life sciences, or renewable energy. Publicly tradable corporations are not eligible.

The amount of the tax rebate is 35% of eligible investments, up to the maximum annual rebate amount of $35,000.

The corporation must apply for a Share Purchase Tax Credit certificate indicating the cost of the share, among other information, which is then provided to the individual investor. To apply for the tax rebate, the individual must submit the certificate from Innovation PEI with his or her income tax return.

CRA Guide 5002-PC, Form PE428

¶121100 — Saskatchewan

¶121110 — Liability for Tax

Saskatchewan personal income tax is imposed under the Saskatchewan *The Income Tax Act, 2000* (SITA). The CRA is responsible for administration of the SETA.

Saskatchewan income tax is payable by individuals resident in the province on the last day of the taxation year and non-residents of the province who have earned income in the province during the year.

An individual's Saskatchewan tax is determined based on taxable income reported for federal income tax purposes, and allocated to the province under the federal allocation rules. For reporting purposes, Saskatchewan tax is based on federal taxable income as shown on the T1 return, which is carried to Form SK428, where Saskatchewan tax is calculated.

SITA 5(1), 6, 7

¶121120 — Tax Rates

The 2018 Saskatchewan budget announced that personal tax rates will remain at 2018 levels, and that previously announced reductions in personal tax rates for 2019 and 2020 will not proceed. Saskatchewan's tax rates for 2017 and 2018 are as follows:

Taxable Income	2017	2018
Taxable income up to $45,225	10.75%	10.50%
Taxable income over $45,225 up to $129,214	12.75%	12.50%
Taxable income over $129,214	14.75%	14.50%

SITA, 8, 51, CRA Guide 5008-PC

¶121130 — Tax on Split Income (Form SK428: Line 44)

Where federal tax must be paid on split income, a Saskatchewan tax must also be paid. The Saskatchewan tax on split income is calculated as the amount of split income imposed under ITA 120.4 multiplied by the highest Saskatchewan tax rate.

The tax on split income is calculated on federal Form T1206, and is reported on Form SK428. The dividend tax credit and the foreign tax credit are the only credits that may be deducted against tax on split income.

See ¶14210 for a detailed discussion of the tax on split income.

SITA 48, CRA Guide 5008-PC, Form SK428, Form T1206

¶121140 — Additional Minimum Tax (Form SK428: Line 51)

Individuals who are subject to federal minimum tax under ITA 127.5 will be subject to Saskatchewan minimum tax at the rate of 50% of the federal minimum tax amount. Individuals who are entitled to a minimum tax carryover for federal purposes under ITA 120.2 may be eligible for a provincial minimum tax credit. The amount of the credit is calculated by multiplying the federal credit amount on Schedule 1 by 50%.

Federal minimum tax is calculated on Form T691. Saskatchewan minimum tax is reported on Form SK428.

SITA 37, 47, CRA Guide 5008-PC, Form SK428, Form T691

¶121150 — Non-Refundable Tax Credits

Saskatchewan has adopted many of the personal non-refundable tax credits offered by the federal government:

- Basic personal amount
- Spouse or common-law partner amount
- Age amount
- Disability amount
- Caregiver amount
- Pension income amount
- Medical expenses
- Donations and gifts

Although the eligibility rules for Saskatchewan's non-refundable tax credits are generally the same as the corresponding federal tax credits, the amounts and method for calculation generally differ.

Saskatchewan's non-refundable tax credit amounts are multiplied by Saskatchewan's lowest tax rate to arrive at the amount of the deduction. There is an exception for donations and gifts, such that the amount of donations and gifts exceeding $200 are multiplied by Saskatchewan's highest tax rate.

See the tax reference tables in the Appendix for a complete listing of non-refundable tax credits available in Saskatchewan.

SITA Divisions 2, 3, CRA Guide 5008-PC, Form SK428

¶121151 — *Amount for Dependent Children Under 18 (Form SK428: Line 5821)*

This non-refundable tax credit is available to individuals who were resident in Saskatchewan at the end of tax year and who had a dependent child to whom all of the following conditions apply:

- the child was less than 18 years of age at any time during the tax year;
- the child lived with the individual claiming the tax credit at the end of the tax year or on the date of death, if the child died during the tax year;

- no one has received a special allowance under the *Children's Special Allowances Act* for the child; and

- no one claimed the child as an eligible dependant or as a spouse or common-law partner for the tax year.

If an individual has a spouse or common-law partner, only one spouse or common-law partner can claim the tax credit. If both spouses or common-law partners are eligible to make the claim and one spouse or common-law partner has a lower taxable income, the spouse or common-law partner with the lower taxable income must make the claim. If the entire credit is not needed to reduce the spouse or common-law partner claiming the credit's Saskatchewan income tax to zero, the other spouse or common-law partner can claim the unused amount.

The amount of the tax credit is $6,094 for each eligible child for the 2018 tax year.

SITA 19, 29, CRA Guide 5008-PC, Form SK428

¶121152 — *Senior Supplementary Amount (Form SK428: Line 5822)*

This non-refundable tax credit is available to individuals who were 65 years of age or older in the tax year and who were resident in Saskatchewan at the end of the tax year. The credit is not income-tested. This credit is non-refundable; however, excess amounts may be transferred to a spouse or common-law partner by completing T1 Schedule SK(S2).

The amount of the tax credit is $1,292 for the 2018 tax year.

SITA 20, 29, CRA Guide 5008-PC, Form SK428

¶121153 — *Home Buyers' Amount (Form SK428: Line 5837)*

This non-refundable tax credit is designed for first-time home buyers.

To be eligible, an individual or his or her spouse or common-law partner must have acquired a qualifying home in the tax year and must not have lived in another home owned by either the individual or his or her spouse or common-law partner in the tax year or in any of the four preceding years.

Qualifying homes includes single-family houses, semi-detached houses, townhouses, mobile homes, condominium units and apartments in duplexes, triplexes, fourplexes, or apartment buildings.

The qualifying home must be registered in the individual and/or his or her spouse or common-law partner's name with the Land Titles Registry, and must be located in Saskatchewan.

The amount of the tax credit is $10,000 for the purchase of a home after December 31, 2011.

The tax credit amount can be shared between an individual and his or her spouse or common-law partner, or between co-owners, but the total amount claimed cannot exceed $10,000.

SITA 19.2, CRA Guide 5008-PC, Form SK428

¶121154 — *Saskatchewan Farm and Small Business Capital Gains Tax Credit (Form SK428: Line 6355)*

This tax credit is available to individuals resident in Saskatchewan at the end of the tax year who have capital gains arising from the disposition of qualified farm property or qualified small business corporation shares.

The tax credit effectively removes the capital gain from the individual's income and recalculates the individual's Saskatchewan income tax payable with the capital gain taxed at Saskatchewan's lowest tax rate.

To apply for the tax credit, individuals must complete Form T1237.

SITA 31, *Saskatchewan Farm and Small Business Capital Gains Credit Regulations*, CRA Guide 5008-PC, Form SK428, Form T1237

¶121155 — *Provincial Foreign Tax Credit (Form SK428: Line 53)*

If an individual's federal foreign tax credit for foreign non-business income is less than the tax paid to a foreign country related to that income, the individual may be entitled to an additional provincial foreign tax credit. A Saskatchewan foreign tax credit may be claimed by an individual who resided in Saskatchewan on the last day of the taxation year, and paid non-business-income tax to a foreign country.

Generally, the Saskatchewan foreign tax credit is equal to the lesser of:

- foreign taxes paid on foreign non-business income but not claimed for purposes of the federal foreign tax credit; and

- the proportion of Saskatchewan income tax equal to the ratio of: net foreign non-business income/net income allocated to Saskatchewan

For purposes of calculating the provincial foreign tax credit, net income is subject to the same adjustments as for federal purposes in claiming the federal non-business foreign tax credit.

The foreign tax credit is calculated on federal Form T2036 and claimed on Form SK428.

SITA 35, CRA Guide 5008-PC, Form SK428, Form T2036

¶121156 — *Political Contribution Tax Credit (Form SK428: Lines 55 to 57)*

This non-refundable tax credit is available to individuals who made contributions in the tax year to:

- a registered Saskatchewan political party; or

- an independent candidate in a Saskatchewan provincial election.

The maximum amount of the tax credit is $650. To calculate the tax credit, the first $400, or portion thereof, of contributions is multiplied by 75%, the next $350, or portion thereof, of contributions is multiplied by 50%, and the next $525, or portion thereof, of contributions is multiplied by 33.33%. The maximum tax credit will be reached when contributions total $1,275.

Contributions can only be claimed if an individual has an official receipt. Official receipts can only be issued for contributions of $25 or more.

SITA 67.1, CRA Guide 5008-PC, Form SK428, Saskatchewan Provincial Worksheet

¶121157 — *Labour-Sponsored Venture Capital Tax Credit (Form SK428: Lines 58 to 60)*

> The Saskatchewan Labour-Sponsored Venture Capital Tax Credit has been decreased from 20% to 17.5%, beginning in the 2018 taxation year. As a result, the maximum individual annual tax credit has decreased from $1,000 to $875, beginning in 2018.

This non-refundable tax credit is available to individuals who were resident in Saskatchewan at the end of the tax year and who made an eligible investment in a labour-sponsored venture capital corporation (LSVCC) that invests in small and medium-size businesses in the tax year or within 60 days of the end of the tax year.

If an RRSP for a spouse or common-law partner was the first registered holder of the LSVCC share, either the contributor or the annuitant may claim the credit for the share.

For 2018 and later taxation years, the maximum total Saskatchewan tax credit that can be claimed in a tax year for investments in both provincially and federally-registered LSVCCs is $875 ($1,000 for taxation years before 2018).

The Saskatchewan tax credit is equal to 17.5% (20% for taxation years before 2018) of the investment. Therefore, the maximum credit amount will be reached when investments total $5,000.

SITA 34, *Saskatchewan Labour-Sponsored Venture Capital Corporations Act*, VD 2005-0153771E5, CRA Guide 5008-PC, Form SK428

¶121158 — *Saskatchewan Mineral Exploration Tax Credit (Form SK428: Lines 69 to 71)*

This tax credit is available to individuals who purchased shares from a mining exploration corporation in the tax year that had exploration expenses in Saskatchewan.

The amount of the tax credit is equal to 10% of eligible expenses.

The tax credit is non-refundable; however, unused amounts can be carried forward for 10 years or carried back for 3 years.

Eligible individuals should receive a Slip SK-METC indicating the amount of the tax credit they are entitled to.

SITA 34.1, *The Mineral Resources Act 1985*, *The Mineral Exploration Tax Credit Regulations*, CRA Guide 5008-PC, Form SK428

¶121159 — *Saskatchewan Graduate Tuition Tax Credit (Form SK428: Line 73)*

This non-refundable tax credit is available to individuals to whom all of the following conditions apply:

- resident in Saskatchewan at the end of the tax year;

- met the necessary qualifications for completing an eligible program at an eligible educational institution; and

- applied for and obtained a Graduate Retention Program Eligibility Certificate from the Saskatchewan Ministry of Advanced Education.

To be eligible, a program must:

- be equivalent to at least 6 months of full-time study at an eligible institution;

- result in a certificate, diploma, or undergraduate degree; or

- provide journeyperson certification.

Eligible institutions are those recognized for Canada-Saskatchewan student loan purposes or by the Apprenticeship and Trade Certification Commission, and are not limited to institutions located in Saskatchewan.

The tax credit is available beginning the year the Graduate Retention Program Eligibility Certificate is obtained, provided that the individual files an income tax return as a resident of Saskatchewan each year. Unused credits can be carried forward for up to 10 years.

For individuals who graduated in 2010 or later, the lifetime maximum credit amount is:

- $3,000 for a 1 year certificate or diploma, or a journeyperson program;

- $6,400 for a 2 or 3 year certificate or diploma;

- $15,000 for a 3 year undergraduate degree; and

- $20,000 for a 4 year undergraduate degree.

SITA 37.1, 39.1, 39.11, CRA Guide 5008-PC, Form SK428, Form RC360

¶121160 — Other Tax Credits, Benefits and Incentives

¶121161 — *Saskatchewan Low-Income Tax Credit*

This is a non-taxable amount designed to help Saskatchewan residents with low and modest incomes.

The 2017 Saskatchewan budget announced enhancements to the low-income tax credit to increase the maximum credits and the benefit clawback rate, effective July 1, 2017. The amount of the tax credit for July 2018 to June 2019 is as follows:

- $346 for the individual claiming the tax credit;

- $346 for a spouse or common-law partner, or for an eligible dependant; and

- $136 per child for a maximum of two children.

The maximum amount of the tax credit is $964 per family. Families with adjusted family net income of $32,643 or less are eligible for the full credit amount. The credit is then reduced by 2.75% of adjusted family net income in excess of $32,643.

To receive the Saskatchewan low-income credit, an individual and his or her spouse or common-law partner must file a personal tax return. The credit is paid quarterly with the federal GST/HST credit.

SITA 39, 40, CRA Guide 5008-PC, CRA Guide RC4210, Form SK428

¶121200 — Yukon

¶121210 — Liability for Tax

Yukon personal income tax is imposed under the Yukon *Income Tax Act* (YITA). The CRA is responsible for administration of the YITA.

Yukon income tax is payable by individuals resident in the province on the last day of the taxation year and non-residents of the province who have earned income in the province during the year.

An individual's Yukon tax is determined based on taxable income reported for federal income tax purposes, and allocated to the province under the federal allocation rules. For reporting purposes, Yukon tax is based on federal taxable income as shown on the T1 return, which is carried to Form YT428, where Yukon tax is calculated.

YITA 1(1)"individual", "taxable income", 3(1), 6

¶121220 — Tax Rates

Yukon's tax rates for the 2017 and 2018 tax years are as follows:

2018 Taxable Income	2018 Tax Rates	2017 Taxable Income	2017 Tax Rates
first $46,605	6.40%	first $45,916	6.40%
over $46,605 up to $93,208	9.00%	over $45,916 up to $91,831	9.00%
over $93,208 up to $144,489	10.90%	over $91,831 up to $142,353	10.90%
over $144,489 up to $500,000	12.80%	over $142,353 up to $500,000	12.80%
over $500,000	15.00%	over $500,000	15.00%

Yukon's tax brackets are indexed annually for inflation using the federal inflation rate.

YITA 6, 7, CRA Guide 5011-PC

¶121230 — Tax on Split Income (Form YT428: Line 44)

Where federal tax must be paid on split income, a Yukon tax must also be paid. The Yukon tax on split income is calculated as the amount of split income imposed under ITA 120.4 multiplied by the highest Yukon tax rate.

The tax on split income is calculated on federal Form T1206, and is reported on Form YT428. The dividend tax credit and the foreign tax credit are the only credits that may be deducted against tax on split income.

See ¶14210 for a detailed discussion of the tax on split income.

CRA Guide 5011-PC, Form YT428, Form T1206

¶121240 — Additional Minimum Tax (Form YT428: Line 51)

Individuals who are subject to federal minimum tax under ITA 127.5 will be subject to Yukon minimum tax at the rate of 42.67% of the federal minimum tax amount. Individuals who are entitled to a minimum tax carryover for federal purposes under ITA 120.2 may be eligible for a provincial minimum tax credit. The amount of the credit is calculated by multiplying the federal credit amount on Schedule 1 by 42.67%.

Federal minimum tax is calculated on Form T691. Yukon minimum tax is reported on Form YT428.

CRA Guide 5011-PC, Form YT428, Form T691

¶121250 — Non-Refundable Tax Credits

Yukon has adopted many of the personal non-refundable tax credits offered by the federal government, including the following:

- Basic personal amount
- Spouse or common-law partner amount
- Age amount
- Disability amount
- Caregiver amount
- Pension income amount
- Medical expenses
- Donations and gifts
- Canada employment amount
- Public transit amount

Although the eligibility rules for Yukon's non-refundable tax credits are generally the same as the corresponding federal tax credits, the amounts and method for calculation may differ.

Yukon's non-refundable tax credit amounts are multiplied by Yukon's lowest tax rate to arrive at the amount of the deduction. There is an exception for donations and gifts, such that the amount of donations and gifts exceeding $200 are multiplied by Yukon's highest tax rate.

See the tax reference tables in the Appendix for a complete listing of non-refundable tax credits available in the Yukon.

YITA 6, CRA Guide 5011-PC, Form YT428

¶121251 — *Territorial Foreign Tax Credit (Form YT428: Line 53)*

If an individual's federal foreign tax credit for foreign non-business income is less than the tax paid to a foreign country related to that income, the individual may be entitled to an additional territorial foreign tax credit. A Yukon foreign tax credit may be claimed by an individual who resided in Yukon on the last day of the taxation year, and paid non-business-income tax to a foreign country.

Generally, the Yukon foreign tax credit is equal to the lesser of:

- foreign taxes paid on foreign non-business income but not claimed for purposes of the federal foreign tax credit; and

- the proportion of Yukon income tax equal to the ratio of: net foreign non-business income/net income allocated to Yukon

For purposes of calculating the provincial foreign tax credit, net income is subject to the same adjustments as for federal purposes in claiming the federal non-business foreign tax credit.

The foreign tax credit is calculated on federal Form T2036 and claimed on Form YT428.

YITA 6(54), 6(55), CRA Guide 5011-PC, Form YT428, Form T2036

¶12152 — *Yukon Political Contribution Tax Credit (Form YT428: Line 56)*

This non-refundable tax credit is available to individuals who made contributions in the tax year to:

- a registered Yukon political party; or

- a candidate seeking election to the Yukon Legislative Assembly.

For 2016 and later taxation years, the Yukon political contribution tax credit was increased to match, on an ongoing basis, the federal political contribution tax credit (see ¶11020). Therefore, Yukon resident individuals can claim a Yukon tax credit for political contributions up to a maximum of $650. The credit available is equal to 75% of the first $400 of contributions, plus 50% of the next $350 of contributions, plus 33 1/3% of the next $525 of contributions. The maximum credit is reached with contributions of $1,275.

YITA 11, CRA Guide 5011-PC, Form YT479

¶12153 — *Small Business Investment Tax Credit (Form YT479)*

This tax credit is available to individuals who were a resident of Yukon and 19 years of age or older at the end of the tax year and who invested in eligible shares or subordinated debt of an eligible Yukon business in the tax year or within 60 days of the end of the tax year.

The amount of the tax credit is equal to 25% of eligible investments, up to the maximum annual credit amount of $25,000.

The tax credit is non-refundable; however, unused amounts can be carried forward for 7 years or carried back for 3 years.

Individuals who are eligible for the tax credit should receive a Certificate YSBITC-1 from the Yukon government.

YITA 13, CRA Guide 5011-PC, Form YT479, www.cra-arc.gc.ca/E/pub/tg/5011-pc/5011-pc-12e.html#P135_4913

¶121254 — *Labour-Sponsored Venture Capital Corporation Tax Credit (Form YT479)*

This tax credit is available to individuals who made eligible investments in the Fireweed Fund Corporation in the tax year or within 60 days of the end of the tax year.

If the investment was made into a spousal or common-law partner RRSP, either the contributor or the annuitant can claim the tax credit for the investment.

The amount of the tax credit is equal to 25% of eligible investments, up to the maximum annual credit amount of $1,250.

The tax credit is non-refundable; however, unused amounts can be carried forward for 7 years or carried back for 3 years.

YITA 14, CRA Guide 5011-PC, Form YT479

¶121260 — Other Tax Credits, Benefits and Incentives

¶121261 — *Research and Development Tax Credit (Form YT479)*

This refundable tax credit is available to individuals who were a resident of Yukon at the end of the tax year and who have eligible expenditures for the tax year for scientific research and experimental development in Yukon.

Expenditures are eligible if they qualify for the federal scientific research and experimental development tax credit.

The amount of the tax credit is equal to 15% of eligible expenditures. An additional 5% is available for amounts paid or payable to the Yukon College.

To claim the tax credit, individuals must complete Form T1232.

YITA 15, CRA Guide 5011-PC, Form YT479

¶121262 — *Yukon First Nations Income Tax Credit (Form YT479)*

This tax credit is available to individual residing on Yukon First Nations settlement lands of the following First Nations:

- Champagne and Aishihik
- Kluane
- Little Salmon/Carmacks
- Nacho Nyak Dun
- Selkirk
- Tesling Tlingit
- Tr'ondek Hwech'in
- Vuntut Gwitchin
- Ta'an Kwach'an
- Kwanlin Dun

The tax credit forms a part of a tax sharing arrangement with the above First Nations. The credit is designed to abate the Yukon tax of individuals who are resident on settlement lands so that the total amount of tax payable remains the same.

The amount of the tax credit is 95% of Yukon tax.

To claim the tax credit, individuals must file a tax return, complete Form YT479, and identify the First Nations settlement lands they reside on.

YITA 12, *First Nation Income Tax Credit Regulation*, CRA Guide 5011-PC, Form YT479, Form YT432

¶121263 — *Yukon Child Benefit*

This is a non-taxable monthly payment to help low- and middle-income families with the cost of raising children under 18 years of age.

The maximum annual amount of the tax credit is $820 for each child. The maximum credit amount is available to families with adjusted family net income of $35,000 or less. The credit is phased out at a rate of 2.5% of adjusted family net income in excess of $35,000 for families with one child, and 5% of adjusted family net income in excess of $35,000 for families with more than one child.

The tax credit is paid together with the federal Canada Child Benefit in a single monthly payment.

YITA 9, *Yukon Child Benefit Regulation*, CRA Guide 5011-PC, CRA Guide T4114

¶121264 — *Yukon Children's Fitness Tax Credit (Form YT 479)*

The children's fitness tax credit is available to Yukon parents who paid fees in the tax year to register a qualifying child in a prescribed program of physical activity. To be eligible, the child must be 16 years of age or younger at the beginning of the taxation year. The maximum base claim for a child is $1,000, or the total eligible fitness expenses relating to that child, whichever is less. Parents may claim an additional $500 in respect of a qualifying disabled child if the parent incurs a minimum of $100 in eligible expenses relating to that child. A qualifying disabled child means a child of the individual who is under the age of 18 at the beginning of the taxation year and who qualifies for the federal disability tax credit (see ¶10120).

Section 9400 of the federal Regulations defines prescribed programs of physical activity for purposes of the Yukon credit.

More than one parent may claim the credit; however, the total amounts claimed by both parents cannot exceed the maximum amount that would be allowed if only one parent were claiming the credit for that child.

The Yukon children's fitness tax credit was converted to a refundable credit for 2015 and later taxation years, consistent with the changes made to the federal children's fitness tax credit. The 2016 Yukon budget announced that the Yukon children's fitness tax credit will be maintained, despite the elimination of the federal children's fitness tax credit.

Chapter 13 — Completing the Québec Income Tax Return (Form TP-1)

Contents

¶13000 Introduction

  ¶13010 Overview and New for 2018

  ¶13020 Who Must File a Québec Income Tax Return

  ¶13030 Definition of Spouse

  ¶13040 Definition of Business Establishment

  ¶13050 Residency

  ¶13060 Filing Deadline and Penalties

  ¶13070 Solidarity Tax Credit

¶13100 Calculating Total Income (Form TP-1: Lines 96–199)

  ¶13105 Overview

  ¶13110 Income from Transferred Property

  ¶13115 Employment Income (Form TP-1: Line 101)

  ¶13120 Retirement Income Transferred by a Spouse (Form TP-1: Line 123)

  ¶13125 Dividends from Taxable Canadian Corporations (Form TP-1: Lines 128, 166, 167)

  ¶13130 Interest and Other Investment Income (Form TP-1: Line 130)

  ¶13135 Rental Income (Form TP-1: Lines 136, 168)

  ¶13140 Capital Gains (Form TP-1: Line 139)

  ¶13145 Support Payments (Form TP-1: Line 142)

  ¶13150 Income Replacement Indemnities and Net Federal Supplements (Form TP-1: Line 148)

  ¶13155 Other Income (Form TP-1: Line 154)

  ¶13160 Business Income (Form TP-1: Line 164)

¶13200 Calculating Net Income (Form TP-1: Lines 201 to 275)

  ¶13205 Deduction for Workers (Form TP-1: Line 201)

  ¶13210 Registered Pension Plan Deduction (Form TP-1: Line 205)

  ¶13215 Employment Expenses and Deductions (Form TP-1: Line 207)

  ¶13220 RRSP Deduction (Form TP-1: Line 214)

  ¶13225 Support Payments (Form TP-1: Line 225)

¶13230 Moving Expenses (Form TP-1: Line 228)

¶13235 Carrying Charges and Interest Expenses (Form TP-1: Line 231)

¶13240 Business Investment Loss (Form TP-1: Line 234)

¶13245 Deduction for Residents of Designated Remote Areas (Form TP-1: Line 236)

¶13250 Deduction for Exploration and Development Expenses (Form TP-1: Line 241)

¶13255 Deduction for Amounts Contributed to the QPP and the QPIP on Income from Self-Employment (Form TP-1: Line 248)

¶13260 Other Deductions (Form TP-1: Line 250)

¶13265 Carry-Over of the Adjustment of Investment Expenses (Form TP-1: Line 252)

¶13270 Adjustment of Investment Expenses (Form TP-1: Line 260)

¶13300 Calculating Taxable Income (Form TP-1: Lines 276–299)

¶13305 Adjustment of Deductions (Form TP-1: Line 276)

¶13310 UCCB and Income from a Registered Disability Savings Plan (Form TP-1: Line 278)

¶13315 Deduction for Strategic Investments (Form TP-1: Line 287)

¶13320 Non-Capital Losses from Other Years (Form T-1: Line 289)

¶13325 Net Capital Losses from Other Years (Form TP-1: Line 290)

¶13330 Capital Gains Deduction (Form TP-1: Line 292)

¶13335 Deduction for an Indian (Form TP-1: Line 293)

¶13340 Deductions for Certain Income (Form TP-1: Line 295)

¶13345 Miscellaneous Deductions (Form TP-1: Line 297)

¶13400 Non-Refundable Tax Credits (Form TP-1: Lines 350–399)

¶13405 Basic Personal Amount (Form TP-1: Line 350)

¶13410 Age Amount, Amount for a Person Living Alone, and Amount for Retirement Income (Form TP-1: Line 361)

¶13415 Amount for Dependants and Amount Transferred by a Child 18 or over Enrolled in Post-Secondary Studies (Form TP-1: Line 367)

¶13420 Union, Professional or Other Dues (Form TP-1: Line 373)

¶13425 Amount for a Severe and Prolonged Impairment in Mental or Physical Functions (Form TP-1: Line 376)

¶13430 Expenses for Medical Services Not Available in your Area (Form TP-1: Line 378)

¶13435 Medical Expenses (Form TP-1: Line 381)

¶13440 Tuition or Examination Fees (Form TP-1: Line 384)

¶13445 Interest Paid on a Student Loan (Form TP-1: Line 385)

¶13450 Tuition or Examination Fees Transferred by a Child (Form TP-1: Line 387)

¶13455 Tax Credit for Volunteer Firefighters (Form TP-1: Line 390)

¶13460 Tax Credit for Workers 65 or Older (Form TP-1: Line 391)

¶13465 Tax Credit for Recent Graduates Working in Remote Resource Regions (Form TP-1: Line 392)

¶13470 Donations and Gifts (Form TP-1: Line 393)

¶13500 Income Tax and Contributions (Form TP-1: Lines 401–450)

¶13505 Income Tax on Taxable Income (Form TP-1: Line 401)

¶13510 Tax Adjustment (Form TP-1, Schedule E: Line 402)

¶13515 Foreign Tax Credit (Form TP-1, Schedule E: Line 409)

¶13520 Tax Credit for the Beneficiary of a Designated Trust (Form TP-1: Line 411)

¶13525 Tax Credit for Contributions to Authorized Québec Political Parties (Form TP-1: Line 414)

¶13530 Dividend Tax Credit (Form TP-1: Line 415)

¶13535 Tax Credit for the Acquisition of Capital Régional et Coopératif Desjardins Shares (Form TP-1: Line 422)

¶13540 Tax Credit for a Labour-Sponsored Fund (Form TP-1: Line 424)

¶13545 Credits Transferred from One Spouse to the Other (Form TP-1: Line 431)

¶13550 Alternative Minimum Tax (Form TP-1: Line 432, Schedule E)

¶13555 Special Taxes (Form TP-1: Line 443)

¶13560 Health Contribution (Form TP-1: Line 448)

¶13600 Calculating Refund or Balance Due (Form TP-1: Lines 451–479)

¶13605 Tax Credit for Childcare Expenses (Form TP-1: Line 455)

¶13610 Tax Credits Respecting the Work Premium (Form TP-1: Line 456)

¶13615 Tax Credit for Home-Support Services for Seniors (Form TP-1: Line 458)

¶13620 QST Rebate for Employees and Partners (Form TP-1: Line 459)

¶13621 — Tax Shield (Form TP-1: Line 460)

¶13625 Other Credits (Form TP-1: Line 462)

¶13630 Refund (Form TP-1: Line 474)

¶13635 Transfer to Spouse (Form TP-1: Lines 476, 477)

¶13700 Assessment

¶13710 Assessment

¶13720 Recourse

¶13000 — Introduction

¶13010 — Overview and New for 2018

¶13011 — *Overview*

This chapter discusses the completion and filing of the Québec TP-1 Income Tax Return (TP-1 return) for Québec resident individuals.

Québec personal income tax is imposed under the Québec *Taxation Act* (QTA). Unlike all of the other provinces and territories, Québec personal income tax is collected and administered by the province of Québec, and not by the CRA. Québec also requires individuals to file a TP-1 return, which is a separate return, in addition to the federal T1 personal tax return.

An individual's Québec tax is determined separately from federal tax, and is based on taxable income reported for Québec income tax purposes. Although there are similarities between the Québec and federal taxation systems, there are several differences that must be considered when filing the Québec TP-1 return, including the following: there are various Québec-specific tax deductions in the calculation of taxable income; Québec offers various additional credits in addition to the federal credits; and transfers of unused non-refundable tax credits between spouses are permitted to a greater extent in Québec than for federal purposes.

¶13012 — *New for 2018*

Amount for a Person Living Alone — The credit for a person living alone has been expanded to include taxpayers who live during the year with a grandchild or great-grandchild who is an eligible student (see ¶13412)

Tax Credit for Experienced Workers — The age of eligibility for the tax credit for experienced workers is lowered and the maximum amount of eligible work income on which the credit is calculated is increased (see ¶13460)

Dividend Tax Credit — The dividend tax credits for both eligible and non-eligible dividends have been changed (see ¶13530)

Tax Credit for Childcare Expenses — The annual limits for childcare expenses eligible for this tax credit have increased for children under age seven and children with a mental or physical impairment (see ¶13605)

Tax Credit for Informal Caregivers — A new component has been added to the tax credit for informal caregivers, applicable to caregivers who help a relative who they neither house nor reside with (see ¶13625.22)

Tax Credit for Volunteer Respite Services — The tax credit for volunteer respite services provided to informal caregivers has been enhanced (see ¶13625.6)

Independent Living Tax Credit for Seniors — The threshold at which the independent living tax credit for seniors may be claimed in respect of eligible expenditures is reduced and the list of eligible expenditures is expanded (see ¶13625.8)

RénoVert Tax Credit — The eligibility period for this temporary refundable tax credit for eco-friendly renovation has been extended to December 31, 2019 (see ¶13625.11)

First-Time Home Buyers' Tax Credit — The first-time home buyers' tax credit is a new credit available as of the 2018 taxation year for the purchase of a qualifying home after December 31, 2017. The maximum value of the tax credit is $750, calculated as 15% of a maximum claim of $5,000.

¶13020 — Who Must File a Québec Income Tax Return

An individual must file a Québec income tax return for the tax year if any of the following situations applies to the individual:

- resident in Québec on the last day of the tax year and required to pay:
  - income tax;
  - a contribution to the Québec Pension Plan;
  - a Québec parental insurance plan premium; or
  - a contribution to the health services fund.

- resident in Québec on the last day of the tax year and:

    - disposed of capital property;

    - realized a capital gain;

    - is reporting a capital gain resulting from a previous tax year reserve; or

    - worked in the restaurant and hotel sector and received tips

- beneficiary of a designated trust

- required to pay the additional contribution for subsidized educational childcare

- required to pay a premium under the Québec prescription drug insurance plan

- resident in Canada, outside Québec, but carried on a business or practiced a profession in Québec and: is required to pay Québec income tax; disposed of capital property; or is reporting a capital gain from a previous tax year reserve

- ceased to reside in Canada in the year and was resident in Québec on the day the individual ceased residence;

- was not resident in Canada at any point in the year and: was employed in Québec; carried on a business in Québec; or disposed of taxable Québec property;

- sole proprietor of a business and required to pay the annual registration fee for the enterprise register

- wishes to transfer retirement income to a spouse, or vice-versa

- wishes, or spouse wishes, to receive the child assistance payment from the Retraite Québec (if this situation applies, both spouses must file an income tax return)

- wishes, or spouse wishes, to receive the shelter allowance under the shelter allowance program (if this situation applies, both spouses must file an income tax return)

- resident in Québec on the last day of the tax year and wishes to receive the solidarity tax credit (if this situation applies and the individual has a spouse, both spouses must file an income tax return)

- no income tax payable for the tax year because:

    - the individual is deducting a loss sustained in a previous year; or

- the individual's spouse on the last day of the tax year is transferring the unused portion of his or her non-refundable tax credits to the individual

- in the tax year, received advance payments of:

    - the tax credit for childcare expenses;

    - any tax credits respecting the work premium;

    - the tax credit for home-support services for seniors;

    - the tax credit for the treatment of infertility; or

    - the tax credit for the restoration of a secondary residence.

- wishes to transfer:

    - the unused portion of the individual's non-refundable tax credits to his or her spouse;

    - an amount as a child 18 or over enrolled in postsecondary studies to the individual's father or mother; or

    - all or part of the individual's tuition or examination fees paid for the tax year to one of the individual's or his or her spouse's parents or grandparents

- wishes to claim:
  - the tax credit for childcare expenses;
  - any tax credits respecting the work premium;
  - the tax credit for home-support services for seniors;
  - the QST rebate for employees and partners;
  - the tax shield; or
  - any credits or refunds on Line 462 (Other credits).

¶13030 — Definition of Spouse

For income tax purposes, an individual's spouse is the person who, at any time during the year:

- was married to the individual;
- was living in a civil union with the individual; or
- was the individual's *de facto* spouse.

A *de facto* spouse is a person of the opposite or same sex who, at any time during the year:

- was living in a conjugal relationship with the individual and was the biological or adoptive parent (legally or in fact) of a child of whom the individual is also the parent; or
- had been living in a conjugal relationship with the individual for at least 12 consecutive months without an interruption of 90 or more days.

An individual's spouse on the last day of the tax year is the person, if any:

- who was the individual's spouse at the end of that day and from whom the individual was not separated at that time because of a breakdown of the relationship. If, on the last day of the tax year, the individual and his or her spouse were separated because of a breakdown of their relationship but the separation lasted for less than 90 days, the individual is considered to have had a spouse on the last day of the tax year; or
- was the individual's spouse at the time of his or her death in the tax year, provided the individual and his or her spouse had not been separated for 90 days or more at that time because of a breakdown of the relationship, and provided the individual did not have a new spouse on the last day of the tax year.

¶13040 — Definition of Business Establishment

An individual resident in Canada must pay Québec tax on business income earned through an establishment in Québec. The concept of an establishment in Québec is similar to the concept of a permanent establishment in Canada. An establishment is a fixed place where an individual carries on business. The place must be permanent or maintained for a significant amount of time and must be used currently or regularly by the individual in carrying on his or her business.

An individual will be deemed to have an establishment in Québec if the individual carries on business through an employee, agent, or mandatary established in a particular place in Québec, provided that the employee, agent, or mandatary has general authority to enter into contracts on behalf of the individual or has a stock of merchandise owned by the individual from which the employee, agent, or mandatary regularly fills orders, or if the individual had use of substantial machinery or equipment in Québec during the tax year.

> If an individual has establishments in Québec and in one or more other provinces, the individual must allocate his or her business income among them on federal Form T2203.

QTA 12, 13, 15, Interpretation Revenu Québec 12-1/R3, Form T2203

¶13050 — Residency

¶13051 — *Factual Residence*

Generally, an individual is resident in the province or territory where he or she has significant residential ties. Where an individual may be considered to be resident in more than one province or territory on the last day of the tax year, the individual will be resident in the province or territory where the individual has the most significant residential ties.

The CRA considers the following factors to almost always be significant residential ties:

- dwelling place
- spouse or common-law partner
- dependants

The CRA's opinion is that the following secondary residential ties should also be taken into account:

- personal property
- social ties
- economic ties
- hospitalization or medical insurance coverage
- driver's license
- vehicle registration
- seasonal dwelling place or leased dwelling place
- memberships in unions or professional organizations

The CRA's opinion is that secondary residential ties must be looked at collectively, and that it would be unusual for a single secondary residential tie to be determinative.

Finally, the CRA's view is that the following residential ties, which may be taken into account, will generally be of limited importance:

- mailing address
- post office box
- safety deposit box
- address on personal stationary such as business cards
- telephone listings
- local newspaper and magazine subscriptions

Folio S5-F1-C1

¶13052 — *Deemed Residence*

An individual is deemed to have been resident in Québec throughout a tax year if at any time during the year the individual:

- was ordinarily resident outside of Canada and sojourned in Québec for a period of, or for periods totaling, 183 or more days;

- was a member of the Canadian Forces and was resident in Québec immediately before leaving Canada on military service in a foreign country;

- was an ambassador, Member of Parliament, officer, high commissioner, minister, servant or senator of Canada, or an agent-general, officer, or servant of a province and was resident in Québec immediately prior to his or her election, employment or appointment, or received representation allowances in respect of the year;

- performed services in a country other than Canada under a prescribed international development assistance program of the Government of Québec of Canada and was resident in Québec at any time during the six month period preceding the day on which those services commenced;

- was a child of, and dependent for support on, an individual to whom any of the three preceding situations apply, and had income of $6,650 or less; or

- was, at any time during the year, under a tax agreement with one or more other countries, entitled to an exemption from an income tax otherwise payable in any of those countries in respect of income from any source, unless all or substantially all of the individual's income from all sources was not exempt because the individual was related to, or a member of the family of, an individual, other than a trust, resident in Québec.

QTA 8

¶13053 — *Non-Residents*

Individuals who are not resident in Canada are taxed on income from employment earned in Québec, business carried on in Québec, and dispositions of Québec property.

An individual who is not resident in Canada is taxed on income from an office or employment reasonably attributable to duties performed in Québec. The income from an office or employment that is reasonably attributable to the duties of the individual performed in Québec is equal to the proportion of the income that the number of days the individual was physically present in Québec for the office or employment is of the total number of days the individual was physically present for the office or employment.

QTA 26, 1089, 1090, Interpretation Revenu Québec IMP 1089-1/R1

¶13054 — *Residence of an Individual who leaves Québec and Canada*

Where an individual leaves Québec and Canada, the following factors will be considered when determining whether or not the individual remains a resident of Québec while outside of Canada:

- the reason for his or her absence;

- the permanence of his or her stay outside of Canada;

- his or her residential ties in Québec and elsewhere;

- the regularity and length of his or her visits to Québec; and

- his or her anticipated return to Québec at the end of his or her stay.

In order for an individual to cease to be a resident of Québec, there must be some permanence to his or her stay outside of Canada. If the individual is outside of Canada for less than two years, there is a presumption that he or she remains a resident of Québec, unless the individual can clearly establish that his or her residential ties in Canada have been severed. If an individual is outside of Canada for more than two years, he or she may still remain a resident of Québec if it is anticipated that he or she will return to Québec.

Interpretation Revenu Québec IMP 22-3/R1

¶13055 — *Resident for Part of the Year*

If an individual ceased to be resident in Canada during the tax year, the last day of the individual's tax year is the last day on which the individual was resident in Canada. If the individual was resident in Québec on that day, he or she will be subject to Québec tax on the income he or she earned during the part of the year he or she was resident in Canada.

If an individual was only resident in Québec for part of the year, the individual's non-refundable tax credits will generally be reduced proportionately based on the number of days in the tax year the individual was resident in Canada. The individual may claim the tax credits for charitable donations, medical expenses, union and professional dues, tuition and examination fees, and interest on student loans, if such expenses were incurred while the individual was resident in Canada.

QTA 23, 24

¶13060 — Filing Deadline and Penalties

An individual's Québec income tax return must generally be filed by April 30th of the year following the tax year. If the individual or his or her spouse carried on a business in the tax year, the individual has until June 15th of the year following the tax year to file his or her return.

> Regardless of the filing deadline, any balance due for the tax year must be paid by April 30th of the year following the tax year, after which interest will be calculated on the unpaid balance.

If an individual does not file his or her income tax return by the filing deadline and has a balance due for the tax year, a 5% penalty will be added to the balance. An additional penalty of 1% will be added for each complete month the individual's return is late, up to a maximum of 12 months.

If an individual wishes to make a change to his or her income tax return, he or she must complete Form TP-1.R-V, *Request for an Adjustment to an Income Tax Return*.

If an individual who was required to file an income tax return did not file one, or filed an incomplete one, he or she can make a voluntary disclosure of the information that was not submitted. The individual will be required to pay the income tax owing and interest, but no penalties will be imposed and Revenu Québec will waive its right to undertake penal proceedings.

Brochure IN-309-V

¶13070 — Solidarity Tax Credit

An individual is entitled to the solidarity tax credit if, at the beginning of a month included in the benefit year beginning on July 1 and ending on June 30, he or she meets the following requirements:

- 18 years of age or older, or, if the individual is under 18 years of age:
  - has a spouse;

- is the parent of a child who lives with him or her; or

    - is recognized as an emancipated minor by a competent authority;

- resident in Québec;

- the individual or his or her spouse is:

    - a Canadian citizen;

    - a permanent resident or protected person under the *Immigration and Refugee Protection Act*; or

    - a temporary resident or holder of a temporary resident permit under the *Immigration and Refugee Protection Act* who has been resident in Canada for the preceding 18 months.

An individual is not entitled to the tax credit for any month if:

- the individual was confined to a prison or similar institution;

- someone received the child assistance payment from the Retraite Québec with regard to the individual; or

- the individual or his or her spouse on the last day of the tax year was exempt from paying income tax because the individual or his or her spouse worked for an international organization, the government of a foreign country, or an office of a political subdivision of a foreign State recognized by the Ministère des Finances.

If an individual ordinarily lives with a spouse, only one of the individual or his or her spouse can claim the tax credit for the couple.

The amount of the tax credit is the total of the amounts the individual is entitled to for the QST component, the housing component, and the component for individuals living in northern villages. The amount of the tax credit may be reduced on the basis of the individual's family income.

An individual may be entitled to the property tax refund component of the tax credit if the individual was resident in Québec on the last day of the tax year and the individual or his or her spouse was the owner, tenant, or subtenant of an eligible dwelling in which the individual was living on the last day of the tax year. Property taxes include school and municipal taxes applicable to the dwelling, which include taxes for water, sewers, garbage collection, and upkeep of roads and streets, taxes for a specific sector to cover public services and facilities, financing taxes levied by municipalities or urban communities, and taxes for the operation of schools, and the tenant's tax. Property taxes do not include transfer taxes.

An individual may be eligible for the northern village component of the tax credit if he or she is a Québec resident and if the individual or his or her spouse is living in an eligible northern village. The amount of the tax credit is based on the number of months in which the individual or his or her spouse lived in the eligible northern village during the year.

The maximum amounts for July 2018 to June 2019 are as follows:

Amounts for the QST:		
• Basic amount	$	287
• Amount for spouse	$	287
• Additional amount for person living alone	$	137
Amounts for housing:		
• Amount for a couple	$	675
• Amount for a person living alone	$	557
• Amount for each dependent child	$	119
Amounts for individuals living in a northern village:		
• Amount per adult	$	1,690
• Amount for each dependent child	$	366
Reduction Threshold	$	34,215

To claim the tax credit, individuals must complete Schedule D of their income tax return, or apply online. New residents must complete Form TP-1029.CS.1-V, *Application for New Residents of Québec*. Individuals must advise Revenu Québec of any changes throughout the benefit year.

The amount of the solidarity tax credit is determined annually, based on the information contained in a taxpayer's income tax return, and will either be paid on a monthly, quarterly or annual basis, depending on the amount of credit determined. The frequency of solidarity tax credit payments varies based on the amount of the credit determined for the year. If the annual amount is $800 or more, the payment is made monthly; if the annual amount is between $240 and $800, the payment is made quarterly (in July, October, January and April); and if the annual amount is $240 or less, the payment is made annually in July.

QTA 1029.8.109.2–1029.8.109.6, 1029.8.114, 1029.8.116.12–1029.8.116.35, Québec Guide TP-1.G, Québec Finance Information Bulletins 2011-2 and 2013-13

¶13100 — Calculating Total Income (Form TP-1: Lines 94–199)

¶13105 — Overview

An individual's total income is comprised of, generally, any amount that is earned by the individual, whatever its source.

The following amounts are not included in an individual's total income:

- the allowance received under the shelter allowance program;
- the value of property received as an inheritance;
- amounts received under a life insurance policy after the death of the insured;
- the child assistance payment from the Retraite Québec;
- the solidarity tax credit;
- any of the tax credits respecting the work premium;
- the GST credit;
- lottery winnings;
- strike pay;
- Canada Child Benefit payments;
- benefits received under a wage loss replacement or income insurance plan to which the individual's employer made a contribution;
- income, gains, and losses from investments held in a tax-free savings account.

Income earned from non-taxable amounts, such as interest, is included in an individual's total income.

¶13110 — Income from Transferred Property

If an individual transferred or loaned property to his or her spouse, or to a person under the age of 18 years old who was the individual's nephew or niece or related to the individual by blood, marriage, or adoption, and the transferee earns income from the property, the income must be reported on the individual's income tax return. An individual is not, however, required to report income from property transferred to his or her spouse for contribution to a tax-free savings account.

¶13115 — Employment Income (Form TP-1: Line 101)

An individual must add the following amounts and enter the total on Line 101:

- the amount in Box A of his or her RL-1 slip;

- the amount in Box R-1 of his or her RL-1 slip; and

- the amount in Box D-1 of his or her RL-25 slip.

¶13116 — *Taxable Benefits*

An individual is required to report the value of taxable benefits including:

- personal use of an automobile;

- in certain circumstances, lodging, transportation, and meals;

- gifts and rewards, subject to exemptions of $500 for non-monetary gifts and non-monetary rewards;

- payment or reimbursement of professional membership dues;

- QPP contributions, QPIP premiums, TFSA contributions, and RRSP contributions;

- loans bearing no or low interest; and

- stock options.

The value of taxable benefits should be indicated in Box A or Box R of the individual's RL-1 slip, or on his or her T4 slip.

QTA 36, Brochure IN-253-V

¶13117 — *Tips*

Individuals must report their tips as income. Individuals who make sales and receive tips and who report tips of less than 8% of their tippable sales will be allocated an amount of tips equal to 8% of their tippable sales.

QTA 42.6–42.15, IMP 42.8-1

¶13120 — Retirement Income Transferred by a Spouse (Form TP-1: Line 123)

If an individual's spouse received eligible retirement income during the year, up to 50% of the eligible retirement income can be transferred by the spouse to the individual, provided that both spouses were resident in Canada at the end of the tax year. To make the transfer, the transferor must complete Schedule Q. The transferred amount must be included on Line 123 of the transferee's Québec income tax return, and can be deducted on Line 250 of the transferor's return. If the transferor was resident in Canada outside of Québec, the amount deducted on his or her federal income tax return must be included in the income of the transferee spouse. The transferee may be entitled to an amount for retirement income as a result of the income included on Line 123.

For the income splitting mechanism to be applicable in a particular taxation year, the transferor spouse (i.e., the person whose income is being split) must have reached 65 years of age before the end of the year. If the transferor spouse died or ceased to be resident in Canada in the year, he or she must have reached 65 years of age on the date of his or her death or on the date on which he or she cased Canadian residency. Eligible retirement income for income splitting purposes includes income on Line 122 of the transferor spouse's tax return (i.e., payments from a pension plan, registered retirement savings plan, registered retirement income fund, deferred profit-sharing plan, or annuities).

QTA 752.0.7.1, 752.0.7.4, 752.0.8, 752.0.10. 776.41.1–776.41.4, IMP. 752.0.8-1/R1, IMP. 752.0.8-2

¶13125 — Dividends from Taxable Canadian Corporations (Form TP-1: Lines 128, 166, 167)

The taxable amount of dividends from taxable Canadian corporations may be reported on an RL-3, RL-15, RL-16 or RL-25 slip. If the individual did not receive one or more of these RL slips, dividends may also be reported on an individual's T3, T4PS, T5, T5013, and T5013A slips.

To report dividends, an individual must enter the taxable amount of all dividends on Line 128, the actual amount of eligible dividends on Line 166, and the actual amount of ordinary dividends on Line 167.

QTA 87(k), 497

¶13130 — Interest and Other Investment Income (Form TP-1: Line 130)

The amount of interest an individual must report is generally shown on his or her RL-3, RL-13, RL-15, and RL-16 slips, or on his or her T3, T5, T5013, and T5013A slips; however, all interest must be reported including interest on income tax refunds and interest on loans made to individuals.

There are three methods for reporting interest from an investment contract, such as a savings bond or term deposit, and a different method may be used for each:

- cash method: the individual must report the interest received by or credited to him or her in the tax year, except to the extent it was reported in previous years. For investment contracts entered into after 1989, the individual must report the interest earned up to the anniversary of the date on which the investment was acquired each year;

- accrual method: each year, the individual must report the amount of interest earned from January 1 to December 31;

- receivable method: each year, the individual must report the interest that falls due in the year.

QTA 87(c), 87(l), 88, 89, 92–92.5, IMP. 88-1/R2, IMP. 92.5-1

¶13135 — Rental Income (Form TP-1: Lines 136, 168)

An individual must report his or her net income from the rental of property on Line 136. The individual's net rental income is his or her gross rental income, less expenses incurred in the tax year to earn the income and capital cost allowance, where applicable. The individual must include a Form TP-128-V, *Income and Expenses Respecting the Rental of Immovable Property*, or a statement of rental income and expenses, for each rental property with his or her Québec income tax return. If the individual incurred labour costs other than salaries and wages paid to employees to maintain, repair, or renovate a rental building, the individual must include Form TP-1086.R.23.12-V, *Costs Incurred for Work on an Immovable*, with his or her return.

If an individual was a member of a partnership with rental income, his or her share of the rental income is shown in Box 3 of his or her RL-15 slip. If the individual did not receive an RL-15 slip, he or she must enclose a copy of the partnership's financial statements with his or her Québec income tax return.

If an individual sustained a rental loss, the amount of the loss must be indicated on Line 136 preceded by the minus sign, and the amount must be subtracted rather than added to the individual's income. Capital cost allowance cannot be included to the extent that it results in a rental loss.

Rental income that is business income is reported on Line 22 of Schedule L, and not on Line 136.

QTA 80–230.0.0.6, Form RL-15, Form TP-128-V, Form TP-1086.R.23.12-V, Brochure IN-100-V, IMP. 81-2/R1, IMP. 128-13, IMP. 130-11/R1, IMP. 130-12/R1

¶13140 — Capital Gains (Form TP-1: Line 139)

If an individual disposed of capital property, such as shares or land, in the tax year and realized greater gains than losses, he or she must report 50% of the excess amount on Line 139 of his or her Québec income tax return as a taxable capital gain.

If the individual's losses from the disposition of capital property are greater than his or her gains, the individual cannot enter a loss on Line 139, but can carry forward 50% of the excess amount to reduce taxable capital gains arising in future tax years. The individual must enclose Schedule G with his or her income tax return. The individual may also carry the net loss back to the previous three tax years by completing Form TP-1012.A-V, *Carry-Back of a Loss*, and filing it separately from his or her income tax return.

An individual can calculate his or her capital gains or losses on the disposition of capital property on Part A of Schedule G. An individual who disposed of resource property must complete Part B. An individual who disposed of qualified fishing property or qualified small business corporation shares must complete Part C.

The following amounts are not included when calculating an individual's taxable capital gains:

- gains arising from the disposition of a principal residence, provided the individual completes Form TP-274-V, *Designation of Property as a Principal Residence*;

- proceeds of disposition for personal-use property of up to $1,000 (note that a loss on the disposition of personal-use property cannot be deducted); and

- proceeds of disposition for precious property of up to $1,000 (note that a loss on the disposition of precious property can only be deducted against gains on the disposition of precious property).

If an individual realized a capital gain on the disposition of shares of a small business corporation and purchased new small business corporation shares, he or she may be able to defer tax on all or part of the gain until the new shares are disposed of.

QTA 231–308.6, Form RL-18, Form TP-274-V, Form TP-1012.A-V, Guide IN-120-V, IMP. 274-2/R1, IMP. 277-1/R1

¶13145 — Support Payments (Form TP-1: Line 142)

An individual must generally report the amount of support payments he or she received in the tax year under a written agreement or judgment where the payments were payable periodically as an allowance for the benefit of the individual or his or her child and where the individual was not living with the payer at the time of the payments. Payments that must be reported include payments received through the support-payment collection system and payments received as arrears.

An individual must also include in his or her income repayments received in the tax year of support paid and deducted in a previous year.

Child support paid under a written agreement or judgment entered into or rendered after April 30, 1997 cannot be deducted by the payer and is not included in the recipient's income. If an individual received non-taxable support, he or she must complete work chart 142.

QTA 312.3–313.0.5, Guide IN-128-V

¶13150 — Income Replacement Indemnities and Net Federal Supplements (Form TP-1: Line 148)

An individual must enter the amount of income replacement indemnities and net federal supplements received on Line 148 and enter the item number corresponding to the source of the income in Box 149.

QTA 311(k.0.1), 311.1, IMP. 28-2/R2

¶13155 — Other Income (Form TP-1: Line 154)

An individual must enter the amount of his or her other income on Line 154 and enter the item number corresponding to the source of the income in Box 153. If the individual has other income from more than one source, he or she must enter the number "66" in Box 153.

¶13160 — Business Income (Form TP-1: Line 164)

If an individual carried on a business in the tax year, as a sole proprietor or a member of a partnership, he or she must use Schedule L to report his or her gross and net income, calculated according to the accrual method. If the individual is a farmer, fisher, or person who earns commissions, he or she can use the cash method to calculate net income.

> An individual who carried on business in the tax year must enclose Form TP-80-V, *Business or Professional Income and Expenses*, or his or her financial statements, with his or her Québec income tax return. If an individual's business was farming or fishing, he or she must enclose his or her financial statements.

If an individual's business has a fiscal period ending other than on December 31st, he or she must add to his or her income the estimated income for the period between the end date of the fiscal period and January 1st of the following year. This amount is calculated on Form TP-80.1-V, *Calculation of Business or Professional Income, Adjusted to December 31*, which must be enclosed with the individual's return.

If the individual's business sustained a loss, he or she must enter the amount of the loss preceded by the minus sign on Schedule L. If the loss is greater than the individual's total income, he or she can carry the loss forward twenty years or carry it back three years to reduce his or her future or past income. If the individual wishes to carry back a loss, he or she must complete Form TP-1012.A-V, *Carry-Back of a Loss*, and file it separately from his or her return.

QTA 80–230.0.0.6, Forms: LM-53-V, RL-15, RL-16, RL-21, RL-27, RL-29, TP-80-V, TP-80.1-V, TP-1012.A-V, TP-1079.6-V, TP-1086.R.23.12-V, Guide IN-120-V, Guide IN-155-V, IMP. 80-8/R1, IMP. 128-13, IMP. 135.2-1/R1

¶13200 — Calculating Net Income (Form TP-1: Lines 201 to 275)

This section discusses the deductions that may be claimed from total income to calculate the net income of an individual for Québec purposes on Line 275. Net income is used to calculate an individual's taxable income, and is used in the calculation of various non-refundable tax credits.

¶13205 — Deduction for Workers (Form TP-1: Line 201)

Individuals can claim a deduction equal to 6% of their eligible work income, up to the maximum deduction of $1,150 for the 2018 tax year.

For these purposes, eligible work income includes employment income, net income earned from a business the individual carried on alone or as a partner actively engaged in the business, the net amount of research grants, Wage Earner Protection Program payments, and amounts received under a work-incentive project.

For these purposes, eligible work income does not include employment income consisting solely of taxable benefits received from previous employment, employment income received as an elected member of a municipal council, employment income received as a member of the council or executive committee of a metropolitan community or a regional country municipality, a municipal utilities commission or corporation, or a school board, or employment income received as a member of the National Assembly, House of Commons, Senate of Canada, or a legislative assembly of another province.

QTA 358.03, work chart 201, www.revenuquebec.ca/en/citoyen/declaration/produire/comment/aideligne/revenu-net/ligne201.aspx

¶13210 — Registered Pension Plan Deduction (Form TP-1: Line 205)

The deduction an individual can claim for contributions to a Registered Pension Plan (RPP) cannot be greater than the amount deducted for such contributions on Line 207 of the individual's federal income tax return. Amounts entered on Line 207 of an individual's federal income tax return with respect to amounts transferred to an RPP should be entered on Line 250 and not Line 205 of the individual's Québec income tax return.

If the individual did not make contributions to an RPP before 1990 and did not make contributions under a retirement compensation arrangement, the individual should enter the amount shown in Box D of his or her RL-1 slip on Line 205.

QTA 70, 965.0.3, Form RL-1, IMP. 71-3/R1, IMP. 317-2

¶13215 — Employment Expenses and Deductions (Form TP-1: Line 207)

If an individual's employment entitles him or her to a deduction, the amount of the deduction must be entered on Line 207 and the item number of the deduction must be entered in Box 206. If the individual is entitled to more than one deduction, the number "22" should be entered in Box 206.

For detailed information on the rules for deducting various employment expenses for Québec purposes, see Guide IN-118-V, *Employment Expenses*. Also see the following Québec Interpretation Bulletins, as applicable:

- IMP. 62-1/R2, *Employee "Required" to Carry on all or Part of His Duties Away From His Employer's Place of Business or in Different Places: Terminology*

- IMP. 62-2/R2, *Office Expenses, Salary to an Assistant or Substitute and Other Supplies — Employee Who Receives Commissions*

- IMP. 62-3/R2, *General Conditions for Deduction of the Expenses of an Employee Who Receives Commissions*

- IMP. 62-4/R2, *Expenses of an Employee Who Receives Commissions*

- IMP. 63-1/R1, *Reasonable Allowance for Travelling Expenses or Motor Vehicle Expenses*

- IMP. 63.1-1/R2, *The Lease Charges Paid for a Motor Vehicle*

- IMP. 63.1-2/R1, *Motor Vehicle Travel Expenses*

- IMP. 64-1/R3, *Capital Cost for a Motor Vehicle*

- IMP. 64-2/R2, *Interest Paid in Respect of a Motor Vehicle*

- IMP. 65-1/R3, *Meal Expenses*

- IMP. 77-1/R3, *Judicial or Extrajudicial Expenses Paid by an Individual*

- IMP. 78-1/R3, *Deduction for Office Rent, Supplies, and Salary of an Assistant or Substitute*

- IMP. 78-2/R1, *Deduction for Supplies Paid by a Forestry Worker*

¶13220 — *RRSP or PRPP/VRSP Deduction (Form TP-1: Line 214)*

An individual may deduct an amount for contributions made to his or her RRSP, to a spousal RRSP or to a pooled registered pension plan (PRPP), including a voluntary retirement savings plan (VRSP), that corresponds to the RRSP or PRPP deduction allowed for such contributions on Line 208 of the individual's federal income tax return for the tax year. If the amount on Line 208 of the individual's federal income tax return includes amounts transferred to an RRSP, such amounts should be entered on Line 250 of the individual's Québec income tax return and not on Line 214.

QTA 339(b), 905.1–933, 935.1–935.8.1, 935.12–935.19, 965.0.19–965.0.37, Form TP-935.3-V

¶13225 — Support Payments (Form TP-1: Line 225)

An individual may be able to deduct support payments made in the tax year as an allowance payable periodically further to a written agreement or judgment, where the payments were made to the individual's spouse or former spouse, the mother or father of the individual's child, or a third party for the benefit of the child.

Child support paid under a written agreement or judgment after April 30, 1997 can generally not be deducted by the payer and is not included in the income of the recipient.

The total amount of deductible support payments must be entered on Line 225 of the individual's Québec income tax return. If the individual paid amounts as support that are non-deductible, the individual should complete work chart 225.

If an individual paid support payment arrears of $300 or more that entitle him or her to a deduction, the amount should be entered on lines 225 and on Line 276 of the individual's Québec income tax return and the individual must check Box 404. The individual may complete Form TP-766.2-V, *Averaging of a Retroactive Payment, Support-Payment Arrears or a Repayment of Support*.

QTA 336.0.2–336.4, Form TP-766.2-V, Guide IN-128-V, IMP. 336.0.2-1, IMP. 336.0.5-1/R1, work chart 225

¶13230 — Moving Expenses (Form TP-1: Line 228)

An individual can deduct moving expenses paid in the tax year if he or she meets both of the following conditions:

- the individual moved in order to take up employment duties, carry on a business, practice a profession, or attend an educational institution at which the individual was enrolled full time in a post-secondary program; and

- the individual's new residence is at least 40 kilometres closer to the individual's new place of study or work.

Generally, only expenses for moving from one location to another in Canada are deductible.

The amount of the deduction is limited to the net income the individual earned in the tax year at his or her new place of work. If the individual is a student, the amount of the deduction is limited to the net income of the research grants he or she received. Unused amounts can be carried forward to future years.

If an individual moved and paid moving expenses in a year following the year of the move, he or she can deduct the expenses in the year of payment.

To claim, individuals must enclose Form TP-348-V, *Moving Expenses*, with their Québec income tax return.

QTA 348–350, Form TP-348-V, IMP. 348-1

¶13235 — Carrying Charges and Interest Expenses (Form TP-1: Line 231)

An individual can deduct the following carrying charges:

- investment management or administration fees, except fees paid with respect to a registered retirement savings plan (RRSP), registered retirement income fund (RRIF), or a tax-free savings account (TFSA);

- amounts paid for the safekeeping of an individual's shares and securities;

- fees, other than commissions, paid to investment counsellors, except fees paid with respect to an RRSP, RRIF, or TFSA; and

- the amount indicated in Box L-4 of the individual's RL-1 slip.

An individual can deduct the interest paid on loans he or she took out to earn investment income if the loans were used to purchase, among other investments, bonds, an interest in a partnership of which the individual was a specified member, or mutual fund units, shares, or preferred shares, up until the time such investments were transferred to an RRSP or TFSA. Interest paid after the sale of investments on loans taken out to purchase the investments may also be deductible in certain circumstances.

An individual can deduct the interest paid on a loan taken out on an insurance policy in order to purchase an investment to earn income. The individual must have his or her insurer complete Form TP-163.1-V, *Interest Paid on a Loan Taken Out on a Life Insurance Policy*, and enclose it with his or her Québec income tax return.

An individual cannot deduct the following expenses:

- the rental charge for a safety deposit box;

- commissions paid to a broker on the purchase or sale of shares or mutual fund units;

- interest paid on loans taken out to make contributions to a registered pension plan (RPP), deferred profit-sharing plan, RRSP, registered education savings plan (RESP), registered disability savings plan (RDSP), or TFSA;

- interest paid on loans taken out in order to purchase Capital régional et coopératif Desjardins shares, shares in the Fonds de solidarité des travailleurs du Québec, or shares in Fondaction, le Fonds de développement de la Confédération des syndicats nationaux pour la cooperation et l'emploi;

- interest paid on loans taken out in order to purchase property transferred to an RPP, RRSP, RDSP, or TFSA as of the date of the transfer;

- interest paid on loans taken out in order to repay amounts withdrawn from an RRSP under the Home Buyers' Plan or the Lifelong Learning Plan;

- management and administration fees, as well as fees paid to investment counsellors, if the fees were paid with respect to an RRSP, RRIF, or TFSA;

- administration fees incurred for the purchase of Capital régional et coopératif Desjardins shares, shares in the Fonds de solidarité des travailleurs du Québec, or shares in Fondaction, le Fonds de développement de la Confédération des syndicats nationaux pour la cooperation et l'emploi; or

- the cost of purchasing specialized publications and journals.

QTA 157(d), 160–163.1, Form RL-1, Form TP-163.1-V, IMP. 128-13, IMP. 160-2/R3, IMP. 234-3, IMP. 487.1-1/R3

¶13240 — Business Investment Loss (Form TP-1: Line 234)

An individual can deduct a business investment loss sustained in the tax year on an investment in a Canadian-controlled private corporation. To calculate the amount of the deduction, the individual must complete Form TP-232.1-V, *Business Investment Loss*, and enclose the Form with his or her Québec income tax return. The total amount of the loss must be entered on Line 233, and the amount of the deduction on Line 234. If the amount of the deduction is greater than the individual's income, the excess amount can be carried back three years or carried forward to future tax years. In order to carry a loss back, the individual must complete Form TP-1012.A-V, *Carry-back of a Loss*, and file it separately from his or her return.

QTA 232.1–233, Form RL-15, Form TP-232.1-V, Form TP-1012.A-V, Guide IN-120-V

¶13245 — Deduction for Residents of Designated Remote Areas (Form TP-1: Line 236)

An individual can deduct the deduction for residents of designated remotes areas if he or she lived in a designated remote area for a period of at least six consecutive months starting or ending in the tax year. The deduction includes a housing deduction and travel deduction. The amount of the deduction is calculated on Form TP-350.1-V, *Calculation of the Deduction for Residents of Designated Remote Areas*, which must be included with the individual's Québec income tax return.

QTA 350.1–350.6, Form RL-1, Form TP-350.1-V, Guide TP-350.1.G-V, IMP. 350.1-1, IMP. 350.1-2

¶13250 — Deduction for Exploration and Development Expenses (Form TP-1: Line 241)

Individuals can deduct Canadian or foreign exploration or development expenses and Canadian oil and gas property expenses. An individual cannot deduct the following amounts on Line 241:

- the deduction for Québec exploration expenses that entitles the individual to an additional deduction (this amount must be entered on Line 250);

- the additional deduction for Québec resources (this amount must be entered on Line 287); or

- the deduction for share and security issues expenses related to Québec resources (this amount must be entered on Line 297).

Individuals claiming a deduction for exploration or development expenses must complete Schedule N.

QTA 359.1.1, 359.2, 359.2.1, 359.3, 359.4, 359.5, Form RL-11, Form RL-15

¶13255 — Deduction for Amounts Contributed to the QPP and the QPIP on Income from Self-Employment (Form TP-1: Line 248)

An individual can deduct an amount for the QPP contribution if he or she earned income from self-employment and the total amounts entered on Line 96 (Canada Pension Plan contribution) and Line 98 (QPP) are less than a prescribed amount. The individual must complete Form LE-35-V, *QPP Contribution on Income from Self-Employment*, to determine the amount of the deduction. Individuals cannot claim this deduction if all of the self-employment income they earned from a business entitled them to a deduction on Line 297 (miscellaneous deductions) or for the QPP contribution an individual responsible for a family-type resource or intermediate resource is required to make on the pensionable earnings entered on Line 40 of Schedule L.

An individual can deduct an amount for the QPIP premium if he or she earned income from self-employment and the amount on Line 97 (QPIP premium) is less than a prescribed amount. The individual must complete Schedule R to determine the amount of the deduction. Individuals cannot claim this deduction if all of the self-employment income they earned from a business entitled them to a deduction on Line 297 (miscellaneous deductions) or 293 (deduction for an Indian) or for the QPP contribution an individual responsible for a family-type resource or intermediate resource is required to make on the pensionable earnings entered on Line 40 of Schedule L.

QTA 339(i.1), Form RL-29, Form LE-35-V

¶13260 — Other Deductions (Form TP-1: Line 250)

An individual claiming a deduction on Line 250 must enter the amount of the deduction on Line 250 and the item number of the deduction in Box 249. If the individual is claiming more than one deduction, enter the number "77" in Box 249. The following other deductions can be claimed on Line 250:

- 03 Deduction for a social benefits repayment

- 04 Deduction for amounts transferred to an RPP, an RRSP, a RRIF, a PRPP/VRSP or an annuity

- 05 Deduction for an amount already included in income (RRSP or RRIF)

- 06 Deduction for a refund of unused RRSP or PRPP/VRSP contributions

- 07 Disability supports deduction

- 08 Deduction for legal fees

- 09 Deduction for Québec exploration expenses that give entitlement to an additional deduction

- 11 Deduction for the purchase of an income-averaging annuity for artists

- 12 Deduction for a repayment of support

- 14 Deduction for a loss in the value of investments in an RRSP, a RRIF or a PRPP/VRSP

- 15 Deduction for the repayment of a QESI amount

- 16 Deduction for amounts transferred to a registered disability savings plan (RDSP)

- 17 Other deductions

For details on these other deductions, see the instructions for Line 250 in the Québec Income Tax Return Guide.

¶13265 — *Carry-Over of the Adjustment of Investment Expenses (Form TP-1: Line 252)*

If, for the tax year, the individual's investment income (Line 36 of Schedule N) is greater than his or her investment expenses (lines 18 and 54 of Schedule N), the individual can reduce his or her investment income by carrying over the unused portion of the adjustment of investment expenses. The unused portion of the individual's adjustment of investment expenses is equal to the total of the amounts indicated since 2004 on lines 40 and 64 of Schedule N, minus the amount already used to reduce the individual's investment income in previous years. The amount deducted on Line 252 cannot be greater than the amount by which the individual's investment income exceeds his or her investment expenses.

¶13270 — *Adjustment of Investment Expenses (Form TP-1: Line 260)*

An individual can deduct an amount for investment expenses that does not exceed the individual's investment income.

An individual must complete Schedule N to calculate the amount to be entered on Line 260 of his or her Québec income tax return if he or she is claiming one or more of the following deductions:

- a deduction for a loss from a partnership of which the individual was a specified member (Line 29 of Schedule L or Line 136 of the return)

- a deduction for carrying charges and interest expenses (Line 231 of the return);

- a deduction for exploration or development expenses (Line 241 of the return);

- a deduction for the following expenses incurred to earn property income:

  - an amount the individual reimbursed for interest received;

  - a deduction for certain films (Line 250 of the return);

  - a deduction for foreign income tax on income from property other than rental property (Line 250 of the return);

  - life insurance premiums deducted with respect to property income that is not rental income; and

  - a deduction for the repayment of an advance on a life insurance policy (Line 250 of the return).

The amount of bad debt deducted in calculating an individual's property income is not taken into account in calculating the adjustment of investment expenses.

Form RL-11, Form RL-15, Form TP-1012.B-V

¶13300 — Calculating Taxable Income (Form TP-1: Lines 276–299)

This section discusses the deductions that may be claimed from net income to calculate taxable income for Québec purposes on Line 299. Taxable income is the amount used to calculate an individual's Québec taxes payable.

¶13305 — Adjustment of Deductions (Form TP-1: Line 276)

An individual must enter the amount of adjustments he or she is required to make with regards to deductions on Line 276 and the item number corresponding with the type of adjustment in Box 277. If the individual is making more than one type of adjustment, he or she must enter the number "28" in Box 277. The following deductions can be claimed on Line 276:

- 01 Repayment of social assistance payments or similar financial assistance

- 02 Repayment of net federal supplements or income replacement indemnities

- 03 Repayment of a scholarship, bursary or similar financial assistance

- 04 Repayment of support

- 05 Support-payment arrears

- 06 Repayment of an amount included in your income for a previous year and deducted from your taxable income for that year

- 07 Recovery of deductions for patronage dividends received from a cooperative

- 09 Adjustment of other investment expenses

For details on these adjustments, see the instructions for Line 276 in the Québec Income Tax Return Guide.

QTA 694.0.1-694.0.2, Form RL-5, Form TP-726.30-V, Form TP-766.2-V, Form TP-1012.B-V, Guide IN-155-V

¶13310 — UCCB and Income from a Registered Disability Savings Plan (Form TP-1: Line 278)

If an individual received the Universal Child Care Benefit, he or she must enter the amount on his or her RC62 slip on Line 278. If the individual had a spouse on the last day of the tax year, the spouse with the lower net income must report the total amount of the Universal Child Care Benefit received by the couple.

If the individual received amounts from a registered disability savings plan, he or she must enter the amount in Box O of his or her RL-1 slip on Line 278.

QTA 694.0.0.1, 694.0.0.3, Form RL-1, Form RC62

¶13315 — Deduction for Strategic Investments (Form TP-1: Line 287)

If an individual is entitled to a deduction for strategic investments, he or she must enter the amount of the deduction on Line 287 and enter the item number that corresponds to the deduction on Line 287. If the individual is entitled to more than one deduction, he or she must enter the number "80" in Box 286.

QTA 726.4, 726.4.0.1, 726.4.9–726.4.17, 726.4.17.1–726.4.17.9, 965.37-965.38, 965.126, QTR 726.4.10R1–726.4.12R2, QTR 726.4.17.4R1, Form RL-11, Form RL-15, Form TP-965.39.4-V, Form TP-965.55-V

¶13316 — *Deduction for the Cooperative Investment Plan (Form TP-1: Line 287, Item 3)*

An individual can claim this deduction if he or she was resident in Québec on the last day of the tax year and purchased qualifying securities from a cooperative or a federation of cooperatives authorized to issue securities. The individual can also claim the unused portion of his or her deductions for the previous five years. The individual can carry forward the unused portion of his or her deduction for the year for five years. To calculate the amount of the deduction, the individual must complete Form TP-965.39.4-V, *Calculation of the CIP Deduction.*

¶13317 — *Additional Deduction for Québec Resources (Form TP-1: Line 287, Item 4)*

An individual entitled to this deduction can calculate the amount of the deduction by following the instructions on his or her RL-11 slip.

¶13320 — Non-Capital Losses from Other Years (Form T-1: Line 289)

An individual can deduct the following losses, provided that he or she did not deduct them in a previous year:

- the non-capital losses the individual sustained after 2005;
- the farm losses and restricted farm losses the individual sustained after 2005;
- the limited partnership losses the individual sustained after 1985.

An individual claiming a deduction for a limited partnership loss must also complete Line 276 and Schedule N.

QTA 727–728.0.4, 728.1-728.2, 731–733, 733.0.0.1, IMP. 727-1/R1, IMP. 1010-4

¶13325 — Net Capital Losses from Other Years (Form TP-1: Line 290)

If an individual is reporting a taxable capital gain on Line 139, he or she can deduct net capital losses sustained in previous years on the disposition of property other than personal-use or precious property, provided that he or she did not deduct the losses in a previous year. To claim the deduction, an individual must complete Form TP-729-V, *Carry-Forward of Net Capital Losses,* and enclose it with his or her Québec income tax return. The individual must also complete Line 276 and Schedule N.

QTA 729–730.2, Form TP-729-V, Guide IN-120-V, IMP. 1010-4

¶13330 — Capital Gains Deduction (Form TP-1: Line 292)

An individual reporting a taxable capital gain on Line 139 may be entitled to a capital gains deduction if he or she meets both of the following conditions:

- the individual realized the gain on the disposition of qualified farm property, qualified fishing property, qualified small business corporation shares, or certain resource property (complete Form TP-726.20.2-V, *Capital Gains Deduction on Resource Property*); and

- the individual was resident in Canada throughout the tax year, or was resident in Canada at some time during the tax year and was resident in Canada throughout the previous tax year or expects to be resident in Canada throughout the next tax year.

To calculate the deduction, the individual must complete Form TP-726.7-V, *Capital Gains Deduction on Qualified Property*.

QTA 726.6–726.20, 726.20.1–726.20.4, QTR 726.14R1-726.15R1, Form TP-726.6-V, Form TP-726.7-V, Form TP-726.20.2-V, Guide IN-120-V, IMP. 1-3/R1, IMP. 726.20.1-1

¶13335 — Deduction for an Indian (Form TP-1: Line 293)

If an individual is an Indian within the meaning of the *Indian Act* such that he or she is registered or is entitled to be registered as an Indian with Aboriginal Affairs and Northern Development Canada, he or she can claim a deduction for his or her income situated on a reserve or premises. Such income includes, for example, employment income situated on a reserve or premises, minus any related deductions, and net business income.

Amounts reported on Line 148, or the amount of a scholarship or bursary on Line 154, should be claimed on Line 295, and not on Line 293.

QTA 725(e)-725.0.2, Form RL-1, IMP. 725-1/R3, IMP. 725-2/R1, IMP. 725-3/R1, IMP. 725-4/R1, IMP. 725-5/R1

¶13340 — Deductions for Certain Income (Form TP-1: Line 295)

If an individual received workers' compensation, compensation for loss of financial support, or indemnities further to a precautionary cessation of work, a traffic accident, an act of good citizenship, or because the individual was the victim of a crime, the individual can enter the amount of the benefit on Line 295 for a deduction, and may be required to enter an adjustment on Line 358.

An individual can also enter on Line 295 the amount of net federal supplements and other income replacement indemnities he or she reported on Line 148 for a deduction. If an individual entered an amount as a social benefits repayment on Line 250 and received net federal supplements, he or she must enter the amount of net federal supplements on Line 148 minus the amount of the repayment of net federal supplements shown on Line 235 of his or her federal income tax return on Line 295.

If an individual received a scholarship, bursary, or similar financial assistance that he or she reported on Line 154, he or she can enter the amount on Line 295 for a deduction. Amounts received under a registered education savings plan do not entitle an individual to this deduction. If the individual entered an amount on Line 250 as a repayment of a scholarship, bursary or similar financial assistance, his or her deduction is equal to the amount included on Line 154 minus the amount of the repayment deducted on Line 250.

If an individual received assistance for the payment of tuition fees that he or she was required to include in his or her income and that do not entitle him or her to an amount for tuition fees on Line 384, the individual can enter the amount on Line 295 for a deduction.

If the individual is under the age of 18 and is required to pay a special tax on Line 443 for the tax year for income derived from income splitting, he or she can claim a deduction for the income subject to the special tax on Line 295.

QTA 725(c)–(c.2), 737.29, Form RL-5

¶13345 — Miscellaneous Deductions (Form TP-1: Line 297)

An individual claiming a miscellaneous deduction must enter the amount of the deduction on Line 297 and the item number corresponding to the deduction in Box 296. If the individual is claiming more than one deduction, he or she must enter the number "88" in Box 296.

The miscellaneous deductions and corresponding item numbers are as follows:

- Item 1: Deduction for a home-relocation loan
- Item 2: Security option deduction
- Item 3: Deduction for foreign researchers
- Item 4: Deduction for foreign experts
- Item 5: Deduction for foreign researchers on a post-doctoral internship
- Item 6: Deduction for foreign specialists
- Item 7: Deduction for foreign producers or foreign individuals holding a key position in a foreign production filmed in Québec
- Item 8: Deduction for employment income earned on a vessel
- Item 9: Deduction for employees of an international financial centre
- Item 12: Deduction for income exempt under a tax treaty
- Item 13: Deduction for share and security issue expenses related to Québec resources
- Item 14: Deduction for employees of certain international organizations
- Item 15: Deduction for employment income earned outside of Canada (Box A of slip RL-17)
- Item 16: Deduction for copyright income
- Item 17: Deduction for shares received in exchange for mining property
- Item 19: Deduction for foreign professors
- Item 20: Deduction for foreign farm workers
- Item 22: Deduction for patronage dividends received from a cooperative
- Item 23: Canadian Forces personnel and police deduction
- Item 24: Deduction for a repayment of the Universal Child Care Benefit
- Item 25: Deduction for a repayment of income from a registered disability savings plan.

For details on these miscellaneous deductions, see the instructions for Line 297 in the Québec Income Tax Return Guide.

¶13400 — Non-Refundable Tax Credits (Form TP-1: Lines 350–399)

> The 2018 Québec budget introduced a new non-refundable First-Time Home Buyers Tax Credit, available as of the 2018 taxation year for the purchase of a housing unit after December 31, 2017. The credit is available to an individual (other than a trust) who is resident in Québec at the end of the taxation year and who acquired a qualifying home located in Québec in the year. The maximum value of the tax credit is $750, calculated as 15% of a maximum claim amount of $5,000. To qualify, the individual or his or her spouse has to intend to inhabit the home as a principal place of residence not later than one year after the time of acquisition and neither the individual nor his or her spouse can have owned and lived in another home in the calendar year of the new home purchase or in any of the four preceding calendar years.

Beginning in 2017, Québec personal tax credit rates were reduced to 15% (from 16%). The rate was previously reduced to 16% (from 20%) by the March 2017 budget. The following tax credits will still use the 20% rate: eligible medical expenses, student loan interest, the first $200 of gifts/donations, and eligible expenses to obtain medical care not provided in the region where an individual lives.

Québec's non-refundable tax credit amounts and related thresholds are indexed annually for inflation using the Québec provincial inflation rate.

Discussed below are the various non-refundable tax credits that an individual can claim for Québec tax purposes.

¶13405 — Basic Personal Amount (Form TP-1: Line 350)

Québec's basic personal amount for the 2018 tax year is $15,012.

QTA 752.0.0.1, Québec Guide TP-1.G, Form TP-1.D-V

¶13410 — Age Amount, Amount for a Person Living Alone, and Amount for Retirement Income (Form TP-1: Line 361)

The age amount, amount for a person living alone, and amount for retirement income are added together and reduced by 18.75% of net family income. Net family income is the total income of both spouses or common-law partners minus $34,030 (for the 2018 tax year).

¶13411 — *Age Amount*

Individuals who are 65 years of age or older on the last day of the taxation year are eligible for the age amount. If an individual had a spouse on the last day of the tax year who was 65 years of age or older on the last day of the tax year, the spouse will also be entitled to the age amount. If one spouse does not claim the full age amount, the unused portion may be transferred to the other spouse.

The age amount can be claimed for an individual who died during the tax year if he or she was 65 years of age or older at the time of death.

The age amount for the 2018 tax year is $3,158. The amount of the credit is reduced by 18.75% of the taxpayer's income in excess of $34,030.

To claim the tax credit, individuals must complete Parts A and B of Schedule B.

QTA 750.2-750.3, 752.0.7.1–752.0.7.6, Québec Guide TP-1.G, Form TP-1.D.B-V (Schedule B, Parts A & B)

¶13412 — *Amount for a Person Living Alone*

An individual may claim a credit for a person living alone if, throughout the tax year, they either lived alone or with a child or children under the age of 18, or over the age of 18 and were a full-time student at a vocational school, college, or university. For 2018 and later taxation years, this credit can also be claimed by a grandparent or great-grandparent who ordinarily lives alone, but who lived during the year with a grandchild or great-grandchild who is an eligible student.

The basic amount of the tax credit is $1,721 for the 2018 tax year. The amount of the credit is reduced by 18.75% of the taxpayer's income in excess of $34,030.

Proof is required that the individual maintained a self-contained domestic establishment, or by completing declaration Form TP-752.0.7.4-V. A self-contained domestic establishment is described as a house; condominium; apartment; or a dwelling or permanent fixture where one ordinarily eats, sleeps, and is equipped with a bathroom and kitchen.

An individual entitled to the tax credit who lived with an eligible student at some time during the tax year and who was not entitled to a child assistance payment from the Retraite Québec for the month of December can claim an additional single-parent amount. An eligible student is a child 18 years of age or older who can transfer to the individual an amount for a child 18 or over enrolled in post-secondary studies, or could have transferred such an amount had he or she not earned income.

The single-parent family supplement is $2,124 for the 2018 tax year. This amount is reduced pro rata by the number of months the individual was entitled to a child assistance payment from the Retraite du Québec during the tax year.

To claim the tax credit, individuals must complete parts A and B of Schedule B.

QTA 750.2-750.3, 752.0.7.1–752.0.7.6, Québec Guide TP-1.G, Form TP-1.D.B-V (Schedule B, Part A & B), Form TP-752.0.7.4-V

¶13413 — *Amount for Retirement Income*

An individual can claim the non-refundable credit for retirement income if the individual or his or her spouse had qualifying pension income in the year that was entered on Line 122 or Line 123 of either spouse's tax return. Qualifying pension income includes life annuity payments from a pension plan, annuity payments from an RRSP or DPSP, and RRIF payments. Amounts that do not qualify as pension for purposes of this credit include OAS payments and QPP/CPP payments. This credit may be split between spouses, if applicable.

The maximum amount of the tax credit is $2,805 for the 2018 tax year. The amount of the credit is reduced by 18.75% of the taxpayer's income in excess of $34,030.

To claim the tax credit, individuals must complete Parts A and B of Schedule B.

QTA 750.2-750.3; 752.07.1–752.0.10, Québec Guide TP-1.G, Form TP-1.D.B-V (Schedule B, Part A & B)

¶13415 — **Amount for Dependants and Amount Transferred by a Child 18 or over Enrolled in Post-Secondary Studies (Form TP-1: Line 367)**

¶13416 — *Child Under 18 Years of Age Enrolled in Post-Secondary Studies*

An individual can claim this amount for a child who was under the age of 18 on the last day of the tax year if, in the tax year, the child was the individual's dependant and was a full-time student pursuing vocational training at the secondary level or post-secondary studies. The amount is also available for infirm dependants who were engaged in vocational training at the secondary level or post-secondary studies part-time.

The amount cannot be claimed if the child had a spouse on the last day of the tax year and the spouse is claiming an amount for credits transferred between spouses on Line 431 of his or her income tax return.

The amount of the tax credit that can be claimed is shown on the RL-8 slip issued by the relevant educational institution. The maximum credit amount that can be claimed in a tax year is $2,884 (for the 2018 tax year) for up to two completed terms that began in the tax year for each child. This credit amount is per term, and up to two terms can be claimed per year. The amount of the credit is reduced by 80% of the child's net income for the tax year, excluding scholarships, bursaries, fellowships, prizes for achievement, and the deduction for residents of designated remote areas.

The tax credit may be split between two eligible individuals.

To claim the tax credit, individuals must complete Part A of Schedule A.

QTA 752.0.1(d)–752.0.3, 752.0.4, 752.0.18.10, Québec Guide TP-1.G, Form TP-1.D.A-V (Schedule A)

¶13417 — *Amount Transferred by a Child 18 or Over Enrolled in Post-Secondary Studies*

A child 18 years of age or older can transfer to his or her parent or parents an amount representing the recognized parental contribution to the child's education if the child was a full-time student enrolled in vocational training at the secondary level or in post-secondary studies and completed at least one term that he or she began in the tax year. The maximum amount that a child may transfer in the 2018 tax year is $10,306. If the child turned 18 during the year, the amount that can be transferred is reduced proportionately by the number of months in the year that the child was under 18.

To claim this credit, the individual must be either the father or mother of the child; the spouse of the child's father or mother; the father or mother of the child's spouse; or have legal custody and fully supported the child immediately before his or her 19th birthday. The amount may be split between both of the child's parents. An individual who claims this amount cannot claim the credit for other dependants 18 years of age or older for the same child. To claim the tax credit, individuals must complete Part B of Schedule A.

To transfer an amount, the child must complete Schedule S and include it with his or her Québec income tax return. The amount may be split between the child's parents.

If a child transfers an amount, he or she will not be able to claim tax credits in respect of the work premium for the year.

QTA 776.41.12–776.41.20, Québec Finance Information Bulletin 2010-8, Québec Guide TP-1.G, Form TP-1.D.S-V (Schedule S)

¶13418 — *Other Dependants*

An individual may claim an amount for other dependants. In order to qualify, a dependant must:

- be 18 years of age or older;
- be related to the individual claiming the amount by blood, marriage or adoption; and
- have ordinarily lived with the claimant during the tax year and was supported by the claimant.

The dependant cannot be:

- the claimant's spouse;
- a child 18 years of age or older and enrolled in post-secondary studies who is transferring an amount; or
- a person whose spouse is deducting an amount on Line 431 of his or her return for credits transferred between spouses.

A dependant may be the individual or his or her spouse's brother, sister, nephew, niece, father, mother, grandfather, grandmother, uncle, aunt or child.

The amount of the tax credit $4,202 per dependant for the 2018 tax year. The amount of the credit is reduced by 80% of the dependant's net income for the tax year excluding scholarships, bursaries, fellowships, prizes for achievement, and the deduction for residents of designated remote areas. If the dependant turned 18 during the tax year, the amount of the credit is reduced pro rata based on the number of months in the tax year preceding the dependant's birthday.

The amount of the tax credit may be split between two eligible individuals.

To claim the tax credit, individuals must complete Part C of Schedule A.

QTA 752.0.1, Québec Guide TP-1.G

¶13420 — Union, Professional or Other Dues (Form TP-1: Line 373)

Individuals may claim a non-refundable tax credit for the amount of union dues or professional fees paid in the tax year that are related to the individual's employment income, as long as none of the individual's income from the employment entitles him or her to a deduction for an Indian or a miscellaneous deduction on Line 293 or 297. These fees are not allowed as a deduction against income as they are for federal tax purposes.

The following dues are deductible for purposes of this credit:

- union dues;
- dues paid to the Commission de la construction du Québec;
- dues paid to the Association professionnelle des chauffeurs de taxi du Québec;
- dues paid to a recognized artists' association or a professional association whose purpose is to maintain a professional status recognized by law;
- compulsory dues paid to a parity committee, advisory committee or similar body;
- the contribution paid to the Office des professions du Québec; and
- annual dues paid to an employee association recognized by the Minister of Revenue. If an individual claimed such dues, he or she cannot claim, for the same employment, the dues paid to a union; to a parity committee, advisory committee or similar body; to the Commission de la construction du Québec; or to the Association professionnelle des chauffeurs de taxi du Québec.

The amount of annual dues claimed by an individual must not include the GST or QST paid on the dues if the individual is entitled to a rebate of the GST and QST.

Individuals may also claim a tax credit for dues paid in the tax year related to employment in the previous tax year, except for professional dues or a contribution to the Office des professions du Québec. However, an individual cannot claim a credit for dues paid in the tax year to an employee association recognized by the Minister of Revenue if the individual claimed a credit in the previous tax year for dues paid in that tax year to any of the following organizations: a parity committee, advisory committee or similar body, a union, the Commission de la construction du Québec, or the Association professionnelle des chauffeurs de taxi du Québec.

Self-employed individuals may also claim a tax credit for annual dues paid in the tax year in certain circumstances. To qualify for the credit, all of the following conditions must apply:

- the dues must be paid to a recognized artists' association or a professional association in order to maintain a recognized professional status, the Office des professions du Québec, or a home childcare providers association recognized under the Act respecting the representation of certain home childcare providers and the negotiation process for their group agreements;
- the dues paid must be related to the operation of the individual's business or the exercise of his or her profession; and
- the individual must not be entitled to a deduction on Line 293 or Line 297 for any of the income he or she earned from his or her business or profession.

The amount of an individual's union or professional dues may be shown in Box F of his or her RL-1 slip (or on his or her T4 slip, if he or she did not receive an RL-1 slip) or in Box 201 of his or her RL-15 slip.

QTA 134.1–134.3; 752.0.18.3–752.0.18.9, Québec Finance Information Bulletin 2000-4, Québec Guide TP-1.G

¶13425 — Amount for a Severe and Prolonged Impairment in Mental or Physical Functions (Form TP-1: Line 376)

This tax credit is available to individuals who had a severe and prolonged impairment in mental or physical functions in the tax year.

An impairment is considered to be severe and prolonged if it has lasted or is expected to last for a consecutive period of at least 12 months, and if one of the following situations applies:

- even with therapy, the appropriate devices, or medication, the individual is always or almost always:

  - unable to perform a basic activity of daily living — seeing, speaking, hearing, walking, eliminating, feeding or dressing him or herself, or functioning in everyday life because he or she does not have the necessary mental functions (basic activities of daily living do not include remunerated work, social activities, recreational activities or housekeeping); or,

  - restricted in more than one basic activity of daily living, if the cumulative effect of the restrictions is equivalent to having a single marked restriction in one basic activity of daily living.

- because of chronic illness, the individual undergoes therapy prescribed by a physician at least twice a week, the therapy is essential to the maintenance of one of the individual's vital functions and requires at least 14 hours per week including time for travel, medical appointments, and post-treatment recovery.

The impairment must be certified by a physician, optometrist, audiologist, speech therapist or speech-language pathologist, occupational therapist, psychologist, or physiotherapist, as applicable.

The tax credit is not available to individuals if:

- remuneration in excess of $10,000 paid to a full-time attendant was used to calculate a medical expenses tax credit on the individual or any other person's income tax return; or

- fees paid for full-time residence in a nursing home were used to calculate a medical expenses tax credit on the individual or any other person's income tax return, unless the nursing home issues a receipt showing the amount relating to remuneration paid to a full-time attendant, the remuneration paid to the full-time attendant does not exceed $10,000, and only the portion of the fees relating to the remuneration paid to the full-time attendant was used to calculate the medical expenses tax credit.

The amount of the tax credit is $3,334 for the 2018 tax year.

The amount of the tax credit is reduced on a pro rata basis if any person received the supplement for handicapped children included in the child assistance payment from the Retraite du Québec for the individual for one or more months during the tax year.

If the individual is claiming the tax credit for the first time and is required to provide certification that his or her impairment is severe and prolonged due to the fact that the individual must undergo therapy meeting the requirements set out above, the individual must file Form TP-752.0.14-V, *Certificate Respecting an Impairment*. Otherwise, an individual may apply for the credit by filing Form T2201 with his or her income tax return. If an individual's health improves after filing a certification of impairment, he or she must advise Revenu Québec.

QTA 752.0.14–752.0.18, Québec Guide TP-1.G, Québec Brochure IN-132-V, Form TP-752.0.14-V, Form T2201

¶13430 — Expenses for Medical Services Not Available in your Area (Form TP-1: Line 378)

This tax credit is available to individuals who paid to obtain medical expenses that were not available in their area in the tax year.

The following expenses are eligible:

- travel and lodging expenses paid in the tax year to obtain, in Québec, medical services that were not available within 200 kilometres (250 kilometres for expenses incurred before July 1, 2016) of the individual's home; and

- moving expenses paid in the tax year to move to within 80 kilometres of a health establishment in Québec, where the health establishment is located 200 kilometres (250 kilometres for expenses incurred before July 1, 2016) or more from the individual's former home.

To be eligible, the expenses must have been paid to obtain medical services for the individual claiming the tax credit, his or her spouse, or a dependant during the year in which the expenses were incurred.

Individuals can claim expenses for which they received or are entitled to receive a reimbursement only if the amount of the reimbursement is included in their income and cannot be deducted elsewhere in their return.

In calculating the amount of expenses for medical services not available in an individual's area, the individual cannot take into account transportation, travel or lodging expenses that the individual or his or her spouse paid to obtain medical or dental services for purely cosmetic reasons. Expenses related to an in vitro fertilization treatment are also excluded in the following circumstances: the expenses are eligible for the tax credit for the treatment of fertility on Line 462; the woman is no longer of child-bearing age; the services are rendered at a centre that is not the holder of a license issued in accordance with the *Regulation respecting clinical activities related to assisted procreation*; or the treatment involves the transfer of more than one embryo (unless in accordance with the decision of a physician, the treatment involves a transfer of two embryos, or a maximum of three embryos in the case of a woman 37 years of age or older).

To claim the tax credit, an individual must file Form TP-752.0.13.1-V *Expenses for Medical Services Not Available in Your Area*, with his or her income tax return.

If the expenses can be included as moving expenses, or if they entitle the individual to the travel deduction (deduction for residents of designated remote areas), it may be to the individual's advantage to claim the expenses on lines 228 or 236, respectively, instead.

QTA 752.0.13.1–752.0.13.5, Québec Guide TP-1.G, Form TP-752.0.13.1-V

¶13435 — Medical Expenses (Form TP-1: Line 381)

The non-refundable medical expense tax credit is available to individuals who paid, or had a spouse who paid, medical expenses for the individual, spouse, or a dependant, during a period of 12 consecutive months ending in the tax year (or, if the individual died in tax year, a period of 24 consecutive months that includes the date of death).

The credit is calculated based on qualifying medical expenses in excess of 3 per cent of family income. Family income is calculated as the total combined income of both spouses or common-law partners.

Expenses do not qualify for the amount for medical expenses if they:

- are being claimed as an amount for medical expenses by another person in his or her income tax return for the tax year;

- have already been used to calculate an amount for medical expenses in an income tax return;

- are included in calculating expenses for medical services not available in the individual's area on Line 378;

- are used to calculate the tax credit for home-support services for seniors on Line 458;

- are used to calculate the independent living tax credit for seniors on Line 462;

- are used to calculate the disability supports deduction on Line 250;

- were paid to obtain services provided for purely cosmetic purposes; or

- were paid to obtain an in vitro fertilization treatment where: the expenses are eligible for the tax credit for the treatment of fertility (Line 462), or the treatment does not comply with the safety standards set by the Québec government.

Following are the most common eligible medical expenses:

- payments made to a doctor, dentist, nurse, nurse practitioner, public hospital or licensed private hospital, for medical, dental or paramedical services;

- payments for drugs prescribed by a physician or a dentist and obtained from a licensed pharmacist;

- the premium paid under the Québec prescription drug insurance plan for the previous or current tax year;

- payments to an insurer or a group insurance plan to cover medical or hospital expenses for the individual, his or her spouse or a dependant, where the payments were made as a premium or contribution, including the value of the benefit related to the employer's contribution;

- payments for eyeglasses (subject to the limit for eyeglass frames of $200 per 12-month consecutive period for each person), contact lenses or other devices for the treatment or correction of a defect of vision, where such items are prescribed by an ophthalmologist or an optometrist;

- reasonable moving expenses of up to $2,000, excluding expenses claimed on Line 228 or Line 378, incurred to enable a person (the individual, his or her spouse, or a dependant) who lacks normal physical development or has a severe and prolonged mobility impairment to move to a dwelling that is more accessible or in which the person is more mobile or functional;

- expenses for the transportation of a person by ambulance to or from a public hospital or licensed private hospital; and

- remuneration paid to an attendant or fees for care in a nursing home.

The amount of any reimbursements an individual or his or her spouse received or is entitled to receive must be deducted from medical expenses unless the reimbursement is included in the individual or his or her spouse's income and not deducted elsewhere.

To claim the tax credit, individuals must complete parts A and C of Schedule B. Medical expenses must be supported by receipts. If an individual is claiming the credit for the first time and must provide certification that the person concerned has a chronic illness requiring the person to undergo therapy essential to one of his or her vital functions at least twice a week and for at least 14 hours a week, the individual must enclose Form TP-752-0.14-V, *Certificate Respecting an Impairment*. Otherwise, the individual may instead enclose Form T2201, *Disability Tax Credit Certificate*. If the person concerned improves, the individual must notify Revenu Québec.

QTA 752.0.11–752.0.13.0.1, 752.0.13.1–752.0.13.5, Québec Guide TP-1.G, Québec Brochure IN-130-V, Form TP-752.0.14.1-V, Form T2201

¶13440 — Interest Paid on Student Loans (Form TP-1: Line 385)

This tax credit is available to individuals if the individual or a related person paid interest after 1997 on a student loan that was granted to the individual under one of the following: the *Act respecting financial assistance for education expenses*, the *Canada Student Loans Act*, the *Canada Student Financial Assistance Act*, the *Apprentice Loans Act*, or a law of a province other than Québec governing the granting of financial assistance to post-secondary students. Interest paid on any other type of loan (such as a line of credit) or on a student loan that was combined with another type of loan is not eligible for this tax credit.

The tax credit is non-refundable; however, unused interest amounts paid after 1997 can be carried forward indefinitely. Unused amounts cannot be transferred to any other person; only the individual to whom the student loan was granted can claim the credit. The interest paid on student loans is converted into a tax credit at the rate of 20 per cent.

To claim the tax credit or carry forward an amount to a future year, individuals must complete Schedule M and enclose it and proof of interest payments with their income tax return.

An individual who claims, for a given taxation year, the non-refundable tax credit with respect to interest paid on a student loan, must include with his or her income tax return for the year, a receipt issued by the financial institution to which the interest was paid.

QTA 752.018.10–752.0.18.14, Québec Guide TP-1.G, Québec Interpretation Bulletin IMP.752.0.18.10-1, Form TP-1.D.M-V (Schedule M)

¶13445 — Tuition or Examination Fees (Form TP-1: Line 398)

This tax credit is available to individuals who paid, or had paid on their behalf, tuition or examination fees for the year, or paid, or had paid on their behalf, tuition or examination fees for the current year, or for previous years, that were not previously used to calculate a tax credit for tuition or examination fees.

The Québec non-refundable tax credit for tuition and examination fees was reduced from a 20% credit rate to an 8% credit rate, effective for fees paid after March 28, 2013.

Tuition and examination fees paid in 2013 qualify for the 20% credit rate if they were: (1) paid before March 28, 2013 to a university, college, or a post-secondary institution for a course of study at the post-secondary level, and they relate to a session that began before March 28, 2013; (2) paid for 2013, to an education institution recognized by the Minister of Revenue for training, for a session in which the individual was enrolled before March 29, 2013; or (2) for examination fees paid for an examination taken prior to May 1, 2013.

All other tuition and examination fees paid in 2013 and later taxation years should be calculated at the 8% non-refundable credit rate. Carryforward amounts from previous years will retain their applicable rates. Fees paid prior to 2013 and those paid in 2013 to which the 20% rate applies will retain their 20% credit rate when applied in future years. To assist taxpayers in calculating unused fee credits, Revenue Québec will indicate on the notice of assessment for the taxation year following 2012, what portion of their unused fees may be converted to a credit at a rate of 20%, and what portion may be converted at a rate of 8%.

An individual cannot claim or transfer tuition or examination fees unless the fees total more than $100 for the year.

Individuals can claim a tax credit for tuition fees paid for the year to:

- an institution at which the individual was enrolled in a post-secondary program;

- an institution recognized by the Minister of Revenue, if the individual was enrolled at the institution for the purpose of acquiring or upgrading skills necessary for a remunerated activity, provided the individual was 16 years of age or older at the end of the year;

- a university outside Canada that the individual attended full time for at least three consecutive weeks, if the course of study leads to a diploma; and

- an institution in the United States at which the individual was enrolled in a post-secondary program, provided the individual lived in Canada near the U.S. border throughout the year and regularly commuted between his or her home and the institution.

The first two types of educational institutions referred to must be located in Canada unless, during the period for which the tuition fees were paid, the individual was temporarily living outside Canada.

The following amounts cannot be claimed as tuition or examination fees:

- the amount from Box A of the individual's RL-8 slip;

- the cost of board and lodging, books, student association fees, travel, parking, or any expenses for which no official receipt was issued;

- tuition or examination fees paid for a year throughout which the individual did not reside in Canada.

The following amounts can be claimed as tuition or education fees:

- application fees (if the individual subsequently enrolls), admission fees and confirmation fees;

- charges for the use of library or laboratory facilities;

- seminar fees;

- co-op fees;

- tuition fees;

- examination fees (including grade review fees);

- charges for issuing a certificate, diploma or degree;

- the cost of books included in the fees paid for a correspondence course or for distance education;

- fees to take the following examinations:

  - an examination that the individual must pass in order to become a member of a professional order named in Schedule I of the *Professional Code*;

  - an examination given by a professional organization in Canada or the United States that the individual must pass in order to obtain a permit to practice issued by a professional order named in Schedule I of the *Professional Code* or a title granted by the Canadian Institute of Actuaries;

  - a preliminary examination that an individual must pass in order to take one of the above examinations; or

  - an examination required to obtain a professional status, a license, or certification to practice a profession or trade.

If an individual's tuition or examination fees were paid or refunded in whole or in part by his or her employer or his or her father's or mother's employer, the individual may claim a credit for the fees the employer paid or refunded, up to the amount included in the individual's income or in his or her father's or mother's income.

An individual may claim a tax credit for tuition or examination fees reimbursed under a vocational training program or a program designed to assist athletes, provided the individual included the amount of the reimbursement in his or her income.

The tax credit is non-refundable; however an individual can transfer the unused portion of his or her tuition or examination fees paid for the year to one of his or her parents or grandparents or one of his or her spouse's parents or grandparents, or carry forward unused tuition or examination fees for 1997 or later years.

To claim, carry forward or transfer tuition or examination fees, an individual must complete Schedule T and enclose it and all receipts for fees paid with his or her income tax return.

QTA 752.018.10–752.0.18.14, Québec Guide TP-1.G, Québec Brochure IN-112-V, Québec Interpretation Bulletin IMP.752.0.18.10-1, Information Bulletin 2005-7, Form TP-1.D.T-V (Schedule T)

¶13450 — Tuition or Examination Fees Transferred by a Child (Form TP-1: Line 398.1)

As discussed above, a student can transfer tuition or examination fees paid for the tax year to his or her parent or grandparent or spouse's parent or grandparent. Only the individual to whom the student transferred tuition or examination fees to can claim the tax credit.

In order for an individual to claim the tax credit, the student must complete Schedule T and designate the individual as the person who can claim the transferred amount. The individual must complete Part D of Schedule A and enter on Line 65 of Schedule A the transferred amount. Schedule T must be enclosed with the student's, and not the individual claiming the credits, Québec income tax return.

QTA 776.41.12–776.41.20, Québec Guide TP-1.G, Form TP-1.D.T-V (Schedule T)

¶13455 — Tax Credit for Volunteer Firefighters and Search and Rescue Volunteers (Form TP-1: Line 390)

An individual who is a volunteer firefighter or a volunteer participating in search and rescue operations, and who performed at least 200 hours of eligible services as a volunteer firefighter or as a volunteer participating in search and rescue operations during the year, can claim a non-refundable credit of $3,000.

Services provided by volunteer firefighters to one or more fire departments offering fire protection on behalf of a government, a municipality or another public authority are eligible services where the services consist of the following: being on call for and responding to firefighting and related emergency calls; attending meetings held by the fire department(s); and participating in required training related to the prevention or suppression of fires. However, the following are not eligible services for the purposes of this credit: replacing permanent firefighters for short periods; being regularly or periodically on duty in a fire station; and periods of on-call duty in the territory. If an individual was also engaged by the same fire department (other than as a volunteer) for the same or similar duties, the individual cannot include any hours related to that department in determining if he or she has met the 200-hour threshold.

Services provided by search and rescue volunteers to one or more eligible organizations are eligible services where the services consist of the following: being on call for and responding to situations requiring search and rescue operations and related emergency calls; attending meetings held by eligible organization(s); and participating in required training related to search and rescue operations. Eligible search and rescue services do not include services provided to an organization if the individual provides search and rescue services to the organization otherwise than as a volunteer.

If an individual provided services as both a volunteer firefighter and as a search and rescue volunteer during the year, add the number of hours of eligible services provided as a volunteer firefighter to the number of hours of eligible services provided as a search and rescue volunteer to determine whether or not the required 200 hours of eligible services have been met.

The individual may have to provide certification from a fire chief or delegated official within the fire department to verify the number of hours of eligible volunteer firefighting services the individual performed for the department, or certification by the team president, or other individual who fulfils a similar role, to verify the number of hours of eligible search and rescue volunteer services the individual performed for the organization.

QTA 752.0.10.0.5, Québec Guide TP-1.G

¶13460 — Tax Credit for Experienced Workers (Form TP-1: Line 391)

The tax credit for experienced workers is available to individuals who live in Quebec, and are 61 years of age or older on the last day of the taxation year, or who are 61 years of age or older on their date of death, if they died in the taxation year. The amount of the credit depends upon the eligible amount of work income. Generally, this is the amount by which the eligible work income of the individual exceeds the base amount of $5,000, to a maximum amount based on age.

The following table shows the maximum eligible work income above the first $5,000 based on a worker's age:

Age of experienced worker	Maximum Eligible Work Income	
	2017	2018 and later
65 and over	$8,000	$11,000
64	$6,000	$9,000
63	$4,000	$7,000

Age of experienced worker	Maximum Eligible Work Income	
	2017	2018 and later
62	n/a	$5,000
61	n/a	$3,000

Eligible work income for the year includes the total of the following amounts:

- salaries, wages and other remuneration, including gratuities, from any office or employment;

- the excess of business income over business losses;

- amounts received under the *Wage Earner Protection Program Act*;

- income supplements received under a project sponsored by a government or government agency in Canada to encourage an individual to obtain or keep employment, or to carry on a business either alone or as a partner actively engaged in the business; and

- grants to carry on research or similar work.

Amounts excluded from eligible work income include:

- income from office or employment which is received or enjoyed in the year because of a previous office or employment;

- amounts deducted in calculating the individual's taxable income for the year (e.g., an individual may not include an amount attributable to the portion of work income deducted in computing taxable income for the year because the income was situated on a reserve, was exempt from income tax under a tax agreement, entitled the individual to a tax holiday for specialized foreign workers, or was related to the exercise of a stock option); and

- as of 2016, income from office or employment where the individual is not dealing at arm's length with the employer or, if the employer is a partnership, with a member of the partnership.

If any portion of the tax credit for experienced workers is unused, it cannot be carried over to another year, and it cannot be transferred to the individual's spouse.

QTA 752.0.10.0.2-752.0.10.0.3

¶13465 — Tax Credit for Recent Graduates Working in Remote Resource Regions (Form TP-1: Line 392)

This tax credit is available to individuals who are recent graduates to whom all of the following conditions apply:

- the individual was resident in a remote resource region of Québec on the last day of the tax year;

- the individual ordinarily worked in a remote resource region for a business carried on in the region;

- the individual's duties were related to the field of specialization in which the individual completed training leading to a recognized diploma; and

- one of the following situations applies to the individual:

  - the individual's employment began in the 24 months following the date on which training leading to a recognized diploma was successfully completed, or, where the recognized diploma was a master's or doctoral degree requiring the individual to write an essay, dissertation or thesis, the date on which the diploma was obtained; or

  - the individual was entitled to the tax credit for a previous tax year and was resident in a remote resource region of Québec throughout the period beginning at the end of that year, and ending on the last day of the tax year.

The tax credit cannot be claimed for self-employment income.

Individuals who were resident in Québec in the tax year and received salary or wages earned in the previous tax year that would have entitled them to the tax credit, had they been received in the previous tax year, may claim the tax credit. The amount of the tax credit is equal to 40% of eligible salary or wages, up to the maximum annual credit amount of $3,000. The maximum lifetime credit amount is $10,000 for individuals in the first situation discussed above, if employment began after March 20, 2012 and the diploma received was for a college or university education. In all other cases, the maximum lifetime credit amount is $8,000.

To claim the tax credit, individuals must complete Form TP-776.1.ND-V, *Tax Credit for Recent Graduates Working in Remote Resource Regions*.

QTA 776.1.5.0.16–776.1.5.0.19, Québec Guide TP-1.G, Form TP-776.1.ND-V

¶13470 — Donations and Gifts (Form TP-1: Lines 393, 395)

Québec resident individuals can claim a non-refundable tax credit for qualifying charitable donations, gifts of cultural property, ecological gifts, and gifts of musical instruments. Generally, an individual can claim a tax credit for donations made in the year for an amount up to 100% (75% for taxation years before 2016) of his or her net income for the year, unless otherwise specified. The donation tax credit is calculated at a rate of 20% of donations up to and including $200, and 24% of donations exceeding $200 (25.75% to the extent that the individual has income that is subject to the 25.75% personal income tax rate). The tax credit is non-refundable; however, unused donations can be carried forward for up to five years. Charitable donations made by both spouses/partners may be totalled and claimed by either person.

Qualifying charitable donations include monetary donations and gifts of property made to the following:

- a registered charity;
- the Government of Canada or a provincial government;
- a Canadian municipality or a municipal or public body performing the function of government in Canada;
- a registered Canadian or Québec amateur athletic association;
- the United Nations or one of its agencies;
- a prescribed foreign university;
- a recognized political education organization;
- the Organisation internationale de la Francophonie or any of its subsidiaries;
- a registered museum;
- a registered cultural or communications organization; or
- a religious order, if the individual making the donation is a member of the religious order and has taken a vow of perpetual poverty.

¶13471 — *Works of Art*

Individuals who donate a work of art to a Québec museum are entitled to a donation tax credit for the fair market value of the gift, multiplied by 125%. Eligible works of art include prints, etchings, drawings, paintings, sculptures, or work of a similar nature, tapestries, hand-woven carpets or appliqués, lithographs, rare folios, manuscripts and books, stamps, or coins.

¶13472 — *Cultural Property & Property with Heritage Value*

The donation tax credit is available to individuals who donate cultural property to a designated public authority or a prescribed institution, as well as to individuals who donate property with heritage value to an accredited museum or certified archival centre.

Form TPF-712.0.1-V, *Certificate of Disposition of Cultural Property*, must be filed with the individual's tax return.

¶13473 — *Ecological Gifts*

The donation tax credit is also available to individuals who make ecological gifts. Ecological gifts are defined as "gifts of land with ecological value or of servitudes encumbering land with ecological value". To be eligible for the donation tax credit, the land must be certified by the Minister of Environment and Wildlife.

¶13474 — *Musical Instruments*

Individuals can claim a gift of a musical instrument to a recognized educational institution in the calculation of the donation tax credit. In order to be considered a recognized educational institution, the institution must be located in Québec and fall into one of the following categories: an elementary or secondary school contemplated by the *Education Act* or by the *Education Act* for Cree, Inuit and Naskapi Native Persons; a college governed by the *General and Vocational Colleges Act*; a private educational institution accredited for purposes of subsidies under the Act respecting private education; a university-level educational institution within the meaning of the Act respecting educational institutions at the university level; or an institution providing instruction in music that is part of the network of the Conservatoire de musique et d'art dramatique du Québec.

QTA 752.0.10.1–752.0.10.3; 752.0.10.5.1–752.0.10.6; 231.2; 725.2.3, Québec Guide TP-1.G, Québec Finance Information Bulletin 2013-6, canada.ca/en/revenue-agency/services/charities-giving/charities.html

¶13500 — Income Tax and Contributions (Form TP-1: Lines 401–450)

¶13505 — Income Tax on Taxable Income (Form TP-1: Line 401)

An individual must complete workchart 401 to calculate his or her income tax payable. Québec's tax rates for the 2017 and 2018 tax years are as follows:

2018 Taxable Income	2018 Tax Rates	2017 Taxable Income	2017 Tax Rates
first $43,055	15.00%	first $42,705	15.00%
over $43,055 up to $86,105	20.00%	over $42,705 up to $85,405	20.00%
over $86,105 up to $104,765	24.00%	over $85,405 up to $103,915	24.00%
over $104,765	25.75%	over $103,915	25.75%

Québec's tax rates are indexed annually for inflation using the Québec provincial inflation rate.

If an individual was resident in Québec on the last day of the tax year and carried on a business in Canada outside of Québec during the tax year, he or she must check Box 403 on his or her Québec income tax return and complete Form TP-22-V, *Income Tax Payable by an Individual Who Carries on a Business in Canada, Outside of Québec*, to calculate his or her income tax.

If an individual was resident in Canada outside of Québec on the last day of the tax year and carried on a business in Québec in the tax year he or she must check Box 403 on his or her income tax return and complete Form TP-25-V, *Income Tax Payable by an Individual Resident in Canada, Outside Québec, Who Carries on a Business in Québec*, to calculate his or her income tax.

QTA 749.1–750.3, Québec Guide TP-1.G

¶13515 — Foreign Tax Credit (Form TP-1, Schedule E: Line 409)

This tax credit is available to individuals who meet the following requirements:

- resident in Québec on the last day of the tax year, or on the day they ceased to be resident in Canada; and

- paid income tax to the government of a foreign country or of a political subdivision of a foreign country, or made a similar contribution to certain international organizations.

An individual's foreign tax credit for non-business income cannot exceed the total foreign income tax paid on non-business income minus the foreign tax credit granted by the CRA on such income.

To claim the tax credit, individuals must enclose Form TP-772-V, *Foreign Tax Credit*, with their income tax return. Foreign income tax paid on non-business income may be shown on Box G of the RL-3 slip, Box 17 of the RL-15 slip, Box L of the RL-16 slip, or Box H of the RL-25 slip. Foreign income tax paid on business income may be shown in Box 18 of the RL-15 slip or Box K of the RL-16 slip.

QTA 772.2–772.13, Québec Guide TP-1.G, Form TP-772-V

¶13525 — Tax Credit for Contributions to Authorized Québec Political Parties (Form TP-1: Line 414)

Contributions made to authorized political parties, independent Members, independent candidates and political party leadership candidates referred to in the Québec *Election Act* can no longer be claimed for purposes of the political contributions tax credit. Only contributions made respecting elections and referendums in municipalities are allowed under the QTA.

For contributions to the official representative of a party or independent candidate authorized to receive such a contribution under the *Act respecting elections and referendums in municipalities*, the credit is the total of: (a) 85% of the lesser of $50 and the total amount of all such contributions; and (b) 75% of the amount by which $50 is exceeded by the lesser of $200 and the amount of all such contributions.

To calculate the credit, complete Work Chart 414. The maximum credit that can be claimed is $155.

QTA 776, Québec Guide TP-1.G, Work Chart 414

¶13530 — Dividend Tax Credit (Form TP-1: Line 415)

Québec has adopted the federal system of separate dividend gross up and tax credit rates for eligible dividends (dividends paid out of a corporation's income taxed at the general corporate rate) and non-eligible or ordinary dividends (dividends paid out of a corporation's income taxed at the reduced corporate income tax rate).

Individuals can claim a tax credit for dividends from taxable Canadian corporations. The amount of the dividend tax credit depends on whether the dividend is an eligible or non-eligible dividend. The 2018 Québec budget reduced the rate of the dividend tax credit for both eligible and non-eligible dividends. No change was made to the dividend gross-up rates. The revised dividend tax credit rates for 2018 and later taxation years are as follows:

Date Dividend Received	Eligible	Non-Eligible
January 1–March 27, 2018	11.90%	7.05%
March 28, 2018–December 31, 2018	11.86%	6.28%
2019	11.78%	5.55%
2020	11.70%	4.77%
2021 and beyond	11.70%	4.01%

QTA 497, 767, Québec Finance Information Bulletin 2006-2, Québec Guide TP-1.G

¶13535 — Tax Credit for the Acquisition of Capital Régional et Coopératif Desjardins Shares (Form TP-1: Line 422)

A taxpayer can claim a non-refundable tax credit of up to $2,000 or 40% of the purchase of up to $5,000 of new shares of the Capital régional et coopératif Desjardins (the CRDC). The purchasing period to which this applies runs from March 1 to the end of February of the following year. So for the 2018 tax year, the period would be March 1, 2018 to February 28, 2019. First-time shares purchased during this period would be available for the credit.

The amount of the tax credit is indicated in Box B of qualifying individuals' RL-26 slips.

The tax credit is non-refundable and unused amounts cannot be carried forward.

QTA 776.1.5.0.11–776.1.5.0.15, Québec Guide TP-1.G, Québec Information Bulletin 2007-8

¶13540 — Tax Credit for a Labour-Sponsored Fund (Form TP-1: Line 424)

This non-refundable tax credit is available to individuals who make certain investments in labour-sponsored funds during the taxation year or in the first 60 days of the following taxation year.

The purchaser must purchase new shares of:

- Class A shares in the Fonds de solidarité des travailleurs du Québec (FTQ); or

- Class A or class B shares in the Fonds de développement de la Confédération des syndicats nationaux pour la cooperation et l'emploi ("Fondaction").

The tax credit cannot be claimed:

- for replacement shares purchased because the individual redeemed his or her shares in a labour-sponsored fund to participate in the Home Buyers' Plan or the Lifelong Learning Plan;

- if the shares were redeemed within 60 days of the individual acquiring them;

- by an individual age 65 or older, or age 45 or older and retired or on pre-retirement leave in the tax year;

- if the shares were transferred to a spousal RRSP or a spousal RRIF and the spouse was age 65 or older, or age 45 or older and retired or on pre-retirement leave in the tax year.

The maximum amount for shares that can be taken into account for the tax credit is $5,000. The credit is calculated by adding the tax credits for the tax year shown on an individual's RL-10 slip and the tax credits not previously used, and then subtracting the cancelled credits shown on the individual's RL-10 slip.

The tax credit is non-refundable; however, unused amounts can be carried forward in some circumstances, such as where the total amounts paid in the tax year to purchase both types of eligible shares, as indicated in boxes A and G of the individual's RL-10 slip, exceeds $5,000.

QTA 776.1.1–776.1.5, Québec Information Bulletins 2008-8, 2009-6 and 2010-6, Québec Guide TP-1.G

¶13545 — Credits Transferred from One Spouse to the Other (Form TP-1: Line 431)

Unlike the federal system, Québec does not provide a specific spousal tax credit; however, an individual may transfer the unused portion of his or her non-refundable credits to his or her spouse after all credits have been taken into account in the calculation of the individual's tax otherwise payable. The transferee spouse must enter the amount transferred to him or her on Line 431 of his or her Québec income tax return.

A Québec taxpayer may claim all of the following unused credits not claimed by a spouse: basic personal amount; age amount; amount for dependants; union or professional dues; amount for a severe or prolonged impairment;

amount for medical services not available in your area; medical expenses; tuition or examination fees; interest paid on a student loan; credit for volunteer firefighters and search and rescue volunteers; credit for recent graduates working in remote regions; donations and gifts; contribution to a political party; dividend tax credit; the tax credit for a labour-sponsored fund; and credit for acquisition of Capital régional et coopérative Desjardins shares.

The Québec definition of spouse is identical to the federal definition of spouse or common-law partner.

QTA 776.41.1–776.41.11, Québec Guide TP-1.G

¶13550 — Alternative Minimum Tax (Form TP-1: Line 432, Schedule E)

The alternative minimum tax limits the advantages an individual can receive in a tax year from tax incentives. An individual may be required to pay this tax if any of the following situations applies to him or her:

- the individual is deducting, on Line 29 of Schedule L, his or her share of a loss sustained by a partnership of which the individual was a specified member;

- the individual is reporting, on Line 139, a taxable capital gain for which he or she is claiming a capital gains deduction on Line 292;

- the individual is deducting a loss with respect to a tax shelter on Line 164;

- the individual is claiming a deduction for interest and carrying charges incurred to acquire flow-through shares, an interest in a partnership as a specified member, a tax shelter, a rental or leasing property, and investment in a film production, or investments in resources;

- the individual is claiming a deduction on Line 241, a deduction for Québec exploration expenses giving rise to an additional deduction on item 9 of Line 250, or a deduction for certain films on Line 250; or

- the individual is claiming a deduction on Line 287, other than the additional deduction for Québec resources or the deduction for the Cooperative Investment Plan where the cost of the securities equals or exceeds the deduction.

If any of the above situations applies, the individual must complete work chart 432 to determine whether or not he or she is required to pay alternative minimum tax.

If an individual does not have to pay alternative minimum tax for the tax year, he or she may be entitled to deduct alternative minimum tax paid in previous years. The individual must complete Form TP-776.42-V, *Alternative Minimum Tax*.

¶13555 — Special Taxes (Form TP-1: Line 443)

If an individual is required to pay any of the following special taxes, he or she must enter the amount on Line 443 and the item number corresponding to the special tax in Box 442:

- 01 Special tax related to the Québec education savings incentive (QESI)

- 02 Special tax related to a registered education savings plan (RESP)

- 03 Special tax related to the non-purchase of replacement shares in a labour-sponsored fund

- 04 Special tax on split income

- 05 Special tax on amounts from an income-averaging annuity for artists

- 06 Other special taxes

For details on these special taxes, see the instructions for Line 443 in the Québec Income Tax Return Guide.

¶13600 — Calculating Refund or Balance Due (Form TP-1: Lines 451–479)

This section discusses the other credits, rebates and payments applied for purposes of calculating an individual's Québec tax refund or tax balance due.

¶13605 — Tax Credit for Childcare Expenses (Form TP-1: Line 455)

¶13606 — *Eligibility for Credit*

This refundable tax credit is available to individuals who paid, or who had a spouse that paid, childcare expenses in the tax year for an eligible child if all of the following requirements are met:

- the individual was resident in Québec on the last day of the tax year, or was resident in Canada on the last day of the tax year and carried on business in Québec in the tax year;

- the childcare expenses were incurred while the individual, or his or her spouse on the last day of the tax year, was:

  - carrying out the duties of an office or employment;

  - actively carrying on a business;

  - practicing a profession;

  - carrying out research under a grant;

  - actively seeking employment;

  - attending an educational institution full time or part time; or

  - receiving benefits under the Québec parental insurance plan or benefits related to a birth or adoption under the Employment Insurance plan.

- the individual or his or her spouse on the last day of the tax year paid the expenses to an individual, daycare centre, holiday and recreation centre, camp, or boarding school;

- the child was living with the individual or his or her spouse on the last day of the tax year at the time the expenses were incurred; and

- the childcare services were provided in Canada by a person resident in Canada, unless the individual was temporarily living outside of Canada.

For 2017 and later taxation years, the definition of "eligible child" was amended for the purposes of calculating the refundable tax credit for childcare expenses. Under the amended definition, an eligible child of an individual for a taxation year means a child of the individual or the individual's spouse, or a child who is a dependent of the individual or the individual's spouse and whose income for the year does not exceed $9,582 if, in any case, at any time during the year, the child is under 16 years of age or is dependent on the individual or the individual's spouse and has a mental or physical infirmity.

The following expenses do not qualify for the tax credit:

- the reduced contribution of $7 per day per child set by the government and paid for childcare services provided by a childcare centre, home childcare provider, daycare centre, or for basic school daycare services;

- amounts paid to the child's mother or father;

- amounts paid to a person with whom the individual was living in a conjugal relationship;

- amounts paid to a person with whom the individual was living, where the child is an eligible child of that person;

- amounts paid to a person under 18 years of age who was related to the individual or a person with whom the individual was living in a conjugal relationship by blood, marriage or adoption, other than a nephew or niece;

- amounts paid to a person for whom the individual (or a person living with the individual whose child, for whom the childcare expenses were paid, is an eligible child) is claiming an amount on Line 367;

- medical expenses and other expenses related to medical and hospital care;

- transportation expenses;

- expenses paid for teaching services;

- clothing and other personal expenses;

- childcare expenses for which another person obtained a tax credit for in relation to the same child;

- expenses that the individual was reimbursed for, or is entitled to a reimbursement for, or that were covered by another Form of financial assistances, unless the reimbursement or assistance was included in an individual's income and cannot be deducted elsewhere;

- expenses reimbursed by the Ministère de l'Emploi et de la Solidarité sociale; and

- the portion of the childcare expenses for which the individual received an allowance from the Ministère de l'Emploi et de la Solidarité sociale.

¶13607 — *Amount of Credit*

The tax credit rate is based on an individual's income, plus the income of his or her spouse, if applicable, on the last day of the taxation year. The amount of the tax credit is 26% to 75% of eligible expenses, depending on the individual's family income. Generally, the tax credit rate decreases as net family income increases.

For 2018 and later taxation years, the maximum amount of expenses eligible for the credit is the lesser of:

- $13,000 for a child of any age who has a severe or prolonged mental or physical impairment, plus $9,500 for a child under the age of 7 at the end of the taxation year, plus $5,000 for a child aged 7 to 16 at the end of the taxation year; and

- The actual child care expenses incurred in the taxation year.

The above annual limits on childcare expenses (i.e., $13,000, $9,500 and $5,000) are indexed for inflation as of the 2019 taxation year.

If childcare expenses were paid to a boarding school or camp, the maximum amount qualifying for the credit is $175 per week for each eligible child under age 7 at the end of the taxation year, and $100 per week for each eligible child aged 7 to 16 at the end of the taxation year. The maximum is $250 per week for a child of any age who has a severe and prolonged impairment in mental or physical functions.

The amount of the tax credit may be split between an individual and his or her spouse on the last day of the tax year.

If the individual is claiming the increased amount for childcare expenses paid for a child with a severe and prolonged impairment in mental and physical functions, the individual must enclose Form TP-752.0.14-V, *Certificate Respecting an Impairment*, with his or her income tax return, unless the individual has already filed it. If the individual is not required to provide certification that the child has a chronic illness requiring him or her to undergo therapy essential to the maintenance of one of his or her vital functions at least twice a week for at least 14 hours a week, the individual can instead enclose Form T2201, *Disability Tax Credit Certificate*. If the child's health improves, the individual must inform Revenu Québec.

If the individual did not receive a RL-24 slip for his or her childcare expenses, the individual must retain a receipt with the childcare provider's social insurance number, address, and signature.

QTA 1029.8.67–1029.8.82, Québec Brochure IN-245-V, Form TP-1.D.C-V, Form T2201, Form TP-752.0.14-V, Brochure IN-103-V

¶13610 — Tax Credits Respecting the Work Premium (Form TP-1: Line 456)

Québec has a series of refundable credits referred to as work premiums. There are three credits: the Basic Work Premium, the Supplement to the Work Premium, and the Adapted Work Premium.

For 2015 and later taxation years, full-time students are not eligible for the work premium or the adapted work premium unless they are, at the end of the year, the parent of a child that lives with them. A full-time student is a student pursuing vocational training at the secondary level or post-secondary studies who is in either of the following situations: (1) in the year, the student begins and completes a term during which he or she must devote a minimum of 9 hours per week to classes or coursework; or (2) the student has a major functional deficiency within the meaning of the *Regulation respecting financial assistance for education expenses*, and he or she begins and completes, in the year, a term during which he or she receives a minimum of 20 hours of instruction per month.

¶13611 — *Basic Work Premium (Form TP-1: Line 456)*

This refundable tax credit is available to individuals who meet all of the following conditions:

- resident in Québec on the last day of the tax year;

- a Canadian citizen, Indian, permanent resident, or refugee;

- at least 18 years of age on the last day of the tax year, or had a spouse, was the parent of a child living with him or her, or was recognized as an emancipated minor by a competent authority;

- was not confined to a prison or similar institution on the last day of the tax year, and did not spend more than 6 months in such an institution during the tax year;

- did not transfer to his or her father or mother an amount as a child 18 or over enrolled in post-secondary studies;

- no one received, with regard to the individual, a child assistance payment from the Retraite du Québec, unless the individual turned 18 years of age before December 1 of the tax year;

- no one designated the individual as a dependent child for the purpose of claiming the work premium tax credit;

- the individual or his or her spouse on the last day of the tax year is reporting, for the purposes of calculating the work premium, employment income, a research grant, Wage Earner Protection Program payments, or income from a business carried on by the individual or his or her spouse, independently or as a partner actively engaged in the business; and

- annual work income is over $2,400 if the individual is a person living alone or a single parent, or over $3,600, combined with that of the individual's spouse, if the individual has a spouse.

An individual is not entitled to the tax credit if the individual or his or her spouse on the last day of the tax year was exempt from paying income tax because the individual or his or her spouse worked for an international organization, the government of a foreign country, or an office of a political subdivision of a foreign State recognized by the Ministère des Finances.

For 2018, the parameters of the work premium are as follows:

	Income excluded	Rate of Increase	Maximum amount
Single individuals	$2,400	9%	$768
Childless couples	$3,600	9%	$1,199
Single-parent families	$2,400	30%	$2,452

	Income excluded	Rate of Increase	Maximum amount
Couples with children	$3,600	25%	$3,189

The basic work premium begins to phase-out at $10,574 of income for single individuals and $16,356 of income for couples.

To apply for the basic work premium, individuals must complete Schedule P to the income tax return. An individual may request that part of the premium be paid in advance in equal monthly instalments, through direct deposit. In order to receive advance payments, an individual must be resident in Québec, in the labour market, and estimate that they are entitled to an annual work premium of more than $500 if a dependent child is designated, or more than $300 if a dependent child is not designated.

To receive such advance payments, an individual must complete Form TPZ-1029.8.P-V, *Work Premium Tax Credit: Application for Advance Payments.*

QTA 1029.8.116.1–1029.8.116.11, Québec Brochure IN-245-V, Form TPZ-1029.8.P-V, Form TP-1.D.P-V

¶13612 — *Supplement to the Work Premium (Form TP-1: Line 456)*

If an individual has stopped receiving last-resort financial assistance or financial assistance under the Alternative jeunesse program and is entitled to the work premium, he or she may also be entitled to the supplement to the work premium. In order to be eligible for the supplement, individuals must meet all of the following conditions:

- resident in Québec on December 31 of the year for which the credit is being claimed;

- a Canadian citizen, Indian, permanent resident, or refugee;

- 18 years of age or older on December 31 of the year, or had a spouse, was the parent of a child living with them, or was recognized as an emancipated minor by a competent authority;

- not confined to a prison or similar institution on December 31 of the year or for more than six months during the year;

- did not transfer to his or her father or mother an amount as a child 18 or over enrolled in post-secondary studies;

- no one received a child assistance program payment from the Retraite du Québec with regard to the individual, unless the individual turned 18 before December 1 of the year;

- no one designated the individual as a dependent child for the purposes of claiming a tax credit respecting the work premium;

- the month for which the credit is being claimed is included in a period of transition to work;

- received last-resort financial assistance or financial assistance under the Alternative jeunesse program during at least 36 of the 42 months preceding the month the individual ceased to receive the assistance due to the individual or his or her spouse earning work income;

- in the first month the individual was no longer eligible for the Social Assistance Program or the Social Solidarity program the individual was entitled to dental and pharmaceutical services under a claim booklet issued by the Ministère de l'Emploi et de la Solidarité socale, unless the individual received financial assistance under the Alternative jeunesse program; and

- the individual has work income of at least $200 for the month.

An individual is not entitled to the supplement if the individual or his or her spouse on the last day of the tax year was exempt from paying income tax because the individual or his or her spouse worked for an international organization, the government of a foreign country, or an office of a political subdivision of a foreign State recognized by the Ministère des Finances.

The amount of the supplement is $200 per individual per month for a maximum of 12 consecutive months, for a maximum credit of $2,400 for a person living alone and $4,800 for a couple.

Individuals may be eligible for advance monthly payments of the credit. To apply, individuals must complete Form TPZ-1029.8.PS-V, *Supplement to the Work Premium: Application for Advance Payments*. Individuals must amend their application if they no longer meet one of the requirements for the credit or become entitled to advance payments.

To claim the tax credit, individuals must complete Schedule P of their income tax return.

QTA 1029.8.116.1–1029.8.116.11, Québec Brochure IN-245-V, Form TPZ-1029.8.PS-V, Form TP-1.D.P-V

¶13613 — *Adapted Work Premium (Form TP-1: Line 456)*

This refundable tax credit is available to individuals who meet, or who had a spouse on the last day of the tax year who meets, the following conditions:

- received, in the tax year or in one of the preceding five years, a severely limited capacity for employment allowance or an allowance under the Social Solidarity Program because of a severely limited capacity for employment; or

- were entitled, in the tax year, to the amount for a severe and prolonged impairment in mental or physical functions.

An individual is not entitled to the tax credit if the individual or his or her spouse on the last day of the tax year was exempt from paying income tax because the individual or his or her spouse worked for an international organization, the government of a foreign country, or an office of a political subdivision of a foreign State recognized by the Ministère des Finances.

The amount of the tax credit is calculated on Schedule P and takes into account the individual and his or her spouse's income and work income, as well as the individual's family situation. The amount of the credit is reduced beyond certain income thresholds.

To apply for the tax credit, individuals must complete Schedule P to the income tax return. An individual may request that part of the premium be paid in advance in equal monthly installments, through direct deposit. In order to receive advance payments, an individual must be resident in Québec, in the labour market, and estimate that they are entitled to an annual work premium of more than $500 if a dependent child is designated, or more than $300 if a dependent child is not designated.

To receive such advance payments, an individual must complete Form TPZ-1029.8.P-V, *Work Premium Tax Credit: Application for Advance Payments*.

QTA 1029.8.116.1–1029.8.116.11, Québec Brochure IN-245-V, Form TPZ-1029.8.P-V, Form TP-1.D.P-V

¶13615 — Tax Credit for Home-Support Services for Seniors (Form TP-1: Line 458)

Québec offers a refundable tax credit to Québec resident seniors who are at least 70 years of age on the last day of the taxation year. If the individual turned 70 years of age during the tax year, only expenses incurred after the individual turned 70 can be claimed.

For 2018, the maximum credit is $6,630, or 34% of a maximum of $19,500 of home support services, per year, per senior, which is reduced by 3% of family income in excess of $57,400 (indexed annually for inflation). For a "dependent senior", the maximum credit is $8,670, or 34% of $25,500 of eligible expenses, per year, per dependent senior. The tax credit reduction based on family income does not apply in the case of a senior who is considered a "dependent senior".

A "dependent senior" is someone over the age of 70 who depends on someone to care for their physical needs as a result of a prolonged impairment, or someone who requires constant care and supervision because of impairment of their mental capacity, or thought activity. To qualify for dependent senior status, certification from a prescribed professional will be required by having them complete Form TPZ-1029.MD.A-V, *Certificate of Dependent Senior Status*.

If both an individual and his or her spouse are eligible for the credit, only one of them can claim it on behalf of the couple, with the applicable maximum annual expense limit deemed equal to the combined total of the individual's annual limit and that of his or her spouse for the year. This means that if each spouse qualifies for the maximum eligible amount of $19,500 for non-dependent seniors, the maximum tax credit is $13,260 (i.e., $39,000 × 34 per cent).

For the purposes of this credit, eligible home-support services generally include the following: housekeeping services; grounds maintenance; personal care services pertaining to dressing, personal hygiene, mobility in the home and eating or drinking; meal delivery services by a community organization; nursing services; supervision and support services; civic support services; laundry services; supplying everyday necessities and running errands; and minor maintenance work outside the dwelling.

The following services are not eligible for this credit: construction, renovation, or repair work; services provided by a spouse or dependant; services provided by a person who is claiming the caregiver tax credit for the senior; services provided outside Québec; hairdressing services; and installation of an alarm or emergency or intercom system.

The eligible expense amount rules differ according to the type of residence the senior lives in. For example, if the senior lives in a private seniors' residence or a condominium, some eligible home-support services may be included in the senior's rent or condominium fees.

Generally, a private seniors' residence is a residential facility where rooms, studios, or apartments intended for seniors are offered for rent, along with services related to security, household tasks, or social activities. The eligible expense amount available to a senior who paid rent to live in a private seniors' residence is calculated using tables which assign values to various services offered by the seniors' residence that are paid as part of the total rent. The total value of the services cannot exceed 65% of the total rent per month, or 75% in the case of a dependent senior.

Expenses included in condominium fees may be eligible for the purposes of this credit. In order to receive this credit for such fees, the condominium administrator must evaluate the cost of eligible services covered by condo fees by completing work chart TPZ-1029.MD.5.C-V, *Cost of Eligible Services Included in Condominium Fees*. Information return Form TPZ-1029.MD.5-V, *Information Return — Tax Credit for Home-Support for Seniors*, must be completed by the condominium administrator and included with the senior's income tax return.

Individuals wishing to receive advance payment of this credit are required to complete Form TPZ-1029.MD.7-V, *Application for Advance Payments Based on Rent and Services Included in Rent*. Form TPZ-1029.MD.9-V, *Application for Advance Payments for Occasional Services*, must be completed for eligible services other than expenses included in rent. Alternatively, expenses may be claimed on the income tax return by completing Schedule J, *Tax Credit for Home-Support Services for Seniors*.

QTA 1029.8.61.1–1029.8.61.7.1, 1086.9–1086.12, Québec Guide TP-1.G, Québec Information Bulletin 2002-8, Québec Brochure IN-102-V, Forms: TPZ-1029.MD.5-V, TPZ-1029.MD.7-V, TPZ-1029.MD.8-V, TPZ-1029.MD.9-V, TPZ-1029.MD.A-V, TP-1.D.J-V

¶13620 — QST Rebate for Employees and Partners (Form TP-1: Line 459)

This rebate is available to individuals who meet the following conditions:

- the individual was an employee or member of a partnership during the tax year;

- the individual paid QST on work-related expenses; and

- expenses were deducted on Line 164 (business income) or on Line 207 (employment expenses and deductions) of the individual's income tax return.

An individual who entered an amount for professional dues on Line 373 of his or her income tax return may also be eligible for the tax credit. A tax credit may also be claimed for dues that could have been claimed on Line 373 if all of the individual's employment income or business income from a partnership had not been excluded or deductible in the calculation of the individual's taxable income.

To claim this tax credit, individuals must complete Form VD-358-V, *Québec Sales Tax Rebate for Employees and Partners*.

Québec *Sales Tax Act*, Form VD-358-V

13621 — Tax Shield (Form TP-1: Line 460)

The tax shield was introduced to encourage individuals to join or remain in the workforce. Individuals who are resident in Québec on the last day of the taxation year, and who are entitled to the tax credit for childcare expenses (see ¶13605), the work premium or the adapted work premium (see ¶13610) may be eligible to claim the tax shield. The maximum work premium component of the tax shield is $450 for a couple. The component related to childcare expenses could represent an increase of several percentage points in the rate of this tax credit. For 2018, the maximum increase in eligible work income from the previous year (for the purposes of calculating the work premium and refundable tax credit for childcare expenses) is $4,000 per worker.

To claim the tax shield, check box 99 of Schedule C or box 5 of Schedule P and Revenu Québec will calculate the credit. Alternatively, individuals can calculate the credit by completing form TP-1029.BF-V, *Tax Shield*. If an individual and his or her spouse are both claiming the tax shield, the amount of the credit will be split evenly between them.

¶13625 — Other Credits (Form TP-1: Line 462)

Other credits that can be claimed on Line 462 are discussed below, and include the following:

- 01 Refundable tax credit for medical expenses

- 02 Tax credit for caregivers

- 03 Tax credit for taxi drivers or taxi owners

- 05 Property tax refund for forest producers

- 06 Tax credit for adoption expenses

- 07 Tax credit for an on-the-job training period

- 08 Tax credit for the repayment of benefits

- 09 Tax credit for income tax paid by an environmental trust

- 10 Tax credit for the reporting of tips

- 11 Tax credit for the treatment of infertility

- 15 Tax credit for scientific research and experimental development

- 18 Tax credit for a top-level athlete

- 19 Tax credit for income from an income-averaging annuity for artists

- 20 Tax credit for volunteer respite services

- 21 Tax credit for respite of caregivers

- 24 Independent living tax credit for seniors

- 25 Tax credit for children's activities

- 28 Tax credit for seniors' activities

- 32 Tax credit for eco-friendly home renovation (RénoVert)

- 33 Tax credit for the updating of residential waste water treatment systems

An individual who is entitled to any of the other tax credits listed above should enter the amount of the credit on Line 462 and the number that corresponds to the credit in Box 461. Individuals claiming more than one of the above tax credits should enter the total amount on Line 462 and "99" in box 461.

¶13625.1 — Refundable Tax Credit for Medical Expenses (Form TP-1: Line 462, Item 1)

This refundable tax credit is available to individuals to whom all of the following conditions apply:

- they were resident in Québec on December 31 of the taxation year;

- they were 18 years of age or older on the last day of the tax year;

- they were resident in Canada throughout the tax year;

- their work income is greater than $3,030 in 2018; and

- they claimed an amount for medical expenses or the disability supports deduction.

The amount of the tax credit is 25% of medical expenses eligible for the non-refundable tax credit, (less the 3% of the family income deducted in arriving at the non-refundable credit), to a maximum credit amount of $1,185 for the 2018 tax year. The credit is reduced by 5 per cent of family net income in excess of $22,910. These amounts are indexed annually.

To claim the tax credit, individuals must complete parts A and D of Schedule B.

QTA 1029.8.117-1029.8.118

¶13625.2 — Tax Credit for Caregivers (Form TP-1: Line 462, Item 2)

A taxpayer may be able to claim a refundable tax credit for caregivers if he or she was a caregiver: (1) of a spouse who is unable to live alone; (2) of an eligible relative who was living with the taxpayer; (3) who cohabitates with an eligible relative who is unable to live alone; or (4) who regularly and continuously helps an eligible relative, but who does not cohabitate with, or house, the relative.

The caregiver credit for caring for a spouse is $1,015 in 2018. To qualify for this credit, the spouse must be 70 years old or older in the tax year; have a severe and prolonged physical or mental impairment as certified by a physician; and have lived with the caregiver for at least 365 days, of which 183 were in the current tax year. The dwelling that they lived in cannot be in a senior citizens' residence. It needs to be a dwelling that the taxpayer owned, rented, or sublet.

The caregiver credit for looking after an eligible relative is up to $1,185 in 2018 for each eligible relative. An eligible relative is a person other than a spouse:

- who is either: (1) over 70 years old and is the taxpayer's or taxpayer's spouse's father, mother, grandfather, grandmother, child, grandchild, niece, nephew, brother, sister, uncle, aunt, great uncle or great aunt; or (2) at least 18 years old and has a severe and prolonged physical or mental impairment (certified by a physician); and

- who either: (1) lived with the taxpayer for a period of at least 365 days with 183 of the days in the current tax year; or (2) did not live with the taxpayer, but regularly and continuously received assistance from the taxpayer for a period of at least 183 days in the current tax year.

A taxpayer can claim the caregiver credit if they were resident in Québec on December 31 of the year and no one else, other than a spouse, is claiming any credits for the taxpayer in a tax year relating to:

- a tax credit respecting dependants (i.e., a tax credit for a child engaged in vocational training or post-secondary studies);

- a tax credit for a dependant with an infirmity;

- a tax credit for an adult child who is a student;

- the non-refundable tax credit for expenses relating to medical care not available in the area of residence;

- the non-refundable tax credit for medical expenses;

- the non-refundable tax credit for moving expenses relating to medical care.

For each eligible relative, the $1,185 tax credit consists of a universal basic amount of $652 plus a supplement amount of $533 that will be reduced based on the eligible relative's income for the year for which the tax credit is being claimed. The reduction rate is 15 per cent for every dollar of income of the eligible relative in excess of $23,700.

To claim the tax credit for caregivers, the individual must complete Schedule H, *Tax Credit for Caregivers*, and enclose Form TP-752.0.14-V, *Certificate Respecting an Impairment*, and Form TP-1029.8.61.64-V, *Tax Credit for Caregivers*, where applicable.

QTA 1029.8.61.61–1029.8.61.70, Québec Guide TP-1.G, TP-752.0.14-V, TP-1029.8.61.64-V, TP-1.D.H-V, TP-752.0.14-V

¶13625.3 — *Tax Credit for Taxi Drivers and Taxi Owners (Form TP-1: Line 462, Item 3)*

The refundable tax credit for taxi drivers is available to individuals who were resident in Québec on the last day of the tax year, and held a taxi driver's permit at some point during the tax year. If the individual also held one or more taxi owner's permits on the last day of the tax year, the individual must have borne less than 90 per cent of the fuel costs for each taxi covered by a permit.

The refundable tax credit for taxi owners is available to individuals who meet the following conditions:

- held at least one valid taxi owner's permit on the last day of the tax year, and, if the permit was issued in the name of more than one person, was designated as the sole permit holder; and

- bore at least 90% of the fuel costs for the taxi covered by the permit during the period of the tax year the individual held the permit.

For the 2017 and 2018 taxation years, the tax credit is subject to an increase of up to $500 per year, from a maximum of $569 to $1,069 in 2017, and from a maximum of $574 to $1,074 in 2018.

To claim the tax credit, individuals must complete Form TP-1029.9-V, *Tax Credit for Taxi Drivers or Taxi Owners*. This tax credit is not taxable to the recipient.

QTA 1029.9–1029.9.4, Form TP-1029.9-V

¶13625.4 — *Adoption Expenses (Form TP-1: Line 462, Item 6)*

This refundable tax credit is available to individuals who incurred eligible adoption expenses and who meet the following conditions:

- resident in Québec on the last day of the tax year; and

- a legal bond of filiation between the individual and the child was recognized in the tax year.

The second requirement will be met if:

- an adoption judgment establishing a bond of filiation was rendered in the tax year by a court having jurisdiction in Québec;

- an adoption judgment rendered outside of Québec received legal recognition in Québec in the tax year; or

- a certificate of compliance was issued in accordance with the Convention on Protection of Children and Co-operation in Respect of Intercountry Adoption, and was notified to the Director de l'Etat civil by the Minister of Health and Social Services or the clerk of the Court of Québec.

An individual is not entitled to the tax credit if the individual or his or her spouse on the last day of the tax year was exempt from paying income tax because the individual or his or her spouse worked for an international organization, the government of a foreign country, or an office of a political subdivision of a foreign State recognized by the Ministère des Finances.

The following expenses are eligible adoption expenses:

- judicial or extrajudicial expenses incurred to obtain an adoption judgment in Québec, legal recognition in Québec of an adoption judgment, or a certificate of compliance with the Convention on Protection of Children and Co-operation in Respect of Intercounty Adoption;

- travel expenses of the child incurred to reach the adoptive parents' residence;

- travel expenses of the child's escort incurred to bring the child to the adoptive parents' residence, if the adoptive parents did not accompany the child;

- travel and living expenses incurred by the adoptive parents to adopt the child;

- fees for the translation of adoption documents;

- fees charged by an organization certified by the Minister of Health and Social Services;

- fees charged by a foreign institution that took care of the child;

- expenses related to the psychological assessment of the adoptive parents; and

- expenses arising from a requirement imposed by a government authority respecting the adoption of a child.

The tax credit for adoption expenses now covers eligible adoption expenses paid by adoptive parents after they file an application to register with the Ministère de la Santé et des Services sociaux or with an organization certified by the Ministère, in addition to expenses that adoptive parents paid once their adoption file has been opened by the Ministère or other organization.

Expenses used to calculate a medical expenses tax credit for the individual or his or her spouse are not eligible. An individual cannot claim expenses for which her or she, or his or her spouse, were reimbursed or are entitled to reimbursement, unless the reimbursement is included in the individual or his or her spouse's income and not deducted elsewhere.

The amount of the tax credit is equal to 50% of eligible adoption expenses, up to the maximum credit amount of $10,000 per child.

To claim the tax credit, individuals must enclose Form TP-1029.8.63-V, *Adoption Expenses*, with their income tax return.

QTA 1029.8.62–1029.8.66, Québec Information Bulletin 2013-7, Form TP-1029.8.63-V

¶13625.5 — *Tax Credit for the Treatment of Infertility (Form TP-1: Line 462, Item 11)*

Individuals who are resident in Québec on the last day of the taxation year can claim a credit for eligible expenses paid in the year for an in vitro fertilization treatment that enables the individual or his/her spouse to have a child.

In the case of expenses incurred after November 10, 2015, neither the individual nor the spouse can have had a child before the start of the in vitro fertilization treatment for which the expenses are paid, and a physician must certify in the appropriate section of Form TP-1029.8.66.2M-V, *Certificate Respecting the Treatment of Infertility*, that neither the individual nor the spouse has undergone surgical sterilization by vasectomy or tubal ligation, as applicable, other than for strictly medical reasons.

To be eligible, the expenses must be related to an in vitro fertilization treatment that meets all of the following conditions:

- The cost of the treatment is not covered by a health insurance plan and cannot be reimbursed to the person undergoing the treatment;

- The treatment involves the transfer of a single embryo or, in accordance with a decision made by a physician:

  - a maximum of two embryos, in the case of a woman 36 years of age or under, or a maximum of three embryos, in the case of a woman 37 years of age or over, if the transfer is carried out *before* November 11, 2015; or

  - a maximum of two embryos, in the case of a woman 37 years of age or over, if the transfer is carried out *after* November 10, 2015; and

- The treatment is carried out in Québec at a centre for assisted procreation that holds a licence issued in accordance with the *Regulation respecting clinical activities related to assisted procreation* (this condition does not apply if the centre is located outside Québec and the person undergoing the treatment lived outside Québec when the expenses were incurred).

Specifically, the following are eligible expenses for this credit:

- expenses paid for an in vitro fertilization activity carried out by a physician;

- expenses paid for an assessment carried out by a member of the Ordre des psychologues du Québec or the Ordre des travailleurs sociaux et des thérapeutes conjugaux et familiaux du Québec;

- expenses paid for drugs that are prescribed by a physician and whose purchase is registered by a pharmacist, and that are not covered by a health insurance plan;

- expenses paid to a business for the transportation of a person undergoing an in vitro fertilization treatment (and, if the person cannot travel without assistance, of the person who accompanies him or her) from the locality where the person lives to a centre for assisted procreation located at least 40 kilometres away, if treatment is not offered in the person's locality;

- travel expenses incurred for a person (and, if the person cannot travel without assistance, of the person who accompanies him or her) so that the person can undergo an in vitro fertilization treatment at a centre for assisted procreation located at least 80 kilometres away from the locality where the person lives, if treatment is not offered in the person's locality; and

- travel and lodging expenses incurred for a person (and, if the person cannot travel without assistance, of the person who accompanies him or her) so that the person can undergo an in vitro fertilization treatment at a centre for assisted procreation located in Québec, if, as certified by a physician (by completing the appropriate section of Form TP-1029.8.66.2M-V, *Certificate Respecting the Treatment of Infertility*), there are no centres for assisted procreation in a radius of 250 kilometres from the locality where the person lives.

The maximum amount of eligible in vitro fertilization expenses that can be claimed by an individual or his/her spouse is $20,000 per year. The credit rate is 20–80%, depending on income level. For couples, the maximum 80% rate of the tax credit will be allowed up to net family income of $50,000, after which it is gradually decreased, to a minimum of 20% for net family income of $120,000 or more. For individuals living alone, the maximum 80% rate of the tax credit will be allowed for individuals with income up to $25,000, after which it will be gradually decreased, to a minimum of 20% for income of $60,000 or more.

To apply for the tax credit, individuals must complete and file Form TP-1029.8.66.2-V, *Tax Credit for the Treatment of Infertility*, with their income tax return.

For more information on the changes to the tax credit for the treatment of infertility, see Québec Information Bulletins 2015-6 and 2014-10 and Québec Bill 20.

QTA 1029.8.66.1–1029.8.66.5, Québec Information Bulletin 2010-8, Form TP-1029.8.66.2-V

¶13625.6 — *Tax Credit for Volunteer Respite Services (Form TP-1: Line 462, Item 20)*

The tax credit for voluntary respite of caregivers is available to eligible individuals who meet the following conditions:

- The individual was resident in Québec on December 31 of the taxation year;

- The individual provided, as a volunteer, home respite services to the informal caregiver of a person with a significant long-term disability;

- The caregiver provided the individual with an RL-23 slip documenting the services provided;

- The individual is not the spouse of the care recipient; and

- The individual is not the father, mother, child, brother or sister of the care recipient, or the spouse of any of these people.

For 2018 and later taxation years, the maximum amount that may be attributed by an informal caregiver, in relation to a care recipient, to an eligible individual for a taxation year, will be adjusted based on the number of hours of volunteer respite services provided to the informal caregiver as follows: $250 for a minimum of 200 hours, $500 for a minimum of 300 hours, and $750 for a minimum of 400 hours. In addition, the maximum amount that may be attributed by an informal caregiver in relation to each care recipient of whom the person is an informal caregiver for the year has been increased to $1,500 (from $1,000) for 2018 and later taxation years.

QTA 1029.8.61.71–1029.8.61.75, Form RL-23

¶13625.7 — *Tax Credit for Respite of Caregivers (Form TP-1: Line 462, Item 21)*

Informal caregivers resident in Québec are eligible for a tax credit of 30% of the total expenses paid for specialized respite services, up to a maximum of $5,200, which equals a maximum credit of $1,560 per year. The maximum amount is reduced by 3 per cent for every $1 of family income in excess of $57,400 (indexed annually for inflation).

The specialized respite services are with respect to the care and supervision of a person who, at the time the expenses were incurred, ordinarily lived with the taxpayer and had a significant disability. Only the individual who is the principal person providing support to the care recipient will be considered the informal caregiver for the purposes of this credit.

To be considered a person with a significant disability for the purposes of this credit, an individual must be at least 18 years of age at the time the expenses are incurred; ordinarily live with the caregiver; require constant supervision because of the disability; and have a severe and prolonged impairment in physical or mental functions or receive palliative care.

The caregiver may be any of the following:

- the taxpayer's spouse;

- the taxpayer's child, grandchild or spouse;

- the taxpayer's brother, sister, nephew or niece, or those of the taxpayer's spouse;

- the spouse of the taxpayer's brother or sister, or spouse of the brother or sister of the taxpayer's spouse;

- the taxpayer's father, mother or any other direct ascendant, as well as any direct ascendant of the taxpayer's spouse; or

- the taxpayer's uncle, aunt, great-uncle, great-aunt or those of the taxpayer's spouse.

The person providing respite services must hold one of the following recognized diplomas:

- Diploma of Vocational Studies in Home Care and Family and Social Assistance, or in Home Care Assistance;

- Diploma of Vocational Studies in Assistance to Patients or Residents in Healthcare Establishments, or in Assistance in Healthcare Establishments;

- Diploma of Vocational Studies in Health, Assistance and Nursing;

- Diploma of College Studies in Nursing;

- Bachelor's degree in Nursing; or

- any other diploma or degree enabling a person to be a visiting homemaker, home-support worker, family and social auxiliary, nursing attendant, healthcare aide, beneficiary care attendant, nursing assistant or nurse.

Expenses claimed by an informal caregiver or another person with respect to another refundable or non-refundable credit cannot also be claimed under this credit. Expenses for which a taxpayer is entitled to a refund or other form of assistance are also ineligible for this credit, unless the expenses are required to be included in the calculation of the taxpayer's income and are not deductible.

To claim the credit, complete Schedule O, *Tax Credit for Respite of Caregivers.*

QTA QTA 1029.8.61.76–1029.8.61.82

¶13625.8 — *Independent Living Tax Credit for Seniors (Form TP-1: Line 462, Item 24)*

This refundable tax credit is available to individuals to whom all of the following conditions apply:

- resident of Québec on the last day of the tax year;

- 70 years of age or older on the last day of the tax year;

- incurred expenses for the purchase, lease and installation of equipment or fixtures used to maintain the individual's autonomy in his or her place of residence, or for one or more stays in a functional rehabilitation transition unit, that were paid by the individual or his or her spouse.

Eligible equipment and fixtures include person-focused remote monitoring devices; GPS devices for tracking persons; devices designed to assist a person in getting on or off a toilet or into or out of a bathtub; walk-in bathtubs and showers; mechanized, rail-mounted chair lifts designed to carry a person up or down stairs; hospital beds; alert systems for persons with hearing impairments; hearing aids; walkers, rollators; canes; crutches and non-motorized wheelchairs.

The equipment or fixtures must be intended for use in the individual's principal place of residence.

An individual cannot claim the tax credit for expenses for which the individual or any other person was reimbursed, or entitled to be reimbursed, unless the reimbursement was included in the individual or other person's income and cannot be deducted elsewhere; or for expenses included in the calculation of another refundable or non-refundable tax credit claimed by the individual or any other person.

The amount of the tax credit is equal to 20% of expenses incurred for the purchase, lease and installation of equipment or fixtures in excess of $250 ($500 for taxation years before 2018), plus 20% of expenses incurred for one or more stays in a functional rehabilitation transition unit. The credit can be claimed for a maximum of 60 days per each stay in a functional rehabilitation transition unit.

To claim the tax credit, individuals must complete Part E of Schedule B.

QTA 1029.8.61.97–1029.8.61.99; 1029.8.61.100–1029.8.61.102

¶13625.9 — *Tax Credit for Children's Activities (Form TP-1: Line 462, Item 25)*

This refundable tax credit is available to individuals who paid fees in the tax year for eligible activities for their children aged 5 to 16 at the beginning of the tax year. Expenses paid for activities for children 16 and 17 years of age at the beginning of the tax year are also eligible if the child has a severe and prolonged mental or physical impairment. To be eligible for the tax credit, an individual must have a household income of $136,195 or less.

The amount of the tax credit is 20% of eligible expenses paid in the tax year. The maximum amount of eligible expenses that can be claimed is $500 per eligible child, or $1,000 per child with a disability.

The credit may be claimed in respect of an individual's own child or the child of his or her spouse or common-law partner. If more than one individual is eligible to claim the credit in respect of the same child, the total of amounts claimed by each individual may not exceed the maximum credit amount.

Qualifying expenditures for the purposes of the credit include eligible expenses incurred during the year for enrollment of a child in an eligible activity. Eligible expenses include registration and membership fees, as well as fees paid to cover the cost of uniforms, equipment used in common, incidental supplies, facility rentals, referees and judges, instruction, and administration.

Expenses not eligible for the credit include fees paid to cover costs of accommodation, travel, food and beverages, or the purchase or rental of equipment for exclusive personal use, as well as fees paid to an individual's spouse or common-law partner or directly to anyone under 18 years of age. In addition, expenditures eligible for other tax credits, such as the charitable donations credit or political contributions credit, are not eligible for the credit. Expenses that are eligible for the child care expenses deduction must first be claimed under that deduction, with any unused qualifying portion being eligible for the credit.

Eligible activities for the credit include fitness activities, as well as certain non-fitness activities, designed for children. Fitness activities eligible for the credit include those that contribute to the cardiorespiratory endurance and development of one or more of the following aptitudes: muscle strength, muscle endurance, flexibility, and balance. It specifically included horseback riding. Artistic, cultural, and recreational development activities that are eligible are those that develop creative skills or expertise, acquire and apply knowledge or improve dexterity or coordination in an artistic or cultural discipline, including: literary arts, visual arts, performing arts, music, media, languages, customs, and heritage. It also includes programs that provide a substantial focus on the wilderness and natural environment, assist with the development and use of intellectual skills, including structured interaction among children where supervisors teach or assist children to develop interpersonal skills.

QTA 1029.8.66.6–1029.8.66.10

¶13625.10 — Tax Credit for Seniors' Activities (Form TP-1: Line 462, Item 28)

This is a refundable tax credit of up to $40 per year to support the participation of low or middle-income seniors in physical, artistic, cultural and recreational activities. The tax credit is calculated as 20 percent of eligible expenses not exceeding $200 a year, and targets seniors 70 and over with an individual income of $41,505 or less.

An eligible expense of a senior for a particular taxation year will be any amount paid by the senior in the year to a person (other than a person that, at the time of the payment, is the operator of a private seniors' residence where the individual lives, or is related to the individual and does not hold a registration number assigned under the Act respecting the Québec sales tax), to the extent that the amount is attributable to the cost of the individual's registration or membership in a recognized program of activities offered by the person. The cost of registration or membership in a program includes the cost to the person with respect to the program's administration, instruction, rental of required facilities, and uniforms and equipment that are not available to be acquired by a participant in the program for an amount less than their fair market value at the time they are acquired. However, the cost does not include the cost of accommodation, travel, food or beverages.

To qualify for the tax credit, an activity:

- must be engaged in weekly for at least eight consecutive weeks or for five consecutive days, and

- must be structured (i.e., it must enable seniors to participate in an activity in a specific setting).

A physical activity must also enable seniors to develop or maintain their cardiorespiratory endurance, their muscular strength or endurance, their flexibility or their balance. Examples of structured physical activities eligible for the tax credit include dance, curling, swimming, tai chi, aquafitness, and bowling.

An artistic, cultural or recreational activity must enhance seniors' ability to develop or improve their dexterity, coordination, cognitive skills, social integration, or psychological well-being. Examples of structured artistic, cultural and recreational activities eligible for the tax credit include computers, singing (e.g., choir), arts and crafts, chess, painting, and knitting.

¶13625.11 — *Tax Credit for Eco-Friendly Home Renovation (RénoVert) (Form TP-1: Line 462, Item 32)*

The RénoVert tax credit is a temporary refundable tax credit for eco-friendly home renovation, available for the 2016 to 2019 tax years. Eco-friendly renovation work recognized for the purposes of the tax credit include renovations pertaining to insulation, sealing, doors that access the exterior, windows, and heating, air conditioning, water heating and ventilation systems, as well as to water quality and soil quality, provided the work relates to existing parts of an individual's eligible dwelling. Note that, applicable to renovation agreements entered into after March 31, 2017, the construction, renovation, modification or rebuilding of a system for the discharge, collection and disposal of waste water, toilet effluents or grey water does not qualify for the RénoVert tax credit, since the Waste Water Treatment Tax Credit applies to such work as of April 1, 2017 (see below).

Eligible costs are for work done by a qualified contractor under a contract entered into after March 17, 2016 and before April 1, 2019. Qualified expenditures must be paid by an individual by December 31, 2019. The work must have a positive environmental impact or improve the dwelling's energy efficiency. Both principal residences and cottages are eligible dwellings for the tax credit, provided the cottage is suitable for year-round occupancy. The initial construction of the dwelling must have been completed before January 1, 2016.

The tax credit applies at the rate of 20% of eligible expenditures in excess of $2,500, up to a maximum cumulative tax credit of $10,000 per eligible dwelling. Co-owners of an eligible dwelling can split the tax credit. The maximum credit is achieved at renovation expenses totalling $52,500 or more.

For additional details on this temporary refundable credit, see the Revenu Québec website at: www.revenuquebec.ca/en/citoyen/credits/renovert/default.aspx. For a list of recognized eco-friendly renovation work, see: www.revenuquebec.ca/en/citoyen/credits/renovert/liste-travaux-reconnus.aspx.

¶13625.12 — *Tax Credit for the Upgrading of Residential Waste Water Treatment Systems (Form TP-1: Line 462, Item 33)*

The 2017 Québec budget introduced a new temporary refundable tax credit to financially assist home owners who must undertake work to upgrade their septic systems. The waste water treatment tax credit applies at the rate of 20% of qualified expenditures in excess of $2,500, up to a maximum tax credit of $5,500 per eligible dwelling. Qualified expenditures are those paid by an individual to have recognized work carried out to upgrade the waste water treatment system of an eligible dwelling located in Québec that is owned by the individual as the individual's principal place of residence or a cottage suitable for year-round occupancy that is normally occupied by the individual. As well, for the purposes of this credit, the initial construction of the dwelling must be complete before January 1, 2017, and the dwelling must be an isolated dwelling within the meaning of the *Regulation respecting waste water disposal systems for isolated dwellings.*

For the purposes of this credit, recognized work includes the construction, renovation, modification, rebuilding, relocation or enlargement of a system for the discharge, collection and disposal of waste water, toilet effluents or grey water of an eligible dwelling. Recognized work will also include necessary site restoration work. However, work may be recognized only if the carrying out of the work is awarded to a qualified contractor under the terms of an agreement entered into after March 31, 2017 and before April 1, 2022. At the time the agreement is entered into, the contractor must be a person or a partnership with an establishment in Québec. In addition, the contractor must hold an appropriate licence issued by the Régie du bâtiment du Québec and the licence security at the time the work is carried out.

Qualified expenditures must be paid in the year and include the cost of permits necessary to carry out the work (including the cost of studies carried out to obtain the permits), the cost of services provided by the contractor to carry out the work, and the cost of movable property that is used in carrying out the work, subject to certain limitations. Expenditures that cannot be claimed for the purposes of this credit include any portion of an individual's costs attributable to the carrying out of recognized work provided for in a service agreement in relation to an eligible dwelling that is: used to finance the cost of recognized work, attributable to goods or services supplied by a non-arm's length person (unless the person holds a QST registration number), deductible in the calculation of an individual's business or property income, or included in the capital cost of depreciable property.

To claim the waste water treatment tax credit, an individual must enclose, with his or her tax return for the year, a completed information return, *Tax Credit for the Upgrading of Residential Waste Water Treatment Systems* (TP-TP-1029.AE.D-V), indicating the description of the work carried out, its cost, the QST registration number assigned to the contractor that carried out the work or, if there is no such number, the contractor's business number or social insurance number and, if applicable, the licence number issued to the contractor by the Régie du bâtiment du Québec. Supporting documents (bids, invoices, etc.) must be kept for the purpose of subsequent verifications by Revenu Québec. Co-owners of an eligible dwelling can split the tax credit.

¶13630 — Refund (Form TP-1: Line 474)

Revenu Québec may use part or all of an individual's refund to pay a debt owed by the individual to the government under a law administered by the government or one of the following laws:

* *Act respecting the Société d'habitation du Québec*;
* *Individual and Family Assistance Act*;
* *Act to facilitate the payment of support*;
* *Act respecting financial assistance for education expenses*;
* *Act respecting family benefits*;
* *Act respecting parental insurance*;
* *Health Insurance Act*.

A refund of less than $2 is not required to be paid out.

If an individual is entitled to an income tax refund, interest will be calculated beginning as of the later of June 15th of the year following the tax year and the 46th day after the day the individual's income tax return was filed.

¶13635 — Transfer to Spouse (Form TP-1: Lines 476, 477)

An individual can transfer all or part of his or her refund to his or her spouse by entering the amount on Line 476. The amount transferred cannot exceed the balance due by the spouse on Line 475 of his or her Québec income tax return. The amount transferred must be entered on Line 477 of the transferee spouse's return.

¶13700 — Assessment

¶13710 — Assessment

After an individual files his or her income tax return, a cursory review is conducted and the individual is sent a Notice of Assessment.

Revenu Québec generally has three years from the date of the Notice of Assessment to conduct a more thorough review and issue a Notice of Reassessment. Individuals should keep all documents supporting the information provided in their income tax return in case a review is carried out. Individuals carrying on a business should keep supporting documents for at least six years from the date they file their income tax return.

¶13720 — Recourse

¶13721 — *Complaint*

An individual may file a complaint with the Direction du traitement des plaintes. The Direction has no decision-making power, but ensures that problems are directed to the appropriate administrative unit.

A complaint must include the following information:

- the individual's name, address and telephone number, and the name, address and telephone number of the individual's representative, if applicable;

- the individual's social insurance number;

- the individual's Québec enterprise number and identification and file numbers, if applicable;

- the taxation period or year covered by the complaint;

- a full description of the problem;

- a detailed list of steps taken by the individual with Revenu Québec including dates of telephone calls, letters sent, names of persons spoken to, etc.; and

- the results obtained to date.

¶13722 — *Cancellation of Interest, Penalties, or Charges*

Interest, penalties, or charges that an individual must pay pursuant to a tax law may be cancelled if:

- after a complete financial analysis of the individual's situation, Revenu Québec determines that the individual is unable to repay his or her debt and a significant portion of this debt is made up of interest, penalties, or charges;

- the individual incurred the interest, penalty, or charges as a result of an error in documentation or information provided to the individual from Revenu Québec; or

- an exceptional situation beyond the individual's control, such as a fire or serious illness, prevented the individual from meeting his or her tax obligations.

To apply for the cancellation of interest, penalties, or charges, the individual must send Revenu Québec a letter explaining his or her situation, or complete one of the following forms: Form MR-94.1-V, *Application for the Cancellation of Interest, Penalties or Charges*; Form FP-4288-V, *Application for the Cancellation of Interest, Penalties or Charges Related to the GST or QST*; or Form MR-94.1.R-V, *Application for the Cancellation of Penalties Related to the Sommaire Périodique des Ventes*.

If the individual is not satisfied with the decision made, he or she can request a review by sending Revenu Québec a letter explaining why he or she believes the decision is unfair or unfounded, or may use one of the forms listed above. The Minister's review decision is final.

¶13723 — *Objection*

If an individual is not satisfied with the results obtained after contacting Revenu Québec, the individual may contest a Notice of Assessment or a Notice of Determination by serving a Notice of Objection.

Serving a Notice of Objection is necessary to safeguard the right of appeal. The Notice of Objection must be served within 90 days of the date on which the Notice of Assessment or Notice of Determination was issued. There is no fee for an objection.

If, at the time of an objection to a Notice of Assessment, the individual has an unpaid balance relating to an amount in dispute, Revenu Québec will not take measures to recover the amount while the individual's file is under review, unless the unpaid amount relates to source deductions or consumption taxes. Interest will, however, continue to accrue.

To file an objection, the individual must send Revenu Québec a letter setting out the facts and reasons for the objection and including the number of the Notice of Assessment or Notice of Determination being contested and the date on which it was issued. Alternatively, an individual may use Form MR-93.1.1-V, *Notice of Objection* or Form FP-159-V, *Notice of Objection (GST/QST)*. All supporting documents and a copy of the notice being contested must be included with the letter or objection.

¶13724 — *Appeal*

If an individual is not satisfied with a decision regarding a Notice of Objection, the individual may file an appeal with the Civil Division of the Court of Québec.

An individual may also go to the courts if Revenu Québec fails to render a decision within the time period required by the *Tax Administration Act* or the *Excise Tax Act*.

In certain cases, an individual may contest a decision by filing a summary appeal with the Small Claims Division of the Court of Québec.

Chapter 14 — Assessments, Audits, and Avoidance Rules

Contents

¶14000 Adjustments, Assessments, and Objections

    ¶14010 Adjusting a Filed T1 Return

    ¶14020 Assessments and Reassessments

    ¶14030 Assessment Checklist

    ¶14040 Waivers

    ¶14050 Objections

¶14100 Audits and Investigations

    ¶14110 Tax Audits

    ¶14120 Books and Records

    ¶14130 Investigations and Inspections

    ¶14140 Solicitor-Client Privilege

¶14200 Income Splitting and the Attribution Rules

    ¶14210 Tax on Split Income (TOSI)

    ¶14220 Transfers and Loans to Spouse or Common-Law Partner and Minors

    ¶14230 Attribution of Gains/Losses to Spouse or Common Law Partner

    ¶14240 Transfers and Loans to a Trust

    ¶14250 Transfers and Loans to a Corporation

    ¶14260 Transfers of Property to a Reversionary Trust

    ¶14270 Income Splitting Strategies

¶14300 Other Avoidance Rules

    ¶14310 Benefit Conferred (Indirect Payments or Transfers)

    ¶14320 Transfer of Income Rights

    ¶14330 Non-Arm's Length Loans

    ¶14340 Inadequate Consideration

    ¶14350 Shareholder Benefits and Loans

    ¶14360 Non-Arm's Length Sale of Shares (Surplus Stripping)

¶14400 General-Anti Avoidance Rule (GAAR)

    ¶14410 Consequences of GAAR Applying

¶14420 Series of Transactions

¶14430 Post-Canada Trustco GAAR Cases

¶14000 — Adjustments, Assessments, and Objections

¶14010 — Adjusting a Filed T1 Return

There is no specific provision in the ITA to allow individuals to amend a T1 return after filing. However, the CRA administratively allows individuals to make changes to filed T1 returns by filing Form T1-ADJ, T1 *Adjustment Request*, or by sending a signed letter with the details of the adjustment request. Form T1-ADJ requires the taxpayer to set out information regarding the nature of the change, the affected T1 return line item (or items), and the amount of the change to each line item. Taxpayers should include documents to support an adjustment request, including receipts, statements, or other information. Individuals should wait to file an adjustment until they receive their notice of assessment for the return.

The CRA generally accepts adjustment requests for as far back as ten years if the adjustment results from an error or omission. However, adjustments relating to discretionary deductions, such as depreciation, are generally accepted only within the normal objection period (see ¶14050). The adjustment request should be sent to the taxation centre where the individual files his or her return (see ¶1121). Individuals can also make adjustment requests using My Account at: canada.ca/en/revenue-agency/services/e-services/e-services-individuals/account-individuals.html.

¶14020 — Assessments and Reassessments

¶14021 — *Initial Assessment*

The CRA processes T1 returns at the applicable CRA Tax Centre. The CRA is required by the ITA to examine "with all due dispatch" all T1 returns that have been filed and to send a Notice of Assessment to the individual. When the return is assessed, the CRA will mail a Notice of Assessment and, if applicable, an explanation of any changes made to the T1 return.

Once an assessment is made, subject to an appeal, it is valid and binding on the individual notwithstanding any error or defect. However, it is not the assessment itself that creates the liability for tax; rather, it is the operation of the ITA as a whole. Thus, an incorrect assessment does not relieve an individual from liability for tax under the provisions of the ITA. Also, the Courts have generally found that the scheme of taxation presumes that a reasonable person would make inquiries if something were clearly amiss in an assessment.

Once the Notice of Assessment is received, it should be compared to the filed return and the CRA should be contacted to clarify or explain any part of the assessment that is contentious. For CRA contact information, visit: canada.ca/en/revenue-agency/corporate/contact-information.html.

The Federal Court considered the meaning of "with all due dispatch" in *Ficek v. Attorney General of Canada*, 2013 CarswellNat 1465 (FC). The issue was whether the Minister had satisfied the duty to assess "with all due dispatch" under ITA 152(1) where it was not assessing the tax returns of taxpayers who participated in a certain tax shelter donation program until after it had audited the tax shelter. The court found that the term "with all due dispatch" is the equivalent of "with all due diligence" or "within a reasonable time". The time period for performance of the duty to assess is not fixed; it is a question of fact. The Minister is given discretion in respect of the "good administration of the Act"; however, discretion is not unfettered and must be reasonable. The purpose of ITA 152(1) is to bring some certainty to a taxpayer's financial affairs at the earliest reasonably possible time. Accordingly, the Court concluded that the Minister failed to comply with the duty to assess "with all due dispatch". In *McNally v. Canada*, 2015 FC 767, the court followed the reasoning in *Ficek*, holding that the phrase "with all due dispatch" does not imply a specific time period before which the Minister must make an assessment; however, while the Minister has broad discretion in assessing taxpayers, it is not unfettered. The court ultimately concluded that the Minister had failed to assess the taxpayer's tax return "with all due dispatch."

ITA 152(1), (3), (3.1), (4), (4.01), (4.1), (7), (8), *Ginsberg*, [1996] 3 C.T.C. 63 (FCA), *Sabharwal*, 2010 CarswellNat 170 (TCC), *Imperial Oil*, [2003] 4 C.T.C. 177 (FCA), *Jolicoeur*, [1960] C.T.C. 346 (Exch. Ct.), *Merlis Investments*, [2001] 1 C.T.C. 57 (FCTD), *Western Minerals*, [1962] C.T.C. 270 (SCC), VD 2007-0243351C6

¶14022 — *Reassessment*

The CRA can reassess a T1 return or make additional assessments of tax, interest, and penalties within the "normal reassessment period". The normal reassessment period for individuals is within three years from the earlier of: (1) the date the CRA *sent* the original notice of assessment for the tax year; and (2) the date the CRA sent the notification that no tax is payable. Effective December 15, 2010, the date of an assessment or determination is deemed to be the date of "sending" (as opposed to the date of "mailing") of the Notice of Assessment or the Notice of Determination. CRA correspondence that is mailed or sent electronically is presumed to be mailed or sent on the date of the notice or notification.

A Notice of Assessment or no tax payable notice is sent only if an individual has filed a T1 return. As a result, there is no time limit for an assessment or reassessment of tax where no return is filed. Where an individual is notified in writing that no tax is payable for the taxation year, CRA has not actually assessed tax, interest, or penalties. Thus, a notification of no tax payable is not an assessment, and there is no right of objection or appeal for this type of notice. As a result, after the normal reassessment period has expired, CRA may continue to issue notices indicating that no tax is payable. Where a notification of no tax payable is issued, any factor that determines the amount of tax for a taxation year is open to review by CRA. As a result, an individual may be open for reassessment of a loss for much longer than the normal reassessment period.

The normal reassessment period can be extended for an additional three years for any of the following reasons

- The individual wants to carry back a loss or credit from a later tax year;

- A non-arm's length transaction between the individual and a non-resident affects the individual's tax;

- The individual pays an amount or receives a refund of foreign income or profits tax;

- A reassessment of another taxpayer's tax for any of the above listed reasons affects the individual's tax;

- A reassessment of another tax year (it must be a prior tax year if the reassessment relates to a loss or credit carryback) for any of the above reasons affects the individual's tax;

- To give effect to the application of the non-resident trust rules in ITA 94, or the foreign investment rules in ITA 94.1 and 94.2;

- The transaction involves a tax shelter or a "reportable transaction" (ITA 237.3(1)) and the information return that is required for the tax shelter or reportable transaction is not filed as and when required; or

- The individual failed to report income from a "specified foreign property" (ITA 233.3(1)) on his or her return and Form T1135 was not filed on time, or a specified foreign property was not identified, or was improperly identified, on Form T1135.

The CRA can reassess a T1 return *at any time* (i.e., no time limit applies) in the following situations:

- The individual has made a misrepresentation because of neglect, carelessness, wilful default, or fraud in either filing the return or supplying information required by the ITA (the CRA's general position is that a misrepresentation has occurred if there is an incorrect statement on the T1 return that is material to the purposes of the return and to any future reassessment);

- The individual filed Form T2029, *Waiver in Respect of the Normal Reassessment Period or Extended Reassessment Period*, with a CRA Tax Services Office before the normal reassessment period expires (the time during which a waiver can be filed is extended an additional three years after the end of the normal reassessment period if the waiver applies to one of the situations described above);

- The reassessment is to carry back losses or certain tax credits and deductions where a prescribed form requesting the amendment has been filed on a timely basis; or

- A court instructs the CRA to reassess.

If the reassessment is after the three-year limit, the CRA may only revise the individual's income to the extent that it may reasonably be considered to relate to those matters set out in the related waiver or misrepresentation.

In addition, where it is necessary as a result of an assessment or an appeal of a taxpayer to adjust a "balance" that is relevant for another taxation year, ITA 152(4.3) allows the CRA to reassess the other taxation year beyond its normal reassessment period. This is known as a "consequential reassessment". Such reassessments apply only to subsequent taxation years. For example, adjustments to a 2014 balance may be used only to reassess the T1 return for 2015 and subsequent years. A "balance" for a taxation year includes an individual's income, taxable income, taxable income earned in Canada, loss, or tax payable or refundable for the year. The CRA is effectively given one year to make a conforming reassessment for a subsequent taxation year.

ITA 152(1), (3), (3.1), (4), (4.01), (4.1), (7), (8), *Riendeau*, [1990] 1 C.T.C. 141 (FCA), *Simard-Beaudry Inc.*, 1971 CarswellNat 239, *Optical Recording Laboratories Inc.*, [1986] 2 C.T.C. 325 (FCTD), *M.N.R. v. Leung*, [1993] 2 C.T.C. 284 (F.C.T.D.), *Blackburn Radio Inc.*, 2012 TCC 255, *Hevey*, [2005] 1 C.T.C. 2848 (TCC); *Bulk Transfer Systems Inc.*, [2004] 2 C.T.C. 2995 (TCC); aff'd [2005] 2 C.T.C. 87 (FCA); *Sherway Centre Ltd.*, [2003] 1 C.T.C. 123 (FCA), VD 2010-0378861I7, 2010-0374771I7, VDs 2011-0404471C6, 2009-0343601I7, IC 75-7R3

¶14023 — *Applying for a Loss Determination*

The objection and appeal process normally does not apply to loss amounts under dispute because there is no tax, interest, or penalty involved. A notification that no tax is payable is considered an "assessment"; however, a nil assessment cannot be appealed, even if the appeal is about something other than losses. As well, a taxpayer cannot object to a notification that no tax is payable, which may be relevant where the taxpayer wishes to change a filing position. However, if a taxpayer does not agree with the losses that the CRA has assessed, the taxpayer can request the CRA to make a loss determination, and the taxpayer may object to such a determination. A loss determination request can be made in respect of a non-capital loss, a net capital loss, a restricted farm loss, a farm loss, or a limited partnership loss. In order to make a loss determination request, the CRA must first have ascertained that the amount of the individual's loss is different from the amount reported by the individual. A request for a loss determination should be made in writing, and sent to the taxpayer's CRA Tax Services Office or Tax Centre. There is no prescribed form for such requests.

When a loss determination request is made, the CRA will officially determine the amount of the loss and confirm it in writing by sending Form T67AM, *Notice of Determination/Redetermination of a Loss*. Once a taxpayer has received this form, he or she can appeal the loss determination as though it were a Notice of Assessment. The determination is binding on both CRA and the individual, subject to an objection or appeal by the individual or a redetermination by the CRA within the normal reassessment period.

With respect to the loss determination process, in VD 2011-0401241I7, the CRA states:

> In the Canadian Tax Court decision *Inco Limited v. HMQ*, 2004 D.T.C. 2847, the court confirmed that three steps are required for a loss determination:
>
> > [13] ... On the other hand, subsection 152(1.1) of the Act clearly contemplates and establishes a procedure involving sequential steps or events that must take place in order for there to be a valid loss determination. These steps are: (a) the Minister ascertains the amount of a taxpayer's non-capital loss for a taxation year in an amount that differs from the one reported in the taxpayer's income tax return; (b) the taxpayer requests that the Minister determine the amount of the loss; (c) the Minister thereupon determines the amount of the loss and issues a notice of loss determination to the taxpayer.
>
> Paragraph 4 of Interpretation Bulletin IT-512 (cancelled), *Determination and Redetermination of Losses*, also clarifies the CRA's position on the requirements for a loss determination to be issued:
>
> > 4. Where at the initial assessing stage or as a consequence of a reassessment arising from an audit or other investigative action by the Department the Minister ascertains a loss in an amount other than that reported by the taxpayer, a notice of assessment or reassessment (including a notice of "nil" assessment or reassessment) will be issued with an explanation of the changes. As well, the notice will inform the taxpayer that upon request the

Minister will make a determination of the loss so ascertained and issue a notice of determination/redetermination. In this context, the Minister will not be considered to have ascertained that the amount of a loss differs from an amount reported by the taxpayer where the difference fully reflects a change requested by the taxpayer as a result of amended or new information.

Therefore, where the difference in the amount of a loss for the year reflects an amendment by the taxpayer, this is not considered to be "ascertained" by the Minister, and therefore, on its own, does not meet the requirements for subsection 152(1.1) loss determination. Therefore, in this case, because the taxpayer is requesting the changes and the Minister would not be "ascertaining" the amount of the loss, the taxpayer cannot request a loss determination.

ITA 152(1.1), (1.2), (3.1), *Interior Savings Credit Union*, [2007] 4 C.T.C. 55 (FCA), *Clibetre Exploration*, [2003] 1 C.T.C. 106 (FCA), VD 2008-0284301I7, IT-512: *Determination and Redetermination of Losses*

¶14030 — Assessments Checklist

The table below summarizes factors to consider in determining whether a taxation year or balance (such as loss carryforwards) of a taxpayer may be subject to reassessment or adjustment by the CRA.

Topic	Comments	Reference
Multiple assessments	A reassessment does not "restart the clock" for purposes of determining the statute-barred period. Except for cases in which the reassessment period is extended by virtue of a waiver or a misrepresentation, a reassessment must be issued within the time frame as established by the first notice of assessment issued.	ITA 152(3.1), (4)
Assessments outside normal assessing period	If there is a misrepresentation or fraud of the type described in ITA 152(4)(a)(i), a reassessment can be made to the extent that the adjustments may reasonably be considered to relate to the misrepresentation. There is no time limit for reassessment in such a case.	ITA 152(4)(a)(i), 152(4.01)
Misrepresentation	Generally, case law has established that any error is tantamount to a misrepresentation and a misrepresentation includes an incorrect statement; see, for example, *Foot*, [1964] C.T.C. 317 (SCC), *Taylor*, [1961] C.T.C. 211 (Ex Ct), *Nesbitt*, 1996 CarswellNat 1916 (FCA), and *Ridge Run Developments*, [2007] 3 C.T.C. 2605 (TCC).	VDs 2005-0113241I7, 2009-0343601I7
Misrepresentation attributable to neglect or wilful carelessness	For the extended reassessment period under ITA 152(4)(a)(i) to apply, there must be a misrepresentation and that misrepresentation must be attributable to neglect, carelessness or wilful default (unless there is fraud). *McKellar*, [2007] 4 C.T.C. 2399 (TCC), in which an investor who consulted a chartered accountant before claiming partnership losses, is an example of a case in which the Court found that a misrepresentation was not attributable to neglect. See also P. Friedlan et al., "Reassessments When an Accountant Was Negligent", *Tax for the Owner-Manager*, Vol. 14-3, July 2014.	150(4)(a)(i), *Boucher*, [2004] 2 C.T.C. 179 (FCA), *O'Dea*, 2009 CarswellNat 1443 (TCC)
Establishing negligence	Generally, negligence is established under ITA 152(4)(a)(i) if it is shown that the taxpayer has not exercised reasonable care. If a taxpayer has made a misrepresentation but the misrepresentation is not attributable to neglect, the CRA cannot reassess under ITA 152(4)(a)(i). Generally, when a taxpayer files a T1 return on what it believes to be the proper method, after thoughtful, deliberate and careful assessment, there can be no misrepresentation attributable to neglect, carelessness or wilful default; see, for example, *Regina Shoppers Mall Ltd.*, [1991] 1 C.T.C. 297 (FCA).	*Venne*, [1984] C.T.C. 223 (FCTD), *Froese*, 1981 CarswellNat 319 (TRB), VD 2005-0113241I7, 9220357

Topic	Comments	Reference
Aggressive filing positions	The CRA may be able to reassess outside the normal limitation period when a contentious filing position was taken in the applicable T1 return filed. However, a filing position taken in respect of an uncertain issue (such whether a gain is on account of income or capital) the CRA does not agree with will not, in and of itself, give rise to a misrepresentation. The CRA generally must prove at least one instance of misrepresentation by the taxpayer/registrant that, while it may have been made in good faith, was nevertheless not one that a normally wise and cautious taxpayer/registrant would have committed.	*Labow*, 2010 CarswellNat 2619 (TCC), Chapter 11 of the CRA's Audit Manual
Reliance on an accountant	A taxpayer cannot escape the consequences of ITA 152(4)(a)(i) merely by stating that a professional accountant was relied upon in filing a return; *Snowball*, [1996] 2 C.T.C. 2513 (TCC).	*College Park Motors*, 2009 CarswellNat 2405 (TCC)
Reliance on a valuator	*Bona fide* reliance on a professional valuator in respect of an amount reported in a T1 return provides a potential defence against an ITA 152(4)(a)(i) assessment.	*Petric*, [2006] 4 C.T.C. 2450 (TCC)
Misrepresentation in statute-barred years	A misrepresentation in a particular taxation year is also a misrepresentation in all subsequent years in which the misrepresented amount is relevant.	VD 2009-034360I7
Onus of proof	Where a reassessment is made outside the statutory reassessment period under ITA 152(4)(a)(i), the onus is upon the Minister to establish the existence of a misrepresentation or fraud.	*Taylor*, [1961] C.T.C. 211 (Ex ct)
CRA detection of errors	In applying ITA 152(4)(a)(i), it is irrelevant whether or not the CRA should have detected the error when the return was filed.	*Nesbitt*, 1996 CarswellNat 1916 (FCA)
Gross negligence penalties	A gross negligence penalty does not necessarily apply where a taxpayer has been reassessed under ITA 152(4)(a)(i); see, for example, *Angus*, [1996] 3 C.T.C. 2618 (TCC). A higher degree of culpability is required for imposing such penalties. Also, the actions of a taxpayer's accountant or other tax advisor may assist in a defence against such penalties; see *Snowball* and *College Park Motors*. In *Knight*, 2012 CarswellNat 1127 (TCC), the Court held that penalties for omissions under ITA 163(1) can be greater than those for gross negligence under ITA 163(2). See also Marlene Cepparo, "Right To Assess After the Normal Period", *Canadian Tax Highlights*, Vol. 22-8, Aug. 2014.	ITA 163(2), *Venne*, [1984] C.T.C. 223 (FCTD), *Chaumont*, 2009 CarswellNat 3798 (TCC)), VD 2013-050905I7
Reassessments outside the normal assessment period	Several provisions of the ITA provide that assessments can be made "notwithstanding subsections 152(4) to (5)", thus overriding the normal reassessment period. Such reassessments can apply, for example, to deemed outlays or expenses, illegal payments, situations involving inadequate consideration and tax shelters.	152(4), (5), 12(2.2), 67.5(2), 69(12), 143.2(15), 184(4)

Topic	Comments	Reference
Adjustments to carryforward tax balances	Generally, the CRA's position, which is supported by various court decisions, is that audit adjustments that do not result in additional taxes payable and only impact the ascertainment of tax account balances (such as non-capital loss and ITC carryforward balances) can be carried out after the normal reassessment period (VDs 2015-0575921I7, 2011-0425501E5, 2013-0475621I7, 2009-0343601I7, 2008-0284301I7, 2006-0185291E5, 2002-0157005). It should also be possible for a taxpayer to make similar adjustments to carryforward balances to correct an error reported in a previous year or to recognize a loss that was previously not reported (*Leola Purdy Sons Ltd.*, [2009] 4 C.T.C. 2041 (TCC)). However, the CRA generally does not permit a re-characterization of expenses from statute-barred years (see VD 2010-0352901I7).	*New St James Ltd*, [1966] C.T.C. 305 (Exch), *Papiers Cascades Cabano Inc.*, [2007] 5 C.T.C. 26 (FCA), VDs 2012-0442961C6, 2013-0479161E5 and 2013-0514331I7
Withholding taxes	There is no assessment limitation period applicable to employee source deductions, non-resident withholding taxes, withholding obligations under ITA 116 in respect of a disposition of taxable Canadian property by a non-resident, or a director's liability for unpaid source deductions.	ITA 227(4), (4.1), (8.4), (10), (10.1)
Consequential assessments	The CRA can reassess beyond the normal reassessment period where it is necessary to recalculate a taxpayer's "balance" for that year as a result of an assessment or a decision on appeal therefrom for a previous taxation year requiring an adjustment to an amount deducted or included in computing the "balance" of the taxpayer for that previous taxation year.	¶14022, ITA 152(4.3), VD 2012-0463681I7
Notification that no taxes are payable	A notification that no tax is payable is considered an "assessment" for purposes of establishing the normal reassessment period and determining whether a particular taxation year is statute-barred. However, a nil assessment cannot be appealed even if the appeal is about something other than losses. Also, a taxpayer cannot object to a notification that no tax is payable, which may be relevant where the taxpayer wishes to change a filing position.	ITA 152(3.1), *Interior Savings Credit Union*, [2007] 4 C.T.C. 55 (FCA), 2008-0284301I7
Loss determinations	Where the CRA ascertains that the amount of a taxpayer's loss for a particular year is different from the amount reported in the taxpayer's T1 return for that year, the taxpayer may request that the CRA determine the amount of the taxpayer's loss for that year. A determination of losses is separate from a notice of assessment and can be objected to by a taxpayer. An appeal can also be made in a year a loss carryforward from a statute-barred year is denied.	¶14023, ITA 152(1.1), 165, IT-512, *Clibetre Exploration*, [2003] 1 C.T.C. 106 (FCA), 2014-0550351C6
Waivers	Where a taxpayer has filed a prescribed waiver with the CRA (Form T2029), the CRA can reassess the taxpayer in respect of those matters set out in the waiver. However, the Minister cannot reassess if the waiver has been revoked with 6 month's notice to the CRA.	¶14040 152(4)(a)(ii), (4.1)

Topic	Comments	Reference
GAAR reassessments	It is not clear whether a taxpayer can file a T1 return on the basis that the GAAR applies, and thus whether the CRA can apply ITA 152(4)(a)(i) where a taxpayer fails to self-assess under GAAR. The CRA's position is that a statute-barred taxation year can be reassessed under ITA 152(4)(a)(i) on the basis that the taxpayer should have determined that GAAR applied. In *Quinco Financial Inc.*, 2016 CarswellNat 4708 (TCC), the Court stated in *obiter* that a taxpayer is permitted to self-assess under the GAAR (paras. 42, 43). Also, in *J.K. Read Engineering*, 2014 CarswellNat 4126 (TCC), the Court held that interest on a GAAR assessment runs from the original balance-due day, stating that "nothing" in ITA 245 "suggest[s] that the application of the GAAR is suspended until an assessment is issued" (para. 43). See also Hogan, "Does a GAAR Assessment Extend the Normal Assessment Period?", *Canadian Tax Focus*, Vol. 7-2, May 2017, Kearl "GAAR Assessments: Still No Penalties Allowed nor Self-Assessment Permitted", *Corporate Structures* (Federated Press), V. XIV-2, 2017, Flood, "Must a Taxpayer Self-Assess Under GAAR?", CTH, Vol. 24-11, Nov. 2016.	245(7), *Copthorne Holdings Ltd.*, 2007 CarswellNat 2808 (TCC), *S.T.B. Holdings Ltd.*, [2003] 1 C.T.C. 36 (FCA); aff'g [2002] 1 C.T.C. 2814 (TCC)
Extended reassessment period	Generally, an extended reassessment period of an additional 3 years after the taxpayer's normal reassessment period applies where the assessment relates to: a loss carryback, adjustments to the losses of another taxpayer; a transaction between the taxpayer and a non-arm's length non-resident person; additional income tax payments to or reimbursements from the government of a foreign country; reductions of amounts renounced in respect of flow-through shares; or gifts of non-qualifying securities.	152(4)(b), *Labow v. R.*, 2010 CarswellNat 2619 (TCC), *Shaw-Almex Industries*, 2009 CarswellNat 3556 (TCC), 2015-061416I7
"Quick" assessments	The issuance of a "quick" assessment by the CRA (i.e., a standard assessment issued shortly after a return is filed) qualifies as an "assessment" under the ITA; see *Provincial Paper Ltd.*, [1954] C.T.C. 367 The CRA is not subject to a specific period of time for the issuance of an initial assessment.	VDs 2008-028430117, 2007-0243351C6
Favourable court decisions received by another taxpayer	After the notice of objection period has lapsed, the CRA's policy is that it will not reassess a taxation year under ITA 152(4) to recognize a favourable court decision received by another taxpayer.	IC 75-7R3 (para. 4), VDs 2004-0085251E5, 2013-0513401M4
Adjustments to assessed amounts	The CRA and the courts may increase or adjust an amount included in an assessment that is under objection or appeal at any time, provided that the total amount of the assessment does not increase.	152(9) Joint Committee Submission 2015-06-19B

¶14040 — Waivers

In addition to the CRA's power to reassess after the normal reassessment period in the event of misrepresentation, the power to reassess at any time is also provided for where the taxpayer has filed a waiver using Form T2029: *Waiver in Respect of The Normal Reassessment Period*, within the normal reassessment period for the taxpayer. In Form T2029, a taxpayer identifies the matters in respect of which the time limit is being waived. Any subsequent reassessment by the CRA must be restricted to the matters identified in the waiver.

A waiver may be revoked by a taxpayer on 6 month's notice by filing Form T652 at the applicable tax services office. Where a taxpayer has filed a notice of revocation in respect of a waiver for a particular taxation year, the CRA's position is that the taxpayer can file another waiver for that taxation year if the year is not statute-barred at the time of filing the second waiver. Thus, although the CRA's long standing position is that a notice of revocation of waiver cannot be withdrawn once it has been filed, if the taxation year involved is not statute-barred, the taxpayer can file another waiver in respect of that taxation year.

A wavier that did not specify the matters being waived was nonetheless held to be valid in *Fietz v. R.*, 2011 CarswellNat 4115 (TCC); aff'd 2013 FCA 32. In the case, the Court generally found that the waiver was valid since the intention of the taxpayer was clear despite the lack of information in the filed waiver form. Also, in *Noran West Developments*, 2012 CarswellNat 4953, a waiver was found to be valid despite the taxpayer's claims that the waiver was not intended to apply to the subject matter in question. Proposing to assess gross negligence penalties if a taxpayer does not sign a waiver breaches an auditor's duty of care and may make the CRA liable for damages (see *Leroux*, 2014 CarswellBC 1179 (BCSC) (paras. 349–351)).

Generally, a taxpayer should only provide a waiver if doing so benefits the taxpayer (the CRA may also benefit from the waiver, but the waiver should not be signed merely to accommodate the CRA). For example, a taxpayer should generally not sign a waiver at the CRA's request solely to prevent a taxation year from becoming statute-barred. It is important for a taxpayer to protect his or her statutory rights, including assessment limitation periods.

ITA 152(4)(a)(ii), (c), 152(4.01)(a)(ii), (4.1), VD 2010-0379511I7

¶14050 — Objections

Where the CRA reassesses a taxpayer's tax liability, a formal objection can be made if the taxpayer does not agree with the amount of tax, interest, or penalties assessed or reassessed by the CRA. A taxpayer has 90 days from the date of the assessment or reassessment to file the objection. After receiving a Notice of Objection, the CRA may reassess tax for a particular year regardless of whether the normal reassessment period has otherwise expired.

A taxpayer can file an objection by: (1) using the Register my formal dispute in My Account (canada.ca/en/revenue-agency/services/e-services/e-services-individuals/account-individuals.html); (2) filing Form T400A, *Objection — Income Tax Act*, or (3) sending a letter to the Chief of Appeals at the taxpayer's CRA Tax Services Office (cra-arc.gc.ca/tso/) or Tax Centre (see ¶1121). With respect to options (2) and (3), a failure to address a Notice of Objection to the Chief of Appeals and/or deliver the objection to the proper place can result in the objection being considered invalid (see, for example, *McClelland*, 2003 CarswellNat 3142 (TCC) and *Mohammed*, [2006] 4 C.T.C. 2191 (TCC)). Form T400A is addressed to the Chief of Appeals and contains instructions to send the objection to the taxpayer's Tax Services Office or Tax Centre.

The reasons for a Notice of Objection must be explained and all relevant facts must be outlined. When drafting a Notice of Objection, it is critical to gather all the relevant facts and to obtain a clear understanding of the CRA's position. The Notice of Objection forms part of the record to be filed with the Tax Court of Canada (if necessary) and statements of fact made in the notice are binding upon the taxpayer on appeal. All the grounds which the taxpayer may bring before the Tax Court should be fully detailed in the Notice of Objection.

It is not necessary to send a Notice of Objection by registered mail. As a best practice, a taxpayer should request the CRA to confirm in writing the receipt of the Notice of Objection or, if delivered by courier, obtain an acknowledgement of courier delivery. In *Hamer*, 2014 CarswellNat 2408 (TCC), the Court granted an application for an extension to file a notice of objection where the Crown failed to produce sufficient evidence to verify that the notice of reassessment in question had been mailed. See also John Sorensen, "Time To Object Extended", *Canadian Tax Highlights*, Vol. 22-8, Aug. 2014.

The CRA may issue more than one Notice of Reassessment in respect of a taxation year. The new Notice of Reassessment will normally cancel and replace a previous Notice of Assessment or Reassessment when the reassessment relates to the same Part of the ITA. In such a case, a new Notice of Objection must be served by the taxpayer with respect to any issue to which the taxpayer previously objected if the taxpayer wants to object to the revised assessment.

In the absence of a statutory provision to the contrary, the law governing the right of appeal is that which was in effect at the time an assessment is made and not that which was in effect for the year in respect of which the assessment was made.

Once the CRA receives the objection, an appeals officer at the applicable CRA Tax Services Office or Tax Centre will review the assessment or reassessment in dispute. The appeals officer will then contact the taxpayer or his or her authorized representative to try to resolve the dispute. If the differences in how the CRA interpreted or applied the law are not resolved, the taxpayer can appeal the assessment or reassessment to the Tax Court of Canada. Once a valid Notice of Objection has been filed, the CRA must reconsider the assessment and with all due dispatch vacate, confirm, or vary the assessment or reassessment, and notify the taxpayer in writing.

A taxpayer does not have to pay the disputed amount of tax, interest, or penalty while waiting for the outcome of the CRA's or the Tax Court of Canada's review. However, once the objection or appeal is settled, normal interest charges will apply to any tax, interest, or penalties outstanding. Interest charges are calculated from the balance-due day.

A taxpayer may apply to the CRA, or in certain circumstances, to the Tax Court of Canada, for an extension of time for filing a Notice of Objection. An application for extension must be made within one year after the expiry of the time limit for filing an objection or making a request. The taxpayer must demonstrate it was unable to act or to instruct another to act in the taxpayer's name during the limitation period or that the taxpayer had a *bona fide* intention to object to the assessment or to make the request within that time. The taxpayer must also demonstrate that it would be just and equitable for the CRA to grant the extension application and that the application was made as soon as circumstances permitted. An application for an extension for filing a Notice of Objection can be made to the CRA through the Chief of Appeals in a District Office or a CRA Taxation Centre. If the extension is granted, the Notice of Objection is considered to have been filed on the day when the CRA's decision is mailed. If the CRA refuses to grant the taxpayer's application for an extension to file a Notice of Objection under ITA 166.1, or fails to notify the taxpayer of its decision to grant or refuse an extension within 90 days following the date on which the application was served on the CRA, the taxpayer is entitled under ITA 166.2(1) to apply to the Tax Court of Canada to have the application granted. ITA 166.2(5) places the same mandatory limits on the Court's discretion to grant an extension application as those placed on the CRA. An extension was granted, for example, in *Carcone*, [2012] 2 C.T.C. 2043 (TCC), when the CRA failed to discharge the onus of showing that the Notices of Assessment in question had been sent at the time alleged and to the correct address of the taxpayer.

ITA 165, 166.1, 166.2, 225.1(7), *CIBC World Markets Inc.*, 2012 CarswellNat 33 (FCA), *Ocean Nutrition Canada Ltd. v. Nova Scotia*, [2012] 3 C.T.C. 110 (NS SC) (a corporation was allowed to appeal against a "nil" assessment), *Interior Savings Credit Union*, [2007] 4 C.T.C. 55 (FCA) (a nil assessment cannot be appealed, even if the appeal is not about losses but about refundable credits), *Newmont Canada*, [2006] 2 C.T.C. 148 (FCA) (a corporation was not permitted to appeal an issue not previously raised in a notice of objection); *Galway*, [1974] C.T.C. 313 (FCTD), *Cohen*, [1980] C.T.C. 318 (FCA), CRA Pamphlet P148: *Resolving Your Dispute: Objections and Appeal Rights Under the Income Tax Act*, IC 71-14R3, IC 75-7R3, IC 00-1R4, ITTN-32, VD 2005-0164681C6, Diep et al., "The Continued Pursuit by Taxpayers for Judicial Review in Canada", *Blakes on Canadian Tax Controversy & Tax Litigation* (Carswell), Stratas, "Writing Position Letters: Some Tips from an FCA Justice", *Canadian Tax Focus*, Vol. 2, No. 3, August 2012, Gibson et al., "The Art of Resolving Tax Disputes," *2011 Prairie Provinces Tax Conference*, (Toronto: Canadian Tax Foundation, 2011), 5:1–25

¶14051 — *Settlements*

The general policy of the CRA and Department of Justice is that there must be a legal basis for a settlement amount in respect of a tax dispute. For example, a compromise may be reached with respect to a valuation issue; however, the CRA will generally not agree to settle for a percentage of a disputed tax amount in respect of a yes/no issue. The CRA states comments on the tax disputes settlement process at: canada.ca/en/revenue-agency under "The Settlement Process".

In *Rosenberg*, 2016 CarswellNat 6765 (FC), the Court held that a negotiated agreement between a taxpayer and the CRA in which the CRA agreed not to proceed with any reassessment for certain taxation years was binding (see paras. 17, 88). See also Walker et al., "Deals with the CRA", CTH, Vol. 25-3, March 2017.

The Court held that the taxpayer was bound by a settlement offer accepted by counsel in *Granofsky*, 2016 CarswellNat 5269 (TCC) (specifically, the condition (ITA 169(3)) that the taxpayer provides "consent in writing" was satisfied by counsel acting on behalf of the taxpayer).

ITA 169, Aprile, "Settlement Offers and Qualifying for Cost Awards", *Canadian Tax Focus*, Vol. 3, No. 1, 2013, Grenon et al., "The Use of Access to Information Processes in Tax Disputes," *Report of Proceedings of the Sixty-Fourth Tax Conference, 2012 Conference Report* (Toronto: Canadian Tax Foundation, 2013), 33:1–37, Macdonell, "Settlement of Tax Disputes at the Appeals and Audit Stage," *2012 Tax Dispute Resolution, Compliance, and Administration Conference Report*, (Toronto: Canadian Tax Foundation, 2013), 6: 1–14

¶14100 — Audits and Investigations

The CRA is responsible for the administration of the ITA and is accountable to the Minister of National Revenue and the Parliament of Canada. The ITA sets out a number of administrative rules concerning the duties of the Minister and officials of the CRA. The ITA also vests the CRA with sweeping powers of inquiry into a taxpayer's affairs and governs the manner in which such inquiries or investigations may be carried out. The CRA's basic objective in conducting an audit is to ensure compliance with tax laws. The CRA's goals include being thorough (i.e., identification of all material issues) and efficient (the CRA has limited resources and is interested in maintaining a timely audit cycle to avoid taxation years becoming statute-barred).

Normally, if a taxpayer is selected for audit, the audit period will cover the most recent T1 filing year and the preceding year (commonly referred to as the one-plus-one policy). In addition to income tax, if the taxpayer is a GST/HST registrant, the CRA will normally perform a compliance review of such taxes, which may lead to a comprehensive GST/HST audit. If there are no adjustments assessed in the course of an audit, the auditor will normally issue a letter indicating no changes to the taxation year are required. If there are adjustments, the auditor will send a proposal letter providing details of the proposed adjustments; a taxpayer typically has 30 days to respond to the letter. The CRA's administrative policy is not to issue a proposal letter less than 30 days prior to the date when the relevant taxation year becomes statute-barred.

¶14110 — Tax Audits

¶14111 — *CRA Information Requests*

At the start of an audit, the CRA will typically send a taxpayer an initial request letter asking for general information related to a particular taxation year or transaction. Significant documentation is typically requested at the initial request stage, including financial statements, account printouts, emails, letters, memos, etc. When a taxpayer receives a CRA information request, generally, the taxpayer can comply with the request, negotiate to reduce the scope of the request or, where the request is considered overly burdensome or unfair, apply to the Federal Court for judicial review of the validity of the request. Normally, a taxpayer will comply with an information request.

When an initial audit request letter is received, it is often beneficial to request a meeting with the CRA to determine the scope of the audit and the purpose of the information requested. After determining the particular audit areas of interest, it may be possible to refine the information provided, thereby reducing audit compliance costs. In the course of negotiating information to be provided, it should be considered that Chapter 10.0 of the CRA's Audit Manual states: "When requesting books and records for audit purposes, auditors should be as specific as possible. The specific records available will depend on the industry involved, the nature of the taxpayer/registrant's business and the size of the business."

As well, CRA Investigation Policy 2010-06 provides as follows:

> Taxpayers and their representatives are encouraged to discuss material differences of opinion regarding the relevancy of information being requested with the official requesting that information. Where taxpayers or representatives continue to have concerns, they are encouraged to raise the issue with that official's supervisor, and to move progressively to higher levels of management as appropriate. The annex to this policy also discusses the legal recourse available, in terms of

requests for judicial review under civil procedures in the *Federal Courts Act*, and procedures for resolving claims that involve solicitor-client privilege.

Other than in cases of seeking a defense with respect to privilege (privilege may be used as a defense against a Crown's application for the provision of documents or information; see *Moodys LLP*, 2011 FC 713 for a discussion of solicitor-client privilege in this context), applying for judicial review of a CRA information request is fairly uncommon. Even if a taxpayer is successful at Court, the CRA is likely to issue a new slightly modified request. Application for judicial review must be made within 30 days in respect of a named person's requirement (see subsection 18.1(2) of the *Federal Courts Act*), 15 days in respect of an unnamed person's requirement, and 90 days in respect of a foreign-based requirement.

Delays in providing the CRA with information may result in the CRA seeking a compliance order under ITA 231.7 (see, for example, *Cornfield*, 2007 FC 436, *Jourdain*, 2007 FC 739, and *Morton*, 2007 FC 503). On summary application by an auditor in the Federal Court or superior court, a judge may order a person to provide any access, assistance, information, or document sought by the CRA under ITA 231.1 or 231.2. The decision in *Norris*, [2002] 3 C.T.C. 346 (FC), discussed the process relating to compliance orders.

A tax professional can submit certain documents to the CRA electronically using the CRA's "submit documents" service which can be accessed directly through Represent a Client (see: canada.ca/en/revenue-agency under "Represent a Client Overview").

ITA 231.7, *Cameco Corporation*, 2017 CarswellNat 3791 (FC) (CRA's application to compel taxpayer to produce employees for interviews was denied), *Lee*, 2016 CarswellNat 330 (FCA) (demand addressed to individual requiring information about his corporations held to be valid), *Money Stop Ltd.*, [2013] 3 C.T.C. 1 (FC), *Black Sun Rising Inc.*, 2013 CarswellNat 2332 (FC), CRA Guide RC4188, *What You Should Know About Audits*, Antel, "Disclosing Information to the CRA About Unnamed Non-Target Persons", *Canadian Tax Focus*, Vol. 3, No. 1, Feb. 2013, CPA Tax Blog, "Audit query replies & access to audit documentation — What are the CRA's guidelines?", Nov. 24, 2016 (cpa-canada.ca/en/connecting-and-news/blogs/tax-blog)

¶14112 — *Requesting CRA Audit Working Papers*

In the course of an audit, filing of a Notice of Objection, or filing of a Notice of Appeal to the Tax Court of Canada, a taxpayer may request information in the possession of the CRA, such as the auditor's working papers, or the report of the Appeals Officer. The CRA's audit report (i.e., Form T20) and working papers typically contain useful information, such as details of assumptions made by the CRA and cases the CRA has relied upon in forming its conclusions. Normally, the CRA will provide its audit reporting and working papers upon making an informal request. If necessary, a formal request can be made under the *Access to Information Act*. The CRA discusses the appropriate procedure for requesting access to such information in VD 2011-0403751C6.

ITA 241(5)(a), *Hanna and Dorion*, 2010 CarswellNat 4344 (FC), CRA Audit Manual section 3.4.7, Guide RC4067: *Protocol between auditors and appeals officers*, RC4415: *2010-2011 Annual Report to Parliament — The Administration of the Access to Information Act*, VD 2008-0285441C6

¶14120 — Books and Records

Taxpayers are required to keep adequate books or accounts in order that income subject to tax may be properly determined. Paper and electronic records are required to be retained for a period of 6 years from the end of the last taxation year to which they relate. Failure to meet the requirement to keep books and records is a punishable offence. The ITA does not require taxpayers to keep their books and records in paper format; the statutory requirement to keep books and records can be met provided the content and the quality of electronic records is sufficient to enable the taxes payable to be determined.

Specifically, ITA 230(1) requires that: "[e]very person carrying on business and every person who is required, by or pursuant to this Act, to pay or collect taxes or other amounts shall keep records and books of account (including an annual inventory kept in prescribed manner) at the person's place of business or residence in Canada or at such other place as may be designated by the Minister, in such form and containing such information *as will enable the taxes payable under this Act or the taxes or other amounts that should have been deducted, withheld or collected to be determined*" (commonly referred to as the "tax determination standard"). Such records must also substantiate and allow verification of all deductible expenses and they must be supported by vouchers or other source documentation in order to permit verification.

Information Circular 78-10R5: *Books and Records Retention/Destruction* discusses CRA views on what should be included in books and records (see in particular para. 29). If a taxpayer wishes to destroy records before the required retention period is over, Form T137: *Request for Destruction of Records* should be filed with the CRA.

In *Holotnak*, [1987] 2 C.T.C. 217 (FCTD); aff'd [1990] 1 C.T.C. 13 (FCA) at p 223, Mr Justice Cullen made the following statement that has been cited in numerous cases: "Section 230 of the Act requires taxpayers to keep adequate books and records. "Adequate" is not defined but it would seem that these records should support whatever the taxpayer is claiming for tax purposes".

Regarding CRA views of what is required for records and books of account to be adequate, see paragraphs 5 to 6 of IC 78-10R5 and Chapter 10 of the CRA's Audit Manual.

Methods and ways of keeping records are also discussed in IC 78-10R5 and in the case of electronic record-keeping, IC 05-1R1: *Electronic Record Keeping*.

ITA 230, 239, 248(1)"record", ITR 5800, *Freitag*, 5 Tax A.B.C. 54, *P X Cossette & Fits Inc*, 23 Tax A.B.C. 65, *Empire House (London) Limited*, [1966] C.T.C. 681, *Pytel*, [2010] 2 C.T.C. 2429 (TCC), *Keating*, [2001] 4 C.T.C. 2043 (TCC), *Archambault*, 2000 CarswellNat 3212 (TCC) IC 78-10R5, Guide RC4409, cra.gc.ca/records, VDs 2014-0526121E5, 2012-0461301E5, 2010-0384481I7

¶14130 — Investigations and Inspections

Pursuant to ITA 231.1(1), tax officials are authorized to inspect, audit, and examine books, records, and property of a taxpayer. Pursuant to ITA 231.2(1), the CRA may require that any person provide any information or any document for any purpose related to the administration or enforcement of the ITA. This requirement is broad, limited only to any purpose related to the administration or enforcement of the ITA. The general intention of ITA 231.2(1) is to provide the CRA the necessary inspection powers to govern a self-reporting tax system.

ITA 231.1(1)(a) specifically provides that an auditor may review "books or records" of a taxpayer or "documents" of the taxpayer or any other person. For this purpose, "documents" include money, a security, and a "record". A "record" is defined in the ITA to include an invoice, account, book, agreement, chart or table, diagram, image, map, memorandum, plan, return, voucher, letter, telegram, statement (financial or otherwise), and any other thing containing information (whether in written or any other form), and also includes computerized information. An auditor is also permitted to examine property in an inventory or any property, process or matter relating to a taxpayer or any other person that may assist in determining the accuracy of inventory of the taxpayer or in ascertaining the information that should be in the books or records of the taxpayer or any amount payable by the taxpayer under the ITA.

By virtue of ITA 231.2(2), the CRA may require a person to provide information or documents relating to unnamed persons only where prior judicial authorization has been given. Once the judicial authorization is obtained, it must be served on the third party together with the requirement to produce information. Formerly, ITA 231.2(3) provided that the CRA could apply *ex parte* to a judge for an order authorizing such a requirement, and after the requirement was served, the affected party had 15 days to apply for judicial review of the *ex parte* authorization. However, applicable to applications made by the CRA after June 26, 2013, the *ex parte* element of third party information applications was eliminated. A third party is now required to make any representations it chooses to make at the hearing of the application for the order. The third party information request rules were generally amended in response to *RBC Life Insurance Co*, 2013 CarswellNat 324 (FCA) and *Lordco Parts*, 2013 CarswellNat 323 (FCA), in which the CRA had its authorization revoked because the taxpayers successfully argued that the CRA had not disclosed all relevant information in its *ex parte* application to the court.

In *KPMG LLP*, 2016 CarswellNat 6263 (FC), the CRA obtained an order on an *ex parte* basis, imposing requirements on KPMG to disclose confidential information relating to certain of its unnamed clients, including their identities and documentation relating to their participation in an offshore company tax structure. A motion to quash the order was dismissed, as the Court found an accountants' Code of Professional Conduct, barring it from disclosing confidential information concerning affairs of clients subject to listed exceptions, did not prevent the CRA from requiring and obtaining information described in an order issued by court pursuant to ITA 231.2(3).

In *Cormark Securities Inc*, [2012] 3 C.T.C. 49 (FC), the Court refused to quash an *ex parte* order for information related to technology company loss trading transactions. At paragraph 49 of *Cormark*, the Court noted the effect of 1996 amendments to ITA 231.2 is to permit a type of fishing expedition for the purpose of facilitating the CRA's access to information. Furthermore, at paragraph 50 the Court stated:

> [T]he Minister no longer needs to show that the Requirement Order relates to a "genuine and serious inquiry" into the tax liability of a specific person or persons, or, for that matter, each and every person or entity targeted by the Order. Rather, it is appropriate to grant an ex parte application for a Requirement Order where the judge is satisfied that the information or documents relating to one or more unnamed persons is required to verify compliance with the *Income Tax Act* through a tax audit that is conducted in good faith …

In *Redeemer Foundation*, [2007] 1 C.T.C. 280 (FCA), the Court allowed the CRA to use a donor list obtained from the foundation to reassess donors whose contributions were not eligible for donation receipts. The foundation appealed the decision but in a 4-3 split, the Supreme Court of Canada dismissed the foundation's appeal (*Redeemer Foundation v MNR*, [2008] 5 C.T.C. 135 (SCC)), finding that the CRA's request for donor information was made for the legitimate purpose of investigating the validity of the foundation's status as a registered charity. The Court noted that requiring the CRA to obtain judicial authorization whenever an audit of a charity entails a possibility that its donors might be investigated and reassessed would be illogical and potentially require judicial authorization in a variety of other circumstances. See also W. Adams, et al., "Canada Revenue Agency Round Table," Report of Proceedings of Sixty-Second Tax Conference, 2010 Tax Conference (Toronto: Canadian Tax Foundation, 2011), 4:1-33, response 14.

In its Policy Statement, *Acquiring Information from Taxpayers, Registrants and Third Parties*, the CRA states:

> There is no need to issue a requirement under subsection 231.2(1) of the ITA, or to obtain judicial authorization under subsection 231.2(2) of the ITA, where the information being sought regarding unnamed persons relates solely to the audit of a named taxpayer. This information can be requested under the inspection powers of section 231.1 of the ITA, and this applies even if it is possible that the unnamed persons may become subject to a review as result of the audit of the named taxpayer.

In *Chambre des notaires*, 2016 CarswellQue 4460 (SCC), the Court held that the requirements provisions under the ITA, including ITA 231.2(1) and ITA 231.7, are unconstitutional and of no force or effect for notaries and lawyers acting as legal counsel. Additionally, in *Chambre des notaires* and *Thompson*, 2016 CarswellNat 1933 (SCC), the Court held that the exception for a lawyer's accounting records as set out in the "solicitor-client privilege" definition in ITA 232(1) is unconstitutional and invalid. In accordance with these decisions, lawyers and Quebec notaries are not required to respond to CRA information requests regarding their clients, and no person is required to provide the CRA with a notary's or lawyer's "accounting record[s]". See also Carbone et al., "Solicitor-Client Privilege and the Québec Court of Appeal", *Blakes on Canadian Tax Controversy & Tax Litigation* (Taxnet Pro), Sept. 2017, Ling et al., "SCC Upholds Solicitor-Client Privilege", *Canadian Tax Focus*, Vol. 6-3, Aug. 2016 and Taylor "Solicitor-client privilege vs the Canada Revenue Agency: the SCC speaks", Stewart McKelvey, June 10, 2016.

In *Rosenberg*, 2016 CarswellNat 6765 (FC), the Court held that a negotiated agreement between a taxpayer and the CRA was binding (see paras. 17 and 88). In the agreement, the CRA had agreed not to proceed with any reassessment for certain taxation years. As a result, the Court held that a demand for information issued by a new auditor against the terms of the agreement made with the former auditor was invalid. See also Walker et al., "Deals with the CRA", CTH, Vol. 25-3, March 2017.

ITA 231–231.5, 238, VD 2009-0316711C6, canada.ca/en/revenue-agency under "Acquiring Information from Taxpayers, Registrants and Third Parties", *Tower and Kitsch*, [2003] 4 C.T.C. 263 (FCA), *1144020 Ontario Ltd.*, [2005] 3 C.T.C. 310 (FC); *Nadler Estate*, [2006] 1 C.T.C. 128 (FCA), *Capital Vision Inc. v. Canada*, 2002 FCT 1317; *James Richardson & Sons, Ltd*, [1984] C.T.C. 345, Kroft et al., "Some Recent Canadian Cases on Issues in Canadian Tax Dispute Resolution", *Blakes on Canadian Tax Controversy & Tax Litigation* (Carswell), Sept. 2013

¶14131 — *Access to Foreign Information*

The CRA may obtain foreign-based information or documentation from a taxpayer relevant for the administration or enforcement of the ITA. By definition, this includes any information or document available or located outside Canada.

Specifically, the CRA may, by notice served whether personally or by registered or certified mail, require the information of any person resident in Canada or of a non-resident who carries on business in Canada. The notice must contain a reasonable period of time for production of information (at least 90 days), a description of the information or document required, and the consequences of failing to provide the information within the time stipulated. A person who receives notice may apply to a judge for a review of the requirement. The application must be made within 90 days of service of the notice. The judge may confirm the requirement, vary the requirement as considered appropriate in the circumstances, or set aside the requirement if it is considered to be unreasonable. A requirement will not be considered unreasonable if the information is under the control of or available to a non-resident that, although not controlled by the person served, is related to the person. When an application for review has been made, the period of time between making the application and the day when the decision is handed down is not counted in the period of time for response to the notice (as the notice stipulates), nor is it counted in the statutory limit for making tax assessments relating to foreign transactions between non-arm's length taxpayers.

ITA 231.6, *Cameco Corporation*, 2017 CarswellNat 3791 (FC) (ITA 231.7 request denied), Reid, "Documents Not Produced" (2011) vol. 19, no. 5 *Canadian Tax Highlights*, 2-3, Toaze, "Some Issues Arising in Transfer Pricing Audits & Disputes," *2006 British Columbia Tax Conference*, (Vancouver: Canadian Tax Foundation, 2006), 7:1–23

¶14140 — *Solicitor-Client Privilege*

When a lawyer is requested by the CRA, or any person duly authorized by the CRA, to provide information or to produce a document relating to a client, the lawyer and client are able to refuse to disclose the information or document if it is protected by solicitor-client privilege.

ITA 232 is designed to ensure that, in the face of the extensive powers of investigation and search provided by ITA 231.1 to 231.5, the protection afforded communications between client and lawyer is preserved. This is accomplished by establishing a method whereby a claim of a solicitor-client privilege in respect of any information or document in the possession of a lawyer that is about to be inspected, examined, or seized by the CRA can first be dealt with by a court. In the ITA, "solicitor-client privilege" is defined as the right, if any, that a person has in a superior court in the province where the matter arises to refuse to disclose an oral or documentary communication on the ground that the communication is one passing between the person and the person's lawyer in professional confidence, except that an accounting record of a lawyer, including any supporting voucher or cheque, is deemed not to be such communication. A lawyer is defined in the ITA to mean a barrister or solicitor, except in Quebec where the term means an advocate or notary.

Solicitor-client privilege includes "solicitor-client communication privilege" and "litigation privilege". "Solicitor-client communication privilege" is privilege that results from confidential communications in the course of the solicitor-client relationship for the purpose of giving or receiving legal advice. "Litigation privilege" protects communications from disclosure and communications that relate to an existing or expected ligation (litigation privilege may include communications made with parties other than the client's lawyer and can apply to non-confidential communications). Litigation privilege generally begins when there is a tangible litigation risk, such as when the CRA challenges a filing position.

Solicitor-client privilege is a substantive right and not just a rule of evidence. The classic definition of solicitor-client privilege can be found in *Wigmore on Evidence* (McNaughton rev. 1961) at paragraph 2292: "Where legal advice of any kind is sought from a professional legal advisor in his capacity as such, the communications relating to that purpose, made in confidence by the client, are at his instance permanently protected from disclosure by himself or by the legal advisor except the protection be waived". It is not necessary that communications protected by solicitor-client privilege occur in relation to litigation, actual or contemplated; it is required that there be a communication between a client and a solicitor that involves the seeking or giving of legal advice and that is intended to be confidential. In *Descôteaux c. Mierzwinski*, [1982] 1 S.C.R. 860 (S.C.C.), the Court stated:

> In summary, a lawyer's client is entitled to have all communications made with a view to obtaining legal advice kept confidential. Whether communications are made to the lawyer himself or to employees, and whether they deal with matters of an administrative nature such as financial means or with the actual nature of the legal problem, all information which a person must provide in order to obtain legal advice and which is given in confidence for that purpose enjoys the privileges attached to confidentiality. This confidentiality attaches to all communications made within the framework of the solicitor-client relationship, which arises as soon as the potential client takes the first steps, and consequently even before the formal retainer is established.

In *The Fundamentals of Canadian Income Tax* (Thomson Reuters Canada), Vern Krishna states:

> For tax purposes, "privilege" means the right that a person has to refuse to disclose an oral or documentary communication on the ground that the communication is one passing between client and lawyer in a professional confidence. In general terms, the following types of documents are covered by solicitor-client privilege: Correspondence between solicitor and client; Opinion letters; Tax plans, reorganizations, agreements of purchase and sale and other agreements.

The existence of solicitor-client privilege in any particular case depends upon the applicable provincial law. Privilege is a right belonging to the client who alone may waive the right. It is important to note that the waiver of privilege may be implied, such as when a document is disclosed to a third-party (discussed below; exceptions to this rule generally apply if disclosure is made under the compulsion of a third-party).

There is a distinction between a lawyer's ethical duty to keep matters concerning a client confidential and solicitor-client privilege. A document is not privileged merely because it is in the possession of a lawyer. In *Solosky* (1979), [1980] 1 S.C.R. 821, 50 C.C.C. (2d) 495 (S.C.C.), the Court stated (p. 502) ". . . it is not every item of correspondence passing between solicitor and client to which privilege attaches, for only those in which the client seeks the advice of counsel in his professional capacity, or in which counsel gives advice, are protected". Also, In *B. v. Canada* (1995), 3 B.C.L.R. (3d) 363, [1995] 5 W.W.R. 374 (B.C. S.C.), the Court stated (paras. 26 and 27):

> I find helpful the following passage from Sopinka, Lederman and Bryant, *The Law of Evidence in Canada* (Toronto: Butterworths, 1992) [pp. 626-27]:
>
> > Although confidentiality is the cornerstone for the protection of communications within particular relationships, confidentiality alone is not sufficient to attract privilege. Confidentiality may well attract other legal and ethical rights and obligations but it does not have its foundation in the evidentiary doctrine of privilege.
> >
> > Evidence law does not concern itself with the ethical requirement upon a professional such as a lawyer to hold in strict confidence all information acquired in the course of his or her professional relationship concerning the business and affairs of a client. The lawyer has a professional duty not to divulge such information without the client's approval or unless required by law to do so. This ethical rule is wider than the evidentiary solicitor-client privilege and applies without regard to the nature of the source of the information or the fact that others may share the knowledge. Where there is a stronger public interest in disclosure, it will override the professional duties of confidence. [Footnotes omitted.]
>
> In spite of the difficulty in defining the concepts of confidentiality as distinct from privilege, I am satisfied that there is a distinction. It is not enough, in my opinion, to establish only confidentiality in order to effect non-disclosure. It is only those documents that are privileged that are subject to non-disclosure.

Two recent Supreme Court of Canada decisions concluded that requirements to provide documents or information issued under the ITA to lawyers or notaries with respect to their clients' affairs constitute unreasonable seizures contrary to section 8 of the *Canadian Charter of Rights and Freedoms*, and consequently, that ITA 231.2(1), 231.7, and the accounting records exception in ITA 232(1) are unconstitutional and of no force or effect for lawyers and notaries acting as legal counsel. In *Chambre des notaires du Québec*, 2016 SCC 20, the Supreme Court concluded that the "requirement" scheme in the ITA is unconstitutional insofar as it applies to lawyers and notaries because it is an unreasonable seizure, and that the lawyers' accounting records exception in the "solicitor-client privilege" definition in the ITA is unconstitutional. Similarly, in *Thompson*, 2016 SCC 21, the Supreme Court applied its reasoning in *Chambre des notaires*, deciding that, because the lawyers' accounting records exception to the definition of "solicitor-client privilege" in ITA 232(1) is unconstitutional, the taxpayer had no obligation to disclose withheld client documentation.

ITA 232, *Iggillis Holdings Inc.*, 2018 CarswellNat 702 (FCA; appeal to SCC dismissed)), *Jakabfy*, 2013 CarswellNat 2237 (FC), *Welton Parent Inc.*, [2006] 2 C.T.C. 177 (FC), *Nesathurai*, [2008] G.S.T.C. 45 (FC), *Banque Nationale et Ouellette*, 2008 CarswellNat 1426 (FC), *MIL (Investments) S.A.*, [2006] 3 C.T.C. 2509 (TCC), *Richard A. Kanan Corp.*, 2011 CarswellNat 1193 (TCC), *Bank of Montreal v. Tortora*, 2010 BCSC 1430, Kroft, "Recent Developments in CRA's Reach for Information: Questions You Want Answered," 2011 British Columbia Tax Conference, (Vancouver: Canadian Tax Foundation, 2011), 5:1–88

¶14141 — *Establishing Privilege*

Recognition of the solicitor-client communication privilege is subject to certain basic conditions. The document or the communication must be a communication between the client and the lawyer under the professional relationship between the client and the lawyer (communications from a lawyer's assistant, student, or articling student are also privileged). Privilege does not apply to accounting records of a lawyer, including any supporting voucher or cheque. Statements of accounts are privileged in respect of the description of the legal work; as such, lawyers should create a separate document for the description of legal services.

For privilege to apply, the communication generally must be confidential. A lawyer meeting with a client in the presence of third parties (other than agents) may jeopardize privilege, as may providing a third party with the legal advice (for example, providing the document to banks or members of a partnership). Documents that constitute legal advice or a legal opinion should be clearly identified as "Privileged and Confidential" (copy of documents kept under the designation of "privileged" documents does not, however, in and of itself, make the documents privileged). As an exception to the above mentioned rules, a limited waiver of privilege is generally available where an accountant is permitted to review privileged documents for the purposes of auditing financial statements. Another example of a limited waiver of privilege may arise where it is necessary to disclose certain details to a CRA auditor to justify the deduction of legal fees in computing income for tax purposes.

Under the concept of common interest privilege, privilege in respect of a legal opinion will also generally not be waived if the opinion is merely exchanged between the parties to a business transaction (the interest must be common, but need not be identical, and the shared document must be intended to aid in the completion of the transaction for the benefit of all parties).

Kroft et al., "Principles Relating to Privilege Claims in a Discovery", *Blakes on Canadian Tax Controversy and Tax Litigation (Taxnet Pro)*, April 2016 (discusses *CIBC*, 2015 CarswellNat 6447 (TCC))

¶14142 — *Accountant Working Papers and Privilege*

In Canada, communications involving tax advice between an accountant and client, including audit working papers and tax files, are not privileged. In *Tower v. MNR*, 2003 FCA 307, the Federal Court of Appeal confirmed that there is no "class privilege" between accountants and their clients in Canada. The court concluded that accountants should not be allowed a class privilege since, unlike lawyers, accountants are not legally and ethically required to uphold and protect the public interest in the administration of justice, nor do they provide legal advice.

In *BP Canada Energy Company*, 2017 FCA 61, the Federal Court of Appeal considered whether or not the Federal Court (2015 CarswellNat 2117) was correct in ordering BP Canada to produce internal tax accrual working papers to the Minister pursuant to ITA 231.7(1) for purposes of assisting the Minister in conducting an ongoing audit of the taxpayer. The Federal Court of Appeal reversed the Federal Court's decision, and held that that corporate taxpayers cannot be required to produce their internal tax accrual working papers to the Minister for use in current and future audits of the taxpayer. The Federal Court of Appeal ruled that "the documents ordered to be produced, given the purpose for which they were sought, are beyond the reach of the Minister" (para 4). It is important to note that the Court did not foreclose the possibility that tax accrual working papers might be producible at the audit stage in specific cases; however, the Court concluded that the CRA could not invoke its audit powers to obtain general and unrestricted access to tax accrual working papers, and that those audit powers should be used with restraint when dealing with these types of documents.

There are certain specific circumstances where clients' communications with accountants may be privileged in Canada. The courts have held that communications from a lawyer to a client's agent, such as an accountant, are privileged if the function of the agent is essential to the giving or receiving of legal advice, as well as communications from the agent to the client's lawyer if made in order to assist the lawyer in providing legal advice. This is sometimes referred to as the "agent doctrine", since the accountant is acting as an agent of the client for purposes of obtaining legal advice. However, the mere fact that an accountant forwards documents to the solicitor at the client's request would be insufficient to rely on the agent doctrine to make the documents protected by privilege.

ITA 232, *Copthorne Holdings*, [2005] 4 C.T.C. 2085 (TCC), *Susan Hosiery Ltd.*, [1969] C.T.C. 353 (Ex Ct), *Tower and Kitsch*, [2003] 4 C.T.C. 263 (FCA), *Cineplex Odeon Corporation v The Attorney General of Canada*, [1994] 2 C.T.C. 293

¶14200 — Income Splitting and the Attribution Rules

Since Canadian federal and provincial income tax is levied at progressive rates, taxpayers often attempt to find ways to income split with lower-income family members in order to reduce the overall amount of income tax payable by the family unit as a whole. Income splitting generally refers to the diversion of taxable income from high-income individuals to family members in a lower tax bracket, thereby allowing for the utilization of multiple graduated tax brackets and basic personal tax credits. By virtue of the dividend tax credit, an individual with no other income can receive approximately $50,000 of eligible dividend income without being subject to personal tax in most provinces (eligible dividends are discussed under ¶3112).

There are various rules contained in the ITA that are intended to prevent income splitting strategies, including the tax on split income rules in ITA 120.4, the attribution rules in ITA 74.1 to 74.5, and the reversionary trust rule in ITA 75(2).

¶14210 — Tax on Split Income (TOSI)

ITA 120.4 imposes a special tax on split income (TOSI) at the highest individual marginal rate on certain passive income of a "specified individual". The TOSI was introduced to prevent income splitting with minor children by way of dividend sprinkling, which involves the acquisition of shares of a private corporation by low-income members of the family of a high-income principal shareholder. The rules apply to income from private business arrangements, such as dividends on private company shares, or income in the form of trust or partnership distributions derived from a business or rental activity of a related individual. In cases where the TOSI applies, the income is subject to tax at the highest individual marginal rate in the hands of the "specified individual", and personal tax credits (with the exception of the dividend tax credit, foreign tax credit, and after 2017, the disability tax credit) are denied with respect to the amounts. The TOSI does not apply to income received by a specified individual as salary or wages (i.e., employment income). The TOSI takes precedence over other anti-avoidance rules that apply to income sprinkling, meaning that, to the extent that an amount is subject to the TOSI, the other rules do not apply (e.g., ITA 56(5), 74.4(2)(g), 74.5(13)).

The TOSI rules were significantly amended, applicable to 2018 and later taxation years. Under the amended rules, the definition of a "specified individual" was expanded to include adult individuals who receive "split income". However, the TOSI generally only applies to adults to the extent that the relevant amount received is unreasonable in the circumstances, based on the individual's labour contribution, invested capital and previous returns and remuneration. A more stringent reasonableness test applies for persons between the ages of 18 and 24. The amended definition of "split income" includes dividends or interest paid by a private corporation directly or indirectly to an individual from a "related business" in respect of the individual and certain capital gains, unless the amount falls within a specific exclusion. Generally, a related business is a business from which split income is derived. There are also various exclusions from the application of the TOSI rules.

Note that an individual's split income is included when determining whether the individual qualifies for certain income-tested benefits, including personal tax credits, the age credit, the GST/HST credit, the Canada Child Benefit, the Working Income Tax Benefit and OAS benefits.

For the CRA's guidance on the amended TOSI rules, see "Guidance on the Application of the Split Income Rules for Adults" at: canada.ca/en/revenue-agency/programs/about-canada-revenue-agency-cra/federal-government-budgets/income-sprinkling/guidance-split-income-rules-adults.html. Also see the *Technical Backgrounder on Measures to Address Income Sprinkling* at: fin.gc.ca/n17/data/17-124_2-eng.asp.

¶14211 — Application of the Tax on Split Income

ITA 120.4 imposes the TOSI at the top marginal rate (33 per cent for 2016 and later taxation years) on "split income" of a "specified individual". For taxation years before 2018, a "specified individual" was an individual under 18 years of age who was a Canadian resident throughout the year with at least one Canadian resident parent at any time in that year. For 2018 and later taxation years, the definition of a "specified individual" is expanded to include Canadian resident adults aged 18 and over who receive "split income".

For 2018 and later taxation years, the "split income" of a specified individual for a taxation year is the aggregate of the following types of income:

1. Amounts required to be included in the specified individual's income for the year in respect of taxable dividends received in respect of shares of a corporation (other than shares listed on a designated stock exchange or shares of a mutual fund corporation) (ITA 120.4(1)"split income"(a)(i));

2. Amounts required to be included in the specified individual's income by virtue of the shareholder benefit rules in ITA 15 in respect of shares of a corporation (other than shares listed on a designated stock exchange or shares of a mutual fund corporation) (ITA 120.4(1)"split income"(a)(ii));

3. Income received from a trust or partnership that is income derived from the provision of property or services by the trust or partnership to, or in support of, a business carried on by: (i) a person related to the specified individual; (ii) a corporation of which a person who is a "specified shareholder" (i.e., a person who holds at least 10 per cent of the shares of any class) of the corporation is related to the specified individual; or (iii) a professional corporation of which a shareholder of the corporation is related to the specified individual (ITA 120.4(1)"split income"(b)(ii)(A));

4. Applicable only to specified individuals under age 18, taxable capital gains from the disposition of shares (other than shares listed on a designated stock exchange or shares of a mutual fund corporation) that are transferred to a non-arm's length person (specifically, twice the amount that would otherwise have been the specified individual's taxable capital gain in respect of the disposition is deemed to be a taxable dividend received by the specified individual) (ITA 120.4(4));

5. Income that is paid or allocated to a specified individual from a partnership or trust, and derived from a business of, or from the rental of property by, the partnership or trust, if a person related to the specified individual: (i) is actively engaged on a regular basis in the activities of the partnership or trust of earning income from a business or the rental of property, or (ii) has, in the case of a particular partnership, an interest in the particular partnership, whether directly or indirectly through one or more other partnerships (ITA 120.4(1)"split income"(b)(ii)(B) and (c)(ii)(D));

6. Income (such as interest) received by a specified individual in respect of a debt obligation of a corporation (other than a publicly-listed corporation or a mutual fund corporation), partnership or trust (other than a mutual fund trust) if other amounts (such as dividends) received by the specified individual from the debtor would be split income (ITA 120.4(1)"split income"(d); however, the following exclusions are provided in subpara. (ii): certain debts of, or debts guaranteed by, governments, which are described in para. (a) of the definition "fully exempt interest" in ITA 212(3); publicly-listed or traded debt; and a deposit standing to the individual's credit at a bank or credit union);

7. Taxable capital gains and income from the disposition of property that is not otherwise split income in situations where income from the underlying property would be split income in the hands of the specified individual (ITA 120.4(1)"split income"(e); specifically, an amount will be split income pursuant to para. (e) when the following two conditions are met: (1) the amount must either be a gain realized by the individual from the disposition of property or income derived by the individual through a trust that is attributable to the disposition of a property; and (2) the property referred to in the first condition must generally be property, the income from which would be split income if received by the specified individual. This would be the case for shares of a corporation (other than a publicly-traded corporation or mutual fund corporation), a debt obligation, or an interest in a partnership or trust. For property other than shares of a corporation, the property must also be a property in respect of which an amount was included in the individual's split income for the year or a previous year, or all or part of its FMV immediately before the disposition was attributable to a share of a corporation (other than a publicly-traded corporation or mutual fund corporation)).

If a particular amount of income is considered to be split income of a specified individual for a taxation year as outlined above, the TOSI will apply and the amount will be taxed at the highest marginal tax rate, unless an exclusion from the TOSI applies, as discussed below.

¶14212 — Exclusions from the Tax on Split Income

There are various exclusions from the application of the TOSI rules. The TOSI does not apply to taxable dividends received on shares listed on a designated stock exchange (i.e., publicly-listed shares) or to salary received by an individual. As well, in order the align the TOSI rules with the pension income splitting rules, the TOSI does not apply to any income from property, or taxable capital gains from the disposition of property, where either: (i) the individual's spouse or common-law partner attained the age of 64 before the year and the income would have been excluded from the spouse or common-law partner's split income if it was earned by them; or (ii) the individual's spouse or common-law partner has died and the income would have been excluded from the spouse or common-law partner's split income if it was earned by them in their last taxation year. Generally, this exclusion allows business owners aged 65 and over to split income with a spouse or common-law-partner who has made no meaningful contribution to the family business, as long as the business owner has made a sufficient contribution to the family business and would therefore qualify for an exclusion under the TOSI rules.

The TOSI will not apply to income designated under ITA 104(14) (preferred beneficiary election), unless a 104(19) designation is made in respect of the elected amount (VD 2018-0759521E5).

The TOSI also does not apply to any income that is an "excluded amount" of a specified individual. An "excluded amount" in respect of a specified individual for a taxation year includes the following (ITA 120.4(1)"excluded amount"(a)–(g)):

(a) *For individuals under age 25*, income from a property acquired by, or for the benefit of, the individual received as a consequence of the death of: (i) a parent of the individual, or (ii) any other person, if the individual is a full-time student at a post-secondary institution during the year or is eligible to claim the disability tax credit in the year;

(b) Income from a property acquired by the individual pursuant to a court order or a written separation agreement where, at the time of the transfer, the individual and his or her spouse or common-law partner were separated and living apart as a result of the breakdown of their marriage or common-law partnership;

(c) Taxable capital gains arising as a result of the deemed disposition on the individual's death under ITA 70(5);

(d) Taxable capital gains from the disposition of qualified farming or fishing property or qualified small business corporation shares (not including taxable capital gains from the disposition of certain shares to a non-arm's length person when the individual is under the age of 18);

(e) *For individuals age 18 and over*, amounts received by the individual from an "excluded business" of the individual that is not a "related business" of the individual;

(f) *For individuals between the ages of 18 and 24*, an amount that is: (i) a "safe harbour capital return" of the individual, or (ii) a "reasonable return" in respect of the individual, having regard only to the contributions of "arm's length capital" to the business by the individual; and

(g) *For individuals age 25 and over*, an amount that is: (i) income from, or a taxable capital gain from the disposition of, "excluded shares" of the individual, or (ii) a "reasonable return" in respect of the individual.

The following examples illustrating the exclusions from the TOSI are contained in the December 14, 2017 Technical Backgrounder (fin.gc.ca/n17/data/17-124_2-eng.asp):

Excluded business

Example 1:

Frances worked for her parents' manufacturing business on a full-time basis throughout the year in which she turned 22 to the year in which she turned 28. Frances then stepped back from being involved in the business for three years.

Frances received dividend income from her parents' manufacturing business during the years she worked for the business, as well as the three years when she did not participate in the business.

The TOSI would not apply in respect of any of the dividends Frances receives. With respect to the dividends received by Frances in the years she was working full-time, the TOSI would not apply, on the basis that she was actively engaged in the business on a regular, continuous and substantial basis in the year that the dividend was received (she would also satisfy the "bright-line" test of working an average of 20 hours per week). With respect to the dividends received by Frances in the years after she stepped back from the business, the TOSI would not apply as the business would be an "excluded business" on the basis that she was actively engaged in the business on a regular, continuous and substantial basis for at least five prior years.

Example 2:

Jeff and Charles are spouses. Jeff is a doctor practicing family medicine through a professional corporation on a full-time basis. Charles is not a doctor. He runs Jeff's medical clinic and he works four days a week for eight hours a day, taking six weeks of vacation per year (including all of July). The rest of the time, Charles runs a part-time consulting business. Both Jeff and Charles own shares in the professional corporation. Each year, the professional corporation pays Jeff and Charles salaries. The retained earnings in the professional corporation are then paid out as dividends to Jeff and Charles on a 50/50 basis.

Both Jeff and Charles would be considered to be actively engaged on a regular, continuous and substantial basis in the business carried on by the professional corporation. Jeff and Charles would have certainty that they satisfy this condition because they both satisfy the 20-hour deeming rule. Therefore, the TOSI would not apply to Jeff or Charles' dividend income.

Excluded shares

Example 3:

Two sisters, Anaya and Saanvi, are seniors. Each of them owns 50 per cent of the common shares of a corporation, which earns investment income and does not have any other source of income. There are no other classes of shares of the corporation. The money in the corporation was originally sourced from the proceeds of a sale of land by their father in the 1970s. Each year, the corporation pays Anaya and Saanvi dividends.

The application of the TOSI would not need to be considered on the dividends received by Anaya and Saanvi because each sister owns capital stock representing at least ten per cent of the value of the corporation, and the corporation neither earns income from the provision of services nor meets the definition "professional corporation" (nor is all or substantially all of the corporation's income derived from a related business).

Retirement and inherited property

Example 4:

Casey is 70 years old and owns shares of a corporation that carries on a consulting business. Prior to her retirement, she worked on a full-time basis for thirty years in the business. Due to her significant labour contributions over the years, Casey meets the five-year deeming rule and the business is an excluded business for her.

The business would also be an excluded business for Casey's 60-year-old spouse, Charlie, who has not worked in the business.

Example 5:

Gary dies at the age of 50. Immediately prior to his death, he owned a 20 per cent interest in a corporation that operates a restaurant. Gary was not involved in the business. The shares owned by Gary qualified as excluded shares before his death because he owned 10 per cent or more of the shares of the corporation and the corporation does not carry on a services business. Gary leaves all of his shares to his 22-year-old niece, Alex. Alex works full time as a painter and does not intend to work in the business.

The shares can be excluded shares for Alex even though she has not attained the age of 25 (which is a requirement for the excluded shares test) because Gary had attained the age of 25.

¶14212.1 — Excluded Business ("excluded amount"(e))

A specified individual aged 18 and over will not be subject to the TOSI on amounts received in the year from an "excluded business" of the individual that is not a "related business" of the individual. An excluded business of an individual is a business in which the individual is "actively engaged" on a regular, continuous and substantial basis in the taxation year in which an amount is received or in any five previous taxation years. A "related business" in respect of an individual includes any business of a corporation where a related individual owns at least 10 per cent of the fair market value of the shares of the corporation (or property, the value of which is derived from shares of the corporation). A related business in respect of an individual can also include a business of a sole proprietorship, corporation, partnership, or trust where a related individual is actively engaged on a regular basis in the operation of the business.

An individual is deemed to be "actively engaged" on a regular, continuous and substantial basis for the year if the individual works in the business at least an average of 20 hours per week during the year or meets that requirement for any five prior years. If an individual does not meet the 20-hour threshold, then it will be a question of fact as to whether the individual was actively engaged in the business on a regular, continuous and substantial basis. However, even if an individual aged 25 or older does not meet the regular, continuous and substantial threshold, the TOSI will apply to amounts derived from a related business only to the extent that they are unreasonable (i.e., only the unreasonable excess will be subject to the TOSI).

Where a corporation operates two separate businesses, and the spouse of the business owner works 25 hours per week in the company's property management business, but does not work in the company's construction business, income received by the spouse from the property management business will be income from an "excluded business". However, any income of the spouse that is derived from the construction business will not meet the excluded business exception and will be subject to TOSI, unless another exception applies. Separate accounting for each business will be required to properly trace the source of the income (VD 2018-0761601E5).

¶14212.2 — Safe Harbour Capital Return or Reasonable Return ("excluded amount"(f))

A specified individual between the ages of 18 and 24 years will not be subject to the TOSI on an amount that is either (i) a "safe harbour capital return" of the individual, or (ii) a "reasonable return" in respect of the individual, having regard only to the contributions of "arm's length capital" to the business by the individual.

A "safe harbor capital return" of a specified individual between the ages of 18 and 24 means a return up to a prescribed rate based on the fair market value of property contributed by the individual in support of a related business. Accordingly, the "safe harbour capital return" test reduces the income includable in TOSI by a notional amount calculated by the prescribed rate of interest multiplied by the fair market value of property contributed by the individual in support of the related business.

Generally, a "reasonable return" is an amount derived directly or indirectly from a related business in respect of the specified individual that is reasonable having regard to the contributions of the specified individual to the related business, relative to other family members who have contributed to the business. For the purposes of the exclusion in paragraph (f) of "excluded amount" for a specified individual between the ages of 18 and 24 years, only the contributions of "arm's length capital" to the business by the individual can be considered when determining whether the amount is a "reasonable return" in the circumstances. Generally, "arm's length capital" of a specified individual between the ages of 18 and 24 years means property of the individual, other than property: (a) that is derived from property income in respect of a related business, (b) that is borrowed by the specified individual under a loan or other indebtedness, or (c) that is transferred to the specified individual from a related person (other than as a consequence of death) (i.e., "arm's length capital" is essentially property inherited or earned by the individual, such as salary).

¶14212.3 — Excluded Shares or Reasonable Return ("excluded amount"(g))

A specified individual aged 25 years and over will not be subject to the TOSI in respect of (i) income from, or a taxable capital gain from, the disposition of "excluded shares" of the individual, or (ii) a "reasonable return" in respect of the individual.

Shares of a corporation will qualify as "excluded shares" of a specified individual where the following conditions are met:

1. the individual has attained the age of 25 years in or before the year;

2. the individual owns at least 10 per cent of the shares of a corporation in terms of votes and value; and

3. the corporation meets the following conditions: (i) it earns less than 90 per cent of its income from the provision of services; (ii) it is not a professional corporation (i.e., a corporation that carries on the professional practice of an accountant, dentist, lawyer, medical doctor, veterinarian or chiropractor); and (iii) all or substantially all of its income is not derived from a "related business" in respect of the specified individual (this is intended to prevent a service business from accessing this exclusion by interposing a non-service entity between it and the intended recipient of the income; e.g., a professional corporation pays rent for the building in which the professional business is carried on to a corporation owned by the adult children of the professional).

The CRA has provided the following administrative guidance with respect to the meaning of "excluded shares": shares of a corporation that has no business income cannot qualify as "excluded shares" (VDs 2018-0744031C6, 2018-0745871C6); shares of a holding corporation or shares held by a family trust will generally not qualify as "excluded shares" (VDs 2018-0743971C6, 2018-0745871C6, 2018-0761601E5); the reference to "business income" and "income" in the excluded shares definition generally means gross income (2018-0743961C6); and the 10 per cent ownership requirement will be met where a taxpayer owns two classes of shares that in the aggregate satisfy the 10 per cent votes and value threshold (VD 2018-0771811E5).

If an individual aged 25 years or older receives amounts that are not derived from excluded shares (or from an excluded business), the TOSI will apply only to amounts derived from a related business to the extent that the amounts exceed a "reasonable return". A "reasonable return" is defined as an amount that is reasonable having regard to the contributions of the specified individual to the related business relative to other family members who have contributed to the business. The contributions that are relevant to this analysis include labour contributions, capital contributions, risks assumed, as well as any other relevant factors. What constitutes a reasonable return is also determined with regard to previous amounts received from the business. An amount will not qualify as a reasonable return from a related business only in cases where it is evident that an amount received by an individual from the business is disproportionate relative to the contributions to, and amounts received from, the business by them and other family members. It is not meant to second-guess a *bona fide* exercise of business judgment by the participants in a business.

At the 2018 STEP-CRA Roundtable, the CRA provided the following guidance regarding claiming the TOSI exclusion for "excluded shares" and a "reasonable return" (VD 2018-0743961C6):

> Where a corporation has income from the provision of both services and non-services (including a service business that also involves a sale of property such as a business carried on by plumbers, mechanics or other contractors that supply replacement parts or building materials), the income from the provision of services and non-services should be computed separately and the non-service income should generally be taken into account in determining whether shares of a corporation are excluded shares of an individual unless such income can reasonably be considered to be necessary but incidental to the provision of the services (for instance as would be the case in an office cleaning service if it billed separately for the cleaning supplies used). In determining gross income, payments that can reasonably be considered reimbursements of expenses (including reimbursement for the supply of goods) will be ignored.

> In general, the safe harbour for excluded shares is intended as a bright line test for situations where amounts received by individuals would otherwise be considered a reasonable return. In some cases, the requirement of a corporation to compute the income from the provision of services and non-services separately for purposes of determining whether the income of a specified individual is excluded from the tax on split income ("TOSI") as income from excluded shares may give rise to additional compliance requirements. In some of these circumstances, consideration can be given to whether it may be better for taxpayers to determine whether the amount is excluded from the TOSI because it is a reasonable return of the individual based on the factors applicable in the circumstances.

¶14213 — Determining the Amount of Tax on Split Income

The TOSI imposes federal tax in the amount of 33 per cent of the specified individual's split income. ITA 120.4(3) provides that a specified individual's Part I tax cannot be less than the TOSI minus any dividend tax credits, foreign tax credits and disability tax credit (after 2017) in respect of the individual's split income for the year. Any other tax credits and deductions otherwise available, such as the basic personal credit or losses from current and previous years, cannot offset this minimum amount of tax. The specified individual also cannot apply any refundable minimum tax carry-over balance against the TOSI.

To ensure that income that is subject to the TOSI is not subject to ordinary Part I tax, the specified individual's split income for the year is deducted from his or her income from a business or property (ITA 201(1)(ww); see Line 424 at ¶11070). However, as mentioned, income that is subject to TOSI is not eligible for any deductions or credits other than any dividend tax credits, foreign tax credits and the disability tax credit (after 2017). Dividend tax credits and foreign tax credits are available since they are attributable to the character of the income and not the particular person on whom Part I tax liability is imposed. As well, ITA 120.4(3) was amended applicable to taxation years after 2017 to provide that the TOSI does not reduce or eliminate a specified individual's ability to claim the disability tax credit.

ITA 120.4, www.fin.gc.ca/n17/17-124-eng.asp, Keung, "The Income Sprinkling Trilogy — V3 of the Tax on Split Income Proposals", March 26, 2018 (tinyurl.com/moodys-v3tosi); Tehranchian, "Revised Rules on Income Sprinkling and Planning Considerations", 11(1) *Taxes & Wealth Management* (Carswell) 2–4 (March 2018); Ratnam, "How the New TOSI Rules Impact your Family", XXIII(1) *Insurance Planning* (Federated Press) 14–17 (2018); Santia, "Revisiting Planning for Private Company Shareholders", 66(2) *Canadian Tax Journal* 421–45 (2018).

¶14220 — Transfers and Loans to Spouse or Common-Law Partner and Minors

ITA 74.1 is designed to prevent an individual from splitting income with family members to reduce the total amount of tax otherwise payable on income from property. ITA 74.1(1) applies where an individual lends or transfers property to or for the benefit of his or her spouse or common-law partner, or a minor who does not deal with the individual at arm's length or is the individual's niece or nephew. The income derived from that property, or from property substituted therefor, will be taxed not in the hands of the recipient but in the hands of the individual for so long as he or she resides in Canada, and in the case of property lent or transferred to the individual's spouse or common-law partner, the recipient continues to be his or her spouse or common-law partner. Where property is lent or transferred to a minor, attribution of income to the individual under this provision will cease commencing with the taxation year in which the recipient attains the age of 18 years; however, see ITA 56(4.1) at ¶14330 for rules concerning certain loans to individuals with whom the taxpayer does not deal at arm's length.

ITA 74.1(1) deals with transfers or loans of property by an individual (whether such transfers or loans are made directly or indirectly, by means of a trust, or by any other means whatever) *to or for the benefit of* a person who is the individual's spouse or common-law partner, or who has since become his or her spouse or common-law partner. Any income or loss of that person for a taxation year from a property (or from property substituted therefor) for the period throughout which the individual is resident in Canada and is the person's spouse or common-law partner is deemed to be income or a loss of the individual and not of that person. For example, if an individual lends or transfers an interest-bearing bond to his or her spouse (or lends or transfers the funds to acquire the bond, which would be a substituted property), the interest income earned by the spouse would be taxed in the individual's hands so long as the individual continues to be a resident of Canada and the holder of the bond continues to be the individual's spouse. The spouse would not be taxed on the interest income.

In *Lipson*, [2009] 1 C.T.C. 314, the Supreme Court of Canada held 4-3 that using ITA 74.1(1) to allow a husband to claim his wife's interest deduction, as part of a scheme to make mortgage interest deductible, violated GAAR. However, in *Evans*, [2006] 2 C.T.C. 2009 (TCC), GAAR did not apply to a series of surplus stripping transactions in which the tax planning relied in part upon the exemption to the attribution rules contained in ITA 74.5(1)(b) for transfers for fair market value consideration.

Income or loss derived from the investment or other use of the income from transferred property (i.e., "second generation income") is not attributed to the transferor, and thus for income tax purposes is income or loss of the recipient. For example, interest on any interest allowed to accumulate is not attributed to the transferor and is income of the recipient. Thus, the income derived from the reinvestment of the bond interest in the above example would be considered to be income of the individual's spouse.

With respect to the meaning of transfer, the CRA provides the following comments in VD 2010-0366301I7:

> As noted in the *Estate of David Fasken*, [1948] C.T.C. 265, 49 D.T.C. 491, at p.497:
>
> > The word "transfer" is not a term of art and has not a technical meaning. It is not necessary to a transfer of property from a husband to his wife that it should be made in any particular form or that it should be made directly. All that is required is that the husband should so deal with the property as to divest himself of it and vest it in his wife, that is to say, pass the property from himself to her. The means, by which he accomplishes this result, whether direct or circuitous, may properly be called a transfer.
>
> The Tax Court of Canada recently confirmed the principle that the shift in value resulting from an undervaluation of exchanged common shares is a transfer of share rights attributable to existing equity from the former holders of common shares to the new common shareholders: *Garron et al*, [2010] 2 C.T.C. 2346. Consistent with the reasoning in *Kieboom*, [1992] 2 C.T.C. 59 #2, this is a transfer of property.

The CRA does not consider ITA 74.1 to apply to conventional estate freeze transactions. In *Romkey v. R.*, [2000] 1 C.T.C. 390 (FCA), shares in a family-owned company were issued to trusts for children. The Court found that the owners were forgoing the right to receive future dividends and this was a "transfer of property" such that ITA 74.1(2) applied to later dividends (the company had no value at the time of the transfer of shares to the trust). In VD 2001-0072705, the CRA states:

> We do not plan to make any changes to our current assessing practices with respect to estate freezes. More specifically, some practitioners have expressed concern that as a result of the *Romkey* decision, subsection 74.1(2) might be applied to an estate freeze transaction. It is our view that subsection 74.1(2) will generally not apply to attribute, to a freezor, dividends paid on shares held by a trust for minor children as part of a typical estate freeze, provided that the shares held by the trust are issued for an amount equal to their fair market value and are paid for with funds that are not obtained from the freezor.

Krauss v. R., [2010] 2 C.T.C. 2023 (TCC); aff'd on other grounds 2010 CarswellNat 3951 (FCA), *Lafontaine*, 2007 CarswellNat 492 (TCC) and *St-Pierre*, [2008] 5 C.T.C. 2706 (TCC); both aff'd [2008] 5 C.T.C. 271 (FCA), *Kaiser*, [2008] 5 C.T.C. 2001 (TCC), *Muio*, [2008] 2 C.T.C. 2308 (TCC), IT-510: *Transfers and Loans of Property made after May 22, 1985 to a Related Minor*, IT-511R: *Interspousal and Certain Other Transfers and Loans of Property*, VDs 2006-0173711E5, 2006-0198071E5, 2006-0199361E5, 2007-0233801C6, 2010-0365581E5, 2010-0366301I7, 2010-0373361C6, 2011-0405071E5, Shane Brown & Brandon Wiener, A Practical Look at the Attribution Rules", 2011 Cdn Tax Foundation conference report, 38:1–60; Lucinda Main, "Income Attribution Rules and Trusts" (2011) vol. 1, no. 2 *Canadian Tax Focus*, 5-6; Irene Jacob *et al*, "Income-Splitting Strategies: Selected Aspects" in "Personal Tax Planning," (2010), vol. 58, no. 4 *Canadian Tax Journal*, 1005–1023; Martin J Rochwerg *et al*, "Freezing, Thawing, and Refreezing: The Intricacies of an Estate Freeze," *2009 Ontario Tax Conference*, (Toronto: Canadian Tax Foundation, 2009), 12:1–29

¶14221 — *Exceptions*

ITA 74.1 does not apply to the following circumstances:

- Child Tax Benefit payments placed on account for the child (ITA 74.1(2), 2007-0233761C6; however, this exclusion does not extend to the Quebec child tax benefit: see VD 2007-0219801E5);

- Transfers of property for fair market consideration (ITA 74.5(1));

- Loans of property that bear a commercial rate of interest if the annual interest is paid within 30 days of each year-end (ITA 74.5(2));

- With regards to attribution of income resulting from property transferred to a spouse or common-law partner, during that period throughout which the spouses or common-law partners are living separate and apart because of a breakdown of their marriage or common-law partnership (ITA 74.5(3)(a); it is not required that the individuals are living separate and apart for a period of 90 days or more: VD 2012-0438021E5; see also Manu Kakkar, "The Attribution Rules and Living Separate and Apart" (2009) vol. 9, no. 3 *Tax for the Owner-Manager*, 9-10);

- A loan or transfer of property effected to artificially take advantage of the attribution rules (ITA 74.5(11));

- A transfer of property that is a payment of a premium under a spousal or common-law partner registered retirement saving plan or "specified pension plan" (i.e., the Saskatchewan Pension Plan), to the extent that the payment is deductible in computing the individual's income (ITA 74.5(12)(a));

- A transfer of property that is a payment of a contribution under a registered disability savings plan (ITA 74.5(12)(a.2));

- Transfers of property that are deductible in computing the transferor's income and are included in computing the income of the recipient (ITA 74.5(12)(b));

- Transfers of property to the individual's spouse or common-law partner while the property (or property substituted for it) is held under a TFSA of which the spouse or common-law partner is the "holder", to the extent that the spouse or common-law partner does not have an "excess TFSA amount" at the time of the contribution (ITA 74.5(12)(c); in VD 2010-0354491E5, the attribution rules applied when money which was gifted to a spouse to contribute to a TFSA was subsequently withdrawn from the TFSA).

- Where an amount is included in computing the split income of a specified individual's split income for a taxation year under ITA 120.4 for a taxation year (ITA 74.5(13));

- Income earned with business assets transferred or loaned (since such income is business income and not income from property);

- Second generation income (i.e., income on income earned from the property transferred) (ITA 248(5));

- The assignment of a retirement pension under the Canada Pension Plan, Quebec Pension Plan, or any prescribed provincial pension plan to a spouse or common-law partner;

- Educational assistance payments from a RESP (VD 2004-0064551E5); and

- The provision of collateral for a joint line of credit (see VD 2009-0317041E5; however, if the taxpayer who contributed most of the capital is obligated to ensure the repayment of the loan or the interest payable on the loan, either in whole or in part, the taxpayer would be deemed to have made the loan to his or her spouse pursuant to ITA 74.5(7) and the attribution rules would apply, subject to the exemption for commercial loans).

¶14222 — Repayment of Existing Indebtedness

Certain provisions in the ITA extend the application of ITA 74.1(1) and (2) to loans or transfers of property which might otherwise have been used to circumvent the attribution rules. One such provision is ITA 74.1(3), which applies where an individual has lent or transferred property to or for the benefit of a person and the property (or property substituted therefor) is used either to repay, in whole or in part, borrowed money that was used to acquire other property or to reduce an amount payable for other property. The income from the other property is required to be included in computing the income from the lent or transferred property under ITA 74.1(1) and (2). In the absence of ITA 74.1(3), it is possible that no amount would be attributed to the individual because the lent or transferred property was directly used to reduce an obligation which itself does not generate any income.

The amount of income or a loss from the lent or transferred property that may be attributed to the individual by virtue of ITA 74.1(3) is that proportion of the income or loss derived from the other property after the loan or transfer was made and used as indicated above that the fair market value of the lent or transferred property is of the cost to the person of the other property at the time of its acquisition. For example, if an individual were to borrow $50,000 from a financial institution to acquire common shares, the individual would be subject to tax on the dividends received on the shares. If that individual's spouse subsequently transfers $25,000 to the individual which is used to pay down the original loan, the spouse would be subject to tax on one-half of the dividends received by the individual after the date of the transfer.

ITA 74.1(3) will not apply to the extent that ITA 74.1(1) or (2) otherwise applies to any income or loss derived from the other property, or from property substituted therefor. Where an individual makes an interest-free loan to a spouse or common-law partner, any income or loss derived from property acquired with the loan proceeds will be taxed in the individual's hands under ITA 74.1(1). If the individual were to subsequently make a commercial-basis loan (within the meaning of ITA 74.5(2)) to his or her spouse or common-law partner to enable the spouse or common-law partner to repay the original interest-free loan, ITA 74.1(3) will not terminate the attribution of income to the individual under ITA 74.1(1).

¶14223 — *Fair Market Value Transfers*

ITA 74.5(1) provides that ITA 74.1(1) and (2) do not apply to certain transfers for fair market value. No income or losses derived from the transferred property (or from property substituted therefor) in a particular taxation year will be attributed to the transferor if the following conditions are satisfied:

1. The transferor received, *at the time of the transfer*, consideration having a fair market value at least equal to the fair market value of the transferred property (ITA 74.5(1)(a));

2. Where the consideration received by the transferor included indebtedness, interest at a commercial rate was charged *at the time the indebtedness was incurred* and was paid annually as described in ¶14224 (ITA 74.5(1)(b)); and

3. For transfers of property to or for the benefit of the transferor's spouse or common-law partner, the transferor elected in his or her return of income for the taxation year of the transfer not to have the rollover provisions of ITA 73(1) apply (ITA 74.5(1)(c)).

All of the above conditions must be met when the property is transferred; otherwise the exclusion in ITA 74.5(1) will not apply. There is no apportionment of income or losses where consideration is received by the individual which has a fair market value less than that of the lent or transferred property.

Where fair market consideration is received by the individual that includes indebtedness, failure to pay the interest in respect of a particular year within 30 days after the end of the year would result in attribution for that year and each succeeding year. The CRA's position is that interest at a rate not less than the prescribed or a commercial rate of interest in effect at the time the loan or indebtedness was incurred must be charged and paid not later than 30 days after the end of each calendar year in which the loan is outstanding (paying interest within one year of incurring the debt will not suffice).

IT-511R: *Interspousal and Certain Other Transfers and Loans of Property* (para. 21), VDs 2009-0330081C6, 2008-0274221I7

¶14224 — *Loans for Value*

ITA 74.5(2) provides an exception to the application of the attribution rules in ITA 74.1(1) and (2) in respect of lent property (or property substituted therefor) where the loan bears a commercial rate of interest and the annual interest is paid within 30 days after the year-end. The following conditions must be met in each taxation year for any income or loss derived in that year from the lent property (or from property substituted therefor) to be excluded from the attribution rules:

1. Interest was charged on the loan at a rate not less than the lesser of the prescribed rate in effect at the time the loan was made and the rate that would have been agreed upon at that time between parties dealing with each other at arm's length, having regard to all the circumstances (ITA 74.5(2)(a)). Presumably an arm's length interest rate would be represented by that which a financial institution would charge considering such factors as the creditworthiness of the borrower, any security available and the prevailing market interest rate;

2. The amount of interest payable for the particular year was paid not later than 30 days after the end of that year (as mentioned above, considered to mean not later than 30 days after the end of the calendar year by the CRA) (ITA 74.5(2)(b)); and

3. The condition in (2) above was met for each taxation year preceding the particular year (ITA 74.5(2)(c)).

ITA 74.5(2) applies to property that is loaned rather than transferred and consequently, a lender is not required to elect out of the rollover in ITA 73(1) to avoid the attribution rules when a loan for value is made.

The prescribed rate in effect at the time the loan was made is the rate determined under ITR 4301(c). The prescribed rate of interest is available at: canada.ca/en/revenue-agency/services/tax/prescribed-interest-rates.html. Where an inter-family loan is made at the prescribed rate in effect at the time the loan is made, for as long as the loan is outstanding, the attribution rules can be avoided regardless of the amount of investment income earned with the loaned proceeds.

The commercial rate of interest must be charged at the time the loan is made and the annual interest must be paid within 30 days after the year-end in each year that the loan is outstanding. Failure to pay the interest in respect of a particular year within 30 days after the end of the year will result in attribution for that year and each succeeding year. A loan of property that does not satisfy the conditions under ITA 74.5(2) will always be subject to the attribution rules in ITA 74.1(1) and (2). A subsequent loan made on commercial terms to replace that loan will not be an excluded loan under ITA 74.5(2) by virtue of ITA 74.1(3). However, if property was acquired with a loan that met the requirements of ITA 74.5(2) and the loan is repaid, the attribution rules will not apply after the repayment to income earned on the property or capital gains arising on the disposition.

In a May 2008 Alberta/Saskatchewan CAs roundtable discussion with the CRA (Member Advisory, Jan 2009, albertacas.ca, q 8), the CRA was asked whether it would accept a loan as meeting the exception from the attribution rules if the loan provided that any interest not physically paid within 30 days after year-end was deemed to be paid by an advance from the lender to the borrower bearing interest at the prescribed rate at that time. The CRA responded that such a loan would not qualify for the exception from the attribution rules, taking the position that "a loan created in the event of unpaid interest does not constitute payment of interest but would represent a deferral of the payment so required".

Splitting income with family members via loans for value is a common income splitting strategy. Tax savings may be achieved where the investment income earned from the loan proceeds is taxed in the hands of a lower-income family member. An inter-family loan is typically made to a spouse or to a trust the beneficiaries of which are children of the taxpayer. Where such a strategy is employed, it is important to ensure that interest at the prescribed rate at the time the loan is made (or at a higher rate) is paid within 30 days of the end of each calendar year. An inter-family loan is typically structured as a demand loan that allows the borrower the right to repay the loan at any time without penalty. Legal counsel should generally be consulted to draft the terms of the loan and ensure it is properly executed.

IT-511R: *Interspousal and Certain Other Transfers and Loans of Property* (para. 22), VD 2009-0330081C6

¶14225 — *Back-to-Back Loans and Transfers*

ITA 74.5(6) ensures that the attribution rules apply where an individual loans or transfers property indirectly, through the use of intermediaries, to or for the benefit of a specified person with respect to the individual. "Specified person", which is defined in ITA 74.5(8), includes a "designated person" in respect of the individual, which in turn is defined in ITA 74.5(5) to mean the individual's spouse or common-law partner or a person under 18 years of age who either does not deal with the individual at arm's length or who is the individual's niece or nephew.

ITA 74.5(6) applies in two situations. First, ITA 74.5(6)(a) deals with a loan or transfer of property by an individual to another person where that property, or property substituted therefor, is subsequently lent or transferred by *any* person (a "third party") directly or indirectly to or for the benefit of the specified person. Second, ITA 74.5(6)(b) applies where an individual has lent or transferred property to another person on condition that property (not necessarily *the* property) be lent or transferred by *any* person (a "third party") directly or indirectly to or for the benefit of a specified person. Where an individual has lent or transferred property under either of these circumstances, for the purposes of ITA 74.1 to 74.4, the property lent or transferred by the third party is deemed to have been lent or transferred, as the case may be, by the individual to or for the benefit of the specified person. Furthermore, in determining whether a transfer of property would be exempt from the attribution rules under ITA 74.5(1) as a transfer for fair market consideration, the individual is deemed to have received any consideration received by the third party for the transfer of the property.

¶14226 — *Guarantees*

ITA 74.5(7) ensures that the attribution rules cannot be avoided where an individual is obligated, either absolutely or contingently, to effect any undertaking to ensure that any or all principal repayments or interest payments are made in respect of a loan made by any person (the "third party") to a specified person rather than making the loan directly. The undertaking may be provided by way of a guarantee, covenant or other agreement. In such circumstances, the property lent by the third party to the specified person is deemed to have been lent by the individual to or for the benefit of the specified person for the purposes of ITA 74.1 to 74.4. Any income or losses derived from the lent property (or from property substituted therefor) may not be subject to attribution if the specified person is charged and pays a commercial rate of interest. For this purpose, any interest paid in respect of the loan by the individual to the third party is deemed by ITA 74.5(7)(b) not to be interest paid by the specified person under ITA 74.5(2)(b) and (c).

If a child under the age of 18 years borrows funds from a financial institution and the loan is guaranteed by the child's father, ITA 74.5(7)(a) deems the loan to be made by the father to the child. Any income or loss derived from property acquired by the child with the loan proceeds would be attributed to the father under ITA 74.1(2) unless the child made the principal and interest payments with his or her own funds. Although the loan should qualify as a commercial-basis loan under ITA 74.5(2), if the father paid any of the interest in respect of a particular year, attribution of income and losses to the father would result for that year and each succeeding year by virtue of ITA 74.5(7)(b) and 74.5(2)(b) and (c). If the father made any principal repayments in respect of the loan, some portion of the income or losses derived from the property acquired with the loan proceeds would be attributed to him under ITA 74.1(2) by virtue of ITA 74.1(3).

¶14230 — Attribution of Gains/Losses to Spouse or Common Law Partner

ITA 74.2(1) complements ITA 74.1(1) (see ¶14220) by imputing to an individual any taxable capital gains and allowable capital losses realized by the individual's spouse or common-law partner on the disposition of property that was lent or transferred by the individual to or for the benefit of the spouse or common-law partner, whether directly or indirectly, by means of a trust or by any other means whatever. This provision also applies in respect of gains or losses realized on the disposition of property substituted for such loaned or transferred property. ITA 74.2(1)(e) provides that, where any taxable capital gains or allowable capital losses from the disposition of property are attributed under ITA 74.2(1) to the individual who lent or transferred the property, the amount so attributed is deemed not to be a taxable capital gain or an allowable capital loss, as the case may be, of the recipient. Unlike ITA 74.1(2) with respect to income and losses derived from lent or transferred property, there is generally no attribution of capital gains and losses in respect of transfers and loans to minors.

By virtue of ITA 248(5), property substituted for the original property transferred is deemed to include any property acquired as a result of one or more further transactions after the first substitution. Where a stock dividend has been declared and received in respect of a particular share of a corporation, ITA 248(5) deems the share received in payment of the stock dividend to be property substituted for the particular share. Consequently, where an individual has transferred shares to his or her spouse, any taxable capital gains or allowable capital losses from the disposition by the spouse of shares received as stock dividends in respect of the transferred shares (unless declared on or before that date) may be attributable to the individual under ITA 74.2.

> Where taxable capital gains or allowable capital losses are attributed to an individual for a taxation year under ITA 74.2(1), any such gains and losses are included in computing the individual's entitlement to the lifetime capital gains exemption, provided that the attributed gains or losses may reasonably be considered to relate to the disposition of a property by another person in the year (ITA 74.2(2)(a)). ITA 74.2(2)(b) provides that such property shall also be deemed to have been disposed of by the individual in the year.

ITA 74.2(3) provides that attribution under ITA 74.2(1) does not apply to a deemed disposition of property upon the emigration of the recipient spouse under ITA 128.1(4)(b), unless the transferor and recipient spouse jointly elect, in their tax returns for the taxation year that includes the subsequent disposition of the property, for it to apply. Hence, ITA 74.2(3) allows the choice of having the gain from the deemed disposition upon emigration taxed in either the recipient's hands or, if the joint election is filed, in the transferor's hands. There is no prescribed form for purposes of making this election.

The following rules and exceptions contained in ITA 74.5 that apply to ITA 74.1 also apply to ITA 74.2: fair market value transfers (ITA 74.5(1); see ¶14223); loans for value (ITA 74.5(2); see ¶14224); back to back loans and transfers (ITA 74.5(6); see ¶14225); guarantees (ITA 74.5(7); see ¶14226); artificial transactions (ITA 74.5(11); see ¶14221); contributions to spousal RRSPs and prescribed pension plans, RDSP payments, deductible/includable payments and TFSA transfers (ITA 74.5(12); see ¶14221), and amounts taxed as split income (ITA 74.5(13)).

ITA 74.2, IT-511R: *Interspousal and Certain Other Transfers and Loans of Property*

¶14240 — Transfers and Loans to a Trust

ITA 74.3(1) contains rules that determine the amount of any income or taxable capital gains that may be attributed to the individual under ITA 74.1 (see ¶14220) and ITA 74.2 (see ¶14230), where the individual has transferred or lent property to a trust in which his or her spouse or common-law partner or certain minors have a beneficial interest at any time. ITA 74.3(1) provides that, where an individual has transferred or loaned property to a trust in which a designated person in respect of the individual is beneficially interested, then any income or loss from the property (or property substituted therefor) or any capital gains realized from a disposition of the property (or property substituted therefor) that would be included in computing the income of the beneficiary as a result of a distribution from the trust, is attributed to the individual who has transferred or loaned the property to the trust. A "designated person" in respect of an individual means the individual's spouse or common-law partner, his or her minor nieces and nephews, and any minor (under 18 years of age) who does not deal at arm's length with the individual. Persons who are related to each other are considered not to deal at arm's length. Essentially, ITA 74.3(1) is a deeming provision which determines the amount of the income or the taxable capital gains of the designated person in respect of the lent or transferred property that may be imputed to the individual under ITA 74.1 or 74.2 respectively.

ITA 74.3 should be read in conjunction with two related provisions concerning transfers or loans of property to a trust. First, ITA 74.5(9) provides that, where a taxpayer has lent or transferred property by any means whatever to a trust in which another taxpayer has a beneficial interest, the taxpayer is deemed, for the purposes of ITA 74.1 to 74.5, to have lent or transferred the property to or for the benefit of the other taxpayer. This ensures that the attribution rules will apply where property is lent or transferred to a spouse or common-law partner or minor through a transfer or loan to a trust in which the spouse or common-law partner or minor has an interest. Secondly, ITA 248(25) provides that a person is beneficially interested in a trust if that person has any right whatsoever to receive any income or capital of the trust, either directly from the trust or indirectly through one or more other trusts, either immediate or future, absolute or contingent, or conditional on or subject to the exercise of any discretionary power.

ITA 74.3(1)(a) allocates all income derived in a year from the lent or transferred property (or property substituted therefor) to the beneficiaries of the trust that are designated persons in respect of the individual, to the extent that their income from the trust for the year is equal to or greater than that income. The income which is so allocated to the designated person may be attributed to the individual under ITA 74.1. For example, consider a trust that has four beneficiaries, two of whom are designated persons in respect of an individual who transferred an income-producing property to the trust. If one-half of the trust's income is derived from that property, the two beneficiaries that are designated persons will be deemed to have earned all the income from that property for the purposes of ITA 74.1, which in turn may deem the income to be that of the individual and not taxable to the beneficiaries. Income of the trust that is not paid or payable to a beneficiary would be taxed in the trust at the highest marginal individual tax rate and would not be subject to the attribution rules.

ITA 74.3(1)(b) determines the amount of the taxable capital gains from the disposition of property which may be imputed to an individual under ITA 74.2, where the individual has lent or transferred that property (or property for which it was substituted) to a trust in which his or her spouse or common-law partner has a beneficial interest. The amount which is deemed by ITA 74.3(1)(b) to be a taxable capital gain of the individual's spouse or common-law partner for the year from the disposition of lent or transferred property is the lesser of: the amount designated under ITA 104(21) for the spouse or common-law partner in the trust's return of income for the year; and the net taxable capital gains for the year of the trust from the disposition of the loaned or transferred property (or property substituted therefor). That amount may be attributed to the individual under ITA 74.2.

The following rules and exceptions in contained in ITA 74.5 that apply to ITA 74.1 and 74.2 also apply to ITA 74.3: fair market value transfers (ITA 74.5(1); see ¶14223); loans for value (ITA 74.5(2); see ¶14224); back to back loans and transfers (ITA 74.5(6); see ¶14225); guarantees (ITA 74.5(7); see ¶14226); artificial transactions (ITA 74.5(11); see ¶14221); contributions to spousal RRSPs and prescribed pension plans, RDSP payments, deductible/includable payments and TFSA transfers (ITA 74.5(12); see ¶14221), and amounts taxed as split income (ITA 74.5(13).

ITA 74.3, IT-510: *Transfers and Loans of Property made after May 22, 1985 to a Related Minor*, IT-511R: *Interspousal and Certain Other Transfers and Loans of Property*

¶14250 — Transfers and Loans to a Corporation

ITA 74.4(2), known as the corporate attribution rule, applies where an individual lends or transfers property to a corporation (other than a small business corporation), in which his/her spouse or common-law partner or certain minors have an interest, if one of the main purposes of the loan or transfer may reasonably be considered to reduce the income of the individual and to benefit, either directly or indirectly, a "designated person" who is a "specified shareholder" of the corporation. A "designated person" in respect of an individual means the individual's spouse, his or her minor nieces and nephews, and any minor (under 18 years of age) who does not deal at arm's length with the individual. A "specified shareholder" of a corporation is a person who holds at least 10% of the shares of any class of the corporation or a related corporation.

If the conditions of ITA 74.4(2) are satisfied, the transferor is deemed to have received an amount of interest in the taxation year computed at the prescribed rate on the "outstanding amount" of the loaned or transferred property. In the case of a transfer of property, the outstanding amount is equal to the fair market value of the property at the time of the transfer less the consideration received from the corporation by the transferor (other than consideration that is "excluded consideration"). In the case of a loan, the outstanding amount is the principal amount of the loan of money or the fair market value of the loaned property. "Excluded consideration" includes indebtedness, shares, or a right to receive indebtedness or shares.

Corporate attribution does not apply if the transferee corporation is a small business corporation. Generally, a small business corporation is a Canadian-controlled private corporation, all or substantially all of the fair market value of the assets of which are attributable to assets that are either assets used principally in an active business carried on primarily in Canada by the corporation or a corporation related to it (or shares or debt instruments of other "connected" small business corporations). See ¶4620 for more information on the definition of a small business corporation. The requirements for the application of ITA 74.4(2) must be satisfied on an annual basis. This means that, if at any time subsequent to the original loan or transfer, the corporation fails to meet the requirements of a small business corporation, the rules in ITA 74.4(2) may apply.

Where the designated person is a beneficiary of a trust, the person is deemed to own that proportion of the shares of the corporation owned by the trust that the fair market value of the person's interest in the trust is of the total fair market value of all interests in the trust. Where a beneficiary's share of the income or capital of the trust is dependent upon the exercise of a discretionary power, the beneficiary is deemed to own each share of the corporation which is owned by the trust. Therefore, any time shares of a corporation which is not a small business corporation are owned or acquired by a trust (e.g., when implementing an estate freeze), one must ensure that the corporate attribution rules do not apply. To avoid the corporate attribution rules when undertaking estate planning involving a corporation that is not a small business corporation, an estate freeze may be implemented by transferring property between corporations (ITA 74.4 does not apply to intercorporate transfers of property). Alternatively, if an amount is transferred or lent to a corporation, it must be ensured that one of the main purposes of the transfer or loan is not to reduce the individual's income and to benefit a designated person. Finally, corporate attribution will not apply to minor children who are beneficiaries of a trust where the trust specifically states that no income will be allocated to the minor children until they are of majority. However, this relieving rule does not apply to a spouse; therefore, where a spouse is a shareholder in the company, the corporate attribution rules could apply.

Based on VD 2005-0126381E5, to avoid the application of ITA 74.4(2) in an estate freeze transaction in which a designated person is involved, the terms of the trust should clearly state that the designated person may not receive or obtain the use of the income or capital of the trust while being a designated person.

In VD 2002-0147325, the CRA states "generally speaking, in situations where a controlling shareholder/director of a particular corporation approves a transfer or loan of property by the particular corporation to another corporation and the property transferred or loaned may be considered to come from the particular corporation's retained earnings (for example, internally generated cash or investments of the particular corporation) such that the property would not represent property paid or transferred to the particular corporation, directly or indirectly, by the individual, it is our view that the transfer or loan of property to the other corporation would not be considered to have been made, indirectly, by the individual for the purposes of subsection 74.4(2) of the Act".

ITA 74.4, IT-511R: *Interspousal and Certain Other Transfers and Loans of Property*, IT-510: *Transfers and Loans of Property made after May 22, 1985 to a Related Minor*, IT-440R2: *Transfer of rights to income*, Paul Festeryga, "Corporate Attribution: The "Anti-freeze" Rule" (2010), Vol 58, No 3, *Canadian Tax Journal* p 675

¶14260 — Transfers of Property to a Reversionary Trust

A trust described in ITA 75(2) is commonly referred to as a "reversionary trust" or a "revocable trust". To come within ITA 75(2), property must be held by a trust created in any manner, and be subject to the condition that the corpus may ultimately or at some future date or as a result of some contingency revert to the donor or some person with whom the donor is connected, or that the corpus remain within the power and disposition of the donor or the donor's nominee. Where the latter conditions are met, ITA 75(2) provides that income, losses, taxable capital gains and allowable capital losses from the property which is the subject of the trust (or property substituted therefor) and is held on such conditions, shall be deemed to belong to the person who creates the trust. ITA 75(2) ceases to apply on the death or change of residence of the transferor.

In *R. v Sommerer*, 2012 CarswellNat 2441 (FCA), the Court stated the following with respect to the purposes of ITA 75(2) (at para. 34): "[b]roadly speaking, subsection 75(2) is intended to ensure that a taxpayer cannot avoid the income tax consequences of the use or disposition of property by transferring it in trust to another person while retaining a right of reversion in respect of the property or property for which it may be substituted, or retaining the right to direct the disposition of the property or substituted property".

ITA 75(2) does not contain a purpose test and care must be taken to avoid inadvertently triggering the provision. If ITA 75(2) applies, the tax consequences can be harsh, including the attribution of income and gains and an inability of the trust to distribute property to most beneficiaries on a tax-deferred basis. Specifically, ITA 107(4.1) provides that a trust to which ITA 75(2) applies cannot transfer property on a rollover basis under ITA 107(2) to any beneficiary, other than the person from whom the property was received (or that person's spouse or former spouse or common-law partner). ITA 107(4.1) ceases to apply upon the death of the person who contributed property to the revocable trust. It is important to note that when ITA 75(2) applies to any property held by a trust, the denial of the rollover pursuant to ITA 107(4.1) applies to all of the trust's property, not just the property to which ITA 75(2) applies.

The CRA's general position, as stated in paragraph 10 of IT-369R (see also VDs 2005-0140951C6 and 2002-0127085), is that when the income of a trust is attributed to a contributor under ITA 75(2), the attributed amount is excluded from the amount included under ITA 104(13) in the income of the beneficiary to whom it was paid or payable in the year, and from the income of the trust in cases in which the income was not paid or payable to a beneficiary in that year. The CRA has noted that paragraph 10 of IT-369R represents an "administrative concession" that may not be applied in all circumstances.

At the 2006 APFF Conference Round Table, the CRA stated that if ITA 75(2) is utilized to attribute a dividend to a corporation which claims an inter-corporate dividend deduction with the intention of allocating the dividend proceeds to a trust beneficiary on a tax-free basis, the GAAR or ITA 56(2) may be applied (VDs 2006-0196231C6, 2011-0401951C6 and 2011-0423291E5). Additionally, at the 2011 STEP Conference, the CRA indicated it would challenge arrangements "structured to invoke ITA 75(2) in a manner which purports to insure that neither the trust nor the beneficiaries are taxable on the income" (see VD 2011-0401951C6). The CRA also provided the following comments on these structures at the 2014 STEP/CRA Roundtable (VD 2014-0523001C6):

> We have reviewed a variety of tax structures of this type in recent years. As was noted in our discussion of these arrangements at the 2011 STEP Conference, the common elements that they share are that a trust is used to invoke subsection 75(2) in an attempt to have neither the trust nor its beneficiaries liable for tax on the corporate dividends declared . . . . In some of these arrangements, the facts have led to a conclusion that the trust acquired the shares for fair market value consideration . . . . As was noted in our 2013 STEP Conference comments regarding the Federal Court of Appeal decision in *Sommerer*, CRA agrees with the general proposition that where property is transferred to a trust by a beneficiary for fair market value consideration, subsection 75(2) will not apply to attribute income in respect of that property to the beneficiary.
>
> In the alternative, if the facts are such that it may be concluded that the trust did not acquire the shares for fair market value consideration, CRA will typically challenge the arrangement on other grounds. Depending on the particular facts, assessments may be pursued to include the dividend income pursuant to paragraph 12(1)(j) or subsection 104(13), in calculating the income of the trust and/or its beneficiaries. Furthermore, CRA would typically hold the view that a strong GAAR argument would exist in support of an assessing position in such cases.

The term "revert", used in ITA 75(2)(a)(i), is not defined in the Act. In VD 2006-0185571C6, the CRA states that "subparagraph 75(2)(a)(i) of the Act may apply if, under the terms of the trust, there is a possibility, however remote, that the property held by a trust may be returned to the person who contributed the property to the trust".

ITA 75(2), IT-369R: *Attribution of Trust Income to Settlor*, Brender *et al*, "*Sommerer v. The Queen*", XII(1) *Corporate Structures & Groups* (Federated Press) 688–95 (2011); Léger, "Family Trusts and the Reversionary Rules" (2012) Vol. 12, No. 1 *Tax for the Owner-Manager*, 7–9; Elie Roth *et al*, "Subsection 75(2): Is CRA's Interpretation Appropriate?", *2010 Canadian Tax Foundation conference report*, 34:1–57

¶14261 — *Loans and Sales to Trusts*

In *Howson*, [2007] 2 C.T.C. 2225 (TCC), the Court found that ITA 75(2) did not apply in respect of a particular loan to a family trust. The Court noted that "it stands to reason that a *bona fide* loan is, on its face, not subject to reversion by the terms of the Trust" (see at para 15). In the case, the Court found that the particular loan was not a contribution to the corpus or capital of the trust. *Howson* was the first case to confirm that ITA 75(2)(a) does not apply to a loan. In the case, the Court did not accept the CRA's stringent views on what constitutes a loan. Based on this decision, a loan of property other than cash to a trust that is outside and independent of the terms of the trust should not be subject to ITA 75(2)(a). It should, however, be highlighted that a loan of property could give rise to attribution under various provisions, including ITA 56(4) or 74.1 (see also VD 2001-0067745). When asked to comment on the decision in *Howson*, the CRA stated that "absent the particular scenario where a loan to a trust is not outside and independent of the terms of the trust, we are of the view that a loan to a trust falls outside the ambit of subsection 75(2) of the ITA and should rather be dealt with under subsections 56(4.1) and 74.1(1) to (3) of the ITA" (VD 2007-0240421C6).

In VD 2009-0330251C6, the CRA states that ITA 75(2) would not apply in the following situation: Mr X owns all of the common shares of a holding corporation; in the context of an estate freeze, the common shares are converted into preferred shares and at the same time, a discretionary family trust subscribes for common shares of the holding corporation; the income and capital beneficiaries of the trust are Mr X and his two adult children; Mr X makes an interest-bearing loan to the trust to finance its subscription of the common shares of the holding corporation (the interest rate on the loan exceeds the prescribed rate and the loan is outside and independent of the terms of the trust); and in the following months, the holding corporation pays a dividend on the common shares held by the trust and the trust repays its loan to Mr X, with interest.

The CRA has stated ITA 75(2) could apply in the context of an estate freeze involving a family trust that does not take place at fair market value (see VD 2010-036630117).

The CRA has taken the position that ITA 75(2) can apply when property is held by a trust under one or more of the conditions provided for in ITA 75(2)(a) or (b), notwithstanding the fact that the property was acquired by the trust for fair market value consideration (see IT-369R, VDs 2006-0185571C6, 2004-0086941C6 and 2002-0118255). However, in *Sommerer*, 2012 CarswellNat 2441 (FCA), the Court concluded that ITA 75(2) only applies to a settlor or subsequent contributor who could be seen as a settlor of a trust. Furthermore, the Court found that ITA 75(2) does not apply to a beneficiary of a trust that transfers property to the trust by means of a genuine sale. The Court's interpretation of ITA 75(2) in *Sommerer* is significantly narrower than that taken by the CRA. The CRA provided updated guidance on its interpretation of ITA 75(2) after the *Sommerer* decision at the CRA Roundtable at the 2013 STEP Canada National Conference (see VD 2013-0480351C6).

In *Brent Kern Family Trust*, 2014 CarswellNat 4166 (FCA), the taxpayer's family trust was deliberately structured to cause ITA 75(2) to apply. Both the Tax Court and the Court of Appeal followed the reasoning in *Sommerer*, and confirmed that ITA 75(2) was not applicable to the property transferred to the family trust by the beneficiary for valuable consideration. The court stated that ITA 75(2) applies universally absent of intent and subjectivity, although it does not include a genuine transfer for value to a trust by a beneficiary. However, note that it is the CRA's position that where taxpayers set up trust structures designed to purposely invoke attribution pursuant to ITA 75(2) with a view to avoiding the payment of tax on extracted corporate dividends, the CRA may pursue assessments to include the dividend income pursuant to ITA 12(1)(j) or 104(13) in calculating the income of the trust and/or its beneficiaries. Furthermore, CRA generally holds the view that a strong GAAR argument would exist in support of an assessing position in such cases (VD 2014-0523001C6).

IT-369R: *Attribution of Trust Income to Settlor*, Matt Stacey, "Lending to Trusts", Canadian Tax Highlights, Vol. 15 No. 1, January 2007; Theo Michalarias, "2009 Legislative Update — Including Administrative Announcements," 2009 Ontario Tax Conference, (Toronto: Canadian Tax Foundation, 2009), 1:1–39; Jim Yager, "Estate Freeze and Reversionary Trust Rule", Vol 19, No 6, Canadian Tax Highlights, 11-12 (June 2011)

¶14262 — *Settlor as Trustee*

The CRA's position is that where a settlor is the sole trustee, because the trust property could not be disposed of without the settlor's consent or direction, ITA 75(2)(b) would apply (VD 2001-0110425). The CRA would no longer consider ITA 75(2) to apply if the settlor resigned as trustee (however, ITA 107(4.1) would continue to apply in such a case as the trust would be considered by the CRA to be tainted). In VD 2008-0292061E5, the CRA states:

> [W]here the settlor or other contributor is the sole trustee of the trust, none of the trust's property can be disposed of without the settlor's consent or direction. As a result of the settlor's direct control over the property transferred to the trust, it is our view that property transferred to the trust by the settlor is held on the condition described in paragraph 75(2)(b) such that subsection 75(2) would apply even though the settlor's ability to control the disposition of the trust property is maintained by his or her position as a trustee. Likewise, where the terms of the trust allow the trust property to pass to persons determined by the trustee and the person who contributed the property is the sole trustee of the trust, subparagraph 75(2)(a)(ii) will apply.

Certain tax commentators have suggested that the CRA's position on this issue may not be correct (for example, see John Saunders, "Inter Vivos Discretionary Family Trusts: A Potpourri of Issues and Traps," *Report of Proceedings of Forty-Fifth Tax Conference*, 1993 Tax Conference (Toronto: Canadian Tax Foundation, 1994), 37:1–58).

Where the settlor is one of several trustees, the CRA does not necessarily take the position that ITA 75(2) applies. In VD 2008-0292061E5, the CRA states, "[r]ecognizing that it is a question of fact as to whether the terms of a particular trust have been so conditioned as to enable the settlor to determine, after the creation of the trust, who will receive the trust property, the fact that the settlor is one of two or more trustees, acting in their fiduciary capacity to decide issues by majority will not normally, in and by itself, give rise to the application of subsection 75(2) of the Act". On the other hand, if a trust has several trustees, but all decisions made by the trustees must be unanimous, the CRA's position is that ITA 75(2) could apply (see VD 2003-0050671E5).

Further to the above, in VD 1999-0013055, the CRA states:

> Where the contributor is one of two or more co-trustees acting in a fiduciary capacity in administering the trust property and there are no specific terms outlining how the trust property is to be dealt with, but rather the property is subject to standard terms ordinarily found in trust indentures, we accept that paragraph 75(2)(b) will generally not be considered applicable. It could still apply however where the terms and conditions of trust expressly require the contributor's consent to any decision made by the trustees as a whole. This would include the situation where decisions are made by a majority of trustees provided that the trustee-contributor is one of that majority but would not include the situation where the terms of the trust require the decisions of the trustees to be unanimous. Thus a determination of whether this condition is met in respect of any particular property can only be made on a case-by-case basis following a review of all the facts and circumstances surrounding a particular situation.

If the CRA's interpretations are correct, to avoid the application of ITA 75(2), the individual from whom a trust receives property should not be the sole trustee or one of a number of trustees, unless there is a majority rule clause that would allow that person to be outvoted.

VD 2006-0191431R3, Elie Roth, "Subsection 75(2): Is CRA's Interpretation Appropriate?", 2010 Canadian Tax Foundation conference report, 34:1–57

¶14263 — *Settlor as Capital Beneficiary*

CRA takes the position that ITA 75(2) can apply where the settlor of the trust is a discretionary capital beneficiary of the trust. In VD 2005-0140951C6, the CRA states that "the fact that [a] capital interest in [a] trust is subject to a discretion does not hinder the application of subsection 75(2) . . . as the simple fact that the property is likely to return to the person from whom it was directly or indirectly received is enough to meet the condition set forth in subparagraph 75(2)(a)(i)". Certain tax commentators have noted that the latter interpretation may not be correct (for example, see John Saunders, "Inter Vivos Discretionary Family Trusts: A Potpourri of Issues and Traps," *Report of Proceedings of Forty-Fifth Tax Conference*, 1993 Tax Conference (Toronto: Canadian Tax Foundation, 1994), 37:1–58).

A narrower interpretation is implicit in the Federal Court — Trial Division decision of *Fraser*, [1991] 1 C.T.C. 314 (FCTD); aff'd 104 F.T.R. 319 (FCA), where the taxpayer was arguing in favour of the application of ITA 75(2) in order to be able to utilize trust losses. The relationship provided that in the event that the taxpayer requested a redemption of her units in a fund, the fund would not continue making investments until the redemption had taken place; however the CRA successfully argued that ITA 75(2) did not apply because this was not a "true" reversionary interest.

In VD 2004-0080731I7, the taxpayer argued that the conditions described in ITA 75(2) were not met with respect to common shares of a controlled foreign affiliate (CFA) that were transferred to a trust by a Canadian resident because the Canadian resident did not have an absolute right of reversion. The CRA's position was that the Canadian resident's entitlement to a return of the corpus of the trust's property depended on the exercise of discretion by the trustees of the trust. The CRA stated: "Our position that subsection 75(2) will apply when the property held by the trust may revert to the contributor by reason of that contributor being a capital beneficiary of the trust remains unchanged. The *Fraser* case dealt with the application of subsection 75(2) to property held in a commercial investment vehicle and the comments of the court in that case are not applicable to the situation under review."

¶14264 — *Terms of a Will*

There is some contention as to whether the terms of a will can lead to the application of ITA 75(2)(a)(i). In VD 2002-0139205, the CRA states that "if, in accordance with the terms of [a] trust, the assets of the trust are to be distributed to the spouse's estate following the spouse's death such that the property transferred initially by the taxpayer to the trust could return to the taxpayer, but only as property inherited from his spouse, we would not normally consider that subsection 75(2) of the Act would be applicable". Conversely, in VD 2003-0050671E5, the CRA takes the position that if the settlor of a trust is not a beneficiary of the trust but the terms of the trust give the settlor's spouse a power of appointment, exercisable by will, to distribute the trust's property as the spouse chooses, ITA 75(2) would apply. However, the CRA states that if a provision of the trust precludes the settlor from becoming a capital beneficiary of the trust and also precludes the spouse from exercising a power of appointment in favour of the spouse, the condition in ITA 75(2)(a) would presumably not be met.

The two scenarios described above are distinguishable under law. Under the first scenario, the assets which remain in the trust at death become part of the spouse's estate and would be distributed in accordance with the terms of the spouse's will. Under the second scenario, a power of appointment would be exercised under the spouse's will which could result in the settlor being named a capital beneficiary of the trust (generally, under a power of appointment, a person has the power to determine how property held in trust will be distributed at a certain time).

¶14265 — *Pass to Persons to be Determined (ITA 75(2)(a)(ii))*

ITA 75(2)(a)(ii) applies where property is held on condition that it or property substituted therefor may pass to persons to be determined by the settlor "at a time subsequent to the creation of the trust". Where the beneficiaries are named in the deed of settlement and the settlor only maintains discretion over the amount of trust property to be distributed, ITA 75(2)(a)(ii) should not apply (see John Saunders, "Inter Vivos Discretionary Family Trusts: A Potpourri of Issues and Traps," *Report of Proceedings of Forty-Fifth Tax Conference*, 1993 Tax Conference (Toronto: Canadian Tax Foundation, 1994), 37:1–58)). It should, however, be noted that in VD 9213965, the CRA states:

> If the person from whom the property was received by the trust has retained a power to veto distributions of property to beneficiaries, we are of the opinion that paragraph 75(2)(b) of the Act would apply.

> If the person, from whom the property was received by the trust, has the possibility to select beneficiaries among a predetermined class, it is our view that, because of the retention of such a power, the provisions of subparagraph 75(2)(a)(ii) of the Act will apply.

> When the person from whom the property was received by the trust cannot determine the identity of the beneficiaries but can only determine the quantum of the trust property to be distributed to the beneficiaries which have already been identified by the trust documents, we are of the opinion that subparagraph 75(2)(a)(ii) and paragraph 75(2)(b) of the Act may not be applicable.

> However, if the possibility to determine the quantum of the trust property is such that it results in the possibility to determine the beneficiaries to whom the property will pass, it is our view that subparagraph 75(2)(a)(i) and paragraph 75(2)(b) of the Act could apply. This situation may occur, among others, if the settlor retains the possibility to identify which property can be distributed to a beneficiary or if he retains the possibility to fix the quantum (for example, in allocating nothing to a beneficiary) so that he has retained the possibility to identify the beneficiary.

¶14266 — *Summary of CRA Views re: ITA 75(2)*

Below is a Quick Reference Table which summarizes the CRA's interpretations regarding ITA 75(2).

Proposed Situation/Circumstance	Does ITA 75(2) Apply?	Reference
Settlor retains the power to veto distributions of property, to select beneficiaries among a pre-determined class, to identify which property can be distributed to a beneficiary, or to determine the beneficiaries to whom property will pass	Yes	9213965
Trust property can revert to the settlor only by operation of law and not pursuant to any condition under the trust	No	9304585 2002-0116535
Settlor has the power to appoint, remove or replace trustees	Yes	9407905
Settlor is the sole trustee	Yes	1999-0013055
Settlor's letter of wishes may effectively be binding on trustees	Yes	2000-0023997
Transfer from 75(2) trust to second trust	No	2001-0067955
Settlor has a contingent right to use or occupy trust property	Maybe	2002-0118255

Proposed Situation/Circumstance	Does ITA 75(2) Apply?	Reference
Corporation settled a trust with its shares to be held for distribution to persons to be determined by the trustees, who are directors of the corporation	No	2002-0123843
Transfer of spouse trust assets after spouse's death	No	2002-0139205
Trust indenture gives settlor's spouse power to appoint capital beneficiary	Yes	2002-0162855
Settlor's spouse has a power of appointment, exercisable by will, to appoint the settlor as a capital beneficiary	Yes	2003-0050671E5
Non-resident trust deemed resident in Canada and trustees have discretion; application of 95(6) results in the continued attribution of the trust's FAPI	Yes	2004-0080731I7
Settlor is co-trustee without control	No	2004-0086921C6
Freeze shares acquired by trust for nominal fair market value and settlor is a beneficiary	Yes	2004-0086941C6
Settlor's spouse has power to allocate among beneficiaries but cannot add settler	No	2004-0086951C6
Property can revert on termination of trust	Yes	2005-0126261R3
75(2) does not require a "loan" or "transfer"	Yes	2005-0127351E5
Corporation is beneficiary of trust that holds shares in the corporation	No	2007-0243241C6 (reversing 2005-0140951C6)
T3 return is required to be filed if 75(2) applies to attribute income	N/A	2006-0185561C6 2017-0693371C6
Loan of income-producing property other than cash	Yes	2006-0185571C6
Loan of cash	No	2006-0185571C6
Attribution of FAPI under 75(2)	Yes	2006-0185671C6
Merging of three identical family trusts	No	2006-0191431R3
Using 75(2) intentionally may trigger GAAR	N/A	2006-0196231C6
75(2) attributes income to tax-exempt Indian bands	N/A	2006-0201361R3 2008-0282491R3
CCA limitations on rental property when 75(2) applies	N/A	2006-0216491E5 2008-0278801C6
Company issues shares to a trust of which it can become a beneficiary	No	2006-0218501E5 2009-0317641E5
No foreign tax credit on trust's foreign income attributed under 75(2)	N/A	2007-0233701C6
Whether ITR 1100(11) applies to rental property transferred to a trust	N/A	2007-0239951E5
A loan to a trust, where the loan is outside and independent of the terms of the trust	No	2007-0240421C6 2008-0300401E5 2009-0330251C6
Trust buys shares of corporate beneficiary for fair market value	No	2007-0243241C6 2010-0388551I7
Loan to trust falls within *Howson*	Yes	2008-0268121E5
Settlor is a co-trustee	Question of fact	2008-0292061E5
Application to a unit trust in Quebec	Yes	2008-0301241E5

Proposed Situation/Circumstance	Does ITA 75(2) Apply?	Reference
Settlor can become a beneficiary by marrying a named person	Yes	2009-0352711E5
Transfer of growth shares to trust with a price adjustment clause	Yes	2010-0366301I7
First Nations land claim settlement trust, but 75(2) does not apply to secondary income	Yes	2010-0372531E5 2011-0391831R3
Rollout from 75(2) trust to avoid 21-year rule	N/A	2011-04018316
The CRA will challenge dividend-stripping schemes that attempt to use 75(2) to avoid tax	N/A	2011-0401951C6 2014-0523001C6
Funds payable to child are left in the trust and reinvested	Yes	2011-0428661E5
What constitutes a genuine loan to a trust	N/A	2012-0453591C6
Price adjustment clause will be considered in determining whether 75(2) applies	N/A	2012-0453891C6
Settlor contributes a limited partnership interest to a trust that may revert back to the settlor under the terms of the trust	Maybe	2013-0476871E5
Property is transferred to a trust by a beneficiary of the trust in return for fair market value consideration	No	2013-0480351C6 2013-0495721C6
Losses from business or from an adventure or concern in the nature of trade	No	2013-0481651I7 2013-0508841I7
An executor transfers estate property, under the testator's will, to a family trust of which the executor is a beneficiary	No	2013-0500711E5
Income attributed under ITA 75(2) retains its nature	N/A	2014-0538241C6
Property income earned by a U.S. revocable living trust (also called a grantor trust)	Maybe	2014-0560361E5
T3 return is not required to be filed for 75(2) trust that only holds non-income producing property	N/A	2016-0645811C6
Trust indenture requires unanimous agreement of trustees, including the settlor, and settlor can remove and replace co-trustee at any time	Yes	2016-0669881I7
75(2) does not attribute foreign non-business income tax (paid by the trust) to the settlor	N/A	2018-0744161C6

¶14267 — *Exceptions to ITA 75(2)*

ITA 75(3) exempts the following types of trusts from the application of ITA 75(2):

- a trust governed by a deferred profit sharing plan, employee benefit plan, employees profit sharing plan, pooled registered pension plan, registered disability savings plan, registered education savings plan, registered pension plan, registered retirement income fund, registered retirement savings plan, registered supplementary unemployment benefit plan, retirement compensation arrangement or TFSA;

- an employee life and health trust, an employee trust, a private foundation that is a registered charity, a related segregated fund trust, a trust described in the definition of "trust" in ITA 108(1)(a.1), or a trust described by ITA 149(1)(y);

- a qualifying environmental trust; and

- a trust established to hold Canada Child Benefit payments for the benefit of a child for whom the payments were received.

¶14270 — Income Splitting Strategies

Despite the rules in the ITA that are designed to prevent income splitting, there are still various ways in which a taxpayer can split income with a spouse or common law partner, or with a related minor.

A self-employed taxpayer can employ and pay employment income to his or her spouse and children (including minors) for services provided to the taxpayer's business, as long as the amount is reasonable in the circumstances (ITA 67). The work performed by family members should be documented and a taxpayer should be prepared to support the amount paid as being reasonable. Paying a salary to family members can allow for the salary or wages to be taxed at a lower marginal rate and for family members to accrue RRSP contribution room. As well, the remuneration paid is deductible in computing income from the business.

Certain capital gains realized by a minor (for example, on shares listed on a designated stock exchange) are not subject to the attribution rules. As well, the attribution rules do not apply to transfers of property for full fair market consideration, loans of property that bear a commercial rate of interest (if the annual interest is paid within 30 days of each year-end), transfers of property that are deductible in computing the transferor's income and included in computing the income of the recipient, income earned by an RESP or RDSP, or Canada Child Benefit payments for children invested directly in the child's name.

Certain income splitting techniques are specifically permitted under the ITA, including contributing to a spousal RRSP (see ¶9133), pension-income splitting (see ¶8140 and ¶9140), and the exemption from the attribution rules available in respect of TFSAs (i.e., an individual can take advantage of TFSA contribution room available to them by using funds provided by their spouse or common-law partner and the spousal attribution rules will not apply to income earned in the TFSA; see ¶16210).

One common income-splitting technique involves loaning money to a lower-income spouse to make investments (i.e., transferring investment funds from one taxpayer to another so that the investment income is taxed in the hands of the lower-income spouse transferee). To avoid the attribution rules, interest must be charged on the loan at the prescribed rate. Prescribed interest rates are available on the CRA's website at: canada.ca/en/revenue-agency/services/tax/prescribed-interest-rates.html. Where the lower-income spouse acquires investments with the loan proceeds, the attribution rules will not require the lending spouse to report any investment income the lower-income spouse earns on the money lent him or her, provided interest on the loan is paid within 30 days of the end of the year (i.e., by January 30th). This strategy is attractive for individuals who are able to earn a rate of return on investments that is higher than the low current prescribed rate. Normally, legal counsel should draft the terms of the loan. Also, it is useful to set up a separate account to clearly track the source of the investment funds and the income earned by the investments.

Some other common income-splitting techniques include the following: a capital loss can be transferred between spouses where property with an accrued loss is transferred to a spouse and an election is filed under ITA 73(1) for the transfer to occur at fair market value; a higher-income spouse can pay all personal family expenses to allow the lower-income spouse to retain earnings and make investments; and CPP and QPP benefits can be shared with a spouse (visit: www1.canada.ca/en/esdc/service-canada.html).

¶14300 — Other Avoidance Rules

¶14310 — Benefit Conferred (Indirect Payments or Transfers)

ITA 246 requires the monetary value of certain benefits conferred on a taxpayer by another person by one or more sales, exchanges, or other means whatever to be accounted for by the taxpayer for the purposes of Part I or Part XIII tax, as the case may be. The provision applies to the extent that the amount of the benefit has not otherwise been included in the taxpayer's income or taxable income earned in Canada but would have been included in the taxpayer's income if the taxpayer were resident in Canada and the amount of the benefit were a payment made to the taxpayer. ITA 246 generally does not apply where it is established that a *bona fide* transaction was entered into by persons dealing at arm's length.

The CRA was unsuccessful in applying ITA 246 in *Osinski*, 2013 CarswellNat 416 (TCC), *943372 Ontario Inc.*, [2007] 5 C.T.C. 2001 (TCC), *Pelletier*, [2004] 5 C.T.C. 2271 (TCC), and *Shahsavar*, [2005] 2 C.T.C. 2562 (TCC).

ITA 56(2) invokes the principle of "constructive receipt", imputing to a taxpayer income diverted to someone else. Also, ITA 56(4) imputes to a taxpayer any right to income transferred by the taxpayer to someone with whom the taxpayer was not dealing at arm's length. ITA 56(2) generally only applies where a taxpayer desires to confer a benefit on a person (ITA 246 does not have such a test).

In *Neuman*, [1998] 3 C.T.C. 177 (SCC), the Court found that ITA 56(2) cannot apply to redirect dividend income to a taxpayer unless that taxpayer has "a pre-existing entitlement" to the dividend income. In the case, income splitting was achieved by the incorporation of a holding company by a taxpayer and the subsequent payment of dividends to the taxpayer's spouse. The CRA will generally not apply GAAR to dividends paid in family income-splitting structures (see, for example, VD 2016-0626781E5); however, the tax on split income (ITA 120.4) or the attribution rules in ITA 74.4 may apply (see ITTN No. 16).

ITA 56(2) will not generally be applicable in a situation involving a *bone fide* loan since such a loan does not constitute a "payment of transfer of property" within the meaning of the provision.

In VD 2012-0462891C6, the CRA indicated it may seek to apply ITA 56(2) to a trustee in respect of distributions made in favour of discretionary beneficiaries related to the trustee in the context of a fully discretionary trust where the sole trustee is also a discretionary beneficiary of the trust. The CRA stated it was concerned with "elaborate arrangements" designed to divert business income to family members.

ITA 15(1), 56(2), 246, *Massicotte*, [2009] 1 C.T.C. 41 (FCA), IT-453, VDs 2016-0666841E5, 2013-0513221I7, 2013-0506401E5, 2013-0502151E5, 2011-0411491E5, 2006-0175601E5, 2010-0364131E5, 2005-0140961C6, Cameron, "Discretionary Dividend Shares — Beware!", Tax Hyperion (Taxnet Pro), Vol. 13-7, July 2016, Smith et al., "Indirect Shareholder Benefits: Subsections 56(2) and 246(1)," *2009 Ontario Tax Conference*, (Toronto: Canadian Tax Foundation, 2009), 10:1–21, Stilwell, "Subsection 246(1) — All or (Almost) Nothing?", *Tax Hyperion* (Carswell), Vol. 12-1, Jan. 2015, Lang, "Section 246 Catches Tax Payments Made by a US LLC", XVIII(1) *Corporate Finance* (Federated Press) 2084-85 (2012)

¶14320 — Transfer of Income Rights

ITA 56(4) applies where a taxpayer has transferred or assigned to a person with whom the transferor was not dealing at arm's length the right to an amount which, had the right not been so transferred or assigned, would be included in the income of the transferor. Spouses and common-law partners are deemed not to be dealing with each other at arm's length, and thus, ITA 56(4) would usually apply where a right to income is transferred from one spouse or common-law partner to another. The amount that is included in income is the part of the amount that relates to the period in the year throughout which the transferor is resident in Canada. A transfer or assignment includes a sale whether or not the sale is at fair market value. Basically, ITA 56(4) serves as an obstacle to switching income from the transferor to the transferee by providing that the amount arising from the right be included in the transferor's income. For example, ITA 56(4) will apply where a taxpayer attempts to redirect payments to a lower income spouse, where such payments would otherwise be amounts received by the taxpayer and taxed accordingly. ITA 56(4) does not apply where there is an actual transfer of the underlying asset that produces the income paid pursuant to the transferred right.

Where an amount of income to which ITA 56(4) applies is invested or otherwise used by the transferee to earn further income, ITA 56(4) will not apply to include the further amount of income in the income of the transferor.

ITA 56(4) does not apply to any portion of a retirement pension that the taxpayer assigns under the Canada Pension Plan or the Quebec Pension Plan, or to an amount that a spouse or former spouse of the taxpayer receives from the taxpayer's registered pension plan, RRSP or RRIF in settlement of rights arising out of, or on a breakdown of, their marriage. As well, ITA 56(4) does not apply to an amount that is income from property where the transferor has also transferred or assigned the property, provided that the property is separate and distinct from the income which arises from it so that it would be possible to transfer one while retaining the other. For example, a life interest created under a trust or testamentary instrument is considered to be a property separate and distinct from the income which arises from it. Consequently, where a life tenant transfers a life interest in an estate to one or more of the persons entitled to the residual interest in the estate, ITA 56(4) does not apply since there is a transfer of property as well as a transfer of the right to income.

An amount to which ITA 56(4) applies could be included in the income of both the transferor and transferee. However, where the transfer or assignment of the right to an amount that is income does not constitute a deliberate attempt to evade or avoid tax, the amount will be included only in the income of the transferor.

Folio S1-F5-C1: *Related Persons and Dealing at Arm's Length*, IT-440R2: *Transfer of Rights to Income*

¶14330 — Non-Arm's Length Loans

ITA 56(4.1) applies when below-market loans are made to related individuals using a trust. Specifically, ITA 56(4.1) provides that, where an individual loans property to a trust and a beneficiary of the trust is an individual who is 18 years of age or older who does not deal at arm's length with the lender, and it may reasonably be considered that one of the main reasons for the making of the loan was to reduce or avoid tax by causing the income from the loaned property to be included in the income of the beneficiary, any income from the loaned property that would otherwise be included in the income of the beneficiary will be attributed to the lender.

Generally, there is no attribution under ITA 56(4.1) where the attribution rule in ITA 74.1 applies in respect of such income (see ¶14220), or if ITA 75(2) applies in respect of the income (see ¶14260). In addition, ITA 56(4.2) exempts from the application of ITA 56(4.1) loans and other indebtedness bearing a commercial rate of interest where the annual interest is paid within 30 days after the year-end. To qualify for this exemption with respect to income derived in a taxation year, the following conditions must be met in each year:

1. Interest must be charged on the loan or indebtedness at a rate not less than the lesser of the prescribed rate of interest in effect at the time the loan was made or the indebtedness arose; and the rate that, having regard to all circumstances, would have been agreed upon between arm's length parties at the time the loan was made;

2. Interest payable in respect of a particular year must be paid not later than 30 days after the year-end; and

3. Interest payable in respect of each preceding taxation year must have been paid not later than 30 days after each year-end.

Thus, failure to pay interest in respect of a particular year within 30 days after the year-end results in attribution for that year and each succeeding year. Furthermore, a subsequent loan on a commercial basis to replace the original loan or indebtedness would not necessarily end the attribution under ITA 56(4.1).

ITA 56(4.3) provides that, where a property is used to repay (in whole or in part) a loan or indebtedness that enabled or assisted an individual to acquire another property, the whole or a portion of the income or loss derived from that other property (or property substituted therefor) must, for the purposes of the attribution rule in ITA 56(4.1), be included in computing income from the property used as repayment. Absent ITA 56(4.3), it might be possible to avoid attribution under ITA 56(4.1) in these circumstances, since the property used as repayment would not itself generate income, even though ITA 56(4.1) would have applied had the property used for repayment purposes been substituted directly for the other property. The amount to be regarded as income from the property used for repayment purposes (and thus to be included in the lender's income under ITA 56(4.1) if the conditions of that subsection are met) is that proportion of the income derived from the other property (or property substituted therefor) that the repaid amount is of the cost to the individual of the other property. For example, if a 20-year-old individual were to borrow $60,000 from a financial institution to acquire common shares, he or she would be subject to tax on the dividends received. If the individual's father subsequently lends the child $20,000 to pay down the original loan, the father would be subject to tax on 1/3 of the dividends received by the child after the date of the pay-down of the loan.

There are no provisions corresponding to ITA 74.5(6) and (7) (see ¶14225 and ¶14226) to provide specifically against avoidance of the rule in ITA 56(4.1) by means of back-to-back loans or guarantees. There is also no express provision against "reverse attribution" for taking advantage of the attribution rules, such as that found in ITA 74.5(11) for artificial transactions.

IT-511R: *Interspousal and Certain Other Transfers and Loans of Property*

¶14340 — Inadequate Consideration

By virtue of ITA 69(1), when a taxpayer acquires property from a person with whom the taxpayer does not deal at arm's length at a cost in excess of the fair market value of the property at the time of acquisition, the cost is deemed to be that fair market value. However, the vendor's proceeds of disposition are not decreased (i.e., the adjustment is one-sided). If a taxpayer disposes of property to a person with whom the taxpayer does not deal at arm's length for proceeds of disposition that are less than the fair market value of the property at the time of disposition, the proceeds of disposition are deemed to be that fair market value. Again, however, the adjustment is one-sided and the acquirer's cost base in the property is not increased.

One-sided adjustments under the rules described above are punitive in nature. For example, if the non-arm's length transfer occurred for proceeds of disposition in excess of fair market value, tax will have been paid by the transferor on the higher proceeds; however, the transferee will not benefit from a higher cost when the transferee later disposes of the property to a third party. Similar provisions apply to property subject to a leasing agreement that is disposed of.

The fair market value rule applying to "acquisitions" in ITA 69(1)(a) and (c) extends to property acquired by gift, bequest, or inheritance, whereas the rule applying to "dispositions" in ITA 69(1)(b) extends only to property disposed of by gift, to the exclusion of property disposed of on death. Dispositions on death are dealt with in ITA 70 and 72, which adopt other rules of valuation for tax purposes.

ITA 69(1), (1.2), *Deptuck*, [2003] 3 C.T.C. 287, *Madsen*, [2001] 1 C.T.C. 244 (FCA), ITTN-44, IT-405 (archived), IT-169, IT-209R, VDs 2013-0484321E5, 2008-0263891R3, 2006-0176081R3, 2003-0004125, 2007-0228281E5, 2004-0086821C6, 2010-0364131E5

¶14350 — Shareholder Benefits and Loans

¶14351 — *Shareholder Benefits*

Pursuant to ITA 15(1), where, at any time in a taxation year, a benefit has been conferred upon a shareholder or on a person in contemplation of becoming a shareholder, the amount or value of the benefit is included in computing the income of the shareholder for the year. ITA 15(1) is designed to circumvent tax-free distributions of corporation earnings to shareholders. The scope of this provision is broad; a shareholder benefit can include virtually any payment, appropriation of property, or advantage conferred on the shareholder by the corporation. A benefit may be conferred upon a shareholder even if there was no intention to confer a benefit. Also, the shareholder does not have to have knowledge that a benefit was conferred; it is enough that the shareholder should have known, given the facts in a particular situation, that he or she was receiving a benefit. For example, a shareholder benefit may arise where corporate funds are transferred to a personal shareholder account even if the shareholder never withdrew any funds from the account and subsequently reversed the transfer.

Unless otherwise deemed to be a dividend by reason of ITA 84, the amount deemed to be received by a shareholder is not characterized as a dividend and accordingly does not entitle an individual shareholder to a dividend tax credit. Furthermore, the amount of the deemed income does not depend on the existence in the corporation of undistributed income. ITA 15(1) can apply if the corporation has a surplus or a deficit. For individual shareholders, the benefit is income to the shareholder in the calendar year in which it is received; the taxation year of the corporation is not relevant.

A payment made by a corporation to purchase something from a shareholder at a price in excess of fair market value would, to that extent, be income in the hands of the shareholder under ITA 15(1) (also see ¶14340). Also, if property is removed from a corporation by a shareholder at a price below fair market value or for no consideration at all, the shareholder's profit from the transaction is income subject to tax. The corporation will normally be deemed to receive the full market value for the property (see ¶14340). Other examples of shareholder benefits include the personal use of company-owned cars, boats, aircraft, resorts, etc. by virtue of shareholdings rather than employment; the occupation by a shareholder of accommodation paid for by the company (to the extent not paid for by the shareholder); and improvements to the shareholder's personal property paid for by the corporation.

ITA 69(4) is generally intended to prevent corporations from understating their income by distributing assets to their shareholders without proper consideration. The terms of the provision are broad, applying to any corporation, resident or non-resident, and to all types of property including capital property, inventory, etc. In each case, where the property has been so appropriated for no consideration or for a consideration below its fair market value, the corporation is deemed to have sold the property during the year and to have received fair market value consideration if such a sale would have increased the corporation's income for a taxation year (or reduced a loss). Such benefits conferred by corporations on their shareholders while going concerns are taxable in the shareholders' hands under ITA 15(1).

Distributions or appropriations of corporate property for the benefit of shareholders on the winding-up, discontinuance, or reorganization of business are taxable to the shareholders under ITA 84(2) (see ¶3130). ITA 69(4) is silent as to the cost of the property to the shareholder. In some cases, the rules contained in ITA 52 may apply to capital property.

The CRA's general position is that an estate re-freeze transaction does not result in the conferral of a benefit on the common shareholders or the preferred shareholder(s), provided that the decrease in value of the corporation is not the result of the stripping of corporate assets and the fair market value of the new preferred shares issued is equal to the fair market value of the old preferred shares at the time of the re-freeze transactions.

ITA 15(1) applies to benefits provided to an individual in their capacity as a shareholder (i.e., qua shareholder). On the other hand, ITA 6(1)(a) applies to benefits provided in an individual's capacity as an employee (i.e., *qua* employee).

If the person on whom a benefit is conferred by a corporation is both a shareholder and an employee, a determination must be made as to whether the benefit was conferred *qua* shareholder or *qua* employee. If a benefit is granted *qua* shareholder, it will be taxed under ITA 15(1) without regard to any of the exceptions found in ITA 6 and the corporation will normally not be entitled to a deduction. Where ITA 6(1)(a) applies, the employer can normally deduct the value of the benefit and source deductions should be withheld in respect of the benefit.

The CRA's general position is that a benefit is considered to be received *qua* employee if it is reasonable to conclude that it has been provided as part of a reasonable remuneration package for the individual as an employee. Also, when an equivalent benefit is extended to all employees, including employees who are shareholders, the benefit will normally be considered an employment benefit. Where a benefit is conferred upon an individual that is the only employee and shareholder of a corporation, the benefit is not necessarily conferred by virtue of being an employee.

ITA 15(1)–(1.4), (7), (9), 69(1), (4), 248(1)"amount", "specified shareholder", *Laliberté*, 2018 TCC 186, *Golini*, 2016 CarswellNat 3212 (TCC), *Dyck*, [2008] 1 C.T.C. 2070 (TCC), *Gestion Léon Gagnon Inc.*, 2006 CarswellNat 4345 (TCC), *Colubriale*, [2006] 5 C.T.C. 2034 (TCC), *Servais*, [2005] 2 C.T.C. 264 (FCA), *Del Grande*, [1993] 1 C.T.C. 2096 (TCC), *Wong*, [1999] 2 C.T.C. 2173 (TCC), *Mullen*, [1990] 2 C.T.C. 2141 (TCC), *Pillsbury Holdings Ltd*, [1964] C.T.C. 294, *Boardman and Saskan Investments Ltd*, [1986] 1 C.T.C. 103 (FCTD), IT-432R2: *Benefits Conferred on Shareholders*, IT-116R3: *Rights to Buy Additional Common Shares*, ITTN-32, ITTN-31R2, ITTN-25, VDs 2016-0651771C6, 2014-0522261E5, Hennessey, "Another Reason To Avoid Shareholder Benefits", Canadian Tax Focus, Vol. 6-1, Feb. 2016,

Elizabeth Junkin, "Section 15 — Shareholder Benefits Update," *2009 British Columbia Tax Conference*, (Vancouver: Canadian Tax Foundation, 2009), 12:1–18

¶14351.1 — *Shareholder Benefit Exclusions*

Specifically excluded from being a taxable shareholder benefit under ITA 15(1) are the following:

1. Distributions to which other specific provisions apply (i.e., a reduction of PUC under ITA 84(4), the redemption, cancellation or acquisition by a corporation of its shares under ITA 84(3), the winding-up, discontinuance or reorganization of the corporation's business under ITA 84(2), and the winding-up of a wholly-owned taxable Canadian corporation under ITA 88);

2. The payment of dividends or stock dividends;

3. Conferring the same right on all common shareholders to acquire additional shares in the corporation (where a corporation has two classes of common shares, each with different voting rights but otherwise identical, a corporation could confer a right to acquire additional shares of a class upon shareholders of that class without giving rise to a shareholder benefit); and

4. The conversion of contributed surplus into PUC pursuant to ITA 84(1)(c.1), (c.2), or (c.3) in respect of certain corporations (see ¶3130).

The exclusion for stock dividends does not apply where one of the purposes of paying the stock dividend is to significantly alter the value of the interest in the corporation of any specified shareholder of the corporation by virtue of ITA 15(1.1). At the 2013 Annual CTF Tax Conference CRA Roundtable, an example was provided of a series of transactions in respect of which the CRA stated ITA 15(1.1) would apply to a non-resident shareholder (see VD 2013-0507981C6). The CRA indicated that it will apply ITA 15(1.1) where the payment of a stock dividend clearly falls within the ambit of the provision. For examples of rulings in which the CRA stated ITA 15(1.1) would not apply, see VDs 2010-0374141R3, 2003-0004125, and 9805975F.

A payment by a corporation to a shareholder made pursuant to a *bona fide* business transaction is not required to be included in the shareholder's income under ITA 15(1). Whether a transaction is a *bona fide* business transaction is question of fact. Normally, a transaction is considered to be *bona fide* when its terms and conditions are the same as they would be if the transaction were entered into by parties dealing at arm's length.

The Courts have found that genuine bookkeeping errors should not result in a taxable benefit being assessed under ITA 15(1) (i.e., erroneous bookkeeping entries generally do not create a shareholder benefit). For example, a cheque posted in error to a shareholder account without the shareholder's knowledge should not constitute a shareholder benefit. It is important to note, however, that only genuine bookkeeping errors can be used as a defence against an ITA 15(1) assessment. For example, a post-year-end adjustment of a tax planning nature would not be considered a correction of a genuine bookkeeping error. Also, ITA 15(1) can apply in circumstances where the shareholder or corporation ought to have known that a benefit was conferred and actions were not taken to reverse the benefit.

Chaplin, 2017 CarswellNat 5226 (TCC), *Bibby*, [2010] 2 C.T.C. 2001 (TCC), *Chopp*, [1998] 1 C.T.C. 407 (FCA), *Lee*, [1999] 3 C.T.C. 2204 (TCC), *Robinson*, [2000] 2 C.T.C. 236 (FCTD), *9100-2402 Québec Inc.*, 2006 CarswellNat 1859 (TCC), *Maan*, [2007] 1 C.T.C. 2220 (TCC), *Cook*, [2006] 5 C.T.C. 2202 (TCC), *Mastracci*, [2007] 1 C.T.C. 2519 (TCC), *Vialink Inc.*, [2009] 3 C.T.C. 2065 (TCC), *Pereira*, 2009 CarswellNat 2295 (TCC), *Rudolph*, 2009 CarswellNat 2716 (TCC)

¶14351.2 — *Common Shareholder Benefits*

A common shareholder benefit is that of the personal use of a car owned by a corporation. This benefit would be taxable under ITA 15(1), except that a special rule is provided to fix a minimum amount at which the taxable amount will be determined. For this purpose, the ITA levies a standby charge which is the value of the income benefit to the shareholder to the extent the corporation is not reimbursed by the shareholder. The rules in ITA 6(1), (1.1), (2), and (7) applicable to employees in similar circumstances are applicable to determine the taxable benefit received by a shareholder or a person related to the shareholder (see ¶2130 and ¶2455).

Where a company-owned aircraft is used substantially for business purposes but occasionally for personal purposes by a shareholder (other than an officer or employee), a taxable benefit is imputed to the shareholder (see ¶2115 and ¶2455). The benefit is based on the same proportion of the total operating costs of the aircraft for the year (including capital cost allowance or full rental fees if leased), as the flying time when used is of the total flying time for the year. The same proportion of the cost is not considered deductible by the corporation. Where the shareholder is also an officer or employee of the corporation and only moderate personal use is made of the aircraft, the CRA will likely treat the benefit as derived from the employment and may not disallow the amount as a deduction by the corporation. This rule will not apply, however, if the shareholder-employee controls the corporation and makes substantial personal use of the aircraft.

Corporate owned life insurance policies may also give rise to taxable shareholder benefits. Applicable as of January 2010 for new policies and January 2011 for existing policies, the CRA's position is that where a wholly-owned subsidiary is the owner of a life insurance policy, and its parent company is the beneficiary of the policy, the payment of premiums by the subsidiary results in a benefit under ITA 15(1) to the parent company. However, if the insurance policy is owned and paid for by the parent company, with the subsidiary as the revocable beneficiary of the policy, the CRA's view is that the parent company would not be subject to ITA 15(1); however, ITA 246(1) (benefit conferred on a person; see ¶14310) could apply to the subsidiary.

The CRA considers it to be a question of fact as to whether a liability insurance premium paid by a corporation for an employee or a shareholder would constitute a taxable benefit (see VD 2010-0390171E5). Where the liability insurance premium paid by a corporation constitutes a benefit conferred by virtue of a person's employment, the value of the benefit is taxable to the employee pursuant to ITA 6(1)(a) and is generally deductible by the corporation (this general rule is also applicable if the insurance policy is transferred from the corporation to an employee; see, for example, VD 2013-0481421C6). Where the premium constitutes a benefit conferred by virtue of a person's shareholdings, the value of the benefit is included in the shareholder's income under ITA 15(1), and the premium is generally not deductible by the corporation.

For the CRA's position on so-called single-purpose corporations that were commonly used in the past to hold US vacation properties in order to avoid US estate tax, see ITTN-32, ITTN-31R2, and paragraph 10 of IT-432R2. Historically, the CRA did not assess a shareholder benefit in respect of a single-purpose corporation; however, the CRA revised its policy as a result of amendments to Canada-U.S. Tax Treaty:Art. XXIX-B. The CRA's former policy ceased to apply to acquisitions of property after 2004; however, the former policy continues to apply under grandfathering rules generally until the disposition of the US real estate or the corporation's shares. Note that grandfathering status can be lost as a result of a deemed disposition for tax purposes; see VDs 2011-0393401E5, 2010-0386871E5, 2006-0185561C6, and 2004-0106241E5.

ITA 15(1), (5), 20(1)(e.2), *Reakes Enterprises Ltd.*, [2006] 4 C.T.C. 2206 (TCC), IT-160R3 (archived): *Personal Use of Aircraft*, ITTN-44, VDs 2013-0481421C6, 2012-0446491E5, 2009-0347291C6, 2010-0359421C6, 2004-0072971I7, 2007-0257251E5, 2007-0241951C6, Kevin Wark, "The Canada Revenue Agency Announces New Assessing Position", XVI(2) Insurance Planning 1002-04 and XIII(2) *Business Vehicles* (Federated Press) 686–88 (2010)

¶14351.3 — *Value of Benefit*

If ITA 15(1) applies, the value of the benefit must be determined (in particular, the value of any non-monetary benefits conferred must be determined). The CRA's position is that the calculation of the amount or value of the benefit should normally be based on the fair market rent of the property minus any consideration paid to the corporation by the shareholder for the use of the property, unless the fair market rent is not appropriate for measuring the benefit. Where the fair market rent is not appropriate, the CRA has stated the "imputed rent" method should be used. Where the imputed rent method is used, the CRA's position is that any consideration paid to the corporation by the shareholder for the use of the property may be subtracted from the imputed rent. Additionally, the CRA considers that for purposes of computing imputed rent, the greater of the cost or fair market value of the property may be reduced by any outstanding interest-free loans or advances that were made to enable the corporation to acquire the property (as a general rule, the Courts have found that shareholder benefits cannot be offset by unrelated shareholder loans).

When asked at the 2015 APFF Annual Tax conference whether the value of a benefit conferred to a shareholder by a corporation for the personal use of a property owned by the corporation could be computed using the prescribed rate of interest provided in ITR 4301(a)(i) as the normal rate of return, the CRA stated: "The Act does not contain any provision with respect to the normal rate of return used to compute the value of a benefit under subsection 15(1). The CRA does not have any guidelines to determine what constitutes a normal rate of return. It depends on the facts." (VD 2015-0595541C6).

Youngman, [1990] 2 C.T.C. 10 (FCA), *Arpeg Holdings Ltd.*, [2008] 2 C.T.C. 140 (FCA), *Fingold*, [1997] 3 C.T.C. 441 (FCA), *Franklin*, [2002] 2 C.T.C. 88 (FCA), *Dumais*, [2009] 1 C.T.C. 24 (FCA), IT-432R2 (para. 11), VDs 2008-0285281C6, 2008-0267401E5, 2015-0595541C6

¶14351.4 — *Interaction with Other Avoidance Provisions*

ITA 15(1) generally does not apply to an indirect shareholder. For example, ITA 15(1) generally should not apply if an individual held shares of an operating corporation through a holding corporation and a benefit was provided to the shareholder by the operating company (in such a case, however, the avoidance rule in ITA 246(1) may apply; see ¶14310).

ITA 56(2) (see ¶14310) provides that where a taxpayer directs or concurs in the payment of an amount to another person, that amount shall be included in the taxpayer's income where, if it had been paid to him, it would have been so included. ITA 56(2), as opposed to ITA 15(1), normally applies where a shareholder directs a corporation to confer a benefit on another party. Also, ITA 246(1) (see ¶14310) provides that where, at any time, a person confers a benefit, directly or indirectly, in any manner whatever, on a taxpayer, the amount of that benefit, if it is not otherwise included in the taxpayer's income and would have been so included if it had been a payment made directly to the taxpayer and if the taxpayer had been resident in Canada, shall either be included in the taxpayer's income in the taxation year in which the benefit has been conferred or, if the taxpayer is a non-resident, shall be deemed for the purposes of Part XIII to be a payment made to the taxpayer at that time in respect of property, services or otherwise depending on the nature of the benefit.

VDs 2012-0464411I7, 2009-0315531E5, 2001-0098297, 2005-0140961C6, Smith et al., "Indirect Shareholder Benefits: Subsections 56(2) and 246(1)," *2009 Ontario Tax Conference*, (Toronto: Canadian Tax Foundation, 2009), 10:1–21

¶14352 — *Shareholder Loans*

To prevent corporate profits from being advanced as loans to shareholders or to persons connected to a shareholder, a loan to a shareholder or to persons connected to a shareholder is considered income to the shareholder or to persons connected to a shareholder, except in the specific circumstances noted below. This rule applies regardless of whether the corporation has any accumulated surplus.

The general shareholder loan rule in ITA 15(2) is extended to: 1) a loan made (or indebtedness granted) by a particular corporation, 2) a loan made (or indebtedness granted) by a corporation related to the particular corporation, or 3) a loan made (or indebtedness granted) by a partnership of which either or both of the corporations is a member. The provision applies where the loan is received by a person who is a shareholder of the particular corporation, connected with a shareholder of the particular corporation, or a member of a partnership or beneficiary of a trust which is a shareholder of the particular corporation. It is not necessary for the lender or creditor to be resident of or carried on business in Canada. However, this provision does not apply to a loan by one non-resident to another. A person is connected with a shareholder of the particular corporation if the person does not deal at arm's length with the shareholder or is affiliated with the shareholder.

Where ITA 15(2) applies, the amount of the loan must be included in computing the income of the shareholder or connected person for the year in which the loan is received. Thus, where the recipient is an individual, the amount taxable will constitute income for the calendar year in which it is received, without regard for the taxation year of the lender or creditor.

ITA 15(2), (2.1), (2.2), (7), VDs 2015-0601211E5, 2012-0442521E5, 2004-0064811E5, 2006-021516117

¶14352.1 — *Shareholder Loan Income Inclusion Exceptions*

No income is imputed to a shareholder in respect of a loan or equivalent indebtedness if the loan is made or indebtedness incurred:

1) In the ordinary course of the lender's or creditor's business and, in the case of a loan, the lending of money is part of the lender's ordinary business (e.g., a loan by a bank or financial institution) and at the time the indebtedness arose *bona fide* arrangements were made for repayment of the debt or loan within a reasonable time;

2) To an employee (other than a specified employee) of the lender or creditor, or to the employee's spouse or common-law partner, to acquire a dwelling for the individual's habitation (see ¶2238). A dwelling is interpreted as including a country house, summer cottage, a self-contained suite in an apartment block, or a unit in a duplex, provided it is actually occupied by the individual. Where the dwelling is only part of a building, the amount of the loan or indebtedness must not exceed the cost of the portion constituting the individual's dwelling. A specified employee is an employee who is either a specified shareholder (generally, a person who holds at least 10% of the shares of any class of the corporation at any time in the year) or a person who does not deal at arm's length with the corporation;

3) To an employee of the lender (if the lender is a corporation) to assist the employee to acquire from the corporation previously unissued fully paid shares of the corporation, or to acquire from a corporation related to the lending corporation previously issued fully paid shares of that related corporation to be held by the employee for the employee's own benefit;

4) To an employee of the lender or creditor to assist the employee to acquire a motor vehicle needed in the performance of employment; or

5) To a trust where the lender or creditor is a private corporation, the corporation is settlor and sole beneficiary of the trust, and the sole purpose of the trust is to facilitate the purchase and sale of shares at fair market value from and to employees (other than specified employees) of the corporation or of a related corporation.

Even if one of the above exceptions is met, the loan or indebtedness will be income of the shareholder unless, at the time the loan is made or indebtedness incurred, there are *bona fide* arrangements for its repayment within a reasonable time and it is reasonable to conclude that the loan was made or indebtedness incurred by virtue of the employment relationship rather than as a shareholder. The delivery of a promissory note or the assumption of the debt by another person does not constitute repayment. A transfer of property to the corporation will effect repayment, to the extent of the fair market value of the property.

As discussed below, even if one of the above exceptions is not met, a loan to a shareholder will also not be included in income where the loan is repaid within one year after the end of the lenders' taxation year in which it was made. However, the loan will be included in income if it can be established the repayment was part of a series of loans and repayments (see VD 2012-0443581E5).

Paragraph 11 of IT-119R4 describes the CRA's views on whether a loan made to an individual is considered to have been received by the individual in his or her capacity as an employee or as a shareholder. An important factor will be whether or not loans on the same terms and conditions are offered to other employees of the corporation who are not shareholders.

In *Dionne*, [1998] 3 C.T.C. 2610 (TCC), the Court took a flexible approach when interpreting the meaning of *bona fide* arrangements for repayment in a reasonable time, stating (para. 16):

> When a statute describes a reasonable time or any other reasonable measure or conduct, one can be sure that what is meant is not something rigidly specific, eternal, universal or regulating, or even a verity. What is meant is the period of time that is reasonable in the circumstances.

ITA 15(2.3)–(2.6), *Davidson*, [1999] 3 C.T.C. 2159, *Barbeau*, 2006 CarswellNat 4909 (TCC), *Loman Warehousing Ltd.*, [2001] 1 C.T.C. 50 (FCA), IT-119R4, VDs 2003-0047891E5, 2004-0064811E5, 2006-0191881R3, 2007-0238971R3, 2007-0244561R3, 2005-0159061E5, 2008-0270201E5, 2002-0118495

¶14352.2 — *Repayment of Shareholder Loans Included in Income*

Where a loan that has been included in computing the income of a shareholder under ITA 15(2) is repaid in a later year, the amount repaid may be deducted in computing income for that subsequent year. This rule does not apply, however, if the repayment is part of a series of loans and repayments. *Bona fide* repayments of shareholder loans resulting from, for example, the payment of dividends, salaries or bonuses should not be considered part of a series of loans or other transactions and repayments.

Where a series of yearly increases in a loan account is followed by one or more yearly decreases, it is necessary to determine whether the first decrease should be regarded as repayment of an amount otherwise subject to tax in the immediately preceding year, or whether it constitutes a repayment of an older amount and is deductible. Unless it is specifically stated that a certain repayment is made on account of a certain outstanding amount, it is generally considered that a payment should first be applied in settlement of the oldest amount outstanding. Accordingly, unless the corporation instructs to the contrary, the CRA will continue the practice of examining the year-end balances in a shareholder's account with any net increase in such balances being considered a loan made to the shareholder in the year. Each decrease in year-end balances ordinarily will be allowed as a deduction from income of the shareholder in the year the decrease occurs if it otherwise qualifies as a repayment rather than the decrease being applied to reduce an amount that may be subject to tax in the immediately preceding year. If, however, a corporation requests that a repayment or decrease be applied to reduce an amount that may be subject to tax in the immediately preceding year, the CRA will generally agree to the request.

A shareholder loan does not necessarily have to be repaid with cash. For example, an individual shareholder may transfer personal assets to the corporation to offset a shareholder loan account.

ITA 20(1)(j), 148(7), IT-119R4 (paras. 24 to 29), VD 2006-0215161I7, 2002-0127455, 2003-0040145, 2008-0303971E5, 2008-0280041R3, 2007-0241041R3, 2007-0241991R3, 2003-0033915, 2002-0121723, 2001-0068763, *VanNieuwkerk*, [2004] 1 C.T.C. 2577 (TCC), *Meeuse*, [1994] 1 C.T.C. 2737 (TCC), *Attis*, [1992] 1 C.T.C. 2244, *Hill*, [1993] 1 C.T.C. 2021

¶14352.3 — *Offsetting Shareholder Loans and Advances*

If shareholder advances are outstanding, all other factors being equal, the advance should be drawn down rather than taking out a separate shareholder loan. Where a separate shareholder loan and advance are outstanding during the same period, technically, ITA 15(2) applies to the shareholder loan even if the amount of the advance is greater than the amount of the loan.

Wood, [1988] 1 C.T.C. 2312 (TCC), *Gannon*, [[1988] 1 C.T.C. 2422] (TCC), *Wolf*, [1992] 2 C.T.C. 2231 (TCC), *Austin*, [1991] 1 C.T.C. 2533 (TCC), VDs 2003-0033915, 2010-0382361E5

¶14352.4 — *Interest-Free Shareholder or Employee Loans*

Where a loan is made (or other indebtedness is granted) to a shareholder by a corporation without interest, or at a low rate of interest, interest at the prescribed rate is imputed to the shareholder and included in computing the shareholder's income by virtue of ITA 15(1) (this rule does not apply if the whole loan or debt is included in the shareholder's income under ITA 15(2)). Similarly, ITA 80.4(1) and (2) respectively deem a taxable benefit to arise on certain interest-free or low-interest-bearing loans received by employees or individual shareholders (or individuals related to such employees or shareholders) (see ¶2235).

Where a taxable benefit is deemed by ITA 80.4 to have been conferred on a shareholder or related individual, the recipient is deemed by ITA 15(9) to be a shareholder of a corporation and the benefit to be a benefit conferred on a shareholder by the corporation, thus bringing that deemed income within the scope of ITA 15(1), unless the loan is received by virtue of employment and ITA 6(9) or 12(1)(w) applies. The portion of any loan or debt included in computing the income of a person or partnership is excluded from the ambit of ITA 80.4. To the extent, therefore, that any loan or indebtedness is caught by the provisions of ITA 15(1) or (2), for example, the absence of interest thereon will not give rise to a further taxable benefit under ITA 80.4.

Where ITA 80.4(2) applies, the benefit received by the individual or partnership in a taxation year is computed as the excess of: 1) the amount of interest that would be payable on the loan or debt at the prescribed rate for the period in the year during which it was outstanding, over 2) the amount of interest, if any, actually paid on the loan or debt before the expiry of 30 days following the end of the year. A person is deemed to be connected with a shareholder if the person does not deal at arm's length with the shareholder. There is an exception, however, where the person is a foreign affiliate. Similar rules apply where the beneficiary of the interest-free or low interest loan is an officer or employee, rather than a shareholder.

An amount taxed as a benefit under ITA 80.4 may be treated by the recipient as interest paid in the year pursuant to a legal obligation to pay interest on borrowed money, so as to possibly qualify for a deduction under ITA 20(1)(c).

ITA 15(1), (2), (9), 20(1)(c), 80.4, 80.5, ITR 4300(7), *VanNieuwkerk*, [2004] 1 C.T.C. 2577 IT-421R2 (para. 11), VDs 2007-0243331C6, 2008-0280041R3, 9518227

¶14352.5 — *Back-to-Back Shareholder Loans*

In light of the shareholder loan income inclusion rules, there is an incentive to interpose, between a corporation and a shareholder, a third party that is not connected to the shareholder in order to avoid an income inclusion or withholding tax. To counter such planning, ITA 15(2.16) to (2.192) were added, applicable in respect of loans received and indebtedness incurred, and specified rights granted, after March 21, 2016, to provide for back-to-back shareholder loan rules that are modelled on the back-to-back loan rules that were already in place in Part XIII of the ITA. The rules in ITA 15(2.16) to (2.192) are intended to ensure that the application of ITA 15(2), and the related rule in ITA 80.4(2), cannot be avoided where a corporation, rather than providing debt funding directly to its shareholder (or to a connected person or partnership), provides debt funding indirectly through one or more intermediaries. For example, the rules apply where a corporation lends funds to an arm's length person on condition that the person makes a loan to a shareholder of the corporation (i.e., a "back-to-back loan" arrangement). Where the rules apply, they generally deem the corporation to make a loan to its shareholder (or to a connected person or partnership) for the purposes of ITA 15 and 80.4 in an amount equal to the funding indirectly provided by the corporation to the shareholder. A repayment is generally deemed to be made on a loan that was previously deemed to be made under the back-to-back loan rules when the amount of funding indirectly provided by a corporation to its shareholder is reduced.

ITA 15(2.16)–(2.192), Woolford et al., "2016 Federal Budget Proposals — Back-to-Back Rules", Corporate Finance (Federated Press), Vol. XX-2, 2016, O'Neill, "Update on Proposed Expansion of Back-to-Back Loan Rules", McCarthy Tétrault *International Tax Newsletter*, Nov. 2016, Spiro et al., "Expansion of the Back-to-Back Rules", IFA (ifacanada.org/en/resource/past-webinars.html), Oct. 19, 2016, PWC, "Bill C-29 significantly expands back-to-back rules", *Tax Insights*, 2016-53 (pwc.com/ca)

¶14360 — Non-Arm's Length Sale of Shares (Surplus Stripping)

ITA 84.1 is an anti-avoidance provision that is intended to prevent the removal of taxable corporate surplus as a tax-free return of capital through a non-arm's length transfer of shares by an individual resident in Canada to a corporation. ITA 84.1 does not apply to arm's length transactions. The application of ITA 84.1 largely depends upon the arm's length and non-arm's length relationships of both the "subject" and "purchaser" corporations.

An expanded definition of non-arm's length applies for the purpose of evaluating whether the taxpayer and the purchaser corporation deal at arm's length in respect of the disposition of the "subject" corporation shares. This expanded definition significantly extends the scope of the avoidance rule.

Where a taxpayer, other than a corporation, disposes of shares in a Canadian resident corporation to another corporation with which the taxpayer is not dealing at arm's length and with which the first corporation is connected for tax purposes, ITA 84.1 prevents the taxpayer from avoiding tax on any amount in excess of the greater of: 1) the PUC of the shares transferred; and 2) the transferor's arm's length ACB (as defined) of the shares (generally, the ACB of the shares is reduced by the amount of any capital gains exemption used by the non-arm's length vendor). ITA 84.1(1) may trigger an immediate deemed dividend to the transferor in respect of consideration other than shares. But for this avoidance provision, the transfer of shares to a purchaser corporation would permit the surplus of the acquired company to be distributed by way of intercorporate dividends to the purchaser corporation. The funds could then be utilized to the purchaser corporation to pay a note owing to the vendor of the shares.

For purposes of ITA 84.1, the subject corporation would be connected with the purchaser corporation if the subject corporation is controlled by the purchaser corporation. A special definition of control is applicable in determining whether corporations are connected for purposes of ITA 84.1. However, control for this purpose does not include control held by virtue of a right to or to acquire shares, or to control the voting rights of shares, etc., as referred to in ITA 251(5)(b). Rather, control means the control that arises *de jure* from such number of shares as carries with it the right to a majority of votes in the election of the board of directors.

ITA 84.1 deems certain persons that would normally be considered to be dealing at arm's length not to be dealing at arm's length for purposes of the provision. Where, immediately before the disposition, the taxpayer is one of a group of fewer than six persons that controlled the subject corporation whose shares are disposed of, and immediately after the disposition the taxpayer is one of a group of fewer than six persons that controlled the purchaser corporation acquiring those shares, the taxpayer is considered not to deal at arm's length with the acquiring corporation. As a result, ITA 84.1 would apply to the transfer. Shares owned by the taxpayer's child under age 18, spouse, or common-law partner, or by certain corporations or trusts are considered to be owned by the taxpayer and not by the actual owner for the purpose of this rule.

A child in this case is defined to include the taxpayer's grandchild or great-grandchild or any person who before the person attained age 19 was wholly dependent on the taxpayer for support and was under the taxpayer's custody and control. Also included are shares owned by a trust of which the taxpayer, the taxpayer's spouse, common-law partner, or child, or a corporation controlled by the taxpayer is a beneficiary as well as shares owned by a corporation controlled by the taxpayer, the taxpayer's spouse, common-law partner, or child, or a trust of which such person is a beneficiary for the purposes of determining whether the taxpayer is a member of a group. When determining whether a corporation is controlled by a group of persons, a group means any two or more persons each of whom owns shares in the corporation. Since for these purposes a corporation can be considered controlled by a person or group even though the corporation is controlled by another person or group, the same corporation can be controlled at the same time by several persons or group of persons. Finally, even though one member of a group actually controls the corporation, the group is considered to control it.

Where, by reason of one or more transactions between non-arm's length persons, shares of a particular person have become vested in another person, those persons are considered to be not at arm's length for the purposes of ITA 84.1 even though one may not have existed at the same time as the other. As a result, inter-generation transfers may be subject to the non-arm's length rule in ITA 84.1 until a third party transaction takes place.

A trust and a beneficiary of the trust or a person related to the beneficiary will be considered not to be at arm's length when considering whether the taxpayer disposed of shares to a non-arm's length corporation for the purposes of this provision. Accordingly, if a trust disposes of shares to a corporation which is otherwise controlled by its beneficiaries or persons related to the beneficiaries, the trust would be considered to have made a disposition to a non-arm's length corporation.

By reason of the introduction of the capital gains exemption, where ITA 84.1 applies, the provision requires a PUC reduction and, in certain circumstances, the immediate recognition of a dividend. Effectively, a taxpayer can only increase the overall amount of PUC to the extent of the amount by which the greater of the ACB and the PUC of the shares being transferred exceeds any non-share consideration.

The reduction required to the PUC of any particular class of shares issued as consideration is equal to: $(A - B) \times C/A$, where: A is the increase in the legal PUC of all classes of shares of the purchaser corporation as a result of the issue; B is the amount by which the greater of (a) the PUC of the transferred shares, and (b) the arm's length ACB of the transferred shares, exceeds the fair market value of any consideration received by the transferor other than the shares in the purchaser; and C is the increase in the PUC of any particular class of shares as a result of the issuance of new shares without reference to ITA 84.1.

For the purposes of ITA 84.1, the ACB of the shares transferred will depend on when and from whom the shares were acquired. If the shares were acquired prior to 1972, the ITA 84.1 ACB is the actual arm's length cost without any adjustments for V-Day value plus the amount of any tax-deferred dividends received in respect of which an election was made under ITA 83(1). If the shares were acquired in a non-arm's length transaction after 1971 or were shares substituted for such shares, the ACB is the ACB as otherwise determined minus: 1) the fair market value of the share on V-Day minus the aggregate of its actual cost (thereby removing any V-Day adjustment) and the amount of any tax deferred dividends received pursuant to an ITA 83(1) election; and 2) the amount of any post-1984 capital gains of the previous owner of the share unless it can be established that the actual amount of capital gains exemption claimed was less than all previous post-1984 non-arm's length gains. Accordingly, in a non-arm's length transaction, the ACB of the shares (or of substituted shares) for these purposes is increased only to the extent that the transferor was taxed on the capital gains realized. Where the ACB of shares was increased via a crystallization of the capital gains exemption, the basis is commonly referred to as "soft basis" (as opposed to "hard basis"), which reflects the rules in ITA 84.1.

Special rules apply where a capital gains reserve was claimed by the transferor in a non-arm's length transaction. In this case, the transferor is considered to have claimed a capital gains exemption based on the lesser of: 1) the total of the reserve claimed and twice the amount actually deducted by the transferor as a capital gains exemption, and 2) twice of the maximum capital gains exemption that could have been claimed by the transferor if no capital gains reserve had been claimed and if the exemption claimed by the transferor for the year were first applied to gains from the disposition of other property. The ACB of the shares to the transferee would be increased by that amount. The CRA considers ITA 84.1(2.1) to apply even if the taxpayer does not and will not claim any capital gains exemption in respect of the disposition (VD 2015-0594461E5).

ITA 84.1 can apply when taxpayers are not dealing at arm's length on a factual basis. Despite Tax Court decisions to the contrary, the CRA has stated that it may apply ITA 84.1 or GAAR in those situations where a purchaser corporation acts as an accommodator or facilitator for the taxpayer in order to avoid the application of ITA 84.1 (see *McMullen*, [2007] 2 C.T.C. 2463 (TCC), *Brouillette*, [2005] 4 C.T.C. 2013 (TCC), VDs 2007-0243221C6, 2007-0243171C6).

ITA 84.1, 70(1), 85(2.1), 186(2), (4)(a), (7), 110.6(19), *Poulin*, 2016 CarswellNat 2347 (TCC), *Evans*, [2006] 2 C.T.C. 2009 (TCC), *Desmarais*, [2006] 3 C.T.C. 2304 (TCC), *Brouillette*, [2005] 4 C.T.C. 2013 (TCC), IT-489R, IC 88-2, VDs 2016-0655831C6, 2016-0669661C6, 2015-0595561C6, 2013-0479402C6, 2012-0433261E5, 2002-0128955, 2006-0183851E5, 2005-0141061C6, Dergousoff, "Employee Buyco Transactions: Not Arm's-Length?", *Canadian Tax Focus*, Vol. 3-4, Nov. 2013, Dolson et al., "Accessing Surplus: What Works, What Doesn't, What's Left," *2014 Prairie Provinces Tax Conference*, (Toronto: Canadian Tax Foundation, 2014), 9: 1–57, Engel, "A Review of Common Mistakes and Errors Made by Tax Professionals," *2015 Prairie Provinces Tax Conference*, (Toronto: Canadian Tax Foundation, 2015), 7: 1–25, Wilkenfeld, "Crystallization Planning: Less May Be More", *Tax for the Owner-Manager*, Vol. 16-2, April 2016, Dupuis, "Surplus Stripping under CRA's Watchful Eye", *Tax Hyperion* (Taxnet Pro), Vol. 13-3, March 2016

¶14400 — General-Anti Avoidance Rule (GAAR)

The GAAR adds a significant level of uncertainty to advanced corporate tax planning strategies. The GAAR was introduced to discourage and prevent tax avoidance transactions that are considered abusive. To the extent that there is no specific anti-avoidance rule which governs a particular transaction, the GAAR may apply. However, GAAR should not affect transactions that are in compliance with the object and spirit of the ITA and, in particular, that are not considered to be a misuse or abuse of the ITA. The determination of whether the GAAR may apply to a particular series of transactions can be complex.

The application of the GAAR by the Courts has been inconsistent and difficult to predict; GAAR cases involve a significant amount of judicial subjectivity (see, for example, Carvalho et al., "Current Cases," *Report of Proceedings of Sixty-Second Tax Conference, 2010 Tax Conference* (Toronto: Canadian Tax Foundation, 2011), 2:1–20).

The Judges Panel at the 2013 CTF Annual Tax Conference indicated that a judicial "smell test" is not applied in GAAR cases, however, the panel acknowledged that a GAAR analysis involves a high level of subjectivity.

Where a transaction (including an arrangement or event) is an avoidance transaction, pursuant to ITA 245(2) the tax consequences are required to be determined as is reasonable in the circumstances to deny the tax benefit that would otherwise result.

In *Canada Trustco*, [2005] 5 C.T.C. 215 (S.C.C.), the following criteria were set out for the purposes of applying GAAR (para. 66):

1. Three requirements must be established to permit application of the GAAR: 1) a tax benefit resulting from a transaction or part of a series of transactions (ITA 245(1) and (2)); 2) the transaction is an avoidance transaction in the sense that it cannot be said to have been reasonably undertaken or arranged primarily for a bona fide purpose other than to obtain a tax benefit [commonly referred to as the principle purpose test]; and 3) there was abusive tax avoidance in the sense that it cannot be reasonably concluded that a tax benefit would be consistent with the object, spirit or purpose of the provisions relied upon by the taxpayer.

2. The burden is on the taxpayer to refute (1) and (2), and on the Minister to establish (3) [in *Lipson v. R.*, [2009] 1 C.T.C. 314 (SCC), the Court stated that the burden is on the Minister to prove that the avoidance transaction results in abuse and misuse on the balance of probabilities (paras 21–23)].

3. If the existence of abusive tax avoidance is unclear, the benefit of the doubt goes to the taxpayer.

4. The courts proceed by conducting a unified textual, contextual and purposive analysis of the provisions giving rise to the tax benefit in order to determine why they were put in place and why the benefit was conferred. The goal is to arrive at a purposive interpretation that is harmonious with the provisions of the Act that confer the tax benefit, read in the context of the whole Act.

5. Whether the transactions were motivated by any economic, commercial, family or other non-tax purpose may form part of the factual context that the courts may consider in the analysis of abusive tax avoidance allegations under s. 245(4). However, any finding in this respect would form only one part of the underlying facts of a case, and would be insufficient by itself to establish abusive tax avoidance. The central issue is the proper interpretation of the relevant provisions in light of their context and purpose.

An avoidance transaction is defined in ITA 245(3) as a transaction that would otherwise directly or indirectly result in a tax benefit, unless it may reasonably be considered to have been undertaken primarily for *bona fide* purposes other than to obtain a tax benefit. Similarly, an avoidance transaction means any transaction that is part of a series of transactions which would result in a tax benefit, unless undertaken primarily for *bona fide* non-tax purposes. The CRA's general position is that ITA 245(3) should be applied to each step of a series of transactions (see, for example, VD 2006-0195991C6). In *Lipson v. R.*, [2009] 1 C.T.C. 314 (SCC), the Court stated that individual transactions "must be viewed in the context of the series" (para. 34).

The fact that a "tax benefit" (broadly defined in ITA 245(1)) results from a transaction or series of transactions does not necessarily mean that the transaction was not otherwise undertaken primarily for *bona fide* non-tax purposes. The Supreme Court stated the following with respect to the primary purpose test in *Canada Trustco* (para. 21):

> The second requirement for application of the GAAR is that the transaction giving rise to the tax benefit be an avoidance transaction within s. 245(3). The function of this requirement is to remove from the ambit of the GAAR transactions or series of transactions that may reasonably be considered to have been undertaken or arranged primarily for a non-tax purpose. The majority of tax benefits claimed by taxpayers on their annual returns will be immune from the GAAR as a result of s. 245(3). The GAAR was enacted as a provision of last resort in order to address abusive tax avoidance, it was not intended to introduce uncertainty in tax planning.

From a practical perspective, the GAAR has created significant uncertainty for corporations and their advisors. At paragraph 123 of *Copthorne Holdings Ltd.*, 2011 CarswellNat 5201 (SCC), the Supreme Court stated "[w]hile Parliament's intent is to seek consistency, predictability and fairness in tax law, in enacting the GAAR, it must be acknowledged that it has created an unavoidable degree of uncertainty for taxpayers. This uncertainty underlines the obligation of the Minister who wishes to overcome the countervailing obligations of consistency and predictability to demonstrate clearly the abuse he alleges".

The following useful framework provided in *MacKay*, [2008] 4 C.T.C. 161 (FCA), can be used to assist in determining whether the primary purpose test has been met (paras. 78 to 79):

> The Appellants argued that certain criteria have been used in the prior cases to make an objective assessment of the primary purpose of the transactions. They submit the following criteria should be applied in these appeals:
>
> (a) Did the parties start out with a business plan or with a tax plan?
>
> (b) Was the product of the transactions integral to the appellant's business and, where relevant, did the appellant acquire property which it was in the normal course of the appellant's business to acquire?
>
> (c) What was the quality and extent of any due diligence carried out by the parties with respect to the commercial benefits of the transactions?
>
> (d) What quantity of the documentary evidence relates to commercial benefits and what quantity relates to the tax benefits?
>
> (e) Is the subjective evidence of the witnesses regarding the alleged business purpose consistent with the "objective back-drop" of the documents?
>
> (f) Has the appellant called all key witnesses to explain the purpose of the transactions or has the appellant refrained from calling key witnesses?
>
> (g) What is the subjective evidence of the party or parties on the other side of the relevant transactions? Were those parties negotiating a business deal or marketing tax benefits?
>
> (h) Does the evidence of what transpired subsequent to the closing of the transactions support the stated business purpose?
>
> (i) What was the end result when comparing the value of the commercial benefits with the value of the tax benefits? Was there a "significant disparity" between the tax benefits and the commercial return?
>
> The inquiry to determine the primary purpose is a factual inquiry, and the above criteria provide a useful structure to analyze the facts and circumstances of these appeals. The list is not exhaustive and no one factor is determinative. It is open for this Court to employ whatever criteria is appropriate given the circumstances of each case in order to make an objective assessment of the primary purpose of the transactions and those criteria may vary from case to case. In addition, the Court must still assess each individual transaction in a series to ascertain the purpose of each.

Significant cases in which the primary purpose of the transactions in question were found not to be tax motivated include *Spruce Credit Union*, 2014 CarswellNat 1736 (FCA), *McClarty Family Trust*, 2012 CarswellNat 819 (TCC), *MIL (Investments) S.A. v. R.*, [2007] 4 C.T.C. 235 (FCA); aff'g [2006] 5 C.T.C. 2552 (TCC), *Evans v. R.*, [2006] 2 C.T.C. 2009 (TCC), and *Canadian Pacific Ltd. v. Canada*, 2001 CarswellNat 2916 (FCA).

Even though a transaction has been carried out primarily for tax purposes and result in a tax benefit, by virtue of ITA 245(4), the GAAR does not apply if it may reasonably be considered that the transaction would not result directly or indirectly in a misuse or an abuse of the ITA, ITR, the Income Tax Application Rules, a tax treaty or any other relevant enactment as described, read as a whole. Accordingly, certain transactions and incentives otherwise provided in the ITA which would permit transactions undertaken primarily for tax reasons are not subject to GAAR unless, having regard to the ITA read as a whole, there is a misuse of the provisions of the ITA or an abuse with regard to the provisions of the ITA read as a whole. As noted in paragraph 41 of *Canada Trustco*, "[t]he courts cannot search for an overriding policy of the Act that is not based on a unified, textual, contextual and purposive interpretation of the specific provisions in issue".

Determining whether tax avoidance was abusive requires a two-part analysis (*Canada Trustco*; para. 55). The first step is to determine the object, spirit or purpose of the provisions of the ITA that are relied on for the tax benefit, having regard to the scheme of the ITA, the relevant provisions and permissible extrinsic aids. The second step is to examine the factual context of a case in order to determine whether the avoidance transaction defeated or frustrated the object, spirit or purpose of the provisions in issue. The Supreme Court of Canada in Copthorne explained the framework through which the GAAR should be applied (paras. 70–74):

> The object, spirit or purpose can be identified by applying the same interpretive approach employed by this Court in all questions of statutory interpretation — a "unified textual, contextual and purposive approach" (*Trustco*, at para. 47; *Lipson v. R.*, 2009 SCC 1, [2009] 1 S.C.R. 3 (S.C.C.), at para. 26). While the approach is the same as in all statutory interpretation, the analysis seeks to determine a different aspect of the statute than in other cases. In a traditional statutory interpretation approach the court applies the textual, contextual and purposive analysis to determine what the words of the statute mean. In a GAAR analysis the textual, contextual and purposive analysis is employed to determine the object, spirit or purpose of a provision. Here the meaning of the words of the statute may be clear enough. The search is for the rationale that underlies the words that may not be captured by the bare meaning of the words themselves. However, determining the rationale of the relevant provisions of the Act should not be conflated with a value judgment of what is right or wrong nor with theories about what tax law ought to be or ought to do.

> Second, a court must consider whether the transaction falls within or frustrates the identified purpose (*Trustco*, at para. 44). As earlier stated, while an avoidance transaction may operate alone to produce a tax benefit, it may also operate as part of a series of transactions that results in the tax benefit. While the focus must be on the transaction, where it is part of a series, it must be viewed in the context of the series to enable the court to determine whether abusive tax avoidance has occurred. In such a case, whether a transaction is abusive will only become apparent when it is considered in the context of the series of which it is a part and the overall result that is achieved (*Lipson*, at para. 34, per LeBel J.).

> The analysis will then lead to a finding of abusive tax avoidance: (1) where the transaction achieves an outcome the statutory provision was intended to prevent; (2) where the transaction defeats the underlying rationale of the provision; or (3) where the transaction circumvents the provision in a manner that frustrates or defeats its object, spirit or purpose (Trustco, at para. 45; Lipson, at para. 40). These considerations are not independent of one another and may overlap. At this stage, the Minister must clearly demonstrate that the transaction is an abuse of the Act, and the benefit of the doubt is given to the taxpayer.

> When applying this test, there is no distinction between an "abuse" and a "misuse". Instead, there is a single unified approach (*Trustco*, at para. 43).

In *Copthorne*, the Supreme Court acknowledged that in some cases the underlying rationale of a provision is not broader than the text itself (for example, where the text is consistent with and fully explains the underlying rationale of a provision) (para 110).

In *Canada Trustco*, the Court implied that the Crown has the burden of both clearly identifying the object, spirit or purpose of the relevant legislation that is said to be frustrated or defeated and clearly identifying that such purpose was frustrated by the transactions in question. However, in *Copthorne*, the Court removed the burden on the Minister to establish with clarity the object, spirit or purpose of the provisions relied upon to achieve a tax benefit (para 73).

The Courts have emphasized that GAAR is to be used as a provision of last resort (see, for example, para 21 of *Canada Trustco* and para 66 of *Copthorne*). Additionally, the Courts have affirmed that the principle set forth in the *Duke of Westminster* that taxpayers are entitled to arrange their affairs to minimize the amount of tax payable continues to apply (see, for example, para. 13 of *Canada Trustco*).

> The Crown cannot discharge the burden of establishing that a transaction results in the misuse of a provision of the ITA merely by asserting that the transaction was not foreseen by Parliament or that it exploits a previously unnoticed legislative gap (see, for example, para. 37 of *Lehigh Cement*, 2010 CarswellNat 1373 (FCA) and para. 124 of *Landrus*, [2009] 1 C.T.C. 2009 (TCC)).

As a general rule, under Canadian tax law, unless a specific provision of the ITA provides otherwise, legal form governs the taxation of transactions so long as that form is consistent with the actual legal effect of the transaction; economic realities are irrelevant (see *Shell Canada*, 1999 CarswellNat 1808 (SCC), paras. 39, 45, 46). With respect to the extent to which the GAAR incorporates an economic substance test, in *Lipson*, the Supreme Court of Canada stated that "[m]otivation, purpose and economic substance are relevant under s. 245(4) only to the extent that they establish whether the transaction frustrates the purpose of the relevant provisions (*Canada Trustco*, at paras. 57–60)" (para. 38).

Although the relevance of an economic test in applying the GAAR was given minimal importance by the Supreme Court of Canada, in a trilogy of GAAR cases dealing with value shifting arrangements using high-low stock dividends, the FCA generally ruled that both the capital loss and income computation provisions of the ITA contain an unexpressed economic substance test to withstand a GAAR challenge (see *Triad Gestco Ltd.*, 2012 CarswellNat 3853 (FCA), *1207192 Ontario Limited*, 2012 CarswellNat 3894 (FCA), and *Global Equity Fund Ltd.*, [2013] 1 C.T.C. 135 (FCA)).

In *Birchcliff Energy Ltd*, 2012 CarswellNat 5540 (TCC), the Court found that the CRA is required to disclose the relevant tax policy relied upon in reassessing a taxpayer under the GAAR in pleadings filed in a GAAR case. Also, in *Superior Plus*, [2015] 5 C.T.C. 2094 (TCC); affd 2015 FCA 241, the Court held that a taxpayer was entitled to review a wide-range of documents (as well as receive answers to questions) regarding deliberations undertaken by the CRA and Finance leading to a GAAR assessment.

Tax payable pursuant to a GAAR assessment is triggered at the time of the relevant transactions and is not delayed until the time of reassessment by the CRA; as such, arrears interest accrues on tax debts owing after respective balance-due days (*J.K. Read Engineering Ltd.*, 2014 CarswellNat 4126 (TCC); see also Colborne et al., "Current Cases," (2015), vol. 63, no. 1 *Canadian Tax Journal*, 217–244).

Li et al., "GAAR in Action: An Empirical Exploration of Tax Court of Canada Cases," (2013), vol. 61, no. 2 *Canadian Tax Journal*, 321–366, Schwartz et al., "Policy Forum: Defending Against a GAAR Reassessment," (2014), vol. 62, no. 1 *Canadian Tax Journal*, 129–146, Samtani et al., "GAAR Revisited: From Instinctive Reaction to Intellectual Rigour," (2014), vol. 62, no. 2 *Canadian Tax Journal*, 401–428, Krishna, "The Fundamentals of Income Tax Law", Ch. 22, (Thomson Reuters Canada), Dolson, "The GAAR Post-Copthorne: Where We've Come From, and Current Applications", *2017 Prairie Provinces Tax Conference* (Toronto: Canadian Tax Foundation, 2017), 6:1–37

¶14410 — Consequences of GAAR Applying

Where GAAR applies, pursuant to ITA 245(5), the tax consequences of the avoidance transaction are determined as are reasonable in the circumstances to deny the tax benefit. This might include: allowing or denying all or part of any deduction, exemption, or exclusion; allocating any deduction, exemption or exclusion, income, loss, or other amount to any person; recharacterizing the nature of any payment or other amount; or ignoring the tax effects which would result from the application of other provisions of the Act (ITA 245(5)).

In *XCO Investments Ltd. v. R.*, [2006] 1 C.T.C. 2220 (TCC), with respect of ITA 245(5), the Court stated (para. 39):

> It would be wholly unacceptable if in reviewing the Minister's decision on what is "reasonable" the court were fettered by the theory that the Minister's decision was a discretionary one and the rules about reviewing a discretionary act and showing deference to the Minister's decision had to be observed. However far reaching section 245 may be, it does not confer discretionary powers on the Minister, either in the decision to apply it or in the determination of its consequences.

Where GAAR has been applied, a taxpayer may object to or appeal from the determination that there has been an avoidance transaction as well as the recharacterization of the appropriate tax consequences. In addition, any person other than the taxpayer may also request an adjustment of a relieving nature with respect to the same transaction.

The request must be made by such person within 180 days after the sending of the notice of assessment or reassessment to the taxpayer.

ITA 167, 245(5)–(8)

¶14420 — Series of Transactions

A series of transactions is defined in ITA 248(10) to include any related transactions or events completed in contemplation of the series. In *OSFC Holdings Ltd. v. R.*, [2001] 4 C.T.C. 82 (FCA), the Court stated that the extended definition in ITA 248(10) of a series of transactions expands the range of transactions that can be considered to constitute a series beyond that which is described in a line of UK tax avoidance cases (the concept of a series articulated in these cases requires that two or more transactions must be pre-ordained in the sense that there was no practical likelihood that one would have been implemented without the other). In *Canada Trustco*, the Court stated (para. 26):

> Section 248(10) extends the meaning of "series of transactions" to include "related transactions or events completed in contemplation of the series". The Federal Court of Appeal held, at para. 36 of *OSFC*, that this occurs where the parties to the transaction "knew of the . . . series, such that it could be said that they took it into account when deciding to complete the transaction". We would elaborate that "in contemplation" is read not in the sense of actual knowledge but in the broader sense of "because of" or "in relation to" the series. The phrase can be applied to events either before or after the basic avoidance transaction found under s. 245(3). As has been noted:

> > It is highly unlikely that Parliament could have intended to include in the statutory definition of "series of transactions" related transactions completed in contemplation of a subsequent series of transactions, but not related transactions in the contemplation of which taxpayers completed a prior series of transactions.

> > (D. G. Duff, "Judicial Application of the General Anti-Avoidance Rule in Canada: OSFC Holdings Ltd. v. The Queen", 57 I.B.F.D. Bulletin 278, at p. 287).

Also, in *Copthorne Holdings Ltd.*, [2009] 5 C.T.C. 1 (FCA), the Court stated (paras. 45 and 46):

> . . . [T]he language of the Supreme Court of Canada in paragraph 26 of *Canada Trustco* that broadens the meaning of "in contemplation", as used in subsection 248(10), does not lead to the conclusion that the "mere possibility" of a connection between a series of transactions and a related translation is sufficient to include that transaction in the series. On the other hand, I am not persuaded that the indicated broadening of "in contemplation" could . . . require an even closer connection between the transaction and the series than was required under the interpretation offered by Rothstein J.A. in *OSFC*.

> In my view, if a series is a motivating factor with respect to the completion of a subsequent transaction, the transaction can be said to have been completed "in contemplation of the series" and a direct causal relationship between the series and the transaction, as argued by the appellant, need not be established. In my opinion, this standard is reconcilable with the test as stated in *OSFC* and as broadened in *Canada Trustco*.

¶14430 — Post-Canada Trustco GAAR Cases

Since the Supreme Court of Canada decision in *Canada Trustco*, GAAR was found to apply in the following cases:

- *Mathew v. Canada*, [2005] 5 C.T.C. 244 (SCC) (*Mathew* and *Canada Trustco* were both handed down on October 19, 2005): GAAR applied to the acquisition of non-capital losses via a partnership transfer. The Court found that the policy established under ITA 111(5) prohibits the transfer of losses outside of a corporate group;

- *Desmarais*, [2006] 3 C.T.C. 2304 (TCC): GAAR applied to surplus stripping transactions in which the connected corporation rules were abused;

- *Ceco Operations Ltd.*, [2006] 5 C.T.C. 2174 (appeal to FCA discontinued): GAAR applied to the utilization of ITA 97(2) partnership rollover rules to indefinitely defer taxation on the proceeds of the sale of a business;

- *MacKay*, [2008] 4 C.T.C. 161 (FCA, reversing the TCC), ; leave to appeal denied 2009 CarswellNat 19 (SCC): GAAR applied to the transfer of losses to purchasers of a shopping centre;

- *Lipson*, [2009] 1 C.T.C. 314 (SCC): GAAR applied to the utilization of ITA 73(1) and 74.1(1) to attribute loss to spouse, and effectively allow for deduction of personal residence mortgage interest;

- *Antle*, 2009 CarswellNat 2792; affirmed by the FCA 2010 FCA 280: Use of Barbados spousal trust to achieve a step-up in cost base. GAAR was not considered by the Federal Court of Appeal in *Antle*, but the Tax Court stated that GAAR would apply to the transactions in question;

- *Copthorne Holdings Ltd. v. R.*, 2011 CarswellNat 5201 (SCC): GAAR applied to a double-counting of paid up capital;

- *Triad Gestco Ltd.*, 2012 FCA 258 and *1207192 Ontario Limited*, 2012 FCA 259: GAAR applied to an internally generated capital loss created as part of a reverse estate freeze transaction (the transactions relied on the fact that trusts were not included in the "affiliated persons" definition in ITA 251.1 before March 23, 2004);

- *Global Equity Fund Ltd*, [2013] 1 C.T.C. 135 (FCA): In transactions similar to those undertaken in *Triad* and *1207192 Ontario Ltd* above, GAAR applied to a series of transactions in which stock dividends were utilized to shift value and create artificial business losses;

- *Pièces Automobiles Lecavalier Inc.*, 2013 CarswellNat 5815 (TCC): The GAAR applied to a series of transactions structured to avoid the application of the debt forgiveness rules in the context of the sale of shares of a corporation with underwater debt owed to its foreign parent company;

- *Descarries*, 2014 CarswellNat 584 (TCC): The GAAR applied to a series of transactions that were designed to convert a deemed dividend into a capital gain since the transactions abused section 84.1;

- *Barrasso*, 2014 CarswellNat 1758 (TCC): The GAAR applied to a "value shift" similar to *Triad Gestco* and *1207192 Ontario*; the fact that the taxpayer will have a real gain on death did not stop GAAR from applying;

- *Birchcliff Energy Ltd.*, 2015 CarswellNat 4799 (TCC): The taxpayer abusively circumvented the loss streaming restrictions by avoiding the special rule ITA 256(7)(b)(iii) that deems control to have been acquired upon an amalgamation (in *Birchcliff Energy*, 2017 CarswellNat 1821 (FCA) and *High-Crest Enterprises Ltd.*, 2017 CarswellNat 1820 (FCA), the decisions of the Tax Court were nullified since the FCA held that the Chief Justice did not have the power to remove a file from a judge who heard an appeal and reassign it to another Tax Court judge to render the decision);

- *Golini*, 2016 CarswellNat 3212 (TCC): The Court stated that it would have applied the GAAR (had ITA 15(1) not applied) to a series of complex transactions designed to create PUC when there had been no corresponding increase in assets or decrease in liabilities of the relevant company;

- *Gervais*, 2018 CarswellNat 12 (FCA): Transactions undertaken to split a capital gain and allow both spouses to claim respective capital gains deductions was held to abuse the attribution rules such that the GAAR applied;

- *Pomerleau*, 2018 FCA 129: The GAAR applied to a series of surplus stripping transactions that avoided ITA 84.1 by converting soft basis in one class of shares to hard basis in another class of shares by using ITS 40(3.6) and 53(1)(f.2);

- *Fiducie Financière Satoma*, 2018 FCA 74 (leave to SCC requested): The GAAR applied to a surplus stripping scheme that involved intentionally utilizing ITA 75(2) to attribute a dividend received by a trust to a corporation, which claimed a deduction under ITA 112(1);

- *2763478 Canada Inc.*, 2017 CarswellNat 2568 (TCC): The GAAR applied to certain stock dividend value shifting transactions that were implemented in the course of an estate freeze;

- *Oxford Properties*, 2018 FCA 30 (leave to appeal to SCC requested): The GAAR applied to a series of transactions involving the selling of bumped LP interests to tax exempt entities after the time period set forth in ITA 69(11) had elapsed;

- *594710 British Columbia Ltd.*, 2018 FCA 166: The GAAR applied to a series of transactions undertaken to implement reverse loss trading by offending the partnership allocation rules in ITA 96 and ITA 103.

GAAR was found not to apply in the following cases since *Canada Trustco*:

- *Univar Canada Ltd.*, [2006] 1 C.T.C. 2308 (TCC): GAAR did not apply to an avoidance of the foreign affiliate anti-avoidance rule in ITA 95(6)(b);

- *Evans*, [2006] 2 C.T.C. 2009 (TCC): GAAR did not apply to surplus stripping involving the use of a partnership;

- *Overs*, [2006] 3 C.T.C. 2255: GAAR did not apply to the reverse use of the spousal attribution rules to enable a taxpayer to claim losses (see also VD 2006-0195991C6);

- *McMullen*, [2007] 2 C.T.C. 2463: GAAR did not apply to surplus stripping transactions involving the division of a business between two arm's length shareholders;

- *MIL (Investments) S.A.*, [2007] 4 C.T.C. 235 (FCA): GAAR did not apply to treaty shopping;

- *Landrus*, [2009] 4 C.T.C. 189 (FCA): GAAR did not apply to transactions that triggered a terminal loss via a disposition to a related partnership;

- *Remai*, [2010] 2 C.T.C. 120 (FCA): GAAR did not apply to a donation to a private foundation of promissory notes issued by the taxpayer's company, followed by a sale of the notes to the taxpayer's nephew;

- *Lehigh Cement*, 2010 CarswellNat 1373 (FCA, reversing the TCC; application for leave to appeal to SCC dismissed with costs): GAAR did not apply to the restructuring of a loan to access the withholding tax exemption under former ITA 212(1)(b);

- *Collins v. R.*, [2010] 5 C.T.C. 6 (FCA): GAAR did not apply to surplus stripping involving a reorganization followed by a return of capital to non-resident shareholders;

- *Garron*, 2010 CarswellNat 4259 (FCA): GAAR did not apply to the use of a Barbados trust to avoid tax on capital gains. GAAR did not form the basis of the decision in the case but the Court noted that GAAR did not apply to the transactions in question;

- *McClarty Family Trust*, 2012 CarswellNat 819 (TCC): GAAR did not apply to a series of transactions in which the kiddie tax was avoided via the payment of a stock dividend and the creation of a capital gain, on the basis that the primary purpose of the transactions in question was creditor-proofing rather than tax avoidance;

- *MacDonald*, 2012 CarswellNat 1129 (TCC); rev'd on other grounds [2013] 4 C.T.C. 251 (FCA): Neither GAAR, nor ITA 84(2) applied to a series of transactions in which surplus was extracted tax-free from a corporation as a capital gain that was offset by carryforward capital losses;

- *Spruce Credit Union*, 2014 CarswellNat 1736 (FCA): GAAR did not apply where credit unions received dividends from a deposit insurance corporation;

- *Swirsky*, [2013] 3 C.T.C. 2104; aff'd on other grounds 2014 CarswellNat 272 (FCA): GAAR did not apply to the attribution of losses incurred by a wife on borrowed money when buying shares from husband because tax reduction was not one of the main purposes of the transactions (the purpose was creditor-proofing);

- *Gwartz*, 2013 CarswellNat 1266: GAAR did not apply to dividends on high-low shares issued to a family trust, which generated capital gains to avoid the kiddie tax, with the Court finding that there is no general policy against surplus stripping or income splitting in the ITA. Note that the transactions implemented in *Gwartz* would no longer be effective as a result of subsequent amendments to the ITA. With respect to the subsequent amendment of ITA 120.4 that would have thwarted the transactions in question, the Court concluded that it did not inform the policy of the provision as it existed at the time;

- *Univar Holdco*, 2017 FCA 207: The GAAR did not apply to a reorganization intended to allow for stepped-up cross-border PUC by relying on former ITA 212.1(4);

- *1245989 Alberta Ltd.*, 2018 CarswellNat 2778 (FCA): The GAAR did not apply to a series of transactions that effectively utilized the capital gains exemption and the paid-up capital averaging rules to remove surplus from a corporation free of tax (i.e., as a return of capital);

- *Alta Energy Luxembourg*, 2018 CarswellNat 4615 (TCC): The GAAR did not apply where a provision in the Canada-Luxembourg Treaty was used to eliminate capital gains tax in both countries;

- *Bank of Montreal*, 2018 CarswellNat 5103 (TCC): The GAAR did not apply to a complex series of cross-border financing transactions that avoided the application of the dividend stop-loss rules in ITA 112(3.1) since the taxpayer did not receive a "tax benefit" from the transactions.

Chapter 15 — Canadian Taxation of Non-Residents and Deemed Residents

Contents

¶15100 Determining Residency for Tax Purposes

    ¶15110 Common Law Rules

    ¶15120 Deeming Rules

    ¶15130 Ceasing Canadian Residency

    ¶15140 Part-Year Residents

¶15200 Dispositions of Taxable Canadian Property

    ¶15210 Excluded Dispositions

    ¶15220 Certificates of Compliance

¶15300 Payments Subject to Withholding Tax

    ¶15310 Interest Payments

    ¶15320 Dividend Payments

    ¶15330 Rents and Royalties

    ¶15340 Pensions and Other Benefits

¶15400 Filing Requirements for Non-Residents & Deemed Residents

    ¶15410 Elective Returns for Non-Residents

¶15500 Emigration and Immigration

    ¶15510 Emigrating from Canada

    ¶15520 Immigrating to Canada

¶15100 — Determining Residency for Tax Purposes

As discussed earlier in this Guide, an individual's liability for Canadian income tax is based on the individual's residence. Canadian resident individuals are subject to Canadian income tax on worldwide income for the period they are resident or deemed resident in Canada. An individual who is not resident in Canada is generally taxed only on Canadian-source income. If an individual emigrates from, or immigrates to, Canada during the year, the individual may be both a part-year resident and a non-resident during the year. Therefore, the determination of residency is important for Canadian income tax purposes.

¶15110 — Common Law Rules

Residence has a meaning in law separate and distinct from domicile or citizenship. Canada does not tax individuals by reason of Canadian citizenship or domicile in Canada; whether a person is taxable in Canada depends on whether they are a resident of Canada. Subject to specific statutory modifications, since the question of whether a person is resident in a particular place is generally a question of fact, residence does not depend upon the exercise of an act of will or intention as in the case of domicile.

Residence implies physical presence but not necessarily within a particular taxation year. If the primary residence of an individual is in Canada, an extended period of absence from Canada or an absence from Canada either for business or pleasure for the whole year may not result in the individual being considered to cease Canadian residency. This would be the case regardless of whether the taxpayer maintains a fixed place of residence outside Canada. As well, an individual may be resident in Canada if that person visits Canada for a portion of the year as part of a regular habit of life or keeps a place of abode ready for use and occupation. An individual may also be a transient visitor to Canada, in which case they will not be considered a resident unless the person sojourns in the country for a period of 183 days or more during the year.

ITA 250(3) provides that a reference to a person who is "resident in Canada" includes a person who is "ordinarily resident in Canada" at the relevant time. The ITA does not define either "resident in Canada" or "ordinarily resident". Therefore, one must look to the meaning attributed to residence in common law (i.e., case law). The leading Canadian case on the meaning of residency is *Thomson v. M.N.R*, 1945 CarswellNat 23 (SCC)), in which the Supreme Court of Canada stated that residency in a place means to "dwell permanently or for a considerable time, to have one's settled or usual abode, to live, in or at a particular place". As well, with respect to the meaning of "ordinarily resident", the Supreme Court stated that "one is 'ordinarily resident' in the place where in the settled routine of his life he regularly, normally or customarily lives."

Generally, in attempting to apply the basic residency principles enunciated in *Thomson*, the Courts will look at numerous factors that relate to what are often called "residential ties" to Canada. No one or any group of two or three items will in themselves establish that the individual is or is not resident in Canada; however, several factors considered together could establish that the individual is a resident of Canada for Canadian income tax purposes. Some of these factors are as follows:

- Ownership of a dwelling in Canada that is continually available to the taxpayer or rental of a dwelling on a long-term basis (e.g., a lease for a period of one or more years);
- Residence of spouse, common-law partner, children, and other dependent family members in a dwelling maintained by the individual in Canada regardless of whether the individual is in Canada;
- Memberships with Canadian churches, synagogues, other religious institutions, recreational and social clubs, unions, and professional organizations;
- Registration and maintenance of vehicles, including automobiles, boats, and airplanes in Canada;
- Holding credit cards and debit cards issued by Canadian financial institutions and other commercial entities including stores, car rental agencies, etc.;
- Local newspaper, magazines, and other periodical subscriptions sent to a Canadian address;
- Rental of Canadian safe deposit box or post office box;
- Subscriptions for life or general insurance, including health insurance, through a Canadian insurance company;
- Maintaining provincial health insurance;
- Mailing address and telephone listing in Canada;
- Stationery, including business cards, showing a Canadian address;
- Canadian bank accounts, other than a non-resident bank account;
- Active securities accounts with Canadian brokers;
- Canadian driver's licence;

- Membership in a Canadian pension plan;
- Holding directorships of Canadian corporations;
- Membership in Canadian partnerships;
- Frequent visits to Canada for family, social, or business purposes;
- Burial plot in Canada;
- Will and power of attorney prepared in Canada;
- Legal documentation indicating Canadian residence;
- Filing a Canadian income tax return as a Canadian resident;
- Ownership of a Canadian vacation or recreational property;
- Active involvement in business activities in Canada;
- Employment in Canada;
- Maintenance or storage in Canada of personal belongings including clothing, furniture, vehicles, family pets, etc.;
- Obtaining landed immigrant status or appropriate work permits in Canada; and
- Severing substantially all ties with a former country of residence or not establishing residential ties with another country.

¶15120 — Deeming Rules

ITA 250(1) contains a number of provision that can deem an individual to be resident in Canada for a year, even of that individual was not resident or "ordinarily resident" under common law rules. ITA 250(1)(a) deems an individual to be resident in Canada throughout a taxation year if that person "sojourned in Canada in the year for a period of, or periods the total of which is, 183 days or more". Generally, the word "sojourn" is interpreted as being "temporarily present". The CRA provides the following guidance on sojourners in paragraphs 1.32 and 1.33 of Folio S5-F1-C1: *Determining an Individual's Residence Status:*

Sojourners as deemed residents

1.32 An individual who has not established sufficient residential ties with Canada to be considered factually resident in Canada, but who sojourns (that is, is temporarily present) in Canada for a total of 183 days or more in any calendar year, is deemed to be resident in Canada for the entire year, under paragraph 250(1)(a). As a result, an individual who sojourns in Canada for a total of 183 days (or more) is taxed differently under the Act than an individual who is factually resident in Canada throughout the same period of time and has subsequently become a non-resident. In particular, an individual who is factually resident in Canada for part of a year is only taxed on his or her worldwide income for that part of the year, in accordance with the rules under section 114. An individual who is deemed to be resident in Canada pursuant to paragraph 250(1)(a) is liable for tax on his or her worldwide income throughout the year.

1.33 The CRA considers any part of a day to be a day for the purpose of determining the number of days that an individual has sojourned in Canada in a calendar year. However, it is a question of fact whether an individual who is not resident in Canada is sojourning in Canada. An individual is not automatically considered to be sojourning in Canada for every day (or part day) that the individual is present in Canada; the nature of each particular stay must be determined separately. To sojourn means to make a temporary stay in the sense of establishing a temporary residence, although the stay may be of very short duration. For example, if an individual is commuting to Canada for his or her employment and returning each night to his or her normal place of residence outside of Canada, the individual is not sojourning in Canada. On the other hand, if the same individual were to vacation in Canada, then he or she would be sojourning in Canada and each day (or part day) of that particular time period (the length of the vacation) would be counted in determining the application of paragraph 250(1)(a). In distinguishing a commuter from a sojourner, relevance should be placed on the country in which an individual spends his or her time away from work. In other words, an individual who comes to

Canada for work purposes may nevertheless be considered sojourning in Canada if that individual does not leave the country to spend his or her time away from work.

This rule would not apply to an individual who comes to Canada and becomes a factual resident part way through the year, or to a Canadian resident who ceases to be resident part way through a year, even if that individual were resident in Canada for 183 days or more in that year. Rather, in such situation, ITA 114 will apply, and the individual will only be taxed as a resident during the portion of the year that the individual lived in Canada.

Conversely, ITA 250(5) provides that if an individual is treated as a non-resident of Canada and a resident of another country for the purposes of a tax treaty, that individual will be deemed to be a non-resident for the purposes of the ITA. This rule is intended to prevent an individual from retaining the benefits of Canadian residency status for the purposes of the ITA, while at the same time avoiding or reducing Canadian income tax under the treaty.

¶15130 — Ceasing Canadian Residency

Where an individual has been a resident of Canada and leaves to reside in another country, it is necessary to determine whether the individual continues to be a resident of Canada for tax purposes. If, for example, a temporary stay outside Canada is for recreational or health reasons, the individual is normally considered to be resident in Canada. In other cases, where residence in another country has been established, a major factor is whether the individual has retained residential ties with Canada.

For example, if a taxpayer leaves a spouse, common-law partner, and family in Canada or ensures that a Canadian dwelling suitable for year-round occupancy is available for occupation by maintaining it or having it maintained vacant, with or without housekeepers or caretakers, or by leasing it with the right to cancel the lease on short notice or without notice, the individual will normally be considered a continuing resident. If, however, the individual's family leaves Canada and the right to occupy a dwelling is disposed of, either by sale or by long-term lease, the individual will ordinarily be considered to have become a non-resident. Where a Canadian resident is absent from Canada for less than two years, the CRA may administratively take the position that there is a presumption that the individual has retained Canadian residency status unless it can be clearly established that all Canadian residential ties have been severed.

The residential ties of a person who is neither married nor living in a common law relationship are often more tenuous. Generally, if a single person leaves Canada for two years or more and has established a residence elsewhere, it is likely that residence in Canada has ceased unless important other ties to Canada exist. For example, where a single person had been supporting one or more persons connected by blood, marriage, or adoption in a dwelling maintained and lived in by the individual in Canada and the individual continued to maintain it after leaving Canada, ordinarily the individual will be considered to be a continuing resident of Canada.

Where residence has not been established in another country, a person is generally presumed to continue to be a resident of Canada.

The CRA's views regarding the requirements for an individual to cease to be factually resident in Canada for tax purposes are in paragraphs 1.10–1.21 of Folio S5-F1-C1, which provide as follows:

Residential ties in Canada

1.10 The most important factor to be considered in determining whether an individual leaving Canada remains resident in Canada for tax purposes is whether the individual maintains residential ties with Canada while abroad. While the residence status of an individual can only be determined on a case by case basis after taking into consideration all of the relevant facts, generally, unless an individual severs all significant residential ties with Canada upon leaving Canada, the individual will continue to be a factual resident of Canada and subject to Canadian tax on his or her worldwide income.

Significant residential ties

1.11 The residential ties of an individual that will almost always be significant residential ties for the purpose of determining residence status are the individual's: dwelling place (or places); spouse or common-law partner; and dependants.

1.12 Where an individual who leaves Canada keeps a dwelling place in Canada (whether owned or leased), available for his or her occupation, that dwelling place will be considered to be a significant residential tie with Canada during the individual's stay abroad. However, if an individual leases a dwelling place located in Canada to a third party on arm's-length terms and conditions, the CRA will take into account all of the circumstances of the situation (including the relationship between the individual and the third party, the real estate market at the time of the individual's departure from Canada, and the purpose of the stay abroad), and may consider the dwelling place not to be a significant residential tie with Canada except when taken together with other residential ties(see ¶1.26 for an example of this situation and see ¶1.15 for a discussion of the significance of secondary residential ties).

1.13 If an individual who is married or cohabiting with a common-law partner leaves Canada, but his or her spouse or common-law partner remains in Canada, then that spouse or common-law partner will usually be a significant residential tie with Canada during the individual's absence from Canada. Similarly, if an individual with dependants leaves Canada, but his or her dependants remain behind, then those dependants will usually be considered to be a significant residential tie with Canada while the individual is abroad. Where an individual was living separate and apart from his or her spouse or common-law partner prior to leaving Canada, by reason of a breakdown of their marriage or common-law partnership, that spouse or common-law partner will not be considered to be a significant tie with Canada.

Secondary residential ties

1.14 Generally, secondary residential ties must be looked at collectively in order to evaluate the significance of any one such tie. For this reason, it would be unusual for a single secondary residential tie with Canada to be sufficient on its own to lead to a determination that an individual is factually resident in Canada while abroad. Secondary residential ties that will be taken into account in determining the residence status of an individual while outside Canada are:

- personal property in Canada (such as furniture, clothing, automobiles, and recreational vehicles);

- social ties with Canada (such as memberships in Canadian recreational or religious organizations);

- economic ties with Canada (such as employment with a Canadian employer and active involvement in a Canadian business, and Canadian bank accounts, retirement savings plans, credit cards, and securities accounts);

- landed immigrant status or appropriate work permits in Canada;

- hospitalization and medical insurance coverage from a province or territory of Canada;

- a driver's license from a province or territory of Canada;

- a vehicle registered in a province or territory of Canada;

- a seasonal dwelling place in Canada or a leased dwelling place referred to in ¶1.12;

- a Canadian passport; and

- memberships in Canadian unions or professional organizations.

Other residential ties

1.15 Other residential ties that the Courts have considered in determining the residence status of an individual while outside Canada, and which may be taken into account by the CRA, include the retention of a Canadian mailing address, post office box, or safety deposit box, personal stationery (including business cards) showing a Canadian address, telephone listings in Canada, and local (Canadian) newspaper and magazine subscriptions. These residential ties are generally of limited importance except when taken together with other residential ties, or with other factors such as those described in ¶1.16.

Application of term ordinarily resident

1.16 Where an individual has not severed all of his or her residential ties with Canada, but is physically absent from Canada for a considerable period of time (that is, for a period of time extending over several months or years), the Courts have generally focused on the term ordinarily resident in determining the individual's residence status while abroad. The strong trend in decisions of the Courts on this issue is to regard temporary absence from Canada, even on an extended basis, as insufficient to avoid Canadian residence for tax purposes. Accordingly, where an individual maintains residential ties with Canada while abroad, the following factors will be taken into account in evaluating the significance of those ties: evidence of intention to permanently sever residential ties with Canada; regularity and length of visits to Canada; and residential ties outside Canada. For greater certainty, the CRA does not consider that intention to return to Canada, in and of itself and in the absence of any residential ties, is a factor whose presence is sufficient to lead to a determination that an individual is resident in Canada while abroad.

Evidence of intention to permanently sever residential ties

1.17 Whether an individual intended to permanently sever residential ties with Canada at the time of his or her departure from Canada is a question of fact to be determined with regard to all of the circumstances of each case. Although length of stay abroad is one factor to be considered in making this determination (that is, as evidence of the individual's intentions upon leaving Canada), the Courts have indicated that there is no particular length of stay abroad that necessarily results in an individual becoming a nonresident. Generally, if there is evidence that an individual's return to Canada was foreseen at the time of his or her departure, the CRA will attach more significance to the individual's remaining residential ties with Canada (see ¶ 1.11–1.15), in determining whether the individual continued to be a factual resident of Canada subsequent to his or her departure. For example . . . .

Steps taken to comply with the Act

1.18 Another factor that the CRA will consider in determining whether an individual intended to permanently sever all residential ties with Canada at the time of his or her departure from Canada, is whether the individual took into account and complied with the provisions of the Act dealing with the taxation of: individuals ceasing to be resident in Canada; and individuals who are not resident in Canada. For example, upon ceasing to be resident in Canada, an individual is required to either pay, or post acceptable security for, the Canadian tax payable with respect to capital gains arising from the deemed disposition of all of the individual's property (with the exception of certain types of property that are listed in subsection 128.1(4)(b)). Where applicable, the CRA will look at whether this requirement has been met as an indication of the individual's intention to permanently sever his or her residential ties with Canada at the time the individual left Canada.

1.19 Similarly, the CRA will take into account whether the individual informed any Canadian residents making payments to the individual that the individual intended to become a non-resident upon leaving Canada, with the result that certain payments (including interest, dividend, rent and pension payments) made to the individual after that time might be subject to withholding tax under Part XIII. See ¶1.24 for more information relevant to individuals ceasing to be resident in Canada.

Regularity and length of visits to Canada

1.20 Where an individual leaves Canada and permanently severs all of his or her residential ties with Canada, the individual's residence status for tax purposes will not be affected by occasional return visits to Canada, whether for personal or business reasons. However, where such visits are more than occasional (particularly where the visits occur on a regular basis), and the individual has maintained some secondary residential ties with Canada, this factor will be taken into account in evaluating the significance of those remaining ties.

Residential ties elsewhere

1.21 Where an individual leaves Canada and purports to become a non-resident, but does not establish significant residential ties outside Canada, the individual's remaining residential ties with Canada, if any, may take on greater significance and the individual may continue to be resident in Canada. However, because the Courts have held that it is possible for an individual to be resident in more than one place at the same time for tax purposes (see ¶1.40–1.52), the fact that an individual establishes significant residential ties abroad will not, on its own, mean that the individual is no longer resident in Canada.

The CRA requests that individuals who leave Canada submit Form NR73, *Determination of Residency Status (Leaving Canada)*, so that the CRA may make a determination of their residency status based on information provided on that form. However, there is no legal requirement for an individual to submit this form to the CRA for an individual to cease to be a Canadian resident, although there are certain situations where filing Form NR73 may be necessary. For example, if the individual will continue to be employed by a Canadian company, and the Canadian employer requires a determination of non-resident status in order to refrain from withholding Canadian tax, or where the individual wishes to access amounts in a locked-in RRSP or RRIF, and the pension administrator requires determination of non-resident status prior to distributing amounts. As well, Form NR73 may be required if the CRA reviews the individual's tax status, and requests it.

¶15131 — *Taxation of Non-Residents and Deemed Residents*

A person who is not a resident of Canada for any part of the year and visits Canada for less than 183 days in a year is not taxable in Canada unless the individual was either employed or carried on business in Canada at some time during the taxation year, disposed of taxable Canadian property, or had income from certain Canadian sources including dividends, interest, rents, or royalties. A non-resident individual who was a partner in a business carried on in Canada would be considered to be carrying on business in Canada and taxable on his or her share of the partnership profits. Non-residents of Canada who are taxable because of an employment or business in Canada are not taxed on worldwide income but only on the part of income that is derived from that employment or business in Canada. The non-resident may deduct a proportionate amount of the available credits and deductions in respect of such income.

As discussed above, a person who is not a resident of Canada for any part of the year, but who visits Canada for a total of 183 days or more in a year, may be deemed to be a resident of Canada and subject to Canadian income tax on their worldwide income for the entire year.

Non-residents and deemed residents are taxed at the federal tax rate plus a surtax of 48% of the federal tax, unless income was earned from a business with a permanent establishment in Canada — in this case, provincial or territorial tax is paid on that income. Deemed residents and non-residents can claim the federal basic personal tax credit plus other applicable tax credits. The non-refundable tax credits are pro-rated for non-residents using a calculation based on income from Canadian sources divided by total world income. For more information, see CRA Guide 5013-G, *General Income Tax and Benefit Guide for Non-Residents and Deemed Residents of Canada.*

¶15140 — Part-Year Residents

If an individual is resident in Canada for only part of the year, only worldwide income for the period in the year during which the individual resided in Canada, less the proportionate part of the applicable credits and deductions, is subject to Canadian tax. Therefore, where an individual becomes resident in Canada during a year, or ceases to be a resident during a year, tax is payable only on income for the period or periods of residence in Canada, employment in Canada, or carrying on business in Canada, as though such period or periods constituted the whole taxation year. Deductions and credits that would reasonably be considered applicable to the period or periods in respect of which the taxpayer received income in Canada are deductible in the determination of taxable income.

For example, if an individual immigrates to Canada and becomes a resident on October 1, only the income attributable to the period from that date to the end of the year will be subject to tax in Canada. Statutory credits (for self, spouse or common-law partner, married equivalent, etc.) are reduced pro-rata based on the period of residence. Similar restrictions apply to other credits that may be available. The credit for charitable donations is limited to 75% of the income attributable to the period of residency and the deduction for medical expenses will be restricted to those paid during the same period (to the extent in excess of 3% of the income for that period). Business losses incurred in prior years before the individual became a Canadian resident are not deductible.

The same rules apply when an individual ceases to be a Canadian resident during a taxation year, provided the individual is neither employed nor carries on business in Canada after ceasing to be a Canadian resident. The individual is considered a resident of Canada for the period in the year during which the individual was resident, was employed, or carried on business in Canada.

ITA 212, Form NR73, Form NR74, Guide 5013-G, Guide T4056, Guide T4058, Folio S5-F1-C1: *Determining an Individual's Residence Status*

¶15200 — Dispositions of Taxable Canadian Property

Generally, Canadian income tax is payable by a non-resident on taxable capital gains realized on the disposition of taxable Canadian property (TCP) other than treaty-protected property. ITA 116, discussed under ¶15220, establishes rules for the enforcement of such tax obligations of non-residents.

TCP includes Canadian real or immovable property, Canadian resource property, property used or held by the taxpayer in a business carried on in Canada, shares of private corporations (or trust or partnership interests) that derive more than 50% of their value from the latter types of property, certain listed securities (see the discussion below), and certain other special types of property. The residence of a corporation, trust, or partnership is not relevant for purposes of the TCP definition.

Effective after March 4, 2010, the TCP definition excludes shares of private corporations (or trust or partnership interests) that do not derive their value principally from real or immovable property situated in Canada, including Canadian resource property and timber resource property, during the 60-month period ending at the time of determination (this test is commonly referred to as the derived value test). Accordingly, a purchaser should closely examine whether the derived value test was met during the 60-month look-back period when securities of a private corporation are acquired.

In applying the derived value test to determine whether private company shares (or a trust or partnership interest) are TCP by virtue of the 60-month look-back rule, shares can retain their characterization as TCP for a period of 60 months after the Canadian real property or resource property that gave rise to the TCP characterization is disposed of. It is important to highlight that the derived value test applies to the shares; it is not relevant who owned the shares at the time the particular property was held by the taxpayer.

In determining after March 4, 2010 whether shares of a holding company are TCP, the look-through rule under paragraph (d) of the TCP definition does not extend to shares or other interests that are not themselves TCP. If shares of a subsidiary of a holding company meet the definition of TCP, a proportionate value approach should be adopted such that, for example, if 60% of the value of the subsidiaries shares is derived from Canadian real property, 60% of the of the value of the shares should be considered Canadian real property for purposes of determining whether the shares of the holding company are TCP. If the shares of the subsidiary are not TCP, any Canadian real or resource property held by the subsidiary is irrelevant in determining whether the shares of the holding company are TCP (i.e., the entire value of the shares of the subsidiary is considered not to be derived from Canadian real or immovable property). For example, a non-resident may own shares of a Canadian public company that derive most of their value from real or resource property situated in Canada through a private holding company. In such circumstances, the shares of the private holding company would not meet the definition of TCP provided the public company shares are not themselves TCP.

In practice, the derived value test can be difficult to apply as the test covers a 60-month period and involves valuation estimates (i.e., in determining whether the principal value test is met, the fair market value of the assets and liabilities must be measured).

Listed securities are TCP only if both a derived value test (consistent with the test described above) and an ownership threshold test are met. The ownership threshold test is met if 25% or more of the issued shares of any class of the corporation, or 25% or more of the issued units of the trust, were owned by or belonged to one or any combination of the taxpayer and persons with whom the taxpayer did not deal at arm's length during a 60-month look-back period. At the 2011 CTF Conference CRA Roundtable, the CRA confirmed that both tests must be met at the same time for shares to be TCP (see VD 2011-0425931C6). Thus, for example, TCP characterization would not arise if one of the tests was satisfied in month 10 and the other in month 50 during a 60-month look-back period.

Property that was subject to a tax-deferred rollover provision may be deemed to be TCP. Where a TCP deeming rule applies, property that would not otherwise be TCP on the acquisition date may be TCP of the vendor. The general purpose of the TCP deeming provisions is to prevent a non-resident from avoiding tax through a tax-deferred transaction.

The disposition of property that is deemed to be TCP gives rise to a T1 return filing obligation and tax may be payable by a non-resident in respect of such a disposition. However, properties excluded from ITA 116 filing and withholding requirements (see ¶15220) include property that is TCP solely because a provision of ITA deems the property to be TCP.

The TCP deeming rules do not take into account whether the underlying real property (i.e., if real property gave rise to the TCP characterization) has been disposed of after the date at which the deeming rule was triggered. However, effective after March 4, 2010, the deeming rules only apply for a 60-month period after a relevant disposition. Where a relevant property is disposed of after the 60-month deeming period, the property would no longer be deemed to be TCP (also, the deeming rule would not continue to apply to a new shareholder, other than in respect of a tax-deferred transfer).

> Several of Canada's tax treaties exempt gains in respect of properties that may meet the TCP definition (a tax treaty provision may also be important in respect of property that is deemed to be TCP). In particular, the derived value tests in respect of securities contained in several of Canada's treaties do not contain a look-back rule similar to that contained in the TCP definition such that only property held by the entity at the disposition date is relevant under the treaty. Most of Canada's treaties do not exempt gains on sales of Canadian real property or resource property from taxation.

Regarding whether mortgages secured by real property in Canada represent an indirect investment in real or immovable property situated in Canada for purposes of the TCP definition, in VD 2012-0453021C6, the CRA states it is of the view that:

> [T]he fact that at some time during the 60-month period that ended at the determination time, most of the value of the shares of a corporation that is not listed on a designated stock exchange was derived directly from assets consisting of non-defaulted arm's length mortgages secured by real property situated in Canada, would not result in a share of that corporation being TCP. However, if the rights of a particular mortgagee were different from those described in subsection 248(4) of the Act, we would need to examine all of the facts and circumstances relating to that particular mortgage before taking a final position and could conceivably reach a different view.

In determining whether a certificate of compliance under ITA 116 (see ¶15220) is required in respect of an acquisition of TCP, the onus is on the purchaser to determine whether a property is TCP. The lack of a due diligence defence from ITA 116 filing and withholding requirements has hindered the effectiveness of the amendments that were intended to ease compliance burdens (i.e., as the amendments did not change the fact that the purchaser still bears the ultimate risk of determining whether a particular property is TCP).

At the 2010 Annual CTF Conference, the CRA stated it does not review or make a determination of whether a property is TCP in the course of processing an ITA 116 certificate request. Although a certificate may be issued under ITA 116(2) or (4) in respect of property that is not TCP, this fact does not influence the amount that must be paid or security provided by the vendor to qualify for a certificate under ITA 116(2) or (4).

As mentioned above, the onus is on the purchaser of property from a non-resident to determine whether a certificate of compliance under ITA 116 is required because the property is TCP. It is important for a purchaser of property from a non-resident to exercise due diligence when determining whether the property acquired is TCP. If tax is not withheld and it is subsequently determined that property is in fact TCP, the purchaser remains liable for withholdings, which the CRA will rigorously pursue.

ITA 44.1(2)(c), 51(1)(f), 85(1)(i), 85.1(1)(a), 85.1(8)(b), 85.1(5), 87(4), (5), 116(6)(a), 128.1(6.1), 248(25.1), 248(1)"taxable Canadian property", Canada-U.S. Tax Treaty:Art. XIII, VDs 2013-051615117, 2012-0444091C6, 2011-0425901C6, Jack Bernstein et al., "TCP Proposal Overshoots Objective?", *Canadian Tax Highlights*, Vol. 21-8, Aug. 2013

¶15210 — Excluded Dispositions

A non-resident who disposes of TCP is not required to file a T1 return in respect of an "excluded disposition".

A disposition is an "excluded disposition" if:

1) No tax is payable under Part I for the tax year;

2) The taxpayer is not liable to pay any amount under the ITA for any previous tax year (other than an amount covered by adequate security under ITA 116 or 220); and

3) Each TCP disposed of in the tax year is "excluded property" as defined under ITA 116 or property for which a certificate was issued under ITA 116.

"Excluded property" of a non-resident includes: a property that is a TCP solely because a provision of the ITA deems it to be a TCP; inventory of a business carried on in Canada (other than real or immovable property situated in Canada, a Canadian resource property, or a timber resource property); a security that is listed on a recognized stock exchange that is either a share of a corporation or "SIFT wind-up entity"; a unit of a mutual fund trust; a bond, debenture, bill, note, mortgage, hypothecary claim, or similar obligation; property of a non-resident insurer that is licensed to carry on an insurance business in Canada; property of an authorized foreign bank that carries on a Canadian banking business; an option or an interest in respect of property (whether or not such property is in existence) just described; and a property that is, at the time of its disposition, a "treaty-exempt property" of the person.

A "recognized stock exchange" is defined as any stock exchange that is located in Canada or in a country that is a member of the OECD and that has a tax treaty with Canada. Furthermore, recognized stock exchanges are also defined to include designated stock exchanges. The Alternative Investment Market of the London Stock Exchange is an example of a stock exchange that is a recognized stock exchange but is not a designated stock exchange.

A "treaty-exempt property" is defined as a "treaty-protected property" (i.e., a property any income or gain from the disposition of which by the taxpayer at that time would, because of a tax treaty with another country, be exempt from tax under Part I of the ITA) in respect of the disposition of which, where the purchaser and the non-resident person are related at that time, the purchaser provides notice to the CRA (ITA 116(5.02)). Property will not qualify as "treaty-exempt property" unless the vendor is resident in the particular country with which Canada has a tax treaty and that treaty exempts the gain from taxation in Canada.

The notice referred to above must indicate the date of the acquisition; the name and address of the non-resident person; a description of the property sufficient to identify it; the amount paid or payable (as the case may be) by the purchaser for the property; and the name of the country with which Canada has concluded a tax treaty and under which the property is "treaty-protected property" (to provide notice, use Form T2062C: *Notification of an Acquisition of Treaty-Protected Property from a Non-Resident Vendor*). If the purchase price of property includes a contingent component that is not known until after the due date for the notice, the CRA will consider the purchaser to have complied with the notification requirement provided that the purchaser files a notice within the time allowed; the amount set out on the notice as paid or payable by the purchaser includes a portion that has been estimated; the fact that the amount on the notice includes a portion that has been estimated is indicated on the notice; and if the actual amount paid or payable turns out to be different than the estimated amount, a revised notice is filed by the purchaser forthwith.

A notice is not required to be filed with the CRA where the purchaser and the non-resident are not related; however, it may be in the purchaser's best interest to provide notice as the treaty-protected property exception from ITA 116 requirements may protect the purchaser from withholding obligations if it turns out that the TCP is not excluded property (to obtain this protection, the purchaser must file a notice even where the vendor and the purchaser are not related; see ITA 116(5.01)). In VD 2008-0289051E5, the CRA states:

> [S]ubsections 116(5) and 116(5.3) of the Act do not apply to a transfer of excluded property. However, it may be beneficial to a purchaser to file the notice described in subsection 116(5.02) of the Act even if the purchaser believes at the time of the purchase that the vendor qualifies for treaty relief in respect of any Part I taxes arising in respect of the transfer. For, example there may be circumstances where the conditions described in paragraphs 116(5.01)(a) and (b) of the Act are satisfied, but on subsequent audit it is determined that the vendor does not qualify for relief from Part I tax under a tax treaty after all. In such case, if the purchaser has filed the notice described in subsection 116(5.02) of the Act, all the requirements of subsection 116(5.01) will have been met, and no liability in respect of withholdings will lie with the purchaser by virtue of the excepting provisions in paragraphs 116(5)(a.1) and 116(5.3)(a) of the Act.

ITA 2(3), 115(1)(b), 116(5.01), (5.02), (6), (6.1), 248(1)"treaty-protected property", "treaty exempt property", 251(2)(b)(ii), 251(3), 251(5)(b), VDs 2012-0455741E5, 2009-0347711C6

¶15220 — Certificates of Compliance

As mentioned above, ITA 116 establishes procedures for collecting tax from non-resident taxpayers on the disposition of TCP, Canadian resource properties, and certain other properties.

> If the property disposed of is not TCP, ITA 116 does not apply. Also, if the property is TCP but is also "excluded property" (see ¶ 15210), ITA 116 does not apply. For property to be "excluded property" under ITA 116(6)(i) by virtue of meeting the "treaty-protected property" definition in ITA 116(6.1), if the purchaser and vendor are related, the purchaser is required to provide notice to the CRA by filing Form T2062C within 30 days of the disposition (ITA 116(5.02)). Furthermore, even if the purchaser and vendor are not related, it may be beneficial to file this notice to reduce the purchaser's risk with respect to whether the vendor is resident in a treaty country to the standard of "reasonable inquiry" (see ITA 116(5), (5.01), and VDs 2008-0289051E5, 2009-0347711C6).

If a purchaser is not satisfied that a particular property is not TCP, the vendor may submit a request for a certificate of compliance. In such a case, the CRA will process the request on the assumption that the property is TCP (all required fields on the appropriate forms should be completed, all supporting documents with the request for the certificate should be provided, an individual tax number or business number for the vendor should be obtained before the disposition, and any correspondence submitted with the appropriate forms should refer to a request for a certificate of compliance as opposed to a "clearance certificate").

While the term "clearance certificate" is commonly used by tax professionals in reference to certificates issued pursuant to ITA 116, the CRA generally only use the term "clearance certificate" to refer to certificates issued pursuant to ITA 159 (regarding wind-ups). The CRA uses the term "certificates of compliance" in respect of certificates issued under ITA 116.

Generally, a purchaser acquiring TCP from a non-resident is required to withhold part of the purchase price and to remit the funds to the CRA on account of the non-resident's potential Canadian tax liability unless:

1) The non-resident obtains a certificate of compliance (Form T2062: *Request by a Non-Resident of Canada for a Certificate of Compliance Related to the Disposition of a Taxable Canadian Property*) from the CRA in respect of the proposed or actual disposition (which typically requires that the vendor pay an amount on account of the potential tax liability);

2) The property is "excluded property", which includes "treaty-exempt property" where certain conditions are met (see under ¶15210); or

3) The purchaser complies with the CRA notice requirements described under ¶15210 (regardless of whether or not the vendor and purchaser are related), the purchaser concludes after reasonable inquiry (see IC 72-17R6, para. 58) that the non-resident person is resident in a country with which Canada has a tax treaty, and the property would be treaty-protected property of the non-resident person if the non-resident person were, under the tax treaty, resident in the particular country.

> ITA 116 filing and withholding procedures are burdensome and the process of obtaining a certificate of compliance may take months. However, if the process is not followed, significant penalties can apply to both the vendor and purchaser. ITA 116 can apply even if a gain is exempt from tax under a treaty.

On a proposed disposition, the seller may either prepay or provide security for the tax that may be payable. If the non-resident does not notify the CRA of the proposed disposition or if the information about the proposed disposition changed, the seller has 10 days after the disposition to advise the CRA. If no certificate is provided and the non-resident does not prepay or provide security for the tax payable, the purchaser generally becomes liable to the CRA for 25% of the cost of the property acquired, or if the CRA issued a certificate for a proposed disposition under ITA 116(2), the liability is 25% of the cost minus the proceeds of disposition (certificate limit) fixed by that certificate (in the case of depreciable property, the required withholding may be greater). The buyer is required to remit this amount to the CRA no later than 30 days after the end of the month in which the property was acquired. The buyer is entitled to recover the tax paid on behalf of the seller and can withhold amounts from any later payments to the seller. The buyer is not liable for the seller's tax if the CRA issued a certificate under ITA 116(4) to the non-resident seller and the buyer for the actual disposition. If a notification is filed after the deadline, the CRA will typically require that any penalty for late filing be paid before it will begins processing the certificate of compliance request.

The CRA is often not able to process a notification and issue a certificate before the remittance deadline. In practice, if the amount withheld by the purchaser is held in escrow for the Receiver General of Canada and a notification has been filed with the CRA in accordance with ITA 116, the CRA will usually issue a so-called "comfort letter" confirming that the purchaser may continue to retain the withheld funds beyond the statutory remittance date, without incurring any interest or penalties, until the CRA can finalize its review of the notification and determine whether any payment of tax is required. If the withheld amount were remitted, the vendor would need to wait for the CRA to assess its T1 return for that year to receive a refund of the amounts withheld (the practice is generally to rely on the comfort letters although there is no statutory basis for it).

Determining whether property is "treaty-protected property" can be complex. As a practical matter, the inclusion of "treaty-exempt property" in the "excluded property" definition is generally only useful in non-arm's length transactions. In respect of arm's length transactions, the onus is on the purchaser to determine whether a property is "treaty-protected property". If tax is not withheld and it is subsequently determined that property is in fact TCP, the purchaser remains liable for withholdings (reasonable inquiry by the purchaser is not sufficient and the ITA does not provide for a due diligence defence for a potential withholding tax assessment).

If Form T2062 is submitted by the vendor and there is a claim under a tax treaty, in paragraphs 29–35 of IC 72-17R6, the CRA states that the vendor should complete and submit Form NR301, NR302, or NR303 along with Form T2062 (for more information on Forms NR301, NR302 and NR303, see: canada.ca/en/revenue-agency/services/forms-publications/information-on-forms-nr301-nr302-nr303.html).

Regarding the exception from withholdings described in (3) above, the CRA has stated that it generally will accept that the purchaser has made reasonable inquiry if Part D of Form T2062C: *Notification of an Acquisition of Treaty-Protected Property from a Non-Resident Vendor* is completed by the vendor or an equivalent declaration is obtained from the vendor. Where there is doubt as to a vendor's entitlement to an exemption under a treaty other than by reason of the vendor's residence status, a purchaser may require the vendor to obtain an ITA 116 certificate of compliance.

In addition to Form T2062, the following forms may also be required to be filed in accordance with ITA 116 requirements:

1) For dispositions of Canadian resource property, Form T2062A: *Request by a Non-Resident of Canada for a Certificate of Compliance Related to the Disposition of Canadian Resource or Timber Resource Property, Canadian Real Property (Other Than Capital Property), or Depreciable Taxable Canadian Property*, and Form T2062A-SCH1: *Disposition of Canadian Resource Property by Non-Residents*;

2) For dispositions of Canadian real property (other than capital property), Canadian timber resource property, and depreciable TCP, Form T2062A; or

3) For dispositions of a life insurance policy in Canada, Form T2062B: *Notice of Disposition of a Life Insurance Policy in Canada by a Non-Resident of Canada*, and Form T2062B-SCH1: *Certification and Remittance Notice*.

The tax paid under ITA 116(2) is intended to approximate the federal and provincial taxes payable at the highest marginal tax rates. However, similar to ITA 116, the Quebec *Taxation Act* has withholding requirements on dispositions of "taxable Québec property" by certain non-residents (see, for example, VD 2005-0141101C6).

For more information on section 116 requirements, including where to file Form T2062, see the CRA website at canada.ca/en/revenue-agency/services/tax/international-non-residents/information-been-moved/disposing-acquiring-certain-canadian-property.html.

ITA 116, 150(5), 227(9), IC 72-17R6: *Procedures Concerning the Disposition of Taxable Canadian Property by Non-residents of Canada — Section 116*, *Morris*, [2010] 3 C.T.C. 24 (FCA), VDs 2012-0444081C6, 2009-031737117, 2009-0347711C6, 2008-0289051E5, 2005-0141101C6, Chris Falk et al., "Section 116 Clearance Certificates," 2010 British Columbia Tax Conference, (Vancouver: Canadian Tax Foundation, 2010), 12:1–41, Bowman, A. "Taxable Canadian Property", *Canadian Tax Foundation 62nd Tax Conference*, 2010

¶15300 — Payments Subject to Withholding Tax

Withholding tax is levied under Part XIII of the ITA on investment/passive income (including dividends, interest, income from estates or trusts, rents, royalties, patronage dividends, and management or administration fees or charges) paid or credited (or deemed to be paid or credited) to a non-resident by a Canadian resident person. The tax is required to be withheld at source by the Canadian payer from the gross amount paid or credited (without deduction of expenses, if any) and is required to be remitted to the Receiver General pursuant to ITA 215.

ITA 212(1) provides for a withholding tax at a rate of 25%; however, this rate is normally reduced under the provisions of an applicable tax treaty. The onus is on the Canadian payer, whether a corporation, partnership, trust company, bank, agent, or individual, to obtain evidence that the beneficial owner of the income resides in a treaty country before the reduced rate applicable by reason of treaty can be applied. The Canadian resident payer is jointly and severally liable with the non-resident payee if the resident payer fails to deduct or withhold the required tax.

General instructions for the withholding of tax on amounts paid or credited to non-residents and for remitting the amounts withheld to the Receiver General and for the annual reporting of all such amounts to the Minister are contained in IC 77-16R4: *Non-Resident Income Tax*. IC 76-12R6: *Applicable rate of part XIII tax on amounts paid or credited to persons in countries with which Canada has a tax convention*, provides Appendices that may be used as withholding tax rate guides. To ensure accurate withholding rates are used, the applicable treaty should always be consulted. The Department of Finance posts Canada's tax treaties online at: fin.gc.ca/treaties-conventions/treatystatus_-eng.asp (treaties are also available on *Taxnet Pro*). Treaty status updates are also provided at both the Finance website and on *Taxnet Pro*. A "tax treaty" is defined in ITA 248(1) as a comprehensive agreement or convention for the elimination of double taxation on income between the Government of Canada and the government of a foreign country that has the force of law in Canada at that time.

Pursuant to ITA 227(6), if an excessive amount has been withheld, an application can be filed for a refund of the excess amount. To effect the application, the non-resident must file form NR7-R: *Application for Refund of Part XIII Tax Withheld* (see IC 77-16R4: paras. 70–77 and VD 2007-0253901E5). The application for a refund is due no later than 2 years after the end of the calendar year in which the amount was paid. The CRA's position is that the effective interest date for calculating refund interest on Part XIII tax is the later of the date of the assessment and the date on which the payment arose.

Withholding tax under Part XIII applies to a non-resident person making payments to another non-resident person where the non-resident payer's business is carried on principally in Canada, or where the non-resident payer manufactures or processes goods in Canada, operates an oil or gas well in Canada, or extracts minerals from a mineral resource in Canada.

For the purposes of Part XIII tax, a management or administration fee or charge does not include a fee or charge to the extent that it is for services performed in the ordinary course of a business carried on by a non-resident that included the performance of such a service for a fee if the non-resident person and the payer were dealing with each other at arm's length or a specific expense incurred by the non-resident person for the performance of a service that was for the benefit of the payer. IT-468R attempts to clarify what constitutes a management or administration fee or charge (the term is not defined in the ITA).

Form NR4: *Statement of Amounts Paid or Credited to Non-Residents of Canada* and Form NR4 Summary: *Return of Amounts Paid or Credited to Non-Residents of Canada* are required to be filed if an amount subject to withholding tax paid or credited to a non-resident is $50 or more. The forms are due on or before the last day of March following the calendar year to which the information return applies. Note that the requirement to file a Form NR4 is independent from the withholding requirement under Part XIII; therefore, Form NR4 is required to be filed where a resident of Canada pays or credits an amount to a non-resident person, even where the amount paid is not subject to withholding tax under Part XIII (VD 2017-0719491C6).

CRA provides a Non-Resident Tax Calculator at: canada.ca/en/revenue-agency/services/e-services/non-resident-tax-calculator-disclaimer.html.

ITA 212, 215, 227, ITR 105(1), 202(1), *Lord Rothermere Donation*, [2009] 4 C.T.C. 2084 (TCC), *TD Securities (USA) LLC*, [2010] 5 C.T.C. 2426 (TCC), *Peter Cundill*, [1991] 2 C.T.C. 221 (FCA), IC 77-16R4, IC 76-12R6, CRA Guide T4061: *NR4 — Non-Resident Tax Withholding, Remitting, and Reporting*, ITTN-41, IT-468R: *Management or Administration Fees Paid to Non-Residents*, VDs 2012-046018117, 2012-0457591C6, 2011-0427251C6, 2010-0369271C6, 2009-0345351C6, 2009-031849117, 2009-032474117, 2007-0253901E5

¶15310 — Interest Payments

Withholding tax on interest applies to every amount paid, credited, or deemed to be paid or credited by a Canadian resident to a non-resident person, as, on account or in lieu of payment of, or in satisfaction of, interest other than:

1) "fully exempt interest" (i.e., certain Government and other bonds, debentures, notes, mortgages, hypothecary claims, and similar obligations) paid to a non-arm's length person, or

2) "participating debt interest" (generally defined as interest, all or any portion of which is contingent or dependent on the use of or production from property in Canada or is computed by reference to revenue, profit, cash flow, commodity price, or any similar criterion).

Effective March 16, 2011, ITA 212(1)(b)(i) was amended to impose withholding tax on interest that, in addition to not being fully exempt interest, is paid or payable to either: a non-resident recipient with whom the payer does not deal at arm's length; or a non-resident recipient (whether arm's length or not) if the interest is paid or payable on a debt obligation owed by the payer to a non-resident with whom the payer does not deal at arm's length.

Prior to 2008, ITA 212(1)(b) imposed tax on a much broader range of interest payments made to non-residents.

A 25% tax rate is imposed under ITA 212(1)(b) to gross interest payments (without deduction of any expenses incurred by the non-resident in earning such interest); however, as mentioned above, the 25% withholding tax is generally reduced for interest paid to a person resident in a country with which Canada has a tax treaty. Under the Canada-US Tax Treaty, there is no withholding tax on interest payments. Under most of Canada's other tax treaties, the withholding tax rate applicable to interest is 10%.

In *Lewin*, 2012 FCA 279; affirming 2011 CarswellNat 4161 (TCC), the Court found that a trustee declaration that an amount was "payable" to a beneficiary did not make the amount credited for purposes of ITA 212(1). At paragraph 49, the Court stated "I would suggest that subsection 104(13) of the Act refers to the point in time at which a trust incurs the obligation to pay a beneficiary, while both the terms "pays" and "credits" in subsection 212(1) of the Act refer to the moment when the obligation is discharged — that is, when the trust essentially gives up possession of the funds necessary to pay the obligation" (also see paragraphs 56–58 of the decision).

ITA 212(1)(b), 215(1), 227(8.1), ITR 202, CRA Guide T4061, IC 77-16R4 (para. 5)

¶15320 — Dividend Payments

Taxable dividends paid or deemed to be paid (see ¶3130) to non-residents are subject to withholding tax at a rate of 25% unless reduced by the terms of a tax treaty. The withholding rate on dividends under most of Canada's tax treaties is either 5% or 15% depending on the recipient's level of ownership of the dividend payer. In certain circumstances, a nil rate may apply depending generally upon the source of the income of the payer corporation.

Capital dividends elected out of a corporation's capital dividend account are considered dividends that are subject to withholding tax. Withholding tax also applies to all deemed dividends regardless of where in the ITA the deeming occurred (*Placements Serco Ltée*, [1988] 1 C.T.C. 213 (FCA)).

The "dividend" definition in ITA 248(1) merely states that this expression includes stock dividends except stock dividends paid by a non-resident corporation to a corporation or a mutual fund trust. Generally, it would appear that all corporate distributions not made as part of a liquidation or authorized capital reduction are dividends (see for example *Hill v The Permanent Trustee Company of New South Wales Ltd*, [1930] A.C. 720 and *Northern Securities Co v The King*, [1935–37] C.T.C. 23 (Exch)).

In the case of dividends paid in cash, the amount subject to tax is the amount paid. Where a dividend is paid in kind, the amount subject to tax would be the value of the property distributed.

A "stock dividend" is also a dividend for withholding tax purposes. A "stock dividend" is defined in ITA 248(1) as including any dividend paid by a corporation to the extent that it is paid by the issuance of shares of any class of the capital stock of the payer corporation. In the case of a stock dividend, the amount of the dividend would appear to be governed by the definition of the word "amount" in ITA 248(1). That definition provides that the amount of any stock dividend paid by a corporation is the amount of the increase in the paid up capital of the corporation by virtue of the payment of the dividend. In paragraph 25 and 26 of IT-88R2: *Stock Dividends*, the CRA states:

> Where a corporation resident in Canada pays a stock dividend to a non-resident shareholder, Part XIII tax must generally be withheld and remitted pursuant to section 215. However, it is not permissible to remit such tax in the form of shares. One approach to this problem is to declare the dividend partly in shares and partly in cash such that sufficient cash is available to satisfy the Part XIII tax liability.

ITA 212(2), VDs 2010-0364531R3, 2009-0318701E5, 2008-0280041R3, 2007-0241991R3, 2007-0243331C6, 2004-0074241E5, 2004-0072231C6, 2001-0106695, Jack Bernstein, "Refundable Withholding Tax Traps", Vol. 20, No. 8, August 2012

¶15330 — Rents and Royalties

Withholding tax is required to be deducted by Canadian residents from amounts paid or credited to non-resident persons in the nature of rents or royalties (the rate will normally be based on the relevant tax treaty). In particular, the following types of payments are subject to withholding tax:

1) Payments for the use of, or for the right to use, in Canada, any property, invention, trade name, patent, trade mark, design or model, plan, secret formula, process, or other thing whatever;

2) Payments for information concerning industrial, commercial, or scientific experience where the total paid as consideration for those services depends upon the use to be made thereof or benefit to be derived therefrom, or depends upon production sales or profits (e.g., payments for "know-how", which the CRA generally considers to include amounts for special knowledge, skills, or techniques that are considered beneficial in the conduct of a business);

3) Payments for services of an industrial, commercial, or scientific character performed by a non-resident person, subject to the same proviso as in (2) above, but not including a payment for services in connection with the sale of property or negotiation of a contract;

4) Payments pursuant to an agreement between the resident and non-resident under which the non-resident agrees not to use or permit any other person to use the property referred to in (1) above, or the information referred to in (2); and

5) Payments that are dependent upon use of or production from property in Canada, even if described as instalments of its sale price, unless the property sold consists of agricultural land.

Specifically exempted from withholding tax are payments of the following kinds:

1) Royalties or similar payments in respect of a copyright if in respect of the production or reproduction of a literary, dramatic, musical or artistic work (including copyright royalties or similar payments for the right to produce or reproduce computer programs);

2) Payments made under a *bona fide* cost-sharing arrangement under which the payer shares with the payee or one or more other non-residents, on a reasonable basis, research and development expenses in exchange for an interest in any property or thing of value that may result;

3) Rental payments for the use of or the right to use outside Canada any corporeal property;

4) Any payment that the payer is entitled to deduct in computing income under Part I of the ITA from a business carried on outside Canada, provided the payer is dealing at arm's length with the payee; and

5) Any payment made to an arm's length person for the use of an aircraft, attached fixtures or equipment, and spare parts.

In *Syspro Software Ltd.*, [2003] 4 C.T.C. 3001 (TCC), the Court held that computer software is a literary work and that the exemption in ITA 212(1)(d)(vi) applies to the right to reproduce and distribute copies of the software. See also VD 2011-0427181E5 in which the CRA takes the position that a payment for the right to sublicense the right to download and use custom computer software by an end-user in Canada would appear to satisfy the requirements for the exemption from Part XIII tax pursuant to ITA 212(1)(d)(vi).

Also, in VD 2011-0399141R3, the CRA states "[p]ayments for distribution rights are considered copyright royalties as the right to distribution is viewed as a component of the right to reproduce or is ancillary to such a right" such that the exemption in ITA 212(1)(d)(vi) applies. The latter CRA VDs highlight that in certain circumstances, provided contracts are appropriately drafted, withholding tax can be reduced (or eliminated) in respect of cross-border license fees relating to the use of software. See also VD 2012-0462801R3 (ruling that certain custom software distribution fees were copyright royalties as the right to distribute was viewed as a component of the right to reproduce the software).

In VD 2011-0422781E5, the CRA states that a payment to a non-resident vendor for a right to use digital property does not generally constitute a royalty payment described in ITA 212(1)(d)(i); rather, the CRA's view is that a payment to access digital property (subject to certain exceptional cases) generally gives rise to business proceeds. See VD 2007-0246981E5 for the CRA's views on the meaning of the terms "rent" and "royalty".

In *Blais*, [2011] 1 C.T.C. 2240 (TCC), payments made by a satellite TV reseller for de-scrambling services to a non-resident were found not to be royalties. In the case, the Court cited the definition of royalty used in *Hasbro* referred to above.

Most tax treaties contain a definition of "royalties" that is applicable in determining whether a reduction in the withholding tax rate is available; see, for example, Canada-U.S. Tax Treaty:Art. XII (the application of this Article is discussed in VDs 2011-0416821R3, 2011-0431571E5, 2010-0374421E5, 2006-0188131E5, 2008-0284551R3, and 2006-0196191C6).

Rental income derived by a non-resident from a 4-storey apartment building in Canada was held to be income from property, not from a business, in *De Villard*, [1978] C.T.C. 2044 (TRB), and was therefore subject to tax under ITA 212(1)(d) (see also *Ravasi*, [1979] C.T.C. 2808 (TRB)). However, ITA 216 allows a non-resident person to elect to be taxed under Part I of the ITA on net income from Canadian real property and timber royalties in lieu of paying Part XIII tax on the gross amount of such payments.

ITA 216(4) permits an agent of a non-resident person to withhold on the basis of the net amount of such rents or royalties where the non-resident person has filed an undertaking with the CRA to file a tax return for the year under Part I. Where the non-resident fails to fulfil the undertaking or pay the proper amount of tax within the time provided for payment, the agent becomes liable for the Part XIII tax that should have been withheld. See Form NR6: *Undertaking to File an Income Tax Return by a Non-Resident Receiving Rent from Real or Immovable Property or Receiving a Timber Royalty*. See ¶5500 and ¶15411 for more information about electing under section 216.

Where payments for property and services are combined, in VD 2007-0253321E5, the CRA states:

> Where a payment represents in part a royalty and in part business profits for purposes of the Treaty, a taxpayer must make reasonable efforts to separate the two. Where a taxpayer fails to, or is unable to, identify the royalty component and the business profits component, the entire payment will be taxed as a royalty and be subject to withholding tax pursuant to paragraph 212(1)(d) (as reduced by the Treaty). The Canadian resident payer is responsible for withholding and remitting the applicable taxes and filing an NR4 return in respect of the taxes withheld. Failure to withhold and remit the appropriate amount of tax within the time limit specified may result in penalties and interests.

ITA 212(1)(d), (16), *Angoss International Ltd.*, [1999] 2 C.T.C. 2259 (TCC), *Pechet*, 2008 CarswellNat 1013 (TCC), ITTN-23, IT-303: *Know-How and Similar Payments to Non-Residents*, IC 77-16R4 (para. 39), CRA Guide T4144: *Income tax guide for electing under section 216*; IT-393R2: *Election re tax on rents and timber royalties — Non-residents*, VDs 2013-0512921E5, 2012-0457951E5, 2011-0404511C6, 2011-0416181E5, 2011-0416891R3, 2010-0382231I7, 2011-0431571E5, 2011-0399141R3, 2009-0331791E5 QTA 34(1)(b), Peter Jovicic et al., "Blurred Lines: Cross-Border Rents and Royalties in the 21st Century," *2013 Conference Report*, (Toronto: Canadian Tax Foundation, 2014), 22: 1–36, Harry Chana, "Part XIII Withholding Adequate?", *Canadian Tax Highlights*, Vol. 20, No. 11, Nov. 2012

¶15340 — Pension and Other Benefits

Payments of Canadian benefits to a non-resident are subject to 25 percent Part XIII withholding tax. Benefits include old age security (OAS) pension, CPP or QPP benefits, RRSP and RRIF payments, pension benefits, death benefits, employment insurance benefits, retiring allowances, deferred profit-sharing plan payments, and retirement compensation arrangement payments. The 25 percent withholding tax rate may be reduced by tax treaty, if any, between Canada and the individual's country of residence.

The treatment of Canadian benefits under a tax treaty depends on the nature of the income and the provisions of the particular treaty. For example, CPP and OAS payments made to a U.S. resident are not subject to Canadian tax; annual pension payments are often subject to a 15 percent withholding tax; and lump-sum RRSP payments are often subject to a 25 percent withholding tax.

The non-resident withholding tax represents the final Canadian tax obligation on pension and other benefit income. Accordingly, benefits reported on Form NR4, *Statement of Amounts Paid or Credited to Non-Residents of Canada*, or Form NR4(OAS), *Statement of Old Age Security Pension Paid or Credited to Non-Residents of Canada*, do not need to be reported on a T1 return unless the individual elects under ITA 217. The section 217 election allows a non-resident individual to pay Canadian tax on his or her benefits at graduated tax rates instead of the Part XIII rate. See ¶15412 for more information on the section 217 election.

A non-resident individual may be liable to both Part I.2 tax and Part XIII non-resident withholding tax on OAS benefits. However, generally, Part I.2 tax is reduced to take into account the non-resident's Part XIII tax liability. Accordingly, the total Part I.2 tax and Part XIII withholding tax will not exceed the OAS benefits paid to the individual. If a non-resident is not subject to Part XIII withholding tax on OAS benefits (for example, where the non-resident makes a section 217 election), the non-resident's Part I.2 tax is calculated in the same way as a Canadian resident individual.

A non-resident who receives Canadian OAS benefits is required to file Form T1136, *Old Age Security Return of Income*, regardless of whether the individual files a T1 return or makes an election under section 217. A non-resident's Part I.2 tax liability is determined on Form T1136 (rather than on the federal worksheet for Line 235), as well as whether the non-resident is required to pay back all or part of the benefits, based on the non-resident individual's level of income. A non-resident is not required to file Form T1136 if there is no Part I.2 tax liability because the non-resident resides in a country that has a tax treaty with Canada that eliminates or reduces the amount of tax Canada may impose on OAS benefits to an amount less than the Part XIII tax otherwise payable on the benefits.

ITA 180.2, 212(1)(h), 212(1)(j), NR4, NR4-OAS, T4A(OAS), T1136, T1213(OAS), Guide T4155: *Old Age Security Return of Income Guide for Non-Residents*

¶15400 — Filing Requirements for Non-Residents & Deemed Residents

An individual who is a non-resident or deemed resident of Canada should file the T1 General Income Tax and Benefit Return for Non-Residents and Deemed Residents if:

- The non-resident or deemed resident individual has Canadian-source income in the year such as capital gains, scholarship income, or business income with no permanent establishment in Canada; and

- The non-resident or deemed resident individual is NOT reporting any income from a business with a permanent establishment in Canada or employment income earned in Canada.

Non-residents and deemed residents of Canada who are reporting income from a business with a permanent establishment in Canada or employment income earned in Canada are required to complete a regular T1 Return.

The T1 jacket and supporting forms and schedules for non-residents and deemed residents are similar to those for residents. However, non-residents and deemed residents may also be required to file the following additional schedules:

- Schedule A, Statement of World Income

- Schedule B, Allowable Amount of Non-Refundable Tax Credits

- Schedule C, Electing Under Section 217 of the *Income Tax Act*

- Form T1248 (Schedule D), Information About Your Residency Status

- Form T2203, Provincial and Territorial Taxes for 2018 — Multiple Jurisdictions

¶15410 — Elective Returns for Non-Residents

There are elections available to non-residents for certain types of Canadian-source income that would otherwise be subject to Part XIII withholding tax. Generally, these elections allow non-residents to file a separate return for Canadian-source income and claim deductions, so that Canadian tax is paid at Part I ordinary tax rates on net income, as opposed to having non-resident tax withheld on gross income. This may also allow the non-resident to claim non-refundable tax credits.

Elections are available for a non-resident who receives the following types of income:

- Rental income from real or immovable property located in Canada or timber royalties on a timber resource property or a timber limit in Canada;

- Canadian benefits, including pension benefits, retiring allowances, deferred profit-sharing plan payments, registered retirement income fund payments, supplementary unemployment benefit plan payments, retirement compensation arrangement payments, and death benefits; and

- Income for the provision of acting services in a film or video production.

¶15411 — *Section 216 Return*

A non-resident earning rental income that is property income is taxable in Canada under Part XIII of the Act and subject to a 25% withholding tax on gross rental income. If the non-resident is carrying on a business in Canada, net rental income is taxed under Part I at graduated tax rates, and the non-resident must report the net rental income on a T1 return.

The person paying the rents or the owner's agent is required to withhold and remit the tax on behalf of the non-resident and report the gross rents and tax withheld on Form NR4, Statement of Amounts Paid or Credited to Non-Residents of Canada. The filing deadline for Form NR4 is March 31 of the following taxation year.

Non-residents earning Canadian rental income as property income have the following options for fulfilling their Canadian tax liability:

1. The non-resident owner may elect under ITA 216 to file a Canadian T1 return and pay tax at graduated tax rates on net rental income. The election is made by filing Form T1159, *Income Tax Return for Electing Under Section 216* ("section 216 return") within two years from the end of the taxation year in which the rents were received. The agent or tenant is still required to withhold and remit tax from gross rental income at the 25% rate and the agent must also complete Form NR4. However, the withholding tax is credited against the tax liability on the individual's return and any excess tax withheld is refunded. Generally, reasonable expenses that relate to earning the rental income are deductible on the section 216 return (e.g., interest expense, property taxes, repairs and maintenance, capital cost, etc.).

2. The non-resident owner may elect to have the initial 25% withholding tax be based on the anticipated net rent (excluding depreciation) rather than the gross rent. As a result, the tax withheld over the course of the year should more closely approximate the tax on net rent on the return filed on a net basis. To have the withholding tax reduced, the individual must appoint an agent who is resident in Canada and must file the section 216 return within six months from the end of the taxation year in which rents were received. The non-resident owner is required to make an undertaking by filing Form NR6, *Undertaking to File an Income Tax Return by a Non-Resident Receiving Rent from Real or Immovable Property or Receiving a Timber Royalty*, by January 1 of each taxation year (in the first year of rental, on or before the date on which the first rental payment is due). If a non-resident owner files Form NR6 but fails to file a section 216 return within the six-month period, the non-resident is no longer permitted to pay tax on net rental income at graduated rates. For the purpose of completing Form NR6, capital cost allowance cannot be deducted in determining the estimated net rental income or loss for the year.

3. If the non-resident owner does not make either of the above elections, as long as the agent or tenant withholds 25% tax from gross rental income, remits the tax to CRA, and files Form NR4 correctly and on time, the non-resident owner is not required to file a Canadian T1 Return to report the receipt of rental income. However, this option does not allow for any deductions against gross rent so it would not usually be the preferred alternative.

If a non-resident files a section 216 return and reports a net rental loss in one taxation year, that loss cannot be carried forward or back to be applied against net rental income reported in another taxation year; however, the losses may be applied against similar income for the same year from another section 216 property.

Non-residents who earn Canadian rental income should elect under ITA 216 in situations where the total tax on net rental income will be less than the 25% withholding tax on gross rental income.

¶15412 — *Electing Under Section 217*

Non-residents who receive payments of Canadian benefits can elect under ITA 217 to have benefits taxed at incremental Canadian tax rates. Canadian benefits for this purpose include pension benefits, certain government assistance benefits, RRSP and RRIF payments, deferred profit sharing plan payments, supplementary unemployment benefit plan payments, employment insurance benefits, retiring allowances, deferred profit-sharing plan payments, and retirement compensation arrangement payments.

Generally, non-residents are subject to a flat 25% withholding tax under ITA Part XIII (subject to treaty reduction) on gross Canadian benefits. The payer is required to withhold and remit the tax on behalf of the non-resident and report the gross benefits and tax withheld on Form NR4, *Statement of Amounts Paid or Credited to Non-Residents of Canada*, due on or before March 31 of the following taxation year. The 25% tax represents the non-resident's final Canadian tax liability and the non-resident does not have to file a T1 return to report the Canadian benefits. Where an individual is a resident of a treaty country, the withholding rate may be reduced under the treaty.

Alternatively, a non-resident may elect under ITA 217 to report Canadian benefits on a T1 return and pay Canadian tax at graduated tax rates and claim applicable deductions and credits. ITA 217(2) provides that no Part XIII withholding tax is payable in respect of a non-resident person's Canadian benefits for a taxation year, provided the non-resident files a Part I return for the year with the CRA within six months after the end of the year and elects in that return to have ITA 217 apply for the year. The section 217 T1 return is due for filing within six months after the end of the year; however, any income taxes owing are due by April 30th. If an individual is also reporting other income on the return, such as employment income or taxable capital gains, the due date is April 30th. If the return is not filed on time, the section 217 election is invalid and the Canadian benefits are subject to 25% withholding tax (subject to treaty reduction). If a section 217 election is made, all Canadian benefits paid or credited in that year must be reported on the section 217 T1 return. Making the section 217 election may result in a refund of all or some of the 25% tax withheld under Part XIII.

The section 217 election does not relieve a non-resident from withholding tax. The payer is still required to withhold 25% tax, unless the non-resident applies for a reduction in the amount of tax required to be withheld by filing Form NR5, *Application by a Non-Resident of Canada for a Reduction in the Amount of Non-Resident Tax Required to be Withheld*, and CRA approves the request. Part XIII tax that is withheld and reported on Form NR4, *Statement of Amounts Paid or Credited to Non-Residents of Canada*, should be entered on line 437 of the section 217 T1 return (see ¶11240).

Making a section 217 election may or may not make sense, depending on the non-resident's Canadian benefit income, worldwide income, and deductions. For example, a non-resident who has very little Canadian benefit income and significant worldwide income would likely not benefit from a section 217 election because they would not be able to reduce their Canadian tax rate to less than the 25% withholding rate. However, for most non-residents receiving Canadian benefit income, it would be necessary to compute taxes under both methods to determine which option results in less Canadian tax.

Non-residents who receive Canadian benefits should elect under ITA 217 where their benefits total less than the top of the lowest federal tax bracket (approximately $46,000) and they have very little other income because, in these circumstances, the effective tax rate will be less than the 25% flat rate that would otherwise apply.

¶15413 — *Non-Resident Actors*

ITA 212(5.1) requires every person who is either a non-resident individual actor or a corporation related to such an individual to pay an income tax of 23% on every amount paid or credited (or provided as a benefit) to or on behalf of the person for the provision in Canada of the actor's acting services in a film or video production. ITA 216.1(1) enables such recipients to file a Part I return and elect to pay tax at marginal rates on their net income instead of 23% on the gross amount (see Form T1287, *Application by a non-resident of Canada (individual) for a reduction in the amount of non-resident tax required to be withheld on income earned from acting in a film or video production*, and Form T1288, *Application by a non-resident of Canada (corporation) for a reduction in the amount of non-resident tax required to be withheld on income earned from acting in a film or video production*).

It is the CRA's view that the only way to avoid the 23% withholding tax levied on gross acting revenues under ITA 212(5.1) is by filing a timely election under ITA 216.1(1). It is not possible to late file a "regular" income tax return under Part I on the premise that the acting services provided by the actor resulted in a permanent establishment in Canada pursuant to Article VII of the Canada-U.S. Income Tax Convention (VD 2015-0603271E5).

ITA 215, 216, 217, Part XIII; Reg. 202; Form NR4, Form NR5, Form NR6, Form NR7-R, Form T1159, Form T1287, Form T1288, Guide 5013-G, Guide T4056, Guide T4061, Guide T4144, Guide T4145, Guide T4155, IC 72-17R6, IC 77-16R4, IT-393R2, IT-434R

¶15500 — Emigration and Immigration

¶15510 — Emigrating From Canada

Individuals emigrating from Canada are deemed to have disposed of their property at fair market value on the date of emigration and to have re-acquired it for the same amount immediately after (ITA 128.1(4)(b)).

The deemed disposition on emigration applies to all of a taxpayer's property, including taxable Canadian property, except the following:

- Canadian real or immovable property, resource property, and timber resource property;

- Canadian business property (including inventory) if the business is carried on through a permanent establishment in Canada;

- pensions and similar rights, including registered retirement savings plans, registered retirement income funds, registered education savings plans, registered disability savings plans, tax-free savings accounts, and deferred profit-sharing plans;

- rights to certain benefits under employee profit-sharing plans, employee benefit plans, employee trusts, and salary-deferral arrangements;

- trust interests that were not acquired for consideration;

- property the taxpayer owned at the time he or she last became a resident of Canada, or property inherited after the taxpayer last became a resident of Canada, if the taxpayer were a resident of Canada for 60 months or less during the 10-year period before the date of emigration;

- employee security options subject to Canadian tax; and

- interests in life insurance policies in Canada (other than segregated fund policies).

To report the deemed disposition, the taxpayer is required to calculate and include in income the capital gain or capital loss that results from the deemed disposition using Form T1243, *Deemed Disposition of Property by an Emigrant of Canada*, and include on Schedule 3, *Capital Gains (or Losses)*, the capital gain (or loss) reported on Form T1243.

If the fair market value of all the property the taxpayer owned upon emigrating from Canada is more than $25,000, the taxpayer must also include a list of their worldwide property holdings with their income tax return by completing Form T1161, *List of Properties by an Emigrant of Canada*. Any personal-use property valued at less than $10,000 does not have to be listed (e.g., clothing, household items, cars, etc.).

The tax owing on a deemed disposition is due by April 30 of the tax year after the year of emigration. However, taxpayers can elect to defer the payment of tax on income relating to the deemed disposition, regardless of the amount, and pay it later, without interest, upon a later sale or other disposition of the property. The election to defer the payment of tax on income relating to the deemed disposition is made on Form T1244, *Election, Under Subsection 220(4.5) of the Income Tax Act, to Defer the Payment of Tax on Income Relating to the Deemed Disposition of Property*. The election must be filed on or before April 30th of the year after the year of emigration. In certain cases, individuals electing to defer tax owing on the deemed disposition must provide security to cover the taxes owing.

If a taxpayer who previously emigrated from Canada re-establishes Canadian residency at a later date, the taxpayer can elect to make an adjustment to the deemed dispositions reported upon emigration if the individual still owns some or all of the property deemed disposed of upon emigration. The election may result in the reduction or elimination of the tax owing in respect of the gain from the previously reported deemed disposition of property on emigration. A written request to make this election must be submitted in writing on or before the filing-due date for the year the individual immigrates and becomes resident in Canada. A list of the properties owned and the fair market value of each property to which this election applies must also be included. This election should be filed with a taxpayer's T1 Return for the year of immigration.

¶15520 — Immigrating To Canada

When a non-resident individual establishes Canadian residency, the individual is deemed to acquire, at fair market value, all of the property the individual owns at the time of immigration, regardless of the location of the property (ITA 128.1(1)). The deemed disposition on immigration applies to all of a taxpayer's property, except the following:

- Canadian real property;

- Canadian business property (including inventory) if the business is carried on through a permanent establishment in Canada;

- pensions and similar rights, including registered retirement savings plans, registered retirement income funds, registered education savings plans, registered disability savings plans, tax-free savings accounts, and deferred profit-sharing plans;

- rights to certain benefits under employee profit-sharing plans, employee benefit plans, employee trusts, and salary-deferral arrangements;

- property the taxpayer owned at the time he or she last became a resident of Canada, or property inherited after the taxpayer last became a resident of Canada, if the taxpayer were a resident of Canada for 60 months or less during the 10-year period before the date of immigration;

- employee security options subject to Canadian tax; and

- interests in life insurance policies in Canada (other than segregated fund policies).

These rules ensure that capital gains acquired prior to an individual becoming a Canadian resident are not taxed in Canada, but that any gains accrued after the date the individual becomes a Canadian resident are taxable.

¶15521 — *Immigration Trusts*

Previously, in certain circumstances, an individual who immigrated to Canada could set up a non-resident "immigration trust" to avoid Canadian tax on income generated on the trust assets for up to 60 months. However, the 60-month immigrant trust exemption to the non-resident trust rules was eliminated, applicable in respect of trusts for taxation years: (1) that end after 2014, if at any time that is after 2013 and before February 11, 2014, the 60-month exemption applies in respect of the trust, and no contributions are made to the trust on or after February 11, 2014 and before 2015; or (2) that end after February 10, 2014 in any other case.

This means that for immigration trusts that were exempt from Canadian tax under section 94 on February 11, 2014, providing that no further contributions to the trust were made for the remainder of 2014, the exemption was eliminated for taxation years that end after 2014. However, if any contributions were made to the trust on or after February 11, 2014 and before 2015, the exemption ceased to apply retroactively, under ITA 94(3)(a), commencing January 1, 2014. As a result, the trust would be deemed to have disposed of virtually all its assets at their fair market value — in the former case immediately before the end of 2014 and in the latter case immediately before the end of 2013 — and to have reacquired those assets at a cost equal to their fair market value at the beginning of 2015 and of 2014 respectively, pursuant to ITA 94(3)(c).

For future years, where an immigrant to Canada has contributed to a trust that was not resident in Canada before the time of immigration, the trust will be deemed to have become resident in Canada for most purposes, to have disposed of virtually all of its assets for their fair market value immediately before the year of immigration, and to have reacquired those assets for a cost equal to that fair market value at the beginning of the year of immigration. Except where an individual immigrates to Canada on January 1 of the particular year, there will be an element of retroactive taxation of the trust's income. As a result of the elimination of the immigrant trust exemption, pursuant to ITA

94(3)(d), the immigrant individual will be personally liable for Canadian tax payable by the trust that the trust itself does not pay.

For more information, see the CRA's responses to questions regarding the elimination of the 60-month immigrant trust exemption at the 2014 STEP/CRA Roundtable (VDs 2014-0529821C6 and 2014-0529831C6).

Chapter 16 — Tax Planning, Registered Plans, and U.S. Tax Considerations

Contents

¶16100 Tax Planning

    ¶16110 Owner-Manager Remuneration Planning

    ¶16120 Post-Mortem Tax Planning and Elections

¶16200 Registered Plans

    ¶16210 Tax-Free Savings Accounts (TFSAs)

    ¶16220 Registered Education Savings Plans (RESPs)

    ¶16230 Registered Disability Savings Plans (RDSPs)

    ¶16240 Comparing Registered Plans

    ¶16250 Taxes in Respect of Registered Plans

¶16300 U.S. Tax Considerations for Canadians with U.S. Connections

    ¶16310 U.S. Income Tax

    ¶16320 U.S. Estate Tax

    ¶16330 U.S. Filing Due Dates, Forms, Remitting, and Penalties

¶16100 — Tax Planning

¶16110 — Owner-Manager Remuneration Planning

A Canadian-controlled private corporation (CCPC) is defined as a corporation that is a "private corporation" and a "Canadian corporation" that is not controlled, directly or indirectly in any manner whatever, by one or any combination of "public corporations" or non-resident persons (ITA 125(7)). Generally, income up to the small business limit derived from an active business carried on in Canada is eligible for the reduced small business corporate tax rate. Virtually every type of business carried on in Canada qualifies, except a "specified investment business" or a "personal services business." The small business limit is $500,000 in every jurisdiction other than Saskatchewan, where the limit is $600,000. Accordingly, as a general tax-planning measure, CCPCs pay a bonus to the owner-manager of the company to reduce corporate taxable income to the small business limit.

Associated corporations are required to share the small business limit. For taxation years beginning after 2018, the reduction of a CCPC's business limit is equal to the greater of: (a) the reduction based on taxable capital (ITA 125(5.1)(a)); and (b) the reduction based on aggregate investment income (ITA 125(5.1)(b)).

Eligibility for the small business deduction depends on the amount of the corporation's taxable capital employed in Canada. When the taxable capital employed in Canada exceeds $10 million, the business limit of $500,000 is reduced, and is eliminated when taxable capital reaches $15 million. The formula to calculate the business limit reduction is: $500,000 × 0.225% × (taxable capital - $10 million)/$11,250. If the CCPC is associated with one or more other corporations in the year, the phase-out includes the taxable capital employed in Canada of the associated corporations.

For taxation years beginning after 2018, a CCPC's small business deduction limit is reduced when investment income earned by a CCPC and any associated corporations exceeds $50,000. Under these rules, the small business deduction limit is reduced by $5 for every $1 of "adjusted aggregate investment income" above $50,000, such that the small business deduction is reduced to zero when aggregate investment income of a CCPC (and any associated corporations) reaches $150,000. The formula to calculate the business limit reduction is as follows: 5 × (aggregate investment income - $50,000). Accordingly, the investment income of all associated corporations must be considered in determining a CCPC's small business deduction limit. Generally, "adjusted aggregate investment income" for the purposes of these rules is derived from the definition of "aggregate investment income" in ITA 129(4) with various adjustments.

Amounts of salary or bonus payable to an owner-manager are normally deductible on the basis that the owner's expertise, know-how, managerial skills, and effort are responsible for the company's profits (see *Safety Boss Ltd. v. R.*, [2000] 3 C.T.C. 2497, which is generally accepted by the CRA: see for example ITTN-22 and VDs 2004-0092931R3 and 2004-0072741R3). Bonuses and salary paid to the owner's minor children or spouse must be reasonable to be deductible (see, for example, *Mépalex Inc. v. R.*, 2002 CarswellNat 4727 (TCC) and *Costigane v. R.*, [2003] 3 C.T.C. 2087 (TCC)). In *Ambulances B.G.R. Inc. v. R.*, 2004 CarswellNat 1054 (TCC), relatively large bonuses paid to adult children were held to be deductible on the basis that they represented reasonable compensation for exceptional services performed by the individuals.

There are many factors to consider when deciding whether to bonus-down to the small business deduction limit, rather than paying tax at the corporate level and paying an eligible dividend. Some of the considerations that should be kept in mind when determining an owner-manager's remuneration strategy are as follows:

- If the owner-manager does not need personal funds for spending, consider leaving earnings in the corporation to generate additional income and defer the personal tax until a later date when personal funds are needed. Generally, tax is deferred where the corporate tax rate is less than the owner-manager's individual tax rate; however, the new rules governing adjusted aggregate investment income must be considered when funds are retained in the corporation to be reinvested;

- Consider paying the owner-manager a sufficient salary to maximize the owner-manager's RRSP contribution room - $147,222 of earned income is required in 2018 to contribute the maximum RRSP amount of $26,500 for 2019;

- Consider paying the owner-manager a sufficient salary to maximize CPP pensionable earnings and fully utilize deductions and credits (e.g.; child care expenses, donations, etc.);

- Consider paying a reasonable salary to the owner-manager's spouse or children who provide services to the company and who are in a lower personal tax bracket;

- Consider that salary must be earned and received in the calendar year, and that accrued bonuses must be paid within 179 days after the corporation's year-end to be deductible in the year accrued;

- Consider paying eligible and/or non-eligible dividends that trigger a refundable dividend tax on hand (RDTOH) refund where the corporation has a balance in the RDTOH account;

- Consider paying tax-free capital dividends where the corporation has a balance in the capital dividend account.

¶16120 — Post-Mortem Tax Planning and Elections

Under ITA 70(5)(a), a Canadian resident taxpayer is deemed to have disposed of all of his or her capital property immediately before death at fair market value, thus realizing all accrued capital gains and losses. As a result, under ITA 70(5)(b), the deceased's estate receives the property at a cost equal to the fair market value immediately before death, unless the property is transferred to a surviving spouse or qualifying spouse trust and no election is made to override the automatic spousal rollover. To qualify for the tax-deferred rollover, the terms of the spouse trust must provide that the spouse is entitled to all of the trust's income during his or her lifetime, and that no one other than the spouse is entitled to receive any trust capital during his or her lifetime (ITA 70(6)(b)). The spousal rollover is not available where shares bequeathed to a spousal trust are converted from one class to another before the shares are transferred or distributed to, and vest indefeasibly in, the spousal trust (VD 2017-0693331C6).

If the deceased owns shares of a closely-held private corporation at death, double tax can arise as a result of the deemed disposition if the private company shares are left to a beneficiary on a non-rollover basis (i.e., the beneficiary is not a spouse or a qualified spouse trust). In many cases, post-mortem planning can be implemented to eliminate or reduce the double tax at death. Post-mortem planning in general, including post-mortem planning to avoid double tax at death, may involve making elections under the Act. There are a myriad of tax elections under the Act that can be made at a Canadian taxpayer's death. Often there is no provision to late-file an election, and depending on the deceased's circumstances, filing an appropriate tax election may result in significant tax savings. For these reasons, it is imperative that a deceased's executor and tax and legal advisors be aware of the various tax elections that can be made at death and the circumstances in which the elections are applicable so that they can properly carry out their professional obligations. Discussed below is some of the planning that can be implemented to eliminate or reduce double tax at death for individuals who die with private company shares, including any tax elections associated with the double tax planning.

¶16121 — Avoiding Double Taxation on Private Company Shares

Double tax can arise as a result of the deemed disposition on death when appreciated shares of a closely-held corporation are left to a beneficiary on a non-rollover basis. This situation occurs because, although the deemed disposition of the shares will result in a capital gain in the decedent's terminal return and the beneficiary will have an increased cost base in respect of the shares, there is no corresponding adjustment at the corporate level (i.e., there is no resulting adjustment to the tax cost of the assets held by the corporation). This can potentially result in double tax to the decedent's estate because the increase in cost base from the deemed disposition at death is not available to shelter the tax resulting from a later liquidation and distribution of assets from the corporation. In many cases, post-mortem planning can be implemented to eliminate or reduce the double tax at death. The choice of planning used to eliminate or reduce the double taxation will depend on the client's particular circumstances.

¶16121.1 — Subsection 164(6) Loss Carryback

ITA 164(6) allows the executor to elect to report any capital losses (net of capital gains) that are realized in the first year of the estate on the final return of the deceased so that all or part of the estate's capital loss from redeeming the deceased's private company shares within the first taxation year of the estate (provided that the stop-loss rules do not apply) is treated as a capital loss of the deceased taxpayer on his or her terminal return. The loss will offset all or part of the capital gain realized as a result of the deemed disposition at death, thus eliminating or reducing double taxation. If the final return does not have sufficient capital gains to offset the capital loss, excess losses can be deducted against other income (with some restrictions).

To make the subsection 164(6) election, the executor must meet the requirements under ITR 1000 and file an amended final return for the deceased. This means that the planning must be implemented within the first taxation year of the estate, which is normally within 12 months from the date of the decedent's death. Generally, once the first taxation year of the estate has passed, the subsection 164(6) loss carryback cannot be used (it may be possible for the estate to file the election after the deadline pursuant to ITA 220(3.2) and ITR 600; however, the Minister has discretion regarding the acceptance or rejection of a late filed election and the waiver of any interest and penalties). Therefore, it is important for the deceased's executor and advisors to review the deceased's assets in a timely manner after death to determine whether any capital losses can be realized from a disposition of assets in the first taxation year of the estate so that the losses can be carried back to the deceased's terminal return to offset capital gains resulting from the deemed disposition at death.

As a result of changes to the rules for testamentary trusts effective for 2016 and later taxation years, only a "graduated rate estate" (defined in ITA 248(1)) of the deceased can take advantage of the subsection 164(6) loss carryback election. An individual can only have one graduated rate estate, so where an individual has multiple wills, only one estate may be designated as a graduated rate estate. If a non-graduated rate estate incurs the loss but does not have any capital gains to offset it, the loss may never be used. Accordingly, where a taxpayer has multiple wills, the potential tax impact of the graduated rate estate designation must be considered carefully to ensure that post-mortem tax planning is not impacted.

The result of implementing subsection 164(6) planning is that the double tax effect is reduced or eliminated, leaving the estate to be taxed on a deemed dividend. Generally, since tax will be paid on a dividend instead of a capital gain, a subsection 164(6) election should be considered where the corporation has significant refundable dividend tax on hand (RDTOH) or capital dividend account (CDA) balances available and/or is able to designate the deemed dividend as an eligible dividend.

The application of the various stop-loss rules in the Act (ITA 40(3.6) and 112(3), for example) should be considered before disposing of assets for a loss in the estate. If the stop-loss rules apply, such rules reduce the amount of the capital loss resulting from the deemed dividend. In other words, the stop-loss rules "stops the loss" that could be used to reduce the amount of capital gain that resulted from the deemed disposition on death. The stop-loss rule in ITA 40(3.6) provides that if a taxpayer disposes of shares to a corporation and is affiliated (defined in ITA 251.1) with the corporation after the disposition, any resulting capital loss is denied and added to the adjusted cost base of the shares retained by the taxpayer. There is an exception to the loss denial in ITA 40(3.61) where the capital loss is carried back from an estate to a deceased's terminal year under ITA 164(6). Therefore, the stop-loss rule in ITA 40(3.6) will not apply to losses that are carried back from an estate to a deceased's terminal year under ITA 164(6). It is important to be aware though, that the exemption only applies to a loss carried back from an estate. It does not apply if the loss is carried back from a spousal, alter ego, joint spousal, or common law partner trust. Therefore, subsection 164(6) planning may be limited by ITA 40(3.6) where the deceased implemented planning involving the use of trusts.

¶16121.2 — *Redeeming Shares With Life Insurance*

In addition to ITA 40(3.6), the stop-loss rules in ITA 112(3) to (3.32) can apply to reduce the loss from the disposition of a share held as capital property by the amount of tax-free dividends received from the share. The denied loss is limited to the extent that previous taxable dividends were paid on the share and do not permit the denied loss to be added to the adjusted cost base of the remaining shares. As a result, when high adjusted cost base shares owned by an estate are redeemed using the capital dividend account, only 50% of the amount of the loss will be available to carry back (ITA 112(3.3)(a)(iii)) and the denied loss cannot be added to the adjusted cost base of the remaining shares.

Dispositions are grandfathered from the application of these rules where either the disposition of the share occurs pursuant to an agreement in writing made before April 27, 1995, or a life insurance policy existed on April 26, 1995 for the purposes of funding the redemption of a share. Estates that have corporate-owned life insurance but whose shares do not qualify as grandfathered shares will incur capital gains tax on 50% of the capital gain due to the application of the stop-loss rules if the estate receives the entire capital dividend account funded by the life insurance.

To avoid the denial of the loss, the estate can implement the "50 Percent Solution". Under this solution, only 50% of the capital dividend account is used to redeem shares with a high cost base that are held by the estate. The estate takes 50% of the capital dividend account and incurs regular dividend tax on the other 50% of the proceeds. There will be no reduction of the capital loss realized on the redemption by the estate, so the entire capital loss will be available to offset the capital gain realized in the terminal return. The 50 Percent Solution preserves 50% of the capital dividend account for use by the remaining shareholders; however, there is an additional cost to the estate because capital gains rates are lower than regular dividend rates. Note that, for 2016 and later taxation years, the stop-loss rules only apply to an estate that is a graduated rate estate; therefore, this type of planning must be done by the deceased's graduated rate estate.

A redemption of shares can occur tax-free if the deceased's shares pass to a spouse or a qualified spouse trust and the shares are redeemed using the capital dividend account. However, the rollover will not be available if a buy-sell agreement prevents the shares from vesting indefeasibly in a spouse or a spouse trust, unless the buy-sell agreement merely creates a put-call arrangement where the estate or the company may force a sale or repurchase of shares.

¶16121.3 — *Paragraph 88(1)(d) Bump*

A paragraph 88(1)(d) bump can be used to avoid or reduce double taxation on private company shares by removing capital property that has appreciated in value from the company following the death of the controlling shareholder. It can also avoid or greatly reduce the problem associated with inheriting shares with a high cost base and low paid-up capital.

Where capital gains are taxed at a lower rate than dividends, the paragraph 88(1)(d) bump may produce a better tax result than winding up a corporation by redeeming its shares to create a loss that can be carried back under ITA 164(6) to reduce the gain arising on death. If there is a change of control as a consequence of death, the shares of the corporation held at the time of death can be transferred to a new corporation for a promissory note (subject to ITA 84.1(1)), the existing corporation can be merged into the new corporation by way of a winding up under ITA 88(1), and in the course of that transaction, the adjusted cost base of the non-depreciable capital property of the existing corporation can be bumped to its fair market value at the time of the death of the controlling shareholder. These assets can then be used to pay down the promissory note owing to the estate.

To implement a winding up under ITA 88(1), the parent and subsidiary must be taxable Canadian corporations, the parent must own at least 90% of the shares of each class of the subsidiary, and any other shares must be owned by non-arm's-length parties. As well, for property to qualify for the 88(1)(d) bump, it must be capital property of the subsidiary (e.g., real property, shares, a partnership interest, a debt instrument, etc.) and it must not be "ineligible property". Ineligible property includes depreciable property, property transferred as part of a butterfly reorganization, and property that a subsidiary acquired from a parent or person who dealt with the parent on a non-arm's length basis.

There are several limitations to the 88(1)(d) bump strategy that may affect the type of planning chosen in a particular client's circumstances. First, the 88(1)(d) bump cannot be implemented unless the estate controls the deceased's corporation; therefore, to ensure that the bump is available, the owner should retain voting control of the freeze company whenever an estate freeze is implemented. Second, the amount by which a property can be bumped is subject to certain limitations, based on the fair market value of the property and share basis. Finally, bumps are not permitted in conjunction with tax-free divisive butterfly reorganizations; this may cause a problem where a holding company owns a portion of the shares of another holding company.

¶16121.4 — *The Pipeline*

The "pipeline" planning involves stripping surplus (to the extent permitted by ITA 84.1) as a means of avoiding double taxation on death. The pipeline transaction reduces the tax on the removal of corporate surplus to the capital gains rate applicable on the shareholder's death. To implement this planning, the estate would incorporate a holding company and sell the deceased's private company shares to the holding company in consideration for a promissory note. The two companies would then merge (by amalgamation, winding up, or redeeming the private company shares owned by the holding company and paying its assets to the holding company as proceeds for the redemption), leaving the assets of the company available to be paid to the estate in satisfaction of the promissory note. The estate will not pay any tax on the repayment of the promissory note and can distribute the acquired assets to the beneficiaries as tax-free capital distributions. The result is that corporate surplus is extracted at capital gains tax rates.

The key to the pipeline is the basis in shares recognized by ITA 84.1. ITA 84.1 is an anti-avoidance rule designed to eliminate surplus stripping by extracting corporate surplus at capital gains rates rather than as dividends (see ¶14360). ITA 84.1 deems the shareholder to receive a dividend to the extent that the sale proceeds exceed the adjusted cost base of the shares. For these purposes, the cost base of the shares is adjusted to eliminate V-day value and the cost resulting from any previous use of the capital gains exemption. The cost resulting from capital gains realized on the deemed disposition at death is recognized for the purposes of ITA 84.1 unless it is sheltered by the capital gains exemption. Therefore, the history of the shares being sold must be analyzed to determine whether any part of the cost of the shares, or shares for which the shares were substituted, is attributable to V-day value or a previous use of the capital gains exemption.

The paragraph 88(1)(d) bump procedure and the pipeline procedure are only available in respect of certain types of assets. As a result, these procedures may be of limited assistance in certain situations. As well, although the implementation of any one procedure does not necessarily preclude the implementation of any other procedure, their interaction should be considered carefully.

¶16122 — *Post-Mortem Tax Elections*

Discussed below are some of the more common tax elections that can be made after a taxpayer's death.

¶16122.1 — *"Rights or Things" Election*

With certain exceptions, where a taxpayer at the time of death had rights or things which, when realized or disposed of, would have been included in computing income, ITA 70(2) requires the value of such rights or things at the date of death to be included in computing income for the year of death. Rights or things are amounts that have been earned at the time of death, but have not yet been included in income. For example, rights or things include commissions and vacation pay owed to the deceased on the date of death and relating to a pay period that ended before death, Old Age Security benefits that were due and payable before death, uncashed matured bond coupons, unpaid bond interest earned to a payment date before death, unpaid dividends declared before the date of death, and certain work in progress of a professional (for additional examples, see IT-212R3: *Income of Deceased Persons — Rights or Things*). However, rights or things would not include RRSP income, eligible capital property and capital property, or periodic payments, such as interest payments from a bank account.

The deceased's representatives can elect to file a separate return of income to report the value of the deceased's rights or things at the time of death (ITA 70(2)). There is no prescribed form; the election takes the form of a separate return of income. All rights or things must be reported on the return, except those transferred directly to beneficiaries; they cannot be split between the final return and the rights or things return. Since each return is assessed as a separate person, the benefit of filing a separate rights or things return is that it allows for lower overall tax in the year of death because the rights or things income is subject to lower marginal rates and can access a second set of basic personal tax credits.

Where filing a separate rights or things return results in additional tax, an election can be made to pay the additional tax in instalments, although interest continues to be charged on any unpaid amounts from the due date to the date the amount is paid in full (ITA 159(5)). To request a delay of payment, security must be posted and Form T2075, *Election to Defer Payment of Income Tax Under Subsection 159(5) of the Income Tax Act by a Deceased Taxpayer's Legal Representative or Trustee*, must be filed.

¶16122.2 — *Elections in Respect of the Deemed Disposition at Death*

As a result of the deemed disposition at death, the deceased is subject to tax on all accrued capital gains on capital property owned at the date of death. However, where property is transferred as a consequence of death to the deceased's spouse or to a qualifying spouse trust, it will automatically be deemed to be disposed of at the deceased's tax cost rather than the fair market value (ITA 70(6); to qualify for the rollover, the deceased must have been resident in Canada immediately before death, the spouse or the spouse trust must be resident in Canada immediately before the death of the individual, and the property must vest indefeasibly in the spouse or the spouse trust within 36 months of the date of death). For certain types of property, the executor has the ability to elect out of the rollover, thereby realizing any accrued gains (or losses) for that property in the deceased's final return (ITA 70(6.2)).

There may be tax advantages to electing out of the spousal rollover. For example, the executor may want to elect out of the rollover for one or more of the following reasons:

- Fully utilize the deceased's personal credits and low marginal tax rates;

- Utilize net capital losses or non-capital losses that would otherwise expire;

- Utilize any remaining 1994 capital gains exemption room;

- Claim a capital gains deduction for qualified farm property or qualified small business corporation shares;

- Use donation credits or carry forward amounts; or

- Use alternative minimum tax credits carried forward from prior years.

In certain circumstances, the executor may also want to create losses to offset other capital gains realized in the year of death or previous years, or to offset other income in the year of death or in the year immediately preceding death. There is no prescribed form for electing out of the rollover. The election is made in the deceased's final tax return by reporting the disposition of each particular property for the alternate proceeds. The choice of alternate proceeds depends upon the type of property being elected on.

For capital property, the executor has the ability to choose, on a property-by-property basis, to use the fair market value of the property as the proceeds of disposition. There is no ability to choose deemed proceeds less than fair market value but greater than the deceased's tax cost, unless it is farm property which is passing to a spouse, child, or grandchild. In that case, the executor can elect to deem the proceeds of disposition to be any amount between the deceased's cost and fair market value immediately before death (ITA 70(9)–(9.3)). If the deceased owned a Canadian securities portfolio, the executor may want to make an election under subsection 39(4), depending on the accrued gains/losses on the portfolio. This election allows certain taxpayers to treat all their Canadian securities as capital property, thereby ensuring that any gains or losses on disposal will be capital in nature. The election is made by filing form T123, *Election on Disposition of Canadian Securities*, with the deceased's final return. This election is not available if the deceased was a "trader or dealer in securities".

As with other capital property owned at death, the deceased is deemed to dispose of his or her principal residence for proceeds equal to the fair market value of the property immediately before death. The gain, if any, arising on the deemed disposition will generally be eligible for a full exemption from tax pursuant to the principal residence exemption (see ¶4430). However, where the deceased owned more than one property at death that could qualify as a principal residence (such as a vacation cottage), the executor will need to make a designation as to how many years each property will be eligible for the exemption. The designation is made in the deceased's final return for the year of death, and by attaching form T2091, *Designation of a Property as a Principal Residence by an Individual*.

¶16122.3 — *Election to Untaint a Spousal Trust*

Under the terms of a qualifying spousal trust, the executor is allowed to pay "testamentary debt", which includes debts and obligations of the deceased immediately before death (such as prior years' income taxes, and any amount payable by the estate as a consequence of the death, including funeral expenses and compensation to representatives). However, if the terms of a spouse trust provide that the executor may use the income or capital of the trust to pay debts other than testamentary debt, the trust is considered to be "tainted" and will not qualify for purposes of the spousal rollover. ITA 70(7) provides rules under which such tainted spouse trusts may be "untainted" for the purposes of the rollover. To make the election to untaint a spouse trust, the taxpayer's legal representative is required, in the taxpayer's terminal return, to list certain properties that have been transferred to a trust as a consequence of the death, with a value equal to or greater than the taxpayer's total "non-qualifying debts". "Non-qualifying debt" generally means the excess of testamentary debt over the total amount of all death taxes arising on property of the trust and debt secured by a mortgage on property owned by the deceased. If this is done, the rollover will not apply to the listed properties, there will be no deferral of capital gains or losses in respect of such properties (i.e., the gains or losses will be taken into account in computing the deceased's income for the year of death), and the trust will be treated as a qualified spousal trust so as to permit the rollover of other capital properties transferred to the trust. The election must be made by the filing due date of the deceased's final income tax return; there is no provision for late filing under the Act.

The effect of the election is to restrict the rollover treatment to those assets that will be deemed to form part of the spouse trust and to subject to the usual deemed realization rules all other assets in the deceased's estate which are being used to pay debts, succession and similar duties, and other bequests or payments. One of the considerations which should be kept in mind in making the election and specifying properties for purposes of this election is the varying income tax consequences attaching to various assets for which a rollover will not apply. Generally speaking, the "listed properties" would be those with the least amount of inherent gains, since the rollover will not apply to those properties, and the remaining properties, to which the rollover will apply, would be those with larger gains.

Note that if the spouse trust is tainted as a consequence of the ability of the trustee to pay income to someone other than the spouse during the spouse's lifetime, it may be possible to untaint the trust by having the other person execute a disclaimer of his or her interest in ITA 248(8)). The disclaimer must be executed within 36 months of the death.

¶16122.4 — *Loss Carryback — Employee Stock Options Disposed of After Death*

Where a deceased employee owns unexercised stock options at death, the deceased is deemed to have received an employment benefit in the year of death equal to the value of the option immediately after death less the amount, if any, paid by the deceased for the option. Where the value of the option subsequently declines such that the amount that was included in the deceased's income in the terminal return exceeds the benefit actually realized by the estate in its first taxation year upon the exercise or disposition of the option, the executor can make an election to deem a certain amount of the loss in the estate to be a loss of the deceased (ITA 164(6.1)). There is no prescribed form for the election. To make the election, the executor files an amended final return for the deceased to adjust for the loss. ITR 1000.1 provides the manner and time in which the election is to be made. Where an election is made, the loss is deemed to be a loss from employment and will offset the employment income inclusion in the year of death. If an election is not made, the loss will be a capital loss which can only be applied against capital gains.

¶16122.5 — *Election in Respect of Reserves*

No deduction is permitted on a deceased's final return for certain amounts receivable after the end of the taxation year (for example, reserves in respect of property sold in the course of a business or a reserve for unpaid proceeds on the sale of capital property). However, if the right to receive these amounts has been transferred to a spouse or qualifying spouse trust on death, ITA 72(2) permits an election to be made to allow a deduction for a reserve that would have otherwise been allowed to the deceased taxpayer in respect of amounts receivable after the end of the taxation year. To make the election to allow a reserve to be claimed on the deceased's final return, the executor and the transferee jointly elect on form T2069, *Election in Respect of Amounts Not Deductible as Reserves for the Year of Death*.

¶16122.6 — *Election to Include RRSP Proceeds Paid to Estate as Income of Spouse*

If a deceased individual has designated his or her estate as the beneficiary of an unmatured RRSP, and the deceased's spouse is a beneficiary of the estate, the executor and the spouse can jointly elect to have the RRSP proceeds included in the spouse's income instead of the deceased's income for the year of death. The election can be for any amount up to the amount qualifying as a "refund of premiums", and the remainder, if any, would be included in the deceased's income (ITA 146(8.1)). An amount paid out of an RRSP as a consequence of death is a "refund of premiums" if the recipient was, immediately before the death of the RRSP annuitant, a spouse or common-law partner of the annuitant or a financially dependent child or grandchild (ITA 146(1)). Therefore, deferral mechanisms are also available for a financially dependent child or grandchild. See also ITA 146.3(1)"designated benefit" (RRIF election upon death); these elections are discussed in CRA Guide RC4177: Death of an RRSP Annuitant, and CRA Information Sheet RC4178: Death of a RRIF Annuitant. No election is available where the RRSP proceeds are designated to the estate and then, by the terms of the will, directed to a spouse trust or to a testamentary trust benefiting a financially dependent child. In this case, the full amount of the proceeds will be taxable in the deceased's final return.

¶16122.7 — Election for Spouse to Assume Home Buyers' Plan (HBP) or Lifelong Learning Plan (LLP) Balances

Any amounts remaining unpaid under a HBP or LLP must be included in the income of the deceased on the final return. If the deceased made any RRSP contributions during the year, these contributions may be designated as a repayment. A rollover is available where the deceased's spouse has jointly elected with the executor, in which case the unpaid amounts are assumed by the spouse and he or she will continue to make the repayments. The election is made in writing and attached to the deceased's final return for the year of death (ITA 146.01(7) and 146.02(7)).

¶16122.8 — Foreign Elections

If the deceased owned assets located outside of Canada or received income from a foreign business, there may be tax elections (or tax returns) required to be filed in the foreign country. As well, if the Canadian resident deceased is a U.S. citizen, there may be U.S. tax elections (and tax returns) that will need to be filed. A discussion of these is beyond the scope of this guide.

¶16200 — Registered Plans

Income and capital gains earned on investments held in certain registered accounts, including Registered Pension Plans, Registered Retirement Savings Plans, Tax-Free Savings Accounts (TFSAs), and Deferred Profit Sharing Plans, is not subject to taxation until funds are withdrawn from the plan. Income and capital gains earned on investments held in a Registered Education Savings Plan (RESP) or Registered Disability Savings Plan (RDSP) is also tax deferred. TFSAs, RESPs and RDSPs are discussed below. RRSPs are discussed at ¶9130.

¶16210 — Tax-Free Savings Accounts (TFSAs)

TFSAs were introduced in 2009. A TFSA is a general-purpose savings account that allows individuals to make contributions each year and withdraw funds at any time for any purpose. Any individual (other than a trust) who is resident in Canada and 18 years of age or older can establish a TFSA, and an individual is permitted to hold more than one TFSA. Income and capital gains earned within a TFSA are not subject to tax. Unlike RRSPs, TFSA contributions are not deductible in computing taxable income and withdrawals made from a TFSA are not included in the recipient's taxable income.

An individual can make annual TFSA contributions (and not be subject to a penalty) up to the amount of the individual's available TFSA contribution room for a taxation year. Beginning in 2009, TFSA contribution room accrues each year to individuals who are 18 years of age or older and resident in Canada. Unlike the RRSP system, TFSA contribution room is created regardless of an individual's income for a taxation year. The amount of TFSA contribution room that accrued each year to an eligible individual was $5,000 for 2009 to 2012, $5,500 for 2013 and 2014, $10,000 for 2015, and $5,500 for 2016 to 2018. The TFSA annual contribution limits and cumulative total from 2009 to 2018 are illustrated in the following table:

Taxation Year	TFSA Annual Limit	Cumulative Total
2009–2012	$5,000	$20,000
2013-2014	$5,500	$31,000
2015	$10,000	$41,000
2016–2018	$5,500	$57,500

Unused TFSA contribution room is carried forward and may be utilized in any future year. For example, if an individual over 17 years of age in 2009 contributed $3,000 to a TFSA each year from 2009 to 2018 (i.e., total contributions of $30,000), the individual's remaining contribution room in 2018 would be $27,500 ($57,500 - $30,000). There is no limit on the number of years that unused TFSA contribution room can be carried forward.

Available TFSA contribution room also includes the amount of distributions made under the TFSA in the preceding year. Thus, individuals who access their TFSA savings have the ability to recontribute an equivalent amount to a TFSA in the future. For example, if an individual contributed $5,000 to a TFSA in 2009, and by 2020, the value of the TFSA grew to $20,000, the individual could withdraw the $20,000 from their TFSA and then re-contribute the same amount at a later date without affecting their TFSA contribution room. However, note that amounts withdrawn in a taxation year do not increase TFSA room until the subsequent taxation year.

Taxes are imposed on excess contributions made to a TFSA (ITA Part XI.01). Similar to RRSPs, excess contributions are subject to a tax of 1 per cent per month. The amount of TFSA contribution room available to an individual for a year is not specifically defined; rather, contribution room is essentially the amount of contributions that the individual can make in the year without creating an "excess amount". Taxes are also imposed under Part XI.01 on contributions made by an individual to a TFSA while the individual was non-resident, in respect of investing in non-qualified or prohibited investments, and in connection with extending supplementary advantages, including deliberate over-contributions (see discussion under ¶16250). A TFSA is generally permitted to hold the same investments as an RRSP.

ITA 146.2(6) provides that if a TFSA "carries on one or more businesses", then Part I tax is payable on its business income. This has been a focus of CRA audit and reassessment activities targeting taxpayers who are actively trading securities in their TFSA. The CRA provided the following update at the 2017 STEP Canada National Conference regarding these audit and reassessment activities (VD 2017-0693341C6):

> The CRA is committed to maintaining a compliance presence on high risk TFSA transactions to ensure that the provisions of the *Income Tax Act* are respected. To date, the CRA has reassessed more than $75 million in additional taxes resulting from audits of TFSAs.

> In 2016, the CRA released Income Tax Folio S3-F10-C1 *Qualified Investments — RRSPs, RESPs, RRIFs, RDSPs and TFSAs*, which provides information on the tax consequences of a registered plan carrying on a securities trading business. In the Folio it is explained that the determination of whether a particular taxpayer carries on a business is a question of fact that can only be determined following a review of the taxpayer's particular circumstances. Interpretation Bulletin IT-479R, *Transactions in Securities* sets out factors developed by the courts that are relevant in determining whether transactions in securities constitute carrying on a business. There is nothing unique to TFSAs when determining whether transactions in securities constitute carrying on a business.

Some additional features of TFSAs include the following:

- Since TFSA withdrawals are not included in computing income for tax purposes, income, losses and gains in respect of investments held within a TFSA, as well as amounts withdrawn, will not be taken into account in determining eligibility for income-tested benefits or credits (such as, for example, the Canada Child Benefit, the GST credit, OAS benefits, the Guaranteed Income Supplement, or Employment Insurance benefits);

- Funds available in an individual's TFSA can be withdrawn tax-free at any time for any purpose, and an individual is permitted to re-contribute withdrawn amounts. However, an individual can only re-contribute withdrawn amounts in the same year without incurring a penalty if the individual has unused TFSA contribution room — otherwise, the individual is required to wait until the following year to re-contribute a withdrawn amount;

- Interest on money borrowed to invest in a TFSA is not deductible;

- An individual can take advantage of TFSA contribution room available to them by using funds provided by their spouse or common-law partner and the spousal attribution rules will not apply to income earned in the TFSA while the funds remain in the TFSA;

- Generally, a TFSA loses its tax-exempt status upon the death of the holder of the account; however, an individual is permitted to name his or her spouse or common-law partner as the successor account holder and in such a case, the account will maintain its tax-exempt status. Alternatively, the assets of a deceased individual's TFSA may be transferred to a TFSA of the surviving spouse or common-law partner regardless of whether the survivor has available contribution room;

- On the breakdown of a marriage or a common-law partnership, an amount may be transferred directly from the TFSA of one party to the TFSA of the other party on a tax-free basis (the transfer will not re-instate contribution room of the transferor, and will not reduce the contribution room of the transferee);

- An individual who becomes non-resident can maintain his/her TFSA; however, no contributions are permitted while the individual is non-resident and contribution room will not accrue for any year throughout which the individual is non-resident (a non-resident who is the holder of a self-directed TFSA can instruct the TFSA to invest funds that were previously contributed to the TFSA at a time when the holder was resident in Canada, since the reinvestment of existing funds does not constitute a new contribution to the TFSA — VD 2017-0685071E5);

- The CRA reports TFSA contribution room to eligible individuals who file an annual tax return (unused TFSA contribution room is carried forward and accumulates for future years); and

- Generally, financial institutions eligible to issue RRSPs are permitted to issue TFSAs.

146.2, canada.ca/en/revenue-agency/services/tax/individuals/topics/tax-free-savings-account.html, Guide RC4466, Guide RC4477, IC 18-1, Folio S3-F10-C1, Folio S3-F10-C2, Folio S3-F10-C3, Basi, "Treatment of Registered Assets on Death — RESPs and TFSAs", 2015 STEP Canada National Conference, Marino et al, "Typical Issues When a US Person Is Part of the Mix," in *2015 Prairie Provinces Tax Conference* (Toronto: Canadian Tax Foundation, 2015), 3:1–33, Office of the Parliamentary Budget Officer, "The Tax-Free Savings Account", Feb 24, 2015, Reed, "TFSA: US Tax Classification" (2014) vol. 22, no. 7 *Canadian Tax Highlights* 5-6, Friedlan, "Tax Deferral: Old and New," 2009 *Prairie Provinces Tax Conference* (Toronto: Canadian Tax Foundation, 2009), 13:1–44, Bank, "Deferred Income Plans for the Owner Manager," *2009 British Columbia Tax Conference* (Vancouver: Canadian Tax Foundation, 2009), 13:1–37, Kesselman, "Policy Forum: Tax-Free Savings Accounts in a Consumption-Based Personal Tax," (2009), vol 57, no 3 *Canadian Tax Journal* 533–562

¶16220 — Registered Education Savings Plans (RESPs)

Under an RESP, funds provided by the subscriber are set aside in a trust to accumulate investment income that will eventually be used for the higher education of one or more beneficiaries. Contributions to an RESP are not deductible in computing the subscriber's income and are returnable to the subscriber at any time, without tax consequences, as a refund of payments. Neither the subscriber nor the trust is taxed on the income accumulating in trust on the funds; however, accumulated income is taxed in the hands of the recipient (normally a student) when paid out of the plan (normally as an "education assistance payment" (EAP)). The maximum annual amount that can be contributed to an RESP is $50,000. In determining whether the lifetime contribution limit has been exceeded, all contributions for the beneficiary are considered, even if they have been withdrawn. A penalty applies to any excess contributions. The maximum period during which contributions may be made to an RESP and the maximum period during which an RESP may be in existence are 35 years and 40 years respectively.

Generally, an EAP is a payment (other than a refund of contributions) made to a designated beneficiary under an RESP to assist the beneficiary to further his or her post-secondary education. If an RESP beneficiary does not enroll in a qualifying educational program, the subscriber can withdraw the investment income from the RESP provided certain conditions are met. Such withdrawals, referred to as accumulated income payments (AIPs), are subject to an additional tax. The amount subject to this additional tax may be reduced or eliminated where certain conditions are met.

Under the Canada Education Savings Grant (CESG) program, the federal government provides a grant of 20% of the first $2,500 of annual RESP contributions such that the maximum CESG per beneficiary per year is $500. An enhanced CESG is available to low and middle income families. In 2018, for families earning $46,605 or less, the government provides an additional grant of 20% of the first $500 (to a maximum of $100) of annual RESP contributions. For families earning more than $46,605 but not more than $93,208, the government provides an additional grant of 10% of the first $500 (to a maximum of $50) of annual RESP contributions. Contributions must be made prior to the end of the calendar year the beneficiary turns 17 for grants to be received. The maximum lifetime grant that a beneficiary may receive is $7,200. Grants are paid directly to the trustee of the RESP and are paid out to the beneficiary as part of his or her EAPs. A CESG repayment is required in respect of an RESP withdrawal if the beneficiary of the RESP is ineligible for an EAP. Where the maximum grant has not been received in prior years and a catch-up contribution is made, the maximum grant for a high-income family is $1,000, the maximum grant for a middle-income family is $1,050, and the maximum grant for a low-income family is $1,100.

Note that since unused CESG amounts are carried forward, the maximum lifetime grant of $7,200 could be received by a high-income family, for example, by making seven annual contributions of $5,000 and a final contribution of $1,000 over an eight-year period starting in the year in which the child turns 10 ($36,000 × 20% = $7,200).

The special penalty taxes in ITA Part XI.01 were made applicable to RESPs in respect of investments acquired by the trust after March 22, 2017, and investments held by the trust that cease to be a "qualifying investment" after March 22, 2017. "Qualified investments" are defined ITA 146.1(1); generally, the types of investments that are permitted to be held by an RESP are the same as those that may be held by an RRSP; see ¶16250 for more information.

ITA 146.1, canada.ca under "Education Savings", Guide RC4092, Folio S3-F10-C1, Folio S3-F10-C2, Folio S3-F10-C3, RESP Bulletin No 1R1 (January 9, 2017), RESP Bulletin No 2 (May 24, 2011), Basi, "Treatment of Registered Assets on Death — RESPs and TFSAs", 2015 STEP Canada National Conference; Marino et al, "Typical Issues When a US Person Is Part of the Mix," in 2015 Prairie Provinces Tax Conference (Toronto: Canadian Tax Foundation, 2015), 3:1–33, Magee, "Tax Planning for Post-Secondary Education", 58(2) Canadian Tax Journal 393–416 (2010); Friedlan, "Tax Deferral: Old and New," 2009 Prairie Provinces Tax Conference, (Toronto: Canadian Tax Foundation, 2009), 13:1–44; Provenzano and Ross, "RESP Withdrawals Part 1" (2009) vol 17, no 4 Canadian Tax Highlights, 8-9 and "RESP Withdrawals Part 2" (2009) vol 17, no 5 Canadian Tax Highlights, 5-6, Weigl et al, "Estate Planning and RESPs", II(5) Personal Tax and Estate Planning (Federated Press) 90–97 (2009).

¶16230 — Registered Disability Savings Plans (RDSPs)

Registered Disability Savings Plans (RDSPs) were introduced in 2007 with the stated purpose of helping parents and others save for the long-term financial security of a child with a severe disability. An RDSP is a trust arrangement under which the beneficiary qualifies for the credit for mental or physical impairment (i.e., the disability tax credit; see ¶10120). An RDSP may be set up by the beneficiary of the plan where the beneficiary is at least 18 years of age and contractually competent. In respect of minors and beneficiaries who are not contractually competent, the parent or legal guardian of the beneficiary may enter into the arrangement. Contributions can be made to an RDSP by the beneficiaries, their parents or family members, or by other authorized contributors. There is no annual contribution limit to an RDSP; however, contributions (other than certain eligible transfers from another plan) may not be made after the end of the year in which the beneficiary attains 59 years of age. There is a lifetime contribution limit to an RDSP of $200,000.

Under the *Canada Disability Savings Act* (CDSA), government contributions in the form of Canada Disability Savings Grants (CDSGs) and Canada Disability Savings Bonds (CDSBs) may be paid into an RDSP. Without considering carryforward entitlement room, the maximum annual CDSG is $3,500 and the maximum annual CDSB is $1,000. The maximum annual CDSG is available when $1,500 is contributed to an RDSP; however, for families with a net income greater than the second personal tax bracket ($93,208 in 2018), the maximum CDSG is $1,000. The CDSB is not dependent upon contributions (i.e., CDSBs may be received simply by setting up an RDSP account); however, CDSB eligibility is fully phased out when family net income reaches the first personal tax bracket ($46,605 for 2018). In respect of an RDSP beneficiary, the maximum lifetime CDSG is $70,000 and the maximum lifetime CDSB is $20,000. CDSGs and CDSBs will not be paid into an RDSP after the end of the year in which the beneficiary reaches 49 years of age. An RDSP calculator is available at rdsp.com/calculator/.

A 10-year carryforward period applies in respect of CDSG and CDSB entitlements. Upon the settlement of an RDSP, CDSB entitlements are determined and paid into the plan in respect of the preceding 10 years based on the beneficiary's family income in those years (as mentioned above, a contribution to the RDSP is not required). Also, balances of unused CDSG entitlements are maintained and carried forward, and when contributions are made, CDSGs are paid in respect of unused entitlements (up to an annual maximum of $10,500).

The RDSP system is generally based on the RESP system. Income earned in an RDSP, including government grants and bonds, is not subject to tax while held in the trust and contributions to an RDSP are not tax-deductible. Contributions to an RDSP can be withdrawn on a tax-free basis; however, withdrawals from the plan attributable to government grants and to investment income earned on the plans assets are subject to taxation when withdrawn (little or no tax may be payable, however, by the RDSP beneficiary if the beneficiary has limited taxable income). Each payment made from an RDSP is considered to be comprised of a taxable portion (attributable to grants and bonds and investment income) and a non-taxable portion (attributable to contributions). Payments to RDSP beneficiaries are known as disability assistance payments (DAPs). Lifetime disability assistance payments (LDAPs) are DAPs that, once started, are payable at least annually until the plan is terminated or the beneficiary has died. Both types of payments may be composed of a portion that is taxable in the hands of an RDSP beneficiary (grants, bonds and investment earnings) and a portion that is not (contributions). Withdrawals from the plan must begin no later than the year in which the beneficiary turns 60 years of age.

An RDSP is intended to be utilized as a long-term savings vehicle. As such, generally, whenever funds are withdrawn from an RDSP, all grants and bonds paid into the RDSP during the 10 years before the withdrawal must be repaid. Additionally, withdrawals from an RDSP are not permitted if the withdrawals would result in the fair market value of the plan's assets falling below the "assistance holdback amount" (unless the beneficiary has a "shortened life expectancy" of five years or less). A government grant repayment may also be required if the beneficiary loses their eligibility for the disability tax credit, the beneficiary under the plan dies, the RDSP is terminated, or the plan ceases to be an RDSP.

RDSP beneficiaries with shortened life expectancies (five years or less) are allowed to make withdrawals without the requirement to repay the assistance holdback amount, if the taxable portion of the withdrawals does not exceed $10,000 per year. A medical doctor must certify as to the life expectancy, and the holder of the plan can elect for the RDSP to become a specified disability saving plan.

Other important features of RDSPs include the following:

- There cannot be more than one RDSP in respect of a particular beneficiary at any given time;

- There is generally no restriction on who can contribute to an RDSP;

- If the beneficiary of an RDSP either ceases to be eligible for the disability credit or dies, the funds in the RDSP (net of any required government repayments) are required to be paid to the beneficiary or pass to the beneficiary's estate (as the case may be);

- A rollover is available for amounts deposited to an RDSP in respect of proceeds from a retirement savings plan of a deceased parent or grandparent of the RDSP beneficiary (such RDSP contributions do not attract CDSGs and are included in the beneficiary's income when withdrawn from the RDSP);

- Amounts paid out of an RDSP are not taken into account for the purposes of calculating income-tested benefits, including the GST/HST credit and the Canada Child Benefit;

- In all provinces and territories, RDSPs have little or no impact on social assistance payments; and

- RDSP payments do not reduce Old Age Security or Employment Insurance benefits.

The special penalty taxes in ITA Part XI.01 were made applicable to RDSPs in respect of investments acquired by the trust after March 22, 2017, and investments held by the trust that cease to be a "qualifying investment" after March 22, 2017. "Qualified investments" are defined ITA 146.4(1); generally, the types of investments that are permitted to be held by an RDSP are the same as those that may be held by an RRSP; see ¶16250 for more information.

ITA 146.4, Guide RC4460, Folio S3-F10-C1, Folio S3-F10-C2, Folio S3-F10-C3, IC 99-1R1, RDSP Bulletins Nos. 1 (May 24, 2011), 2R2 (2015), 3R1 (2015), 4 (2013), Registered Plans Compliance Bulletin Nos. 6r1 (2012), 7 (2011). Kinnear, "Treatment of registered assets on death — Locked-in accounts, RPPs and RDSPs", 2015 STEP Canada National Conference; Adlington, "RDSP Planning", 10(6) *Tax Hyperion* 4–6 (June 2013); Watson, "RDSP or Henson Trust — Which Is Right for Your Client?", *Tax Hyperion*, Vol 9–12, Dec 2012, Friedlan, "Tax Deferral: Old and New," *2009 Prairie Provinces Tax Conference* (Toronto: Canadian Tax Foundation, 2009), 13:1–44, Golombek, "Planning with Registered Disability Savings Plans", 57(2) *Canadian Tax Journal* 338–360 (2009).

¶16240 — Comparing Registered Plans

Whether an individual should invest in a TFSA, an RRSP, an RESP, an RDSP, or a combination of each depends on many factors, including savings needs, cash flow needs, investment return expectations, and whether the individual has dependents (in particular, a child who is expected to attend secondary school or a disabled child). A common aspect of all registered plans is that investment income that accrues within the plan is sheltered from tax, which provides a significant tax advantage when comparing registered and non-registered investment accounts. TFSAs will normally be attractive for individuals that have used all of their RRSP room (and RESP and RDSP government grant room, where applicable) in a taxation year. Also, TFSAs may be particularly attractive to retirees who no longer have RRSP contribution room or child education savings needs.

Further to the above, unlike RRSPs, payments made out of a TFSA are not included in computing income (also, TFSA withdrawals do not affect income-tested benefits and can be re-contributed to a TFSA without affecting contribution room). However, contributions to a TFSA are not deductible in computing income. RRSP contributions are deductible in computing income (provided sufficient RRSP contribution room is available); however, RRSP withdrawals are included in computing income and can affect income tested benefits. Also, RRSP contributions are subject to withdrawal requirement rules at the end of the year in which the individual attains 71 years of age. Assuming an individual's marginal tax rate will be lower in retirement, investing in an RRSP will normally be more attractive than investing in a TFSA. However, if RRSP contribution room is fully utilized and an individual has additional funds on-hand, investing in a TFSA will generally be beneficial, unless the individual desires to invest in an RESP or an RDSP.

Contributions to TFSAs, RESPs, and RDSPs are not deductible in computing income. Unlike TFSAs, where certain conditions are met, contributions (within certain limits) to RESPs and RDSPs attract government grants. However, investment income earned while investments are held in an RESP or an RDSP, in addition to government grants paid into the plan, are taxable upon withdrawal. Nonetheless, the funds are normally taxable in the hands of a low-income beneficiary and may attract little or no tax. TFSA withdrawals are not included in computing income.

The following table compares various features of RRSPs and TFSAs:

RRSPs	TFSAs
Contributions are tax-deductible	Contributions are not tax-deductible
Withdrawals are taxable	Withdrawals are tax-free
Contribution room is based on earned income	Contribution room is not income-based
Indefinite carry-forward room	Indefinite carry-forward room
Income is sheltered from tax	Income is sheltered from tax
Must roll to RRIF after age 71	Permitted past age 71
Cannot contribute and withdraw (unless HBP or LLP)	Can contribute and withdraw (amounts withdrawn from TFSA in a year is added to TFSA room for the following year)
Intended for retirement savings	Intended for saving for shorter-term goals

¶16250 — Taxes in Respect of Registered Plans

ITA Part XI.01 (207.01–207.07) contains rules that restricts investments that can be held in registered plans, including RRSPs, RESPs, RRIFs, RDSPs and TFSAs. In particular, these registered plans may invest only in property that is a qualified investment and must not invest in property that is a prohibited investment. In addition, they must avoid investments or transactions that are structured so as to artificially shift value into or out of the plan or result in certain other supplementary advantages.

Folio S3-F10-C1, *Qualified Investments — RRSPs, RESPs, RRIFs, RDSPs and TFSAs*, provides information on the most common types of property that constitute a qualified investment and the tax consequences of acquiring, holding and disposing of a non-qualified investment. With respect to what constitutes a qualified investment for an RRSP, RESP, RRIF, RDSP and TFSA, Folio S3-F10-C1 provide as follows:

1.4 The following are common types of qualified investments:

- money, GICs and other deposits;

- most securities listed on a designated stock exchange, such as shares of corporations, warrants and options, and units of exchange-traded funds and real estate investment trusts;

- mutual funds and segregated funds;

- Canada Savings Bonds and provincial savings bonds;

- debt obligations of a corporation listed on a designated stock exchange;

- debt obligations that have an investment grade rating; and

- insured mortgages or hypothecs.

1.5 While the Act and Regulations set out the types of investments that are qualified investments, many firms have internal policies that further limit the types of qualified investments that may be held by the registered plans they administer. The legislation does not prohibit them from having such policies, which reflect the business decisions of the firm.

1.6 Given the numerous and wide variety of investments that exist, the CRA does not maintain a master list of specific investments that are qualified investments, nor does it make determinations as to whether a specific investment qualifies except in the context of an advance income tax ruling or audit.

1.7 Registered plan trustees are responsible for monitoring investments to minimize the possibility of a plan holding a non-qualified investment.

. . .

1.10 The types of property that constitute a qualified investment for an RRSP, RESP, RRIF, RDSP and TFSA are described in the respective definitions of qualified investment in subsections 146(1), 146.1(1), 146.3(1), 146.4(1) and 207.01(1). Those definitions also include by reference certain property described in the definition of qualified investment in section 204. In addition, investments prescribed by section 4900 of the Regulations are qualified investments. It is possible for an investment to qualify under more than one provision. The list of qualified investments is generally the same for all five types of registered plans discussed in this Chapter. Where there are differences, this has been noted in the description of the particular investment. The table in ¶1.100 lists the specific statutory or regulatory authority for each type of qualified investment described in the Chapter.

1.11 Generally, the conditions that must be met for an investment to be a qualified investment apply on an on-going basis. However, several provisions contain conditions that apply only at a point in time, typically on acquisition of the investment by the registered plan. Where this is the case, it has been noted in the section of the Chapter describing that investment.

Non-qualified investments would include, for example, land and general partnership units.

Folio S3-F10-C2, *Prohibited Investments — RRSPs, RESPs, RRIFs, RDSPs and TFSAs*, discusses the meaning of a prohibited investment, as well as the tax consequences of acquiring, holding and disposing of prohibited investments. Folio S3-F10-C2 discusses the definition of a prohibited investment as follows:

2.5 A prohibited investment for a registered plan is defined in subsection 207.01(1) as any of the following:

- a debt of the controlling individual of the plan [i.e., the annuitant of an RRSP or RRIF, the subscriber of an RESP, or the holder of an RDSP or TFSA]

- a debt or share of, or an interest in, a corporation, trust or partnership in which the controlling individual has a significant interest (see ¶2.6 to 2.15)

- a debt or share of, or an interest in, a person or partnership with which the controlling individual does not deal at arm's length

- an interest (or for civil law a right) in, or a right to acquire, a debt, share or interest described in any of the preceding bullets

A prohibited investment also includes certain prescribed property (see ¶2.16). There are also three categories of excluded property, notably insured mortgages or hypothecs (see ¶2.18). The conditions for an investment to be a prohibited investment apply on an ongoing basis.

Significant interest

2.6 The concept of significant interest is relevant in determining whether a particular investment is a prohibited investment for an individual's registered plans. Subsection 207.01(4) sets out the circumstances in which an individual has a significant interest in a corporation, trust or partnership. Each of these is discussed below, but in general, an interest of at least 10% is considered a significant interest.

. . .

Prescribed property

2.16 Property prescribed by subsection 4900(15) of the Regulations is also a prohibited investment. Under this provision, shares of certain small business corporations, venture capital corporations or co-operative corporations that are a qualified investment for an RRSP, RESP, RRIF or TFSA solely because of subsection 4900(14) of the Regulations will become a prohibited investment in the event the qualification conditions in any of subparagraphs 4900(14)(a)(i) to (iii) are no longer met. This could occur, for example, if a specified small business corporation were to stop carrying on an active business.

If an investment is both a non-qualified investment and a prohibited investment, ITA 207.04(3) deems the investment to be a prohibited investment only.

If a registered plan acquires a non-qualified or prohibited investment or an existing investment becomes non-qualified or prohibited, the controlling individual of the plan (i.e., the annuitant of an RRSP or RRIF, the subscriber of an RESP, or the holder of an RDSP or TFSA) is subject to a tax under ITA 207.04 equal to 50 per cent of the fair market value of the non-qualified or prohibited investment at that time. Individuals liable for the tax for any calendar year must file Form RC339, *Individual Return for Certain Taxes for RRSPs or RRIFs, RESPs or RDSPs* or Form RC243, *Tax-Free Savings Account (TFSA) Return*, as applicable. The form, together with any balance due, must be submitted by no later than June 30 of the following year. The 50 per cent tax on non-qualified or prohibited investments is refundable in certain circumstances. To qualify for the refund, the investment must be disposed of before the end of the calendar year following the year in which the tax arose (or such later time as is permitted by the Minister of National Revenue); however, no refund is available if it is reasonable to consider that the controlling individual knew or ought to have known that the investment was, or would become, non-qualified or prohibited.

In addition to the 50 per cent tax on the value of a non-qualified or prohibited investment, the controlling individual of the plan may be subject to a 100 per cent "advantage tax" on specified non-qualified or prohibited investment income. Generally, specified non-qualified investment income is any subsequent generation income or capital gain derived from an amount that was previously taxed in the plan or any other plan of the individual (i.e., income or a capital gain on a non-qualified investment or income from a business carried on by the plan). The advantage tax rules are discussed in Folio S3-F10-C3, *Advantages — RRSPs, RESPs, RRIFs, RDSPs and TFSAs*.

In late 2016, the CRA announced a change in its position with respect to the tax consequences of investment management fees for RRSPs, RRIFs and TFSAs that are paid outside of a registered plan. In the CRA's view, investment management fees represent a liability of the registered plan, and thus would be expected to be paid by the trustee using funds from within the plan. If paid outside of the plan, it is the CRA's view that the resulting indirect increase in value of the plan assets would likely constitute an "advantage" under ITA 207.01(1). However, in October 2018, the CRA announced that it is deferring implementation of this administrative policy, pending completion of a review of the issue by the Department of Finance. Accordingly, paragraph 3.35 of Folio S3-F10-C3, *Advantages — RRSPs, RESPs, RRIFs, RDSPs and TFSAs*, provides that comments on the tax treatment of fees and expenses incurred in connection with a registered plan and its investments will be included in a future update to the Folio (see VDs 2016-0670801C6, 2017-0722391E5 and 2018-0779261E5).

ITA 207.01–207.07, Folio S3-F10-C1, Folio S3-F10-C2, Folio S3-F10-C3, Form RC243, Form RC339

¶16300 — U.S. Tax Considerations for Canadians with U.S. Connections

¶16310 — U.S. Income Tax

Generally, a Canadian individual can be considered a U.S. resident for U.S. income tax purposes if the individual has a green card or meets the "substantial presence" test. An individual will have a substantial presence in the U.S. where the individual spends at least 31 days in the U.S. during a taxation year, and where the result of a prescribed formula for presence in the United States is equal to or greater than 183 days.

The prescribed formula for a taxation year is:

- the sum of an individual's days present in the U.S. in the current year; plus

- 1/3 of the number of days present in the U.S. in the first year before the current year; plus

- 1/6 of the number of days present in the U.S. in the second year before the current year.

Certain days present in the U.S. are excluded for this test, including:

- days an individual spends commuting to his or her workplace in the U.S. for at least 75% of total workdays in the year;

- days an individual remains in the U.S. beyond an intended stay due to a medical emergency; and

- days spent in the U.S. by certain students.

However, an individual who meets the substantial presence test will not be considered a U.S. resident if, for the entire year, the individual has a closer connection to a foreign country (i.e., Canada). To have a closer connection to Canada in a particular year, the individual must:

- Be present in the U.S. for less than 183 days during the calendar year;

- Have a tax home in Canada for the entire year;

- Establish a closer connection to the Canadian tax home compared to the U.S. home; and

- File U.S. Form 8840, *Closer Connection Exception Statement for Aliens*, with the IRS by the tax return due date (including any extensions to file), which is April 15, extended to June 15 for individuals with no U.S. source employment income.

This means that a retired Canadian who regularly spends four months a year in Florida, for example, would be considered a U.S. resident under the substantial presence test, and should file Form 8840 in order to avoid being treated as a U.S. resident and subject to U.S. income tax on worldwide income.

If an individual is considered a resident of both Canada and the U.S. under each country's domestic tax law, double taxation on worldwide income can be avoided by being treated as a resident of either the U.S. or Canada under the Canada-U.S. Tax Treaty. Non-resident individuals taking advantage of the tax treaty to reduce their U.S. tax liability, including those claiming non-resident status under the treaty, are required to file a Treaty-Based Return (Form 8833) with their Form 1040NR, *U.S. Non-resident Alien Income Tax Return*. This return is due on April 15 of the following year for individuals with U.S. source wage income, or June 15 of the following year in all other cases. Failure to file a treaty disclosure return could result in a minimum penalty of US$1,000.

¶16320 — U.S. Estate Tax

Canadian residents may be subject to U.S. estate tax if they die owning U.S. assets, including U.S. real estate and shares of U.S. corporations. In 2018, U.S. estate tax will apply on the value of a Canadian resident deceased's U.S. property only if the deceased's worldwide gross estate exceeds US$11.18 million.

¶16321 — *Assets Subject to U.S. Estate Tax*

Unlike Canadian taxes at death, U.S. estate tax is applied to the fair market value of the assets subject to the tax rather than the accrued capital gain on the property. For Canadian residents (who are not U.S. citizens), U.S. estate tax is imposed on the fair market value of U.S. situs property. U.S. situs property for U.S. estate tax purposes includes:

- U.S. real estate, including vacation properties, rental properties, private homes and business properties;

- Tangible personal property located in the U.S. at death, including cars, boats, jewelry and furnishings;

- Shares and options of private or public U.S. corporations (even if held in a Canadian account, registered or non-registered);

- Debt obligations of U.S. individuals, corporations, partnerships, trusts, or government;

- U.S. mutual funds including money market funds; and

- U.S. pension plans and annuities, including IRA's and 401(k) plans.

However, not all assets associated with the U.S. are considered to be U.S. situs assets. The following assets are excluded from U.S. estate tax for Canadians:

- U.S. publicly traded bonds;

- U.S. Treasury Bills;

- U.S. bank accounts, unless connected with a U.S. business;

- U.S. life insurance policy on the life of a non-resident alien of the U.S.;

- Canadian mutual funds investing in U.S. equities; and

- American depository receipts (ADRs).

For U.S. residents and U.S. citizens (including U.S. citizens resident in Canada), U.S. estate tax is imposed on the fair market value of an individual's worldwide estate at death, which includes "all property, real or personal, tangible or intangible, wherever situated." This is a very broad definition. It includes commonly held assets such as real estate, stocks and bonds, cash, debts held, and insurance on the decedent's life. It also includes the value of certain gifts made by the decedent within three years of the decedent's death, transfers with a retained life estate, transfers taking effect at death, revocable transfers, and property over which the decedent possessed a general power of appointment.

¶16322 — *Deductions and Credits Against U.S. Estate Tax*

Deductions can be taken against the value of the estate subject to estate tax for certain expenses, indebtedness, taxes, and bequests of the decedent. U.S. persons receive a deduction for the full amount of the expense or debt. Canadian residents receive a pro-rated deduction, based on the ratio of U.S. assets to worldwide assets. Allowable deductions include the following: funeral expenses; estate administration expenses (including legal and accounting fees, probate fees, and valuation fees); debts of the decedent; income tax liability at death; unpaid mortgages and other property liens; bequests to a U.S. citizen spouse; and charitable bequests. The gross estate less the above-noted deductions results in an individual's "taxable estate" subject to U.S. estate tax.

U.S. persons receive a unified credit against U.S. estate tax. The unified estate tax credit, exemption amount, and highest marginal estate tax rates applicable to U.S. persons for 2015 to 2018 are illustrated in the table below.

Calendar Year	Unified U.S. Estate Tax Credit (US$)	Exemption Amount (US$)*	Highest U.S. Estate Tax Rate (%)
2015	$2,117,800	$5,430,000	40%
2016	$2,125,800	$5,450,000	40%

Calendar Year	Unified U.S. Estate Tax Credit (US$)	Exemption Amount (US$)[*]	Highest U.S. Estate Tax Rate (%)
2017	$2,141,800	$5,490,000	40%
2018	$4,417,800	$11,180,000	40%

Notes:

* The *Tax Cuts and Jobs Act* (TCJA) increased the U.S. estate tax exemption amount to $11.18 million for 2018 (to be indexed annually), effective for 2018 through 2025.

The unified U.S. estate tax credit amount in the above table is available only to U.S. persons. The estate tax unified credit for Canadian residents is US$13,000, which is equivalent to the U.S. estate tax on a taxable estate of US$60,000. However, the Canada-United States Tax Treaty increases the unified credit for Canadian residents. Under the Treaty, Canadian residents are entitled to the same unified credit as a U.S. person, pro-rated based on the ratio of U.S. situs assets to worldwide assets, as illustrated by the following formula:

[Gross value of the U.S. situs property/Gross value of worldwide assets] × Unified U.S. estate tax credit for U.S. persons (US$4,417,800 in 2018)

> Because of the enhanced unified credit available under the Canada-U.S. Treaty, Canadians with U.S. assets will have a U.S. estate tax liability only if their worldwide assets are valued at more than US$11.18 million in 2018.

The U.S. provides for a marital deduction (i.e., a spousal rollover) where property is transferred to a U.S. citizen spouse or to a qualified domestic trust (QDOT). There is no marital deduction for property transferred to a non-U.S. citizen spouse. There is a marital credit available under the Canada-U.S. Treaty for property transferred to a spouse or to a spousal trust, the terms of which would qualify for the marital deduction if the spouse were a U.S. citizen. This means that the spouse must have a "qualifying income interest for life" in the trust. A qualifying income interest is one in which the spouse is entitled to all the income from the property, payable annually, or at more frequent intervals, and no person has a power to appoint any part of the property to any person other than the spouse, except for a power exercisable only at or after the spouse's death. These terms are similar to the requirements for the spousal rollover for Canadian tax purposes.

¶16323 — *U.S. Estate Tax Filing Requirements*

A U.S decedent is required to file a U.S. Estate Tax Return (Form 706) if the decedent's worldwide assets at death are greater than the estate tax exemption amount in the year of death (i.e., US$11.18 million in 2018). A Canadian resident (non-U.S. citizen) decedent is required to file a U.S. Estate Tax Return (Form 706-NA) if the decedent's U.S. situs assets at death are greater than US$60,000. The estate tax return is due 9 months after the date of death, although the executor can request an automatic six-month extension of the time to file (which does not extend the time to pay). If a deceased is claiming any treaty credits (such as the enhanced unified credit and marital credit), the executor will also be required to file a Treaty Based Return (Form 8833).

> A Canadian decedent with U.S. assets at death greater than US$60,000 is required to file a U.S. Estate Tax Return and a Treaty-Based Return even if the decedent has no U.S. estate tax liability.

¶16324 — *Planning for U.S. Real Estate*

As discussed above, Canadian residents are subject to U.S. estate tax on the value of any U.S. real estate owned at death, regardless of whether the property is a vacation, rental, or business property. Below is a discussion of some ownership and planning alternatives to allow Canadians to minimize, defer, or eliminate estate tax on U.S. real estate.

¶16324.1 — Personal Ownership

Personal Ownership with Will Planning

Personal ownership may be appropriate for a Canadian if the individual's U.S. estate tax liability can be managed or eliminated through the application of the unified and marital credits available under the treaty. Since this mainly depends on the value of the individual's U.S. estate and worldwide estate, it must be determined on a case-by-case basis. Where personal ownership is combined with will planning using a special kind of spousal trust called a "restricted" spousal trust, a spouse's U.S. estate tax liability may also be eliminated. This type of will planning allows the owner to obtain the spousal rollover for Canadian purposes, obtain the marital credit under the treaty, and remove the U.S. property from the spouse's estate for U.S. estate tax purposes. To implement this type of planning, individuals' wills need to be reviewed and revised to ensure that proper will planning is in place to minimize U.S. estate tax and to coordinate Canadian and U.S. taxes at death.

Alternatively, a Canadian who owns U.S. situs property can qualify for a tax-deferred rollover if the property is transferred to a qualified domestic trust (QDOT). A QDOT is a trust that is similar in nature to a Canadian qualified spousal trust. For a trust to qualify as a QDOT: (1) the surviving spouse must receive the income from the trust at least annually, (2) no person other than the surviving spouse can be a beneficiary during the spouse's lifetime, and (3) at least one trustee must be a U.S. citizen or U.S. domestic corporation. U.S. estate tax is imposed at the earlier of the distribution of trust principal to the surviving spouse and the death of the surviving spouse. The QDOT can be structured so that it is a Canadian-resident trust. It is important to understand that the use of a QDOT does not decrease a deceased's estate tax liability, but merely defers it until the spouse's death, and that if a QDOT is used, the deceased's estate will have to forgo the marital credit provided under the treaty.

Personal Ownership with Life Insurance

If the above will planning is not appropriate in an individual's circumstances, personal ownership can be combined with a term life insurance policy to cover an individual's U.S. estate tax liability. Keep in mind that the insurance coverage may need to be adjusted if the value of the property increases or decreases significantly over time. As well, the cost of the insurance should be weighed against the potential estate tax liability. Since insurance proceeds on the life of a Canadian are not U.S. situs property, the proceeds will not be subject to U.S. estate tax; however, the insurance proceeds will reduce the deceased's unified credit amount because the amount will be included in the value of the deceased's worldwide estate for purposes of determining treaty credits.

Personal Ownership with a Non-Recourse Mortgage

Alternatively, personal ownership can be combined with non-recourse debt. For U.S. estate tax purposes, the value of a non-recourse mortgage is netted against the value of the property when determining the value of U.S. situs property. Since U.S. estate tax is based on the amount of equity in U.S. property, obtaining a non-recourse loan (mortgage) to help finance the property can reduce the liability for U.S. estate tax. "Non-recourse" refers to the fact that the only recourse that the lender has upon default of the loan is the actual property itself; the loan is not collectible against any other asset of the individual. Recourse debt does not give rise to a similar reduction in value.

¶16324.2 — Joint Ownership

Ownership as joint tenants with rights of survivorship is not a recommended form of ownership for Canadians who own U.S. real estate for several reasons. First, ownership in joint tenancy may cause unintended U.S. estate and gift tax consequences upon its creation or termination. For example, U.S. gift tax may be imposed on the creation or termination of a joint tenancy in U.S. real property between two non-U.S. spouses, depending on the date of creation or purchase, the relative contribution of funds towards the purchase by each joint tenant, and the proceeds of termination received by each spouse.

In addition, for U.S. estate tax purposes, when there is a spousal joint tenancy and the surviving spouse is not a U.S. citizen, the entire value of jointly held property is included in the decedent's gross estate unless the executor submits facts sufficient to show that the property was not acquired entirely with consideration furnished by the decedent, or was acquired by the decedent and the other joint owner by gift, bequest or inheritance. This means that if sufficient proof cannot be provided, the entire value of the property will be included and taxed at the death of the first spouse to die. As well, the entire value of the property will be taxed again at the death of the surviving spouse (assuming that the surviving spouse continues to own the property at his or her death). As well, since property held in joint tenancy passes by right of survivorship, joint ownership does not allow the spouses to undertake effective will and estate planning for U.S. estate tax.

Finally, for Canadian tax purposes, if the joint tenancy is between spouses, the deemed disposition of the property at death will not occur until the death of the second spouse. This may result in foreign tax credit problems if U.S. estate tax is triggered on the first spouse's death.

If individuals already own U.S. real estate in joint tenancy and both spouses have contributed equally to its purchase, they may want to consider severing the joint tenancy so that they own the property as tenants in common. With this type of ownership, each spouse is only subject to estate tax on 50% of the value of the property. Alternatively, if one spouse has contributed all of the funds towards the purchase of the property, the joint tenancy can be severed, making the contributing spouse the sole owner of the property without giving rise to any U.S. gift tax or Canadian tax implications. Once the property is owned individually, the owner can undertake will and estate planning for U.S. estate tax.

¶16324.3 — Canadian Discretionary Trust

An alternative ownership option is to use an irrevocable Canadian discretionary trust to own U.S. real estate. If the trust is structured properly, no U.S. estate tax will be payable when either spouse dies. Generally, the trust should be set up before the purchase of the property; therefore, it is not an option for real estate that is already owned before the trust is created. This type of trust would generally be established as follows:

- The individual would gift the necessary funds to the trust to allow it to purchase the U.S. property;

- The spouse is the income beneficiary and is given the right to use the property during his or her lifetime;

- The spouse and children can be capital beneficiaries of the trust, and the trustees are given the discretion to encroach on trust capital. The spouse's right to capital should be based on an ascertainable standard such as income payable for health, education, maintenance, and support;

- The spouse can be a trustee of the trust but cannot have a general power of appointment over the trust's property; and

- The trust should be structured such that the contributor is not a beneficiary or a trustee of the trust and does not have a general power of appointment over the assets of the trust.

If this arrangement is set up properly, the U.S. property will not be included in either spouse's estate for U.S. estate tax purposes; however, since the individual cannot be a beneficiary of the trust, this plan essentially requires the individual to give the U.S. property away to his or her family. The family trust structure should be considered in conjunction with, and should be consistent with, an individual's estate plan.

There are some Canadian tax consequences to consider with respect to this type of ownership structure. First, for Canadian income tax purposes, the attribution rules must be considered when property is transferred to a trust for the benefit of family. In the trust described above, the trust's income and capital gains should not be attributed to the contributor, because the contributor is neither a trustee nor a beneficiary of the trust. Secondly, when a beneficiary is given the use of the trust's real estate and the trust pays the upkeep costs, maintenance and taxes relating to the property out of the trust's income, the beneficiary may be considered to have received a taxable benefit equivalent to the amount spent by the trust on these expenses. This provision will not apply if the trust does not earn any income, but to avoid the possible application of a taxable benefit, it may be best to have the spouse pay the operating expenses.

In addition, the trust will be considered to have disposed of its property for proceeds equal to fair market value on the 21st anniversary of the trust's creation. The trust will be subject to tax on any accrued gains on the property at that time. Therefore, planning should be in place to deal with the 21-year deemed disposition rule. For example, the trust can be structured to allow for the distribution of the real estate to the spouse or to the children before the trust's 21st anniversary date. The property can be distributed by the trust to the children at cost if they are Canadian residents at the time of the transfer. As a result, the use of a trust may not be a permanent solution to avoid U.S. estate tax.

If the trust sells the property for a gain, it will be liable for both U.S. and Canadian income tax on the capital gain at the applicable capital gains rate. The trust will receive a foreign tax credit in Canada for U.S. income taxes paid on the sale, so the trust will end up paying tax at the higher rate. Therefore, the taxes will be the same as if the property were owned personally.

¶16324.4 — Single Purpose Corporation (SPC)

A single purpose corporation (SPC) is a corporation set up by a Canadian to hold U.S. real estate in an attempt to avoid U.S. estate tax on the property. Upon death, the individual would be considered to own shares of a Canadian corporation (as opposed to U.S. property directly) and, therefore, would not be subject to U.S. estate tax on the U.S. real estate. As a result of a long-standing administrative position taken by CRA, the shareholders of an SPC were not assessed a taxable benefit for personal use of the property as long as the corporation's only objective is to hold U.S. residential real estate for the personal use or enjoyment of the shareholder. Consequently, for many years SPCs were a common entity used by Canadians to hold U.S. real estate. However, SPCs are no longer a viable structure to hold U.S. real estate since CRA withdrew their administrative position with respect to not assessing a shareholder benefit several years ago (though there is a grandfathering exception for SPC structures that were already in place at the time). As well, the corporate structure imposes a high income tax cost when the property is sold and the proceeds distributed from the corporation, and it can be difficult to unwind without adverse tax consequences, particularly if a gain has accrued on the property.

¶16325 — *Planning for U.S. Portfolio Assets*

Canadians commonly hold U.S. stock in their investment portfolio, which is also subject to U.S. estate tax, as discussed above. Below are some planning options to consider in order to minimize or avoid estate tax on U.S. portfolio assets.

Gifting U.S. portfolio assets — Canadians with shares in U.S. corporations can decrease or eliminate their U.S. estate tax exposure by gifting the shares to members of their family who have a lower net worth. For Canadian purposes, if the shares are gifted to a spouse, there is no deemed disposition and thus no immediate tax on any inherent capital gains. However, if the shares are gifted to a child, the individual will have to realize and pay tax to the extent there are any inherent capital gains. The Canadian attribution rules should also be considered when gifting to a spouse or to minor children. For U.S. purposes, the gift would not be subject to U.S. gift tax because gift tax does not apply to gifts of intangible assets from a Canadian resident (who is not a U.S. citizen).

Canadian mutual fund — Canadians with U.S. shares can decrease or eliminate their U.S. estate tax exposure by holding the assets through a Canadian mutual fund. This option allows an individual to maintain investments in U.S. capital markets, but avoid U.S. estate tax since the individual is holding shares of a Canadian mutual fund at death.

Canadian corporation — Canadians with U.S. portfolio assets can decrease or eliminate their U.S. estate tax exposure by holding U.S. shares through a Canadian corporation. The assets can be transferred to the corporation on a tax-deferred basis under section 85 of the Act. An element of double taxation may arise on the distribution of the sale proceeds from the corporation due to the reduction of the corporation's refundable dividend tax on hand (RDTOH) balance resulting from the foreign tax credit claim for U.S. taxes paid.

¶16326 — Planning for U.S. Citizens or U.S. Residents in the Family

It is becoming more and more common for Canadians to be married to a U.S. citizen, or to have children who live in the United States. Since the U.S. citizen spouse and U.S. resident children will be subject to U.S. estate tax on their worldwide estate, the Canadian's will should consider the tax implications of leaving assets directly to family members who are U.S. citizens or residents.

¶16326.1 — *Spousal Trust*

A U.S. citizen spouse will be subject to U.S. estate tax on their worldwide estate at death, including assets that were inherited from a predeceased Canadian spouse. To avoid having assets left to a U.S. citizen spouse being subject to estate tax at the U.S. spouse's death, a Canadian decedent can leave his assets to a spousal trust, the terms of which remove it from the U.S. spouse's estate for U.S. estate tax purposes. This type of planning will avoid U.S. estate tax at the surviving U.S. spouse's death on assets left to a U.S. spouse from a Canadian decedent.

To accomplish this, the terms of the owner's will would bequeath the residue of his estate to a spouse trust, under which the surviving U.S. spouse is entitled to all the income from the property, and no person has a power to appoint any part of the property to any person other than the spouse, except for a power exercisable only at or after the spouse's death. The terms of the trust are also such that the trust qualifies as a spousal trust for Canadian purposes in order to obtain the spousal rollover under the Act. This means that while the spouse is alive, he or she is entitled to receive all the income earned by the trust, and that no other person may receive or otherwise obtain the use of any of the income or capital of the trust during the spouse's lifetime. However, the trust is different from a traditional Canadian spousal trust in that the spouse can only hold a "limited power of appointment" over the trust assets. This means that the spouse will not have the ability to appoint the entire trust assets to him- or herself, his or her estate, his or her creditors, or the creditors of his or her estate.

The trust would ideally have three trustees, one of which can be the surviving spouse. The three trustees can make decisions by majority vote. If the surviving spouse is named as a trustee, the trust document should provide that the spouse cannot participate in capital distributions to him/herself beyond an ascertainable standard. If the surviving spouse is the sole trustee, provision must be made in the trust for an independent trustee or trustees to make decisions with respect to distribution of capital to the spouse beyond the ascertainable standard. If the children are also U.S. citizens or they live in the U.S. and they are also named as trustees, their discretion as trustees should also be limited to the ascertainable standard. This type of will planning removes the Canadian decedent's assets from the surviving U.S. spouse's estate for U.S. estate tax purposes.

To avoid the U.S. foreign trust rules, it may also be advisable to have a provision in the will that instructs the trustees to distribute all income and capital gains earned in the year. Under the foreign trust rules, income accumulated in the trust has an interest charge applied to it when it is eventually distributed to the U.S. beneficiary. In addition, capital gains that are accumulated in the trust and later distributed by the trust are taxed in the U.S. as ordinary income rather than at more favorable capital gains tax rates. These punitive results can be avoided if the trust distributes its income and capital gains each year.

¶16330 — U.S. Filing Due Dates, Forms, Remitting, and Penalties

The U.S. *Internal Revenue Code* (Code) (and certain other U.S. legislation) imposes many filing and payment requirements on Canadian residents with U.S. connections, and penalties and interest apply in respect of compliance infractions. The U.S. Filing Requirements Quick Reference Table, the U.S. Filing and Remitting Quick Reference

Table, and the U.S. Penalties Quick Reference Table are intended to assist Canadians with U.S. connections meet U.S. tax payment and filing obligations. Forms and Guides are available at www.irs.gov/.

Pursuant to IRS Rev. Proc. 2014-55, U.S. persons are no longer required to file Form 8891, *U.S. Information Reporting for Beneficiaries of Certain Canadian Registered Retirement Plans*, for any year, past or present. Form 8891 was generally required to be filed by U.S. persons to report contributions to, undistributed earnings in, or distributions received from, Canadian registered retirement plans, as well as to make a treaty election to defer U.S. income tax on accrued undistributed income in Canadian registered plans. IRS Rev. Proc. 2014-55 also eliminates the requirement to file Forms 3520 and 3520-A for a Canadian RRSP or RRIF.

¶16331 — *U.S. Filing Requirements Quick Reference Table*

Due Date	U.S. Form	Description	Code Reference	Comments
15-Jan	1040-ES	Fourth tax instalment	6315	Fourth U.S. tax instalment payment for prior year due
15-Mar	3520-A	Annual Information Return of Foreign Trust With a U.S. Owner	6048(b)	Form 3520-A is an annual information return in respect of a foreign (from a U.S. perspective) trust with at least one U.S. owner/grantor. Each U.S. person treated as an owner of any portion of a foreign trust under the U.S. grantor trust rules is responsible for ensuring that the trust files Form 3520-A and furnishes the required annual statements to its U.S. owners and U.S. beneficiaries. Per IRS Rev. Proc. 2014-55, Form 3520-A is not required to be filed for a foreign trust that is a Canadian RRSP or RRIF. Form 3520-A is due on the 15th day of the third month after the end of the trust's tax year (March 15 for a trust with a calendar year). The trust can request an automatic 6 month filing extension by filing Form 7004, *Application for Automatic Extension of Time to File Certain Business Income Tax, Information, and Other Returns*
15-Apr	1040-ES	First Tax instalment	6315	First U.S. tax instalment payment for current year

Due Date	U.S. Form	Description	Code Reference	Comments
15-Apr	1040, 1040NR	Income Tax Return and Remainder of Taxes Payable	6012	A Canadian resident that was an employee in the U.S. and was subject to U.S. income tax withholding is generally required to file Form 1040NR by April 15. Also, A U.S. citizen that either resided in the U.S. in the year or that was employed in the U.S. in the year is generally required to file Form 1040 by April 15. The remainder of any U.S. taxes payable for the prior calendar year are due on April 15. In respect of a U.S. citizen that lives and works in Canada, generally, the filing and payment deadline is automatically extended to June 15
15-Apr	4868	Application for extension of time to file tax return	6081	Where an individual is unable to file Form 1040 or Form 1040NR by the filing due date of April 15, the individual can file Form 4868: *Application for Automatic Extension of Time to File U.S. Individual Tax Return* to apply for a 6 month filing extension (or 4 month extension where the return is otherwise due on June 15). An individual does not have to explain why they are asking for the extension. U.S. taxes due are still due on April 15 where an extension is filed
15-Apr	2555, 2555-EZ	Foreign Earned Income Return	911	U.S. citizens and resident aliens living abroad can generally exclude a certain amount of foreign earnings from taxes (US$104,100 for 2018) and/or claim a housing exclusion. To qualify for the exclusion, the taxpayer must satisfy either (1) a "Bona Fide Residence Test" or (2) a "Physical Presence Test." The physical presence test does not require relocation to a foreign country but does require that the taxpayer live and work outside the U.S. for at least 330 days in a year. The residence (relocation) test is more complex; under the test, the taxpayer does not need to be physically outside the U.S. for a specific number of days. To claim the exclusion, a taxpayer is required to file Form 2555. Form 2555 is due on the same date (with extensions considered) as the individual's U.S. income tax return

Due Date	U.S. Form	Description	Code Reference	Comments
15-Apr	709	Gift Tax Return	6019 (see also 2501(a)(2), 6075)	U.S. citizens and residents may be subject to U.S. gift tax on gifts of any type of property in excess of an annual exclusion amount. Non-resident aliens of the U.S. are may be subject to U.S. gift tax on gifts of U.S. real estate or U.S. tangible personal property located in the U.S. in excess of the annual exclusion amount. The annual exclusion amount for 2018 is US$152,000 for gifts to a non-US citizen spouse and US$15,000 for gifts to any other recipient. U.S. residents and U.S. citizens are allowed a lifetime US$11.18 million exemption from gift tax (note that use of the US$11.18 million lifetime gift tax exemption erodes the estate tax exemption). An unlimited gift tax exemption deduction applies to transfers from one US-citizen spouse to another. Form 709 is due on or before April 15; however, a filing extension is available by filing Form 8892 (automatic six month extension). Also, if a tax return (ie, Form 1040) extension is filed, the extension also applies to the gift tax return. Where an extension applies, taxes are still payable on or before April 15.
15-Apr	3520	Annual Return To Report Transactions With Foreign Trusts and Receipt of Certain Foreign Gifts	6048	U.S. persons (U.S. citizen or U.S. resident) are required to file Form 3520 to report certain transactions with foreign (from a U.S. perspective) trusts and to report the receipt of certain large gifts or bequests from foreign persons. Reportable events include: the formation of a foreign trust by a U.S. person; the transfer of cash or other assets from a U.S. settlor/grantor to a foreign trust; the receipt of any distributions by a U.S. beneficiary from a foreign trust; a gift or bequest to a U.S. person from a non-resident alien individual or foreign estate in excess of US$100,000; and a gift from a foreign corporation or partnership in excess of a certain threshold. A U.S. person that is treated as the owner of any part of the assets of a foreign trust under the grantor trust rules is required to file Form 3520 each year. Per IRS Rev. Proc. 2014-55, Form 3520 is not required to be filed for a foreign trust that is a Canadian RRSP or RRIF. Form 3520 is due on the same date (with extensions considered) as the individual's U.S. income tax return.

Due Date	U.S. Form	Description	Code Reference	Comments
15-Apr	5471	Information Return of U.S. Persons With Respect to Certain Foreign Corporations	6038, 6046	Form 5471 is required to be filed by certain U.S. citizens and residents who are shareholders, officers or directors of a foreign corporation if certain ownership thresholds are met. There are generally four categories of persons that may be required to file this form: (1) a U.S. person who is an officer or director of a foreign corporation in which any U.S. person owns or acquires 10% or more of the stock of the foreign corporation; (2) a person who becomes a U.S. person while owning 10% or more of the stock of the foreign corporation; (3) a U.S. person who had control of a foreign corporation for at least 30 days; and (4) a U.S. shareholder who owns stock in a foreign corporation that is a controlled foreign corporation for at least 30 days and who owned that stock on the last day of the that year. Form 5471 is due on the same date (with extensions considered) as an individual's U.S. income tax return
15-Apr	8833	Treaty-Based Return Position Disclosure	6114, U.S. Regulation 301.7701(b)-7	Form 8833 is required to be filed by taxpayers making a treaty-based return position (ie, a position that a treaty overrules or modifies a provision of the *Internal Revenue Code* and thereby causes (or potentially causes) a reduction of tax on the taxpayer's tax return). A separate form is required for each treaty-based return position taken by a taxpayer. Form 8833 is due on the same date (with extensions considered) as the individual's U.S. income tax return (ie, Form 1040NR)
15-Apr	8858	Information return respecting disregarded entities	6011, 6012, 6031, and 6038	Form 8858: *Information Return of U.S. Persons With Respect To Foreign Disregarded Entities*, is required to be filed by certain U.S. citizens and residents that own a foreign disregarded entity (FDE) directly or indirectly or constructively. The tax owner of the FDE is generally the person that is treated as owning the assets of the FDE for purposes of U.S. income tax law. Form 8858 is due on the same date (with extensions considered) as an individual's U.S. income tax return

Due Date	U.S. Form	Description	Code Reference	Comments
15-Apr	8865	Return of U.S. Persons With Respect to Certain Foreign Partnerships	6038, 6046B	The following U.S. persons (citizen or resident) are generally required to file Form 8865: a U.S. person who controlled a foreign partnership at any time during the partnership's tax year; a U.S. person who at any time during the tax year of the foreign partnership owned a 10% or greater interest in the partnership while the partnership was controlled by U.S. persons each owning at least 10% interests; a U.S. person that contributed property to a foreign partnership and had a 10% or greater interest in the partnership after the transfer (or if the value of the property transferred exceeded US$100,000); or a U.S. person that had a reportable event under section 6046A during that person's tax year. Form 8865 is due on the same date (with extensions considered) as an individual's U.S. income tax return
15-Apr	8891	Information Return for Beneficiaries of Certain Canadian Registered Plans	6001, 6048(d)(4)	Per IRS Rev. Proc. 2014-55, Form 8891 is no longer required to be filed for any year, past or present.
15-Apr	8938	Statement of Specified Foreign Financial Assets	6038D	Form 8938 is required to be filed by U.S. citizens or residents who hold an interest in any specified foreign financial asset if the aggregate value of all the individual's specified foreign financial assets exceeds US$50,000. Form 8938 is due on the same date (with extensions considered) as the individual's U.S. income tax return (ie, Form 1040).
15-Apr	FinCEN Form 114	Report of Foreign Bank and Financial Accounts (FBAR)	*Bank Secrecy Act*	A U.S. citizen or U.S. resident who has a financial interest in, or signature or other authority over, any financial accounts in a country outside the U.S., if the aggregate value of the accounts exceeds US$10,000 at any time during the calendar year, is required to report that relationship each calendar year by filing Form 114 on or before April 15 of the following year. There is an automatic 6-month extension to October 15. Form 114 is not filed with a federal income tax return. Form 114 must be filed electronically. See: bsaefiling.fincen.treas.gov/NoRegFBARFiler.html.
15-Jun	1040-ES	Second tax instalment	6315	Second U.S. tax instalment payment for current year

Due Date	U.S. Form	Description	Code Reference	Comments
15-Jun	1040, 709, 3520, 5471, 8833, 8858, 8865, 2555, 2555-EZ	Income Tax Return (if extension applies)	6081	In respect of a U.S. resident or citizen that lives and works in Canada, generally, the filing deadline for Form 1040 (and related forms due on the same date) is automatically extended to June 15. A statement must be attached to Form 1040 indicating the automatic extension applies
15-Jun	4868	Application for extension of time to file tax return	6081	As mentioned above, in respect of a U.S. citizen that lives and works in Canada, generally, the filing deadline for Form 1040 and for paying U.S. taxes is automatically extended to June 15th (interest, however, is charged in respect of any unpaid taxes beginning on April 15). If, on June 15, the individual requires extra time to file their return, Form 4868 can be filed to apply for an additional 4 month filing extension (taxes are still due on June 15 where an extension is filed)
15-Jun	2350	Application for extension of time to file tax return	6081	Form 2350 may be used by a U.S. citizen or resident in Canada to ask for an extension of time to file a U.S. return if the individual expects to file Form 2555 or 2555-EZ with their return and needs time to meet either the bona fide residence test or the physical presence test to qualify for the foreign earned income exclusion and/or the foreign housing exclusion or deduction. If an extension is granted, it will normally be to a date 30 days after the date on which the individual expects to meet either of the latter tests. However, if the individual needs to allocate moving expenses, the individual may be given an extension to 90 days after the end of the year following the year the individual moved from the U.S.
15-Sep	1040-ES	Third tax instalment	6315	Third U.S. tax instalment payment for current year
15-Sep	3520-A	Information Return of Foreign Trust With a U.S. Owner (if extension applies)	6048(b)	As mentioned above, Form 3520-A is due on the 15th day of the third month after the end of the trust's tax year (March 15 for a trust with a calendar year). However, the trust can request an automatic 6 month extension of time by filing Form 7004, *Application for Automatic Extension of Time to File Certain Business Income Tax, Information, and Other Returns*
15-Oct	709	Gift Tax Return (if an extension applies)	6019 (see also 2501(a)(2), 6075)	See comments above. Generally, Form 709 is due on or before April 15; however, an extension may be filed using Form 8892 (automatic six month extension)

Due Date	U.S. Form	Description	Code Reference	Comments
15-Oct	1040, 1040-NR, 709, 3520, 5471, 8833, 8858, 8865, 2555, 2555-EZ	Income Tax Return (if extension applies)	6081	Where a Form 4868 extension (discussed above under April 15) was filed and accepted, Form 1040 or 1040-NR (and related forms due on the same date) are due on or before October 15
20th day after the transfer	8288, 8288-A	Withholding Tax Return for Dispositions by Foreign Persons of U.S. Real Property Interests	1445(a)	A withholding obligation is imposed on a purchaser or other transferee that acquires a U.S. real property interest (USRPI) from a foreign person. Generally, 10% of the gross proceeds must be withheld (certain foreign interest holders that are beneficiaries or shareholders are subject to federal income tax withholding at a rate of 35%). This withholding serves to collect U.S. tax that may be owed by the foreign person. The purchaser (or withholding agent) is required to file Form 8288 to report and transmit the amount withheld and to send Form 8288-A (Statement of Withholding on Dispositions by Foreign Persons of U.S. Real Property Interests) to each person from whom tax has been withheld. The foreign person subject to withholding must file a U.S. income tax return (Form 1040NR, 1041, 1065, 1065-B, or 1120-F) and to attach Form 8288-A to the return to receive credit for any tax withheld and to report the sale. There are certain exceptions to withholding tax applying, and the amount that must be withheld may be adjusted pursuant to a withholding certificate issued by the IRS. See Form 8288-B, Application for Withholding Certificate for Dispositions by Foreign Persons of U.S. Real Property Interests, for information about withholding certificates

Due Date	U.S. Form	Description	Code Reference	Comments
9 months after date of death	706, 706-NA	Estate (and Generation Skipping Transfer) Tax Return	6018	The estates of U.S. citizens or residents are required to file Form 706 and may be subject to U.S. estate tax if the decedent's gross worldwide estate at death is more than US$11.18 million. The estates of non-resident aliens of the U.S. (i.e., non-U.S. citizens and non-U.S. residents for U.S. transfer tax purposes) are required to file Form 706-NA and may be subject to U.S. estate tax generally if the decedent's gross estate located in the U.S. (including shares in U.S. corporations (ie, shares of corporations organized under U.S. law), U.S. real estate, and U.S. business assets) at death is more than US$60,000. See also Canada-U.S. Tax Treaty:Art. XXIX B. Form 4768: *Application for Extension of Time To File a Return and/or Pay U.S. Estate (and Generation-Skipping Transfer) Taxes*, can be filed to apply for an automatic 6-month extension of time to file Form 706

¶16332 — *U.S. Penalties Quick Reference Table*

U.S. Form	Infraction	Code Reference	Penalty
3520	Failure to file	6677, 6039(F)(c)	The penalties which may be assessed for a failure to file Form 3520 include: (1) a penalty equal to 35% of the gross value of the distributions received from a foreign trust or transferred to a foreign trust, or (2) a penalty equal to 5% per month for the amount of certain foreign gifts (to a maximum of 25%). Additional penalties may be imposed if an infraction continues after the IRS mails a notice of failure to comply with a reporting requirement (this penalty may not exceed the gross reportable amount). Penalties may be waived by the IRS if the taxpayer can show that there was reasonable cause for the failure to file
3520-A	Failure to file	6677	The U.S. owner of the trust assets (the grantor) may be subject to a penalty equal to 5% of the value of the trust assets treated as owned by the U.S. owner/grantor if the trust fails to file a timely Form 3520-A, does not furnish all of the information required, or if the Form includes incorrect information. Additional penalties may be imposed if an infraction continues after the IRS mails a notice of failure to comply with a reporting requirement (this penalty may not exceed the gross reportable amount). Penalties may be waived by the IRS if the taxpayer can show that there was reasonable cause for the failure to file

U.S. Form	Infraction	Code Reference	Penalty
5471	Failure to file	6038	A penalty may be assessed of US$10,000 for a failure to file Form 5471 by the due date. If the taxpayer is notified by the IRS of a duty to file, the penalty is US$10,000 per month up to a maximum of US$50,000. Penalties may be waived by the IRS if the taxpayer can show that there was reasonable cause for the failure to file
8833	Failure to file	6712	Failure to disclose a treaty-based return position may result in a penalty of US$1,000. Penalties may be waived by the IRS if the taxpayer can show that there was reasonable cause for the failure to file
1040, 1040-NR, 706, 706-NA, 709	Failure to file; failure to pay tax	6651, 6662	A late filing penalty of 5% of any tax due is normally applied for each month a return is filed late (to a maximum of 25% of taxes due). Also, a late tax payment penalty of 0.5% of the tax due per month for each month the payment is late, also not exceeding 25% of the total tax, may be imposed. Penalties may be waived by the IRS if the taxpayer can show that the failure is due to a reasonable cause. Penalties may be increased for fraudulent behaviour. Additional penalties may also be imposed in respect of willful attempts to evade or defeat payment of tax and for valuation understatements that cause an underpayment of tax
8288, 8288-A	Failure to file; failure to with-hold	6651, 7202, 1445	A late filing penalty of 5% of any tax due is normally applied for each month a return is filed late (to a maximum of 25% of taxes due). Also, a late tax payment penalty of 0.5% of the tax due per month for each month the payment is late, also not exceeding 25% of the total tax, may be imposed. Penalties may be waived by the IRS if the taxpayer can show that the failure is due to a reasonable cause. If a person is required to withhold tax under section 1445 of the *Internal Revenue Code*, the person may also be liable for the entire amount of the taxes that were not withheld (plus interest). Also, person may be liable to a penalty of US$10,000 for willful failure to collect and pay over the taxes due
8858	Failure to file	6038	A penalty may be assessed of US$10,000 for a failure to file Form 8858 by the due date. If the taxpayer is notified by the IRS of a duty to file, the penalty is US$10,000 per month up to a maximum of US$50,000. Penalties may be waived by the IRS if the taxpayer can show that there was reasonable cause for the failure to file
8865	Failure to file	6038	A penalty may be assessed of US$10,000 for a failure to file Form 8865 by the due date. If the taxpayer is notified by the IRS of a duty to file, the penalty is US$10,000 per month up to a maximum of US$50,000. Penalties may be waived by the IRS if the taxpayer can show that there was reasonable cause for the failure to file. Additional penalties may be imposed on Category 1 and 2 filers (see section 6038(c); there may be a reduction in allowable foreign tax credits respecting the entity)

U.S. Form	Infraction	Code Reference	Penalty
8938	Failure to file	6038D	A penalty may be assessed of US$10,000 for a failure to file Form 8938 by the due date. If the taxpayer is notified by the IRS of a duty to file, the penalty is US$10,000 per month up to a maximum of US$50,000. Penalties may be waived by the IRS if the taxpayer can show that there was reasonable cause for the failure to file.
FinCEN 114	Failure to file; failure to pay tax	U.S. Code of *Federal Regulations*	Failure to file Form 114 may result in a penalty of up to US$10,000 per violation. The penalty can be waived if the person can show reasonable cause for the violation and if the person provides a late-filed Form 114. For any person found to be "willfully violating" the requirements to file, a penalty of up to US$500,000 can also be imposed.

APPENDICES

Medical Expense Credit Quick Reference Table

Appendix A

The Medical Expense Credit Quick Reference Table lists and describes approximately 400 itemized expenses, stating if they do or do not qualify for the medical expense tax credit under section 118.2 of the *Income Tax Act*, and identifying the authority, including sections of the *Income Tax Act* and *Income Tax Regulations*, case law, CRA Views Documents, Interpretation Bulletins, Folio Views, Guides and other relevant CRA publications.

The table is intended to serve as a guideline only. Section 118.2 of the *Income Tax Act* and the *Income Tax Regulations* should be consulted for precise wording, exceptions and restrictions. Also see ¶10190 and ¶10200 of the *Personal Tax Return Guide* for a detailed discussion of the Medical Expense Tax Credit.

At the end of the Medical Expense Credit Quick Reference Table is a list of authorized medical practitioners by province or territory for the purposes of claiming the medical expense tax credit, reproduced from the CRA website. The list summarizes publicly available provincial and territorial information identifying those health care professionals authorized to practice as medical practitioners.

Current to November 2018

Item	Qualifies	Description of Medical Expense	Reference
Acne treatment	Depends	Cosmetic procedures to treat common acne would generally not qualify; however, cosmetic procedures to treat acne that is severe, persistent and disfiguring would be considered to have a medical or reconstructive purpose, and may qualify if the conditions in 118.2(2)(a) are met. See also "Cosmetic surgery"	118.2(2)(a), 118.2(2.1), 2011-0412591E5, S1-F1-C1 (paras 1.143–1.146)
Acoustic coupler	Yes	Amount paid for an acoustic coupler (prescription not required)	118.2(2)(i), CRA Guide RC4064

Item	Qualifies	Description of Medical Expense	Reference
Acupuncturist	Depends	Amount paid to an acupuncturist licensed to practise under the laws of the province or territory as a medical practitioner. The CRA's view is that a person is authorized by the laws a jurisdiction to act as a medical practitioner if there is specific legislation that enables, permits or empowers a person to perform medical services and generally, such specific legislation provides for the licensing or certification of the practitioner as well as for the establishment of a governing body (eg, a college or board) with the authority to determine competency, enforce discipline and set basic standards of conduct. In *Couture*, an acupuncturist in Ontario was held not to be a "medical practitioner" as "authorized to practice" means specifically authorized by legislation, not simply permitted. As well, in *Power*, acupuncture services performed by an unlicensed practitioner in Ontario were not eligible. However, in *Murphy*, an acupuncturist was held to be a "medical practitioner" in 2007 because Ontario had passed the *Traditional Chinese Medicine Act* (Couture was distinguished from Murphy by virtue of the enactment of the TCMA). The CRA looks for specific legislation that enables, permits or empowers a person to perform medical services	118.2(2)(a), S1-F1-C1 (paras 1.20-1.23, 1.131), 2009-0337771E5, *Couture*, [2009] 2 C.T.C. 80 (FCA, reversing the TCC), *Murphy*, [2010] 6 C.T.C. 2341 (TCC), *Power*, 2012 CarswellNat 977 (TCC), 2009-0337771E5
Air conditioner (prescribed)	Yes	Amount paid for an air conditioner to cope with an individual's severe chronic ailment, disease or disorder qualify if prescribed by a medical practitioner. The claimable portion of the expense is limited to the lesser of: 1) $1,000 and 2) 50% of the amount paid for the air conditioner. The cost of electricity used to operate an air conditioner that qualifies for the medical expense credit is not eligible for the medical expense credit. A central air conditioner may qualify under this provision; 2009-0314751E5 (document numbers provided throughout this table refer to CRA Views Documents, available in *Taxnet Pro* and *TaxPartner*)	118.2(2)(m), Reg 5700(c.3), 2007-0251291I7, S1-F1-C1 (para 1.122)

Item	Qualifies	Description of Medical Expense	Reference
Air filter, cleaner, or purifier (prescribed)	Yes	Amount paid for an air filter, cleaner, or purifier for use by an individual who is suffering from a severe chronic respiratory ailment or a severe chronic immune system disregulation to cope with or overcome that ailment or disregulation qualify (prescription required). If an air exchanger and an air purifier are separate units such that each may be purchased separately (ie, the functions of purifying and exchanging the air are not engineered to work together inextricably as one unit), the CRA's view is that only the cost of the air purifier may qualify as a medical expense under 118.2(2)(m) and 5700(c.1). If the device acts as an air exchanger in addition to an air purifier, this fact will not generally preclude it from qualifying for the medical expense credit	118.2(2)(m), Reg 5700(c.1), 2002-0140205, 2010-0379331E5, S1-F1-C1 (para 1.122)
Alberta Health Care Insurance Plan	No	See "Premiums paid to private health services plans (PHSP)"	118.2(2)(q), S1-F1-C1 (para 1.134)
Altered auditory feedback device (prescribed)	Yes	Amount paid for an altered auditory feedback device designed to be used by an individual who has a speech impairment (prescription required)	118.2(2)(m), Reg 5700(z.1), S1-F1-C1 (para 1.122)
Alternative medicine	No	The medications for which the medical tax credit is available must be prescribed by a medical practitioner	118.2(2)(n), *Banman v. R.*, [2001] 2 C.T.C. 2111 (TCC)
Ambulance service fees	Yes	Amount paid for ambulance service fees for transportation to or from a public or licensed private hospital	118.2(2)(f), S1-F1-C1 (para 1.64)

Item	Qualifies	Description of Medical Expense	Reference
Amount claimed under section 64 (disability supports deduction)	No	An amount claimed under section 64 cannot be deducted under section 118.2. Section 64 allows a deduction for various eligible expenditures paid in the year by a disabled individual for services, devices, or supports that enable the individual to perform the duties of an office or employment, carry on a business, attend a designated educational institution or secondary school, or carry on research or similar work for which a grant was received. A section 64 deduction is generally limited to the amount of disability support costs paid in the year to enable a disabled individual to earn certain sources of income less reimbursements and other forms of assistance the disabled individual received in respect of the disability support cost. Individuals do not have to be eligible for the disability tax credit to claim a deduction under section 64 (except in the case of the deduction of part-time attendant care costs). Also, the disability tax credit can be claimed in addition to a deduction under section 64	64(a)A(iv), S1-F1-C3, S1-F1-C1 (para 1.148)
Anaesthetist fees (prescribed)	Yes	Amount paid in respect of anaesthetist fees not covered by provincial health insurance (prescription required)	118.2(2)(o), S1-F1-C1 (para 1.130)

Appendix A — Medical Expense Credit Quick Reference Table

Item	Qualifies	Description of Medical Expense	Reference
Animals (specially trained to assist impaired person)	Yes	The cost of an animal specially trained to assist a patient who is blind or profoundly deaf or has severe autism, severe diabetes, severe epilepsy or a severe and prolonged impairment that markedly restricts the use of the patient's arms or legs may qualify for the credit. The animal must be provided by a person or organization one of whose main purposes is such training of animals. Eligible expenses include amounts paid for the care and maintenance of such an animal, including food and veterinary care; for reasonable travel expenses of the patient incurred for the purpose of attending a school, institution or other facility that trains, in the handling of such animals, individuals who are so impaired; and for reasonable board and lodging expenses of the patient incurred for the purpose of the patient's full-time attendance at a school, institution or other facility just described. A certificate from a medical practitioner that the animal is required by the patient is not required. The cost of acquiring and caring for a service dog to assist an individual with Post-Traumatic Stress Disorder is not an eligible expense (2016-0647181M4). However, certain expenses incurred after 2017 in respect of an animal specially trained to perform specific tasks for a person with a severe mental impairment, to assist them in coping with the impairment, are eligible (e.g., a psychiatric service dog trained to assist with PTSD); see tinyurl.com/cra-animals.	118.2(2)(l), S1-F1-C1 (para 1.92); 2010-0378461E5, 2014-0519971M4
Antiseptic	No	Amount paid for antiseptic	2009-0332141E5
Appointment cancellation fee	No	A fee paid in respect of a missed appointment with a medical practitioner	118.2(2)(a), Zaffino, [2007] 5 C.T.C. 2560 (TCC)
Artecoll injections	Depends	For expenses incurred after March 4, 2010, expenses incurred for purely cosmetic procedures no longer qualify for the credit (unless required for medical or reconstructive purposes). See also "Cosmetic surgery"	118.2(2.1), CRA 2004-0078231I7, S1-F1-C1 (paras 1.143–1.146)
Artificial eye	Yes	Including expenses in respect of (prescription not required)	118.2(2)(i), S1-F1-C1 (paras 1.73-1.74)

Item	Qualifies	Description of Medical Expense	Reference
Artificial kidney machine	Yes	Amount paid for a kidney machine, including the cost of repairs, maintenance, and supplies; additions, renovations, or alterations to a home (the hospital official who installed the machine must certify in writing that the additions, renovations, or alterations were necessary for installation); the portion of the operating costs of the home that relate to the machine (excluding mortgage interest and CCA); a telephone extension in the dialysis room and all calls to a hospital for advice or to obtain repairs; and necessary and unavoidable costs to transport supplies. A prescription is not required	118.2(2)(i), CRA Guide RC4064, S1-F1-C1 (paras 1.73-1.74, 1.82–1.86)
Artificial limbs	Yes	Amount paid for an artificial limb, including the cost of repairs and parts and other expenses in respect of (prescription not required)	118.2(2)(i), S1-F1-C1 (paras. 1.73-1.74)
Assessment, medical	Yes	Costs for a medical assessment qualify if the fee is paid to a medical practitioner. If the fee is not paid to a medical practitioner, it may qualify if it is for diagnostic purposes (2011-0427011E5).	118.2(2)(a), (o), 2011-0427011E5
Assisted breathing device		See "Iron lung"	
Associations	Yes	Payments made to partnerships, societies and associations for medical services rendered by their employees or partners qualify for the credit as long as the person who provided the service is a medical practitioner, dentist or nurse authorized to practice as a medical practitioner (for example, the Victorian Order of Nurses and The Canadian Red Cross Society Home Maker Services). The CRA has stated that "payments qualify only to the extent that they are for the period when the patient is at home. Payments for a period when the nurse is simply looking after a home and children when the patient is in hospital or otherwise away from home do not qualify since these would be personal or living expenses. In some instances, such as that of the Canadian Mothercraft Society, the visiting worker instead of the society may give the receipts but, if the worker can be regarded as a practical nurse, those receipts will be accepted."	118.2(2)(a), S1-F1-C1 (para 1.28)
Athletic or fitness club fees	No	Amounts paid for athletic or fitness club membership	CRA Guide RC4064, 2011-0402881E5, 2010-0361011E5, *Roberts*, 2012 CarswellNat 3320

Item	Qualifies	Description of Medical Expense	Reference
Attendant care (patient qualifies for the disability credit)	Yes	Amount paid as remuneration for one full-time attendant for a patient who qualifies for the disability credit, or the cost of full-time care in a nursing home for such a patient, may qualify for the credit. At the time the remuneration is paid, the full-time attendant cannot be under 18 years of age or be the individual's spouse or common-law partner. It is the CRA's view that a taxpayer's private home would not be considered a "nursing home" for purposes of 118.2(2)(b). The CRA accepts that a particular place need not be a licensed nursing home but is of the view that it must have the equivalent features and characteristics of a nursing home (see 2007-0253621E5). If a patient claims the medical expense credit under 118.2(2)(b), the patient cannot claim the disability tax credit. See also under "Nursing home (full-time care)" and 2011-0418081E5, 2009-0346431E5, 2008-0285321C6, 2005-0142361E5. See also the summary of claimable attendant care expenses in Chapter 8	118.2(2)(b), CRA Guide RC4064, S1-F1-C1 (paras 1.31–1.39)

Item	Qualifies	Description of Medical Expense	Reference
Attendant care at a retirement home, home for seniors, or other institution	Yes	Amounts paid for attendant care at a retirement home, home for seniors, or other institution as remuneration for a full-time attendant may quality. A disability tax credit certificate is required. Also, the CRA requires a detailed statement from the establishment showing the amount paid for staff salaries that apply to attendant care services. Qualifying costs include: food preparation; housekeeping services for a resident's personal living space; laundry services for a resident's personal items; health care (registered nurse, practical nurse, certified health care aide, personal support worker); activities (social programmer); salon services (hairdresser, barber, manicurist, pedicurist), if included in the monthly fee; transportation (driver); and security for a secured unit. Ineligible costs include: rent; food; cleaning supplies; other operating costs (such as the maintenance of common areas and outside grounds); and salaries and wages paid to the following employees: administrators; receptionists; groundskeepers; and janitors or maintenance staff. If a claim is made under 118.2(2)(b) rather than 118.2(2)(b.1) (limited to $10,000; see below), the disability tax credit cannot be claimed. See also the summary of claimable attendant care expenses in Chapter 8	118.2(2)(b), CRA Guide RC4064, S1-F1-C1 (paras 1.31–1.39), 2009-0346431E5

Item	Qualifies	Description of Medical Expense	Reference
Attendant care (part-time)	Yes	Amounts paid as remuneration for part-time attendant care may qualify for the credit, The attendant cannot be the patients spouse or common-law partner and must be over 17 years of age when the amounts were paid. The care must be provided in Canada and a disability tax credit certificate (Form T2201) is required. Where amounts are paid to an establishment, the CRA requires a detailed statement from the establishment showing the amount paid for staff salaries that apply to attendant care services (all amounts paid to a nursing home generally qualify). The claim is limited to $10,000 (or $20,000 if the individual dies in the year). While most claims under 118.2(2)(b.1) will be for a part-time attendant, the CRA acknowledges that expenses for a full-time attendant may also be claimed under 118.2(2)(b.1). The $10,000 limit applies to each person paying for attendant care. A person can claim the disability credit and make a claim under 118.2(2)(b.1); however, where a claim is made under 118.2(2)(b.1), no part of the remuneration can be included in computing a deduction claimed in respect of the patient under section 63 or 64 or 118.2(2)(b), (b.2), (c), (d) or (e) for any taxation year. See under "Attendant care at a retirement home, home for seniors, or other institution" regarding qualifying costs (see also 2004-0101081E5)	118.2(2)(b.1), CRA Guide RC4064, S1-F1-C1 (paras 1.31–1.36, 1.40–1.43), 2006-0172181I7
Attendant care provided at a group home in Canada	Yes	Amounts paid as remuneration for an individual's care or supervision provided in a group home in Canada maintained and operated exclusively for the benefit of individuals who have a severe and prolonged impairment may qualify. A disability tax credit certificate (Form T2201) is required. Also, the CRA requires a detailed statement from the establishment showing the amount paid for staff salaries that apply to attendant care services. A claim under 118.2(2)(b.2) does not preclude a person from claiming the disability credit; however, where a claim is made under 118.2(2)(b.2), no part of the remuneration can be included in computing a deduction claimed in respect of the patient under section 63 or 64 or 118.2(2)(b), (b.1), (c), (d) or (e) for any taxation year. See also the summary of claimable attendant care expenses in Chapter 8	118.2(2)(b.2), CRA Guide RC4064, S1-F1-C1 (paras 1.31–1.36, 1.44–1.46)

Item	Qualifies	Description of Medical Expense	Reference
Attendant care in a self-contained domestic establishment (full-time)	Yes	Amounts paid as remuneration for a full-time attendant at a person's personal residence may qualify for the credit. The attendant cannot be the patients spouse or common-law partner and must be over 17 years of age when the amounts were paid. Additionally, ether: 1) a disability tax credit certificate (Form T2201) is required or 2) a letter from a medical practitioner has to certify that the patient is likely to continue to be dependent on others for his or her personal needs and care for the long-term and needs a full-time attendant because of an impairment in mental or physical functions. Fees claimed must be for salaries and wages paid for attendant care services. If an individual issues the receipt for attendant care services, the receipt must include the attendant's social insurance number. Several attendants can qualify as one full-time attendant as long as there is only one attendant for any given period of time (2007-0253621E5). If a claim is made under 118.2(2)(c) rather than 118.2(2)(b.1) (limited to $10,000), the disability tax credit cannot be claimed. See also the summary of claimable attendant care expenses in Chapter 8	118.2(2)(c), CRA Guide RC4064, S1-F1-C1 (paras 1.31–1.36, 1.47–1.50)

Item	Qualifies	Description of Medical Expense	Reference
Attendant care (full-time at a nursing home; patient lacks normal mental capacity)	Yes	The cost of receiving full-time care in a nursing home is an eligible medical expense not only in respect of a patient with a severe and prolonged mental or physical impairment (see 118.2(2)(b)), but also in respect of a patient who is and will in the foreseeable future continue to be dependent on others for his/her personal needs and care because of a lack of normal mental capacity. Such a condition must be certified by a medical practitioner in either a letter or by completing Form T2201. An individual can generally claim the entire amount paid for full-time care in a nursing home. The care does not have to be provided in Canada. Where a claim is made under 118.2(2)(d), the disability tax credit cannot be claimed (see para 118.3(1)(c)). Though the term "nursing home" in paragraph 118.2(2)(b) does not include a retirement residence even if it provides 24-hour nursing care (see Miles Estate v. R., [2000] 2 C.T.C. 2165), the CRA accepts that where a portion of retirement home costs is identified as being paid for attendant care, it will qualify under paragraph 118.2(2)(b.1) (2005-0142361E5). A taxpayer's home also does not qualify as a nursing home. See also the summary of claimable attendant care expenses in Chapter 8	118.2(2)(d), CRA Guide RC4064, S1-F1-C1 (paras 1.31–1.36, 1.51–1.55), 2005-0149621E5, 2007-0253621E5
Audible signal device	Yes	Amount paid for an audible signal device (prescription not required)	118.2(2)(i), CRA Guide RC4064, S1-F-C1 (paras 1.73-1.74, 1.80)
Autistic child day care, school, institution or other place	Depends	For an institute to qualify, the CRA's view is that certification would need to clearly indicate that the centre has specialized equipment, facilities, or trained personnel to provide care, or care and training, of a person with an autistic disorder	118.2(2)(e), 2010-0403181E5, 2004-0065621E5, S1-F1-C1 (paras 1.31–1.36, 1.56–1.63)
Baby breathing monitor		See "Infants"	
Baby formula (prescribed)	No	Amounts paid for baby formula, even if prescribed by a medical practitioner, do not qualify if it is also available over-the-counter (see also "Over-the-counter medications").	118.2(2)(n), 2011-0399851E5
Baby wipes/moist wipes	No	It is CRA's view that the reference to "other products" in 118.2(2)(i.1) is restricted to the same class of products as diapers, disposable briefs, etc. and would not include baby wipes or moist wipes	118.2(2)(i.1), 2010-0356391E5, 2012-0437351E5, S1-F1-C1 (para 1.87)

Item	Qualifies	Description of Medical Expense	Reference
Balance disorder (prescribed device)	Yes	Amount paid for a pressure pulse therapy device designed to be used by an individual who has a balance disorder (prescription required)	118.2(2)(m), Reg 5700(z.4), S1-F1-C1 (para 1.122)
Bathroom aids		See "Device or equipment (bathtub or shower)"	
Behaviour analyst	Depends	Payments to a behaviour analyst would not qualify as eligible medical expenses unless the amounts were paid for "medical services" performed by a medical practitioner authorized to practise as such pursuant to the laws of the jurisdiction in which the service was rendered. Behaviour analysts are not authorized as medical practitioners in Ontario (2016-0633581E5).	118.4(2)(a), S1-F1-C1 (paras 1.20–1.23)
Bicycle, battery-powered	No	The CRA's view is that a battery powered two-wheeled bicycle cannot be considered a wheelchair	2009-0323571E5
Bicycle, motorized stationary	No	The CRA's view is that a motorized stationary bicycle (designed for people with medical conditions such as Parkinson's disease, muscular dystrophy and arthritis) cannot be considered a device	2012-0440931E5
Bicycle, recumbent exercise	No	The CRA's view is that a recumbent exercise bike prescribed by a medical practitioner cannot be considered a device or equipment	2014-0528671E5
Birth centre	Maybe	Payments made to a birth centre are eligible where the payment is made to a medical practitioner authorized to practise in accordance with the laws of the province or territory (e.g, a midwife)	118.4(2) 2017-0728281M4
Birth control devices	Depends	The CRA has stated that birth control pills which a medical practitioner has prescribed are considered to qualify under 118.2(2)(n) if a pharmacist has recorded the prescription	118.2(2)(n), S1-F1-C1 (para 1.127)
Bite-activated nipples for sippy-cup	No	Amount paid for bite-activated nipples for sippy-cup	2009-0332141E5
Blind individuals (braille note-taker; prescribed)	Yes	Amount paid for a braille note-taker designed to be used by a blind individual to allow them to take notes (that can be read back to them or printed or displayed in Braille) with the help of a keyboard and that is for the individual's use as prescribed by a medical practitioner (prescription required)	118.2(2)(m), Reg 5700(y), S1-F1-C1 (para 1.122)

Item	Qualifies	Description of Medical Expense	Reference
Blind individuals (guide dog)	Yes	The purchase of a guide dog for a blind individual from an institution that trains such dogs, as well as related expenses (for a list of qualifying expenses, see under "Animals")	118.2(2)(l), S1-F1-C1 (para 1.92)
Blind individuals (intervening services)	Yes	Amount paid for deaf-blind intervening services used by a person who is both blind and profoundly deaf and paid to someone in the business of providing such services	118.2(2)(l.44), S1-F1-C1 (para 1.106)
Blind individuals (optical scanner; prescribed)	Yes	Amount paid for an optical scanner (or similar device) designed to be used by a blind individual to enable him to read print (prescription required)	118.2(2)(m), Reg 5700(l), S1-F1-C1 (para 1.122)
Blind individuals (reading software; prescribed)	Yes	Amount paid for a device or software designed to be used to enable the individual to read print and that is for the individual's use as prescribed by a medical practitioner (prescription required)	118.2(2)(m), Reg 5700(l.1), S1-F1-C1 (para 1.122)
Blind individuals (special computer devices; prescribed)	Yes	Amount paid for a device or equipment, including a synthetic speech system, Braille printer and large print-on-screen device, designed exclusively to be used by a person who is blind in the operation of a computer (prescription required)	118.2(2)(m), Reg 5700(o), CRA Guide RC4064, S1-F1-C1 (para 1.122)
Bliss symbol board or similar device (prescribed)	Yes	Amount paid for a bliss symbol board or similar device designed to be used to help an individual who has a speech impairment communicate by selecting the symbols or spelling out words (prescription required). The purchase of an iPad to assist certain special needs children would not qualify for the medical expense credit, nor would a digital camera used to make Bliss symbol boards (*Henschel*, 2010 CarswellNat 1783 (TCC))	118.2(2)(m), Reg 5700(x), 2010-0383021E5, S1-F1-C1 (para 1.122)
Block fees	Yes	Block fee paid to a medical centre to cover the cost of certain ancillary or incidental uninsured medical services	118.2(2)(a), 2014-0540731E5, 2007-0255741I7, S1-F1-C1 (para 1.29)
Blood coagulation monitors (prescribed)	Yes	Prescribed blood coagulation monitor for individuals who require anti-coagulation therapy, including associated disposable peripherals such as pricking devices, lancets and test strips	118.2(2)(m); Reg 5700(s.1), S1-F1-C1 (para 1.122)
Blood pressure monitors	No	Purchase of a blood pressure monitor	CRA Guide RC4064
Blood transfusion (prescribed)	Yes	Amount paid for a blood transfusion (prescription required)	CRA Guide RC4064, 118.2(2)(a)

Item	Qualifies	Description of Medical Expense	Reference
Bone conduction receiver	Yes	Purchase of a bone conduction receiver (prescription not required). See also "Hearing aid"	118.2(2)(i), CRA Guide RC4064, S1-F1-C1 (para 1.80)
Bone marrow transplant	Yes	Reasonable amounts paid to locate a compatible donor, to arrange the transplant including legal fees and insurance premiums, and reasonable travelling costs including board and lodging for the patient, the donor, and their respective companions	118.2(2)(l.1), S1-F1-C1 (paras 1.93, 1.147)
Boots (Orthopaedic)		See "Brace (including related costs)" and "Orthopaedic shoe or boot (and an insert for a shoe or boot)"	
Botox injections	Depends	For expenses incurred after March 4, 2010, expenses incurred for purely cosmetic procedures no longer qualify for the credit (unless required for medical or reconstructive purposes). See also "Cosmetic surgery"	118.2(2.1), 2004-0078231I7, S1-F1-C1 (paras 1.143–1.146)
Brace (for a limb)	Yes	Amounts paid for braces for a limb, including woven or elasticized stockings made to measure, qualify for the credit (prescription not required). The CRA has stated that "a "brace for a limb" does not necessarily have to be something of a rigid nature, although at least one of the functions of the brace must be to impart some degree of rigidity to the limb which is being braced. Accordingly, that phrase is considered to include woven or elasticized stockings where these are of a kind that are carefully fitted to measurement or are made to measure. When a brace for a limb is necessarily built into a boot or shoe in order to permit a person to walk, the brace will be considered to include the boot or shoe. A rehabilitative splinting system to stretch the tissue in the elbow would likely qualify as a "brace for a limb" (2011-0429871E5).	118.2(2)(i), CRA Guide RC4064, S1-F1-C1 (paras 1.73-1.74, 1.77)
Brace (spinal)	Yes	Amount paid for a spinal brace (prescription not required)	118.2(2)(i), S1-F1-C1 (paras 1.73-1.74)
Braille note-taker		See "Blind individuals"	
Braille printer		See "Blind individuals"	
Breast prosthesis		See "External breast prosthesis"	
Breast pump	No	Purchase of a breast pump	2007-0248701E5
Buzzer		See "Hearing aid"	
Canadian Red Cross Society Home Maker Services		See "Associations"	
Cancellation fee		See "Appointment cancellation fee"	

Appendix A — Medical Expense Credit Quick Reference Table

Item	Qualifies	Description of Medical Expense	Reference
Cancer treatment	Yes	Cost of cancer treatments provided by a medical practitioner, including treatment received outside Canada for drugs not approved in Canada.	118.2(2)(a), CRA Guide RC4064
Cannabis		See "Marijuana or marijuana seeds"	
Car seat	No	An infant car seat, even if specially designed for a disabled child	2003-0046145
Cardiograph (prescribed)	Yes	Amount paid in respect of cardiograph tests not covered by provincial health insurance (prescription required)	118.2(2)(o), CRA Guide RC4064
Care or care and training at institutions or other places	Yes	Amounts paid for care at an institution or other place may qualify for the credit. An "appropriately qualified person" (normally a medical practitioner; preferably who does not work for the institution) has to certify in writing that the person has an impairment in mental or physical functions and confirm the person "requires" the equipment, facilities, or personnel available at the establishment. A private home adapted to the needs of its owner/occupant would not qualify as an "other place" for purposes of 118.2(2)(e) (2007-0253621E5). A retirement home was found to qualify in McKinley, [2004] 2 C.T.C. 2672 (TCC), but not in *Lister*, [2007] 1 C.T.C. 137 (FCA) or in *Shultis*, [2007] 1 C.T.C. 2182 (TCC). The expense of renting an accommodation near the school or institution would not qualify; however, transportation expenses to and from the school may qualify under 118.2(2)(g) (2009-0349551E5). A school that provides an allergy-free environment for a severely allergic student does not qualify (2013-0507021E5)	118.2(2)(e), CRA Guide RC4064, S1-F1-C1 (paras 1.31–1.36, 1.56–1.63)

Item	Qualifies	Description of Medical Expense	Reference
Care or care and training at special schools	Yes	Amounts paid for care or training at a school may qualify for the credit. An "appropriately qualified person" (normally a medical practitioner; preferably who does not work for the school) has to certify in writing that the person has an impairment in mental or physical functions and confirm the person "requires" the equipment, facilities, or personnel available at the establishment. Under former 110(1)(c)(vi), private school fees incurred for a child with behavioral problems were held to be ineligible (see *Somers v. MNR*, [1979] C.T.C. 2001 (TRB)) since there was no evidence of mental or physical handicap and the school in question was not an institution of the type specified. Also, in *Flower v. R.*, [2005] 2 C.T.C. 2730 (TCC), fees to an Academy for children with learning disabilities did not qualify. However, in *Rannelli v. MNR*, [1991] 2 C.T.C. 2040, the Court concluded that fees paid to a school for dyslexic children qualified under former 110(1)(c)(vi). Fees paid to a disciplinary school for children with attention disorders were found to qualify in *Marshall*, [2003] 4 C.T.C. 2794 (TCC). Fees paid to the Calgary Academy qualified in *Karn*, 2013 CarswellNat 1382, since the school was only for students with learning disabilities; however, tuition fees paid did not qualify in *Bauskin*, 2013 CarswellNat 342, because there was no evidence of special equipment, facilities or personnel in the school's mainstream program, nor in *Leibovich*, 2016 TCC 6, because the clinical reports failed to establish a need for special equipment, facilities, or personnel and the school did not have special programs for students with learning disabilities.	118.2(2)(e), CRA Guide RC4064, S1-F1-C1 (paras 1.31–1.36, 1.56–1.63), 2006-0213231E5, Scott, [2009] 1 C.T.C. 224 (FCA)
Caregiver training	Yes	An amount paid for reasonable expenses (other than amounts paid to a person who was at the time of the payment the individual's spouse or common-law partner or a person under 18 years of age) to train the individual (or a person related to the individual) if the training relates to the mental or physical infirmity of a person who is related to the individual *and* is a member of the individual's household (or is dependent on the individual for support)	118.2(2)(1.8), S1-F1-C1 (paras 1.113-1.114)

Item	Qualifies	Description of Medical Expense	Reference
Catheters and catheter trays	Yes	Amounts paid for catheters and catheter trays required by the patient by reason of incontinence caused by illness, injury or affliction (including catheter trays, tubing, or other products required for incontinence caused by illness, injury, or affliction); a prescription is not required	118.2(2)(i.1), CRA Guide RC4064, S1-F1-C1 (para 1.87)
Cell phone	No	A medical device or equipment that was not prescribed by a medical practitioner and that is not otherwise described in section 118.2 does not qualify	*Olney*, 2014 CarswellNat 3383 (TCC)
Certificates	Yes	Amount paid to a medical practitioner for completing and providing additional information in regard to Form T2201 and other certificates	118.2(2)(a), CRA Guide RC4064
Chair (power-operated)		See "Power-operated guided chair", "wheelchair", and "Scooter"	
Chiropodist (or podiatrist)	Yes	Amount paid to a chiropodist (or podiatrist) licensed to practise under the laws of the province or territory as a medical practitioner	118.2(2)(a), S1-F1-C1 (paras 1.20–1.23)
Chiropractor	Yes	Amount paid to a chiropractor licensed to practise under the laws of the province or territory as a medical practitioner	118.2(2)(a), S1-F1-C1 (paras 1.20–1.23)
Christian Science practitioner	No	Payments to a Christian Science practitioner where the practitioner is not otherwise a medical doctor or a nurse acting within the scope of his or her profession (none of the provinces or territories license Christian Science practitioners as being medical practitioners). Amounts paid to a Christian Science nurse authorized to practise as a nurse according to the relevant laws referred to in subsection 118.4(2) would qualify. The CRA's view is that a person is authorized by the laws of a jurisdiction to act as a medical practitioner if there is specific legislation that enables, permits or empowers a person to perform medical services and generally, such specific legislation provides for the licensing or certification of the practitioner as well as for the establishment of a governing body (eg, a college or board) with the authority to determine competency, enforce discipline and set basic standards of conduct	118.2(2)(a), 2006-0180991M4, 2005-0126931E5, 2006-0180991M4, 2007-0224311E5, 2009-0337771E5, S1-F1-C1 (paras 1.20–1.23)
Circumcision procedure	Depends	Cost of infant male circumcision would generally qualify if it can be shown that it is not done purely for cosmetic purposes	118.2(1), 118.2(2.1), 2011-0411641E5, S1-F1-C1 (paras 1.143–1.146)

Item	Qualifies	Description of Medical Expense	Reference
Clinic or corporation (amount paid for medical services)	Yes	Amounts paid to a clinic or corporation for medical services provided by or supervised by a medical practitioner	118.2(2)(a), *Mudry*, 2008 CarswellNat 715 (TCC), 2003-0045561E5, 2010-0361011E5, S1-F1-C1 (para 1.28)
Clinical counsellor		See "Counsellor"	
Cochlear implant	Yes	Amount paid for a cochlear implant (prescription not required)	118.2(2)(i), CRA Guide RC4064, S1-F1-C1 (para 1.80)
Colostomy and ileostomy pads	Yes	Amount paid for colostomy and ileostomy pads, including pouches and adhesives (prescription not required)	118.2(2)(i), CRA Guide RC4064, S1-F1-C1 (paras 1.73-1.74, 1.78)
Commodes		See "Device or equipment (bathtub, shower or toilet)"	
Complex Continuing Care Co-payments	Yes	Ontario Complex Continuing Care Co-payments paid to a public hospital by hospital patients who are waiting for placement in a long-term care facility	118.2(2)(a), 2015-0574831E5
Compression stockings	Depends	Cost of compression stockings required to be worn after treatment for varicose veins would qualify if fitted to measurement or made to measure	118.2(2)(i), S1-F1-C1 (para 1.77), 2011-0411181E5
Contact lenses (prescribed)	Yes	Amount paid for contact lenses (prescription required from a medical practitioner or optometrist)	118.2(2)(j), CRA Guide RC4064, S1-F1-C1 (para 1.89)

Item	Qualifies	Description of Medical Expense	Reference
Cosmetic surgery (purely cosmetic procedures)	No	After March 4, 2010, expenses incurred for purely cosmetic procedures no longer qualify for the credit. This generally includes surgical and non-surgical procedures purely aimed at enhancing one's appearance, such as the following: augmentations (such as chin, cheek, lips); body modifications (such as tongue splits); body shaping, contouring or lifts (such as breasts, buttocks, face and stomach); botulinum injections; chemical peels; implants (such as jewellery implanted into an eye or a tooth, or microdermal, transdermal, and subdermal cosmetic implants); filler injections for removal of wrinkles; hair removal and replacement procedures; laser treatments (such as skin resurfacing and removal of age spots); liposuction; reshaping procedures (such as rhinoplasty and otoplasty); rib removal; tattoo removal; and teeth whitening, contouring or reshaping. A cosmetic procedure will continue to qualify if required for medical or reconstructive purposes (see directly below). The CRA's former position was that an amount paid to a medical practitioner for surgery of any kind, whether cosmetic or elective, generally qualified as a medical expense.	118.2(2.1) 2004-0078231I7, 2006-0180991M4, 2010-0362981M4, 2010-0365801E5, 2011-0429431E5, 2012-0448691E5, S1-F1-C1 (paras 1.143–1.146)

Item	Qualifies	Description of Medical Expense	Reference
Cosmetic surgery (for medical or reconstructive purposes)	Yes	After March 4, 2010, expenses incurred for purely cosmetic procedures no longer qualify for the credit. A cosmetic procedure will continue to qualify if required for medical or reconstructive purposes (for example, those that would ameliorate a deformity arising from, or directly related to, a congenital abnormality, a personal injury resulting from an accident or trauma, or a disfiguring disease), including the following: breast implant and related procedures for reconstructive purposes after a mastectomy; breast reduction to reduce back and shoulder pain; dental braces, if required to correct a misaligned bite; dental veneers to correct decayed or misaligned teeth; gastric bypass surgery, gastric sleeve surgery or gastric stapling; laser eye surgery; removal of excess skin after rapid weight loss due to a risk of infection; and the treatment of melasma that is severe, persistent and disfiguring. The cost of sex reassignment surgery and related surgeries would likely qualify (2012-0463201E5). The CRA's former position was that and amount paid to a medical practitioner for surgery of any kind, whether cosmetic or elective, generally qualified as a medical expense.	118.2(2.1) 2004-0078231I7, 2010-0362981M4, 2010-0365801E5, 2010-0378051E5, 2012-0439481E5, 2013-0480831E5, S1-F1-C1 (paras 1.143–1.146)
Counsellor	Depends	The CRA has stated that counselling services are considered to qualify if: 1) the counsellor is working in a recognized mental health clinic, community agency or hospital; 2) the counsellor is a member of an association governing their profession; and 3) the treatment is at the request of, or in association with, a medical practitioner	2002-0171795, 2005-0153591E5, 2006-0213231E5
Courses, pain management	Yes	Expenses related to pain management courses if incurred for diagnosis, therapy or rehabilitation purposes in relation to a pre-existing medical problem and paid to a certified medical practitioner or public or private hospital.	2011-0397731E5
Crutches	Yes	Amount paid for crutches, including related costs (prescription not required)	118.2(2)(i), S1-F1-C1 (paras 1.73-1.74)
Cushion (wheelchair or bath	Depends	Amount paid for a wheelchair cushion would qualify as a medical expense, but amount paid for a bath cushion would not	118.2(2)(i), S1-F1-C1 (paras 1.73-1.74), 2010-0361221E5

Item	Qualifies	Description of Medical Expense	Reference
Cycle monitoring fees (prescribed)	Yes	Amount paid in respect of cycle monitoring fees not covered by provincial health insurance (prescription required), including diagnostic procedures relating to cycle monitoring fees. It is not required that the patient be diagnosed as medically infertile (118.2(2.2), 2017-0699941E5).	118.2(2)(o), 118.2(2.2), S1-F1-C1 (para 1.130), 2011-0401711E5
Deaf individual (intervening services)	Yes	Amount paid for deaf-blind intervening services used by a person who is both blind and profoundly deaf and paid to someone in the business of providing such services	118.2(2)(l.44), S1-F1-C1 (para 1.106)
Deaf individual (teletypewriter; prescribed)	Yes	Amount paid for a teletypewriter or similar device, including a telephone ringing indicator, that enables a deaf or mute individual to make and receive telephone calls (prescription required)	118.2(2)(m), Reg 5700(k), S1-F1-C1 (para 1.122)
Dental appliance (used to treat sleep apnea)	Yes	Amount paid for a dental appliance would qualify as a medical expense if the individual is suffering from a "severe chronic respiratory ailment" and the dental appliance was "designed exclusively for use by" the individual for that ailment.	118.2(2)(m), Reg 5700(c), 2011-0429541E5, S1-F1-C1 (para 1.122)
Dental crowns	Yes	Amount paid to a dentist or medical practitioner for dental crowns	118.2(2)(a), 2010-0362981M4
Dental hygienist	Yes	Amount paid to a dental hygienist licensed to practise under the laws of the province or territory as a medical practitioner	118.2(2)(a), S1-F1-C1 (paras 1.20–1.23)
Dental implants	Yes	Amount paid to a dentist or medical practitioner for dental implants	118.2(2)(a), 2006-0218021E5, 2011-0397151E5
Dentist	Yes	Amount paid for dental services	118.2(2)(a), S1-F1-C1 (paras 1.20–1.23)
Dentures	Yes	Amount paid to a person authorized under the laws of a province to carry on the business of a dental mechanic for the making or repairing of an upper or lower denture, or for the taking of impressions, bite registrations and insertions in respect of the making, producing, constructing and furnishing of an upper or lower denture (prescription not required)	118.2(2)(p), S1-F1-C1 (para 1.132)
Detoxification clinic for a person addicted to drugs or alcohol	Yes	Amount paid to attend a detoxification clinic where a medical practitioner certifies in writing that the person requires the specialized equipment, facilities, or personnel provided. There is no requirement that the detoxification clinic be a public or licensed private hospital	118.2(2)(a), CRA Guide RC4064, S1-F1-C1 (paras 1.56–1.63)

Item	Qualifies	Description of Medical Expense	Reference
Device or equipment (bathtub, shower or toilet; prescribed)	Yes	Amount paid for a mechanical device or equipment designed to be used to assist an individual to enter or leave a bathtub or shower or to get on or off a toilet (prescription required). Eligible devices would include a raised toilet seat. Commodes designed for the purpose of assisting individuals to get on or off a toilet (or enter or leave a bathtub or shower) may also qualify. Bath cushions would not qualify	118.2(2)(m), Reg 5700(g), 2009-0332141E5, 2010-0361221E5, S1-F1-C1 (para 1.122)
Device or equipment (cold therapy; prescribed)	No	Cost of a cold therapy device (such as a Cryo-Cuff or Polar Care Cube) prescribed by a doctor to control and reduce knee swelling	2011-0395281E5 2011-0428191E5
Device or equipment (electrotherapy; prescribed)	Yes	Amount paid for an electrotherapy device designed to be used by an individual with a medical condition or by an individual who has a severe mobility impairment (prescription required). An electrical muscle stimulation (EMS) device used for muscle stimulation and strengthening is an electrotherapy device (2011-0428191E5).	118.2(2)(m), Reg 5700(z.2) 2011-0428191E5, S1-F1-C1 (para 1.122)
Device or equipment (general)	No	A medical device or equipment that was not prescribed by a medical practitioner and that is not otherwise described in section 118.2 does not qualify (see list of eligible expenses in this table; for example, see under "Altered auditory feedback device", "Blind individuals", "Bliss symbol board", "Cell phone", "Diabetics", "Drugs", "Heart disease", "Infants", "Mobility impairment", "Pressure pulse therapy device", "Reading services", "Standing device", "Teletypewriter (or similar device)", "Vibratory signalling device", "Visual signalling device"	118.2(2), *Young*, 2009 CarswellNat 4364 (TCC)
Device or equipment (respiratory ailment; prescribed)	Yes	Amount paid for a device or equipment designed exclusively for use by an individual suffering from a severe chronic respiratory ailment or a severe chronic immune system disregulation (prescription required). An air conditioner, humidifier, dehumidifier, heat pump or heat or air exchanger specifically does not qualify under Regulation 5700(c)	118.2(2)(m), Reg 5700(c), S1-F1-C1 (para 1.122)
Diabetics (blood sugar measure; prescribed)	Yes	Amount paid for a device designed to enable individual to measure blood sugar level (prescription required)	118.2(2)(m), Reg 5700(s), S1-F1-C1 (para 1.122)
Diabetics (infusion pump; prescribed)	Yes	Infusion pump (including disposable peripherals) for the treatment of diabetes (prescription required)	118.2(2)(m), Reg 5700(s), S1-F1-C1 (para 1.122)

Item	Qualifies	Description of Medical Expense	Reference
Diabetics (insulin)	Yes	The cost of insulin or substitutes, as prescribed by a medical practitioner, purchased by a person suffering from diabetes qualifies. The CRA has stated that when such a person has to take sugar-content tests using test-tapes or test tablets and a medical practitioner has prescribed this diagnostic procedure, the tapes or tablets qualify as devices or equipment under 118.2(2)(m) and Part LVII of the Regulations. The cost of insulin pens (both reusable and disposable) also qualifies (2015-062123I7).	118.2(2)(k), (n), S1-F1-C1 (paras 1.90-1.91)
Diabetics (scales)	No	The cost of various kinds of scales, which diabetics frequently use for weighing themselves or their food	S1-F1-C1 (paras 1.91, 1.131)
Diapers	Yes	Diapers required by the patient by reason of incontinence caused by illness, injury or affliction qualify; a prescription is not required. Amounts paid to a diaper service do not qualify	118.2(2)(i.1), CRA Guide RC4064, S1-F1-C1 (para 1.87)
Diathermy	Yes	Amount paid to a medical practitioner or a licensed private hospital	118.2(2)(a), CRA Guide RC4064
Dietician	Depends	Payments to a dietician would not qualify as eligible medical expenses unless the amounts were paid for "medical services" performed by a medical practitioner authorized to practise as such according to the laws of the jurisdiction in which the service was rendered (the CRA's view is that a person is authorized by the laws of a jurisdiction to act as a medical practitioner if there is specific legislation that enables, permits or empowers a person to perform medical services and generally, such specific legislation provides for the licensing or certification of the practitioner as well as for the establishment of a governing body (eg, a college or board) with the authority to determine competency, enforce discipline and set basic standards of conduct)	118.2(2)(a), 2009-0337771E5, S1-F1-C1 (paras 1.20–1.23)
Disposable briefs	Yes	Amounts paid for disposable briefs required by the patient by reason of incontinence caused by illness, injury or affliction; a prescription is not required	118.2(2)(i.1), S1-F1-C1 (para 1.87)
Doctor	Yes	Amounts paid to a medical practitioner (meaning discussed in CRA Guide RC4065 and S1-F1-C1 (paras 20–23) for medical services	118.2(2)(a)
Dogs (guide)		See "Guide dogs"	

Item	Qualifies	Description of Medical Expense	Reference
Doulas	No	Amounts paid for doulas are not eligible since they are not a regulated health care profession in any province or territory	2017-0728281M4
Driveway alterations	Yes	Reasonable amounts paid to alter the driveway of the main residence of a person who has a severe and prolonged mobility impairment to allow easier access to a bus qualify. Also, the CRA has stated that "reasonable expenses relating to alterations to the driveway would also qualify under this provision if they facilitate access to whatever mode of transportation, bus or otherwise, that is ordinarily used by the patient." However, the cost of installing a walkway would generally not qualify as an eligible medical expense (see 2011-0404911E5).	118.2(2)(l.6), 2011-0404911E5, S1-F1-C1 (para 1.108)
Driving lessons for disabled person	No	The cost of tuition fees and exams for driver training for a disabled individual	2007-0244411E5
Drugs bought under Health Canada's Special Access Program	Yes	Drugs and medical devices bought under Health Canada's Special Access Program (ie, amounts paid for drugs and medical devices that have not been approved for use in Canada if they were purchased under this program). Visit Health Canada's Web site at canada.ca/en/health-canada.html	118.2(2)(s), (t), S1-F1-C1 (para 1.137)
Drugs, medicaments or other preparations or substances (over-the-counter)	No	Over-the-counter medications, vitamins, and supplements, even if prescribed by a medical practitioner. Subparagraph 118.2(n)(ii) refers to drugs, medicaments or other preparations or substances "that can lawfully be acquired for use by the patient only if prescribed by a medical practitioner or dentist". See also 2010-0362941E5, 2008-0264631M4, 2008-0270031E5 and 2007-0231171E5	CRA Guide RC4064, 118.2(2)(n), S1-F1-C1 (paras 1.123–1.125), 2014-0529511E5

Appendix A — Medical Expense Credit Quick Reference Table

Item	Qualifies	Description of Medical Expense	Reference
Drugs, medicaments or other preparations or substances (prescribed)	Yes	Amounts paid for drugs, medicaments or other preparations or substances that are manufactured, sold or represented for use in the diagnosis, treatment or prevention of a disease, disorder or abnormal physical state, or its symptoms, or in restoring, correcting or modifying an organic function qualify for the credit if a medical practitioner or dentist prescribed the medication and the medication is purchased from a pharmacist who recorded the prescription in a prescription record. Additionally, such amounts also qualify where they are available without a prescription and a medical practitioner or dentist has prescribed the medication for the patient and the medication is only available with the intervention of a medical practitioner (eg a pharmacist). The cost of drugs, medicaments or other preparations or substances used to lawfully end an individual's life as outlined in the *Criminal Code*, also qualify (2017-0703891C6)	118.2(2)(n), S1-F1-C1 (paras 1.123–1.127), Reg 5701
Elastic support hose (prescribed)	Yes	Amount paid for elastic support hose designed exclusively to relieve swelling caused by chronic lymphedema (prescription required)	118.2(2)(m), Reg 5700(u), S1-F1-C1 (para 1.122)
Elective medical procedures performed by a medical practitioner	Depends	For expenses incurred after March 4, 2010, expenses incurred for purely cosmetic procedures no longer qualify for the credit (unless required for medical or reconstructive purposes). See also "Cosmetic surgery"	2006-0180991M4, 118.2(2.1), S1-F1-C1 (paras 1.143–1.146)
Electric breast pump	No	Purchase of an electric breast pump	2007-0248701E5
Electric shock treatments (prescribed)	Yes	Amount paid for electric shock treatments (prescription required)	CRA Guide RC4064, 118.2(2)(a)
Electrocardiograms (prescribed)	Yes	Amount paid in respect of electrocardiogram tests not covered by provincial health insurance (prescription required)	118.2(2)(o), CRA Guide RC4064
Electrolysis	Depends	Amounts paid to a medical practitioner for electrolysis	CRA Guide RC4064, S1-F1-C1 (paras 1.143–1.146)
Electronic bone healing device (prescribed)	Yes	Amount paid for electronic bone healing device (prescription required)	118.2(2)(m), Reg 5700(z.2), CRA Guide RC4064, S1-F1-C1 (para 1.122)
Electronic speech synthesizer (prescribed)	Yes	Amount paid for a speech synthesizer (electronic) that enables a mute individual to communicate by use of a portable keyboard (prescription required)	118.2(2)(m), Reg 5700(p), S1-F1-C1 (para 1.122)

Item	Qualifies	Description of Medical Expense	Reference
Electrotherapy device (prescribed)	Yes	Amount paid for an electrotherapy device designed to be used by an individual with a medical condition or by an individual who has a severe mobility impairment (prescription required)	118.2(2)(m), Reg 5700(z.2), S1-F1-C1 (para 1.122)
Elevators or lifts (power-operated) (prescribed)	Yes	Amount paid for elevators or lifts designed exclusively for use by a person with an impairment to allow them to access different levels of a building, enter or leave a vehicle, or place a wheelchair on or in a vehicle (prescription required)	118.2(2)(m), Reg 5700(m), CRA Guide RC4064, S1-F1-C1 (para 1.122)
Environmental control system (electronic or computerized) (prescribed)	Yes	Amount paid for environmental control system designed exclusively for the use of an individual with a severe and prolonged mobility restriction (prescription required) (including the basic computer system used by a person with a mobility impairment)	118.2(2)(m), Reg 5700(t), CRA Guide RC4064, S1-F1-C1 (para 1.122)
Exercise equipment (prescribed)	No	Amount paid for exercise equipment that was prescribed by a licensed medical practitioner	2010-0385911E5, 2011-0402881E5
External breast prosthesis (prescribed)	Yes	Amount paid for an external breast prosthesis prescribed by a medical practitioner and that is required because of a mastectomy (prescription required). However, the cost of undergarments used to hold the prosthesis in place would not qualify (2012-0436991E5).	118.2(2)(m), Reg 5700(j), S1-F1-C1 (para 1.122)
Extremity pump (prescribed)	Yes	Amount paid for an extremity pump designed exclusively to relieve swelling caused by chronic lymphedema (prescription required)	118.2(2)(m), Reg 5700(u), S1-F1-C1 (para 1.122)
Eyeglasses (prescribed)	Yes	The cost of eyeglasses qualifies as a medical expense under 118.2(2)(j), including the cost of both the frames and lenses (prescription required from a medical practitioner or optometrist). The CRA has expressed the view that sunglasses prescribed by an optometrist to treat photosensitivity, which causes an individual to suffer from headaches caused by the sun or bright lighting, would not qualify for the credit (2003-0046081E5). The sunglasses in the particular situation were purchased from a retail story and were not prescription sunglasses. See also "Swimming goggles"	118.2(2)(j), S1-F1-C1 (para 1.89)
Eyelid surgery	Depends	For expenses incurred after March 4, 2010, expenses incurred for purely cosmetic procedures no longer qualify for the credit (unless required for medical or reconstructive purposes). See also "Cosmetic surgery"	118.2(2.1), 2004-0078231I7, S1-F1-C1 (paras 1.143–1.146)

Item	Qualifies	Description of Medical Expense	Reference
Feeding tube	No	Feeding tube insertion and an accompanying apparatus	2007-0220531E5
Fertility treatments	Yes	The cost of fertility treatments, including artificial insemination and fertility medications, qualifies as a medical expense. It is not required that the patient be diagnosed as medically infertile (118.2(2.2), 2017-0699941E5).	118.2(2)(a), (n), 118.2(2.2), 2010-0381401E5, S1-F1-C1 (para 1.130)
Fitness club fees		See "Athletic or fitness club fees"	
Full-time attendant care		See "Attendant care in a self-contained domestic establishment (full-time)", "Attendant care (full-time at a nursing home; patient lacks normal mental capacity)", "Attendant care (patient qualifies for the disability credit)", and "Attendant care at a retirement home, home for seniors, or other institution"	
Furnace	Yes	Electric or sealed combustion furnace acquired to replace a furnace that is neither of these types of furnace where the replacement is necessary solely because of a severe chronic respiratory ailment or a severe chronic immune system disregulation and the replacement is prescribed by a medical practitioner	118.2(2)(m), Reg 5700(c.2), S1-F1-C1 (para 1.122)
Glasses (prescribed)		See "Eyeglasses"	
Gluten-free food	Yes	For a patient who has celiac disease, the incremental cost of acquiring gluten-free food products as compared to the cost of comparable non-gluten-free food products generally qualifies. Such costs qualify if the patient has been certified in writing by a medical practitioner to be a person who, because of that disease, requires a gluten-free diet.	118.2(2)(r), 2010-0403181E5, 2011-0427621E5, S1-F1-C1 (para 1.136)
Group home		See "Attendant care provided at a group home in Canada"	
Guide dogs	Yes	The purchase of a guide dog for a blind individual from an institution that trains such dogs, as well as related expenses (for a list of qualifying expenses, see under "Animals")	118.2(2)(l), S1-F1-C1 (para 1.92)
Hair transplant surgery	Depends	For expenses incurred after March 4, 2010, expenses incurred for purely cosmetic procedures no longer qualify for the credit (unless required for medical or reconstructive purposes). See under "Cosmetic procedures"	118.2(2.1), CRA Guide RC4064, S1-F1-C1 (paras 1.143–1.146)

Item	Qualifies	Description of Medical Expense	Reference
Hardwood floors	Depends	The CRA's view is that hardwood flooring would not generally be an eligible medical expense because it would typically be expected to increase the value of a home, or because it would normally be incurred by persons without a severe and prolonged mobility impairment (S1-F1-C1 para. 1.97). However, see *Sotski*, 2013 CarswellNat 3360 (TCC), where the taxpayer was successful in claiming the cost of laminate flooring as a medical expense, since the court found that the new flooring did not necessarily increase the value of the home, and was installed specifically for the purpose of easing the taxpayer's spouse's difficulty with walking on carpeting. In this case, the taxpayer's spouse suffered from Parkinson's disease, arthritis, and postural problems, which made walking on carpeting difficult and unsafe (see also under "Home alterations").	118.2(1.2), (1.21), 2009-0326721I7, 2011-0422991E5, *Hendricks*, 2008 CarswellNat 3091 (TCC), *Sotski*, 2013 CarswellNat 3360 (TCC), S1-F1-C1 (para 1.97)
Health Line Services	No	Amount paid for a personal response system	CRA Guide RC4064, *Mattinson*, 2008 CarswellNat 84 (TCC)
Health plan premiums	Yes	See "Premiums paid to private health services plans (PHSP)"	118.2(2)(q) 2013-0480711M4, S1-F1-C1 (paras 1.133–1.135)
Health plan premiums paid by employer	Depends	Health plan premiums paid by an employer and not included in employment income do not qualify; however, such amounts can qualify if included in computing employment income	118.2(3)(b), CRA Guide RC4064, S1-F1-C1 (paras 1.133–1.135)

Item	Qualifies	Description of Medical Expense	Reference
Hearing aid (general)	Yes	Amount paid for a hearing aid, including the cost of repairs, batteries, parts, moulds, creams, rental costs, and other expenses in respect of the hearing aid qualify for the credit (prescription not required). The CRA has stated that in addition to the more usual hearing aid devices, an "aid to hearing" includes: a device that produces extra-loud audible signals such as a bell, horn or buzzer; a device to permit the volume adjustment of telephone equipment above normal levels; a bone-conduction telephone receiver; and a "Cochlear" implant. When a hearing aid is incorporated into the frame of a pair of eyeglasses, both the hearing aid and the eyeglass frame qualify under 118.2(2)(i). A listening device that is acquired to alleviate a hearing impairment by eliminating or reducing sound distortions for the purpose of listening to television programs, movies, concerts, business conferences or similar events, is also considered to qualify as an "aid to hearing" under 118.2(2)(i). See also see "Vibratory signalling device" and "Visual fire alarm indicator"	118.2(2)(i), CRA Guide RC4064, 2009-0332141E5, S1-F1-C1 (paras 1.73-1.74, 1.80-1.81))
Hearing aid (service contract)	Yes	Amount paid for a service contract for a cochlear implant	118.2(2)(i), 2003-0001495, S1-F1-C1 (paras 1.73-1.74)
Hearing aid (volume control feature)	Yes	Amount paid for a volume control feature (additional) used by a person who has a hearing impairment (prescription required)	118.2(2)(i), CRA Guide RC4064, S1-F1-C1 (para 1.80)
Hearing aid (warranty)	Yes	Cost of an extended warranty for a hearing aid	118.2(2)(i), 2007-0247031E5, S1-F1-C1 (paras 1.73-1.74)
Heart monitor (prescribed)	Yes	Amount paid for a heart monitor including the cost of repairs and batteries (prescription required)	118.2(2)(m), Reg 5700(d), CRA Guide RC4064, S1-F1-C1 (para 1.122)
Herbal medicines		See "Homeopathic medicines" and "Over-the-counter medications"	
Hernia truss	Yes	Amount paid for a hernia truss (prescription not required)	118.2(2)(i), S1-F1-C1 (paras 1.73-1.74)
Hip prosthesis	Yes	Amount paid to a hospital for a hip replacement prosthesis (ceramic femoral head) as part of total hip replacement surgery	118.2(2)(a) 2014-0533671E5

Item	Qualifies	Description of Medical Expense	Reference
Home alterations (addition of bathroom)	No	An amount paid to add a bathroom to a home is not a qualifying home renovation cost where the addition of the bathroom increases the value of the home. In Chobotar, 2009 CarswellNat 1308 (TCC), the credit was denied in respect of a specially designed bathroom for a person in a wheelchair because the bathroom increased the value of the home	*Chobotar*, 2009 CarswellNat 1308 (TCC), S1-F1-C1 (paras 1.94–1.100)
Home alterations (pedestal sink)	No	An amount paid for a pedestal sink	118.2(2)(l.2), (l.21), Young, 2009 CarswellNat 4364 (TCC),S1-F1-C1 (paras 1.94–1.100)
Home alterations (qualifying expenses)	Yes	Amounts paid to make changes to give a person who has a severe and prolonged mobility impairment or who lacks normal physical development access to (or greater mobility or functioning within) the person's home may qualify. The costs may be incurred in building the principal residence of the person, or in renovating or altering an existing home (an RV that is used as a place of residence could be considered a home for this purpose; 2005-0133691I7). Renovation or construction expenses do not qualify unless: 1) they would not typically be expected to increase the value of the home; and 2) they would not normally be incurred by people without a severe and prolonged mobility impairment (ie, items such as hot tubs, swimming pools, and hardwood floors do not generally qualify; although, see *Sotski*, 2013 CarswellNat 3360 (TCC), where the taxpayer was successful in claiming the cost of laminate flooring as a medical expense, since the court found that the new flooring did not necessarily increase the value of the home, and was installed specifically for the purpose of easing the taxpayer's spouse's difficulty with walking on carpeting).	118.2(2)(l.2), (l.21), CRA Guide RC4064, S1-F1-C1 (paras 1.94–1.100), *Hillier v The Queen*, [2000] 3 C.T.C. 2367 (TCC)

Item	Qualifies	Description of Medical Expense	Reference
		Eligible expenses could include, for example: buying and installing outdoor or indoor ramps where stairways impede the person's mobility; enlarging halls and doorways to give the person access to the various rooms of his or her dwelling; lowering kitchen or bathroom cabinets to give the person access to them; power flush toilets; or the cost of installing a stair lift. See also 2007-0251071E5, 2009-0342581E5, 2005-0163161E5, 2007-0251071E5, 2010-0379331E5, 2011-0422991E5, *Hendricks*, 2008 CarswellNat 3091 (TCC), *Totten*, [2005] 3 C.T.C. 2061 (TCC), *Henschel*, 2010 CarswellNat 1783 (TCC) and *Savoy*, 2011 CarswellNat 193 (TCC).	
Home care services (provided by a nurse)	Yes	Amount paid to a licensed nurse for home care services (ie, for private nursing care)	118.2(2)(a), CRA Guide RC4064, 2009-0332141E5
Home construction costs		See "Home Alterations"	
Homeopathic services	Depends	Amount paid to a medical practitioner for homeopathic services qualifies. The CRA's view is that a person is authorized by the laws of a jurisdiction to act as a medical practitioner if there is specific legislation that enables, permits or empowers a person to perform medical services and generally, such specific legislation provides for the licensing or certification of the practitioner as well as for the establishment of a governing body (eg, a college or board) with the authority to determine competency, enforce discipline and set basic standards of conduct. Homeopaths are not authorized as medical practitioners in New Brunswick (2010-0407341E5).	118.2(2)(a), CRA Guide RC4064, Herzig, [2004] 3 C.T.C. 2496 (TCC), 2009-0337771E5, S1-F1-C1 (paras 1.20–1.23)
Homeopathic medicines	No	The cost of vitamins, herbs, organic and natural foods, natural health products and bottled water not recorded by a pharmacist, even if they are prescribed by a medical practitioner (see under "Over-the-counter medications"). See also *Ray*, 2009 CarswellNat 473 (TCC), *Ali v. R.*, [2008] 4 C.T.C. 245 (FCA) and *Leeper*, 2015 CarswellNat 1126 (TCC)	118.2(2)(n), 2011-0391961E5, 2016-0646001M4, S1-F1-C1 (para 1.125)

Item	Qualifies	Description of Medical Expense	Reference
Hospital bed	Yes	Amount paid for a hospital bed for an individual's use as prescribed by a medical practitioner qualifies (including such attachments thereto as may have been included in a prescription therefor). A ceragem massager bed does not qualify (*Reid*, 2008 CarswellNat 2069 (TCC)). Nor does a RIK Fluid Overlay mattress (2009-0318231E5) or a Sleep Country adjustable bed (*Young*, 2009 CarswellNat 4364 (TCC)). A Slumberland adjustable bed qualifies (Crockart, [1999] 2 C.T.C. 2409 (TCC)). Also, the cost of redesigning a bed to be a hospital bed qualifies; Vucurevich, [2000] 1 C.T.C. 3044 (TCC). The cost of an over-bed rolling table does not qualify. Also, a massage chair would not qualify; 2009-0341601E5 (See also under "Mattress")	118.2(2)(m), Reg 5700(h), 2009-0332141E5, S1-F1-C1 (para 1.122)
Hospitals	Yes	Amount paid to a public or private hospital that is designated as a hospital by the province or territory where the hospital is located	118.2(2)(a), CRA Guide RC4064 S1-F1-C1 (paras 1.24–1.30)
Hot tub		See "Whirlpool bath"	
House cleaning services	No	Amounts paid for house cleaning services do not qualify. See however under "Attendant care at a retirement home, home for seniors, or other institution". Also, see Zaffino, [2007] 5 C.T.C. 2560 (TCC) (cleaning costs allowed under paragraph 118.2(2)(b.1) (part-time attendant costs))	2009-0332141E5
Hydrotherapy	Depends	Amounts paid to a medical practitioner for hydrotherapy qualify. The CRA's view is that a person is authorized by the laws of a jurisdiction to act as a medical practitioner if there is specific legislation that enables, permits or empowers a person to perform medical services and generally, such specific legislation provides for the licensing or certification of the practitioner as well as for the establishment of a governing body (eg, a college or board) with the authority to determine competency, enforce discipline and set basic standards of conduct. See also "Hydrotherapy pool".	118.2(2)(a), CRA Guide RC4064, 2009-0337771E5
Hydrotherapy pool (fees for use)	No	Fees paid to access a hydrotherapy pool	2015-0567251E5
Iliostomy pads	Yes	Amount paid for iliostomy pads (prescription not required)	118.2(2)(i), S1-F1-C1 (paras 1.73-1.74, 1.78)

884

Item	Qualifies	Description of Medical Expense	Reference
Immune system dis-regulation or respira-tory ailment (air or water filter; pre-scribed)	Yes	Air or water filter or purifier for use by an individual who is suffering from a severe chronic respiratory ailment or a severe chronic immune system disregulation to cope with or overcome that ailment or dis-regulation (prescription required)	118.2(2)(m), Reg 5700(c.1), S1-F1-C1 (para 1.122)
Immune system dis-regulation or respira-tory ailment (electric or sealed combustion furnace)	Yes	Electric or sealed combustion furnace ac-quired to replace a furnace that is neither an electric furnace nor a sealed combus-tion furnace where the replacement is nec-essary solely because of a severe chronic respiratory ailment or a severe chronic im-mune system disregulation and the replace-ment is prescribed by a medical practitioner	118.2(2)(m), Reg 5700(c.2), S1-F1-C1 (para 1.122)
Incontinence	Yes	Amounts paid for catheters and catheter trays required by the patient by reason of incontinence caused by illness, injury or affliction (including catheter trays, tubing, or other products required for incontinence caused by illness, injury, or affliction); a prescription is not required. Bed clothing, disposable gloves for caregivers and body ointments do not qualify for the credit.	118.2(2)(i.1), 2010-0359861E5, S1-F1-C1 (pa-ras 1.87-1.88)
Inductive coupling osteogenesis stimula-tor (prescribed)	Yes	Amount paid for an inductive coupling os-teogenesis stimulator for treating non-union of fractures or aiding in bone fusion (prescription required)	118.2(2)(m), Reg 5700(v), S1-F1-C1 (para 1.122)
Infants (SIDS device)	Yes	Amount paid for a device designed to be attached to infants diagnosed as being prone to sudden infant death syndrome in order to sound an alarm if the infant ceases to breathe and that is for the in-fant's use as prescribed by a medical prac-titioner (a medical practitioner must certify in writing that the infant is prone to sud-den infant death syndrome)	118.2(2)(m), Reg 5700(r), S1-F1-C1 (para 1.122)
Infusion pump (pre-scribed)	Yes	Amount paid for an Infusion pump, in-cluding the cost of disposable peripherals used in the treatment of diabetes (prescrip-tion required). See also "Diabetics"	118.2(2)(m), Reg 5700(s), S1-F1-C1 (para 1.122)
Insulin and insulin pens	Yes	An amount paid for insulin and insulin substitutes generally qualifies. A medical practitioner must have prescribed the insu-lin, but a pharmacy or any other type of store may sell the insulin without a written prescription and the expense will qualify (ie, provided an initial prescription was given). The cost of insulin pens (both re-usable and disposable) also qualifies (2015-0621231I7). See also "Diabetics"	118.2(2)(k), (m), Reg 5700(b), S1-F1-C1 (paras 1.90-1.91, 1.126)
Insurance		See "Travel medical insurance"	

Item	Qualifies	Description of Medical Expense	Reference
Interest (on bank loan)	No	Interest expense on a bank loan obtained to finance a medical or dental procedure does not qualify because it is paid to a bank instead of a medical practitioner, dentist, nurse, public hospital, or licensed private hospital	2011-0416651I7
In-vitro fertilization procedure (pre-scribed)	Yes	Amount paid in respect of in-vitro fertilization procedure not covered by provincial health insurance (prescription required). Qualifying amounts include daily ultrasound and blood tests once the in-vitro procedure has begun, sperm freezing and egg freezing and storage, but do not include amounts paid to cover the donor's costs. Travel costs incurred for an IVF procedure outside of Canada will likely qualify (2011-0396951E5). It is not required that the patient be diagnosed as medically infertile (118.2(2.2), 2017-0699941E5)	S1-F1-C1 (para 1.130), CRA Guide RC4064, 118.2(2)(a), (o), 118.2(2.2), 2015-0612331I7, 2011-0396951E5, 2011-0415601E5, 2011-0416451E5, 2011-0396951E5, 2009-0311051E5
Iontophoresis device (prescribed)	Yes	Costs for an iontophoresis device that has been prescribed by a doctor for the treatment of hyperhidrosis (excessive sweating)	118.2(2)(m), Reg 5700 (z.2), 2011-0391861E5, S1-F1-C1 (para 1.122)
Iron lung	Yes	Cost of an iron lung, including the cost of repairs, a portable chest respirator that performs the same function, a continuous positive airway pressure machine, or mechanical ventilator, and parts and other expenses in respect of (prescription not required)	118.2(2)(i), CRA Guide RC4064, S1-F1-C1 (paras 1.73–1.75)
Kidney machine (artificial)	Yes	Amount paid for a kidney machine, including the cost of repairs, maintenance, and supplies; additions, renovations, or alterations to a home (the hospital official who installed the machine must certify in writing that the additions, renovations, or alterations were necessary for installation); the portion of the operating costs of the home that relate to the machine (excluding mortgage interest and CCA); a telephone extension in the dialysis room and all calls to a hospital for advice or to obtain repairs; and necessary and unavoidable costs to transport supplies. A prescription is not required	118.2(2)(i), CRA Guide RC4064, S1-F1-C1 (paras 1.73-1.74, 1.82–1.86)
Lab tests (prescribed)	Yes	Amount paid for lab tests, procedures and services, including necessary interpretations (prescription required). See also "Tests"	118.2(2)(o), S1-F1-C1 (para 1.128)

Item	Qualifies	Description of Medical Expense	Reference
Lacrisert (ophthalmic insert)	Depends	Lacrisert may qualify in special cases where it is prescribed by a medical practitioner or optometrist specifically for the treatment or correction of a specified defect of vision (eg; progressive visual deterioration)	118.2(2)(j), 2010-0371881E5
Lap band surgery	Yes	Lap band surgery qualifies as a medical expense and is not considered to be cosmetic surgery where the taxpayer is diagnosed with obesity and related health issues	118.2(2)(a), 2011-0395451E5, S1-F1-C1 (paras 1.143–1.146)
Large-print on-screen device (prescribed)	Yes	Amount paid for a large-print-on-screen device designed exclusively to be used by a person who is blind in the operation of a computer (prescription required). See also "Blind individuals"	118.2(2)(m), Reg 5700(o), S1-F1-C1 (para 1.122)
Laryngeal speaking aids	Yes	A laryngeal speaking aid qualifies for the credit (prescription not required). A laryngeal speaking aid is an electronic type of instrument that assists a person to produce speech sounds. That CRA has stated that an artificial larynx or a similar type of speaking aid for a person who would otherwise be deprived of an effective speech capability also generally qualify for the credit. Qualifying expenses related to these devices include the cost of batteries, maintenance, repairs or replacements	118.2(2)(i), S1-F1-C1 (paras 1.73-1.74, 1.79)
Laser eye surgery	Yes	Amount paid for laser eye surgery	118.2(2)(a), CRA Guide RC4064, 2010-0362981M4, S1-F1-C1 (para 1.89)
Laser hair removal	Depends	Expenses incurred after March 4, 2010 for purely cosmetic procedures no longer qualify for the credit (unless required for medical or reconstructive purposes). Procedures to treat excessive hair growth due to Polycystic Ovarian Syndrome (PCOS) would generally be considered to have a medical or reconstructive purpose (see 2011-0405091E5 and 2011-0401221E5). See under "Cosmetic surgery"	118.2(2.1), 2010-0361271E5, 2012-0462471M4, S1-F1-C1 (paras 1.143–1.146)
Laser therapy (endovenous)	Yes	Cost of endovenous laser therapy (EVLT) used as a treatment for varicose veins	118.2(2)(a), 2011-0411181E5, 2013-0477051E5
Laser treatments (to quit smoking)	Yes	Cost of laser treatments to quit smoking if paid to a medical practitioner (certified laser technicians are not recognized and regulated as medical practitioners in Alberta: 2011-0427631E5)	118.2(2)(a), 118.4(2), 2011-0427631E5

Item	Qualifies	Description of Medical Expense	Reference
Lawn care services provided for an impaired person	No	Amount paid for lawn care services	2009-0332141E5
Learning disability (laptop and digital voice recorder)	No	The cost of a laptop computer and digital voice recorder (with THINK, SAY, WRITE)	2011-0431291E5
Learning disability (reading device; prescribed)	Yes	Amount paid for a device or software designed to be used by blind individuals or individuals with a severe learning disability to enable the individual to read print (prescription required)	118.2(2)(m), Reg 5700(1.1), S1-F1-C1 (para 1.122)
Learning disability (reading services)	Yes	Amount paid for reading services provided to a person who is blind or has a severe learning disability and paid to someone in the business of providing such services (a medical practitioner must certify in writing that these services are necessary)	118.2(2)(l.43), S1-F1-C1 (para 1.105)
Learning disability (software; prescribed)	Yes	Amount paid for software designed to be used by a blind individual, or an individual with a severe learning disability, to enable the individual to read print (prescription required). The software programs WiViK and Read and Write Gold Version 9 qualify, but Dragon Naturally Speaking does not (2011-0431291E5)	118.2(2)(m), Reg 5700(1.1), S1-F1-C1 (para 1.122)
Learning disability (tutoring services)	Yes	Amounts paid as remuneration for tutoring services used by (and which are supplementary to the primary education of) a person with a learning disability or an impairment in mental functions and paid to someone in the business of providing such services who is not related to the person being tutored. A medical practitioner must certify in writing that these services are necessary because of the learning disability or impairment in mental functions	118.2(2)(l.91), S1-F1-C1 (para 1.117)
Legal fees	No	Legal fees incurred to correct medical records or in order to receive medical services, or to pursue health coverage under a provincial health insurance plan (eg; OHIP) do not qualify as a medical expense	118.2(2)(a), 2010-0358201E5, 2010-0389841E5
Legal reports		See "Medical services"	
Lifeline	No	Amount paid for a personal response system	CRA Guide RC4064, *Mattinson*, 2008 CarswellNat 84 (TCC)
Light therapy device	No	Amount paid for a light therapy device for the treatment of Seasonal Affective Disorder	2008-0305071E5

Item	Qualifies	Description of Medical Expense	Reference
Lip reading and sign language training	Yes	Amount paid for reasonable expenses relating to rehabilitative therapy, including training in lip reading and sign language, incurred to adjust for the patient's hearing or speech loss	118.2(2)(l.3), S1-F1-C1 (para 1.101)
Liposuction	Depends	For expenses incurred after March 4, 2010, expenses incurred for purely cosmetic procedures no longer qualify for the credit (unless required for medical or reconstructive purposes). See under "Cosmetic surgery"	118.2(2.1), 2010-0362981M4, S1-F1-C1 (paras 1.143–1.146)
Liver extract injections for a person with pernicious anemia	Yes	Amount paid for liver extract injections for a person with pernicious anemia generally qualifies. A medical practitioner must have prescribed the injections, but a pharmacy or any other type of store may sell the extract without a written prescription and the expense will qualify (ie, provided an initial prescription was given)	118.2(2)(k), S1-F1-C1, (paras 1.90-1.91, 1.131)
Lymphedema		See "Extremity pump" and "Elastic support hose"	
MRI procedure	Yes	Cost of an MRI (magnetic resonance imaging) procedure	118.2(2)(o), 2011-0415671E5
Maintenance expenditures	No	There is no specific provision that would allow maintenance expenditures (such as snow removal or lawn maintenance) as a medical expense, other than when included in costs of a nursing home or when performed by an attendant as part of attendant care	2014-0552351E5
Manitoba Health Plan	No	See "Premiums paid to private health services plans (PHSP)"	118.2(2)(q), S1-F1-C1 (para 1.134)

Item	Qualifies	Description of Medical Expense	Reference
Marijuana or marijuana seeds	Yes	Amounts paid to Health Canada or a designated producer for marijuana plants or seeds, cannabis or cannabis oil for use by a patient authorized under the *Access to Cannabis for Medical Purposes Regulations* (or exempt under section 56 of the *Controlled Drugs and Substances Act*) to possess or use for medical purposes qualify. With the exception of the cost of seeds purchased from Health Canada, expenses incurred by authorized users to grow their own marijuana are not eligible medical expenses (2006-0209581E5). Services provided in relation to the supply of marijuana would have to meet the requirements of 118.2(2)(a) to qualify as medical services provided by an authorized medical practitioner (2011-0405191E5).An amount paid for a vaporization system designed to allow smoke-free inhalation of medical marijuana would not qualify (2012-0432791E5).	118.2(2)(u), S1-F1-C1 (paras 1.139–1.142) 2015-0588751E5
Massage chair	No	Amount paid for a massage chair (see under "Hospital Bed" for qualifying expenses)	2009-0341601E5
Massage therapy	Depends	Payments for massage therapy would not qualify as eligible medical expenses unless the amounts were paid for "medical services" performed by a medical practitioner authorized to practise as such according to the laws of the jurisdiction in which the service was rendered. The Courts have found that the fact massage therapy qualifies for the medical expense credit in Ontario and BC but not in New Brunswick does not violate the Charter of Rights (*Noddin*, [2005] 1 C.T.C. 2287 (TCC)). The CRA's view is that a person is authorized by the laws of a jurisdiction to act as a medical practitioner if there is specific legislation that enables, permits or empowers a person to perform medical services and generally, such specific legislation provides for the licensing or certification of the practitioner as well as for the establishment of a governing body (eg, a college or board) with the authority to determine competency, enforce discipline and set basic standards of conduct	118.2(2)(a), 2009-0337771E5, S1-F1-C1 (paras 1.20–1.23)

Item	Qualifies	Description of Medical Expense	Reference
Mattress (not for a hospital bed)	No	Cost of a specialized mattress (eg; memory foam, orthopedic, non-allergenic) generally does not qualify, even if prescribed by a medical practitioner (See also under "Hospital bed"). Costs for a custom mattress, custom mattress topper and custom pillow prescribed by a medical practitioner for neck & back pain, sleep headaches, jaw disorders, sleep apnea, etc., also do not qualify	2009-0332141E5, 2011-0397731E5, 2017-0724441E5, *Henschel*, 2010 CarswellNat 1783 (TCC)
Medical devices		See "Devices or equipment"	
Medical ointments (prescribed)	Yes	Medical ointments used to treat or prevent infection may qualify (prescription required)	118.2(2)(n)(i), Reg 5701, 2010-0359861E5, S1-F1-C1 (paras 1.87-1.88)
Medical records	Depends	Fees paid for the completion of health and disability forms by a medical practitioner are eligible; however, fees paid to obtain a copy of medical records from a document management company are not	118.2(2)(a), S1-F1-C1 (para 1.26), 2014-0553301E5

Item	Qualifies	Description of Medical Expense	Reference
Medical services (amounts paid to a medical practitioner)	Yes	Amounts paid to a medical practitioner, dentist or nurse or a public or licensed private hospital in respect of medical or dental services. Depending on the laws of the applicable province or jurisdiction, an amount paid to a medical practitioner authorized to practise as medical practitioner in accordance with the laws of the province or territory can include an osteopath; a chiropractor; a naturopath; a therapeutist (or therapist); a physiotherapist; a chiropodist (or podiatrist); a psychoanalyst who is a member of the Canadian Institute of Psychoanalysis or a member of the Quebec Association of Jungian Psychoanalysts; a psychologist; a qualified speech-language pathologist or audiologist such as, for example, a person who is certified as such by The Canadian Association of Speech-Language Pathologists and Audiologists (CASLPA) or a provincial affiliate of that organization; an occupational therapist who is a member of the Canadian Association of Occupational Therapists; an acupuncturist; a dietician; or a dental hygienist (the CRA's view is that a person is authorized by the laws of a jurisdiction to act as a medical practitioner if there is specific legislation that enables, permits or empowers a person to perform medical services and generally, such specific legislation provides for the licensing or certification of the practitioner as well as for the establishment of a governing body (eg, a college or board) with the authority to determine competency, enforce discipline and set basic standards of conduct). See the following chart prepared by CRA summarizing authorized medical practitioners by province or territory: cra-arc.gc.ca/tx/ndvdls/tpcs/ncm-tx/rtrn/cmpltng/ddctns/lns300-350/330/ampp-eng.html?goback=%2Egde_3982304_member_148118619)	118.2(2)(a), S1-F1-C1 (paras 1.20–1.30), CRA Guide RC4064, 2009-0337771E5
Medical services (block fees)	Yes	Block fee paid to a medical centre to cover the cost of certain ancillary or incidental uninsured medical services	118.2(2)(a), 2007-0255741I7, S1-F1-C1 (para 1.29)
Medical services (legal reports)	Depends	Amount paid for medical legal reports and other reports created for the purpose of litigation where the service is performed by a medical practitioner may be deductible: see conflicting views in 2006-0218131E5 and 2011-0436011E5	118.2(2)(a), 2006-0218131E5, 2011-0436011E5

Item	Qualifies	Description of Medical Expense	Reference
Medical services (medical assistance in dying)	Yes	Amounts paid to a medical doctor, nurse practitioner or public or licensed private hospital for medical assistance to lawfully end an individual's life as outlined in the *Criminal Code*, including the cost of medicaments or other preparations or substances used to lawfully end an individual's life	118.2(2)(n) Reg 5701 2017-0703891C6
Medical Services Plan of British Columbia	No	See "Premiums paid to private health services plans (PHSP)"	118.2(2)(q), S1-F1-C1 (para 1.134)
Medicaments		See "Drugs, medicaments or other preparations or substances"	
Membership fee	No	A fee paid to a private medical clinic as a "membership" or "access" fee (the CRA's view is that such a fee is paid for access to medical services rather than for medical services themselves; in the situation considered in the reference herein, the membership fee was not attributable to a particular medical expense)	118.2(2)(a), (q), 2006-0166961E5, S1-F1-C1 (para 1.29)
Metabolism tests (prescribed)	Yes	Amount paid in respect of metabolism tests not covered by provincial health insurance (prescription required)	118.2(2)(o), CRA Guide RC4064
Midwife	Yes	Amounts paid to a midwife authorized to practise as a medical practitioner in accordance with the laws of the province or territory (midwives are authorized in all provinces/territories except PEI and Yukon)	118.2(2)(a), 118.4(2) 2017-0728281M4
Mobility impairment (electrotherapy device; prescribed)	Yes	Amount paid for an electrotherapy device designed to be used by an individual with a medical condition or by an individual who has a severe mobility impairment (prescription required)	118.2(2)(m), Reg 5700(z.2), S1-F1-C1 (para 1.122)
Mobility impairment (vehicle operation device; prescribed)	Yes	Amount paid for a device designed exclusively to enable an individual to operate a vehicle (prescription required). An amount paid for prescribed devices that are designed exclusively to enable an individual with a mobility impairment to operate a Segway, bicycle or tricycle (e.g.; levers, knobs and handles that allow the individual to control steering, speed, braking and signalling) are an eligible medical expense; however, the cost of the Segway, bicycle or tricycle, where the intention is to modify after purchase, is not an eligible medical expense. (2016-0645021C6).	118.2(2)(m), Reg 5700(n), S1-F1-C1 (para 1.122)

Item	Qualifies	Description of Medical Expense	Reference
Mobility impairment (walking device; prescribed)	Yes	The cost of a device that is exclusively designed to assist an individual in walking qualifies (prescription required). To qualify, a device must "provide actual support in the action of walking". In *T. Preugschas v. R.*, [2005] 5 C.T.C. 2315 exercise equipment used by a victim of spinal cord damage was held to be deductible under 118.2(2)(m) where the machine was prescribed by a Swiss neuro-physiotherapist. See also "Devices or Equipment"	118.2(2)(m), Reg 5700(i), 2009-0351441E5, S1-F1-C1 (para 1.122)
Monitoring or tracking expenses	No	Expenses related to the remote monitoring of a person, including the cost of the purchase or rental of a tracking device and expenses for use of the device.	2012-0456201E5
Moving expenses	Depends	Reasonable moving expenses (that have not been claimed as moving expenses on anyone's tax return) to move a person who has a severe and prolonged mobility impairment, or who lacks normal physical development, to housing that is more accessible to the person or in which the person is more mobile or functional, to a limit of $2,000	118.2(2)(l.5), 2011-0403471E5, S1-F1-C1 (para 1.107)
Nasal and sinus rinse	No	Amount paid for a nasal and sinus rinse does not qualify if it is available without a prescription	2012-0433101E5
Nasal bone detection test	Yes	Amount paid for a nasal bone detection test where the tests are done by a medical practitioner or a nurse for the purpose of diagnosing, treating or preventing disease (see 2007-0246741E5)	118.2(2)(a)
Native healing therapist	Depends	Payments to a native healing therapist would not qualify as eligible medical expenses unless the amounts were paid for "medical services" performed by a medical practitioner authorized to practise as such according to the laws of the jurisdiction in which the service was rendered. The CRA's view is that a person is authorized by the laws of a jurisdiction to act as a medical practitioner if there is specific legislation that enables, permits or empowers a person to perform medical services and generally, such specific legislation provides for the licensing or certification of the practitioner as well as for the establishment of a governing body (eg, a college or board) with the authority to determine competency, enforce discipline and set basic standards of conduct	118.2(2)(a), 2007-0224311E5, 2009-0337771E5, S1-F1-C1 (paras 1.20–1.23)

Item	Qualifies	Description of Medical Expense	Reference
Naturopath (amount paid to)	Depends	Payments to a naturopath would not qualify as eligible medical expenses unless the amounts were paid for "medical services" performed by a medical practitioner authorized to practise as such according to the laws of the jurisdiction in which the service was rendered. In *Parent*, [2008] 4 C.T.C. 2094 (TCC), a naturopath was held not to be a medical practitioner in Quebec (see also 2015-0585011I7, 2016-0624871C6). Naturopaths are not authorized as medical practitioners in New Brunswick (2010-0407341E5).	118.2(2)(a), S1-F1-C1 (paras 1.20–1.23)
Naturopath (medicines)	No	Naturopathic medicines do not qualify. In *Bentley*, 2009 CarswellNat 1518 (TCC), the Court found that while a patient appeared to benefit from naturopathic medicines, the requirements of paragraph 118.2(2)(n) were not met as the naturopathic medicines bought at a naturopath's office were not dispensed by a licensed pharmacist	118.2(2)(n) 2011-0426031E5, S1-F1-C1 (paras 1.123–1.125)
Needle or syringe (prescribed)	Yes	Designed to be used for the purpose of giving an injection (prescription required)	118.2(2)(m), Reg 5700(b), S1-F1-C1 (para 1.122)
New Brunswick Medicare Division of Provincial Department of Health	No	See "Premiums paid to private health services plans (PHSP)"	118.2(2)(q), S1-F1-C1, (para 1.134)
Newfoundland Medical Care Plan	No	See "Premiums paid to private health services plans (PHSP)"	118.2(2)(q), S1-F1-C1, (para 1.134)
Northwest Territories Health Insurance Services Agency of Territorial Government	No	See "Premiums paid to private health services plans (PHSP)"	118.2(2)(q), S1-F1-C1, (para 1.134)
Note-taking services	Yes	Amount paid for note-taking services used by a person with an impairment in mental or physical functions and paid to someone in the business of providing such services (a medical practitioner must certify in writing that the service is necessary)	118.2(2)(l.41), S1-F1-C1 (para 1.103)
Nova Scotia Medical Services Insurance	No	See "Premiums paid to private health services plans (PHSP)"	118.2(2)(q), S1-F1-C1, (para 1.134)
Nova Scotia Seniors' Pharmacare Program	Yes	Premiums paid to Nova Scotia Seniors' Pharmacare Program (see 2006-0205931E5)	118.2(2)(q)
Nuchal translucency test	Yes	Amount paid for nuchal translucency tests where the tests are done by a medical practitioner or a nurse for the purpose of diagnosing, treating or preventing disease	118.2(2)(o), 2007-0246741E5

Item	Qualifies	Description of Medical Expense	Reference
Nurse	Yes	Amount paid to a licensed nurse for medical services	118.2(2)(a), CRA Guide RC4064, S1-F1-C1 (paras 1.20–1.30)
Nursing home		See "Attendant care (full-time at a nursing home; patient lacks normal mental capacity)", "Attendant care (patient qualifies for the disability credit)", and "Attendant care at a retirement home, home for seniors, or other institution"	
Occupational therapist	Yes	Amount paid to an occupational therapist who is a member of the Canadian Association of Occupational Therapists	118.2(2)(a), CRA Guide RC4064, S1-F1-C1 (paras 1.20–1.23)
Ontario Health Insurance Plan	No	See "Premiums paid to private health services plans (PHSP)"	118.2(2)(q), S1-F1-C1 (para 1.134)
Optical scanners or similar devices (prescribed)	Yes	Amount paid for an optical scanners or similar devices designed for use by a person who is blind to enable them to read print (prescription required). See also "Blind individuals"	118.2(2)(m), Reg 5700(l), S1-F1-C1 (para 1.122)
Oralist interpreter		See "Sign language services"	
Organ transplant	Yes	Reasonable amounts paid to locate a compatible donor, to arrange the transplant including legal fees and insurance premiums, and reasonable travelling costs including board and lodging for the patient, the donor, and their respective companions qualify for the credit. In *Zieber*, 2008 CarswellNat 1716 (TCC), the Court found that an embryo transplant constituted an "organ transplant"; however, the CRA and subsequent TCC cases disagree (see 2010-0391691E5, *Warnock*, 2014 CarswellNat 2957, *Zanatta*, 2014 CarswellNat 3808, and *Pearen*, 2014 CarswellNat 3809)	118.2(2)(l.1), S1-F1-C1 (para 1.93, 1.147)
Organic foods	No	Amount paid for organic foods (see under "Over-the-counter Medications")	CRA Guide RC4064, Chevalier v. R., [2008] 4 C.T.C. 2009, S1-F1-C1 (paras 1.123–1.125), 2016-0646001M4
Orthodontic work including braces	Yes	Amount paid for orthodontic work	118.2(2)(a), CRA Guide RC4064
Orthopedic chair	No	Amount paid from an orthopedic chair	2010-0389391E5
Orthopaedic shoe or boot and an insert for a shoe or boot (prescribed)	Yes	Amount paid for an orthopedic shoe or boot (and an insert for a shoe or boot) made to order for an individual in accordance with a prescription to overcome a physical disability of the individual (prescription required). Non-customized orthopedic shoes do not qualify (2012-0456201E5). See also "Brace"	118.2(2)(m), Reg 5700(e), S1-F1-C1 (para 1.122)

Item	Qualifies	Description of Medical Expense	Reference
Osteogenesis stimulator (inductive coupling; prescribed)	Yes	Amount paid for an osteogenesis stimulator for treating non-union of fractures or aiding in bone fusion (prescription required)	118.2(2)(m), Reg 5700(v), S1-F1-C1 (para 1.122)
Osteopath	Depends	Payments to an osteopath would not qualify as eligible medical expenses unless the amounts were paid for "medical services" performed by a medical practitioner authorized to practise as such according to the laws of the jurisdiction in which the service was rendered. Osteopaths and orthotherapists are not authorized as medical practitioners in Quebec (2014-0523911E5, 2015-0585011I7)	118.2(2)(a), S1-F1-C1 (paras 1.20–1.23, 2016-0624871C6)
Over-bed rolling table	No	Cost of over-bed rolling table	2009-0332141E5
Over-the-counter medications	No	Over-the-counter medications, vitamins, supplements and natural health products do not qualify for the credit even if they are prescribed by a medical practitioner. Subparagraph 118.2(n)(ii) refers to drugs, medicaments or other preparations or substances "that can lawfully be acquired for use by the patient only if prescribed by a medical practitioner or dentist". See also *Ray*, 2009 CarswellNat 473 (TCC), *Ali v. R.*, [2008] 4 C.T.C. 245 (FCA) and *Leeper*, 2015 CarswellNat 1126 (TCC)	118.2(2)(n), CRA Guide RC4064, 2016-0646001M4, 2014-0529511E5, 2012-0462011E5, 2011-0419231E5, 2011-0391961E5, 2010-0378121M4, 2010-0362941E5, 2008-0284881E5, 2008-0264631M4, 2008-0270031E5, 2007-0231171E5, S1-F1-C1 (paras 1.123–1.125)
Oximeter and probes	No	Amount paid for oximeter and probes	2009-0332141E5
Oxygen (including oxygen equipment or tent)	Yes	Amounts paid for oxygen or for equipment, including an oxygen tent, necessary to administer oxygen qualify (a prescription is required). The CRA has stated that eligible expenses include oxygen face masks and tanks containing oxygen under pressure. The cost of renting equipment for topical pressurized oxygen therapy (TPOT), including an extremity system controller, extremity bag and oxygen concentrator, also qualifies (see 2011-0408941E5)	118.2(2)(i), (k), Reg 5700, S1-F1-C1 (paras 1.73-1.74, 1.90)
Oxygen concentrator	Yes	Amount paid for an oxygen concentrator, including the cost of repairs and parts and other expenses in respect of (such as electricity). A prescription is not required	118.2(2)(i), CRA Guide RC4064 S1-F1-C1 (paras 1.73-1.74)
Oxygen therapy (hyperbaric)	Yes	Hyperbaric oxygen therapy treatment administered by a medical practitioner qualifies when it is offered to an individual for therapeutic or rehabilitative reasons	118.2(2)(a), 2014-0529101E5

Item	Qualifies	Description of Medical Expense	Reference
Pacemakers (prescribed)	Yes	Amount paid for a pacemaker (prescription required)	118.2(2)(m), Reg 5700(d), S1-F1-C1 (para 1.122)
Pads	Yes	Amount paid for Iliostomy or colostomy (prescription not required)	118.2(2)(i), S1-F1-C1 (paras 1.73-1.74, 1.78)
Page turner device (prescribed)	Yes	Amount paid for a page turning device designed to be used by an individual who has a severe and prolonged impairment that markedly restricts their ability to use their arms or hands to turn the pages of a book or other bound document (prescription required)	118.2(2)(m), Reg 5700(z), S1-F1-C1 (para 1.122)
Parking fees	Depends	Parking fees paid while at doctors' appointments do not qualify. Parking fees can be claimed as transportation or travelling expenses under 118.2(2)(g) and (h) if the requirements are otherwise met. See "Transportation and travel expenses for medical purposes"	118.2(2)(g), (h) 2011-0394771E5, 2010-0362981M4, S1-F1-C1 (paras 1.69, 1.72)
Partnerships		See "Associations"	
Part-time attendant care		See "Attendant care (part-time)"	
Personal response systems	No	Amounts paid for personal response systems such as Lifeline and Health Line Services	CRA Guide RC4064, *Mattinson*, 2008 CarswellNat 84 (TCC)
Personal trainer	Depends	The costs of using a personal trainer, even if recommended or prescribed by a medical practitioner, will generally not qualify. However, a personal trainer for a Thalidomide victim qualified in *Olney*, 2014 CarswellNat 3383 (TCC) as therapy under 118.2(2)(l.9)	2009-0342711E5, 2010-0391051E5, 2011-0429001E5
Photodynamic therapy	Yes	The cost of photodynamic therapy to treat rosacea qualifies as a medical expense.	2010-0383831I7, S1-F1-C1 (paras 1.73-1.74)
Phototherapy equipment	Yes	Purchase of phototherapy equipment for the treatment of psoriasis or other skin disorders, including the cost of repairs and parts and other expenses in respect of the equipment, including amounts paid to operate and maintain the equipment (prescription not required)	118.2(2)(i), S1-F1-C1 (paras 1.73-1.74)
Physiotherapist	Yes	Amount paid to a physiotherapist licensed to practise under the laws of the province or territory as a medical practitioner	118.2(2)(a), S1-F1-C1 (paras 1.20–1.23)
Podologue	No	Amount paid to a podologue in the province of Quebec	2009-0337771E5
Pool	No	The costs of a pool does not qualify for the medical expense credit even if recommended by a medical practitioner; see 2009-0342581E5, 2006-0198081E5 and *Barnes*, [2010] 1 C.T.C. 2009 (TCC). See also "Home alterations"	118.2(l.2), (l.21), S1-F1-C1 (para 1.97)

Item	Qualifies	Description of Medical Expense	Reference
Power of attorney fees	No	Fees paid pursuant to provincially prescribed rates for a power of attorney where incurred as a result of an individual's financial incapacity due to medical reasons	2010-0390011E5
Power-operated guided chair installation (prescribed)	Yes	Amount paid for a power-operated guided chair installation (prescription required)	118.2(2)(m), Reg 5700(f), S1-F1-C1 (para 1.122)
Power-operated lift or transportation equipment (prescribed)	Yes	Designed exclusively for use by a disabled individual to allow the individual access to different areas of a building or to assist the individual to gain access to a vehicle or to place the individual's wheelchair in or on a vehicle (prescription required)	118.2(2)(m), Reg 5700(m), S1-F1-C1 (para 1.122)
Premiums paid to private medical clinic as an access fee	No	A fee paid to a private medical clinic as a "membership" or "access" fee (the CRA's view is that such a fee is paid for access to medical services rather than for medical services themselves; in the situation considered in the reference herein, the membership fee was not attributable to a particular medical expense)	118.2(2)(a), (q), 2006-0166961E5, S1-F1-C1 (para 1.29)
Premiums paid to private health services plans (PHSP)	Yes	A "private health services plan" is defined in 248(1) as "(a) a contract of insurance in respect of hospital expenses, medical expenses or any combination of such expenses, or (b) a medical care insurance plan or hospital care insurance plan or any combination of such plans". Specifically excluded is "any such contract or plan established by or pursuant to (c) a law of a province that establishes a health care insurance plan as defined in section 2 of the *Canada Health Act*, or (d) an Act of Parliament or a regulation made thereunder that authorizes the provision of a medical care insurance plan or hospital care insurance plan for employees of Canada and their dependants ...". A qualifying amount may be paid as a premium, contribution or other consideration under a private health services plan in respect of one or more of the individual, the individual's spouse or common-law partner and any member of the individual's household with whom the individual is connected by blood relationship, marriage, common-law partnership or adoption (except to the extent that the premium is deducted under 20.01(1) in computing an individual's income from a business for any taxation year). Where the plan covers over-the-counter drugs, the plan still may qualify	118.2(2)(q), IT-339R2 (Meaning of "Private Health Services Plan"), 2008-0270031E5, 2013-0480711M4, 2014-0524321I7, S1-F1-C1 (paras 1.133–1.135)

Item	Qualifies	Description of Medical Expense	Reference
Premiums paid to provincial or territorial prescription drug plans	Yes	Premiums paid to provincial or territorial prescription drug plans (for example, the Quebec Prescription Drug Insurance Plan, the Nova Scotia Seniors' Pharmacare Program, or the British Columbia Fair Pharmacare Program) qualify. Note, however, that premiums paid under provincial or territorial government medical or hospitalization plans are not eligible	118.2(2)(q), CRA Guide RC4064, S1-F1-C1 (paras 1.133–1.135)
Premiums paid under provincial medical or hospitalization plans	No	Premiums paid under provincial or territorial government medical or hospitalization plans	CRA Guide RC4064, S1-F1-C1 (para 1.134)
Pre-natal classes	No	The cost of pre-natal classes provided by registered nurses to prospective parents	2017-0696851E5
Pre-natal and post-natal treatment	Yes	Amounts paid for pre-natal and post-natal treatment provided by a medical practitioner	118.2(2)(a)
Pressure pulse therapy device (prescribed)	Yes	Amount paid for a pressure pulse therapy device designed to be used by an individual who has a balance disorder (prescription required)	118.2(2)(m), Reg 5700(z.4), S1-F1-C1 (para 1.122)
Prince Edward Island Health Services Payment Plan	No	See "Premiums paid to private health services plans (PHSP)"	118.2(2)(q), S1-F1-C1 (para 1.134)
Print-on-screen device		See "Blind individuals"	
Private health care services	Yes	Amounts paid to an institution is a licensed private hospital (the CRA has stated that "possession of a municipal licence to carry on business does not necessarily qualify the institution. However, if the institution possesses a provincial licence designating it as a "hospital," subject to its meeting and maintaining standards set by local health, building and fire authorities, the institution may qualify as a hospital for income tax purposes."). The institution does not have to be located in Canada	118.2(2)(a), CRA Guide RC4064, S1-F1-C1 (paras 1.24-1.25)
Psoriasis		See "Phototherapy equipment"	
Psychoanalyst	Yes	Amount paid to a Psychoanalyst who is a member of the Canadian Institute of Psychoanalysis or a member of the Quebec Association of Jungian Psychoanalysts	118.2(2)(a), S1-F1-C1 (paras 1.20–1.23)
Psychologist	Yes	Amount paid to a psychologist licensed to practise under the laws of the province or territory as a medical practitioner	118.2(2)(a), S1-F1-C1 (paras 1.20–1.23)

Item	Qualifies	Description of Medical Expense	Reference
Purifier (prescribed)	Yes	Acquired for an individual who is suffering from a severe chronic respiratory ailment or a severe chronic immune system disregulation to cope with or overcome that ailment or disregulation (prescription required)	118.2(2)(m), Reg 5700(c.1), S1-F1-C1 (para 1.122)
Pulse Electromagnetic Technician	Depends	Payments to a pulse electromagnetic technician would not qualify as eligible medical expenses unless the amounts were paid for "medical services" performed by a medical practitioner authorized to practise as such according to the laws of the jurisdiction in which the service was rendered. Pulse electromagnetic technicians are not authorized as medical practitioners in Ontario (2014-0551781M4)	118.2(2)(a), S1-F1-C1 (paras 1.20–1.23)
Quebec Health Insurance Board (including payments made to the Health Services Fund)	No	See "Premiums paid to private health services plans (PHSP)"	118.2(2)(q), S1-F1-C1 (para 1.134)
Radiological services or procedures (prescribed)	Yes	Amount paid in respect of radiological services or procedures not covered by provincial health insurance (prescription required)	118.2(2)(o), CRA Guide RC4064, S1-F1-C1 (para 1.128)
Reading device (prescribed)	Yes	Amount paid for a device or software designed to be used by blind individuals or individuals with a severe learning disability to enable the individual to read print (prescription required)	118.2(2)(m), Reg 5700(l.1), S1-F1-C1 (para 1.122)
Reading services	Yes	Amount paid for reading services provided to a person who is blind or has a severe learning disability and paid to someone in the business of providing such services (a medical practitioner must certify in writing that these services are necessary)	118.2(2)(l.43), S1-F1-C1 (para 1.105)
Real-time captioning services	Yes	Used by a person with a speech or hearing impairment and paid to someone in the business of providing such services.	118.2(2)(l.4), S1-F1-C1 (para 1.102)

Item	Qualifies	Description of Medical Expense	Reference
Registered clinical counsellor	Depends	Payments to a registered clinical counsellor would not qualify as eligible medical expenses unless the amounts were paid for "medical services" performed by a medical practitioner authorized to practise as such according to the laws of the jurisdiction in which the service was rendered. The CRA has stated that a registered clinical counsellor in B.C. does not qualify as a medical practitioner (see 2007-0246011E5 and 2007-0250511E5). The CRA has also stated that counselling services are considered to qualify if: 1) the counsellor is working in a recognized mental health clinic, community agency or hospital; 2) the counsellor is a member of an association governing their profession; and 3) the treatment is at the request of, or in association with, a medical practitioner. The CRA's view is that a person is authorized by the laws of a jurisdiction to act as a medical practitioner if there is specific legislation that enables, permits or empowers a person to perform medical services and generally, such specific legislation provides for the licensing or certification of the practitioner as well as for the establishment of a governing body (eg, a college or board) with the authority to determine competency, enforce discipline and set basic standards of conduct	118.2(2)(a), 2002-0171795, 2005-0153591E5, 2006-0213231E5, 2009-0337771E5, S1-F1-C1 (paras 1.20–1.23)
Reiki practitioner	Depends	Payments to a Reiki practitioner would not qualify as eligible medical expenses unless the Reiki practitioner was authorized as a medical practitioner according to the laws of the jurisdiction in which the service was rendered (see also the comments directly above)	118.2(2)(a), Tall, 2008 CarswellNat 4735 (TCC), S1-F1-C1 (paras 1.20–1.23)
Renovation costs (home)		See "Home Alterations"	
Residential treatment center or out-patient clinic	Yes	Amounts paid to a residential treatment centre for medical treatment (e.g., for an eating disorder, depression, ADHD or addiction) where a medical practitioner certifies in writing that the person requires the specialized equipment, facilities, or personnel provided. There is no requirement that the treatment centre be a public or licensed private hospital.	118.2(2)(e), S1-F1-C1 (paras 1.56–1.63), 2012-0436431E5, 2012-0444341E5
Respiratory ailment		See "Immune system disregulation or respiratory ailment"	
Retirement home		See "Attendant care at a retirement home, home for seniors, or other institution"	

Item	Qualifies	Description of Medical Expense	Reference
Rocking bed	Yes	Amount paid for a rocking bed for poliomyelitis victims (prescription not required)	118.2(2)(i), S1-F1-C1 (paras 1.73-1.74)
Rolf therapy	Depends	Payments for Rolf therapy would not qualify as eligible medical expenses unless the amounts were paid for "medical services" performed by a medical practitioner authorized to practise as such according to the laws of the jurisdiction in which the service was rendered. The CRA's view is that a person is authorized by the laws of a jurisdiction to act as a medical practitioner if there is specific legislation that enables, permits or empowers a person to perform medical services and generally, such specific legislation provides for the licensing or certification of the practitioner as well as for the establishment of a governing body (eg, a college or board) with the authority to determine competency, enforce discipline and set basic standards of conduct	2007-0235861E5, 2009-0337771E5, S1-F1-C1 (paras 1.20–1.23)
Saskatchewan Medical Care Insurance Plan	No	See "Premiums paid to private health services plans (PHSP)"	118.2(2)(q), S1-F1-C1 (para 1.134)
School tuition (for impaired persons)		See under "Care or care and training at special schools"	
Scientology	No	Amount paid to Founding Church Scientology for a course of treatment or for other services	118.2(2)(a), 33 Tax A.B.C. 243
Scooter	Yes	Amount paid for a scooter that is used in place of a wheelchair (prescription not required). The cost of renting a scooter would also qualify. However, an electric scooter only qualifies if it is acquired in substitution for a conventional wheelchair and is used to improve mobility.	118.2(2)(i), CRA Guide RC4064, S1-F1-C1 (para 1.76), 2010-0378071E5, 2009-0332141E5
Second stairway hall hand railing	No	Amount paid for second stairway hall hand railing	2009-0332141E5
Segway	No	A Segway cannot be considered a wheelchair, nor is it "exclusively designed" for individuals with mobility impairments. See also "wheelchair".	118.2(2)(i), Reg 5700 (i), (m), (z.3), 2015-0596311I7
Seniors home		See "Attendant care at a retirement home, home for seniors, or other institution"	

Item	Qualifies	Description of Medical Expense	Reference
Shiatsu therapist, registered	Depends	Payments to a registered shiatsu therapist would not qualify as eligible medical expenses unless the amounts were paid for "medical services" performed by a medical practitioner authorized to practise as such according to the laws of the jurisdiction in which the service was rendered. Registered shiatsu therapists are not authorized as medical practitioners in BC (2015-0571341E5)	118.2(2)(a), S1-F1-C1 (paras 1.20–1.23)
Shoes (orthopedic)		See "Orthopaedic shoe or boot (and an insert for a shoe or boot)"	
Sign language (interpretation services)	Yes	Amounts paid for sign-language interpretation services used by a person with a speech or hearing impairment and paid to someone in the business of providing such services qualify.	118.2(2)(l.4), S1-F1-C1 (para 1.102)
Skating (ice time and coach)	No	A skating coach would not be considered to be administering therapy under the general supervision of a medical doctor or occupational therapist	118.2(2)(l.9), 2010-0355211E5
Skin disorders		See "Phototherapy equipment"	
Sleep evaluation study	Yes	Costs for a sleep evaluation study paid to a private sleep clinic	118.2(2)(a), 118.2(2)(o), 2011-0397231E5
Snow blower	No	The cost of a snow blower does not qualify	2014-0552351E5
Social worker	No	Services provided by a registered social worker do not qualify; see for example *Pickwood v. R.*, [2005] 4 C.T.C. 2314 (TCC)	118.2(2)(a)
Societies (medical)	Depends	Payments made to partnerships, societies and associations for medical services rendered by their employees or partners are qualifying medical expenses as long as the person who provided the service is a medical practitioner, dentist or nurse authorized to practise (for example, the Arthritis Society employs physiotherapists)	118.2(2)(a), S1-F1-C1 (para 1.28)
Software (prescribed)	Yes	Amount paid for software designed to be used by a blind individual, or an individual with a severe learning disability, to enable the individual to read print (prescription required)	118.2(2)(m), Reg 5700(1.1), S1-F1-C1 (para 1.122)
Speaking aid (laryngeal)	Yes	Amount paid for a speaking aid (laryngeal), including the cost of repairs and parts and other expenses in respect of (prescription not required)	118.2(2)(i), S1-F1-C1 (paras 1.73-1.74, 1.79)
Special Access Programme devices		See "Drugs, medicaments or other preparations or substances"	

Item	Qualifies	Description of Medical Expense	Reference
Speech impairment (auditory feedback device; prescribed)	Yes	Amount paid for an altered auditory feedback device designed to be used by an individual who has a speech impairment (prescription required)	118.2(2)(m), Reg 5700(z.1), S1-F1-C1 (para 1.122)
Speech impairment (bliss symbol board; prescribed)	Yes	Amount paid for a Bliss symbol board (or similar device) designed to be used to help an individual who has a speech impairment communicate by selecting the symbols or spelling out words (prescription required). The purchase of an iPad to assist certain special needs children would not qualify for the medical expense credit	118.2(2)(m), Reg 5700(x), 2010-0383021E5, S1-F1-C1 (para 1.122)
Speech synthesizer (electronic; prescribed)	Yes	Amount paid for a speech synthesizer (electronic) that enables a mute individual to communicate by use of a portable keyboard (prescription required)	118.2(2)(m), Reg 5700(p), S1-F1-C1 (para 1.122)
Speech-language pathologist or audiologist	Yes	Amount paid to a speech-language pathologist or audiologist where the province or territory authorizes a pathologist or audiologist as a medical practitioner (such as, for example, a person who is certified as such by The Canadian Association of Speech-Language Pathologists and Audiologists (CASLPA) or a provincial affiliate of that organization). Amounts paid to a speech therapy technician are not eligible unless the therapist's services help the physician or the speech therapist establish a diagnostic or a medical treatment, or they are prescribed and administered under the general surveillance of a physician (2012-0465171E5).	118.2(2)(a), S1-F1-C1 (paras 1.20–1.23)
Spinal brace	Yes	Amount paid for a spinal brace or a spinal support (prescription not required). Amount paid for a seamless T-shirt to be worn underneath is not considered to be paid "in respect of" a spinal brace (2011-0429441E5)	118.2(2)(i), S1-F1-C1 (paras 1.73-1.74)
Spinal fluid tests (prescribed)	Yes	Amount paid in respect of spinal fluid tests not covered by provincial health insurance (prescription required)	118.2(2)(o), CRA Guide RC4064
Standing device (prescribed)	Yes	Amount paid for a standing device designed to be used by an individual who has a severe mobility impairment to undertake standing therapy (prescription required)	118.2(2)(m), Reg 5700(z.3), S1-F1-C1 (para 1.122)
Stem cell therapy	Yes	Amounts paid to a medical practitioner or a licensed private hospital in respect of stem cell therapy. Where the therapy is not available in Canada, travel costs would also likely be eligible (2012-0448971E5)	118.2(2)(a), 2009-0319341E5

Item	Qualifies	Description of Medical Expense	Reference
Stool examinations (prescribed)	Yes	Amount paid in respect of stool examination tests not covered by provincial health insurance (prescription required)	118.2(2)(o), CRA Guide RC4064
Stroller	Depends	The CRA's view is that a stroller designed for a child with special needs would qualify as a wheelchair where the stroller is purchased for a child who would otherwise require a wheelchair	2003-0046145
Sudden infant death syndrome device	Yes	Amount paid for a device designed to be attached to infants diagnosed as being prone to sudden infant death syndrome in order to sound an alarm if the infant ceases to breathe and that is for the infant's use as prescribed by a medical practitioner (a medical practitioner must certify in writing that the infant is prone to sudden infant death syndrome)	118.2(2)(m), Reg 5700(r), S1-F1-C1 (para 1.122)
Sunglasses (prescription)	Yes	The cost of prescription eyeglasses qualifies as a medical expense under 118.2(2)(j), including the cost of both the frames and lenses (prescription required from a medical practitioner or optometrist). The CRA has expressed the view that sunglasses prescribed by an optometrist to treat photosensitivity, which causes an individual to suffer from headaches caused by the sun or bright lighting, would not qualify for the credit (2003-0046081E5). The sunglasses in the particular situation were purchased from a retail story and were not prescription sunglasses	118.2(2)(j), S1-F1-C1 (para 1.89)
Supplements	No	Over-the-counter medications, vitamins, and supplements do not qualify for the credit even if they are prescribed by a medical practitioner. Subparagraph 118.2(n)(ii) refers to drugs, medicaments or other preparations or substances "that can lawfully be acquired for use by the patient only if prescribed by a medical practitioner or dentist". See also *Ray*, 2009 CarswellNat 473 (TCC), *Ali v. R.*, [2008] 4 C.T.C. 245 (FCA), *Berg*, 2011 CarswellNat 4735 (TCC) and *Leeper*, 2015 CarswellNat 1126 (TCC)	118.2(2)(n), CRA Guide RC4064, 2014-0529511E5, 2008-0264631M4, 2008-0270031E5 and 2007-0231171E5, S1-F1-C1 (paras 1.123–1.125)

Item	Qualifies	Description of Medical Expense	Reference
Surrogacy fees	No	Fees paid to a surrogate to carry the embryo and deliver the baby for the biological parents do not qualify. Related expenses, such as medical services provided directly to a surrogate also do not qualify, since the surrogate is not the "patient" as defined in 118.2(2)(a). Expenses relating to in-vitro and embryology services and travel and meal costs incurred for procedures outside of Canada do qualify	2010-0391691E5, 2015-0572891E5, 2015-0589741E5, *Warnock*, 2014 CarswellNat 2957 (TCC), *Zanatta*, 2014 CarswellNat 3808 (TCC), *Pearen*, 2014 CarswellNat 3809 (TCC))
Swimming goggles (prescribed)	Yes	The cost of swimming goggles if prescribed by a medical practitioner or optometrist specifically for the treatment or correction of a specified vision defect	118.2(2)(j) 2017-0690361E5
Swimming pool	No	The costs of a pool does not qualify for the medical expense credit even if recommended by a medical practitioner; see 2009-0342581E5, 2006-0198081E5 and *Barnes*, [2010] 1 C.T.C. 2009 (TCC). See also "Home alterations"	118.2(l.2), (l.21), S1-F1-C1 (paras 1.94–1.100)
Synthetic speech system		See "Blind individuals"	
Syringe (prescribed)	Yes	Designed to be used for the purpose of giving an injection (prescription required)	118.2(2)(m), Reg 5700(b), S1-F1-C1 (para 1.122)
Talking textbook (prescribed)	Yes	Amount paid for a talking textbook for use by an individual with a perceptual disability in connection with the individual's enrolment at an educational institution in Canada (or a designated educational institution) (prescription required)	118.2(2)(m), Reg 5700(w), S1-F1-C1 (para 1.122)
Tape liquid bandage	No	Amount paid for tape liquid bandage	2009-0332141E5
Teeth whitening	Depends	For expenses incurred after March 4, 2010, expenses incurred for purely cosmetic procedures no longer qualify for the credit (unless required for medical or reconstructive purposes). Formerly, an amount paid to a dentist or other medical practitioner for teeth whitening qualified (over-the-counter teeth whitening products did not qualify for the credit; see under "Over-the-counter medications"). See also "Cosmetic procedures"	118.2(2.1), 2003-0012351E5, S1-F1-C1 (paras 1.143–1.146)
Telephone ringing indicator (prescribed)	Yes	Amount paid for a telephone ringing indicator that enables a deaf or mute individual to make and receive telephone calls (prescription required)	118.2(2)(m), Reg 5700(k), S1-F1-C1 (para 1.122)
Teletypewriter or similar device (prescribed)	Yes	Amount paid for a teletypewriter (or similar device) that enables a deaf or mute individual to make and receive telephone calls (prescription required)	118.2(2)(m), Reg 5700(k), S1-F1-C1 (para 1.122)

Item	Qualifies	Description of Medical Expense	Reference
Television signal decoder (prescribed)	Yes	Amount paid for a television signal decoder that decodes special television signals to permit the script of a program to be visually displayed (prescription required). Where a television contains a closed-caption decoder, the cost equivalent of the decoder chip where the chip decodes special television signals to permit the script of a program to be visually displayed would qualify	118.2(2)(m), Reg 5700(q), 2004-0068651I7, S1-F1-C1 (para 1.122)
Tests (prescribed)	Yes	Amount paid in respect of medical tests such as cardiographs, electrocardiograms, metabolism tests, radiological services or procedures, spinal fluid tests, stool examinations, sugar content tests, urine analysis, x-ray services, and digital infrared thermal imaging (see 2009-0307921E5) including the cost of any related interpretation or diagnosis (prescription required)	118.2(2)(o), CRA Guide RC4064
Therapeutist (or therapist)	Depends	Amount paid to a therapeutist (or therapist) licensed to practise under the laws of the province or territory as a medical practitioner qualifies. The Court found that a thalassotherapy centre in Quebec did not qualify for the credit in *Roy v. R.*, 2004 CarswellNat 4481 (TCC)	118.2(2)(a), S1-F1-C1 (paras 1.20–1.23)
Therapy (see also "Therapy plan")	Depends	The cost of therapy received by a person who qualifies for the disability credit is generally eligible for the medical expense credit to the extent that the therapy is provided by someone other than the person's spouse or common-law partner (and who is 18 years of age or older when the amounts are paid) and the therapy has been prescribed and supervised by a doctor, a psychologist (for a mental impairment) or an occupational therapist (for a physical impairment). The CRA's general position is that monitoring by a medical doctor would not meet the requirement that the therapy be administered under the general supervision of a medical doctor	118.2(2)(l.9), CRA Guide RC4064, S1-F1-C1 (paras 1.115-1.116), 2008-0291501E5

Item	Qualifies	Description of Medical Expense	Reference
Therapy plan (individualized)	Depends	Applicable to expenses incurred after 2013, costs for designing an individualized therapy plan are eligible for the medical expense credit if: (1) the therapy set out in the plan is prescribed and supervised by a doctor, a psychologist (for a mental impairment) or an occupational therapist (for a physical impairment); (2) an individualized therapy plan is required to access public funding for specialized therapy, or a doctor, a psychologist (for a mental impairment) or an occupational therapist (for a physical impairment) prescribes an individualized therapy plan; (3) the plan is designed for an individual who is eligible for the disability tax credit; and (4) the amounts are paid to persons ordinarily engaged in the business of providing such services to unrelated individuals	118.2(2)(l.92), S1-F1-C1 (para. 1.117.1)
Toilet seat (raised)		See "Device or equipment (bathtub, shower or toilet)"	
Traditional Chinese medicine (TCM) practitioner	Depends	Payments to a TCM practitioner would not qualify as eligible medical expenses unless the amounts were paid for "medical services" performed by a medical practitioner authorized to practise as such according to the laws of the jurisdiction in which the service was rendered. Amounts paid to a TCM practitioner in Ontario currently do not qualify; however, the TCM profession is was in the process of establishing self-regulation to meet requirements under the *Regulated Health Professions Act, 1991* at the time of writing	118.2(2)(a), 2010-0359241E5, S1-F1-C1 (paras 1.20–1.23)
Training		See "Caregiver training", "Sign language training", "Lip reading training", and "Care or care and training at special schools, institutions, or other places"	
Transplant costs		See "Bone marrow transplant", "Organ transplant", and "Hair transplant"	

Item	Qualifies	Description of Medical Expense	Reference
Transportation expenses for medical purposes (generally)	Yes	If medical treatment is not available locally (within 40 kilometres), an individual may be able to claim the cost of travelling to get the treatment where it is reasonable to do so. Travel costs are not allowed where "substantially equivalent medical services" are "available" locally, even if it is more expensive locally (see *Tokarski*, 2012 CarswellNat 985 (TCC) and *Ismael*, 2014 CarswellNat 1817 (TCC)). Travel costs can include a spouse's daily visits to the patient, not just when travelling to the hospital with the patient (*Bell* [2010] 1 C.T.C. 2433 (TCC) and *Jordan*, 2012 CarswellNat 4419 (TCC). Three 60 km daily round trips do not qualify because is less than 40 km one way (2013-0483171E5). Travel costs for winter travel to a warmer climate to alleviate taxpayer's severe chronic pain were not allowed in *Tallon*, 2015 CarswellNat 2823 (FCA, reversing the TCC). The CRA agrees that travel expenses incurred to travel to a warmer climate, even if for health reasons, are not eligible medical expenses (2015-0610741C6). Travel expenses of an orthodontist paid by a taxpayer to receive dental services do not qualify because only travel expenses incurred in respect of the patient are allowed (2016-0624871C6).	118.2(2)(g), CRA Guide RC4064, S1-F1-C1 (paras 1.64–1.72), 2015-0584181E5, 2014-0520551E5, 2013-0510121E5, 2013-0478271E5, 2012-0463351E5, 2012-0435931E5, 2012-0437281E5, 2012-0457461E5, 2012-0461911E5
Transportation expenses (travel to a school or institution attended for medical purposes)	Yes	Where an individual's tuition costs qualify as a medical expense under paragraph 118.2(2)(e) (see under "Care or care and training at institutions or other places"), travel costs to transport the individual to the school (or other institution) and the travel costs home from the school qualify as medical expenses provided the conditions contained in paragraph 118.2(g) described above are met. The expense of renting an accommodation near the school and travel expenses incurred to come home for holidays would not qualify.	118.2(2)(g), 2009-0349551E5, 2010-0385321M4, 2011-0395911E5, S1-F1-C1 (paras 1.64–1.72)

Item	Qualifies	Description of Medical Expense	Reference
Transportation expenses for medical purposes (vehicle; detailed method)	Yes	If medical treatment is not available locally (within 40 kilometres), an individual may be able to claim the cost of travelling to get the treatment somewhere else where it is reasonable to do so (see for example *Sienema*, 2010 CarswellNat 3305 (TCC)). Note that although 118.2(2)(g) refers to transportation provided by a person engaged in the business of providing transportation services (eg taxi, bus or train), this requirement is waived by 118.2(4) where, because such transportation is not readily available, a private vehicle is used. In this case a reasonable mileage charge will be recognized as a qualifying medical expense under 118.2(2)(g). The individual can use a detailed method or a simple method for calculating the travel expenses. Under the detailed method, the individual must keep all receipts and records for the vehicle expenses paid. The individual also must keep track of the total number of kilometres driven during the period and the number of kilometres driven specifically for the purpose of medical expenses. An individual's claim for travel expenses is the percentage of total vehicle expenses that relate to the kilometres driven for medical reasons.	118.2(2)(g), CRA Guide RC4064, S1-F1-C1 (paras 31–34), *Patton v. R.*, [2006] 1 C.T.C. 2293 (TCC), S1-F1-C1 (paras 1.64–1.72)
Transportation expenses for medical purposes (vehicle; simple method)	Yes	As mentioned above, if medical treatment is not available locally (within 40 kilometres), an individual may be able to claim the cost of travelling to get the treatment somewhere else. If an individual uses the simple method to calculate vehicle expenses, the individual must keep track of the kilometres traveled for medical reasons during the 12-month period. Kilometers driven for medical reasons are then multiplied by a flat rate per kilometer for each province or territory.	118.2(2)(g), CRA Guide RC4064, S1-F1-C1 (paras 1.64–1.72)
Transportation expenses for medical purposes (frequent flyer points)	Yes	If an individual is required to travel by air to obtain treatment, the value of Aeroplan points used to purchase an airline ticket can be claimed as a medical expense where the trip is for the purposes of obtaining medical treatment	118.2(2)(g), *Johnson v. R.* 2010 CarswellNat 1647 (TCC), S1-F1-C1 (paras 1.64–1.72)
Transportation and travel expenses for medical purposes (parking fees)	Yes	Parking fees can be included in transportation or travelling expenses under 118.2(2)(g) and (h) if the requirements are otherwise met. See also "Parking fees"	118.2(2), (g), (h), 2011-0394771E5, S1-F1-C1 (paras 1.64–1.72)

Item	Qualifies	Description of Medical Expense	Reference
Travel expenses for medical purposes (meals and accommodations)	Yes	If an individual has to travel more than 80 kilometres (one way) for medical treatment, in addition to travel costs, the individual may be able to claim the cost of meals and accommodations (such as hotel costs) as a medical expense credit. An individual can also claim travel expenses for someone to accompany them if a medical practitioner certifies in writing that the individual is unable to travel without assistance. (Travel expenses cannot be claimed for more than one accompanying person: 2011-0423231E5). Travel costs can include a spouse's daily visits to the patient, not just when travelling to the hospital with the patient (*Bell* [2010] 1 C.T.C. 2433 (TCC) and *Jordan*, 2012 CarswellNat 4419 (TCC)). Travel costs for winter travel to a warmer climate to alleviate taxpayer's severe chronic pain were allowed in *Tallon*, 2014 CarswellNat 1886 (TCC, under appeal to FCA). Note that an 80km limit applies to transportation expenses claimed under 118.2(2)(h) whereas a 40km limit applies to travel expenses claimed under 118.2(2)(g). If the detailed method to calculate meal expenses is used, the individual must keep receipts. If the simple method is used, a flat rate of $17 a meal, to a maximum of $51 per day, per person, without receipts, may be claimed (see IC 73-21R9). All receipts must be kept for accommodation expenses. It is generally a question of fact whether an expense that meets the criteria set out in 118.2(2)(h) may be considered a "reasonable" travel expense.	118.2(2)(h), CRA Guide RC4064, S1-F1-C1 (paras 1.64–1.72), 2015-0584181E5, 2014-0520551E5, 2013-0510121E5, 2013-0507301C6, 2013-0478271E5, 2012-0463351E5, 2012-0435931E5, 2012-0437281E5, 2012-0457461E5, 2012-0461911E5, 2010-0391871M4, 2010-0391371M4, 2010-0385321M4, 2010-0377291M4, 2010-0353251M4, 2009-0337761E5, 2007-0255831E5
Travel insurance		See "Travel medical insurance"	
Travel medical insurance	Depends	Amounts paid to acquire certain travel medical insurance policies can qualify as a medical expense if the amount is paid as a premium, contribution or other consideration to a private health services plan ("PHSP")	118.2(2)(q), S1-F1-C1 (paras 1.133–1.135), 2007-0229901E5
Truss for hernia	Yes	Amount paid for a truss for a hernia (prescription not required)	118.2(2)(i), S1-F1-C1 (paras 1.73-1.74)
Tubing	Yes	Amounts paid for catheters and catheter trays required by the patient by reason of incontinence caused by illness, injury or affliction (including catheter trays, tubing, or other products required for incontinence caused by illness, injury, or affliction); a prescription is not required	118.2(2)(i.1), S1-F1-C1 (para 1.87)

Item	Qualifies	Description of Medical Expense	Reference
Tutoring services	Yes	Amounts paid as remuneration for tutoring services that are supplementary to the primary education of a person with a learning disability or an impairment in mental functions and paid to someone in the business of providing such services (who is not related to the person being tutored) qualify for the credit if a medical practitioner certifies in writing that the services are necessary because of the learning disability or impairment in mental functions. In 2011-0429701I7, salary paid to a teacher for special education services for a disabled child qualified.	118.2(2)(l.91), *Hoare*, [2007] 4 C.T.C. 2283 (TCC), S1-F1-C1 (para 1.117)
US Medicare Plan B	Depends	The CRA has stated that they "are not able to confirm whether or not the payment of such premiums would qualify as a "medical expense" under paragraph 118.2(2)(q) of the Act". The CRA further stated that "based on the information that we have, it appears that amounts paid for Medicare Plan B are merely "set-off" against an individual's entitlement to US Social Security benefits. In such a situation, if the premiums paid by way of a "set-off" do otherwise satisfy the criteria in paragraph 118.2(2)(q) of the Act, the full amount "set-off" would be a "medical expense" for the purposes of the Act"	118.2(2)(q), 2001-0109875, 2007-0254661E5
Ultrasound tests	Yes	The cost of ultrasound tests generally qualifies. Amounts paid by an individual to a "medical practitioner" (including a nurse) or to a "public or licensed private hospital" (ie, a hospital is licensed by the jurisdiction in which it operates) to obtain medical services qualify. Also, qualifying expenses include amounts paid for laboratory, radiological or other diagnostic procedures or services, with necessary interpretations, for maintaining health, preventing disease or assisting in the diagnosis or treatment of an injury, illness or disability as prescribed by a medical practitioner	118.2(2)(a), (o), 2009-0349731E5, S1-F1-C1 (para 1.130)
Umbilical cord blood collection/storage	No	Amount paid for collection and storage of umbilical cord blood	*Shapiro*, 2014 CarswellNat 594 (TCC), 2005-0137781E5, 2010-0390981E5, 2011-0422941E5
Urine analysis (prescribed)	Yes	Amount paid in respect of urine analysis test not covered by provincial health insurance (prescription required)	118.2(2)(o), CRA Guide RC4064

Item	Qualifies	Description of Medical Expense	Reference
Vaccines and vaccinations	Yes	Amounts paid for a vaccine generally qualify for the credit. A medical practitioner or dentist must have prescribed the vaccine and the vaccine must be purchased from a pharmacist who has recorded the purchase	118.2(2)(n), CRA Guide RC4064
Van for wheelchair	Yes	20% of the amount paid, up to a maximum claim of $5,000, for a van that has been previously adapted, or is adapted within six months of the date of purchase, to transport a person who needs to use a wheelchair may be claimed as a medical expense. Expenses related to the operation of the van rather than to costs incurred for the acquisition or adaptation of the van do not fall within scope of 118.2(2)(l.7); *Scully*, [2009] 2 C.T.C. 2225 (TCC). In 2011-0420021E5, a portion of the cost to acquire a van and adapt it with power-operated lift and hand controls for a quadriplegic individual qualified.	118.2(2)(l.7) 2011-0420021E5, (S1-F1-C1 (paras 1.109–1.112, 1.122)
Vasectomy reversal	Yes	An amount paid for a vasectomy reversal qualifies since it relates to the "existing medical condition" of infertility	118.2(2)(a), 2014-0529901E5
Vehicle modification (prescribed)	Yes	Amounts paid to modify a vehicle to permit a person confined to a wheelchair to gain independent access to and drive the vehicle (prescription required)	118.2(2)(l.7), 118.2(2)(m), 5700(m), CRA Guide RC4064, 2011-0420021E5, S1-F1-C1 (paras 1.109–1.112, 1.122)
Vibratory signalling device (prescribed)	Yes	Amount paid for a vibratory signalling device For an individual with a hearing impairment (prescription required)	118.2(2)(m), Reg 5700(q.1), S1-F1-C1 (para 1.122)
Victorian Order of Nurses		See "Associations"	
Visual fire alarm indicator (prescribed)	Yes	Amount paid for a visual fire alarm indicator for an individual with a hearing impairment (prescription required)	118.2(2)(m), Reg 5700(q.1), S1-F1-C1 (para 1.122)
Visual or vibratory signalling device (prescribed)	Yes	Amount paid for a visual or vibratory signalling device for use by an individual with a hearing impairment (prescription required)	118.2(2)(m), Reg 5700(q.1), S1-F1-C1 (para 1.122)
Vitamin B12 injections for pernicious anemia	Yes	An amount paid for vitamin B12 injections for pernicious anemia generally qualifies. A medical practitioner must have prescribed the injections, but a pharmacy or any other type of store may sell the vitamin B12 without a written prescription and the expense will qualify (provided an initial prescription was given)	118.2(2)(k), 2011-0426031E5, S1-F1-C1 (paras 1.90, 1.131)

Item	Qualifies	Description of Medical Expense	Reference
Vitamins	No	Over-the-counter medications, vitamins, and supplements do not qualify for the credit even if they are prescribed by a medical practitioner. Subparagraph 118.2(n)(ii) refers to drugs, medicaments or other preparations or substances "that can lawfully be acquired for use by the patient only if prescribed by a medical practitioner or dentist". See also *Ray*, 2009 CarswellNat 473 (TCC), *Ali v. R.*, [2008] 4 C.T.C. 245 (FCA) and *Leeper*, 2015 CarswellNat 1126 (TCC)	118.2(2)(n), CRA Guide RC4064, 2014-0529511E5, 2010-0378121M4, 2008-0264631M4, 2008-0270031E5, 2007-0231171E5
Voice recognition software	Yes	Amount paid for voice recognition software used by a person who has an impairment in physical functions (a medical practitioner must certify in writing that the expense is necessary because of a physical impairment)	118.2(2)(l.42), S1-F1-C1 (para 1.104)
Walking aids (prescribed)	Yes	The amount paid for a walking aid designed exclusively to help a person who has a mobility impairment to walk (prescription required). To qualify, a device must provide actual support in the action of walking	118.2(2)(m); Reg 5700(i), CRA Guide RC4064, 2009-0351441E5, S1-F1-C1 (para 1.122)
Water filter, cleaner, or purifier (prescribed)	Yes	Acquired for an individual who is suffering from a severe chronic respiratory ailment or a severe chronic immune system disregulation to cope with or overcome that ailment or disregulation (prescription required) (a water softener may qualify; 2007-0255191E5)	118.2(2)(m); Reg 5700(c.1), S1-F1-C1 (para 1.122)
Water well	No	Costs for a "water well" used for warm water therapy	2011-0392871E5
Weight loss program/clinic	Depends	Amounts paid for a weight loss program to a person licensed to practise under the laws of the province or territory as a medical practitioner will qualify as a medical service where the program is offered for therapeutic or rehabilitative reasons (eg; the treatment of obesity)	118.2(2)(a), (o), 2011-0402881E5, 2010-0358421E5, 2010-0361011E5, 2011-0429001E5, S1-F1-C1 (para 1.28)

Item	Qualifies	Description of Medical Expense	Reference
Wheelchair	Yes	Amount paid for a wheelchair, including cost of repairs and parts and other expenses in respect of qualify (prescription is not required). The CRA has stated that the term "wheelchair" is not restricted to the conventional arm-powered or battery-powered wheelchairs, but also includes scooters and wheel-mounted geriatric chairs" (see para 1.76 S1-F1-C1), a standing wheelchair (2015-0596311I7), and a tricycle wheelchair (2009-0351781E5). The cost of renting a wheelchair would also qualify, as would the cost of a cushion for a wheelchair. However, a "wheelchair" does not include: a battery-powered bicycle (2009-0323571E5), a power-lift armchair (2014-0524211E5), a Segway (2015-0596311I7), or a standard bicycle or tricycle (2016-0645021C6).	118.2(2)(i), CRA Guide RC4064, 2009-0332141E5, 2010-0361221E5, 2011-0395531E5, S1-F1-C1 (paras 1.73-1.74, 1.76)
Whirlpool bath (installed in home)	No	The cost of a hot tub a person installs in their home, even if prescribed by a medical practitioner, does not qualify (see the Supplementary Information (Annex 8) to the 2005 Federal Budget (2005-3) and 2006-0198081E5). In *Johnston*, the cost and installation of a hot tub for a severely disabled individual was denied because it does not satisfy 118.2(2)(l.2). It should, however, be noted that the CRA has stated that if a medical practitioner prescribes treatments in a hot tub or a whirlpool bath the cost of the treatment qualifies as a medical expense under 118.2(2)(a) if paid, for example, to a public or licensed private hospital	118.2(2)(a), (l.2), (l.21), CRA Guide RC4064, S1-F1-C1 (paras 1.97, 1.131), *Johnston*, 2012 CarswellNat 1636 (TCC), *Anthony*, 2012 CarswellNat 3538 (TCC)
Whole body vibration (WBV) unit (prescribed)	Yes	Amount paid to purchase, or for the use of, a whole body vibration (WBV) unit will qualify as a medical expense if the unit is prescribed by a medical practitioner to undertake standing therapy in the treatment of a severe mobility impairment (prescription required)	118.2(2)(m), Reg 5700(z.3), 2010-0358821E5, S1-F1-C1 (para 1.122)
Wig (prescribed)	Yes	Amount paid for a wig made to order for individuals who have suffered abnormal hair loss owing to disease, medical treatment or accident (prescription required)	118.2(2)(m); Reg 5700(a), S1-F1-C1 (para 1.122)
Window film (3M)	No	The application of 3M window film on all interior windows of a house to filter out UV rays does not qualify as a medical expense	2010-0379331E5
X-ray services (prescribed)	Yes	Amount paid in respect of x-ray services not covered by provincial health insurance (prescription required)	118.2(2)(o), CRA Guide RC4064

Item	Qualifies	Description of Medical Expense	Reference
Yoga fees	No	Amount paid for yoga fees, even if recommended or prescribed by a medical practitioner	2011-0423231E5
Yukon Territorial Insurance Commission premiums	No	See "Premiums paid to private health services plans (PHSP)"	118.2(2)(q), S1-F1-C1 (para 1.134)

List of Authorized Medical Practitioners by Province or Territory

Reproduced below from the CRA website is a list of authorized medical practitioners by province or territory for the purposes of claiming the medical expense tax credit (see list at tinyurl.com/cra-medprac). The list summarizes publicly available provincial and territorial information identifying those health care professionals authorized to practice as medical practitioners. The CRA highlights that the list is not an all inclusive list of every profession that is authorized by each province or territory.

Acupuncturist: Alberta, British Columbia, Newfoundland and Labrador, Ontario and Quebec.

Audiologist: Alberta, British Columbia, Manitoba, New Brunswick, Newfoundland, Ontario, Quebec, and Saskatchewan.

Chiropodist: Manitoba, New Brunswick, and Ontario.

Chiropractor: Alberta, British Columbia, Manitoba, New Brunswick, Newfoundland and Labrador, Nova Scotia, Ontario, Prince Edward Island, Quebec, Saskatchewan, and Yukon.

Combined lab and x-ray technologist: Alberta.

Counselling therapist: Nova Scotia

Criminologist: Quebec

Dental assistant: Alberta, Manitoba, New Brunswick, Newfoundland and Labrador, Nova Scotia, Prince Edward Island, and Saskatchewan.

Dental hygienist: all provinces and territories.

Dental nurse: Manitoba.

Dental technician or technologist: Alberta, British Columbia, Manitoba, New Brunswick, Newfoundland and Labrador, Nova Scotia, Ontario, Quebec, and Saskatchewan.

Dental therapist: Newfoundland and Labrador, Northwest Territories, Nunavut, Saskatchewan, and Yukon.

Dentist: all provinces and territories.

Denturist, dental mechanic, denturologist: all provinces and territories.

Dietician: Alberta, British Columbia, Manitoba, New Brunswick, Newfoundland and Labrador, Nova Scotia, Ontario, Prince Edward Island, Quebec, and Saskatchewan.

Emergency medical technician: Alberta, British Columbia, Prince Edward Island, and Saskatchewan.

Hearing aid practitioner: Alberta, British Columbia, Manitoba, Newfoundland and Labrador, and Quebec.

Homeopath: Ontario

Kinesiologist: Ontario

Licensed or registered practical nurse: all provinces and territories.

Marriage and family therapist: Quebec

Medical laboratory technologist: Alberta, Manitoba, New Brunswick, Newfoundland and Labrador, Nova Scotia, Ontario, Quebec, and Saskatchewan.

Medical radiation technologist: Alberta, New Brunswick, Nova Scotia, Ontario, Quebec, and Saskatchewan.

Midwife: Alberta, British Columbia, Manitoba, New Brunswick, Newfoundland, Nova Scotia, Northwest Territories, Nunavut, Ontario, Quebec, and Saskatchewan.

Naturopath: Alberta, British Columbia, Manitoba, Nova Scotia, Ontario, and Saskatchewan.

Occupational therapist: Alberta, British Columbia, Manitoba, New Brunswick, Newfoundland and Labrador, Nova Scotia, Ontario, Prince Edward Island, Quebec and Saskatchewan.

Ophthalmic medical assistant: Northwest Territories and Nunavut.

Optician: Alberta, British Columbia, Manitoba, New Brunswick, Newfoundland and Labrador, Nova Scotia, Ontario, Prince Edward Island, Quebec, and Saskatchewan.

Optometrist: all provinces and territories.

Pharmacist: all provinces and territories.

Physician: all provinces and territories.

Physiotherapist or physical therapist: Alberta, British Columbia, Manitoba, New Brunswick, Newfoundland and Labrador, Nova Scotia, Ontario, Prince Edward Island, Quebec, Saskatchewan, and Yukon.

Podiatrist: Alberta, British Columbia, Manitoba, New Brunswick, Ontario, Quebec, and Saskatchewan.

Professional technologist in orthoses/prostheses: Quebec

Psychological associate: British Columbia, Manitoba, and Ontario.

Psychologist: Alberta, British Columbia, Manitoba, New Brunswick, Newfoundland and Labrador, Nova Scotia, Northwest Territories, Nunavut, Ontario, Prince Edward Island, Quebec, and Saskatchewan.

Psychoeducator: Quebec

Registered massage therapist or massage therapist: British Columbia, New Brunswick, Newfoundland and Labrador, and Ontario.

Registered nurse (including nurse practitioner): all provinces and territories.

Registered nursing assistant: Northwest Territories, and Quebec.

Registered nutritionist: Alberta, New Brunswick, Nova Scotia and Quebec.

Registered psychiatric nurse: Alberta, British Columbia, Manitoba, Saskatchewan, and Yukon.

Registered psychotherapist: Ontario

Respiratory therapist: Alberta, Manitoba, New Brunswick, Newfoundland and Labrador, Nova Scotia, Ontario, Quebec, and Saskatchewan.

Sexologist: Quebec

Social worker: Alberta, British Columbia, Manitoba, New Brunswick, Newfoundland and Labrador, Nova Scotia, Ontario, Prince Edward Island, Quebec, and Saskatchewan.

Speech language pathologist: Alberta, British Columbia, Manitoba, New Brunswick, Newfoundland, Ontario, Quebec, and Saskatchewan.

Surgeon: all provinces and territories.

Traditional Chinese medicine practitioner: British Columbia and Ontario.

Vocal guidance counsellor: Quebec

Tax Reference Tables

Appendix B

Tables provided by KPMG LLP[1]

Appendix B-1 — Federal and Provincial/Territorial Income Tax Rates and Brackets — 2018

	Tax Rates	Tax Brackets	Surtax Rate	Surtax Threshold
Federal[a]	15.00%	Up to $46,605		
	20.50	46,606–93,208		
	26.00	93,209–144,489		
	29.00	144,490–205,842		
	33.00	205,843 and over		
British Columbia[b]	5.06%	Up to $39,676		
	7.70	39,677–79,353		
	10.50	79,354–91,107		
	12.29	91,108–110,630		
	14.70	110,631–150,000		
	16.80	150,001 and over		
Alberta[c]	10.00%	Up to $128,145		
	12.00	128,146–153,773		
	13.00	153,774–205,031		
	14.00	205,032–307,547		
	15.00	307,548 and over		
Saskatchewan[d]	10.50%	Up to $45,225		
	12.50	45,226–129,214		
	14.50	129,215 and over		
Manitoba[e]	10.80%	Up to $31,843		
	12.75	31,844–68,821		
	17.40	68,822 and over		
Ontario[f, g]	5.05%	Up to $42,960		
	9.15	42,961–85,923	20%	$4,638
	11.16	85,924–150,000	36	5,936
	12.16	150,001–220,000		
	13.16	220,001 and over		
Québec[g]	15.00%	Up to $43,055		

	Tax Rates	Tax Brackets	Surtax Rate	Surtax Threshold
	20.00	43,056–86,105		
	24.00	86,106–104,765		
	25.75	104,766 and over		
New Brunswick[i]	9.68%	Up to $41,675		
	14.82	41,676–83,351		
	16.52	83,352–135,510		
	17.84	135,511–154,382		
	20.30	154,383 and over		
Nova Scotia[d]	8.79%	Up to $29,590		
	14.95	29,591–59,180		
	16.67	59,181–93,000		
	17.50	93,001–150,000		
	21.00	150,001 and over		
Prince Edward Island[d, g]	9.80%	Up to $31,984		
	13.80	31,985–63,969		
	16.70	63,970 and over	10%	$12,500
Newfoundland & Labrador[j]	8.70%	Up to $36,926		
	14.50	36,927–73,852		
	15.80	73,853–131,850		
	17.30	131,851–184,590		
	18.30	184,591 and over		
Northwest Territories[i]	5.90%	Up to $42,209		
	8.60	42,210–84,420		
	12.20	84,421–137,248		
	14.05	137,249 and over		
Nunavut[i]	4.00%	Up to $44,437		
	7.00	44,438–88,874		
	9.00	88,875–144,488		
	11.50	144,489 and over		
Yukon[i]	6.40%	Up to $46,605		
	9.00	46,606–93,208		
	10.90	93,209–144,489		
	12.80	144,490–500,000		
	15.00	500,001 and over		

Notes:

a. The federal tax brackets are indexed each year by a calculated inflation factor, which is based on the change in the average federal inflation rate over the 12-month period ending September 30 of the previous year compared to the change in the rate for the same period of the year prior to that. The federal inflation factor is 1.5% for 2018.

b. British Columbia indexes its tax brackets using the same formula as that used federally, but uses the provincial inflation rate rather than the federal rate in the calculation. The province's inflation factor is 2.0% for 2018. Residents of British Columbia are also required to make monthly payments under the province's Medical Services Plan (MSP). However, the province's 2018 budget proposed to eliminate MSP premiums effective January 1, 2020.

c.   Alberta indexes its tax brackets using the same formula as that used federally, but uses the provincial inflation rate rather than the federal rate in the calculation. The province's inflation factor is 1.2% for 2018.

d.   Saskatchewan, Nova Scotia and Prince Edward Island do not index their tax brackets or, where applicable, surtax thresholds.

e.   Manitoba indexes its tax brackets using the same formula as that used federally, but uses the provincial inflation rate rather than the federal rate in the calculation. The province's inflation factor is 1.2% for 2018.

f.   Ontario indexes its tax brackets and surtax thresholds using the same formula as that used federally, but uses the provincial inflation rate rather than the federal rate in the calculation. The province's inflation factor is 1.8% for 2018. Ontario resident individuals with taxable income over $20,000 are also required to pay a Health Premium each year. Ontario's 2018 budget proposed to eliminate the province's surtax and adjust the personal income tax brackets and rates, effective January 1, 2018. The new incoming government of Ontario, however, has confirmed that it does not intend to proceed with the changes to the personal income tax rates, brackets and surtax that were presented in the province's 2018 budget on March 28, 2018.

g.   Ontario and Prince Edward Island have a surtax system where surtax applies to the provincial income tax (before surtax) in excess of the threshold noted in the table. For example, Ontario surtax of 20% applies to the provincial income tax (before surtax) in excess of $4,638. Ontario surtax of 36% applies in addition to the 20% surtax (i.e., a total surtax of 56%) to the provincial income tax (before surtax) in excess of $5,936. The surtax effectively increases the top marginal tax rate for residents of Ontario and Prince Edward Island to 20.53% (13.16% × 156%) and 18.37% (16.70% × 110%), respectively.

h.   Québec indexes its tax brackets using the same formula as that used federally, but uses the provincial inflation rate, excluding changes in liquor and tobacco taxes, rather than the federal rate in the calculation. The province's inflation fact or is 0.82% for 2018. Residents of Québec are required to make payments to the province's Health Services Fund.

i.   New Brunswick and the territories (Northwest Territories, Nunavut and the Yukon) index their tax brackets using the same formula as that used federally. The inflation factor is 1.5% for 2018.

j.   Newfoundland and Labrador indexes its tax brackets using the same formula as that used federally, but uses the applicable provincial inflation rate rather than the federal rate in the calculation. Newfoundland and Labrador's inflation factor is 3.0% for 2018.

Appendix B-2 — Federal and Provincial/Territorial Non-Refundable Tax Credit Rates and Amounts for 2018[a]

	Federal	B.C.	Alta.	Sask.	Man.	Ont.
Tax rate applied to credits	15.00%	5.06%	10.00%	10.50%	10.80%	5.05%
Indexation factor[b]	1.50%	2.00%	1.20%	n/a	1.20%	1.80%
Basic personal[c]	$11,809	$10,412	$18,915	$16,065	$9,382	$10,354
Spousal/partner and wholly dependent person[d, e]	11,809	8,915	18,915	16,065	9,134	8,792
Net income threshold	—	892	—	1,607	—	879
Dependants[e]						
18 and over and infirm	See	See	10,949	9,464	3,605	See
Net income threshold	Caregiver	Caregiver	7,233	6,715	5,115	Caregiver
Caregiver[e]	6,986	4,556	10,949	9,464	3,605	4,881
Net income threshold	16,405	15,419	17,409	16,164	12,312	16,696
Child (max)[f]	—	—	—	6,094	—	—
Adoption[g]	15,905	15,905	12,936	—	10,000	12,632
Disability[h]	8,235	7,809	14,590	9,464	6,180	8,365
Disability supplement[i]	4,804	4,556	10,949	9,464	3,605	4,878
Pension (max)[h]	2,000	1,000	1,456	1,000	1,000	1,432
Age 65 and over[h, j]	7,333	4,669	5,271	4,894	3,728	5,055
Net income threshold	36,976	34,757	39,238	36,430	27,749	37,635
Medical expense threshold[k]	2,302	2,165	2,445	2,268	1,728	2,343
Employment[l]	1,196	—	Ref.[*]	—	—	—
Canada Pension Plan contributions (max)[m]	2,594	2,594	2,594	2,594	2,594	2,594
Employment Insurance premiums (max)[m]	858	858	858	858	858	858
Children's fitness (max)[n] and arts[o]	—	—	—	—	500	—
Home buyers (max)[p]	5,000	—	—	10,000	—	—
Home accessibility (max)[q]	10,000	Ref.[*]	—	—	—	—
Tuition fees[r]	Yes	Yes	Yes	No	No	No
Education[r]						
Full-time — per month	—	200	735	—	400	—
Part-time — per month	—	60	221	—	120	—
Charitable donations[s]						
Credit rate on first $200	15.00%	5.06%	10.00%	10.75%	10.80%	5.05%
Credit rate on balance	29.0/33.0%	16.80%	21.00%	14.75%	17.40%	11.16%

	N.B.	N.S.	P.E.I.	Nfld.	NWT	Nunavut	Yukon
Tax rate applied to credits	9.68%	8.79%	9.80%	8.70%	5.90%	4.00%	6.40%
Indexation factor[b]	1.50%	n/a	n/a	3.00%	1.50%	1.50%	1.50%
Basic personal[c]	$10,043	$8,481	$8,660	$9,247	$14,492	$13,325	$11,809
Spousal/partner and wholly dependent person[d, e]	8,528	8,481	7,431	7,556	14,492	13,325	11,809
Net income threshold	853	848	693	756	—	—	—
Dependants[e]							

	N.B.	N.S.	P.E.I.	Nfld.	NWT	Nunavut	Yukon
18 and over and infirm	4,743	2,798	2,446	2,936	4,803	4,803	See
Net income threshold	*6,730*	*5,683*	*4,966*	*6,311*	*6,816*	*6,816*	*Caregiver*
Caregiver[e]	4,743	4,898	2,446	2,937	4,804	4,804	6,986
Net income threshold	*16,198*	*13,677*	*11,953*	*14,351*	*16,405*	*16,405*	*16,405*
Child (max)[f]	—	1,200	1,200	—	—	1,200	—
Adoption[g]	—	—	—	12,116	—	—	15,905
Disability[h]	8,131	7,341	6,890	6,240	11,753	13,325	8,235
Disability supplement[i]	4,743	3,449	4,019	2,937	4,804	4,804	4,804
Pension (max)[h]	1,000	1,173	1,000	1,000	1,000	2,000	2,000
Age 65 and over[h, j]	4,904	4,141	3,764	5,903	7,089	9,994	7,333
Net income threshold	*36,507*	*30,828*	*28,019*	*32,348*	*36,976*	*36,976*	*36,976*
Medical expense threshold[k]	2,273	1,637	1,678	2,014	2,302	2,302	2,302
Employment[l]	—	—	—	—	—	—	1,196
Canada Pension Plan contributions (max)[m]	2,594	2,594	2,594	2,594	2,594	2,594	2,594
Employment Insurance premiums (max)[m]	858	858	858	858	858	858	858
Children's fitness (max)[n] and arts[o]	—	—	—	—	—	—	1,000/500
Home buyers (max)[p]	—	—	—	—	—	—	—
Home accessibility[q]	Ref.*	—	—	—	—	—	—
Tuition fees[r]	No	Yes	Yes	Yes	Yes	Yes	Yes
Education[r]							
Full-time-per month	—	200	400	200	400	400	—
Part-time-per month	—	60	120	60	120	120	—
Charitable donations[s]							
Credit rate on first $200	9.68%	8.79%	9.80%	8.70%	5.90%	4.00%	6.40%
Credit rate on balance	17.95%	21.00%	16.70%	18.30%	14.05%	11.50%	12.80%

Notes:

* "Ref." indicates a refundable credit — see the applicable note.

a. The table shows the dollar amounts of federal and provincial non-refundable tax credits for 2018 (except for Québec). In order to determine the credit value, each dollar amount must be multiplied by the tax rate indicated, which is the lowest tax rate applicable in the particular jurisdiction. For example, the Ontario basic personal credit amount of $10,354 is multiplied by 5.05% to determine the credit value of $523. Income earned by the taxpayer or dependant, as applicable, in excess of the net income thresholds shown in the table serves to reduce the availability of the credit on a dollar-for-dollar basis. The only exception to this is the age credit, which is reduced by 15% of the taxpayer's net income in excess of the threshold.

b. The indexation factors indicated in the table are used to index the credits in each jurisdiction. The calculation of these factors is based on the change in the average federal or provincial inflation rate over the 12-month period ending September 30 of the previous year compared to the change in the rate for the same period of the year prior to that. British Columbia, Alberta, Manitoba, Ontario and Newfoundland and Labrador use the applicable provincial inflation rate in their calculations, while Saskatchewan and New Brunswick use the federal inflation rate. Nova Scotia and Prince Edward Island do not index their credits. Saskatchewan announced a temporary suspension of the personal income tax indexation factor starting with the 2018 taxation year. The Northwest Territories, Nunavut and Yukon use the federal inflation rate.

c. Nova Scotia provides an additional basic personal amount of $3,000 where a taxpayer's income is $25,000 or less. This amount will decrease proportionately if the taxpayer's income is between $25,000 and $75,000.

d. The spousal/partner and wholly dependent person amounts are calculated by subtracting the spouse/partner and wholly dependant's net income from the maximum amount. The spousal/partner credit may be claimed for a common-law partner as well as for a spouse. Taxpayers who are single, divorced or separated, and who support a dependant in their home may claim the wholly dependent person credit. The credit can be claimed for dependants under the age of 18 who are related to the taxpayer, for the taxpayer's parents or grandparents, or for any other infirm person who is related to the taxpayer (see note (e)). Nova Scotia provides an additional non-refundable tax credit for spousal/partner and wholly dependant person in the year if their income is $25,000 or less. The amount for 2018 is $3,000. This amount will decrease proportionately if their income is between $25,000 and $75,000.

e. The Canada caregiver credit is available to taxpayers who care for a related dependant. Generally, the dependant must be over the age of 18 and infirm, or, in the case of a parent or grandparent, over the age of 65 (except for federal and Ontario purposes, where the credit is not available in respect of non-infirm dependants). For the federal Canada caregiver credit, the credit amount is $6,986 in respect of infirm dependants who are parents, grandparents, brothers/sisters, aunts/uncles, nieces/nephews, adult children of the claimant or of the claimant's spouse or common-law partner, and $2,182 in respect of an infirm dependent spouse or common-law partner in respect of whom the individual claims the spouse or common-law partner amount, an infirm dependant for whom the individual claims an eligible dependant credit, or an infirm child who is under the age of 18 years at the end of the year. For Ontario, the credit amount is $4,881 in respect of relatives who are infirm dependants, including adult children of the claimant or of the claimant's spouse or common-law partner. British Columbia's 2018 budget replaced the infirm dependant credit with a new Caregiver Tax Credit effective for 2018 and subsequent tax years, and will follow the same rules as the federal credit. Yukon also replaced the infirm dependant credit with a new Caregiver Tax Credit effective for 2018 and subsequent tax years, and will follow the same rules as the federal credit.

f. Nova Scotia and Prince Edward Island provide a credit for children under the age of 6. If certain conditions are met, an individual can claim $100 per eligible month for a maximum of $1,200 per year. Unused credit amounts may be transferred between spouses. Saskatchewan provides a credit for children under the age of 18 if certain conditions are met. Unused credit amounts may be transferred between spouses.

g. The adoption credit is available on eligible adoption expenses incurred in the year and not reimbursed to the taxpayer, up to the maximum amount indicated in the table.

h. The disability, pension and age credits are transferable to a spouse or partner. The amounts available for transfer are reduced by the excess of the spouse's or partner's net income over the basic personal credit amount. The disability credit is also transferable to a supporting person other than a spouse or partner; however, the amount of the credit is reduced by the excess of the disabled person's net income over the basic personal credit amount.

i. The disability supplement may be claimed by an individual who is under the age of 18 at the end of the year. The amount in the table represents the maximum amount that may be claimed, and is reduced by certain child and attendant care expenses claimed in respect of this individual.

j. Saskatchewan provides an additional non-refundable tax credit for individuals aged 65 or older in the year, regardless of their net income amount. The amount for 2018 is $1,292. Nova Scotia provides an additional non-refundable tax credit for individuals aged 65 or older in the year if their taxable income is $25,000 or less. The amount for 2018 is $1,465. This amount will decrease proportionately if their income is between $25,000 and $75,000.

k. The medical expense credit is calculated based on qualified medical expenses exceeding 3% of net income or the threshold shown in the table, whichever is less. Medical expenses incurred by both spouses/partners and by their children under age 18 may be totalled and claimed by either spouse/partner. Taxpayers can also claim medical expenses for other eligible dependants to the extent the amount exceeds the lesser of 3% of net income of the dependant or the threshold shown in the table. Ontario is currently the only province with a maximum allowable medical expense for other eligible dependants. The limit is $12,632 for 2018.

l. The federal employment credit may be claimed by individuals based on the lesser of the amount indicated in the table and the amount of employment income earned in the year. Alberta offers a refundable family employment credit for Alberta residents with children under the age of 18 who meet the income eligibility criteria. The credit is paid out in January and July of each year. Yukon also provides a non-refundable tax credit for the Canada employment amount. The tax credit is calculated the same way as the federal credit, but using the lowest Yukon tax rate.

m. Self-employed taxpayers can deduct 50% of their Canada or Québec Pension Plan premiums in calculating net income. The balance is claimed as a non-refundable tax credit. Self-employed taxpayers can also claim Employment Insurance premiums paid.

n. Taxpayers in Manitoba can claim a maximum of $500 for fees paid on registration or membership for an eligible program of physical activity for children under the age of 18 at the end of the year, spouse or common-law partner aged 18 to 24 at the end of the year, and self if under 25 years of age at the end of the year. For children or young adults eligible for the disability tax credit, taxpayers can claim an additional $500 if a minimum of $100 is paid for registration or membership fees for a prescribed program of physical activity. Yukon also provides a children's fitness tax credit. In Yukon, taxpayers can claim a maximum of $1,000 for fees paid for the cost of registration or membership in a prescribed program of physical activity for children under the age of 16 (or 18 if eligible for the disability tax credit) at the beginning of the year. Parents may claim an additional $500 in respect of a child eligible for the disability tax credit if the parent incurs a minimum of $100 in eligible expenses relating to that child. British Columbia eliminated the fitness tax credit effective January 1, 2018.

o. Taxpayers in Manitoba and Yukon can claim a maximum of $500 for fees relating to the cost of registration or membership in an eligible program of artistic, cultural, recreational, or developmental activity for children under the age of 16 (or 18 if eligible for the disability tax credit) at the beginning of the year. For children under 18 years of age at the beginning of the year eligible for the disability tax credit, taxpayers can claim an additional $500 if a minimum of $100 is paid for registration or membership fees for an eligible artistic program. British Columbia eliminated the children's arts tax credit effective January 1, 2018.

p. First-time home buyers who acquire a qualifying home during the year may be entitled to claim a federal non-refundable tax credit up to $5,000 and worth up to $750 ($5,000 × 15%). To qualify, neither the individual nor his or her spouse or common-law partner can have owned and lived in another home in the calendar year of the new home purchase or in any of the four preceding calendar years. The credit can be claimed by either the purchaser or by his or her spouse or common-law partner. The credit will also be available for certain home purchases by or for the benefit of an individual eligible for the disability tax credit. Saskatchewan's First-Time Home Buyers Tax Credit provides a non-refundable income tax credit of up to $1,075 (10.75% × $10,000) to eligible taxpayers. There are also provisions to allow persons with a disability to qualify for the purchase of more accessible homes, with eligibility rules similar to those for the existing federal incentive for first-time home buyers. The credit generally applies to qualifying homes acquired after December 31, 2011.

q. The home accessibility tax credit provides a credit for qualifying expenses incurred for work performed or goods acquired in respect of a qualifying renovation of an eligible dwelling of someone who is 65 years or older before the end of the taxation year or eligible for the disability tax credit. British Columbia and New Brunswick provide a refundable credit of up to $1,000 for similar expenses.

r. The eligible portion of the tuition and education tax credits are transferable to a spouse or common-law partner, parent or grandparent. Any amounts not transferred may be carried forward indefinitely by the student. The federal government eliminated the education tax credits effective January 1, 2017. British Columbia's 2018 budget eliminated the province's education tax credits effective January 1, 2019. The elimination of the federal education tax credit automatically cancels this credit for all of the territories, unless legislative changes are made. The Northwest Territories and Nunavut have both passed legislation to retain the education tax credit; however, Yukon has not.

s. Charitable donations made by both spouses/partners may be totalled and claimed by either person. The maximum amount of donations that may be claimed in a year is 75% of net income. However, all donations may be carried forward for five years if they are not claimed in the year made. The federal donation tax credit rate of 33% applies to charitable donations made after 2015 over $200 to the extent of the claimant's income that is subject to the top tax bracket (over $205,843 for 2018). Otherwise, the rate of 29% applies to the donations over $200.

Appendix B-3 — Québec Non-Refundable and Refundable Tax Credit Rates and Amounts for 2018

Québec Non-Refundable Tax Credit Rate and Amounts for 2018

Tax rate applied to credits[a]	15.0%
Indexation factor[b]	0.82%
Basic personal amount	$15,012
Amounts for dependants:	
Child under 18 engaged in full-time training or post-secondary studies[c]	2,884
Child over 17 who is a full-time student[d]	See note[d]
Other dependants over 17[e]	4,202
Person living alone or with a dependant:[f, g]	
Basic amount	1,721
Single-parent amount (supplement)	2,124
Age 65 and over[f]	3,158
Experienced workers (age 61 and over)[h]	
Age 61	3,000
Age 62	5,000
Age 63	7,000
Age 64	9,000
Age 65 and over	11,000
Pension (max)[f]	2,805
Disability	3,334
First-time home buyers[i]	5,000
Union and professional dues[j]	10%
Tuition fees[k]	8%
Interest paid on student loans[l]	20%
Medical expenses[m]	20%
Charitable donations:[n]	
Credit rate on first $200	20%
Credit rate on balance	24/25.75%

Notes:

a. In order to determine the credit value, each dollar value must be multiplied by Québec's tax credit rate. For example, the basic personal credit amount of $15,012 is multiplied by 15% to determine the credit value of $2,252. The unused portion of all non-refundable credits may be transferred from one spouse/partner to another, but only after all credits have been taken into account in the calculation of the individual's income tax otherwise payable.

b. Québec indexes its tax credits each year by using an inflation factor that is calculated based on the provincial rate of inflation, excluding changes in liquor and tobacco taxes. The Québec inflation factor is 0.82% for 2018. For the purpose of calculating the basic personal amount and personal tax credits, Québec's tax legislation stipulates automatic indexation.

c. This credit is available for a dependent child who is under the age of 18 and is engaged in full-time professional training or post-secondary studies for each completed term, to a maximum of two semesters per year per dependant. It is also available for infirm dependants who are engaged in such activities part-time.

d. An eligible student is able to transfer to either parent an amount relating to an unused portion of their basic personal credit amount for the year (transfer mechanism for the recognized parental contribution). Each taxation year, the amount that can be transferred must not exceed the limit applicable for that particular year ($10,306 for 2018).

e. This credit is available if the dependant, other than the spouse, is related to the taxpayer by blood, marriage or adoption and ordinarily lives with the taxpayer. In order to be eligible for the tax credit, the taxpayer must also not have benefited from a transfer of the recognized parental contribution from this dependant.

f. The total of the credit amounts for being 65 years of age or over, for living alone or with a dependent, and for receiving retirement income is reduced by 18.75% of the amount by which net family income exceeds $34,030.

g. Québec's 2018 budget extended this tax credit to grandparents and great -grandparents. However, the rules are not broadened for the purpose of the single-parent family supplement amount. Therefore, for the 2018 and subsequent taxation years, the basic amount is available if the individual lives in a self-contained domestic establishment that he/she maintains and in which no other person, other than himself/herself, a minor person, or an eligible student lives of whom the individual is either the father, mother, grandfather or grandmother, or the great-grandfather or great-grandmother. If an individual (i.e., father or mother) is living with an eligible student (i.e., a person who is 18 or over and is a post-secondary or vocational training student who transferred or could have transferred an amount to the single parent (see note (d)), the individual may be able to add an amount for a single-parent family of $2,124 to the basic amount for a person living alone.

h. Québec's 2018 budget lowered the eligibility age from 62 to 61 for 2018. The province also increased the maximum amount of "eligible work income" to $11,000 for all workers age 65 and over effective in 2018. For 2018, this credit is available for workers who are 61 years of age or older. For workers age 61, the credit applies at a 15% rate to $3,000 of "eligible work income" in excess of $5,000. For workers age 62, the credit applies at a 15% rate to $5,000 of "eligible work income" in excess of $5,000. For workers age 63, the credit applies at a 15% rate to $7,000 of "eligible work income" in excess of $5,000. For workers age 64, the credit applies at a 15% rate to $9,000 of "eligible work income" in excess of $5,000. For workers age 65 and over, the credit applies at a 15% rate to $11,000 of "eligible work income" in excess of $5,000. The credit for workers age 61 or older is reduced by 5% of eligible work income over $34,030. Eligible work income includes salary and business income, but excludes taxable benefits received for a previous employment as well as amounts deducted in computing taxable income, such as the stock option deduction. Any unused portion of the tax credit may not be carried forward or transferred to the individual's spouse.

i. Québec's 2018 budget introduced a new first-time home buyers non-refundable tax credit of up to $5,000 and worth up to $750 ($5,000 × 15%) for a housing unit located in Québec and that is acquired after December 31, 2017. To qualify, the individual or his or her spouse has to intend to inhabit the home as a principal place of residence not later than one year after the time of acquisition and neither the individual nor his or her spouse can have owned and lived in another home in the calendar year of the new home purchase or in any of the four preceding calendar years.

j. The credit for union and professional dues is calculated based on the annual fees paid in the year. The portion of professional dues relating to liability insurance is allowed as a deduction from income and therefore not included in calculating the credit amount.

k. The tuition credit is calculated based on tuition, professional examination and mandatory ancillary fees paid for the calendar year. Tuition fees qualify for an 8% non-refundable credit for Québec tax purposes. The student may transfer the unused portion of the tuition credit to either one of his/her parents or grandparents. The portion of this credit that is not transferred will be available for future use by the student.

l. Interest paid on student loans is converted into a tax credit at a rate of 20%. Interest not claimed in a particular year may be carried forward indefinitely.

m. The medical expense credit is calculated based on qualified medical expenses in excess of 3% of family income. Family income is the total income of both spouses/partners. Eligible medical expenses and eligible expenses to obtain medical care not provided in the region where an individual lives will continue to be converted into a tax credit at the rat e of 20%.

n. Charitable donations made by both spouses/partners may be totalled and claimed by either person. The maximum amount of donations that may be claimed in a year is 100% of net income. However, all donations may be carried forward for five years (or 10 years for certain particular donations) if they are not claimed in the year made. Québec's tax credit is 20% on the first $200 of eligible gifts. If the individual taxpayer's income exceeds $104,766 in 2018, then he/she may be eligible f or a 25.75% donation credit on the lesser of eligible gifts made in excess of $200 and his/her income in excess of $104,766. All other donations that do not fall into either the 20% or 25.75% category will receive a 24% tax credit on donations.

Québec Refundable Tax Credit Rate and Amounts for 2018[a]

	Tax Rate	Maximum expense	Maximum credit
Medical expenses[b]	25%	certain eligible medical expenses	$1,185
Reduced by 5% of family income in excess of $22,910[c]			
Child care expense credit[d]	from 26 to 75%		
The lesser of the expenses incurred or:			
For a child who has a severe or prolonged mental or physical impairment		$13,000	
For a child under the age of seven		9,500	
For a child under the age of seventeen		5,000	
Adoption expense credit[e]	50%	20,000	10,000
Infertility treatment credit[f]	from 20% to 80%	20,000	16,000
Informal caregivers of related adults[g]			
Basic amount			652/1,015[c]
Supplement			533[c]
Reduced by 16% of the eligible relative's income over $23,700[c]			
Respite of caregivers[h]	30%	5,200	1,560
Reduced by 3% of the caregiver's family income in excess of $57,400[c]			
Home support of elderly persons living alone[i]			
Not recognized as dependant seniors	35%	19,500	6,825
Recognized as dependant seniors	35%	25,500	8,925
Reduced by 3% of the individual's family income in excess of $57,400[c]			
Short-term transition of seniors in rehabilitation centre[j]	20%	costs incurred in maximum 60-day period	
Safety equipment for seniors[k]	20%	costs incurred in excess of $500	
Eco-friendly renovations[l]	20%	costs incurred in excess of $2,500	10,000
Residential waste water treatment system[m]	20%	costs incurred in excess of $2,500	5,500

Notes:

a. Québec's credit rate, maximum expense eligible and method of calculation of the credit varies from one type of refundable credit to another. Québec's credit rate is applied to the dollar amounts in the table to determine the maximum credit value. For example, the adoption expense credit amount of $20,000 is multiplied by 50% to determine the maximum credit value of $10,000. Some refundable credits are reduced when thresholds are exceeded.

b. Québec provides a refundable tax credit equal to the total of 25% of medical expenses eligible for the non-refundable credit and 25% of the amount deducted for disability support products and services. A minimum amount of earned income has to be earned in order to claim the refundable tax credit: $3,030 for 2018.

c. Québec indexes various tax credits each year by using an inflation factor that is calculated based on the provincial rate of inflation, excluding changes in liquor and tobacco taxes. The Québec inflation factor is 0.82% for 2018.

d. Unlike the federal treatment of qualifying child care expenses, which are eligible for a deduction in computing net income, Québec provides a refundable tax credit for such expenses. The rate of credit falls as net family income rises. Québec's 2018 budget announced an increase to the maximum amount applicable to childcare expenses paid in respect of a child with a severe or prolonged mental or physical impairment to $13,000 (from $11,000) and in respect of a child under the age of seven to $9,500 (from $9,000), as of the 2018 taxation year. The province's budget also proposed to automatically index the annual limits on childcare expenses as of the 2019 taxation year. In general, the maximum amount of expenses eligible for the credit in 2018 is the lesser of:

-   $13,000 for a child of any age who has a severe or prolonged mental or physical impairment, plus $9,500 for a child under the age of seven, plus $5,000 for a child under the age of 17, or

-   the actual child care expenses incurred in the year.

The definition of eligible expenses includes costs incurred during the period an individual receives benefits under the Québec Parental Insurance Plan or the Employment Insurance Plan. The child care expenses are not limited by the earned income of the parent. For the purpose of calculating the refundable tax credit for childcare expenses, the definition of "eligible child" o f an individual means a child of the individual or the individual's spouse, or a child who is a dependant of the individual or the individual's spouse and whose income for the year does not exceed $10,306, if, in any case, at any time during the year, the child is under 16 years of age or is dependent on the individual or the individual's spouse and has a mental or physical infirmity.

e. Qualifying expenses include court and legal fees paid to obtain the final adoption order, travel and accommodation expenses for foreign adoptions, translation expenses, and fees charged by foreign and domestic social agencies.

f. The applicable credit rate varies from 20% to 80% of eligible infertility expense, depending on family situation and income. The credit can be claimed on infertility expenses of up to $20,000.

g. There are three components to this credit. The first component applies to caregivers who house an eligible relative in their home where the relative is 70 years of age or older or is an adult with a severe and prolonged mental or physical impairment. The second component applies to informal caregivers who live in an eligible relative's home and a physician has attested that the relative is unable to live alone due to a severe and prolonged mental or physical impairment. Finally, the third component applies to caregivers whose spouse is 70 years of age or older, or has a severe and prolonged mental or physical impairment, and the couple lives in their own home other than in a seniors' residence. Québec's 2018 budget introduced a fourth component to the refundable tax credit for informal caregivers as of the 2018 taxation year. The fourth component will be for informal caregivers who, without housing or co-residing with an eligible relative, provide support to the relative on a regular and continuous basis. The new component of the tax credit will consist of $533 for each eligible relative. Additionally, the province's 2018 budget added nurse practitioners to the list of medical practitioners authorized to issue certifications for the purposes of the refundable tax credit for informal caregivers to attest that the individual is unable to live alone or needs assistance in carrying out basic activity of daily living due to a severe and prolonged mental or physical impairment. The amount of the basic credit increases to $1,015 for 2018 if the caregiver cares for an elderly spouse. Note that caregivers caring for an elderly spouse are not entitled to the supplement amount. For the purposes of this credit, an eligible relative is a child, grandchild, nephew, niece, brother, sister, uncle, aunt, great-uncle, great-aunt or any other direct ascendant of the individual or the individual's spouse.

h. Caregivers can also claim a refundable tax credit for respite services. Qualifying expenses include specialized respite services respecting the care and supervision of an eligible person. If the expense has been used in calculating another refundable or non-refundable credit, it cannot be claimed for this credit as well.

i. The home support tax credit can be claimed by persons age 70 and over living in their home. For seniors recognized as dependant, and when this credit is determined in respect of a couple as soon as one of the members of the couple is recognized as dependant, no reduction is allowed. If the expense also qualifies for the non-refundable medical expense credit, it cannot be claimed for this credit as well.

j. The rehabilitation centre tax credit can be claimed by seniors age 70 or older in respect of costs incurred for the first 60 days of any given stay in a public or private "functional rehabilitation transition unit". There is no limit to the number of stays that can be claimed.

k. The safety equipment tax credit can be claimed by seniors age 70 or older for the purchase or rental of equipment (including installation costs) used to improve their safety and security in their principal residence. Examples of qualifying equipment include remote monitoring systems, GPS tracking devices for persons, and walk-in bathtubs or showers.

l. The RénoVert tax credit has been introduced on a temporary basis, for qualified eco-friendly home renovations done by a qualified contractor under a contract entered into after March 17, 2016 and before April 1, 2019 (the province's 2018 budget extended the eligibility period to March 31, 2019, from March 31, 2018). Examples of eco-friendly renovation work include insulation, sealing, doors that access the exterior, windows, and heating, air conditioning, water heating and ventilation systems, as well as to water quality and soil quality. Eco-friendly renovation work excludes any work eligible for the credit for the upgrading of residential waste water treatment system, since a new refundable tax credit applies to such work since April 1, 2017 (see note (m)). The work must relate to existing parts of an individual's eligible dwelling.

m. The temporary refundable tax credit for the upgrading of residential waste water treatment systems of a principal residence or a cottage which includes the construction, renovation, modification or rebuilding of a system for the discharge, collection and disposal of waste water, toilet effluents or grey water, can be claimed if the work is carried out by a qualified contractor and paid under a service agreement entered into after March 31, 2017 and before April 1, 2022.

Appendix B-4 — Combined Top Marginal Tax Rates for Individuals — 2018[a]

	Interest and Regular Income	Capital Gains[a]	Eligible Dividends	Non-Eligible Dividends[b]
British Columbia[c]	49.80%	24.90%	34.20%	43.73%
Alberta	48.00	24.00	31.71	41.64
Saskatchewan[d]	47.50	23.75	29.64	39.60
Manitoba	50.40	25.20	37.79	45.92
Ontario[e]	53.53	26.76	39.34	46.84
Québec[f] — Amounts received before March 28, 2018	53.31	26.65	39.83	43.94
— Amounts received after March 27, 2018	53.31	26.65	39.89	44.83
New Brunswick[g]	53.30	26.65	33.51	46.88
Nova Scotia	54.00	27.00	41.58	47.33
P.E.I.	51.37	25.69	34.23	44.26
Newfoundland & Lab.	51.30	25.65	42.62	43.81
Northwest Territories	47.05	23.53	28.33	35.98
Nunavut	44.50	22.25	33.08	36.78
Yukon	48.00	24.00	28.92	41.42

Notes:

a. The lifetime capital gains exemption limit for qualified farm property, qualified fishing property and qualified small business corporation shares increased to $848,252 (from $835,716) for 2018. An additional lifetime capital gains exemption of $151,748 is available for qualified farm or fishing property disposed of in 2018.

b. The federal dividend tax credit (DTC) rate that applies to non-eligible dividends decreased to 10.03% (from 10.52%) of taxable dividends beginning January 1, 2018. The dividend gross-up factor that applies to non-eligible dividends also decreased to 16% (from 17%) beginning January 1, 2018.

c. British Columbia announced an increase to the province's DTC rate that applies to eligible dividends to 12% (from 10%), effective January 1, 2019.

d. Saskatchewan increased the province's DTC rate that applies to eligible dividends to 11% (from 10.75%) of taxable dividends effective January 1, 2018. Saskatchewan's 2018 budget increased the province's DTC rate that applies to non-eligible dividends to 3.333% (from 3.196%) of taxable dividends effective January 1, 2018. The rate will further increase to 3.362% effective January 1, 2019.

e. Ontario decreased the province's DTC rate that applies to non-eligible dividends to 3.12% (from 4.29%) of taxable dividends effective January 1, 2018.

f. Québec's 2018 budget proposed to decrease the DTC rate that applies to eligible dividends received after March 27, 2018 to 11.86% (from 11.9%) of taxable dividends. The rate will further decrease to 11.78% effective January 1, 2019 and 11.7% effective January 1, 2020. The budget also proposed to decrease the DTC rate that applies to non -eligible dividends received after March 27, 2018 to 6.28% (from 7.05%) of taxable dividends. The rate will further decrease to 5.55% effective January 1, 2019, 4.77% effective January 1, 2020 and 4.01% effective January 1, 2021.

g. New Brunswick decreased the province's DTC rate that applies to non-eligible dividends to 2.853% (from 3.245%) of taxable dividends effective January 1, 2018. The rate will further decrease to 2.75% effective January 1, 2019.

Appendix B-5 — Retirement and Savings Plans — Contribution Limits

	2015	2016	2017	2018
Money Purchase Registered Pension Plans				
Contribution limit[a]	$25,370	$26,010	$26,230	$26,500
Pensionable earnings[b]	140,945	144,500	145,722	147,222
Registered Retirement Savings Plans				
Contribution limit[c]	24,930	25,370	26,010	26,230
Previous year's earned income[d]	138,500	140,945	144,500	145,722
Deferred Profit Sharing Plans				
Contribution limit[e]	12,685	13,005	13,115	13,250
Pensionable earnings[f]	70,472	72,250	72,861	73,611
Tax-Free Savings Account				
Annual contribution limits[g]	10,000	5,500	5,500	5,500
Registered Education Savings Plans				
Annual limit[h]	N/A	N/A	N/A	N/A
Lifetime limit[i]	50,000	50,000	50,000	50,000
Registered Disability Savings Plans				
Annual limit[j]	N/A	N/A	N/A	N/A
Lifetime limit[k]	200,000	200,000	200,000	200,000

Notes:

a. The money purchase registered pension plan (RPP) contribution limit indicated in the table is the maximum limit applicable each year. The contribution limit is the greater of the limit for the preceding year, and the 2009 contribution limit of $22,000 adjusted for inflation. In general, the 2009 contribution limit will be indexed by an inflation factor equal to the average wage for the applicable year divided by the average wage for 2009.

b. The total of all employer and employee contributions to an RPP is limited to the lesser of the current year's contribution limit and 18% of the employee's pensionable earnings for the year. The amount of pensionable earnings that generates the contribution limit is indicated in the table.

c. The registered retirement savings plan (RRSP) contribution limit is equal to the RPP contribution limit for the preceding year.

d. The total of all contributions to an RRSP is limited to the lesser of the current year's contribution limit and 18% of an individual's earned income for the preceding year, plus any carry-forward contribution room. The amount of earned income that generates the contribution limit is indicated in the table.

e. The deferred profit sharing plan (DPSP) contribution limit is equal to one-half of the RPP contribution limit for the year.

f. The total of all employer contributions to a DPSP is limited to the lesser of the current year's contribution limit and 18% of an employee's pensionable earnings for the year. The amount of pensionable earnings that generates the contribution limit each year is indicated in the table.

g. Canadians age 18 and over can earn tax-free income in a Tax-Free Savings Account (TFSA) throughout their lifetime. Income, losses and gains on investment in the account, as well as amounts withdrawn, are not taxable and are not taken into account for determining eligibility for certain income-tested benefits or credits. Each calendar year, a taxpayer can contribute up to the TFSA limit, plus any unused TFSA contribution room from the previous year. The annual contribution limit increased to $10,000 (from $5,500) for 2015, however, it was reduced back to $5,500 effective January 1, 2016. The annual contribution room limit is indexed for inflation and rounded to the nearest $500. Generally, amounts withdrawn from a TFSA will be added to the individual's contribution room for future years. TFSA contributions are not tax -deductible.

h. Retirement education savings plans (RESPs) are commonly used by parents and other guardians to save for a child's post-secondary education. Like TFSAs, contributions to RESPs are not tax-deductible, but investment income can be earned in the plan tax-free. While there is no annual limit, contributions into the plan should be carefully considered in order to maximize government assistance payments under the Canada Education Savings Grant and Canada Learning Bond programs.

i. For each beneficiary there is a lifetime limit of $50,000, regardless of the number of plans in place for that beneficiary.

j. A registered disability savings plan (RDSP) is a savings plan to help parents and others save for the long-term financial security of a person who is eligible for the disability tax credit. Like RESPs, contributions to RDSPs are not tax-deductible, but investment income can be earned in the plan tax-free. While there is no annual limit, contributions into the plan should be carefully considered in order to maximize government assistance payments under the Canada Disability Savings Grant and Canada Savings Bonds programs.

k. Contributions on behalf of any one beneficiary are capped at a lifetime maximum of $200,000. Contributions can continue to be made until the end of the year the beneficiary turns 59, or until the beneficiary ceases to be a resident of Canada, dies or ceases to qualify for the disability tax credit.

Appendix B-6 — Automobiles — Deductions and Benefits

	2018	2017	2016	2015	2013-14
Deduction limits:[a]					
Maximum cost for capital cost allowance purposes[b]	$30,000	$30,000	$30,000	$30,000	$30,000
Maximum deductible monthly lease payment[c]	$800	$800	$800	$800	$800
Maximum deductible monthly interest cost on automobile loans[d]	$300	$300	$300	$300	$300
Maximum deductible allowances paid to employees[e]					
First 5,000 employment-related kilometres	55¢	54¢	54¢	55¢	54¢
Each additional employment-related kilometre	49¢	48¢	48¢	49¢	48¢
Taxable benefits:					
Standby charge benefit					
Employer-owned automobile		2% per month of original cost			
Employer-leased automobile		$2/3$ of monthly lease cost			
Operating cost benefit per kilometre of personal use[f]	26¢	25¢	26¢	27¢	27¢
Allowances[g]		Taxable with certain exceptions			

Notes:

a. When a motor vehicle is purchased or leased for the purpose of earning income, certain expenses may be deducted. The more common types of motor vehicle expenses include fuel, insurance, maintenance and repairs, licence and registration fees, capital cost allowance, lease payments, and interest. The expenses also include all applicable federal and provincial sales taxes (GST, HST, PST and QST) to the extent the taxpayer is not a sales tax registrant and does not claim an input tax credit (input tax refund in Québec) for the taxes paid.

b. The maximum amounts shown in the table are determined before all applicable sales taxes, and are based on the automobile's year of purchase. Each automobile with a cost in excess of the limit is allocated to a separate capital cost allowance (CCA) Class 10.1. The maximum capital cost of each automobile that may be included in Class 10.1 is $30,000 plus all applicable federal and provincial sales taxes. A Class 10.1 automobile is not subject to the normal recapture or terminal loss rules, and is eligible for a 15% CCA claim in the year of disposition. Motor vehicles having a cost equal to or less than the limit are included in Class 10. The normal rules for recapture, terminal loss and CCA apply to the se vehicles. The CCA rate for both classes is 30% declining balance (15% in the year of acquisition).

c. The maximum amounts shown in the table are determined before all applicable sales taxes, and are based on the year the lease was entered into. In general, the maximum deductible monthly lease charge is computed as the lesser of:

- the actual lease payments paid or incurred in the year (including insurance, maintenance and taxes if they are part of the actual lease payment);

- the prescribed monthly rate; or

- the annual lease limit, which is equal to the monthly pre-tax lease cost multiplied by the ratio of [CCA cost limit ÷ (85% × greater of the prescribed limit and the manufacturer's suggested list price)]

d. The maximum deductible monthly interest cost is based on the automobile's year of purchase.

e. For the Northwest Territories, Nunavut and Yukon, the tax-exempt allowance is set 4 cents higher (in 2018, 59 cents for the first 5,000 kilometres and 53 cents for each additional kilometre).

f.   Operating expenses include items such as gasoline and oil, maintenance charges and licences and insurance. Operating expenses do not include items such as interest, lease costs for a leased automobile or parking costs. For taxpayers who are employed principally in selling or leasing automobiles, a reduced rate of 22 cents per kilometre in 2017 and 23 cents per kilometre in 2018 applies.

g.   An "allowance" is generally defined as an amount paid for which the employee does not have to account (by providing receipts, vouchers, etc.) to the employer for its actual use. This can be contrasted to a "reimbursement" for which the employee must usually provide the employer with receipts and that the employer repays to the employee on a dollar -for-dollar basis.

Index

Note: All index references are to sections of the book.

A

Actors

- non-resident withholding tax, 15413

Adjusted cost base

- additions to, 4120
- bonds, 4124
- calculation, 4120
- deductions from, 4120
- identical properties, 4121
- negative, 4128
- partnership interest, 4123
- shares, 4122

Adjustments

- to filed T1 return, 14010

Adoption

- expenses tax credit, 10090

Advance Income Tax Rulings, 1010

Advances to employees, 2110

Adventure or concern in the nature of trade, 4015

Advertising

- business expense deduction, 6130.1
- in non-Canadian media, 6140.1
- non-deductible from business income, 6140.1
- rental expense deduction, 5220.2

Affiliated persons

- defined, 4811
- transfers between, 4812

Age amount

- tax credit, 10020

Aircraft

- expense deduction, 2455
- personal use of, 2115

Alberta, *see* Provincial and territorial taxes and credits

Alimony and maintenance, *see* Support payments made/received

Allowable business investment loss (ABIL)

- claiming and filing, 9191
- deductibility, 4610
- generally, 4600, 9190
- small business corporation definition, 4620

Allowance for survivor, 8332

Allowances to employees, 2120

- motor vehicle, 2122, 2130
- travel, 2121, 2123

Alternative minimum tax

- adjusted taxable income, 11101
- basic exemption, 11102
- basic minimum tax credit, 11102
- calculating, 11100

Alternative minimum tax *(cont'd)*

- carryforward, 11100, 11104

- claiming and filing, 11105

- liability for payment, 13550

- special foreign tax credit, 11103

Annuities, 3305

- capital element in, 3306

Appeals

- deduction from business income, 6130.4

Appraisal costs, 6140.2

Apprentice

- apprentice mechanics' tools deduction, 2345, 2410

- completion grant, 8262

- incentive grant, 2125, 2415, 8262

- investment tax credit, 11030

Artists

- employment expense deductions, 2420

- project grants, 8261, 8261.1

Assessments, *see also* Reassessments

- checklist, 14030

- initial, 14021

- loss determination application, 14023

- notice of objection, 14050

- reassessment, 14022

- waivers, 14040

Attendant care

- medical expense deduction, 10123

- summary of claimable expenses, 10195.2

Attribution rules, *see also* Income splitting

- attribution of gains/losses to spouse or common-law partner, 14230

- defined, 14200

- generally, 14200

- interest-free or low interest loans, 14220

- transfers to spouse or minors, 14220

- transfers to a trust or corporation, 14240, 14250, 14260

Auditing and accounting fees, 6130.5

Audits, *see* Tax audits

Automobiles

- allowance, 2122, 2130

- deductions and benefits table, Appendix B-6

- deduction from business income, 6130.6, 6140.16

- deduction from employment income, 2455

- deduction from professional income, 6230

- deduction from rental income, 5220.13

- luxury passenger vehicles, 7160

- operating costs benefit, 2132

- standby charge, 2131

Available-for-use rules

- depreciable property, 7125

Awards and prizes

- taxation of, 2205, 2280, 8261.4

B

Bad debts

- business expense deduction, 6130.7

- capital account, 4520

- personal use property, special rules, 4573

Balance-due day, 1230

Balance owing, 11350

Bank charges

- dedution from business income, 6130.8

Basic personal amount

• tax credit, 10010

Benefit conferred, 14310

Blended payments, 3235

Board and lodging

• special work site, 2136

• taxable employment benefit, 2135

Bonds and debentures

• accrual rules, 3205

• adjusted cost base (ACB), 4124

• proceeds of disposition, 4350

• when transferred between interest dates, 3230

Bonuses

• deduction from business income, 6130.9

Books and records, 14120

Borrowing money expenses

• deduction from business income, 6130.10, 6130.23

British Columbia, *see* Provincial and territorial taxes and credits

Bursaries

• taxation of, 8261

Business income

• calculating, 6113

• definition of business and carrying on a business, 6112

• determining, 6110

• expenses, limits on deductibility, 6120

• expense deductions, allowable, 6130

• expense deductions, non-allowable, 6140

Business investment loss, *see* Allowable business investment loss (ABIL)

C

CRA, *see* Canada Revenue Agency

Canada child benefit

• generally, 10005

• income splitting, 14270

Canada employment amount

• tax credit, 10230

Canada Pension Plan (CPP)/Quebec Pension Plan (QPP)

• additional contributions, 10062

• claiming and filing, 8121, 11211

• contributions through employment credit, 10060

• contributions on self-employment and other earnings, 9230, 10070, 11210

• excess contributions, 10061, 11260

• generally, 8120

• taxation of benefits received, 8100

Canada Revenue Agency

• administration of income tax, 1000

• mailing addresses, 1121

• publications, 1010

• Tax Centres, 1121

Canada savings bonds, 3215

Canadian-controlled private corporation (CCPC)

• owner-manager remuneration planning, 16110

• stock option benefits to employees, 2315, 2510, 9330

Canadian development expenses (CDE), 7410

Canadian exploration expenses (CEE), 7405

Canadian Forces personnel

• employment income deduction, 2425, 9310

Canadian oil and gas property expenses (COGPE), 7415

Canadian residents, *see also* Emigrating from Canada; Immigrating to Canada; Non-residents; Residency

- deemed, 15120, 15400
- determination of residency, 15110
- part-year, 15140
- taxation of, 15131

Capital cost allowance, *see also* Depreciable property

- accelerated CCA, 7006
- available-for-use rules, 7125
- claiming for rental purposes, 5121, 5240
- claiming for business, 6150, 7110
- classes, 6151
- • summary table 7005
- depreciable property additions for year, 7115, 7120
- depreciable property quick reference table, 7000
- general rules, 7105
- half-year rule, 7140
- luxury passenger vehicle, 7160
- recapture, 7145
- rental properties, 7165
- revising CCA claims, 7170
- separate class property, 7155
- terminal loss, 7150
- transferred or misclassified property, 7134

Capital dividends

- generally, 3125

Capital gains

- defined, 4005
- determining, 4200
- exemption, *see* Capital gains exemption
- gifts of qualifying securities, 4600

- inclusion in income, 4100
- lifetime exemption, 4210, 9380
- listed personal property, 4571
- personal-use property, 4571
- principal residence disposition, 4430
- proceeds of disposition, 4110
- qualified small business corporation (QSBC), 4220
- replacement property, 4700
- reserve, 4140
- Schedule 3, 4005, 4130
- security gains or losses, 4011
- special rules, 4700
- vs. income, 4010

Capital gains exemption/deduction

- lifetime capital gains exemption, 9380
- principal residence, 4430
- qualified farm or fishing property, 4231
- qualified small business corporation shares, 4220

Capital loss

- business investment losses, 4600, 9190
- calculating, 4100
- carryback/carryforward, 9370
- claiming and filing, 9374
- loss application rules summary, 9373
- net capital losses of other years, 9372
- superficial losses, 4812

Capital property

- adjusted cost base, 4120
- charitable donation of, 10214
- costs of disposition, 4120

Caregiver

- tax credit, 10055, 10110, 10260

Carrying charges

- deduction from investment income, 3710

Cellular phone, computers, internet

- employer provided, 2140

Carrying on a business, 6112

Change in use

- generally, 4434

- principal residence, 4435, 5410, 5420

Charitable donations

- calculation of tax credit, 10211

- capital property, 4330

- carryforward of credit, 10211.2

- claiming and filing, 10215

- direct beneficiary designations, 10214.3

- generally, 6140.4, 10210

- gift defined, 10212

- property donations, 10214

- split-receipting rules, 10212.2

- to U.S. charities, 10213

Child care expenses

- eligible expenses, 9173.1

- employer paid, 2145

- generally, 9170

- maximum deductible, 9171

- non-eligible expenses, 9173.2

- who may claim, 9172

Child support

- taxation of support paid, 9211

- taxation of support received, 8241

Child tax benefit

- tax planning, 3200, 8210

Children's arts tax credit

- generally, 10280

Children's fitness tax credit

- generally, 10250, 11325

Clean energy equipment

- depreciation classes, 7235

Clergy

- residence deduction, 2430, 9260

Club dues

- business expense non-deductible, 6140.5

- employer provided, 2295

Commission salespersons

- expenses deductible, 2435, 6130.13

Common-law partner, *see* Spouse or common-law partner

Conditional sales repossessions, 4560

Contingent liabilities, 6140.3

Contractors

- completed method, 6172

Conventions

- expenses deduction, 6130.14, 6230

Cost base, *see* Adjusted cost base

Counselling services, 2155

Cultural property

- gift to charity, 10214.1

Cumulative eligible capital

- generally, 6161

Cumulative net investment loss (CNIL)

- defined, 4240

Cumulative net investment loss (CNIL) *(cont'd)*
- effect on capital gains exemption, 4240
- investment expenses, 4241
- investment income, 4242

Customer lists
- deduction from business income, 6140.17

D

Damages
- deduction from business income, 6130.15
- taxation of, 3250, 4110

Death Benefits
- payment to non-residents, 8265
- taxation of benefits received, 8265

Deceased taxpayers
- loss carryback, 16121.1
- medical expenses, 10192
- T1 return due date, 1140
- tax planning, 16120, 16122

Deductions from net income, *see also under* specific items
- other payments deduction, 9340

Deductions from total income, *see also under* specific items
- other deductions, 9270

Deductions, personal tax
- quick reference table, 9010

Deemed disposition
- at death, elections, 16121.1, 16122.5
- change in use rules, 4434
- emigration, 15510

Dependants
- caregiver credit, 10055, 10260
- eligible dependant credit, 10040
- medical expense deduction, 10193, 10200

Depreciable property
- available-for-use rules, 7125
- capital cost allowance, 7100, 7115, 7120
- CCA class summary table, 7005
- dispositions, *see* Dispositions
- generally, 4400, 4420
- grants, subsidies, and rebates, 7132
- non-arm's length transactions, 7133
- personal use of property, 7131
- quick reference table, 7000

Depreciation, *see* Capital cost allowance

Digital currency
- disposition of, 4315

Directors
- fees, employment income, 2165

Disabled persons
- attendant care expenses, 10123
- disability supports deduction, 9180
- disability tax credit, 10120
- • calculation of, 10124
- • certification requirements, 10122
- • claiming and filing, 10126, 10141
- • transferring to supporting individual, 10125, 10140
- employment benefits, 2170, 2490
- medical expenses, 10123
- registered disability savings plans, 8230, 16230
- requirements for eligibility, 10121

Discounts on merchandise/commission from personal sales, 2175

Discounts

- deduction from business income, 6130.16

Dispositions

- bonds, debentures, promissory notes, 4510
- depreciable property, 4420, 7135
- generally, 4400
- land and buildings, 4410
- principal residence exemption, 4430

Dividend income, 3100

- capital, 3125
- capital gains, 3150
- deemed, 3130
- from Canadian corporations, 3110
- from non-resident corporations, 3115
- in kind, 3135
- meaning of, 3105
- payments to non-residents, 15320
- received by spouse or common-law partner, 3120
- rental arrangements, 3165
- reporting, 11081
- securities lending arrangement, 3160
- stock, 3140
- taxation, 11081, 11080

Dividend rental arrangements, 3165

Dividend stop-loss rules, 4820

Dividend tax credit

- claiming and filing, 11081
- generally, 11080

Donations, *see* Charitable donations

E

Earned income

- calculation for RRSP purposes, 9132
- defined for child care expenses, 9170

Education and textbook credits, *see* Tuition, education, and textbook credits

EFILE, 1123

Eligible capital expenditures (ECE), *see also* Intangible assets

- generally, 7300

Eligible educator school supply tax credit, 11330

Emigrating from Canada

- deemed disposition on emigration, 15510
- generally, 15510

Employee benefit plans, 2180

- flexible, 2200

Employee health and welfare trusts, 2185

Employee profit sharing plans (EPSP), 2190

- tax on excess amounts, 11062

Employment benefits and allowances, 2100, *see under* specific items

Employment deductions

- apprentice mechanics tools, 2410
- artists and musicians, 2420
- commissioned employees, 2435
- GST/HST rebate, 2401
- limits on deductibility, 9250
- other, deduction for, 9250
- professional and union dues, 2406, 2407, 9150
- profit sharing plans, 2445
- transport employees, 2525

Employment deductions *(cont'd)*
- travel and residence, 2525

Employment income

- employee vs. independent contractor, 2015

- generally, 2005

- salary deferral arrangements, 2020, 2160

- tax-free benefits, 2100

- taxable benefits, 2100

Employment Insurance (EI)

- benefits, 2195

- benefits repayment, 9281

- claiming and filing, 8222

- lump-sum payments, 8221

- overpayments through employment premiums, 10080, 11270

- premiums on self-employment, 10130, 11230

- repayment, 11221

- taxation of, 8220

- tax credit for premiums paid, 8220

Entertainment

- expenses deductible, 6140.6

Exploration and development expenses

- deduction for, 9240

F

Family tax cut credit, 11065

Farming and fishing income

- calculating income, 6310

- capital gains exemption, 6330

- definition, 6320

- instalment payment of tax, 1214

- inventory, optional treatment of, 6310

- losses (farming), 6350, 9361

- net income stabilization account (NISA), 6340

- qualified farm property, 4230

- qualified fishing property, 4230

- taxation of, 6310

Fellowships

- taxation of, 8261

Filing due dates, 1140

- deceased persons, 1140

- generally, 1140

- requirements quick reference table, 1410

- self-employed taxpayers, 1140, 1410

Fines and penalties

- deduction not allowed, 6140.9

- quick reference table, 1420

First-time home buyers

- tax credit, 10270

Fishers, *see* Farming and fishing income

Foreign accrual property income (FAPI), 3520

Foreign exchange gains/losses

- capital account, 4530, 6171

- deduction from business income, 6130.17, 6171

Foreign investment income

- income information reporting, 1310, 3530

- offshore investment fund property, 3510

Foreign tax credit

- business, 11012

- claiming and filing, 11013

- deduction for excess amount, 9273.5

- foreign non-business income tax paid, 9273.6

- generally, 9273.5, 11010

- non-business, 11011

G

GST/HST credit

- application, 1153

GST/HST rebate

- employee and partner, 2401, 11320
- included in employment income, 2401

General anti-avoidance rule (GAAR)

- cases, 14430
- consequences of GAAR applying, 14410
- generally, 14400
- series of transactions, 14420

Gifts, *see* Charitable donations; Awards and prizes

Goodwill, 6140.10

Government grants, 2210, 2301, 7132

Gratuities and tips, 2215

Guaranteed income supplement (GIS)

- generally, 8331
- reporting of, 8331

Guarantees and warranties

- deduction from business income, 6130.19, 6140.11

H

Half-year rule

- capital cost allowance, 7140

Health services plan premiums, 2275, 2290, 6140.21

Home accessibility tax credit, 10300

Home buyers' tax credit, 10270

Home Buyers' Plan, *see also* Registered retirement savings plans

- Schedule 7 reporting, 9137
- withdrawal and repayment to RRSP, 8251

Home office

- business expense deduction, 6130.20
- expense deduction by employee, 2470

Home relocation loan (employee)

- deduction, 2440, 9320

I

Illegal payments, 6140.12

Immigrating to Canada

- generally, 15520

Inadequate consideration, 14340

Income, *see under* specific type of income (e.g., Business, Investment, etc.)

Income rights, transfer of, 14320

Income splitting

- attribution of gains and losses to spouse or common-law partner, 14230
- attribution rules, 14200
- defined, 14200
- pension income splitting, 8140–8143, 9140, 10102
- strategies, 14270
- tax on split income, *see* Tax on split income
- transfer and loans to spouse or common-law partner or minors, 14220
- • back-to-back loans and transfers, 14225
- • exceptions, 14221
- • fair market value transfers, 14223
- • guarantees, 14226
- • loans for value, 14224

Income splitting *(cont'd)*
• • repayment of existing indebtedness, 14222

• transfers and loans to a corporation, 14250

• transfers and loans to a trust, 14240

• transfers of property to a reversionary trust, 14260

Income tax deducted

• withheld at source, 11240

Income Tax Folios, 1010

Income Tax Technical News, 1010

Indexed debt obligations, 3226

Indirect payments or transfers, *see* Benefit conferred

Inducement payments

• deduction from business income, 6130.21

Infirm, *see* Disabled persons

Information Circulars, 1010

Information returns

• generally, 1310

Instalments, 1200, 11340

• balance-due day, 1230

• interest on late or deficient, 1220

• methods, 1210

• My Account service, 1240

Insurance, *see also* Life insurance

• deduction from business income, 6130.22, 6140.13

• supplemental unemployment benefit plan, 2195

Intangible assets

• generally, 7205

Interest

• credit, paid on student loans, 10150

• deductibility rules, 3720, 6140.14

• expenses, deduction for, 3720

• income, *see* Interest income

Interest income, 3200

• accrual rules, 3205

• blended payments, 3235

• damage awards, 3250

• definition, 3210

• generally, 3200

• on tax refunds, 3250

• paid to non-residents, 15310

• reporting, 3200, 3205

Interpretation Bulletins, CRA, 1010

Inventory

• distinguished from capital property, 4010

• farming or fishing, 6310

Investment income

• annuities, *see* Annuities

• carrying charges, deduction, 3710, 5256

• deductions in computing, 3700

• • carrying charges, 3710

• • interest expense, 3720

• dividends, *see* Dividend income

• foreign-source, 3500

• interest, *see* Interest income

• mutual fund, *see* Mutual funds

• royalties, *see* Royalties

• taxation of, 3700

• transfer of right to income, 3340

Investment tax credit

• apprenticeship expenditures, 11034

• eligible child care space expenditures, 11035

• flow-through mining expenditures, 11033

• generally, 11030

Investment tax credit *(cont'd)*
- qualified property, 11031
- qualified SR&ED expenditures, 11032
- refund of, 11300

K

Kiddie tax, *see* Tax on split income

L

Labour-sponsored funds
- federal tax credit, 11040
- reporting, 11000

Labour-sponsored funds tax credit
- claiming and filing, 11041
- generally, 11040

Land
- adjusted cost base (ACB), 4125

Landscaping costs
- business income, deduction from, 5253
- rental income, deduction from, 5250, 5253

Lease transactions
- lease-leasebacks, 7222
- options, 7221
- vs. sale, 7220

Leasehold inducements
- tax treatment, 5254.2

Leasehold interests
- depreciable asset, 7210

Leasing properties
- CCA, 7211
- defined, 7211

- specified, 7215

Legal fees
- deductible from business income, 6130.24, 6140.15
- deductible from employment income, 2300, 2450
- deductible from rental income, 5220.6
- general deductibility, 9271
- support payments, re, 9213, 9271

Liability for Canadian tax, 1020

Life insurance premiums (group), 2220

Licences, *see also* Intangible assets
- deduction from business income, 6130.25

Life insurance, 3310

Lifelong learning plan (LLP)
- Schedule 7 reporting, 9137
- withdrawal and repayment to RRSP, 8251

Limited partnership, *see also* Partnership
- losses of other years, 9350

Listed personal property, *see* Personal-use property

Loans
- employee, interest-free and low-interest, 2235, 2440, 14352.4
- employee home purchase and relocation, 2238
- non-arm's length persons, 3335, 14330
- shareholder, 3330, *see also* Shareholder loans
- spousal, income splitting, 14220

Losses
- business investment, 4600, 9190
- capital loss, *see* Capital loss
- carryback, 9370
- cumulative net investment, 4240
- farm, 6350, 9361

Losses *(cont'd)*
- generally, 4005
- limited partnership, 9350
- non-capital, *see* Non-capital loss
- office or employment, 2010
- rental, 5300
- summary table, 9373
- superficial, 4812

Loyalty and points programs, 2240

M

Manitoba, *see* Provincial and territorial taxes and credits

Meals and entertainment
- deductibility, business income, 6130.26
- deductibility, employment income, 2245, 2530
- employee, 2245
- golf club, 6130.26, 6140.5

Medical expenses
- amount claimable, 10190
- attendant care/nursing home expenses, 10123, 10195.2
- authorized medical practitioners, list of, Appendix A
- deceased persons, 10192
- dependants, 10193, 10200
- eligible, 10195
- payment and reimbursement of, 10191
- quick reference table of allowable and non-allowed medical expenses, Appendix A
- receipts, 10194
- refundable medical expense supplement, 11280
- time of, 10192

Membership fees
- deduction from business income, 6130.3, 6130.27

Minimum tax, *see* Alternative Minimum Tax

Mining projects
- depreciation class, 7225

Mortgage foreclosures, 4560

Motor vehicles, *see* Automobiles

Moving expenses
- claiming and filing, 9204
- deduction from income, 6130.28, 9200
- eligible expenses, 9203
- students, 9202

Municipal officer's expense allowance, 2265

Musicians
- employees' instrument expense deduction, 2460

Mutual funds
- disposition of, 4310
- income, 3315
- segregated funds, 3316

N

Net-capital loss, *see* Capital loss

Net federal tax calculation
- generally, 11000

NETFILE, 1122

Net income, *see* type of income (e.g., Business, Employment, Investment, Professional, Rental, etc.)

Net income stabilization account (NISA), 6340

New Brunswick, *see* Provincial and territorial taxes and credits

Newfoundland and Labrador, *see* Provincial and territorial taxes and credits

Non-arm's length sale of shares, *see* Surplus stripping

Non-capital loss

- carryback/carryforward, 9360

- generally, 9360

Non-refundable tax credits, *see also* specific items

- generally, 10000

- personal tax credits quick reference table, 10005

Non-residents

- elective returns, 15410

- filing requirements, 15400

- payments to, 11240

- taxation of, 11240, 15131

Northern residents deduction

- residency deduction, 2465, 9390

- travel benefits deduction, 2467

Northwest Territories, *see* Provincial and territorial taxes and credits

Notice of objection, *see* Assessments

Nova Scotia, *see* Provincial and territorial taxes and credits

Nunavut, *see* Provincial and territorial taxes and credits

O

Objections

- filing, 14050

Office, income from, *see* Employment income

Oils sands projects

- depreciation classes, 7230

Old Age Security (OAS) benefits

- claiming and filing, 8113

- clawback, 8112

- generally, 8110

- non-resident, payment to, 8113, 15340

- repayment, 9282, 11222

- voluntary deferral, 8111

- withholding, 11222.1

Ontario, *see* Provincial and territorial taxes and credits

Options to buy or sell property, 4540

Organization expenses, 6140.18

Other income, *see* under specific items

Overseas employment

- tax credit, 11090

Owner/managers

- remuneration planning, 16110

P

PRPP employer contributions, 9105

Parking

- employer-provided, 2270

Part-year residents

- taxation of, 15140

Partnership

- adjusted cost base of partnership interest, 4123

- defined, 3600

- limited partnership income, 3600

- - at-risk amount, 3620

- - definition, 3610

- limited partnership losses, 9350

- reporting, limited partnership income, 3600

Patents, *see* Intangible assets

Payment of tax

- generally, 1200
- instalments, 1200
- reporting taxes paid, 11340

Penalties

- deductibility from business income, 6140.9
- failure to file, 1420
- generally, 1420
- information returns, 1420
- quick reference table, 1420
- third party, 1430

Pension adjustment

- generally, 9110
- reporting, 9110
- RRSP deduction limit, 9131

Pension benefits/income, *see also* Canada Pension Plan (CPP)/Quebec Pension Plan (QPP), Old Age Security (OAS) Pension

- claiming and filing, 10105
- credit amount claim, 10100
- eligible pension income, 8141, 10101
- foreign, 8134, 10103
- generally, 8100
- income-splitting between spouses, 8140, 9140, 10102
- legal fees, 9271
- lump-sum payments, 8263
- non-resident, payment to, 10104, 15340
- registered plans, 8132
- registered retirement income funds (RRIFs) and annuities, 8133
- reporting, 8136
- service pension or allowance, 2320
- superannuation or pension benefits, 8131

- tax credit, 10100
- U.S. social security, 8135

Personal or living expenses

- non-deductible from business income, 6140.19

Personal tax credits, *see also* specific items

- quick reference table, 10005

Personal tax deductions

- quick reference table, 9010

Personal use property

- $1,000 rule, 4572
- bad debts, 4573
- excluded property, 4572
- generally, 4570
- listed personal property, 4571

Police force personnel

- employment income deduction, 2425

Political contributions

- business non-deductibility, 6140.20
- federal tax credit, 11020, 11021

Post-mortem tax planning and elections, 16120, 16122

Power saw operators

- deduction from income, 2480

Prescribed debt obligations, 3228

Prescribed international organization

- deduction from employment income, 9404

Prince Edward Island, *see* Provincial and territorial taxes and credits

Principal residence

- calculating exemption, 4433
- change in use, 4434, 5410, 5420, 5430

Principal residence *(cont'd)*

• defined, 4431

• designation, 4432

• exemption, 4430

• qualifying as, 4431

Prizes, *see* Awards and prizes

Professional and union dues, 2406, 2407, 9150

Professional income, *see also* Business income

• determination of, 6210

• expenses, 6230

• incorporation of practice, 6240

• service and management corporations, 6250

• work in progress, 6220

Provincial and territorial taxes and credits

• Alberta, 12100

• • liability for tax, 12110

• • non-refundable tax credits, 12150

• • other tax credits, 12160

• • tax rate, 12120

• British Columbia, 12200

• • liability for tax, 12210

• • non-refundable tax credits, 12250

• • other tax credits, 12260

• • tax rates, 12220

• Manitoba, 12300

• • liability for tax, 12310

• • non-refundable tax credits, 12350

• • other tax credits, 12360

• • tax rates, 12320

• New Brunswick, 12400

• • liability for tax, 12410

• • non-refundable tax credits, 12450

• • other tax credits, 12460

• • tax rates, 12420

• Newfoundland and Labrador, 12500

• • liability for tax, 12510

• • non-refundable tax credits, 12550

• • other tax credits, 12560

• • tax rates, 12520

• Northwest Territories, 12600

• • liability for tax, 12610

• • non-refundable tax credits, 12650

• • other tax credits, 12660

• • tax rates, 12620

• Nova Scotia, 12700

• • liability for tax, 12710

• • non-refundable tax credits, 12750

• • other tax credits, 12760

• • tax rates, 12720

• Nunavut, 12800

• • liability for tax, 12810

• • non-refundable tax credits, 12850

• • other tax credits, 12860

• • tax rates, 12820

• Ontario, 12900

• • liability for tax, 12910

• • non-refundable tax credits, 12950

• • other tax credits, 12960

• • tax rates, 12920

• overview, 12010

• • administration and enforcement, 12050

• • credits, 12040

• • residence, 12020

• • taxes, 12030

• Prince Edward Island, 121000

• • liability for tax, 121010

• • non-refundable tax credits, 121050

• • other tax credits, 121060

Provincial and territorial taxes and credits *(cont'd)*
- • tax rates, 121020
- Quebec, *see* Quebec
- Saskatchewan, 121100
- • liability for tax, 121110
- • non-refundable tax credits, 121150
- • other tax credits, 121160
- • tax rates, 121120
- Yukon, 121200
- • liability for tax, 121210
- • non-refundable tax credits, 121250
- • other tax credits, 121260
- • tax rates, 121220

Public transit
- tax credit, 10240

Q

Qualified farm or fishing property
- capital gains exemption, 4231
- definition, 4231, 4232
- *inter vivos* transfer to child, 4235
- share of capital stock of family farm or fishing corporation, 4233

Qualified small business corporation
- capital gains exemption, 4220
- defined, 4221
- purification of, 4223
- special rules, 4224

Quebec taxes and credits
- abatement, 11250
- assessment, 13700
- calculating net income, 13200
- calculating refund or balance due, 13600
- calculating taxable income, 13300
- calculating total income, 13100
- filing deadlines and penalties, 13060
- income tax and contributions, 13500
- non-refundable tax credits, 13400
- non-refundable and refundable tax credits table, Appendix B-3

R

Railway employees' expenses
- deduction from income, 2485

Reassessments
- generally, 14022
- objections, 14050
- waivers, 14040

Recapture
- of CCA, 7145

Recreational facilities
- employer provided, 2295

Refund due, 11351

Registered disability savings plan (RDSP)
- claiming and filing, 8231
- generally, 8230, 16230
- receipts from as income, 8230
- transfers to on a rollover basis, 9273.8

Registered education savings plan (RESP)
- accumulated income payments (AIPs), 8266.2, 11061
- Canada Education Savings Grants, 16220
- contribution limits, 16220
- educational assistance payments (EAPs), 8266.1
- generally, 8266, 16220
- Part X.5 tax, 11061
- taxation of, 8266

Registered pension plans

- deduction, 9120

Registered retirement income fund (RRIF)

- excess transfers to, 9273.4

- reporting, 8133

Registered retirement savings plan (RRSP)

- borrowing to contribute, 9136

- deduction, 9130

- deduction limit, 9131

- defined, 8250

- earned income for RRSP purposes, 9132

- employer-provided, 9136

- excess transfers to, 9273.4

- Home Buyers' Plan, 8251

- income, 8250

- Lifelong Learning Plan, 8251

- overcontributions, 9135

- qualified and prohibited investments, 16250

- Schedule 7 reporting, 9137

- spousal plans, 8252, 9133

- tax planning points, 9136

Rental income

- business or property income, 5110

- calculating, 5120

- capital cost allowance, 5121, 5240

- change-in-use rules, 5410

- current vs. capital expenses, 5210

- deductible expenses, 5200, 5210, 5220

- Form T776, 5600

- generally, 5000

- landscaping costs, 5253

- lease cancellation payments, 5254

- leasehold inducements, 5254

- non-residents, 5124, 5500, 15330

- reporting, 5600

- soft costs, 5255

- tax consequences, 5120

- undeveloped or vacant land, 5256

- U.S., 5005

Rental losses, 5300

Rent expense

- deduction from business income, 6130.29

Replacement property rules

- deferring gains, 4700

- former business property, 4710

- generally, 4700

- involuntary dispositions, 4720

- land and building reallocation of proceeds, 4740

- rollover rules where election filed, 4730

Research grants, 2301

Reserves

- deduction from business income, 6130.31

Residency

- ceasing Canadian, 15130

- clergy, residence deduction, 2430

- common law rules, 15110

- deeming rules, 15120

- generally, 15100

- indication of, 15110

- part-year, 15140

- principal, *see* Principal residence

- taxing non-residents and deemed residents, 15131

Resource pools (expenses), 7400, *see also* Canadian exploration expenses; Canadian development expenses; Canadian oil and gas property expenses

Restrictive convenants, 7320

Retirement compensation arrangements (RCA)

- employment income, 2305, 2500, 9273.2

Retirement plan contribution limits table, Appendix B-5

Retiring aliowances

- generally, 8264
- legal fees, 9271
- taxation of, 8264
- transfers to RRSP or RPP, 8264.1

Returns

- amending, 14010
- EFILE, 1123
- elections filing, 1130
- filing due date, 1140
- filing requirements, 1100, 1410
- information returns, 1310
- NETFILE, 1122
- paper, 1121
- who must file, 1110

Royalties

- investment income, 3325
- non-residents, 15330

S

Salaries and wages

- business expense deduction, 6130.32
- paid to spouse/children, 6140.22
- salary deferral arrangements, 2020, 2160
- taxation of, generally, 2005, 6130.32

Salespersons

- commission income, 2150

- travelling expenses, 2530

Saskatchewan, *see* Provincial and territorial taxes and credits

Scholarships, fellowships, and bursaries

- taxation of, 2310, 8261

School supply tax credit, *see* Eligible educator school supply tax credit

Search and rescue volunteers tax credit, 10290

Securities lending arrangements, 3160

Scientific research expenditures

- deduction from business income, 6130.33

Section 216 election, 5500

Security options, *see* Stock options

Self-employment income, *see* Business Income; Professional income

Settlements, 14051

Shareholder benefits

- common examples of, 14351.2
- exclusions, 14351.1
- generally, 14351
- interaction with other avoidance provisions, 14351.4
- value of, 14351.3

Shareholder loans

- generally, 14352
- income inclusion exceptions, 14352.1
- interest-free, 14352.4
- offsetting, 14352.3
- repayment of included in income, 14352.2

Shares

- adjusted cost base (ACB), 4122
- bankrupt corporation, of, 4360

Shares *(cont'd)*

- convertible shares or debt, 4370

- proceeds of disposition, 4350

Small business corporation (SBC)

- capital gains deferral, 4340

- capital gains exemption, 4220

- defined, 4620

Social assistance

- claiming and filing, 8321

- taxation of benefits received, 8320

Social events

- employer provided, 2325

Soft costs

- land or buildings, deductibility, 5255

Solicitor-client privilege, 14140

- accountant working papers and, 14142

- establishing, 14141

Specified investment flow-through trusts (SIFTs), 3320

Specified leasing property, 7215

Split income

- deduction from business income, 6130.34

Spouse or common-law partner

- amounts transferred from, 14220

- defined, 10032

- eligible dependent amount, 10040

- loan to, income splitting, 14220

- net income, 10031

- pension income splitting, 8140

- RRSP for, 8252, 9133

- support payments, 8240, 9210

- tax credit, 10030

Standby charge, *see* Automobiles

Start-up expenses, 6140.7

Stock options

- cash-out payments, 2512, 4321

- employee deduction, 2510, 9330

- employment benefit, 2315

- exercise of, 4320

Stop-loss rules, dividend, 4820

Strike pay, 2340

Students

- child care expense deduction, 9170

- interest paid on student loan, 10150

- moving expenses, 9202

- tuition credit, 10160

Superannuation or pension benefits, 8131

Supplies

- deduction from employment income, 2515

Support payments made

- claiming and filing, 9215

- generally, 9210

- legal fees, 9213, 9271

- lump-sum payments, 9212.3

- prior payments, 9212.1

- shared custody and tax credits, 9214

- specific purpose and third-party payments, 9212.2

- taxation of, 9211

Support payments received

- claiming and filing by recipients, 8245

- defined, 8240

- legal fees paid to collect, 8244

- lump-sum payments, 8242, 8242.3

Support payments received *(cont'd)*

- payments from non-residents, 8243

- payments to third party, 8242.2

- taxation of, 8241

Surplus stripping

- generally, 4250, 14360

T

Tax audits

- access to foreign information, 14131

- books and records, 14120

- generally, 14100

- information requests by CRA, 14111

- investigations and inspections, 14130

- requesting CRA audit working papers, 14112

- solicitor-client privilege, 14140

Taxable Canadian property (TCP) dispositions

- certificates of compliance, 15220

- excluded dispositions, 15210

- generally, 15200

Tax avoidance

- reporting transactions, 1320

Taxes (business)

- deduction from business income, 6130.11, 6130.35

Taxes (income)

- non-deductibility from business income, 6140.23

Tax-free savings accounts (TFSAs)

- generally, 16210

Tax law, sources, of, 1010

Tax on split income

- application of, 14211

- claiming and filing, 11071

- determining amount of tax, 14213

- exclusions, 14212

- generally, 14210

Taxpayer relief

- generally, 1520

Tax planning

- income splitting, 14200

- owner-manager remuneration, 16110

- post-mortem, 16120, 16122

- registered plans, 16200

- U.S. estate tax, 16320

Tax rates

- tax rates and brackets table, Appendix B-1

- tax credit rates and amounts table, Appendix B-2

- top marginal tax rates table, Appendix B-4

Tax reference tables, Appendix B

Tax returns, *see* Returns

Tax shelters

- claim for loss/deduction, 1330

Tax treaty, *see* Treaty

Terminal loss

- generally, 7150

Tips, 2215

Tools, tradesperson, 2520

Travel expenses

- between home and work, 2352

- deduction from employment income, 2525, 2530

- transportation passes (employer-provided), 2351

Treasury bills, 3220

Treaty

- conflicting with Act, 1010
- income exempt under, 9401

Trust and estate income

- capital distributions, 3412
- flow through of income, 3413
- non-resident trusts, 3430
- income distributions, 3411
- non-resident beneficiaries, 3420

Trusts

- non-resident, 3430
- tax credit, Part XII.2, 11310

Tuition, education and textbook credits

- carryforward of unused credits, 10165
- certificate to support claim, 10167
- claiming and filing, 10168, 10181
- designated educational institution, 10161
- educational institution, 10161
- education and textbook credits, 10164
- eligible fees, 10162
- employer-provided tuition and fees, 2355
- generally, 10160
- occupational, trade, or professional examinations, 10162.4
- qualifying educational program, 10161
- tuition fess, eligible, 10162
- transfer of unused credits
- - from a child, 10166, 10170
- - from a spouse, 10166, 10180

U

U.S. Social Security

- taxation of benefits received, 8135

U.S. taxes

- estate tax, 16320
- filing requirements, 16331
- income tax, 16310
- penalties, 16332
- substantial presence test, 16310

Uniforms and special clothing, 2360

Union dues

- deduction, 2407, 9150

Universal Child Care Benefit (UCCB)

- generally, 8210
- repayment, 9160
- taxation, 8210

V

Vacation and sick leave credits, 2105

Vacations

- employer provided, 2365

V-Day value

- adjusted cost base (ACB), 4127

Voluntary Disclosure Program

- generally, 1510

Volunteer firefighters' tax credit

- generally, 10220

Vow of perpetual poverty

- deduction of income and benefits, 9402

W

Waivers, 14040

Withholding taxes

- dividend payments, 15320

- generally, 15300

- income tax withheld at source, 11240

- interest payments, 15310

- payments to non-residents, 11240, 15300

- pension and other benefits, 15340

- rents and royalties, 15330

Work in progress

- election by professionals to exclude, 6220

Workers' compensation

- claiming and filing, 8311

- taxation of benefits received, 2370, 8310

Working income tax benefit

- advance payments, 11050

- generally, 11290

- claiming and filing, 11051

Y

Yukon, *see* Provincial and territorial taxes and credits